Handbook of Industrial
and Organizational Psychology

Contributors

Walter C. Borman, *University of South Florida*

John W. Boudreau, *Cornell University*

René V. Dawis, *University of Minnesota*

Irwin L. Goldstein, *University of Maryland, College Park*

Robert M. Guion, *Bowling Green State University*

Robert J. Harvey, *Virginia Polytechnic Institute & State University*

Joyce C. Hogan, *University of Tulsa*

Robert T. Hogan, *University of Tulsa*

John R. Hollenbeck, *Michigan State University*

William C. Howell, *Rice University
    & U.S. Air Force Human Resources Laboratory*

Charles L. Hulin, *University of Illinois, Champaign-Urbana*

Daniel R. Ilgen, *Michigan State University*

Robert G. Lord, *University of Akron*

Karen J. Maher, *University of Akron*

Sara L. Rynes, *University of Iowa*

Handbook of Industrial and Organizational Psychology

SECOND EDITION

Volume 2

Marvin D. Dunnette and Leaetta M. Hough
Editors

Consulting Psychologists Press, Inc.
Palo Alto, California

Library of Congress Cataloging-in-Publication Data
(Revised for vol. 2)

Handbook of industrial and organizational
   psychology

   Includes bibliographical references and index.
   1. Psychology, Industrial. 2. Organizational
behavior. I. Dunnette, Marvin D. II. Hough,
Leaetta M.
HF 5548.8.H265   1990   158.7   90-2294
ISBN 0-89106–041–3 (v. 1)
ISBN 0-89106-042-1 (v. 2)

Printed in the United States of America

Dedicated to our fathers,
Rodney A. Dunnette, attorney,
and
Mervin B. Hough, master builder.
They set standards of
quiet excellence and uncommon wisdom
that challenge us still.

Contents

Figures

CHAPTER 9   Training in Work Organizations   507

CHAPTER 10   Utility Analysis for Decisions in Human Resource Management   621

Tables

Preface

As we mentioned in our preface to the first volume of this *Handbook*, the basic structure has not changed much from the structure of the first edition published in 1976. Thus, the section headings for this edition are similar to those of the first edition:

- Theory in Industrial and Organizational Psychology

- Measurement and Method in Industrial and Organizational Psychology

- Individual Behavior and Organizational Practices

- Attributes of Individuals in Organizations

- Work Roles, Work Functions, and Consumer Responses

- Social Group Processes, Organizational Factors, and Other Facets of Organizational Functioning

- Industrial and Organizational Psychology in the Cross-cultural Context

Our intent was that the new *Handbook* be seen as an extension of the first *Handbook*. Accordingly, scholars invited to contribute to the volumes of this second edition were assured that they would not be constrained by what was in the first *Handbook* but that they should also not feel compelled to make their contributions so new and different that no links with the first were recognizable. The hope was that the content of the two editions of the *Handbook* would play an important role in reflecting the nature of the growth and development of industrial and organizational psychology during the last 35 to 40 years of this century.

Although the basic structure of the two editions has been retained, changes in content were inevitable. Several chapters have been added to reflect the emergence of new areas of knowledge and concern in industrial and organizational psychology. These are reviewed briefly below:

- *Theory in Industrial and Organizational Psychology*
This section has been expanded to include chapters on individual differences theory, decision making theory, and cognitive theory. In fact, the first chapter of this volume is the one contributed by R. Lord and K. Maher, titled *Cognitive Theory in Industrial and Organizational Psychology*. Their chapter describes revolutionary developments in cognitive science, developments that propel us toward thinking about old issues in our field in new, more systematic and flexible ways.

- *Measurement and Method in Industrial and Organizational Psychology*
A separate chapter on item response theory has been added. Two chapters on research strategy have been included—one on what might be called the *phenomenology* of discovery in science and the other on the broad domain of research strategies and tactics available to researchers in industrial and organizational psychology. The distinction between laboratory and field research methods has been de-emphasized by *not* including separate chapters on each. Multiple methods in research and replication of significant findings are important and are, of course, emphasized along with many other strategies and tactics discussed in Chapters 7 and 8.

- *Individual Behavior and Organizational Practices*
New chapters have been included on work structure and the design of jobs and roles, recruitment and organizational entry processes, and methods of utility estimation in human resources practices and functions. Issues related to job satisfaction are considered within the somewhat broader context of organizational socialization and persistence.

- *Attributes of Individuals in Organizations*
A separate chapter on physical abilities has been added.

- *Work Roles, Work Functions, and Consumer Responses*
A new chapter on employee compensation has been added.

- *Social Group Processes, Organizational Factors, and Other Facets of Organizational Functioning*
New chapters have been added on organizational design, intergroup issues in organizational and group performance, and the measurement of productivity in work settings.

- *Industrial and Organizational Psychology in the Cross-cultural Context*
Cross-cultural issues in industrial and organizational psychology have been expanded from one chapter in the 1976 *Handbook* to sixteen chapters in the present *Handbook*. This expansion has taken the form of asking each contributor to write about his or her own research interests and activities and to present them in the context of issues seen as most salient to organizational psychology in her or his particular country. In addition to writing the introductory chapter for this section, Harry Triandis has served as a coeditor for these chapters.

Chapters in this section constitute the content of volume 4, which will contain contributions by industrial and organizational psychologists from Australia, France, Germany, Hong Kong, India, Israel, Japan, the Netherlands, the People's Republic of China, the Soviet Union, Spain, Sweden, and the United Kingdom.

After deciding on the major content areas to be included in the four volumes of this *Handbook*, a tentative plan was developed for each of the intended chapters. This took the form of a series of one-page documents, each containing the suggested title for a particular chapter, a paragraph describing the desired content, and a listing of three or four possible authors considered to be well suited for writing such a chapter. Here is an example of what was said on one such page:

> *Training in Work Organizations.* This chapter should include all that is known about the practical realities of designing, conducting, and evaluating personnel training and development programs in work settings. The chapter should be extended beyond what has been traditionally called training to include longer term development procedures such as job rotation, special assignments, and job design. Research in the area of career development should be included here. The revised chapter should take account of training in the military, of early intervention programs, remedial education, goal-setting research, and all other areas relevant to the design, development, and evaluation of training systems in work organizations.

These statements of probable content were then sent along with letters of invitation to persons who had been suggested as possible authors. After an individual had accepted the invitation to write a chapter, a second more detailed letter was sent describing the structure of the new *Handbook* as described earlier. In addition, the following guidance was given about the type of emphasis we hoped the authors would give to their chapters. These suggestions were stated as follows:

> As with the previous *Handbook*, the emphasis in your chapter should *not* be like an Annual Review chapter. Summarize what is known, of course, but please extend it and develop the implications for theory and practice for the future of what is known now. As before, the plan is to produce a handbook that is broad in its coverage giving strong emphasis to theoretical, conceptual, methodological, and practical issues. The major view you should have in writing your chapter is to assure that what you say is not only up-to-date, but also ahead of its time—a chapter that is pace-setting and which will, in fact, guide the development of Industrial and Organizational Psychology well into the next century.

Ultimately, authors were selected for a total of 44 chapters. (At that time, we had not yet decided to develop volume 4.) Several of the authors asked colleagues to coauthor their chapters; some authors contributed to more than one chapter. Thus, the total number of authors who agreed eventually to write or to cowrite one or more of the 44 chapters is 65. Surprisingly, only 10 of these authors had been involved in writing for the 1976 *Handbook*. In this sense, the present *Handbook* cannot really be regarded as a revision or even a second edition of the earlier *Handbook*. It is, in fact—both in content and in authorship—a *Second Handbook of Industrial and Organizational Psychology*. These 65 authors include scholars of diverse training and institutional affiliation. They are from 41 different institutions; 60 are in academic departments (37 in psychology, 22 in departments of business or management, and 1 in sociology); 5 are with consulting firms. The 21 additional authors of chapters in volume 4 represent 18 different institutions located in 13 different countries.

It is unfortunate but true that the press of other commitments must be expected to cause a few authors, initially enthusiastic about doing a chapter, to decide that they must withdraw from the project. For the 27 chapters in these first two volumes, only four of the initial authors withdrew. Fortunately, we were able to identify and persuade others to step in on short notice and under even greater time pressure. We deeply appreciate their willingness to join the enterprise under such circumstances.

More vexing is the fact that people—even world-class scholars—differ from each other. We have come to believe that one of the most profound of these differences is the time taken to complete handbook chapters. We estimate that time to completion for such chapters is distributed across scholars with a standard deviation of about 180 days. The distribution is markedly skewed such that the median and the third quartile are both substantially below the mean. Amazingly, four of this *Handbook*'s manuscripts were in our hands within six months after the authors' initial acceptances. We leave to the reader the task of deducing from our estimate of the standard deviation the likely outer limits of this incredible distribution. As a result, publication of this *Handbook* has been delayed, as was the case with the first *Handbook*, far more than we like.

Even so, the overall effort has most definitely been fulfilling. Best of all, the level of scholarship shown by all these contributors has been superb. Even those who overshot their target dates did send completed manuscripts that were clearly worth waiting for. It is apparent that each author worked hard and long to produce the best possible statement of current research and thinking in his or her area of expertise. We are fully convinced that the hundreds of industrial and organizational psychologists who have joined our ranks over the last 15 years, as well as the next several generations of entering industrial and organizational psychology and organizational behavior students, will profit greatly from what is contained in the pages of these volumes.

From the very beginning of this project, indispensable assistance has been provided by Kim Downing. She has handled the mountain of correspondence with authors of these chapters and with a vast number of other authors and publishers during the process of obtaining required permissions. She most certainly deserves a medal of honor for diligence and perspicacity. Kim tackled problems as they appeared and solved them quickly and efficiently. The editorial "struggle" was eased considerably by her quickness, her persistence, and, on occasion, her friendly audacity in being able to cope with the occasional contentious individual who seemed to be standing in the way of the *Handbook*'s progress.

After some brief period of negotiation, we were gratified to sign a publishing agreement with Consulting Psychologists Press. We appreciate the helpfulness of Bob Most, John Black, and, in particular, CPP's president and CEO, Lorin Letendre, for their support and enthusiasm in choosing this project as a major vehicle for their expansion into publishing state-of-the-art contributions in industrial and organizational psychology.

A very special advantage in working with Consulting Psychologists Press has been the privilege of working with the director of their book division, Lee Langhammer Law. She has managed the entire project through all phases of production; she and her staff have carefully and delightfully edited these manuscripts from beginning to end. This has been done with wisdom, patience, and without rancor. Lee is truly a rarity. There is no way in which one could properly acknowledge the level of excellence she has demonstrated throughout this project.

The so-called incidental expenses involved in a project of this magnitude can grow far beyond what one would ever reasonably estimate. Hundreds of phone calls, thousands of pages of copying costs, and a seemingly endless stream of letters and packages requiring substantial amounts of postage, air express fees, and other special delivery charges accumulate over the days, weeks, months, and years. These costs have been borne by grants made to the project by Personnel Decisions Research Institute. It is fair to say that the financial feasibility of this undertaking might be very difficult to justify purely on the basis of sound business reasoning. The generosity of PDRI's Board of Trustees is deeply appreciated for their willingness to grant facilities and funds to help in handling the substantial incidental expenses accumulated over the lifetime of this effort.

We are delighted that we are now putting the second volume to bed. The other volumes are on their way. We look forward to future travels with less weighty luggage.

MARVIN D. DUNNETTE
LEAETTA M. HOUGH
St. Paul, Minnesota
April 1991

CHAPTER 1

Cognitive Theory in Industrial and Organizational Psychology

Robert G. Lord
Karen J. Maher
University of Akron

Recent developments from the cognitive science literature are examined, and applications of these developments to industrial and organizational psychology are discussed. Information processing can be conceptualized as occurring within theoretical systems called cognitive architectures. These architectures define (a) the nature and organization of memory, (b) primitive (easily performed) cognitive operations, and (c) a control structure that sequences information processing steps. Symbolic architectures describe processing in terms of serial manipulations of symbols (e.g., language) as a way of understanding environments or solving problems. Connectionist architectures describe processing at a more basic, neurologically based level. Connectionist architectures conceptualize processing in terms of the flow of activation and inhibition between networks of neuronlike processing units.

Recent thinking about human memory is also summarized. Key issues include the operation of memory in storing and retrieving information, implicit and explicit memory, growing support for a multiple rather than unitary conceptualization of working memory, and the role of memory in controlling the sequencing of thought. We also discuss schemas and their role in guiding memory and information processing. Performance on any task is viewed as depending on the interaction between information processing and task-relevant knowledge.

This conceptualization is applied to problem solving, expert-novice differences, and social perceptions. Finally, we show that the distinction between automatic and controlled processing is a more complex issue than is commonly recognized. This distinction involves a number of related constructs, including the role of intentionality and the load on attentional resources created by processing tasks.

The Role of Cognitive Theory in Our Field

TO MANY OBSERVERS in the field, it may appear as if numerous areas of industrial and organizational psychology have been transformed by the "cognitive revolution." A cognitive orientation is common in our field, as illustrated by research in performance appraisal, decision making, leadership perceptions, and human factors that seeks to explain work behavior in terms of cognitive operations dealing with attention, encoding, retrieval, and transformation of information. A cognitive science approach is process oriented. Such an approach defines processes, measures them, and ties the measured processes to theoretical models. Although industrial and organizational researchers often espouse a process orientation, our assessment is that the field has not taken full advantage of the opportunities presented by recent developments in cognitive science. There has been a revolution in industrial and organizational terminology, but only a minor revolt in theory development and methodology refinement. Yet recent advances in cognitive science are truly revolutionary. The implications of these advances for our field are much more profound than one would infer from reading much of the literature of industrial and organizational psychology.

The purpose of this chapter is to go beyond the more common social-cognitive applications by discussing some fundamental concepts in cognitive science in a way that emphasizes their implications for our field. We also describe some new developments that may have the potential to advance our thinking and

methodology. We do not intend to review comprehensively the portion of the industrial and organizational literature that is cognitively oriented. This work has recently been reviewed elsewhere (Ilgen & Klein, 1989; Lord & Maher, 1989). Nor do we provide a comprehensive coverage of cognitive science or recent developments in that literature. Anderson (1990) provides an excellent introductory text, while Posner's (1989) *Foundations of Cognitive Science* provides a broad treatment of cognitive science at a more advanced level.

Rather, this chapter is intended to be a survey of some of the developments and topics in cognitive science. The reader looking for an integrative framework answering all cognitive questions relevant to our field may be disappointed. In many areas of cognitive science, needed answers have not yet been developed and important problems are just beginning to be addressed. Cognitive science is a relatively new field, which is still developing a coherent perspective and set of underlying principles. Moreover, there is sometimes disagreement even among experts in cognitive science about particular issues. Therefore, any attempt on our part to draw conclusions about debated issues would be presumptuous. However, there are topics in cognitive science where theory and research are sufficiently developed that they are worth summarizing, and the potential application of these topics to industrial and organizational psychology is worthy of consideration. We have tried to identify implications by developing examples of broad relevance to industrial and organizational psychology, but many examples are simply illustrations that were convenient or easily available. We encourage the reader to overcome this limitation by considering the implications of our discussion for areas of personal interest.

Relevance of Cognitive Science

A cognitive science approach can provide insight into problems that are typically investigated by industrial and organizational researchers and yield considerable benefits if applied to the field. For example, much performance appraisal literature has focused on the problem of halo in performance ratings. Suggested solutions to this problem have ranged from rater training (Borman, 1975; Pulakos, 1984) to statistical correction for halo (Holzbach, 1978; Landy, Vance, Barnes-Farrell, & Steele, 1980). However, even though much work on halo has had a cognitive orientation, there has been no consistent theoretical system to identify the microlevel processes that produce halo and other rating phenomena. If researchers attempted to model the cognitive processes that produce halo at a very detailed micro level, understanding of halo may increase and more appropriate interventions may be designed. Alternatively, attempts at modeling rating behavior may show that halo is a natural result of the manner in which our cognitive systems are structured and that it is related to social intelligence applied in work settings.

Skill acquisition and transfer of training are other issues that have puzzled researchers in our field. Learning principles are usually technique-oriented and include such issues as stimulus variability, identical elements, and conditions of practice. The principles typically applied to organizational training situations have not been tied to a coherent information processing theoretical framework. Training research could benefit from focusing on the cognitive processes involved in skill acquisition (Howell & Cooke, 1989). The research that has been conducted by cognitive

psychologists (Anderson, 1983a, 1987) on how knowledge is acquired, structured, and integrated into a cognitive system has important implications for how training should proceed or whether training will transfer to new situations. The importance of knowledge for training is exemplified by research demonstrating differences between expert and novice schemas, which illustrate that the form of knowledge representation changes with experience (Chi, Glaser, & Farr, 1988).

Leadership and other social perceptions provide another example of the rich source of information that can be tapped by focusing on cognitive systems. Two related problems gaining increased attention are the differing perceptions of male and female managers (Heilman, Block, Martell, & Simon, 1989; Lord & Maher, 1991) and the very small number of women in management and leadership positions (Morrison & Von Glinow, 1990). Part of these problems may stem from basic perceptual processing that depends on knowledge structures learned through experience. The dearth of female executives may not be the result of a conscious bias or intentional discrimination. Rather, it may reflect the way perceivers organize information about gender, managers, and leaders in memory; how information in memory is automatically accessed; and how this organization influences judgment and decisions (Lord & Maher, 1991).

Paradigm of Cognitive Science

To appreciate how cognitive science can influence industrial and organizational psychology, one must understand that a fundamental goal of cognitive science is to develop a theoretical system that specifies how people function. The term *theoretical system* simply describes a model used to explain how information processing works. Different theoretical systems may be used for different problems or situations, but each should be coherent and provide an acceptable explanation of the phenomenon in question. Theoretical systems involve specifications of basic cognitive operations that transform input information into new and more useful forms. These systems involve assumptions about how memory systems are organized and operate, and they also specify a system's control structure, which determines the sequence of cognitive operations. More specifically, a *control structure* determines how mental representations and rules are invoked while generating thought or action. Much of the potency of cognitive science stems from viewing information processing as a coherent and functionally sufficient system, rather than from simply examining the isolated effects of certain cognitive operations or ways to conceptualize memory, as is often the case in applied work. Much of the current excitement in cognitive science pertains to questions of what type of theoretical system should be used as a basis for cognition.

Like many information processing studies in industrial and organizational psychology, research in cognitive science often begins with a flow diagram of underlying processes. However, work in cognitive science often goes beyond flow diagrams. Typical cognitive research collects detailed measures of cognitive processes gathered while subjects perform their tasks, whereas measures of cognitive processes are relatively rare in applied work (Lord & Carpenter, 1986). Process measures may come from protocol analyses, strategic choices, information search behaviors, errors, or reaction times. An additional step common in cognitive research, but rare in the industrial and organizational field, is to compare process measures to predictions from simulations of underlying processes. Simulations force researchers to be specific about how mechanisms in flow diagrams operate, because they require the development of a functionally adequate model that will work using a computer and the logic of a specific programming language. Comparing a simulation to real subjects determines whether the model

is complete enough to fully account for the obtained process and outcome data.

The differences in theory and methodology between cognitive science and industrial and organizational psychology reflect differences in basic strategies that might be used to address the same issue in each field. For example, if researchers in both fields were concerned with explaining typing performance, industrial and organizational psychologists would attempt to predict performance from a work sample or aptitude measure. Cognitive scientists might begin with similar strategies to predict typing performance, but they would also aim to understand the processes underlying that performance. A simulation model of the underlying processes would be developed and compared to the behavior of human subjects at a very detailed level, perhaps tying reaction times to patterns of error. Rumelhart and Norman (1982) developed such a theoretical model to simulate typing behavior, and they showed that this model predicts the errors and finger movements of experienced typists. Not only does this type of research offer the potential to increase ability to predict typing performance, but it may also lead to more effective interventions to increase performance.

In short, we think some of the work in cognitive science offers a very different paradigmatic approach for theory and research that can be of considerable value. Both methodology and theory focus on developing an integrated understanding of how cognitive processes produce intelligent behavior.

In the major sections of this chapter, some advances and issues in cognitive science that have particularly compelling implications for our field are highlighted. Developments in many areas of cognitive science are discussed, but the focus is on three issues: (a) cognitive architectures, (b) the operation of memory in task performance, and (c) the joint role of prior knowledge and current processing as fundamental factors that determine how human information processing systems operate. Such issues must be understood to address more general concerns such as explaining skilled task performance, social cognitions, or the automatic versus controlled processing distinction.

Cognitive Architectures

Many cognitive scientists have recently argued that to fully understand the functioning of intelligent systems, one must model how information is processed within a coherent theoretical system. This goal can be accomplished at many levels of analysis, ranging from those that are based directly on neuroscience, to those that are "neurally inspired," to those that are highly symbolic and involve the use of language. Currently, many researchers suggest that cognitive science is in the midst of a paradigm shift. Traditional theory is more symbolically oriented, concerned with conscious processes that operate on symbol structures stored in long-term memory (e.g., Newell & Simon, 1972), while much of the newer theory is focused at a more micro, neurologically based level. These different perspectives correspond to symbolic and connectionist architectures, respectively, which we describe in the following two sections. The issue of which cognitive architecture is more appropriate for explaining cognition is crucial, since cognitive architectures provide a metastructure within which information processing can operate. To the extent that alternative cognitive architectures imply different information processing requirements, the applications to industrial and organizational psychology would vary as well. But more importantly, symbolic and connectionist architectures provide different ways of thinking about problems that may be of concern to industrial and organizational psychologists.

A *cognitive architecture* can be defined as a "fixed system of mechanisms that underlies and produces cognitive behavior" (Newell, Rosenbloom, & Laird, 1989, p. 93). A cognitive architecture (a) specifies the nature of memory within a functional system, (b) defines the basic or primitive operations used by the system, and (c) specifies the type of control structure that organizes and sequences the primitive operations that produce intelligent behavior. In computer science, *architecture* roughly refers to the underlying structure that can be programmed (e.g., hardware and associated primitive built-in operations). The concern with cognitive architectures relates to the underlying nature of the "human computing machine" and the manner in which its hardware structure constrains the types of programs that people can use. Different architectures can be thought of as qualitatively different types of computer models that can be used to simulate human behavior. But they can also be thought of as different levels of analysis for representing human cognitive functioning that imply different types of memory, elementary cognitive processes, and control structures.

Most readers are probably familiar with a "standard" cognitive architecture, which consists of very short-term visual and auditory sensory stores, a limited capacity short-term memory, and a long-term memory with limitless capacity (Atkinson & Shiffrin, 1968; Simon & Kaplan, 1989, pp. 9–10). This architecture emphasizes symbolic processing, which allows people to represent the world in terms of an internal mental model to which they can apply rules to form inferences (Johnson-Laird, 1989). Within this standard architecture, information processing involves a sequence of serial operations that take information from sensory stores or memories, transform it, and store this updated information. For example, when interpreting the behavior of a familiar co-worker, we may access a knowledge structure related to the co-worker that is stored in memory, note that she seems unusually happy this morning, and store this transformed knowledge structure in long-term memory. Such *fetch-operate-store* cycles are common in conventional computing. In conjunction with an overarching control structure, these cycles have been successfully used to model human information processing in many tasks.

However, this standard symbolic system is just one of many possible cognitive architectures. Alternatively, one could attempt to explain psychological processes at a neural rather than symbolic level. Since different architectures may be functionally equivalent and can accomplish the same tasks, differences in cognitive architectures may not seem that important at first glance. But as Pylyshyn (1989) notes, "devices with different functional architectures cannot in general directly execute the same algorithms" (pp. 72–73). A basic and very simple operation in one architecture may involve a complex sequence of steps that takes more time and computational resources and is more prone to error in another architecture. What conventional computer-based architectures do well (rapid, symbolic processing based on sequences of relatively simple operations), people often find very difficult; conversely, what people can do easily (recognize complex patterns or produce fluid and skilled motor movement), computer-based architectures find difficult. The implications of such differences for industrial and organizational psychology become apparent when we intervene to change work behavior. Training programs based on an inappropriate cognitive architecture may be difficult for people to learn and to apply to their jobs, and they may not generalize very well to other situations. Moreover, a consequence of inappropriate training programs may very well be increased error both in training and on the job.

In the following sections, we will describe in some detail the two major architectures—symbolic and connectionist—that cognitive science theorists propose as representations of human cognitive capacities. Understanding the differences in these two architectures is useful to industrial and organizational psychologists in at least three ways. First, alternate architectures imply different ways of processing information, which suggests very different principles for explaining topics of traditional concern to industrial and organizational psychologists, topics such as motivation, learning, task or social perception, and problem solving. Second, an understanding of these distinctions is needed to appreciate major shifts in cognitive science that are presently occurring and are being reinforced by shifts in funding priorities in the federal government. (For example, the 1990s have been characterized as the "decade of the brain" by President Bush.) Third, and perhaps most important, since behavior in real situations involves simultaneous coordination of activities at many levels, it may require the use and coordination of activities involving different architectures. For example, cognition using a symbolic architecture may be influenced in part by knowledge that is activated by a connectionist architecture. It is the interplay of these two types of architectures that may be of most relevance to industrial and organizational psychologists.

Symbolic Cognitive Architectures

There are a variety of symbolic cognitive architectures, but in general, they represent a high level of analysis, since they are defined in terms of functions rather than neurological mechanisms (Newell et al., 1989, p. 102). Symbols are patterns with the special property that they designate structures outside themselves (Simon & Kaplan, 1989, p. 13). For example, the word *leader* is a symbol that designates a structure in memory (e.g., a category) that has a rich and personal meaning to most of us. The elements of symbolic architectures can be conceptualized as symbols held in one or more memories (Simon & Kaplan, 1989, p. 8). Operators transform these symbols to interpret information from sensory stores, to generate motor responses, or to create knowledge. All this must be done on a time scale that is compatible with environmental requirements, or in "real time." Typically, we think of symbolic systems as operating using a standard model of cognition described previously (visual and auditory sensory buffers, short-term memory, long-term memory, and serial information processing). Such systems permit the flexible use of language to represent an infinite number of ideas in terms of a much smaller number of symbols (words) as well as rules that operate on these symbols (e.g., grammar).

While this description is rather abstract, its application to industrial and organizational psychology can be seen more easily if we realize that people have internal mental models or symbol systems of the world that guide processing on many tasks, such as strategic decision making or social perception. Models represent abstractions of the world that are symbolic rather than literal translations of the world. As Johnson-Laird (1989) notes,

> We seem to perceive the world directly, not a representation of it. Yet this phenomenology is illusory: what we perceive depends on both what is in the world and what is in our heads—on what evolution has "wired" into our nervous systems and what we know as a result of experience. The limits of our models are the limits of our world. (pp. 470–471)

Thus, workers with different mental models—for example supervisors compared to supervisees, people trained in different functional specialties, or people of different cultures or genders—may not experience the "same" organizational world. One function of a common organizational culture is to create fairly similar mental models for organizational members (Lord & Maher, 1991, chap. 8). The importance of this point cannot be overstated. Since many cognitive operations involve managing these mental models in a rule-based fashion, different symbolic

representations will create different cognitions related to the same task. Issues that seem as straightforward as interpreting the meaning of language or describing the steps in a specific job actually involve translation into an internal symbolic form by listeners. Thus, the simple act of a supervisor giving feedback to a subordinate may easily be interpreted by a subordinate in ways not intended by the supervisor, because the subordinate may be relating it to different internal models or applying different operations to the feedback (for example, the subordinate may be thinking, what does this mean in terms of my next raise?). Similarly, descriptions of the basic duties in a job may differ when job analysts have internal models that differ in terms of action identification levels (Herbert & Lord, 1989).

Simon (1990) persuasively argues that many aspects of intelligent human behavior, such as intuition or expert skills, are explained very well by cognitive science theories based on symbolic architectures. Most models of work behavior used by industrial and organizational psychologists implicitly involve a symbolic architecture. Thinking, problem solving, reasoning, communicating with others, or calculating subjective expected utilities all involve operations that we apply to internal symbols. Similarly, difficulties encountered by people in performing such operations may be understood in terms of the constraints of human symbolic architectures, such as the very limited capacity working (short-term) memory. Theories explaining social perceptions or social interactions also emphasize symbolic architectures. Trait concepts provide a widely understood language for describing the qualities of others. Researchers concerned with social perceptions have focused on the meaning of traits to perceivers (Mischel, 1973) and perceiver attributional (Kelley, 1973; Taylor & Fiske, 1978) or categorization (Cantor & Mischel, 1979) processes. Attempts to develop more detailed symbolic explanations of social cognitions (e.g., Wyer & Srull, 1980) often implicitly describe a symbolic cognitive architecture because they specify the nature of memory, define primitive operations, and specify the control structure that organizes and sequences primitive operations.

It should be stressed that symbolic architectures are memory-based. That is, they retrieve symbols from memory locations, operate on them, and store these new symbols, perhaps writing over old symbols or storing them in new locations. For example, in the Wyer and Srull (1980) model, information is retrieved from or dumped into various memory bins. This basic fetch-transform-store operation implies that many of the problems people have in performing tasks will involve problems in retrieving or storing information. Consistent with this implication, Anderson (1987) finds that many of the errors made in early stages of skill acquisition reflect memory failures.

Connectionist Cognitive Architectures

Symbolic architectures are based, in part, on an analogy to modern computers, but people, of course, have some characteristics that distinguish them from computers. This difference has led many cognitive psychologists to posit architectures based on a brain metaphor rather than a conventional computer metaphor. Connectionist architectures use neurobiological evidence as a source of constraints on what is plausible and as a metaphor suggesting how cognitive processes might operate. Three characteristics of human brains are particularly noteworthy since they provide the logic for important aspects of connectionist architectures. First, brains consist of a very large number of interconnected neurons that can be mutually excitatory or inhibitory. For example, Anderson (1990) notes that

> the human brain itself contains roughly 100 billion neurons, each of which may have roughly the processing capability of

a medium-sized computer. A considerable fraction of the 100 billion neurons are active simultaneously and do much of their information processing through interactions with one another. (p. 20)

This organization suggests that many cognitive processes are not directly controlled by a central executive component. Instead, in a connectionist system, executive functions are inherent in the operations of systems of processing units. A separate central executive is not a part of connectionist systems, but it is usually required in symbolic systems.

Second, the principle of relating processing units (analogous to groups of highly connected neurons) by activation or inhibition is also closely related to physiological aspects of human brains since neurons activate or inhibit other neurons. This principle is crucial in connectionist architectures, as activation or inhibition from one unit to another is the only basic operation in connectionist architectures.

Third, the physiology of neurons makes them slow compared to a computer. Neurons operate on a time scale of milliseconds, whereas computers operate on a scale of nanoseconds, which is about 10^6 faster. As Rumelhart, Hinton, and McClelland (1986, p. 75) note, many of the human processes with which we are concerned—perception, memory retrieval, speech processing, and sentence comprehension—are completed in a few milliseconds. Therefore, these processes cannot involve more than about 100 elementary sequential operations. In fact, connectionist architectures do not use the very fast sequential search of modern computers. Instead, they rely on slower operations involving networks of neurons that process information simultaneously (parallel processing). Rumelhart, Hinton, and McClelland's "neurally inspired" architecture directly reflects a *parallel distributed processing* (PDP) or *connectionist* cognitive architecture that is very different from the classical symbolic architecture discussed above.

We should note that, technically, the issue of levels of analysis (symbolic versus neural) is distinct from the issue of serial versus parallel processing, but for our purposes, in this chapter the contrast between symbolic serial and connectionist parallel models will be stressed.* Most research in industrial and organizational psychology is based on the classic symbolic serial model. The parallel processes in connectionist models suggest alternative ways of thinking about many issues of concern to industrial and organizational psychologists. At an applied level, we must also understand how these two models interface.

It should be stressed that connectionist and symbolic architectures need not be competitive theories about knowledge, but rather theories that apply at different levels. As noted by Rumelhart, Hinton, and McClelland (1986), connectionist theories specify the *microstructure* of cognition. Because they use parallel processes, connectionist architectures accomplish tasks very quickly, even though each single operation is relatively slow. Rumelhart, Hinton, and McClelland (1986, p. 57) suggest that processes which occur in less than .25 to .5 seconds should be described in terms of parallel models; longer processes have a serial component and may be described better in terms of sequential symbolic information processing models. It is useful to think of the "gaps" in symbolic architectures as being filled in by connectionist theories and principles. For example, how we move from bin to bin (Wyer & Srull, 1980), how we activate person or script schemas, or how the schema construct can be defined may be best explained by a connectionist architecture.

The three physiologically based principles discussed above—processing occurring in diffusely represented networks of units, processing only involving the spread of activation or inhibition, and processing occurring in parallel—are fundamental aspects of connectionist architectures. A greatly simplified example of a three-level network that translates an input pattern into an output response is shown in Figure 1. In this network, processing occurs in parallel as input units activate or inhibit internal units, which in turn activate or inhibit output units. Conceptualizing information processing as being produced by such networks produces a very different understanding of key information processes, such as knowledge, learning, memory retrieval, or pattern recognition, than an understanding based on symbolic architectures. For example, in connectionist systems, knowledge is represented by the *pattern* of activation among units. This pattern is equivalent to a set of weights that specifies the connections among units. Thus, connectionists often think of knowledge as being reflected in a set of weights. Learning then corresponds to changes in the weights that reflect knowledge. New learning occurs very slowly as the result of experience with the input stimulus and feedback from output responses. Such differences are explained in the next few sections.

Hidden Units, Modularity, and Symbolic Capacity. Many discussions of connectionist architectures acknowledge only two levels—sensory input and motor output. However, more sophisticated models allow for additional layers of "hidden units" between inputs and outputs. Hidden units are often conceptualized as being semantically meaningful. They can also be thought of as categories used to interpret stimulus information or as scripts used to generate motor responses. Hidden units can also be organized into more aggregate, interconnected units or modules, which can be conceptualized as knowledge relevant to a given domain.

---

* Clearly, some symbolic systems (those making use of symbolic network models) incorporate a substantial amount of parallel processing, but most other symbolic models are assumed to operate serially (Simon & Kaplan, 1989, p. 13). Similarly, most work on connectionist architectures emphasizes parallel processing capacity, but an important aspect of connectionist architectures is that they can also produce serial processes. In fact, if connectionist models could not generate serial processes, the argument that they provide a microstructure for symbolically based cognitions would be implausible.

FIGURE 1

A Multilayer Connectionist Network

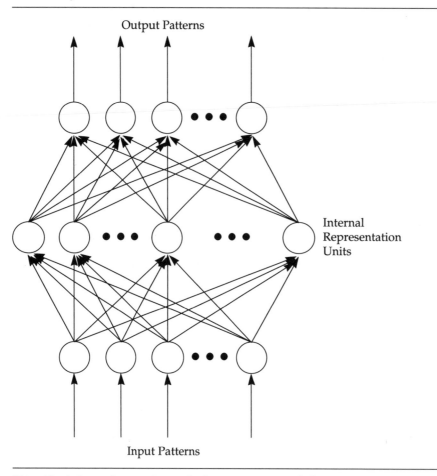

Note: The information coming to the input units is recoded into an internal representation, and the outputs are generated by the internal representation rather than by the original pattern.

From "Learning Internal Representations by Error Propagation" by D. E. Rumelhart, G. E. Hinton, and L. McClelland. In *Parallel Distributed Processing: Explorations in the Microstructure of Cognition* (p. 320) by D. Rumelhart, J. McClelland, and the PDP Research Group, 1986, Cambridge, MA: MIT. Copyright 1986 by MIT. Reprinted by permission.

Such groups of hidden units produce a "modularity" in information processing, since units within modules can be readily accessed when a module is currently active. One can have many layers of connections between sensory input and   internal concepts; similarly, many layers may exist between internal units and motor responses. Hidden units also allow connectionist theorists to explain many properties of symbolic architectures as by-products of such layers of connections.

Knowledge Representation.   Connectionist architectures conceive of knowledge as being represented in the weighted *connections among neurons,* not in a value stored at some specific memory location—hence the term *distributed* in PDP models. In such systems, a mental state corresponds to a pattern of activation among neurons, and this activation pattern is the content of memory. Alternative contents are simply alternative patterns of activation, and information is retrieved from memory by re-instatement of prior patterns of activation (Rumelhart, 1989). This conceptualization of knowledge contrasts with symbolic architectures that represent knowledge as the content of a particular memory location or bin that must be accessed to be used. Interestingly, symbolic architectures imply that memory content exists irrespective of the activating source. For example, co-worker behaviors are preserved in symbolic form in an observer's memory after they are observed and interpreted. Connectionist architectures, on the other hand, imply that the contents of memory may exist only in the presence of an appropriate activating source. Thus, some memory patterns may be accessible only through external cues, some may require internal cues, and others may require a combination of internal and external cues. Since accessing information in memory may often require the presence of appropriate external cues, it may be difficult for workers to mentally simulate or describe some aspects of their job, yet these same aspects can be easily performed in their normal context of work activities.

Implicit Versus Explicit Knowledge. In connectionist models, knowledge is *implicit* in the structure of the devices that carry out information processing tasks, that is, in the pattern of interrelationships among units. Implicit knowledge is diffusely represented in the processing system itself and may be used without any awareness of this knowledge. In

contrast, *explicit* knowledge pertains to knowledge that is consciously retrieved or transformed by mental operations.

The implicit versus explicit knowledge distinction has a direct analogy to industrial and organizational psychologists' concern with the perceived intercorrelations of rating dimensions, or in other terms, illusory halo. Such work posits that through the process of rating traits or behaviors, raters produce ratings that are more similar than actual stimulus covariances would justify (Cooper, 1981a). Halo is often thought to be produced by explicit or conscious symbolic activity of raters. For example, it has been attributed to naive theories of personality, which are typically defined as beliefs about which personality dimensions are highly correlated. A related explanation of halo is in terms of subjects' ratings of the conceptual similarity among dimensions (Cooper, 1981b), which is also a symbolic process. We suggest that halo can be produced by a different process—knowledge (connections) implicit in the processing mechanism, that is, knowledge implicit in raters' interpretive and memory structures. When making ratings, factors, such as goals, context, stimulus characteristics, or individual differences in raters, that activate one concept will also tend to activate closely connected concepts, and these same factors will inhibit concepts that are not usually associated, thereby producing illusory halo.

Our suggestion that halo is produced by properties implicit in the human processing mechanism is consistent with several findings from the industrial and organizational literature. Recent work shows that illusory correlations can overestimate the associations in stimulus dimensions that are weakly correlated, or illusory correlations can underestimate the correlations in highly correlated stimulus material (Murphy & Jako, 1989; Murphy & Reynolds, 1988). In connectionist architectures, interrelations among units are built up with experience so that the pattern of connections that exists in memory could be stronger or weaker than the pattern present in any specific stimulus being rated. Explaining halo in terms of implicit connections implies that rating distortions may (Cooper, 1981b) or may not (Kozlowski & Kirsch, 1987; Murphy & Jako, 1989) be predicted by subjects' *explicit* (symbolically based) ratings of conceptual similarity, because implicit and explicit knowledge may often be independent (Schacter, 1987, 1989), arising from distinct memory systems and perhaps even from cognitive architectures that involve different levels of organization. Another implication of connectionist explanation for halo is that we would expect implicit correlations to match actual correlations only when raters have extensive experience with situations similar to those being rated. This matching should occur because connectionist units can be "tuned" to a specific pattern of inputs with extensive experience and feedback (Rumelhart, 1989). Consistent with this expectation, Kozlowski and Kirsch (1987) found that job knowledge and familiarity with a ratee were significantly correlated with several measures of accuracy. But halo has also been found to *increase* as raters become more familiar with the individual being rated (Jacobs & Kozlowski, 1985). These results may reflect different consequences of learning in connectionist architectures. For familiar patterns, receptor units can amplify activation in memory, producing a kind of recognition response. The same process also fills in missing parts or distorts the input pattern toward the stored pattern (Rumelhart, 1989, p. 148), which would produce greater halo.

Since implicit knowledge is built up over time and is diffusely represented in the processing system itself, one would expect people to have little awareness and little direct control of this knowledge. Thus, we may not know how or even that we generalize from one dimension to another; we may have no awareness that we automatically relate categories such as male and leader, thereby attributing being male as a characteristic of leadership. Similarly, we may often rely on implicit processes like intuition to make decisions (Isenberg, 1989) or to make social and task-related evaluations. Limitations in awareness are quite consistent with connectionist architectures because they do not assume people have any conscious access to the microlevel operations that connect one unit or one layer of units to another. Instead, conscious access is gained only when an entire pattern is activated. Limitations in awareness are more difficult to explain by symbolic architectures because these architectures imply people have conscious access to the operations producing cognitions (retrieval, transformation, and storage of symbol structures).

Accessing Information in Memory.   Thinking in terms of connectionist architectures is helpful for understanding how we might access information in memory using pattern recognition processes. Since connectionist units have "gap filling" capacities and can complete partially presented patterns through a process called *settling-in* or *relaxing* (which is described in more detail in a later section on memory schema), memory cues that only approximate the pattern the module is tuned to detect can still be effective. Imperfect cues can activate memory, but they may also take longer to settle in or activate a more appropriate pattern. Thus, when cues are imperfect, memory may be less "available" than when better fitting cues are used. We have not seen any discussion of availability (Tversky & Kahneman, 1974) in terms of this settling-in process, but it seems likely that connectionist principles pertain to this issue as well. This settling-in process also produces a built-in *goodness-of-fit* measure, which is the extent to which a cue creates the maximum possible activation in a receiving module (Rumelhart, Smolensky, McClelland, & Hinton, 1986, pp. 16–17). As will later be discussed, goodness of fit may be important in explaining how people categorize, or select among several potentially appropriate memory units.

Another key notion in explaining memory search is the idea of content-addressable memory—features of a person such as voice quality or facial features can directly activate a memory store corresponding to that person, allowing us to recognize instantly the person with no apparent search through memory. Content-addressable memories are found in both symbolic architectures, such as Wyer and Srull's (1980) bin model or Anderson's (1983a, 1987) ACT* architecture, as well as in connectionist architectures. However, symbolic architectures can explain this process only in a general way, that is, by acknowledging that certain cues automatically access the correct memory locations. Connectionist architectures provide a more specific way to conceptualize content-addressable memory, which works for both symbolic and nonsymbolic types of cues, and that is as a spreading of activation from sensory units activated by a stimuli such as a face to a *module* "tuned" to respond to this pattern of activation. Retrieval involves the completion of a pattern initiated by an external stimulus. When a unit is sufficiently activated, it captures attention and also activates or inhibits other related memory information, affecting the availability of this information.

Consequences of Parallel Processing. Researchers concerned with connectionist architectures emphasize that, as compared with serial processing, parallel processing allows rapid performance on complex tasks. However, the notion of parallel processing has broader implications for understanding how cognitions interrelate in producing organizational behaviors. The assumption that parallel processing can occur raises the possibility that multiple types of inputs are used simultaneously in producing organizational behaviors.

This possibility contrasts with explanations based on symbolic architectures and suggests new ways of thinking about many practical topics. For example, when interacting with a co-worker, one may simultaneously process verbal behavior, nonverbal behavior, affective cues, task information, cultural norms, past experience, and current attitudes in producing cognitions or behavior. Furthermore, perceivers may not be aware that all of these sources of information influence processing.

Another important consequence concerns the impact of cognitive architectures on theory development. Researchers tend to develop explanations of organizational phenomena based on their understanding of how people process information. Serial symbolic processing models implement cognitive operations in discrete steps, implying that theoretical explanations of such processes should specify how one step leads to another. For example, some theories of problem solving posit that there are discrete steps such as problem definition, generation of alternatives, evaluation of alternatives, choice of solutions, and implementation planning. Understanding problem solving, then, involves understanding how individuals move from one step to another. Similarly, theories attempting to explain turnover intentions (e.g., Mobley, Griffeth, Hand, & Meglino, 1979) might posit that task perceptions based on objective task (or social) information produce affective reactions such as satisfaction or organizational commitment. These affective reactions, in turn, lead to turnover intentions. Such theoretical explanations often treat dissatisfaction as a mediating process (Michaels & Spector, 1982; Williams & Hazer, 1986), though Farkas and Tetrick (1989) suggest that reciprocal or cyclical relationships are also important.

Connectionist processing, however, implies that the cognitive operations producing many behaviors in organizations may occur simultaneously, thus providing an alternative theoretical perspective. For example, in problem solving, problems may be defined while alternative problem solutions are constructed and evaluated (Eisenhardt, 1989; Nutt, 1984), particularly when experts solve problems (Glaser, 1989). Similarly, turnover intentions, job perceptions, and affective reactions may all emerge through reciprocal, mutually activating, parallel processes because they are connected to each other in memory. It is not the symbols that are connected, but the numerous neural-like units that form the basis for the symbols that are richly connected through multiple paths. If this interpretation is correct, separation of job perceptions, affect, and intentions into independent constructs may be an artificial and misleading description of underlying processes. The description of these processes is at the wrong (symbolic) level. The strong relationship between job perceptions, affect, and turnover intentions may reflect connections at a much deeper, neurally based level. Following this logic, attempts to use affect as a critical mediating variable may be misdirected.

One consequence of treating simultaneously interacting constructs as being independent and serially related is the potential for causality to operate in directions counter to one's underlying serially based theory, which assumes that job perceptions cause affect, which in turn causes turnover intentions. Interestingly, several studies show that manipulated affect influences job perceptions (Adler, Skov, & Salvemini, 1985; Kraiger, Billings, & Isen, 1989) and that turnover intentions of new hires influences later job satisfaction (Doran, Stone, Brief, & George, 1991). Rather than illustrating "reverse causality" in an otherwise appropriate symbolic serial model, such effects might reflect the operation of highly integrated parallel processes at a much more micro level.

Expert versus novice differences in processing can also be better understood by considering the implications of parallel processing for how cognitions are sequenced.

Novices emphasize symbolic processes that involve a large portion of working memory, and so they must proceed sequentially to maximize use of limited working memory. Use of surface features to categorize a problem may be temporally separated from the processes that use categorization to generate problem responses (Glaser & Chi, 1988). Experts, however, may simultaneously use surface features, deeper principles, or response dimensions (Glaser, 1989) to characterize a problem and often simultaneously solve it. Much more information is brought to bear on problem interpretation, so problem solving becomes more of a perceptual process than an analytical activity. Experts are able to bring together diverse types of information and responses automatically because these types of information are interrelated through connections built up through experience.

In short, the parallel processing suggested by connectionist architectures has some very general implications for conceptualizing cognitive activities. Cognitive processes driving human activities are not always packaged in discrete, symbolic (higher level) units that cleanly segment perceptions, affect, cognitions, or motor activities into separate components that either affect or are affected by each other in a sequential manner, as suggested by a symbolic architecture. Instead, perceptions, affect, cognitions, and motor activities may simultaneously be active and interact in producing cognitive activities, as suggested by a connectionist architecture. For example, theories of emotion assert that cognitive, physiological, perceptual, and motor components interact in producing affective experience (Leventhal, 1984). We expect that people will have difficulty developing introspective explanations of such parallel processes and may prefer more ambiguous labels such as feelings or intuition. People may also be unable to describe in symbolic terms many of the factors involved in forming an intention or affective reaction. Thus, our ability to explain such processes using symbolically based self-descriptive measures may be inherently limited. On the other hand, some issues may be better addressed at a symbolic level, such as reasoning, problem solving on unfamiliar tasks, and conscious monitoring and control of cognitive processes. However, the issue of what types of activities are better explained at a symbolic versus connectionist level is as yet unresolved and is at the heart of the debate between these two views of cognitive science.

Sequential Control of Activity.   Though connectionist architectures emphasize parallel processing, the same principles used to explain parallel processing can produce serial behavior when serial activities are required by a task. Sequential control of behavior or thoughts can be explained in connectionist architectures in terms of a pattern of activation or inhibition flowing from early activities to later activities. This pattern, of course, is based on connections learned from past experience. Sequential activities are often required due to physical and motor constraints that force us to do one activity after another rather than simultaneously—for example, we cannot turn a door knob until we have grasped it; we cannot say two words at the same time. Thus, to adequately control behavior, a cognitive system must be able to sequence behaviors and appropriately integrate each behavior with environmental perceptions. (See Allport, 1989, for a more comprehensive discussion of this issue in relation to selective attention.) In addition to explaining how behavior unfolds over time, we suggest that the delaying, or inhibiting, aspect of earlier activities on later activities is a general control device that can also explain why pursuing one goal *automatically* inhibits the pursuit of another goal (Kuhl, 1986) or why classifying an individual using one construct (honest) might inhibit classification in partially contradictory terms (greedy).

This sequencing capability of connectionist systems is most easily illustrated by work modeling motor activities. Rumelhart and Norman (1982) simulated a skilled typist using the system shown in Figure 2, which explains how one would type the word *very*. Such systems have shown considerable success in predicting different times for keystrokes and also for predicting errors that are likely to be made.

As explained by McClelland, Rumelhart, and Hinton (1986, pp. 14–16), the system in Figure 2 assumes that the decision to type a word activates a unit for that word, which in turn activates units for each letter. However, the letters are not all typed at once because the first letter also inhibits the units for the second, third, and fourth letters, and so on. As a result of this combination of activation and inhibition among letters, the first letter is most highly activated, and units for other letters are only partially activated. The actual keypress for a letter causes a strong inhibition signal to be sent to the unit for the letter just typed, which both removes this letter from further consideration and removes the inhibition on successive letters. This makes the unit for the next letter highest in activation, producing a motor activity corresponding to the appropriate keystroke, deactivating that unit, and increasing the activation of successive units. The system repeats, successively activating appropriate letters and words.

It is important to note that while the motor activities are serial, the pattern of activation of units is a parallel process. If such processes did not occur in parallel, skilled typists would not be able to achieve speeds in excess of 80 words per minute. This speed translates roughly into 125 milliseconds per keystroke, which is too fast for a serial system. More detailed analyses of motor activity also show this parallel effect. For example, since *v* and *er* correspond to different rows on the typewriter keypad, the hand movement towards the *v* in *very* is less than if *v* is typed in isolation. This is because the hand movement for *v* is inhibited by the partial activation of *er*, which requires the hand to move in the opposite direction.

FIGURE 2

The Interaction of Activations in Typing the Word "Very"

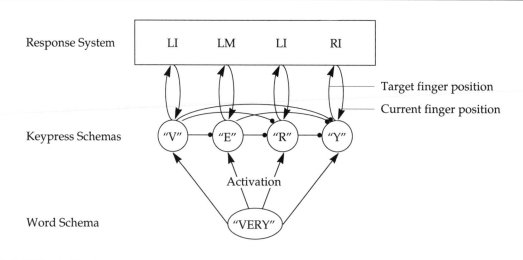

Note: The "very" unit is activated from outside the model. It in turn activates the units for each of the component letters. Each letter unit specifies the target finger positions, specified in a keyboard coordinate system. L and R stand for the left and right hands, and I amd M for the index and middle fingers. The letter units receive information about the current finger position from the response system. Each letter unit inhibits the activation of all letter units that follow it in the word. Inhibitory connections are indicated by the lines with solid dots at their terminations.

From "Simulating a Skilled Typist: A Study of Skilled Motor Performance" by D. E. Rumelhart and D. A. Norman, 1982, *Cognitive Science, 6*, p. 12. Copyright 1982 by Ablex Publishing Corporation. Adapted by permission.

Because these analyses show that all letters in a word have a simultaneous effect on the motor movements involved in typing each letter, an explanation of typing based on parallel processing is superior to explanations based on serial symbolic architectures.

This example, based on the work of Rumelhart and Norman (1982), illustrates how connectionist architectures that are parallel processing devices can be used to control motor activities that occur in a serial manner. The implications of such capacities are more general, however, for they suggest that many other processes that occur in a serial fashion, such as motor activities, eye movements, attention, thinking, intentions, and behaviors,

could be similarly controlled by a connectionist architecture. Thus, the microstructure of cognitive processes involved in using scripts to generate behavior in familiar contexts (Gioia & Poole, 1984; Lord & Kernan, 1987) may be a parallel, connectionist architecture. Similarly, motivational processes may be controlled by such a parallel device. One issue in understanding how we maintain motivation on a specific task is how we suppress attention to other competing tasks or goals. Suppressing attention to low priority goals until higher priority goals have been attained can be explained in a manner analogous to Rumelhart and Norman's (1982) model of how we suppress the finger movements required to type a particular letter until the prior letter has been typed. That is, the suppression occurs through inhibitory connections from high to low priority goals. Thus, maintaining motivation on a specific task does not require an explanation based on symbolic processes such as valence-instrumentality-expectancy (VIE) theory.

In general, connectionist architectures have proved to be very successful in such areas as modeling motor movement like typing, perceptions, and some types of learning (Kehoe, 1988) and in using constraint satisfaction networks to define and model schemas (Rumelhart, Hinton, & McClelland, 1986). The value of connectionist architectures in explaining higher level activities is not so clear, but even the critics of connectionist architectures (Fodor & Pylyshyn, 1988) recognize their value as an explanation of the *microstructure* underlying symbolic cognitive architectures.

Relevance to Industrial and Organizational Psychology. Issues pertaining to microstructures of cognition may not appear important to industrial and organizational psychologists concerned with more global issues. However, if we take a deeper look at most areas of applied interest, we frequently find that problems of practical concern pertain to issues that involve microstructures. For example, work on strategic decision making in organizations employs many constructs that may be explainable in terms of the type of microstructures already discussed. Brief and Downey (1983) discuss the effects of implicit theories of CEOs; Hambrick and Mason (1984) discuss the effects of processes such as limited attention, selective perceptions, and idiosyncratic interpretations of environments on strategic choice of top management; Dutton and Jackson (1987) show how cognitive categories associated with threats or opportunities can influence many processes related to strategic decision making; and Porac and Thomas (1990) link strategic decision making to

categorizations of competitors. Each of these processes may involve the very fast, automatic, and intuitive aspects of cognition associated with connectionist architectures. In other words, when decision makers intuitively solve problems, it may be that their understanding of the problem activates a potential solution because of the numerous connections between microlevel problem features and aspects of solutions, not because explicit conscious operations link representations to solutions at the symbolic level. This implies that conscious control has a smaller role in producing strategic decisions than is typically assumed.

Another important consequence of cognitive architecture research is the recognition that information processing reflects the joint influence of symbolic and connectionist architectures as they functionally interface with the task and social environments. Work behavior takes place in situations that activate connectionist as well as symbolic processing. Yet symbolic processes have received primary emphasis by industrial and organizational psychologists in attempts to understand behavior in work situations. Topic areas such as motivation, attitude-behavior research, and training are often based on symbolically oriented techniques. We suspect that techniques emphasizing only the symbolic perspective will have limited applied value—motivational theories will not predict well, behavior will not be closely related to attitudes, and training will not be optimal or applied back on the job. In a more general sense, the attitude-behavior paradox may simply reflect the fact that conscious attitudes occur at a symbolic level but behavior is produced by both symbolic and connectionist processes. In short, industrial and organizational techniques that emphasize only symbolic processes may be insufficient to understand or predict behavior in organizations.

A clear example of this problem can be seen in individual differences research, which relies heavily on symbolically based self-assessment techniques. The low predictability of individual differences has been attributed to strong situations (Weiss & Adler, 1984), but it is also understandable if symbolically based personality assessment techniques miss many aspects of connectionist processes that affect behavior in most work situations. For example, we might expect executives who have a high tolerance for ambiguity to function better in uncertain organizational situations than executives who have a low tolerance. However, the types of events labeled ambiguous by executives depend on connectionist level processes. For experienced executives, factors associated with strategic change may be obvious, whereas for less experienced executives, these same factors may be very ambiguous. If researchers try to predict executive performance solely on the basis of tolerance for ambiguity, they will not predict behavior very well.

Motivational research could also benefit from work designed to bridge the gap between symbolic and connectionist architectures. Many motivational theories posit "multilevel" explanations of behavior, which may involve processing best described by symbolic and connectionist architectures. For example, Vallacher and Wegner (1987) posit that task behaviors are defined (identified) at multiple levels, with the level that receives conscious attention (the prepotent level) varying both with task experience and with momentary disruptions in performance. Similarly, control theories (Carver & Scheier, 1981; Klein, 1989; Lord & Hanges, 1987; Powers, 1973) posit that hierarchies of control loops are involved in explaining behavior. Like action identification theory, control theories usually posit that attention moves down levels when lower level discrepancies are addressed (e.g., Lord & Kernan, 1987), but conscious control is never pushed all the way down to the bottom of such hierarchies. For example, we rarely consciously control skeletal movements in doing tasks, and we do not think of the muscle tensions required for such movements.

It is convenient to argue that motivational processes at lower hierarchical levels are simply handled automatically as a result of practice, but we think this is an inadequate explanation. It is more reasonable to suggest that at some point a transition to a connectionist architecture occurs. This assertion implies that at some lower level in hierarchies, sensory inputs and potential responses are processed in parallel, learning and practice are reflected in appropriately weighted (connected) hidden units, basic cognitive operations differ, and activation-based control structures are used. We have already shown how patterns of activation and inhibition could sequentially activate appropriate steps in well-learned schema (recall our description of Rumelhart & Norman's, 1982, connectionist model of typing behavior). Such elementary control structures, when coupled with basic operations such as content-addressable memory, may lead to quite different views of motivation at more neurally related levels than the symbolically based explanations (e.g., Klein, 1989) typically applied to higher levels.

Symbolic Versus Connectionist Architectures

Considerable debate currently exists concerning which type of architecture is more appropriate to represent human cognition (Fodor & Pylyshyn, 1988). But as illustrated by the previous discussion, we see no reason to assume that human cognitive capacities involve only one architecture. A point that is often ignored by individuals debating the issue of the "correct" architecture for understanding human cognition is that human cognitive abilities have evolved to include many specific and functionally unique systems (Sperry & Schacter, 1987). Thus, *multiple* cognitive architectures may be appropriate for understanding human behavior. It seems reasonable to assert that symbolic and connectionist architectures coexist and correspond to different physical phenomena and different time scales. Both may be required to accomplish different functional requirements in human behavior. For example, simultaneous accomplishment of some actions using controlled processes and others using automatic processes may be accomplished by simultaneous use of different architectures. The distinction between automatic and controlled processing depends on the relative importance of symbolic and connectionist level operations, with controlled processing emphasizing more symbolic processes and automatic processing emphasizing more connectionist processes. Thus, the level of analysis may be critical in explaining phenomena of interest.

The assertion that there are multiple architectures to consider implies that behavior in organizational and social settings may involve a blend of cognitive activity types. It further suggests that debate over which architecture is *the* correct architecture for understanding information processing activity should be replaced with a concern for how processes using different architectures might interact and how this could facilitate or impede intelligent behavior. Cognitive psychologists have not adequately considered this possibility, and there has been little work concerned with how different architectures may interrelate (Norman, 1986; Simon & Kaplan, 1989, p. 8). This issue needs to be addressed by cognitive scientists, and it is central to understanding how people working in organizations accomplish multiple work and social activities.

Assessing Cognitive Architectures

The distinction between symbolic and connectionist architectures is provocative, and yet there is a danger for our field if these distinctions are used as theoretical constructs with no concern for how they can be operationalized. Assessing a particular type of cognitive architecture is very challenging methodologically, but Newell et al. (1989, p. 101) have provided some useful suggestions. They observe that a system's cognitive architecture is an important, but often hidden, determinant of behavior and assert that cognition is always the result of the architecture plus the contents of memory, combined under a press to be adaptive in a specific task environment. But the inner structure is often hidden and only knowledge-level behavior is revealed. This makes appreciation or assessment of cognitive architectures difficult, but not impossible.

Cognitive architectures are revealed in many ways—speed of processing, memory errors, linguistic slips, perceptual illusions, failures of rationality in decision making, and interference effects of learned material, to name a few (Newell et al., 1989, p. 101). Since some of these types of "errors" are often the direct concern of industrial and organizational psychologists, we assert that our field needs to consider more carefully the cognitive architecture underlying the human competencies with which they are concerned.

Newell et al. offer several strategies for analysis of architectures. First, observe reaction times and identify behaviors that are very fast. If there is little time to process information, then the results are more likely to reflect the system's underlying architecture, rather than a series of processing steps. They also suggest that automatic behavior is more likely to reflect primitive operations indicative of the system's underlying architecture. A second approach is to look for universal regularities or phenomena that occur over a wide range of situations. One such regularity is that performance on any task improves according to the power law of the number of trials, which can be explained by an underlying architecture (Rosenbloom & Newell, 1986).

We should emphasize that complex behaviors are often the result of multiple factors that include both connectionist and symbolic architectures as well as complexity resulting from the adaptation to a complex task environment. As Simon (1990) notes, "human rational behavior (and the rational behavior of all physical symbol systems) is shaped by a scissors whose two blades are the structure of task environments and the computational capabilities of the actor" (p. 7). If one can specify the complexity of a task in terms of the information processing requirements it places on individuals, one should also be able to specify the computational capabilities of individuals by observing the extent to which they behave intelligently on standardized tasks. For example, Campbell (1988) developed a typology of characteristics that can be related both to task complexity and the cognitive demands of the person performing the task. He suggests that three factors—amount of information load, diversity, and rate of change—can be used to describe task complexity and cognitive demands using corresponding terms. Such frameworks may help researchers identify both the characteristics of task environments and the abilities of individuals that lead to intelligent behavior.

Memory

Understanding memory is important to industrial and organizational psychologists for three reasons. First, memory provides a storehouse of information that is crucial in performing organizational tasks. Thus, understanding how we store or retrieve information from memory is required to improve practice in areas such as performance appraisal, training, and decision making. Second, memory provides a work space for performing cognitive tasks. Ways in which memory limits task performance, and ways to overcome memory limitations are important to our field. Third, the internal operation of memory processes may provide a control structure that guides information processing activities. In any task, be it rating behavior, problem solving, or motor activity, the sequencing of perceptions, thoughts, and overt behaviors is highly

dependent on the information and goals that are currently active in working memory and on the knowledge structures that can be most easily accessed from this information.

In this section research related to three areas of concern in memory are covered— memory as a data storage device, memory as a resource used in task performance, and memory as an aspect of a control structure. Research that questions conventional thinking in these areas and research that is relevant to industrial and organizational psychologists is also summarized.

Before continuing this discussion, two terms need to be addressed—*activation* and *networks*. *Activation* is a momentary process based on an energy analogy that is closely related to the idea of attention (Kahneman, 1973). Information with high activation can be found quickly and reliably in memory. Activation must be maintained either from environmental information entering memory through sensory stores or through processes such as rehearsal; otherwise, information fades from attention. Long-term memory is often conceptualized as a *network* linking concepts or propositions (Anderson, 1983b; Collins & Quillian, 1969). In such networks, information is retrieved by the parallel spread of activation from highly activated to less activated nodes in a memory network. Thus, sensory input and the contents of working memory, which are highly activated long-term memory nodes, affect what can be easily accessed from long-term memory. This idea is similar to the notion of activation spreading through a connectionist architecture.

Anderson (1983b) found that the time to retrieve information depends on its level of activation. Anderson's thinking focuses on the effects of explicit, conscious processing on spreading activation. However, implicit memory effects, as well as other nonconscious effects such as priming (Higgins & Bargh, 1987), suggest that activation may spread through networks in an implicit, unconscious manner. For example, several studies show that nonconscious search through memory networks may be an important component in producing many motor activities (Jordon & Rosenbaum, 1989; Sternberg, Monsell, Knoll, & Wright, 1978).

Input and Retrieval of Information From Memory

Input and retrieval functions of memory are important for our field because our predominant methodology is to use people as measuring devices. Self-report measures, evaluations of others in leadership or performance appraisal areas, descriptions of behaviors or organizational characteristics, and numerous other types of measures require accurate retrieval from memory. Recognizing that accuracy in rating is dependent on memory processes, industrial and organizational psychologists have developed many techniques that are based on the logic that more extensive processing of social or task-relevant information will produce more accurate memory for this information. For example, diary keeping (Bernardin & Walter, 1977; DeNisi, Robbins, & Cafferty, 1989), traditional use of behaviorally anchored rating scales (BARS; Bernardin & Smith, 1981; Smith & Kendall, 1963), prototype anchored rating scales (PARS; Hauenstein & Foti, 1989), frame-of-reference training (Athey & McIntyre, 1987; Bernardin & Buckley, 1981; Pulakos, 1984, 1986), and rater observational training (Thornton & Zorich, 1980) all attempt to produce more elaborate (and/or better quality) encoding of stimulus material, which is to be rated at a later time.

The effectiveness of such techniques is supported by many memory studies that show that more extensive encoding of stimulus material aids retrieval. Having subjects elaborate information more thoroughly at encoding may generally be effective because more potential retrieval cues are provided and subjects are allowed to infer information that

cannot be remembered (Anderson, 1990, pp. 181–182). For example, techniques such as having subjects complete a sentence or rate the pleasantness of work can enhance recall. Such effects are also consistent with Craik and Lockhart's (1972) notion that information would be recalled better if it were processed at a deeper, more meaningful level. This idea has been directly incorporated into industrial and organizational psychological research concerned with rater accuracy. Athey and McIntyre (1987) suggest that frame-of-reference training is more successful than other types of training because it produces a "cognitively more elaborate and meaningful source of information for raters" (p. 571). Similar thinking has guided concern with more automatic processes such as categorization as being a source of rating error, in part, because it involves superficial or incomplete processing of observed behavior (DeNisi & Williams, 1988; Ilgen & Feldman, 1983; Lord, 1985). Such thinking also implies that more controlled, effortful encoding processes will produce greater accuracy.

Though this research is correct in noting that encoding affects later memory, it is an incomplete explanation of the process. Another theoretical approach to understanding retrieval was developed by Tulving (e.g.,Tulving & Thompson, 1973), which helps us qualify the effects of encoding, or elaboration, on memory. Tulving argued that *encoding-retrieval interactions* were the key issue in understanding memory accuracy. Memory researchers have consistently found that retrieval of information from long-term memory is much more likely when the retrieval conditions, or cues, match the conditions under which information was encoded. (Schacter, 1989, provides a thorough review of this research.) This encoding-retrieval interaction is important for understanding when we can accurately retrieve factual information, such as remembering whether an employee exhibited a particular behavior. This interaction implies that more elaborate encoding of information will be beneficial only to the extent that retrieval cues are able to reinstate the encoding context. Thus, intervention techniques that attempt to align encoding and retrieval processes should be much more effective than techniques that merely attempt to produce more extensive or more meaningful encoding. Intervention techniques should be most effective if they create encoding frames that match frames used when making social judgments, as has been shown for diary-keeping (DeNisi, Robbins, & Cafferty, 1989) and frame-of-reference training (Hauenstein & Foti, 1989). However, the potential for such interventions is inherently limited because such retrieval techniques provide only symbolic level cues, whereas both symbolic and connectionist level processes create the encoding context.

Encoding-retrieval interactions are quite robust, pertaining to the effects of mood, physical features, or semantic meaning of the information to be remembered. Bower (1981), for example, consistently finds that information is recalled better if the mood at recall matches the mood at encoding. This research suggests that supervisors who are in a good mood when appraising their subordinates may be better able to access favorable behavioral or performance information, while those in a bad mood may have relatively greater access to unfavorable information. Physical (Fisher & Craik, 1977; Morris, Bransford, & Franks, 1977) or phonetic (Stein, 1978) features of words can also serve as powerful retrieval cues when subjects encode information in terms of physical or phonetic features; similarly, semantic cues can help subjects retrieve information that is semantically encoded. While we know of no information generalizing such findings to work situations, we expect that physical features of people are so salient that they would provide a powerful set of indexing cues. Such rich cues would be absent when we complete a behavioral description questionnaire because the individuals being rated are unlikely to be present. Thus, descriptions (or expectations) about workers may be dependent on context. The superiority of physical or phonetic encoding, when paired with similar retrieval cues, provided devastating evidence against Craik and Lockhart's (1972) depth of processing theory, which posited that information that was encoded more deeply (semantically) should always be better recalled. Semantic encoding is superior only when retrieval cues are semantically based. (See Nelson, 1977, for other criticisms of Craik and Lockhart's theory.)

The implications of this line of memory research are nicely illustrated in a study by McKelvey and Lord (1986). They found that encoding processes designed to increase elaboration (periodic breaks to take notes) resulted in improved memory accuracy only when matched with very similar retrieval cues (having subjects write out summaries of the interaction prior to making behavioral ratings). Contrary to their initial hypotheses, McKelvey and Lord (1986) also found that less effortful procedures, such as encoding in terms of context-appropriate categories, produced memory that was generally *more accurate*, particularly when matched with similar retrieval conditions. This encoding-retrieval interaction suggests that naturally occurring schemas may provide a powerful aid to accurate memory if they relate to schemas used during retrieval. However, inappropriate schemas can be a major source of distortions in memory. Retraining that produces more normative schemas may be an effective means to create consensus in social judgments, as suggested by work on retraining performance appraisal prototypes (Hauenstein & Foti, 1989).

Though not phrased in such terms, encoding-retrieval interactions are also relevant to topics other than rating behavior. For example, the literature on decision making and problem solving often characterizes information processing as using a very small sample of potentially relevant information that is cued by task or contextual features. This notion of bounded rationality has existed in the work on organizational decision making (March & Simon, 1958) for a number of years. Framing (Tversky & Kahneman, 1981) involves similar effects. One interpretation of decision frames (Beach, 1990) is that they are task-specific knowledge domains cued by relevant aspects of tasks or contexts. Thus, framing or bounded rationality in decision making can also be conceptualized as an encoding-retrieval interaction. In other words, limitations in the information that can be accessed given currently salient retrieval cues are the source of framing effects and part of the reason for bounded rationality.

Task Performance and Memory

A second reason for industrial and organizational psychologists to be interested in memory is that working memory provides a general workspace that is used in a variety of tasks related to job performance: problem solving, decision making, social interaction, and other symbolic processing operations. Most research in these areas focuses on the processing constraints associated with the limited attentional capacity of human memory or the limited amount of information that can be held in a short-term store. More recent work has emphasized *working memory*, which is defined as that portion of long-term memory that is currently active, rather than as a separate limited-capacity central memory register.

Awareness of memory constraints has served as a basis for several types of research in industrial and organizational psychology. It is associated with concerns over resource-dependent versus resource-independent tasks (Ackerman, 1987), motivational research that focuses on allocation of attentional capacity (Kanfer & Ackerman, 1989), and interest in heuristic versus "rational" decision-making processes (Lord & Maher, 1990; Nisbett & Ross,

1980; Tversky & Kahneman, 1974). Another relevant line of research focuses on individual differences in this limited memory capacity, suggesting such differences may provide a basis for personnel selection for resource-dependent tasks. Concern with memory constraints also relates to the debate on whether the validities of measures of general ability are stable over time (Ackerman, 1987; Barrett, Caldwell, & Alexander, 1989; Fleishman & Mumford, 1989; Henry & Hulin, 1987; Murphy, 1989). Arguments that general ability becomes less critical as skill develops are directly based on the idea that limited cognitive resources (working memory capacity) become less critical as skill develops. In short, working memory capacity is an issue germane to a substantial body of industrial and organizational work in our field.

Three developments in the literature on memory and information processing lead us to question the utility of viewing short-term memory as having a limited, unitary attentional capacity. First, research arising from both an evolutionary and a physiological perspective suggests that the human brain is not aptly described as a homogenous, single-capacity processing mechanism. The brain is better characterized as a network of processing devices that are dedicated to particular types of tasks or particular functions. Most tasks, especially complex tasks, are performed through communication and cooperation among these subprocessing units. For example, relying on neurobehavioral evidence, Allport (1989) states that "spatial attention is a distributed function in which many functionally differentiated structures participate, rather than a function controlled uniquely by a single center" (p. 644). Second, considerable research indicates that there are separate implicit and explicit memory capacities (Schacter, 1987), which are both used to perform tasks. Third, recent theorizing by Baddeley (1986) and Allport (1989) suggests that more complex conceptualizations of working memory are required. Particularly important is their argument that working memory is not a unitary capacity system. In this section, we review research related to each of these three developments and discuss the implications of this work for industrial and organizational psychology.

Multiprocessor Views of Human Processing Capacity.   Much of the information processing work in the past 25 years has emphasized explicit, conscious symbolic processing, and therefore emphasized the reliance on a limited-capacity working (short-term) memory in performing cognitive tasks. However, other lines of thinking suggest that cognitive capacities involved in processing tasks are much more diffuse. Working from an evolutionary perspective, Sperry and Schacter (1987) argue that the human brain has developed by adding new components and processing capacities that perform the specific functional requirement of adaptive tasks. The consequence is that people have many fairly specific processing capacities rather than a single uniform processing capacity implied by a symbolic system. Biologically based research (Allen, 1983; Sejnowski & Churchland, 1989) has developed a similar view of human processing capacity. Allen argues that the brain is best characterized as comprised of many *subprocessors,* which interact in a cooperative manner when people perform complex tasks. Because some of these processing capacities developed early in evolutionary terms, we should not expect all subprocessors to be geared toward symbolic processing capacity.

To the extent that task performance relies on nonsymbolic processing, which does not use our limited attentional capacities, it should not be constrained by the type of processing capacities on which much industrial and organizational work has focused (e.g., general intellectual ability or verbal intelligence). In addition, to the extent that jobs can be designed to use multiple processing capacities

rather than a single one, tasks can be made less resource dependent. This possibility has already been applied in much of the engineering psychology research (e.g., Wickens, 1984); however, this work has emphasized the trade-offs between visual and auditory processing at the *symbolic* level. The major trade-off in work tasks may be between symbolic-level and connectionist-level processing, which may depend on experience. The capacity for nonsymbolic-level processing also leads one to question whether selection based on general intellectual ability may be necessary. Work showing the importance of implicit as well as explicit memory processes in task performance, which is covered in the next section, is also consistent with this view of distributed rather than unitary information processing capacities.

Explicit and Implicit Memory.   Most memory research, such as that reviewed in the prior section on input and retrieval of information, requires that subjects explicitly reference and consciously recollect prior material. Such procedures involve *explicit memory.* However, recent research indicates that people (and other animals) also possess implicit memories. *Implicit memory* does not involve conscious recollections or explicit references to prior experience. Instead, it is usually inferred from the facilitation of performance on a memory or skill-related task (e.g., priming effects). Schacter (1987, 1989) presents several types of evidence that indicate that explicit and implicit memories are functionally distinct (dissociated) and that performance related to implicit and explicit memories is independent.

Currently there is considerable debate as to the underlying causes of the functional independence of explicit and implicit memory. Schacter (1989) argues that research is most consistent with the interpretation that explicit and implicit memories are supported by physically distinct information processing systems. One interesting line of research consistent with this view shows that amnesic patients, whose explicit memory is severely impaired because of disease or physical trauma, have more normally functioning implicit memory, which allows the gradual learning of many skills. However, Roediger (1990) takes a contrary position, arguing that many dissociations can be understood by using general principles (encoding-retrieval interactions) that apply to both explicit and implicit memory.

Researchers have labeled the explicit memory *declarative memory* (Schacter, 1989) and the implicit, skill-related memory *procedural memory.* Declarative memory involves the outcome of processing operations that are consciously available (Schacter, 1989, p. 702). Declarative memory is associated more closely with symbolic processing and the operation of working memory. Procedural memory involves the on-line processing involved in performing a task in which knowledge is represented implicitly. Further, such knowledge may not be accessible unless the task is actually being performed. In other words, a person may have a skill or an ability to perform a task but cannot translate this knowledge into symbolic form.

Anderson's work suggests that skill acquisition involves transferring knowledge from declarative to procedural memory. One consequence of this transfer is that with skill development, task performance becomes less dependent on the limitation of working memory. However, with skill development, knowledge may also become less available outside of the actual task performance context. For example, a novice typist may be able to easily state which letters are typed by which fingers, but a skilled typist may no longer be able to articulate this information, although the information is present in memory. Such information may only be accessible when fingers are placed on a keyboard or when one physically simulates key strokes. This example

illustrates that many skilled tasks may be highly dependent on implicit memory that is accessible and can be used only in very specific situations. In these situations, people may have difficulty articulating task-relevant knowledge, though they can use this knowledge to perform tasks.

Roediger (1990) emphasizes a slightly different distinction between explicit and implicit memory. He asserts that the mode of processing required by memory tests—perceptual (data-driven) versus meaning (concept-driven)—is a more important determinant of explicit or implcit memory than the procedural-declarative distinction. His findings show that memory tests that require different modes of processing produce dissociations even when both tests involve procedural or both involve declarative information. Thus, according to Roediger, the perceptual versus meaning mode of processing distinction is actually the crucial factor. Interestingly, Roediger's perceptual-meaning distinction is quite close to the difference between connectionist and symbolic cognitive architectures.

In short, we think explicit knowledge such as verbal information corresponds closely to the capacities of symbolic architectures. Implicit knowledge such as intuition may be more aptly explained by connectionist architectures. Despite these differences, one can think of similar principles as applying to explicit and implicit memory. Both rely on activation levels that vary in strength flowing through networks of connections, and both show encoding-specificity effects.

The distinction between explicit and implicit memory is also of direct relevance to training. Specifically, the notion of implicit learning can provide insight into how training programs can fail or succeed. Many training techniques require the use of a symbolic architecture to process information. Such techniques include lecture, discussion, video, and case histories. These training interventions are often a step removed from actual task performance, which provides experience in the work setting. But such training may miss the component of job performance related to implicit processes (which Berry and Broadbent, 1988, suggest are dependent on general overall pattern-matching processes) that are data-driven. Explicit instruction may direct attention away from crucial inputs necessary to implicit learning, or it may suggest strategies that are less effective than intuitive ideas about how a task should be performed. Berry and Broadbent (1988) stress the role of salience in distinguishing between explicit and implicit learning. They investigated and supported the hypothesis that explicit learning was effective for salient relationships, but nonsalient relationships were learned in an implicit manner. Surprisingly, they also found that explicit cues had *detrimental* effects on transfer of learning across two conceptually similar tasks.

The implications of these findings for training are that explicit and implicit knowledge may have to be created by different processes, and these two types of knowledge may have very different consequences for transfer of training. Formal, symbolically oriented training techniques, such as lectures, may be useful in transferring explicit knowledge, but implicit knowledge may require more experience-based, context-specific training. Berry and Broadbent's (1988) work implies that explicit training may be appropriate for the more salient aspects of jobs, but that less salient aspects may be learned best through on-the-job experience. Attempts to train implicit knowledge with declarative instructions are unlikely to be effective for several reasons. First, it may be difficult to identify the implicit content that needs to be trained, for as Reber (1989) notes, what is held or stored in implicit memory exceeds what can be articulated. Second, and perhaps more important, is the likelihood that trainers may not be able to communicate symbolically information that can be more effectively learned implicitly. In such cases, explicit training may actually

inhibit learning and transfer. As already noted, Berry and Broadbent (1988) found that explicit cues had detrimental effects on transfer of training.

However, symbolically oriented information does not always inhibit transfer. In an influential article, Campione, Brown, and Ferrara (1982) argue that transfer of training is related to subjects' *metacognitive* knowledge. Metacognitive knowledge refers to subjects' conscious knowledge of their own cognitive resources and the fit of these resources with varying task requirements. An additional aspect of metacognitive knowledge concerns people's ability to self-regulate cognitive activities during ongoing problem-solving activities. In terms of the perspective developed in the present chapter, domain-specific skills may involve learning at a connectionist level, but metacognitive skills are primarily symbolic. We expect that experts at the highest levels have appropriate connectionist-level recognition systems, but they also have highly developed metacognitive knowledge, and they may also have superior *reflective* access, which is the ability to consciously mention, as well as use, components of their information processing system. Thus, at the most advanced skill levels, explicit and implicit knowledge are effectively integrated by connectionist and symbolic level systems. Discovering what training approaches best develop such integrated knowledge is an important challenge for future research.

Understanding the complexities involved in learning and learning transfer are particularly important because jobs are increasing in cognitive complexity (Goldstein & Gilliam, 1990; Howell & Cooke, 1989) and so training techniques must change to reflect this increasing complexity. As Howell and Cooke (1989) note, "successful performance increasingly depends on what people contribute at the cognitive juncture between observable inputs and outputs" (p. 124). These authors argue for an emphasis on a cognitive orientation to training, rather than an orientation based on traditional behaviorism principles. We agree with this assessment and suggest that the distinction between explicit and implicit knowledge can illustrate the importance of such a cognitive approach to training as long as it incorporates concepts at both the symbolic and connectionist level.

Working Memory.   Most current cognitive research conceptualizes working memory as that portion of long-term memory that is currently active. Understanding working memory is important practically because (a) we need to maintain activation in working memory while information is encoded, indexed, and stored in long-term memory; (b) working memory is often thought of as a limited work space, a limited attentional capacity, or a processing resource that must be allocated among competing tasks; and (c) the information currently active in working memory is a source of activation for other information or productions, making it an important component of control structures that guide information processing.

Thinking about the nature of working memory has changed substantially from the 1960s to the 1990s. Earlier views were consistent with the notion of a short-term memory of fixed capacity that served as a central register in a symbolic processing device. Short-term memory limitations were seen as a bottleneck that limited the processing capacity of the entire human information processing system. For example, filter theories (Broadbent, 1958) posited highly selective attention to sensory information, with the nonattended stimuli being excluded from further processing. Though it was later recognized that nonattended stimuli could receive some processing, revisions of filter theories retained the basic concept of limited central-processing capacity as the fundamental constraint causing selectivity (Allport, 1989). However, this notion of a central memory unit with fixed capacity was severely

criticized in the 1970s and 1980s by work from a number of researchers. It did not fit well with Craik and Lockhart's (1972) depth-of-processing theory, nor did the notion of fixed capacity hold up in research focusing on dual-task phenomena.

Dual-task work investigates subjects' performance on both a *primary* task such as reading or problem solving, and a simultaneous *secondary* task that presumably also requires working memory capacity, such as rehearsing and recalling a small set of digits. If working memory has a fixed, unitary capacity, the secondary task should reduce performance on the primary task. Yet very often, the concurrent load of the secondary task does not disrupt subjects' performance on a primary task (Baddeley & Hitch, 1974).

Baddeley's (1986) work provides an alternative interpretation of working memory for explicit knowledge; because of its broad implications, we cover this work in some detail. He conceptualizes working memory as involving a central executive, which is a limited-capacity processor involved in control and selection functions, and two "slave "subsystems, which serve to maintain activation. One slave subsystem, the *articulatory loop*, maintains activation by verbal rehearsal. This system can maintain activation only for a limited number of syllables, since each syllable takes time to articulate and information in the articulatory loop decays rapidly with time. Therefore, when words or digits have many syllables (e.g., Afghanistan), activation can be maintained for fewer words than when there are fewer syllables (e.g., Chad or Cuba). Baddeley calls the second slave subsystem a *visuospatial scratch pad*—a mental work space that allows the temporary storage and manipulation of visual and spatial information. Dual-task experiments generally show disruption of performance only when the primary and secondary tasks employ the same subsystem.

Baddeley's discussion of the central executive in working memory is related to how we integrate or resolve inconsistencies from information in different subsystems. For example, Baddeley (1986, p. 228) views the central executive as having limited capacity for explicit processing of information. It is called into play when (a) tasks require planning or decision making, (b) automatic processing is difficult, (c) novel or poorly learned actions are involved, (d) situations are dangerous or technically complex, or (e) suppression of habitual responses is required. In general, these are situations where we cannot sequence or control processing using schemas stored in long-term memory. Thus, this executive system provides an alternative to simple schema-directed processing.

Baddeley's (1986) conceptualization of working memory still involves a limited capacity system, but his work rejects the notion of working memory as being a single, unitary, short-term information storage system. This line of thinking is carried further in recent work by Carpenter and Just (1989) on working memory constraints in reading. They see working memory as being a limited resource that is shared by the component processes involved in complex tasks such as language comprehension, but this resource is used in an active and flexible manner by subjects. Thus, they view working memory in terms of operational capacity, which depends on the tradeoffs made among component processes and an individual's *task-specific* pool of resources. They assert that there is no absolute measure of memory capacity. Carpenter and Just also assert that individual differences in memory capacity for one type of task will differ from memory capacity in another task, in part because capacity reflects how subjects allocate memory resources, which may differ from task to task.

Such findings raise a fundamental question concerning limitations of working memory. If the limitations do not arise from a specific bottleneck in a central-processing mechanism, where do they come from? Allport (1989)

directly addresses this question based on work in the area of visual attention. He argues that selectivity in attention arises not from limitations in processing capacity, but instead from the need to produce coherence in behavior in the face of environmental cues for conflicting behaviors. In other words, selectivity occurs as a consequence of constraints on behavioral *output*, not as a consequence of severe limitations in processing information *inputs*. Selectivity in attentional engagement partially reflects what Allport calls *selection-for-action*. Selective processing is necessary to map just those aspects of a visual array onto just those parameters needed to control action. Allport asserts that as long as streams of information related to appropriate output can be appropriately segregated (there is no unwanted "crosstalk" between different channels), information related to different effector systems can be processed concurrently.

Allport notes that all perceptually guided activities need time to be completed. Motor activities, speech articulation, and visual fixations required for many tasks can only be done in a serial fashion—for example, we can't move in two directions at the same time. Hence, the system that controls behavior excludes information that is not relevant to high-priority goals as a way to protect these important activities. Thus, selectivity in information processing is as much a function of inhibiting information related to low-priority goals as it is a function of limitations in working memory capacity. In other words, selective attention is motivational as well as cognitive. Allport (1989, p. 654) further suggests that control of attention is exercised indirectly through a mechanism of competing priority assignments that is implemented by a parallel distributed processing system.

Though somewhat esoteric for an industrial and organizational psychologist, this view of working memory and attentional processes has some interesting implications. Part of the well-known motivational effects of goal setting may arise from the capacity of high-priority goals to inhibit attention to information not related to the execution of goal-related activity. Further, when difficult goals are set, learning on complex tasks may be inhibited by the same types of selection-for-action principles discussed by Allport (1989). For example, Shalley (in press) found that creativity was lower when goals for high productivity were assigned unless creativity goals were also assigned. One plausible explanation of such results is that information related to creativity was not attended to unless creativity was also a high-priority goal.

We think the demise of a fixed-capacity unitary working memory construct has many important applied implications. Much current thinking in social cognition, skill development (Ackerman, 1987), and motivation (Kanfer & Ackerman, 1989) is based on the idea of a fixed-capacity attentional resource. This work shows that secondary tasks such as preparing to recall information or planning a speech (Gilbert, Pelham, & Krull, 1988), self-regulation (Gilbert, Krull, & Pelham, 1988), or goal setting (Kanfer & Ackerman, 1989) interfere with primary task performance. To be fair, most of these researchers who examine dual-task phenomena acknowledge problems with a unitary attentional resource perspective, but they still base their theories on this conceptualization. Yet application of Baddeley's (1986) or Allport's (1989) formulations implies that interference would generally not occur when different memory subsystems could maintain segregation of information input and appropriately match it with separate effector mechanisms. For example, in Kanfer and Ackerman's (1989) simulation of air traffic controllers, what appear to be problems in allocating working memory resources may stem from the facts that all inputs were visual and linguistically represented and all outputs were keyboard responses. If auditory as well as keystroke output were allowed *and* if multiple channels of input were provided, "attentional resources"

might be much less limiting. This example illustrates an important general point: Information processing problems may stem at least as much from the structure of a particular task as from the limits of the person performing the task.

Activation and Control of Information Processing

As noted earlier, a third reason for being interested in how memory functions is that memory activation is an important input to the control structures that sequence cognitive operations. We noted earlier that one function of cognitive architectures is to specify the sequence with which information processing operations are performed, that is, its control structure. Understanding control is important in understanding how cognitive processes unfold over time; control structures link sensations, perceptions, interpretations, and overt responses. Such links may occur directly (automatically) in a manner that produces minimal drain on attentional resources. Alternatively, they may occur indirectly (through controlled processing), being linked by paths that demand attention and working memory operations. (See the work of Cohen, Dunbar, & McClelland, 1990, for elaboration of this point.)

Anderson (1983a) describes the problem of control of cognitions as follows:

> Human cognition at all levels involves choosing what to process. Alternatives present themselves, implicitly or explicitly, and our cognitive systems choose, implicitly or explicitly, to pursue some and not others. We orient our senses to only part of the environment; we do not perceive everything we sense; what we do perceive we do not recognize in all possible patterns; only some of what we recognize do we use for achieving our goals; we follow only some ways of pursuing our goals; and we choose to achieve only some of the possible goals. (p. 126)

The point we wish to make is simple—control, however explained, is closely tied to the operation of human memory. This point illustrates the general value of understanding memory and its relation to other aspects of a cognitive architecture.

To illustrate how memory and control interact, we will describe in the remainder of this section one architecture that has been widely applied by cognitive psychologists, Anderson's ACT* architecture. ACT stands for adaptive control of thought, and the ACT* model is the newest version of an architecture that has had a long period of development. This architecture posits two separate but connected memories, comprised of discrete symbol structures, that are used in producing task activities—declarative and procedural memory. Both memories have strengths associated with each element and are accessed when activation levels for elements are sufficiently high. An overview of ACT* architecture is provided in Figure 3.

In ACT*, working memory is the currently active portion of declarative memory plus the declarative structures activated by the operation of procedural memory. Working memory also contains goals that serve as important and general sources of activation, and elements that are activated by environmental perceptions or motor feedback. Activation spreads automatically through working memory and then to other connected nodes in declarative or procedural memories. Sufficient activations allow the firing of a production (a condition-action operation) in procedural memory or the inclusion of a declarative element in working memory.

In this system, the sequence of operations is memory-dependent because the firing of productions or the inclusion of declarative elements in working memory occurs when activation levels exceed some threshold. Thus, control is spread over an extensive associative memory network, and when declarative or procedural information is sufficiently activated, it "captures" conscious attention and is "popped" into working memory. This highly activated information then serves as a source of activation for other information, and the process is repeated. ACT* illustrates the central role of working memory in controlling actions, since working memory is the portion of long-term memory that currently has high activation levels. It is from these nodes that activation flows to productions or other information in declarative memory. In this sense, working memory helps control what we do and what we think. However, control also depends on how long-term memory networks function and on whether the units accessed are themselves aggregates of highly connected memory units (i.e., schemas).

This ACT* control structure contrasts with more common control procedures used by most symbolic systems in which control is passed directly from one processing step, or subgoal, to another as in a typical computer program (Pylyshyn, 1989, pp. 66–68). In ACT*, control reflects the ebb and flow of activation levels as determined by the general operation of working memory and long-term memory networks, not the very narrowly defined relation between two steps in a logical sequence of information processing operations. We think the more general conceptualization of control in ACT* fits better with an intelligent system, and it is also quite consistent with a connectionist architecture.

While somewhat complex, the focus on how memory and control interrelate is a generally important issue for understanding cognitive processing and human behavior. It deserves much more careful attention in applied settings. We illustrate the general importance of this issue by briefly showing its relevance to a long-standing issue in psychology—whether behavior is internally or externally controlled. Internal control is associated with highly activated goals in

FIGURE 3

Overview of Anderson's ACT* Cognitive Architecture

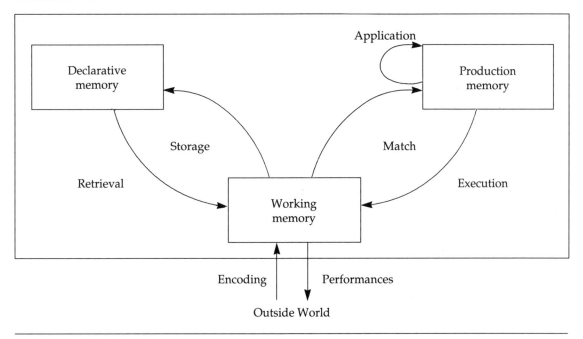

working memory where these goals are strongly connected to other elements in long-term memory that plan for actions, as when goals related to familiar scripts are activated by personal values. External control is associated with salient environmental stimuli, producing high levels of activation that are strongly related to other elements in working memory. For example, an external stimulus configuration might elicit a familiar categorical schema that is richly connected in long-term memory and activates appropriate behavioral responses. In either case, we would expect the issue of internal versus external control to be a momentary event, with most work tasks involving many instances of internal control and many other instances of external control.

Rather than attempting to understand issues like internal or external control of behavior in terms of general personality dimensions, we think it is more useful to think of it as reflecting the functioning of a particular cognitive architecture in the context of a particular task. The individual component of most importance in such situations is the relative strength and size of the cognitive structures associated with goal schemas or schemas used to interpret environmental information and how easily these particular schemas are activated. The topic of memory schemas is discussed in a subsequent section.

Methods for Studying Memory

Ecological Studies of Memory.   Most of the research on memory reviewed to this point has been laboratory-based and has focused on identifying the mechanisms responsible for temporary and enduring memory. Such work has been criticized by Neisser (1976, 1982) because it often has very little meaning outside of a particular theoretical framework (e.g., depth-of-processing research). When theoretical winds shift, much of the prior work on memory loses its relevance. Neisser argues that studying memory in natural contexts has a much more enduring value. Such work may also satisfy concerns in industrial and organizational psychology that information processing work should have applied relevance.

Neisser (1982) also argues that the truly important questions in memory have been avoided by psychologists. He argues that naturally occurring memories that address issues such as how we develop a sense of self, how we learn from mistakes, how we plan and integrate information into activities of our daily lives, and how we extract the underlying meaning from information should be given much more emphasis. We think these are precisely the types of issues that should be important to industrial and organizational psychologists concerned with information processing in organizations. Rather than merely borrowing from memory research, industrial and organizational psychologists could make important contributions to our understanding of memory processes by investigating memory in naturally occurring situations. We would hope that researchers interested in this potential would investigate implicit as well as explicit memory processes and conceptualizations of memory grounded in connectionist as well as symbolic architectures. In explaining social interactions at work, is all the information that guides interactions symbolically mediated and conscious? Or are more implicit processes important determinants of social interactions?

Techniques used to study memory require substantial technical sophistication. We briefly mention common techniques here and provide references to more detailed sources describing each technique. Different approaches have been used to study limitations of working memory and the operation of long-term memory.

Working Memory.   Current conceptualizations of working memory as involving attentional resources or currently active long-term memories have led to an emphasis on investigating resource allocation using dual-task techniques. As already noted, such tasks often involve a primary and a secondary task that are performed concurrently. Sperling and Dosher (1986) provide a good discussion of dual-task methodology. We mention only that this approach is tied to the assumption of a unitary short-term memory of limited capacity. Baddeley's (1986) work makes this assumption untenable, limiting the general applicability of dual-task methodology. Researchers using dual-task techniques need also to consider the loads of each task on the articulatory loop and the visuospatial scratch pad, since these are relatively independent working memory subsystems. When primary and secondary tasks create a concurrent load on different subsystems, they will cause minimal disruption or interference. When they create processing loads on the same subsystem, interference can be substantial, particularly if the load is on the visuospatial subsystem (Schacter, 1989, pp. 688–689). Allport's (1989) work suggests that output constraints also affect the information that is available in working memory.

Long-term Memory.   There are several excellent discussions of methodological issues related to studying long-term memory (Bower & Clapper, 1989; Puff, 1982; Srull, 1984). The three major categories of measures used are recall, recognition, and reaction time. Recall measures seem somewhat less relevant to general measurement issues in industrial and

TABLE 1

**Classification of Possible Responses
for SDT Analysis of Recognition Memory Task**

	Recognition Item's Status in Stimuli	
Subject Response	*Present*	*Not Present*
Present	Hit	False alarm
Not Present	Miss	Correct rejection

organizational psychology, but measures of clustering in recall (Murphy & Puff, 1982) have been successfully used to assess the extent of script processing (Foti & Lord, 1987). More typical of most industrial and organizational concerns are recognition measures because they are closely related to the type of processes used in questionnaire rating techniques. A key issue in using such measures is controlling for individual differences in leniency or stringency of criteria. Experimental control can be created by using forced-choice techniques, but a more common and general approach is to assess response sets using statistical procedures such as signal detection theory (SDT).

We should stress that the SDT paradigm is a very general and well-developed approach to independently assess sensitivity and response bias in ratings. It predates the recognition in our field that accuracy and biases such as halo error are independent (Murphy & Balzer, 1989) and is particularly useful since it can be used to help understand the consequences of raters basing their ratings on cognitive categories (see Lord, 1985). It can also be applied to judgments that are not directly concerned with memory. For example, Borman and Hallam (1991) applied the technique to examine pass/fail judgments of work samples made by experts and novices. Because of its broad applicability, we explain signal detection theory in a bit more detail.

Signal detection theory, which has been extensively developed during the last 20 years, can be applied to dichotomous or continuous choice ratings. In typical applications, subjects observe stimulus materials, and they respond to recognition based questions in a yes-no format. As shown in Table 1, this yields four possibilities: hits, false alarms, misses, or correct rejections. But only two probabilities, hits and false alarms, are needed to represent all the unique information, since the probability of a miss is equal to 1 minus the hit rate, and the probability of a correct rejection is equal to 1 minus the false alarm rate. Thus, SDT analyses only focus on hit rates (HR) and false alarm rates (FAR).

From information on HR and FAR, indices of both memory sensitivity (accuracy) and response bias can be developed. Memory discrimination is a function of HR minus FAR, and response bias is a function of HR plus FAR (Macmillan & Creelman, 1990). Various indices of memory discrimination have been theoretically analyzed by Swets (1986), and indices of bias have been compared by Macmillan and Creelman (1990). Snodgrass and Corwin (1988) used simulation techniques to empirically evaluate alternative measures, focusing on the requirement that memory discrimination and bias should be independent.

Reaction-time measures are frequently used to assess search behavior in memory networks, to examine the effects of priming on memory, and to assess the effects of repeated practice on retrieval. Reaction time provides a measure of accessibility of information in memory and, thus, should be related to use of heuristics such as availability (Tversky & Kahneman, 1974). Reaction times may also be helpful in differentiating automatic from controlled processing in memory search or in differentiating symbolic and connectionist architectures. Srull (1984) provides a particularly useful discussion of such measures. We mention only two issues researchers should consider. First, one must take account of speed-accuracy tradeoffs in interpreting reaction times. Second, reaction times frequently need to be transformed using logarithmic functions to facilitate interpretation. Such transformations minimize the effects of occasional responses that are very slow, and they also "straighten out" power functions that are quite common in memory research.

One methodological problem that cuts across many information processing areas is that the effects of cognitive schemas can be demonstrated experimentally, but there are no convenient measures to assess individual differences in the extent to which people rely on schema-based processing while doing a task. One possibility is to develop recognition-memory measures as a way of operationalizing schema use (Cellar & Barrett, 1987; Cellar & Wade, 1988; Lord, 1985). For example, Cellar and Wade (1988) reasoned that people using a particular type of schema would commit schema-consistent false alarms on recognition memory measures. They developed a recognition memory measure of intrinsic-extrinsic orientation by assessing FAR for intrinsic and extrinsic questionnaire items, and found this measure explained significant amounts of incremental variance in intrinsic motivation even after the effects of perceived locus of causality and perceived competence had been statistically controlled. Presumably, individuals who relied on intrinsic as compared to extrinsic scripts while doing the task

found it to be more intrinsically motivating, and they also made recognition errors consistent with intrinsic, but not extrinsic, scripts.

Representation of Knowledge and Information Processing

One very general advancement in cognitive science in the past 20 years is the recognition that intelligent behavior is not simply the result of variables related to current processing. Instead, intelligent performance on many tasks results from efficient processing applied to appropriately organized knowledge (Feigenbaum, 1989; Glaser & Chi, 1988; Simon, 1990). This dual emphasis on knowledge and processing to explain performance complements interest in knowledge structures or schema that originated from research explaining how information is interpreted, stored, or retrieved from memory. Because this topic is of general importance, the role of memory schema from both symbolic and connectionist perspectives will be discussed in the next section. The role of schema in helping to develop general explanations of information processing or more comprehensive theories in specific topical areas will also be emphasized. The joint effects of knowledge and processing activities in developing adequate theories in several domains of the field— person-situation interactions, problem-solving behavior, and social cognitions—will then be considered. The chapter will be concluded with a discussion of automatic and controlled processing.

Cognitive Schema

A common notion linking information processing in many areas is the idea that with experience in a particular domain, information is organized into larger interconnected units. These aggregate structures permit experts to use different processes than novices, resulting in generally superior expert performance.

In fact, recent thinking in both artificial intelligence (Feigenbaum, 1989) and human information processing systems (Chi et al., 1988; Simon, 1990) explains skilled performance in human (Anderson, 1987) and expert systems (Harmon & King, 1985) in terms of information processes applied to domain-specific knowledge. Aggregate units or "packages of knowledge" can also be conceptualized as data structures used to represent generic concepts stored in memory (McClelland et al., 1986, p. 19). These structures help us interpret, store, and retrieve task or social information.

With minor variations in meaning, these aggregations are referred to by many names—chunks (Simon & Kotovsky, 1963), schemas (or schemata) (Bartlett, 1932; Piaget & Inhelder, 1969), knowledge structures (Galambos, Abelson, & Black, 1986), scripts (Schank & Abelson, 1977), categories (Rosch, 1978), and frames (Beach, 1990; Minsky, 1975). Psychomotor schemas also exist and control activities such as talking and walking. We will use the term schema(s) in our discussion. In industrial and organizational psychology, schemas have been used to explain social classifications in performance appraisal (Borman, 1987; Feldman, 1981; Nathan & Lord, 1983), leadership perceptions (Lord, Foti, & De Vader, 1984), threat versus opportunity labels in strategic decision making (Dutton & Jackson, 1987), classification of competitors (Porac & Thomas, 1990), organizational culture (Harris, 1989; Lord & Maher; 1991; Rentsch, 1990), goal-related cognitions (Gioia & Poole, 1984; Lord & Kernan, 1987), plan schema (Earley & Shalley, in press), and framing effects in decision making (Beach, 1990). Yet how schema are defined and precisely how they affect information processing require further specification.

Schemas and Symbolic Architectures. Schemas can be defined at either symbolic or connectionist levels. We will first discuss schemas at the symbolic level, then show how viewing schemas from a connectionist perspective can

> take us beneath the surface of schemata, to a level of description that allows us to see how we can preserve the desirable characteristics of schemata and at the same time make them more flexible, more sensitive to context, more adaptable. (McClelland, Rumelhart, &the PDP Research Group, 1986, p. 1)

At a symbolic level, schemas can be defined as packages of data that form "natural units" (Anderson, 1980). These units are highly interconnected and are retrieved from memory in an all-or-none manner. Schemas may be relatively small, such as a propositional structure representing information contained in a sentence, or they may be much larger, corresponding to themes or passages in a story. The critical issue is unitization rather than the size of a unit. As Anderson (1980, p. 147) notes, the key idea is that we form units when the elements in working memory correspond to elements in existing knowledge structures.

From the perspective of a symbolic architecture, schemas can also be thought of as internal models of the outside world. They give meaning to patterns of sensory stimuli, allow inference (Abelson & Black, 1986; Minsky, 1975), and allow efficient but flexible information processing (Rosch, 1978). One schema can also be embedded within another, allowing people to form larger organized knowledge representations. This ability to use schemas in a flexible manner is a major source of the information processing effectiveness and adaptive capacity of humans. However, reliance on schemas is also a major source of limitations. Schemas related to problem solving, called *problem spaces* by Newell and Simon (1972), create powerful limitations on the comprehensiveness of symbolic problem-solving activities. For example, bounded rationality is a more accurate portrayal of how people solve problems than optimization (Simon, 1990).

Research on schemas has emphasized their role in guiding data storage and retrieval. Schacter (1989) reviews considerable research showing that schemas affect encoding through selection of schema-relevant information, by providing a means to interpret information, and through providing a basis for integrating information. Schemas can be activated through exposure to sets of features that are highly associated with schemas (Cantor & Mischel, 1979; Rosch, 1978; Srull, 1983), by labels that identify schemas, or by goals subjects are pursuing when exposed to information (Foti & Lord, 1987; Hoffman, Mischel, & Mazze, 1981; Jeffery & Mischel, 1979).

In conjunction with our previous discussion of working memory and control, we can now appreciate how schemas can lower the demands for conscious control of information processing. Schemas, which are activated through recognition processes based on pattern-matching, have high activation levels that pop them into working memory when appropriate stimulus configurations are encountered in the environment. Once in working memory, schemas serve as sources of activation for related information as well. Given control structures that make use of activation level, as was illustrated with the ACT* architecture, schema activation and associated connections can control the sequences of thoughts to which we attend. Thus, schemas can be very potent retrieval devices and can provide convenient means to interpret and elaborate information during encoding.

The general effects of schemas in priming related constructs are particularly interesting. Social stereotypes can be thought of as affecting many perceptions and expectations through such priming processes. As suggested by the work of Heilman et al. (1989), classification as female may make leadership categories less available, whereas classification as

male may make leadership categories more accessible. Schemas can have fairly general effects on how task-related information is processed: Using a "play" script may make interpretations related to intrinsic motivation more available, whereas using a work script activates extrinsic motivation (Cellar & Barrett, 1987; Cellar & Wade, 1988); learning goals elicit very different types of strategy development and evaluation processes than do performance goals (Elliott & Dweck, 1988); the prospects of loss trigger very different risk-taking behaviors than do the prospects of gain (Kahneman & Tversky, 1979); and classifying situations as threats as opposed to opportunities produces very different strategic responses (Dutton & Jackson, 1987). The considerable effects of schemas on decision making (Lord & Maher, 1991, chap. 13; Walsh, 1989) are also consistent with the idea that schemas organize information and serve as a general source of activation, thereby affecting the retrieval of other information from long-term memory.

One difficulty with the application of schema concepts, particularly in industrial and organizational psychology, is that we have tended to define schemas in terms of content—leadership, gender, or threat-opportunity schema. This tendency may have developed because people interested in specific content domains developed theories specific to their area of interest. However, we see no reason to assume schemas are so homogeneous. Knowledge about goals may be integrated with knowledge about people or knowledge about contexts, particularly in work situations. For example, Borkenau's (1990) empirical research shows that trait constructs are more closely tied to differences in the personal *goals* of perceivers than they are to central tendencies in the attributes of the people perceivers have encountered over time. Thinking about a task that needs to be done may simultaneously activate information about how the task should be done, who may be able to perform the task, and the type of situation in which a task is likely to be completed. This idea is consistent with suggestions that person-in-situation schemas are more useful than either person or situation categories (Cantor, Mischel, & Schwartz, 1982), that many schemas are really ad hoc categories (Barsalou,1983, 1985), or that schemas gain some of their specificity by incorporating general world knowledge (Medin, 1989).

Schemas are also used as a general explanation of information processing. However, we need to specify how schemas fit with a general control structure or permit the use of simpler operations to fully develop our understanding of schema functioning. For experts in a given domain, schemas allow the use of recognition processes as a substitute for more elaborate heuristics (Logan, 1989; Simon, 1990) and allow us to solve problems using much more limited search processes (Lord & Maher, 1990; Simon 1990). Expert schemas may also be organized around deeper, response-oriented principles as opposed to surface features (Chi et al., 1988; Day & Lord, in press; Glaser, 1989). Thus, we might expect experts to be oriented toward solution rather than problem features, as shown by applied studies of managerial problem solving (e.g., Nutt, 1984). Extending this type of research offers a promising area for integrating cognitive and applied knowledge.

Schemas and Connectionist Architectures. Schemas can also be viewed from a connectionist perspective. Rumelhart, Smolensky, McClelland, and Hinton (1986) posit that schemas, like other knowledge in connectionist architectures, correspond to the activation of a set of highly interconnected units and that they

> emerge at the moment they are needed from the interaction of large numbers of much simpler elements all working in concert with one another. Schemata are not explicit entities, but rather are implicit in our knowledge and are created

by the very environment that they are trying to interpret—as it is interpreting them. (p. 20)

Rumelhart, Smolensky, McClelland, and Hinton (1986) define schemas as a constraint network. Each processing unit in such networks is simply an expectation or hypothesis that some sort of feature (acoustic, semantic, visual, etc.) is present in a stimulus input, and each connection in the network represents a constraint among the hypotheses. Thus, one can think of a feature as activating a specific receptor unit, and this unit, in turn, activates or inhibits other units to which it is connected. If connections (weights) among two units in the network are weak, the constraint between them is weak; if connections are strong, constraints are strong. If weights are positive (one unit activates another), strong connections simply mean that if feature A is present, feature B is expected to be present. Strong negative constraints mean just the opposite; if A is present, B is expected *not* to be present.

An interesting feature of such constraint networks is that if they are allowed to iterate through multiple cycles or steps of activation, they settle in to a stable, locally optimum state in which as many of the constraints are satisfied as possible. This "solution" to the network can be thought of as a schema interpreting input or recognizing a pattern. An important aspect of such networks is that they always move from a state that satisfies fewer constraints to a state that satisfies more constraints (Rumelhart, Smolensky, McClelland, & Hinton, 1986 p. 16). They can also produce overall goodness-of-fit measures, which indicate how well the schema satisfies the input constraints. Furthermore, the networks can be described as carrying out their information processing by climbing into states of maximal satisfaction of the constraints implicit in the network.

According to Rumelhart, Smolensky, McClelland, and Hinton (1986), the connective strengths that comprise a schema define its default values. For example, if a feature is not present in a stimulus input, but its corresponding unit is strongly connected to other units that are present, this feature's unit will quickly be activated as the network settles in to an interpretation of the stimulus. This function of schema helps us understand how we can recognize category members that possess only some of the defining features of a category. Categories can be based on fuzzy concepts like family resemblance (Rosch, 1978), because settling in processes help to remove this fuzziness and activate an appropriate category from a partially fitting stimulus. The same process also explains why minor discrepancies from schemas are generally ignored.

Schemas can embed smaller structures in larger ones, creating treelike structures. Because schemas have these features, Rumelhart, Smolensky, McClelland, and Hinton (1986) argue that they can represent knowledge at all levels. They also suggest that goals can be represented as patterns of activation that provide an input to thinking processes, and that PDP networks "learn" to establish specific subgoal patterns in response to specific inputs and superordinate goals. Thus, we expect that representations of goal schemas could also be developed by conceptualizing them as constraint networks.

Schemas are also active processing devices that recognize input patterns based on the goodness-of-fit of the schema to the data being processed. This quality is very important for two reasons. First, it suggests how an appropriate (best fitting) memory structure can capture control at an appropriate time in a diffusely operating control structure such as that of ACT*. Second, it solves the problem of adequately defining similarity which has been an issue for symbolically based interpretations of categories (Medin, 1989), because similarity or goodness of fit is an output of the constraint satisfying network.

Rumelhart, Smolensky, McClelland, and Hinton (1986) also explain how such multiple constraint networks can be configured into mental models, suggesting a natural bridge between connectionist and symbolic architectures. People can use such mental models to settle in to solutions of problems using three refined abilities: pattern matching, forming expectations based on mental models, and skill at manipulating the environment and evaluating feedback. Rumelhart et al. (1986) suggest that as we become more skilled in an area, we become better at reducing problems to pattern-matching tasks. They assert that perceiving solutions to problems through settling in processes is easy to explain in terms of constraint networks, but is quite difficult to explain in terms of symbolic processing models.

The work of Rumelhart, Smolensky, McClelland, and Hinton (1986) has been presented to give readers a feeling for the type of model of schemas that connectionist theorists develop. Other researchers have also investigated these issues. For example, Gluck and Bower (1988) have used similar models based on adaptive network theory to show that categories can be learned from associative learning principles in which the weights of connecting units correspond to strengths of associations in terms of classical learning theory. Their model fit subjects' data better than predictions derived from probability matching, exemplar retrieval, or simple prototype models of category learning. Estes (1988) has also shown how relatively simple network-based models can learn categories in an active, self-adjusting manner that overcomes weaknesses in extant exemplar-memory and prototype models of categorization.

Though such work is admittedly esoteric, when viewed from the perspective of an industrial and organizational psychologist it has some important applied implications. The first is simply that schemas may be learned and applied implicitly, like any other type of knowledge depicted in a connectionist framework. In fact, symbolically coded information might interfere with the efficient application of implicit processes that would otherwise be used, as suggested by the work of Berry and Broadbent (1988). This recognition raises questions concerning exclusively symbolic-based interventions aimed at changing schema.

A second implication is that we should expect difficulties when nondeclarative (implicit) schematic information must be communicated to other individuals. If individuals have learned to perform a task by themselves using schemas or other processes closely related to connectionist architectures, they will have difficulty translating information into a symbolic form for communication to others. Consider, for example, the task of flying an airplane. Many perceptions, motor responses, and interpretations of situations may be quite rapid and closely tied to schemas activated in parallel by the many sources of information available to a pilot. When flying solo, experienced pilots may have little difficulty relating perceptions to appropriate decisions and motor responses, but they may experience substantial difficulty doing the same task as part of a team. It may be difficult to encode their implicit understanding into symbolic terms and effectively communicate it to other crew members while flying a plane, particularly in crisis situations. Thus, many of the communication and coordination difficulties of cockpit crews, which on the surface seem to be problems of communication or group processes (see Foushee, 1984, for an alarming description of such problems), may also be problems in group members' inability to make implicit knowledge explicit in their verbal communications.

Many of the coordination difficulties of organizational work groups may be related to bridging knowledge in connectionist and symbolic architectures. Thus, considering the problems of spanning cognitive architecture provides a complement to understanding coordination difficulties in terms of social skills, power structures, or lack of a team orientation in work groups. Such cognitive interpretations of difficulties in group processes should be considered along with the more traditional social explanations to optimally improve group functioning.

Joint Effects of Knowledge and Processes

In this section, we will concentrate on three more general issues that illustrate the value of emphasizing both processing and underlying knowledge structures. First, we will show how this approach could lead to more adequate understanding of such issues as how person and situational factors interact in explaining behavior, particularly when we recognize that processing may involve either symbolic or connectionist architectures. Second, we will illustrate how this line of thinking pertains to the general topic of problem solving, helping us to understand expert-novice differences. Third, we will discuss the general issue of social-information processing from this perspective, explaining why this area is particularly challenging to understand from a cognitive science perspective.

Person-Situation Interactions. The general issue of how personal qualities affect behavior can be put in a broader perspective by considering recent discussions of whether the person, the situation, or person-situation interactions determine behavior. Symbolically based explanations of individual differences (e.g., Cantor & Kihlstrom, 1987, 1989) suggest that people logically operate on perceptions of environmental information as a means to achieve their own goals. Such approaches view complexity in behavior as arising from the goals, plans, strategies, and knowledge of perceivers as applied in a particular environment. Goals, plans, strategies, knowledge, and even biases in perceiving environments may be relatively stable, producing the cross situation consistencies in behaviors associated with personality effects.

An alternative view is to emphasize person-situation interactions in terms of a connectionist architecture. This view stresses the parallel activation of neural-like units from task or social information in the environment and from internal goals, values, or cognitions that are momentarily activated. Units in memory "tuned" to combinations of environment and person-based activation would automatically "capture" attention when their activation level was sufficiently high, directing subsequent processing and behavior in ways that are specific to certain person-situation combinations. Such an explanation would emphasize a "recognize and act" aspect of behavior that is highly dependent on specific environmental information to which a person has learned to respond. Thus, person-situation interactions involve more than just symbolic level processes. They also reflect the connectionist structures that exist for automatically responding to certain types of environmental information. This perspective provides a very different notion of social intelligence or goal directedness. It allows for tacit knowledge and automaticity to have a much greater impact, particularly when coupled with a parallel memory system and a control structure in which highly activated units capture attention, even if unrelated to current goals, plans, or intentions.

A connectionist view has another advantage for understanding person-situation interactions. As noted by Mitchell and James (1989, p. 405), one of the key issues to understanding person-situation interactions is to see how the person side of the interaction provides coherence across situations, yet still explains the dynamic aspects that produce variability in behavior either over situations or over time. One common approach to this issue is to posit that individuals have schemas that serve various information processing functions, such as organizing incoming information and providing meaning (e.g., categorical schemas) or integrating and sequencing the behavior output by a person (e.g., scripts).

As noted earlier, connectionist views of how schemas operate are helpful in seeing how the same knowledge structure (the same set of weights) can be equally activated by slightly different input patterns. Settling-in patterns based on the internal connections in such structures quickly activate aspects of a schema that were not activated by environmental information. Thus, many different patterns of environmental information can activate the same schema as long as there is a sufficient match to initiate this settling-in process. Such processes could produce consistency in interpretations of similar but nonidentical environments, or at a deeper level, they could produce consistency in responding to similar but nonidentical interpretations.

The settling-in procedure can also explain how people exhibit variability in interpretations and behavior across situations. Settling-in procedures produce higher activation levels as more and more of the input connections are matched by sensory information—the better the fit, the higher the activation level. This process allows one to make goodness-of-fit judgments as a function of activation levels for a particular schema, but it also provides an automatic mechanism for selecting the most appropriate schema for interpreting input information—the schema with the highest level of activation. Applying different schemas is one means to explain variability, either over time or over situations. Thus, when conflicting schemas are simultaneously activated and are "popped" into working memory, activation levels may provide a heuristic for intuitive judgments as to which is more appropriate. If only one schema is sufficiently activated to capture attention, then choice processes occur automatically with no load on working memory. In either case, one can easily conceive of changes across situations as producing a shift from one schema to another. Such shifts can produce discontinuities in perceptions or behavior (Hanges, Braverman, & Rentsch, 1989; Lord & Maher, 1991).

Problem Solving and Expert-Novice Differences.   As noted by VanLehn (1989), problem-solving work can be partitioned into work on knowledge-lean and knowledge-rich task domains. *Knowledge-lean* problem solving occurs where very little information is used to solve problems, typically only information contained in brief problem descriptions and general knowledge. Concern with this type of problem solving was popular in the 1960s and 1970s and culminated with Newell and Simon's (1972) influential book *Human Problem Solving.* Newell and Simon conceptualized problem solving as occurring within a symbolic architecture and involving two basic processes—understanding and search. Understanding allows the construction of an internal symbolic model of the problem based on problem instructions, or the development of a *problem space.* Problem spaces specify initial states in a problem, operators that can change the initial states into new states, and tests as to whether the problem has been successfully solved. Search involves using the potential operators to create a sequence of steps that solves a problem. Search processes involve symbolic manipulations and are heavily dependent on working memory capacity.

The actual search processes used depend heavily on guesswork combined with a number of heuristics, such as working forward from an initial state *(forward chaining),* working backward from the end state *(backward chaining),* or selecting particular operators and finding ways to create the conditions required for their use *(operator subgoaling).* As subjects work through problems, they both progress toward solutions and create new, problem-specific procedures that can be used more efficiently. A considerable body of scientific work is concerned with describing and explaining the development of problem-specific procedures, and a number of these learning mechanisms have been identified. For example, *compounding* takes two separate operators and combines them to create a new macro-operator, and *tuning* adjusts the operator selection mechanism based on the success of specific operators in advancing problem solving. An important learning mechanism in ACT* is *proceduralization,* which creates efficient task-specific productions from general-purpose productions.

As a whole, research on knowledge-lean problem solving has been very successful, with Newell and Simon's (1972) approach explaining the problem-solving steps taken by subjects, subjects' verbal comments, latencies between steps, and even eye movements (VanLehn, 1989, p. 528). But in the late 1970s, attention shifted to knowledge-rich problem solving. *Knowledge-rich* problem solving pertains to domains such as algebra, chess, physics, bridge, medical diagnosis, computer programming, and public policy formulation, where very extensive knowledge is required for solving even simple problems. Such work is also called *schema-based* problem solving because it emphasizes the organized knowledge stored in long-term memory rather than working memory processes.

Knowledge-rich problem solving involves very different kinds of mental activities. Subjects generally recognize problems as a familiar type, retrieve solution procedures from memory, and follow these procedures (VanLehn, 1989). Further, problem solving involves more recognition processes and much more limited search procedure (Simon, 1990). Knowledge-rich problem solving also depends heavily on various types of learning that occur as one gains experience in an area. This gradual learning has proved much more difficult to explain and simulate than the search procedures used in knowledge-lean situations.

A number of important empirical findings, summarized by VanLehn (1989), have emerged

TABLE 2

Characteristics of Expert Cognitive Processing

1. Experts excel mainly in their own domains.
2. Experts perceive large meaningful patterns in their domain.
3. Experts are fast; they are faster than novices at performing the skills of their domain, and they quickly solve problems with little error.
4. Experts have superior short-term and long-term memory.
5. Experts see and represent a problem in their domain at a deeper (more principled) level than novices; novices tend to represent a problem at a superficial level.
6. Experts spend a great deal of time analyzing a problem qualitatively.
7. Experts have strong self-monitoring skills.

From "Overview" by R. Glaser and M. T. H. Chi in *The Nature of Expertise* (pp. xvii–xx) by M. Chi, R. Glaser, and M. Farr (Eds.), 1988, Hillsdale, NJ: Erlbaum. Copyright 1988 by Lawrence Erlbaum Associates. Adapted by permission.

from this problem-solving work. Perhaps most important is the role of learning in all types of problem solving. Even in knowledge-lean problem solving, tactical learning occurs very quickly, and processes such as compounding, tuning, and chunking allow problem solving to improve dramatically with even limited practice. Such improvements substantially reduce the demands that problem solving places on working memory, but these improvements need not be interpreted as automating problem-solving processes.

For most complex real-world tasks, experts are defined as individuals with several thousand hours of experience in a domain, and "world-class" expertise typically takes at least 10 years of concentrated experience (at least 20,000 hours). Novices typically have only a few hundred hours experience in an area, and prenovices have only a few hours experience. Research comparing experts and novices has become increasingly common in the last decade, and a number of general findings have emerged. Glaser and Chi (1988) list seven characteristics of experts, which are summarized in Table 2. Particularly interesting is the work that shows superior memory of

experts. Ericsson and Polson (1988) explain this superiority in terms of the memory management skills of experts that allow them to use already existing encoding and retrieval structures that exist in long-term memory. These structures can be flexibly applied to incorporate information from a task environment.

The idea that experts have superior self-monitoring skills is also quite interesting. Experts can monitor their progress toward solutions better than novices can, and they are less likely to get stuck for long time periods in ineffective approaches to problem solving. To illustrate, Schoenfeld (1981) notes that expert problem solvers frequently (about once a minute) make a comment concerning their current direction or amount of progress, while novices may follow an approach for twenty minutes without considering whether to abandon it. VanLehn (1989, p. 563) suggests that this difference is partially explainable in terms of the greater number of potential schemas that experts could apply to a problem-solving task.

Lesgold et al. (1988) suggest additional reasons that experts have greater self-monitoring skills. One is that they have more working memory capacity available to keep track of problem-solving processes because of the many more efficient problem-solving operations they can perform and because of their memory management skills just noted. An additional factor noted by Lesgold et al. in their work on X-ray diagnosis is the more refined perceptual skills of experts. They perceive features of X-rays more accurately than novices or intermediates (third- or fourth-year medical students), and more importantly, the diagnosis task for experts was more of a pattern-matching recognition task than an inferential task. It should be recalled that pattern-matching processes are handled particularly well by the parallel processes of connectionist architectures. It also seems likely that experts' superior skill involves the use of implicit knowledge and processes, which may also free up symbolic processing capacity. These interpretations illustrate a general point made several times in this chapter—that high levels of performance stem from the integration of *both* symbolic and connectionist architectures.

We think understanding of changes in problem solving with experience, particularly the development of expertise, is an important applied issue. We suggested elsewhere (Lord & Maher, 1990) that expert problem solving has both strong prescriptive value and strong theoretical utility compared to other types of information processing models. Indeed, some recent work in the management area (Eisenhardt, 1989), though not labeling the process as expert information processing, shows that expertise can lead to more effective, more comprehensive, and faster decisions than more deliberate, analytic decision-making processes.

Understanding the development and use of expert knowledge is also practically important from the perspective of training and selection. We have already suggested that use of nonsymbolic or implicit knowledge presents substantial problems for training. The domain specificity of expert skills also suggests general training programs cannot create domain-specific expertise. Training programs must be both task-specific and extensive. However, it may also be true that some types of practice or experience may be more efficient than others for developing expertise. One approach worth considering that is directly tied to self-monitoring skills is to give learners experience with mistakes and errors, as has been suggested by Frese and Altmann (1989).

When approached from a selection perspective, work on expert problem solving leads one to caution against an overemphasis on general intelligence measures (Hunter, Schmidt, & Judiesch, 1990). There may be a general aptitude for acquiring information, but that may be quite different from an aptitude for acquiring a specific type of information (e.g., information about computer programming). We think the sustained interest in an area for 10 years or more requires a motivational as well as a cognitive explanation, as suggested by Posner (1989) and Murphy (1989). While it may also be true that the rate of learning as one progresses toward expert status (which is a critical issue in applied areas) may vary across individuals, acquiring expertise may be more of a motivational than a cognitive capacity issue. However, if efficient performance of work tasks involves both explicit and implicit processes, we doubt whether symbolically oriented tests, particularly paper-and-pencil tests, would tap all the relevant capacities of potential workers. Instead, motivational factors in developing expertise should also be emphasized.

Social Information Processing. Social information processing is a particularly challenging issue to explain from a cognitive science perspective. Social perceptions are based on both implicit and explicit factors, and individuals may have little insight into the implicit processes affecting social cognitions. Moreover, social information processing also has a strong affective component. Unlike most of the experimental work on social cognitions, which investigates perceptions in low cognitive load situations, social cognitions in applied settings are formed and modified in high load conditions. High cognitive load makes implicit processes more important because many explicit symbolic level processes (e.g., causal analysis) are precluded by the concurrent cognitive demands of work situations. As a consequence, in applied settings we generally do not use explicit, symbolic processes to form social perceptions, though we certainly can when highly motivated or when we are passive observers rather than interacting with others. Social perception processes are often like the processing of secondary tasks in most dual-task experiments. They may interfere with primary tasks, but they may also be formed using implicit processing capacities that minimize interference. Thus, a critical issue in understanding social cognitions in applied settings concerns how perceptual processes change with increasing cognitive load on perceivers. In this section we focus on the critical issue of cognitive load, focusing on the effects of cognitive load on attributional processes, the reliance on nonverbal behavior to form perceptions, and the role of affect in social perceptions.

Social psychologists are just beginning to investigate how cognitive load affects social perceptions. Theories of social perceptions in the 1960s and 1970s emphasized rational, quasi-scientific processes, with much attention devoted to attribution theory processes. However, later research depicted the social perceiver as being a "cognitive miser" who uses limited-capacity processes and "top-of-the-head" reasoning to form causal attributions (Taylor & Fiske, 1978). Other work emphasized limited-capacity categorization processes rather than explicit causal analysis (Feldman, 1981; Lord, Foti, & De Vader, 1984; Smith & Miller, 1983) as explanations of social perceptions. Gilbert has a more comprehensive theory that includes all of these factors, but he suggests that some processes are ignored under high load conditions. The work of Gilbert and his colleagues (Gilbert, Krull, & Pelham, 1988;

Gilbert, Pelham, & Krull, 1988) suggests that a crucial determinant of the type of processes used to form social perceptions is the degree of cognitive load or "cognitive busyness" of perceivers. Gilbert, Pelham, and Krull (1988) argue that person perception involves three steps: categorization (identifying actions), characterization (identifying traits implied by the actions), and correction (identifying situational constraints that may have caused the actions). Gilbert, Pelham, and Krull (1988) argue that under high cognitive load conditions, perceivers may categorize persons but do not take into account situational considerations that may explain behavior. Perceivers may appropriately consider situational constraints in forming social perceptions under low load conditions, but this "correction" step tends to be skipped when perceptions are formed while perceivers are cognitively busy with other tasks. We suggest that categorization and characterization reflect pattern-matching processes that rely more on capacities associated with connectionist than symbolic architectures. Correction, on the other hand, may require symbolic attributional reasoning in order to discount categorization if a target's behavior can be situationally explained. This type of reasoning process requires substantial working memory capacity, and it can be prevented by tasks that use the same working memory capacity. Thus, cognitive load affects how thoroughly social perceptions are processed.

Gilbert's work is both compelling and relevant to applied psychology. His major focus is on the consequences for the correction step in social perception of reducing symbolic processing capacity by having subjects perform a concurrent task. But equally interesting is how subjects can form social perceptions without extensive reliance on symbolic processing capacities. Less cognitively demanding processing of social information could occur in at least two ways. First, perceivers may more readily attend to nonverbal rather than verbal cues in forming social perceptions. Second, perceivers may depend on the affective nature of perceptions to help them form social judgments. Both of these processes may lead us to form on-line judgments (Hastie & Park, 1986), where summary judgments (e.g., categories) are produced and retained in memory but many of the details of the original stimulus information are forgotten. Perceivers may then use the category and settling-in processes to "fill-in" information that is consistent with the category when called upon to make a judgment.

In short, nonverbal cues and the influence of affective components may play significant roles in social perception. Nonverbal and affective processes are usually not addressed in much applied work. The operation of these processes may be explained, in part, by the notion of multiple processing capacities. Exactly what these multiple processing capacities are is not clear. They may be physically identifiable brain systems, or they may simply be the result of processing at a connectionist level. However, the implications stemming from either possibility are the same—nonverbal and affective capacities for social perceptions occur in parallel with more symbolically based capacities. Usually, perceivers would integrate the information from each of these sources through higher level symbolic processing. But when this higher level capacity is used for other tasks, perceivers can still base social judgments directly on affective and physical information.

Nonverbal Cues.   Gilbert, Pelham, and Krull's (1988) work also shows the importance of nonverbal information in forming social perceptions. They found that when perceivers were cognitively busy, they tended to rely on a target's nonverbal behavior to form judgments. In that study, those subjects who were cognitively busy (performing another task while simultaneously perceiving social information) were less likely than nonbusy subjects to attribute the nonverbal behavior of a target person to situational constraints and were more likely to attribute the nonverbal behavior to dispositional characteristics of the target. In other words, under high cognitive load situations, perceivers can easily assimilate trait-related nonverbal information but do not always make use of situational information to correct dispositional judgments. An additional series of studies by Gilbert and Krull (1988) showed that under high load conditions people make less use of linguistic information in forming impressions. Instead, they place more emphasis on nonverbal behaviors when required to perform a concurrent task.

Extending this logic, perceivers may have a separate processing capacity to perceive and interpret nonverbal behavior of others. One capacity may be our implicit understanding of others based on visual or nonverbal behavior. Brewer (1988) asserts that many social categories are "pictoliteral," with race, age, and gender being visually distinct social categories within which other finer classifications occur. In other words, perceivers likely attend to gender or age information immediately and perhaps use this information to influence subsequent judgments and decisions without awareness.

Affect.   Social cognitions may also be highly influenced by their affective relevance. Feelings and emotions are important components of most social relationships. Social processes in work situations have additional affective consequences because dyadic relations with superiors, work assignments, promotions, raises, hiring, and continued employment all depend on the way we are perceived by others.

It has been recognized for many years that affect is a major dimension of social perceptions (e.g., Osgood, Suci, & Tannenbaum, 1957), and current work on social perceptions also emphasizes affective components (Srull & Wyer, 1989). Dual-code theories of social cognitions (Srull & Wyer, 1989) posit that perceivers form separate representations of people in terms of trait and evaluative concepts (e.g., like-dislike). Leventhal (1984) provides a general theory, asserting that we have separate systems that operate in parallel for controlling objective, problem-oriented behavior and emotional affect-oriented behavior. Zajonc (1984) reviews extensive physiological and psychological research demonstrating that affect and cognition are separate systems, though others (Izard, 1990) emphasize the interdependence of these systems. Zajonc also argues that affect is primary in an ontological and evolutionary sense.

We favor the position that affective and cognitive processing involves distinct, parallel systems that are highly interactive, which is consistent with an emphasis on connectionist architectures. An interesting implication of this perspective is that one would expect high cognitive load to reduce our capacity to form cognitive assessments while leaving much of our capacity for emotional judgments intact. Consistent with this idea, Bargh (1990, p. 94) identifies several studies indicating that perceivers have a preconscious capacity to classify others as being "good" or "bad." In addition, recent work on the development of emotional regulation (Kopp, 1989; Tronick, 1989) indicates that affective communication between a mother and infant—at ages when symbolic ability is not well developed—is a crucial step in developing self-regulatory capacities and effective goal-directed activities. Given our characterization of social cognitions in work situations as being secondary tasks, one might expect affective components (and affective communication) to be particularly important factors in social perceptions in organizational settings. Interestingly, Wayne and Ferris (1990) found that the extent to which a supervisor liked a subordinate was a major determinant of exchange quality between supervisors and subordinates, particularly in field settings.

Affective reactions are also a major determinant of performance appraisal processes (Cardy & Dobbins, 1986; Smither, Collins, & Buda, 1989; Tsui & Barry, 1986), but to date we know of no research directly examining the consequences of cognitive load on affective processes. This question seems to be crucial for understanding social perceptions in work settings as well as for understanding many other types of applied perceptions (e.g., leadership, job perceptions, or organizational climate).

We expect social perception in work situations to be based on nonsymbolic, limited-capacity processing that is strongly influenced by nonverbal, affective, and implicit processes. Such an interpretation suggests why processes like performance appraisal are enduring problems to practitioners, since in performance appraisal symbolic explanations are emphasized. This interpretation also contrasts significantly with the type of processes typically investigated by social cognitive researchers (e.g., the verbal components of category prototypes). Concerns over the applied relevance of some social-cognitive research (Banks & Murphy, 1985; Ilgen & Favero, 1985) underscore this difference. For example, performance appraisal ratings may be based more on affect cues than on observed behaviors.

In addition to social cognitions, many other types of perceptions are formed during normal work activities. For example, job perceptions and perceptions of organizational climate may be formed under "cognitively busy" conditions. Generalizing from our analysis of social cognitions, we would expect such perceptions to depend on nonverbal, affective, and implicit processes. One interesting possibility is that such perceptions have a strong affective component, which would be explained by our assertion that affective judgments conflict less with symbolic processing capacity. Consistent with this line of thinking, James and James (1989) found a strong latent, emotionally relevant, personal climate factor to underlie perceptions of role stress and harmony, job and work group characteristics, and leadership. They suggest that "the underlying cognitive structures pertaining to emotionally relevant cognitions of work environments are more integrated and parsimonious than has been realized" (p. 748). One possibility is that cognitions in each of these separate domains are inferred from or co-occur with affective reactions. Thus, such perceptions may be constructed based on implicitly produced affective information rather than being derived solely from descriptively accurate environmental cognitions. A similar possibility is that affective reactions activate such personal climate perceptions, making them more likely to be used to understand organizational environments during encoding processes. Interestingly, much work on job perceptions shows that they can be affected by social (Thomas & Griffin, 1983) and affective (Adler, Skov, & Salvemini, 1985; Kraiger, Billings, & Isen, 1989) cues.

We have stressed that information processing in organizations, whether related to problem solving, social perception, or reactions to tasks, occurs under high cognitive load conditions. To understand how people function effectively in such situations requires an explanation of how knowledge complements processing capacity in producing intelligent behavior. To some extent, knowledge speeds up and expands our capacity for symbolic information processing, but we believe that its major advantage is to allow us to use alternative types of information processing not available to individuals who lack the needed content specific knowledge. For example, pattern recognition processes tied closely to operations at a connectionist level may be critical in explaining information processing in many types of organizational activity. Similarly, knowledge may permit many tasks to be performed using automatic as compared to controlled processing. This difference is discussed in the final section of this chapter.

Automatic and Controlled Processing

Applications in Industrial and Organizational Psychology

The distinction between automatic and controlled processing has become increasingly significant in the industrial and organizational field over the past decade. The automatic versus controlled concept has been most frequently applied by industrial and organizational psychologists to the areas of social perception and skill acquisition. In social perception, the concept has served as a useful explanation for biases in rating behavior (Feldman, 1981; Lord, 1985) and leadership perceptions (Lord et al., 1984), where biases and errors are thought to result from automatic processing. Automatic and controlled processing concepts have also been used to describe changes in cognitive load as skills develop (Ackerman, 1987), often with the assumption that automatic processing is superior to controlled processing.

The automatic versus controlled processing distinction corresponds roughly to the concepts of low and high cognitive load on working memory. *Controlled processing* is thought to be demanding of attentional capacity, serial in nature, and able to be disrupted by concurrent cognitive load. *Automatic processing* is well learned in long-term memory, operates in parallel, and is virtually unaffected by load (Shiffrin & Schneider, 1977). Automaticity in social perception has implications not only for rating behavior in performance appraisal but also for daily interaction with others where communications and reciprocal responses depend on social perceptions. Much of our social interaction with supervisors, subordinates, and peers in organizations occurs simultaneously with, or is part of, task performance and so may proceed relatively automatically. We rely on automatic processes in some instances to help make sense of the organizational world.

One of the most influential articles in the industrial and organizational field applying the automatic versus controlled distinction to social perception was Feldman's (1981) treatment of cognitive processes in performance appraisal. In that widely cited paper, Feldman argued that both automatic and controlled processes operate in social interaction; automatic processes serve to categorize individuals who match a particular prototype, while controlled processes described by attribution theory operate when information is inconsistent with prior information. Subsequent research efforts were focused largely on making the rating process more "controlled" in order to minimize rating error, by using diary keeping and rater-observational training (e.g., Athey & McIntyre, 1987; DeNisi, Robbins, & Cafferty, 1989). Because automaticity is often associated with bias, the goal here is often to decrease the level of automatic processing—to reduce "errors" in perceptions.

Additionally, automaticity plays a major role in skill acquisition, with fairly obvious implications for training (Ackerman, 1987). Ackerman's (1987) framework is a model of skill acquisition based largely on the automatic versus controlled distinction. In his model, cognitive resources are assumed to have a fixed or limited capacity. One of the basic assumptions of this model is that the constraints of fixed resources can be overcome through automation. Interestingly, the goal in social perception is often to decrease the level of automaticity used in making ratings or forming judgments, whereas the goal in skill acquisition is typically to increase the level of automaticity in performance. Though these goals differ, the applications of the automatic versus controlled constructs to industrial and organizational psychology have common

roots in the work of Shiffrin and Schneider (1977).

Shiffrin and Schneider's (1977) seminal article has served as the conceptual basis for many discussions of automatic and controlled processing by industrial and organizational psychologists (Ackerman, 1987; Feldman, 1981; Lord, 1985). It is important, however, to discuss recent developments and criticisms related to this construct. On the surface, the distinction between automatic and controlled processing seems critically important for understanding any information processing task, but there are both operational and definitional problems with the distinction suggested by Shiffrin and Schneider (1977). Yet this distinction continues to be applied, and sometimes misapplied, by by industrial and organizational psychologists. For this reason, we think the automatic controlled processing construct needs to be critically evaluated in light of recent work by cognitive scientists. In addition, we need to evaluate carefully how it has been applied in our field.

Shiffrin and Schneider (1977) differentiated between automatic and controlled processing and showed how these processing modes could be applied to a single type of information processing task—visual search for specific targets. Their definitions of these constructs have been applied to much more complicated cognitive tasks in industrial and organizational psychology and many other areas. In their theory of attention and visual search, Shiffrin and Schneider (1977) provide the following definitions:

> Controlled search is highly demanding of attentional capacity, is usually serial in nature with a limited comparison rate, is easily established, altered, and even reversed by the subject, and is strongly dependent on load. Automatic detection is relatively well learned in long-term memory, is demanding of attention only when a target is presented, is parallel in

nature, is difficult to alter, to ignore, or to suppress once learned, and is virtually unaffected by load. (p. 127)

Shiffrin and Schneider also suggested that automatic processing was very slow in developing; tasks could become automatized only after thousands of trials, and then only in conditions where subjects search for the same target items in all conditions.

Shiffrin and Schneider's framework has certainly had a broad impact—their model showed how processes change with experience on a task, clearly demonstrating that learning proceeds differently under consistent versus variable mapping conditions. However, several aspects of Shiffrin and Schneider's model have been criticized in the cognitive science and social cognitive literatures. In this section, we review the major criticisms of the model and discuss the implications of these criticisms for industrial and organizational psychology. We also offer alternative views of automatic and controlled processing that we think will be useful, then provide directions for future research in our field.

Allport (1989) criticizes the Shiffrin and Schneider model because of its assumption of a unitary resource of fixed capacity, which is closely related to the amount of attentional resources available for task execution. In other words, according to Shiffrin and Schneider, automatic processing can free up a portion of this resource; the extra resources can then be allocated to concurrent tasks. However, Allport argues that humans may have multiple, specific resources, where certain computational functions may be limited by attentional capacity while others are not. Sperry and Schacter (1987) make a similar argument concerning memory functions. (See also Allen, 1983.) They argue that specific capacities are developed through evolution that are highly specialized and cannot be used for other functions; these capacities therefore create minimal attentional demands

on other resources. This argument is consistent with the point made above that both connectionist and symbolic architectures may appropriately represent human information processing. For example, our ability to judge frequency of occurrence of stimulus events, time, and space (Hasher & Zacks, 1979) may stem from a separate resource, which makes them seem as if they are functions that do not limit our capacity for other tasks (i.e., they are automatic).

Other criticisms of the Shiffrin and Schneider definition of automatic and controlled processing are raised by Ryan (1983). He argues that operational procedures used to distinguish automatic and controlled processing break down when carefully examined. Ryan notes that more than one so-called controlled process can run without interference between the concurrent tasks. For example, simultaneous serial scans of semantic and formal information, physical and categorical codes, or visually and auditorily presented memory sets have been empirically demonstrated. Similarly, reaction time for scanning a set of information may not vary with set size in the way suggested by Shiffrin and Schneider (Ryan, 1983, p. 175). Additionally, Sanders, Gonzales, Murphy, Liddle, and Vitina (1987), in their investigation of criteria for automatic processing, found that automatic frequency processing is subject to interference and requires some minimal capacity.

An additional cause for concern is the manner in which the automatic-controlled processing construct has been used in industrial and organizational psychology. The automatic versus controlled dichotomy may have been overgeneralized and applied to tasks that require many cognitive steps and are much more complex than Shiffrin and Schneider's visual search task. For example, performance appraisal involves the dynamic interplay of people over time in a highly complex work environment. Factors that are not important in the Shiffrin and Schneider paradigm are very important in work settings, and to characterize the entire process as being automatic or controlled misses many other important cognitive operations (e.g., role of intention, goals, priming, affect, memory look-ups, and social feedback).

One critical distinction that is often not acknowledged is that it makes sense only to speak in terms of automatic or controlled *processes,* but many industrial and organizational psychologists imply that entire *tasks* are performed in either an automatic or controlled manner. That is, tasks are comprised of many specific processes, each of which may be characterized along an automatic-controlled continuum. Therefore, it is misleading to characterize an entire task as either automatic or controlled.

In short, the distinction between automatic and controlled processing and the parallel notion of a limited attentional resource is not as straightforward as many believe. Further, use of this construct to explain information processing in work settings is quite difficult. Despite these substantial difficulties, there are some useful ideas embedded in the Shiffrin and Schneider framework. They involve (a) the central role of consciousness and intention in understanding information processing and (b) the notion that experience or learning can reduce the cognitive load of a task. These are really two distinct components of Shiffrin and Schneider's framework, and therefore we address them separately in the following sections. The reader may recognize that these issues also require an appreciation of the issues of level of cognitive architecture and unitary versus multiple memory resources, which were covered earlier in this chapter.

Automaticity, Intention, and Consciousness.
One important issue involves the matter of intention and consciousness. This issue has considerable applied relevance because goals exist on multiple levels, only some of which are appropriately conceptualized as being cognitive or involving conscious attention

(Powers, 1973). Moreover, sometimes goals directly result in organizational behavior, while at other times behavior occurs without a clear goal or intention. The role of automaticity can, in part, explain these phenomena. Consciousness and intentions link organizational behavior and information processing because they directly link motivation and cognitive operations. Bargh's (1989, 1990) work is particularly relevant to our discussion because he links antecedent cognitions and environmental events to conscious goals and cognitions. Conscious goals and cognitions, in turn, have both intended and unintended consequences.

Bargh's (1989) different varieties of automaticity depend on whether there is awareness of an activating event, whether a specific processing goal is in place, or whether the effect of the processing is intentional (pp. 10–11). These issues relate to the more general question of how a control structure in a cognitive architecture might operate. Bargh (1989) identifies three varieties of automaticity: preconscious, postconscious, and goal dependent.

Preconscious automaticity requires some type of triggering event that occurs prior to any conscious awareness of that event. One of the most interesting characteristics of preconscious automaticity is that the perceiver is not aware that any preconscious factors are influencing judgments and, therefore, is unaware of any biases that operate in a preconscious fashion. Preconscious interpretations of stimulus events, though outside of awareness, influence subsequent judgments or evaluations that may be made on a more conscious level (pp. 11–12). Affective judgments may play a preconscious role in many domains, as suggested by our previous discussion of social cognitions and job perceptions. Another example of preconscious automaticity is automatic categorization, which merely involves matching a pattern to some preexisting knowledge structure or schema, a process that our previous discussion shows can be appropriately explained at a connectionist level.

Categorization can involve schemas (scripts or person categories) that are closely related to current goals. Alternatively, categorization can result from chronically accessible social constructs. When such constructs are used to interpret social and task environments, activation does not require the presence of goals, intention, or awareness that the stimulus information has been categorized. The presence of salient physical features of individuals (e.g., gender, race, age) may also activate group stereotypes at a preconscious level. In short, there are many ways by which preconscious cognitive activities can influence subsequent interpretations and behaviors. Many of these preconscious activities seem to be better explained at a connectionist, rather than a symbolic, level.

Postconscious automaticity depends on some recent conscious experience and attentional processing for its occurrence. Bargh (1989) describes postconscious automaticity as "the nonconscious consequences of conscious thought" (p. 14). In other words, the person is intentionally or consciously processing some information, but some of the consequences or side effects of this intentional processing come from unintentional intrusions. The primary difference between postconscious and preconscious processing is that awareness of the activating event is necessary for postconscious processing to occur; such awareness is not necessary for preconscious processing to influence interpretation (p. 19).

Bargh's (1989) third major variety of processing, *goal-dependent automaticity*, requires that the person have a specific, conscious processing goal. There are two types of goal-dependent automaticity: unintended and intended. Unintended automaticity occurs when there are unintended consequences of intentional thought processes (p. 20). One example of this phenomenon involves subjects being asked to make behavioral ratings of stimuli. They may spontaneously make trait inferences from the behavioral stimuli when such inferences are not required (and may even interfere

with accurate behavioral ratings). Managing unintended consequences of goals may be an important issue in applied settings. Intended goal-dependent automaticity is intentional, yet still considered a form of automaticity because the processes do not need to be controlled once they are started; the processes can become autonomous. Examples of intended automaticity include scripts and well-learned complex action sequences (shifting gears or steering) involved in driving. Motor activity that is highly practiced, such as familiar processes in operating machinery, would also fall into this category.

Bargh (1989) suggests that these different types of automatic processing do not occur in isolation, but occur simultaneously with other automatic and controlled processing. Of particular interest to researchers in the industrial and organizational field may be ways in which conscious experience is influenced by preconscious and postconscious processing. Many work behaviors, judgments, and evaluations are probably undertaken consciously, with a goal in mind. However, such conscious activities may well be substantially influenced by preconscious and postconscious processing activity. "Mindlessness" (Langer, Blank, & Chanowitz, 1978) in social behaviors and script-based task behaviors (Gioia & Poole, 1984) has also been attributed to automatic processing. Bargh's framework provides greater insight into such mindless organizational phenomena, particularly since he also recognizes (Bargh, 1990) that goals themselves may be automatically activated by environmental stimuli.

We presented Bargh's (1989) model for two reasons. The different varieties of automaticity certainly illustrate that the automatic-controlled concept is much more complex than a simple either/or situation. The model also suggests that all types of automaticity are produced by an underlying control structure and an implicit memory system which may be appropriately described in connectionist terms.

Bargh's discussion of automatic processing is certainly interesting and seems to illustrate the need to explain how automatic and controlled processes are integrated. We suggest that the issues he raises can be better understood as examples of the interplay between connectionist (automatic) and symbolic level (controlled) activities. Because connectionist activities provide the microstructure for cognitions, they occur simultaneously with symbolic activities—connectionist activities precede, follow, and co-occur with symbolic processing. Thus, we think that Bargh's discussion emphasizes the mutual influence between connectionist and symbolic level processing, which we have argued has to occur in any intelligent system.

Automaticity and Cognitive Load.   A second important contribution of Shiffrin and Schneider's (1977) model was the notion that the cognitive load created by a task can be reduced by learning. They suggested that with extensive practice (often a thousand trials or more), visual search processes could be performed automatically. However, many interpretations in the industrial and organizational field of this phenomenon suggest that any reduction in the cognitive demands of a task that occur through experience should be explained in terms of automatic processes. A major section of this chapter emphasized that task performance depends jointly on knowledge and processes. Thus, knowledge can substitute for processing in many ways. One aspect of skill development may involve substituting knowledge for processing. This is quite different than arguing that serial controlled processes have become automated. A related argument is that the development of knowledge allows one to use different but more efficient processes, such as more selective search or reliance on pattern recognition (Simon, 1990). (For a more detailed explanation of skill acquisition, see Weiss, 1990.)

A third aspect of skill acquisition may involve the development of metacognitive skills, which improve the strategic use of cognitive resources in performing tasks. Metacognitive skills may develop because prior learning and increased efficiency free up symbolic capacity to address metacognitive issues. Thus, "cascading" processes in skill development may permit learning to occur at increasingly higher levels of abstraction as lower-level activities are performed more efficiently. The use of more efficient processes with experience is a critical component of Logan's theory of automaticity. Logan (1988, 1989) developed a model of automaticity with particular relevance to skill acquisition. Similar to the views of Bargh (1989), Logan believes it is misleading to view automatic and controlled processing as a dichotomy. In fact, Logan (1989) argues that automatic processing may be controlled in the sense that certain automatic processes can be overridden by conscious processes; automatic processing does not simply involve the withdrawal of attention.

According to Logan (1988), automaticity involves direct access retrieval from memory. On the other hand, nonautomatic processing involves the use of algorithms to respond to a stimulus. For example, when first required to solve a problem or make a response, people make use of an algorithm. With experience, however, people are able to directly retrieve the solution from memory without requiring the use of algorithms. Automatization, then, reflects the development of a knowledge base that can be used for direct access memory retrieval; the smaller the relevant knowledge base, the more likely it is necessary to use an algorithm. This process is precisely what is thought to occur as expertise develops; experts in a domain can directly access the relevant knowledge held in memory.

It is also worth repeating that viewing automatic processing as reducing cognitive load is directly tied to a unitary, fixed resource view of cognitive capacities. Multiple resource views of cognitive capacities suggest another very effective way of reducing the cognitive load of a task—relying on an alternative processing capacity. For example, rather than basing social perceptions on verbal information, Gilbert and Krull's (1988) work suggests that perceivers may rely on nonverbal information under high load conditions. Such shifts reduce cognitive load by trading off one resource for another, rather than automating processes. We expect that on complex tasks there are many similar tradeoffs workers can make to manage cognitive demands. This again suggests that all reductions in the processing load created by a task shouldn't be interpreted in terms of automatic processing.

The two issues discussed above—how we move from preconscious to postconscious to goal-dependent thoughts and how limited cognitive resources are used in performing work activities—are typically thought of as symbolic level questions, yet they can also be addressed at the level of a connectionist architecture. Cohen et al. (1990) discuss automaticity in terms of a parallel distributed processing framework, or connectionist model, which was described earlier in this chapter. In their model, the degree of automaticity depends on the strength of processing pathways. Here, as in Logan's model, automaticity is tied to retrieval from memory, but Cohen et al.'s explanation occurs at a deeper connectionist level. Direct pathways in memory correspond roughly to automatic processing; indirect pathways in memory correspond to a more controlled type of processing. Cohen et al. also suggest that multiple attentional resources exist and serve to activate or inhibit (mod-ulate, in their terms) pathways in order to minimize interference among tasks.

Despite difficulties with some components of the Shiffrin and Schneider conceptualization of automatic and controlled processing,

we think the construct still has considerable relevance to the field of industrial and organizational psychology. However, its utility lies in guiding a careful examination of issues with general relevance to our field, such as how goals and conscious thoughts relate to behavior or how automaticity and cognitive load are related. Yet these questions cannot be comprehensively addressed without a fundamental understanding of issues such as the nature of memory resources (unitary versus multiple-capacity views) and how connectionist and symbolic level cognitive architectures are integrated.

Conclusions

In this chapter, we covered much complex material, yet several basic points serve to summarize key issues:

- First, we asserted that the best cognitive science work attempts to explain information processing within a coherent theoretical system called a cognitive architecture.

- Second, cognitive architectures can be specified at two complementary levels—symbolic and connectionist. While cognitive scientists may debate the appropriateness of each of these levels, we maintain that most intelligent behavior depends on processing at both levels. To produce intelligent, adaptive behavior, connectionist level and symbolic level processes must be integrated. We provided practical examples showing how industrial and organizational psychology has overemphasized symbolic compared to connectionist level activities, and we suggested ways that connectionist thinking could benefit the field.

- Third, we reviewed memory research that showed pervasive encoding-retrieval interactions.

- Fourth, memory research suggests that people have multiple rather than a unitary capacity for processing information.

- Fifth, a diffusely operating memory system provides an important component of the control structure that guides information processing.

- Sixth, we suggested that skilled behavior involves the integration of current processing capacity and knowledge gained through experience.

- Finally, we presented some alternative perspectives on the automatic-controlled processing continuum. We also suggested that this continuum may reflect the relative emphasis on symbolic versus connectionist level processing.

These seven points stem from developments in cognitive science that are indeed revolutionary. These developments force us to think about old issues in new, more systematic and flexible ways. We hope this chapter provides the reader with an opportunity to learn more about cognitive science and to understand how a cognitive science perspective can be applied to issues central to industrial and organizational psychology. A cognitive revolution in the industrial and organizational field requires continual interplay between cognitive science and industrial and organizational psychology. What such advancement requires is that industrial and organizational psychologists undergo a process of continued learning about cognitive science and attempt to apply this knowledge to theoretical issues in the field. However, the field of industrial and organizational psychology also has much to offer to cognitive science. Many of the real-world tasks or issues we are concerned with are ideal vehicles for developing and testing cognitive principles. For example, we have argued that domain-specific expertise produces qualitative

changes in the type of processes that people use. Applied contexts provide both samples of people with extensive task experience and tasks important enough to warrant intensive investigation.

We would like to thank Rosalie Hall, Donald Perlis, Ray Sanders, Marty Murphy, Roseanne Foti, Neil Hauenstein, Mona Moths-Strean, Mary Kernan, Michael Lehman, James Farrell, and Krista Neltner for their careful reading and helpful comments on earlier versions of this manuscript.

References

Abelson, J. A., & Black, J. B. (1986). Introduction. In J. Galambos, R. Abelson, & J. Black (Eds.), *Knowledge structures* (pp. 1–18). Hillsdale, NJ: Erlbaum.

Ackerman, P. L. (1987). Individual differences in skill learning: An integration of psychometric and information processing perspectives. *Psychological Bulletin, 102,* 3–27.

Adler, S., Skov, R. B., & Salvemini, N. J. (1985). Job characteristics and job satisfaction: When cause becomes consequence. *Organizational Behavior and Human Decision Processes, 35,* 266–278.

Allen, M. (1983). Models of hemispheric specialization. *Psychological Bulletin, 93,* 73–104.

Allport, A. (1989). Visual attention. In M. Posner (Ed.), *Foundations of cognitive science* (pp. 631–682). Cambridge, MA: JAI Press.

Anderson, J. R. (1980). Concepts, propositions, and schemata: What are the cognitive units? In J. Flower (Ed.), *Nebraska symposium on motivation* (pp. 121–162). Lincoln: University of Nebraska Press.

Anderson, J. R. (1983a). *The architecture of cognition.* Cambridge, MA: Harvard University Press.

Anderson, J. R. (1983b). Retrieval of information from long-term memory. *Science, 20,* 25-30.

Anderson, J. R. (1987). Skill acquisition: Compilation of weak-method problem solutions. *Psychological Review, 94,* 192–210.

Anderson, J. R. (1990). *Cognitive psychology and its implications.* New York: Freeman.

Athey, T. R., & McIntyre, R. M. (1987). Effect of rater training on rater accuracy: Levels-of-processing theory and social facilitation theory perspectives. *Journal of Applied Psychology, 72,* 567–572.

Atkinson, R. C., & Shiffrin, R. M. (1968). Human memory: A proposed system and its control processes. In K. Spence & J. Spence (Eds.), *The psychology of learning and motivation* (Vol. 2, pp. 89–163). New York: Academic Press.

Baddeley, A. (1986). *Working memory.* Oxford: Clarendon Press.

Baddeley, A., & Hitch, G. J. (1974). Working memory. In G. Bower (Ed.), *Advances in learning and motivation* (Vol. 8, pp. 47–90). New York: Academic Press.

Banks, C. G., & Murphy, K. R. (1985). Toward narrowing the research-practice gap in performance appraisal. *Personnel Psychology, 38,* 335–345.

Bargh, J. A. (1989). Conditional automaticity: Varieties of automatic influence in social perception and cognition. In J. Uleman & J. Bargh (Eds.), *Unintended thought* (pp. 3–51). New York: Guilford.

Bargh, J. A. (1990). Auto-motives: Preconscious determinants of social interaction. In E. T. Higgins & R. Sorrentino (Eds.), *Handbook of motivation and cognition: Vol. 2. Foundations of social behavior* (pp. 93–130). New York: Guilford Press.

Barrett, G. V., Caldwell, M. S., & Alexander, R. A. (1989). The predictive stability of ability requirements for task performance: A critical reanalysis. *Human Performance, 2,* 167–181.

Bartlett, F. C. (1932). *Remembering.* London: Cambridge University Press.

Barsalou, L. W. (1983). Ad hoc categories. *Memory and Cognition, 11,* 211–227.

Barsalou, L. W. (1985). Ideals, central tendency, and frequency of instantiation as determinants of graded structure in categories. *Journal of Experimental Psychology: Learning, Memory, and Cognition, 11,* 629–654.

Beach, L. R. (1990). *Image theory: Decision making in personal and organizational contexts.* Chichester, England: Wiley.

Bernardin, H. J., & Buckley, M. R. (1981). Strategies in rater training. *Academy of Management Review, 6,* 205–212.

Bernardin, H. J., & Smith, P. C. (1981). A clarification of some issues regarding the development and use of behaviorally anchored rating scales (BARS). *Journal of Applied Psychology, 66,* 458–463.

Bernardin, H. J., & Walter, C. S. (1977). Effects of rater training and diary-keeping on psychometric error in ratings. *Journal of Applied Psychology, 62,* 64–69.

Berry, D. C., & Broadbent, D. E. (1988). Interactive tasks and the implicit-explicit distinction. *British Journal of Psychology, 79,* 251–272.

Borkenau, P. (1990). Traits as ideal-based and goal-derived social categories. *Journal of Personality and Social Psychology, 58,* 381–396.

Borman, W. C. (1975). Effects of instructions to avoid halo error on reliability and validity of performance evaluation ratings. *Journal of Applied Psychology, 60,* 556–560.

Borman, W. C. (1987). Personal constructs, performance schemata, and "folk theories" of subordinate effectiveness: Explorations in an army officer sample. *Organizational Behavior and Human Decision Processes, 40,* 307–322.

Borman, W. C., & Hallam, G. L. (1991). Observation accuracy for assessors of work sample performance: Consistency across task and individual differences correlates. *Journal of Applied Psychology, 76,* 11–18.

Bower, G. H. (1981). Emotional mood and memory. *American Psychologist, 36,* 129–148.

Bower, G. H., & Clapper, J. P. (1989). Experimental methods in cognitive science. In M. I. Posner (Ed.), *Foundations of cognitive science* (pp. 245–300). Cambridge, MA: MIT Press.

Brief, A. P., & Downey, H. K. (1983). Cognitive and organizational structures: A conceptual analysis of implicit organizing theories. *Human Relations, 36,* 1065–1090.

Brewer, M. B. (1988). A dual process model of impression formation. In T. K. Srull & R. S. Wyer (Eds.), *Advances in social cognition* (Vol. 1, pp. 1–36). Hillsdale, NJ: Erlbaum.

Broadbent, D. E. (1958). *Perception and communication.* London: Pergamon.

Broadbent, D. E. (1971). *Decision and stress.* London: Academic Press.

Campbell, D. J. (1988). Task complexity: A review and analysis. *Academy of Management Review, 13,* 40–52.

Campione, J. C., Brown, A. L., & Ferrara, R. A. (1982). Mental retardation and intelligence. In R. Sternberg (Ed.), *Handbook of human intelligence* (pp. 392–490). New York: Cambridge University.

Cantor, N., & Kihlstrom, J. F. (1987). *Personality and social intelligence*. Englewood Cliffs, NJ: Prentice-Hall.

Cantor, N., & Kihlstrom, J. F. (1989). Social intelligence and cognitive assessments of personality. In R. Wyer, Jr., & T. Srull (Eds.), *Advances in social cognition* (Vol. 2, pp. 1–59). Hillsdale, NJ: Erlbaum.

Cantor, N., & Mischel, W. (1979). Prototypes in person perception. In L. Berkowitz (Ed.), *Advances in experimental social psychology*. New York: Academic Press.

Cantor, N., Mischel, W., & Schwartz, J. C. (1982). A prototype analysis of psychological situations. *Cognitive Psychology, 14*, 45–77.

Cardy, R. L., & Dobbins, G. H. (1986). Affect and appraisal accuracy: Liking as an integral dimension in evaluating performance. *Journal of Applied Psychology, 71*, 672–678.

Carpenter, P. A., & Just, M. A. (1989). The role of working memory in language comprehension. In D. Klahr & K. Kotovsky (Eds.), *Complex information processing: The impact of Herbert A. Simon* (pp. 31–68). Hillsdale, NJ: Erlbaum.

Carver, C. S., & Scheier, M. F. (1981). *Attention and self-regulation: A control-theory approach to human behavior*. New York: Springer-Verlag.

Cellar, D. F., & Barrett, G. V. (1987). Script processing and intrinsic motivation: The cognitive sets underlying cognitive labels. *Organizational Behavior and Human Decision Processes, 40*, 115–135.

Cellar, D. F., & Wade, K. (1988). Effect of behavioral modeling on intrinsic motivation and script-related recognition. *Journal of Applied Psychology, 73*, 181–192.

Chi, M. T. H., Glaser, R., & Farr, M. J. (Eds.). (1988). *The nature of expertise*. Hillsdale, NJ: Erlbaum.

Cohen, J. D., Dunbar, K., & McClelland, J. L. (1990). On the control of automatic processes: A parallel distributed processing account of the Stroop effect. *Psychological Review, 97*, 332–361.

Collins, A. M., & Quillian, M. R. (1969). Retrieval time from semantic memory. *Journal of Verbal Learning and Verbal Behavior, 8*, 240–247.

Cooper, W. H. (1981a). Ubiquitous halo. *Psychological Bulletin, 90*, 218–244.

Cooper, W. H. (1981b). Conceptual similarity as a source of illusory halo in job performance ratings. *Journal of Applied Psychology, 66*, 302–307.

Craik, F. I. M., & Lockhart, R. S. (1972). Levels of processing: A framework for memory research. *Journal of Verbal Learning and Verbal Behavior, 11*, 671–684.

Day, D. V., & Lord, R. G. (in press). Expertise and problem categorization: The role of expert processing in organizational sense-making. *Journal of Management Studies*.

DeNisi, A. S., Robbins, T., & Cafferty, T. P. (1989). Organization of information used for performance appraisals: Role of diary-keeping. *Journal of Applied Psychology, 74*, 124–129.

DeNisi, A. S., & Williams, K. J. (1988). Cognitive approaches to performance appraisal. In K. Rowland & G. Ferris (Eds.), *Research in personnel and human resource management* (Vol. 6). Greenwich, CT: JAI Press.

Doran, L. I., Stone, V. K., Brief, A. P., & George, J. M. (1991). Behavioral intentions as predictors of job attitudes: The role of economic choice. *Journal of Applied Psychology, 76*, 40–45.

Dutton, J. E., & Jackson, S. E. (1987). Categorizing strategic issues: Links to organizational action. *Academy of Management Review, 12*, 76–90.

Earley, P. C., & Shalley, C. E. (in press). New perspectives on goals and performance: Merging motivation and cognition. In G. Ferris & K. Rowland (Eds.), *Research in personnel and human resource management* (Vol. 9). Greenwich, CT: JAI Press.

Eisenhardt, K. M. (1989). Making fast strategic decisions in high-velocity environments. *Academy of Management Journal, 32*, 543–576.

Elliott, E. S., & Dweck, C. S. (1988). Goals: An approach to motivation and achievement. *Journal of Personality and Social Psychology, 54*, 5–12.

Ericsson, K. A., & Polson, P. G. (1988). A cognitive analysis of exceptional memory for restaurant orders. In M. Chi, R. Glaser, & M. Farr (Eds.), *The nature of expertise* (pp. 23–70). Hillsdale, NJ: Erlbaum.

Estes, W. K. (1988). Toward a framework for combining connectionist and symbol-processing models. *Journal of Memory and Language, 27*, 196–212.

Farkas, A. J., & Tetrick, L. E. (1989). A three-wave longitudinal analysis of the causal ordering of satisfaction and commitment on turnover decisions. *Journal of Applied Psychology, 74,* 855–868.

Feigenbaum, E. A. (1989). What hath Simon wrought? In D. Klahr & K. Kotovsky (Eds.), *Complex information processing: The impact of Herbert A. Simon* (pp. 165–182). Hillsdale, NJ: Erlbaum.

Feldman, J. M. (1981). Beyond attribution theory: Cognitive processes in performance appraisal. *Journal of Applied Psychology, 66,* 127–148.

Fisher, R. P., & Craik, F. I. M. (1977). The interaction between encoding and retrieval operations in cued recall. *Journal of Experimental Psychology: Human Learning and Memory, 3,* 701–711.

Fleishman, E. A., & Mumford, M. D. (1989). Abilities as causes of individual differences in skill acquisition. *Human Performance, 2,* 201–223.

Fodor, J. A., & Pylyshyn, Z. W. (1988). Connectionism and cognitive architecture: A critical analysis. *Cognition, 28,* 3–71.

Foti, R. J., & Lord, R. G. (1987). Prototypes and scripts: The effects of alternative methods of processing information. *Organizational Behavior and Human Decision Processes, 39,* 318–341.

Foushee, H. C. (1984). Dyads and triads at 35,000 feet. *American Psychologist, 37,* 885–894.

Frese, M., & Altmann, A. (1989). The treatment of errors in learning and training. In L. Bainbridge & S. Ruiz Quintanilla (Eds.), *Developing skills with information technology* (pp. 65–86). Chichester, England: Wiley.

Galambos, J. A., Abelson, R. P., & Black, J. B. (1986). *Knowledge structures.* Hillsdale, NJ: Erlbaum.

Gilbert, D. T., & Krull, D. S. (1988). Seeing less and knowing more: The benefits of perceptual ignorance. *Journal of Personality and Social Psychology, 54,* 193–202.

Gilbert, D. T., Krull, D. S., & Pelham, B. W. (1988). Of thoughts unspoken: Social inference and the self-regulation of behavior. *Journal of Personality and Social Psychology, 55,* 685–694.

Gilbert, D. T., Pelham, B. W., & Krull, D. S. (1988). On cognitive busyness: When person perceivers meet persons perceived. *Journal of Personality and Social Psychology, 54,* 733–740.

Gioia, D. A., & Poole, P. P. (1984). Scripts in organizational behavior. *Academy of Management Review, 9,* 449–459.

Glaser, R. (1989). Expertise and learning: How do we think about instructional processes now that we have discovered knowledge structures? In D. Klahr & K. Kotovsky (Eds.), *Complex information processing: The impact of Herbert A. Simon.* Hillsdale, NJ: Erlbaum.

Glaser, R., & Chi, M. T. H. (1988). Overview. In M. Chi, R. Glaser, & M. Farr (Eds.), *The nature of expertise* (pp. xv–xxviii). Hillsdale, NJ: Erlbaum.

Gluck, M. A., & Bower, G. H. (1988). From conditioning to category learning: An adaptive network model. *Journal of Experimental Psychology: General, 117,* 227–247.

Goldstein, I. L., & Gilliam, P. (1990). Training system issues in the year 2000. *American Psychologist, 45,* 134–143.

Hambrick, D. C., & Mason, P. A. (1984). Upper echelons: The organization as a reflection of its top managers. *Academy of Management Journal, 9,* 103–206.

Hanges, P. J., Braverman, E. P., & Rentsch, J. R. (1989). *Changes in raters' impressions of subordinates: A catastrophe model.* Manuscript submitted for publication.

Harmon, P., & King, D. (1985). Expert systems: *Artificial intelligence in business.* New York: Wiley.

Harris, S. G. (1989). *A schema-based perspective on organizational culture.* Paper presented at the annual meeting of the Academy of Management, Washington, DC.

Hasher, L., & Zacks, R. T. (1979). Automatic and effortful processes in memory. *Journal of Experimental Psychology: General, 108,* 356–388.

Hastie, R., & Park, B. (1986). The relationship between memory and judgment depends on whether the judgment task is memory-based or on-line. *Psychological Review, 93,* 258–268.

Hauenstein, N. M. A., & Foti, R. J. (1989). From laboratory to practice: Neglected issues in implementing frame-of-reference training. *Personnel Psychology, 42,* 359–378.

Heilman, M. E., Block, C. J., Martell, R. F., & Simon, M. C. (1989). Has anything changed? Current characterizations of men, women, and managers. *Journal of Applied Psychology, 74,* 935–942.

Henry, R. A., & Hulin, C. L. (1987). Stability of skilled performance across time: Some generalizations and limitations on utilities. *Journal of Applied Psychology, 72,* 457–562.

Herbert, G. R., & Lord, R. G. (1989). *Cognitive representations of job information.* Unpublished manuscript, University of Akron, OH.

Higgins, E. R., & Bargh, J. A. (1987). Social cognition and social perception. In M. Rosenzweig & L. Porter (Eds.), *Annual review of psychology* (Vol. 38, pp. 369–425). Palo Alto, CA: Annual Reviews.

Hoffman, C., Mischel, W., & Mazze, K. (1981). The role of purpose in the organization of information about behavior: Trait-based versus goal-based categories in person perception. *Journal of Personality and Social Psychology, 40,* 211–225.

Holzbach, R. L. (1978). Rater bias in performance ratings: Superior, self-, and peer ratings. *Journal of Applied Psychology, 63,* 579–588.

Howell, W. C., & Cooke, N. J. (1989). Training the human information processor: A review of cognitive models. In I. Goldstein (Ed.), *Training and development in organizations* (pp. 121–182). San Francisco: Jossey-Bass.

Hunter, J. E., Schmidt, F. L., & Judiesch, M. K. (1990). Individual differences in output variability as a function of job complexity. *Journal of Applied Psychology, 75,* 28–42.

Ilgen, D. R., & Favero, J. L. (1985). Limits in generalization from psychological research to performance appraisal processes. *Academy of Management Review, 10,* 311–321.

Ilgen, D. R., & Feldman, J. M. (1983). Performance appraisal: A process focus. In L. Cummings & B. Staw (Eds.), *Research in organizational behavior* (Vol. 5, pp. 141-197). Greenwich, CT: JAI Press.

Ilgen, D. R., & Klein, H. J. (1989). Organizational behavior. In M. Rosenzweig & L. Porter (Eds.), *Annual review of psychology* (Vol. 40, pp. 327–351). Palo Alto, CA: Annual Reviews.

Isenberg, D. J. (1989). How senior managers think. In W. H. Agor (Ed.), *Intuition in organizations: Leading and managing productively* (pp. 91–110). Newbury Park, CA: Sage.

Izard, C. (1990). Facial expressions and the regulation of emotions. *Journal of Personality and Social Psychology, 58,* 487–498.

Jacobs, R., & Kozlowski, S. W. J. (1985). A closer look at halo error in performance ratings. *Academy of Management Journal, 28,* 201–212.

James, L. A., & James, L. R. (1989). Integrating work environment perceptions: Explorations into the measurement of meaning. *Journal of Applied Psychology, 74,* 739–751.

Jeffery, K., & Mischel, W. (1979). Effects of purpose on the organization and recall of information in person perception. *Journal of Personality, 47,* 397–419.

Johnson-Laird, P. N. (1989). Mental models. In M. Posner (Ed.), *Foundations of cognitive science* (pp. 469–499). Cambridge, MA: MIT Press.

Jordan, M. I., & Rosenbaum, D. A. (1989). Action. In M. Posner (Ed.), *Foundations of cognitive science* (pp. 727–767). Cambridge, MA: MIT Press.

Kahneman, D. (1973). *Attention and effort.* Englewood Cliffs, NJ: Prentice-Hall.

Kahneman, D., & Tversky, A. (1979). Prospect theory: An analysis of decision under risk. *Econometrica, 47,* 263–291.

Kanfer, R., & Ackerman, P. L. (1989). Motivation and cognitive abilities: An integrative/aptitude-treatment interaction approach to skill acquisition. *Journal of Applied Psychology, 74,* 657–690.

Kehoe, E. J. (1988). A layered network model of associative learning: Learning to learn and configuration. *Psychological Review, 95,* 411–433.

Kelley, H. H. (1973). The processes of causal attribution. *American Psychologist, 28,* 107–127.

Klein, H. J. (1989). An integrated control theory model of work motivation. *Academy of Management Review, 14,* 150–172.

Kopp, C. B. (1989). Regulation of distress and negative emotions: A developmental view. *Developmental Psychology, 25,* 343–354.

Kozlowski, S. W. J., & Kirsch, M. P. (1987). The systematic distortion hypothesis, halo, and accuracy: An individual-level analysis. *Journal of Applied Psychology, 72,* 252–261.

Kraiger, K., Billings, R. S., & Isen, A. M. (1989). The influence of positive affective states on task perceptions and satisfaction. *Organizational Behavior and Human Decision Processes, 44,* 12–25.

Kuhl, J. (1986). Motivation and information processing: A new look at decision making, dynamic change, and action control. In R. M. Sorrentino & E. T. Higgins (Eds.), *Handbook of motivation and cognition: Foundations of social behavior* (Vol. 1, pp. 404–434). New York: Guilford Press.

Landy, F. J., Vance, R. J., Barnes-Farrell, J. L., & Steele, J. W. (1980). Statistical control of halo error in performance ratings. *Journal of Applied Psychology, 65,* 501–506.

Langer, E., Blank, A., & Chanowitz, B. (1978). The mindlessness of ostensibly thoughtful action: The role of "placebic" information in interpersonal interaction. *Journal of Personality and Social Psychology, 36,* 635–642.

Lesgold, A., Rubinson, H., Feltovich, P., Glaser, R., Klopfer, D., & Wang, Y. (1988). Expertise in a complex skill: Diagnosing x-ray pictures. In M. Chi, R. Glaser, & M. Farr (Eds.), *The nature of expertise* (pp. 311–342). Hillsdale, NJ: Erlbaum.

Leventhal, H. (1984). A perceptual-motor theory of emotion. In L. Berkowitz (Ed.), *Advances in experimental social psychology* (Vol. 17, pp. 117–182). Orlando, FL: Academic Press.

Logan, G. D. (1988). Toward an instance theory of automatization. *Psychological Review, 95,* 492–527.

Logan, G. D. (1989). Automaticity and cognitive control. In J. Uleman & J. Bargh (Eds.), *Unintended thought* (pp. 52–74). New York: Guilford Press.

Lord, R. G. (1985). An information processing approach to social perceptions, leadership and behavioral measurement in organizations. In B. M. Staw & L. L. Cummings (Eds.), *Research in organizational behavior* (Vol. 7, pp. 87–128). Greenwich, CT: JAI Press.

Lord, R. G., & Carpenter, M. (1986). *Measuring cognitive processes.* Paper presented at the annual meeting of the Academy of Management, Chicago.

Lord, R. G., Foti, R., & De Vader, C. (1984). A test of leadership categorization theory: Internal structure, information processing, and leadership perceptions. *Organizational Behavior and Human Performance, 34,* 343–378.

Lord, R. G., & Hanges, P. J. (1987). A control system model of organizational motivation: Theoretical development and applied implications. *Behavioral Science, 32,* 161–178.

Lord, R. G., & Kernan, M. C. (1987). Scripts as determinants of purposeful behavior in organizations. *Academy of Management Review, 12,* 265–277.

Lord, R. G., & Maher, K. J. (1989). Cognitive processes in industrial and organizational psychology. In C. Cooper & I. Robertson (Eds.), *International review of industrial and organizational psychology, 1989.* New York: Wiley.

Lord, R. G., & Maher, K. J. (1990). Alternative information processing models and their implications for theory, research, and practice. *Academy of Management Review, 15,* 9–28.

Lord, R. G., & Maher, K. J. (1991). *Leadership and information processing: Linking perceptions and performance.* New York: HarperCollins.

Macmillan, N. A., & Creelman, C. D. (1990). Response bias: Characteristics of detection theory, threshold theory, and "nonparametric" indexes. *Psychological Bulletin, 107,* 401–413.

March, J. G., & Simon, H. A. (1958). *Organizations.* New York: Wiley.

McClelland, J. L., Rumelhart, D., & Hinton, G. E. (1986). The appeal of parallel distributed processing. In D. Rumelhart, J. McClelland, & the PDP Research Group (Eds.), *Parallel distributed processing: Explorations in the microstructure of cognition: Vol. 1. Foundations* (pp. 3–44). Cambridge, MA: MIT Press.

McClelland, J. L., Rumelhart, D., & the PDP Research Group (Eds.). (1986). *Parallel distributed processing: Vol. 2. Explorations in the microstructure of cognition: Psychological and biological models.* Cambridge, MA: MIT Press.

McKelvey, J. D., & Lord, R. G. (1986, April). *The effects of automatic and controlled processing on rating accuracy.* Paper presented at the annual meeting of the Society for Industrial and Organizational Psychology, Chicago.

Medin, D. L. (1989). Concepts and conceptual structure. *American Psychologist, 44,* 1469–1481.

Michaels, C. E., & Spector, P. E. (1982). Causes of employee turnover: A test of the Mobley, Griffeth, Hand, and Meglino model. *Journal of Applied Psychology, 67,* 53–59.

Minsky, M. (1975). A framework for representing knowledge. In P. H. Winston (Ed.), *The psychology of computer vision* (pp. 211–277). New York: McGraw-Hill.

Mischel, W. (1973). Toward a cognitive social learning reconceptualization of personality. *Psychological Review, 80,* 252–283.

Mitchell, T. R., & James, L. R. (1989). Conclusions and future directions. *Academy of Management Review, 14,* 401–407.

Mobley, W. H., Griffeth, R. W., Hand, H. H., & Meglino, B. M. (1979). Review and conceptual analysis of the employee turnover process. *Psychological Bulletin, 86,* 493–522.

Morris, C. D., Bransford, J. D., & Franks, J. J. (1977). Levels of processing versus transfer appropriate processing. *Journal of Verbal Learning and Verbal Behavior, 16*, 519–533.

Morrison, A. M., & Von Glinow, M. A. (1990). Women and minorities in management. *American Psychologist, 45*, 200–208.

Murphy, K. R. (1989). Is the relationship between cognitive ability and job performance stable over time? *Human Performance, 2*, 183–200.

Murphy, K. R., & Balzer, W. K. (1989). Rater errors and rating accuracy. *Journal of Applied Psychology, 74*, 619–624.

Murphy, K. R., & Jako, R. (1989). Under what conditions are observed intercorrelations greater or smaller than true intercorrelations? *Journal of Applied Psychology, 74*, 827–830.

Murphy, K. R., & Reynolds, D. H. (1988). Does true halo affect observed halo? *Journal of Applied Psychology, 73*, 235–238.

Murphy, M. D., & Puff, C. R. (1982). Free recall: Basic methodology and analyses. In C. Puff (Ed.), *Handbook of research methods in human and cognition* (pp. 99–128). New York: Academic Press.

Nathan, B. R., & Lord, R. G. (1983). Cognitive categorization and dimensional schemata: A process approach to the study of halo in performance ratings. *Journal of Applied Psychology, 68*, 102–114.

Neisser, U. (1976). *Cognitive and reality: Principles and implications of cognitive psychology.* San Francisco: Freeman.

Neisser, U. (1982). *Memory observed: Remembering in natural contexts.* San Francisco: Freeman.

Nelson, T. O. (1977). Repetition and depth of processing. *Journal of Verbal Learning and Verbal Behavior, 16*, 151–171.

Newell, A., & Simon, H. A. (1972). *Human problem solving.* Englewood Cliffs, NJ: Prentice-Hall.

Newell, A., Rosenbloom, P. S., & Laird, J. E. (1989). Symbolic architectures for cognition. In M. Posner (Ed.), *Foundations of cognitive science* (pp. 93–131). Cambridge, MA: MIT Press.

Nisbett, R., & Ross, L. (1980). *Human inference: Strategies and shortcomings of social judgment.* Englewood Cliffs, NJ: Prentice-Hall.

Norman, D. A. (1986). Reflections on cognition and parallel distributed processing. In J. McClelland, D. Rumelhart, & the PDP Research Group (Eds.), *Parallel distributed processing: Vol. 2: Explorations in the microstructure of cognition: Psychological and biological models* (pp. 531–546). Cambridge, MA: MIT Press.

Nutt, P. C. (1984). Types of organizational decision processes. *Administrative Science Quarterly, 29*, 414–450.

Osgood, C. E., Suci, G. J., & Tannenbaum, P. H. (1957). *The measurement of meaning.* Urbana: University of Illinois Press.

Piaget, J., & Inhelder, B. (1969). *The psychology of the child.* New York: Basic Books.

Porac, J., & Thomas, H. (1990). Taxonomic mental models in competitor definition. *Academy of Management Review, 15*, 224–240.

Posner, M. I. (1988). Introduction: What is it to be an expert? In M. Chi, R. Glaser, & M. Farr (Eds.), *The nature of expertise* (pp. xxix-xxxvi). Hillsdale, NJ: Erlbaum.

Posner, M. I. (Ed.). (1989). *Foundations of cognitive science.* Cambridge, MA: MIT Press.

Powers, W. T. (1973). Feedback: Beyond behaviorism. *Science, 179*, 351–356.

Puff, C. R. (Ed.). (1982). *Handbook of research methods in human and cognition.* New York: Academic Press.

Pulakos, E. D. (1984). A comparison of rater training programs: Error training and accuracy training. *Journal of Applied Psychology, 69*, 581–588.

Pulakos, E. D. (1986). The development of training programs to increase accuracy with different rating tasks. *Organizational Behavior and Human Decision Processes, 38*, 76–91.

Pylyshyn, Z. W. (1989). Computing in cognitive science. In M. Posner (Ed.), *Foundations of cognitive science* (pp. 51–91). Cambridge, MA: MIT Press.

Reber, A. S. (1989). Implicit learning and tacit knowledge. *Journal of Experimental Psychology: General, 118*, 219–235.

Rentsch, J. R. (1990). Climate and culture: Interaction and qualitative differences in organizational meanings. *Journal of Applied Psychology, 75*, 668–681.

Roediger, H. L., III (1990). Implicit memory: Retention without remembering. *American Psychologist, 45*, 1043–1056.

Rosch, E. (1978). Principles of categorization. In E. Rosch & B. B. Lloyd (Eds.), *Cognition and categorization.* Hillsdale, NJ: Erlbaum.

Rosenbloom, P. S., & Newell, A. (1986). The chunking of goal hierarchies: A generalized model of practice. In R. Michalski, J. Carbonell, &

T. Mitchell (Eds.), *Machine learning: An artificial intelligence approach* (Vol. 2). Los Altos, CA: Morgan Kaufman.

Rumelhart, D. E. (1989). The architecture of mind: A connectionist approach. In M. Posner (Ed.), *Foundations of cognitive science* (pp. 133–159). Cambridge, MA: MIT Press.

Rumelhart, D. E., Hinton, G. E., & McClelland, L. (1986). A general framework for parallel distributed processing. In D. Rumelhart, J. McClelland, & the PDP Research Group (Eds.), *Parallel distributed processing: Vol. 1 Explorations in the microstructure of cognition: Foundations* (pp. 45–76). Cambridge, MA: MIT Press.

Rumelhart, D. E., & Norman, D. A. (1982). Simulating a skilled typist: A study of skilled motor performance. *Cognitive Science, 6,* 1–36.

Rumelhart, D. E., Smolensky, P., McClelland, J. L., & Hinton, G. E. (1986). Schemata and sequential thought processes in PDP models. In J. McClelland, D. Rumelhart, & the PDP Research Group (Eds.), *Parallel distributed processing: Vol. 2 Explorations in the microstructure of cognition: Psychological and biological models* (pp. 7–57). Cambridge, MA: MIT Press.

Ryan, C. (1983). Reassessing the automaticity-control distinction: Item recognition as a paradigm case. *Psychological Review, 90,* 171–178.

Sanders, R. E., Gonzalez, E. G., Murphy, M. D., Liddle, C. L., & Vitina, J. R. (1987). Frequency of occurrence and the criteria for automatic processing. *Journal of Experimental Psychology: Learning, Memory, and Cognition, 13,* 241–250.

Schacter, D. L. (1987). Implicit memory: History and current status. *Journal of Experimental Psychology: Learning, Memory, and Cognition, 13,* 501–518.

Schacter, D. L. (1989). Memory. In M. Posner (Ed.), *Foundations of cognitive science* (pp. 683–725). Cambridge, MA: MIT Press.

Schank, R. C., & Abelson, R. P. (1977). *Scripts, plans, goals, and understanding.* Hillsdale, NJ: Erlbaum.

Schoenfeld, A. H. (1981). *Episodes and executive decisions in mathematical problem solving.* Paper presented at the annual meeting of the American Educational Research Association, Los Angeles.

Sejnowski, T. J., & Churchland, P. S. (1989). Brain and cognition. In M. Posner (Ed.), *Foundations of cognitive science* (pp. 301–356). Cambridge, MA: MIT Press.

Shalley, C. E. (in press). The effects of productivity goals, creativity goals, and personal discretion on individual creativity. *Journal of Applied Psychology.*

Shiffrin, R. M., & Schneider, W. (1977). Controlled and automatic human information processing: Perceptual learning, automatic attending, and a general theory. *Psychological Review, 84,* 127–190.

Simon, H. A. (1990). Invariants of human behavior. In M. Rosenzweig & L. Porter (Eds.), *Annual review of psychology* (Vol. 41, pp. 1–19). Palo Alto, CA: Annual Reviews.

Simon, H. A., & Kaplan, C. A. (1989). Foundations of cognitive science. In M. Posner (Ed.), *Foundations of cognitive science* (pp. 1–47). Cambridge, MA: MIT Press.

Simon, H. A., & Kotovsky, K. (1963). Human acquisition of concepts for serial patterns. *Psychological Review, 70,* 534–546.

Smith, E. R., & Miller, F. D. (1983). Mediation among attributional inferences and comprehension processes: Initial findings and a general method. *Journal of Personality and Social Psychology, 44,* 492–505.

Smith, P. C., & Kendall, L. M. (1963). Retranslation of expectations: An approach to the construction of unambiguous anchors for rating scales. *Journal of Applied Psychology, 47,* 149–155.

Smither, J. W., Collins, H., & Buda, R. (1989). When ratee satisfaction influences performance evaluations: A case of illusory halo. *Journal of Applied Psychology, 74,* 599–605.

Snodgrass, J. G., & Corwin, J. (1988). Pragmatics of measuring recognition memory: Applications to dementia and amnesia. *Journal of Experimental Psychology: General, 117,* 34–50.

Sperling, G., & Dosher, B. (1986). Strategy and optimization in human information processing. In K. Boff, L. Kaufman, & J. Thomas (Eds.), *Handbook of perception and performance* (Vol. 1). New York: Wiley.

Sperry, D. F., & Schacter, D. L. (1987). The evolution of multiple memory systems. *Psychological Review, 94,* 439–454.

Srull, T. K. (1983). Organizational and retrieval processes in person memory: An examination of processing objectives, presentation format, and the possible role of self-generated retrieval cues. *Journal of Personality and Social Psychology, 44,* 1157–1170.

Srull, T. K. (1984). Methodological techniques for the study of person memory and social cognition. In R. Wyer & T. Srull (Eds.), *Handbook of social cognition* (Vol. 2, pp. 1–72). Hillsdale, NJ: Erlbaum.

Srull, T. K., & Wyer, R. S., Jr. (1989). Person memory and judgment. *Psychological Review, 96,* 58–83.

Stein, B. S. (1978). Depth of processing reexamined: The effects of precision of encoding and test appropriateness. *Journal of Verbal Learning and Verbal Behavior, 17,* 165–174.

Sternberg, S., Monsell, S., Knoll, R. L., & Wright, C. E. (1978). The latency and duration of rapid movement sequences: Comparisons of speech and typewriting. In G. E. Stelmach (Ed.), *Information processing in motor control and learning* (pp. 117–152). New York: Academic Press.

Swets, J. A. (1986). Form of empirical ROCs in discrimination and diagnostic tasks: Implications for theory and measurement of performance. *Psychological Bulletin, 99,* 181–198.

Taylor, S. E., & Fiske, S. T. (1978). Salience, attention, and attribution: Top of the head phenomena. In L. Berkowitz (Ed.), *Advances in experimental social psychology.* New York: Academic Press.

Thomas, J. G., & Griffin, R. (1983). The social information processing model of task design: A review of the literature. *Academy of Management Review, 8,* 672–682.

Thornton, G. C., III, & Zorich, S. (1980). Training to improve observer accuracy. *Journal of Applied Psychology, 65,* 351–354.

Tronick, E. Z. (1989). Emotions and emotional communication in infants. *American Psychologist, 44,* 112-119.

Tsui, A. S., & Barry, B. (1986). Interpersonal affect and rating errors. *Academy of Management Journal, 29,* 586-599.

Tulving, E., & Thompson, D. M. (1973). Encoding specificity and retrieval processes in episodic memory. *Psychological Review, 80,* 352–373.

Tversky, A., & Kahneman, D. (1974). Judgment under uncertainty: Heuristics and biases. *Science, 185,* 1124–1131.

Tversky, A., & Kahneman, D. (1981). The framing of decisions and the psychology of choice. *Science, 211,* 453–458.

Vallacher, R. R., & Wegner, D. M. (1987). What do people think they're doing? Action identification and human behavior. *Psychological Review, 94,* 3–15.

VanLehn, K. (1989). Problem solving and cognitive skill acquisition. In M. Posner (Ed.), *Foundations of cognitive science* (pp. 527–579). Cambridge, MA: MIT Press.

Walsh, J. P. (1989). *Knowledge structures and the management of organizations: A research review and agenda.* Unpublished manuscript.

Wayne, S. J., & Ferris, G. R. (1990). Influence tactics, affect, and exchange quality in supervisor-subordinate dyads. *Journal of Applied Psychology, 75,* 487–499.

Weiss, H. M. (1990). Learning theory and industrial and organizational psychology. In M. D. Dunnette & L. Hough (Ed.), *Handbook of industrial and organizational psychology* (2nd ed., vol. 1, pp. 171–221). Palo Alto, CA: Consulting Psychologists Press.

Weiss, H. M., & Adler, S. (1984). Personality and organizational behavior. In B. Staw & L. Cummings (Eds.), *Research in organizational behavior* (Vol. 6, pp. 1–50). Greenwich, CT: JAI.

Wickens, C. D. (1984). *Engineering psychology and human performance.* Columbus, OH: Merrill.

Williams, L. J., & Hazer, J. T. (1986). Antecedents and consequences of satisfaction and commitment in turnover models: A reanalysis using latent variable structural equation methods. *Journal of Applied Psychology, 71,* 219–231.

Wyer, R. S., Jr., & Srull, T. K. (1980). The processing social stimulus information: A conceptual integration. In R. Hastie, T. Ostrom, E. Ebbesen, R. Wyer, Jr., D. Hamilton, & D. Carlston (Eds.), *Person memory: The cognitive basis of social perception* (pp. 227–300). Hillsdale, NJ: Erlbaum.

Zajonc, R. B. (1984). On the primacy of affect. *American Psychologist, 39,* 117–123.

Individual Behavior
and Organizational Practices

Production of goods and services by the institutions and organizations of society forms the basis for the employment of individuals. Industrial and organizational psychologists study the structure of work and the systems of production as a means of assuring a good match between individuals' attributes (as discussed later in the five chapters of Section II) and the nature of their work assignments. The nine chapters in this section provide in-depth coverage of both the science and technology of practices instrumental to accomplishing optimum use of human resources—use that affords productive matches for both individuals and the work organizations of society.

Chapters 2 and 3 describe methods of studying jobs and work roles, and Chapter 4 discusses human factors considerations in the design of tools, equipment, and work systems. Chapter 5 provides extended treatment to methods of measuring employee performance—methods of criterion development and criterion measurement. Next steps in building an effective work force involve recruitment, discussed thoroughly in Chapter 7, and personnel assessment and selection, covered in Chapter 6. After persons have been selected by an organization, a proper match between individuals' attributes and organizational and work requirements can be made more certain by designing and implementing job-focused training systems, covered in Chapter 9, and by attending to employees' work role expectations and attitudes, as discussed in Chapter 8. Finally, Chapter 10 presents theory and methods of utility analysis—strategies that have been developed to determine the ultimate usefulness of the foregoing methods oriented toward assuring a good match between individuals' attributes and the nature of their work assignments. Taken together, the nine chapters of this section of the *Handbook* form an in-depth account of traditional methods and practices in industrial and organizational psychology. The paragraphs below provide somewhat greater detail about the content of each of the chapters in this section.

R. J. Harvey in Chapter 2 [Job Analysis] states that significant progress has occurred over the 15 years since publication of the first *Handbook of Industrial and Organizational Psychology*. Impetus for such progress has come from the explosive growth and greatly enhanced sophistication of computer technology and from the continuing challenge of seeking to forge an empirical link between the domain of individual differences constructs and the domain of job behavior constructs. Harvey has structured his discussion of job analysis into six broad topics: basics, philosophies, collecting job analysis data, legal issues, uses of job analysis information, and the dimensionality of work. Throughout, Harvey expresses strong views about the status of both past and current research, concepts, and various job analysis methods according to their relative usefulness in accomplishing a variety of human resources applications.

D. R. Ilgen and J. R. Hollenbeck in Chapter 3 [The Structure of Work: Job Design and Roles] point out that *jobs* and *roles* both represent prescribed patterns of behavior for organizational members, but that very little overlap exists between the research literatures on the two topics. They note that topics related to *jobs* emphasize primarily the *content* of elements comprising jobs whereas topics related to *roles* emphasize primarily the *processes* whereby sets of behaviors come to be labeled as roles. Ilgen and Hollenbeck develop an approach they call *job-role differentiation* to define the boundary between jobs and roles. They then proceed to apply notions of *content* and *objectivity* from the job literature to the role literature, and, in turn, to apply notions of *process* from the role literature to the job literature. Their approach results in new perspectives on many issues, including such factors as the nature of jobs, the dimensionality of job characteristics, the measurement of role conflict, and several other issues of equal interest. They note that their conceptualization of these issues is a first step toward integrating these two large but primarily separate literatures. Even so, they are optimistic that their review and reinterpretation of these literatures will provide a springboard for developing further integration of concepts and research results related to *jobs* and *roles* as they are dealt with by industrial and organizational psychologists.

W. C. Howell in Chapter 4 [Human Factors in the Workplace] describes human factors as an interdisciplinary field of science and application concerned with user-oriented design. Its focus is on the design of systems no matter how simple or complex. Howell notes that the system concept is the same as the open system model of organizations on which much of modern industrial and organizational psychology rests. Even so, industrial and organizational psychology and human factors have not often shown the type of cooperative integration implied by their shared model. Perhaps because of this, Howell has shrewdly, I believe, written a primer that compellingly conveys exactly what human factors is about, where it is headed, and what it has to offer to work organizations and society. I guarantee that anyone who reads this chapter will view the contrivances of his or her world much more critically. No one will come away from Howell's chapter without having gained a good amount of "human factors religion."

W. C. Borman in Chapter 5 [Job Behavior, Performance, and Effective-
ness] reviews methods for the development and measurement of criteria
of individual job performance. After presenting a brief history of major
thoughts, observations, and conceptions of criteria, Borman provides a
comprehensive review of methodological advances, research results, and
personnel research applications of performance ratings. His review is
exceptionally thorough, including the evaluations of different rating
forms, results of training directed toward reducing rating errors, and
questions and research results related to such matters as accuracy and the
convergent and discriminant validities of ratings. Borman also gives
critical attention to so-called objective criteria such as turnover, sales
volume, error rates, and work samples. He also presents examples of how
structural and latent variable modeling has been used in studying performance constructs as a means of enhancing scientific understanding of the
underlying dimensionality of individual performance in work settings. In
summing up the chapter, Borman comments on the contrast between
conceptual advances in criterion understanding, which have been impressive, and the more problematic state of actual criterion measurement.
Even though problems of measurement are still far from being solved,
Borman expresses optimism that advances are being made, and he
strongly urges that efforts toward developing the perfect criterion measurement system be rigorously pursued because "criteria provide the
foundation of industrial and organizational psychology and the practice of
applied personnel research in organizations."

R. M. Guion in Chapter 6 [Personnel Assessment, Selection, and
Placement] states that a *predictive hypothesis* is central to processes of
personnel selection and selection research. This hypothesis requires an
understanding of the job, an exact knowledge of the aspect of job behavior
that is to be predicted, and one or more applicant characteristics that are
hypothesized to predict that behavior. Guion elaborates on this theme
throughout the chapter—placing primary emphasis on the need for
scientific foundations and understanding as elaborated by professional
judgment, and research designs for use in developing evidence bearing on
the evaluation of predictive measures. Guion preaches against letting
one's guard down. He emphasizes strongly the need for continued
surveillance to guard against opening the door to shoddy practices, snap
judgments, or falling into simplistic habit patterns that rely on unfounded
claims or the pride of past successes. *Professional judgment* is systematic,
informed, and based on understanding and research.

Sections of the chapter are devoted to all aspects of selection research,
including learning about the job, the choice of dependent (*criterion*)
measures, methods of assessment, and special considerations such as bias
and fairness, adverse impact, validity generalization, utility analysis,
multivariate procedures, and methods that may be employed in evaluating
psychometric validity and job relatedness. The breadth of information

presented in this chapter is impressive. Guion's final words of advice are short, direct, and imperative: "The days of personnel research have not ended."

S. L. Rynes in Chapter 7 [Recruitment, Job Choice, and Post-hire Consequences: A Call for New Research Directions] notes that the 1976 edition of this *Handbook* devoted only one page to organizational recruiting. Since then, Rynes reports that the empirical literature on recruiting has expanded considerably and has made many conceptual advances. Recruitment research has concentrated on three topics: recruiters, recruitment sources, and realistic job previews. Sadly, Rynes finds little basis for integration across these three research streams because each of the topic areas has, to a large degree, developed in isolation from the others. Given what she perceives to be a piecemeal approach to recruitment research, Rynes determined that the time was ripe to develop a new research agenda for studying many important questions bearing on the role of recruitment in *attracting* applicants to organizations. Accordingly, the final third of her chapter is devoted to an alternative model for recruitment research—one that takes account of many more contextual, independent, dependent, and process variables than had been accomplished in previous research. In closing, Rynes reminds the reader that the importance of recruitment will expand greatly in the years ahead as predicted labor shortages materialize and current trends toward ever increasing diversity of the labor force intensify.

C. Hulin in Chapter 8 [Adaptation, Persistence, and Commitment in Organizations] provides an incredibly comprehensive overview of attitude-behavior models as they relate to job satisfaction/job dissatisfaction and organizational adaptation, persistence, and commitment. Both theoretical analyses and empirical results suggest that patterns of work role behaviors, both positive and negative, are predictable from a knowledge of work role attitudes. Such attitudes arise, in turn, from individuals' frames of reference, personal utilities (evaluations) of both direct and indirect costs of work role membership, and individual dispositional factors. Hulin concludes that *behavioral patterns* such as changes in job inputs, job outcomes, the nature of work roles, or work role involvement form the legitimate *dependent* variables in studies of organizational withdrawal, persistence, and adaptation. As mentioned, Hulin supports this conclusion throughout this chapter with an abundance of evidence drawn from both theory and empirical results.

I. L. Goldstein in Chapter 9 [Training in Work Organizations] emphasizes that training systems will be of greatly increased importance in the years immediately ahead as fewer persons enter the work force and increasingly sophisticated and complex technology becomes more and more prevalent. The decade of the 1980s witnessed many advances in research and theory in training systems. In keeping with these advances, Goldstein provides in these pages a most comprehensive and superbly comprehensible account of state-of-the-art principles in training theory, practice, and technology. Early sections of the chapter discuss training needs analysis and how job tasks may be linked with required knowledges, skills, and abilities in the development of training programs. Emphasis is given to research results in cognitive and instructional psychology that relate to trainee readiness and motivation to learn. Extended attention is given to methods of training program evaluation. Final sections of the chapter describe a variety of fairly recent training methods, such as behavior role modeling and self-management methods. Goldstein devotes the last sections of the chapter to recent social issues that pose new challenges to training design issues, such as aging, fair employment practice, technical obsolescence, career change, and increasingly complex production methods and systems. Goldstein's chapter provides knowledge that should stimulate training researchers and practitioners to exert increased effort toward successfully coping with the rapid pace of organizational and societal change in the years immediately ahead.

J. W. Boudreau in Chapter 10 [Utility Analysis for Decisions in Human Resource Management] discusses utility analysis as a family of theories and measures designed to describe, predict, and/or explain what determines the usefulness or desirability of decision options (e.g., improved selection, training, performance appraisal, internal staffing, and compensation) and to examine how information affects such decisions. Boudreau's approach to his subject is encyclopedic. He covers it in nine major areas as follows: (a) fundamental concepts of utility as it fits within the broader domain of decision models; (b) historical review of the utility model and assumptions fundamental to understanding utility analysis; (c) a review and summary of studies wherein industrial and organizational psychologists have used utility estimates to evaluate the consequences of their interventions; (d) a critical review of research aimed at estimating or measuring the dollar value of the variability of employee performance; (e) a discussion of the role of risk and uncertainty in utility analysis—showing that such analysis may, in fact, improve decisions even when only meager information is available; (f) a persuasive argument in support of perceiving utility analysis as a framework where interdisciplinary approaches (e.g., industrial and organizational psychology and labor economics) can be used to advantage in taking account of such issues as equal employment opportunity, affirmative action, capital budgeting, variable costs, human resource accounting, and a wealth of other labor market considerations; (g) consideration of how utility analysis can be used to evaluate the impact of programs (such as training, compensation, and employee involvement) undertaken for the purpose of improving employee performance; (h) formulation of a unified utility model that takes account of employee flow into, through, and out of organizations—thereby showing how the model may be used to define and optimize links between recruitment, selection, turnover, and internal staffing; and, finally, (i) suggestions for needed future utility research that will yield broader understanding of human resource management decision making.

As mentioned, Boudreau's coverage of *utility analysis* is truly encyclopedic. Boudreau is hopeful that readers of this chapter will be rewarded with a vast array of ideas to aid in further development of decision tools that truly reflect a partnership between applied social science research and managerial decisions regarding human work behavior. I am convinced that his hopes are well founded.

–MARVIN D. DUNNETTE

CHAPTER 2

Job Analysis

Robert J. Harvey
Virginia Polytechnic Institute &
State University

Significant progress has occurred since McCormick's (1976) review of job analysis, particularly regarding instrumentation. Standardized "worker-oriented" instruments capable of comparing task-dissimilar jobs on a common metric have undergone significant evolution, and many such questionnaires now exist. Advances in computer technology have allowed the development of integrated personnel systems to manage the vast amounts of data generated during the job analysis process. Applications of artificial intelligence and expert-systems technology promise to further reduce the cost and labor-intensiveness of the job analysis process.

Two primary challenges face the field. First, we must increase our knowledge of the job analysis rating process. Our understanding of the cognitive aspects of rating jobs lags far behind our ability to construct comprehensive work measurement instruments; the issue of job analysis ratings validity has scarcely been addressed. Second, we must begin in earnest to assemble an empirical data base that links the domain of human individual differences constructs (e.g., mental abilities, interests, personality traits) with the domain of job behavior constructs (e.g., delegating/coordinating, exchanging information, operating machines); industrial psychologists have for decades been calling for such research (e.g., Dunnette, 1976). Armed with this information, great progress toward solving the problems of employee selection and placement can be made.

The Basics of Job Analysis

Background

HISTORICALLY, JOB ANALYSIS has been a relatively soporific area of industrial and organizational psychology, characterized by neither heated controversy nor prominent visibility in the research literature. Technologies for identifying and rating job tasks have been refined by decades of use in military, government, and industry settings and can be applied to analyze new jobs using a step-by-step, cookbook approach (e.g., see Christal, 1974; Gael, 1983; Morsh, 1964). For much of this century, there was little governmental regulation of personnel practices in general, or job analysis in particular; thus, few constraints were placed on using job analysis data to solve practical personnel problems.

The state of job analysis when McCormick (1976) performed his review for the previous edition of this *Handbook* was quite different then than it is today: Task analysis was the dominant job analysis technique; President Gerald Ford was distributing "Whip Inflation Now" buttons; many psychologists had yet to comprehend the importance of the revolutionary "worker-oriented" concept of job analysis taken by the then-novel *Position Analysis Questionnaire* (PAQ; McCormick, Jeanneret, & Mecham, 1972), which for the first time allowed meaningful comparisons to be drawn between task-dissimilar jobs; and the *Albemarle Paper Co. v. Moody* (1975) case, which firmly established job analysis as a necessary part of a test validation effort, was just being decided by the Supreme Court. In short, it was a period in which few people gave much thought to the topic of job analysis.

Since then, however, much has changed. Job analysis has grown far beyond its previous emphasis on task analysis; instead, compliance with external regulations, the avoidance of discrimination lawsuits, and the need to closely link job analysis data with specific personnel functions have become major concerns to organizations. Standardized job analysis questionnaires applicable to many different organizations and jobs have increased dramatically in number and popularity (e.g., the *Professional and Managerial Position Questionnaire,* or PMPQ, of J. Mitchell & McCormick, 1979; the *Job Element Inventory,* or JEI, of Harvey, Friedman, Hakel, & Cornelius, 1988; the *Occupation Analysis Inventory,* or OAI, of Cunningham, Boese, Neeb, & Pass, 1983; the *General Work Inventory,* or GWI, of Cunningham & Ballentine, 1982, and the *Common-Metric Questionnaire,* or CMQ, of Harvey, 1990a).

The debate over validity generalization has focused newfound attention and importance on the process of describing and grouping jobs for test validation and validity transportability purposes. Similarly, the comparable worth issue has generated heightened interest in describing jobs for compensation purposes. Even the mundane area of task analysis has been the subject of research interest, as in, for example, selecting task rating scales, assessing the reliability of ratings, and applying artificial intelligence techniques to reduce the labor-intensiveness of collecting task data.

Given that industrial and organizational psychologists have been analyzing jobs for the better part of this century, one would think that by now we would have been able to agree on a definition of job analysis and its key terms. Unfortunately, we have not; if anything, confusion as to what the term *job analysis* means is greater today than ever before. To put this issue into perspective, Kershner offered an interesting assessment:

> As is patently evident, job analysis has been a sort of handmaiden serving in various ways a variety of needs and all the while floundering in a morass of semantic confusion.

No, this is not a recent observation; it was made in 1955 and was cited by McCormick (1976, p. 654) in the previous edition of this *Handbook*. What is striking is that, decades later, it is still accurate. As Kershner indicated, job analysis as an area of research and practice has many problems due in large part to a state of basic terminological confusion. Remedial action is needed on three fronts.

First, as Schmitt (1987) noted, significant gaps abound in the job analysis research base; consequently, practical prescriptions for collecting and using job analysis data are often based on little or no empirical justification. As Prien (1977) noted, by 1971 "research on job analysis had approximated little more than a pilot effort" (p. 169). Much additional research must be conducted to remedy current gaps in the literature, especially regarding the information processing aspects of the job analysis rating process.

Second, what Kershner called a "morass of semantic confusion" is worse than ever, and conflicting definitions of key terms are rampant. With respect to the term *job analysis,* many industrial and organizational psychologists confuse the process of *collecting* job descriptive data with the process of *applying* it to solve personnel problems (e.g., employee selection). For example, T. W. Mitchell (1986) proposed an "understanding-based" method for identifying personal life history events, or *biodata,* hypothesized to determine subsequent job performance; Mitchell considered the process of writing biodata items to be job analysis. In a similar vein, others have used the term *job analysis* to denote the process of identifying personality traits, dispositional adjectives, and other personal traits thought to be required for successful job performance (e.g., Arneson & Peterson, 1986; Hughes & Prien, 1989).

The position taken in this chapter is that it is critical that the term *job analysis* be applied only to procedures that *collect* information describing verifiable job behaviors and activities; it should *not* be used to denote the wide assortment of procedures that make inferences about people or otherwise *apply* job analysis data (e.g., to infer personal traits that might be necessary for successful job performance).

Third, progress must be made to address the "image problem" facing job analysis; little progress has been made with respect to changing the widespread "handmaiden" (handperson?) perception that Kershner described over 35 years ago. Prien (1977) described this phenomenon, observing that

> although job analysis is an essential feature of almost every activity engaged in by industrial-organizational psychologists, the subject is treated in textbooks in a manner which suggests that any fool can do it and thus it is a task which can be delegated to the lowest level technician. This is quite contradictory to the position taken ... in the EEOC Selection Guidelines. (p. 167)

Cunningham (1989) made a similar observation, noting that

> when I first started back in the sixties, job analysis was a very lonely area to work in. Over the years, it has not been very popular relative to some of the more glamorous activities in I/O psychology. Job analytic research and development is expensive, time-consuming, and laborious. It is sometimes difficult to publish, and it does not seem to hold a strong attraction for students. In short, job analysis might be characterized as the Rodney Dangerfield of I/O psychology: it doesn't get a lot of respect. (p. 7)

I hope that this chapter will generate interest in solving these problems, many of which stem directly or indirectly from confusion regarding what job analysis is—and is not. I first address the issue of defining key terms.

Terminology

Job analysis has its own somewhat unique vocabulary, and some confusion results from the fact that many of these terms are used in everyday language (e.g., *job, duty*) and their meaning differs when used in a job analysis context. However, much of our current semantic confusion is self-inflicted, being caused by inconsistent usage of terms in the research literature, texts, and relevant professional standards documents. Surprisingly, one of the most troublesome issues concerns the definition of job analysis.

What is Job Analysis?   The McCormick (1976) chapter is perhaps the most widely cited and influential recent treatment of this topic. McCormick (pp. 652–653) defined job analysis as the collection of data on (a) "job-oriented" behaviors, such as job tasks and work procedures; (b) more abstract "worker-oriented" behaviors, such as decision making, supervision, and information processing; (c) behaviors involved in interactions with machines, materials, and tools; (d) methods of evaluating performance, such as productivity and error rates; (e) job context, such as working conditions and type of compensation system; and (f) personnel requirements, such as skills, physical abilities, and personality traits.

Building on McCormick's definition, I define *job analysis* as the collection of data describing (a) observable (or otherwise verifiable) job behaviors performed by workers, including both *what is accomplished* as well as *what technologies are employed* to accomplish the end results and (b) verifiable characteristics of the job environment with which workers interact, including physical, mechanical, social, and informational elements. Job behaviors or contextual characteristics can be observed both directly (e.g., physical actions performed, tools and machines used, people contacted, materials modified, services provided, or sources of data used as input) as well as indirectly, through the use of what McCormick et al. (1972, p. 384) termed *strong inference* from other observable job behaviors. For example, an activity like making managerial decisions regarding investments and cash flow may be described in terms of the work products involved or produced by the decision, the kinds of data used as input

or produced by the decision maker, or the consequences of incorrect decisions.

My definition of job analysis parallels McCormick's by emphasizing the description of work behaviors, work products, and job context, including the informational and social context in which the work is performed. It differs, however, by excluding the process of inferring hypothetical worker traits or abilities (variously termed *job specifications, worker specifications,* or *personnel specifications*) presumed to be required for job performance (e.g., "general cognitive ability," "leadership," "dominance," "sociability"). Inferring required personal traits—though admittedly an important part of the employee selection process—is excluded because it fails to meet the following three criteria that I maintain should characterize a job analysis method.

First, job analysis methods should have as their goal the description of *observables*. This view parallels the position taken in the *Uniform Guidelines on Employee Selection Procedures* (1978, often termed the *Guidelines* or *Uniform Guidelines*), particularly regarding the meaning of the term *work behavior:*

> Job analysis ... includes an analysis of the important work behavior(s) required for successful performance and their relative importance and, if the behavior results in work product(s), an analysis of the work product(s). Any job analysis should focus on the work behavior(s) and the tasks associated with them. If work behavior(s) are not observable, the job analysis should identify and analyze those aspects of the behavior(s) that can be observed and the observed work products. (section 1607.14.C.2)

Thus, even behaviors that some might consider unobservable, such as coordinating, deciding, or planning, can be objectively described in terms of the observables that result from their performance, such as people contacted in the course of making the decision, kinds of supplies ordered, or consequences of the decision. All work behaviors, no matter how abstract they may appear at first, must have an observable component and will eventually result in an observable action, state, or product.

If a work behavior does *not* have an observable component, then by definition it cannot be described in a job analysis. As the *Guidelines* note, an *observable* is something "able to be seen, heard, or otherwise perceived by a person other than the person performing the action" (section 1607.16.N). Describing observables should be the sole goal of a job analysis.

Second, a job analysis should involve the description of work behavior *independent of the personal characteristics or attributes of the employees who perform the job.* That is, the work itself is being described, not the personal traits or performance effectiveness of the people who currently attempt to perform the job. A job analysis describes *how* a job is performed and must not be colored by whether or not the employees currently hired to perform the job are doing so successfully or not. The unit of analysis in job analysis is the *job* or the *position* (defined below), *not* the *incumbents* who perform the work. Techniques that describe the level of effectiveness of individual employees are called *performance appraisals*, not job analyses.

Third, and of critical importance, job analysis data must be *verifiable* and *replicable*. That is, should the accuracy or validity of a job analysis be challenged, the organization must be able to justify every job analysis rating in terms of observable behaviors, actions, work products, information used or produced, and the like. The importance of restricting job analysis to the domain of verifiable observables cannot be overemphasized. Key to the ability to demonstrate the validity of job analysis data is the requirement of *replicability*—that is, independent observers with adequate job familiarity should produce functionally equivalent ratings.

Obviously, some degree of inference is involved in most rating processes; to the extent they are present, inferences in job analysis should be of the "strong" variety defined by McCormick et al. (1972). That is, less observable behaviors (e.g., "making decisions") can be described in terms of their observable, manifest aspects. "Weak" inferences—in particular, inferring the hypothetical human constructs presumed necessary for personal success on the job—should not be termed job analysis.

Knowledge/Skills Versus Abilities/"Others" and Job Specifications Versus Job Analyses. Other than the term job analysis, the phrase *job knowledge, skills, abilities, and other characteristics* (KSAs or KSAOs) has probably caused more semantic confusion than any other. Because of the fundamental differences that exist between job knowledge and skill (KS) versus ability and "other" (AO) specifications, I find it much more useful to replace the term KSA/KSAO with a discussion of KS versus AO requirements.

When the component K, S, A, and O terms are defined, it is readily apparent that KSs are specified directly in terms of observable job behaviors, whereas AOs are only indirectly—if at all—linked to the actual job behaviors identified in a job analysis. In the case of KS requirements, the 1978 *Guidelines* define job *knowledge* as "a body of information applied directly to the performance of a function" (section 1607.16.M), and a job *skill* as "a present, observable competence to perform a learned psychomotor act" (section 1607.16.T). In contrast, AO requirements are couched in terms of much more abstract *hypothetical constructs.* To quote the APA *Standards* (1985), in this context a construct is

> a psychological characteristic (e.g., numerical ability, spatial ability, introversion, anxiety) considered to vary or differ across individuals. A construct

(sometimes called a latent variable) is not directly observable; rather it is a theoretical concept derived from research and other experience that has been constructed to *explain observable behavior patterns.* (p. 90, emphasis added)

Although "behavior" is common to KS and AO specifications, the *kind* of behavior being referenced differs sharply. Skills are defined in terms of learned, observable, psychomotor acts; the behaviors used to define a skill-based job specification are precisely the same ones identified in the job analysis (e.g., interacting with specific machines, equipment, or other physical aspects of the job environment). For job knowledge specifications, job analysis items specifying the kinds of information used (e.g., knowledge of traffic laws, APA style rules, chemical reactions involving chlorine, or the value of Art Deco furniture) directly define the required knowledge domains.

Although a "skill" or a "knowledge" cannot be directly observed, the fact that a given body of knowledge must be used as input, or produced as output, on a job, or that a specific psychomotor skill is involved in accomplishing a given observable job behavior, *can* be unambiguously specified in terms of observable job activities. Thus, the link between job analysis data and KS specifications should be very close. To the extent that inferences are required, they are of the strong type discussed by McCormick et al. (1972)—that is, using the listing of activities and sources of information contained in the job analysis to derive a listing of associated psychomotor skill and knowledge demands.

Identifying AO requirements is a qualitatively different matter. The behaviors referenced when defining general human abilities and individual differences traits are typically *not* the job behaviors detailed in the job analysis; the former kind of behaviors involve responding to standardized test stimuli designed to assess the level of the hypothetical trait possessed by a testee (e.g., the items on a paper-and-pencil IQ or personality test). Accordingly, it is unlikely that any significant overlap will exist between the work behaviors identified in the job analysis and the test-taking behaviors exhibited by the testee when responding to the test items that purport to measure a given ability or trait. AO requirements are typically expressed in terms of hypothetical traits (e.g., cognitive ability, dominance, introversion, leadership) on which *people* presumably differ; they are not properties or characteristics of *jobs.*

KSs and AOs additionally differ in terms of the degree to which an individual's *level* of job knowledge or a learned psychomotor skill can be altered. Because they are task-specific and learned by definition, job skills can be sharpened via practice, and job knowledge can be increased via training or other educational efforts (of course, the maximum attainable level of proficiency will likely differ across individuals). In contrast, although there is some debate on this question, AO traits are often viewed as relatively stable and enduring personal characteristics that defy efforts at change (e.g., general intelligence, extraversion).

To further complicate matters, researchers have employed inconsistent definitions of these terms. Regarding skills, much confusion has been caused by authors who overgeneralize the term *ability* to include learned psychomotor skills and knowledge-usage requirements. Schmitt (1987) cited examples of this ability-skill confusion, including the "ability to type a paper in APA format," the "ability to balance an account," and the "ability to sort mail by zipcode" (p. 4). Such activities are much better described in terms of knowledge and skill requirements, not "abilities."

In a related example, Hughes and Prien (1989) stated that developing selection tests involves constructing a job analysis questionnaire "consisting of task statements and perhaps knowledge, skill, and ability statements

(KSAs, herein referred to as job skills)" (p. 284, emphasis added). Further, these "skills" were as diverse as

> ability to listen, ability to read…agility, leg strength…ability to think logically… ability to remember, ability to follow oral orders, color vision, lower body strength… ability to read gauges… ability to bend, ability to work in confined spaces, sense of direction, observation skill, knowledge of physics…ability to apply facts, deduction, reaction time, ability to analyze information, ability to make decisions…and claustrophobia. (p. 289)

Clearly, there are large differences in the size of the inferential leap necessary to conclude that each of these "skills" are necessary for successful job performance based on a job analysis. Additionally, some are presumably much more amenable to improvement on the part of job applicants (e.g., leg strength, ability to read) than others (e.g., color vision, reaction time).

My insistence on differentiating between a job analysis and a KS- or AO-based job specification is hardly novel or unprecedented; indeed, only in relatively recent years has this fundamental distinction become blurred. The 1978 *Uniform Guidelines* draw sharp distinctions between behavior-based job analyses and trait-based job specifications, defining *job analysis* as an examination of work behaviors, and noting that *work behavior* is

> an activity performed to achieve the objectives of the job. Work behaviors involve observable (physical) and unobservable (mental) components. A work behavior consists of the performance of one or more tasks. *Knowledges, skills, and abilities are not behaviors,* although they may be applied in work behaviors. (section 1607.16.Y, emphasis added)

Other authors (e.g., Gael, 1983; Siegel & Lane, 1987) have taken similar positions. As Gael noted, job analysis

> means breaking a job down into tasks performed by job incumbents, synthesizing those tasks into job functions, and obtaining data and studying those tasks and functions…. A distinction can be drawn between: *information pertaining to the work itself*—the specific tasks and attributes of those tasks, such as importance, difficulty, and frequency; and *information associated with, but not directly involved in, the work itself*—the skills and abilities needed to perform the work adequately. (1983, pp. 11–12, italics in original)

Similarly, Siegel and Lane (1987) held that

> job analysis is a systematic procedure for identifying the duties entailed in performing a job and the surroundings (both physical and social) in which these duties are performed…. When a job analysis is undertaken preliminary to initiating selection, placement, or training programs, it is the basis for *inferring* personnel specifications ("specs"); that is, the knowledge, skills, abilities, and other personal qualifications (KSAOs) prerequisite to satisfactory job performance. (1987, p. 83, italics added)

Unfortunately, some authors have completely blurred the distinction between a job analysis and a set of job specifications. For example, the *Standards for Educational and Psychological Testing* (1985) defined job analysis as "any of several methods of identifying the tasks performed on a job or the knowledge, skills, and abilities required to perform that job" (p. 92). The SIOP (1987) *Principles for the Validation and Use of Personnel Selection Procedures* noted that in addition to describing work behavior, *job analysis is the identification of worker specifications* which include a description of the general level of skill or knowledge required to perform the job duties. Inferences about the worker characteristics are made by the researcher or job experts by combining knowledge of the work performed and what workers have to do to perform the work. (p. 6, italics added)

Because job or worker specifications make inferences about the employment potential of job candidates on the basis of their personal characteristics, they function as *selection tests;* that is, applicants are not hired if they do not meet the characteristics listed in the job specifications. Indeed, in listing the kinds of selection tests that *must* be validated, the SIOP *Principles* include virtually every kind of data contained in job specifications:

Such selection procedures include, but are not limited to, standardized paper-and-pencil tests, performance tests, work samples, personality inventories, interest inventories, projective techniques, tests of honesty or integrity including polygraph examinations, assessment center evaluations, biographical data forms or scored application blanks, interviews, educational requirements, experience requirements, reference checks, physical requirements such as height or weight, physical ability tests...or any other selection instrument, whenever any one or a combination of them is used or assists in making a personnel decision. (p. 1)

It is important to clearly differentiate between job analyses and job specifications for a number of reasons. First, they describe different things: Job specifications describe *people* in terms of characteristics that are presumably necessary for successful job performance; job analyses describe *job behaviors,* independent of the characteristics of the specific people who

perform them. Thus, the unit of analysis (personal traits vs. job behavior) is different. Although KS-oriented job specifications are much more closely tied to the job analysis (depending on the philosophy of job analysis used, the content of the KS specifications may be taken directly from the job analysis), the unit of analysis will always be different.

Second, different judgment and inference processes are used, especially with respect to AO requirements. AO-oriented job specifications involve the weak inference that hypothetical constructs or other personal characteristics are necessary for job performance, based on an examination of job behaviors that may have little or no overlap with the test-taking behaviors used to measure the abilities. It is a long inferential leap from a description of observable job tasks to a listing of general ability and trait requirements. Particularly if one allows for the possibility that people with *different* ability profiles may be able to perform the job equally well, this inference process may become vastly more complicated.

Although developing KS-based job specifications involves much less of a logical leap, some degree of translation, restating, or abstraction from the behaviorally oriented information contained in the job analysis itself is still involved. That is, when moving from a job analysis of the form "the worker performs behaviors A and B using information about X and Y to accomplish outcome Z" to a job specification of the form "the successful applicant will be able to exhibit the skills necessary to perform behaviors A and B and possess content mastery of knowledge domains X and Y," varying degrees of inference will be required.

Third, demonstrating the validity of AO-based job specification inferences involves some form of construct-oriented strategy (e.g., see Schmitt, 1987, p. 4) and/or criterion-oriented validity evidence. As Schmitt (1987, p. 4) noted, if one operationalizes KS-based job specifications directly in terms of the job tasks (the approach endorsed above), a relatively simple content-oriented strategy can be used to validate KS inferences.

Organizational Structure Terms. Moving on to relatively less troublesome terms, the *position* is the most basic structural entity in an organization, representing the collection of work tasks, activities, responsibilities, and associated contextual characteristics that are assignable to a single person; this person is termed the *position incumbent*. The distinction between the position and its incumbent is important: An incumbent is a real person holding the position, whereas the position is a convenient organizational abstraction (a hypothetical construct, if you will) that can be created, modified, or eliminated at the discretion of the employing organization.

A position exists whether or not an actual person is employed to perform its work activities, a fact that highlights the earlier distinction between a job analysis and an employee/worker/job specification. That is, a position may be analyzed to produce a job analysis, whether or not it currently has an incumbent. Assuming that people with different profiles of skills, abilities, and personal traits may be able to successfully perform the tasks assigned to the position (i.e., a *compensatory* model in which high standing on some traits may compensate for lower scores on others), several possible employee specification profiles for a single position can be constructed.

Like the position, the job is an organizational abstraction, although it is not as easily defined. At a conceptual level, a job is a collection of positions similar enough to one another in terms of their important work behaviors to share a common job title. Henderson (1979) defined a job to be "work consisting of responsibilities and duties that are sufficiently alike to justify being covered by a single job analysis" (p. 134).

Thus, a job is made up of one or more similar positions, each of which is functionally interchangeable with the others in terms of job activities. Although simple enough at the conceptual level, a number of difficulties arise with this definition in practice. For example, when are positions similar enough to one another to be considered a single job, given that there is almost always some degree of within-title variability? Similarly, what are the important work behaviors that should be considered when determining position similarity?

Positions and jobs are the entities, or units of analysis, that are studied in a job analysis. As discussed earlier, job incumbents are *not* the object of study in a job analysis, although they frequently serve as sources of information about the activities performed in the positions or jobs being studied. The organizational entities (positions, jobs) are described in the job analysis process, not the characteristics of the incumbents who occupy them.

In the same manner as a job is a collection of similar positions, a *job family* is a collection of jobs similar enough in terms of their important work activities to be grouped together and treated as interchangeable *for a given personnel purpose.* For example, jobs may be grouped to form job families for the purpose of obtaining a sufficient sample size for a test validation or validity generalization project (e.g., Cornelius, Schmidt, & Carron, 1984), or for the purpose of developing a performance appraisal form that can be shared by a number of different jobs (Cornelius, Hakel, & Sackett, 1979).

Some authors use specialized terms to describe different kinds of job families. For example, Henderson (1979) defines a *class* as "all jobs sufficiently similar as to kinds of subject matter, education and experience requirements, level of difficulty and responsibility, and qualification requirements" (p. 134). Moving up, a *class-series* is defined as "a grouping of classes having similar job content but differing in degree of responsibility, level of skill, knowledge, and qualification requirements." Henderson defined a *family* to be "two or more class-series within a business that have related or common work content" and an *occupation* as "a grouping of jobs or job classes within a number of different businesses that require similar skill, effort, and responsibility." This definition of occupation is essentially the one used by the U. S. Department of Labor (DOL) in its *Dictionary of Occupational Titles;* in essence, an occupation is a job or job family found across a number of organizations.

Although these more specialized terms certainly have their place, in the interest of simplicity I will label these various abstractions *job families* because the basic issue is the same in all cases: determining the degree of work similarity between a number of jobs or aggregates of jobs. The problems encountered when making these higher-level aggregations of jobs are similar to those faced when identifying job groupings. For example, what kinds of job analysis information should be used? How much similarity is enough? To what degree can within-group variability be tolerated? Is similarity on some job analysis attributes more important than similarity on others? To what degree do the job family groupings differ as a function of the purpose for grouping jobs?

In view of the questions and ambiguities involved in identifying jobs and job families, it should be apparent that jobs and job families are at best imprecise abstractions used to reduce the confusion involved in describing and comparing work activities within and across organizations. In one sense, the only personnel entity that is "real" is the position, in that a single human performs it and its activities can be unambiguously delineated in a job analysis. All higher-level organizational constructs—(jobs, families, occupations)—necessarily involve aggregating across, and thereby ignoring and deeming unimportant, a potentially sizable number of both large and small behavioral differences that exist between positions. It is easy to fall into the trap of treating jobs and job families as if they are monolithic, "real" entities, and thereby lose sight of the fact that there is invariably a nontrivial degree of within-title or within-family variability in job

behavior. In some cases, this within-classification variability may be unimportant; in others, it may be highly significant. The problem of within-classification variability is discussed further in a later section.

Job classification is the term used to describe the process by which decisions regarding position or job similarity are made for a particular personnel purpose. As such, it involves the application of job analysis data to group positions into jobs and jobs into families. Although the position-to-job grouping process has received comparatively little attention, the formation of job families has emerged as a highly controversial issue due to its central role in the process of generalizing test validities from setting to setting or job to job.

Summary

Attaining agreement on the semantic meaning of common job analysis terms is a surprisingly complicated activity. Even with respect to defining job analysis, we see sharp disagreement: In addition to the traditional view that job analysis is the description of work behavior and the objective work environment, some authors have attempted to include various methods for inferring required human abilities, traits, vocational interests, personality characteristics, and even biodata events under the label of job analysis. Similar semantic problems exist regarding related terms, particularly KSAs/KSAOs. I maintain that the term job analysis should be applied only to methods whose goal is the description of work behavior, independent of the characteristics of the employees who attempt to perform the job. The various methods for doing so are examined in the next section.

Philosophies of Job Analysis

Once the purpose for collecting job data is identified, the most basic task when conducting a job analysis is to identify the *kind* of descriptive questions that should be asked about the work being performed, what Cornelius, Carron, and Collins (1979) termed the *job analysis philosophy*. The core issue is whether we desire highly technological, job-specific listings of job behavior versus descriptions that locate jobs on a common metric that is constant across even task-dissimilar jobs.

A Taxonomy of Job Analysis Methods

The conventional method for categorizing job analysis methods and techniques employs taxonomies that classify each into one of a number of mutually exclusive, essentially *nominal* categories. For example, Cornelius, Carron, and Collins (1979) used a task- and worker- versus ability-oriented taxonomy; McCormick (1976) used a job- versus worker-oriented taxonomy.

Alternatively, one can view job analysis techniques as varying with respect to one or more underlying dimensions; this is the approach taken here. I use two dimensions: (a) the degree of technological/behavioral specificity manifest in the job descriptors and (b) the kind of item-rating metric produced by the instrument's rating task. These factors are crossed to define my taxonomy of job analysis methods.

Behavioral Specificity of Job Descriptor Items. The specificity dimension indicates the degree of behavioral and technological detail provided by the job analysis items; a method's location on this dimension is determined by the type of item content included in, or produced by (in the case of derived job ratings), the instrument. Behavioral specificity can range from very low (e.g., a narrative job description or a holistic characterization of an entire job using descriptors like "clerical" versus "managerial") to high (e.g., the task- and element-based techniques discussed below).

Existing taxonomic approaches have been primarily sensitive to this single dimension of behavioral specificity. For example, the basic difference between McCormick's (1976) job-versus worker-oriented classification is one of specificity: Job-level data focus on highly molecular, results-oriented task statements, whereas worker-level items concentrate on the more behaviorally abstract processes involved in performing the tasks.

The specificity dimension exerts a strong influence on the degree to which meaningful cross-job comparisons are possible. It is self-evident that if jobs are rated on nonoverlapping sets of behavioral/contextual descriptors, the only comparative conclusion possible is a rather trivial one: that the jobs are "not the same." It is perhaps less obvious that a similar limitation exists on the kinds of comparisons that can be made even when a *common* pool of items is used to describe all jobs being compared. The reason for this is that even when a single job analysis instrument is used, a non-trivial percent of items will probably be rated "Does not apply" (DNA) for any given job (e.g., Harvey & Hayes, 1986). This DNA effect is more pronounced to the extent that (a) the jobs are task-heterogeneous and/or (b) the job analysis items have high behavioral or technological specificity.

The problem is, jobs with high similarity in their DNA profiles may be very similar on a quantitative profile-similarity index (i.e., they are nearly identical in terms of what they *do not* perform), yet may be very dissimilar in terms of the relatively small number of non-DNA activities. With a sufficient number of DNA agreements, a high baseline for profile similarity is built in, and one may erroneously conclude that the jobs are in fact similar enough to be grouped together.

Because the meaningfulness of cross-job comparisons is determined in large part by the kind of job analysis items rated, the behavioral and technical specificity dimension has important implications for job classification. Job grouping analyses are frequently conducted to address a very simple question: namely, whether jobs are the same or different for some purpose (e.g., to determine whether test validities can be generalized to a new situation, or assess whether an organization has violated the Equal Pay Act). There is a sort of theory of relativity for job analysis and cross-job comparisons that must be remembered in such cases: Quantitative job similarity or difference can only be specified *relative to the behavioral or technological specificity of the job descriptive items selected for study.*

That is, jobs that may be highly dissimilar at one level of behavioral specificity may be found to be identical in another. If the job analysis items are written at a highly molecular level, very minor task technology differences between jobs can lead to the potentially misleading conclusion that the jobs are totally dissimilar. This possibility has often been cited as a criticism of the job analysis process in general (e.g., Schmidt, Hunter, & Pearlman, 1981) and was a primary motivating force behind the development of worker-oriented job analysis inventories (e.g., McCormick et al., 1972).

Rating Scale Metric.   In sum, the degree of behavioral or technological specificity represented by the job analysis items exerts a powerful effect on the end result of cross-job comparisons, and the degree of specificity must therefore be carefully matched with the purpose for comparing jobs. However, job analysis methods also vary on a second dimension that influences the meaningfulness of cross-job comparisons—namely, the kind of metric produced by the rating scales and rater instructions.   Of issue here is the degree to which the item rating process produces numbers that lie on a common *metric*, or scale. This dimension is essentially independent of the behavioral specificity dimension.

As was discussed earlier, it should be obvious that rating jobs on nonoverlapping sets of job-descriptive items prevents one from drawing meaningful cross-job comparisons (or cross-position ones as well, for that matter;

I will use the former term to describe all cross-entity comparisons, be they among positions, jobs, occupations, families, etc.). It should likewise be obvious that if different rating *scales* are used to describe each job being studied, meaningful cross-job comparisons will also be impossible. In both cases, this is due to the fact that the *metric* is incomparable between jobs. In the first case, jobs are described using incomparable behavioral items; even if the rating scale is the same, there is no overlap in the items being rated, and the metric defined by the job activity content domain is incomparable. In the second case, even though a common set of behavioral descriptors may be used, the question asked by the rating scale is effectively different across jobs, producing a different rating scale metric (e.g., as would happen if Job A were rated on the amount of time spent on each activity, and Job B were rated on the amount of training time required to be proficient on each job activity). In either case—incomparable content domain or incomparable rating scales—meaningful comparisons between jobs are not possible; only when both the job content metric and the rating scale metric are common across jobs can we meaningfully compare jobs.

The difference between whether ratings are *cross-job-relative* versus simply *within-job-relative* determines an instrument's location on this second, scale-metric dimension. Operationally, if the rating scales, instructions to raters, or subsequent score transformations cause a job analysis item's numerical rating to be expressed *relative to the other items performed on that job*, the item ratings will be deemed to be only within-job-relative.

If ratings are only within-job-relative, when comparing a job analysis item's numerical rating on Job A versus Job B, one cannot determine whether Job A has more of, the same amount of, or less of the characteristic being rated than Job B. Indeed, meaningful comparisons may not even be possible between positions holding the *same* job title when ratings are within-job-relative, due to the fact that different incumbents may (a) use different "benchmark" tasks (when making direct ratings on scales like relative-time-spent or relative importance that couch ratings in terms of whether the item is more or less than the "typical" item performed on the job) or (b) differ in the number or makeup of items rated as applicable (in the case of scores produced by rescaling items relative to the total number, or sum of, a job's item ratings, such as is done when percent-time-spent ratings are formed by dividing each task rating by the sum of the ratings given by that rater).

An example should help clarify this point. Consider the Importance rating scale used by the PAQ, in which 1 = *very minor*, 2 = *low*, 3 = *average*, 4 = *high*, and 5 = *extreme*; similar relative-importance (RI) and relative-time-spent (RTS) scales are commonly used in job analysis questionnaires (e.g., the JEI uses the RTS scale). Suppose that people in two positions at a major corporation, CEO and head janitor, rate an item "Negotiate with others to reach an agreement" as 4 on Importance. The CEO gives this rating because her contract negotiations with suppliers, banks, labor unions, customers, and others affect the financial well-being of the corporation; the head janitor bases her rating on the fact that she must negotiate with other janitors to determine the days and shifts that each will work, keeping everyone as satisfied with the schedule as possible to reduce turnover and grievance problems.

In a strictly within-job-relative sense, the *relative* importance of "negotiating with others" to each position may indeed be identical and may cause the item to receive the same numerical rating. However, is it correct to conclude that because both positions receive a rating of 4 that they require the same *amount* of negotiating, that the negotiating is equally sophisticated or demanding, that the effects of improper negotiating are identical, or otherwise infer that negotiating is equally important to both positions? Of course not!

All that may be concluded in such a case is that *to some unknown degree* the activity "negotiating" is performed on the job.

This example illustrates a serious problem confronting many job analysis instruments, both standardized and custom developed: Statistical analyses of job ratings cannot discern the difference between a within-job-relative versus a cross-job-relative frame of reference. Statistical methods used to quantify and assess work similarity are founded on the assumption that the numbers on the scale mean the same thing for every entity rated. Thus, a rating of 4 is interpreted to mean that the two positions possess *identical levels or magnitudes of the characteristic being rated*. As a consequence, profile comparisons computed between the head janitor and CEO would offer the completely erroneous conclusion that these two positions involve *identical levels* of negotiating.

It should be clear that meaningful cross-job comparisons cannot be made when the job analysis items are rated in a within-job-relative fashion. Relative-time-spent, the Air Force's percent-time-spent (e.g., Carpenter, 1974; Christal, 1974; Pass & Robertson, 1980) transformation used in the CODAP system, relative-importance, all varieties of ranked data, and other "relative" ratings provide essentially *ipsative* information. At best, all they tell us is that *for that given job* a certain item has relatively more of the attribute being rated than other items *on that job* that receive lower ratings, and relatively less of the attribute than items *on that job* that receive higher ratings. If ratings are within-job standardized or centered in this fashion, it can easily be the case that for a given item one job will receive a lower numerical rating than a second job, *even if the first job performs the item at a higher absolute level* (e.g., if the first job performs more items, and the items are rescaled by dividing each one by the sum of each job's ratings).

Solely within-job-relative information is potentially extremely misleading if one attempts to take its numerical ratings at face value and subject them to statistical analyses that make level-based comparisons between positions or jobs. That is, jobs with identical "relative" profiles can have wildly different absolute levels of the items, just as jobs with very different "relative" profiles can have identical absolute levels of the items! It is therefore disconcerting to note the widespread use of job analysis methods that either (a) directly collect only within-job-relative data (e.g., most task inventories use RTS or RI scales) or (b) transform ratings to produce a within-job-relative metric (e.g., the CODAP percent-time-spent transformation). For the many uses of job analysis data that involve making level-sensitive comparisons between jobs, data of this type are of little use.

Only with cross-job-relative ratings can one make meaningful level-based comparisons between jobs. Cross-job-relative ratings are obtained when items are rated on a common rating scale metric; that is, an item's rating scale is constant across positions, and more important, the numbers on the scale *mean the same thing* in terms of the frequency or amount of the characteristic being measured, regardless of the job rated or person making the ratings. Within-job-relative ratings effectively define a unique metric for *each* position or job, making cross-job comparisons meaningless and misleading.

The problems associated with using rating procedures that produce data having largely ipsative properties are not unique to job analysis; for example, in the area of measuring social or interpersonal power, Schriesheim, Hinkin, and Podsakoff (1991) recently identified serious psychometric problems facing popular instruments for measuring power. Hicks (1970) provided a general discussion of this problem.

Fortunately, cross-job-relative scales are widely available, although for reasons unknown they appear to have been much less popular than within-job-relative scales like relative-importance and RTS. For example, absolute frequency scales (e.g., "This activity is performed: *hourly, daily, weekly, monthly, quarterly, yearly*"), criticality-of-error scales (e.g., "If this activity is performed incorrectly, the consequences will be: *no injury, minor injury not requiring medical attention, injury requiring medical attention, permanent disability, death*"), and similar scales provide a metric that has a constant meaning regardless of the job being rated. Simply instructing raters to attempt to rate on a metric that is constant across all jobs, while providing them with a rating scale phrased only in within-job-relative terms, is highly unlikely to produce data that meet this criterion.

A New Taxonomy. Combining these two dimensions—specificity of information and the degree to which items are rated on a common metric—produces the taxonomy of job analysis methods presented in Table 1; each discrete type of method in Table 1 has been given a number to facilitate discussion. For present purposes, the scale-metric dimension is given three levels: (a) At the lowest level, there is essentially no metric (i.e., the items provide only qualitative data); (b) at the intermediate level, items are rated on scales that provide only within-title-relative data; and (c) at the highest level, a cross-job-relative metric is produced that allows meaningful level-based comparisons to be made.

As an aside, I must note that the decision to categorize this dimension into these three levels was made for purposes of simplicity of exposition; in no way do I wish the reader to infer that there are rigid lines of demarcation between the various categories, especially between scales providing cross-job-relative versus only within-job-relative data. As will become obvious from the discussion below, rating formats should be judged based on the *degree* to which they allow cross-job-meaningful level comparisons; this determination is not an all-or-nothing matter and

TABLE 1

A Taxonomy of Job Analysis Methods, Including Examples of Each Type

	Behavioral/Technological Specificity		
Kind of Scale Metric	*High*	*Moderate*	*Low*
Cross-job-relative; meaningful level-based comparisons frequency scale	Type 1 Task inventory rated using absolute scale Task inventory rated using "do you perform" checklist	Type 2 CMQ items rated on absolute frequency frequency data Dichotomous CMQ, JEI item ratings	Type 3 CMQ dimension scores based possible JEI dimension scores based on dichotomized data FJA ratings of Data, People, Things
Within-job-relative; ratings expressed relative to the other activities performed on job or rated on scales that are not anchored in terms of verifiable job behavior	Type 4 Task inventory rated using relative-time, relative-importance, percent-time scales	Type 5 JEI item ratings using relative-time scale Duty ratings on relative-time, relative-importance	Type 6 JEI dimension scores based on relative-time ratings
Qualitative; no numerical ratings, or no quantitative comparisons possible between jobs	Type 7 Job-specific listings of tasks Behaviorally specific critical incidents	Type 8 Long narrative job description Behaviorally abstract critical incidents	Type 9 Holistic job grouping judgments Short narrative job description

will likely be affected by factors extraneous to the instrument itself (e.g., characteristics of the rater, such as training and instrument familiarity).

For the sake of simplicity, Table 1 also categorizes the behavioral and technological specificity dimension into three levels: (a) low specificity, offering a very abstract view of work that describes little in the way of job behaviors or task technologies; (b) moderate specificity, typified by items that attempt to be insensitive to fine-grained task behavior/technology differences yet still convey meaningful data regarding general job behaviors;

and (c) high specificity, characterized by items that are closely tailored to the individual jobs or occupations studied, and that are therefore capable of revealing significant differences between jobs that might be found to be similar at a more abstract level of analysis. The same caveats regarding the undesirability of viewing these categories as having rigid boundaries discussed with respect to the rating scale-metric dimension also apply here.

The following sections examine each of the major types of job analysis methods. Organizationally, the discussion will progress across Table 1 by columns (i.e., levels of specificity).

High-Specificity, or "Task-Oriented," Methods

Terminology and Techniques.   These approaches to job analysis describe work in technologically and behaviorally explicit terms, what McCormick (1976) labeled the *job-oriented*—and others call the task-oriented—philosophy. In task-oriented analysis, the *element* is the most basic descriptive unit of work activity, consisting of behaviors that are too specific to be labeled tasks (as defined below). Cascio (1987) described an element as "the smallest unit into which work can be divided without analyzing separate motions, movements, and mental processes" (p. 185). Thus, elements are the behavioral building blocks of tasks. Elements are not directly useful for many personnel purposes, although they are valuable in other functions, such as industrial engineering.

The *task* is the next higher level of abstraction used to describe work behavior, although as Gael (1983, pp. 8–9) noted, it has been defined in a staggering number of different ways. These various definitions have some common ground, such that (a) tasks involve an action or series of actions or elements, (b) these actions are performed closely in time and usually in the same order, (c) the task has an identifiable starting and stopping point, (d) task performance results in a meaningful and identifiable goal, outcome, or objective, and (e) tasks are assignable to individual positions. The task action verb is critical and should be as observable and behaviorally explicit as possible. Table 2 presents Gael's (1983) listing of desirable action verbs.

Sidney Fine's *Functional Job Analysis*, or FJA (e.g., Fine, 1989; Fine & Wiley, 1971), is a highly structured variant of the task-oriented approach. FJA mandates several components of a good task statement: (a) the action verb, which describes in observable detail the activity performed; (b) the result of the action, specified in terms of the observable things that

are accomplished as a result of task performance; (c) the tools, equipment, and other work aids used; and (d) the degree of discretion given the worker to determine the way in which the task is executed. The FJA system for identifying and rating tasks is quite detailed, and texts like Fine (1989) offer a much more detailed description of the process by which task statements are written and rated. A listing of sample FJA task statements is presented in Table 3.

The FJA approach is usually applied to one job at a time, producing listings of tasks tailored to each job. In contrast, the *task inventory* approach analyzes a number of different jobs at once using a single questionnaire. As popularized by the military, particularly the Air Force (e.g., Morsh, 1964), this variant of the task-based approach describes jobs in terms of their involvement with a number of task statements, each of which being rated in questionnaire format. In the task inventory approach, only a subset of the total listing of tasks will likely apply to any given job, as the inventory contains all tasks thought to be a part of any job included in the study.

In addition to the military and other governmental agencies, the task inventory approach has achieved popularity among some of the larger private-sector employers; given the amount of labor and cost involved in developing custom task inventories, however, it is infrequently seen in smaller or less well-funded organizations. Gael (1983) provided a detailed treatment of the planning, conduct, and analysis of task inventory projects.

Table 4 presents a sample of the tasks included in a 698-item inventory I constructed for a city government. A comparison of Tables 3 and 4 illustrates how FJA tasks tend to be more detailed than the typical task inventory item. The term *activity* is sometimes used to refer to the kinds of task statements found in inventories.

One of the advantages claimed for the task-based approach is that each task can be

TABLE 2

Suggested Action Verbs for Task Statements

Accumulate	Code	Erect	Join	Place	Rewire
Adjust	Collect	Estimate	Judge	Plan	Rework
Advise	Compare	Evaluate		Post	Route
Aid	Complete	Examine	List	Prepare	
Align	Compute	Explain	Loan	Prescribe	Scan
Amend	Conduct	Extract	Locate	Probe	Schedule
Analyze	Connect		Log	Process	Secure
Approve	Contact	Fabricate	Lubricate	Program	Select
Arrange	Control	Figure			Set
Assemble	Coordinate	File	Maintain	Qualify	Set-up
Assign	Copy	Formulate	Measure	Quote	Signal
Audit	Correct		Modify		Solder
Authorize	Count	Gather	Monitor	Ready	Sort
		Give		Reassemble	Store
Balance	Date	Group	Name	Recall	Survey
Batch	Deliver	Guard	Notify	Receive	
Buy	Demonstrate	Guide		Recondition	Tabulate
	Describe		Observe	Record	Test
Calculate	Design	Help	Obtain	Refer	Trace
Calibrate	Diagnose	Hold	Open	Regulate	Transcribe
Cancel	Direct		Operate	Reject	Transmit
Certify	Disconnect	Identify	Order	Relay	Troubleshoot
Change	Dispatch	Inform	Organize	Remove	Tune
Charge	Dispose	Initiate	Overhaul	Repair	Type
Check	Divide	Insert		Replace	
Choose	Document	Inspect	Paint	Reproduce	Verify
Cite		Install	Patch	Request	
Classify	Edit	Instruct	Phone	Review	Weigh
Clean	Encode	Interview	Pick	Revise	Write
Clear	Enter				

From *Job Analysis: A Guide to Assessing Work Activities* (p. 60) by S. Gael, 1983, San Francisco: Jossey-Bass. Copyright 1983 by Jossey-Bass, Inc. Reprinted by permission.

described in terms of a number of attributes, and the attributes rated can be matched to the purpose for collecting job data. Gael (1983, p. 98) suggested several possible rating scales, including importance, relative time spent, frequency, and difficulty. The *Guidelines* require that the job analysis identify the work behaviors important for success on the job, a directive many have interpreted to mean that tasks should be rated on criticality, importance,

or a combined criticality/importance scale. Figure 1 shows examples of Gael's (1983) suggested rating scales for task inventories.

Cross-Job-Relative Methods. When items on highly specific job analysis inventories are rated using a scale that is not within-job-relative (e.g., absolute frequency), a common metric is obtained, and meaningful cross-job, level-sensitive item and profile comparisons are

TABLE 3

Functional Job Analysis Task Statements

Searches for/brings together/collects agency records (financial, legal, medical, etc.) on specified client in order to assemble sources of information to supplement/corroborate information on application form

Reads/scans city street map, selecting, according to estimated closeness to client's home, those agencies listed on referral guide which deliver services requested by client, in order to list available, convenient services

Classifies/assigns/arranges, by categories of services offered, agencies listed in community services catalog in order to prepare services referral guide

Visually checks inventory of foodstuffs, suggested menus, and household supplies in home, using discretion as to need, quantity, and brand; and noting those items which must be purchased for meal preparation and house maintenance, in order to prepare (write) shopping list

Informs child caretaker of the decision for type of exam needed by child and reviews with caretaker arrangements necessary to obtain it in order that caretaker may make appointment with appropriate docotor/health facility

Writes/composes letter to physician, following agency procedures and, as necessary, using agency resources for clarification, in order to request information concerning recipient's use of medical services

Asks questions; listens to responses of complainant, clarifying vague emotionally charged statements about complaint; and records information on form questionnaire in order to specify source, nature, and scope of the complaint

From *An Introduction to Job Analysis* (p. 46) by S. Fine and W. Wiley, 1971, Washington, DC: Upjohn Institute for Employment Research. Copyright 1971 by S. Fine. Reprinted by permission.

possible. Instruments of this type are classified into Type 1 of the taxonomy presented in Table 1. With such data, cross-job comparisons are sensitive to both (a) the binary information conveyed by the tasks performed in common between jobs and (b) elevation differences between profiles of task ratings.

However, even if jobs are rated on a common rating scale metric, because of the high level of behavioral and technological specificity of the tasks, comparisons using such data may fail to detect more abstract similarities between jobs that are masked by minor technological differences. This situation may or may not be desirable, *depending on one's purpose for comparing jobs.* For example, when grouping jobs for the purpose of developing technical training programs, fine-grained differences may be very meaningful; conversely, when grouping jobs to share a general ability-oriented predictor test, task differences that obscure broader behavioral similarities may be very undesirable.

Unfortunately, there are comparatively few examples of such instruments. In task inventories, the use of "relative" rating scales like RTS and relative-importance appears to be much more common (e.g., see Christal,

TABLE 4

Sample Task Inventory Items and Duties

Inspecting

Conduct field inspections.
Conduct building inspections.
Perform on-site inspections.
Participate in preplanning.
Inspect and enforce adherence to city codes and specifications.
Check sites for compliance with approved plans and contract documents.
Ensure compliance by contractor.
Check for compliance with traffic codes.
Examine, replace water flow charts.
Read meters.
Check water plant for sanitary conditions.
Collect water samples.
Ensure thorough completion of job activities.
Monitor changing conditions of job site, patrol area, emergency scene.
Patrol streets to control animals.
Check records to ensure that information is in accordance with laws and
    ordinances.
Examine equipment before purchase.
Inspect food preparation areas to determine degree of cleanliness.
Conduct home safety inspections.

Investigating

Research penal code, traffic code, code of criminal procedure, city ordinances,
    election code, local government code, etc.
Gather, maintain resource information from public and private sectors.
Research, assemble, and present material for new ordinances.
Gather information for preparation of reports.
Develop cases against suspects leading to arrest.
Conduct searches.
Survey crime scenes for evidence.
Determine crucial events related to emergency situations.
Investigate illegal drugs and controlled substances.
Investigate spills and points of discharge pollution.
Investigate offenses, complaints.
Investigate the occupants and contents of suspicious vehicles.
Engage in surveillance of suspects, locations, vehicles.

1974; Gael, 1983; Morsh, 1964). And, for those who follow the Air Force's suggested practice (e.g., Christal, 1974) of transforming task ratings from their original metric into the percent- based metric used in the CODAP system (i.e., by dividing each rating by the sum of the ratings given to that specific position or job), data that exhibit only within-job-relative

FIGURE 1

Typical Task Inventory Rating Scales

Directions for Responding to a Question About Task Time

Part C of this survey is about the time you spend on each task.

You have already identified the tasks that are part of your job by circling a number from 1 to 7 in the *Significance* column. Now you should judge the amount of time you spend on each task and *write your response* alongside the task in the Part C—Time Spent column. For this survey, "time" means the overall amount of time you devote to performing a task—over the long haul, not each separate performance of a task, nor to just the last few weeks.

Use the time guide shown below to indicate your estimate of the time you spend on each task you perform.

0   =   I spend no time on this task.

1   =   I spend a very small amount of time on this task as compared with most tasks I perform.

2   =   I spend less time on this task than I spend on most other tasks I perform.

3   =   I spend slightly less time on this task than I spend on most other tasks I perform.

4   =   I spend as much time on this task as I spend on most other tasks.

5   =   I spend slightly more time on this task than I spend on most other tasks.

6   =   I spend more time on this task than I spend on most other tasks I perform.

7   =   I spend a very large amount of time on this task as compared with most other tasks I perform.

The number you select should be your best estimate of the total amount of time you spend performing the task as compared with other tasks you perform. Again, the larger the number you select, the more time you feel you spend performing the task.

properties will unavoidably be produced, *even if the original task rating scale had meaningful cross-job-relative properties.*

Within-Job-Relative Methods.   Due to the popularity of "relative" rating scales for task inventories, Type 4 of the job analysis taxonomy (see Table 1) is much more populated than the common-metric Type 1. Given that the only practical difference between cross-job-relative versus within-job-relative task inventory data is the rating scale format, it is difficult to understand why job analysts would dramatically reduce the kinds of cross-job comparisons that are possible by choosing the latter kind of scale.

With only within-job-relative task data, meaningful comparisons between jobs are quite limited. Because level-based differences will be arbitrary and therefore misleading, only the binary data conveyed by the fact that a task applies or does not apply should be used to make cross-job comparisons. For example, the CODAP approach (Christal, 1974) reports the percent of tasks in common (PTC) between pairs of jobs, a statistic that assesses at least some degree of quantitative cross-job similarity. CODAP also produces a statistic termed

FIGURE 1

Typical Task Inventory Rating Scales (continued)

Directions for Responding to a Question About Task Significance

Read each task statement carefully and decide whether or not the task is part of your present job. You are not expected to perform all the tasks listed, nor are all tasks performed in every business service center. It is important that you think only of your present job, not previous jobs. Some tasks you perform are more significant for your job than others. Consider the following factors in judging the significance of a task to your job:

a. *Importance*   –   The contribution of the task to effective operation in your office.

b. *Frequency*   –   How often you perform the task

c. *Difficulty*   –   How hard the task is to do or to learn to do effectively

Combine these factors in your mind to determine the significance of a task, and choose an appropriate rating according to the following:

0   =   Definitely not a part of my job; I never do it.

1   =   Under unusual or certain circumstances may be of a minor significance to my job

2

3

4   =   Of substantial signicance to my job

5

6

7   =   Of most significance to my job

---

percent task overlap (PTO) that is based on the numerical percent-transformed ratings described earlier; because this individually restandardized data cannot convey meaningful level-based information, PTO similarity statistics are much less informative than the dichotomously based PTC values and must therefore be interpreted with great caution.

Nonmetric Methods.   Like the within-job-relative techniques, job analysis methods in Type 7 of the Table 1 taxonomy are also commonplace. To be classified as a nonmetric method, a technique must (a) not collect

quantitative ratings on the job tasks (e.g., by simply listing a job's tasks or ranking the tasks in terms of some criterion like time-spent or importance) or (b) produce listings of tasks that vary across the jobs being studied (e.g., as a typical application of the FJA technique will do, producing a relatively unique set of tasks tailored to each individual job). In either case, cross-job comparisons are not particularly informative, and only qualitative similarities between jobs can be identified.

The critical-incident technique (Flanagan, 1954) can also be classified into this category, although for reasons described below, critical

FIGURE 1

Typical Task Inventory Rating Scales (continued)

Directions for Responding to a Question About Task Frequency

Instructions for Part B

Part B of the questionnaire is about how often you perform various tasks.

1. Read these instructions carefully before going on.

2. Read each task staement carefully and decide whether or not you now perform the task—it is important that you think only of your present job, not previous jobs. If you do not perform a task, write a zero (0) alongside the task in the column headed "Frequency." If you perform a task, choose the closest number (from 1 to 7 in accordance with the guide presented below) to describe how often you perform the task. Write that number in the "Frequency" box alongside the task.

Frequency Guide

I perform this task:

      7 = about once each hour or more often
      6 = about every day or more often (not each hour)
      5 = about every other day
      4 = about once each week
      3 = about once each month
      2 = about once every six months or less
      1 = about once every year
      0 = I do not perform this task on my current job

The number you select should be your best estimate of your average frequency of performing the task. As you can see, the larger the number you select, the more frequenty you perform the task.

From *Job Analysis: A Guide to Assessing Work Activity* (pp. 100–103) by S. Gael, 1983, San Francisco: Jossey-Bass. Copyright 1983 by Jossey-Bass, Inc. Adapted by permission.

incidents have their drawbacks when used to analyze jobs. According to Flanagan (1954), a *critical incident* is composed of three parts: (a) a description of the *setting* in which a job behavior occurred, (b) a description of the *behavior* itself, which is usually a highly effective or ineffective act (i.e., it has a clearly identifiable *valence*), and (c) a description of the positive or negative *consequences* that resulted from the behavior. Figure 2 shows a behaviorally anchored rating scale developed from critical incidents.

Critical incident data are usually collected by asking subject matter experts (SMEs) to recall examples of particularly effective or ineffective job behavior they have witnessed or performed. Critical incidents are written using a three-step procedure in which the setting, the behavior, and the consequences are described. By pooling incidents from several SMEs, a detailed picture of job performance can be obtained.

The critical incidents approach has achieved popularity in the performance appraisal area,

FIGURE 2

Using Critical Incidents in a BARS Format

	9	Could be expected to conduct a full day's sales clinic with two new sales personnel and thereby develop them into top sales people in the department.
Could be expected to give his sales personnel confidence and a strong sense of responsibility by delegating many important jobs to them.	8	
	7	Could be expected *never* to fail to conduct training meetings with his people weekly at a scheduled hour and to convey to them exactly what he expects.
Could be expected to exhibit courtesy and respect toward his sales personnel.	6	
	5	Could be expected to remind sales personnel to wait on customers instead of conversing with each other.
Could be expected to be rather critical of store standards in front of his own people, thereby risking their developing poor attitudes.	4	
	3	Could be expected to tell an individual to come in anyway even though she/he called in to say she/he was ill.
Could be expected to go back on a promise to an individual whom he had told could transfer back into previous department if she/he didn't like the new one.	2	
	1	Could be expected to make promises to an individual about her/his salary being based on department sales even when he knew such a practice was against company policy.

Note: Figure represents a scaled expectations rating scale for the effectiveness with which the department manager supervises sales personnel.

From "The Development and Evaluation of Behaviorally Based Rating Scales" by J. P. Campbell, M. D. Dunnette, R. D. Arvey, & L. V. Hellervik (1973), *Journal of Applied Psychology 57*, 15–22. Copyright 1973 by the American Psychological Association. Reprinted by permission.

where it is used to identify the BARS and related scales. However, the critical incidents method is of questionable desirability as a general-purpose job analysis method. First, although it focuses on observable job behaviors, it does not describe the job as it *should* be performed; both effective and ineffective behaviors are included in the descriptions. Second, critical incident data are often not replicable—that is, different employees holding the same job will likely manifest different methods for correctly and incorrectly performing their assigned tasks; this may translate in to completely nonoverlapping sets of critical incidents for different positions performing the same job. Thus, although behaviorally rich, critical incidents leave much to be desired as a job analysis method, running the risk of being both deficient (in the sense that each important job behavior may *or may not* be represented by a critical incident) and contaminated (in the sense that the content of the incidents is influenced by characteristics of both the job as well as the specific individuals who perform it).

The critical incidents approach is perhaps best viewed as a useful adjunct to traditional task-oriented methods of job analysis. After first obtaining and reviewing a listing of *all* of a job's important tasks, SMEs could then generate critical incidents for *each* task. This technique for generating incidents is likely to be more thorough than the informal approach typically seen when generating critical incidents during BARS development (e.g., Smith & Kendall, 1963) in that the domain of task performance is defined first, and all raters make use of a comprehensive list of task information when generating incidents. Developed in this fashion, critical incidents can provide an effective vehicle for illustrating successful versus undesirable strategies for performing each of a job's tasks, as well as communicating the organization's standards for assessing individual effectiveness in task performance.

Moderate-Specificity, or "Worker-Oriented," Methods

Terminology and Techniques.   The job *duty* occupies the next higher level of behavioral abstraction; a duty describes a collection of tasks that are similar in terms of having a common objective or focus. Cascio (1987) defined a duty as "a large segment of the work performed by an individual and may include any number of tasks" (p. 185). Duties play a vital role by expressing the information contained in a large number of individual tasks in terms of a much smaller number of more easily communicated general work activities. They are used heavily in the task inventory approach, such that tasks are often grouped and rated by duty category (e.g., see Table 4).

The term *worker-oriented* job analysis was coined by McCormick (e.g., McCormick, 1976) to describe a method that describes even task-dissimilar jobs on a common set of descriptors that tend to be more behaviorally and technologically abstract than task statements. Such instruments represent a great improvement over the highly specific task-oriented approach if one's purpose is making cross-job comparisons that are relatively insensitive to the task technologies involved in each job.

Although task similarity measures (e.g., percent of tasks in common) can be constructed from task inventory data to quantify the degree of similarity between jobs, such measures can present a misleading picture of job similarity. That is, two jobs may be quite similar in terms of their general work behaviors and objectives, yet may demonstrate very little task overlap (e.g., police chief and fire chief, police sergeant and fire lieutenant). Worker-oriented job analysis seeks to describe these more behaviorally abstract general categories of job activity.

As outlined by McCormick et al. (1972), the basic idea behind the worker-oriented approach is that (a) relatively few general work behaviors exist and (b) all jobs can be described in terms of how much of each general work behavior they involve. Unfortunately, conflicting terminology creeps into our discussion at this point: The term *element* is used (e.g., McCormick, 1976, p. 673) in worker-oriented analysis to describe the general work behaviors rated in a worker-oriented job analysis. This use of this term is very different from its use in task-oriented job analysis, in which case it refers to the very specific behaviors that are the building blocks of tasks.

In contrast to the task inventory approach, in which questionnaires containing many hundreds of items are custom-made for each set of jobs to be analyzed, one should be able (in theory, at least) to construct a single worker-oriented inventory made up of a relatively small number of moderate-specificity items that would be capable of describing all jobs in all situations. Examples of questionnaires that have attempted to achieve this ideal include the PAQ, JEI, OAI, GWI, and CMQ discussed earlier.

Moderate-specificity, worker-oriented items seek to describe the general human behaviors involved in performing a job's tasks rather than the technologies involved in performing the tasks themselves (Fleishman & Quaintance, 1984, p. 107). In McCormick et al. (1972) terms, a worker-oriented item "refers to a generalized class of behaviorally related job activities, including the behavioral adjustment required to features of the work context" (p. 349). Examples of worker-oriented items from the JEI are presented in Figure 3.

Conceptually, worker-oriented items are more behaviorally abstract and less technologically specific than task statements. However, it is difficult to specify a practical decision rule that would allow one to unambiguously classify a given item as a "task" versus a "worker-oriented" item; this distinction is more one of degree than one of kind. As McCormick et al. (1972) noted,

job-oriented elements are descriptions of job content that have a dominant association with, and typically characterize, the "technological" aspects of jobs and commonly reflect what is achieved by the worker. On the other hand, worker-oriented elements are those that tend more to characterize the generalized human behaviors involved; if not directly, then by strong inference. Although the job-oriented and worker-oriented job-element concepts have certain parallels, respectively, to the work fields and worker functions set forth by Fine ... there is also a difference in these two frames of reference. The job-oriented concept typically would be reflected by the use of specific task statements such as those embodied in job inventories.... In turn, the worker-oriented concept typically would be reflected by the use of descriptions of reasonably definitive human behaviors of many kinds. (p. 348)

In practical terms, the rigid distinction that some authors draw between the task- and worker-oriented approaches is more illusory than real, although it does provide a convenient shorthand notation to describe the somewhat different goals of the two methods. As a rule of thumb, for any given worker-oriented item one should be able to identify several more behaviorally specific task statements that illustrate the performance of the item. The content of these tasks would vary, depending on the job being described.

However, this rule is not infallible, as many task statements can also be divided into a number of more specific task statements. This situation is frequently encountered when using the task inventory approach. The reason for the existence of these more general task statements is that, on purely practical grounds, the number of items in an inventory must be kept within certain limits (e.g., less

FIGURE 3

Sample Worker-oriented Items From the JEI

Rating Scale: Relative Time Spent

1	2	3	4	5
Very little	Below average	Average	Above average	Very much

If the job element is not appropriate, leave it blank.

In doing your job, you...

			CC
17.	Work outdoors	____	(31)
18.	Work in an enclosed area that is hot	____	(32)
19.	Work in an enclosed area that is cold	____	(33)
20.	Work in polluted air (dust, toxic fumes)	____	(34)
21.	Are subjected to vibration	____	(35)
22.	Work under improper lighting conditions (too dark, too glaring)	____	(36)
23.	Work where you easily become dirty	____	(37)
24.	Work in a cramped or uncomfortable space	____	(38)
25.	Work in a quiet area	____	(39)
26.	Work in an area of moderate noise (office with typewriters)	____	(40)
27.	Work in an area of loud noise	____	(41)
28.	Are responsible for the safety of the general public	____	(42)
29.	Are responsible for the safety of members of the Coast Guard	____	(43)
30.	Judge distances	____	(44)
31.	Tell the difference in colors	____	(45)
32.	Notice different patterns of sound (Morse code, engines not running right)	____	(46)
33.	Notice differences or changes in sound through loudness, pitch or tone quality	____	(47)
34.	Sense body position and balance (walking on I beams, walking on deck)	____	(48)

From "A Study to Develop an Improved Enlisted Performance Evaluation System for the U.S. Coast Guard" (p. B–6) by E. T. Cornelius and M. D. Hakel, 1978, Washington, DC: U.S. Coast Guard. Copyright 1978 by U.S. Coast Guard. Reprinted by permission.

than 1,000 statements). Thus, when the number of jobs covered by a task inventory increases, the tasks become shorter, more general, less technologically specific, and therefore bear increased similarity to worker-oriented items.

Conversely, some items in worker-oriented questionnaires appear sufficiently behaviorally specific to be labeled "tasks," at least in the task-inventory model of task specificity. For example, the PAQ contains items dealing with using long-handled tools, operating air and space vehicles, and contacting special interest groups. Items of this nature often appear in task inventories.

Clearly, in practical terms, there is some degree of overlap between task- and worker-oriented items. The essential difference between task- and worker-oriented methods lies in the purpose to be served when collecting job analysis information: Worker-oriented instruments seek to describe jobs in such a fashion that broad cross-job behavioral similarities can be identified, unobscured by fine-grained task differences that may exist.

Cross-Job-Relative Methods. Methods that seek to describe and compare task-dissimilar jobs, as do the moderate-specificity techniques in Type 2 of the taxonomy presented in Table 1, rate a common set of job descriptors using cross-job-relative rating scales. However, due to the use of predominantly within-job-relative rating scales, most existing worker-oriented questionnaires fall some degree short of this ideal and are more accurately classified as Type 5 methods having only limited ability to make cross-job-meaningful, level-based comparisons.

For example, one of the most widely used worker-oriented questionnaires is the PAQ (McCormick et al., 1972). Most items on the PAQ are rated on the Importance scale discussed earlier in this section (112 of the 187 items describing job behavior use this scale);

regarding the operational definition of importance, even the instrument's authors acknowledge that "the concept of 'importance' is admittedly a rather ambiguous one" (Jeanneret, McCormick, & Mecham, 1977, p. 5). Although the job analysis manual for the PAQ (Jeanneret et al., 1977, p. 5) at one point cautions against making within-job-relative ratings, many inducements to use a within-job-relative frame of reference are present.

Specifically, the manual instructs raters to "consider whatever aspects seem to relate to the importance of the item *to the job in question*" (p. 5, emphasis added), and directs that "if an activity is performed very frequently, takes up a large amount of the worker's time, and is critical for adequate job performance, it usually should receive a rating of 5" (Jeanneret et al., 1977, p. 5), the maximum Importance rating. The instructions contained in the PAQ booklet direct raters to simply judge "how important the activity described in the item is to the completion of the job" and to "consider such factors as amount of time spent, the possible influence on overall job performance if the worker does not properly perform this activity, etc." (Form B, p. 6). Such instructions encourage Importance ratings that express the item's criticality only with respect to the job's other applicable items, and not the degree of importance vis à vis other jobs in the economy.

Other PAQ items are rated on scales that are defined in terms of similarly behaviorally ambiguous anchors. For example, one of the items defining the Decision, Communication, and General Responsibility factor is item 185, which rates the amount of "general responsibility" a job possesses; the rating anchors are *very limited, limited, intermediate, substantial, and very substantial*. The job analysis manual (Jeanneret et al., 1977, pp. 61–62) lists sample job titles to illustrate each anchor (e.g., the CEO of a medium- or large-sized organization is *very substantial*, a power-plant operator is *intermediate,* and a sewer-pipe cleaner is *very limited*). It is very difficult to justify highly abstract ratings of this type in terms of concrete job behaviors.

By using its rating scales and instructions for illustrative purposes, I do not mean to imply that the PAQ is the only worker-oriented instrument that suffers from concerns regarding within-job-relative ratings; indeed, the majority of standardized job analysis instruments that have appeared since the introduction of the PAQ (e.g., the PMPQ, PDQ, OAI, and GWI) also contain rating scales, rater instructions, and/or item wordings that allow or encourage the making of only within-job-relative ratings (including an instrument with which I have been closely involved, the JEI). As was noted earlier, using "relative" scales like RTS to rate task inventory items produces similar problems. Only by using less subjective and within-job-relativistic scale anchors can this problem be solved; doing so would also greatly improve the defensibility and replicability of the item ratings given to such instruments.

Type 2 instruments do exist, however, differing from other standardized worker-oriented instruments primarily by their use of rating formats that are more behaviorally explicit and absolute. For example, Lozada-Larsen (1988) developed the *Executive Checklist* (EXCEL) for use in describing executive, managerial, and supervisory jobs. In addition to being rated on within-job-relative scales (e.g., relative importance), the 249 EXCEL items are described on an absolute frequency scale (e.g., the activity is performed *once a day to several times a day, once a week to four times a week*, etc.) that allows unambiguous cross-job comparisons of item ratings and ratings profiles.

In contrast to EXCEL, the CMQ (Harvey, 1990a) was designed to be applicable to all jobs. The CMQ employs a number of rating scales for each item, including an absolute frequency scale (e.g., the activity is performed

hourly to many times each hour, daily, etc.). Other CMQ item rating scales have a high level of behavioral specificity to facilitate the rating process and ensure that a given rating "means the same thing" across different jobs (e.g., when describing interactions with other people, each kind of person contacted is described according to the actions performed with them, including *take information from them, coordinate/schedule their activities, sell to them or persuade them, train/instruct/educate them, etc.*). Behaviorally referenced scales of this sort provide less subjectivity when assigning ratings and allow ratings to be independently verified if distortion is suspected. They also provide a common metric that allows cross-job-meaningful comparisons to be drawn.

Type 2 instruments are capable of providing some of the most useful kinds of job analysis information, as their job-descriptive items are general enough to identify broad similarities between jobs (e.g., for validity generalization purposes), yet specific enough to provide the basic descriptive data needed to drive many personnel functions (e.g., item-level data can be used for performance appraisal purposes). Much additional effort needs to be spent developing and refining instruments of this type, as most comparisons we seek to make between jobs will benefit from having information about both the *kind* of activities performed on a job as well as level-based data denoting *how much* (relative to other jobs) of the activity is present.

Within-Job-Relative Methods. As noted above, because of the limited cross-job-meaningful comparisons possible using their rating scale formats, most existing standardized worker-oriented questionnaires are classified as Type 5 methods. An additional example can be found in duty ratings obtained using "relative" scales. In task-inventory job analyses, it is common to group task statements by duty category and rate both the task statements as well as the abstract duty categories; if a within-job-relative scale like RTS or relative-importance is used, the duty ratings will suffer the same cross-job limitations as do the task ratings.

However, ways for dealing with some of the limitations of "relative" scales do exist. For cases in which the scale contains a DNA option (e.g., as many RTS scales do, indicating that no time is spent on the item), the binary judgment of whether the item is performed or not can be used to construct percent-items-in-common statistics that allow some degree of cross-job-meaningful comparison; these statistics are most useful when one is primarily concerned with identifying groups of jobs that share certain work activities, regardless of the *amount* to which the activity is performed or its level of sophistication.

Additionally, dichotomized responses can be scored to produce dimension scores that have common-metric properties. Harvey (1989) demonstrated this technique with the JEI, using a 3-parameter logistic item response theory (IRT) model to produce cross-job-meaningful dimension scores. Factor analytic methods based on dichotomized data can also be applied in such situations. In these cases, the possible loss of information produced by dichotomizing is probably far outweighed by the increased confidence that one can place in the substantive meaning of the item ratings.

Nonmetric Methods. Job analysis methods that employ moderate-specificity items, yet do not produce item-level quantitative data (Type 8), are relatively limited in usefulness, as they do not allow numerical comparisons to be made between jobs. Examples include critical incident items written at a higher-than-usual level of behavioral generality (e.g., as might be seen in performance appraisal instruments designed to apply to many different jobs), as well as the qualitative data contained in short narrative job descriptions.

Low-Specificity Methods

Terminology and Techniques. At the highest level of behavioral abstraction, *job dimensions* describe jobs in terms of general constructs—typically, factor or principal component scores—that are themselves defined in terms of item ratings made at a higher level of behavioral specificity. All of the moderate-specificity instruments discussed above combine item ratings to form estimates of these latent variables (e.g., clerical activities, operating machines).

Because of their low specificity, job dimensions are valuable when comparing jobs that differ at a more behaviorally specific level of analysis. The problems inherent in identifying these job dimensions are discussed in a later section on the dimensionality of work.

Cross-Job-Relative Methods. Type 3 job analysis methods describe jobs in terms of scores on very abstract dimensions of work, each of which is scaled on a metric that allows meaningful level-based comparisons between jobs to be drawn. Such data are extremely useful for applications that require comparisons between jobs to be made on a highly task-insensitive metric (e.g., grouping jobs for validity generalization purposes).

Cross-job-relative dimension scores can only be computed using item ratings that are themselves made on a cross-job-relative rating scale. If the job analysis items are not scaled on a metric that is comparable across jobs, there is simply no way that any composite variable computed from such item ratings can lie on a common metric. Factor-scoring techniques are critically dependent on the validity of the assumption that a given numerical item rating denotes the same amount of the characteristic being rated regardless of the job in question.

Because their item ratings lie on a common metric, Type 2 instruments can be scored to produce job dimension scores that also lie on a cross-job-meaningful metric. As was noted earlier, if it is possible to meaningfully dichotomize the within-job-relative item ratings for Type 5 instruments, cross-job-meaningful comparisons may be made using composite scores (e.g., factor scores, latent trait estimates) derived from the dichotomized data; however, the dimension scores based on dichotomized within-job-relative rating scales will probably be sensitive to more gross kinds of cross-job similarities when compared against job dimension scores based on Likert-type, cross-job-relative item rating scales.

Within-Job-Relative Methods.   Although scoring schemes based on dichotomized item ratings are one way to make instruments based on within-job-relative rating scales produce dimension scores that are comparable across jobs, the best way to solve the measurement problems of these instruments is to revise their rating format. In some respects, the problems involved in interpreting and using dimension scores computed from nondichotomized, within-job-relative item ratings are even more severe than those encountered at the item level. At least with item-level data, one has confidence that the amount of the characteristic being rated is significantly different for items given the lowest rating (typically, DNA) versus those given higher ratings (i.e., the item applies to some degree). With dimension scores computed from nondichotomized, within-job-relative data, however, the option of dichotomizing the dimension scores into a "Dimension applies/Dimension does not apply" format is not available, as the factor scores are expressed as continuous variables that lie on a standardized metric. That is, a score of 0 on a job dimension indicates that the job is located at the mean of the reference distribution of jobs used to standardize the instrument; it does not indicate that the job has zero amount of the dimension. Indeed, this is the fundamental appeal of job dimensions: Each dimension represents general

kinds of work activity that are presumed to characterize *all jobs* to a greater or lesser degree.

Sophisticated factor analytic or IRT-based scoring systems cannot improve the quality or precision of the original item-level ratings; just because numerical dimension scores may be expressed to three decimal places does not mean that they actually measure jobs with this degree of precision or that the scale of the factor is constant across jobs. In the best possible case, the use of imprecise, within-job-relative rating scales only introduces unsystematic noise into the dimension scores that serves to attenuate the degree to which they can predict other criteria of interest (e.g., compensation rates); in the worst case, both random and nonrandom, rater- or job-specific noise is added, further calling into question the validity of the dimension scores.

Nonmetric Methods.   The final cell in the job analysis typology—Type 9—consists of highly abstract methods that do not produce quantitative data. Based on these characteristics, one might be tempted to conclude that these techniques are of limited usefulness in solving job analysis problems; however, considerable recent interest has been generated in them, and they will therefore be examined here.

Narrative Methods.   The most obvious example of a Type 9 job analysis method is the narrative approach; often termed a *job description*, it typically consists of several sentences describing general duties, behaviors, responsibilities, working conditions, reporting relationships, and other characteristics. I prefer to think of narrative job descriptions as being a *use* of job analysis data, not a method of job analysis per se, especially because they often contain worker-specification-oriented data as well as a description of job activities (e.g., required abilities, interests, experience); accordingly, job descriptions are examined more closely in a later section covering uses of job analysis data.

Holistic Ratings. The *holistic* or *whole-job* approach to rating jobs has been proposed as a means for producing job analysis data; holistic techniques have attracted attention in recent years due to the efforts of some validity generalization researchers (e.g., Pearlman, 1980; Pearlman, Schmidt, & Hunter, 1980; Schmidt, Hunter, & Pearlman, 1981). These authors have concluded that in many instances a job analysis need involve only the most cursory, nonbehavioral, and nonquantitative description of work activities.

Only recently of interest to most industrial psychologists, the holistic approach to rating jobs is not new, having been used for years in the area of job evaluation. If one considers the procedures employed to describe and group jobs using the whole-job compensation methods (e.g., ranking, classification, market pricing) to be job analysis, the holistic approach has been around for a long time. Although many in the compensation area reject holistic data as being unacceptably subjective, imprecise, and not demonstrably job-related (e.g., Henderson, 1979, p. 212), within industrial and organizational psychology these methods have been enthusiastically embraced in some quarters as a cost-effective method for describing and grouping jobs (e.g., Cornelius, Schmidt, & Carron, 1984; Pearlman, 1980; Sackett, Cornelius, & Carron, 1981).

With respect to analyzing jobs for test validation purposes, Pearlman et al. (1980) claimed that "recent research has shown that…a job analysis need not be extremely detailed or complex; it is only necessary to be able to assign a job to its general occupational grouping (e.g., clerical work)"(p. 376). This quote illustrates an unusual aspect of the holistic approach: It is both a method for describing jobs *and* a technique for making job grouping decisions.

In addition to the task-worker-ability taxonomy of job analysis methods described by Cornelius, Carron, and Collins (1979), Pearlman (1980) proposed a fourth job analysis philosophy that describes

the *overall nature of the job* by broadly characterizing jobs in terms of their job titles or general descriptions of the nature of work or groups of activities performed…. Moreover, descriptors reflecting the overall nature of the job may often represent what amounts to an implicit, simultaneous consideration of some combination of the other three categories. (p. 11, italics in original)

As Schmidt et al. (1981) elaborated,

fine-grained, detailed job analyses tend to create the appearance of large differences between jobs that are not of practical significance in selection. Our results show that such molecular job analyses, so heavily emphasized in personnel selection research in recent years, are unnecessary in practice. Instead, much broader methods, such as those that permit the grouping of jobs on the basis of their broad content structure or their similarity in inferred ability requirements—*without reference to specific tasks, duties, or behaviors*—are the most appropriate and powerful techniques. (p. 175, italics added)

It is important to note that data-based techniques are available (e.g., the Type 2 and 3 methods) to achieve the Schmidt et al. (1981) objective of describing and grouping jobs for test validation and validity generalization purposes; such behaviorally abstract job descriptors were developed explicitly for the purpose of identifying job similarities that are masked by task differences. Indeed, there are many reasons to prefer a data-based job analysis method over the nonempirical holistic approach. Among them, (a) worker-oriented item ratings and job dimension scores are expressed in terms of *quantitative* data that allow numerical job-similarity statistics to be computed (e.g., to justify aggregating jobs for validity generalization purposes) and (b) the job ratings are based on verifiable job behavior and can be independently verified if necessary (holistic judgments are made in the absence of such data).

To perform holistic job analysis, one need only make a rational, nonempirical determination regarding the kind of "broad job content" involved in the work (e.g., "this is a clerical job" versus "this is a managerial job"). Thus, there are no time-consuming interviews to conduct, no tedious or costly observations of job incumbents to perform, no burdensome questionnaires to construct or score—in short, *one need not collect any data at all* beyond the minimal information contained in the job title.

According to its proponents, the usefulness of the holistic approach extends far beyond the area of test validation using general cognitive ability tests as predictors. Schmidt et. al (1981, pp. 175–177) claimed that holistic job analysis should be used in validity generalization, criterion construction, performance appraisal, and any other area of industrial and organizational psychology that has fallen prey to the influence of "behaviorist assumptions introduced into personnel psychology in the early 1960s... that, in retrospect,... can be seen to be false" (p. 166).

The holistic approach represents a radical departure from traditional job analysis methods, to the point that its proponents argue that for many purposes it is unnecessary to collect *any* data describing job activities in order to justify a personnel decision. Before we discard traditional methods of job analysis, however, a careful examination of the arguments advanced in favor of holistic job ratings is in order, especially the central claim that rating "behavior" is not the appropriate focus for a job analysis.

Should Job Analyses Describe Behavior?

The goal of job analysis has traditionally been the description of job behavior. The job analysis methods considered earlier differ primarily in terms of the *degree* to which their descriptors are technologically specific, as well as the cross-job meaningfulness of the information produced by their rating scales; all share the premise that observable, verifiable job behavior—and a description of objective characteristics of the work environment—is the proper focus of a job analysis. In contrast, the holistic approach involves the *absence* of a job analysis as the term is usually defined.

At the heart of the issue lies the question of whether one believes that industrial and organizational psychology in general—and job analysis in particular—should concern itself with "behavior." The position advanced by holistic job analysis proponents (e.g., Schmidt et al., 1981) is that "the field of personnel psychology came to be so far off base" because during the "late 1950s and early 1960s... behaviorist influences began to make themselves felt" (pp. 178–179).

According to Schmidt et al., among the dire consequences that befell industrial and organizational psychology as a result of behaviorist influences was the rise in popularity of behavior-oriented job analysis. Based upon their claim that "it is now widely recognized in most areas of psychology that basic behaviorist assumptions are conceptually flawed" (1981, p. 180), they deduced that holistic job analysis should be used to reverse the damage caused by behaviorist influences, particularly behavior-based job analysis.

Key among the behaviorist fallacies Schmidt et al. (1981) identified is the notion, "virtually set in concrete in the federal government's *Uniform Guidelines*" (p. 180), that behaviorally oriented job analysis is appropriate for employee selection, criterion development, performance appraisal, and related purposes. Their argument that behavior should not be the focus of a job analysis is based on the following observation:

There are two central claims to the modern behavioristic beliefs as they are manifested in the field of personnel psychology: that [human] abilities are not observable and that behavior is observable. Both claims are false to fact.... Consider the supposed observability of behavior. Suppose that a worker is to screw a certain bolt into a certain hole in each automobile as it passes on the assembly line. Is "screwing in the bolt" an observed behavior in the worker? Certainly not. (p. 181)

In addition to the position that job behaviors are unobservable, Schmidt et al. (1981) noted that physical aspects of the work environment

are no more observable than [human ability] traits. Furthermore, physiology has established similar facts about the [work] response or behavior. A motor act such as screwing in a bolt is known to be a highly complex pattern of time-sequenced patterns of neural impulses to thousands of muscle fibers, to postural muscles, to eye muscles, and so forth. Thus, it is well known that no response ever repeats itself either. Thus, any equivalence of successive acts must be an internal *perceptual* process carried out by the brain. Therefore, responses [i.e., worker behaviors] too are events in the observing psychologist's mind and hence not directly observable.... Thus the response (i.e., the behavior) of behaviorism is no more observable than is an ability; both are hypothetical constructs in the minds of those who use them as theoretical devices. (p. 181)

Thus, the argument that holistic judgments should replace behaviorally oriented job analysis for test validation and criterion-development purposes is based on the following logic. First, the behaviors performed by a worker on a job (e.g., screwing a bolt into a hole) are unobservable, hypothetical events that exist only in an observing psychologist's mind. Much like the proverbial tree that falls in the forest, presumably if no one is there to watch, work behavior does not exist. Second, physical aspects of the work environment (e.g., the bolt being inserted, the cars on the assembly line, the other workers on the line, the employee's supervisor) are also hypothetical events that are not directly observable, existing only in the minds of those who attempt to observe them. Third, workers *never* repeat a job behavior (even our assembly line employee who screws the same bolt into the same hole in each car that passes during an 8-hour shift); only the *perception* that these activities are repetitions exists, and then only in the mind of an observer.

A number of reasons exist for doubting these conclusions. First, there can be little reason to question the fact that the behavior of humans when performing their jobs is both "real" and observable. Only by attempting to restrictively define behavior exclusively in terms of neurons, synapses, muscle fibers, neurotransmitters, and the like can one conclude that the domain of job behavior is intrinsically unobservable or nonrepeatable. Although psychologists employ theories to explain *why* some job applicants have different likelihoods of job success, and in the process use hypothetical explanatory constructs (e.g., drives, goals, abilities, interests, values), we do *not* have to appeal to a theory to tell us that the job behavior actually occurred. *Behavior is not a hypothetical construct;* it is the observable reality that psychological theories seek to explain.

Second, the work environment in which the incumbent performs the specified job behaviors is similarly "real" and observable. Although one may debate the degree to which the abstract characteristics rated in organizational climate or culture inventories have a basis in objective reality, it is difficult to deny the physical reality of the bolt that the worker screws into the car on the assembly line. *The physical, informational, and interpersonal work environment is not a hypothetical construct,* and its existence does not depend on the presence of an external observed to "perceive" it. To quote the APA Standards, a construct is

> a psychological characteristic (e.g., numerical ability, spatial ability, introversion, anxiety) considered to vary or differ across individuals. A construct (sometimes called a latent variable) is not directly observable; rather it is a theoretical concept derived from research and other experience that has been constructed *to explain observable behavior patterns.* (1985, p. 90, emphasis added)

By any standard definition of the term *construct*, the job behaviors and objective environmental characteristics rated in task- and worker-oriented inventories are *not* constructs, they are observable phenomena. As the *Standards* note, abilities are hypothetical constructs and therefore cannot be directly observed. Psychologists *observe* behavior and then *infer* the action of traits or abilities; these inferences may *or may not* be useful to us in explaining observed behavior. Only by making the radical assumption that behavior is an introspective or perceptual event that exists solely in the mind of an observer can one justify the conclusion that job behaviors and job-required human abilities and traits are equally observable.

In sum, holistic job ratings and criticisms of the appropriateness of behavior-oriented job analysis are based on the highly unconventional belief that job behavior is unobservable and that job ability and trait requirements *are* observable (or at least, are as observable as job behavior). Since its inception, job analysis has had as its goal the description of verifiable aspects of work behavior. Notwithstanding

recent claims to the contrary, job behavior and the associated work environment remain observable and should continue to be the focus of the job analysis process.

Summary

To provide a means for categorizing existing job analysis methods, as well as guiding the future development of currently underutilized—but potentially very useful—techniques, I presented a taxonomy that characterizes job analysis methods based on their degree of behavioral specificity and kind of rating scale metric used. When viewed from this perspective, a number of limitations facing existing task- and worker-oriented job analysis methods were identified. These problems concern the ability to make meaningful cross-job comparisons and are caused by the use of rating scales and instruction sets that encourage a within-job-relative rating strategy.

Arguments advocating the abandonment of traditional behavior-oriented methods of job analysis were also considered; on closer examination, they were found to rest upon the questionable premise that job behavior and the physical work environment are unobservable, hypothetical constructs and that human ability requirements are directly observable. Describing job behavior has been and should continue to be the focus of the job analysis process; methods of collecting such data are considered in the next section.

Collecting Job Analysis Data

Sources of Job Data

One of the most critical decisions made in the course of conducting a job analysis is identifying the people who will describe the job and provide the job ratings. As Thompson and Thompson (1982) noted, the safest strategy is to collect information from as many informed sources as possible. Although the qualifications for being termed an SME are vague, a minimum condition is that the person have direct, up-to-date experience with the job for a long enough time to be familiar with all of its tasks (Thompson & Thompson, 1982).

Incumbents.   Job incumbents, given that they are involved in the day-to-day performance of the job in question, are among the most frequently used sources of job information. Although nagging questions remain regarding the degree to which job analysis results are colored by the personal characteristics of the incumbents selected to provide data (e.g., sex, job tenure, or performance level), incumbents are certainly one of the most credible sources of job data. Because of their questionable job mastery, newly hired and probationary employees are not good choices as SMEs.

An important practical limitation of using job incumbents is that many lack sufficient verbal ability to perform certain job rating and description tasks, particularly task inventories that cover a mix of high- and low-level jobs. For example, lower-level employees may misunderstand the task statements that characterize higher-level jobs. A lack of verbal ability may also hamper performance on standardized worker-oriented job analysis questionnaires (e.g., the PAQ). As Ash and Edgell (1975) noted, because of its very high reading level, the PAQ is unsuitable for completion by most job incumbents; according to the PAQ's authors (*PAQ Newsletter*, August 1989), "use job analysts (rather than incumbents or supervisors) to collect PAQ data. When possible, training of the persons to be [job] analysts by an *experienced* PAQ analyst is recommended" (p. 2).

There are additional drawbacks to the use of incumbents. As Gatewood and Feild (1987, p. 184) noted, incumbents may lack the motivation to participate, may have a difficult time communicating their job activities in a systematic and complete fashion (in either a questionnaire format or verbally to an interviewer), or may harbor motives that are in conflict with the goal of obtaining an accurate and complete description of the work. For example, incumbents may perceive an advantage to exaggerating their duties, particularly when the data will be used for compensation puposes.

Supervisors.   Because they play a key role in determining what job incumbents do on their jobs, supervisors often serve as SMEs. Although on average supervisors may possess higher levels of verbal ability than incumbents, they share many of the same drawbacks, particularly in terms of their motivations. In general, incumbents and supervisors are undoubtedly among the best *sources* of job descriptive information, particularly when the information is obtained using focused interviews, observation, or related techniques that allow the analyst to probe or otherwise assess the validity of their statements. However, they may not be the best prepared to produce the actual job analysis *ratings*, particularly when more behaviorally abstract kinds of items are judged.

Job Analysts.   The use of trained job analysts to collect job data and provide job analysis ratings has a number of advantages. Because of their familiarity with job analysis methods, analysts should be able to produce the most cross-job-consistent and reliable ratings. This is especially true for standardized worker-oriented job analysis questionnaires that use terms that may be unfamiliar to employees or supervisors (e.g., "near-visual differentiation").

Drawbacks to the use of job analysts exist, however. The use of external job analysts can be quite expensive: For cases in which job analysts initially have little or no familiarity with the job being rated, considerable time and effort must be expended by the analyst to become sufficiently familiar with the activities of the job (e.g., by using the interview or observational methods discussed below).

An effort-saving strategy used by some job analysts is to require incumbents or supervisors to complete a short, open-ended questionnaire in which they describe their job prior to being interviewed by the analyst. Although this can be a useful tool to break the ice and provide a starting point for more focused and probing questions, this technique has potential drawbacks. If important activities are omitted from the SME's initial narrative, this fact may not be discovered in the subsequent interview.

Additionally, when analysts have had experience with jobs that appear to be similar to the one being analyzed (e.g., based on job title similarity), the potential exists for the analyst to rely on preexisting job stereotypes that may or may not accurately describe the job being rated. Although some studies (e.g., Harvey & Lozada-Larsen, 1988) have suggested that stereotypes invoked by a job title are not a determinant of job ratings when unfamiliar jobs are rated (probably because *no* substantive stereotype exists), the situation may be very different when more common titles—or even uncommon titles with which the analyst has had prior experience—are rated.

Even if additional data are collected, analysts may selectively attend to only information that is consistent with their preexisting job stereotype and discount inconsistent information; similar maladaptive information processing strategies are frequently seen in the employment interview (e.g, McDonald & Hakel, 1985) and performance appraisal (e.g., Feldman, 1981) process. In such cases, job analysts may demonstrate high interrater agreement (i.e., if they share the stereotypes, which is likely if the analysts have previously analyzed similar jobs), yet their ratings may have very low validity.

Although supervisors and others may similarly fall victim to overreliance on stereotypes, the problem would appear to be much more likely for job analysts that deal with a large number of different jobs and who work under tight time pressures. In a large job analysis project, each analyst may interview several SMEs in a single day and only later make the actual job ratings, relying on their notes and recollection of the earlier observations. Given the degree to which we might expect suboptimal information processing in such situations (e.g., Feldman, 1981), it is unfortunate to note the lack of research conducted in realistic settings that examines the information processing aspects of the job analysis rating process.

Other sources of information may also be used in a job analysis. For example, archival sources of data may be useful, such as training manuals, job descriptions, results of previous job analyses, and performance evaluation devices. Alternatively, other kinds of SMEs (e.g., personnel officials familiar with the job) may be able to provide useful descriptive information.

Methods of Collecting Data

Have Analysts Observe the Job.   A number of different techniques for collecting job information may be used to extract data from the sources described above. One of the most informative is to observe workers as they perform the job. This observation can take the form of physical measurement in which quantifiable aspects of the work are recorded, such as weights of objects moved, distances objects are moved, or temperature ranges in which the work is performed.

More often, information is collected by observing workers as they engage in their job activities. Such observation can range from the informal to the highly structured, that is, video- and audiotaping workers as they perform the job, or having job analysts themselves perform the job in a participant observer role.

Ask SMEs to Describe the Job.   We also can simply ask SMEs to describe the activities they perform on the job. This often takes the form of an *interview* in which analysts follow either a structured or open-ended strategy for obtaining data. Less frequently seen, but of value in some situations, workers can be requested to keep *diaries* describing the activities they perform on the job; this approach is especially useful for jobs that involve highly time-variable activities or that are otherwise difficult to observe.

Questionnaires are an effective data collection technique when a number of jobs are being analyzed or when there are a large number of incumbents in a job. These inventories can be developed for the specific sample of jobs in question (e.g., as in the task inventory approach), or standardized worker-oriented inventories can be used. Standardized questionnaires are much more economical to use than custom inventories, particularly when they can be completed by the incumbent to avoid the time and expense required for job analysts to make the ratings.

In many job analysis projects, a combination of data collection methods is used. For example, interviews and observation of a sample of employees from each job can be used to develop a task inventory, which is subsequently administered to all employees. For worker-oriented analysis, job analysts may conduct interviews and observations and later complete a standardized questionnaire.

Rating Process Questions

Operationalizing Criticality. Obtaining information denoting the criticality of individual work activities is important for a number of reasons. Unfortunately, documents like the *Uniform Guidelines* do not specify how criticality is to be operationalized. Two general strategies for identifying critical tasks have emerged: (a) direct ratings, in which SMEs use a rating scale (e.g., Importance, Criticality of Errors) to judge each task, and (b) composite indexes, in which task ratings are combined to form a single criticality

value (e.g., by multiplying Time Spent x Importance).

Schmidt and Sulzer (1989) surveyed industrial and organizational psychologists regarding the ways in which criticality was assessed, finding considerable variability in both the kind of rating scales and methods used to form criticality ratings (15 different task rating scales were identified). Considerable variability also exists with respect to the methods for using these ratings. For example, for methods based on a single Importance rating, definitions for criticality included receiving a rating of 3 or better on a 4-point scale; ratings of 1 or better on the same scale; items rated applicable by 50 percent or more of incumbents; and all items rated higher than the bottom 25 percent of the distribution of ratings.

Methods identified by Schmidt and Sulzer (1989) that involved the use of multiple rating scales for each task included (2 x Importance + Frequency); (Frequency x Criticality of Errors); (Difficulty x Criticality of Errors + Time Spent); and (Time Spent x Importance). The most complicated methods involved conditional judgments, as in, for example, (Importance rating of 3 or better out of 5 and a Frequency rating of 3 or better out of 5), or (50% or more of incumbents say the task is performed, and the Importance and Frequency ratings for the item exceed the grand mean).

Given the diversity of methods for combining rating scale information to obtain a criticality judgment, it is obvious that different methods may produce different rankings of critical tasks. This is particularly important in view of the fact that in the Schmidt and Sulzer (1989) survey, 52 percent of the industrial and organizational psychologists indicated they "almost always" or "frequently" eliminate tasks that do not achieve criticality cutoffs from subsequent uses of the job analysis data. Research is needed to identify the degree to which different measures of criticality identify different tasks and the degree to which these differences produce different personnel decisions.

Redundancy Between Task Rating Scales.
A related question concerns the required number of task rating scales. In the *integrated personnel system* approach (e.g., Avner & Mayer, 1986; Harvey, 1986b; J. Mitchell & Driskill, 1986; Wilson, 1987), a number of different personnel functions are linked by the use of a master job analysis data base. To allow a single set of tasks to serve a variety of personnel functions, some authors (e.g., Gael, 1983) have advised that each task be rated on a number of different rating scales.

The problem is, adding additional rating scales to a task inventory *multiplicatively* increases the number of ratings that are necessary; beyond a certain point, adding more scales makes completing the task inventory unmanageable. Thus, researchers need to know the minimum number of rating scales that can be used to provide sufficient task data to drive a variety of personnel functions. Practically speaking, if the ratings on two scales are sufficiently highly correlated, one of the pair can be eliminated from the inventory.

Several studies have examined task rating scale correlations (e.g., Cragun & McCormick, 1967; Sanchez & Levine, 1989, Wilson, 1989), the general conclusion being that many scales are correlated at a moderate to high level, with the highest correlations occurring when job-level rating profiles are examined (i.e., for each rating scale, means across all incumbents are computed for each item and these mean vectors are correlated). For example, Sanchez and Levine (1989) compared mean ratings of Overall Importance, Task Criticality, Task Responsibility, Difficulty of Learning, and Relative Time Spent ratings, finding high correlations (.60s to .90s) between many pairs of scales; only Relative Time Spent and Task Responsibility exhibited consistently low correlations with the others.

These findings need to be interpreted cautiously. For example, it may be argued that in many cases the wrong unit of analysis has been examined. Instead of using aggregate job-mean profiles computed across a number of different positions holding a common title, I would argue that the individual raters should be studied without any aggregation. Before it is appropriate to analyze job mean profiles, it must first be demonstrated that the individuals within each job do not significantly differ in terms of the ways in which they use the scales (see James, 1982). It is entirely possible that different raters holding the same job may differ in their degree of scale intercorrelation; removing cross-rater differences before computing the scale correlations may present a completely misleading picture of the way in which the scales are used.

Studies that used individual raters instead of job means as the unit of analysis (e.g., Friedman, 1988, 1990; Wilson, 1989) reported results very different from the job-mean results of Sanchez and Levine (1989). In particular, they found that (a) the mean interscale correlations (for each job, averaging the rs across raters) are *much* lower than those reported in job-level studies and (b) the degree of variability around these means is large (i.e., individual raters within each job differ considerably in terms of the degree to which their ratings on the different scales are correlated). Clearly, significant individual differences in the use of rating scales exist that preclude aggregation.

Although their study focused on aggregated ratings, Sanchez and Levine (1989) also reported data indicating sizable individual differences in rating scale use. Job-mean rs between scales ranged from −.22 to .91, whereas individual-rater rs ranged from −.60 to .96. They noted that for many subjects, the overall importance rating was predicted at "only moderate" levels from the other scales; for the remaining subjects, overall importance was highly predictable (1989, p. 342).

The phenomenon of *aggregation bias* (James, 1982) can be used to explain the very high interscale correlations observed when analyzing mean profiles. That is, true interrater differences in scale correlations are eliminated when aggregate profiles are formed; the resulting unrepresentative mean profiles may indeed correlate very strongly and positively, even when many raters produced *negatively* correlated or even completely uncorrelated ratings. The issue of aggregation bias and within-title variability is discussed in more detail below.

In sum, based on the large degree of cross-rater variability in the degree of task rating scale intercorrelation, it appears that reductions in the number of task rating scales required to serve a variety of personnel applications cannot be achieved. Additional research addressing the question of *why* there are such large individual differences in rating scale use is needed to resolve this issue.

The Role of Dichotomous Ratings. A finding reported in many settings (e.g., Carpenter, 1974; Pass & Robertson, 1980; Wilson & Harvey, 1990) concerns the degree of redundancy between dichotomous do-you-perform (DYP) task judgments and the presumably more informative relative-time-spent (RTS) ratings. In short, when job-level mean profiles are analyzed, correlations between the percent of incumbents performing a task and the corresponding mean RTS rating are *very* high: Wilson and Harvey (1990) reported *r*s in the high .80s and .90s; Pass and Robertson (1980) and Carpenter (1974) also reported *r*s in the .90s.

On the basis of such findings, Pass and Robertson (1980) concluded "no practical gain in information is achieved from the continuous Relative Time-Spent scale" (p. vii). Carpenter (1974) concluded that "in groups of five or more individuals, dichotomized task performance data... is the most critical component of the resultant group job description" (p. i). Wilson and Harvey (1990) reached a similar conclusion.

To some degree, it appears counterintuitive to find that simply knowing the percent

of raters who indicate they perform a task explains 80 to 90 percent of the variance in mean RTS ratings. For example, one might expect that variability on the dichotomous rating would be severely limited (i.e., shouldn't positions holding the same title agree on the tasks that are part of the job?); such a situation would sharply attenuate the *r* between RTS and DYP ratings.

The explanation advanced by Wilson and Harvey (1990) centers on the role of within-title variability in the RTS and DYP judgment. Namely, without variability in both sets of ratings, correlations of the magnitude reported in the examples I have cited are simply not possible. Figure 4 presents a scatterplot between the mean RTS and DYP ratings for one of the jobs reported in Wilson and Harvey (1990); the data in this figure (each point represents a single task; only tasks that at least one incumbent rated as applicable were included) indicate that RTS and DYP means vary across a full range of scores and that the association between mean RTS and DYP ratings is even higher than that conveyed by the *r*s (i.e., due to nonlinearity).

High RTS-DYP correlations reflect the disconcerting fact that a high level of disagreement often exists between incumbents *within the same job title* regarding the tasks they perform. The results reported to date on a variety of jobs suggest that high within-title disagreement is commonplace; indeed, it is often the case that *over half of a job's tasks are performed by less than 50 percent of the job's incumbents.* Thus, the issue of within-title variability in job analysis results is one that must be confronted.

Dealing With Within-Title Variability. Traditional wisdom holds that some degree of within-title variability in job analysis ratings is inevitable; the source of this variance is typically seen to be simple unreliability (e.g., Cranny & Doherty, 1988). The standard response is to eliminate this variability by computing job mean profiles and then using

FIGURE 4

Scatterplot of Mean RTS Versus the Percent of Incumbents Indicating They Perform a Task

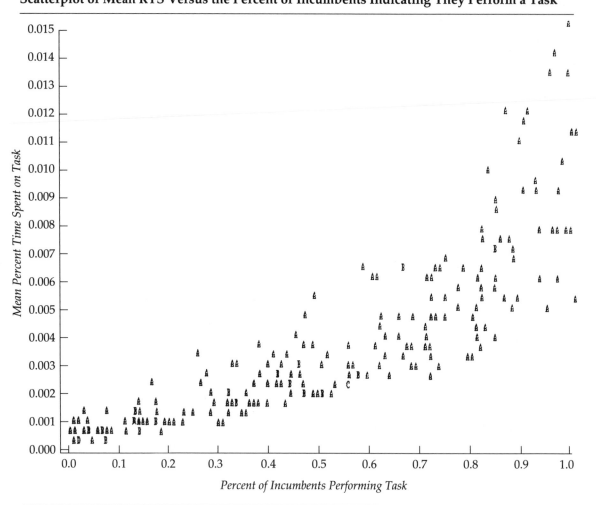

Note: A = 1 task, B = 2 tasks, C = 3 tasks

means for subsequent applications of the job data. As Sanchez and Levine (1989) noted, "this aggregation process is typically done in job analysis, because it is assumed that individual biases are overcome by aggregating the data across subjects" (p. 338).

The underlying logic for eliminating within-title variability is based on classical test theory (e.g., Nunnally, 1978)—namely, that (a) a single "true" profile of task ratings exists for each job, (b) rating differences between positions are random error "noise," and therefore (c) the mean profile for each job computed across multiple positions is the best estimate of the "true" job profile. The corollary of this conclusion is that position ratings themselves should *not* be used or studied, as they are not as reliable as the mean profiles computed across several positions that nominally perform the same job.

There are many reasons to question the validity of the conclusion that aggregate job mean profiles are always the most reliable form of job analysis data and that within-title variability is noise that must be summarily eliminated. First, the argument for aggregating ignores a growing body of research (e.g., Green & Stutzman, 1986; Harvey, 1982, 1986a; Schmitt & Cohen, 1989; Stutzman, 1983) indicating that nontrivial rating differences are at least in part caused by the presence of meaningful subgroups of positions within existing job titles.

Second, the argument in favor of eliminating within-title rating variability is based on the assumption that no "true" variability exists between positions sharing a job title (e.g., Cranny & Doherty, 1988). In other words, the existing job title system is assumed to be perfect, and any failure of incumbents to perfectly agree on the task ratings is due to an inability to properly understand the rating task.

Many theories of work and organizational processes (e.g., Dansereau, Graen, & Haga, 1975; Graen, 1976; Katz & Kahn, 1978) predict that a number of systematic processes exist that cause true task differences to occur between job incumbents. As part of the ongoing negotiation process that occurs in supervisor-subordinate dyads, a subordinate's aspirations, past level of performance, specific job skills, degree of liking by the supervisor, job tenure, and other factors combine to cause true cross-position differences in the tasks assigned to employees that nominally hold the same job title.

The problem of within-title variability is intimately tied to the aggregation bias phenomenon discussed by James (1982). In short, although the practice of computing mean profiles is certainly effective at eliminating within-title rating differences, the validity and representativeness of these aggregate profiles depends on the *kind* of variability being discarded—that is, is it random noise, in which case it is appropriate to remove it, or does it reflect systematic variance, in which case it is *not* appropriate to aggregate? Sufficient empirical and theoretical evidence exists to justify the conclusion that a significant portion of observed within-title variability is due to systematic factors and thus should not be aggregated away.

To the extent that systematic variance is discarded, James (1982) demonstrated that the aggregate profile is increasingly unrepresentative of individual positions; in extreme cases, the aggregate profile may not adequately describe any of the positions contained in a job. Industrial and organizational psychologists can no longer simply assume that disagreement between positions is noise that must be removed by computing means.

Assessing the Quality of Job Analysis Data. *Rating Source Convergence.* Although it is well known that interrater agreement does not prove that the ratings are valid, in many cases users of job analysis data rely solely on interrater agreement statistics to demonstrate the quality of job analysis ratings. In terms of agreement between trained job analysts, research data indicate generally good agreement (.70s to .90s) when tasks (e.g., Cragun & McCormick, 1967; Wilson, Harvey, & Macy, 1990) and worker-oriented items (e.g., Harvey & Hayes, 1986) are rated. Interrater rs in the .90s are common for worker-oriented instruments using trained job analysts.

However, caution should be used when interpreting reliabilities for worker-oriented instruments and task inventories. Harvey and Hayes (1986) demonstrated that because a high percentage of PAQ items are likely to receive DNA ratings, interrater reliabilities computed on the full profile of PAQ ratings provide an overly optimistic view of rating agreement (i.e., the numerous DNA ratings provide a built-in level of "reliability" that can mask serious disagreements on the items that *are* part of the job). Similar results can occur for task inventories, which can contain a vast number of DNA ratings for individual jobs. Reliabilities for such instruments should be reported for both the overall profile and the reduced profile formed by eliminating DNA items.

Reliabilities for the more abstract worker-function scales of FJA (Data, People, and Things) and the various scales used in the *Dictionary of Occupational Titles* (DOT) have been mixed (e.g., Cain & Green, 1983; Geyer, Hice, Hawk, Boese, & Brannon, 1989). Some scales achieved levels of reliability (.80s and .90s) seen in task- and worker-oriented item ratings (e.g., the worker-function scales), whereas others demonstrated highly questionable results (e.g., reliabilities under .50 were seen for many temperament and criticality-of-physical-demands items). Particularly for these more holistic ratings, which in many cases involve inferences regarding AO requirements (e.g., the DOT worker temperament ratings), the distinction between interrater reliability and the *validity* of these inferences must be kept in mind. Simply showing agreement between judges proves little when worker requirements involving hypothetical personal traits—as opposed to observable job behaviors—are rated.

Regarding ratings convergence, results using raters who are not professional job analysts have been even less encouraging. Using the PAQ, Smith and Hakel (1979) found that supervisors and incumbents consistently produced higher ratings when compared to job analysts, although the *shapes* of the rating profiles were similar. In some instances (e.g., when one is concerned solely with identifying the items that are part of the job and not the *degree* to which they are part of the job), this kind of profile elevation bias is not important; for many situations, however, it is a very important bias.

Other studies have raised serious questions regarding the degree to which incumbents and supervisors are able to agree among themselves when describing a job. Meyer (1959) found only 58 percent agreement between incumbents and their supervisors when rating 77 job activities (foremen and general foremen were studied). In a study of Air Force finance and accounting jobs, Hazel, Madden, and Christal (1964) found that on average only 63 percent of tasks that subordinates indicated they performed were also rated as applicable by their supervisor; conversely, only 59 percent of tasks rated applicable by supervisors were rated similarly by the subordinates. In a study of 59 supervisor-subordinate dyads in a municipal government organization, Harvey (1990b) reported that on average incumbents rated as applicable 4 percent of the tasks that supervisors said were *not* performed; of greater concern, on average incumbents failed to rate as applicable 30 percent of the tasks that supervisors said *were* part of the job.

Although it is at times difficult to determine who is correct when analyzing disagreements between incumbents and supervisors, it is obvious that when levels of disagreement like those reported above exist, *someone* is providing an incorrect description of the job. Whenever possible, multiple raters, supervisory reviews of ratings, and lie scales (discussed below) should be used to improve the quality of job analysis data.

Effect of Amount of Information on Ratings Quality. A number of studies have examined the effectiveness of techniques that reduce the cost and intrusiveness of the job analysis process by reducing the amount of job data collected by the rater. For example, Jones, Main, Butler, and Johnson (1982) proposed using only a short narrative job description as the basis for making PAQ ratings, thereby avoiding the time and expense involved in having job analysts first become familiar with the jobs (e.g., by interviews with incumbents and observation).

Studies examining such techniques (Cornelius, DeNisi, & Blencoe, 1984; DeNisi, Cornelius, & Blencoe, 1987; Friedman & Harvey, 1986; Harvey & Hayes, 1986; Harvey & Lozada-Larsen, 1988) have consistently supported the validity of the common-sense notion that people who are less familiar with a job cannot rate it as well as those who are intimately familiar with it. Specifically, both interrater reliability as well as convergence with known "true" profiles were inadequate when rating on the basis of only cursory job descriptive information.

Assessing the Validity of Job Ratings. The issue of the validity of job ratings has received even less attention than the interrater agreement question. With respect to the validity of the popular RTS task rating scale, the most common strategy has been to compare RTS ratings to independent estimates of the actual amount of time spent on various activities. Results using this method have not been encouraging (e.g., Carpenter, Giorgia, & McFarland, 1975; Hartley, Brecht, Pagery, Weeks, Chapanis, & Hoecker, 1977). In such studies, the RTS ratings were first transformed to PTS values by dividing each RTS rating by the sum of the ratings given by that rater. When comparing actual percent-time and PTS ratings, Carpenter et al. (1975) found that they differed by about one percentage point on average. Although this might appear to be a very small error, even tasks that receive the maximum RTS rating typically have a PTS value of only 0.5 percent to 1 percent! Thus, these differences are quite large.

Similarly disconcerting results have been obtained by examining the performance of *lie scales* or other devices to identify careless or invalid responding. Green and Stutzman (1986) included a number of task statements known *not* to be part of the job and computed a *carelessness index* based on the number of bogus items endorsed. Although one might be able to excuse a small percentage of careless

responses, Green and Stutzman found that 50 percent of the raters indicated that at least one bogus task was performed!

A second strategy for identifying careless raters was used by Wilson, Harvey, and Macy (1990). In this approach, several task statements were repeated, and consistency indices were formed by examining differences in rating the repeated items (both present–not present, and the change in ratings given applicable tasks). Wilson et al. found that although most raters were consistent, a nontrivial subset of raters were highly inconsistent (e.g., rating a task highly the first time and rating it DNA the second).

A widespread technique for demonstrating the validity of a job analysis questionnaire involves asking incumbents to estimate the percentage of their job that is described by the items on a 0 to 100 percent scale (e.g., Page & Gomez, 1979), or by computing the percentage of incumbents who indicate that the inventory adequately described their job (e.g., Cragun & McCormick, 1967). Two difficulties are present in this approach. First, how high must the percent-coverage ratings be before one can conclude that the inventory is "valid"? For example, Cragun and McCormick reported mean percent-coverage ratings in the 70 percent range; is that good, bad, or indifferent?

Second, Wilson (1990) examined the effect of manipulating task content on percent-coverage ratings and reported a highly troubling finding. Wilson used a test-retest design on a single job, with 100 tasks in a full task questionnaire administered first, and a 30-item subset of tasks administered at a follow-up testing. The tasks in both inventories received virtually identical mean ratings on Importance, Significance, Frequency, and Difficulty, indicating that the subset was composed of the same kinds of tasks contained in the full inventory; thus, a sizable reduction in percent-coverage ratings was expected for the shortened inventory. Instead, incumbents gave the 30-item subset (which represented a 70 percent reduction in task coverage) a mean percent-coverage rating of 77 percent; the full inventory attained a mean coverage rating of 93 percent. If the percent-coverage scale had worked as expected, the ratings of the 30-item inventory should have been much lower, ideally, 30 percent.

Taken together, the evidence on interrater agreement, lie scales, and percent-performing judgments paints a troubling picture regarding the reliability and validity of job analysis ratings. Although some lack of agreement between job incumbents is expected due to true differences in job activities, the lie-scale data indicate that individual incumbents often provide highly inconsistent and invalid ratings. Regarding validity, the one study to examine the sensitivity of percent-coverage statistics to actual variations in task coverage suggests that direct judgments of an instrument's content-sampling validity may provide a misleading picture.

Effect of Rater Characteristics on Job Ratings.   Conclusions regarding the degree to which job analysis ratings vary as a function of characteristics of the rater have come full-circle recently. For years, industrial and organizational psychologists seemed content to rely on a handful of studies (e.g., Arvey, Davis, McGowen, & Dipboye, 1982; Arvey, Passino, & Lounsbury, 1977; Wexley & Silverman, 1978) whose findings were interpreted to indicate that rater sex and job effectiveness do not influence job analysis ratings. Even in the absence of recent research findings to the contrary, however, examination of these studies reveals a number of reasons for skepticism.

Studies that have been cited as indicating that the PAQ is not sensitive to bias (e.g., Arvey et al., 1977, 1982) suffer from questions regarding external validity: Small samples of raters were used, the raters were college students participating for course credit (not actual job analysts), and they did not conduct their own background data collection (e.g., they watched short video presentations in which the sex of a simulated "worker" was manipulated). The dissimilarity between such situations and the conditions in which actual PAQs are given by job analysts is large.

Wexley and Silverman (1978) is frequently cited as indicating that the performance effectiveness level of incumbents does not influence job analysis ratings; however, it also suffers from external generalizability problems, as the job analysis questionnaire used was quite different than the typical task- or worker-oriented inventory. The *Store Manager Description Questionnaire* (SMDQ) used in the study consisted of only seven behavior-oriented items (e.g., personnel management, expense control, building maintenance and security), plus 30 "worker characteristics" (e.g., decisiveness, cooperation, leadership ability, open mindedness, logical judgment). In short, the seven work-oriented items were holistic *duty* ratings, not task judgments; the remaining 30 items involved inferring KS and AO requirements, not the description of job behavior.

The criterion measures used to assess the level of job effectiveness of the store managers who rated the SMDQ were gross store sales and net profit, adjusted for the number of store employees (presumably, these criteria were under the control of the store manager). Based on a failure to find significant differences between the job mean profiles computed on the highest third versus the lowest third of store managers (segmented by sales and profit criteria), Wexley and Silverman (1978) concluded that:

> both high and low performers can be used in job analysis studies, since both groups respond to questionnaires in a similar manner. These findings seem to suggest that all incumbents can represent a reliable source for obtaining job analysis information. (p. 649)

The generalizability of this conclusion, based on raters from a single organization rating a single job on an atypical questionnaire and whose level of performance effectiveness was defined solely in terms of the profitability of their entire store, is questionable. Indeed, subsequent research has produced opposite conclusions.

Mullins and Kimbrough (1988) and Ronan, Talbert, and Mullett (1977) reported differences in the critical incidents generated by police patrol officers as a function of the rater's level of performance effectiveness. Aamodt, Kimbrough, Keller, and Crawford (1982) reported race-based differences in critical incident generation. Additionally, Hauenstein and Foti (1989) found differences in police officer ratings of the effectiveness level of critical incidents as a function of the performance effectiveness level of the raters.

Studies of task- and worker-oriented job analysis ratings have also reported significant effects due to race, sex, job tenure, and other factors. Schmitt and Cohen (1989) reported both race and sex subgroup differences in task ratings made by incumbents. Ferris, Fedor, Rowland, and Proac (1985) reported sex-based differences in mean task significance ratings under some rating conditions. Sanchez (1990) found differences in the degree of correlation between various task rating scales as a function of job experience; correlations increased with increased experience. Sanchez also found experience-based differences in the mean level of task ratings, such that incumbents with less experience tended to give higher ratings of task importance and difficulty than more experienced raters. Feldman's (1981) theory of cognitive processes in the performance appraisal process was used to explain these findings. Finally, Hayes (1988) found that worker-oriented ratings on the JEI differed as a function of a number of rater characteristics, including whether or not the worker had previously filed a workman's compensation claim.

In sum, one cannot simply assume that job analysis ratings will be unaffected by characteristics of the rater; studies conducted in realistic settings have reported differences on the basis of race, sex, job tenure, performance level, and other factors. Additional research incorporating theory-based attempts to explain ratings differences (e.g., Sanchez, 1990) is needed to determine the extent of these biases and to develop practical prescriptions for detecting and reducing them.

Holistic Job Ratings. A number of reasons exist to question the quality of holistic job ratings; by *holistic,* I refer to strategies that judge the job as a single undivided entity (e.g., Schmidt et al., 1981) or that rate a relatively small number of behaviorally abstract categories (e.g., the seven general work behaviors used by Wexley & Silverman, 1978). In this sense, directly rating job duties would be considered a holistic task; similarly, direct estimation of AO requirements when developing job specifications involves holistic judgments (e.g., Wexley & Silverman's ratings of decisiveness, leadership ability, and open mindedness).

On theoretical grounds (e.g., Feldman, 1981; Tversky & Kahneman, 1974), we would predict questionable accuracy for holistic job ratings, as the same cognitive processes operative in performance appraisal settings should apply to the job analysis rating process as well. For example, if the duty categories rated in a job analysis do not correspond to the cognitive schemata employed by the job analyst when the relevant job information was initially observed and stored, undesirable judgment heuristics (e.g., representativeness or availability) may influence the duty ratings. Specifically, features of the prototype elicited by the duty category name—which may *not* accurately describe the job in question—may effectively determine the duty rating.

Given that a large amount of recall and subsequent integration of information is required to make holistic duty and KS/AO ratings, such ratings may be significantly less valid than those requiring less integration or recall (e.g., behaviorally specific task ratings). Likewise, holistic ratings may be highly reliable in an interrater sense—yet lack validity—if the analysts making them share prototypes of the job being rated (e.g., if the raters are job analysts who have had similar prior experiences rating jobs). In short, simply finding that job analysts agree among themselves when making holistic ratings offers no evidence that the ratings are valid.

Empirical data regarding the effectiveness of holistic ratings is scarce, and most studies suffer from a failure to use an independent standard against which the validity of the holistic ratings can be judged (e.g., Cornelius & Lyness, 1980; Cornelius, Schmidt, & Carron, 1984). For example, Cornelius et al. (1984) claimed that "simple holistic job classification judgments perform as well as (if not better than) [an] elaborate statistical procedure" involving more detailed job analysis ratings (p. 255). However, the "elaborate statistical procedure" cited in this study involved using discriminant analysis to predict *holistic job category membership ratings* from detailed job analysis data and did *not* involve comparing holistic job classification judgments against an independently derived job classification structure. The fact that the holistic job classification judgments made by one group of employees agree with the holistic job classification judgments made by a second group of employees at the same plant says nothing about the *validity* of these judgments. The important question—which the Cornelius et al. (1984) study failed to address—concerns the degree to which holistic job grouping judgments agree with the job classification structures produced from analysis of detailed job data.

In another study that claimed benefits for holistic job classification ratings, Sackett, Cornelius, and Carron (1981) found similarity between the hierarchical cluster analysis groupings produced from holistic paired-comparison judgments versus a 237-item task inventory. However, the Sackett et al. study involved only eight relatively task-heterogeneous foreman jobs in the chemical processing industry, raising questions about its generalizability to larger samples of jobs.

Evidence indicating that holistic job ratings are not interchangeable with the results obtained from traditional detailed job analyses was reported by Hartman and Kromm (1989), who compared holistic job grouping judgments with empirically derived groupings using 810 school superintendents, principals, and business officials. Based on ratings of 78 job descriptors, their results indicated that empirically derived groupings were significantly more predictable than the holistic groupings. (Discriminant analyses in holdout samples were performed, using the job analysis ratings as predictors and the holistic or empirical grouping structures as the categorical criterion). Predictability in the derivation samples was also superior in the empirically derived groups. Hartman and Kromm also found that the empirical grouping analyses revealed a number of cases in which individuals holding the same job title demonstrated different job analysis profiles; the holistic procedure did not uncover this fact.

With respect to direct ratings of abstract job characteristics, Butler and Harvey (1988) examined the ability of raters to directly judge the 32 job dimension scores produced by the PAQ; results indicated that even professional job analysts who were employees of a consulting firm specializing in PAQ job analysis demonstrated virtually no convergence between holistic PAQ dimension ratings and the factor analytic dimension scores produced from their individual PAQ item ratings. Although the sample of professional analysts used was small, the conditions for being able to demonstrate similarity between holistic and decomposed ratings were near-optimal in terms of rater familiarity with the instrument: That is, if professional analysts cannot produce holistic ratings that converge with traditionally derived dimension scores under these conditions, it is unlikely raters less familiar with the instrument would be able to do so.

Reducing the Costliness of Collecting Task-level Job Data. Although the technologies involved in collecting task-oriented job analysis information have been refined over decades of use (e.g., see Christal, 1974; Fine, 1989; Gael, 1983) and can be applied in a straightforward fashion, collecting task-based job data remains a very costly undertaking. For job-specific methods of task analysis like FJA, in which each job is analyzed separately, considerable employee and analyst time is devoted to interviewing, observing, and otherwise collecting the information needed to write the task statements; additional time is then required to rate the tasks (e.g., using the Data-People-Things functional level scales). The process of developing task inventories is similar, with the addition that analyst effort is required to assimilate and edit the tasks generated from different jobs into a single inventory; once developed, incumbent time is required to complete the inventory (e.g., by rating each task statement using a frequency rating scale).

Consequently, the task analysis process can be quite costly in terms of time and resources; in even a small-to-moderate sized organization, hundreds or thousands of person-hours of effort may be required to collect the task data, and additional time will subsequently be required to keep the task information up-to-date as jobs change. Although precise statistics are not available, it has been my experience that only a relatively small percentage of organizations collect and maintain a comprehensive task-level job analysis data base; this lack of task-based data is probably due in large part to the high costs involved.

Fortunately, advances in computer hardware and software technology hold the promise of significantly reducing the cost and labor-intensiveness of this approach to job analysis.

Improvements in computer hardware have been dramatic: In the period in which McCormick (1976) wrote the previous *Handbook* chapter on job analysis, expensive mainframe computer systems were required to manage a large task data base (e.g., the CODAP system descibed by Christal, 1974). The amount of data that must be managed is considerable, even in smaller organizations. For example, I developed and administered a task inventory for a 120-position organization that produced over 106,000 individual task ratings; in another organization with 3,600 employees, a similar task inventory produced over 1.8 million task ratings! Clearly, some degree of automation is necessary to deal with this amount of data.

Today, desktop personal computers costing under $10,000 can match the performance of the million-dollar mainframe systems that only 15 years ago were required to run programs like CODAP. Thus, the computing power required to manage job analysis data bases is within the reach of even the smallest organization. Efforts to develop computerized integrated personnel systems (IPS) have increased dramatically in recent years (e.g., Avner & Mayer, 1986; Harvey, 1986b; Mitchell & Driskill, 1986; Wilson, 1987).

Although computerized integrated personnel systems can make the process of managing and using large amounts of task-based job analysis data practical for both large and small organizations, the problem of *collecting* the task information remains. Fortunately, advances in computerized artificial intelligence (AI) and expert systems technologies offer a means for addressing this problem. With respect to generating task statements, Coovert (1985, 1986; Vance, Coovert, & Colella, 1989) has employed AI technology to develop computer software systems that reduce the labor-intensiveness—especially regarding the need for job analysts—of the task-statement generation process. Wilson (1991) developed a software system for collecting job analysis data describing the physical activities and requirements of jobs; instead of using trained job analysts to observe and interview incumbents prior to making such ratings, Wilson's system simply requires incumbents to sit at a personal computer and answer the questions posed by the software.

An alternative approach to reducing the labor-intensiveness of developing a pool of task statements can be found in what I have termed the *generic task inventory* method. Instead of developing task inventories essentially from scratch for each organization, it should be possible to assemble pools of tasks for general occupational categories (e.g., clerical, managerial, retail sales, legal, computer programming, or public safety) based on integrating past job analysis work in each general occupational category. These pools of tasks could potentially be quite large; although many tasks would probably be DNA for specific organizations and some new tasks would likely need to be written for each new organization, dramatic reductions in the time and cost involved in developing an organization-specific task inventory could be achieved if a generic task inventory were capable of capturing 80 to 90 percent of the task content in advance.

In sum, the primary obstacles to the widespread collection and use of task-based job analysis data—namely, the labor-intensiveness of writing and rating task statements and the administrative problems associated with managing large volumes of task data—may soon be overcome. Increased computerization, combined with efforts to build and apply data bases of task statements for general occupational categories, offer the promise of making detailed, task-based job analysis techniques available to all organizations, regardless of size. Although standardized worker-oriented questionnaires are useful for many personnel functions, there are some applications of job analysis data, such as development of training programs, that can only be solved with task-oriented job analysis data: Making such methods cost effective is a critical goal.

Summary

A limited range of choices exists with regard to selecting the sources of data used in the job analysis process; typically, some combination of incumbents, supervisors, or observer/analysts serve as sources of data. Little is known, however, about the factors that influence the quality of job analysis ratings, and research on the performance appraisal and employment interview processes gives rise to substantial concerns regarding the degree to which suboptimal information processing strategies may contribute to job analysis ratings.

The empirical studies that have examined the job analysis rating process do not form the basis for optimism: Significant job rating differences have been observed as a function of incumbent sex, tenure, and performance level; incumbents and supervisors often provide dramatically different descriptions of jobs; different incumbents holding the same job can produce sharply divergent task ratings; incumbents often endorse tasks that are known *not* to be part of their jobs and inconsistently rate repeated tasks; and it is likely that the various information processing biases and effects seen in the performance appraisal and employee interview processes occur in the job analysis process as well. The solution to the problem of job analysis ratings disagreement is not to simply compute a mean and hope that errors will cancel out. Much additional research on the process issues involved in collecting job analysis data is needed so that we may be able to clarify the conditions under which we may be confident in the quality of the job analysis ratings produced by different data collection strategies.

Legal Issues in Collecting and Using Job Analysis Data

Although I would like to think that organizations collect and use job analysis data because it is the right thing to do and will result in more effective human resource management, the reality is that many employers conduct job analyses primarily to defend against potential employment discrimination lawsuits from employees or job applicants. In such instances, the overriding desire is to limit legal liability; at times, little attention is given to actually using the job data.

Indeed, among some there is the perception that simply conducting a job analysis—*any* job analysis—is all that is required to protect an organization from a discrimination lawsuit. As Schmitt (1987) noted, "sometimes it seems the job analysis has become an end in itself and the necessary linkage [to personnel functions] is absent" (p. 2). For reasons presented below, simply collecting job analysis data is not an effective strategy, viewed from either a legal-defensibility or a sound personnel management perspective.

Laws and Court Decisions

Laws. Title VII of the Civil Rights Act of 1964 ("Title VII") has been the prominent piece of legislation having implications for job analysis; most employment discrimination court decisions are based on it. In short, Title VII prohibits employment practices based on race, sex, color, religion, or national origin.

The key concept arising from judicial interpretation of Title VII has been that of *job relatedness,* or the ability to demonstrate that challenged employment practices are significantly related to successful job performance.

When demonstrating job relatedness, job analysis data are useful in showing that the job has been systematically studied and that specific selection tests, appraisal instruments, or other personnel decisions are based on the data contained in the job analysis.

Although not as influential as Title VII, a number of other laws have implications for the collection and use of job analysis data. For example, the *Age Discrimination in Employment Act* of 1967 prohibits age-based discrimination in employment practices; in terms of job analysis, this has implications for both test validation (e.g., demonstrating that work activities of older and younger workers are not significantly different) and for performance appraisal (e.g., appraisal systems that have adverse impact with respect to older employees must be job-related).

Similarly, the *Equal Pay Act* of 1963 bars sex-based discrimination in awarding compensation; this is relevant to job analysis in two ways. First, job analysis data are commonly used to develop compensation systems and must be free of sex-based biases in the initial description of job activities. Second, the Equal Pay Act states that jobs involving comparable skill, effort, responsibility, and working conditions should be paid comparably; job analysis data can be used to determine whether this condition is met.

Court Decisions. Most laws do not directly deal with job analysis techniques or specify *how* job analysis data should be collected and used. Instead, the role of job analysis has largely been defined by the courts as they have attempted to interpret the laws. Several Supreme Court decisions have had an influence on job analysis, beginning with *Griggs v. Duke Power Co.* (1971), which established the importance of the concept of job relatedness.

Albemarle Paper Co. v. Moody (1975) was one of the most important of the Supreme Court decisions pertaining to job analysis, as it spelled out in detail the role of job analysis in demonstrating job relatedness. Although not legally binding themselves, the court stated that the test validation guidelines developed by the EEOC (currently manifest as the 1978 *Uniform Guidelines*) are "entitled to great deference" as an interpretation of the goals of Title VII. As was discussed earlier, behavior-based job analysis figures prominently in the *Guidelines*.

Albemarle established job analysis as something that virtually *must* be done to defend challenged employment practices, particularly in the area of validity transportability or generalization. According to *Albemarle*, without a systematic analysis of both the original and target jobs, validity generalization cannot be justified. This principle was recently upheld in *EEOC v. Atlas Paper Box Co.* (1989), in which the U.S. Sixth Circuit Court of Appeals rejected a validity generalization argument involving the use of a general cognitive ability test for clerical jobs. Although Atlas made errors in the use of the ability test, the court repeatedly criticized the lack of a systematic job analysis. For example,

> the expert witness offered by defendant, John Hunter, failed to visit and inspect the Atlas office and never studied the nature and content of the Atlas clerical and office jobs involved. The validity of the generalization theory utilized by Atlas with respect to this expert testimony under these circumstances is not appropriate. Linkage or similarity of jobs in dispute in this case must be shown by such on site investigation to justify application of such a theory.

The courts usually interpret Title VII to mean that an on-site job analysis must be conducted, that it must comprehensively describe the domain of job behaviors, and that it must identify the most important behaviors. For example, in *Jones v. Human Resources Administration* (1975), the job analysis was ruled unacceptable because it "did not cover the full spectrum of tasks performed by those in this position" (Thompson & Thompson, 1982).

Some court decisions have made it clear that job analysis and the development of job specifications are two distinct processes. For example, in *U.S. v. State of New York* (1979), the court rejected a procedure that directly rated KS and AO requirements (in this case, using the job element technique popularized by Primoff, 1975), noting that "a task-oriented analysis was not done" and that the KS/AO-oriented job element technique "does not focus on what [employees] actually do on the job, but only on the underlying traits or characteristics that [employees] believe characterize successful job performance" (Thompson & Thompson, 1982). Although obtaining KS and AO requirements is important, such ratings must be based on a prior systematic analysis of the important job behaviors.

A number of performance appraisal employment discrimination cases have also been decided by the courts. When adverse impact is involved, the courts have rejected performance appraisal systems involving supervisory ratings that are not based on a formal analysis of job behaviors and performance standards (e.g., *Sledge v. J. P. Stevens & Co*, 1978). Although the means by which employers must "validate" appraisal systems are far from clear (e.g., Barrett & Kernan, 1987; Kleiman & Durham, 1981), performance appraisal systems are consistently termed "tests" by the courts and subjected to the validation standards applied to traditional selection procedures.

This principle of holding subjective techniques like supervisory performance appraisals to the same standards as those applied to more formal assessment and testing procedures was recently upheld in the Supreme Court's *Watson v. Fort Worth Bank & Trust* (1988) decision. In Watson, however, the justices differed regarding the employer's burden of proof in demonstrating the job relatedness of the appraisal system; opinions among the justices ranged from requiring the use of traditional empirical test validation strategies on the one hand, to allowing defendants to simply argue that the appraisals have a "manifest relationship to the job in question" (cited in Bersoff, 1988) on the other. In any event, job analysis data will continue to play a pivotal role in documenting the job relatedness of employee performance appraisals, whether or not a separate "validation study" is necessary to document the link between job analysis and performance appraisal.

Professional Standards Documents

The third piece of the regulatory triad consists of professional standards documents developed by various organizations (e.g., APA and SIOP) and regulatory guidelines issued by governmental entities (e.g., the EEOC). Although such documents lack the force of law, the courts have relied heavily on them as indicators of the professional state of the art in validation procedures (e.g., as the justices in the *Albemarle* decision used the APA *Standards*).

The *Uniform Guidelines* (1978).   The courts have relied heavily on the *Guidelines*, which assert the necessity of (a) conducting a job analysis that describes work tasks, regardless of whether content-, construct-, or criterion-oriented validation strategies are used (e.g., section 1607.14.D2) and (b) demonstrating via job analysis that jobs "perform substantially the same major work behaviors" as justification for generalizing test validities (section 1607.7.B2). However, the job classification question of how one demonstrates substantial similarity in work behaviors was not addressed in the *Guidelines*.

The *Guidelines* are fairly specific regarding one other use of job analysis data—the development of criterion measures and performance

appraisal systems. In this regard, the *Guidelines* state that job analysis data should be used to demonstrate that "whatever criteria are used... represent important or critical work behavior(s) or work outcomes" identified in the job analysis (section 1607.14.3).

The approach to collecting and using job analysis data adopted in the *Guidelines* has not been greeted with universal acclaim by industrial and organizational psychologists, at times being subjected to hostile criticism. Some authors (e.g., Guion & Gibson, 1988; Landy, 1986) contend that the *Guidelines* are too rigid regarding their requirement of conducting a detailed job analysis in all settings and in recognizing only three test validation strategies: content-, construct-, and criterion-oriented. Others (e.g., Schmidt et al., 1981) have been even more critical, charging that the behavior-oriented job analysis approach advocated in the *Guidelines* has prevented the field of industrial and organizational psychology from advancing—for example, by precluding the presumption of validity for a new test-job combination in the absence of job analysis data demonstrating behavioral similarity between the new job and the jobs for which validation data exists.

The APA *Standards* (1985).   Various editions of the APA *Standards* have been cited frequently in court decisions involving job analysis, although they are not very specific concerning job analysis procedures or definitions of key terms. For example, the definition of job analysis used in the current edition of the *Standards* fails to recognize the difference between describing job behaviors versus inferring KS- and AO-based job specifications. Similarly, although they discuss the need to identify KSAs, the *Standards* do not define what KSAs are.

The *Standards* are similar in many ways to the *Guidelines*. For example, they identify the same three strategies for demonstrating test validity, and specify that the content-oriented strategy must be restricted to situations in which a "singular and direct" link exists between the test and the job content identified in a job analysis. The *Standards* and *Guidelines* are also consistent in requiring the demonstration that "critical job content factors are substantially the same (as is determined by a job analysis)" (*Standards,* p. 61) prior to generalizing the validity of a test in a new situation.

Regarding construct validity, the *Standards* make it clear that two inferences must be validated: (a) the test measures the ability construct in question and (b) there is evidence that the construct is a causal determinant of "major factors of job performance" (p. 61). The latter process concerns the validation of AO-based job specifications and requires a job analysis (e.g., to identify the job performance factors that must be shown to be related to the tests via criterion-related data). The *Standards* specifically warn that "expert judgment alone should not be used to substantiate a claim of construct-related evidence" (p. 61), agreeing with the *Guidelines* regarding the necessity of job analysis to support a construct validity claim.

The SIOP *Principles* (1987).   The *Principles* represent the most recently revised standards document, the one most directly under the control of industrial and organizational psychologists and the one least similar to the 1978 *Uniform Guidelines*. Despite the stated goal of making the *Principles* "consistent with the *Standards*" (1987, p. 1), many important differences exist.

Perhaps the most dramatic departure taken by the *Principles* concerns the need for a job analysis when past validity results are generalized or transported to new settings. Although the *Guidelines, Standards,* and numerous court decisions have held that some form of on-site systematic job analysis must be performed in each new situation, the *Principles* allow that

a less detailed job analysis may be all that is required... because past research on the job allows the generation of sound hypotheses concerning predictors, and *criteria can be developed with little reference to a specific job analysis* in a particular organization. When a systematic new job analysis is not completed, the researcher should compile *reasonable evidence* which establishes that the jobs in question are similar in terms of work behavior and/or *required knowledge, skills, and abilities.* (1987, p. 5, emphasis added)

This statement raises a number of questions. First, if a traditional job analysis of the new job is not conducted, where will the "reasonable evidence" that the new job is sufficiently similar to the old jobs be obtained? Presumably, the holistic job rating method critiqued earlier in this chapter would be acceptable for this purpose. For example, Pearlman et al. (1980) claimed that to generalize validities to new settings and jobs, "all that would be necessary is *sufficient job analysis information* to insure that the job in question is indeed a member of the occupation or job family on which the validity distribution was based" (p. 376, emphasis added).

In practice, the phrase "sufficient job analysis information" has an unusual translation: Pearlman (1980) indicated that such a "job analysis" involves "broadly characterizing jobs in terms of their *job titles*" (p. 11, emphasis added). Cornelius et al. (1984) made a similar observation, noting that "a simple informed judgment by job experts (incumbents or supervisors) is enough to determine whether a test can be transported from one setting to another" (p. 257). Such a "job analysis" does not meet standard definitions of the term; indeed, the courts have been quite clear in explicitly rejecting cursory techniques of this nature (e.g., *EEOC v. Atlas Paper Box Co.,* 1989; Thompson & Thompson, 1982).

Second, in contrast to the *Guidelines* and *Standards*, which maintain that job *behaviors* must be analyzed when assessing work similarity for validity generalization purposes, the *Principles* allow the substitution of estimated KS/AO requirements. Regarding the selection of a job analysis method, the *Principles* note only that "several job analysis procedures exist, each differing in its possible contribution to the objectives of a validity study" and that "whatever job analysis method is used, it should be used carefully" (p. 5).

Third, it is unclear how much past research is needed to justify the conclusion that "a less detailed job analysis" is adequate. The *Principles* can in effect be interpreted to conclude that job analysis is *optional* if the job analyst deems it unnecessary. Some authors (e.g., Schmidt & Hunter, 1981) have already claimed that sufficient data exist to show that "professionally developed cognitive ability tests are valid predictors of performance on the job and in training *for all jobs... in all settings*" (p. 1128, emphasis added).

With respect to the identification and validation of KS/AO requirements, the *Principles* again depart from the *Guidelines* and numerous court decisions (e.g., *U.S. v. State of New York*, 1979) and allow great flexibility in determining job specifications. With respect to judging KS and AO requirements, they caution only that

> any scales used to evaluate tasks and knowledges, skills, and abilities (KSAs) should have reasonable psychometric characteristics. Lack of consensus among job experts regarding tasks and KSAs should be noted and carefully considered. Current job descriptions or other documents may or may not serve the immediate research purpose. (p. 5)

The *Principles* thus do not *require* an analysis of job behaviors prior to judging estimated KS and AO requirements as do the *Guidelines*;

all that is required is for "the researcher or job experts [to combine] knowledge of the work performed and what workers have to do to perform the work" (p. 6). The choice of an appropriate job analysis method to identify this "knowledge of the work," how "reasonable psychometric properties" or "consensus among job experts" is operationalized, or what one should do after "carefully considering" poor agreement between SMEs is left to the discretion of the practitioner.

In another departure from the *Guidelines*, which require that criterion measures "represent important or critical work behavior(s) or work outcomes" identified in the job analysis (section 1607.14.B.3), the *Principles* appear to make job analysis optional when constructing a criterion measure as well. The *Principles* state only that "the results of a formal job analysis are *helpful* in criterion construction" (p. 9, emphasis added). Similar flexibility is granted in developing employee appraisal forms, as they note that "the development of rating procedures should *ordinarily* be guided by job analyses if, for example, raters are expected to evaluate several different aspects of performance" (p. 10, emphasis added).

With respect to the issue of content validation, the *Principles* agree with previous standards documents and court decisions that require a detailed task-based analysis of job behaviors. Similarly, with respect to construct-oriented strategies, the *Principles* stress that they must be based on "a thorough understanding of the work and of what the worker is expected to accomplish" (p. 26). In particular, they note that "the practice of asking subject matter experts to list the constructs that they believe are required for successful performance does not, without further evidence, provide a basis for a claim of construct validity" (p. 26). However, the form that this further evidence would take is unspecified.

Summary

Although the regulatory climate in which job analysis data are collected and applied is constantly changing, some general principles have remained relatively constant. First, behaviorally specific job analysis is the only effective strategy for identifying and (content) validating KS-based job specifications; demonstrable links to such data are also vital for developing and defending criterion measurement and appraisal systems.

Second, the techniques for identifying and validating AO-based job specifications are qualitatively distinct from those used to validate KS-based requirements. Although many types of job analysis data can be used in the process of (construct) validating inferences of general ability and trait requirements, specifications of ability requirements must be based on something more than just the "professional judgment" of the analyst.

Third, a job analysis is needed to justify validity generalization or transportability decisions, although the specificity of this information is open to debate. To the extent that behaviorally specific predictor tests are used (e.g., work samples), it is likely that more specific job analysis data should be used to assess job similarity.

Uses of Job Analysis Information

Job analysis data form—or at least *should* form—the foundation for nearly all important personnel decisions. This section will examine the link between job analysis data and the uses to which it may be put. On the positive side, a number of the links between job analysis data and specific personnel functions are quite clear and effective, such as developing performance appraisal instruments and predicting compensation rates; conversely, some of these links are highly controversial and in need of significant additional research before clear guidelines can be given to practitioners, such as in using job analysis data to set ability- and trait-based worker specifications for employee selection purposes.

Job Classification

Perhaps the most basic and direct use of job analysis information is to determine what constitutes a *job* or a *job family*. That is, which groupings of positions or jobs are similar enough to be treated interchangeably for a specified personnel purpose? Job classification decisions have become increasingly important as a consequence of recent interest in validity generalization techniques; specifically, to justify the generalizability of previous validation results, one must be able to show that new jobs are sufficiently similar to the ones on which validation data exist. Several distinct steps are involved in arriving at such a determination.

Theoretical Models.   As a first step in making a job classification decision, one must decide which conceptual view of jobs and job families is to be taken. Until recently, this decision was implicit, as only one view of the underlying structure of work was commonly encountered in personnel psychology.

The traditional view of work is based on what numerical taxonomists and factor analysts have termed an *independent-cluster structure* (e.g., see Coombs & Satter, 1949; Harris & Kaiser, 1964; Sokal, 1974). In independent-cluster structures, each of the entities to be grouped is classified into one *and only one* class or grouping (numerical taxonomists refer to these as *taxons*). In the context of job classification, this means that when positions are grouped to form jobs, each position will be assigned to one and only one job title grouping, and there will be no overlap between titles. Similarly, when grouping jobs to form job families, each job will be placed into one and only one job family cluster, and no overlap will exist between job families. A pictoral view of these links is presented in Figure 5.

I have questioned this conceptual view of work (e.g., Harvey, 1982, 1986a); specifically, when grouping jobs, one often encounters patterns of job similarity that simply do not behave according to these simple rules. When grouping jobs to form job families, instead of finding independent-cluster structures, the data often indicate that family membership can best be represented as *overlapping* clusters of jobs. That is, some jobs belong to multiple families. Similarly, when grouping positions to form jobs, positions often are classified into multiple jobs; put another way, there is overlap between the job clusters.

Researchers in the field of numerical taxonomy have long been aware of such phenomena; indeed, some (e.g., Sokal, 1974) have concluded that overlapping-cluster structures frequently provide a more realistic representation of the similarity of objects than the simplistic independent-clusters model. For similar reasons, I contend that the traditional independent-cluster model is usually a fundamental oversimplification of the interrelations between positions, jobs, and job families. For example, in the case of grouping jobs to form families, only in cases in which there is effectively no overlap between jobs in terms of having important job activities in common can independent-cluster job families be produced; such findings are empirically unlikely, especially when worker-oriented items or job dimensions are used to assess job similarity.

Under the overlapping-clusters view of job similarity, jobs will (a) vary with respect to a number of general dimensions of work activity, (b) be similar to one another in requiring some dimensions and dissimilar regarding others, and (c) typically each involve a *number* of general dimensions of work activity. For example, one job family might be characterized by dimensions like external contacts, supervising nonsupervisory employees, and operating stationary machines, including jobs like loading dock supervisor—whereas a second family might be composed of jobs involving external contacts, operating light highway vehicles, hazardous working conditions, supervising nonemployees, and supervising nonsupervisory employees, including such jobs as police sergeant and fire lieutenant. These two families overlap in terms of both having external contacts and supervising nonsupervisory employees, but are nonoverlapping on their other important dimensions.

In essence, this is the conceptual view of work that underlies the *job component validity* technique (e.g., McCormick, DeNisi, & Shaw, 1979). That is, even highly task-heterogeneous jobs can be found similar in terms of sharing one or more general dimensions of work, and dissimilar on other general dimensions of work.

Techniques for Making Job Classification Decisions. A second decision that must be made when grouping jobs is to select a grouping procedure. This involves selecting from among the numerous quantitative techniques for analyzing multivariate data that have been proposed as vehicles for identifying job similarity. Although some authors have claimed that holistic job grouping judgments (e.g., Pearlman, 1980) can be used to make such decisions, I would argue that the limitations of holistic techniques—in particular, the job-relatedness issue and the lack of adequate demonstrations of results-similarity between holistic and empirical job grouping methods—are at present sufficient to remove them from consideration.

With regard to selecting a statistical job grouping technique, the descriptive, dimension-oriented techniques (e.g., Q-factor analysis, three-mode factor analysis) offer significant advantages over both inferential methods (e.g., MANOVA) and hierarchical cluster analysis (HCA; see Harvey, 1986a, for further discussion). The superiority of dimension-oriented techniques is enhanced to the degree that the overlapping-clusters

FIGURE 5

Traditional View of the Link Between Positions, Job, and Job Families

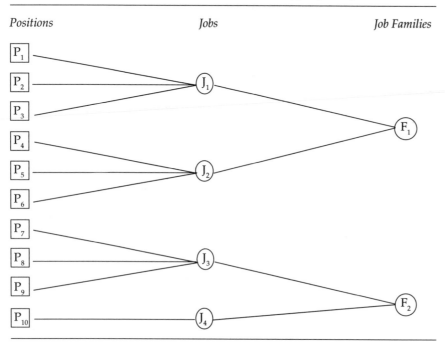

model of job similarity is more appropriate for the data than the independent-clusters model. Regarding the inferential job-grouping methods, limitations include (a) the critical role of statistical power (i.e., with a large enough sample of job descriptors or raters, virtually *any* pair of jobs can be found to be "significantly different" because of the power to detect even trivial differences; with a small enough sample, any set of jobs can be found to be "the same" due to lack of power to detect even large true differences); (b) the lack of effect size guidelines to guide decision making when significance tests are not used; and (c) testing a null hypothesis that few would ever expect to be true (i.e., if measured with sufficient precision, it is unlikely that two jobs would ever demonstrate *exactly equal* job analysis profiles).

Limitations of hierarchical cluster analysis include (a) HCA can *only* produce independent-cluster solutions, regardless of the actual latent structure of the data; (b) the decision rules for identifying the correct number of clusters in HCA have never been definitive and are almost certainly going to be incorrect when the independent-clusters assumption is violated (i.e., if the jobs truly do not form independent clusters, the concept of a "correct" number of independent clusters is meaningless); and (c) numerous algorithms for computing HCA solutions exist, and different computational methods often produce very different cluster solutions (e.g., Milligan, 1981). In short, there is little point in forcing an overly simplistic conceptual model onto a set of job similarity data. Indeed, if independent clusters *are* actually present, dimension-oriented techniques like Q-factor analysis are capable of recovering them; the reverse is not true of hierarchical cluster analysis (i.e., if overlapping clusters are present, it is highly unlikely that HCA could recover them).

The important question to be addressed when grouping positions or jobs is *on which attributes* do they differ and on which attributes are they similar—not are they the "same" or "different." Particularly when grouping jobs from different plants, geographical areas, or industries (e.g., to conduct a consortium-style test validation study), it is inevitable that *some* degree of difference on some job dimensions will be observed. What is needed is research that will determine the amount and kinds of differences that can be tolerated before validities or other personnel decisions are moderated by cross-job behavior differences. Although initial efforts toward this goal have been promising (e.g., Gutenberg, Arvey, Osburn, & Jeanneret, 1983), much additional research remains to be conducted.

Selecting the Job Analysis Data. A third decision that must be made when conducting job classification analyses is to select the appropriate job analysis philosophy when describing the positions or jobs to be grouped. Although only a few studies have varied the type of job analysis data to assess the degree to which job classification structures differ (e.g., Cornelius, Carron, & Collins, 1979; Harvey, 1988), common sense and the available empirical data indicate that the kind of job descriptors chosen will exert a powerful effect on the resulting job groupings. As Harvey (1988) reported, more behaviorally and technologically abstract descriptors (in this case, JEI versus task-oriented data) produced more abstract and overlapping job families. Consistent with the conceptual foundation of the worker-oriented approach, its descriptors are less sensitive to task differences between jobs, and job groupings identified using worker-oriented

data will be based on similarity in terms of more generalized work behaviors.

Even when holding the job analysis philosophy constant, different job similarity statistics—as well as ways of centering and/or standardizing the data matrix—will produce different job classification conclusions (e.g., Hamer & Cunningham, 1981; Harvey, 1985a; Harvey & Wilson, 1985). Some statistics are based solely on dichotomous similarity (e.g., percent tasks in common), some equate individual job profiles for different total rating scores prior to computing similarity (e.g., the CODAP percent-task-overlap statistic), some are sensitive only to similarity in profile shape and eliminate profile elevation differences (e.g., correlations), and others retain information on shape, elevation, and dispersion differences (e.g., profile distance statistics).

Given that different types of job analysis data and different methods for computing similarity statistics will yield different solutions, it is important to match the purpose for grouping jobs with the job analysis philosophy. For applications in which a high degree of technological detail and homogeneity are desired (e.g., training, performance appraisal, job title assignment, developing job descriptions, and other functions that use the *job* as the basic unit of analysis), job grouping analyses should be conducted using more specific, task-oriented job descriptors as input. Conversely, for purposes that desire groupings that are similar in terms of generalized work behaviors (e.g., job component validity, test validation using general ability tests, career path planning), worker-oriented items or job dimension scores would be preferred. The choice of the profile similarity statistic will be most strongly influenced by the degree to which cross-job differences in profile elevation are meaningful: If within-job-relative rating scales are used to rate the job analysis items, statistics sensitive to either binary profile similarity (e.g., percent items in common) or relative profile shape (but not elevation) should be used (e.g., profile correlations). In either case, interpretations of the job groupings must be made in the context of the lack of meaningful elevation information (i.e., jobs that group together may differ significantly in the actual levels of the job behaviors involved, which may or may not be appropriate). If cross-job level comparisons are interpretable (e.g.. Type 2 or 3 job analysis data are used as input), elevation-sensitive statistics may be used instead and will provide a more comprehensive description of job similarity.

Job Descriptions

Another direct use to which job analysis information may be put is the formation of job descriptions. However, what is meant by *job description* is quite variable; for example, the popular *narrative job description* is often only loosely based on a systematic job analysis. Figure 6 presents an example of a narrative job description.

Job descriptions need not be strictly narrative; Figure 7 presents an example of a job description developed from a task-oriented job analysis data base; computerized integrated personnel systems are capable of automatically generating such descriptions from current personnel data and updating the descriptions as job tasks and duties change. The increased job relatedness and specificity of job descriptions of this sort are powerful inducements to prefer this approach over subjectively developed job narratives.

Performance Appraisal

As noted earlier, the courts have for some time required employers to demonstrate the job relatedness of appraisal systems (e.g., *Brito v. Zia*, 1973; *Watson v. Fort Worth Bank & Trust*, 1988). In practical terms, demonstrating the job relatedness of an appraisal system

means showing that a job analysis was performed and identifying the link between the job analysis data and the appraisal procedures.

An assessment of whether two key errors are present should also occur. *Criterion contamination* is said to occur when the appraisal procedure involves the rating of factors that are not demonstrably part of the job (e.g., Cascio, 1987). For example, rating an employee on the dimension "dealing with the public" is only appropriate if the job actually requires the employee to engage in public contact. *Criterion deficiency* occurs when the appraisal system fails to rate aspects of performance that *are* part of the job. Both errors concern the content validity of the appraisal system, the former involving rating of dimensions that are not in the domain of job activities, the latter involving inadequate domain sampling.

Using job analysis information in the performance appraisal process would seem to be a very straightforward issue. However, a number of different strategies for linking job analysis data to the appraisal process exist, and they vary in terms of the strength of this link.

Holistic Methods.   Schmidt et al. (1981) concluded that individual effectiveness on the job must be defined as a single holistic score and that ratings on a number of behaviorally specific performance dimensions are unnecessary and potentially misleading. The basis for this prescription is the claim that:

> correlations between criterion dimensions, after correction for attenuation due to unreliability, typically approach 1.00, indicating that different behavioral dimensions are virtually collinear at the true score level (Schmidt & Hunter, 1978). Under these circumstances, it is obvious that only a measure of overall job performance is needed in validity studies. (Schmidt et al., 1981, p. 175)

FIGURE 6

Narrative Job Description

City Architect I

Nature of Work

This is professional and technical work in the preparation of architectral plans, designs, and specifications for a variety of municipal or public works building projects and facilities.

Minimum Qualifications

Education and Experience—Graduation from an accredited college or university with a specialization in architecture or architectural engineering; or equal.

Knowledge, Abilities, and Skills—Considerable knowledge of the principles and practices of architecture; ability to make structural and related mathematical computations and make recommendations on architectural problems; ability to design moderately difficult architectural projects; ability to interpret local building codes and zoning regulations; ability to secure good working relationships with private contractors and employees; ability to train and supervise the work of technical and other subordinates in a manner conducive to full performance; ability to express ideas clearly and concisely, orally and in writing; skill in the use of architectural instruments and equipment.

Illustration of Duties

Prepares or assists in the preparation of architectural plans and designs all types of building projects constructed by the City, including fire stations, park and recreation buildings, office buildings, warehouses, and similar structures; prepares or supervises the preparation of final working drawings including architectural drawings, such as site plans, foundations, floor plans, elevations, section details, diagrams, and schedules rendering general features and scale details; prepares or supervises some of the engineering calculations, drawings and plans for mechanical details, such as plumbing, air-conditioning phases, and lighting features; writes construction standards and project specifications; prepares sketches including plans, elevations, site plans, and renderings and makes reports on feasibility and cost for proposed City work; writes specifications for all aspects of architectural projects including structural, mechanical, electrical, and air-conditioning work; confers with engineering personnel engaged in the preparation of structural plans for a building, making recommendations and suggestions as to materials, construction, and necessary adjustments in architectural designs to fit structural requirements; inspects construction in the field by checking for conformity with plans and material specifications; inspects existing structures to determine need for alterations or improvements and prepares drawings for such changes; performs related work as required.

Supervision Received

General and specific assignments are received and work is performed according to prescribed methods and procedures with allowance for some independence in judgment in accomplishing the assignments.

Supervision Exercised

Usually limited to supervision of technical assistants in any phase.

FIGURE 7

Task-based Job Description

Job Description Profile Scores for TM Pay Grade E-7

D-Tsk	Task Title	Percent Members Performing	Avg % Time Spent by Members Performing	Avg % Time Spent by All Members	Cum. Sum of Avg % Time Spent by All Members	No. Duties or Tasks
B 1	Write enlisted performance evaluations	80.00	2.46	1.97	1.97	
A 1	Review enlisted performance evaluations	82.86	2.32	1.93	3.90	
C 18	Maintain logs (pass down log [PDL] etc.)	62.86	3.01	1.89	5.79	
B 4	Ensure work assigned to subordinates is completed	82.86	2.27	1.88	7.66	
C 6	Update publications/instructions (pen and ink and page changes)	80.00	2.28	1.82	9.49	5
B 5	Coordinate work within division	68.57	2.56	1.76	11.25	
C 17	Fill out work requests/work orders	62.86	2.42	1.52	12.77	
A 11	Evaluate operational commitments in order to schedule workload	60.00	2.35	1.41	14.18	
A 5	Screen messages, bulletins, etc. for appropriate action	74.28	1.84	1.36	15.54	
A 2	Make personnel assignments	80.00	1.68	1.34	16.88	10
A 3	Assign work priorities	71.43	1.78	1.27	18.15	
C 7	Maintain correspondence/message files	62.86	1.94	1.22	19.38	
A 24	Receipt for weapons	71.43	1.68	1.20	20.58	
B 2	Make work assignments	74.28	1.56	1.16	21.74	
A 25	Ensure readiness of command for inspections (administrative operational, material, etc.)	68.57	1.66	1.14	22.88	15
A 15	Prepare weekly discrepancy report	54.28	2.01	1.09	23.97	
C 25	Prepare reports of unsatisfactory/defective torpedoes, or equipment	65.71	1.64	1.08	25.05	
A 27	Review and submit status reports (performance, inventory, casualty, etc.)	62.86	1.64	1.03	26.08	
F 21	Inspect weapons handling gear (slings, hoist, etc.)	68.57	1.37	0.94	27.02	
C 5	Maintain tickler file	48.57	1.88	0.91	27.93	20
Z 9	Attend meetings, seminars, conferences, etc.	54.28	1.68	0.91	28.84	
A 9	Monitor training program	57.14	1.54	0.88	29.72	
E 12	Inspect all material upon receipt for damage, quality, quantity, etc.	42.86	2.02	0.87	30.58	
Z 4	Stand inspections	60.00	1.42	0.85	31.44	
C 11	Route correspondence/publications/instructions, etc.	51.43	1.65	0.85	32.28	25

Task-based Job Description (continued)

Job Description Profile Scores for TM Pay Grade E-7

D-Tsk	Task Title	Percent Members Performing	Avg % Time Spent by Members Performing	Avg % Time Spent by All Members	Cum. Sum of Avg % Time Spent by All Members	No. Duties or Tasks
A 18	Coordinate weapon overhaul and repair within own command and/or between other ships and stations	51.43	1.64	0.84	33.12	
A 20	Recommend personnel for formal training	65.71	1.26	0.83	33.95	
D 11	Sign off practical factors	71.43	1.14	0.81	34.76	
F 32	Turn in torque wrenches for calibration	51.43	1.55	0.80	35.56	
C 39	Prepare/update 3M schedules (cycle, quarterly, weekly)	54.28	1.42	0.77	36.33	30
C 1	Draft naval messages	48.57	1.58	0.76	37.09	
A 14	Sign requisitions requiring approval	54.28	1.39	0.76	37.85	
C 8	Type correspondence/forms	40.00	1.82	0.73	38.58	
A 10	Represent command at conferences and meetings	45.71	1.56	0.71	39.29	
Z 1	Hold field days, sweepdowns, etc.	42.86	1.60	0.68	39.97	35
C 20	Update recall bill	37.14	1.84	0.68	40.66	
Z 6	Counsel personnel on personal/military matters	54.28	1.25	0.68	41.34	
D 2	Update individual training records	45.71	1.48	0.68	42.01	
D 1	Prepare individual training records	45.71	1.48	0.68	42.69	
C 35	Maintain torpedo record book	51.43	1.32	0.68	43.36	40
A 7	Coordinate with military activities as required	48.57	1.37	0.66	44.03	
F 62	Destroy classified materials in accordance with current instructions	51.43	1.29	0.66	44.69	
C 15	Draft instructions/notices	45.71	1.45	0.66	45.35	
D 3	Schedule training lectures	54.28	1.22	0.66	46.01	
C 24	Maintain log/file of report of unsatisfactory/defective torpedoes or equipment	57.14	1.14	0.65	46.66	45
C 16	Review/chop outgoing correspondence/messages	34.28	1.89	0.64	47.31	
A 22	Maintain liaison with personnel of other departments to prevent or correct interface problems	45.71	1.41	0.64	47.95	
B 7	Complete weapons firing reports	45.71	1.40	0.64	48.58	
C 13	Maintain status boards	57.14	1.10	0.63	49.21	
Z 5	Attend general drills	48.57	1.28	0.62	49.83	50
A 19	Determine expendable materials (surveys, disposal, etc.)	51.43	1.19	0.61	50.44	
A 16	Evaluate and take appropriate action on reports from torpedo readiness acceptance (TRAT) inspection	51.43	1.16	0.60	51.04	
F 53	Perform weapons receipt inspection	54.28	1.09	0.59	51.63	
A 4	Write billet/job descriptions	45.71	1.28	0.58	52.22	
E 17	Pack/unpack weapons/components	48.57	1.20	0.58	52.80	55

FIGURE 7

Task-based Job Description (continued)

Job Description Profile Scores for TM Pay Grade E-7

D-Tsk	Task Title	Percent Members Performing	Avg % Time Spent by Members Performing	Avg % Time Spent by All Members	Cum. Sum of Avg % Time Spent by All Members	No. Duties or Tasks
J 41	Perform quality assurance checks on weapons	17.14	3.37	0.58	53.37	
C 19	Maintain leave schedules	45.71	1.23	0.56	53.94	
C 29	Make entries in daily work log	40.00	1.40	0.56	54.50	
F 61	Participate in weapons firefighting procedures	45.71	1.22	0.56	55.06	
C 14	Distribute safety material (publications, posters, etc).	51.43	1.06	0.55	55.60	60
E 1	Order parts, tools, supplies, etc.	57.14	0.95	0.54	56.14	
C 12	Maintain division officer's notebook	31.43	1.67	0.52	56.67	
A 23	Organize departmental/division security	42.86	1.20	0.52	57.18	
F 1	Test weapons security alarm systems	51.43	1.00	0.51	57.70	
C 2	Draft naval letters	34.28	1.46	0.50	58.20	65
F 44	Remove/install weapons/components in shipping containers	42.86	1.16	0.49	58.69	
D 22	Develop on-the-job training (OJT) program	45.71	1.07	0.49	59.18	
Z 8	Conduct inspections (zone,personnel, safety, etc.)	48.57	1.01	0.49	59.66	
F 8	Chip, preserve, and paint topside areas	11.43	0.76	0.08	95.28	
F 24	Operate forklift	5.71	1.50	0.08	95.37	
H 17	Install battery power supplies	14.28	0.60	0.08	95.45	
F 7	Handle and fire pyrotechnic devices	17.14	0.50	0.08	95.53	
D 20	Prepare and administer feedback reports for the purpose of updating training	11.43	0.71	0.08	95.61	230
C 26	Prepare corrective action request (NAVORD form 4855/18)	11.43	0.70	0.08	95.69	
F 25	Maintain/use hydraulic RAM	11.43	0.70	0.08	95.77	
G 22	Electrically zero synchros/servos	8.57	0.98	0.08	95.85	
G 10	Remove/replace components on printed circuit boards	8.57	0.96	0.08	95.93	
G 9	Repair cables (splices, etc.)	8.57	0.94	0.08	96.01	235
F 14	Perform emergency de-fueling procedures on weapons	11.43	0.67	0.08	96.09	
J 30	Overhaul and repair pneumatic actuated valves	5.71	1.38	0.08	96.17	
C 32	Prepare work request customer service form (OPNAV form 4790/36A)	8.57	0.88	0.07	96.24	
D 10	Prepare test/examinations	11.43	0.64	0.07	96.31	
D 16	Construct training aids	11.43	0.64	0.07	96.38	240

FIGURE 7

Task-based Job Description (continued)

Job Description Profile Scores for TM Pay Grade E-7

D-Tsk		Task Title	Percent Members Performing	Avg % Time Spent by Members Performing	Avg % Time Spent by All Members	Cum. Sum of Avg % Time Spent by All Members	No. Duties or Tasks
F	5	Maintain small arms(clean, lubricate, etc.)	14.28	0.51	0.07	96.45	
J	18	Test weapons homing control logic unit	5.71	1.25	0.07	96.52	
J	23	Test weapons velocity switches	11.43	0.62	0.07	96.66	
H	33	Maintain torpedo tube electrical system	11.43	0.61	0.07	96.73	245
F	33	Calibrate torque wrenches	14.28	0.50	0.07	96.79	
J	57	Test missile igniter	8.57	0.78	0.06	96.86	
C	37	Review/update casualty reports (CASREPTS)	8.57	0.78	0.06	96.92	
F	42	Operate forward/aft capstan	11.43	0.57	0.06	96.99	
J	10	Service weapons hydraulic systems	5.71	1.16	0.06	97.05	250
J	43	Fuel/defuel weapons	14.28	0.46	0.06	97.11	
D	21	Prepare programmed instructions	8.57	0.74	0.06	97.17	
F	48	Inspect/test-operate magazine de-watering systems	8.57	0.70	0.06	97.23	
H	11	Perform final preparation of complete torpedo (MK-16)	17.14	0.35	0.06	97.29	
D	25	Train instructors in OJT methods	8.57	0.66	0.06	97.35	255
J	31	Overhaul and repair mechanical depth mechanisms	2.86	2.00	0.06	97.41	
J	17	Remove/replace weapons propulsion battery	8.57	0.70	0.06	97.46	
J	14	Overhaul and repair weapon turbine propulsion unit	2.86	2.00	0.06	97.52	
F	79	Install safety wire	8.57	0.69	0.06	97.58	
J	33	Overhaul and repair mechanical steering units	2.86	2.00	0.06	97.63	260
J	20	Repair weapons gyros	2.86	2.00	0.06	97.69	
H	19	Remove/replace thrust reversal nozzle plug	11.43	0.50	0.06	97.74	
H	13	Perform abort procedures on weapons	14.28	0.42	0.06	97.80	
F	78	Neutralize electrolyte spillage (acid, alkaline)	8.57	0.65	0.05	97.85	
Z	14	Stand special sea detail watches (helmsman, after steering, line handler, etc.)	8.57	0.62	0.05	97.90	265
F	65	Clean/repair liquid stowage tanks	5.71	0.88	0.05	97.95	
J	49	Install electrolyte in weapons batteries	8.57	0.60	0.05	98.00	
J	9	Perform torpedo receiver sensitive test	5.71	0.86	0.05	98.05	

From *Methods to Evaluate Scales and Sample Size for Stable Task Inventory Information* by J. Pass and D. Robertson, 1980, San Diego, CA: Navy Personnel Research and Development Center (NPRDC TR No. 80–28). Reprinted by permission.

There is reason to be skeptical of the generality of this conclusion. In a test of the Schmidt-Hunter unidimensionality hypothesis, Butler and Harvey (1986) examined the corrected and raw correlations between the dimensions contained in a behaviorally specific appraisal system developed for police patrol officers. Although the dimensions were correlated to some degree, there was no evidence of the high levels of redundancy claimed by Schmidt et al. (1981).

It seems reasonable to predict that rating dimension correlations will be lower to the extent that the appraisal dimensions—and the rating points on each dimension—are defined in terms of observable job behaviors (e.g., see Feldman, 1981); conversely, high correlations may result when vague traits are rated. Thus, when a traditionally specific job analysis is conducted and behaviorally explicit dimensions are developed, the problem of excessive correlation cited by Schmidt et al. (1981) as justification for using a single global effectiveness rating should not occur. Unfortunately, few research studies conducted in realistic settings have addressed this question.

Trait-oriented Methods.   The most salient characteristic of the trait approach is that a number of worker traits judged necessary for successful job performance are listed, and the amount of each trait possessed by the worker is judged. Worker performance is deemed more effective to the degree that employees possess higher levels of the traits. Figure 8 presents an instrument based on this approach.

The main problems with trait-oriented appraisal instruments concern criterion contamination and deficiency. Basically, in the absence of a job analysis that defines the domain of important job behaviors, it is impossible to demonstrate that a trait-oriented instrument spans the domain of job performance fully and does not include extraneous dimensions. Even if a job analysis has been performed, the process by which the developer accomplishes the

inferential leap from job analysis to a set of trait listings must be fully documented; depending on the traits chosen, this may not be a trivial task.

Task-oriented Methods.   Task-oriented approaches to performance appraisal differ from the trait-based methods primarily in terms of the way in which performance dimensions are identified. In trait systems, job descriptive data are used to infer the general traits that characterize successful job performance in much the same way as job specifications are developed for selection purposes. Task-based systems employ a much more direct link to the job analysis data (e.g., Harvey, 1986b; Thompson & Thompson, 1985).

Once the task-based job analysis is completed and duty categories have been indentified, a task-based appraisal instrument can be constructed by using the duties as the appraisal dimensions and using the tasks performed under each duty to define the dimension. For administrative purposes, only duty ratings need be collected; for purposes of employee development, the job tasks themselves may also be rated and these ratings summarized for each dimension. A portion of a task-based developmental appraisal form for the job of computer programmer is presented in Figure 9. Advantages of this approach to using job analysis data for performance appraisal center on the ease of demonstrating the job relatedness of the rating forms as well as being able to justify dimension ratings in terms of actual job behaviors.

Critical Incident Methods.   There are three primary means by which critical incident data may be used in the appraisal process: (a) behaviorally anchored rating scales (BARS; e.g., Smith & Kendall, 1963) and their derivatives, (b) weighted behavior checklists, and (c) a hybrid "task-BARS" approach involving the use of critical incidents to define performance

FIGURE 8

Trait-based Appraisal Instrument

Worker Requirements Study Ratings Sheet

Circle Appropriate Number

1. Quality of Work (accuracy, neatness, thoroughness)

Inferior Work	Rather Careless	Meets Requirements	Highly Accurate	Exceptional

0 1 2 3 4 5 6 7 8 9 10 11 12 13 14 15

2. Quantity of Work (volume, amount, speed)

Very Slow	Insufficient Work	Moderate	Rapid Worker	Highly Productive

0 1 2 3 4 5 6 7 8 9 10 11 12 13 14 15

3. Knowledge of Work

Almost None	Limited	Adequate	Good Understanding	Excellent Comprehension

0 1 2 3 4 5 6 7 8 9 10

4. Adaptability (adjustment to change, ability to learn)

Unable To Adapt	Slow in Learning	Satisfactory	Adapts Readily	Rapid Learner

0 1 2 3 4 5 6 7 8 9 10

5. Dependability (reliability)

Needs Constant Supervision	Needs Frequent Checking	Usually Dependable	Seldom Needs Checking	Highly Reliable

0 1 2 3 4 5 6 7 8 9 10

6. Cooperation (working with other employees)

Troublemaker	Has Difficulty	Generally Cooperative	Gets Along Well	Excellent Relations

0 1 2 3 4 5 6 7 8 9 10

From *Establishing Valid and Fair Worker Requirements: Claims Examiner I* (Project Report, p. 39) by R. Klimoski and S. Gravenkemper, 1982, Columbus, OH: Bureau of Disability Determination.

standards in a task-oriented appraisal instrument (e.g., as was used by Butler & Harvey, 1986). In the BARS approach, a pool of critical incidents is generated, the mean effectiveness rating of each incident is determined, incidents are grouped by SMEs into clusters to form the appraisal dimensions, and a subset of the scaled incidents is used to define the various levels of performance for each dimension. Figure 2 presents a typical BARS dimension rating scale.

The *BARS approach* is useful in that the appraisal dimensions are described in explicit behavioral terms. Unfortunately, it has several drawbacks. First, gaps may exist in the rating scales for each dimension (i.e., there are usually areas in which no critical incidents have scale values); thus, raters must interpolate between incidents. Second, there is often considerable task heterogeneity within BARS dimensions regarding critical incident content; that is, for a single dimension, the critical incidents used as anchors may describe the performance of very different job tasks (e.g., in Figure 2, the most effective incident deals with providing training to new employees, an intermediate incident deals with criticizing store standards, and the least effective incident deals with lying to employees about salary policies). It is entirely possible that a single employee could demonstrate *all* of these behaviors during the rating period, as they exemplify good and bad ways of performing what are basically *different tasks;* which incident should be chosen as the most representative? Conversely, what if the employee has performed *none* of the incidents defining the dimension?

Third, questions about the job relatedness of BARS can be raised, due to the fact that the BARS method *discards* critical incidents at nearly every step of the development process—for example, if SMEs can't agree on the effectiveness rating, if SMEs can't agree on the performance dimension measured by the incident, or if several incidents with the same scale value exist for a given dimension. Systematically ignoring parts of the job analysis is the operational definition of criterion deficiency.

The second critical incident method— *weighted checklists*—avoids these problems by presenting raters with the entire list of critical incidents generated from the job analysis. By weighting each checked behavioral incident by its scale value, numerical dimension ratings can be obtained. However, the degree to which the pool of critical incidents spans the domain of job tasks can be questioned for both the incident checklist and BARS approaches; that is, if the job analysis conducted in the course of appraisal instrument development consists solely of the generation of critical incidents, it is possible that job tasks exist for which there are no corresponding critical incidents. Again, potentially serious criterion deficiency could exist.

The third approach—what I have termed the *task-BARS technique*—is a hybrid combining features of both the task-based and BARS techniques, using critical incidents as rating anchors in the general context of a task-based appraisal format. In short, instead of using a Likert-type rating scale to rate employee effectiveness on the tasks or dimensions (e.g., with anchors like *Far below expectations, Below expectations, At the expected level, Above expectations, Far above expectations*), appraisal dimension anchors are composed of critical incidents representing *all possible levels* of dimension/task performance. Thus, critical incidents serve as the behavioral anchors for task-identified rating dimensions. Because the task-based rating dimensions are generated first, and critical incidents are formed to define each of the various possible levels of task effectiveness, the problems with gaps in the rating scales and task heterogeneity within dimensions seen in traditional BARS scales can be reduced. A sample dimension from the instrument used by Butler and Harvey (1986) is presented in Figure 10.

FIGURE 9

Task-based Performance Appraisal Dimension

Duty Category	Does Not Apply	Performance on This Task	
		Needs Improvement	*Is Acceptable*
Writing, Completing Reports			
Complete standard forms for city, state, federal authorities	_____	_____	_____
Draft written evaluations of subordinate's performance	_____	_____	_____
Complete monthly activity report	_____	_____	_____
Write letters, memos	_____	_____	_____
Write specifications, plans	_____	_____	_____
Complete request form for checks	_____	_____	_____
Complete suspect booking, custody, control forms, contact, and fingerprint cards	_____	_____	_____
Prepare service requests, job orders	_____	_____	_____
Make written record of information supplied to police officers	_____	_____	_____
File charges with appropriate agency	_____	_____	_____
Prepare monthly, quarterly, annual reports	_____	_____	_____
Prepare purchase requisitions	_____	_____	_____
Prepare service requests for vehicle repairs	_____	_____	_____
Complete offense reports	_____	_____	_____
Complete accident reports	_____	_____	_____
Complete vehicle maintenance checklists	_____	_____	_____
Prepare reports for supervisor	_____	_____	_____
Recordkeeping			
Process requests for vehicle repair	_____	_____	_____
Maintain records of maintenance needs on equipment	_____	_____	_____
Record mileage and amount of gas used	_____	_____	_____
Maintain records of attendance, time off, sick, vacation leaves	_____	_____	_____
Input data into computer	_____	_____	_____
Record arrest information	_____	_____	_____
Record statements of witnesses, suspects, victims	_____	_____	_____
Record arrival of units at scene	_____	_____	_____
Receive and record alarms	_____	_____	_____
Log types and kinds of evidence	_____	_____	_____
Record types of injuries suffered by victims	_____	_____	_____
Note sighted water leaks	_____	_____	_____
Keep notes on employee performance for evaluation purposes	_____	_____	_____
Record daily activities	_____	_____	_____
Record work, hours on time sheet	_____	_____	_____
Maintain daily contact sheet	_____	_____	_____
Complete vehicle check list	_____	_____	_____
Process unpaid violations	_____	_____	_____
Maintain records of vehicle maintenance needs	_____	_____	_____
Videotape bookings	_____	_____	_____
Record sworn affidavits	_____	_____	_____

FIGURE 10

Task-BARS Rating Dimension

Patrol Officer

Preparing for Duty

 (1) Late for roll call majority of period, does not check equipment or vehicle, does not have necessary equipment to go to work.

 (2) Late for roll call, does not check equipment or vehicle for damage or needed repairs, unable to go to work from roll call, has to go to locker, vehicle, or home to get necessary equipment.

 (3) Not fully dressed for roll call, does not have all necessary equipment.

 (4) On time, has all necessary equipment to go to work, fully dressed.

 (5) Early for work, has all necessary equipment to go to work, fully dressed.

 (6) Always early for work, gathers all necessary equipment to go to work, fully dressed, checks activity from previous shifts before going to roll call.

 (7) Always early for work, gathers all necessary equipment to go to work, fully dressed, uses time before roll call to review previous shift's activities and any new bulletins, takes notes of previous shift's activity mentioned during roll call.

In summary, performance appraisal and criterion construction methods vary considerably in terms of the ease with which they may be demonstrated to be job related. For both legal defensibility and sound personnel management reasons, techniques that are based on specific, observable job behaviors (i.e., the task and critical incident methods) should be easier to use and defend than methods having only a weak or indirect link to a job analysis (e.g., trait-based and holistic methods).

Employee Selection

Identifying KS and AO Requirements. In traditional approaches to test validation, employers are faced with the need to make two separate kinds of inferences when linking job analysis data to the employee selection process. First, the behavioral descriptions of job activities obtained from the job analysis must be converted to a listing of required KS and AO requirements; this is the process of developing job specifications examined earlier. Second, the KS/AO specifications must be tied to the practical processes by which job candidates are assessed with respect to their levels of the necessary KS and AO constructs (i.e., a test development or employee assessment question). Figure 11 diagrams these processes.

Identifying Required KSs and AOs. When developing KS/AO specifications, the courts and most professional standards documents require a detailed analysis of important job activities, regardless of whether a content- or construct-oriented strategy is followed. When task-oriented data are used, the first problem is to identify a job's *critical* or *important* tasks.

FIGURE 11

**Inferential Steps in Using Job Analysis Data
to Develop Employee Selection Techniques**

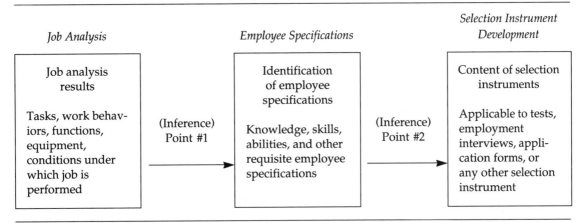

From *Human Resource Selection* (p. 192) by R. Gatewood and H. Feild, 1989, Orlando, FL: Harcourt, Brace, Jovanovich. Copyright 1989 by Harcourt, Brace, Jovanovich. Reprinted by permission.

Combining task-oriented data with critical incidents information can also be useful in identifying critical tasks (e.g., *Davis v. Washington*, 1972). Once critical job behaviors have been identified, SMEs can be used to identify the KSs and AOs required to perform the critical tasks—ideally, with as much direct reference to specific job tasks as possible, especially for the KS items—and assess their relative importance as determinants of job success (e.g., see *Contreras v. City of Los Angeles*, 1981; *Guardians Association of NYC Police Dept. v. Civil Service Commission of New York*, 1980).

If a worker-oriented job analysis has been conducted, one may instead rely on empirical links between worker-oriented scores and KS/AO requirements identified previously to predict KS/AO requirements for the job at hand (e.g., using the job component validity approach developed by McCormick, DeNisi, & Shaw, 1979; McCormick et al., 1972). Once sufficient empirical data exist to link the dimensions of work behavior (identified via worker-oriented instruments) with the

dimensions of human knowledge, ability, and skill (identified via standardized ability and achievement tests, as appropriate), the empirical-linking approach will undoubtedly be preferred over the potentially highly subjective processes involved in using SMEs to infer job specifications (e.g., see Dunnette & Borman, 1979, pp. 484–485).

With respect to the use of SMEs to identify KS and AO requirements, considerable variability in the strategies used to link job analysis data to KS/AO inferences exists. For example, *threshold traits analysis* (TTA; Lopez, Kesselman, & Lopez, 1981) uses job supervisors to directly rate the skills, job knowledge, specific abilities, abstract abilities, and personality traits they feel are required to perform the job. A listing of the traits rated in TTA is presented in Figure 12.

To support the claim that TTA ratings of KS and AO constructs are job-related, Lopez et al. noted that in one study they conducted, the median interrater reliability computed across the 33 traits was .86 (however, it is not clear

FIGURE 12

KS and AO Traits Rated in Threshold Traits Analysis

	Area	Job Functions	Trait	Description—**Can:**
Threshold Traits Analysis	*Physical*	Physical exertion ⟶	1. Strength	Lift, pull, or push physical objects
			2. Stamina	Expend physical energy for long periods
		Bodily activity ⟶	3. Agility	React quickly: has dexterity, coordination
		Sensory inputs ⟶	4. Vision	See details and color of objects
			5. Hearing	Recognize sound, tone, and pitch
	Mental	Vigilance and attention ⟶	6. Perception	Observe and differentiate details
			7. Concentration	Attend to details amid distractions
			8. Memory	Retain and recall ideas
		Information processing ⟶	9. Comprehension	Understand spoken and written ideas
			10. Problem-solving	Reason and analyze abstract information
			11. Creativity	Produce new ideas and products
	Learned	Quantitative computation ⟶	12. Numerical computation	Solve arithmetic and numerical problems
		Communications ⟶	13. Oral expression	Speak clearly and effectively
			14. Written expression	Write clearly and effectively
		Action selection and projection ⟶	15. Planning	Project a course of action
			16. Decision-making	Choose a course of action
		Application of information and skill ⟶	17. Craft knowledge	Apply specialized information
			18. Craft Skill	Perform a complex set of activities
	Motivational	Unprogrammed ⟶	19. Adaptability—change	Adjust to interruptions and changes
		Cycled ⟶	20. Adaptability—repetition	Adjust to repetitive activities
		Stressful — Working ⟶	21. Adaptability—pressure	Adjust to critical and demanding work
		Secluded — Conditions ⟶	22. Adaptability—isolation	Work alone or with little personal contact
		Unpleasant ⟶	23. Adaptability—discomfort	Work in hot, cold, noisy work places
		Dangerous ⟶	24. Adaptability—hazards	Work in dangerous situations
		Absence of direct supervision ⟶	25. Control—dependability	Work with minimum of supervision
		Presence of difficulties ⟶	26. Control—perseverance	Stick to a task until completed
		Unstructured conditions ⟶	27. Control—initiative	Act on own, take charge when needed
		Access to valuables ⟶	28. Control—integrity	Observe regular ethical and moral codes
		Limited mobility ⟶	29. Control—aspirations	Limit desire for promotion
	Social	Interpersonal contact ⟶	30. Personal appearance	Meet appropriate standards of dress
			31. Tolerance	Deal with people in tense situations
			32. Influence	Get people to cooperate
			33. Cooperation	Work as a member of the team

From "An Empirical Test of a Trait-oriented Job Analysis Technique" by F. Lopez, G. Kesselman, and F. Lopez, 1981, *Personnel Psychology, 34*, p. 484. Copyright 1981 by *Personnel Psychology*, Inc. Reprinted by permission.

whether these values were computed before or after raters were allowed to discuss and resolve differences in their trait ratings). Lopez et al. (1981) acknowledged that "some traits may be more reliably assessed than others" (p. 486); however, they did not report reliabilities for individual traits, and the seriousness of this problem for the TTA rating method has yet to be determined.

Other approaches to inferring KS and AO requirements do not rely at all on a prior analysis of job tasks or behaviors. For example, the adjective checklist approach method advocated by Arneson and Peterson (1986) requires job incumbents to simply "identify the kind of personal characteristics that make for an excellent worker" (p. 3). This is accomplished by checking personal trait adjectives (see Figure 13) that the incumbent feels are required; these ratings are then converted to personality trait specifications (i.e., intellectence, adjustment, prudence, ambition, sociability, and likability).

At a minimum, methods that directly rate KS and AO requirements must be able to demonstrate substantial agreement across raters regarding the traits deemed necessary. Unfortunately, the data reported by Arneson and Peterson indicated less-than-perfect agreement among their raters. One-hundred percent agreement on ratings of the trait-based adjectives (i.e., required vs. not required) was obtained on only 25 of the 80 items; using a less stringent 90 percent criterion of interrater agreement, only 59 of the 80 adjectives were agreed upon.

Even methods for identifying KS/AO specifications that *are* based on a rigorous job analysis may fail to produce acceptable interrater agreement. For example, Hughes and Prien (1989) first performed a detailed task analysis, which was followed by rating the KS/AO items listed in Table 5.

Although Hughes and Prien explicitly attempted to link the job analysis data to KS/AO ratings, their results indicated a distressing lack of agreement among judges. As the interrater agreement statistics reported in Table 5 indicate, there was considerable variability in trait ratings, and the overall level of agreement was quite low. Similarly disconcerting results were found when interrater agreement correlations were examined: Regarding the Importance ratings, the mean interrater r was only .31 ($S = .12$), and rs ranged from a low of $-.03$ to a high of only .50. Interater reliability judgments regarding the "difficulty to acquire" each KS/AO construct were even lower: The mean r was only .16 ($S = .34$), and values ranged from a low of $-.40$ to a high of .64. When one considers that these interrater agreement correlations are only sensitive to the *shape* of the profile of KS/AO requirement ratings, and *not* sensitive to differences across raters in terms of the *level* or *amount* of each trait needed (including that source of variance would likely further reduce the magnitude of interrater agreement), one can easily agree with Hughes and Prien that "the problem indicated by the interrater correlations is quite serious" (p. 287).

Ironically, Hughes and Prien (1989) scrupulously followed the prescriptions outlined in the *Guidelines:* (a) Raters were given a detailed job analysis (343 task statements); (b) job-knowledgeable raters were used as SMEs; and (c) a systematic step-by-step process of linking KS/AO employee specifications to the job analysis was attempted. If SMEs demonstrate massive interrater disagreement under these very favorable conditions, what can be expected when on-site job analysis data are not collected, or when raters judge even more abstract traits (e.g., personality or biodata items)?

Even if KS/AO rating methods that produce higher levels of interrater agreement can be developed, the truly important question—whether the inference that the trait is required for successful job performance is *valid*—cannot be addressed by interrater agreement statistics. In addition, such methods appear to implicitly assume that there is a *single* profile of

FIGURE 13

Adjective Checklist Approach to Rating AO Constructs

Hogan Descriptive Adjective Inventory

Directions: Think of the kinds of personal qualities that make for an excellent worker in this position. Listed below are a number of adjectives. Read each one and decide whether or not it describes this ideal worker.

		Yes	No				Yes	No
1.	Simple	❏	❏		28.	Assertive	❏	❏
2.	Calm	❏	❏		29.	Charming	❏	❏
3.	Careless	❏	❏		30.	Impatient	❏	❏
4.	Ambitious	❏	❏		31.	Good with numbers	❏	❏
5.	Talkative	❏	❏		32.	Pessimistic	❏	❏
6.	Irritable	❏	❏		33.	Inconsistent	❏	❏
7.	Well-educated	❏	❏		34.	Complacent	❏	❏
8.	Self-doubting	❏	❏		35.	Likes to be alone	❏	❏
9.	Responsible	❏	❏		36.	Friendly	❏	❏
10.	Unassertive	❏	❏		37.	Reads a lot	❏	❏
11.	Introverted	❏	❏		38.	Happy	❏	❏
12.	Tactful	❏	❏		39.	Dependable	❏	❏
13.	Slow learner	❏	❏		40.	Hard working	❏	❏
14.	Cheerful	❏	❏		41.	Show-off	❏	❏
15.	Unconventional	❏	❏		42.	Cold	❏	❏
16.	Forceful	❏	❏		43.	Complex	❏	❏
17.	Sociable	❏	❏		44.	Anxious	❏	❏
18.	Hot-tempered	❏	❏		45.	Careful	❏	❏
19.	Many interests	❏	❏		46.	Lazy	❏	❏
20.	Tense	❏	❏		47.	Quiet	❏	❏
21.	Team player	❏	❏		48.	Good natured	❏	❏
22.	Noncompetitive	❏	❏		49.	Poorly educated	❏	❏
23.	Reserved	❏	❏		50.	Confident	❏	❏
24.	Diplomatic	❏	❏		51.	Unreliable	❏	❏
25.	Poor memory	❏	❏		52.	Leaderlike	❏	❏
26.	Depressed	❏	❏		53.	Extraverted	❏	❏
27.	Impulsive	❏	❏		54.	Blunt	❏	❏

TABLE 5

KS/AO Constructs and Reliabilities

Cohen's Kappa Values for Task to Job Skill Linkage Analysis

	Job Skill	Kappa	Significance
2.	Ability to listen	.2337	.0084
3.	Ability to read	.1988	.1074
8.	Mechanical comprehension	.4077	.0000
12.	Agility	.3122	.0026
13.	Leg strength	.4145	.0003
14.	Arm strength	.4498	.0000
15.	Upper body strength	.4609	.0000
16.	Ability to think logically	.1774	.0359
19.	Ability to visualize spatially	.3236	.0271
21.	Ability to remember	.0171	.8013
22.	Ability to follow oral orders	.0208	.7544
27.	Color vision	.0203	.8442
30.	Lower body stregth	.4615	.0000
31.	Total body stregth	.4720	.0000
40.	Ability to balance	.3407	.0158
42.	Arithmetic ability	.3759	.0750
43.	Ability to read gauges	.3887	.0171
44.	Hand dexterity	.1900	.0882
45.	Eye/hand coordination	.2080	.0569
48.	Ability to bend	.3580	.0001
49.	Ability to work in confined spaces	.2411	.1172
53.	Sense of direction	.3104	.0587
54.	Observation skill	.1403	.1252
57.	Knowledge of physics	.3679	.0195
58.	Endurance	.3649	.0012
60.	Ability to reach compartments	.4536	.0013
63.	Ability to apply facts	.0145	.8306
71.	Deduction	.2111	.0177
78.	Reaction time	.3836	.0044
79.	Ability to analyze information	.3337	.0066
81.	Ability to make decisions	.2737	.0026
85.	Knowledge of chemistry	.4461	.0143
86.	Hand strength	.2577	.0004
P11.	Claustrophobia	.4098	.1529

From "Evaluation of Task and Job Skill Linkage Judgments Used to Develop Test Specifications" by G. Hughes and E. Prien, 1989, *Personnel Psychology, 42,* p. 289. Copyright 1989 by *Personnel Psychology,* Inc. Reprinted by permission.

KS and AO traits that will be required to achieve successful criterion performance; the possibility that a compensatory model in which low levels of some traits can be offset by high levels on other traits does not appear to be considered.

Assessing KSs and AOs in Individuals.   The second aspect of using job analysis data in the course of dealing with KS/AO requirements involves assessing the degree to which individual job candidates or employees possess the constructs (i.e., an individual assessment issue), and/or developing assessment methods to quantify applicant standing on the constructs of interest (e.g., assessment centers or work samples). The role of job analysis data in this process depends on whether KS versus AO characteristics are assessed; in the case of KSs, job analysis data can be directly used when developing assessment techniques to measure these characteristics, such as in specifying the behaviors to be sampled in work samples, performance tests, or job knowledge tests. In the case of AO requirements (e.g., honesty, leadership, dominance, intelligence, and need for achievement), job behaviors are typically not directly used in the assessment process and standardized tests or assessment exercises usually do not employ job-specific content.

Identifying Job Similarity for Validation Purposes.   Court decisions and the *Uniform Guidelines* indicate that a behavior-based job analysis should be used when assessing job similarity for consortium-validation and validity generalization purposes (i.e., demonstrating that the jobs in question perform essentially the same profile of activities under similar conditions). An alternative method to solve the problem of validating tests in small organizations was advocated by Guion (1965) and consists of grouping jobs based on their similarity with respect to *individual dimensions* of work instead of the full profile of job activities.

This *synthetic validity* strategy consists of (a) collecting job analysis data on several different jobs, (b) identifying work dimensions that are to some degree common across the jobs, and (c) validating tests for groups of jobs that share individual work dimensions—previous validation data may be used, or the organization can collect its own. In terms of the kind of job analysis data that should be used, the method must be able to identify common dimensions of work behavior; although a task-based analysis to identify common duty areas can be conducted, standard worker-oriented instruments offer an efficient means of identifying common worker-oriented items or job dimensions.

Compensation

Although there is no lack of litigation regarding the area of employee compensation (particularly based on the Equal Pay Act), in comparison to employee selection there are more degrees of freedom in using job analysis data to make compensation administration decisions. These uses take two main forms: (a) determining whether the Equal Pay Act criteria of equal skill, effort, responsibility, and working conditions are present when comparing jobs (i.e., a job classification question) and (b) using job analysis data to predict compensation rates.

Measuring Skill, Effort, Responsibility, and Working Conditions.   In interpreting the Equal Pay Act, the courts are called on to decide whether jobs that currently receive differential pay require equivalent skill, effort, responsibility, and are performed under similar working conditions. If so, a violation of the act exists. Typically, the jobs in question differ in terms of their relative proportion of male and female incumbents.

Job analysis data have been called on to facilitate the determination of whether jobs require equal skill, effort, responsibility, and working conditions (e.g., see Henderson, 1979).

Unfortunately, the question of measuring abstract constructs like effort and responsibility has parallels to the problems faced in determining KS/AO requirements. That is, considerable abstraction is required to make the inferential leap from job behaviors to a listing of skill, effort, and responsibility requirements. As was the case for identifying KS and AO requirements, a popular solution is to have SMEs directly judge these traits; alternatively, the kinds of job dimensions measured by worker-oriented job analysis questionnaires can be categorized into skill, effort, responsibility, and working condition clusters to allow quantitative comparisons between jobs. This latter approach is preferable from the standpoint of being able to demonstrate job relatedness.

Measuring Compensable Factors. Standardized worker-oriented job analysis questionnaires have been highly successful in the area of compensation; by using the job dimension scores produced by these instruments as *compensable factors*, or the abstract job characteristics on which organizations base compensation decisions, impressive levels of prediction of market compensation rates have been achieved. Indeed, these instruments have achieved levels of predictive efficiency that are virtually unparalleled in other areas of industrial and organizational psychology.

Much of this research has involved the PAQ (e.g., McCormick, Mecham, & Jeanneret, 1977; Robinson, Wahlstrom, & Mecham, 1974), and more recently, the JEI (Harvey et al., 1988). Procedurally, jobs are analyzed using worker-oriented methods, general job dimension scores are produced, and these work dimension scores are used as predictors of market compensation rates for the jobs in question. Once market pay policies with respect to each job dimension are captured using multiple regression, a predicted compensation value termed *points* can be determined for any new job by simply applying the regression weights in new samples of jobs.

One of the most notable aspects of this research concerns the magnitude of the multiple correlations obtained using these policy-capturing techniques on compensation data: Using the relatively primitive JEI, Rs in the .70s and .80s predicting existing compensation rates have been obtained (e.g., Harvey et al., 1988). Studies using the PAQ have reported even higher levels of predictive efficiency. For example, McCormick et al. (1977) reported an R of .85.

There have been a few clouds on this otherwise sunny horizon, however, particularly concerning the ability of worker-oriented instruments like the PAQ and JEI to predict pay rates for managerial, professional, and executive jobs. The PAQ's authors have agreed (e.g., McCormick et al., 1977; J. Mitchell & McCormick, 1979) that it lacks sufficient coverage of the work activities of higher-level jobs and does not predict pay rates for these jobs as effectively as it does for blue collar jobs. Other instruments (e.g., EXCEL, PMPQ, PDQ) have subsequently been developed to remedy the lack of coverage of managerial and executive work dimensions seen in general-purpose instruments like the PAQ and JEI.

Some have criticized the use of policy-capturing approaches in general, charging that they serve to capture and perpetuate sex-based discriminatory pay policies that may exist in the labor market (e.g., Schwab, 1984, p. 87). In defense of market-capturing techniques, however, one must note that instruments like the PAQ and JEI did not *create* the market conditions being captured by these regression coefficients; there is little reason to kill the messenger that simply describes prevailing market policies.

Of perhaps greater importance, when one considers the fact that most holistic rating methods used for compensation purposes (e.g., the Hay system, described by Bellak, 1984) rate jobs on highly abstract, nonbehavioral compensable factors (e.g., "know how," "accountability"), the behaviorally verifiable job analysis item ratings that worker-oriented instruments use to define compensable factors represent a quantum improvement in measurement precision and defensibility. One can easily hypothesize that far more pay inequity is caused by reliance on sex-stereotype-influenced, non–job-related holistic compensable factor ratings than is caused by capturing market pay policies.

Finally, research (e.g., Harvey, 1985b) comparing unit weights and rational weights—which presumably cannot perpetuate past sex-based pay discrimination—with market-based policy-capturing equations has suggested that the jobs that benefit most from *not* using market policies tend to be stereotypically male jobs, such as heavy equipment operator or police officer. Stereotypically female titles—secretary, receptionist—often receive *fewer* points using nonmarket equations. Additional research is needed to determine the generalizability of these finings.

Summary

Many personnel applications (e.g., performance appraisal, training, work samples, performance tests, job descriptions, developing KS-based job specifications) require moderate- or high-specificity job data (tasks, behaviorally defined worker-oriented items, critical incidents), both to facilitate the development of quality products as well as demonstrate job relatedness. Other uses (e.g., compensable-factor compensation systems, test validation using more abstract AO-based constructs) that require a relatively task-insensitive common metric on which to compare jobs are better served by using low- specificity data (e.g., job dimension scores).

In view of the poor levels of interrater reliability—to say nothing of the ultimate issue of validity—that to date have characterized methods that infer KS/AO-based employee

specifications on the basis of direct SME ratings, there is little reason for optimism regarding the future of such methods. Researchers should focus on identifying empirically defined links between the domain of job activity constructs and the domain of human KS and AO characteristics, using job component or synthetic validity methods, for example.

The Dimensionality of Work

Background

The central concept in worker-oriented job analysis is that a number of general dimensions of work behavior underlie all jobs and that even task-heterogeneous jobs can be described and meaningfully compared in terms of their scores on these dimensions. The majority of research directed toward identifying general dimensions of work behavior has been conducted by factor analyzing structured job analysis questionnaires composed of worker-oriented items (e.g., Cunningham et al., 1983; Harvey et al., 1988; McCormick et al., 1972). However, the identification of general work dimensions is an issue facing more behaviorally specific, task-oriented job analysis methods as well; for example, Fine's FJA seeks to compare even highly dissimilar tasks in terms of their involvement with a small number of very general work behaviors. In short, the issue of defining the dimensionality of work centers on the question of identifying *general job behavior constructs.*

Identifying the dimensionality of work behavior is critical for two reasons. First, describing jobs in terms of general work dimensions is important for personnel functions in which it is critical to identify behavioral similarities between jobs that may be masked by task technology differences. Second, efforts designed to identify the basic dimensions on which *people* vary, or to identify general "types" of people, have been carried out by psychologists concerned with identifying and measuring individual differences. The general dimensions of concern to such researchers include cognitive abilities (e.g., Guilford, 1967), physical abilities (e.g., Fleishman & Quaintance, 1984), personality traits (e.g., Hogan, 1990), and biodata (e.g., Owens, 1971).

Industrial and organizational psychologists have for many years been calling for research to link the dimensional system defining general work behaviors with the dimensional system defining general human characteristics or types. Dunnette (1976) characterized these two domains as "the two worlds of human behavioral taxonomies" (p. 477) and highlighted the theoretical and practical importance of being able to systematically match the characteristics of people with the characteristics of jobs.

Unfortunately, research on the human dimensionality side of the equation appears to have advanced much further than research aimed at defining the dimensionality of work behavior. Since the turn of the century, individual differences psychologists have been attempting to span the dimensionality of human traits, particularly cognitive and perceptual abilities (e.g., Spearman, 1927). Systematic empirical work dimensionality research did not begin to emerge until the 1960s (e.g., Cunningham, 1964; Jeanneret, 1969; Palmer & McCormick, 1961).

Task-oriented Work Dimensions

Functional Job Analysis. Although typically viewed as a task-oriented method, FJA has at its core a theoretical statement regarding the general dimensionality of work activities. FJA is based on the position that all tasks can be described and compared in terms of three fundamental work dimensions termed *worker functions*: Data, People, and Things. Figure 14 lists these dimensions and the hierarchy of activities hypothesized by Fine to define each.

By determining a task's involvement, termed its *functional level*, with respect to the Data, People, and Things dimensions, a common content and rating scale metric is obtained that allows even highly dissimilar tasks to be compared meaningfully. Although the way in which functional level ratings are computed in FJA is quite different than that used in worker-oriented instruments (i.e., FJA rates tasks and then summarizes across tasks to form overall Data, People, and Things scores, whereas worker-oriented instruments apply factor scoring coefficients to worker-oriented item ratings to obtain dimension scores), the conceptual foundation of FJA directly addresses the issue of identifying general dimensions of work activity. At a conceptual level, then, a job's overall functional-level ratings would comprise Type 3 data in the taxonomy of methods presented in Table 1.

At a practical level, however, because FJA's Data–People–Things dimensions were developed through largely nonempirical means, little is known about the measurement properties or construct validity of these dimensions. One study that addressed these issues (McCulloch & Francis, 1989) raised questions about the validity of the hierarchical ordering of activities defining these scales. Using confirmatory factor analysis of a pool of items measuring each of the seven levels of the People scale (e.g., persuading, supervising, mentoring), McCulloch and Francis found that although the seven constructs themselves were empirically justified, there was no support for the predicted hierarchical relationship among them.

Dimensionality of Task Inventories. A similar lack of information exists regarding the dimensionality of task inventory data. Given that task inventories typically include hundreds of individual task statements—making a factor analysis difficult using even

FIGURE 14

FJA Functional Level Rating Scales

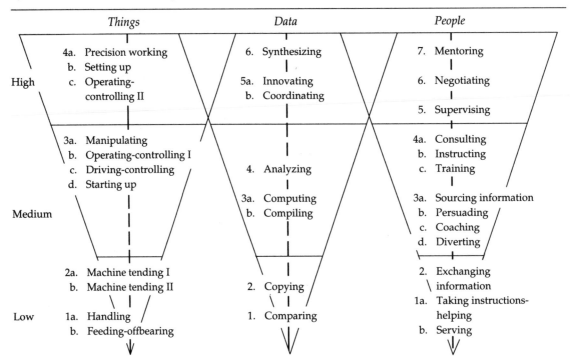

1. Each hierarchy is independent of the other. It would be incorrect to read the functions across the three hierarchies as related because they appear to be on the same level. The definitive relationship among functions is within each hierarchy, not across hierarchies. Some broad exceptions are made in the next note.
2. Data is central since a worker can be assigned even higher data functions although Things and People functions remain at the lowest level of their respective scales. This is not so for Things and People functions. When a Things function is at the third level, e.g., Precision working, the Data function is likely to be at least Compiling or Computing. When a People function is at the fourth level, e.g., Consulting, the Data function is likely to be at least Analyzing and possibly Innovating or Coordinating. Similarly for Supervising and Negotiating. Mentoring in some instances can call for Synthesizing.
3. Each function in its hierarchy is defined to include the lower numbered functions. This is more or less the way it was found to occur in reality. It was most clear-cut for Things and Data and only a rough approximation in the case of People.
4. The lettered functions are separate functions on the same level, separately defined. The empirical evidence did not support a hierachial distinction.
5. The hyphenated functions, Taking instructions-helping, Operating-controlling, etc. are single functions.
6. The Things hierarchy consists of two intertwined scales: Handling, Manipulating, Precision working is a scale for tasks involving hands and hand tools; the remainder of the functions apply to tasks involving machines, equipment, vehicles.

today's computers—it is not surprising that limited research has been conducted in this area.

Harvey, Wilson, and Blunt (1989) examined the convergence between the factors extracted from a 521-item insurance company task inventory and direct incumbent ratings of 37 job duty categories. Their results indicated that (a) the task factors were not interpretable as general dimensions of work, tending to be highly technology-specific (e.g., paying claims, writing computer programs, setting premium rates), and (b) there was very low numerical convergence between the direct duty ratings and the empirically derived factor scores.

In terms of the relation between dimensions underlying task- and worker-oriented data, Harvey and Hayes (1988) correlated factor scores obtained from a task inventory given to city government employees with PAQ dimension scores obtained on the same positions. Their results indicated very little convergence between task- and worker-oriented dimensions. As was the case in the Harvey, Wilson, and Blunt (1989) study, the task factors were quite technology-specific (e.g., fire fighting, police patrol, public works) and not readily interpretable as general dimensions of work sought by Type 3 methods.

Although there have not been many empirical studies in this area, it seems unlikely that the Type 3 common-metric dimensions of work that underlie worker-oriented instruments (see Table 1) can be obtained by factoring task inventories. Indeed, because of the close mathematical relationship between the *item-mode* factors described above and the *rater-mode* factors obtained by factoring the raters-by-raters correlation matrix computed from the transposed item data (e.g., see Ross, 1963, 1964; Stephenson, 1952), we would expect that task-inventory factors will be useful primarily for fine-grained job classification purposes, such as when attempting to identify clusters of positions or jobs that perform similar work activities. Analysis of less technology-

specific items appears to be necessary to recover general dimensions of work activity.

Worker-oriented Dimensions

General-Purpose Instruments. *The PAQ.* The pioneering research aimed at defining the domain of worker-oriented dimensions was performed by McCormick and colleagues at Purdue University during the 1960s and early 1970s (e.g., Cunningham, 1964; Jeanneret, 1969; McCormick, Jeanneret, & Mecham, 1972). One result of this process—the PAQ—has been factor analyzed by Jeanneret (1969) for Form A (producing the System I factors) and Mecham, McCormick, and Jeanneret (1977) for Form B (producing the System II structure). Table 6 summarizes the overall factors of the PAQ obtained from these studies.

Alternative Views of the PAQ's Dimensionality. Using a different factor model and rotation procedure, Harvey (1987) reanalyzed the Jeanneret (1969) Form A data using the common factor analysis model and oblique Harris-Kaiser rotation (the PAQ had initially been analyzed using the principal components model and orthogonal varimax rotation). These results (also presented in Table 6) indicated that although more overall factors were retained than in the System I and II analyses (19 versus 5 and 13, respectively), these factors were interpretively quite similar to those reported by Mecham et al. (1977) for the Form B data.

Because these first-order factors were to some degree intercorrelated, a second-order factor analysis was conducted on the correlation matrix of the 19 first-order factors. The results of this analysis indicated that three second-order factors were present, named as follows (examples of first-order factors loading on each are presented in parentheses): (a) Working With People and Data (Decision/ Communication/Social Responsibility; Dealing With the Public; Direct Supervision;

Clerical/Information Processing), (b) Working With Things (Graphic/Measurement/Technical Duties; Operate/Adjust/Tend Machines/Tools/Equipment; Precise/Repetitive/Vigilant Duties; Using Miscellaneous Senses/Tools), and (c) Physical Work Environment (Unpleasant/Hazardous Work Environment; Outdoor Work).

Although speculative, it is interesting to observe the parallels between these second-order PAQ factors and the conceptually derived Data–People–Things dimensions of Fine's FJA. In these second-order factors of the PAQ, the Data and People dimensions are combined, suggesting that the sources of data dealt with on many jobs are primarily interpersonal in nature (e.g., people supervised, dealing with customers or the public, interacting with other employees). With the addition of a work environment/context dimension, FJA's Data–People–Things framework provides an elegant and parsimonious conceptual organization for the numerous first-order PAQ dimensions.

Additional General-Purpose Instruments. In addition to the PAQ, a number of general-purpose worker-oriented questionnaires have been developed to date; these instruments have various qualities that make them desirable for certain situations and purposes. The *Job Element Inventory* (JEI; Cornelius & Hakel, 1978; Harvey et al., 1988) was developed to parallel the item content of the PAQ, yet it has a much lower reading level, allowing it to be administered to job incumbents, supervisors, or other SMEs. As was noted earlier, the high reading level of the PAQ precludes its use by the typical job incumbent or supervisor. The dimensions of the JEI obtained from factor analysis are summarized in Table 6.

Cunningham's GWI and OAI represent a somewhat different approach to identifying general dimensions of work activity. In contrast to the PAQ and JEI, which rate items that are predominantly phrased in terms of technology-independent, general work

behaviors, the GWI and OAI are composed of a mix of what would traditionally be classified as task- and worker-oriented items. In the case of the OAI, considerably more items are included (617) than are present in the PAQ (194) or JEI (153). The GWI is essentially a short form of the OAI designed to assess similar work behavior constructs.

Managerial Instruments. In contrast to the approach taken by the PAQ, JEI, GWI, and other general-purpose instruments that seek to analyze any job in any setting, some worker-oriented instruments have been targeted solely at managerial, supervisory, executive, and professional (MSEP) jobs. One of the first examples of such instruments was the PMPQ of J. Mitchell and McCormick (1979), although others have subsequently been developed (e.g., Lozada-Larsen's [1988] EXCEL and Page & Gomez' [1979] *Position Description Questionnaire*). A summary of the work dimensions identified by these instruments is presented in Table 7.

Unfortunately, little effort has been devoted to linking dimensions identified from MSEP instruments with the dimensions obtained from the general-purpose instruments discussed earlier. Additionally, the most widely known of the MSEP-specific instruments—the PMPQ—suffers from a number of drawbacks, including (a) a limited number of items (98), only a limited subset of which (42) describe work behaviors; (b) highly behaviorally abstract items (e.g., there are only one or two items each to describe activities as complex as supervising/directing, oral communications, judgments involving people, and written communications); and (c) highly behaviorally abstract item rating scales for the 42 behavioral items (although 10 numerical rating points are provided, only 5 of these are anchored, plus a "Does not apply" zero anchor). Because of the high level of behavioral abstraction in its items and rating scales, difficulty in documenting or justifying PMPQ item ratings in terms

TABLE 6

Summary of Dimensions From General-Purpose Worker-Oriented Instruments

PAQ System I	Alternative PAQ System I	PAQ System II	Dichotomous JEI
Decisions/ communication/social responsibility (1)	Decisions/ communication/social responsibility (1)	Decisions/ communication/social responsibility (1)	Supervise/direct/ evaluate others (2)
Skilled job activity (2)	Operate/adjust/tend machines/tools/ equipment (5)	Operate/adjust/tend machines/tools/ equipment (2)	Operate/adjust/tend machine/tools/ equipment (1)
Information processing (5)	Clerical/information processing (4)	Clerical/information processing (3)	Clerical equipment usage (8)
	Graphic/ measurement/ technical (2)	Graphic/ measurement/ technical (4)	Routine information exchange (6) Process quantitative information (10)
		Personal service (5)	Personal service (9)
	Regular work hours (17)	Regular work schedule (6)	
	Precise/repetitive/ vigilant (11)	Repetitive duties (7)	Repetitive/vigilant (16)
Equipment/vehicle operation (4)	Operate machines requiring continuous attention (3)	Operate machines requiring continuous attention (8)	Operate nonprecision machine/tools (7)
Physical activities (3)	Gross body movement while stationary (7) Gross body movement while mobile (15)	Gross body movements/activities (9)	Gross body movement/activities (11)
	Direct supervision of others (10)	Direct supervision of others (10)	
	Deals with public (12) Sales/buyer contacts (19)	Public/customer contact (11)	External contacts (5)
	Personally demanding situations (14)		
	Unpleasant/hazardous work environment (6)	Unpleasant/hazardous work environment (12)	Unpleasant work environment (12) Risks/hazards (13)

TABLE 6

Summary of Dimensions From General-Purpose Worker-Oriented Instruments (continued)

PAQ System I	Alternative PAQ System I	PAQ System II	Dichotomous JEI
		Optional apparel/ nontypical work schedule (13)	
			Plan/schedule/ resolve/organize (3)
	Visual/auditory sensing/judging (8)		Visual/auditory sensory information/judging (4)
	Estimating/judging physical characteristics of objects (9)		
			Internal contacts (14)
	Using miscellaneous senses/tools (18)		Taste/odor/touch sensory information/ judging (15)
	Outdoor work (13)		
	Balance/agility (16)		

Note: PAQ System II names have been modified in some cases in order to more fully describe their item content. Alternative System I analyses are from Harvey (1989). Numbers in parentheses are the original factor numbers.

of actual job behaviors would be expected. Similarly, by virtue of using rating scales that include several completely unanchored rating points, the degree to which PMPQ item scores can be seen to lie on a metric that allows cross-job level-sensitive comparisons to be made can be called into question.

Integrating General-Purpose and Managerial Dimensions. Although general-purpose and managerial instruments have developed along largely nonoverlapping paths, it is possible to identify areas of similarity between these instruments. Table 8 attempts to integrate the dimensions uncovered from general-purpose and managerial instruments

into a general structure of work activity constructs.

The structure presented in Table 8 borrows liberally from Fine's Data–People–Things theory of work and the results of the Harvey (1987) second-order factor analysis of the PAQ. It should be noted that not all dimensions identified in previous studies were included because some of them are not truly worker-oriented in nature. That is, they are too close to the actual task technologies involved in performing the work to function as Type 3 dimensions. Examples of such dimensions include activities involved in dealing with the department-specific technologies of various organizational units (e.g., research and

TABLE 7

Summary of Dimensions From Managerial Worker-oriented Instruments

PDQ	PMPQ	EXCEL
Supervising	Interpersonal activities Communicating/instructing	Employee relations: Supervise/lead/instruct Human resources management: Policy/programs
Strategic long-range planning Monitor business indicators	Planning/decision making (split)	Planning/goals/budgeting
Controlling	Planning/decision making (split)	Finance: Fixed assets/cash Human resource management: hiring Finance: Administration
Products/services (split) Consulting (split)	Processing information/data	Products/services: R&D/technical support
Products/services (split) Customer relations/marketing (split) Consulting (split)	Technical activities	Products/services: Marketing/sales/advertising Production management
Customer relations/marketing (split) External contacts (split)		Customer relations Contract management
External contacts (split)		External contacts: Professional/industrial
External contacts (split)		External contacts: Legal/government External contracts: Public relations
Coordinating		Internal contacts: Consult/communications
	Personal job requirements	
	Relevant experience	
	Special training	
	Second-language usage	

TABLE 8

Taxonomy of General-Purpose and Managerial Dimensions

Interpersonal (FJA's "People")
    Internal contacts
    Communication/instruction/consulting/coordinating
    Supervision/direction of employees
        – Lower-level
        – Mid/upper-level
    External contacts
        – Public/customers
        – Professional/industrial
        – Legal/regulatory
    Personally demanding situations
    Personal services for others

Information Processing (FJA's "Data")
    Resources/assets/financial
    Planning/scheduling/budgeting
    Production/operations/systems analysis/management
    Physical environment sensing/judging
    Decision making/conflict resolution
    Policies/procedures
    Multiple language use
    Contract management
    Taking/exchanging information
    Clerical activities

Mechanical/Technical/Physical Activities (FJA's "Things")
    Adjust/tend/repair equipment
    Operate equipment
        – Office
        – Production/manufacturing
        – Light vehicles
        – Heavy vehicles
        – Tools
    Gross body activities
        – Strength/endurance
        – Coordination/balance
    Graphic/quantitative/measurement activities

Work Context

Apparel	Task/skill variety, repetitive activities
Work schedule	Task significance
Reward system	Feedback
Unpleasant physical environment	Task identify
Risks and hazards	Licensing/certification
Autonomy	Training/education experience

development, marketing, accounting). Similar dimensions characterize some general-purpose instruments, particularly the OAI (e.g., its dimensions include biological/health-related activities, botanical activities, electrical-electronic repair, working with animals, and food preparation/processing). Although useful at a more task-specific level of analysis, such dimensions are of limited use when comparing across task-dissimilar jobs.

The evolution of worker-oriented instruments is continuing as standardized questionnaires are being developed that attempt to (a) more comprehensively span the dimensionality of both exempt and nonexempt job activity, (b) provide greater behavioral specificity and verifiability of the item ratings, and (c) allow untrained incumbents or supervisors to provide the item ratings. For example, the CMQ (Harvey, 1990a) was written using items having an 8th grade (or lower) reading level to allow completion by incumbents and supervisors and uses a matrix type of response format that produces (a) a much larger number of data points on each position than is typically seen in worker-oriented questionnaires and (b) much greater behavioral specificity in item ratings.

For example, with respect to job dimensions dealing with external contacts, the CMQ response matrix describes 13 types of people contacted (e.g., customers, regulatory officials, contractors, executives of other organizations) as the rows of the matrix, and uses dichotomous ratings of multiple columns to describe the kinds of behaviors performed with each type of external contact (e.g., take information from them, schedule their activities, resolve disputes involving them, provide treatment or therapy to them). Thus, instead of obtaining only 13 rating points to describe external contacts—as would be the case if a single Likert-type rating scale had been used—the standardization version of the CMQ rates each contact on 20 scales, producing 260 data points from this single grid.

By using a grid-type format, the CMQ avoids the problems faced by methods that assign only a single number to describe each kind of personal contact. For example, in FJA, a single functional-level value (e.g., consulting) would be assigned on the People scale for each external contact; in contrast, the CMQ allows for the possibility that a job may indeed involve consulting, yet may *not* perform other activities at a lower level in the FJA People hierarchy (e.g., serving, taking instructions, coaching). Fine (1989) acknowledged this possibility, noting that although "each function in its hierarchy is defined to include the lower numbered functions," this hierarchical relationship "was most clear-cut for Things and Data and only a rough approximation in the case of People" (p. 6).

Summary

Building on the pioneering empirical and conceptual work undertaken by McCormick, Fine, and colleagues, much progress has been made toward the goal of identifying the domain of worker-behavior and work-context constructs on which jobs vary. Additional research is now needed to improve the degree to which standardized worker-oriented job analysis questionnaires are capable of accurately measuring these constructs, as most existing instruments have problems with respect to (a) assessing only a limited subset of the total number of job dimensions that have been identified and/or (b) using rating scales and instruction sets that have questionable psychometric properties (e.g., behaviorally vague anchors, within-job-relativistic formats, or assumptions of unidimensional, hierarchical relationships among potentially multidimensional rating anchors). Armed with the ability to make meaningful cross-job comparisons on a comprehensive set of work-behavior constructs, we will finally have the tools needed to develop the empirical link to bridge Dunnette's "two worlds of human behavioral taxonomies" (1976, p. 477).

References

Aamodt, M. G., Kimbrough, W. W., Keller, R. J., & Crawford, K. J. (1982). Relationships between sex, race, and job performance level and the generation of critical incidents. *Journal of Educational and Psychological Research, 2*, 227–234.

Albemarle Paper Co. v. Moody (1975). 422 U.S. 405.

American Educational Research Association, American Psychological Association, & National Council on Measurement in Education (1985). *Standards for educational and psychological testing.* Washington, DC: American Psychological Association.

Arneson, S., & Peterson, S. (1986, April). *An adjective checklist approach to job analysis.* Paper presented at the annual meeting of the Southwestern Psychological Association convention, Fort Worth, TX.

Arvey, R. D., Davis, J. A., McGowen, S. L., & Dipboye, R. L. (1982). Potential sources of bias in job analytic processes. *Academy of Management Journal, 25*, 618–629.

Arvey, R. D., Passino, E. M., & Lounsbury, J. N. (1977). Job analysis results as influenced by sex of incumbent and sex of analyst. *Journal of Applied Psychology, 62*, 411–416.

Ash, R. A., & Edgell, S. L. (1975). A note on the readability of the Position Analysis Questionnaire (PAQ). *Journal of Applied Psychology, 60*, 765–766.

Avner, B. K., & Mayer, R. S. (1986, August). Developing an integrated personnel system and split-role performance appraisal. In W. Tornow (Chair), *State-of-the-art applications of job analysis:*

Integrated personnel systems. Symposium presented at the annual meeting of the American Psychological Association , Washington, DC.

Barrett, G. V., & Kernan, M. C. (1987). Performance appraisal and terminations: A review of court decisions since Brito v. Zia with implications for personnel practices. *Personnel Psychology, 40*, 489–503.

Bellak, A. O. (1984). Comparable worth: A practitioner's view. In *Comparable worth: Issue for the 80's* (Vol. 1). Washington, DC: U. S. Commission on Civil Rights.

Bersoff, D. N. (1988). Should subjective employment devices be scrutinized? It's elementary, my dear Ms. Watson. *American Psychologist, 43*, 1016–1018.

Brito v. Zia (1973). 478 F.2d 1200.

Butler, S. K., & Harvey, R. J. (1986, April). *Testing the Schmidt-Hunter performance appraisal unidimensionality hypothesis.* Paper presented at the annual meeting of the Southwestern Psychological Association, Fort Worth, TX.

Butler, S. K., & Harvey, R. J. (1988). A comparison of holistic versus decomposed rating of Position Analysis Questionnaire work dimensions. *Personnel Psychology, 41*, 761–771.

Cain, P. S., & Green, B. F. (1983). Reliabilities of selected ratings available from the Dictionary of Occupational Titles. *Journal of Applied Psychology, 68*, 155–165.

Carpenter, J. B. (1974). *Sensitivity of group job descriptions to possible inaccuracies in individual job descriptions* (AFHRL-TR-74-6). Lackland AFB, TX: Air Force Human Resources Laboratory, Occupational Research Division.

Carpenter, J. B., Giorgia, M. J., & McFarland, B. P. (1975). *Comparative analysis of the relative validity for subjective time rating scales* (Tech. Rep. AFHRL-TR-75-63). San Antonio, TX: Air Force Human Resources Laboratory.

Cascio, W. F. (1987). *Applied psychology in personnel management.* Englewood Cliffs, NJ: Prentice-Hall.

Christal, R. E. (1974). *The United States Air Force occupational research project* (AFHRL-TR-73-75). Lackland AFB, TX: Air Force Human Resources Laboratory, Occupational Research Division.

Contreras v. City of Los Angeles (1981). 25 FEP 867.

Coombs, C., & Satter, G. A. (1949). A factorial approach to job families. *Psychometrika, 14,* 33–42.

Coovert, M. D. (1988). *The use of mental models to affect quality in human-computer interactions.* Unpublished doctoral dissertation, Ohio State University.

Coovert, M. D. (1986, April). Altering artificial intelligence heuristics to provide data for specific applications. In S. Gael (Chair), *Advances in tailoring job analysis methods for specific applications.* Symposium presented at the annual conference of the Society for Industrial and Organizational Psychology, Chicago.

Cornelius, E. T., Carron, T. J., & Collins, M. N. (1979). Job analysis models and job classification. *Personnel Psychology, 32,* 693–708.

Cornelius, E. T., DeNisi, A. S., & Blencoe, A. G. (1984). Expert and naive raters using the PAQ: Does it matter? *Personnel Psychology, 37,* 453–464.

Cornelius, E. T., & Hakel, M. D. (1978). *A study to develop an improved enlisted performance evaluation system for the U.S. Coast Guard.* Washington, DC: Department of Transportation, USCG.

Cornelius, E. T., Hakel, M. D., & Sackett, P. R. (1979). A methodological approach to job classification for performance appraisal purposes. *Personnel Psychology, 32,* 283–297.

Cornelius, E. T., & Lyness, K. S. (1980). A comparison of holistic and decomposed judgment strategies in job analyses by job incumbents. *Journal of Applied Psychology, 65,* 155–163.

Cornelius, E. T., Schmidt, F. L., & Carron, T. (1984). Job classification approaches and the implementation of validity generalization results. *Personnel Psychology, 37,* 247–260.

Cragun, J. R., & McCormick, E. J. (1967). *Job inventory information: Task reliabilities and scale interrelationships* (PRL-TR-67-15). Lackland AFB, TX: Personnel Research Laboratory. (NTIS No. AD–681–509)

Cranny, C. J., & Doherty, M. E. (1988). Importance ratings in job analysis: Note on the misinterpretation of factor analyses. *Journal of Applied Psychology, 73,* 320–322.

Cunningham, J. W. (1964). *Worker-oriented job variables: Their factor structure and use in determining job requirements.* Unpublished doctoral dissertation, Purdue University, West Lafayette, IN.

Cunningham, J. W. (1989, August). Discussion. In R. J. Harvey (Chair), *Applied measurement issues in job analysis.* Symposium presented at the annual meeting of the American Psychological Association, New Orleans.

Cunningham, J. W., & Ballentine, R. D. (1982). *The general work inventory.* Raleigh, NC: Authors.

Cunningham, J. W., Boese, R. R., Neeb, R. W., & Pass, J. J. (1983). Systematically derived work dimensions: Factor analyses of the Occupation Analysis Inventory. *Journal of Applied Psychology, 68,* 232–252.

Dansereau, F., Graen, G., & Haga, W. (1975). A vertical dyad approach to leadership in formal organizations. *Organizational Behavior and Human Performance, 13,* 46–78.

Davis v. Washington (1972). 5 FEP 293.

DeNisi, A. S., Cornelius, E. T., & Blencoe, A. G. (1987). Further investigation of common knowledge effects on job analysis ratings. *Journal of Applied Psychology, 72,* 262–268.

Dunnette, M. D. (1976). Aptitudes, abilities, and skill. In M. D. Dunnette (Ed.), *Handbook of industrial and organizational psychology.* Chicago: Rand McNally.

Dunnette, M. D., & Borman, W. C. (1979). Personnel selection and classification systems. *Annual Review of Psychology, 30,* 477–525.

EEOC v. Atlas Paper Box Co. (1989). 868 F.2d 1487.

Feldman, J. M. (1981). Beyond attribution theory: Cognitive processes in performance appraisal. *Journal of Applied Psychology, 66,* 127–148.

Ferris, G. R., Fedor, D. B., Rowland, R. M., & Proac, J. F. (1985). Social influence and sex effects on task performance and task perceptions. *Organizational Behavior and Human Performance, 36,* 66–78.

Fine, S. A. (1989). *Functional job analysis scales: A desk aid.* Milwaukee, WI: Sidney A. Fine.

Fine, S., & Wiley, W. W. (1971). *An introduction to functional job analysis.* Washington, DC: Upjohn

Institute for Employment Research.

Flanagan, J. C. (1954). The critical incident technique. *Psychological Bulletin, 51,* 327–358.

Fleishman, E. A., & Quaintance, M. K. (1984). *Taxonomies of human performance.* Orlando, FL: Academic Press.

Friedman, L. (1988, April). Rating tasks on importance, frequency, significance, and difficulty: does it make a difference? In R. J. Harvey (Chair), *Troublesome questions in job analysis.* Symposium presented at the annual conference of the Society for Industrial and Organizational Psychology, Dallas.

Friedman, L., & Harvey, R. J. (1986). Can raters with reduced job descriptive information provide accurate Position Analysis Questionnaire (PAQ) ratings? *Personnel Psychology, 39,* 779–789.

Gael, S. (1983). *Job analysis: A guide to assessing work activities.* San Francisco: Jossey-Bass.

Gatewood, R. D., & Feild, H. S. (1987). *Human resource selection.* New York: CBS College Publishing.

Geyer, P. D., Hice, J., Hawk, J., Boese, R., & Brannon, Y. (1989). Reliabilities of ratings available from the Dictionary of Occupational Titles. *Personnel Psychology, 42,* 547–560.

Graen, G. (1976). Role making processes within complex organizations. In M. D. Dunnette (Ed.), *Handbook of industrial and organizational psychology.* Chicago: Rand McNally.

Green, S. B., & Stutzman, T. (1986). An evaluation of methods to select respondents to structured job-analysis questionnaires. *Personnel Psychology, 39,* 543–564.

Griggs v. Duke Power Co. (1971). 401 US 424.

Guardians Association of NYC Police Dept. v. Civil Service Commission of New York (1980). 23 FEP 909.

Guilford, J. P. (1967). *The nature of human intelligence.* New York: McGraw-Hill.

Guion, R. M. (1965). *Personnel testing.* New York: McGraw-Hill.

Guion, R. M., & Gibson, W. M. (1988). Personnel selection and placement. *Annual Review of Psychology, 39,* 349–374.

Gutenberg, R. L., Arvey, R. D., Osburn, H. G., & Jeanneret, P. R. (1983). Moderating effects of decision-making/information-processing job dimensions on test validities. *Journal of Applied Psychology, 68,* 602–608.

Hamer, R. M., & Cunningham, J. W. (1981). Cluster analyzing profile data confounded with interrater differences: A comparison of profile association measures. *Applied Psychological Measurement, 5,* 63–72.

Harris, C. W., & Kaiser, H. F. (1964). Oblique factor analytic solutions by orthogonal transformations. *Psychometrika, 29,* 347–362.

Hartley, C., Brecht, M., Pagery, P., Weeks, G., Chapanis, A., & Hoecker, D. (1977). Subjective time estimates of work tasks by office workers. *Journal of Occupational Psychology, 50,* 23–26.

Hartman, E. A., & Kromm, G. M. (1989, April). *A comparison of rationally and empirically derived job families.* Paper presented at the annual conference of the Society for Industrial and Organizational Psychology, Boston.

Harvey, R. J. (1982). A new approach to job classification using two-mode factor analysis. *Dissertation Abstracts International, 43,* 1649-B. (University Microfilms No. 82-22-098)

Harvey, R. J. (1985a, August). A comparison of data analysis techniques in job analysis. In E. T. Cornelius (Chair), *Comparative job analysis research.* Symposium presented at the annual meeting of the American Psychological Association, Los Angeles.

Harvey, R. J. (1985b, November). Comparable worth compensation systems: Implications for the bottom line. In R. J. Harvey (Chair), *Comparable worth: Employment issue of the 80s?* Symposium presented at the convention of the Texas Psychological Association, Houston.

Harvey, R. J. (1986a). Quantitative approaches to job classification: A review and critique. *Personnel Psychology, 39,* 267–289.

Harvey, R. J. (1986b, April). Computerized dedication and mapping of job analysis data for managerial level positions. In S. Gael (Chair), *Advances in tailoring job analysis methods for specific applications.* Symposium presented at the annual conference of the Society for Industrial and Organizational Psychology, Chicago.

Harvey, R. J. (1987, April). Alternative factor structures for the Position Analysis Questionnaire (PAQ). In M. D. Hakel (Chair), *The dimensionality of work: Future directions, applications, and instrumentation.* Symposium presented at the annual conference of the Society for Industrial and Organizational Psychology, Atlanta.

Harvey, R. J. (1988, April). Does the choice of worker- versus task-oriented job analysis data influence job classification results? In R. J. Harvey (Chair), *Troublesome questions in job analysis.* Symposium presented at the annual conference of the Society for Industrial and Organizational Psychology, Dallas.

Harvey, R. J. (1989). Latent-trait versus factor scoring of the Job Element Inventory. In R. J. Harvey (chair), *Applied measurement issues in job analysis.* Symposium presented at the annual meeting of the American Psychological Association, New Orleans.

Harvey, R. J. (1990a). *The common-metric questionnaire for the analysis and evaluation of jobs* (field test version 1.12). San Antonio, TX: The Psychological Corporation.

Harvey, R. J. (1990b, April). Incumbent versus supervisor perceptions of job tasks. In K. Kraiger (Chair), *Cognitive representations of work.* Symposium presented at the annual conference of the Society for Industrial and Organizational Psychology, Miami.

Harvey, R. J., Friedman, L., Hakel, M. D., & Cornelius, E. T. (1988). Dimensionality of the Job Element Inventory (JEI), a simplified worker-oriented job analysis questionnaire. *Journal of Applied Psychology, 73,* 639–646.

Harvey, R. J., & Hayes, T. L. (1986). Monte carlo baselines for interrater reliability correlations using the Position Analysis Questionnaire. *Personnel Psychology, 39,* 345–357.

Harvey, R. J., & Hayes, T. L. (1988, March). *Task- versus worker-oriented job analysis factors.* Paper presented at the meeting of the Southeastern Psychological Association, New Orleans.

Harvey, R. J., & Lozada-Larsen, S. R. (1988). Influence of amount of job descriptive information on job analysis rating accuracy. *Journal of Applied Psychology, 73,* 457–461.

Harvey, R. J., & Wilson, M. A. (1985, April). *Impact of job analysis data specificity on job classification results.* Paper presented at the convention of the Southwestern Psychological Association, Austin.

Harvey, R. J., Wilson, M. A., & Blunt, J. H. (1989). *A comparison of rational versus empirical methods of deriving job analysis dimensions.* Manuscript under review.

Hauenstein, N. M. A., & Foti, R. J. (1989). From laboratory to practice. Neglected issues in implementing frame-of-reference rater training. *Personal Psychology, 42,* 359–378.

Hayes, T. L. (1988, April). Do demographic and experience characteristics of incumbents predict job analysis ratings? In R. J. Harvey (Chair), *Troublesome questions in job analysis.* Symposium presented at the annual conference of the Society for Industrial and Organizational Psychology, Dallas.

Hazel, J. T., Madden, J. M., & Christal, R. E. (1964). Agreement between worker-supervisor descriptions of the worker's job. *Journal of Industrial Psychology, 2,* 71–79.

Henderson, R. (1979). *Compensation management.* Reston, VA: Reston.

Hicks, L. E. (1970). Some properties of ipsative, normative, and forced-choice normative measures. *Psychological Bulletin, 74,* 167–184.

Hogan, J., & Arneson, S. (1987, April). *Using the "Big Five" personality dimensions in job analysis.* Paper presented at the annual conference of the Society for Industrial and Organizational Psychology, Atlanta.

Hogan, R. (1990). Personality and personality measurement. In M. D. Dunnette (Ed), *Handbook of industrial and organizational psychology* (2nd ed.). Palo Alto, CA: Consulting Psychologists Press.

Hughes, G. L., & Prien, E. P. (1989). Evaluation of task and job skill linkage judgments used to develop test specifications. *Personnel Psychology, 42,* 283– 292.

James, L. R. (1982). Aggregation bias in estimates of perceptual agreement. *Journal of Applied Psychology, 67,* 219–229.

Jeanneret, P. R. (1969). *A study of the job dimensions of "worker-oriented" job variables and of their attribute profiles.* Unpublished doctoral dissertation, Purdue University (University Microfilms number 70-8908), West Lafayette, IN.

Jeanneret, P. R., McCormick, E. J., & Mecham, R. (1977). *Job analysis manual for the Position Analysis Questionnaire (PAQ).* West Lafayette, IN: University Book Store.

Jones v. Human Resources Administration (1975). 12 FEP 265.

Jones, A. P., Main, D. S., Butler, M. C., & Johnson, L. A. (1982). Narrative job descriptions as potential sources of job analysis ratings. *Personnel Psychology, 35,* 813–828.

Katz, D., & Kahn, R. L. (1978). *The social psychology of organizations.* New York: Wiley.

Kershner, A. M. (1955). *A report on job analysis.* Washington, DC: Office of Naval Research, ONR Report ACR-5. (Cited in McCormick, 1976)

Kleiman, L. S., & Durham, R. S. (1981). Performance appraisal, promotion, and the courts: A critical review. *Personnel Psychology, 34,* 103–121.

Landy, F. J. (1986). Stamp collecting versus science: Validation as hypothesis testing. *American Psychologist, 41,* 1183–1192.

Lopez, F. M., Kesselman, G. A., & Lopez, F. E. (1981). An empirical test of a trait-oriented job analysis technique. *Personnel Psychology, 34,* 479–502.

Lozada-Larsen, S. R. (1988). *Going beyond criticism: Management work theory and research.* Unpublished doctoral dissertation, Rice University, Houston.

McCormick, E. J. (1976). Job and task analysis. In M. D. Dunnette (Ed.), *Handbook of industrial and organizational psychology* (pp. 651–696). Chicago: Rand McNally.

McCormick, E. J., DeNisi, A., & Shaw, B. (1979). Use of the Position Analysis Questionnaire for establishing the job component validity of tests. *Journal of Applied Psychology, 64,* 51–56.

McCormick, E. J., Jeanneret, P. R., & Mecham, R. C. (1972). A study of job characteristics and job dimensions as based on the Position Analysis Questionnaire (PAQ). *Journal of Applied Psychology, 56,* 347–367.

McCormick, E. J., Mecham, R. C., & Jeanneret, P. R. (1977). *Technical manual for the Position analysis questionnaire (PAQ) (System 2).* West Lafayette, IN: University Book Store.

McCulloch, M. C., & Francis, D. J. (1989, August). Analyzing the social content of jobs: Testing the social scale of Functional Job Analysis. In T. W. Mitchell (Chair), *Theory, instrumentation, applications, and consequences in recent job analysis research.* Symposium presented at the annual meeting of the American Psychological Association, New Orleans.

McDonald, T., & Hakel, M. D. (1985). Effects of applicant race, sex, suitability, and answers on interviewers' questioning strategy and ratings. *Personnel Psychology, 38,* 321–334.

Meyer, H. H. (1959). Comparison of foremen and general foremen conceptions of the foreman's job responsibility. *Personnel Psychology, 12,* 445–452.

Milligan, G. (1981). A review of monte carlo tests of cluster analysis. *Multivariate Behavioral Research, 16,* 379–407.

Mitchell, J. L., & Driskill, W. E. (1986, August). Optimizing integrated personnel system training decisions and development. In W. Tornow (Chair), *State-of-the-art applications of job analysis: Integrated personnel systems.* Symposium presented at the annual meeting of the American Psychological Association, Washington, DC.

Mitchell, J. L., & McCormick, E. J. (1979). *Development of the PMPQ: A structural job analysis questionnaire for the study of professional and managerial positions. (Report No. 1).* West Lafayette, IN: Occupational Research Center, Department of Psychological Studies, Purdue University.

Mitchell, T. W. (1986). Specialized job analysis for developing rationally-oriented biodata prediction systems. In S. Gael (Chair), *Advances in tailoring job analysis methods for specific applications.* Symposium presented at the annual conference of the Society for Industrial and Organizational Psychology, Chicago.

Morsh, J. E. (1964). Job analysis in the United States Air Force. *Personnel Psychology, 17,* 717.

Mullins, W. C., & Kimbrough, W. W. (1988). Group composition as a determinant of job analysis outcomes. *Journal of Applied Psychology, 73,* 657–664.

Nunnally, J. (1978). *Psychometric theory.* New York: McGraw-Hill.

Owens, W. (1971). A quasi-actuarial basis for individual assessments. *American Psychologist, 26,* 992–999.

Page, K. C., & Gomez, L. R. (1979). *The development and application of job evaluation systems using the Position Description Questionnaire* (Personnel Research Report No. 162-79). Control Data Corporation.

Palmer, G. J., & McCormick, E. J. (1961). A factor analysis of job activities. *Journal of Applied Psychology, 45,* 289–294.

PAQ Newsletter (1989, August).

Pass, J. J., & Robertson, D. W. (1980). *Methods to evaluate scales and sample size for stable task inventory information* (NPRDC TR 80-28). Navy Personnel Research and Development Center:

Pearlman, K. (1980). Job families: A review and discussion of their implications for personnel selection. *Psychological Bulletin, 87,* 1–27.

Pearlman, K., Schmidt, F. L., & Hunter, J. E. (1980). Validity generalization results for tests used to predict job proficiency and training success in clerical occupations. *Journal of Applied Psychology, 65,* 373–406.

Prien, E. P. (1977). The function of job analysis in content validation. *Personnel Psychology, 30* 167–174.

Primoff, E. S. (1975). *How to prepare and conduct job element examinations.* Washington, DC: U. S. Government Printing Office.

Robinson, D. D., Wahlstrom, O. W., & Mecham, R. C. (1974). Comparison of job evaluation methods: A "policy capturing" approach using the Position Analysis Questionnaire. *Journal of Applied Psychology, 59,* 633–637.

Ronan, W. W., Talbert, T. S., & Mullett, G. M. (1977). Prediction of job performance dimensions—police officers. *Public Personnel Management, 6,* 173–180.

Ross, J. (1963). The relation between test and person factors. *Psychological Review, 70,* 432–443.

Ross, J. (1964). Mean performance and the factor analysis of learning data. *Psychometrika, 29,* 67–73.

Sackett, P. R., Cornelius, E. T., & Carron, T. J. (1981). A comparison of global judgment vs. task oriented approaches to job classification. *Personnel Psychology, 34,* 791–804.

Sanchez, J. (1990, April). *The effects of job experience on judgments of task importance.* Paper presented at the annual conference of the Society for Industrial and Organizational Psychology, Miami.

Sanchez, J. I., & Levine, E. L. (1989). Determining important tasks within jobs: A policy capturing approach. *Journal of Applied Psychology, 74,* 336–342.

Schmidt, F. L., & Hunter, J. E. (1981). Employment testing: Old theories and new research findings. *American Psychologist, 36,* 1128–1137.

Schmidt, F. L., Hunter, J., & Pearlman, K. (1981). Task differences as moderators of aptitude test validity in selection: A red herring. *Journal of Applied Psychology, 66,* 166–185.

Schmidt, G. R., & Sulzer, J. L. (1989, April). *Defining the criticality of job content: A survey of job analysis procedures.* Paper presented at the annual conference of the Society for Industrial and Organizational Psychology, Boston.

Schmitt, N. (1987, April). *Principles III: Research issues.* Paper presented at the annual conference of the Society for Industrial and Organizational Psychology, Atlanta.

Schmitt, N., & Cohen, S. A. (1989). Internal analysis of task ratings by job incumbents. *Journal of Applied Psychology, 74,* 96–104.

Schriesheim, C. A., Hinkin, T. R., & Podsakoff, P. M. (1991). Can ipsative and single item measures produce erroneous results in field studies of French and Raven's (1959) five bases of power? An empirical investigation. *Journal of Applied Psychology, 76,* 106–114.

Schwab, D. (1984). Using job evaluation to obtain pay equity. In *Comparable worth: Issue for the 80's* (Volume 1). Washington, DC: U. S. Commission on Civil Rights.

Siegel, L., & Lane, I. M. (1987). *Personnel and organizational psychology.* Homewood, IL: Irwin.

Sledge v. J. P. Stevens & Co. (1978). 585 F. 2d 625.

Smith, J., & Hakel, M. D. (1979). Convergence among data sources, response bias, and reliability and validity of a structured job analysis questionnaire. *Personnel Psychology, 32,* 677–692.

Smith, P. C., & Kendall, L. M. (1963). Retranslation of expectations: An approach to the construction of unambiguous anchors for rating scales. *Journal of Applied Psychology, 47,* 149–155.

Society for Industrial and Organizational Psychology, Inc. (1987). *Principles for the validation and use of personnel selection procedures* (3rd ed.). College Park, MD: Author.

Sokal, R. R. (1974). Classification: Purposes, principles, progress, prospects. *Science, 185,* 1115–1123.

Spearman, C. (1927). *The abilities of man.* New York: Macmillan.

Stephenson, W. (1952). Some observations on Q technique. *Psychological Bulletin, 49,* 483–498.

Stutzman, T. M. (1983). Within classification job differences. *Personnel Psychology, 36,* 503–516.

Thompson, D. E., & Thompson, T. A. (1982). Court standards for job analysis in test validation. *Personnel Psychology, 35,* 865–874.

Thompson, D. E., & Thompson, T. A. (1985). Task-based performance appraisal for blue-collar jobs: Evaluation of race and sex effects. Journal of *Applied Psychology, 70,* 747–753.

Tversky, A., & Kahneman, D. (1974). Judgment under uncertainty: Heuristics and biases. *Science, 185,* 1124–1131.

Uniform guidelines on employee selection procedures (1978). *Federal Register, 43,* 38290–38315.

U.S. v. State of New York (1979). 21 FEP 1286.

U. S. Department of Labor (1977). *Dictionary of occupational titles* (4th ed.). Washington, DC: U. S. Employment Service.

Vance, R. J., Coovert, M. D., & Colella, A. (1989). *An expert system for job analysis: An evaluation.* Paper presented at the third annual meeting of the Society for Industrial and Organizational Psychology, Dallas.

Watson v. Fort Worth Bank & Trust (1988). 487 U.S. 108 S.Ct. 2777.

Wexley, K. N., & Silverman, S. B. (1978). An examination of the difference between managerial effectiveness and response patterns on a structured job analysis questionnaire. *Journal of Applied Psychology, 63,* 646–649.

Wilson, M. A. (1987). Work dimensionality and integrated personnel systems. In M. D. Hakel (Chair), *The dimensionality of work: Future directions, applications, and instrumentation.* Symposium presented at the annual conference of the Society for Industrial and Organizational Psychology, Atlanta.

Wilson, M. A. (1989). *An examination of significance ratings of job tasks and duties.* Manuscript under review.

Wilson, M. A. (1990). *Respondent estimates of task inventory validity.* Manuscript under review.

Wilson, M. A. (1991). An expert system for abilities-oriented job analysis: Are computers equivalent to paper-and-pencil methods? In R. J. Harvey (Chair), *Measurement issues in job analysis: New approaches to old problems.* Symposium presented at the sixth annual conference of the Society for Industrial and Organizational Psychology, St. Louis.

Wilson, M. A., & Harvey, R. J. (1990). The value of relative time-spent ratings in task-oriented job analysis. *Journal of Business and Psychology, 4,* 453–461.

Wilson, M. A., Harvey, R. J., & Macy, B. (1990). Repeating items to estimate the test-retest reliability of task inventory ratings. *Journal of Applied Psychology, 75,* 158–163.

CHAPTER 3

The Structure of Work:
Job Design and Roles

Daniel R. Ilgen
John R. Hollenbeck
Michigan State University

Jobs and roles both represent prescribed patterns of behaviors for organizational members. It is not surprising that the nature of jobs and roles has attracted much attention in industrial and organizational psychology. Yet in spite of the similarities between the functions of jobs and roles, there is surprisingly little overlap between the literatures on each topic. It is argued here that this lack of overlap is due, in part, to the fact that the two topics are addressed by those who come to industrial and organizational psychology from different orientations so that the definitions of jobs and roles in use fail to clearly differentiate the two constructs. This chapter presents a perspective that more clearly delineates the boundary between jobs and roles. The approach, termed job–role differentiation (JRD), *uses Blau and Scott's (1962) idea of prime beneficiaries, combined with a universe of task elements, to define the boundary between jobs and roles. Once a framework for isolating the domains of jobs and roles is presented, jobs and roles are explored in terms of the characteristics of each domain in an effort to highlight the functions of each and the value of job and role constructs for structuring behavior in organizational settings.*

Introduction and Overview

Elements of Organizational Structure

ORGANIZATIONS ARE STRUCTURED systems. Virtually all large organizations specify and legitimatize their structure by developing elaborate organizational charts and communicating the elements of the charts to all concerned. At the organizational level, the elements of structure may be defined in terms of a number of companies, divisions, plants, departments, or some other aggregate of positions. These elements are then linked by rules of association typically based on authority relationships. Thus, at an abstract level, organizational structures are described in terms of a set of elements and a set of associative rules that describe the nature of the relationships among the elements.

Although widespread agreement exists on the fact that organizations are structured systems, there is little agreement on the specific elements that constitute structure. Two general systemic perspectives are used—task/functional systems and social systems.

Task/functional systems view organizational structure in terms of the functions that must be accomplished. Functions are further divided into tasks. Tasks are then grouped or clustered and labeled positions or jobs. The basic unit of analysis in the structure is that of jobs or positions. The relationships among units in such systems often get far less attention than the units themselves. To the extent that the relationships are delineated, they are often dictated by the coordination requirements among positions for the accomplishment of general tasks or goals. Relationships among jobs or positions are also dictated by power and authority differences among positions linked to maintain control through lines of authority and responsibility.

A second structural perspective on organizations examines the *social system*. Social systems consist of individuals and relationships among individuals. Individuals represent the elements of social systems, and the interactions among individuals functioning alone or in clusters or groups are the focus of attention. Theories of social systems are not interested in particular persons that make up the organizational structure. When individuals are addressed, often they are viewed in terms of attributes of either individuals or members of identifiable groups (e.g., union members, blue collar or white collar workers, minorities, women, or older workers). Whereas task/functional systems place much emphasis on the *elements* of the structure, social systems focus more on the nature of the *relationships among elements.* At the most general level, these relationships are ones of status as reflected in power and influence differentiations among persons and groups.

Although organizational structures can be described in terms of organizational level characteristics, our concern in this chapter is more at the individual level than at that of the organization, plant, or division. In particular, we are concerned with the nature of structural characteristics that filter down to the everyday work environment of employees. At this level, our interest is in the dynamic interaction between characteristics of the physical and social environments of individuals with the persons themselves and with the behavioral and attitudinal consequences of such interactions. We shall argue that these interactions between the individual's immediate task/physical environment and the social environment have been addressed most frequently in two relatively nonoverlapping literatures, the literature of jobs and the literature of roles. The lack of overlap is not because of an absence of a shared domain but because research and writing in one domain tends to ignore that in the other. It is our intention in this chapter not to isolate the two.

Before becoming immersed in the specifics of organizational structures from within either the job or role perspective, some consideration should be given to the permanence and/or concreteness of structures defined by jobs or roles. At any given time, the structure of an organization appears relatively objective and well defined from either the job or the role perspective. That is to say, if multiple observers were asked to describe the structure in terms of some system, such as a set of jobs, there would be a great deal of agreement about what jobs exist in the organization. There may also be a great deal of agreement on the duties and responsibilities that define these jobs. Finally, when viewed over time, there also tends to be a great deal of stability; jobs comprising an organization normally do not change radically from year to year and neither do the duties and responsibilities attached to most jobs. Obviously, there are exceptions; some jobs change a great deal, a few are eliminated, and a few are added. However, most of the time changes over adjacent years are modest.

This stability gives permanence to the organizational structure. The permanence is quite useful. Without some relative constancy in the nature of organizational jobs and roles, it would be extremely difficult to function in organizations. For example, selection of new employees assumes that the jobs into which these new employees will be placed will remain relatively stable so that persons with personal attributes matching the job requirements can be selected. However, the stable appearance of organizational structures often masks the arbitrary nature of the structures. Jobs and roles evolve over time as the result of the interaction of physical and social systems in the organization and often stabilize for very arbitrary reasons. The arbitrariness is often overlooked when examining an already existing system staffed by employees who have held their positions for some time. The very existence of the jobs and roles and the existence of people in them who have been in them for some time often leads both the incumbents and independent observers to conclude that there is some inherent goodness or correctness to the structure that exists. At this point, we simply caution the reader of the tendency to

see jobs and roles as having more credibility than they deserve.

Jobs and Roles: Definitions, Comparisons, and Contrasts

Jobs. The study of jobs and the study of roles have long but divergent histories. The study of jobs has been dominated by industrial engineers and psychologists interested primarily in description and in the development of taxonomies. Understanding the critical knowledge, skill, and ability requirements of jobs is necessary to select, place, and train employees for particular jobs and to design new jobs or redesign existing ones. Systems for comparisons among jobs are needed for evaluating financial compensation for particular jobs and for developing equitable compensation systems. Elements and physical and psychological demands are necessary to construct new or alter already established jobs to fit the people who fill them. These are just a few of the many demands for information about the nature of jobs that necessitate the development of taxonomic systems and measurement techniques for describing jobs according to the taxonomies.

Like all taxonomic systems, those for describing and analyzing jobs are arbitrary, with their value depending on the extent to which they are useful for the purposes to which they are applied. Ideally, one taxonomic system for classifying jobs could be devised that would meet everyone's needs for information about jobs. Unfortunately, no such system exists, nor is one likely to emerge in the near future. Fleishman's monumental work (summarized in Fleishman & Quaintance, 1984) began as an attempt to develop an overarching taxonomy of tasks that would provide a way to classify all kinds of tasks, especially those that are an integral part of most jobs in the workplace. This broad-based effort led to the conclusion that more than one taxonomic system was necessary to capture the important dimensions of tasks and meet the needs of the various constituencies interested in knowledge about tasks. The five taxonomic systems Fleishman and Quaintance settled on were the (a) criterion measures approach, (b) information-theoretic approach, (c) task strategies approach, (d) ability requirement approach, and (e) task characteristics approach. The same conclusion—that it is impossible to design one broad taxonomic system that meets the wide range of purposes that exist for its use—is equally relevant at the aggregate level of jobs as it is for tasks. The demands on a job taxonomic system are simply too diverse to be met by one system.

In part, the wide variety of approaches to jobs is due to the fact that there are diverse groups interested in jobs. These groups can be combined into three relatively homogeneous clusters. One cluster is represented by *industrial engineering* or *human factors*. Here the concern is primarily with the design of jobs and the distribution of tasks required by the system to the human and nonhuman elements in order to maximize system effectiveness. The focus is on individual jobs within systems and the implications of human performance capabilities for the design of jobs in those systems. This approach can be characterized as deductive, in that it begins with a normative theory about how jobs should be designed to maximize reliability and efficiency of performance from a physical requirements perspective.

Another focus on jobs is that of *job analysts*. Here the concern tends to be more with developing descriptive taxonomies for existing jobs than with designing new jobs. Through structured observation systems, taxonomies of jobs are developed and measurement systems devised to aid in the selection, placement, and training of people at work as well as to develop integrated structures or job families. This approach is inductive; it begins by collecting data on the job via observation, interviews, or question-

naires and then develops conceptions about what the job entails. It is also passive. The primary criterion is fidelity of description rather than increasing efficiency of performance or increasing task motivation.

Finally, jobs have also been approached from a *motivational perspective*. From this perspective, the ability of job incumbents to accomplish job requirements is assumed. Concern is with the willingness of job incumbents to invest time and effort over extended periods of time in the job to perform it effectively. In contrast to the other two approaches, the motivational approach often makes assumptions about the needs and values of job incumbents, and these assumptions guide or influence the taxonomic systems developed for jobs.

This motivational approach, like the human factors approach, is deductive because it begins with a normative theory about how new jobs should be designed to maximize some outcome. Rather than reliability and efficiency of performance, this approach attempts to maximize job incumbents' motivation to work on the job for reasons associated with the job itself. Such motivation is commonly labeled *intrinsic motivation* to imply that task motivation stems from intrinsic properties of the task or job rather than from incentives or rewards attached to holding the job or to job performance. Historically, this approach represented an alternative to the human factors approach and clearly attempted to distance itself from that earlier perspective. Nevertheless, the motivational approach shared, with human factors and industrial engineering, an interest in designing jobs to accomplish particular ends. It did not share the job-analytic concern with developing taxonomic systems of jobs for selection, placement, training, and financial compensation.

Roles.   Research on roles developed primarily in the fields of sociology and social psychology from interest in the nature of social systems and the interrelationships among people comprising those systems. At its most basic level, a *role* is often described as an expected pattern or set of behaviors (Biddle, 1979). This expected pattern of behavior is labeled in the everyday language of the people in the social system. These labels may correspond to terms that are identical to jobs (e.g., bookkeeper, systems analyst, or accountant), but they also may not map directly onto jobs (e.g., parent or friend).

The simplicity of the role definition as a set of expected behaviors masks the complexity and ambiguity that is discovered as one probes more deeply into the underlying assumptions behind the definition. Each behavior in the expected set can be described along two dimensions, a quality dimension and a quantitative one (Naylor, Pritchard, & Ilgen, 1980). That behaviors differ qualitatively and quantitatively is obvious. Typing a letter is very different from composing the letter. In addition, within any given qualitative behavioral category, different amounts of that behavior exist. Thus, we might expect that roles are sets of expectations about the amount and type of behavior expected of a person holding a particular role. This is only partially the case. Roles tend to be much more precisely defined in terms of types of behaviors than in terms of amounts. Moreover, with a few exceptions (e.g., J. S. Jackson, 1965), more of each particular type of behavior expected in the role is presumed to be better. Thus, roles are often only partially bounded quantitatively on any particular qualitative dimension, with the quantitative limits being imposed by the finite amount of time and effort that the individual can devote to the total set of behaviors constituting the role.

Although the definition of a role deals with the particular pattern of behavior expected of persons in that role, most of the interest in roles has not been with the patterns per se but with the way in which the patterns develop, are changed, and interact with other patterns of behaviors (roles) over time. By definition, expectations are beliefs or cognitions held by individuals. Therefore, roles exist in the minds of people. In all work with roles, at least one of those persons of concern regarding a role is the person who holds the role and acts out behaviors as a holder of that role. Yet there may be a number of others who are linked in various ways to the role holder and who also hold expectations about the pattern of behavior that should be displayed to perform the focal person's role. Most of the research on roles and role phenomena addresses the degree of agreement and disagreement in beliefs and expectations about role behaviors among different individuals.

Comparisons and Contrasts.   Although the literature on jobs and roles developed relatively separately, a closer examination of each reveals considerable overlap in the theoretical domains that each attempts to span. For example, both literatures suggest that the nature of each gets mapped into the individual job–role holder through learning and that similar motivational constructs influence compliance with the learned jobs or roles. Likewise, both literatures are interested in the effectiveness of job or role behavior and judge effectiveness by comparing the behavior exhibited by a person in a given job or role to some standard(s) of performance. In addition, the conclusions drawn about behavior in jobs and in roles are often quite similar in both literatures. However, the differences in focus between the two sometimes lead to conclusions that, at least on the surface, appear to conflict. The major points of divergence are mentioned below.

The greatest difference between job and role orientations toward work is in the primary focus of each. Job literature focuses on the behavioral *content* of the elements called jobs, and the role literature focuses on the *process* that establishes the expected set of behaviors labeled a role. As we mentioned earlier, the actual content of jobs, or even the taxonomic systems on which to describe the content, differs for different investigators and different purposes addressed by the job information. However, there is not disagreement on the fact that it is the content of the job that is important. How that content is defined, learned, or changed often is of interest, but that interest is subordinated to the content itself; it is of interest only after the content itself is understood. In contrast, role theorists put much less emphasis on content. Rather, they are concerned about how the content, any content, is communicated, or learned, or how compliance to the content is enforced.

A second difference in orientation between the two views is that the origins of job characteristic perceptions are often traced to physical characteristics of the job, whereas the origins of role characteristics are traced to the social domain in which the person is located. The physical domain of job characteristics requiring direct responses to physical conditions is obvious, such as the grocery cashier's responses triggered by the items placed on the conveyer belt and the need to register the price of these items in some fashion. Less obvious are more abstract job characteristics such as job scope or task uncertainty. These can be traced less easily to particular physical demands of the task and are likely to be influenced by the opinions of others in the workplace (O'Reilly & Caldwell, 1979; Weiss & Shaw, 1979; White & Mitchell, 1979). Nevertheless, from a relative emphasis standpoint, descriptions of jobs are more likely to look at the physical job demands than to the social environment for the definition of "reality" regarding the job. Role theorists are more likely to do the reverse. For them, expectations are communicated to role incumbents through others or through observing others. Roles are seen as existing in the shared perceptions of people. Thus, role theorists concentrate more on social sources when searching for sources of role expectations than do those with a job focus.

Finally, when comparing the motivational dynamics suggested by one motivational view of jobs, termed the *job characteristics model*, to that of role theories, the two differ somewhat in the psychological mechanisms they emphasize. Job characteristic theories posit motivational states that are positively oriented and deal with feelings of responsibility, meaningfulness, and knowledge of results, the latter of which allows for learning the job and for feelings of accomplishment when the feedback indicates that the job was done well (Hackman & Oldham, 1976, 1980). Role theorists, however, are primarily concerned about the uncertainty and stress felt when job incumbents feel they cannot accomplish all role demands (D. Katz & Kahn, 1978). These motivational states are primarily aversive and therefore are to be avoided or reduced.

Toward an Integration of Jobs and Roles. The time has come for an integration of theory and research on jobs and roles. Such an integration is desirable for several reasons. Clearly there is much overlap in the functions of jobs and roles as well as in the outcomes with which each of the literatures is concerned. Scientific parsimony would suggest that integration is preferred over separation in the case of high overlap. Yet, in spite of the overlap, there are a number of issues where the orientations of the two are quite different and the conclusions drawn appear to be in conflict. Any integration of job and role orientation has to address directly the apparent inconsistencies in the two independent literatures that now exist.

We found that the development of an integrative view of jobs and roles was complicated by two factors. First, as already stated, there are three distinct schools of thought on jobs— industrial engineering/human factors, job analytical, and motivational. A comprehensive integration of roles and jobs would need to integrate the three schools of thought on jobs themselves and integrate the three with the theory and literature on roles. Yet such an extensive undertaking is beyond the scope of this chapter. Thus, we will be integrating the theory and literature on roles with the theory and literature on one school of thought on jobs, the motivational approach.

This choice was made for two reasons. First, an integration of the three schools of thought in jobs is already under way in a program of research by Campion (Campion, 1988, 1989; Campion & Thayer, 1985). Second, of the three schools of thought on jobs, the motivational approach has most recently generated the greatest amount of attention in industrial and organizational psychology and organizational behavior. Although we shall place the emphasis on the motivational approach, the conceptual framework developed here will draw from, and hopefully add to, the other two schools of thought on jobs. Where this occurs, it is noted.

It is somewhat paradoxical that the second factor that hindered an integration of the job and role literature is that there is currently a *lack* of differentiation between the two concepts as they are defined in their respective literatures. That is, despite the fact that separate literatures are recognizable for jobs on one hand and work roles on the other, most researchers would, in our opinion, be hard-pressed to identify which of the two constructs was being defined if the definition were removed from the context of the text in which the definition was embedded. For example, does the definition, "Behaviors and activities that are directly associated with achieving a specific objective" (Herbert, 1976, p. 316) define a job or a work role? If you guessed job, you were wrong; so were we. In the remainder of the chapter, we will first develop a framework that draws a clearer distinction between jobs and roles. Admittedly, to gain this distinction we will have to force the two apart somewhat more than even we will be willing to tolerate in the end. However, once we have created a system for separating

the two, we shall map each back onto the system in a way that we feel more clearly develops the similarities and differences between jobs and roles than is frequently done at the present time. The presentation of the integrating model will then be followed by a discussion of the job characteristics and the role literature, taking into account the implications of the integrative model for each. In the final section of the chapter, some remaining steps for further development of a unitary job–role perspective will be outlined.

Job–Role Differentiation: A Task Elements Approach

Before launching into the task elements approach to job–role differentiation, we should stress that the following discussion is not meant to describe the ways in which these issues *are* currently being treated. Rather, what follows is a description of how we have chosen to construe the issues at this point. In order to understand the distinction we wish to draw between jobs and work roles, we must first discuss two concepts: *prime beneficiaries* and *universe of task elements*. The former is borrowed from organization theory and the latter from the job-analytical approach to task description.

Prime Beneficiary

Any discussion of jobs or work roles must first come to terms with the fact that neither can be divorced from the organizational context within which it exists. Organizations typically originate to meet the needs of an individual or group of individuals whose needs cannot be met without the creation of a social organization. Blau and Scott (1962) developed a typology of organizations that was based on the notion of who benefited from the social structure, and they differentiated organizations by their prime beneficiaries.

According to Blau and Scott, there were four basic categories of prime beneficiaries. The four organization types were: (a) mutual benefit associations, (b) service organizations, (c) commonweal organizations, and (d) business concerns.

Mutual benefit associations are organizations where the members or rank-and-file participants are the prime beneficiaries (Blau & Scott, 1962). These organizations include such groups as labor unions or professional organizations. In *service organizations*, the prime beneficiary is the public in direct contact with the organization. The members of the public are people who are not technically members of the organization, yet who interact with it. Public hospitals or elementary schools are examples, with patients and local families, respectively, as the prime beneficiaries.

Commonweal organizations' prime beneficiary is the public at large—that is, the members of the society in which the organization operates. Examples of this type of organization would include military organizations or protective services such as police or fire departments.

Finally, the most common organizations are *business concerns*. Here the owners of an organization are the prime beneficiaries. Any privately held corporation or small business would fall under this heading.

Although the prime beneficiaries are certainly not the only beneficiaries of a social organization, Blau and Scott emphasized that the prime beneficiaries should be singled out in any typological scheme because they create the primary reasons for the organization's origin and existence. The approach to job–role differentiation taken here will assume that a group can be identified that functions as prime beneficiaries of an organization and that this group can be differentiated from other beneficiaries.

The framework developed here begins with the assumption that, to meet the goals or expectations of the prime beneficiaries, certain functional operations or jobs must be accomplished. Some of these jobs may be performed by the prime beneficiaries, but more often individuals other than the prime beneficiaries must be recruited to perform them. The fact that the prime beneficiaries have to enlist others to perform the majority of jobs within the organization creates the need to formally define the jobs. Without the existence of a priori definitions, it would not be possible to recruit and select the people needed to accomplish the organization's objectives.

It should be stressed that the prime beneficiaries are rarely those who run the organization on a day-to-day basis. Yet the most important jobs that need to be filled are those associated with running the organization. Administrative agents of the prime beneficiaries are often charged with the duty of defining and monitoring day-to-day performance in the remaining jobs. In mutual benefit associations, service organizations, and commonweal organizations, the administrative agents are either elected or appointed by agents who were elected by the prime beneficiaries. In business concerns, these administrative agents are often appointed by the prime beneficiaries at least at the time that the organization is formed. The lasting impact of these founding decisions on organizational structure and functions should not be underestimated (Boeker, 1989). After that point, administrative agents are usually selected by administrative agents already with the organization.

Universe of Task Elements

It will also be useful to recognize that jobs can be broken down into smaller job elements or tasks. We will use the term *task element* to represent these job components. The universe of task elements represents a relatively finite set of generic job components beyond which further reduction is unnecessary—that is, the elements are expressed at a relatively low level of abstraction. Thus, the word *element* is employed within this conceptual framework in much the same way that the word *element* is used in chemistry. Several different approaches to the specification of such generic task elements exist, including those developed by McCormick and his colleagues (McCormick, 1979; McCormick, Jeanneret, & Mecham, 1972), Fleishman (1975), Campion and Thayer (1985), and Fine and Wiley (1974). For our purposes, the two most important aspects shared by each of these approaches are that, first, the elements they describe are *generic*. That is, they are not job specific. All jobs can be defined with the elements represented in the universe. Second, the elements are meant to be *comprehensive*. That is, no additional elements are needed to describe all jobs.

The practice of breaking down tasks into generic elements and then working with the elements is certainly not unique here. For example, virtually all approaches to synthetic validation in the area of personnel selection rely on such a practice (Hollenbeck & Whitener, 1988; Mossholder & Arvey, 1984; Primoff, 1959). Job evaluation also is based on the assumption that such elements can be described and comparisons on these generic elements be made across jobs (Schwab, 1984).

A Definition of Jobs

For the purpose of developing a theory of job–role differentiation, jobs will be defined as *a set of task elements grouped together under one job title and designed to be performed by a single individual*. The task elements that comprise the job are characterized by the following four attributes:

- *Jobs are created by the prime beneficiaries* (or their agents), in the sense that it is this group that originally has responsibility for grouping the task elements

into the eventual collection that constitutes the job.

- *Jobs are objective*, where *objective* implies only that there is a shared consensus about the elements comprising the job. (No claim is made here that the jobs are "real" in any positivistic sense.) This shared consensus results primarily from the fact that the elements comprising the job are formally described and are typically written into various organizational documents.

- *Jobs are bureaucratic*. The elements comprising the jobs exist independently of job incumbents. In fact, more often than not, the existence of the jobs predates the presence of the job incumbents.

- *Jobs are quasi static*. It is assumed that, while not immutable, jobs do not change on a day-to-day basis, but rather are relatively constant over time.

For purposes here, task elements that meet the four criteria just listed will be referred to as *established task elements*. Although this definition of jobs is not meant to reflect a consensual definition, it should be noted that this definition and characterization of jobs is not completely alien to the literature on tasks and jobs. The definition for established task elements and jobs is highly similar, although not identical, to what has been referred to in the past as *official tasks* (Pepinsky & Pepinsky, 1961), *tasks qua tasks* (McGrath & Altman, 1966), *objective tasks* (Roby & Lanzetta, 1958), and *defined tasks* (Hackman, 1969). Despite the similarity to past conceptualizations, this definition may sound highly unconventional to some, particularly those who have become accustomed to the blurred distinction between jobs and work roles existing in the scientific literature.

Whereas we can arbitrarily define jobs as being objective, bureaucratic, and quasi static, the fact remains that jobs exist in an environment that is *subjective, personal,* and *dynamic.* Moreover, there exists in this environment a number of *diverse constituencies* other than the prime beneficiaries. Members of these constituencies have a great deal at stake in these jobs. This manifest incongruence between jobs on one hand and work environments on the other severely limits the viability of jobs, as restricted by our definition, in ongoing work organizations. Moreover, the complexity (and sometimes the remoteness) of the work environment makes it virtually impossible for the prime beneficiaries to anticipate all the task elements that will be necessary to make jobs work in the environment for which they are designed.

Thus, to make jobs work in their environment, an extra set or collection of task elements needs to be added to those that originally constituted the job. It is important to note that this does not expand the universe of task elements that we have chosen to call jobs and have defined as finite. Rather, it adds some elements from another domain onto the job that did not exist until there was the necessity of enacting the job in a particular work setting. These additional task elements are specified by a variety of social sources, not the least of which is the incumbent. Such elements will be referred to as *emergent task elements.* Emergent task elements are differentiated from the established ones defined by the prime beneficiaries; emergent task elements are by definition subjective, personal, dynamic, and specified by a variety of social sources other than the prime beneficiaries. The notion of emergent task elements is similar though not identical to what other writers on tasks have referred to as *private tasks* (Pepinsky & Pepinsky, 1961), *subjective tasks* (Roby & Lanzetta, 1958), or *redefined tasks* (Hackman, 1969).

In the conceptual framework drawn here, emergent task elements are mapped into roles. Thus, the framework proposed differentiates work roles from jobs by relegating to jobs only established task elements, and to roles both established task elements and emergent ones. *Roles* are larger sets containing emergent task elements plus those elements of the jobs that are communicated to the job incumbent through the social system and maintained in that system. We are suggesting by this system that the boundaries of a job can be relatively precisely defined by limiting job elements to those that are formally established. The boundaries for roles, on the other hand, are less precise both in the sense of the total set of elements in the role and in the sense of the interface between jobs and roles. Ignoring the precise boundaries for a moment, it is reasonable to say that the individual's role in the organization consists not only of his or her formal job but also of informal task elements that are either self-generated or are thrust upon the role occupant by other people in the social network in which the job is enacted.

Because the established task elements that comprise the job are usually written down, the point where the job elements end and the role as distinguished here begins is usually quite clear from within the job framework. This does not mean, however, that the job is permanently fixed. To allow for change, we defined jobs as quasi static rather than static. Whereas the emergent task elements or role elements are never written down, over time the prime beneficiaries, knowingly or not, may incorporate these elements into the formal job itself. When this occurs (and job analysis methods based on job incumbents' perceptions virtually assure that it will when the job analyses are used to develop job descriptions), these elements cease to be emergent and become established; they are transferred from the domain of the role to that of the job.

Various Job–Role Combinations

To illustrate this distinction more concretely, Figure 1 depicts several different job–role combinations. At one extreme is the classic

FIGURE 1

**Examples of Different Combinations
of Established and Emergent Job–Role Elements**

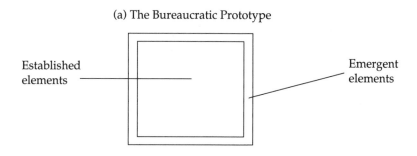

(a) The Bureaucratic Prototype

Established elements

Emergent elements

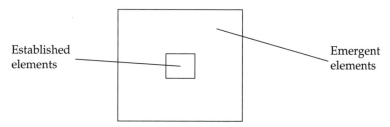

(b) The Loose Cannon Prototype

Established elements

Emergent elements

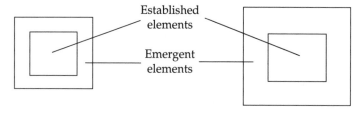

(c) The Job Similarity–Role Difference Prototype

Established elements

Emergent elements

Bureaucratic Prototype, shown in panel *a*. For these positions, virtually all the task elements are established and there is very little, if any, room for expansion or emergent elements. In this condition, the job and the role become synonymous. Many low-scope jobs, such as a hydraulic pallet unloader at a canning factory, hand packager at a small chemical manufacturing firm, or part assembler in an electronics manufacturing plant, would fit this category well, although as a prototype, no organizational work role would fit perfectly.

Panel *b* depicts the Loose Cannon Prototype. Here the work role is comprised of few established elements; instead, it is almost wholly made up of emergent task elements. In this type of job, there is little, if any, formal job description, and the incumbent (or those in his or her role set) is free to choose the tasks to be undertaken. The incumbent has the latitude to build his or her role. Ross Perot's tenure at General Motors or Oliver North's role in the National Security Council are examples that fit this category.

The Job Similarity–Role Difference Prototype, shown in panel *c*, deals with situations where two individuals who share the same job have very different roles. In this situation, although the formal descriptions of the jobs are identical, special characteristics of the incumbents in each job have expanded the role. On a football team, for example, a rookie and a 10-year veteran could both occupy the job of outside linebacker. The established duties of an outside linebacker could be identified for both (e.g., contain the outside run, cover backs coming out of the backfield). Thus, the inner box representing the job is identical in size for each player. However, the veteran, because of his additional experience, would more than likely have an expanded role, with a number of emergent task elements (e.g., calling the defensive formation, making formal decisions regarding penalties, serving as a team leader) that may not be present in the rookie's role. Therefore, the outer box for the veteran player is much larger than the corresponding box for the rookie.

Job-role differences could also originate because of differences in the supervisor (an important person in the role set) rather than the incumbent. The role of research assistant as supervised by an assistant professor who happens to be short on time and high in need for cognitive structure may differ substantially from the role of research assistant as supervised by a full professor who happens to be low in need for cognitive structure and

more interested in student development. Again, although the established task elements associated with the job of research assistant are given (and published in the appropriate handbooks and bylaws), the role of research assistant could vary greatly across situations on a person-by-person basis.

With the distinction between jobs and roles (i.e., established vs. emergent task elements) in place, we will now review the literature on job and role characteristics in light of this distinction. Although existing job and role research was obviously not conducted within the present conceptual framework, we nevertheless feel that applying this system to this research in a post hoc fashion will illuminate several important issues associated with each literature.

Theory and Research on Job Characteristics

Job Characteristics Theory

We described earlier three general orientations toward jobs represented by industrial engineers and human factors psychologists, job analysts, and those focusing on motivational characteristics. The first and last of these are primarily concerned with the design of jobs; the job analysts concentrate on describing and clustering jobs already in existence. Furthermore, we indicated that the initial focus on job design was primarily that of industrial engineering and human factors. The motivational perspective grew out of frustration with limitations of the initial approach. A great deal of research in the industrial and organizational psychology literature in the last few years has addressed job design from the motivational perspective. In addition, much of that research has addressed one particular theory, the *job characteristics theory* (JCT), either by testing tenets of the theory, extending it, or criticizing it. We shall turn our attention to that model.

Development.   JCT has its origins in a major study by Turner and Lawrence (1965) that examined the relationship between attributes of tasks and employees' reactions to their work. These authors constructed measures of six task attributes predicted to be positively related to employee satisfaction and attendance. With a sample of 47 jobs, they empirically derived a summary index, the *requisite task attribute index*, based on a linear combination of the attributes and used the index to predict satisfaction and attendance. The most striking results of the research were the findings implying that responses to specific job characteristics systematically varied with the cultural backgrounds of employees.

Hackman and Lawler (1971) followed up Turner and Lawrence's work, narrowing the set of six requisite task attributes to four and suggesting a reductionist view that cultural differences could be mapped into the value systems of employees. They proposed that individuals who desired growth and involvement in their work would respond more favorably toward jobs that were high on the four dimensions just mentioned than would employees who did not value growth and involvement in their work.

Hackman and Oldham (1976, 1980) further extended and refined JCT. It is their version of the theory that we will explore in detail in the pages that follow. The basic Hackman-Oldham job characteristics theoretical model is presented in Figure 2. At the most general level, five job characteristics are seen as prompting three psychological states, which in turn lead to a number of personal and work-relevant outcomes. The links between the variables in the model are shown as moderated by several individual differences characteristics. We shall discuss each of the major classes of variables in the model in more detail.

Psychological States.   Three psychological states—experienced meaningfulness of the work, experienced responsibility for the outcomes of the work, and knowledge of results of the work activities—are the core of the model. It is postulated that an employee experiences positive affect to the extent that the three states are present. The positive affect created by the presence of these psychological states is believed to be reinforcing and to serve as an incentive for continuing to try to perform the task. The result is a self-perpetuating cycle of positive work motivation that is predicted to continue until one or more of the psychological states is no longer present or until the individual no longer values the internal rewards that derive from high performance.

Job Characteristics.   Of the five characteristics of jobs shown in Figure 2 as fostering the emergence of the psychological states, three are expected to contribute to perceptions about the meaningfulness of the work and one each to experienced responsibility and to knowledge of results.

The three job characteristics that are predicted to combine additively to determine the psychological meaningfulness of the job are as follows:

- *Skill variety*—the degree to which a job requires a variety of different activities to carry out the work; in addition, the activities must require the use of a number of different skills and abilities of the person

- *Task identity*—the degree to which a job requires completion of a whole and identifiable place of work

- *Task significance*—the degree to which the job has a substantial impact on the lives or work of other people, whether in the immediate organization or outside the organization

FIGURE 2

The Job Characteristics Model of Hackman and Oldham

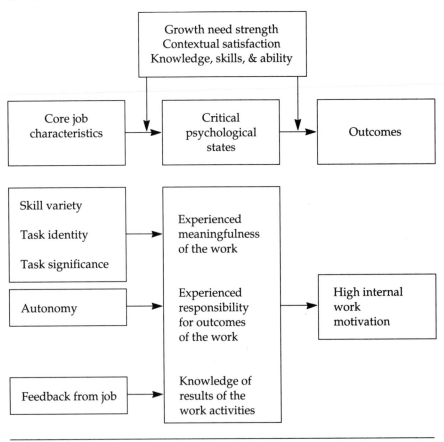

From "Motivation Through the Design of Work: Test of a Theory" by J. R. Hackman and G. R. Oldham, 1976, *Organizational Behavior and Human Decision Processes, 16*, p. 256. Copyright 1976 by Academic Press, Inc. Adapted by permission.

The job characteristic predicted to prompt employee feelings of personal responsibility for the work outcomes is autonomy. *Autonomy* is defined as the degree to which the job provides substantial freedom, independence, and discretion to the individual in scheduling the work and in determining the procedures to be used in carrying it out.

Knowledge of results is predicted to be prompted by the amount of *feedback* the employee receives from doing the work. Feedback, in turn, is seen as the degree to which carrying out the work activities required by the job provides the individual with direct and clear information about the effectiveness of his or her performance. Initially, feedback was seen as solely a characteristic of the task or job itself. More recently it has been expanded to include job performance information available both from doing the job and from others in the job environment.

Motivational Potential.   According to the job characteristics model, the overall potential of a job to prompt self-generated motivation is highest when all of the following are true: (a) The job is high on the job characteristics expected to lead to experienced meaningfulness, (b) the job is high on autonomy, and (c) the job is high on feedback. The *motivating potential score* (MPS) is a measure of the degree to which these conditions are met. MPS is computed by combining the scores on the five characteristics as follows:

$$\text{Motivating potential} = \left[\frac{\text{skill variety} + \text{task identity} + \text{task significance}}{3} \right]$$
$$\times \text{autonomy} \times \text{feedback}$$

Moderators.   Job characteristics theory predicts that three characteristics of people are especially important for understanding who will and who will not respond positively to jobs that are high in motivating potential. These three characteristics are identified as moderators in Figure 2 and will be discussed separately.

The theory posits that the strength of an employee's needs for growth can be critical in determining how vigorously a person responds to a job high in motivating potential. It is expected that those employees with strong needs for personal growth and self-direction at work are most likely to appreciate and respond positively to increased opportunities for personal accomplishment provided by a job high in motivating potential. Employees' reactions to jobs high in motivating potential are expected to be affected by their satisfaction with aspects of the work context, such as pay, job security, co-workers, and supervisors. When employees are not satisfied with one or more of these contextual factors, their ability to respond positively to a high-MPS job may be severely

diminished according to the theory. Finally, JCT suggests that employees must have sufficient knowledge and skill to perform effectively on jobs high in motivating potential.

Outcomes.   Also shown in Figure 2 are several variables that are predicted to be affected by job-based motivation. When a job is high on MPS, employees are expected to be satisfied with the nature of the tasks in the job and also with opportunities they have for personal learning and growth at work. In addition, internal work motivation is expected to be affected by the characteristics of jobs. Finally, the model specifies that employee work effectiveness is likely to be high when jobs are high in MPS.

Job Characteristics Theory From a Job–Role Differentiation Perspective

If the framework developed earlier to differentiate jobs from roles is applied to job characteristics theory, our taxonomy would place JCT more in the role than the job domain. There are two primary reasons for this. First, the core job dimensions tend to be those that evolve out of the informal social environment rather than from the physical environment or from formal task descriptions. This is particularly true with respect to the three job dimensions that impact most directly on psychological meaningfulness—task identity, task significance, and skill variety. The first two in particular are primarily defined by the cultural values to which the job holder prescribes, at least in the sense that they are important to the perception of meaningfulness. Task identity, the extent to which the job incumbent works on a complete task and produces an identifiable product, could be defined external to the job holder by reference to the nature of the task. However, in the theory, the dimension is treated from the perspective of the job incumbent. Its meaning is not attached to the job in any absolute sense but is based on the job holder's interpretation. This interpretation is likely to be strongly influenced by other individuals with whom the job holder identifies (Salancik & Pfeffer, 1977). These persons may or may not be coworkers. In a similar fashion, task significance is highly subjective and very likely to be dependent on the social environment or culture that provides some basis for judging whether the job in question is likely to be perceived as significant. Skill variety, on the other hand, could be referenced in the more objective characteristics of the tasks rather than social perceptions. However, it should be noted that the measurement instrument developed to address JCT usually is completed by the job incumbent as the source for the description of skill variety and all other job characteristics.

There is a distinct difference between the JCT approach to skill variety and the approach to skill variety taken by those who design jobs from an industrial engineering or human factors perspective. The former looks at skill variety as a condition that stimulates the job incumbent to invest or not invest time and effort in the job through the perceptions of the meaningfulness of the work. The latter tends to view skill variety in terms of the extent to which the human abilities of the job incumbent are or are not overextended. In JCT, human abilities of job incumbents are assumed to be sufficient to accomplish the task—that is, abilities are taken as given.

A second way in which JCT tends to share more with roles than with jobs is in terms of its focus on the job incumbent rather than on the job. In general, differences in descriptions of the job obtained from persons sharing the same job title in the same organization can be attributed to two sources: (a) measurement error or (b) true task differences attributable to the fact that some individuals who hold the jobs have negotiated additional (or fewer) task elements in the social system in which they are located. JCT is much more likely than other views of jobs to take these differences at face value, as if they do indeed represent true differences in jobs when the incumbents see them as such. This focus is understandable because theory is concerned with individuals' reactions to their jobs, and it is assumed that the most immediate precursors of individual responses are the beliefs and expectations of the responders. The effect of this orientation is that, whereas other job views may focus on standardization and homogeneous clustering of responses across people to create jobs and job families, JCT pays little attention to job systems.

Two primary concerns are always raised with respect to research on jobs. These are (a) the nature of jobs in terms of their objectivity and dimensionality and (b) the impact of jobs on job incumbents' behavioral and socioemotional outcomes. An examination of the jobs literature, much of which has been focused on the job characteristics theory of Hackman and Oldham (1976), clearly reveals these two major areas of focus.

The Nature of Jobs in Terms of Objectivity. A great deal of controversy in the JCT literature has developed around the issue of whether incumbents' ratings of jobs provided on the *Job Diagnostic Survey* (JDS) are based on objective characteristics of jobs or on extraneous social or personal influences. The questions have been framed both theoretically and practically and have tended to be addressed in one of three ways. Framed theoretically, the concern is with whether or not ratings of job characteristics obtained from job incumbents on the JDS can be influenced by factors other than the objective properties of the job; framed practically, the issue is one of determining the extent to which such ratings obtained from job incumbents are isomorphic with objective properties of the job. Research on these issues can be clustered into studies (a) that have explored the degree of agreement between incumbents' ratings and the ratings of others, (b) those that have addressed the impact of social cues on job perceptions, and (c) those that have assessed the affects of incumbents' job experience on their perceptions of the key job characteristics of the model.

One set of research addressing objectivity focuses on the associations between incumbents' ratings of a job's characteristics and ratings of those characteristics made by others, such as peers, supervisors, job analysts, or researchers. Results of research on this topic are inconclusive. Correlations between job incumbents' ratings of their jobs and others' ratings of the same job have been as low as .16 (Brief & Aldag, 1978) and .36 (Birnbaum, Farh, & Wong, 1986) on one hand, to as high as .90 (Stone & Porter, 1975) and .91 (Griffin, 1983) on the other. Similarly, in some instances the correlations between the ratings of external agents and incumbents' reactions were lower than the correlations between incumbent ratings of jobs and incumbent reactions (Kigundo, 1980; Spector, 1987), but in most cases these correlations were the same or higher (Algera, 1983; Brief & Aldag, 1978; Oldham, Hackman, & Pearce, 1976; Stone & Porter, 1975).

The second approach to objectivity is the research that contrasted the effects of objective task characteristics with task information provided by social sources. In all cases, raters were exposed to tasks with known characteristics, or at least characteristics that were held constant across raters and then presented with social cues about task characteristics that vary in some way among raters. Again, results across studies appear inconsistent. Some studies indicate job ratings are affected by social informational cues only (O'Reilly & Caldwell, 1979), others indicate that objective task conditions explain nearly all the variance in perceptions (White & Primoff, 1979), and still others find social information effects that are contingent on third variables such as task experience or field dependence (Weiss & Shaw, 1979).

A final theme involving objectivity deals with the effects of incumbents' characteristics and experiences on their ratings of task characteristics. In these studies, correlations between employees' job ratings and their personal characteristics are examined for individuals who perform the same task. Since the task is supposedly invariant, any significant correlations obtained point to a lack of objectivity. Results from some studies indicate personal factors do influence ratings (O'Reilly, Parlette, & Bloom, 1980; Stone, 1979), whereas other studies suggest they either do not affect perceptions (Caldwell & O'Reilly, 1982) or do so in relatively weak fashion compared to objective characteristics (Ganster, 1980).

The most parsimonious conclusion to be drawn from these three sets of research is that the objectivity question remains undecided both theoretically and practically. Yet, in our opinion, this inconclusiveness may be due as much to asking the wrong question as to ambiguities in the research. At the theoretical level, there would appear to be two types of questions that could be asked about the extent to which incumbents' ratings of job characteristics map objective characteristics of the tasks themselves. The first of these asks whether factors other than objective characteristics of the jobs themselves, such as verbal statements by others in the work setting about the job characteristics or personal characteristics of the perceiver, can influence job incumbents' perceptions of job characteristics. The answer to this question is clear. Of course they can. This has been demonstrated for JDS ratings (O'Reilly & Caldwell, 1979; White & Mitchell, 1979) and is entirely consistent with a long history of research that shows that the perception of any stimulus is a function of characteristics of the stimulus itself, of the context in which the stimulus is placed, and of the perceiver. Thus, there is no need to continue to ask whether JDS ratings *can* be affected by factors other than the objective characteristics of the job itself.

Once it is accepted that job incumbents' perceptions of job characteristics can be affected by factors other than the objective characteristics of the job itself, the more interesting questions address the contribution of factors other than objective characteristics of the job to variance in perceptions of job characteristics. These questions can be framed in the strong or weak sense. The strong form asks how much variance in job characteristics perceptions is attributable to other variables of interest. The weak form asks whether a particular variable not considered part of the objective job contributes to the variance in job characteristics perceptions.

Unfortunately, both of these types of questions are flawed. The strong question suffers from practical limitations. As a theoretical question, it is a question about explained variance in perceptions in the population of jobs that are of interest to the job characteristics theory. This population of jobs is very large, so large that it is extremely unlikely that research on jobs will be able to adequately sample the population in a way that will allow for an acceptable empirical answer to the population question. Certainly past research that has calculated the percent of variance in perceptions due to social cues or personal characteristics of raters with as few as one job has not provided a reasonable answer to the population question. However, when the question is limited to estimating the percent of variance in job characteristics ratings due to particular nonjob variables for a particular job or a particular situation, the question can be answered, but it is of little interest beyond the particular setting under study. Even studies that do adequately sample the jobs, such as studies relying on large-scale, national data bases, rarely sample or adequately measure the kinds of contextual or personal factors most likely to affect perceptions.

The weak form of the question involves identification of variables not included as part of the objective characteristics of the task that contribute to variance in rated perceptions of job characteristics by job incumbents.

This question can be addressed empirically and is of interest. That is to say, if one is interested in using incumbents' ratings of job characteristics to indicate the nature of the job, then it is important to know what variables other than those in the job itself may affect the ratings. The weak form of the question simply attempts to demonstrate that a particular variable does, under certain conditions, affect such ratings. Observations of such effects are both theoretically and practically interesting.

Practical and theoretical limits in observing variance due to social or personal variables yields very little information related to the primary purpose for which all this research was undertaken—that is, the purpose of understanding the correspondence between incumbents' ratings of job characteristics and *objective* properties of the job. In spite of the differences in findings reported in the three areas of research on job perceptions reported earlier, the evidence is clear that incumbents' perceptions are often affected by other factors. However, whether or to what extent the variance is due to objective job characteristics cannot be addressed directly without clear standards for what is or is not an objective characteristic of the job, and such standards or criteria do not and will not exist. The absence of such standards is particularly the case for some of the job dimensions of the JDS which are, by their very nature, subjective. For example, the assessment of whether a job is significant cannot be defined independently of the value system of the person or persons making the rating. At a normative level, it is reasonable to say that certain jobs should be seen as significant by most people in a particular culture or subculture, but beyond that, there really is little basis for making any absolute claims about the significance level of the dimension. Thus, strictly speaking, questions about the objectivity of job incumbents' perceptions are unanswerable.

The approach of job-role differentiation (JRD) outlined in this chapter obviates the objectivity issue by noting that both jobs and roles are socially constructed and neither is objective. Jobs are social constructions of the prime beneficiaries or their agents, and roles are social constructions of the actors in the job incumbents' role set, including him or herself. The meaning attributed to consensus or agreement between job incumbents' perceptions of job characteristics will vary depending on whether job or role elements are being addressed. For example, for jobs where prime beneficiaries or their agents have formalized the job characteristics and described them in some written document, agreement between job incumbents' perceptions and the public descriptions may be attributed to the accuracy of incumbents' perceptions. However, if the job characteristics are ones that fit the role definition and have emerged from the dynamic interaction among individuals in a particular work setting, then the incumbents' perceptions should be just as valid as those of any other of a number of actors in that setting. Also, a lack of agreement between incumbents' self-reports of task characteristics and some specific group of others (e.g., coworkers) may not reflect lack of agreement with other sources (e.g., supervisors). Moreover, lack of agreement may not reflect inaccuracy of perceptions inherent in one party or another as much as it reflects the recognition of power differentials; incumbents may conform to the emergent task elements thrust upon them from a more powerful source but may ignore task elements emerging from less powerful ones.

With respect to roles, social and personal influences on perceptions can hardly be treated as error; they represent legitimate sources of emergent task elements. JRD helps to suggest where such influences will be most pronounced. Given the formality with which established elements are treated, we would expect that it is primarily the emergent elements of the role that will be susceptible to this kind of influence.

The O'Reilly et al. (1980) study, for example, dealt with a role (public health nurse working in the field) where there was likely to be significantly more variance in emergent task elements. The nature of the work, the supervision (or lack thereof), and the context in which it took place were highly conducive to role expansion or contraction. Under these conditions, characteristics of the person and the context were likely to profoundly influence responses to the JDS, such that different incumbents were likely to rate the job differently. Rather than interpreting the differences as perceptual bias, however, JRD suggests that these differences may be real and could be traced to differences in emergent task elements.

However, the Ganster (1980) study, which dealt with assembly tasks in a lab setting with college students, was not very conducive to role expansion or contraction. Under these conditions, only established task elements (which do not vary across individuals) affected responses to the JDS, and there was little in the way of emergent task elements to create variation among respondents.

In this discussion we do not mean to imply that the established job elements constitute the "true score" or are unchangeable. Rather, the research questions raised now turn to the amount and nature of the influence going from one social source to the other. Power differences and the fact that established elements are formalized and written down ensures influence of the prime beneficiaries on incumbents.

However, a great deal of influence also goes the other way because of the remoteness of the prime beneficiaries to the environment in which the jobs must be enacted. This occurs most dramatically when interviews, observations, or questionnaires of job incumbents are used to "update" job analyses. It is here where the JRD approach is also relevant for the job-analytic approach to jobs. The job-analytic approach to jobs, because it is completely inductive, will inevitably capture both established and emergent task elements in the process of collecting data on the jobs. Although obviously not using the terms that we are using here, researchers in the job-analytic school have hardly been insensitive to the fact that the source of the data can affect the description of the job. It is not surprising, therefore, that a parallel literature dealing with agreement among raters on job ratings (e.g., incumbents, supervisors, or external agents) appears in that literature (Cornelius, DeNisi, & Blencoe, 1979; Hazel, Madden, & Christal, 1964; Meyer, 1959; Smith & Hakel, 1979). This line of research, however, is rarely cited by investigators doing essentially the same work in the area of job characteristics theory.

Over time, job-analytic practices inevitably lead to changes in the classification of emergent task elements, such that emergent elements often become established elements that are written into formal job descriptions. It could also be the case that former elements that might have been established by the prime beneficiaries may disappear altogether. The conditions under which this is most likely to occur and when it is most likely to enhance organizational effectiveness would seem a critical matter to pursue. Under certain conditions this may be a very adaptive response which allows a large organization to stay in tune with its environment and thus promote the goals sought by the prime beneficiaries. In other instances, it could become a form of abdication on the part of the prime beneficiaries that may eventually lead to severe goal conflicts among organizational subgroups and organizational declines. A redirection of research along lines of exploring the movement of elements from jobs to roles and vice versa would seem very informative. It would also promote the use of research techniques such as archival analysis and content analysis (e.g., of formal job descriptions at various times in an organization's history),

which to date have received little attention in this area.

Job Dimensionality.   There has been much research directed at the dimensionality of jobs (Campion & Thayer, 1985; McCormick et al., 1972; and Wood, 1986, to name a few). This has been no less true with the research spawned by the job characteristics theory.

Unlike many theories of jobs, the presentation of JCT occurred simultaneously with that of a measurement instrument developed for the theory, the *Job Diagnostic Survey* (JDS; Hackman & Oldham, 1976). The availability of the instrument had a strong impact on subsequent research. First, it restricted the types of issues that were researched. For example, there have been over 30 empirical tests of *growth need strength* (GNS) as a moderator of the relationship between characteristics of jobs and job incumbents' responses to them, but there have been few tests of other individual differences variables that might affect these relationships, such as contextual satisfaction or ability. The JDS contains a measure of GNS but not of these other measures. Thus, almost all questions regarding possible effects of individual differences in job settings involved GNS as the individual difference.

A second effect of the simultaneous occurrence of the theory and the measure was the tendency to confound criticisms of the theory with criticisms of the measure. This was particularly true regarding objectivity and dimensionality. Regarding objectivity, the theory was often criticized for purporting to deal with objective properties of the job when in fact, from the outset, it was addressing incumbents' perceptions of jobs (Roberts & Glick, 1981).

Similarly, care must be taken in reading the literature to disentangle theoretical issues from measurement ones with respect to the nature and number of job dimensions. Fortunately, dimensionality research has also been conducted on the *Job Characteristic Inventory*

(JCI; Sims, Szilagy, & Keller, 1976), a widely used alternative to the JDS.

Factor-analytic studies of the dimensionality of the JDS and JCI have failed to converge on any one factor solution. While a few studies have confirmed the presence of the five dimensions suggested by the theory (Brass, 1979; R. Katz, 1978; Lee & Klein, 1982), most have not (Champoux, 1978; Dunham, 1976; Dunham, Aldag, & Brief, 1977; Gaines & Jermier, 1983; O'Reilly et al., 1980; Pierce & Dunham, 1978; Pokorney, Gilmore, & Beehr, 1980; Rousseau, 1977; Sekaran & Trafton, 1978), and for the ones that have not, there was little consistency in the factors that were obtained. Explanations for the inconsistency have been traced both to characteristics of the items of the measuring instruments, such as the presence of negatively loaded items (Idaszak & Drasgow, 1987; Kulik, Oldham, & Langer, 1988) and to sample characteristics such as age, education, and status (Fried & Ferris, 1986).

The research on the dimensionality as viewed from the standpoint of JCT is one of the clearest areas for which a distinction between jobs and roles would be beneficial. In spite of the fact that the factor-analytic studies investigating dimensionality were interested in the dimensions of jobs, almost without exception (e.g., Birnbaum et al., 1986) these studies have used *persons* rather than *jobs* as the unit of analysis. That is to say, job incumbents' ratings of job characteristics were factor analyzed without regard for the jobs held by those job incumbents. In some cases, job incumbents all were in the same job or were from as few as two or three jobs (Evans, Kiggundu, & House, 1979; Orpen, 1979; Pokorney et al., 1980). In the worst case, when only one job is used, the intercorrelations among the ratings of job dimensions are likely to be highly dependent on the idiosyncratic nature of that job. Thus, little or no information is gained about the dimensionality of jobs in any population that would be of interest to those concerned

about job design or work motivation. Given the inattention that has been paid to the sampling of jobs, it is not surprising that the literature on dimensionality is inconclusive.

Although making a clear distinction between jobs and roles as has been suggested in this chapter does not provide clear answers to the specific content of job dimensions or to the number of dimensions that is most appropriate, it does structure the approach to job and role dimensionality. Most importantly for asking questions about the dimensionality of jobs, the unit of analysis must be the job. Each case in the analysis should be a job, and each job should be represented once and only once in the analysis. To be consistent with JRD as developed here, we would also suggest that the content of job dimensions should consist of those elements that are used to create the formal job system by the prime beneficiaries or their agents. Dimensions of roles, on the other hand, could be explored within jobs. In this case, the individual differences in perceptions of role dimensions when on jobs with identical job elements provide the basis for role dimensions, although the variance between individuals may be due to things other than the roles, such as response styles or rating errors.

Job–role differentiation (JRD) moves the focus away from the five core characteristics of jobs by placing the emphasis on a universe of elements partitioned into two groups and labeled jobs and roles. Once the universe of task elements is defined, determining the number of dimensions may be useful in terms of parsimony of description. However, most of the factors will be a function of the choice of instrument used to delineate the elements. For example, McCormick et al. (1972) described a universe with 194 elements and 33 dimensions, and Campion and Thayer (1985) described a universe with 70 elements and 4 dimensions. Whether one system of condensation is a better representation of the universe described by the instrument than another is much less important than the comprehensiveness of the instrument itself. Moreover, for certain purposes (e.g., increasing satisfaction), because of the strong relationship between the core characteristics and satisfaction, it may be useful to aggregate various task elements by the core characteristics they influence. The purpose under such conditions is one of control rather than description, and the condensed structure best suited for one purpose is unlikely to be the best for other purposes. If the goal is mapping individuals' implicit theories about job characteristics, other factor schemes will prove more useful (e.g., Stone & Gueutal, 1985). If the goal is job evaluation, still another scheme may be best (Hay, 1981). Any system for reducing the number of elements is simply a taxonomy, and the "goodness" of the taxonomy is judged in terms of its usefulness for the purpose for which it was proposed.

One final point regarding the dimensionality of jobs and JCT is that the whole issue takes on less importance for JCT when two points are considered. First, the five core characteristics have typically been combined into a unitary composite, or the *motivational potential score* (MPS) through either a simple additive formula or the multiplicative formula; the empirical evidence suggests that it does not matter a great deal which linear combination is used (Arnold & House, 1980; Ferris & Gilmore, 1985; Hackman & Oldham, 1976; Umstot, Bell, & Mitchell, 1976). Second, no differential predictions are made for any one core characteristic and outcomes. For these reasons, the integrity of any one core characteristic is simply not that critical.

Impact of Jobs on Job Incumbents

Impact of Jobs on Socioemotional Outcomes. JCT originally predicted that job characteristics affect employees' satisfaction with the work, intrinsic motivation, and performance. Without question, the evidence for a relationship between perceived task scope and satisfaction

is strong (Fried & Ferris, 1986; Stone, 1986), often accounting for over 50 percent of the variance in various facets of satisfaction.

One theme of research within this area dealt with exploring the degree to which this strong relationship was artifactual—that is, a function of *common method variance* (Roberts & Glick, 1981) or *priming effects* (Salancik & Pfeffer, 1977). The literature in this area has not been highly supportive of these alternative explanations. For example, as already mentioned, several studies indicate that observers' ratings of job characteristics explain about as much variance in incumbents' satisfaction as do incumbents' own ratings (Birnbaum et al., 1986; Oldham et al., 1976; Stone & Porter, 1975). Moreover, the observed relationships between task characteristics and satisfaction were no higher in field settings than in laboratory settings where tasks were manipulated (Stone, 1986). This finding questions the impact of common method variance, since this source of variance should be inflated in field relationships (where measures of task characteristics and outcomes were both obtained from self-reports) relative to those in the laboratory (where outcomes were measured with self-reports, but task characteristics were manipulated). Research exploring the impact of priming as an explanation for task characteristics–satisfaction relationships has also been unsupportive (Brief & Aldag, 1978; Spector & Michaels, 1983; Stone & Gueutal, 1984).

Another theme in the literature on satisfaction and task characteristics deals with the potential reciprocal relationship between job characteristics and satisfaction. Several studies have examined the possibility that satisfaction could cause enhanced perceptions of task characteristics, and results from these studies are generally supportive of this position (Adler, Skov, & Salvemeni, 1986; Caldwell & O'Reilly, 1982; Hogan & Martell, 1987; James & Jones, 1980; James & Tetrick, 1986; O'Reilly & Caldwell, 1979). From a JRD perspective, one way this could result is from a process whereby individuals who are satisfied with the work tend to take on more emergent elements, resulting in the eventual development of a role with increased task scope.

The final and most pervasive theme regarding affective outcomes deals with the moderating influences of GNS on the relationship between task characteristics and satisfaction. The evidence here has been reviewed elsewhere in no fewer than seven articles: four traditional narrative reviews (Graen, Scandura, & Graen, 1986; Griffen, Welsh, & Moorehead, 1981; O'Brien, 1982; Roberts & Glick, 1981) and three meta-analytic ones (Fried & Ferris, 1986; Loher, Noe, Moeller, & Fitzgerald, 1985; Spector, 1987). The four narrative reviews all concluded that there was at best very weak support for the moderating effects of GNS. The three meta-analytic reviews were more supportive of the proposed moderating effect; however, each of these reviews came to slightly different conclusions regarding specifics about the nature of the interaction.

Viewed from the perspective of JRD, GNS is a variable that would be more likely to directly affect task scope, as opposed to functioning as a moderator variable of the task scope–outcome relationship. The direct affect also would be true for knowledge, skills, and abilities (KSA), moderators that were proposed in the original theory but which received much less attention than GNS. Specifically, given that within jobs the established task elements are fixed, individuals with high GNS and high KSA would be more likely to take on additional emergent task elements. Although such main effects have not been the focus of JCT researchers, it is often the case that the main effects for GNS on outcomes are stronger empirically than their moderating effects (Champoux, 1980; Pierce, Dunham, & Blackburn, 1979; Pokorney et al., 1980).

The Impact of Job Characteristics on Performance. The proposition that job characteristics would be related to performance has received much weaker empirical support (Fried & Ferris, 1987; Stone, 1986). Fried and Ferris (1987) note that the strongest relationship between task characteristics and performance deals with task identity, where the 90 percent credibility value for the average correlation is a mere .13. Fried and Ferris divided the 13 studies that examine the task characteristics performance relationship into two subgroups: cross-sectional (or what they refer to as nonmanipulative) and longitudinal (manipulative).

Looking at research reviewed by Fried and Ferris from a JRD perspective suggests that the performance studies might better be divided into three subgroups: cross-sectional with single job categories, longitudinal with a single job, and cross-sectional with multiple jobs. Currently the tasks characteristics literature does not recognize the conceptual difference underlying these three types of studies. However, the approach to JRD developed here highlights their difference. Moreover, JRD highlights the fact that the divisions among these studies are not just methodological, but instead reflect fundamental differences in how jobs are conceptualized.

First, turning to the longitudinal or manipulative studies, it would appear that researchers here are interpreting JCT as a theory of what JRD refers to as jobs. The rationale for a task complexity–performance relationship comes directly from JCT. That is, according to JCT, the scope of the job has a positive impact on the psychological state of the incumbent and in turn motivates the person's performance motivation (Griffin, 1981). It is an approach to jobs that is consistent with JRD theory because the task is reestablished for all job incumbents in a similar fashion.

However, when one looks at the cross-sectional studies with single job categories, it appears that researchers have interpreted JCT as a theory of what JRD refers to as roles. That is, within a single job category, there is no variation in established task elements, and thus the only source of task scope variations is through emergent elements. The same rationale that JCT uses to explain why increased task scope may increase performance in a job that has been manipulated could still apply to studies of this variety. However, JRD offers an alternative explanation. In the JRD framework, differences in reported levels and job scope across people in the same job are viewed as a result of an ongoing negotiation between the job incumbent and members of his or her role set. This raises the possibility that the direction or causation may be reversed—that is, job incumbent performance may affect job scope or, to be more technically accurate, role scope. In this case, those persons who perform their role well may have their role altered in such a way that the role at time $t + 1$ has greater scope than at time t. This effect of role negotiations and expansion for those that perform well has been observed by Graen and his colleagues in the leadership domain (Graen & Scandura, 1987).

Comparing the results for cross-sectional studies versus longitudinal studies, Fried and Ferris found that the task scope–performance relationship increased ($r = +.23$) when longitudinal studies were removed from the analysis. Since the JCT rationale for a scope–performance relationship predicts such a relationship only for the longitudinal studies, it would be tempting to interpret this research as supporting the JRD prediction regarding reverse causality.

The third set of studies that looked at task scope—performance relationships—were cross-sectional with multiple jobs. A severe limitation of such research is the absence of a common performance metric across jobs. Performance units, both qualitative and quantitative, vary as a function of the value of the job, making it difficult to obtain high-quality measures that compare performance on different jobs. Some significant advances have recently been made in this area (e.g., Pritchard, Jones, Roth, Stuebing, & Ekeberg, 1988), but most past research has not provided very good ways

for combining performance data across tasks and removing the task effects on performance.

Theory and Research on Role Characteristics

In contrast to the work on jobs where there are major differences in the three schools of thought on the construct itself, views of roles all share the same overall perspective. At the most basic level, roles exist in the belief system of one or more persons. The beliefs that comprise the role, at the very minimum, relate to the behaviors of persons with whom the role is associated. In addition, although roles themselves are patterns of individual behaviors where the behaviors can be described in quantitative and qualitative terms (Naylor et al., 1980), role theories or models have focused less on the content of the roles than on the process by which roles are developed, transmitted, and enforced. The discussion of roles that follows will first present common models of roles, followed by a description and evaluation of research on roles in light of the job–role differentiation perspective adopted here.

Role Theory

The classic role process is the role episode described in the works of Kahn and his colleagues (Kahn, Wolfe, Quinn, Snoek, & Rosenthal, 1964; D. Katz & Kahn, 1978) and depicted here in Figure 3. This model is based on the assumption of an interaction between two persons—the person performing in the role (focal person) and another person who holds a set of beliefs that constitute the role (role sender). The role sender communicates this set of beliefs (termed the *sent role* in Figure 3) to the focal person. The focal person receives this communication in the form of the perceived role and responds to it by taking some action (role behavior). Finally, that behavior is fed back to the role sender and serves as

FIGURE 3

The Central Features of the Role Episode

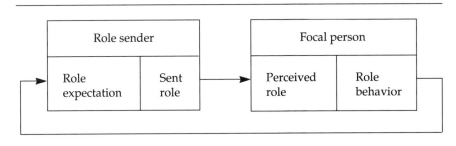

From *The Social Psychology of Organizations* (p. 196) by D. Katz & R. L. Kahn, 1978, New York: Wiley. Copyright 1978 by John Wiley & Sons, Inc. Adapted by permission.

an input into the role sender's belief system. A role sender's perceptions of the role behavior are then compared to some standard or expectation held by the role sender for the focal's behavior, and the result of that comparison may influence the sender's expectations for future behaviors. The role expectations, in turn, are the basis for the sent role as the whole process recycles. This basic process has been elaborated on by adding individual and organizational variables likely to influence it (e.g., D. Katz & Kahn, 1978) and also by recognizing that the role sender may represent a number of persons, including the focal person.

Graen (1976) termed the role episode a role-taking model and contrasted it with role making. The primary difference between the two models, according to Graen, was the passivity of the focal person. As depicted in Figure 3, focal persons are presented with role behaviors from the role senders, and they react to them. Graen and his colleagues (Dansereau, Graen, & Haga, 1975; Graen, 1976; Graen & Scandura, 1987) argued that focal persons are much more active than this. Typically, focal persons are highly motivated to possess roles in which they can perform successfully. As a result, they do not sit passively by and receive whatever roles role senders decide to give them; rather, focal persons actively attempt to influence role senders as they try to build a role that will be mutually satisfactory to role senders and to themselves. Graen has labeled this more active process role making.

Most recently, Graen (Graen & Scandura, 1987) incorporated role taking into an expanded three-phased longitudinal model of role making that he calls a *theory of dyadic organizing.* This model is presented in Figure 4. The behaviors of interest to the theory cover a time sequence beginning with the focal person's entry in the organization and ending when the roles and the focal person are well established. Although the model is directed at leader-member dyads, the descriptive phases need not be so restrictive. Phase 1 is the role-taking phase that is nearly identical to the role episode of Figure 3. It is seen as little more than the initial encounter between role senders and focal persons when the latter attempt to get some idea of what is to be done in the role. This phase is followed immediately by the second phase, in which focal persons' roles are developed through a series of behaviors involving sampling various behaviors, negotiating, persuading, and in general working out the nature of the role.

FIGURE 4

**The Role-making Model Adapted From
Graen and Scandura's Theory of Dyadic Organizing**

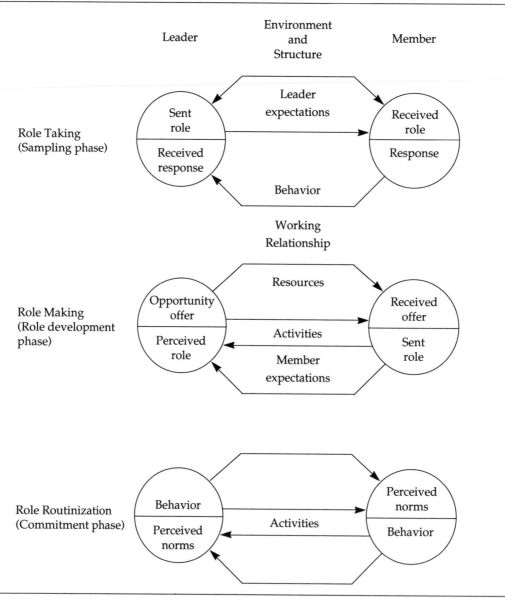

From"Toward a Psychology of Dyadic Organizing" by G. B. Graen and T. A. Scandura, 1987. In L. L. Cummings and B. M. Staw (Eds.),
Research in Organizational Behavior, Vol. 9, Greenwich, CT: JAI Press. Copyright 1987 by JAI Press. Adapted by permission.

According to Graen and Scandura (1987), the second phase varies in length as a function of both the nature of the tasks incorporated into the role and the persons involved in the role-making process. Eventually it ends, and when it does, it is followed by the third and final stage, role routinization. Here the relationships between role senders and focal persons stabilizes as both commit themselves to the expected patterns of behavior (roles) that the focal persons are to perform. Interdependencies are established that are understood by both parties and allow for an effective interaction between the parties without investing large amounts of effort defining and maintaining those understandings. If no understanding or commitment can be reached, either the role process remains in the role-making stage or the role relationship breaks down. In the latter case, one or the other breaks off the interaction necessary to maintain the role relationship. Figure 4 presents a schematic of the role-making process for the dyadic interaction between a supervisor (role sender) and a member of his or her work group (focal person).

The theory of dyadic organizing provides an excellent framework for understanding the dynamic nature of the role process. It captures the interaction between role senders and focal persons, and it provides a recognition of the active involvement of the focal persons and dynamic shifts in role behaviors. In particular, the final stage implies that role behavior can continue for extended periods without much investment on the part of either the focal person or the role sender in monitoring behaviors. The classic role episode suggests constant monitoring. Yet the cognitive demands of such a high level of awareness are not consistent with the more recent views of habitual autonomic responding (e.g., Gersick & Hackman, 1990; Mitchell & Beach, 1990).

Like all general models in the role area, Graen's model is more a heuristic structure for viewing role issues than a testable model of role

behavior. He has conducted research within the general framework of a model, the results of which are consistent with that framework (e.g., Graen & Cashman, 1975; Graen, Liden, & Hoel, 1982; Graen, Novak, & Sommerkamp, 1982). Yet this research is best viewed as a series of topics within the role domain, with data that are consistent with the overall view of roles; the research is not, nor was it intended to be, a critical test of the model itself.

Role Ambiguity and Conflict

Although the potential importance of roles and the complex processes represented by the role episode and its logical expansion into a role-making sequence has been well accepted within the organizational sciences, the attention given to roles has been limited to two particular role constructs: role ambiguity and role conflict. *Role ambiguity* refers to the level of uncertainty or lack of clarity surrounding expectations about a single role. Expectations about specific behaviors that are to be performed in the role may be unclear, and so may be expectations or beliefs about the outcomes likely to result from the behaviors (Cook, Hepworth, Wall, & Warr, 1981). Role conflict involves an incompatibility of demands facing the focal person (Cook et al., 1981). This incompatibility can originate from any number of sources, one of whom may be the focal person him or herself. For example, there may be conflict between the way the focal person believes he or she should perform a role and the beliefs of that person's supervisor or spouse. Likewise, there may be conflict between co-workers' and supervisors' or co-workers' and customers' expectations for how a particular person's role should be performed. The nature of the conflicting expectations is of two types: time conflicts and logical or ethical inconsistencies (Naylor et al., 1980).

There are a number of definitional issues that may influence the anticipated antecedents and consequences of role ambiguity and conflict. Unfortunately, these are rarely addressed. For the most part, research on these role constructs pays little attention to presenting precise definitions of what is meant by role ambiguity or conflict in the research. In fact, in a recent meta-analysis by Jackson and Schuler (1985), which provided an excellent review of antecedents and consequences of role ambiguity and conflict, the authors launched into the review before offering any discussion of the construct or operational definitions of role ambiguity or role conflict. Their approach was not atypical for role conflict and ambiguity research. Apparently it is assumed among researchers in this area that labels are so clear, or that the readers are so well informed, that definitions are unnecessary.

The failure to define constructs may be due in part to the fact that the vast majority of studies in organizational settings rely on a single measure of the two variables. The measure is that of House and Rizzo, (1972a, 1972b). Given its popularity, its psychometric properties and other characteristics have been investigated, and it has held up well to such scrutiny (Schuler, Aldag, & Brief, 1977). However, these investigations have focused on the factor structure and various estimates of reliability rather than on the construct validity of the scale.

Research.   Jackson and Schuler (1985) provided a good inductive review of the role ambiguity and conflict literature. Tables 1 and 2 summarize the literature of Jackson and Schuler's (1985) meta-analysis. For both ambiguity and conflict, the authors used identical sets of antecedent variables clustered into those that were derived from the organizational setting and those from the focal person. The same sets of consequence variables for ambiguity and conflict were focal persons' affective reactions and their behaviors. In contrast to other overall reviews (e.g., Van Sell, Brief, & Schuler, 1981), the contents of the

sets were empirically determined from an analysis of the literature rather than from some theoretical framework.

In Table 1, three sets of organizational context antecedent variables frequently correlated with role ambiguity are ordered in terms of their proximity to the focal person and his or her job context. At the most distant level, the organization, both formalization and level in the organization were found to correlate significantly with feelings of role ambiguity. The difference in magnitude of the relationship is consistent with the nature of the constructs addressed. Formalization at the organizational level refers to the extent that work practices are guided by rules, regulations, practices, and policies that make clear what is expected of persons in the organization. Presumably, the formalization also is likely to incorporate the nature of the role expectations sent to focal persons. The size of the estimated population correlation is consistent with the prediction. However, job level is believed to impact on roles more indirectly. In this case, it is assumed that, in general, jobs are more complex and less completely specified at higher levels of the organization. It is therefore assumed that the roles sent to role senders should also be more ambiguous. However, at least two conditions must hold for levels to relate to reports of ambiguity; job complexity must relate closely to role complexity, and levels must be closely related to job complexity. These assumptions are consistent with the data, but the likely slippage at each juncture means that high correlations between organizational level and role ambiguity should not be expected.

The remaining two categories or clusters of antecedents within the immediate work environment are those associated most directly with elements of the jobs or tasks of the focal persons and those associated with interpersonal interactions, primarily with the supervisors. With one exception, the correlations are consistent with the generalization that

TABLE 1

Summary of Meta-analysis Results for Correlates of Role Ambiguity

Correlates	Number of Studies	Number of Cases	$\bar{r}$	SD_r	"True $\bar{r}$"
Antecedents					
Organizational context					
Organizational level					
Formation	9	1300	−.31	.21	−.49*
Level	5	1675	.08	.07	.11*
Immediate task environment					
Task					
Task/skill variety	11	4089	−.06	.15	−.11
Autonomy	12	4196	−.23	.12	−.39*
Task identity	8	1992	−.27	.08	−.47*
Feedback from task	8	2195	−.22	.12	−.41*
Task/interpersonal					
Feedback from others	8	2194	−.35	.24	−.58*
Leader initiating structure	31	3705	−.28	.16	−.43*
Leader consideration	25	2854	−.30	.15	−.44*
Participation	18	2880	−.36	.17	−.55*
Individual characteristics					
Locus of control	8	2059	.17	.09	.28
Tenure	8	1663	−.12	.09	−.16*
Age	6	1421	−.17	.07	−.23*
Education	5	1227	.11	.11	.15*
Self-esteem	7	2918	−.21	.09	−.34*
Consequences					
Affective reactions					
Role conflict	47	10217	.27	.16	.42*
Job satisfaction					
General	56	10489	−.30	.16	−.46*
Supervision	17	3619	−.36	.09	−.53*
Work itself	28	4313	−.33	.11	−.52*
Co-workers	14	3579	−.25	.11	−.37*
Pay	18	4237	−.17	.12	−.26*
Advancement	16	3365	−.25	.10	−.40*
Tension/anxiety	43	7570	.30	.19	.47*
Commitment	12	2890	−.27	.10	−.41*
Involvement	11	2460	−.28	.10	−.44*
Propensity to leave	25	4974	.18	.14	.29*

TABLE 1

**Summary of Meta-analysis Results
for Correlates of Role Ambiguity (continued)**

Correlates	Number of Studies	Number of Cases	$\bar{r}$	SD_r	"True $\bar{r}$"
Behavioral reactions					
Absence	5	834	.09	.08	.13*
Performance					
Objective	9	1300	−.08	.15	−.10
Others' ratings	17	3320	−.08	.10	.12*
Self-ratings	11	1312	−.24	.13	−.37*

Note: $\bar{r}$ is the weighted average correlation; SD_r is the standard deviation for $\bar{r}$: "True $\bar{r}$" is the average weighted correlation corrected for the reliabilities of the variables and restriction of range in the predictors, using methods described by Hunter, Schmidt, and Jackson, (1982); *indicates that the 90 percent confidence interval does not include the value of 0.00.

From "A Meta-analysis and Conceptual Critique of Research on Role Ambiguity and Role Conflict in Work Settings" by S. E. Jackson and R. S. Schuler, 1985, *Organizational Behavior and Human Decision Processes, 36*, pp. 22–23. Copyright 1985 by Academic Press. Adapted by permission.

the more that social and task conditions in focal persons' immediate environments provide clear cues about what should and should not be done on the job, the lower the level of role ambiguity reported.

The relationship between role ambiguity and the variables typically labeled consequences of role ambiguity are very consistent. The parsimonious conclusion is that role ambiguity is an unpleasant state. For behavioral variables, the results are less clear; there was a low positive relationship between absenteeism and ambiguity. The relationship was negative for performance when the measures of performance were ratings but not when they were objective measures.

The most obvious impression from Table 2 is that these data look a lot like those of Table 1. From an empirical standpoint, the similarity is not surprising, given the fact that the two role constructs have been estimated to correlate between .37 (Fisher & Gitelson,

1983) and .42 (Jackson & Schuler, 1985) in the population when sample correlations are corrected for unreliability and range restriction. For antecedents, only ratings of the formal structure of the organization and task autonomy differed from those found for role ambiguity. For consequences, the pattern of results was nearly the same, with somewhat lower relationships between conflict and behavioral variables than was the case for ambiguity.

Methodological Limitations of Research. On one hand, a certain degree of comfort could be gained from the convergence across reviews of the literature and between role constructs. In particular, both role ambiguity and role conflict are frequently associated with negative affective states or with states in the environment that, a priori, are judged to produce uncertainty either about what the person is supposed to do or about the consequences of displaying given role behaviors.

TABLE 2

Summary of Meta-analysis Results
for Correlates of Role Conflict

Correlates	Number of Studies	Number of Cases	$\bar{r}$	SD_r	"True $\bar{r}$"
Antecedents					
Organizational context					
Organizational level					
Formalization	9	1300	−.07	.20	−.11
Level	5	1675	−.05	.06	−.07*
Immediate task environment					
Task					
Task/skill variety	8	3275	.10	.11	.17*
Autonomy	8	3275	.00	.16	.00
Task identity	5	1178	−.25	.05	−.44*
Feedback from task	5	1381	−.13	.09	−.25*
Task/interpersonal					
Feedback from others	5	1381	−.18	.12	−.31*
Leader initiating structure	10	1839	−.17	.09	−.27*
Leader consideration	9	1709	−.28	.09	−.42*
Participation	14	2287	−.24	.18	−.37*
Individual characteristics					
Locus of control	5	1806	.16	.07	.27*
Tenure	7	1571	.02	.10	.02
Age	6	1421	−.05	.13	−.06
Education	5	1227	.14	.14	.19
Self-esteem	0	–	–	–	–
Consequences					
Affective reactions					
Job satisfaction					
General	37	6314	−.31	.13	−.48*
Supervision	14	3440	−.36	.08	−.53*
Work itself	22	4022	−.30	.08	−.49*
Co-workers	11	2893	−.28	.07	−.42*
Pay	14	3399	−.20	.08	−.31*
Advancement	14	3287	−.23	.11	−.38*
Tension/anxiety	23	4035	.28	.13	.43*
Commitment	11	2583	−.24	.14	−.36*
Involvement	10	2326	−.16	.07	−.26*
Propensity to leave	13	1915	.21	.11	.34*

TABLE 2

Summary of Meta-Analysis Results
for Correlates of Role Conflict (continued)

Correlates	Number of Studies	Number of Cases	$\bar{r}$	SD_r	"True $\bar{r}$"
Behavioral reactions					
Absence	3	424	−.01	.12	−.02
Performance					
Objective	3	769	.01	.02	.02
Others' ratings	14	3119	−.07	.08	−.11*
Self-ratings	7	1037	−.02	.12	−.03

Note: $\bar{r}$ is the weighted average correlation; SD_r is the standard deviation for $\bar{r}$; "True $\bar{r}$" is the average weighted correlation corrected for the reliabilities of the variables and restriction of range in the predictors, using methods described by Hunter, Schmidt, and Jackson (1982); *indicates that the 90 percent confidence interval does not include the value of 0.00.

From "A Meta-analysis and Conceptual Critique of Research on Role Ambiguity and Role Conflict in Work Settings" by S. E. Jackson and R. S. Schuler, 1985, *Organizational Behavior and Human Decision Processes, 36*, pp. 24–25. Copyright 1985 by Academic Press. Adapted by permission.

In addition, the relationship between role constructs and affect tends to be stronger with ambiguity than with conflict, and neither construct relates very strongly to behaviors.

On the other hand, a closer look at much of this research raises some concerns. The most serious of these relates to the self-report nature of the data. As has already been mentioned, both role ambiguity and role conflict have been measured on the same scale—a scale in which the initial development was aimed at creating two relatively independent dimensions. Yet, as has been mentioned, the estimate of the population correlation between the two constructs is approximately .40. Furthermore, if one compares the similarity in the pattern of relationships between role conflict and various outcomes with the same relationships for role ambiguity (i.e., the data of Table 1 with that of Table 2), it is clear that the discriminant validity of the two scales is extremely low. As a rough index of their similarity, we correlated the two sets of correlations from Jackson and Schuler (1985) reported in Tables 1 and 2 and found a correlation of .87. Thus, either the constructs are not independent or there is a great deal of method variance confounding much of the research using the House and Rizzo (1972b) scale. We suspect both conclusions are reasonable.

The self-report nature of the data raises another well-recognized limitation of the research when attempts are made to interpret the data of Tables 1 and 2. With the exception of two of the performance measures, all the remaining variables, both antecedents and consequences, were measured by questionnaire items that were administered to the same persons who completed the role ambiguity and conflict scales. Furthermore, with few exceptions, the antecedent or consequent variables were measured at the same time as the role measures, making the inference of causation implied in the labels antecedent and consequent extremely tenuous.

The solution to the problem of self-report measures is less apparent than its recognition. For task characteristics such as task variety and autonomy, a straightforward reommendation is that others besides focal persons provide assessments of these variables to reduce common method biases and tendencies for individuals to respond to all items in a consistent manner. Both method bias and consistent responding tend to inflate the observed correlation between attributes of tasks assessed in this manner and role constructs. However, subjective reports from focal persons are appropriate for measuring constructs that are themselves subjective states of the persons of interest. If role ambiguity and role conflict are construed as constructs of the focal persons' belief systems, they, too, are best measured directly using self-report measures. Therefore, those measures that appear most appropriate both theoretically and practically for each set of constructs are inherently flawed when used together.

Conceptual Limitations of Research.   In response to the common method problem, some have suggested that the role constructs themselves be measured by assessing role characteristics independent of focal persons (e.g., Jackson & Schuler, 1985). Yet the source for obtaining estimates of role characteristics is less a measurement issue than a conceptual one. Recall that earlier it was pointed out that role ambiguity has been defined as the degree of clarity or certainty surrounding expectations about a single role. Referring back to the role episode of Figure 3, such expectations are located in the received role box and clearly are part of the domain of the focal person. Therefore, the appropriateness of the answer to the source problem is dictated by the theory, and the theory implies that ambiguity is a perceptual construct residing within the cognitive framework of the focal person. We caution

that, in reaching this conclusion, we do not deny that certain conditions in the external environment of the individual are more likely than others to produce feelings of role ambiguity. Clearly, there are. Furthermore, learning about these conditions is both interesting and important with respect to role ambiguity. In particular, knowing that role ambiguity is associated with negative affective states and desiring to attempt to minimize role ambiguity requires that one understand the environmental variables believed to influence role ambiguity. Accepting such interest, however, does not imply that role ambiguity is a condition of the role environment but only that conditions in the role environment create behavioral expectation cues that vary in clarity.

The issue of external conditions versus internal states also is relevant to role conflict. Here, however, the response to the internal-external dilemma is complicated by the incompatibility between the stated definition of role conflict and the definition in use. We stated earlier that role conflict, if defined by researchers, is defined as an incompatibility of demands facing the focal person. Strictly speaking, according to this definition, role conflict could be defined external to the individual in terms of the number of roles that are being sent to him or her. However, clearly, from the way in which role conflict is treated in the literature, the conflict of interest is the focal person's perceptions of the incompatibility of the role demands. Just as was the case for role ambiguity, if role conflict is going to be a construct that can be addressed by changing conditions in the role set outside the focal person, for practical reasons it is hoped that some correspondence exists between perceptions of incompatibility and actual incompatibility in sent roles.

Redefining role conflict as the focal person's perceived incompatibility between role demands brings the definition more in line with the definition in use in the literature reviewed earlier, but, according to Naylor et al.

(1980), it still lacks one critical element for the experience of conflict. Omitted is the inclusion of perceptions about valued outcomes associated with compliance with one or more of the roles and noncompliance with the others. These authors stress that the primary interest in role conflict is in the effect of perceptions of conflict on the focal person. Furthermore, this effect cannot be anticipated without some knowledge about the magnitude of the value of the outcomes associated with each role and about the similarity of the outcomes.

To illustrate Naylor et al.'s point, consider two roles with a particular level of incompatible demands on the focal person, and assume that the person is well aware of the incompatibilities. Consider the following three sets of perceptions about the nature of the valued outcomes that the focal person believes are associated with compliance with each role:

Case	Compliance
1	Outcomes associated with neither A nor B are valued.
2	Outcomes associated with A are highly valued; those associated with B are not.
3	Outcomes associated with both A and B are both highly valued.

According to the commonly stated definition of role conflict, all three of the situations listed above are equal in the degree of role conflict they produce; under all conditions, the incompatibility of role demands was the same. According to Naylor et al. (1980), conflict is greatest in Case 3. In this situation, the choice of compliance with one role and noncompliance with the other should be difficult; for others it should not. These authors also pointed out the House and Rizzo (1972b) scale for measuring role conflict and ambiguity does not take into account the compatibility and magnitude of rewards associated with alternative roles. This omission may be one of the reasons that role conflict research findings are less consistent than research on role ambiguity. Although it would be valuable at this point to go back to the literature on role conflict to see whether the issues of outcome value may have influenced the empirical findings, it is not possible because of the fact that almost all of the literature used a single scale to assess conflict, a scale that does not take outcome values into account.

It is also the case that defining role conflict and role ambiguity exclusively in terms of the incumbents' subjective experience weakens ties between the role theory and interventions aimed at ameliorating role problems. That is, there were very strong links in JCT between the theory, the measurement device (JDS), and interventions based on all these (i.e., job enrichment). Thus far, we have noted that the link between role theory as expressed by either D. Katz and Kahn (1978) and the measurement device (the House & Rizzo, 1972b, scales) has not been as strong. Moreover, there seems to be no intervention efforts stemming from either role theories or measures that would be analogous to job enrichment's relationship to JCT and the JDS.

Conclusions About Role Ambiguity and Conflict.   All three major reviews of role ambiguity to which we have frequently referred (i.e., Fisher & Gitelson, 1983; Jackson & Schuler, 1985; Van Sell et al., 1981) concluded that, although there were some consistent findings across studies, a great need exists for theory development and more theory-driven research. All recommended that role ambiguity and role conflict constructs be embedded in a more fully developed role theory and research guided by this more richly articulated theory. Van Sell et al. (1981) made explicit their choice of theory in their elaboration of Kahn et al.'s (1964) extended role episode. Jackson and Schuler (1985) were less explicit as to the specific theory but suggested six ways to address future research (see Table 3). It is interesting to note, however, that none of the calls for extended theory raised questions about

TABLE 3

Recommended Issues for Future Research on Role Ambiguity and Conflict

1. The search for moderators of the relationship between antecedents and consequences of role ambiguity and conflict should be theory driven.

2. Causal designs should be used.

3. The relationship between objective and subjective role ambiguity and conflict must be explored.

4. Role ambiguity and role conflict should be viewed as separate constructs, and separate hypotheses should be generated for each.

5. More rigorous parsimonious theory should be developed for the antecedents and consequences of role ambiguity and conflict.

6. Role ambiguity and conflict must be more closely linked to related issues of task and reward ambiguity and conflict.

From "A Meta-analysis and Conceptual Critique of Research on Role Ambiguity and Role Conflict in Work Settings" by S. E. Jackson and R. S. Schuler, 1985, *Organizational Behavior and Human Decision Processes, 36.* Copyright 1985 by Academic Press. Adapted by permission.

the constructs themselves, particularly as they are operationally defined by the scales currently in use for assessing them.

We, too, agree wholeheartedly with the call for greater theoretical development and more theory-driven research. However, we differ from others in one respect: We feel that the theoretical development needs to begin with the constructs themselves before addressing the network of relationships with other constructs. To illustrate our position, consider the list of recommendations in Table 3. Rather than consider recommendations three through six as issues associated with role ambiguity and conflict, we have argued that these are part of the very nature of the constructs themselves. According to our position, objective conditions in the focal person's environment (3), the independence of the two constructs (4), parsimony (5), and links to rewards (6) must be assessed with respect to the nature of the theoretical constructs themselves. The first two conditions, a search for theory-driven moderators and causal research designs, can and should be pursued only after construct development has been addressed. The final suggestion, that the

two role constructs be linked to tasks, will be addressed in the next section as we bring together jobs and roles. In the section that follows, we suggest that the job–role differentiation perspective offers some means of guiding role research.

Roles From a Job–Role Differentiation Perspective

It was pointed out earlier that the role literature, in contrast to the job literature, focuses almost exclusively on the processes by which roles are developed and communicated and ignores the specific content of the roles. When content is mentioned, it is usually described in general terms, with little or no information about the elements composing the set. A second way of suggesting content is to infer it from some global label for the role. Examples of the latter are the inferred content of roles with labels such as manager, spouse, parent, or blue collar worker. Although a little more specific than the first, this second method is also extremely imprecise regarding role content.

Measuring Roles

We also noted earlier that existing measures of role conflict and role ambiguity show less evidence of discriminant validity than should be the case. In addition, we argued that since, theoretically, these constructs are subjective states of the role incumbent, subjective measures of each may be completely appropriate. This does not mean that these measures cannot be supplemented, however. Finally, we also noted that the current lack of emphasis on content in role theory resulted in a dearth of applied interventions for dealing with role problems. JRD's emphasis on content (i.e., in terms of task elements) helps suggest methods of measurement that would serve as useful supplements to existing measures. In addition, since these measures move us closer to the environment (as opposed to internal subjective experience), it also helps suggest interventions appropriate for redressing role problems.

Because of its focus on lack of knowledge, role ambiguity as measured in light of JRD could be assessed by asking incumbents how certain they are that various task elements were part of the incumbent's role. The ratings could be made on a scale anchored by "certain that it is" and "certain that it is not." The number of responses that the incumbent makes near the midpoint of the scale would give an indication of the amount of experienced role ambiguity. To measure role conflict, the same ratings could be made by members of that person's role set. Here, the magnitude of discrepancies between (a) the incumbent's description of the role and the description of the role provided by others, as well as (b) one role sender's description and the description of some other role sender, would provide an index of the amount of role conflict. Perceived uncertainties on the part of the incumbent that are not accompanied by differences in role senders reflect ambiguity caused by lack of information, whereas uncertainties

accompanied by discrepancies reflect ambiguity caused by conflicts in information.

The type of measurement procedure just described has several advantages, not the least of which is that it may increase the empirical discriminability of two constructs that seem to overlap more than they should in conventional measures. That is, since the index of role conflict is derived at least partially from sources external to the incumbent, this method should reduce the likelihood that response styles are the explanation for associations between these two constructs and may help establish a valid causal link between them.

Another advantage of the measurement approach suggested by JRD is that it could identify the specific social sources that are creating the conflict and thus allow for all assessment of critical contingencies. For example, the role senders that make up the incumbents' social environment may differ greatly in their ability to reward or punish incumbents. Thus, conflict between high-power role senders on the one hand (e.g., the prime beneficiaries or their agents who control pay or continued employment) and low-power role senders on the other, while technically creating a role conflict, does not create role conflict that affects the incumbent in any significant way. The same is the case for conflict among low-power role senders. Role conflict only becomes an issue when it originates from two powerful role senders. Perhaps the failure to distinguish between low-contingency or technical role conflicts and high-contingency or substantive role conflicts is one of the reasons that the role conflict research findings are more variable than the findings for role ambiguity.

By explicitly addressing the beliefs of other members of the role set about the role, JRD allows for the possibility that role ambiguity of the incumbent could be shared by the other members of the role set. Under these conditions, it seems less likely that role ambiguity would lead to low performance ratings.

Similarly, role conflicts could be recognized by others in the role set, and they may adjust their ratings of performance accordingly. Thus, JRD would not make predictions about the relationship of the role incumbent's perceptions of role ambiguity or conflict without simultaneously addressing the expectations of others in the role set. Conflict and ambiguity would seem to have their most deleterious effects on performance ratings when the incumbent is the only one who is experiencing the ambiguity or is the only one sensitive to the conflict.

A final advantage of the measurement we have suggested for JRD is that it provides the content and hence provides the direction for change. The method, when it uncovers role ambiguity or role conflict, simultaneously isolates the social source and task element creating the problem. Also, by distinguishing the relative importance of the element to the role, the procedure goes beyond distinctions of mere presence and absence. Thus, one can identify ambiguities or conflicts that may arise not because of the presence or absence, but because of uncertainty or inconsistencies in the relative importance of a given element. That is, in some cases, all role senders may agree that a given element belongs in an individual's role but may disagree on its overall centrality to the role. These kinds of disagreements regarding level of an element in the role may create much role ambiguity and conflict that may not be discernible in meaures that only emphasize presence or absence. Hopefully, by increasing the link between the theory (which specifies the task elements), the measures (which obtain ratings of the elements from different sources), and the practice of changing role elements based on this information, role theory may begin to have an impact on applied contexts that is consistent with the interest it has generated among researchers.

As has been mentioned, both role conflict and role ambiguity ignore the content of particular roles. Job–role differentiation retains content in the elements that comprise a role. In particular, from the job–role differentiation perspective, the elements of the role are both the bureaucratic elements described by the job and those behaviors that are over and above those specified by the formal job description; they are the elements of the job resulting from the interaction between the focal person (job incumbent) and others to create the set of duties and responsibilities perceived to constitute the role of the focal person.

Although this perspective still does not provide cues to what will or will not be the qualitative dimensions of roles (i.e., content), we feel that job–role differentiation does offer some useful ways to look at roles. For example, it suggests that, when descriptions are obtained of the actual behaviors displayed by a number of persons all holding the same job, these descriptions can be expected to differ for valid reasons. That is to say, the differences in descriptions should not be attributed primarily to error variance in the measures of the role behaviors for the role in question. Such differences would be expected as each individual role holder and the members of his or her role set negotiate a role for the job holder. If these differences are indeed valid differences due to the construction of each individual role, then the differences should be predictable from variables known to affect the role process. Research aimed at understanding and predicting these differences should be of interest. Furthermore, this perspective implies that job-analytic work that treats all within-job differences as error variance by calculating mean dimensions per job may in this way lose some valuable information about the nature of behavior in the jobs and may also generate central tendency estimates of behaviors on the job that may not fit well many of the jobs in the set. The extent to which variance in job behaviors within jobs exists and is predictable is an empirical issue that the job–role differentiation perspective suggests is important to investigate.

Converting Roles to Jobs

Combining (a) the job–role differentiation perspective on the nature of elements that are seen as part of a job and (b) those that are relegated to roles with Graen's (Graen & Scandura, 1987) three-stage model of role making suggests that different types of elements are exchanged at different times in the role-making process. We would hypothesize that, in the first stage, the *initial role episode*, established elements are exchanged between supervisors and subordinates (or any other focal person–role sender pair). These elements will tend to be the standard elements of the job as it was described to the applicant both as part of the hiring process and by the supervisor in the initial encounter with the new employee. In Graen's second stage, the *working-it-out stage*, emergent elements that we would classify in the role domain are added. Here the specific actors who have an interest in what the focal person does, the stakeholders, work with the focal person to establish the role as it is to be performed in that setting. Finally, in the third and final stage, the *investigation stage*, some of what were formerly emergent task elements become formalized and transcribed into actual job descriptions. At the same time, some formerly established elements may be dropped if the need for them fails to emerge regularly. This conversion of role elements into job elements is likely to occur (a) when there is a great deal of consensus on the part of all members in the role set that the element is required by all who hold that job and/or (b) if the prime beneficiaries decide that an element that "emerged" for one jobholder should be formally established for all. This conversion of emergent elements into established elements will also result from inductive job-analytic techniques used to describe the behaviors of particular jobs. Such techniques employ interviews or structured job-analytic instruments such as the *Position Analysis Questionnaire* (McCormick, 1979) to identify

the critical behaviors of a representative sample of job incumbents. The behaviors common to the sample of persons on a particular job are then used to describe the job. To the extent that behaviors emerging from the role-making process become common over all or apply to most of the people in a particular job, these behaviors will get added to the job domain when inductive procedures are used to establish job descriptions.

Conclusion

We argue that there are two systemic perspectives on what constitutes organizational structure as experienced by individual organizational members: the task/functional system and social system approaches. In line with this view, interactions between the individual's immediate task/physical environment and the social environment have been addressed most frequently in two nonoverlapping literatures: that of jobs and that of roles. Despite the separateness of these approaches and these literatures, the fact remains that both jobs and roles evolve over time as a result of the interaction of both physical and social forces. Today, both of these literatures encompass much of the same theoretical domain.

In addressing this theoretical domain, however, each of these two frameworks sees the interaction of organizational members and structure in slightly different ways. The job characteristics literature places a greater emphasis on content of the elements called jobs, whereas the role literature emphasizes the process whereby the expected set of behaviors labeled a role are established. The job characteristics literature stresses the physical demands of the task in terms of defining the reality of the job, and much of the empirical research conducted from the job characteristics framework attempts to establish the nature and objectivity of job perceptions.

The role literature focuses more on the subjective experience resulting from the process of sharing expectations among role occupants and role senders. The empirical research emanating from this is devoted almost exclusively to the constructs of role ambiguity and role conflict.

We attempted in this chapter to initiate an integration of these two literatures. The first step in bridging these two literatures was to more clearly differentiate between the two constructs of jobs and roles, since in our opinion no consensus currently exists regarding how these two relate. For us, the notion of prime beneficiary and the universe of task elements form the basis for integration we label job–role differentiation. Jobs are viewed as a set of established task elements that are objective, bureaucratic, quasi static, and grouped together by the prime beneficiaries or their agents. The requirement that these jobs operate in an environment that is subjective, personal, dynamic, and filled with many constituencies other than the prime beneficiaries, however, demands that an extra set of task elements be incorporated. These additional task elements are seen as emergent elements, and in the framework drawn here, these constitute roles.

This conceptualization of job–role differentiation was then used as a bridge to link theory and empirical research on jobs and roles. In doing so, notions of content and objectivity from the job literature were applied to the role literature. At the same time notions of process and social diversity in task expectations from the role literature were applied to the job literature. We then showed how our conceptualization offers a new perspective on issues such as (a) the nature of jobs in terms of their objectivity, (b) the dimensionality of job characteristics, (c) the impact of jobs on incumbents' socioemotional outcomes and performance levels, (d) the measurement of role conflict and ambiguity, (e) applied interventions aimed at ameliorating role problems, and (f) the nature of task elements exchanged at various stages of the role-making process.

Clearly, ours is no more than a first step in the process required to fully integrate these two long-standing literatures. Moreover, even in taking this first step, we realize that we have oversimplified and pulled roles and jobs apart more than researchers in either domain may feel is warranted. If, in coming to grips with this distinction, both sets of researchers begin to examine the other perspective more carefully, then we will have at least partially succeeded in our objective. A formal, well-developed theory of jobs and roles would need to go beyond job–role differentiation as presented here and deal explicitly with other issues, such as the explication of the universe of task elements. The approach as presented here assumes the existence of such elements without developing or adopting any one approach specifically. We have noted that such approaches exist and that the notion of generic task elements is pervasive in other areas of industrial and organizational psychology, but this is clearly not the same as specifying the universe itself.

In addition, a formal theory of jobs and roles also has to deal explicitly with the nature of rewards associated with jobs. Some of these will be inextricably linked to the task elements themselves; others may be connected arbitrarily. A formal theory must also deal with quantitative goals or expectations that may exist for performance on certain established or emergent task elements. These goals may not be formalized, even for bureaucratic elements, and thus could create additional problems for role conflict and ambiguity in terms of ends instead of means.

Although the development of an integrated approach to jobs and roles represents a large undertaking, we feel that the conceptual payoff from such an endeavor warrants the effort. We hope this review and reinterpretation of issues in the job and role literatures provides the springboard for such an effort.

The authors would like to thank Arthur Brief, Yitzhak Fried, Richard Hackman, Howard Klein, and Patrick Wright for helpful comments on earlier drafts of this manuscript. We are also indebted to Douglas Sego and Patricia Walz, who assisted in the preparation of this manuscript. Finally, special acknowledgment is given to Greg Oldham for his valued comments and insights on the job design literature.

References

Adler, S., Skov, R., & Salvemeni, V. (1986). Job characteristics and job satisfaction: When cause becomes consequence. *Organizational Behavior and Human Decision Processes, 35,* 266.

Algera, J. A. (1983). "Objective" and perceived task characteristics as a determinant of reactions by task performers. *Journal of Occupational Behavior, 56,* 95–105.

Arnold, H. J., & House, R. J. (1980). Methodological and substantive extensions to the job characteristics model of motivation. *Organizational Behavior and Human Performance, 25,* 161–183.

Biddle, B. J. (1979). *Role theory: Expectations, identities and behaviors.* New York: Academic Press.

Birnbaum, P. H., Farh, J. L., & Wong, G. Y. (1986). The job characteristic model in Hong Kong. *Journal of Applied Psychology, 71,* 598–605.

Blau, P. M., & Scott, R. S. (1962). *Formal organizations: A comparative approach.* New York: Chandler Publishing.

Boeker, W. (1989). Strategic change: The effects of founding and history. *Academy of Management Journal, 32,* 489–515.

Brass, D. J. (1979). *Effects of relationships among task positions on job, interpersonal variable, and employee satisfaction and performance.* Unpublished doctoral dissertation, University of Illinois, Urbana-Champaign.

Brief, A. P., & Aldag, R. J. (1978). The job characteristic inventory: An examination. *Academy of Management Journal, 21,* 659–670.

Caldwell, D. F., & O'Reilly, C. A., III. (1982). Task perceptions and job satisfaction: A question of causality. *Journal of Applied Psychology, 67,* 361–379.

Campion, M. A. (1988). Interdisciplinary approaches to job design: A constructive replication with extensions. *Journal of Applied Psychology, 73,* 467–481.

Campion, M. A. (1989). Ability requirement implications of job design: An interdisciplinary perspective. *Personnel Psychology, 42,* 1–24.

Campion, M. A., & Thayer, P. W. (1985). Development and evaluation of an interdisciplinary measure of job design. *Journal of Applied Psychology, 70,* 29–43.

Champoux, J. E. (1978). A preliminary examination of some complex job scope-growth need strength interactions. *Proceedings of the Academy of Management, 38,* 59–63.

Champoux, J. E. (1980). A three sample test of some extensions to the job characteristic model of motivation. *Academy of Management Journal, 23,* 466–479.

Cook, J. D., Hepworth, S. J., Wall, T. D., & Warr, P. B. (1981). *The experience of work.* London: Academic Press.

Cornelius, E. T., DeNisi, A. S., & Blencoe, A. (1979). Expert and naive raters using the PAQ: Does it matter? *Personnel Psychology, 34,* 791–804.

Dansereau, F., Graen, G. B., & Haga, W. J. (1975). A vertical dyad linkage approach to leadership within formal organizations. *Organizational Behavior and Human Performance, 13,* 46–78.

Dunham, R. B. (1976). The measurement and dimensionality of job characteristics. *Journal of Applied Psychology, 61,* 404–409.

Dunham, R. B., Aldag, R. J., & Brief, A. P. (1977). Dimensionality of task design as measured by the job diagnostic survey. *Academy of Management Journal, 20,* 209–223.

Evans, M. G., Kiggundo, M. N., & House, R. J. (1979). A partial test and extension of the job characteristics model of motivation. *Organizational Behavior and Human Decision Processes, 24,* 354–381.

Ferris, G. R., & Gilmore, D. C. (1985). A methodological note on job complexity indices. *Journal of Applied Psychology, 70,* 225–227.

Fine, S. A., & Wiley, W. W. (1974). An introduction to functional job analysis. In E. A. Fleishman & R. A. Bass (Eds.), *Studies in personnel and industrial psychology.* Homewood, IL: Irwin.

Fisher, C. D., & Gitelson, R. (1983). A meta-analysis of the correlates of role conflict and ambiguity. *Journal of Applied Psychology, 68,* 320–333.

Fleishman, E. A. (1975). Toward a taxonomy of human performance. *American Psychologist, 30,* 1127–1149.

Fleishman, E. A., & Quaintance, M. K. (1984). *Taxonomies of human performance.* New York: Academic Press.

Fried, Y., & Ferris, G. R. (1986). The dimensionality of job characteristics: Some neglected issues. *Journal of Applied Psychology, 71,* 419–426.

Fried, Y. C., R. Ferris, G. R. (1987). The validity of the job characteristics model: A review and meta-analysis. *Personnel Psychology, 40,* 287–322.

Gaines, J., & Jermier, J. M. (1983). Functional exhaustion in a high stress organization. *Academy of Management Journal, 26,* 567–586.

Ganster, D. C. (1980). Individual differences in task design: A laboratory experiment. *Organizational Behavior and Human Performance, 26,* 131–148.

Gersick, C. J. G., & Hackman, J. R. (1990). Habitual routines in task-performing groups. *Organizational Behavior and Human Decision Processes, 47,* 65–97.

Graen, G. B. (1976). Role making processes within complex organizations. In M. D. Dunnette (Ed.), *Handbook of industrial and organizational psychology* (pp. 1201–1245). Chicago: Rand McNally.

Graen, G. B., & Cashman, J. (1975). A role-making model of leadership in formal organizations: A developmental approach. In J. G. Hunt & L. L. Larson (Eds.), *Leadership frontiers* (pp. 143–166). Kent, OH: Kent University Press.

Graen, G. B., Liden, R., & Hoel, W. (1982). The role of leadership in the employee withdrawal process. *Journal of Applied Psychology, 67,* 868–872.

Graen, G. B., Novak, M., & Sommerkamp, P. (1982). The effects of leader–member exchange and job design on productivity and job satisfaction: Testing a dual attachment model. *Organizational Behavior and Human Performance, 30,* 109–131.

Graen, G. B., & Scandura, T. A. (1987). Toward a psychology of dyadic organizing. In L. L. Cummings & B. A. Staw (Eds.), *Research in Organizational Behavior, 9,* 175–208.

Graen, G. B., Scandura, T. A., & Graen, M. R. (1986). A field experimental test of the moderating effects of growth need strength on productivity. *Journal of Applied Psychology, 71,* 484–491.

Griffin, R. W. (1981). A longitudinal investigation of task characteristics relationships. *Academy of Management Journal, 24,* 99–113.

Griffin, R. W. (1983). Objective and social sources of information in task redesign: A field experiment. *Administrative Science Quarterly, 28,* 184–200.

Griffin, R. W., Welsh, A., & Moorhead, G. (1981). Perceived task characteristics and employee performance: A literature review. *Academy of Management Review, 6,* 655–664.

Hackman, J. R. (1969). Toward understanding the role of tasks in behavioral research. *Acta Pychologica, 31,* 97–128.

Hackman, J. R., & Lawler, E. E., III (1971). Employee reactions to job characteristics [Monograph]. *Journal of Applied Psychology, 55,* 255–286.

Hackman, J. R., & Oldham, G. R. (1976). Motivation through the design of work: Test of a theory. *Organizational Behavior and Human Performance, 16,* 250–279.

Hackman, J. R., & Oldham, G. R. (1980). *Work redesign.* Reading, MA: Addison-Wesley.

Hay, E. (1981). *The guide chart-profile method of job evaluation.* New York: Hay Associates.

Hazel, J. T., Madden, J. M., & Christal, R. E. (1964). Agreement between worker–supervisor descriptions of the worker's job. *Journal of Industrial Psychology, 2,* 71–79.

Herbert, T. T. (1976). *Dimensions of organizational behavior.* New York: Macmillan.

Hogan, E. A., & Martell, D. A. (1987). A confirmatory structural equations analysis of the job characteristics model. *Organizational Behavior and Human Decision Processes, 39,* 242–263.

Hollenbeck, J. R., & Whitener, E. (1988). Criterion-related validation for small sample contexts: An integrated approach to synthetic validity. *Journal of Applied Psychology, 73,* 536–544.

House, R. J., & Rizzo, J. R. (1972a). Role conflict and ambiguity as critical variables in a model of organizational behavior. *Organizational Behavior and Human Performance, 7,* 467–505.

House, R. J., & Rizzo, J. R. (1972b). Toward the measure of organizational practices: Scale development and validation. *Journal of Applied Psychology, 56,* 388–396.

Idaszak, J. R., & Drasgow, F. (1987). A revision of the Job Diagnostic Survey: Elimination of a measurement artifact. *Journal of Applied Psychology, 72,* 69–74.

Jackson, J. S. (1965). Structural characteristics of norms. In I. D. Steiner & M. Fishbein (Eds.),

Current studies in social psychology. New York: Holt, Rinehart & Winston.

Jackson, S. E., & Schuler, R. S. (1985). A meta-analysis and conceptual critique of research on role ambiguity and role conflict in work settings. *Organizational Behavior and Human Decision Processes, 36,* 16–78.

James, L. R., & Jones, A. P. (1980). Perceived job characteristics and job satisfaction: An examination of reciprocal causation. *Personnel Pychology, 33,* 97–135.

James, L. R., & Tetrick, L. E. (1986). Confirmatory analytic tests of three causal models relating job perceptions to job satisfaction. *Journal of Applied Psychology, 71,* 77–82.

Kahn, R. L., Wolfe, D. M., Quinn, R. P., Snoek, J. D., & Rosenthal, R. A. (1964). *Occupational stress: Studies in role conflict and ambiguity.* New York: Wiley.

Katz, D., & Kahn, R. L. (1978). *The social psychology of organizations* (2nd ed.). New York: Wiley.

Katz, R. (1978). Job longevity as a situational factor in job satisfaction. *Administrative Science Quarterly, 23,* 204–223.

Kiggundo, M. N. (1980). An empirical test of the theory of job design using multiple job ratings. *Human Relations, 33,* 339–351.

Kulik, C. T., Oldham, G. R., & Langer, P. H. (1988). Measurement of job characteristics: Comparison of the original and the revised job diagnostic survey. *Journal of Applied Psychology, 73,* 462–466.

Lee, R., & Klein, A. R. (1982). Structure of the Job Diagnostic Survey for public service occupations. *Journal of Applied Psychology, 67,* 515–519.

Loher, B. T., Noe, R. A., Moeller, N. L., & Fitzgerald, M. P. (1985). A meta-analysis of the relation of job characteristics to job satisfaction. *Journal of Applied Psychology, 70,* 280–289.

McCormick, E. J. (1979). *Job analysis: Methods and applications.* New York: American Management Association.

McCormick, E. J., Jeanneret, P. R., & Mecham, R. C. (1972). A study of job characteristics and job dimensions as based on the Position Analysis Questionnaire (PAQ) [Monograph]. *Journal of Applied Psychology, 56,* 347–368.

McGrath, J. E., & Altman, I. (1966). *Small group research: A synthesis and critique of the field.* New York: Holt, Rinehart & Winston.

Meyer, H. H. (1959). Comparison of foreman and general foreman conceptions of the foreman's job responsibility. *Personnel Psychology, 12,* 445–452.

Mitchell, T. R., & Beach, L. R. (1990). Do I love thee? Let me count… Toward an understanding of intuitive and automatic decision making. *Organizational Behavior and Human Decision Processes, 47,* 1–20.

Mossholder, K. W., & Arvey, R. D. (1984). Synthetic validity: A conceptual and comparative review. *Journal of Applied Psychology, 69,* 322–333.

Naylor, J. C., Pritchard, R. D., & Ilgen, D. R. (1980). *A theory of behavior in organizations.* New York: Academic Press.

O'Brien, G. E. (1982). Evaluation of the job characteristics theory of work attitudes and performance. *Australian Journal of Psychology, 34,* 383–401.

Oldham, G. R., Hackman, J. R., & Pearce, J. L. (1976). Conditions under which employees respond positively to work. *Journal of Applied Psychology, 61,* 395–403.

O'Reilly, C. A., & Caldwell, D. (1979). Informational influence as a determinant of task characteristics and job satisfaction. *Journal of Applied Psychology, 64,* 157–165.

O'Reilly, C. A., Parlette, G. N., & Bloom, J. R. (1980). Perceptual measures of task characteristics: The biasing effects of different frames of reference and job attitudes. *Academy of Management Journal, 23,* 118–131.

Orpen, C. (1979). The effects of job enrichment on employee satisfaction, motivation, involvement, and performance: A field experiment. *Human Relations, 32,* 189–217.

Pepinsky, H. P., & Pepinsky, P. N. (1961). Organization, management strategy, and team productivity. In L. Petrillo & B. M. Bass (Eds.), *Leadership and interpersonal behavior.* New York: Holt.

Pierce, J. L., & Dunham, R. B. (1978). The measurement of perceived job characteristics: The job diagnostic survey versus the job characteristics inventory. *Academy of Management Journal, 21,* 123–128.

Pierce, J. L., Dunham, R. B., & Blackburn, R. S. (1979). Social systems structure, job design, and growth need strength: A test of a congruency model. *Academy of Management Journal, 22,* 223–240.

Pokorney, J. J., Gilmore, D. C., & Beehr, T. A. (1980). Job Diagnostic Survey dimensions: Moderating effect of growth needs and correspondence with dimensions of Job Rating Form. *Organizational Behavior and Human Performance, 26,* 222–237.

Primoff, E. S. (1959). Empirical validations of the J-coefficient. *Personnel Psychology, 12,* 413–418.

Pritchard, R. D., Jones, S. D., Roth, P. L., Stuebing, K. K., & Ekeberg, S. E. (1988). Effects of group feedback, goal setting, and incentives on organizational productivity [Monograph]. *Journal of Applied Psychology, 73,* 337–358.

Roberts, K. H., & Glick, W. (1981). The job characteristics approach to task design: A critical review. *Journal of Applied Psychology, 66,* 193–217.

Roby, T. B., & Lanzetta, J. T. (1958). Considerations in the analysis of group tasks. *Psychological Bulletin, 55,* 88–101.

Rousseau, D. M. (1977). Technological differences in job characteristics, job satisfaction, and motivation: A synthesis of job design research and sociotechnical systems theory. *Organizational Behavior and Human Performance, 19,* 18–42.

Salancik, G. R., & Pfeffer, J. (1977). An examination of need-satisfaction models of job attitudes. *Administrative Science Quarterly, 23,* 521–540.

Schuler, R. S., Aldag, R. J., & Brief, A. P. (1977). Role conflict and ambiguity. *Organizational Behavior and Human Performance, 20,* 111–128.

Schwab, D. P. (1984). Using job evaluation to obtain pay equity. In *Comparable worth: Issues for the 1980s. A consultation of the U.S. Commission on Human Rights* (pp. 83–92). Washington, DC: U.S. Civil Rights Commission.

Sekaran, U., & Trafton, R. (1978). The dimensionality of jobs: Back to square one. *Proceedings of the Midwest Division Academy of Management, 21,* 249–262.

Sims, H. P., Szilagy, A. D., & Keller, R. T. (1976). The measurement of job characteristics. *Academy of Management Journal, 19,* 195–212.

Smith, J. E., & Hakel, M. D. (1979). Convergence among data sources, response bias and reliability and validity of a structured job analysis questionnaire. *Personnel Psychology, 32,* 677–692.

Spector, P. E. (1987). Method variance as an artifact in self-reported affect and perceptions at work: Myth or significant problem. *Journal of Applied Psychology, 72,* 438–443.

Spector, P. E., & Michaels, C. E. (1983). A note on item order as an artifact in organizational surveys. *Journal of Occupational Psychology, 56,* 35–36.

Stone, E. F. (1979). Field independence and perceptions of task characteristics: A laboratory investigation. *Journal of Applied Psychology, 64,* 305–310.

Stone, E. F. (1986). Job scope–job satisfaction and job scope–job performance relationships. In E. A. Locke (Ed.), *Generalizing from laboratory to field settings* (pp. 189–206). Lexington, MA: Lexington Books.

Stone, E. F., & Gueutal, H. G. (1984). On the premature death of need satisfaction models: An investigation of Salancik and Pfeffer's views on priming and consistency artifacts. *Journal of Management, 10,* 237–258.

Stone, E. F., & Gueutal, H. G. (1985). Am empirical derivation of the dimensions along which characteristics are perceived. *Academy of Management Journal, 2,* 376–396.

Stone, E. F., & Porter, L. W. (1975). Job characteristics and job attitudes: A multivariate study. *Journal of Applied Psychology, 60,* 57–64.

Turner, A. N., & Lawrence, P. R. (1965). *Industrial jobs and the worker.* Boston: Harvard Graduate School of Business Administration.

Umstot, D., Bell, C. H., & Mitchell, T. R. (1976). Effects of job enrichment and task goals on satisfaction and productivity: Implications for task design. *Journal of Applied Psychology, 61,* 371–394.

Van Sell, M., Brief, A. P., & Schuler, R. S. (1981). Role conflict and role ambiguity: Integration of the literature and directions for future research. *Human Relations, 34,* 43–71.

Weiss, H. M., & Shaw, J. B. (1979). Social influences on judgments about tasks. *Organizational Behavior and Human Performance, 24,* 126–140.

White, S. E., & Mitchell, T. R. (1979). Job enrichment versus social cues: A comparison and competitive test. *Journal of Applied Psychology, 64,* 1–9.

Wood, R. E. (1986). Task complexity: Definition of the construct. *Organizational Behavior and Human Decision Processes, 37,* 60–82.

CHAPTER 4

Human Factors in the Workplace

William C. Howell
Rice University and
U.S. Air Force Human Resources Laboratory

Human factors is an interdisciplinary field of science and application concerned broadly with user-oriented design. It is founded on the premise that integration of human and physical components is essential if the combination, viewed as a coherent system, is to function safely and effectively. Thus, its focus is on incorporating knowledge of human capabilities and tendencies into the design of systems as simple as hand tools or as complex as space stations. This system concept is essentially the same as the open system *model of organizations on which modern industrial and organizational psychology rests. In fact, work organizations constitute the environmental context for many important person-machine systems. In practice, however, human factors and industrial and organizational psychology have shown little of the cooperative integration implicit in their shared model.*

This chapter illustrates a variety of design issues to which human factors research and applications are being directed, as well as some of the more common human factors techniques. Featured are applications of direct relevance to the modern workplace, those involving advanced technologies, and those derived from cognitive psychology and related sciences.

Introduction

Historical Background and Development

FOR OUR PURPOSES, the human factors concept can be described as an adoption of both human and physical perspectives when designing things for people to use, whether they be simple hand tools or computer hardware and software, sophisticated weapons systems or entire office complexes and space stations.

The premise that one should consider human characteristics when creating devices to extend human capabilities or to increase safety and comfort seems almost too obvious to mention; indeed, it is as old as recorded history (Christensen, 1987). Like liberty and justice, however, "design for the user" has proved far more elusive to implement than one might expect. Consider, for example, the once popular three-wheeled all-terrain vehicle (ATV), the manufacture of which was halted in 1987. Thousands of serious injuries and deaths failed to convince its manufacturers that the design was unstable, while special reports pinpointing its deficiencies had little effect, nor did prominent coverage on national television. Corrective action was prompted only by the prospect of massive losses through litigation, and even then there was little indication that the defendants really believed the design was defective! The reason? Because the ATV met its engineering specifications, and in the hands of an alert and skilled user, it could be operated safely. Any problem, therefore, was largely the fault of the user, whose manifold and notorious deficiencies combine to undermine effective engineering through so-called human error. Similar justification was expressed in support of a game called "Lawn Darts," banned by the Consumer Protection Agency in 1988 after a long history of serious injuries, as well as unstable jeep-type vehicles, still on the market as of 1988, and countless other products.

This machine-oriented, or "blame the user," design philosophy runs counter to the human factors philosophy. Anecdotal evidence supported by systematic studies of design professionals (Eastman, 1968; Lintz, Askren, & Lott, 1971; Meister, Sullivan, & Askren, 1968) suggests that preoccupation with technical standards remains deeply ingrained in the belief system of the design community. Until recently, it was rarely challenged by the public either, the prevailing attitude seeming to be that ordinary people are in no position to question the wisdom of technical experts. To err, after all, is human, not "professional." More recently, however, prompted by several widely publicized design failures, such as the Three Mile Island nuclear power plant accident and the Challenger space shuttle disaster, multimillion-dollar lawsuits, and Ralph Nader's crusades, public confidence in the infallibility of design professionals is starting to wane. In any case, the balance still tilts strongly toward what Meister (1987) calls the engineer's "obsession with hardware" (p. 37). Consideration of the user cannot be taken for granted if design is left entirely up to design professionals.

The human factors philosophy, then, holds that the design process should include a systematic effort to consider how people are likely to respond to particular design features, even if that response constitutes misuse or error from a purely technical standpoint. Since predicting human reactions is the province of psychology, it is therefore no surprise that the principal body of knowledge necessary to implement this philosophy comes from psychologists.

The catalyst that first transformed concept into practice was World War II (Mark, Warm, & Huston, 1987; K. U. Smith, 1987). Problems posed by the massive buildup in personnel needed to operate increasingly sophisticated military hardware threw psychologists and engineers together on project-oriented task forces. Numerous instances were found in which equipment design virtually assured operator error. The B-25 aircraft, for example, had identical and adjacent controls for landing gear and flaps, a design guaranteed to produce its share of belly landings (Christensen, 1958). The B-29, "supposedly engineered with high precision," had similar problems in its computerized gun system (K. U. Smith, 1987, p. 2). Correction of such flaws, and the resulting improvements in system effectiveness, led eventually to the idea that operator and machine should be viewed as partners in a common goal-directed enterprise: the man-machine system.[1] Strengths, weaknesses, and tendencies of both human and machine components must be taken into account if the enterprise is to function safely and effectively. The best design is the one that maximizes the fit (Mark, Warm, & Huston, 1987).

Following World War II, the Department of Defense (DoD) continued to recognize the value of what was then called *human engineering*, or *engineering psychology*, and the concept spread to the large contractors (particularly in the aircraft industry) who supplied the military with its advanced technology. To this day, through its research laboratories, external funding, and general influence on our national research and development agenda, DoD remains the foremost advocate for the human factors philosophy (Meister, 1985).

But the field is no longer limited to military applications—nor, for that matter, to psychology. What began chiefly as an applied branch of experimental psychology assumed new dimensions, attracting converts from medicine, other sciences, and such design fields as engineering and architecture. By the late 1950s, it had acquired all the institutional trappings of a formal discipline, with its own journals (e.g., *Human Factors, Ergonomics*), organizations (e.g., Society of Engineering Psychologists, Human Factors Society, Ergonomics Society), and academic programs (e.g., the graduate psychology programs at Ohio State University, University of Wisconsin, University of Michigan, Johns Hopkins University, University of Illinois, Purdue University, and Tufts University).

Today, though psychologists still constitute the largest identifiable component of the field's membership (49%), they represent a minority; the majority of the 57 graduate training programs are now found in engineering schools (Sanders, 1985). Of the more than 4,000 members of the Human Factors Society, only about 47 percent hold doctorates (Knowles, 1986).[2] One can view these trends with alarm—as an indication that the foundation in psychological science is eroding—or with satisfaction in the belief that the gospel is now reaching the heathens. Regardless of interpretation, the current situation has exacerbated the inevitable controversies that have plagued the field since its inception.

One of these controversies has to do with a name: The field has had trouble agreeing on one (Howell & Goldstein, 1971). Some authorities, including most of the field's founders (e.g., Chapanis, 1976) and several more recent authors (e.g., Howell, 1985; Meister, 1984; Wickens, 1984) distinguish *engineering psychology*, a specialty deeply rooted in the scientist-practitioner model of psychology, from *human factors* or *ergonomics*, a larger multidisciplinary field that includes the former. Other writers, such as Sanders and McCormick (1987), make little or no distinction and use the terms interchangeably, with an apparent preference for *human factors*.

A second important issue concerns the emphasis of the field: Should it emphasize research and theory, or should it emphasize practice? Most "engineering psychologists" see themselves as applied researchers interested in the fundamental theories of human performance. So do many "human factors specialists," although a growing number may consider traditional theory-based research, particularly that of a psychological nature, irrelevant or at best an expensive luxury (Simon, 1987). Such practitioners would probably prefer a discipline rooted in detailed handbook-type prescriptions consistent with the model that guides the engineering professions (L. L. Smith, 1987).

It is no accident, then, that Alfonse Chapanis' (1976) excellent chapter in the first edition of this *Handbook* was entitled "Engineering Psychology," while this one is called "Human Factors." This reflects the real change within the field and the growing acceptance of the latter term. While conceding the title, I shall not concede the trend toward deemphasizing psychological research and theory. In the following pages, I hope to reinforce the old truism that there is nothing so practical as a good theory, while emphasizing that psychology is still the best (though certainly not the only) source of theories on human performance.

One other historical thread is worth noting. In the early part of this century, a mechanical engineer, Frederick Taylor (see Copley, 1923), and an industrial psychologist and her husband, Lillian and Frank Gilbreth (see Gilbreth, 1911), introduced industry to the concept of improving worker efficiency through systematic analysis, simplification, and standardization of work methods. *Scientific management*, as it became known, was the conceptual forerunner of modern task and job analysis techniques and may therefore be considered an early application of the human factors philosophy to the workplace. Though clearly adopting a man-machine system perspective, however, these early efforts were far more consistent with engineering than with modern human factors objectives: The aim was to make the human being more machinelike and reliable, not to adapt the machine to human characteristics. The focus was on the work rather than the worker, and thus important human characteristics were overlooked.

Nonetheless, the thread that began with scientific management is woven throughout the history of work design efforts. The analytic approach remains the cornerstone of all attempts to improve the fit between humans and technology; efficiency, particularly as it relates to productivity, remains prominent among systems criteria. What has changed is our understanding of human performance and the factors that control it, and we realize that often there are tradeoffs between short-term efficiency and long-term productivity. The cost of a technically efficient but humanly unacceptable design can far outweigh its benefits once accident rates, insurance and litigation costs, perceived stress, turnover, and deliberate disuse or misuse are factored in. Modern human factors applications in the workplace, therefore, take a broader view of human strengths, limitations, and tendencies as well as a more comprehensive outlook on criteria. Performance, ease of learning, safety, and user acceptance are now considered legitimate goals of human factors research and practice.

Human Factors in the Present Day

As noted earlier, human factors is no longer the exclusive province of the military. Clearly what is foremost to the field are its applications to high technology: designing human-computer interfaces (displays, controls), conducting human-computer interaction (HCI) research to resolve software development and expert systems issues (including those involving the interface), and contributing in a variety of ways to the evolution of robotics. Obviously, these applications extend to a host of nonmilitary domains, including space and air-traffic control systems, commercial and industrial systems, and consumer products design. In view of their growing prominence, high-technology applications and research will be featured more in this chapter than in its first edition counterpart.

Changes in the workplace brought about by technological advance have many implications for human factors above and beyond those associated with machine design. In particular, as the capability of machines expands, decisions regarding allocation of functions between human and machine become increasingly difficult. And as machines assume more of the intellectual and physical work load, the human's role must be continually redefined.

As we shall see, the human factors discipline has contributions to make in both function-allocation decisions and in the structuring of tasks that remain a human responsibility. For example, as humans become less involved in direct manual control operations and increasingly responsible for supervisory control over semiautonomous machine systems (Sheridan, 1987), they are relieved of the more routine and predictable aspects of work and are left to grapple with the more unpredictable and poorly defined aspects. Moreover, it gives them executive control over an increasingly powerful and complex array of "subordinates," the functioning of which must be well understood if they are to be managed effectively (Davis, 1987). Paradoxically, therefore, increasing the scope of machine responsibility and capability often increases rather than reduces demands on the human operator. Human factors researchers have consequently given considerable attention to human performance in monitoring, inference, diagnosis, judgment, decision making, process control, and other largely cognitive tasks (Christensen, 1987).

Though design, rather than training or selection, constitutes the principal thrust of the human factors approach, neither of these alternative strategies for improving system performance can be ignored in implementing the design strategy (Meister, 1987). Firstly, any design carries with it personnel and training requirements that must be considered when estimating or evaluating overall effectiveness. For example, menu-driven computer programs may be easier to learn—and therefore pose fewer selection or training constraints—than those using more sophisticated commands, but at a substantial cost in speed. Which design is better depends on the available labor pool, training costs, and the eventual importance of processing speed for the anticipated uses and users. Secondly, a major class of design "products" consists of training devices and systems themselves. If one

is to design a simulator or intelligent instructional system for maximum effectiveness, one must attend to both initial learning and transfer characteristics. In short, "design for the user" is impossible without some indication of which user one is referring to and what the ultimate purpose of the design is. However, since selection and training are well covered in other chapters of this *Handbook*, we shall omit further discussion of these topics here.

Another important comment on the nature of modern human factors thinking and practice centers around the system concept, alluded to earlier and addressed later in this chapter. The general notion that human and machine constitute interacting components, or *subsystems,* of a goal-oriented entity referred to as the *human-machine system* is fundamental to the entire human factors enterprise (Sanders & McCormick, 1987). As shown in Figure 1, it is often depicted as a prototypic model in which energy and information flow serially through machine and human components in the order *sensor-central processor-effector,* with the two components interacting at the sensory and response *interfaces.* At the *display* interface, human receptors receive or extract information/energy from the machine output; at the *control* interface, human response is transformed into the machine's input. Effective integration of the two major subsystems, hence effective performance of the entire system, is heavily dependent on interface design—the extent to which displays and controls are consistent with human capabilities.

This is, of course, a very incomplete account of a model that is itself only a partial representation of reality. For example, the whole system interacts with a surrounding environment; there are many places where feedback loops permit an element's output to influence its input; some processes operate simultaneously or in parallel; and information flow is subject to top-down (executive) as well as bottom-up (data-driven) control.

FIGURE 1

Schematic Representation of the Person-Machine System

Work Environment

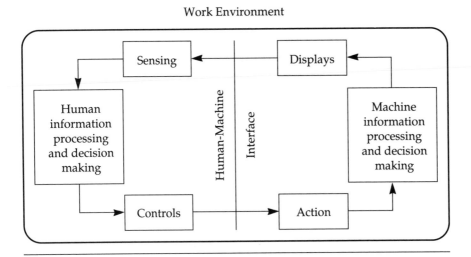

Nevertheless, the prototypic model is sufficient to convey several critical concepts:

- Systems comprise multiple interacting components.

- Interface design is of extreme importance.

- The human and the machine are reasonable candidates for many similar functions, such as information processing.

- Systems are usually hierarchical in that they consist of elements that are themselves systems, that is, subsystems of the whole.

The fourth point suggests that one may analyze system functions at various levels—the entire system, the human or machine subsystem, the display subsystem of the machine component, the visual system of the human component, and so on (Meister, 1987). In fact, this hierarchical arrangement also links the human-machine system to the larger system that encompasses the entire work organization: The former is simply a subsystem of the latter. Each operates as an *open* system in that it receives input from and returns output to its environment (Katz & Kahn, 1978). Thus, the work organization constitutes a principal facet of the human-machine system's environment. Since interaction with an environment is critical to the definition of system objectives—recall that systems are goal-directed entities—the work organization helps to define and monitor the performance of the human-machine system.

It is also this link between system levels that ties together human factors and industrial and organizational psychology. The objectives of the larger system (e.g., productivity, stability, safety, public responsibility, and acceptance) that allow it to function in its environment may be met through a variety of means, including personnel selection and training, organizational design and development, public relations, political activity, and of course human factors. As a practical matter, human factors considerations represent a relatively small portion of the total financial and psychological investment of most organizations, even in high-technology industries and military organizations in which the human factors profile is highest. Likewise, human factors plays a fairly minor role in industrial and organizational psychology. One survey of industrial and organizational psychologists, for example, revealed that only about five percent of the respondents reported human factors activities as among their job responsibilities (Prien, 1981).

To some extent, the low reported involvement by industrial and organizational psychologists may be explained by the relative autonomy of the human factors specialty: Organizations that take human factors seriously assign those responsibilities to specialists in the field. However, when one considers that human factors specialists constitute only about two-tenths of one percent of the U.S. engineering population and that only about 600 such professionals are actually employed in applications work (Alluisi, 1987), the specialization argument loses credibility. The only plausible conclusion is that despite its current growth, the human factors perspective is sorely underrepresented in most work organizations relative to other strategies for attaining goals.

If organizations and industrial and organizational psychologists subscribe to the "open systems" view, and indeed most seem so inclined, it is both strange and unfortunate that they accord both the human-machine subsystem and the substantive human factors knowledge base so little attention. If the substantiality of the knowledge base seems doubtful, I offer as evidence the *Handbook of Human Factors* (Salvendy, 1987), a 1,874-page volume filled with facts and theory, as well as a number of other excellent texts, such as those of Kantowitz and Sorkin (1983), Wickens (1984), Meister (1985), and Sanders and McCormick (1987).

Similarly, it is equally strange and unfortunate that the human factors community pays the larger system—the work organization—so little heed because of its preoccupation with the human-machine subsystem, though a notable exception is Meister (1985). Certainly it would enjoy a stronger position were it more cognizant of the facets of that environment to which industrial and organizational psychologists and organizational behaviorists are most attuned. Work redesign efforts occasioned by the current organizational interest in creating intrinsically rewarding jobs and expanding participatory management would appear highly relevant to human factors specialists. Only with difficulty, however, does one find such content discussed in the typical human factors curriculum, journal, or textbook. Fortunately, it does receive some attention in Meister (1985) and in Salvendy's (1987) *Handbook*.

The point is that human factors and industrial and organizational psychology, though sharing a common conceptual model, move in largely different orbits when it comes to work organizations. The reasons, traceable to differences in lineage and tradition coupled with modern guild issues, seem to have little rational basis and considerable maladaptiveness, especially since neither has made serious inroads into the long-standing dominance of organizations by financial, marketing, legal, engineering, and other nonpsychological—in some cases, antipsychological—interests. Neither "design for the user" nor "organizations are human" has yet replaced "watch the bottom line" in the Book of Organizational Slogans. Until they do, neither industrial and organizational psychologists nor human factors psychologists can afford the luxury of ignoring their common interests and values.

One final note concerns the predominantly theoretical orientation of the human factors specialty in psychology. As in much of psychology, the emphasis has shifted from the behaviorist to the cognitive paradigm (Shuell,

1986; Van Cott, 1984; White & Zsambok, 1987; Wickens & Kramer, 1985), and this will be reflected in the content of the present chapter. It is perhaps worth noting also that, under the leadership of such pioneering individuals as Franklin Taylor, Paul Fitts, Alfonse Chapanis, Donald Broadbent, J. C. R. Licklider, K. U. Smith, and others, the human factors discipline was instrumental in affecting this paradigm shift. Broadbent's (1958) "filter theory" of attention and Garner's (1962) information-theory conceptualization of human information processing were among the more influential early attempts to model human mental processes. Both grew out of research aimed at solving human factors problems at a time when the rest of psychology was at the height of its behaviorist preoccupation.

It is also worth noting that modern cognitive theory, much of it derived from basic laboratory experimentation, has proved quite useful in high-technology applications, such as in the design of interfaces, data base management software, and intelligent computer-assisted instruction (ICAI) systems (Eberts & Brock, 1987; Fotta, 1987; Kramer & Shumacher, 1987; Norman, 1984). Likewise, advances in computer science have been instrumental in the evolution of the cognitive models themselves, and most notably advances in artificial intelligence (AI). One recently developed program, *Soar*, illustrates clearly how far mental modeling has progressed since the 1950s. Based on fundamental principles of human perception, memory, learning, language, and reasoning, plus a growing recognition of how content experts function, *Soar* seeks to model the entire domain of human cognition within a common framework. Unlike the task-specific programs typical of AI, or the function-specific models typical of cognitive psychology, this model is theoretically capable of dealing in a humanlike fashion with any information processing situation a person might encounter in the real world!

While having some distance to go before realizing this lofty goal, tests of *Soar*'s performance in comparison to that of humans on a number of cognitive tasks have proved encouraging (Waldrop, 1988a, 1988b). Cognition, of course, has an identifiable locus as a subsystem in the overall human-machine system model.

Strategies, Tactics, and Methods

Roles in Human Factors

Human factors professionals assume a number of roles in the interest of improved human-machine system operation. Unfortunately, actual design, in the sense of participation at the earliest conceptual stage of system development, is rarely among them. Meister (1987) distinguishes five sequential but overlapping phases in system development:

- System planning
- Preliminary design
- Detail design
- Testing and evaluation
- Production

Following development, the system is returned to its sponsor or purchaser, where it enters a sixth phase and becomes operational. In each phase, there is a legitimate human factors function. However, even in the military, where DoD directives explicitly mandate inclusion of human factors considerations in the planning phase and elaborate programs have been articulated to promote this policy—e.g., the Navy's *Hardman* (1979), the Army's *Manprint* (Strub, 1987), and the Air Force's *Impacts* (Mohney, 1989) programs—actual development generally proceeds with little, if any, human factors input (Meister, 1987). When such consideration is incorporated, it is usually only after physical parameters and performance characteristics have already been set.

More typically, human factors specialists are called upon when testing and evaluation, or worse, operational performance of the system, show a high incidence of failure, particularly if that failure appears to involve human error, at which point they assume a system diagnosis or consultant role. The proverbial pound of cure at this stage can be extremely costly relative to the developmental ounce of prevention, and the system need not be particularly sophisticated for this generalization to hold. Increasingly, for example, consultants are being hired in conjunction with product liability and industrial accident litigation to offer testimony regarding defects of a purely human factors nature (Christensen, 1987). I once testified on behalf of a plaintiff whose prize bull had been killed by insecticide. Misleading instructions for product use and insufficient warnings against recognized hazards, including death, led to an award of $8 million in damages against the manufacturer. Labeling, of course, is an important part of the human-machine interface in consumer products.

Perhaps in the future the courts will succeed where appeals to rationality have failed, and organizations will show more inclination to incorporate human factors in the early stages of product and system development. Meanwhile, the job of most human factors professionals remains to identify and correct design mistakes—before or after litigation—but only after the damage has already been done.

Another major role of the human factors professional is that of researcher as defined in terms ranging from the basic theory-driven study of human performance characteristics to the task-specific, mission-oriented testing of particular designs. As noted earlier, debate over the appropriate orientation for human factors research—often couched in terms of the usefulness of the resulting research products—has always been vigorous. Some argue that virtually nothing generated by standard psychological research paradigms can be interpreted precisely enough to be of much use (Meister, 1985; Rouse, 1987; Simon, 1987; L. L. Smith, 1987); others claim that it is only through the kind of general understanding yielded by such research that we can hope to make progress in design (Wickens, 1984). Some take an intermediate position. Foley and Moray (1987), for example, argue that it is unrealistic and even misleading to expect factual material on human sensory and perceptual capabilities to be structured in simple tables from which one can predict how an observer will respond to a particular design feature. Yet they clearly believe such information is useful since they provide it in their discussion of sensory and perceptual capabilities.

The debate will never be resolved, and it is probably healthy that it continue in order to exert a sort of "checks and balances" influence on the field. We need the full range of research activities under the same disciplinary roof in order to ensure that important practical issues are addressed at a basic level and that extant basic knowledge is made available in some useful form (Mark, Warm, & Huston, 1987), even if that form is not the standard table some might prefer. Different levels of research are also called for at different stages in the design process. One might find broad theoretical concepts useful in planning and preliminary design phases, but empirical testing of alternative design prototypes necessary in the later phases.

Each of the three major roles—designer, consultant, and researcher—requires a different mix of human factors tools. The remainder of this section illustrates these techniques as applied to each role, which range from broad strategies to specific methodologies.

Human Factors Role in Design. The principal concern here is simply to gain a voice in the design process early enough to do some good. The techniques of greatest salience are strategic, but guidance along these lines is by no means easily accessible. Meister (1985) is perhaps the best source of ideas, most of which are drawn from a lifetime of personal experience. Alluisi (1987) suggests that the field as a whole should use leverage in the evolving computer-assisted design (CAD) and manufacturing (CAM) fields to promote the use of human factors expertise: Since "CAD/CAM capabilities are revolutionizing the design and development process" (Alluisi, 1987, p. 288), but are still in their formative years, the human factors discipline has an opportunity to influence the entire design infrastructure. The only difficulty, according to Alluisi, is that we lack the kind of data and data bases necessary to make that impact. Meister (1985, 1987) has voiced similar concerns and appears to concur with Alluisi in arguing for "a human factors engineering database with units of measure and formats that can be used by the design engineers 'at the bench'" (p. 288). However, this is exactly the kind of data base that Foley and Moray (1987) seem to be warning us against.

In sum, there are conflicting responses as to how best to overcome neglect of human factors considerations in system design. Given the discipline's small numbers (Alluisi, 1987) and lack of clout in most organizations (Meister, 1985), a brute force approach, which we might call the "beat 'em" strategy, seems to hold little promise. The alternative suggested by Alluisi and Meister, a "join 'em" strategy in which human factors data bases are generated according to the rules and preferences of those in control, has not happened despite 25 years of advocacy, and to some observers would constitute a serious misrepresentation of such data even if it had. Perhaps enlightenment will come without any strategy at all: merely as a by-product of that great consciousness-raiser, threat of litigation! What it once did for selection and training, it may soon do for human factors.

Human Factors Role in Consulting.   Once a basic design is in place, human factors specialists have less difficulty registering their input. In fact, their consultation may be actively sought on such details as where to locate a display, what kind of seating to provide, or how to position various controls. If serious human error problems have surfaced, human factors consultants are almost certain to be charged with a portion of the detective work. Among the most noteworthy instances of such failure diagnosis was the investigation following the Three Mile Island nuclear power plant accident in 1979 (Kemeny, 1979; Rasmussen & Rouse, 1981; Rubenstein & Mason, 1979). Analysis of the system and the task facing plant operators revealed myriad violations of human factors design principles that almost certainly contributed to the near-disaster. Needless to say, attention was paid to human factors consultants in the resulting modifications.

Applying human factors to an existing system or to a well-defined design is heavily dependent on analytic techniques, particularly those involving task demands of both a molar (e.g., sequence of operations) and molecular (e.g., display legibility) nature. A few examples shall be cited here to illustrate the point.

Function Analysis.   According to Laughery and Laughery (1987), three approaches are available for describing functional relations between system components: (a) flow analysis, (b) time-line analysis, and (c) network analysis. *Flow analysis* involves qualitative description of event or operation sequences that together comprise a function or process, irrespective of temporal or agent considerations. Ordinary flowcharts used in computer programming constitute familiar examples of flow analysis. *Time-line analysis* is principally concerned with the temporal and agent considerations lacking in flow analysis, the purpose being to describe how functional requirements are distributed over time for the particular agents. It is frequently used in the planning stages of systems or projects to help determine how to allocate work load among human and machine components. *Gantt charts*, which depict time along a horizontal axis and activities assigned to particular agents as bars arranged vertically at appropriate positions on this common time line, are representative of this type of analysis. Finally, *network analysis* includes dependencies and interactions between components and is considerably more useful for representing the actual complexities of many of the current systems. PERT (Program Evaluation and Review Technique) charts, popular in project management circles, are representative of this category.

More typical of the network analysis techniques used in human factors applications, however, is *link analysis*, which is used to evaluate layout or configuration options, such as in displays, work space, and office design. This approach focuses on the relations between design elements—displays, controls, workstations, and so on—associated with particular tasks so as to identify configurations most conducive to critical aspects of task performance. If a task requires throwing two switches in sequence, for instance, response speed would be enhanced by positioning them in close proximity to one another; accuracy, however, would require that they be clearly distinguishable and perhaps positioned in accordance with a common sequence rule. A good illustration of link analysis is shown in a study by Fitts, Jones, and Milton (1950) aimed at improving the location of aircraft instruments. In this early application of human factors, these researchers indexed the relations between instruments during execution of particular aircraft maneuvers by recording pilot eye fixations. From link diagrams of the sort illustrated in Figure 2, they were able to determine the arrangement of instruments that would minimize required movement time, that is, by locating functionally linked instruments close together. Although links can

represent many other kinds of relations, and determination of the best design can involve use of elaborate mathematical procedures and computer programs, the logic is essentially the same: The task is analyzed according to operations that must be performed relative to a set of physical elements, and the operational relations are used to identify the best arrangement for some specified criterion.

Network analysis assumes many forms and serves purposes other than those illustrated through use of PERT charts and link analysis. For instance, one sophisticated technique is SAINT (Systems Analysis of Integrated Networks of Tasks), used primarily in simulation development. Rule-based activities are represented with sufficient precision to permit modeling of entire tasks as illustrated in Figure 3. From this description, one can develop programs to automate components of the total task, simulators with specified levels of fidelity, and optimization models against which to compare human performance. Unlike simpler network models, SAINT and its generation of software-based techniques can be used to portray timing, sequencing, and decision characteristics of relatively complex and dynamic systems. Thus, it has proven useful in a variety of research, training, and design applications (Chubb, 1981).

Molecular Analysis. Human factors evaluation of isolated components of a system, such as the legibility of a display or the feel of a control, is usually accomplished by expert judgment or some type of narrowly focused "quick and dirty" research. Expert judgment may be reinforced by handbook data, much of which consists of basic performance functions obtained under carefully controlled laboratory conditions (e.g., basic psychophysical functions, threshold data, etc.). As noted earlier, the fact that one must often extrapolate extensively from such data and ignore a host of potentially biasing factors in the operational context has led some to question the value of basic human

FIGURE 2

**Eye-Movement Link Values Between Instruments
During a Climbing Maneuver**

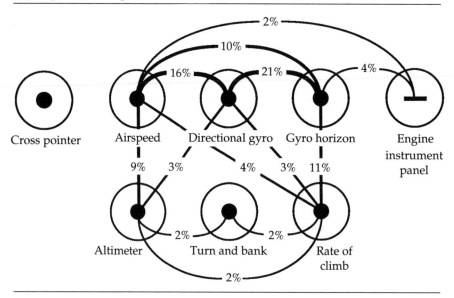

performance data. Others argue that we simply don't have enough of it in the right format. In any case, few contest the point that the "expert" must frequently rely on his or her judgment, or that even unaided, such judgment is likely to be far superior to the alternative—total disregard of human factors.

In those rare instances where time, money, and management support are sufficient to permit it, specific design issues may be subjected to empirical testing. Such study may take any number of forms, ranging from a survey of potential users for acceptability or ease of use, for example, to experimental comparison of performance on alternative designs using whatever subject population is handy. Naturally, the meaningfulness of results will vary accordingly.

The consultant role, then, requires a complete set of analytic and research tools, together with liberal application of ingenuity, informed judgment, and at least a passable

facility in the art of organizational politics. Problem solving, frequently in a pressure-filled atmosphere, is probably the best way to describe the job.

Human Factors Role in Research.   As indicated earlier, the nature of human factors research covers the entire basic-applied spectrum. At the basic end, many of the problems addressed and methods used are indistinguishable from those of traditional experimental psychology. Psychophysical methods and reaction time paradigms are still commonly used to provide human performance information for display design. Simple factorial experiments are conducted to answer questions about perceptual, attentional, memorial, judgmental, or motor capabilities and tendencies. Since the emphasis in modern experimental psychology is on human cognitive processes—the metaphor of choice being the digital computer—and the emphasis in human factors is

FIGURE 3

SAINT Activity Sequence Analysis for Dialing a Telephone

Enter the Network

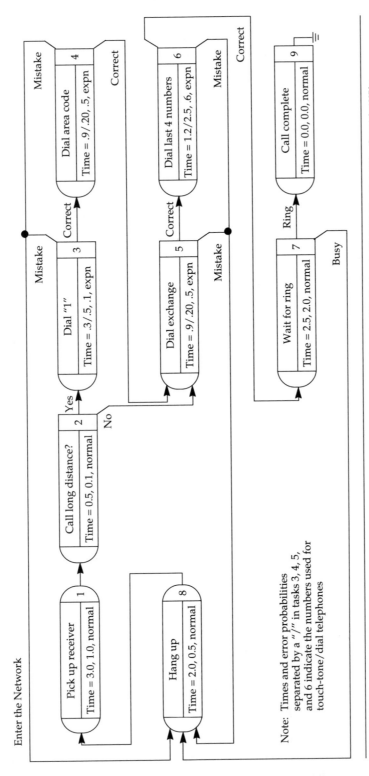

Note: Times and error probabilities separated by a "/" in tasks 3, 4, 5, and 6 indicate the numbers used for touch-tone/dial telephones

From "Simulating Manned Systems" by G. P. Chubb, K. R. Laughery, and A. A. B. Pritsker in *Handbook of Human Factors* (p. 1303), G. Salvendy, Ed. (1987), New York: Wiley. Copyright 1987 by John Wiley & Sons, Inc. Reproduced by permission.

on human-computer interaction (HCI), the compatibility of the specialties has never been closer. Consider, for example, the central concern of memory theorists for some time: the question of how information is represented and organized in human long-term memory. This question becomes vitally important in designing data base software for human access (Landauer et al., 1982). At the same time, implementation and testing of theoretical concepts in the actual system context permits a kind of external validation undreamed of in times past.

Not all design problems, however, are as amenable to the direct application of basic human performance concepts as that of database access. If for no other reason, the sheer complexity of real world contexts makes direct translation of laboratory data extremely tenuous (Meister, 1985). Multiple interacting variables are the rule rather than the exception; hence, factorial experiments, or even quasi-experimental approximations, are usually out of the question. On the other hand, simple applied experiments involving the direct comparison of multivariable design alternatives are inefficient due to lack of generalizability: Each new alternative requires a new test. The nature of this dilemma has been recognized for some time, and compromise solutions have been proposed. Among the most promising is Williges' (1973) adaptation of *response-surface methodology*, a technique for determining the most useful combinations of conditions to include in any empirical test involving realistically complex systems. Unfortunately, this methodology has never seen much use (Meister, 1985). In practice, the preferred solution remains the ad hoc kind of applied research that, while having little generalizability, at least answers the question at hand—preferred, that is, when research is considered at all; as noted earlier, the overwhelming preference favors expert judgment alone.

The human factors researcher, even at the more basic or theoretical end of the spectrum, is nonetheless guided by potential systems

applications. As problems become more mission oriented, practical considerations in addition to the applicability-generalizability dilemma assume greater importance. For example, one must be able to demonstrate the value-added potential of the research from some salient aspect of the resulting "product." Evaluation of outcomes may be more appropriately defined in terms other than traditional scientific significance criteria. An 80 percent chance that one design will prove superior to another, though statistically far short of significance, may be a substantial improvement over no information at all (50%), particularly if percentage points mean potential savings of multimillion-dollar costs or human life.

Finally, unlike so-called pure science, in which understanding is never sufficient and every report ends with the caveat that "more research is needed," applied research has finite—often practically defined—limits. The question becomes, "How much can be learned in x time with y dollars, and is it worth the expenditure?" instead of "How much remains to be learned?" Often, projects are terminated when the knowledge is sufficient for the problem at hand, irrespective of the scientific merit of continuation. Such is the reality facing most human factors researchers and the source of frustration for those not properly attuned to it.

Research methodology, then, ranges from traditional laboratory techniques to quasi experimentation to ad hoc applied designs. Promising compromise techniques have been largely ignored, and practical considerations severely limit the scientific acceptability of much of the applied research work. However, based on my unsystematic observation of recent literature, it would seem that human factors researchers are much more inclined to use multivariate techniques such as multivariate analysis of variance, multiple regression analysis, multidimensional scaling, structural equation modeling, and factor analysis than was the case earlier. If true, this trend would represent some progress toward dealing more effectively with the complexity of real systems. The limitations of the simple one- or two-variable designs that previously dominated human factors research are both well recognized and serious.

Contextual Influences in Human Factors

Implicit in the previous discussion is the assumption that the way human factors is practiced depends to some extent on the context. Mandated by DoD directive, for example, the nature of human factors participation in the development of a new weapons system may be quite different from that found in the design of a consumer product. In the latter instance, the involvement might be at the level of convincing a busy executive who has never heard of human factors that such research is worth spending time and money on—usually against the best advice of more firmly entrenched marketing, engineering, financial, operational, and even personnel management groups competing for the same resources. While there is little need to belabor so obvious a point, several issues associated with particular settings deserve mention.

Traditional DoD and Aerospace Contexts. As noted earlier, the chief problem here lies in translating official policy into action. Human factors is well recognized at top management levels, but control of the design process is largely in the hands of those who subscribe to a different philosophy. There are, however, some encouraging signs. For example, the National Aeronautics and Space Administration (NASA), despite a long history of resistance to the human factors philosophy, has solicited human factors input in planning the manned space station targeted for the mid-1990s (Sheridan, Kruser, & Deutsch, 1987).

Other Public and Semipublic Contexts. Two other domains in which the human factors discipline has enjoyed some visibility are transportation and electric power. The Department of Transportation, the National Highway Safety Commission, the Federal Aviation Administration, the Department of Energy, the Nuclear Regulatory Commission, and the various industries overseen by them have come to recognize—somewhat grudgingly in most cases—the inevitability of human involvement in such systems. Unfortunately, it generally takes some catastrophic or near-catastrophic event such as the Three Mile Island accident to make the point.

The problem is that the systems in question are already in place and, in the not entirely unbiased opinion of those responsible for them, are reported to be functioning well. System modifications in the interest of improved operator performance or safety are likely to be expensive, and even if successful in the long run, are likely to produce short-term transfer problems. At the very least, the cost of retraining an entire work force can be substantial. The result is an inertia that can only be overcome by some clear indication that the system has failed. Even then, the solution is likely to be sought first in an expanded role for the machine (i.e., more automation) rather than a more congenial task environment for the human (i.e., better human factors).

For example, consider the well-documented plight of the air-traffic controller. As the density of air traffic has mushroomed, the mental work load in this high-stress, well-paid, but essentially dead-end job has increased, probably up to the danger point (Morganthau, Cohn, Sandza, & Murr, 1987). The incidence of reported near-collisions has escalated, as has the number of stress-related symptoms experienced by the controllers, such as burnout, diabetes, hypertension, and ulcers (Finkleman & Kirschner, 1980). Still, the emphasis continues to be on improving the machine capability (Wiener, 1980). Nothing short of a rash of mid-air collisions is likely to force a rethinking of the total system, including the proper role for the human controller.

In the case of the nuclear power industry, a near-disaster did produce a significant increase in attention paid to human-machine interfaces, operating procedures, and training (Moray & Huey, 1988). Important changes were also implemented in the administrative structure of the Nuclear Regulatory Commission, with the result that human factors was accorded formal recognition in the setting of requirements and conduct of compliance reviews (Woods, O'Brien, & Hanes, 1987). Most recently, the Nuclear Regulatory Commission sponsored an 18-month study of human factors research needs that targeted (a) human-system interface design, (b) personnel subsystems, (c) human performance, (d) management and organization, and (e) the regulatory environment as areas deserving major attention (Moray & Huey, 1988). Clearly, a lesson in human factors was learned as a result of Three Mile Island.

One recent success story occurred without the threat of impending disaster and involves automobile safety. The now familiar high-mounted rear brake light, required on all passenger cars manufactured since 1985, is the direct result of human factors research dating to the 1960s. The work that finally sold the idea consisted of three field studies involving over 8,000 taxicabs and company vehicles driven normally with one of four alternative brake light designs in place, including the then-standard configuration as a control. In all three studies, the incidence of rear-end collisions with the addition of the high-mounted brake light was reduced by about 50 percent relative to the conventional design. This small design change is estimated to prevent 1.7 million accidents per year in the United States—at a savings of over $1.4 billion (Malone, 1986)!

Why was this project successful? Is there a lesson to be learned about strategies for effecting change in well-entrenched systems? Probably not. Consider first that the change was unobtrusive and relatively cheap to implement: A single light was added to the automobile, and drivers did not have to learn new driving habits. Second, a massive, rigorous field test was implemented with relative ease

under normal operating conditions. Third, the results were overwhelming and unequivocal. Finally, despite all this, it still took more than 20 years for this simple, cheap, and effective idea to be implemented! Such is the inertia in existing systems and the challenge facing those who would seek to effect human factors improvements after the fact.

Workplace Context. The situation here would be similar to that of the transportation and power domains were it not for the computer revolution. Almost overnight, organizations of all sizes were forced to rethink the ways they made decisions, processed and stored information, carried on communications, related to the outside world, and managed their work flow. Maintaining the status quo is no longer an option; the question becomes not whether to change, but how. For this reason, as Alluisi (1987) suggested, the atmosphere would seem extremely conducive to the application of human factors knowledge and research techniques.

The point of greatest impact, however, has not been the user organizations themselves; management remains largely ignorant of human factors issues. Rather, it has been the setting in which advanced systems are conceived and developed: the high-technology computer hardware, software, and robotics industries and the host of peripheral supporting industries that have sprung up. Those who develop such systems or system components are increasingly aware that *user friendliness*[3] is an important selling point and that understanding the tasks faced by users and the objectives of particular work organizations is necessary to produce competitive products. We shall have ample opportunity to explore illustrations of these high-technology applications in a later section. Suffice it to say here that the workplace is being systematically reshaped by those who create our advanced technologies, but the broader implications of such changes for human performance and well-being are only beginning to come to the forefront.

Consider, for example, the case of the video display terminal (VDT), fast becoming a universal office fixture (Giuliano, 1982), and the evolution of which profited from years of developmental research on anthropometry (body measurements), legibility, and other human performance functions (Sanders & McCormick, 1987). However, no one anticipated the range of complaints, from eyestrain to skin rashes to miscarriages, that would arise once VDTs started replacing conventional displays in large numbers throughout the work force. By 1983, the complaints were so vociferous that the National Academy of Sciences convened a "blue ribbon" panel to investigate the apparent crisis. The panel's conclusion was that while VDTs per se involve no demonstrable occupational hazards, how they are integrated within the physical and task environment may pose real problems (Leeper, 1983). In other words, it is not enough to incorporate human factors into the design of a system component; its subsequent role in the organizational system must also be examined from a user standpoint. To quote the final report, "when understanding has advanced to the level that [VDT] guidelines are feasible, the most likely course will be development of different sets of guidelines for different jobs" (p. 2). As a postscript, an official set of guidelines did appear during the final editing of this chapter (ANSI/HFS 100-1988 [1988]). The scope is somewhat broader than the quotation predicted, but still limited to text processing, data entry, and data inquiry tasks.

To date, most work organizations are reluctant to conduct the kinds of studies that would show how best to incorporate technical innovations into their particular milieu, preferring instead to rely on product developers who cannot possibly anticipate the ramifications of particular usage patterns and whose best interests are served by the widest possible distribution of their wares. Until this point becomes generally recognized, we can expect to see more cases like that of the VDT in other technologies and other workplace settings around the world.

One facet of the workplace showing a growing sensitivity to human factors consideration is that involving health and safety (hence the quick response to the VDT scare). Ideally, I would report that this trend represents a new spirit of humanism, altruism, or even morality on the part of modern work organizations, but unfortunately, there is little evidence to support such optimism. Instead, it seems, "the principal motives for safety developments in the 20th century have arisen from litigation— much of it due to worker's compensation laws" (Huston, 1987, p. 181). Also, "private employers have sponsored health promotion activities for their employees in the hope of reducing the annual increase in health related costs" (Cohen, 1987, p. 161). Passage of legislation such as the Occupational Safety and Health Administration (OSHA) Act of 1970— which mandates for employees a safe working environment, safe tools, knowledge of hazards, competent fellow employees and managers, and safety rules (Hammer, 1976)—has had a tremendous impact on employer awareness of health and safety issues. The merits of the 1970 OSHA legislation are perhaps arguable, but no one can deny that the costs associated with neglecting employee well-being went up dramatically, or that employers took their responsibility much more seriously, in the aftermath of this legislation. It has also prompted much research on accident and hazard analysis, development of safety devices and safer machine designs, warning techniques, protective clothing, stress measurement and reduction, and a host of other human factors issues connected with the workplace (Mark, Warm, & Huston, 1987).

Consumer Products Context. In much the same vein, over much the same period, for many of the same nonaltruistic reasons, organizations have become increasingly sensitive to the populations for whom they manufacture, distribute, and sell consumer goods. It no longer makes good economic sense to "let the buyer beware." Tough state and federal laws and even tougher courts have made all parties involved increasingly cognizant of their responsibility to minimize the risks of hazard, malfunction, and foreseeable misuse of the products they offer the public. Quite often, product liability litigation hinges on such human factors issues as the following:

- Were systematic hazard analyses performed in relation to the design?

- Was proper attention paid to special characteristics of the user population?

- Were labels and warnings sufficient to inform the user of known hazards so as to avoid them?

- Was the consumer instructed or trained properly at point of sale?

- Was a safer design alternative feasible?

In such cases, the courts often recognize testimony of human factors experts to help explain the human-product relations involved—the extent to which the product in question was or was not conceived in accordance with human factors principles and standards. Naturally, purveyors of consumer products are becoming increasingly interested in what those principles and standards are, and what, in fact, *human factors* is—particularly after losing multimillion-dollar lawsuits.

Some 600 human factors specialists are currently engaged in this sort of legal work (Sanders & McCormick, 1987), and most are in great demand. These include university professors, scientists, or consultants whose primary employment is quite different in orientation: seeking and dispensing knowledge in as unbiased a fashion as possible, rather than helping attorneys with the inherently biased task of persuading courts. Regrettably, litigation is considerably more lucrative than many other pursuits, so the rapid growth in this area may be at the expense of primary employers. It is

difficult to see, for example, how full-time academics can earn the larger part of their salaries through part-time legal work without some sacrifice in scholarship. Consequently, some individuals have reduced their primary employment to part time; others have moved into the expert testimony business full time. I know one individual who, after resigning his professorship, quickly became so successful that he was able to limit his practice to a single product—and more than quadrupled his academic salary in the process! How far this trend will continue and whether it will advance the field is anyone's guess. In my opinion, the short-term outlook is good: Both society and the field can only benefit from the awakening interest in human factors. In the longer run, however, the field could lose both substance and credibility if it fails to exercise self-restraint.

While one may find some satisfaction in the success litigation has had in promoting awareness of human factors, it seems a sad commentary that so rational and noble an idea as concern for the consumer or user requires such drastic measures to gain acceptance within our industrial institutions. Equally disconcerting is society's response as reflected in legislation and jurisprudence, which so often constitutes an equally irrational and selfish overreaction. No bull is worth $8 million, but public outrage against cavalier disregard for the consumer can make it so.

Models of the Human Component

As noted earlier, the human-machine model is often used to depict the central concepts underlying the human factors discipline (see Figure 1). This level of abstraction is adequate for descriptive purposes, but falls short of the precision required to move either the science or the practice forward in a meaningful way. Whether the aim is to generate knowledge that can be transferred to some operational context, to develop a training simulator, or to optimize the design of the operational system itself, it is helpful to have an explicit representation or model of the operator's role.

There is no clear consensus on what form such models should take. Chubb, Laughery, and Pritsker (1987), for example, distinguish three categories that are now in common use: (a) task-network models, (b) control-theory models, and (c) cognitive models. The task-network approach has already been discussed in relation to analytic techniques: It provides a detailed account of the dynamic aspects of human performance in particular system contexts. The control-theory approach applies primarily to skilled psychomotor performance[4] in which the individual is depicted as a servo mechanism operating to minimize the discrepancy between the system's present and desired state in a closed-loop or feedback-controlled fashion. Obviously, this model was dominant in an era when most systems were under direct manual control and operators dealt with continuous (analog) rather than digital input or error functions. While this type of control is far from extinct, it is giving way rapidly to the supervisory control required by semiautomated systems (Sheridan, 1987). Here, the individual sets initial conditions, monitors performance, and makes periodic adjustments in the largely autonomous operation of the machine (computer-controlled) component. In short, the feedback-control loop linking the system to the environment may be closed in varying degrees at the machine rather than the human level. At the extreme, fully automatic control removes the individual from the loop entirely. Figure 4 illustrates this progression of concepts.

Finally, the cognitive approach follows directly from the trend in modern work toward supervisory control and reflects the point made earlier that as the individual's burden of routine activities lightens, the cognitive work load often increases—usually to an indeterminate net level. Measuring that level is itself an important topic of current research and one not easily accomplished. Whatever the level, the qualitative nature of mental operation required of people in the workplace has become the central focus of modern human performance research. Thus, cognitive models have come to dominate the human factors literature.

The discussion of human factors that follows is heavily influenced by modern conceptions of human cognition. First, many of the concepts used—attentional capacity, automatic processing, working memory, declarative and procedural knowledge, and so on—are drawn directly from the cognitive literature. Second, the tasks used to illustrate these concepts, such as monitoring, troubleshooting, and data base access, are representative of the cognitive emphasis in modern work. Finally, the organization of topics follows roughly the sequence depicted in most cognitive stage models as the predominant direction of information flow: input (sensory, attentional, "early" perceptual processes), central processing (comprehension, memory, reasoning, judgment, choice), and output (execution, overt action).

Problems and Research

Because it is impossible in a single chapter to do justice to even a fraction of the problems addressed by human factors, the illustrations presented in this section represent only a sampling from a selected portion in the field and reflect my personal biases. Selection was based on whether the problem was directly relevant to the modern workplace, whether the information was current, and whether the work was theoretically based in psychology, most notably, cognitive psychology. Human performance issues were given priority over those with a more physical, physiological, or total-system orientation. Although important work has appeared on such topics as the design of hand tools (Mital, 1986), bathroom fixtures (Kira, 1976), anthropometric measurements (NASA, 1978), and a host of narrowly defined computer design issues (e.g., Schneiderman, 1987), it will not be discussed as such here.

FIGURE 4

Supervisory Control as Related to Direct Manual Control and Full Automation

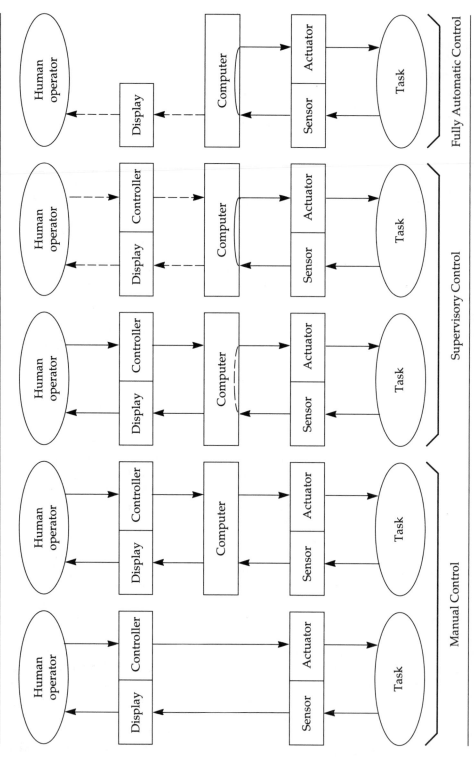

From "Supervisory Control" by T. B. Sheridan in *Handbook of Human Factors* (p. 1245), G. Salvendy, Ed. (1989), New York: Wiley. Copyright 1987 by John Wiley & Sons, Inc. Adapted by permission.

Vigilance and Monitoring

One of the oldest topics in human factors is the question of how human operators function under conditions of low-input signal rates—a *signal* being defined as some event, usually critical to system performance, to which the operator is supposed to respond. Obviously, in the supervisory control mode typical of modern systems, watching for and recognizing the occasional malfunction or critical condition is a key aspect of the individual's role and is often shared with a computer. The so-called human-computer monitoring concept is now commonplace in commercial aircraft, air traffic control, industrial inspection, medical settings (Beatty, Ahern, & Katz, 1977), and process control contexts (Parasuraman, 1987).

The reason for the continuing interest in this topic, which in its 40-year history has been the subject of more than 1,000 studies, is the suspicion that people are rather poor at responding to low-frequency inputs over sustained periods of "watchkeeping" (Mackie, 1987). The original task involved detection of faint signals amid the visual clutter or "noise" endemic to the primitive radar systems of World War II. Detection rates were found to decline dramatically after as little as 30 minutes of sustained vigil. A very similar function was obtained in the laboratory using a quite different task, for example, the "clock test" in which subjects reported occasional double-jumps in discrete movements of a pointer (Mackworth, 1950), and in many subsequent experiments using a variety of other research vehicles (Buckner & McGrath, 1963). The phenomenon became known as the *vigilance decrement*, and considerable effort was directed toward finding ways to combat it (Wickens, 1984).

In time, competing theories evolved that emphasized arousal, sensitivity loss or fatigue, expectancy, and reinforcement explanations, together with associated remedies. As the data accumulated, however, complications arose.

First, it became apparent that even in its classic form, the decrement was no simple matter. Application of the emerging signal detectability theory (TSD)[5] methodology suggested that both d' (or sensory) and β (or decision criterion) shifts can occur under certain circumstances (Broadbent & Gregory, 1965; Welford, 1968). Second, some conditions—notably those involving complex tasks and signals well above threshold—produced no decrement at all in the classic sense, even over very long watch periods, although the overall level, latency, or variability of performance might vary (Adams, Humes, & Stenson, 1962; Howell, Johnston, & Goldstein, 1966; Williges, 1976). One series of studies suggested that attention becomes more erratic as the watch progresses (Howell et al., 1966), yet the nature of attention at that time was very poorly understood (Adams, 1987).

The upshot of this increasingly complicated picture, made more so by the growing complaints about the generalizability of laboratory data, led some to dismiss the entire vigilance effort as irrelevant and the decrement as a pseudoproblem (Adams, 1987; Kibler, 1965). Some invoked the engineer's dictum that if humans have trouble, automate. But the problem has not disappeared: It is abundantly clear that people are unlikely to abandon their supervisory role in semiautomated systems and that they will continue to function as monitors far into the future, even if they share this role with machines. Therefore, the problem remains along with questions concerning the adequacy of what we know about it that is applicable to real systems.

One issue of *Human Factors* (Warm & Parasuraman, 1987) was devoted entirely to this dilemma. Although various opinions were expressed, several conclusions may be drawn. First, if our laboratory-based generalizations are valid, then they must be demonstrated in realistic settings. Second, more needs to be known about the specific nature of those settings—obviously, a prerequisite for any test or rational application of existing generalizations. Third, advances in cognitive theory, notably in the area of attention, offer considerable promise as a foundation on which to build bridges between the laboratory and the field.

Two lines of research illustrate progress consistent with the conclusions drawn above. Drury and his colleagues (Czaja & Drury, 1981; Drury, 1975; Drury & Sinclair, 1983) analyzed industrial quality control tasks from the standpoint of human/machine function allocation and distinguished four function categories:

- Monitoring continuous processes

- Examining items for defects

- Measuring items on critical features

- Patrolling or supervising and spot-checking the work of other inspectors

Arguing that monitoring and measurement are best handled by machines and patrolling by humans, Drury and Sinclair (1983) focused on examining as the function most worthy of study. When they compared human and machine performance under realistic circumstances in an inspection task—detecting nicks and dents, tool marks, scratches, and spots in small steel cylinders—they found that humans significantly outperformed the prototype machine in terms of accuracy "largely because of the more sophisticated decision-making capabilities of humans" (p. 391). The tests were conducted over a four-to-six hour period with rest breaks each hour, so the time parameter was realistic even though no attempt was made to examine the course of performance over time. Illustrative results are shown in Figure 5.

While obviously not intended as an indictment of machine inspection nor a quixotic attempt to defend humanism against the onslaught of the machine, Drury's work illustrates how meaningful questions about

FIGURE 5

Inspector and Machine Performance on Nicks and Dents

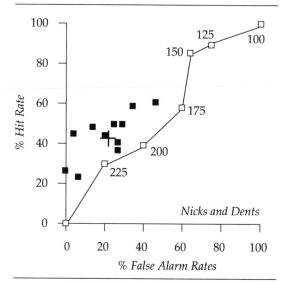

Note: Individual inspectors: filled squares; average for inspectors: large cross; inspection device: open squares (connected); threshold values for device: numbers on data points.

From "Human and Machine Performance in an Inspection Task" by C. G. Drury and M. A. Sinclair, 1983, *Human Factors, 25,* pp. 391–399. Copyright 1983 by The Human Factors Society, Inc. Reproduced by permission.

detection task design can be posed and answered in a realistic setting. The question was how well alternative strategies, both reasonable on a priori grounds, accomplish the inspection task; the answer in this case favored the human over the machine. The work also sheds light on how human and machine perform this task, thereby providing useful information and a better understanding of the operational problem.

The second illustration involves the test of an idea for maintaining monitoring performance that stems directly from a currently popular attention theory. In an influential paper on human information processing,

Schneider and Shiffrin (1977) distinguished between two types of cognitive function: automatic processing, which involves highly overlearned skills such as driving a car, and controlled processing, which is conscious, intentional, requires effort, and interferes with other mental activities (Posner & Snyder, 1975). In this model, attention is viewed as a limited processing resource only partially allocable by the individual that determines to a great extent how adequately controlled mental activities are carried out. Different tasks require different amounts of attention and draw differentially upon the limited store; automatic processing, however, is "free" or at least cheap in its demands on the resource. Finally, most skills begin in the controlled state, but may become progressively more automatic with practice. Two critical variables in this process are (a) the consistency with which stimulus and response elements of a task are paired during practice and (b) the amount of such practice.

Drawing on these principles, Fisk and Schneider (1981) were able to show that the vigilance decrement is attributable almost exclusively to controlled processing. Consistent pairing of to-be-detected target stimuli with detection responses and feedback over 4,000 training trials was sufficient to automatize the subject's detection response. Transfer to a standard vigilance paradigm in which only 18 of 6,000 presentations contained the target stimulus resulted in virtually no decrement over time. By contrast, similar training in which only some of the 4,000 trials contained target stimuli (variable mapping) produced a typical vigilance decrement over the 6,000-trial (50-minute) test session as illustrated for hit rate by the open data points in Figure 6. What decrement did occur under consistent mapping (closed data points) could be accounted for entirely by a shift in the subject's decision criterion. That is, subjects did not become less vigilant over time in the sense of losing sensitivity, although they did become somewhat less prone to report the

FIGURE 6

Hit Rate for Consistently Mapped (CM) and Variably Mapped (VM) Conditions

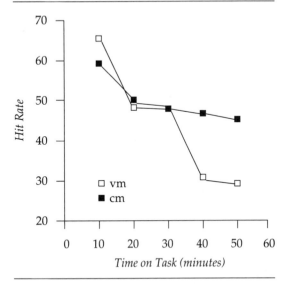

From "Control and Automatic Processing Tasks Requiring Sustained Attention" by A. D. Fisk and W. S. Schneider, 1981, *Human Factors*, 23, pp. 737–750. Copyright 1981 by The Human Factors Society, Inc. Reproduced by permission

occurrence of a signal whether or not it was actually present.

A particularly noteworthy aspect of these findings is that the ineffective variable-mapping paradigm was the one in which training conditions most closely approximated the transfer conditions. However, consistent mapping, which offered seemingly unrealistic preparation for a task whose most salient feature is low target frequency relative to nontarget events, produced sustained performance. Based on the traditional consideration of similarity between training and transfer conditions, one would have predicted opposite results. Only through understanding the cognitive processes involved—automatic versus controlled processing—was it reasonable to predict such counterintuitive findings.

The message, of course, extends well beyond the vigilance phenomenon and suggests that intensive training on certain procedural elements of a task—-training designed to make the subroutines cognitively automatic and thereby freeing up capacity for handling more unpredictable or creative task demands— is a potentially useful strategy for training people to deal with complex work assignments. The trick is to identify those elements of the task amenable to automatization. And even if all suitable elements are so trained, the remaining elements would still require controlled processing and thus the attention of the operator.

Mental Work Load

If infrequent inputs pose a problem for the human operator in today's advanced systems, the opposite condition—excessive task demands—may constitute an even greater one. To make matters worse, it is not always possible to tell from observing behavior or analyzing the task in a conventional way what the work load actually is. Automation designed to reduce the tasks of the operator sometimes increases perceived demands and lowers performance, as noted earlier. Similarly, seemingly difficult tasks may produce higher than expected performance with or without feelings of excessive pressure. Since work load has serious implications for safety, efficiency, wage setting, and health, however, finding ways to measure it is vitally important (Moray, 1982).

Literally hundreds of empirical and theoretical papers have addressed this issue over the past decade (Wickens & Kramer, 1984), and the interest shows no signs of fading. Unfortunately, no simple answers have emerged—only a multitude of poorly correlated behavioral, physiological, and subjective indexes (Wierwille & Williges, 1978). Moreover, even within these categories, agreement among measures has not been high. The prevailing interpretation is that work load is a multifaceted construct

rather than the hoped-for "scalar quantity" (Kramer, Sirevaag, & Braune, 1987), and the various indexes are measuring different of its facets. Thus, "only through the joint use of a number of measurement techniques can we expect to elucidate the mental work load of human operators" (p. 159), a thought that if literally true is depressing from the standpoint of practical applications. As we shall soon see, however, the situation may not be all that bleak.

While a complete account of the various measures is beyond the scope of this chapter, it would be well to examine a few of the more common of each type. The principal *behavioral* index is simply performance on some reference task—either the primary task itself, on the theory that there is a direct relation between work load and performance, or a secondary task in a dual-task or time-sharing paradigm. The latter is based on a more complex model involving competition for resources necessary to perform cognitive functions: The more resource the subject must spend on the primary task—that is, the greater its mental work load—the less he or she has for allocation to the secondary task. Thus, secondary task performance should suffer in proportion to primary task work load and thereby serve as an index of it.

Both kinds of behavioral indexes have serious theoretical and practical shortcomings that limit their usefulness. The most obvious shortcomings are the heavy reliance on disputable theoretical assumptions (e.g., see Kantowitz, 1985) and the impracticality of adding to an operator's already excessive work load simply to measure it. Personally, I would prefer not to be on board the aircraft for which the dual-task paradigm was being used to index the pilot's or controller's mental work load during, say, a difficult landing in heavy traffic!

Physiological measures enjoy the same intuitive appeal that they have elsewhere in psychology, that is, the idea that what they reveal is somehow more fundamental or real than behavioral or introspective measures. But they suffer from the same drawbacks in terms of cost, artifacts, and interpretation problems. Their real advantage lies in their potential unobtrusiveness: One can take records continuously without interfering with the operator's mental state or performance (Wickens & Kramer, 1984). Moreover, their reliability and interpretability seem to be improving, particularly in the case of heart-rate variability, pupilometry, and ERP (event-related brain potentials; Kramer, Sirevaag, & Braune, 1987). Heart-rate variability seems particularly sensitive to response load, pupil diameter to overall task demands, and the P300 component of the ERP to perceptual/cognitive demands (Wickens, 1987).

The measures most commonly used in today's applied settings, however, are undoubtedly the *subjective* ones. Ironically, they may be the most defensible on the grounds that ultimately it is what the operator perceives, not some abstract concept of reality, that must be dealt with in the workplace (Moray, Johanssen, Pew, Rasmussen, Sanders, & Wickens, 1979). Fortunately, these are also the easiest measures to obtain and are the ones with the highest face validity (Gopher & Braune, 1984). Their principal shortcomings are their intrusiveness, if gathered during actual performance of the primary task, or their retrospectiveness, if gathered afterward, plus all the usual problems associated with self-report measurements.

Foremost among the latter is the problem of deciding exactly what items to include on the scale. The most popular approach in current use, the SWAT technique, requires subjects to rate tasks on three dimensions—something they are able to do quite reliably (Boyd, 1983; Reid, Shingledecker, & Eggemeier, 1981). If subjective mental work load (SML) is a multidimensional construct, however, then such decisions matter a great deal in the interpretation of any obtained scores. However, the content of the many rating scales in current use suffers from

lack of uniformity, the bases of choice having been informal intuitions rather than a formal theory of SML. This charge has, in fact, been leveled against SWAT by Gopher and Braune (1984). But the picture is changing, and it is to these recent developments that our attention is now directed.

Rediscovery of Stevens' psychophysical law and the direct scaling techniques upon which it rests led Gopher and Braune (1984) to propose an adaptation of the simple magnitude estimation method for measuring SML. Briefly, subjects indicate the experienced "load or demand imposed on them by the task" using an unlimited numerical scale anchored at 100 by a task of intermediate difficulty. Properly instructed in this method, people have been shown to produce reliable scales having approximate ratio properties for complex social stimuli as well as the traditional psychophysical dimensions (Stevens, 1966).

Gopher and Braune had subjects make such estimates following each of 21 single- and dual-task laboratory problems of various composition and difficulty levels. As shown in Table 1, the results produced clear discrimination among the tasks in rated load.

Further, several different estimates of reliability produced values in the high .90s. Thus, irrespective of its underlying complexity, SML can be judged consistently as "a coherent and potent psychological attribute" (p. 529) using this simple method. The approach, therefore, has considerable practical merit, a point that has been verified in subsequent applications to simulated air traffic control (Yeh & Wickens, 1988) and pilot (Kramer, Sirvaag, & Braune, 1987) tasks.

Another recent development in the mental work load field is the appearance of theoretical concepts that may serve to tie some of the empirical loose ends together. By and large, these efforts are based on modern attention theories, particularly the multiple resource model in which mental activities are seen as dependent on specialized attentional resources

TABLE 1

Average Raw and Transformed Scores for the 21 Experimental Conditions

		Test 1			Test 2		
		Raw Score	Transformed		Raw Score	Transformed	
	Experimental Task	$\overline{X}$	$\overline{X}$	SD	$\overline{X}$	$\overline{X}$	SD
1.	Sternberg visual-verbal 2	54.5	0.057	0.012	59.0	0.052	0.014
2.	Sternberg auditory-verbal 2	60.5	0.081	0.012	62.3	0.069	0.016
3.	Sternberg visual-verbal 4	65.9	0.111	0.017	79.3	0.166	0.018
4.	Sternberg auditory-verbal 4	75.0	0.139	0.018	80.7	0.172	0.026
5.	Sternberg visual-spatial 2	77.5	0.150	0.022	83.8	0.184	0.032
6.	Hidden pattern	95.2	0.223	0.038	84.3	0.180	0.033
7.	Card rotation	118.8	0.315	0.041	97.8	0.242	0.038
8.	1-dimensional compensatory tracking	100*	0.283	0.032	100*	0.302	0.035
9.	Maze tracing	120.4	0.325	0.036	113.6	0.329	0.032
10.	Sternberg auditory-spatial 2	148.1	0.415	0.034	115.6	0.344	0.056
11.	Sternberg visual-spatial 4	118.4	0.334	0.034	118.1	0.368	0.045
12.	Critical tracking	109.2	0.290	0.046	122.8	0.424	0.052
13.	Dual, tracking and auditory-verbal 2	163.8	0.488	0.028	132.4	0.431	0.040
14.	Dual, tracking and visual-verbal 2	156.9	0.481	0.031	132.8	0.442	0.035
15.	Delayed digit recall	156.6	0.465	0.054	141.5	0.473	0.037
16.	Dichotic listening	175.0	0.505	0.061	146.7	0.482	0.052
17.	Track and visual-verbal 4	170.1	0.523	0.032	146.0	0.512	0.033
18.	Dual, tracking* and auditory-verbal 4	170.4	0.514	0.026	150.6	0.516	0.037
19.	Dual, tracking and visual-spatial 2	184.6	0.576	0.033	144.6	0.490	0.038
20.	Dual, tracking and visual-spatial 4	212.5	0.686	0.033	176.7	0.667	0.040
21.	Dual, tracking and delayed digit	280.9	0.921	0.026	243.8	0.894	0.025

Note: $N = 55$; * denotes the reference task.

From "On the Psychophysics of Work load: Why Bother With Subjective Measures?" by D. Gopher and R. Braune, 1984, *Human Factors, 26*, pp. 519–532. Copyright 1985 by The Human Factors Society, Inc. Reproduced by permission.

that exist in limited supply in multiple stores. Different tasks make different demands on the various stores, and performance is explained by the pattern of supply, demand, and usage that exists across stores at any given time. Time-sharing performance, for example, depends on the extent to which primary and secondary tasks draw from the same resource pools, how much resource each requires, how much is available, how efficiently the resource is used, and so on. Although not without its

detractors (e.g. Kantowitz, 1985), the multiple resource model has had considerable success in predicting specific interference effects among laboratory tasks in the dual-task paradigm (Wickens, Mountford, & Schreiner, 1981).

Recently, Yeh and Wickens (1988) added to this model a notion from the verbal report literature, which suggests that introspection makes particular demands on working memory. With this addition, they were able to account for many of the previously mentioned inconsistencies between performance-based and subjective measures of mental work load, the problem now known as the *dissociation phenomenon*. More specifically, they identified conditions under which one can expect these measures to "dissociate" and the precise kinds of inconsistency characteristic of each. Apart from the obvious scientific value of this conceptualization, it has the practical virtue of indicating how the practitioner should use and interpret subjective work load measures in real-world applications. For example, if a task imposes demands on working memory in excess of its capacity, one should not trust subjective measures and should look instead to primary task performance. Conversely, whenever exhortations or incentives are used to increase performance through motivation, one should take subjective measures very seriously since they may expose hidden costs that will surface later on.

It takes no great stretch of the imagination to see how, in matters of task-related demands, human factors researchers and industrial and organizational psychologists may well be exploring the same territory under different banners. Good theoretically anchored measures of mental work load might offer some badly needed perspectives on such standard problems as job-related stress, work motivation, and job satisfaction. And the variables traditionally studied in these latter contexts must certainly have some bearing on mental work load, as the Yeh and Wickens model implies.

Display Design Issues

One of the traditional human factors concerns, the information display interface, still occupies a prominent position in research and application. However, the focus has shifted in keeping with the changing configuration of systems for doing work. Literal "dial reading" and the fairly limited set of human factors issues associated with it have given way to

CRTs, computer-based tasks, and the overwhelming array of questions that each new development introduces. Anyone wishing to find out what sort of dial to use, how to position it, and what specifications to build into it for best performance under specified task conditions can get reasonably satisfactory answers from available handbooks (e.g., Van Cott & Kinkade, 1972). Nor is there a shortage of handbook advice on CRT design (e.g., Smith & Aucella, 1983; Smith & Mosier, 1986). However, one would be hard-pressed to find clear, definitive, empirically based answers to most of one's questions in such sources. This is in no sense an indictment of either the handbook authors or the human factors research establishment; it merely reflects the primitive state of our knowledge when it comes to tasks and capabilities that could only be found in science fiction a decade or so ago.

Today there are simply very few absolute constraints on what information one can display or how. Information on virtually any aspect of system and environmental operation—past, present, or projected future—can be presented in near real-time or summarized form; it can be cross-tabulated, analyzed, edited, or otherwise processed; it can be coded tabularly, graphically, acoustically, pictorially, in color, in animation, or in multiple dimensions; key items can be highlighted, zoomed in on, isolated for special attention, or accompanied by bells and whistles; the viewer can control what is viewed, or not, or both under prescribed conditions; the list goes on and on. The only real limitation is cost.

And display variables constitute only half the story. The other half is the task. It is a well-established principle that for almost any set of tasks and display variables one can expect a task x display interaction. Since the nature of tasks assigned to the human is changing—indeed is itself often a variable in system design—data produced using any research task can be expected to have a very short half-life. To appreciate more fully the variety of task possibilities that exist at the user-computer interface, one need only scan the taxonomy in Table 2.

Since most problems in the design of modern display interfaces stem from the almost limitless number of options available and the knowledge that almost any human performance data has limited generalizability, it is little wonder that handbooks offer such minimal guidance or that design decisions are so often based on cost or engineering rather than human factors criteria. For this reason also, I have chosen to feature approaches rather than data in illustrating modern display research. Two recent lines of investigation are presented, each having broad implications for current work.

Alphanumeric Formatting.   The first example concerns the question of how one should structure the alphanumeric material on a standard CRT screen. Since such displays are now a part of most clerical jobs and the amount of time people spend working before them is enormous, even a small improvement in the facility with which operators extract information can translate into a substantial savings in time and money. Tullis (1983), for example, estimated that a 1-second savings in average extraction time would save 55 person years annually in just one of the computerized systems of the (pre-divestiture) Bell System!

Recognizing the ad hoc nature of most of the structured formats then in existence, Tullis saw improved formatting as a potential target for enhancing performance. As reflected in Table 3, his research addressed this issue by first deriving from the existing theoretical and empirical literature a set of general parameters (and accompanying measures) that seemed to capture most of the variance in format design. He then conducted a series of laboratory studies exploring the relation of search time and user acceptance to systematic manipulation of the six characteristics. From these data, he generated empirical regression equations which

he hoped would constitute a general means of evaluating any actual or proposed format design without the necessity for conducting an actual test. Finally, he cross-validated the prediction equations on both performance and acceptance criteria using both laboratory tasks and data reported in the literature.

The results were extremely encouraging. Cross-validated r's were about .80 for both performance and user acceptance criteria (the former showing sensitivity to only four of the six format variables). Particularly interesting is that the prediction equations for the two criteria are in no sense comparable (see Table 3). Apparently, there is little correspondence between formats people like and the ones that they perform best on. This discrepancy has been verified in two subsequent studies that have extended and supported the Tullis models (Fontenelle, 1988; Schwartz, 1986).

Tradeoffs between objective and subjective criteria are not uncommon in the human factors literature, and the practical difficulties that they pose for the system designer or organizational decision maker are far from trivial. Yet they are rarely followed up with research designed to help the decision maker out of the dilemma. This case is no exception. It would be useful to know, for example, why people prefer the features they do, whether (or how easily) they could be trained to accept the high-performance features, what the potential long-term costs might be for choosing the optimal-performance features over the user-preferred ones, and whether task or user population differences moderate the discrepancy.

Reading in Narrative Format.   Whereas the Tullis work focused on common data base query or search tasks, an equally common use of CRT displays is presenting text material for reading and editing. It has been known for some time that people read more slowly in this mode than they do from paper. Despite much research, however, the reasons for this costly discrepancy—and thus the possibilities for

TABLE 2

User Action Subtaxonomies for User-System Interface Actions

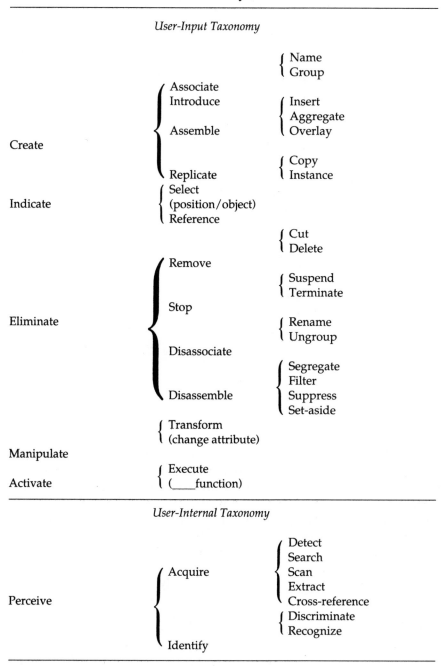

User-Input Taxonomy

- Create
  - Associate
    - Introduce
      - { Name
      - Group }
    - Assemble
      - { Insert
      - Aggregate
      - Overlay }
    - Replicate
      - { Copy
      - Instance }
- Indicate
  - { Select
  - (position/object)
  - Reference }
- Eliminate
  - Remove
    - { Cut
    - Delete }
  - Stop
    - { Suspend
    - Terminate }
  - Disassociate
    - { Rename
    - Ungroup }
  - Disassemble
    - { Segregate
    - Filter
    - Suppress
    - Set-aside }
- Manipulate
  - { Transform
  - (change attribute) }
- Activate
  - { Execute
  - (___function) }

User-Internal Taxonomy

- Perceive
  - Acquire
    - { Detect
    - Search
    - Scan
    - Extract
    - Cross-reference }
    - { Discriminate
    - Recognize }
  - Identify

TABLE 2

User Action Subtaxonomies for User-System Interface Actions (continued)

User-Internal Taxonomy (cont.)

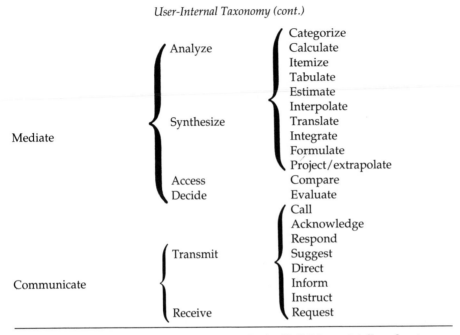

Mediate	Analyze	Categorize
		Calculate
		Itemize
		Tabulate
		Estimate
	Synthesize	Interpolate
		Translate
		Integrate
		Formulate
		Project/extrapolate
	Access	Compare
	Decide	Evaluate
Communicate	Transmit	Call
		Acknowledge
		Respond
		Suggest
		Direct
		Inform
		Instruct
	Receive	Request

eliminating it—remained a mystery. Hypotheses ran the gamut from visual to cognitive to emotional causes.

Gould and his colleagues seem now to have produced some definitive data on this issue (Gould, Alfaro, Finn, Haupt, & Minuto, 1987). After failing to isolate the causal factors in a series of single-variable experiments (Gould, Alfaro, Barnes, Finn, Grischowsky, & Minuto, 1987), these investigators undertook six more studies using multiple variables which in combination controlled the physical approximation of the CRT to a normal "paper display." The results were quite conclusive: The closer the image quality came to that of paper, the more comparable became the reading performance. Figure 7 shows the relationship as a function of resolution (the distribution of points at each level reflects the effect of other variables). Although the task used throughout these experiments was proofreading, the authors cite other work using a comprehension task that produced consistent findings.

While pinpointing the source of the discrepancy as purely visual may seem anticlimactic, it is nonetheless an important finding because it rules out cognitive and emotional explanations. Thus, remedies can be found readily, if not cheaply, in better image quality. Yet the story is by no means complete in that we still do not know how the component

TABLE 3

Variables That Predict Format Effects and the Prediction Equations for Search Time and Preference Criteria

Variable	Definition
Overall density *(D)*	Number of character spaces used (percent of those available)
Local density *(L)*	Number of filled character spaces within 5° (visual angle) of each character weighted by distance
Grouping *(G)*	Number of well-defined perceptual groups formed by displayed characters (Gestalt-based algorithm)
Size of groups *(S)*	Average visual angle subtended by perceptual groups
Number of items *(I)*	Number of data items where a data item is a set of characters on a line separated by no more than one blank space
Item uncertainty *(U)*	Entropy in any item's location based on the number of unique horizontal and vertical starting positions

Prediction Equations

1. Search time = $1.6696 - .0209\,D + .0286\,L + .0201\,G + .09175$
2. Subjective preference = $-3.1627 - .0801\,D + .0522\,L + .0184\,G + .07295 + .0194\,I + .4121\,U$

variables (polarity, resolution, font, anti-aliasing) "trade off," or indeed what the visual processes are by which they affect reading. As our understanding of these mechanisms grows, the possibilities for ameliorating the disadvantages of CRT text in more practical ways should increase.

Compatibility and Stereotypes.   Considerations relevant to information displays also involve human information processing and output, or response, functions, but neither can be conceptualized meaningfully independent of the input. Extending the point made earlier about the task dependence of display variables, one arrives at an even broader generalization that encompasses multiple component interactions: stimulus-response (S-R) or stimulus-cognition-reponse (S-C-R) compatibility. This notion, which comes as close to a guiding principle as human factors has to offer, holds that it is the *relationship* between

input and output variables, rather than either set alone, that is critical for human performance. Some display-control relations, for example, such as turning a steering wheel in a particular direction and seeing it go there, are obviously more effective than others. But not all relations are as obvious as in this physical correspondence relation. Researchers must use empirical evidence to determine which combinations produce the best performance or fewest errors. This often involves measuring population stereotypes, as in the case of determining the clearest way to represent hazard information on warning signs, for example (Ryan, 1987).

In considering and trying to measure display-control relationships, it is apparent that the changing nature of work has shifted attention from a peripheral to a more central locus. Thus, rather than the fairly straightforward kinds of S-R relations that are important in say, vehicular control, we must

FIGURE 7

**Mean Within-Participants Reading Speeds on
CRT Displays and Paper as a Function of Displays Resolution**

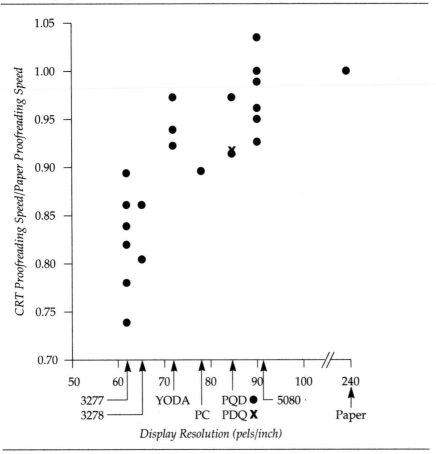

look for the conceptual, semantic, or logical re- lations that make it easier to troubleshoot a system, retrieve something from a database, integrate information, or solve problems under one configuration or another. The more com- patible the input and output aspects are in cognitive terms, the more effective the design— hence, the substitution of S-C-R for S-R in the compatibility designation (Wickens, 1984).

Often research on the C aspect of compat- ibility involves identifying stereotypical men- tal models or schemata that a defined popula- tion uses in conceptualizing such tasks;[6] the dominant paradigm for describing these mod- els is that of information processing and the computer. Thus, attention, as we saw, is described as a partially allocable, capacity- limited information processing resource;

pattern recognition, perception, memory, language, reasoning, and problem solving are described in terms of information coding, storage, working memory, classification, retrieval, and other symbol manipulation operations (Lachman, Lachman, & Butterfield, 1979; Wickens, 1984). The reference group for which cognitive stereotypes are defined can be as broad as the general population or as narrow as a targeted user group for a particular system. One population distinction of particular relevance to the design of computers and computer-based systems is that of novice and expert. It appears that the mental models characteristic of these groups are often qualitatively different, a fact of great significance for both systems design and training. Indeed, much of the work in the closely related fields of human-computer interaction, expert systems, and artificial intelligence centers around identification of cognitive stereotypes for purposes of making the machine more compatible with the human, the user more like an expert, or the machine more like a human in certain respects (Fotta, 1987; Kramer & Schumacher, 1987; Waldrop, 1988a, 1988b).

Human Computer
Interaction (HCI) Issues

Function Allocation. We have frequently referred to the changes in work that have occurred over the past decade or so due to technology, and to the continuing growth in opportunities for automation—particularly in the domain of cognitive functions. An obvious by-product of these trends is the growing significance of decisions regarding which functions to automate: More options mean more consequences, more criteria, and more tradeoffs to be considered, and thus more difficult choices to be made (Westin, Schweder, Baker, & Lehman, 1985). Since those choices often involve organizational policy as well as system design considerations, the process whereby functions are allocated

to humans and machines seems a particularly appropriate topic for discussion here.

Recent works by Kantowitz and Sorkin (1987) and Meister (1985) provide excellent summaries of the alternatives and issues involved in function allocation; the following discussion draws heavily from both sources. The central theme is that it is a mistake to take too literally the traditional systems notion that human and machine are competing candidates for a list of rigorously defined functions, with each task going to the better qualified. Relative capabilities, particularly as expressed in quantitative terms, quickly become outdated as more sophisticated machines overtake and surpass the human on function after function. A more promising view is to recognize that "machines and people are not really comparable subsystems" (Kantowitz & Sorkin, 1987, p. 359). A fundamental difference is that "people are flexible and inconsistent whereas machines are consistent but inflexible" (p. 361). Therefore, they should be thought of in complementary rather than comparative terms. Of course, as sophisticated models such a *Soar* become more commonplace, even this argument may vanish since the model will capture human flexibility and inconsistency along with everything else.

Accepting this distinction for the moment, however, two allocation strategies can be identified. The first, which enjoys considerable popularity in both management and engineering circles, is to automate everything that can feasibly be automated. While defensible on reliability and often on cost effectiveness grounds, the strategy fails to recognize less obvious system costs associated with inflexibility. As noted earlier, what is left for the individual to do may constitute extremely inappropriate or difficult tasks, with consequent increases in human error, training requirements, and stress. Moreover, failures—though perhaps rare—will always occur in automated systems, and their effects can be devastating. Modern mass transit systems, for example, have become increasingly dependent on so-phisticated automation for control. However, from the introduction of the San Francisco Bay Area's BART system to the Miami area's Metro-rail, malfunctions have represented a continu-ing threat and occasionally a major problem. Wiener (1987) makes this point using the fol-lowing graphic quotations from the *Miami Herald*:

> "No longer do drivers handle a train's speed. No longer do they bring it to a precise stop at station platforms. That's all done now by a high-tech package of coils and antennae—known as ATO—that have reduced drivers to little more than push-button doormen." However, accord-ing to Driver Pam Walden, about every 10 stations...ATO fails to receive the signal to stop, forcing her to hit the red button that slams on the brakes. "Usually you end up overshooting the station, so you have to backtrack to let people out," Walden said, noting that without her, the train would keep going to the next station. (p. 725)

Merely finding the problem in automated systems can be time-consuming and frustrat-ing, and the resulting loss of confidence in the automated system can be incalculable. And finally, there is the problem of maintaining human "stand-by" proficiency on rarely used skills that become critical when the machine goes down (Kantowitz & Sorkin, 1987).

A dramatic illustration of how these condi-tions can lead to system failure despite great technological sophistication is found in the 1988 *Vincennes* tragedy. During operations in the Persian Gulf, the USS *Vincennes*—which was equipped with one of the most "intelligent" weapon systems in our fleet—accidentally shot down an Iranian airliner mistakenly ident-ified as a hostile F-14. Many lives were lost, and the United States suffered a serious blow to its credibility and reputation. In the course of sub-sequent investigations, it was discovered that the crew not only misidentified the aircraft,

but believed that it was descending when it was actually ascending. A panel of psycholo-gists testified before the House Armed Services Committee that the "intense stress compound-ed by complex technology clearly contribut-ed" to the tragedy (*Science Agenda*, 1988, p. 4). Indeed, as one panelist pointed out, automated systems can be a "mixed blessing" because as operators become less involved and increas-ingly dependent on the computer system, they become poorly prepared to make critical judg-ments when the situation arises. How to deal with such crises and thus avert future disasters is among the issues sorely in need of human factors research.

The second, more balanced approach to automation follows from the complementary components view introduced above. In this approach, policy considerations, such as the inevitability of human supervision and the primacy of human values, and pre-existing system requirements, such as the necessity for performing certain calculations that are clear-ly beyond human capability, are identified ex-plicitly and used in the initial assignment of functions. Next, consideration is given to alter-native configurations for implementing the re-maining functions, with attention paid both to "relative ability lists" such as that illustrated in Table 4, and to interactive features.

The result is that humans and machines are given those functions for which each is quali-fied by one or another criterion, and the rest are assigned to some interactive combination. For example, determination of organizational goals and values is necessarily a human func-tion; massive calculations and strict adher-ence to logic are clearly appropriate for ma-chines. With these initial assumptions in mind, one considers various options for allocating a particular decision function. Rather than asking whether human or machine is better equipped to handle it, the focus shifts to the kind of interaction that can make best use of the capabilities of both. Some form of decision aiding becomes the obvious solution; it

TABLE 4

**Functional Advantages and Disadvantages of Men and Machines
(Modified From Lyman and Fogel, 1961)**

Functional Area	Man	Machine
Data sensing	Can monitor low probability events not feasible for automatic systems because of number of events possible	Limited program complexity and alternative; unexpected events cannot be handled adequately
	Absolute thresholds of sensitivity are very low under favorable conditions	Generally not as low as human thresholds
	Can detect masked signals effectively in overlapping noise spectra	Poor signal detection when noise spectra overlap
	Able to acquire and report information incidental to primary activity	Discovery and selection of incidental intelligence not feasible in present designs
	Not subject to jamming by ordinary methods	Subject to disruption by interference and noise
Data processing	Able to recognize and use information, redundancy (pattern) of real world to simplify complex situations	Little or no perceptual constancy or ability to recognize similarity of pattern in spatial or temporal domain
	Reasonable reliability in which the same purpose can be accomplished by different approach (corollary of reprogramming ability)	High reliability may increase cost and complexity; particularly reliable for routine repetitive functioning
	Can make inductive decisions in new situations; can generalize from few data	Virtually no capacity for creative or inductive functions
	Computation weak and relatively inaccurate; optimal game theory strategy cannot be routinely expected	Can be programmed to use optimum strategy for high-probability situations
	Channel capacity limited to relatively small information throughput rates	Channel capacity can be enlarged as necessary for task
	Can handle variety of transient and some permanent overloads without disruption	Transient and permanent overloads may lead to disruption of system
	Short-term memory relative poor	Short-term memory and access times excellent

TABLE 4

**Functional Advantages and Disadvantages of Men and Machines
(Modified From Lyman and Fogel, 1961) (continued)**

Functional Area	Man	Machine
Data transmitting	Can tolerate only relatively low imposed forces and generates relatively low forces for short periods	Can withstand very large forces and generate them for prolonged periods
	Generally poor at tracking though satisfactory where frequent reprogramming required; can change to meet situation. Is best at position tracing where changes are under 3 radians per second	Good tracking characteristics over limited requirements
	Performance may deteriorate with time because of boredom, fatigue, or distraction; usually recovers with rest	Behavior decrement relatively small with time; wear maintenance and product quality control necessary
	Relatively high response latency	Arbitrarily low response latencies possible
Economic properties	Relatively inexpensive for available complexity and in good supply; must be trained	Complexity and supply limited by cost and time; performance built in
	Light in weight, small in size for function achieved; power requirements less than 100 watts	Equivalent complexity and function would require radically heavier elements, enormous power and cooling resources
	Maintenance may require life support system	Maintenance problem increases disproportionately with complexity
	Nonexpendable; interested in personal survival; emotional	Expendable; nonpersonal; will perform without distraction

From "The Human Operator in Control Systems" by G. A. Bekey in *Systems Psychology* (pp. 248–277), K. B. DeGreene (Ed.), (1970), New York: McGraw-Hill. Copyright 1970 by McGraw-Hill. Reproduced by permission.

remains to be decided which form, since aiding can be carried out in a number of ways. Thus, the conceptual options are laid out and reviewed against performance and user-acceptance criteria. Studies or surveys might be necessary at this point to resolve the issue, or the superiority of one scheme may become obvious. In any event, the final configuration will in all likelihood be more useful than had the choice process been governed by the attitude that it is better to automate everything or that it is strictly human versus machine. Comparative advantages are considered, but in a cooperative rather than competitive framework.

Meister (1985) offers explicit guidance for carrying out the function-allocation process, using an approach consistent with the so-called

FIGURE 8

Important Elements of Computer Systems

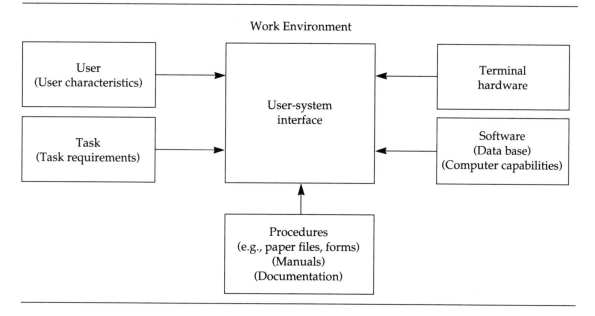

Work Environment

complementary view but strongly influenced by formal decision logic. It consists of delineating all the allocation options for each function, specifying criteria, assigning weights to both options and criteria by some standard means, multiplying weights, and summing over each option to determine the best solution. This procedure is essentially an adaptation of multi-attribute utility theory.

One final approach with a host of futuristic implications is what Kantowitz and Sorkin (1987) refer to as *dynamic allocation* (p. 365). The basic concept is to provide the user with the facility and discretion to alter the allocation on-line as, for example, in such familiar illustrations as cruise control and automatic pilot. Naturally, in the context of "smart" computer systems, the concept would extend to applications much more sophisticated than servo control. For example, some advanced military C^{3}I (command, control, communication, and intelligence) systems offer the human operator a fully automated information processing and decision capability for choosing targets and firing weapons, which can then be overridden or altered in various ways during the course of a battle (Department of the Army, 1983). Of course, such responsibilities, coupled with the massive amount of information now available to the operator, can greatly increase mental work load (Wohl, 1981). Kantowitz and Sorkin (1987) even raise the possibility of using physiological measures to monitor work load and initiate appropriate task adjustments automatically as the burden becomes excessive.

Function allocation issues are not limited to those involving human and machine components. As illustrated in Figure 8, computer-based systems can be represented as comprising user, task, procedural, software, and hardware elements, all coming together at the invisible integrating surface known as the *user-system interface* within a common work environment. Designing an effective interface requires simultaneous consideration of all these elements, their interactions, and allocation of functions among them. Within either the user or machine categories, one generally has considerable latitude for assigning functions (e.g. hardware vs. software or user judgment vs. rigid procedures). Discussion of such options is well beyond the scope of this chapter. To illustrate a few of those available in one aspect of the hardware domain, Table 5A presents a summarized comparison of alternative input devices, and 5B of output devices.

The problem to which we now turn, capturing user knowledge, bears on the functions intervening between input and output, and indirectly on the allocation of those functions to human or software components.

User Knowledge, Expert and Otherwise. Whether one's purpose is to automate some task, simulate human performance in the task, train people to do it better (with or without the help of a computer), or improve the person-machine dialogue, an essential precondition is understanding how people perceive the task or the system of which it is a part. Accordingly, much research effort has been directed toward describing the mental models held by various users of computer-based systems. Generalizations such as Card, Moran, and Newell's (1983) classic attempt to model the user's cognitive interaction with the computer have helped stimulate and direct work in this area.

Armed with a better understanding of the systems themselves—better *conceptual models*, to use Norman's, 1987, term—resulting from better task analysis procedures, what knowledge we have of mental models is beginning to pay dividends in a number of applications (Baecker & Buxton, 1987). Still, that knowledge is limited by one of psychology's longest standing problems: the difficulty of gaining access to private events. The most commonly used method for eliciting knowledge in both cognitive psychology and artificial intelligence consists of analyzing verbal protocols obtained from the user in the course of performing the task (Ericsson & Simon, 1984). However, such verbalizations have notorious limitations in both the accuracy and completeness with which they represent actual thought processes (Nisbett & Wilson, 1977), and they are enormously difficult to analyze objectively.

Another approach involves structuring tasks in such a manner that different kinds of errors necessarily reflect particular modes of thought. Though useful in certain well-defined contexts such as troubleshooting (e.g., Gitomer, 1988), this technique is limited by the requirement that all cognitive options be mapped unambiguously onto identifiable response patterns. Such experimental control is rarely possible.

A third technique just beginning to gain recognition is based on multidimensional scaling and cluster analysis (Butler & Corter, 1986; Cooke & McDonald, 1986, 1987). Users are asked to make relatedness judgments for a large number of knowledge items, and scaling techniques are applied to the judgments in constructing a structural representation of that knowledge domain. The approach has been used successfully to distinguish experts from novices in professions as diverse as fighter pilots and computer programmers (Schvaneveldt, Durso, Goldsmith, Breen, Cooke, Tucker, & DeMaio, 1985; Cooke & Schvaneveldt, 1986).

Despite these advances, systematic elicitation of user knowledge is still a primitive science, and most design decisions are based instead on the designer's intuitive conceptualization of user models. Nevertheless, however they are arrived at, the ultimate programs defining system interactions can be subjected to human factors evaluation after the fact.

TABLE 5A

Computer Input Devices With Some of Their Principal Features and References

Input Device	Features	References
Keyboard	The vast majority of past research on input devices has dealt with keyboards. Reasonable and fairly detailed guidelines exist with respect to the physical properties of keys and keyboards and—to a lesser extent—their layout, logical properties, operating procedures, etc. Guidelines for alphabetic keyboards are particularly good, and those for numeric keypads are reasonable. Function keyboards are rather system-dependent; guidelines can specify their physical properties but can only suggest methods and basic principles for function selection and layout. It is not clear that chorded keyboards are viable except in highly specialized situations.	Alden et al. (1972) Siebel (1972)
Light pen, light gun—a wand with a light-detecting tip used to determine the specific point on a display it touches.	Light pens can be used effectively for cursor placement and text selection, command construction, and for interactive graphical dialogs in general, including drawing. There is evidence, however, that greater accuracy may be possible with a mouse in discrete tasks and with a trackball in drawing tasks. Mode mixing, as by alternating use of light pen and keyboard, can significantly disrupt performance, since the light pen must be picked up and replaced with each interval of use. Continuous use of a light pen, at least on commercially available Cathode ray tube (CRT) terminals with vertical display surfaces, can be quite fatiguing. There has been no known research on desirable physical and logical properties for light pens.	English et al. (1967) Goodwin (1975) Irving et al. (1976)
Joystick—a vertical stick generally used to move a display cursor in a direction corresponding to the direction of stick movement.	There are many studies of the use of joysticks for continuous tracing tasks, but few studies of their use for discrete or continuous operand selection or graphical input tasks. The studies that have been performed have found the mouse, light pen, and trackball preferable in terms of speed, accuracy, or both. Joysticks are sometimes used for windowing and zooming control in graphical displays. No research on this topic was found, although the results of tracking studies may be applicable here. Otherwise, no clear recommendations for joystick properties have emerged, even with respect to basic issues like position versus rate versus acceleration control. These issues may be fairly task-specific.	Card et al. (1978) English et al. (1967) Irving et al. (1976)

TABLE 5A

Computer Input Devices With Some of Their Principal Features and References (continued)

Input Device	Features	References
Trackball—a partially exposed ball rotated by the hand generally used to move a displayed cursor in a direction corresponding to the movement of ball rotation.	The trackball appears to be effective for both discrete and continuous operand selection and graphical input tasks, and it may yield the best performance when graphical inputs must be alternated with keyboard input. No empirical data on physical properties were found, but some such data are thought to exist in the tracking literature.	Irving et al. (1976)
Mouse—a small device rolled by hand on a surface generally used to move a displayed cursor in a direction corresponding to the direction of movement of the mouse.	Although the mouse is not in widespread use, there is evidence that it is an effective device for text selection. No data are known concerning its physical properties or its use in other tasks.	Card et al. (1978) Engelbart (1973) English et al. (1967)
Graphical input tablet—a flat surface which detects the position and movement of a hand-held stylus generally used to generate a drawing on a display.	Graphical input tablets are capable of fairly high pointing accuracy (within 0.08 cm, according to one study). They are commonly used for freehand drawing but may be inferior for discrete position input tasks. They may also involve a performance decrement due to low stimulus-response compatibility when the drawing surface is separate from the display surface.	English et al. (1967) Myer (1968)
Touch panel—a device which overlays the display and senses the location touched by a finger or stylus.	No empirical performance data were found dealing with the touch panel. While its inherent resolution limits may preclude serious use for fine discrete position and continuous position input, it feels natural and may become a common device for more coarse positioning and selection from lists.	Hlady (1969) Johnson (1977)
Knee control	A knee control has been used in one research study for discrete position input. It is not known to be in use otherwise and seems unlikely to see serious use.	English et al. (1967)

TABLE 5A

Computer Input Devices With Some of Their Principal Features and References (continued)

Input Device	*Features*	*References*
Thumbwheels, switches, potentiometers	These have been studied primarily outside the computer systems domain and are discussed in standard human factors reference sources. They are not often used as input devices for interactive computer systems.	Chapanis (1972)
Tactile input devices	Although some tactile input devices have been proposed, little human factors research has been done on them other than that concerned with prosthetics.	Noll (1972)
Psychophysiological input devices	Electromyographic signals have provided superior performance in some control tasks to joysticks and other manual control devices. Use of heart rate, keyboard response latency, electroencephalographic input, etc. is technologically feasible, although sophisticated input is not yet achievable via these methods. There are ethical and legal problems as well as technological difficulties. Significant human factors data were not found with respect to computer-related use of these techniques.	Slack (1971) Wargo et al. (1967)
Automated speech recognition	The current state of this technology limits its use to relatively simple input tasks. Even in these there are problems with different speakers, noise, etc. Although speech input seems like a very desirable and natural input mode and is clearly preferred over other communication modes for interpersonal communication, it is not clear whether it will prove to be widely applicable for human-computer interaction tasks. Very little information was found that would assist the designer in recognizing tasks for which speech input is appropriate or in selecting an appropriate speech input device.	Addis (1972) Bezdel (1970) Braunstein & Anderson (1961) Chapanis (1975, 1981) Turn (1974)
Hand printing—for optical character recognition (or for subsequent entry by typists)	The constrained hand printing required for optical character recognition (OCR) input results in low input rates and sometimes high recognition-error rates as well. Although manual transcription of such data clearly cannot be avoided in many cases, the preponderance of evidence suggests that direct keyboard entry yields better performance than printing, with a little practice, even when users are not skilled typists. Some error and input rate data on hand printing exists, along with some information about the effect of various printing constraints on input performance.	Apsey (1976) Devoe (1967) Masterson & Hirsch (1962) L. B. Smith (1967) Strub (1971)

TABLE 5A
_____

Computer Input Devices With Some of Their Principal Features and References (continued)

Input Device	Features	References
Mark sensing	As with hand printing, this form of transcription results in lower input rates than does practiced but unskilled typing. Some error and input rate data exists. May be slightly faster than constrained hand printing.	Devoe (1967) Kulp & Kulp (1972)
Punched cards	Keypunching performance differs significantly from ordinary typing because of differences in both the machine and the typical data to be keyed. Some reasonably good data exist on keypunch timing and error rates.	Neal (1977)
Touch-tone telephone	Several studies suggest that the touch-tone telephone is a satisfactory device for occasional use as a computer terminal, even by naive computer users. It seems clear, though, that it is not a satisfactory device for prolonged interaction or for significant amounts of nonnumeric input.	Miller (1974) Smith & Goodwin (1970) Witten & Madams (1977)

TABLE 5B
_____

Computer Output Devices With Some of Their Principal Features and References

Type of Display	Features	References
Refreshed CRT	The ordinary, refreshed Cathode ray tube (CRT) is currently the basic computer display. A good deal of data exists concerning appropriate visual properties of CRT displays. Studies that have compared user performance using CRTs with performance using other display devices, however, do not provide a satisfactory basis for selection decisions.	Shurtleff (1990)
Storage tube CRT	For some graphical applications, direct-view storage tubes may be preferable to refreshed displays. The storage tube allows very high-density, flicker-free displays but imposes significant constraints on interactive dialog. Although information exists concerning the basic functional advantages and disadvantages of such displays, no empirical data pertaining to human factors concerns were found.	Steel (1971)
Plasma panel	Plasma panel displays are inherently "dot" or punctuate displays, and studies of symbol generation methods are relevant. Little empirical information exists on human performance aspects of plasma displays per se.	

TABLE 5B

Computer Output Devices With Some of Their Principal Features and References (continued)

Type of Display	Features	References
Teletypewriter	Reasonable guidelines exist with respect to the design of tele-typewriter terminals, including both physical and functional properties. See the discussion of keyboards in Table 5A.	Dolotta (1970)
Line printer	Research on typography is voluminous and directly applicable. Research dealing directly with the line printer used in computer output is scanty but consistent with findings of typographic research (e.g., mixed upper-lower case is best for reading comprehension). Guidelines are not known to exist but could be constructed with additional survey of typographic research literature. Use of line printers for "pseudographic" displays is common but little discussed in the literature. Pseudographics is an inexpensive way to convey simple graphical information and should probably be used more widely in batch applications.	Cornog & Rose (1967) Lewis (1972) Ling (1973) Poultron & Brown (1968)
Laser displays	Reasonable human factors guidelines with respect to visual properties have been proposed, but these displays are not widely used.	Gould & Makous (1968)
Tactile displays	Although some tactile displays have been proposed or even developed, little human factors research has been done other than that concerned with prosthetics.	Noll (1972)
Psychophysiological displays	Psychophysiological input is technically feasible now, but psychophysiological displays are still only a topic for research.	
Large-screen displays	There is conflicting evidence with respect to the performance effects of large-group versus individual displays. The main advantage of large-screen displays are a larger display area and the existence of a single display that is clearly the same for all viewers. Unfortunately, higher display content is not achievable due to the resolution limits of existing technology (e.g., light valve displays) and may be unachievable in principle, since the large-screen display usually subtends a smaller visual angle than an individual display located close to the user.	Landis et al. (1967) Smith & Duggar (1965)
Speech and synthetic speech	Although speech output clearly has many advantages over output modes for interpersonal communication, there is essentially no information on the conditions for which speech would be an appropriate computer output.	Chapanis (1975, 1981)

FIGURE 9

Feature Description of Nine Text Editors

Editor [Ref.]	Display	Auto Line Wrap[a]	Strong Line Concept[b]	Text Units	Command Invocation	Insert Mode	Means of Addressing[c]	Addressing Hardware	Computer Processor[d]
					Feature				
TECO [20]	TTY[e] style	No	Yes	Characters, lines	1-letter mnemonic	Yes	Relative to current position	Keyboard	PDP-10 equivalent, via 3Mb net
WYLBUR [24]	TTY[e] style	No	Yes	Characters, lines	English-like, abbreviated	Yes	Absolute line numbers	Keyboard	IBM 370, 1200 baud
EMACS [23]	Partial page	Yes	Yes	Characters, words, lines, sentences, paragraphs	1-letter mnemonic, control keys	No	Relative to current position	Keyboard	PDP-10 equivalent, approximately 1200 baud
NLS [18,19]	Partial page	Yes	No	Characters, words, paragraphs	1-letter English-like on keyboard or 5-key chordset	Yes	Screen position	Mouse	PDP-10 with local processor
BRAVOX [21]	Full page	Yes	No	Characters, words, lines, paragraphs	1-letter mnemonic, menu, function keys	No	Screen position	Mouse	Xerox Alto personal computer
BRAVO [22]	Partial page	Yes	No	Characters, words, lines, paragraphs	1-letter mnemonic	Yes	Screen position	Mouse	Xerox Alto personal computer

FIGURE 9

Feature Description of Nine Text Editors (continued)

Editor [Ref.]	Display	Auto Line Wrap[a]	Strong Line Concept[b]	Text Units	Command Invocation	Insert Mode	Means of Addressing[c]	Addressing Hardware	Computer Processor[d]
					Feature				
WANG [26]	Partial page	Yes	No	Characters	Function keys	Yes	Screen position	Step keys[f]	Stand-alone Wang word processor
STAR [27]	Full page	Yes	No	Characters, words, sentences, paragraphs	Function keys, menus	No	Screen position	Mouse	Xerox 8000 processor
GYPSY [25]	Partial page	Yes	No	Characters, words, paragraphs	Function keys	No	Screen position	Mouse	Xerox Alto personal computer

[a] Automatic line wrap means that during type-in a new line is automatically begun when a word overflows the old line, without any intervention from the user.

[b] This refers to editors that require the user to type RETURN at the end of each line of text. Usually, this also means that there is an explicit CARRIAGE-RETURN character at the end of each line in the internal representation of the document.

[c] This refers to the primary means of addressing (all editors have the ability to search).

[d] Time-sharing computers were used under conditions of light load. Terminals and computer displays were all CRTs, except that one WYLBUR user preferred her own hardcopy terminal.

[e] A TTY (teletype) style display is one that does not continuously show the state of the document, but only shows the sequence of commands entered by the user. Snapshots of pieces of the document are displayed when the user explicitly asks for them.

[f] Four keys with arrows on them, which move the cursor up, down, left, and right (see [2]).

From "The Evaluation of Text Editors: Methodology and Emperical Results" by T. L. Roberts and T. P. Moran, 1983, *Communications of the ACM, 26* (4). Copyright, 1983 by the Association for Computing Machinery. Reproduced by permission.

One good example of this approach is a comprehensive evaluation of text editors as reported by Roberts and Moran (1987). No interactive computer system is more widely used in the workplace than the text editor, and none has appeared in as wide a variety of forms. Since it is intended to be a flexible tool, applicable to a variety of tasks by many different kinds of users, any overall evaluation represents an ambitious undertaking. The Roberts and Moran study attempted such an appraisal for nine of the most diverse text editors and word processors available at that time (1982). As shown in Figure 9, the criteria consisted of both actual performance measures, (time, error, learning ease) and functionality ratings using a sample of 53 common or benchmark tasks drawn from a comprehensive taxonomy of 212 (see Figure 10). Four experts were used to obtain the functionality ratings, normative time, and error scores; four novices produced the learning data. As shown in Figure 11, the programs differed markedly on the various indexes. GYPSY was efficient and easy to learn, but low in functionality; NLS was very functional but generated a high error rate; TECO was poor in all respects; BRAVOX was good overall; and so on.

Obviously, this is not the final word on text editors, and one can question certain aspects of the test (e.g., see Baecker & Buxton, 1987). Nonetheless, the general approach—to start with a taxonomy, select representative tasks, gather subjective as well as performance and learning data from novice and expert users, and draw conclusions from those data—seems infinitely superior to relying on a designer's intuition. Keep in mind that the programs identified as very poor by Roberts and Moran must have been consistent with some designer's intuition!

Other HCI Research.   Text editing is just one of many HCI functions to which human factors research has been directed. Graphics,

manual input devices, speech input and display characteristics, programming, documentation, and a number of other system design elements have all received their share of attention. Often, however, the work is narrowly focused, atheoretical, and all too often proprietary. While this literature does contain some information of interest to the industrial and organizational community, its primary audience is the design specialist. For the interested reader, Schneiderman (1987), Gould and Lewis (1983), a number of chapters in Salvendy (1987), and the annual special issues of the *SIGCHI Bulletin* devoted to human factors in computing systems represent excellent sources.

Office Automation Issues

Up to this point, our discussion of human factors has centered around specific facets of the advanced systems revolutionizing work and the workplace. Before leaving the topic, it might be well to take a somewhat broader view of these systems, examining their collective impact on one particular work setting: the office. Office automation is itself a system design problem, one over which organization management exercises considerable control and around which a knowledge base is developing. Our discussion draws liberally on the excellent summaries of this literature provided by Czaja (1987), Giuliano (1982), and Helander (1985).

White-collar occupations have now surpassed blue-collar occupations as the predominant form of work in America, and the trend continues as shown in Figure 12. Computer technologies have narrowed the distinction even further: Office and professional work has assumed many of the structural features of production work, such as specialization, higher speed-accuracy requirements, shift work, and so forth, while production workers are performing more officelike and professional tasks, such as keyboard operations and fault diagnosis. It is easy to see why automation of office

FIGURE 10

Taxonomy of Editing Tasks on Which the Evaluation Methodology Is Based

Modify Document
    Content and structure of text
        Characters, words, numbers, sentences, paragraphs, lines, sections, document
        References (e.g., keep up-to-date references to section numbers in the document)
        Sources for text or attributes (e.g., make the text layout be the same as in another
        document)
    Layout of running text and structure
        Inside paragraphs (e.g., indent the first line of a paragraph so far from the left margin)
        Headings, random lines (e.g., center)
        Interparagraph layout (e.g., leave so much space between paragraphs)
        General (e.g., lay out document in so many columns)
    Page layout
        Every page (e.g., print a page heading that includes the current section number)
        Non-mainline text (e.g., position footnotes at the bottom of the page)
    Attributes of characters
        Line break (e.g., automatic hyphenation)
        Shape (e.g., boldface)
    Tables
        Column beginning (e.g., columns are equally spaced)
        General alignment (e.g., align the column on the decimal points)
        Modify alignment (e.g., swap the positions of two columns)
        Treatment of table entries (e.g., line up the left and right edges of [justify] each table entry)
    Summary of text (e.g., table of contents)
    Special applications (e.g., mathematical formulas)

Locate Change (Addressing)
    Text (e.g., find text which has specified content)
    Structure (e.g., find the next section heading)
    Layout/Attributes (e.g., find a boldface character)
    Misc.

Program Edits (Control)
    Command sequences (e.g., invoke a sequence of commands with parameters)
    Control structure (e.g., repeat a sequence of commands a specified number of times)
    Tests (e.g., compare strings for alphabetical order)
    Storage (e.g., store pointers to places in documents)
    User control (e.g., ask user for parameters during execution)
    Preexisting composite commands (e.g., sort a sequence of text strings)

Find Task or Verify Change (Display)
    Display text and layout (e.g., show the outline structure of the text)
    Display system state (e.g., show where the selection is relative to the whole document)

Miscellaneous
    Hardcopy
        Draft copy [e.g., print with extra space between lines)
        Misc. (e.g., print on envelopes)
    Intermediate Input/Output (e.g., save away the current version of a document)
    Other (e.g., perform arithmetic on numbers in the document)

FIGURE 11

Overall Evaluation Scores for Nine Text Editors

Editor[a]	Time[b] $M \pm CV^f$ (sec/task)	Error[c] $M \pm CV$ (% Time)	Learning[d] $M \pm CV$ (min/task)	Functionality[e] (% tasks)
		Evaluation Dimensions		
TECO	49 ± .17	15% ± .70	19.5 ± .29	39%
WYLBUR	42 ± .15	18% ± .85	8.2 ± .24	42%
EMACS	37 ± .15	6% ±1.16	6.6 ± .22	49%
NLS	29 ± .15	22% ± .71	7.7 ± .26	77%
BRAVOX	29 ± .29	8% ±1.03	5.4 ± .08	70%
BRAVO	26 ± .32	8% ± .75	7.3 ± .14	59%
WANG	26 ± .21	11% ±1.11	6.2 ± .45	50%
STAR	21 ± .18	19% ± .51	6.2 ± .42	62%
GYPSY	19 ± .11	4% ±2.00	4.3 ± .26	37%
$M(M) \; M(CV)$[g]	31 .19	12% .98	7.9 .26	54%
$CV(M)$[g]	.31	.49	.53	.25

[a] The evaluations for TECO, WYLBUR, NLS, and WANG are from the first author's thesis [11]; the first author also evaluated STAR. The evaluations of the other editors were done in the second author's laboratory.

[b] The Time score is the average error-free expert performance time per benchmark task on the given editor. A difference between editors with mean values M_1 and M_2 is statistically reliable (95% confidence) if $[M_1 - M_2] > 0.33° (M_1 + M_2)/2$.

[c] The Errors score is the average time, as a percentage of the error-free performance time, that experts spend making and correcting errors on the given editor. A difference between editors with mean values M_1 and M_2 is statistically reliable (95% confidence) if $[M_1 - M_2] > 20\%$. Thus, no differences between editor means are reliable in this data.

[d] The Learning score is the average time for a novice to learn how to do a core editing task on the given editor. A difference between editors with mean values M_1 and M_2 is statistically reliable (95% confidence) if $[M_1 - M_2] > 0.45° (M_1 + M_2)/2$.

[e] The Functionality score is the percentage of the tasks in the task taxonomy (Figure 10) that can be accomplished with the given editor.

[f] The *Coefficient of Variation (CV) = Standard Deviation / Mean* is a normalized measure of variability. The CVs on the individual scores indicate the amount of between-user variability.

[g] The M(CV)s give the mean *between-user* variability on each evaluation dimension, and the CV(M)s give the mean *between-editor* variability on each dimension.

FIGURE 12

U.S. Employment Trends

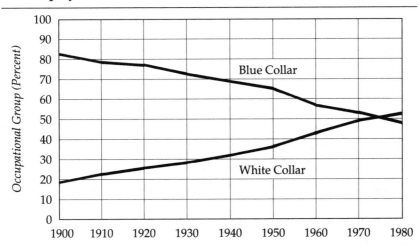

systems is such a critical target for human factors input.

Giuliano (1982) distinguishes three overall office design concepts—preindustrial, industrial, and information age—as illustrated in Figure 13. The preindustrial form is paper-intensive, loosely structured, and heavily dependent on individual performance; the industrial form relies heavily on specialization, simplification, and structured work flow in the classic organization theory sense; the information age concept is oriented around individual workstations, data bases, and networking. One theoretical advantage of the information age concept, apart from its obvious efficiency, is its potential for reducing the psychological distance between managers and subordinates and for restoring meaningfulness to the work performed.

Unfortunately, the transition from the industrial to information age design has been slow and painful. Most large organizations seem stalled somewhere in the middle, superimposing elements of the technology, such as VDTs,

on a relatively unchanged structure. Thus, as discussed earlier, automation has made the work more demanding in some respects and more trivial in others; skill requirements have increased, but the human role has in many ways diminished.

Part of the transition problem is undoubtedly a reflection of the normal resistance to change that characterizes most organizational constituencies. This may resolve itself in time as the technologies become more familiar and certain key elements of the information age become more commonplace. However, part of the problem stems also from our lack of understanding and hard evidence in support of the information age concept and its implementation. It is not altogether clear how the concept should be implemented or how different configurations actually perform on the various system functions. Most importantly, we have yet to understand how to gain user acceptance at the outset so that whatever potential benefits the concept has to offer can be realized (Czaja, 1987; Gould & Lewis, 1983).

FIGURE 13

Graphic Representation of Preindustrial, Industrial, and Information-Age Office Concepts

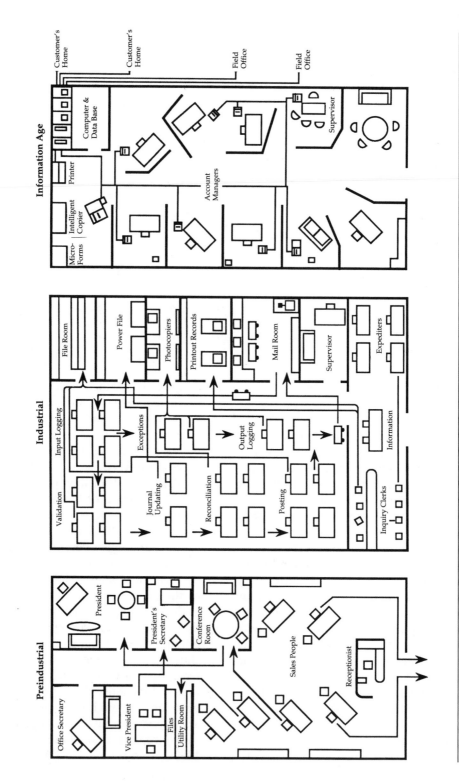

When one considers the nature of these system evaluation and implementation problems, it becomes clear that we are in a realm where the traditional human factors orientation alone will not suffice. To use the open-system metaphor from the beginning of this chapter, it is a realm where the interaction of person-machine subsystems with the larger organizational systems becomes critical; hence, the cooperative effort of industrial/organizational and human factors specialties is required. Consider, for example, the acceptance problem. Certainly factors such as organizational climate, prevailing management style, and the reward system have a lot to do with how readily any automation concept is received. No matter how efficient the concept may be in principle, or how well it has shown in simulations or in other organizational contexts, its acceptance and consequent success can never be taken for granted.

Office automation must therefore be carefully planned with regard for the kinds of organizational variables industrial and organizational psychologists have been worrying about since the days of Hawthorne. If trust in management is lacking and the proposed changes appear to threaten valued personal outcomes, then even involving end users in the planning, which is the strategy for promoting acceptance most favored by human factors, may fail to produce total cooperation. Further repercussions are likely later on. Changes of the magnitude involved in the transition from industrial to information age extend well beyond the procedural level: They constitute a serious alteration in a complex sociopolitical system, a replay of the classic Tavistock discovery. The human factors and design communities know little about such sociological or sociopsychological processes. However, as awareness of the need for this type of input appears to be growing (Czaja, 1987; Westin et al., 1987), the time has never been better for strengthening the ties between these two specialties.

The essential components of the information age (or true office automation [OA]) concept are (a) the decentralization and autonomy afforded by individual multifunction workstations (VDTs), (b) the information capability afforded by data bases to which the workstations have easy access, and (c) the integration afforded by local area networking (LAN). Perhaps its most critical feature, however, is the fact that it encompasses virtually all levels and functions represented in the typical office, not just clerical workers, word and data processing, or communication. As Czaja (1987) notes, "OA has come to imply an *integrated* office system (IOS) or office information system (OIS)...designed to aid office personnel in a wide range of activities which include document preparation, information management, and *decision making*" (p. 1592, italics added).

Each element of the system offers a variety of options, and the technology changes so rapidly that whatever list one might offer would be outdated by the time it reached readers. In view of its central role in the all-important integrating function, however, the LAN concept deserves a bit of elaboration. It is also the technical component most often blamed for the somewhat slower than anticipated transition to full information age automation during the early 1980s.

As of 1985, the three major LAN configurations were those illustrated in Figure 14. The *star* network connects all workstations to a central controlling device; the *ring* circulates all information among all workstations; and the *tree* (or "bus") design provides multiple frequency bands, each of which can be dedicated to particular use. Each configuration arose from a particular communication application (e.g., the star from the familiar PBX telephone system concept), but adaptation to the multifunction, computer-based requirements of the true automated office was retarded by limitations in the capacity of certain components and lack of standardization among manufacturers—particularly for ring and tree

FIGURE 14

Three Local Area Network Configurations

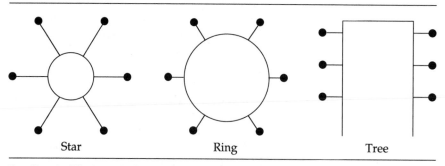

Star   Ring   Tree

From "Emerging Office Automation Systems" by M. G. Helander, 1985, *Human Factors, 27*, pp. 3–20. Copyright 1985 by The Human Factors Society, Inc. Reproduced by permission.

configurations (Helander, 1985). Writing in 1987, Czaja continued to cite the standardization problem, but many of the other technical limitations seemed to be disappearing. As we saw in our evaluation of particular machine elements, the best design often is heavily dependent on task and user characteristics. Thus, it becomes important to analyze and classify tasks involved in office work before attempting a systematic evaluation. And in this area there has indeed been some progress. One of the several useful taxonomies (see Table 6) is based on a massive study of 1,200 white-collar positions in 11 companies at 40 different sites. Another, integrating several lines of research, provides a more functional conceptualization as illustrated in Figure 15. Each major task category has produced some human factors data (including some we have already encountered) for use in the office design process. However, comparative studies of entire systems are extremely rare and much needed (Helander, 1985). In fact, despite his own efforts along these lines, Helander cites the absence of "a generic taxonomy that can be validated for different types of tasks and organizations" (p. 18) as a pressing need.

What we do have are rather global recommendations for carrying out the design process, and they are essentially the same ones encountered earlier for system design in general:

- Form a design team

- Define the system

- Assess needs

- Select components

- Implement a prototype

- Evaluate the prototype

- Feed the evaluation results back into the design cycle

In addition, there should be early and continuing involvement of users in the entire process, the purpose being to promote acceptance and to make use of their considerable insights (Czaja, 1987; Gould & Lewis, 1983; Helander, 1985). Finally, care should be taken to ensure adequate training on the prototype system and to use an appropriate evaluation scheme, preferably a pre-post repeated measures design with a control group, over reasonable time

TABLE 6

Taxonomy of Office Tasks and Time Distributions for Management and Nonmanagement

Task Descriptors	Percentage of Time	
	Management	Nonmanagement
Advising, counseling, assisting, recommending, problem solving, instructing, acting as liaison	12.9	5.3
Bookkeeping, accounting, calculating, inventorying, invoicing	2.0	48.1
Deciding, authorizing, approving	12.8	2.5
Evaluating, auditing, controlling, coordinating	17.7	11.6
Completing forms, filing, recording, logging	—	7.7
General administration, paperwork	3.1	—
Human relating, supervising, appraising performance, staffing, motivating	21.1	7.3
Informing, reporting	4.4	4.2
Interactive formal meetings	3.0	—
Orders, requests, invoices, bills	—	3.0
Planning, budgeting, analyzing	16.2	2.5
Arranging/scheduling of meetings, appointments	—	7.3
Selling, convincing, persuading, advertising	8.2	1.7
Typing, transcribing, copying, writing	—	4.5
Total	101.4	102.7

From "The Office Activities in Two Organizations" by C. J. Thachenkary and D. W. Conrath in *Office Information Systems* (pp. 453–467), N. Naffah, Ed. (1982), Amsterdam: Elsevier. Copyright 1982 by Elsevier Science Publishers. Reproduced by permission.

periods, say, over 3, 6, and 12 months (Czaja, 1987).

Office automation, along with the other computer-based changes in the workplace (CAD, CAM, robotics, etc.) are happening so rapidly we scarcely have time to digest the implications of one innovation before the next one is upon us. With the entire world as a source of and potential market for these innovative products, the competitive pressure can only accelerate the process in the years ahead. The risk is that measurably superior products at one level of analysis—purely engineering or traditional human factors—may prove less useful at such higher levels as organizational and societal unless thought is given to longer range consequences at the outset. At each level, however, the complexity and cost of conducting the necessary research goes up; the time required to get meaningful answers increases. One can only wonder, therefore, whether the call for more global research efforts such as Helender proposed and we have echoed here is a somewhat quixotic hope. We may instead be headed for a period of Darwinian evolution in these systems, which may put entire organizations and social institutions at risk. The whole office concept may fail the test of survival.

Conclusions

We have explored an extremely small sample of the problems, concerns, and research issues

FIGURE 15

Taxonomy of Office Interactions and Office Tasks

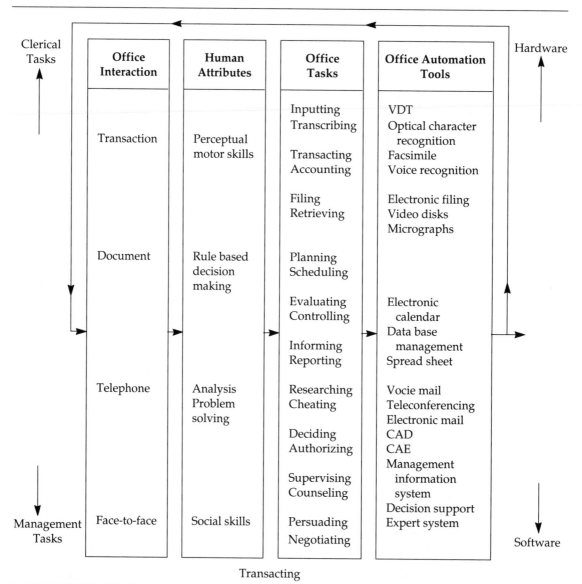

From "Emerging Office Automation Systems" by M. G. Helander, 1985. *Human Factors, 27,* pp. 3–20. Copyright 1985 by The Human Factors Society, Inc. Adapted by permission.

endemic to human factors. Notable among the omissions are such traditional topics as control devices, human response capabilities, the ambient environment, and simulation—all still very active areas. Training and decision making, currently receiving much attention due to the changing personnel requirements of advanced systems, are also missing since they are well represented in other chapters of this *Handbook*.

These omissions, however, are consistent with the aim of this chapter, the intent of which was not to provide comprehensive or even representative coverage, but rather to convey a sense of what human factors is about, where it is headed, and what it has to offer work organizations and society. As we have seen, it is an attempt to make sure that our technology doesn't proceed without us, in the belief that "human engineering" results in safer, more acceptable, more efficient systems. And since systems that are coming to dominate the workplace—and thus, to a great extent, to define work—are growing in sophistication at an amazing rate, including or neglecting human factors at the design stage has obvious implications for the overall functions of the entire work organization. Poor design of a hand tool affects a small fraction of the work force and perhaps results in some marginal increase in labor costs; once discovered it can easily be corrected. By contrast, poor design of the human-computer interface or the automated office, or poor allocation of functions to humans and machines, undermines organizations in a more profound way. The consequences are likely to be massive and extremely difficult to reverse—so much so that their resolution must be found elsewhere in the organizational system: selection, training, work scheduling, supervision, or when all else fails, employee assistance programs!

The increasing scope of systems design decisions has another important implication that human factors specialists are only beginning to appreciate. As semiautomated work systems become larger and more sophisticated, the list of psychological variables to be considered becomes longer and more complex. It used to consist mainly of factors involved in perceptual-motor proficiency; now it encompasses a growing array of cognitive variables; tomorrow, it will undoubtedly include affective, emotional, motivational, and social considerations. Design questions will not end with the demonstration of superior performance, but will extend into the realm of consequences for human interactions, morale, motivation, and quality of work life. In a word, human factors will be obliged to grapple with many of the same problems and variables that are today the preoccupation of industrial and organizational psychologists.

All of which brings us back to the point at which we started: Conceptually, the human-machine system cannot be divorced from the organizational system of which it is a part. Human factors and industrial and organizational psychology are being forced into closer concordance by the dramatic evolution of computer technology, although it is not yet clear whether either fully realizes it, nor indeed, whether even the combined efforts of our disciplines will be sufficient to channel technological development into the directions that will most benefit society.

Notes

1 The sexist designation is used here only in the interest of historical accuracy.
2 Although training models vary considerably within as well as across major disciplines, the most common routes to a career in human factors are master's degree programs in industrial engineering and doctoral degree programs in psychology. In both cases, human factors represents a specialty or concentration. The IE programs tend to have a more technical-professional emphasis, whereas the psychology programs tend to be more research (scientist-practitioner) oriented. Both the Human Factors Society and Division 21 of the American Psychological Association have

formulated "training guidelines" (see Howell, Colle, Kantowitz, & Wiener, 1987), and the former is in the process of instituting a certification procedure. As of 1990, however, virtually anyone can represent him or herself as a human factors professional!

3 Computer scientists and human factors specialists have come to abhor this term; they prefer *compatibility* or *dialogue effectiveness*.

4 This holds true for human factors. In industrial and organizational psychology, it is beginning to be used in a more general sense (see Lawler, 1976).

5 TSD theory suggests that all detection tasks, including those of classical psychophysics, involve identification of a "signal" against a background of "noise" based on both sensory (d') and decision (β) considerations. When a signal is presented, the observer interprets the experience in terms of its likelihood of representing the noise-alone or signal-plus-noise condition, both of which are defined probabilistically (see Swets, 1964).

6 The terms *mental model* and *schema* refer to somewhat different constructs, but for present purposes may be considered together.

References

Adams, J. A. (1987). Criticisms of vigilance research: A discussion. *Human Factors, 29,* 737–740.

Adams, J. A., Humes, J. M., & Stenson, H. H. (1962). Monitoring of complex visual displays III: Effects of repeated sessions on human vigilance. *Human Factors, 4,* 149–158.

Alluisi, E. A. (1987). Human factors technologies—past promises, future issues. In L. S. Mark, J. S. Warm, & R. L. Huston (Eds.), *Ergonomics and human factors: Recent research.* New York: Springer-Verlag.

ANSI/HFS 100–1988. (1988). *American National Standard for human factors engineering of visual display terminal workstations.* Santa Monica, CA: Human Factors Society.

Baecker, R. M., & Buxton, W. A. S. (1987). *Human-computer interaction.* Los Altos, CA: Morgan Kaufmann.

Beatty, J., Ahern, S., & Katz, R. (1977). Sleep deprivation and the vigilance of anesthesiologists during simulated surgery. In R. R. Mackie (Ed.), *Vigilance: Theory, operational performance, and physiological correlates* (pp. 511–535). New York: Plenum.

Boyd, S. (1983). Assessing the validity of SWAT as a work load measurement instrument. In A. Pope & L. Haugh (Eds.), *Proceedings of the Human Factors Society 27th annual meeting.* Santa Monica, CA: Human Factors Society.

Broadbent, D. E. (1958). *Perception and communication.* London: Pergamon Press.

Broadbent, D. E., & Gregory, M. (1965). Effects of noise and signal rate upon vigilance as analyzed by means of decision theory. *Human Factors, 7,* 155–162.

Buckner, D. N., & McGrath, J. J. (Eds.). (1963). *Vigilance: A symposium.* New York: McGraw-Hill.

Butler, K. A., & Corter, J. E. (1986). The use of psychometric tools for knowledge acquisition: A case study. In W. Gale (Ed.), *Artificial intelligence and statistics.* Reading, MA: Addison-Wesley.

Card, S. K., Moran, T. P., & Newell, A. (1983). *The psychology of human-computer interaction.* Hillsdale, NJ: Erlbaum.

Chapanis, A. (1976). Engineering psychology. In M. D. Dunnette (Ed.), *Handbook of industrial and organizational psychology.* Chicago: Rand McNally.

Christensen, J. M. (1958). Trends in human factors. *Human Factors, 1,* 2–7.

Christensen, J. M. (1987). The human factors profession. In G. Salvendy (Ed.), *Handbook of human factors.* New York: Wiley.

Chubb, G. P. (1981). SAINT, a digital simulation language for the study of manned systems. In J. Moraal & K. R. Kraiss (Eds.), *Manned system design: Methods, equipment, and applications.* New York: Plenum.

Chubb, G. P., Laughery, K. R., & Pritsker, A. A. B. (1987). Simulating manned systems. In G. Salvendy (Ed.), *Handbook of human factors.* New York: Wiley.

Cohen, A. (1987). Overview paper: Health, stress, and workload in an era of workplace change. In L. S. Mark, J. S. Warm, & R. L. Huston (Eds.), *Ergonomics and human factors.* New York: Springer-Verlag.

Cooke, N. M., & McDonald, J. E. (1986). A formal methodology for acquiring and representing expert knowledge. *IEEE Special Issue on Knowledge Representation, 74,* 1422–1430.

Cooke, N. M., & McDonald, J. E. (1987). The application of psychological scaling techniques to knowledge elicitation for knowledge-based systems. *International Journal of Man-Machine Studies, 26*, 533–550.

Cooke, N. M., & Schvaneveldt, R. W. (1986, June). *The evolution of cognitive networks with computer programming experience.* Paper presented at the Workshop on Empirical Studies of Programmers, Washington, DC.

Copley, F. B. (1923). *Frederick W. Taylor,* Vol. I. New York: Harper.

Czaja, S. J. (1987). Human factors in office automation. In G. Salvendy (Ed.), *Handbook of human factors.* New York: Wiley.

Czaja, S. J., & Drury, C. G. (1981). Training programs for inspection. *Human Factors, 23,* 473–484.

Davis, R. (1987). Robustness and transparency in intelligent systems. In T. B. Sheridan, D. S. Kruser, & S. Deutsch (Eds.), *Human factors in automated and robotic space systems: Proceedings of a symposium* (pp. 211–233). Washington, DC: National Research Council.

Department of the Army (1983). *PATRIOT: Information and coordination control, guided missile system, truck mounted: AN/MSQ-116* (Tech. Rep. No. TM9-1430-602-10-1). Washington, DC.

Drury, C. G. (1975). Inspection of sheet materials—model and data. *Human Factors, 17,* 257–265.

Drury, C. G., & Sinclair, M. A. (1983). Human and machine performance in an inspection task. *Human Factors, 25,* 391–399.

Eastman, C. M. (1968). *Exploration of the cognitive process in design* (Tech. Rep. AFOSR-68-1374). Madison, WI: University of Wisconsin Environmental Design Center.

Eberts, R. E., & Brock, J. F. (1987). Computer-assisted and computer-managed instruction. In G. Salvendy (Ed.), *Handbook of human factors.* New York: Wiley.

Ericsson, K. A., & Simon, H. A. (1984). *Protocol analysis: Verbal reports as data.* Cambridge, MA: MIT Press.

Finkelman, J. M., & Kirschner, C. (1980). An information-processing interpretation of air traffic control stress. *Human Factors, 22,* 561–567.

Fitts, P. M., Jones, R. E., & Milton, J. L. (1950). Eye movements of aircraft pilots during instrument landing approaches. *Aeronautical Engineering Review, 9,* 24–29.

Fisk, A. D., & Schneider, W. (1981). Controlled and automatic processing during tasks requiring sustained attention: A new approach to vigilance. *Human Factors, 23,* 737–750.

Foley, P., & Moray, N. (1987). Sensation, perception, and system design. In G. Salvendy (Ed.), *Handbook of human factors.* New York: Wiley.

Fontenelle, G. (1988). *A contrast of guideline recommendations and Tullis's prediction model for computer displays: Should text be left-justified?* Unpublished doctoral dissertation, Rice University, Houston, TX.

Fotta, M. E. (1987). Artificial intelligence: An introduction and applications to the human-computer interface. In L. S. Mark, J. S. Warm, & R. L. Huston (Eds.), *Ergonomics and human factors.* New York: Springer-Verlag.

Garner, W. R. (1962). *Uncertainty and structure as psychological concepts.* New York: Wiley.

Gilbreth, F. B. (1911). *Motion study.* Princeton, NJ: Van Nostrand.

Gitomer, D. H. (1988). Individual differences in technical troubleshooting. *Human Performance, 1,* 111–131.

Gopher, D., & Braune, R. (1984). On the psychophysics of work load: Why bother with subjective measures? *Human Factors, 26,* 519–532.

Gould, J. D., Alfaro, L., Barnes, V., Finn, R., Grischkowsky, N., & Minuto, A. (1987). Reading is slower from CRT displays than from paper: Attempts to isolate a single-variable explanation. *Human Factors, 29,* 269–299.

Gould, J. D., Alfaro, L., Finn, R., Haupt, B., & Minuto, A. (1987). Reading from CRT displays can be as fast as reading from paper. *Human Factors, 29,* 497–517.

Gould, J. D., & Lewis, C. (1983). Designing from usability—key principles and what designers think. *Proceedings CHI '83 conference: Human factors in computing systems* (pp. 50–53). Boston.

Giuliano, V. E. (1982). The mechanization of office work. *Scientific American, 247,* 148–165.

Hammer, W. (1976). *Handbook of systems and product safety.* Englewood Cliffs, NJ: Prentice-Hall.

Hardman Project Office, Chief of Naval Operations (OP-112). (1979, July). *Documented description of the weapon system acquisition process* (Tech. Rep. HR 79-01). Washington, DC.

Helander, M. G. (1985). Emerging office automation systems. *Human Factors, 27*, 3–20.

Howell, W. C., Colle, H. A., Kantowitz, B. H., & Wiener, E. L. (1987). Guidelines for education and training in engineering psychology. *American Psychologist, 42*, 602–605.

Howell, W. C. (1985). Engineering psychology. In E. M. Altmaier & M. E. Meryer (Eds.), *Applied specialties in psychology*. New York: Random House.

Howell, W. C., & Goldstein, I. L. (1971). *Engineering psychology: Current perspectives in research*. New York: Appleton-Century-Crofts.

Howell, W. C., Johnston, W. A., & Goldstein, I. L. (1966). Complex monitoring and its relation to the classical problem of vigilance. *Organizational Behavior and Human Performance, 1*, 129–150.

Huston, R. L. (1987). An overview of safety engineering in human factors. In L. S. Mark, J. S. Warm, & R. L. Huston (Eds.), *Ergonomics and human factors: Recent research*. New York: Springer-Verlag.

Kantowitz, B. H. (1985). Stages and channels in human information processing: A limited review and analysis of theory and methodology. *Journal of Mathematical Psychology, 29*, 135–174.

Kantowitz, B. H., & Sorkin, R. D. (1983). *Human factors: Understanding people-system relationships*. New York: Wiley.

Kantowitz, B. H., & Sorkin, R. D. (1987). Allocation of functions. In G. Salvendy (Ed.), *Handbook of human factors*. New York: Wiley.

Katz, D., & Kahn, R. L. (1978). *The social psychology of organizations*. New York: Wiley.

Kemeny, J. G., et al. (1979). *The President's commission on the accident at Three Mile Island*. Springfield, VA: National Technical Information Services.

Kibler, A. W. (1965). The relevance of vigilance research to aerospace monitoring tasks. *Human Factors, 7*, 93–99.

Kira, A. (1976). *The bathroom* (rev. ed.). New York: Viking Press.

Knowles, M. (Ed.). (1986). *Human Factors Society 1986 directory and yearbook*. Santa Monica, CA: Human Factors Society.

Kramer, A. F., & Schumacher, R. M. (1987). Human-computer interaction: A brief glimpse of an emerging field. In L. S. Mark, J. S. Warm, &

R. L. Huston (Eds.), *Ergonomics and human factors* (pp. 213–224). New York: Springer-Verlag.

Kramer, A. F., Sirevaag, E. J., & Braune, R. (1987). A psychophysiological assessment of operator work load during simulated flight sessions. *Human Factors, 29*, 145–160.

Lachman, R., Lachman, J. L., & Butterfield, E. C., (1979). *Cognitive psychology and information processing: An introduction*. Hillsdale, NJ: Erlbaum.

Landauer, T. K., Duamis, S. T., Gomez, L. M., & Furnas, G. W. (1982). Human factors in data access. *Bell System Technical Journal, 61*, 2487–2509.

Laughery, K. R., Sr., & Laughery, K. R., Jr. (1987). Analytic techniques for function analysis. In G. Salvendy (Ed.), *Handbook of human factors*. New York: Wiley.

Lawler, E. E., III. (1976). Control system in organizations. In M. Dunnette (Ed.), *Handbook of industrial and organizational psychology*. Chicago: Rand McNally.

Leeper, P. (1983). VDTs and vision: Work place design is the key. *Human Factors Bulletin, 26*, 1–3.

Lenorovitz, D. R., Phillips, M. D., Ardrey, R. S., & Kloster, G. V. (1984). A taxonomic approach to characterizing human-computer interfaces. In G. Salvendy (Ed.), *Human-computer interaction* (pp. 111–116). Amsterdam: Elsevier.

Lintz, L. M., Asken, W. B., & Lott, W. J. (1971). *System design trade studies: The engineering process and use of human resources data* (Tech. Rep. AFHRL TR-71-24). Wright-Patterson Air Force Base, OH: Air Force Human Resources Laboratory.

Mackworth, N. H. (1950). *Researches on the measurement of human performance* (Medical Research Council Special Report Series 268). London: HM Stationery Office.

Mackie, R. R. (1987). Vigilance research—are we ready for countermeasures? *Human Factors, 29*, 707–723.

Malone, T. B. (1986). The centered high-mounted brake light: A human factors success story. *Human Factors Bulletin, 29*, 1–4.

Mark, L. S., Warm, J. S., & Huston, R. L. (Eds.). (1987). *Ergonomics and human factors: Recent research* (pp. 1–7). New York: Springer-Verlag.

Mark, L. S., Warm, J. S., & Huston, R. L. (Eds.). (1987). An overview of ergonomics and human factors. In L. S. Mark, J. S. Warm, & R. L. Huston (Eds.),

Ergonomics and human factors: Recent research (pp. 1–7). New York: Springer-Verlag.

Meister, D. (1984). Dear editor. *Human Factors Society Bulletin, 27,* 3.

Meister, D. (1985). *Behavioral analysis and measurement methods.* New York: Wiley.

Meister, D. (1987). System design, development, and testing. In G. Salvendy (Ed.), *Handbook of human factors.* New York: Wiley.

Meister, D., Sullivan, D. J., & Askren, W. N. (1968). *The impact of manpower requirements and personnel resources data on system design* (Tech. Rep. AFHRL TR-68-44). Wright-Patterson Air Force Base, OH: Air Force Human Resources Laboratory.

Mital, A. (Ed.). Special issue: Hand tools. *Human Factors, 28* (Whole No. 3).

Mohney, J. D. (1989). IMPACTS: How to get more out of what you've got. *Impacts Bulletin, 1,* 1–5.

Moray, N. (1982). Subjective mental work load. *Human Factors, 23,* 25–40.

Moray, N. P., & Huey, B. M. (Eds.). (1988). *Human factors research and nuclear safety.* Washington, DC: National Academy Press.

Moray, N., Johannsen, G., Pew, R., Rasmussen, J., Sanders, A., & Wickens, C. (1979). Final report of the experimental psychology group. In N. Moray (Ed.), *Mental work load: Its theory and measurement.* New York: Plenum.

Morganthau, T., Cohn, B., Sandza, R., & Murr, A. (1987), July). Year of the near miss. *Newsweek,* 20–27.

National Aeronautics and Space Administration (NASA). (1978). *Anthropometric source book: Vol. 1. Anthropometry for designers. Vol. 2. A handbook of anthropometric data.* (NASA Reference Publication 1024).

Nisbett, R., & Wilson, T. (1977). Telling more than we know: Verbal reports on mental processes. *Psychological Review, 84,* 231–259.

Norman, D. A. (1984). Stages and levels in human-machine interaction. *Interactional Journal of Man-Machine Studies, 21,* 365–375.

Norman, D. A. (1987). Design principles for human-computer interfaces. In R. M. Baecker & W. A. S. Buxton (Eds.), *Human-computer interaction.* Los Altos, CA: Morgan Kaufmann.

Prien, E. (1981). *I/O psychologist job analysis.* Washington, DC: American Psychological Association, Division of Industrial and Organizational Psychology.

Parasuraman, R. (1987). Human-computer monitoring. *Human Factors, 29,* 695–706.

Posner, M. I., & Snyder, C. R. R. (1975). Attention and cognitive control. In R. L. Solso (Ed.), *Information processing and cognition: The Loyda symposium.* Hillsdale, NJ: Erlbaum.

Rasmussen, J., & Rouse, W. B. (1981). *Human detection and diagnosis of system failures.* New York: Plenum.

Reid, G., Shingledecker, C., & Eggemeier, T. (1981). Application of conjoint measurement to work load scale development. In R. Sugarman (Ed.), *Proceedings of the Human Factors Society 25th annual meeting.* Santa Monica, CA: Human Factors Society.

Roberts, T. L., & Moran, T. P. (1987). The evaluation of text editors: Methodology and empirical results. In R. M. Baecker & W. A. S. Buxton (Eds.), *Human-computer interaction.* Los Altos, CA: Morgan Kaufmann.

Rouse, W. B. (1987). Much ado about data. *Human Factors Society Bulletin, 30,* 1–3.

Rubenstein, T., & Mason, A. F. (1979, November). The accident that shouldn't have happened: An analysis of Three Mile Island. *IEEE Spectrum,* 33–57.

Ryan, J. P. (1987). Cognitive aspects of hazard warning labels. In L. S. Mark, J. S. Warm, & R. L. Huston (Eds.), *Ergonomics and human factors: Recent research.* New York: Springer-Verlag.

Salvendy, G. (Ed.). (1987). *Handbook of human factors.* New York: Wiley.

Sanders, M. S. (1985). Human factors graduate education: An update. *Human Factors Society Bulletin, 28,* 1–3.

Sanders, M. S., & McCormick, E. J. (1987). *Human factors in engineering and design.* New York: McGraw-Hill.

Schneider, W., & Shiffrin, R. M. (1977). Control and automatic human information processing: I. Detection, search, and attention. *Psychological Review, 84,* 1–66.

Schneiderman, B. (1987). *Designing the user interface.* Reading, MA: Addison-Wesley.

Schvaneveldt, R. W., Durso, F. T., Goldsmith, T. E., Breen, T. J., Cooke, N. M., Tucker, R. G., & DeMaio, J. C. (1985). Measuring the structure of expertise. *International Journal of Man-Machine Studies, 23,* 699–728.

Schwartz, D. R. (1986). *Formatting effects on the use of computer-generated alphanumeric displays: The moderating effects of task characteristics.* Unpublished doctoral dissertation, Rice University, Houston, TX.

Science Agenda. (1988, Fall). The Vincennes incident: Congress hears psychologists. Washington, DC: *American Psychological Association, 1,* 4–5.

Sheridan, T. B. (1987). Supervisory control. In G. Salvendy (Ed.), *Handbook of human factors.* New York: Wiley.

Sheridan, T. B., Kruser, D. S., & Deutsch, S. (Eds.), (1987). *Human factors in automated and robotic space systems: Proceedings of a symposium.* Washington, DC: National Research Council.

Shuell, T. J. (1986). Contributions of cognitive psychology to learning from instruction in Air Force training. In *Learning research laboratory: Proposed research issues* (Tech. Rep. AFHRL-TP-85-54, pp. 29–44). Brooks Air Force Base, TX: Manpower and Personnel Division, Air Force Human Resources Laboratory.

Simon, C. W. (1987). Will egg-sucking ever become a science? *Human Factors Society Bulletin, 30,* 1–4.

Smith, K. U. (1987). Origins of human factors science. *Human Factors Society Bulletin, 30,* 1–3.

Smith, L. L. (1987). Whyfore human factors? *Human Factors Society Bulletin, 30,* 6–7.

Smith, S. L., & Aucella, A. F. (1983). *Design guidelines for the user interface to computer-based information systems* (Tech. Rep. ESD-TR-83-122). Bedford, MA: Mitre.

Smith, S. L., & Mosier, J. N. (1986). *Guidelines for designing user interface software* (Tech. Rep. ESD-TR-278). Bedford, MA: Mitre.

Stevens, S. S. (1966). On the operation known as judgment. *American Scientist, 54,* 385–401.

Strub, M. H. (1987, August). *Manprint: The challenge for applied experimental and engineering psychology.* Presentation at the annual meeting of the American Psychological Association, New York.

Swets, J. A. (Ed.). (1964). *Signal detection and recognition by human observers: Contemporary readings.* New York: Wiley.

Tullis, T. S. (1983). The formatting of alphanumeric displays: A review and analysis. *Human Factors, 25,* 657–682.

Tullis, T. S. (1984). *Predicting the usability of alphanumeric displays.* Unpublished doctoral dissertation, Rice University, Houston, TX.

Van Cott, H. P. (1984). From control systems to knowledge systems. *Human Factors, 26,* 115–122.

Van Cott, H. P., & Kinkade, R. D. (Eds.). (1972). *Human engineering guide to equipment design.* Washington, DC: U.S. Superintendent of Documents.

Waldrop, M. M. (1988a). Toward a unified theory of cognition. *Science, 241,* 27–29.

Waldrop, M. M. (1988b). Soar: A unified theory of cognition? *Science, 241,* 296–298.

Warm, J. S., & Parasuraman, R. (Eds.). (1987). Vigilance: Basic and applied research. *Human Factors, 29* (Whole No. 6).

Welford, A. T. (1968). *Fundamentals of skill.* London: Methuen.

Westin, A. F., Schweder, H. A., Baker, M. A., & Lehman, S. (1987). Office technology and managerial excellence. In R. M. Baecker & W. A. S. Buxton (Eds.), *Human-computer interaction.* Los Altos, CA: Morgan Kaufmann.

White, R. H., Jr., & Zsambok, C. (1987). An overview of cognitive psychology. In L. S. Mark, J. S. Warm, & R. L. Huston (Eds.), *Ergonomics and human factors* (pp. 71–78). New York: Springer-Verlag.

Wickens, C. D. (1984). *Engineering psychology and human performance.* Columbus, OH: Merrill.

Wickens, C. D. (1987). Information processing, decision making, and cognition. In G. Salvendy (Ed.), *Handbook of human factors.* New York: Wiley.

Wickens, C. D., & Kramer, A. (1985). Engineering psychology. *Annual Review of Psychology, 36,* 307–348.

Wickens, C. D., Mountford, S. J., & Schreiner, W. (1981). Multiple resources, task hemispheric integrity, and individual differences in time sharing. *Human Factors, 23,* 211–229.

Wiener, E. A. (1980). Special issue preface. *Human Factors, 22,* 517–519.

Wiener, E. A. (1987). Application of vigilance research: Rare, medium, or well done? *Human Factors, 29,* 725–736.

Wierwille, W., & Williges, R. (1978). *Survey and analsis of operator work load assessment techniques* (Tech. Rep. S-78-101). Blacksburg, VA: Systemetrics, Inc.

Williges, R. C. (Ed.). (1973). Response surface methodology: Special issue. *Human Factors, 15,* 293–354.

Williges, R. C. (1976). The vigilance increment: An ideal observer hypothesis. In T. B. Sheridan & G. Johannsen (Eds.), *Monitoring and supervisory control.* New York: Plenum.

Wohl, J. G. (1981). Force management decision requirements for Air Force tactical command and control. *IEEE Transactions on Systems, MAN, & Cybernetics,* SMCII, 618–639.

Woods, D. D., O'Brien, J. F., & Hanes, L. F. (1987). Human factors challenges in process control: The case of nuclear power plants. In G. Salvendy (Ed.), *Handbook of human factors.* New York: Wiley.

Yeh, Y-Y., & Wickens, C. D. (1988). Disassociation of performance and subjective measures of work load. *Human Factors, 30,* 111–120.

CHAPTER 5

Job Behavior, Performance, and Effectiveness

Walter C. Borman
University of South Florida

This chapter is about criterion development and criterion measurement. Major topics include important views and concepts related to criteria, recent developments in methods of measuring criterion performance, conceptual and methodological advantages and disadvantages of various kinds of criterion measures, and conclusions about criterion development and measurement. Because performance ratings are so often used as criteria in personnel research applications, considerable attention is focused on ratings. Areas discussed include design and evaluation of rating forms, analysis of ratings from different sources (e.g., peers or supervisors), identification of training treatments to reduce rating error and enhance the accuracy of performance ratings, examination of the performance judgment process to aid in understanding and improving ratings, and analysis of strategies for evaluating performance ratings, including assessment of psychometric properties, interrater reliability, convergent and discriminant validity, and accuracy. Also critically reviewed as criteria are turnover, absences, production rates, job level and salary, sales, disciplinary cases, performance tests or work samples, and job knowledge tests. Parallel to what has been accomplished with predictor domains such as cognitive abilities and personality, the development and evaluation of criterion models is offered as a promising direction for criterion research. Structural and latent variable modeling may be used to identify and confirm performance constructs in order to enhance the scientific understanding and usefulness of criteria.

MEASURES OF CRITERION perform-ance are necessary for almost all competently conducted personnel research applications in organizations. If we are to assess empirically the impact of any personnel action on individual or group performance, criteria are essential. Criteria are needed to assess the effectiveness of personnel selection procedures, organizational training programs, job design efforts, and many other personnel-related actions and interventions. In personnel selection, for example, we may develop an experimental selection test, administer it to applicants for a job, and later assess the performance of those hired to evaluate the test's validity by correlating test scores with performance scores. This naturally requires some measure of performance that fairly and accurately depicts actual performance levels. In sum, criterion measures have great importance for practical applications in personnel research.

Criteria and criterion measures are, however, of considerable interest in their own right. Much has been made of learning as much as possible about what tests measure and how test scores should be interpreted, based especially on the scientific principles of construct validation (Cronbach & Meehl, 1955). A similar framework is appropriate for learning about criterion measures. To echo the work of others such as James (1973) and P. C. Smith (1976), researchers need to apply the same degree of effort and rigor to develop criteria and criterion measures that they used to develop predictor tests.

Views and Observations on Criteria

In this section, we review and discuss several important issues relevant to criteria and criterion measurement.

The Concept of Criterion Relevance and Other "Criteria for Criteria"

The most important standard for criteria is relevance. *Relevance* refers to the correspondence between criteria and the actual performance demands of the target job. A criterion measure should assess one or more of the job's important performance requirements; as a set, criterion measures should provide comprehensive coverage of all important performance requirements of the job.

The terms "contamination" and "deficiency" have been useful in assessing criterion relevance. *Contamination* is said to exist when a criterion measure taps variance irrelevant to the performance requirements. For example, a sales-per-month criterion for a computer software salesperson may be a function of this person's sales ability *and* the ease of software sales in his or her region. This measure is contaminated. Criterion *deficiency* becomes an issue when a set of criteria for a job fails to measure one or more of its important performance areas. For example, a work sample performance test for a typist position may very faithfully reflect technical proficiency on that job but completely fail to tap important interpersonal requirements. This measure is therefore deficient. A totally relevant set of criterion measures is thus neither contaminated nor deficient.

In practice, it may be possible to correct for criterion contamination where the source and degree of contamination can be identified, such as in adjusting for unequal opportunity to perform effectively, but nothing can be done about deficiency, short of obtaining or creating additional criterion measures. This issue will be discussed in more detail later in this chapter.

Early writings about criteria for criteria describe several standards in addition to relevance. A brief discussion of these historic statements should be useful here, not only to understand standards for criteria themselves, but to help provide a sense of the history of criterion development and measurement.

Some time ago, Bellows (1941) listed accessibility and cost, acceptability to the sponsor, and predictability as three important criteria for criteria. The first two reflect an emphasis on the practical, use-what's-available approach to criterion measurement, an approach many (e.g., P. C. Smith, 1976) have argued against. The third criterion illustrates the logical fallacy of selecting criteria in personnel selection research according to the magnitude of predictor-criterion relationships, no matter what the particular nature of the criteria (e.g., their relevance) may be. This is a classic case of misunderstanding the criterion development process and ignoring the issue of relevance in criterion measurement.

Some time later, Toops (1944) advanced a relatively sophisticated treatise on criteria for criteria and related problems. He provided an in-depth analysis of criterion contamination, including such problems as the effects of teamwork on individual productivity, the issue of equal pay for both sexes based on equal levels of productivity, and problems with environmental constraints, such as relatively slow machine speed affecting criterion scores (production in this case).

Jenkins (1946), reviewing then-recent advances in applied testing practices, noted that from 1920 through 1940 considerable progress was made on the predictor development side, but almost no attention was given to criteria. He observed that during the twenties and thirties much was learned about the validation of tests, *given a criterion,* but that was exactly the problem: Criteria were considered "given of God or just to be found lying around" (p. 93). Jenkins then discussed advances in thinking about and working with criterion measures on the part of American psychologists during

World War II, including quite a sophisticated discussion of such problems as criterion unreliability and deficiency, low correlations between training and job performance, and the sometimes dynamic nature of job performance requirements over time.

Fiske (1951) argued that an "ideal" approach to criterion development was to determine the contributions of each criterion behavior to the goals of the organization in assessing individual performance, urging that empirical research be used instead of "value judgments" in developing criteria. It is unclear how values about effectiveness can be divorced from operational definitions of performance.

Wherry (1957) referred to criteria for criteria by observing that psychometricians (like himself) should be depressed about the state of the art in criterion development compared to predictor test development. This was an early call for more rigorous criteria for criterion measures.

Weitz (1961), in his often-cited criteria for criteria paper, listed time, type, and level as "criterional dimensions" to be considered in developing and better understanding criterion measures. *Time* refers to when the criterion measure is taken, *type* has to do with the specific kind of criterion measure selected, and *level* pertains to the cutoff score for acceptable or unacceptable performance. Level is not actually important if criterion scores are treated as continuous variables, as they often are.

Wallace (1965) argued that the criterion for criteria of relevance to the total job might be less important than relevance to a particular research hypothesis that would lead to greater understanding of predictor-criterion relationships. He offered an example in the life insurance industry of considering as criteria total sales, which may be very relevant to the overall performance of an insurance salesperson, *or* a measure of number of calls made to potential clients (per unit time), which is presumably a behavioral element contributing to sales success but perhaps not as relevant to overall sales performance. If we had a test that was hypothesized to predict this latter call-willingness/reluctance criterion, then Wallace's suggestion is to utilize this criterion because it is most pertinent to the predictor-criterion hypothesis.

The Ultimate Criterion Model

Thorndike (1949) proposed what is essentially a *hypothetical criterion construct*. For each situation in which criteria are required, we might conceive of an ultimate criterion, a single measure that would optimally summarize all relevant performance requirements in that situation. If such a criterion could be developed, it would presumably be a weighted linear composite of all important criterion elements. Thorndike offers an example: A person displaying maximum performance on the ultimate criterion for an insurance sales job might be one who sells the maximum amount of insurance it is possible to sell, allows none of these policies to lapse, and continues at this maximum performance level for many years.

The ultimate criterion concept can best be thought of as hypothetical and as a special case of composite criteria. More will be said about composite criteria in the next subsection.

Multiple and Composite Criteria

We might ask the following question about criteria: For the typical job, should we have a single criterion measure, or is it more appropriate to identify multiple criteria? Supporters can be found for both positions. Advocates of a composite criterion (e.g., Brogden & Taylor, 1950; Nagel, 1953) view the criterion as basically economic in nature, whereas those favoring multiple criteria (e.g., Dunnette, 1963; Guion, 1961; P. C. Smith, 1976; Wallace, 1965) believe criteria should represent behavioral or psychological constructs.

The central issue is to identify the purpose of criterion measurement (Schmidt & Kaplan, 1971). In making personnel selection decisions, for example, it is necessary at some point to combine multiple criteria to form a composite. Qualities such as overall success, worth as an employee, and contribution to the organization must be determined in order to select persons with the highest predicted overall performance. If the goal is increased understanding of predictor-criterion links, then multiple criteria are more appropriate. Continuing with the selection example, if individual criterion elements refer to very different kinds of performance (e.g., technical and interpersonal), different predictors (e.g., ability tests for the former and temperament construct measures for the latter) are likely to correlate with performance in each of these areas. Combining such criteria in a composite masks relationships between individual predictors and criteria, relationships that could increase understanding of predictors, criteria, and the relationship between them.

In addition to the question of research goals and strategies bearing on the use of composite or multiple criteria, there is the empirical question of how multidimensional the criteria *are* for jobs. If criterion measures are highly correlated in a job, then combining them to form a composite seems appropriate. Studies by Rush (1953), Seashore, Indik, and Georgopoulos (1960), Peres (1962), Ronan (1963), and others empirically demonstrate the multifactor nature of job performance. More recent work confirms the multidimensionality of job performance (e.g., J. P. Campbell, 1986).

This empirical question concerning the multidimensionality of criteria becomes complicated, however. Low correlations between criterion measures can be due to unreliability (Marks, 1967). In addition, method-specific variance may lead to low relationships between criteria tapped using different methods (e.g., work sample or knowledge test scores correlated with ratings). The method variance issue is even more complex because method is easily confounded with the actual content of criterion elements. For example, job sample tests are said to tap maximum performance, the "can-do," technical proficiency aspects of job performance. Ratings, on the other hand, may reflect more the typical performance over time, "will-do" elements of performance. Accordingly, low relationships between such criterion indices might be a function of the different criterion constructs being focused on and the different methods being used. Thus, measurement issues including reliability of criterion measures and method variance associated with these measures when multiple methods are used cloud the empirical question regarding the multidimensionality of job performance. Interestingly, factor analyses of rating data, a *single method* in the context of this discussion, have also revealed multiple dimensions of job performance (cf. Pulakos, Borman, & Hough, 1988), which helps to confirm the multidimensional nature of performance.

Finally, it may be useful to consider the *expected correlation* between criterion elements in jobs. Cooper's (1981) thesis is relevant here. He argues that different dimensions of performance for individual jobs are likely to be correlated because of the way jobs are structured. A job usually requires incumbents to perform on a reasonably homogeneous set of tasks—that is, tasks that have similar knowledge, skill, and ability (KSA) requirements. If this were not the case, positions would be difficult to fill, with widely divergent KSAs necessary for successful performance. Because the KSA requirements are typically similar across tasks for a job, performance on the different dimensions of job performance will usually be correlated.

On balance, performance requirements for jobs are likely most faithfully represented by multiple criteria, with these criteria positively correlated to some extent. Later we will discuss the notion of developing models of job

performance to reflect explicitly the nature and structure of multiple criterion constructs for a job or family of jobs. The model-building effort directly addresses this difficult problem of attempting to identify and then represent multiple criteria using fallible job performance measures.

Astin's Distinction Between Conceptual Criteria and Criterion Measures

Astin (1964) provided definitions and a useful discussion of different concepts pertinent to criteria. He defined the term *conceptual criterion* as a verbal statement of the important or socially relevant outcomes related to a particular problem. *Criterion measures,* in turn, refer to operational definitions of the conceptual criteria (e.g., performance rating scales or job sample tests). This distinction is important because it implies a logical sequence for identifying or developing criterion measures that are suitable for indexing criterion performance. First, conceptual criteria should be carefully identified to include all important dimensions of performance. This exercise will typically involve detailed articulation of the important performance requirements for the target job—articulations made with considerable help from the sponsor organization. *After* the conceptual criterion has been developed, attempts can be made to identify or develop operational measures related to each component of the conceptual criterion.

The ordering of these two steps is important. It prevents the common practice of using criterion measures simply because they are available or easily developed. It also ensures that, while criterion measures are being identified or developed, the researcher can assess the extent of conceptual criterion coverage provided by the criterion measures and thus estimate the deficiency of the measures. If a set of measures is very deficient in reflecting important conceptual criteria, then more work is needed to increase this coverage. In fact, Astin argued that the validity of criterion measures can only be evaluated rationally—not empirically—by a logical analysis of these measures' relevance to the conceptual criteria.

The Campbell et al. Distinction Between Behavior, Performance, and Effectiveness

J. P. Campbell, Dunnette, Lawler, and Weick (1970) defined behavior as what managers actually do. Behaviors, with no evaluative component, might include tasks managers perform and activities that involve them. Performance criteria are developed by determining the value of behaviors to important organizational outcomes. Performance, then, reflects members' contributions to organizational goals—behaviors that lead to or detract from a position's contribution to organizational effectiveness. Performance criteria in this system are equivalent to Astin's *criterion measures;* they are operational definitions of important performance requirements that permit assessments of individual differences in performance levels.

Effectiveness has to do with outcomes. In the J. P. Campbell et al. model, global outcome measures such as promotion rate, salary level, and productivity indices are differentiated from performance measures because the effectiveness indices reflect not only the individual's contribution to effectiveness but also reflect factors beyond his or her control. J. P. Campbell et al. argued that the appropriate focus in their model for criterion development efforts is within the *performance* domain.

More recent conceptual and empirical work confirms the potential of external factors to influence the effectiveness of individuals in organizations. Peters and O'Connor (1980) hypothesized that constraints on performance, such as lack of proper tools, absence of required help from supervisors or co-workers, or insufficient job information, may lead to lower effectiveness levels and in turn reduce ability-

effectiveness relationships. In a series of laboratory experiments, Peters, O'Connor, and colleagues demonstrated that constraints on performance can adversely affect outcome measures of effectiveness (Peters, Chassie, Lindholm, O'Connor, & Kline, 1982; Peters, O'Connor, & Rudolf, 1980). Field studies correlating severity of constraints with performance ratings show a reduced effect for constraints on performance (O'Connor, Peters, Rudolf, & Pooyan, 1982; Olson & Borman, 1989). In any case there is some support for the concern that outcome effectiveness measures are confounded in the sense that they reflect both the skill and effort of organization members *and* factors beyond their control.

Ghiselli's Concepts of Dynamic Criteria and Criterion Dimensionality

Ghiselli (1956) observed that the nature of criterion performance requirements may change over time as employees learn and develop on the job. He suggested that this *dynamic criterion* phenomenon could cause certain abilities or personal characteristics to be good predictors of performance at one point in an employee's tenure but not at another. For example, early in a salesperson's career, an aggressive search for clients may be important for success, while later on, maintaining warm and cordial relationships with customers might become more critical. Thus, it is conceivable that the rank order of salespersons' effectiveness could change with changes over time in the job's performance requirements.

Fleishman's laboratory experiments (Fleishman & Fruchter, 1960; Fleishman & Hempel, 1954) focused on a similar phenomenon. A major finding was that ability, psychomotor, and perceptual skill requirements for performing motor tasks change as learning progresses. The very nature of the task is transformed as learning changes the way persons approach performance on the task. With different abilities and skills becoming necessary as time spent on the task increases, the rank order of subjects' performance levels changes, and the patterns of validity of these skill and ability predictors change over time. In particular, for novel perceptual-psychomotor tests, for example, general cognitive ability seems to better predict early task performance, while perceptual speed and psychomotor ability are better at predicting later performance (Ackerman, 1987).

However, much remains to be learned about the extent of this phenomenon in jobs and careers. Barrett, Caldwell, and Alexander (1985) reviewed 12 studies with data bearing on the existence (or not) of dynamic criteria and found little evidence for the phenomenon. They concluded that the dangers for personnel selection practice posed by dynamic criteria are not so serious as was feared, and that more concern should be focused on improving the reliability of criterion measures. The critical analysis of Barrett et al. is interesting, but the dynamic criterion concept remains of considerable theoretical and conceptual interest. Researchers should keep in mind the possibility that job requirements could change sufficiently over time to alter the patterns of validities for predictors of job performance.

Criterion dimensionality of the individual is another intriguing—and complicating—concept in the area of criterion measurement (Ghiselli, 1956). The notion is that two or more persons on the same job may be equally effective but may reach that level of performance very differently in behavioral terms. In a management job, for example, one manager may lead with charisma and flair, while another may incorporate a participative, caring style; both approaches can result in effective managerial performance. Thus, different dimensions of performance are relevant for assessing the effectiveness of these two managers, and different measures will likely be successful in predicting the performance of these two

managers. In jobs where very different behavioral patterns are possible for success, this could be a significant criterion problem; however, research is needed to examine the extent of this phenomenon in actual organizational settings.

Evaluating Variability in Job Performance

Current instruments for performance rating provide estimates of *modal* performance. That is, rating forms require raters to estimate typical performance, essentially ignoring any variation in performance levels. From a measurement perspective, this translates into making judgments about a ratee's modal level of performance on each dimension. Yet it seems obvious that employees' performance on individual dimensions varies over time and across different situations on the job. In fact, such performance is probably more faithfully characterized by a distribution than it is by a single number. And if performance distributions for individual ratees could be accurately determined, considerable information appropriate for theoretical and practical purposes might be revealed. In addition to the mode, the variance and the skewness of the distribution, for example, could prove useful.

Consider the two performance distributions graphed in Figure 1. Although these employees have the same modal performance on this dimension, A performs at close to his or her minimum level most of the time, whereas B performs closer to his or her maximum level and is more consistent than A in performing on this dimension. In addition, it may be possible to draw inferences about the abilities and motivation of the two employees. A is capable of performing at the highest level but generally performs in the average range; B is perhaps more limited regarding capabilities in this aspect of the job but performs close to his or her own highest level most of the time.

FIGURE 1

Performance Distributions for Two Employees

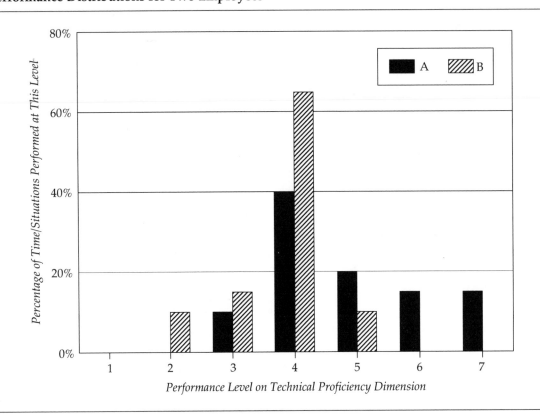

Performance Level on Technical Proficiency Dimension

An attempt has been made to develop a rating system that yields certain useful parameters of a ratee's performance distribution. Kane (1986) derived what he calls a *distributional measurement model,* in which variability in effort or motivation and external constraints beyond the control of the ratee are viewed as important and are addressed through his *performance distribution assessment method* (PDA).

With the PDA method, the rater is asked to record for each performance dimension the percentage of time that each level of performance cannot be attained because of factors beyond the ratee's control, then to note the percentage of time the ratee performed at or above each successive performance level. Kane (1986) provides formulas that allow computation of an average performance score, a consistency-in-performance score, and what he calls a *negative-range avoidance score,* an index of how successfully the ratee avoids poor performance. Thus, in Kane's system, variability in performance is explicitly addressed and indexed. Unfortunately, the usefulness of the system is not well known; for example, can raters make reliable judgments of the percentages? Nonetheless, the PDA system is a bold initiative to obtain estimates of performance distribution parameters.

An alternative way to depict variability in job performance is to consider even more directly performance levels over time. Mapping performance levels of individuals or groups, as in time-series analyses (Glass, Willson, & Gottman, 1975; McCain & McCleary, 1979), allows a picture to emerge of modal performance and variability in performance. In addition, this method provides a display of performance slope—that is, whether performance levels are ascending, descending, or remaining steady, as is shown in Figure 2.

Komaki, Collins, and Penn (1982) used time-series analysis to evaluate safety performance in a food processing plant before and after training to decrease accident rates. Although these researchers were focusing on work group performance, the same strategy could be applied to individual performance. Of course, a major disadvantage of this method is that several measures of performance over time must be generated for individual employees.

In addition to the scientific merit of obtaining these more refined pictures of employee performance, the degree of variability or consistency of job performance is of considerable practical importance for some jobs. For example, a power plant operator should display very consistent high levels of performance on dimensions such as technical competence and decision making. A high modal level of performance with considerable variability is not acceptable. The point, then, is that performance distributions may provide comparatively rich descriptions of individuals' performance, giving us substantially greater understanding of that performance, along with its causes and consequences.

Recent Developments in "Enlarging the Criterion Space"

Equal employment opportunity considerations have led to increased concern that performance

FIGURE 2

Time-Series Performance Data for an Employee

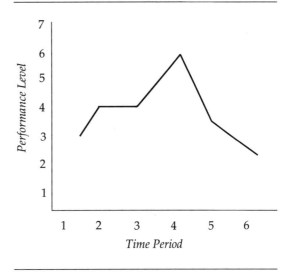

criteria be *job-related*, especially in personnel selection research (*Uniform Guidelines*, 1978). This is as it should be. However, a question might be raised about the boundaries of what is considered job-related. Some recent research and thinking has defined job performance much more broadly.

C. A. Smith, Organ, and Near (1983) have discussed what they call *organizational citizenship behavior* (see also Organ, 1988), which refers to behavior beyond task proficiency. In their conceptual and empirical work, they identified two factors: (a) altruism—day-to-day, prosocial behaviors toward others in the organization that help these others perform more effectively and (b) generalized compliance—"good-soldier," conscientiousness behaviors that demonstrate concern for doing things properly for the good of the organization. An intriguing finding is that job satisfaction–job performance relationships where performance is defined more broadly in the manner of the first citizenship factor are substantially higher than satisfaction–performance correlations in general. A possible explanation is that high job satisfaction leads to more interest in, and tendency to carry out, altruistic prosocial initiatives at work.

Similarly, Borman, Motowidlo, Rose, and Hanser (1987), in identifying the performance requirements of enlisted soldiers in the U.S. Army, developed a model of soldier performance that included dimensions related to organizational commitment and socialization (e.g., adjustment to the Army and following orders and regulations). Their position was that such behavioral elements can be considered performance criteria as long as unit members' increased performance in these areas increases organizational effectiveness. It appears that citizenship, commitment, and socialization behaviors may contribute to an organization's effectiveness, especially in a team-oriented environment.

Related also to criterion areas beyond task proficiency, Brief and Motowidlo (1986) provide a comprehensive treatment of prosocial behavior in organizations—that is, behavior on the part of organization members that is intended to promote the welfare of the individual, group, or organization. Their discussion distinguishes between role-prescribed and extra-role activities in the prosocial domain. In some cases, this kind of behavior is explicitly required. For example, in the Borman et al. model, "supporting and providing guidance to other unit members" is one of the performance dimensions and is thus a role-prescribed behavior. In other cases, it is outside the formally *required* job role and is behavior that goes beyond the call of duty to help out an individual, a group, or the entire organization. Interestingly, Brief and Motowidlo point out that prosocial behavior may at times be dysfunctional to the organization, as when a unit member helps a co-worker with a personal problem and in the process fails to complete an important job-related task.

Nonetheless, in most cases, organizational effectiveness is probably enhanced by prosocial behavior.

It seems clearer, however, that *task performance* is linked to organizational performance. More empirical research is needed to assess individual performance–organizational effectiveness relationships for these additional non–task-related elements of performance. If such links are found to be substantial, it would provide more justification for considering these less obvious elements as legitimate performance criteria for individual organization members.

Methods of Measuring Criterion Performance

Four major types of measures are used to assess criterion performance. The most often used are ratings—estimates of individuals' performance made by supervisors, peers, or others familiar with the incumbent's work behavior. Objective measures of performance or of other criterion behavior (e.g., absences or turnover) are also frequently used as criterion measures. Performance tests or job sample simulations are sometimes applied to measure task proficiency on jobs. Finally, written job knowledge tests are often used to evaluate success in training and, on occasion, the technical knowledge component of job performance. Descriptions of these measures and related research follow.

Performance Ratings

The emphasis in this section will be on ratings gathered for research only as criteria for personnel research applications. Although ratings can be generated for purposes of salary administration, promotion and termination decisions, or employee feedback and development, and although performance appraisal systems to address these administrative functions are extremely important to individual and organizational effectiveness (cf. DeVries, Morrison, Shullman, & Gerlach, 1981), they are beyond the scope of this chapter.

Performance ratings are indeed the most often used criterion measure in industrial and organizational psychology. Landy and Farr (1980) refer to several surveys intended to assess how frequently ratings are used as criterion measures in research reports. The percentages reach 75 percent and higher, suggesting that considerable attention should be paid to this criterion measurement method.

Issues in using ratings as performance criteria include (a) design of the rating form to be used, (b) advantages and disadvantages of ratings from different sources (e.g., supervisors or peers), (c) type of training to provide to raters, (d) examination of the performance judgment process to aid in understanding and improving ratings, and (e) evaluation of ratings in relation to psychometric properties (e.g., halo, reliability, validity, and accuracy). Because the fifth issue is relevant to each of the first four, evaluation of ratings will be discussed first, followed by discussions of the other four issues.

Evaluation of Ratings. The following subsections describe various approaches to evaluating job performance ratings.

Psychometric Properties. Ratings of job performance often suffer from psychometric errors. These can be classified as:

- *Distributional errors.* These errors involve raters misrepresenting the distributions of performance across persons they are evaluating. Misrepresentations can occur both in the means of ratings they provide (leniency/severity) and in the variance of ratings that result (restriction of range). Regarding leniency/severity, a rater may provide evaluations that are higher than

warranted by actual performance levels (leniency) or lower (severity). This bias can be caused by raters having inaccurate frames of reference or norms that result in inflated or deflated ratings. With restriction of range, a rater may rate two or more ratees on a dimension such that the variance of these ratings is lower than the variance of the actual performance levels for those ratees. Raters who commit this error fail to differentiate sufficiently between ratees on individual dimensions.

- *Illusory halo.* A rater might make ratings on two or more dimensions such that the correlations between the dimensions are higher than between-dimension correlations of the actual relevant behaviors. This halo effect arises when the rater fails to differentiate sufficiently between performance *on different dimensions* for individual ratees. It is also possible that raters might underestimate the relationships between dimensions and provide ratings that correlate lower than the actual behaviors (Fisicaro, 1988).

- *Other errors.* Not as commonly referred to are such perceptual and rating errors as the similar-to-me error (Latham, Wexley, & Pursell, 1975), the first impression error (Latham et al., 1975), and error due to systematic distortion (Kozlowski & Kirsch, 1987), similar to the logical error of Guilford (1954). The *similar-to-me error* refers to an unwarranted projection of a rater's own personal characteristics onto a ratee. *First impression error* occurs when the rater allows early experiences with a ratee to be weighted more than they should be. *Systematic distortion* is an error characterized by a rater making evaluations of ratees on multiple dimensions such that the pattern of correlations between dimensions more closely reflects the semantic similarity of the dimension names than the actual correlations between behaviors relevant to those dimensions. Systematic distortion is said to occur when the rater makes assessments based on assumptions about what behaviors *should* go together instead of according to the actual covariation of the behaviors (Shweder, 1975).

Interrater Reliability. Interrater agreement in performance evaluations *within* rating source (e.g., between peers) or *across* sources (e.g., between supervisors and peers) is sometimes offered as indirect evidence for the accuracy of ratings. From a logical perspective, this is of course a problem. Raters within *or* across sources may agree closely in their evaluations of ratees but may still be inaccurate. They may, for example, *all* focus on ratee characteristics (such as likability) that are irrelevant to job performance.

Campbell, Dunnette, Lawler, and Weick (1970) and Borman (1974) made the further point that high interrater reliability between raters at different organizational levels (e.g., peers versus supervisors) should not necessarily be expected. Members of different organizational levels may have different orientations and perspectives regarding ratee performance because of differences in roles related to the ratees, and they may observe significantly different samplings of ratee behavior as a result. Accordingly, raters from different levels may not agree very closely in their evaluations, but each may be providing valid performance data based on relevant but somewhat different performance information.

On balance, good interrater agreement is desirable, especially between raters at a single organizational level. Such agreement suggests that at least they are focusing on similar samples of job behavior, although, as mentioned, care must be taken in interpreting lower interrater reliabilities.

Convergent and Discriminant Validity. Kavanagh, MacKinney, and Wolins (1971) presented an ANOVA approach for evaluating the convergent and discriminant validity of ratings. A main effect and an interaction term in the ANOVA model are especially useful for these purposes. The ratee effect indexes convergent validity or overall interrater agreement collapsed across dimensions. The ratee x dimension interaction indicates the degree of discriminant validity, or the agreement between raters in the *patterns* of individual ratees' performance levels on the different dimensions. Kavanagh et al. described intraclass indices that can be used to compare levels of convergent and discriminant validity across different studies.

As Schmitt and Stults (1986) point out, a limitation of the ANOVA approach is that trait intercorrelations and method intercorrelations cannot be estimated. More recent developments, using path analysis (e.g., Althauser, 1974) or confirmatory factor analysis (e.g., Kenny, 1979; Widaman, 1985), overcome this limitation and, further, allow evaluation of convergent and discriminant validity hypotheses at both the matrix and individual measure levels.

The main thrust of the Widaman approach, for example, is to compare the fit of different hierarchically nested models to estimate in a multitrait-multimethod matrix of ratings (a) convergent validity (a model with dimension or trait factors fits better than one with no such factors present); (b) discriminant validity (a model with two or more interpretable trait factors fits better than a model with a single trait factor); and (c) method variance—that is, different rating instruments or rating sources (a model with method factors fits better than one with no method factors). A distinct advantage of this strategy is that variance-accounted-for estimates can be computed to index precisely the extent of convergent validity and method bias in the ratings. The general approach has been described and applied to performance rating data by Vance, MacCallum, Coovert, and Hedge (1988).

Accuracy. Some have argued that *accuracy* is the most important criterion for evaluating the quality of performance ratings (e.g., Bernardin & Pence, 1980; Borman, 1977; Murphy, Garcia, Kerkar, Martin, & Balzer, 1982).[1] Investigating psychometric properties, interrater agreement, and convergent/discriminant validity of ratings certainly yields useful information about such measures; but these are only indirect methods of assessing accuracy. The argument is similar to preferring information about a test's validity to such qualities as its reliability or item characteristics. The correct rank ordering of ratees on a performance dimension and/or on overall performance is, for example, needed to ensure that test validities are properly estimated. In fact, for any application in personnel research that requires evaluation of performance at the individual level, validity or accuracy of criterion measurement is very important.

It should be mentioned that this requirement for validity or accuracy of performance scores in personnel research is somewhat in contrast to what is needed for performance appraisal systems intended to serve administrative purposes such as promotion decisions and employee feedback and development. In those cases, evaluative criteria such as acceptance by users (e.g., Banks & Murphy, 1985) and usefulness in meeting organizational and individual objectives (DeVries et al., 1981) become equally important. As a concrete example, when evaluating a sensitive employee who is performing poorly but has excellent potential for effective performance and seems to need some encouragement to realize that potential, accuracy in rating the poor performance seems less important than providing positive feedback on some of the tasks performed well, thus enhancing the employee's future performance. More generally, when an administrative performance appraisal system is not accepted as fair and useful by employees, accuracy of the ratings made with the system appears to be less important than gaining system credibility. However, in the case of performance rating for personnel research applications, the requirement for accuracy (or validity) is more evident.

Unfortunately, evaluation of accuracy or validity requires external criterion target scores of some type against which to compare the ratings. Such scores are almost never available in organizational environments. Therefore, accuracy research has largely proceeded in laboratory settings.

To evaluate accuracy, written or videotaped vignettes have been developed and target performance scores for the vignettes have been derived. With the "paper-people" approach to vignette development (e.g., DeCotiis, 1977), behavioral examples scaled according to effectiveness level are woven together to create descriptions of hypothetical employees performing on jobs. Typically included in each vignette is one behavioral example representing each performance dimension for the job, selected to reflect the intended performance level. Ratings of the hypothetical employees' performance can then be compared dimension by dimension to the effectiveness scale scores of the behavioral examples in the vignettes.

Videotaped vignettes of employees performing tasks or jobs can also be developed to help investigate accuracy in ratings (Borman, 1977; Murphy et al., 1982). Target scores are typically assigned to videotaped performances on each dimension, using "experts" thoroughly familiar with the task or job to provide performance judgments. The procedure involves giving the expert judges considerable exposure to the taped behavior so their ratings are as well informed as possible. High convergent and discriminant validity across judges is usually offered as evidence for the quality of the means of the experts' target scores (e.g., Borman, 1977;

Murphy et al., 1982). Once target scores are assigned to the paper-people or videotaped vignettes, these stimulus materials can be employed in rating research, and the accuracy of performance ratings can be assessed, as appropriate.

Regarding actual measures of accuracy, many years ago Cronbach (1955) greatly clarified the issue of indexing interpersonal accuracy by demonstrating that the often-used difference score measure (*D:* Sum of the differences between ratings of persons on two or more traits or dimensions and the target criterion scores for those same persons and dimensions) decomposes into four separate components of accuracy, each with a different psychological interpretation. He argued against use of the *D* or *D*^{2} measures of accuracy because they confound the four components. The first component, *elevation,* refers to how closely a rater's grand mean of his or her ratings (across ratees and dimensions) agrees with the grand mean of the target scores. *Differential elevation* relates to accuracy in differentiating between different ratees' mean target scores (collapsed across dimensions). *Stereotype accuracy* reflects how correctly raters differentiate between dimension target score means (collapsed across ratees). Finally, *differential accuracy* is the degree to which raters correctly rank order ratees on each dimension, controlling for ratee and dimension effects (see Cronbach, 1955, or Murphy et al., 1982, for the actual mathematical definitions of the four accuracy components).

Differential elevation *(DE)* and differential accuracy *(DA)* seem especially useful for applications in performance rating research, *DE* because it indexes a rater's accuracy in assessing different ratees' overall performance and *DA* because it provides an index of skill in differentiating between different ratees' performance levels in individual aspects of the job. Stereotype accuracy might be useful in assessing a group's training needs by accurately describing the group's strong and weak performance areas averaged across its members.

In addition to the *D* or *D*^{2} measure and Cronbach's component scores, other accuracy or validity indices have been used. Borman (1975) and Athey and McIntyre (1987) correlated ratings with criterion target scores on several dimensions *by individual ratees* and then averaged these correlations across the ratees evaluated. This is a validity index of how correctly raters can identify strong and weak performance areas for each ratee, and may be especially appropriate for evaluating interpersonal diagnostic skill in performance counseling and management development settings. Gordon (1970) and Thornton and Zorich (1980) have studied what might be called observational accuracy, or success in recognizing and recalling behaviors that have occurred in performance.

Still another way to study accuracy is to use signal detection theory (Baker & Schuck, 1975; Lord, 1985). Lord, for example, argued that estimating hit rates (proportion of observed items correctly identified as exhibited by the target ratee) and false-alarm rates (proportion of items falsely so identified) provides data that allow inferences to be made about the accuracy of the information processing strategies used by individual observers. The basic notion is that raters may be quite accurate using a Cronbach index but still be inaccurate in the ratee behavior they actually process in arriving at their ratings. In this sense, signal detection theory provides a more precise, fine-grained assessment of rating accuracy.

In sum, there are two major issues in studying accuracy in ratings. The first is establishing criterion target performance scores against which to compare ratees' ratings. This is an extremely difficult problem. Target criterion scores are simply very hard to justify in settings that are at all realistic. The most realistic rating task designed to include target scores would seem to involve the videotaped performances of individuals on jobs, but even this task is obviously very different from the typical performance rating task faced by persons in organizations (even from a for-research-only rating task). To increase the realism of the rating task, Feldman (1981) suggested giving subject raters in videotape research other responsibilities besides viewing and rating ratees. Favero and Ilgen (1989) implemented this suggestion by requiring raters in a videotape lab study to perform other duties in addition to evaluating the videotaped performers (e.g., working on organizational problems presented in an in-basket). Further, Bernardin and Villanova (1986) described a "modal rating situation" typically faced by persons in organizations actually responsible for performance appraisal. More attention must be paid to realism and generalizability issues.

The second issue is how to compute accuracy. This is less problematic. Cronbach's (1955) early insights in the field of interpersonal perception have provided good choices of accuracy indices. The researcher need only select an index or indices conceptually appropriate for the research being conducted.

Relations Between Accuracy and Rating Errors.   Intuitively, we would think psychometric errors in ratings should be correlated negatively with accuracy. The greater the error in a set of ratings, the less accuracy to be expected. If this relationship is high, we might even employ indices of psychometric error as substitute measures of (in)accuracy. This would be very useful because, as we have seen, accuracy is difficult to study.

However, two kinds of research results suggest that reducing psychometric error in ratings may not enhance their accuracy. In studies where both psychometric errors *and* accuracy scores could be computed for individual raters, correlations between accuracy and rating errors such as leniency, halo, and restriction of range are near zero (Murphy & Balzer, 1989). Low *positive* correlations between halo error and accuracy have actually been reported (Cooper, 1981). In the other type of study, when raters are trained successfully to

reduce psychometric error, accuracy is either not affected (Borman, 1979a) or actually decreases (Bernardin & Pence, 1980).

Recent work has shed more light on rater error–accuracy relationships. Becker and Cardy (1986) demonstrated that relationships between halo and accuracy vary according to the particular measures of halo and accuracy used, and counterintuitive relationships between these measures (i.e., positive correlations between halo and accuracy) can be partially explained by the way the halo and accuracy indices are defined statistically. Fisicaro (1988) found that when halo was defined as an absolute difference between dimension interrelations of ratings and dimension interrelations of actual target performance scores (i.e., taking into account "negative halo" as well as "positive halo"), correlations between this conception of halo error and accuracy were more negative—as one would intuitively expect. Regarding the halo measures, note that the variance-across-dimensions, within-ratee index of halo was found to be flawed in that, unlike the mean intercorrelations of ratings on the dimensions, it is influenced by characteristics of the ratings irrelevant to halo (Pulakos, Schmitt, & Ostroff, 1986). In any case, although motivation is considerable for using estimates of psychometric error as proxy measures of accuracy, relationships between these rating errors and accuracy are not sufficiently well specified for this approach to be feasible.

Often, research on performance ratings has properly focused on ways to improve their usefulness as criteria. This effort has proceeded in four principal areas of research: (a) rating format design and empirical comparisons between formats, (b) selection of raters, (c) rater training, and (d) rating process research. Each will be discussed in turn.

Research on Rating Formats.   Over the years, many different types of rating formats have been developed and used in research and practice. Table 1 lists many of these formats. Refer

TABLE 1

Performance Rating Formats

- Graphic scales (Paterson, 1922–23)
- Man-to-man scales (Guilford, 1954)
- Ranking forms (Ghiselli & Brown, 1955)
- Forced choice scales (Bartlett, 1983; Sisson, 1948)
- Summated scales (J. P. Campbell, Dunnette, Arvey, & Hellervik, 1973)
- Critical incidents checklist (Flanagan, 1954)
- Behaviorally anchored rating scales—BARS (P. C. Smith & Kendall, 1963)
- Behavior observation scales—BOS (Latham & Wexley, 1981)
- Behavior summary scales (Borman, 1979a)
- Mixed standard scales (Blanz & Ghiselli, 1972)
- Behavioral checklist (Komaki, 1981)
- Frequency of behavior scale (Kane, 1986)

to Bernardin and Beatty (1984) and Whisler and Harper (1962) for descriptions of most rating formats.

It has seemed compelling to believe that characteristics of rating formats are important determinants of rating accuracy. There have been certain very creative and conceptually sound ideas about format development. Here are some highlights:

- The notion of supervisors or peers providing numerical scores for employees on job-relevant traits or performance areas is an interesting idea. Ideally, it provides well-informed observers with a means of quantifying their perceptions of individuals' job performance. This is highly preferable to verbal descriptions of performances because individuals can now be compared in a reasonably straightforward way. The notion can be viewed as analogous to developing

structured job analysis questionnaires to take the place of verbal job descriptions for purposes of comparing jobs (McCormick, 1976; see also Harvey, this volume). In each case, quantification of perceptions clears the way for scientific study of an area that could not previously be studied in this manner.

- Development of forced choice scales was an ingenious attempt to overcome problems with raters' subjectivity and bias in making performance evaluations. The main idea was to eliminate the *opportunity* for raters to slant ratings according to their own subjective biases. One version of the scales developed to evaluate Army officers presented descriptive behavioral items in groupings of four (Sisson, 1948). Two relatively favorable, positive items were matched in rated social desirability, but one of the items was judged very descriptive of effective performers and the other judged less so. Likewise, there appeared two items with relatively low (and equal) rated social desirability, but one was judged substantially more descriptive of poor performers than the other. An example tetrad grouping is presented as follows:

	Most Descriptive	Least Descriptive
A. Cannot assume responsibility	❑	❑
B. Knows how and when to delegate authority	❑	❑
C. Offers suggestions	❑	❑
D. Changes ideas too easily	❑	❑

The rater was asked to review the items in each grouping and to check which of the four items was most descriptive and which was least descriptive of the ratee. A score of +1 was given for responding "most descriptive" to the positively keyed item or "least descriptive" to the negatively keyed item, and a score of −1 was given for responding "least descriptive" to the positively keyed item or "most descriptive" to the negatively keyed item. Responding either most or least descriptive to the nonkeyed items earned a score of zero.

Proponents of this kind of scale argue that the hidden-key feature of the scale design prevents raters from assigning higher (or lower) ratings than warranted. One criticism of the format is that a single overall performance score is obtained from the ratings rather than a score for each different performance dimension [although King, Hunter, & Schmidt (1980) constructed multidimensional forced choice scales]. A second problem is a consequence of the scale's main advantage: Raters have expressed dissatisfaction about not having control over the outcomes of their ratings. Nonetheless, this format represents a bold initiative to create a relatively objective rating instrument.

P. C. Smith and Kendall (1963) extended the notion of critical incidents (Flanagan, 1954) by designing a rating format they referred to as behavioral expectation scales, now generally labeled *behaviorally anchored rating scales* (BARS). P. C. Smith and Kendall reasoned that different effectiveness levels on job performance rating scales might be anchored using behavioral examples of incumbent performance. Accordingly, they developed performance rating dimensions with scaled behavioral examples anchoring the appropriate effectiveness levels on the

dimensions. The high and low segments of a rating dimension with two behavioral anchors for the safety-mindedness dimension on the job of power plant maintenance worker (Bosshardt, Rosse, & Peterson, 1984) appear in the example that follows:

7 — ▪ This employee stopped another employee from "air lancing" coal dust from a pulverizer without wearing proper eye protection. As a result, possible eye damage was prevented.

1 — ▪ This employee was replacing a pipe union on an acid line without wearing any protective equipment. The union broke with pressure on the line, and his face received an acid burn.

Essentially, the rater's task is to compare observed job behaviors of the ratee with the behavioral anchors on the scale to assign a rating on that dimension. This was seen as preferable to evaluating a ratee without guidance regarding the effectiveness levels of different scale points. The BARS idea is more than a format; it is a system, or even a philosophy (Bernardin & Smith, 1981). For example, ideally raters should record examples of employee work behavior throughout the appraisal period to aid in assigning performance ratings.

Another positive feature of BARS is that users of the system typically participate in scale development, enhancing the credibility of the format. Further, from a domain sampling perspective, BARS development steps provide an excellent vehicle with which to identify all important performance dimensions for a job (J. P. Campbell, Dunnette, Arvey, & Hellervik, 1973). Having persons knowledgeable about a job generate many actual behavioral examples of performance on that job should result in an exhaustive listing of its performance requirements and provide an operational way to define comprehensively the *conceptual criterion*, in Astin's (1964) nomenclature.

- Blanz and Ghiselli (1972) introduced the mixed standard scale (MSS), a rating format with several appealing features. The MSS consists of three behavioral statements, essentially BARS anchors, for each performance dimension. One reflects relatively effective performance, a second represents midlevel or average performance, and a third depicts lower-level performance. Typically, the behavioral statements across dimensions and effectiveness levels are randomly ordered on the scale, and the rater is asked to indicate whether the ratee's performance is worse than, the same as, or better than the performance represented in each statement. A score for a ratee on each dimension can then be derived according to the following rules for these logically consistent rating combinations, where a plus sign means "better than" ratings, zero means "the same as" ratings, and a minus sign means "worse than" ratings:

Effective Statement	Average Statement	Ineffective Statement	Derived Rating
+	+	+	7
0	+	+	6
−	+	+	5
−	0	+	4
−	−	+	3
−	−	0	2
−	−	−	1

Actually, there are 27 possible patterns of ratings for a dimension; the other 20 represent illogical combinations. For example, 0, −, + is not a logical set of ratings. How can a ratee be at the same level of performance as the high effectiveness statement but perform worse than the midlevel statement? This feature of the MSS can be viewed as a distinct advantage, because the number of illogical response patterns can be scored for each rater, ratee, and dimension, and useful inferences can be made from these scores. For example, if such scores are high for a rater they may indicate incompetently completed ratings by that rater; high scores for a ratee may suggest that the ratee is difficult to evaluate; and high scores for a dimension may mean that the statements associated with the dimension are ambiguous. This diagnostic information can then lead to useful interventions, such as rater training for inconsistent raters, a search for alternate raters for ratees scored inconsistently, and further scale development work for high error dimensions. Another potential advantage of the MSS format with behavioral statements randomly ordered instead of grouped by dimension is that halo might be reduced because the dimensions are disguised from raters, although a recent study found no decrease in halo as a function of this feature of the MSS format (Dickinson & Glebocki, in press).

This format thus represents an unusual and potentially effective way to generate performance information. The judgments a rater is asked to make are somewhat more straightforward than is the case with BARS, for example. The rater must simply compare the effectiveness of observed ratee behavior to the effectiveness reflected in a single behavioral statement, without reference to dimensions of performance or continua of effectiveness.

Format Comparison Studies. A reasonable empirical question concerning these and other rating formats is, Which ones are better? Format comparison studies have been conducted to address this issue, usually employing psychometric criteria as the dependent variables. Early studies (e.g., Blumberg, DeSoto, & Kuethe, 1966; Madden & Bourdon, 1964; Taylor, Parker, & Ford, 1959) focused on relatively narrow considerations—number of scale points, vertical versus horizontal scales, and the like. More recent work compared entire formats and used such criteria as halo, leniency, restriction of range, and interrater reliability. As an example of such a study, Bernardin (1977) had college student raters evaluate their college professors on BARS and two carefully developed summated rating scales. The latter had positively and negatively worded behavioral statements and required raters to indicate how frequently (from never to always) each ratee exhibited them. Results showed no significant differences between formats on the psychometric properties of interrater reliability, halo, leniency, and discrimination between ratees.

Reviews of format comparison studies (e.g., Landy & Farr, 1980; Schwab, Heneman, & DeCotiis, 1975) suggest the following conclusions: The psychometric superiority of BARS is questionable. Some studies show ratings on BARS have better psychometric properties than ratings made on other formats (e.g., J. P. Campbell, Dunnette, Arvey, & Hellervik, 1973), but other studies show no such differences

(e.g., Bernardin, Alvares, & Cranny, 1976). The most important consideration in format development may be that rigorous scale development procedures are followed (Bernardin, 1977). Landy and Farr (1980) estimate that as little as 4 percent of the variance in psychometric quality may be accounted for by format, although Guion and Gibson (1988) argue that it is premature to give up on format-related research.

A useful way to view performance rating formats is as mechanisms for helping raters (a) conduct an organized and efficient search for ratee performance-related behavior, (b) translate these behavioral observations into evidence pertinent to assessing ratee performance on each dimension, and then (c) make accurate judgments about ratee effectiveness levels on each dimension. Ideally, formats should be configured so that the operations required of raters reflect natural cognitive processes leading to efficient and effective processing of performance information. Characteristics of rating scales should provide a clear presentation of standards to help raters evaluate observed work behavior. Thus, it should be useful to identify and then use those features most compatible with effective observation and evaluation of behaviors.

Feldman (1986) explores these fundamental rating format characteristics in an essay in which he distinguishes between performance measurement systems with dimensions permitting *analytic* processing and those with dimensions requiring *intuitive* processing. In the analytic case, performance on the dimensions can be objectively defined, with relatively few alternatives to a specified way of performing the job on those dimensions. Feldman (1986) offers the example of the machinist job, where the frequency and magnitude of errors largely define performance on the technical skill dimensions. In this case, a format might be best designed to require recall or estimation of the frequency, rate, or intensity of behaviors that job analysis indicates are important for successful performance.

In the intuitive case, performance on the job must be assessed according to dimensions based on value systems not as objectively specifiable as in the analytic case. Managerial jobs represent a good example of where intuitive assessment of performance is required. The role of the rater is then to interpret ratee behavior according to these values as they are depicted on the rating instrument. Thus, in such a case, formats should be designed to define in observable, behavioral terms the performance dimensions highly valued by the organization.

In sum, minor rating format manipulations are not likely to make much difference in improving the accuracy of performance ratings. However, in the design of rating instruments, it is useful to consider how best to depict a job's performance requirements on the instrument in a way that is easily understandable by raters as well as cognitively compatible with the rating task to help raters make accurate performance judgments.

Selection of Raters. A second attempt to improve the psychometric properties and accuracy of ratings concerns attention paid to the source of those ratings (e.g., supervisor, peer, or self). Logically, each of these and other sources has advantages in providing valid performance information. Experienced supervisors have reasonably good norms for performance, because typically they have seen relatively large numbers of employees working on the job and thus have well-calibrated views of different performance levels. Peers are usually privy to the most performance information regarding their fellow workers; lay wisdom suggests that it is difficult to hide your actual performance level from co-workers. Self-ratings have a similar advantage in that, clearly, considerable performance-related information should be available from these ratings.

Other rating sources are used less often, but have certain inherent advantages.

Supervisees are likely to have especially relevant information about their supervisors' leadership skills. An outside observer sampling on-the-job behavior is free from the possible biasing effects of organizational and personal roles related to the ratee.

There are disadvantages to each of these rating sources as well. Supervisors may not actually observe much of the day-to-day work performance of supervisees. Co-workers and supervisees often lack experience in making formal performance evaluations, and the latter are typically in a position to see only a relatively small portion of their supervisors' job performance. Self-ratings may be distorted due to inflated evaluations of the rater's own performance. Finally, an observer will not usually view a sufficient sample of ratee performance to obtain an accurate picture of typical performance over time. The previous statements depend to some extent on the structure of the ratee's organization and the particular interactive work roles practiced by supervisors, co-workers, and supervisees in the organization.

Research on this topic seeks to determine which source or configuration of sources provides the most accurate, error-free evaluations of performance. Accordingly, studies have been conducted to (a) assess the psychometric properties and reliability of ratings from each source, (b) examine the interrater agreement between sources, and (c) evaluate the predictive validity of peer and self-assessments.

Regarding the first type of study, conclusions are that self-ratings are generally more lenient than peer or supervisor ratings (e.g., Kirchner, 1965; Parker, Taylor, Barrett, & Martens, 1959) but contain less halo than do ratings from those sources (e.g., Heneman, 1974; Kirchner, 1965). Results are mixed regarding comparative levels of interrater reliability within the peer and supervisor sources, but on balance, supervisory ratings tend to be more reliable (Klieger & Mosel, 1953; Pulakos & Borman, 1988; Springer, 1953).

In relation to interrater agreement between sources, peer and supervisor ratings typically agree more closely with ratings from either of the other two sources than do self-ratings (Harris & Schaubroeck, 1988; Klimoski & London, 1974). Yet interrater reliability between peers and supervisors is usually only moderate, with agreement within rating source greater than agreement across the two sources (e.g., Berry, Nelson, & McNally, 1966; Borman, 1974; Gunderson & Nelson, 1966).

Although high interrater reliability is desirable in ratings, suggesting that different raters are focusing on similar, presumably job-related factors, close agreement across rating sources may be unrealistic, as I mentioned earlier. Thus, low to moderate across-source agreement in ratings may not be so much a sign of unreliability as an indicator that somewhat different aspects of performance are being observed and reported on (Borman, 1974; J. P. Campbell et al., 1970).

Finally, peer and self-assessments have been used to predict future performance. This can be conceived of as a kind of validity check on ratings from these sources. Among others, Hollander (1954, 1965), Downey, Medland, and Yates (1976), and Waters and Waters (1970) have evaluated relationships between peer assessments and later performance in both military and civilian samples. Kane and Lawler (1978) summarized this work and found a mean validity coefficient of .43 when peer nominations (i.e., identification of the best and worst performers) were used to predict subsequent performance and a somewhat lower validity when peer ratings were used. These results are impressive in a sense, but interpreting the magnitude of the correlations as indicators of validity is problematic. They may underestimate validity where the constructs reflected in the peer assessments and subsequent criteria are dissimilar (e.g., ratings of present performance on technical proficiency against a criterion of supervisory performance). They may overestimate validity if the criteria for the ratings are also ratings and the predictors and criteria share invalid method variance. Nonetheless, there is evidence that peer assessments are tapping important performance-related variance (Kane & Lawler, 1978).

Mabe and West (1982) performed a meta-analysis of relationships between self-assessments on traits or competency dimensions and criteria relevant to those assessments, including objective test scores, academic grades, and supervisor ratings. The mean correlation was .29, indicating moderate validity for self-ratings.

On balance, however, peer and supervisor ratings of performance appear to hold the most hope for providing accurate depictions of job performance. Leniency in self-ratings and (perhaps worse yet) differential leniency, in which some raters inflate their self-ratings more than others, are especially problematic with self-assessment.

Rater Training. Rater training provides a promising approach to improving the quality of performance ratings. Two general kinds of training programs have emerged to help raters generate more error free and accurate ratings (Bernardin & Buckley, 1981; D. E. Smith, 1986). *Rater error training* seeks simply to alert raters to certain psychometric or perceptual errors such as leniency/severity, halo, restriction-in-range, and similar-to-me effects. Training often takes the form of a brief lecture on or demonstration of the error and a plea to avoid such errors when making performance ratings (Bernardin & Buckley, 1981). *Frame-of-reference training* (Bernardin & Pence, 1980) attempts to convey to raters that performance is multidimensional and to familiarize them thoroughly with the actual content of each performance dimension. Regarding familiarization, examples of different levels of performance on individual dimensions are typically reviewed with raters, along with the "correct" or actual performance levels the examples reflect (e.g., Pulakos, 1984).

Researchers have conducted studies comparing the psychometric properties and accuracy of ratings made by raters trained using one of the approaches just discussed and ratings generated by untrained raters. Results suggest the following conclusions:

- Error training is usually successful in reducing the target psychometric error (e.g., Latham, Wexley, & Pursell, 1975).

- Error training does not improve the quality of ratings when interrater reliability or accuracy is used as a criterion (e.g., Borman, 1979a).

- Frame-of-reference training increases rating accuracy (McIntyre, Smith, & Hassett, 1984; Pulakos, 1984).

In addition, practice in making ratings and feedback about rating errors and accuracy are important components of training programs (Latham, 1986; D. E. Smith, 1986). The five frame-of-reference studies identified by D. E. Smith (1986) all employed practice and feedback in their successful programs.

A useful observation has been offered by Bernardin and Pence (1980): Rater error training is successful in reducing the target psychometric response set or error (e.g., halo), but essentially *new response sets* are forced on raters (e.g., to eliminate halo, spread out your ratings across dimensions), resulting in either no change in accuracy or a reduction in it. Similarly, Borman (1979a) suggested that to direct persons to adjust their rating distributions in some manner is relatively easy for training to accomplish; it is much more difficult to train raters to be more accurate. Frame-of-reference training appears to be the best bet to attain this worthwhile goal.

Research is needed now to identify the elements responsible for rater training success (e.g., Athey & McIntyre, 1987). This will allow streamlining and refinements of frame-of-reference programs to enhance their efficiency and effectiveness in improving rating accuracy.

Rating Process Research. Arguably, the so-called process approach to studying performance ratings began with Wherry's treatise on ratings (appearing in Landy & Farr, 1983, and Wherry & Bartlett, 1982). This ambitious effort presented a "theory of ratings," which included a kind of "job analysis of the rating process" (Landy & Farr, 1983, p. 285). Using applied measurement theory along with principles from the areas of human learning and memory, Wherry fashioned a series of propositions to help better understand this process.

Regarding attempts to illuminate the performance rating process, the basic rationale has been that we should "get beyond" manipulations of rating formats and other psychometric concerns with ratings to study in detail the entire sequence that raters follow in making performance judgments. Rating process research could then inform us enough to be able to intervene in order to reduce rater errors, biases, and inaccuracies. The reasoning goes that a scientific examination of performance rating requires a rigorous sequencing of theory development, hypothesis or proposition generation, and hypothesis testing. Cognitive psychology has been the source of models relating to the now familiar steps of observing, encoding, storing in memory, retrieving from memory, judgment, and rating (e.g., De Nisi, Cafferty, & Meglino, 1984; Landy & Farr, 1980). Personality and social psychology contributed additional concepts, such as implicit personality theory, attribution theory, and personal construct theory, to be considered when further conceptualizing and studying the performance rating process (e.g., Borman, 1983; Feldman, 1981; Ilgen & Feldman, 1983). These models and concepts will be reviewed next; then research applications will be discussed.

Rating Process Models. Two kinds of rating process cognitive models with somewhat different emphases have emerged in the performance rating literature. The first are termed *process models*, depicting the rating sequence presented in the previous paragraph, along with factors hypothesized to influence that process (Cooper, 1981; DeCotiis & Petit, 1978; De Nisi et al., 1984; Landy & Farr, 1980, 1983). The second kind of model emphasizes and elaborates on the encoding step in that sequence to consider in some depth categorization in processing performance-related information (Feldman, 1981; Ilgen & Feldman, 1983; Lord, 1985).

To provide a more detailed view of these two types of models, prototypes of each will be described. Then, the potential influences of implicit personality theory, attribution processes, and personal construct theory on performance judgments will be discussed briefly.

The De Nisi et al. (1984) model is comparatively detailed in specifying the cognitive steps that presumably take place during the rating process (see Figure 3). Performance information is sought and encoded and stored first in "individual memory bins" and then in longer-term memory. Before a performance evaluation is made, the rater makes judgments about possible external influences on the performance and how typical this performance is of the ratee. De Nisi et al. emphasize the rater as an active seeker of performance information; they also note the central importance of memory in the rating process. Thus, De Nisi et al.'s model contains the basic steps of observing, encoding, storing, retrieving, judging, and rating, as presented in several additional models (Cooper, 1981; Landy & Farr, 1980, 1983).

Each of these other process models has unique and useful features as well. For example, Cooper's formulation carefully attends to how different steps in his sequential process model influence both accuracy and illusory halo in ratings. Essentially, random error in the process sequence decreases accuracy, and systematic error in the sequence increases halo. Landy and Farr view performance rating as dependent upon "highly filtered information." The actual ratee behavior observed is influenced by several factors before emerging as a performance judgment about the ratee.

Feldman (1981) and Ilgen and Feldman (1983) provide prototypes of a somewhat different kind of rating process model. Although the cognitive-based information processing sequence described previously is incorporated into their models, two additional features are emphasized. First, these authors elaborate considerably on categorization processes, referring to that part of the process model where encoding is taking place. Confronted with a barrage of performance-related information about ratees, the rater simplifies the information by categorizing it into dimensions that represent in relatively simple form the complexity of the "raw" behavior observed. Categories are selected for a ratee behavior via a matching process between features of the behavior and the category (e.g., hard-working, slacking off), and when work-related information about the ratee is to be recalled, often the category is brought up rather than the specific behavior.

A second difference between this type of model and those discussed previously is that automatic and controlled attentional processes are distinguished. These authors make the point that when the patterns of ratee behavior conform with previous impressions, then that behavior is "automatically" categorized without much conscious effort. However, when an unexpected or otherwise noteworthy behavior is observed, more active categorizing, including changing categories for a ratee (e.g., from conscientious to careless at times), is likely to occur.

Categorizing performance-related behavior to simplify the large amount of performance information observed is an important process

FIGURE 3

De Nisi, Cafferty, and Meglino (1984) Model of Performance Rating

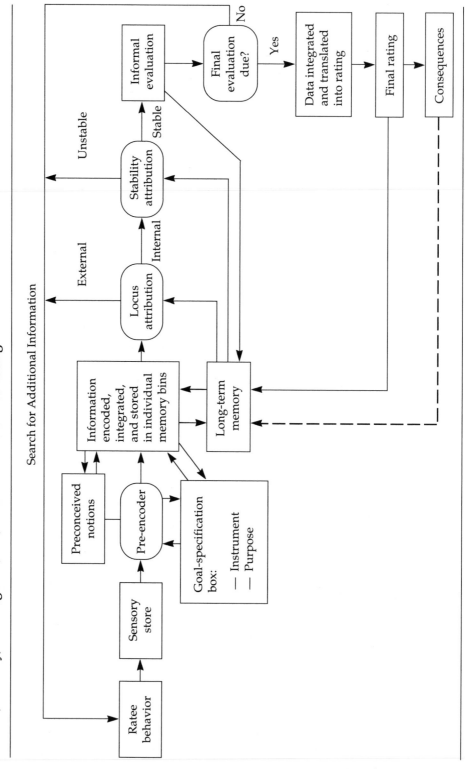

From "A Cognitive View of the Appraisal Process: A Model and Research Propositions" from *Organizational Behavior and Human Performance* by A. S. De Nisi, T. P. Cafferty, and B. M. Meglino, 1984, *Organizational Behavior and Human Performance, 33*, p. 363. Copyright 1984 by Academic Press, Inc. Adapted by permission.

to understand. Research in cognitive psychology has confirmed the heuristic usefulness of some kinds of knowledge structures. Besides categories (similar to *dimensions* in performance rating parlance) as aids in this simplification process, schemata, prototypes, stereotypes, and scripts have been discussed as important in social perception.

Briefly, schema is a generic term that subsumes several other hypothesized cognitive structures. *Schemata* are virtually synonymous with categories, both referring to reference concepts used by raters to help make judgments about other persons (e.g., Cantor & Mischel, 1977; Wyer & Srull, 1980). *Prototypes* highlight modal or typical features of a category (e.g., Hastie, 1981) and can be thought of as good examples of schemata. An examplar of a prototype is, "Al is a perfect example of what I think of as sociable." *Stereotypes* are similar to prototypes but refer to groups of people rather than individuals (Hamilton & Gifford, 1976). In addition, stereotypes tend to carry a significant affective component, usually negative. Finally, *scripts* are events or event sequences that are remembered as being representative of a person's actions (Abelson, 1981). They are often abstracted versions of actual events, with gaps filled in to create a coherent story. In filling these gaps, actions and other made-up parts of the story are included to be consistent with what is remembered about the event sequence related to the person being evaluated.

Thus, basically, schemata and associated hypothesized knowledge structures are used to reduce complexity in social perception. Loss of specific behavioral detail may lead to errors and biases in perception and judgment.

Relevant Personality/Social Psychology Concepts. Person perception concepts from the areas of personality and social psychology have also been useful in contributing to thought and research on the performance judgment process. Implicit personality theory (IPT), personal construct psychology (PCP), and attribution processes have provided alternative framworks from which to view performance ratings.

Marked similarities are evident between certain features of IPT and PCP and the concept of a schema. IPTs (Schneider, Hastorf, & Ellsworth, 1979) have to do with assumptions a person makes about how personal characteristics (or work behaviors) covary in people, whether these assumptions are right or wrong. The personal characteristics in IPTs are then similar to schemata, but the *relationships between* different schemata are the focus here. Some research shows that relationships between personal characteristics based on ratings of others well known to the raters are quite similar to assumed relationships between these personal characteristics, suggesting in turn that ratings are made on the basis of *assumed* relationships between personal characteristics rather than according to *actual* relationships (Hakel, 1974; Passini & Norman, 1966). Another possible effect IPT may have on perceptions and ratings of personal characteristics (or performance-related behavior) involves individual differences between different raters' IPTs. Such differences in assumed correlations between dimensions could contribute to interrater disagreement.

Personal constructs (Adams-Webber, 1979; Kelly, 1955) are defined as content categories used to organize and simplify information. In particular, as part of his ambitious psychological theory, Kelly (1955) observed that individuals develop personal construct systems to judge events (or the activities of other people) and to make predictions about future events. Importantly, some of these categories are imposed on their person perceptions. These interpersonal filters may influence observations and judgments about other people by providing frames of reference or sets that make perceivers look for selective kinds of interpersonal information and interpret this information according to their own constructs (Duck, 1982). Accordingly, in the domain of social perception, personal constructs are very similar to schemata.

The social cognition literature (e.g., Ostrom, Pryor, & Simpson, 1980; Wyer & Srull, 1986) is compelling in arguing for the existence in some form of these knowledge structures, schemata, IPTs, or personal constructs. However, the question might be asked, "How do these categories function in the performance evaluation setting?" How can the heuristic notions discussed in this literature be put into practice to determine more clearly the importance of these notions for influencing performance judgments? One possibility is to consider what might be referred to as "folk theories" of job performance (Borman, 1983). *Folk theories* are performance constructs used naturally by persons familiar with a job to describe its performance requirements and to differentiate between effective and ineffective performers. Two examples from job analysis interviews are (a) a secretarial supervisor stating that a key to effectiveness in his or her secretary's job is "maximizing time on task, staying with work tasks until they are completed," and (b) a sales manager reporting that a critical factor to successful performance in sales positions within the district is "knowing the products inside out." These firm opinions about job performance requirements, or folk theories, may be examples of categories or schemata that influence the ways organization members view and interpret work behavior of persons performing on the job. Accordingly, these categories or schemata could affect performance ratings made by supervisors or peers.

To test the importance of considering schemata in studying performance ratings, it is crucial to investigate relationships between the content and/or structure of categories and actual rating behavior. For example, do raters with very different schemata regarding the performance requirements for a job tend to disagree in their performance ratings? A related consideration is the stability of these categories and their structure over time and in different work contexts. Are categories difficult to change? Can "valid" categories from a job analysis be trained so that raters possess an effective category system?

Attribution theory is also relevant to our concerns about the performance rating process. *Attribution* refers to observers or raters assigning *causes* to behavior (Kelley, 1967). Specifically, the fundamental attribution error (Ross, 1977) occurs when individuals interpret their own behavior as caused primarily by situational factors, yet interpret behavior of others as influenced more by their personal characteristics or internal dispositional factors. This effect has been demonstrated in many studies (cf. Kelley & Michela, 1980).

Results from attribution research most germane to performance rating are, first, that consistent behavior (performance) is more likely to be attributed to dispositional factors than is inconsistent behavior (Frieze & Weiner, 1971). Second, and related to this finding, unexpected performance outcomes are attributed more to chance or luck than to ability on the part of the ratee (Zuckerman, 1979). Third, observing behavior consistent with what is expected tends to be interpreted as dispositionally caused, whereas unexpected behavior is thought to be more situationally determined.

Two studies that demonstrate the usefulness of attribution theory for understanding performance ratings are, first, Deaux and Emswiller's (1974) study, in which they found that men's successful performance is more likely attributed to their own doing than to chance, while the opposite pattern of attributions is evident for women. The second study, by Scott and Hamner (1975), required raters to evaluate the performance of videotaped actors exhibiting equal mean levels of performance, but with some showing ascending (improving) levels of performance and others descending levels. The actors who showed ascending levels were rated relatively high on motivation and effort and lower on ability as compared to their descending-levels counterparts.

More generally, attribution theory raises the question of what factors raters use in making performance judgments and how those factors influence ratings. For example, when raters attribute poor performance to situational causes, do they give "extra credit," providing higher ratings than warranted on the basis of actual effectiveness, thus allowing for these situational influences? Attribution theory provides some alternative ways of thinking about and studying the performance rating process.

Field Research on Rating Process Issues. Three related process-oriented research approaches address the basic question of what factors "cause" or influence performance ratings and what cues influence raters when they make judgments about others' work performance. These approaches include (a) investigations focused on the effects of rater and ratee characteristics on ratings, (b) exploratory policy capturing research to evaluate the importance of various cues to making summary performance judgments, and (c) confirmatory path analysis studies investigating the impact of selected factors on performance evaluations.

Studies on rater and ratee characteristics reviewed by Landy and Farr (1983), as well as subsequent research, show, first, that rater gender, age, and education have no significant effects on ratings. Second, raters with more experience and knowledge about the job, and also better job performers, provide higher-quality ratings (Mandell, 1956). Third, certain evidence suggests that raters provide somewhat higher ratings for ratees whose race is the same as their own (Kraiger & Ford, 1985; Schmitt & Lappin, 1980), although at least one recent study (Pulakos, White, Oppler, & Borman, 1989) does not confirm this effect. Finally, person perception studies on accuracy in interpreting and predicting the behavior of others (cf. Funder, 1987; Taft, 1955) and studies investigating rater individual difference correlates of performance rating accuracy (Borman, 1979b; Cardy & Kehoe, 1984) suggest that general

cognitive ability and field independence, as well as certain temperament constructs such as tolerance, personal adjustment, and self-control, correlate positively with rating accuracy.

Some studies of *ratee* characteristics indicate a sex role stereotype effect for gender, with men being evaluated more highly than women on traditionally male jobs, and a similar advantage for women on female-oriented jobs (Schmitt & Hill, 1977; Schneier & Beusse, 1980). Ratee race findings are as discussed previously, with some evidence of higher evaluations by raters for same-race ratees. Ratee age does not appear to be a significant factor in rating levels. Tenure on the job typically correlates positively with ratings, although not strongly so.

Most of the factors just discussed can affect the *level* of ratings, but another way of examining the influence of these factors is to study differences in *patterns of cues* that raters employ in making ratings. An example would be to evaluate the relative importance attached to factors such as technical competence, interpersonal skill, and position tenure when female workers are being rated compared to ratings of the same factors for their male counterparts. In this example, differences in the patterns of how these factors are used would imply that the judgment processes associated with rating men and women in turn differ.

Two related methods are well suited to investigating this aspect of rating processes. *Policy capturing* (e.g., Christal, 1968; Hobson & Gibson, 1983) and *path analysis* (e.g., James, Mulaik, & Brett, 1982) are appropriate paradigms when scores for ratees are available on both "cue variables," or potentially important factors that might influence ratings, *and* some overall job performance rating for each of these same ratees. In both approaches, scores on the rating factors or independent variables are essentially regressed against the overall performance ratings, and an importance weight for each factor is computed—based on standardized beta weights in the case of policy capturing and on unstandardized regression weights (structural parameters) or standardized weights (path coefficients) in the case of path analysis.

When policy capturing is employed, analysis is often at the level of the individual rater. A prototype study of this type is that of Hobson, Mendel, and Gibson (1981), who developed 100 profiles of hypothetical professors, each described by scores on 14 dimensions thought to be relevant to performance as a professor (e.g., lecturing delivery and obtaining research funding). Psychology faculty members then rated the overall effectiveness of each hypothetical professor, and regression analyses were conducted for each of these faculty subjects. Conclusions were that different subgroups of faculty subjects had substantially different patterns of regression weights for the dimensions. For example, one subgroup had a reasonably well-balanced set of importance weights across instructional and research aspects of the job, whereas a second subgroup's highest weights were all in the instructional areas, especially lecturing delivery and knowledge of field.

Thus, policy capturing may be useful for identifying the importance that individual raters actually place on different factors when making summary judgments such as overall job performance ratings. One intriguing direction for research with policy capturing would be to group raters initially according to similarities in their patterns of importance weights—that is, presumably, similarities in approaches to integrating this information to make performance judgments. Then these rater "judgment styles" could be related to individual differences, organizational characteristics, or other variables with a theory-driven link so that reasons for similarities and differences in judgment strategies could be explored. Zedeck and Kafry (1977) attempted to examine such a link by grouping nurses according to similarities in patterns of importance weights on performance rating dimensions; then, organization (i.e., hospital) and individual

differences (e.g., verbal ability) relationships with rating strategy were examined. No significant relationships were found, but other such attempts to assess links between rater style and individual or organizational variables may shed considerable light on the performance rating process.

A similar approach to uncovering the factors or cues raters may use to make performance judgments employs path analysis or causal modeling. For example, Hunter (1983) conducted a meta-analysis of 14 studies that used causal analysis to identify relationships between supervisory ratings and (a) general cognitive ability scores, (b) work sample test performance, and (c) job knowledge test scores on the part of ratees. Results suggest that of the three, ratee job knowledge has the largest direct effect on ratings and that cognitive ability has an indirect effect on ratings through its influence on job knowledge.

Responding to Hunter's study, Guion (1983) suggested that other variables besides ratee cognitive ability, job knowledge, and task proficiency might be investigated as having potential effects on performance ratings. Guion saw two sets of variables as especially good candidates for research: interpersonal relationship factors and ratee personal characteristics.

Borman, White, Pulakos, and Oppler (submitted for publication) recently addressed the Guion challenge. Using LISREL VI (Joreskog & Sorbom, 1981), Borman et al. tested the model shown in Figure 4 for a sample of U. S. Army soldiers in nine different jobs. Results of a meta-analysis across the jobs indicated that self-reports of ratee personal characteristics (achievement orientation and dependability) influenced supervisory ratings directly, as well as through their effects on certain performance indicators (number of awards and disciplinary actions received). As in Hunter (1983), general cognitive ability based on *Armed Services Vocational Aptitude Battery* scores for ratees influenced ratings

FIGURE 4

Performance Rating Model Across Nine Army Jobs

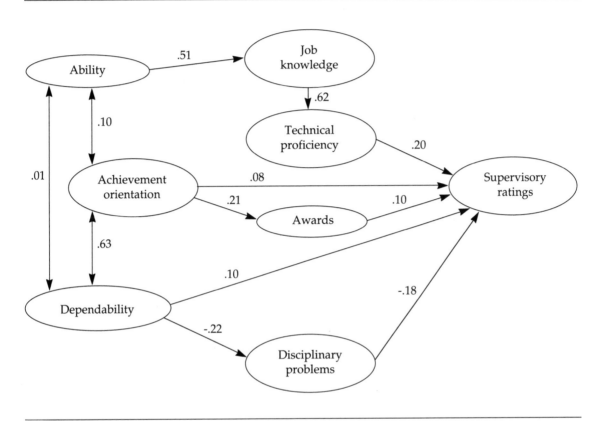

Note: *N* = 4,362

indirectly through its effect on ratee job knowledge as measured by multiple-choice job knowledge tests. Job knowledge in turn contributed to ratee technical proficiency (work sample performance test scores), with technical proficiency having a direct effect on the supervisors' ratings. Significantly, the variance accounted for in the ratings more than doubled when the variables not included in Hunter's model were added. Thus, we gain more understanding of the determinants of ratings from the extended model here. Models with additional, different variables are

needed to more completely map the cues raters use in making performance judgments.

Causal modeling to test hypotheses about relationships between factors potentially influencing performance judgments and the performance ratings themselves seems useful as a strategy for learning more about rating processes. Of course, care should be taken to satisfy measurement requirements in this kind of research. The most important is to avoid including rater perceptions as independent variables in the models (Billings & Wroten, 1978). As an example, strong relationships between raters' evaluations of ratee characteristics and their performance ratings can be misleading because of common method (the rater) variance between these two measures.

Another contribution of the research into the rating process is that several propositions or hypotheses have emerged from theory-building efforts or surveys of process-related research. Those of most general interest for criterion measurement are:

- Assessment of behavior is a function of the theory and meaning attached by a rater to that behavior and situation. Differences in theory/meaning lead to differences between raters within groups (e.g., supervisors) and between groups (e.g., supervisors vs. self) regarding the interpretation and evaluation of performance, which in turn leads to low interrater agreement.

- Effectiveness of performance appraisal may be enhanced by having observation and recording done by one assessor, and evaluation per se done by an independent assessor; this is in contrast to having one person observe, record, *and* evaluate.

- There is more consistency in the behavior of middle-level performers than there is in the behavior of high- or low-level performers.

- A rater's personal constructs influence the behaviors that are noticed, recorded, and evaluated; behaviors that are not part of or are inconsistent with the rater's personal construct theory are ignored, distorted, or discounted.

- A rater encountering information inconsistent with expectations will be more likely to seek additional information to confirm those expectations.

- Raters will be more likely to recall overall impressions of ratees and the evaluations associated with those impressions than the specific behaviors which gave rise to them.

The first four items in this list appear in Landy, Zedeck, and Cleveland (1983); the fifth and sixth are from De Nisi, Cafferty, and Meglino (1984). These propositions provide a sampling of the kinds of research questions that emerge from the so-called process approach to studying performance ratings. On one hand, they represent basic questions about observation, attention, memory for behavior, integration of performance information, and evaluation. On the other hand, it is hoped that investigating these kinds of questions may also lead to improvements in criterion development and performance measurement procedures.

Enthusiasm for more basic research into rating process issues and hope that the research will result in more error-free and accurate performance measurement is not uniformly shared. Voices of caution and criticism have been heard. Of special concern is the difficulty of generalizing laboratory findings to actual organizational performance rating settings. Ilgen and Favero (1985) identify factors that limit generalizability of most current process-oriented research to *on-line performance appraisal* settings—ratings for purposes of feedback and counseling, for example. However, some of these limitations apply also to our present concerns with criterion development and measurement, typically conducted on a for-research-only basis. Factors relevant here include the following:

- Behavioral observations are not usually made over time on multiple trials in either paper-people or videotape research.

- Situational factors that may reduce (or enhance) performance levels are not well represented in laboratory research.

- Rater-ratee interaction is not properly simulated in paper-people studies or in videotape research.

- Typically, behavior only, not behavior *and* organizational outcomes, is viewed by raters in laboratory rating studies.

According to this analysis, the laboratory context is substantially different from the situation most likely faced by a rater making criterion performance evaluations. More effort is clearly necessary to improve the realism of laboratory research directed toward the study of rating process and related performance rating topics.

It might be noted that the major strategies for examining rating processes do have some similarity in context to real-world personnel evaluation procedures. Subjects working with paper-people protocols are in situations similar to those of supervisors several levels up reviewing behavioral performance reports on employees and making evaluations. Viewing videotape presentations of brief performances places subject raters in conditions similar to those of assessors in an assessment center making effectiveness judgments about performance. The main points remain, however: (a) Caution is in order with respect to generalizing laboratory research on performance ratings, especially to questions of performance appraisal for counseling, feedback, and related administrative purposes, but also to ratings for research only; (b) similar to what has been accomplished for interviewing research (Bernstein, Hakel, & Harlan, 1975), and following Murphy, Herr, Lockhart, & Maguire (1986) in the performance rating area, research should go forward to assess similarities and differences in results between laboratory and field settings; (c) effort and ingenuity should be applied to make laboratory research settings better reflect the organizational settings intended for the research questions asked; and (d) attempts to bring important performance rating research issues out into field settings should continue, with incumbent organization members as subjects.

Objective Criteria

A second major measurement method for criterion performance involves use of objective criteria. Objective criteria employed in personnel research include turnover, absences, production rates, job level and salary, sales, disciplinary cases, and any other directly countable record or index. At first glance, one may presume that objective criteria are better than ratings, which are inherently subjective. Unfortunately, judgment often enters into the assignment of objective criterion scores. Also, objective measures are notoriously deficient as criteria because they typically tap only a small proportion of the job's performance requirements (e.g., Guion, 1965). Contamination can be a problem with some of these criteria as well. Problems such as opportunity bias beyond the assessee's control may influence these outcome measures. Nonetheless, when they are relevant to important conceptual criteria and are reasonably reliable and uncontaminated—or when corrections can be made to reduce contamination—objective measures can be useful in indexing some criterion dimensions.

Turnover. Turnover or attrition is often an important prima facie criterion because the cost of training replacement personnel is usually high; also, having people, especially key people, leave the organization can be disruptive and can adversely affect organizational effectiveness. Turnover is sometimes treated as a single dichotomous variable—a person is either a "leaver" or a "stayer." This treatment fails to distinguish between very different reasons for leaving the organization (e.g., being fired for a disciplinary infraction vs. leaving voluntarily for health reasons). Clearly, turnover for such different reasons will have different patterns of relationships with individual difference or organizational factor predictors. Prediction of turnover with any substantive interpretation requires a look at the categories of turnover.

Some have advocated two turnover categories, voluntary and involuntary, but in many organizational settings this division is too coarse. Where sample sizes permit, it seems preferable to create a dichotomous variable for each turnover category and then compare on the predictor variable(s) of interest those who left for that reason to all those who stayed. It may be, for example, that employees fired for disciplinary reasons have reliably different scores on certain personality scales—say, lower socialization—compared to stayers, whereas prior health status is the only predictor of leaving the organization for health reasons. This approach to dealing with turnover as a dependent criterion variable, along with research based on turnover models (see Hulin, this volume), appears to offer the most hope for learning more about why individuals leave organizations and what can be done to reduce unwanted turnover.

Absences.   For most jobs, having employees at work regularly is important for individual and organizational effectiveness. Accordingly, issues of absences and attendance are legitimate criteria to consider. Unfortunately, three problems plague measures of absences or attendance (Hammer & Landau, 1981). First, criterion contamination is often a factor in measuring absences. Distinctions should be made between involuntary and voluntary absence, for example, with the latter being the more important to predict and then reduce. However, researchers may group involuntary absences for reasons such as legitimate illnesses together with willful, voluntary absences for reasons such as being upset with a supervisor. Making the voluntary-involuntary distinction is often difficult without asking each employee why he or she was absent in each case; even then, one is left with possibly slanted self-reports.

A second problem with absence measures is that they are unstable. In the case of voluntary absences, such factors as the organizational environment can influence absence rates differently for different organization members and can lead to criterion unreliability with absence measures (Hammer & Landau, 1981). One way to reduce this instability is to measure attendance rather than absences. Latham and Pursell (1975) demonstrated that attendance was a more reliable measure than number of absences in a sample of loggers. However, attendance measures necessarily confound voluntary and involuntary absences. A second approach to reducing criterion instability here is to collect absence data over longer time periods (Ilgen & Hollenback, 1977). However, a potential problem is that the antecedent variables or events hypothesized to affect absences may decline in relevance to absences as time goes on, rendering conclusions regarding such hypotheses more and more tenuous over time (Harrison & Hulin, 1989).

Another problem in measuring absences is serious skewing of distributions. Severe truncation, with many sample members having *no* absences, causes difficulties when absences are correlated with scores on another variable such as a predictor measure. Difficulties especially take the form of reduced power for significance tests and depressed correlations with other variables.

A hopeful sign is that emerging alternative strategies for treating absence data, such as event history models, may improve prediction of absences (Harrison & Hulin, 1989) and increase our understanding of the absence-taking process (Fichman, 1989). In sum, voluntary, illegitimate absences should be the focus of study regarding absences in criterion development. This class of absence is presumably a function of employee motivation and willingness to work. Accordingly, it should be predictable from measures of individual differences in employees and organizational factors. Involuntary absences are caused by events beyond the employee's or organization's control, are typically unpredictable, and are therefore outside the personnel research domain.

Production Rates. For jobs that have observable, countable products that result from individual performance, a production rate criterion is a compelling bottom-line index of performance. However, as often noted (e.g., Guion, 1965; P. C. Smith, 1976), considerable care must be taken in gathering and interpreting production data. For example, work-related dependencies on other employees or on equipment for determining production rates may create bias in these rates. Also, production standards and quota systems (e.g., in data entry jobs) create problems for criterion measurement.

As with absences, instability of production rates is another potential problem. Rothe's (1978) extensive research on production workers doing piecework shows that week-to-week production rates are only moderately reliable. Correlations between successive weeks' production average .75 with incentives, and .53 with no incentives, for increased production (Rothe, 1978). Longer periods for data collection may be necessary to ensure stable criterion production rates. Most importantly, researchers attempting to derive production criteria should pay special attention to possible contaminating influences whereby employees have unequal opportunities to produce at the same rate.

Job Level and Salary. These criteria are intuitively appealing for management and some professional jobs. If in these jobs an organization rewards employees with promotions and salary increases strictly according to their overall performance and worth to the organization, such criteria seem quite appropriate, when adjustments are made for years of service or some similar tenure-related indicator. Regarding adjustments for tenure, Hulin

(1962) provided perhaps the most refined treatment, correcting increases in salary for the expected salary rise as predicted by length of service.

Regardless of the corrections made, promotion rate and salary criteria are susceptible to contaminating influences. Situational factors such as timing of higher-level position openings and market value of a particular specialty can adversely affect measures of these criteria. In addition, politics within the organization, when it results in promotion and salary decisions based on factors other than merit, can introduce error into these criterion measures. Finally, as a practical restriction, it is difficult to compare individuals who enter the organization at very different levels and salaries. Promotion rate and salary criteria are best applied in organizations that promote from within.

Nonetheless, provided proper corrections for tenure or experience level can be accomplished and that contaminating factors are not a serious problem, promotions and salary do provide reasonable summary indices of an employee's total worth to the organization. In fact, it might be argued that these criteria reflect a consensus perception (across several supervisors) of an employee's performance in all aspects of the job, weighted according to the organization's value placed on each of these aspects. To increase understanding of work performance per se and to enable evaluation of performance on individual job dimensions, it would of course be preferable to obtain multiple criterion scores for each important dimension of the job.

Sales. Initially, sales jobs may seem ideally suited for the use of objective criteria as performance measures. Total sales volume for a fixed period, number of sales per unit time, or some similar index of bottom-line sales volume appear compelling as global, overall performance measures. Upon closer inspection, however, significant criterion contamination issues are evident for objective sales criteria.

First, summary sales volume measures are a function of both individual skill and effort *and* environmental factors beyond the control of the salesperson. In the context of the J. P. Campbell et al. (1970) behavior-performance-effectiveness model, objective sales volume is an effectiveness measure; where environmental influences are both important and unequal in their effect on salespeople, criterion measurement will be contaminated.

One way to remove contamination is to adjust sales data for factors such as market potential (e.g., Cravens & Woodruff, 1973). A practical strategy for making these adjustments is to create norms for stores, sales territories, or for whatever the appropriate comparison unit is. Then criterion scores for each salesperson can be compared to scores for other salespersons with roughly the same selling-related environment and thus similar opportunities to produce sales.

Unfortunately, an inherent problem with this approach has to do with the norming process itself. For example, if large sales territories with many salespersons are used to accomplish the norming, there may be meaningful differences within territories with respect to opportunity to perform. If smaller territories are used, then the norms tend to be unstable because the mean sales performance comparison indices are based on too few salespersons. Thus, *how* one does the adjusting may be as important as whether or not to adjust. However, the development of norming strategies that overcome these types of problems is likely to be quite useful in criterion development efforts.

Interestingly, sales quotas established for compensation purposes as standards for individual salespersons, or groups of them, can represent an attempt to allow for all environmental contaminants in creating an expected sales performance index. Accordingly, sales volume compared to assigned quota—if the quotas are established with great wisdom about all likely unequal environmental influences that might affect sales but that are beyond the salespersons' control—could actually provide a reasonable global index of sales performance. In practice, quotas are not likely to attain this degree of fairness, and researchers should certainly examine quota development procedures carefully before using them in this manner.

As with most other objective performance measures, sales criteria suffer from problems of deficiency in that global measures of sales volume will often fail to tap important parts of the job. For example, identifying new customers and maintaining good relations with existing customers are important aspects of sales but would not be directly indexed by objective sales measures.

Disciplinary Cases. In the military and in certain highly structured organizations, records of disciplinary actions may provide an index of troublemaking behavior detrimental to the individual's performance and to organizational effectiveness. Care should be taken in interpreting such indices because different supervisors and/or units may have different policies regarding the assignment and recording of disciplinary actions, making comparisons across units difficult. Also, as with absences, the base rate of such actions may be very low and the distributions skewed.

Despite these potential difficulties, some construct validity was obtained for a disciplinary-actions-per-unit-time measure on U.S. Army enlisted personnel early in their careers. The disciplinary actions measure correlated considerably higher with peer and supervisor ratings on dimensions related to personal discipline than it did with ratings of technical skill or physical fitness and military appearance (J. P. Campbell, 1986).

Work Sample Tests

Work sample or performance tests are sometimes developed to provide criteria, especially for training programs. For example, to help evaluate the effectiveness of training, work samples may be used to assess performance on important tasks before and after training. Such tests can also be used for other personnel research applications, such as criteria in selection studies. Work samples used as criteria should be distinguished from work samples used as predictors of performance in selection. Asher and Sciarrino (1974) and Cascio and Phillips (1979) have reviewed and discussed work samples as selection devices.

Some argue that work sample tests have the highest fidelity for measuring criterion performance. In a sense, the argument is compelling: What could be more direct and fair than to assess employees' performance on a job by having them actually perform some of the most important tasks associated with it? The performance can then be evaluated for level of competence. Yet evaluation of work samples as criteria is not quite so simple, and their use involves several issues—test development issues, conceptual issues regarding their appropriateness, and validity issues. Each is discussed below.

Test Development Issues.   The most convincing rationale and procedures for developing work sample tests incorporate the sequence of defining for a job (a) the job content universe, (b) the job content domain, (c) the test content universe, and (d) the test content domain (Guion, 1978). The *job content universe* may consist of an exhaustive list of all tasks and activities carried out by job incumbents in the course of performing the job. A list of these tasks, along with a breakdown of all steps included in each task, provides a good working definition of the job content universe. Next, the *job content domain* is sampled from the content universe. Subject matter experts (SMEs), typically incumbents and/or their supervisors, rate the importance of the tasks in the content universe, and the content domain is identified to contain a workable number of the most critical tasks reflecting all important aspects of the job.

As Guion (1978) points out, the *test content universe* is a theoretical concept intended to include (a) all tasks that might be used in testing, (b) all conditions that might be created for testing individual tasks, and (c) all procedures that could be used to obtain performance scores for testees. From this universe, the *test content domain* is selected, containing not only the tasks to be tested but the context in which each task is to be presented for testing; procedures for generating test scores are also specified. The main issues with testing conditions and context is one of generalizability: Will the testing conditions elicit testee performance that generalizes to actual on-the-job performance? Regarding context, should the task be tested in a work sample or in some other testing mode (e.g., paper-and-pencil job knowledge test or performance ratings)?

As an example of this test development sequence, C. H. Campbell, Campbell, Rumsey, and Edwards (1986) developed a work sample test for evaluating the performance of medical specialists in the U.S. Army. A thorough task-based job analysis first provided a working definition of the job content universe, in which 239 tasks were identified in an exhaustive description of all job content. Also, the tasks were clustered into homogenous groupings on the basis of content. Then SMEs rated the importance of each task for satisfactory performance as a medical specialist, and 30 of the most important tasks, also representative of the task clusters, formed the job content domain.

In addition, the test content universe took into account contextual features that might be built into the testing conditions to make them realistic. Finally, Campbell et al. reviewed components or steps of all surviving tasks to decide on the appropriateness of the performance test mode for tasks. In particular, each task was examined to determine if some hands-on work sample test could be developed to measure performance on the whole task or at least some important components of the task. Fifteen of the 30 tasks could be tested in the hands-on mode, and Campbell et al. designed performance tests, including appropriate equipment specifications, a scoring system for SMEs to use in evaluating performance on each component or step of each task, and a scorer training program to standardize the assessment of performance on each task. Three example tasks from the performance test for medical specialists are: (a) assemble needle and syringe and draw medication, (b) administer an injection, and (c) initiate an intravenous infusion.

Table 2 then presents six of the eleven task steps for a task in another performance test developed for motor transport operators in the Army (Campbell et al., 1986). A testee's performance on each of these task steps is graded pass or fail based on relatively objective standards, and a percent pass score is used as the total performance test score across all steps.

Another issue in performance test development concerns process versus product: Should the test be focused on the *process* of performing a task or on the *product* that results from completing the task? In general, tasks associated with products (e.g., troubleshooting a problem with a radio) can be oriented toward either product or process; tasks with no resulting products (e.g., interviewing a job candidate) must be scored according to process considerations only. An advantage to scoring products over process is that assessment is typically more objective. However, if the procedures taken to arrive at the product are also important, process assessment is clearly necessary.

Other test development issues relevant to scoring of work samples are germane here. Unscorable or difficult-to-score process steps are to be avoided. For example, checking and inspecting steps are difficult, if not impossible, to observe. Ill-defined steps, such as "adjust protective mask" for the medical specialist example (to what standard?) and complex steps where a testee can do well on one part of the step but poorly on another, should also be avoided. Even for those evaluators who are expert at a job for which a performance test has

TABLE 2

Task Steps 3–8 for the Motor Transport Operator Task: Perform Vehicle Emergency and Recovery Procedures

3. Position wooden block on the ground under the axle.

4. Position jack on wooden block.

5. Position jack under the axle housing.

6. Turn out screw jack until jack touches axle housing.

7. Close bleeder valve with jack handle.

8. Raise wheel assembly off the ground.

been developed, training in scoring is critical. The scoring system must be unambiguously understood at an operational level, and evaluators should be instructed to offer the same stimulus set to all testees—that is, to provide the same opportunity for successful performance to each person being tested. Often, for example, evaluators are tempted to coach testees, and this practice should be forbidden.

Still another issue with scoring work samples as part of test development is the relative merits of pass-fail marks versus performance level ratings on test steps. Guion (1978) argues for test step performance ratings because they provide more information. Indeed, many steps seem amenable to a continuous performance scale where such ratings as "more skillful," "faster," and "less waste" may have meaning for evaluating performance. For certain very simple task steps or steps that have definite, straightforward standards, pass-fail may suffice; but it will usually be desirable to develop continuous performance scales for use in work sample testing.

Finally, certain practical concerns with performance test development should be mentioned. Time available for testing will almost always be limited, so tasks that take a long time to complete may be impractical to test. However, steps from the task may be strategically selected such that they take considerably less time to test as long as the knowledge, skills, and abilities required for the shortened task are highly similar to those required by the entire task. Also, and more obviously, limitations are sometimes posed by unavailability of equipment or impracticality of its use. Very expensive equipment or equipment that might create dangerous conditions (e.g., for a nuclear power plant operator job) make it difficult to develop performance tests for jobs requiring such equipment.

Issues About the Criterion Space Measured by Work Sample/Performance Tests. A second major issue with performance or work sample tests is that researchers may erroneously come to see them as ultimate criteria— that is, these tests are sometimes considered *the* criterion of choice for accurately assessing performance in certain jobs, especially those that require complex motor skills. Performance tests should not be thought of in this light. First, they are clearly maximum performance rather than typical performance measures. As such, they tap the "can-do" more than the "will-do" performance-over-time aspects of effectiveness. Yet "will-do" longer-term performance is certainly important for assessing effectiveness in jobs. Accordingly, these measure are deficient when used exclusively in measuring perforrance.

In summary thus far, inherent shortcomings of work samples for measuring some aspects of performance, as well as practical limitations such as time and equipment constraints, argue against relying on such tests to provide a comprehensive index of overall performance. An important theme of this chapter is that whenever possible, more than one kind of criterion measure should be used, each focusing on that aspect of the criterion it measures best.

Validity Issues. It is beyond the scope of this section to discuss in any depth the different types of validity and their relative merits for evaluating the usefulness of work samples or job knowledge tests. Nonetheless, the view embraced is Dunnette's (Dunnette, 1966): that validation is a process of learning about the meaning of a test's scores and evaluating that meaning.

Content, criterion-related, and construct validity can all take a role in helping to understand what work samples are measuring. For example, content validity notions are relevant to assessing the validity of the tests (Guion, 1978). That is, how closely does a particular test share important content—tasks, components of tasks, conditions—with the content reflected on the job? Actually, content validity can be virtually assured if the work sample test development sequence just outlined is followed conscientiously.

Construct validity principles are more useful in evaluating the meaning of work sample criterion test scores. Examining relationships between these scores and data from other criterion measures can be useful in evaluating the validity of work sample tests. Perhaps the most important construct validation principle applicable in this case is to seek disconfirming evidence for test score validity. For example, strong positive correlations between test scores and ratings of scorer-testee friendship would cast doubt on the validity of work sample scores; likewise, small differences in mean scores between known masters and nonmasters on a target job would certainly reflect poorly on the usefulness of such scores as measures of job proficiency. On the positive side, lack of disconfirming evidence after a series of studies and analyses of this type provides more optimism on the meaning of criterion measures. This, along with evidence of hypothesized positive relationships with other variables, is of course important in building a nomological net in support of construct validity for such measures (Cronbach & Meehl, 1955).

Perhaps an even more compelling framework, seemingly tailor-made for studying the meaning of criterion work sample test scores, is generalizability theory (Cronbach, Rajaratnam, & Gleser, 1963). Generalizability theory can be viewed as an extension of classical psychometric theory. Classical test theory recognizes only a single, undifferentiated source of error; in contrast, generalizability theory recognizes distinct sources of error in measurement. It replaces the reliability coefficient with the coefficient of generalizability, the true score with a more precisely defined universe score, and undifferentiated error variance with specific sources of variance. The universe score is the expected value of the observed score for a person over the universe of items. The coefficient of generalizability is the ratio of universe score variance to observed score variance. In generalizability theory, there may be several different sources of error variance and several coefficients of generalizability, depending on the universe to which the researcher wishes to generalize.

Thus, for any particular measure, it is possible to evaluate the limits of generalizability over different items and conditions of administration. Glaser and Klaus (1962) identified a number of possible elements detrimental to generalizability in performance testing: (a) variations in the testing environment (e.g., with a driving test, variations in weather conditions), (b) instability in the testing equipment (e.g., automatic versus stick shift), and (c) testee attitudes or reactions toward being tested (e.g., varying levels of anxiety concerning the testing). Generalizability designs can be used to evaluate separately each of these possible sources of measurement error in performance testing.

Job Knowledge Tests

Still another major category of criterion measures is the job knowledge test. Job knowledge tests, like work samples, are used primarily as criteria to assess the outcomes of training in organizations. As with work samples, they may also serve as criterion measures for other personnel research purposes. Part of the same content validation sequence, discussed in the last section on work sample/performance tests, can be applied to job knowledge test development (Guion, 1978; Lammlein, 1986). Defining the job content universe with an exhaustive list of nontrivial tasks and identifying the most important tasks using expert judgment is a reasonable way to focus on a workable set of tasks for item writing.

Once the target tasks are identified, items can be prepared, typically in a multiple-choice format, although other kinds of items such as the essay type are of course possible. Just as in writing any other multiple-choice items, care should be taken to ensure that the item stems and response alternatives are clearly stated and that distractor responses are definitely wrong but plausible. Osborn and Campbell (1976) suggest an approach for writing job knowledge items based on important target tasks in the job content domain. For each important task, they suggest asking why the worker fails to perform behaviors correctly on the task. Possibilities are that he or she (a) doesn't know *where* to perform (e.g., where objects, pieces are located), (b) doesn't know *when* to perform a step (problems with sequencing), (c) doesn't know *what* the result should be, or (d) doesn't know *how* to perform individual steps or the entire task. From this framework, items with correct responses, and especially distractor responses, can be productively generated.

An issue with job knowledge test development is when the paper-and-pencil knowledge test medium is appropriate for evaluating job performance. When a task is procedural, requiring primarily knowledge about steps to complete it, and not complex motor skills for performing each step, a job knowledge format seems clearly to be as appropriate as a work sample format. Tasks requiring certain skills and operations are probably not amenable to job knowledge testing, requiring instead a performance test treatment. Such tasks include (a) those that require finely tuned acts of physical coordination (e.g., a police marksmanship task), (b) those that require quick reaction (e.g., typing a letter under time pressure), and (c) those that require complex time-sharing psychomotor performance (e.g., aircraft cockpit simulator tasks) (Osborn & Campbell, 1976).

As with work sample tests, validity issues for job knowledge tests focus both on the content validity of the test itself and on the validity of inferences made from test scores. Content validity of knowledge tests is aided by a systematic selection of tasks toward which items are then written. The job content universe–content domain–test universe–test domain sequence provides a specific workable procedure for this task selection (Guion, 1978). As discussed, however, care should be taken to represent with job knowledge items only those tasks that can be reasonably tested in a knowledge test mode.

Regarding validity of test scores, one strategy for evaluating their meaning in the spirit of construct validation is to examine empirically alternative hypotheses about relationships between job knowledge test scores and scores on other variables. For example, test items that involve high reading difficulty levels may be biased in favor of persons with better reading skills as opposed to simply measuring job knowledge.

This last example points to a significant potential problem with job knowledge tests targeted toward jobs with low reading level requirements. The reading level of the test should be no higher than that required on the job. Two ideas that have addressed this problem are the "walk-through" testing procedure and an approach to designing picture items for job knowledge tests.

Briefly, the *walk-through test* (Hedge & Teachout, 1986) requires testees to describe what they *would do* in a series of job situations important

to the successful conduct of that job. Appropriate equipment is generally available for the testee to "show and tell," thus eliminating the reading requirements present with job knowledge tests. This procedure also allows for the testing of tasks that can't be used in a work sample mode because of problems with safety or inconvenience in actual performance (e.g., certain emergency procedures for a power plant operator).

Regarding the *picture-item test*, Osborn and Ford (1977) developed two interesting versions that replace multiple-choice responses with pictures of equipment. In one version, a picture of a correctly repaired aircraft generator was shown along with pictures of several incorrectly repaired generators, with instructions to select the one that had been correctly repaired. In the second version, testees were asked to identify errors in a picture of an incorrectly completed task. Evaluation studies of the knowledge test component of the walk-through procedures and of knowledge tests using picture items should be carried out.

Developing and Evaluating Models of Job Performance

Considerable theoretical and empirical effort has been dedicated to developing and evaluating individual differences models of predictors. For example, factor analytic studies have led to explication of the aptitude (Guilford, 1967; Thurstone, 1938), personality (Hogan, 1983; Tupes & Christal, 1961), and vocational interest (Rounds & Dawis, 1979) domains. In each of these individual differences areas, the models derived from factor analysis represent attempts to parsimoniously characterize the important dimensions of the domain. With personality, for example, Eysenck's (1947) work suggests that three summary dimensions—introversion/extroversion, neuroticism, and psychoticism—explain much of the variation in temperament. Fiske (1949), Norman (1963), and more recently Digman and Inouye (1986) report that a five-factor personality dimension system consistently summarizes self-reports and ratings of personality.

With all the effort expended on model development and evaluation on the predictor side, almost no theoretical or empirical work has focused on models of job performance, reflecting the bias of concern in our field for predictors over criteria.

We should now specify what a performance model might look like and how such models could benefit the science and practice of our discipline. A criterion model for a particular job family, for example, might first identify in summary form the important performance requirement constructs for those jobs. The model would also specify relationships between the constructs. In structural modeling terms, the latent structure of the criterion variables would be hypothesized, with one (or preferably more than one) indicator measure identified for each performance construct.

An Example Job Performance Model: The Case of Project A

A characterization of such a model appears in Figure 5. This model, derived from a long-term, large-scale study to improve the selection and classification system for enlisted persons entering the U.S. Army (Project A: J. P. Campbell, 1986; see Hakel, 1986 for a critical review), specifies hypothesized latent criterion variables, along with their respective indicator measures, for nine Army enlisted jobs (J. P. Campbell, McHenry, & Wise, 1990; Wise, Campbell, McHenry, & Hanser, 1986).

The form of this model allows testing it for goodness of fit using confirmatory factor analysis (James, Mulaik, & Brett, 1982; Schmitt & Stults, 1986). It is also possible with the LISREL confirmatory factor analysis program (Joreskog & Sorbom, 1981) to test the generality of a performance model across jobs—in this case,

how consistently the hypothesized model was confirmed across the nine jobs. This is the kind of model development effort possible for specifying a summary multidimensional view of the criterion performance requirements for groupings of jobs.

Continuing with the example above, Table 3 shows the main performance indices finally confirmed to measure the five performance constructs. In this example, several of the performance measures were themselves summary indices derived from pilot and field tests of the ratings, work sample, job knowledge, and administrative criterion measures.

In particular, for the 30 job knowledge tasks reflected in the job knowledge test domain for each job (the 15 work sample tasks for each job were a subset of the 30 job knowledge tasks), tasks were grouped according to similarity of task content within each of the nine jobs. The grouping of tasks resulted in from 8 to 15 functional categories for individual jobs (e.g., providing first aid and firing weapons). There was considerable but by no means complete overlap in functional categories across the nine jobs. At this point, work sample test scores and job knowledge test scores were separately generated for each functional category within the jobs by computing a percent passed score for the steps on tasks assigned to that category (work samples) and a percentage-of-items-correct score for steps on the tasks assigned to that job knowledge test category. Then, within each job and type of measure, factor analyses were conducted.

Results showed that some factors consistently emerged across several or even all jobs (e.g., communications/radio operation and vehicle maintenance), and a smaller number of factors were unique to individual jobs. In all, five common work sample and job knowledge test content categories were identified, using a combination of factor analysis results and rational/practical considerations. One technical skills category was retained as unique to each job. At this point, each of the six content

FIGURE 5

Summary Preliminary Model of Enlisted Soldier Performance

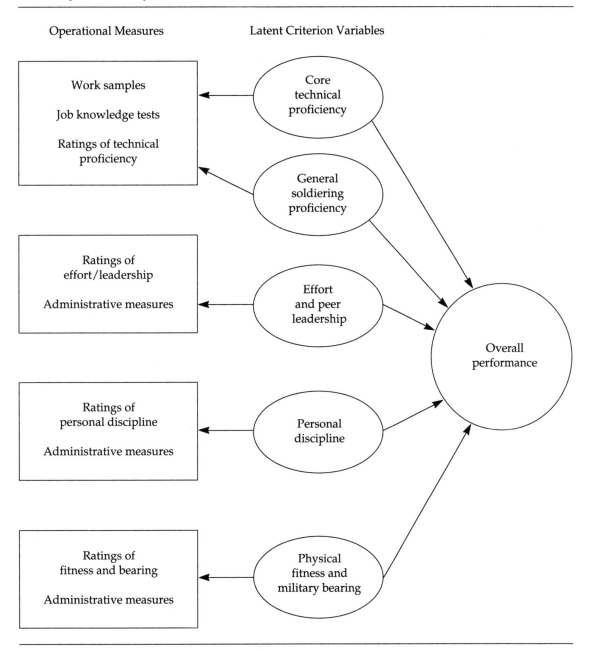

TABLE 3

Performance Measures for Each of Five Criterion Constructs

1.   Core Technical Proficiency
       Work samples for specific job
       Job knowledge test on specific job

2.   General Soldiering Proficiency
       Work samples for parts of job in common with other jobs
       Job knowledge test on parts of job in common with other jobs

3.   Effort and Peer Leadership
       Peer and supervisory ratings, effort/leadership factor
       Peer and supervisory ratings, job-specific rating scale factors
       Administrative awards and certificates measure

4.   Personal Discipline
       Peer and supervisory ratings, personal discipline factor
       Administrative disciplinary problems measure (–)
       Administrative promotion rate measure

5.   Physical Fitness and Military Bearing
       Peer and supervisory ratings, fitness/bearing factor
       Administrative physical readiness measure

categories could be scored for most of the jobs and the work sample and job knowledge test domains were scored separately, employing respectively the percentage of task steps performed correctly for tasks in that category and the percentage of items correct for items in that task category.

For the performance ratings, peer and supervisor ratings on the scales developed to be in common across all jobs (Army-wide scales: e.g., maintaining equipment, following regulations) were first pooled, then intercorrelated and factor analyzed. An interpretable three-factor solution resulted:

- Effort/Leadership—including effort and technical skill in performing the job, peer leadership, and self-development

- Personal discipline—including self-control, integrity, and following regulations

- Military bearing—including physical fitness and military appearance

This three-factor solution reflected very adequately the structure associated with each of the nine jobs. Unit-weighted composites of ratings on the three factors were accordingly computed to represent the Army-wide rating scales in criterion model development efforts. Factor analyses of job-specific rating scales were likewise conducted within each of the nine jobs. Consistently emerging were two factors representing job performance central to the specific content of each job and performance less central to the job content. Unit-weighted composites of pooled peer and supervisor ratings were computed for these two factors as well.

Finally, four administrative measures were judged relevant for performance measurement. Criterion development work suggested that number of awards and certificates per year in the Army, promotion rate, physical readiness test scores, M-16 rifle qualifying scores, and number of disciplinary actions divided by months in the Army should be target criterion variables. Further, field tests showed that self-reports of these administrative indicators are remarkably accurate. Thus, self-reports of the five indices in Table 3 were employed in the subsequent criterion model development work.

The final set of criterion variables entering into the performance modeling phase for each of the nine jobs appears as follows: [2]

- Two to six work sample content category scores

- Two to six job knowledge content category scores

- Three Army-wide rating category scores

- Two job-specific rating category scores

- One overall effectiveness rating score

- Five administrative measure scores

At this point, correlations between these criterion variables were computed for each job separately. Table 4 displays the intercorrelations for the radio operator job. Exploratory factor analyses were also conducted within each job. One consistent finding across all jobs was that written job knowledge and rating method factors emerged. A second consistent result was that the administrative measures and Army-wide rating factors combined in a conceptually satisfactory way. The awards and certificates variable linked with the effort/leadership rating factor; the disciplinary actions and promotion rate measures clustered together with the Army-wide discipline factor; and the physical readiness test scores and military bearing factor consistently loaded on the same factor. A third finding was that the job-specific rating scale factors loaded more highly on the effort/leadership construct factor than on either of the two proficiency construct factors.

Thus, correlation matrices for each job, follow-up exploratory factor analyses of each of these matrices, and a preliminary model of soldier job performance developed previously (J. P. Campbell & Harris, 1985) led to a target model as shown in Figure 5, except for the inclusion of a written test and a rating factor *and* the adjustment of tying the job-specific rating factors to the effort/leadership factor rather than to the two proficiency factors. This model was tested within each job using the LISREL confirmatory factor analysis procedure.

To summarize the results, chi-square goodness-of-fit tests within each job suggested that the model accounted for the obtained correlations between criterion measures. Further, a LISREL option to test this model across all nine jobs simultaneously showed that the fit was satisfactory. Wise et al. (1986) and Campbell et al. (1990) point out that the model development procedures employed precluded a completely "fair" confirmatory test here. The target model was posited in part on the basis of observed empirical relationships between criteria. Nonetheless, this work remains a very useful illustration of performance model development.

Accordingly, the five-construct, multidimensional representation of job performance appearing in Table 3 seems warranted for each of these jobs. This differentiated depiction of performance was subsequently shown to be important when test validation results demonstrated that cognitive predictors had substantial relationships with the two proficiency factors, and personality predictors correlated more highly with the effort/leadership and discipline factors.

This example shows how a performance model might be derived, tested, and then used in personnel research. How much more widely the model would apply to other jobs is unclear, although it is important to note that the nine jobs studied in this research were selected to be representative of the more

TABLE 4

Correlations Between Criterion Measures for Radio Operators

	1	2	3	4	5	6	7	8	9	10	11	12	13	14	15	16	17	18	19	20	21
1. Work sample—technical	—																				
2. Work sample—common tasks	25	—																			
3. Work sample—safety	25	18	—																		
4. Work sample—communications	28	27	28	—																	
5. Work sample—vehicle	09	08	16	01	—																
6. Job knowledge—technical	42	31	10	34	11	—															
7. Job knowledge—common tasks	21	31	21	29	09	60	—														
8. Job knowledge—safety	23	18	13	21	10	59	36	—													
9. Job knowledge—communications	21	15	09	38	02	60	50	50	—												
10. Job knowledge—vehicle	22	05	06	21	-06	37	23	28	32	—											
11. Overall performance rating	20	24	15	15	-02	24	17	09	14	03	—										
12. Rating—effort/leadership	24	21	21	15	02	30	28	14	16	06	83	—									
13. Rating—discipline	10	14	07	10	-01	20	15	04	15	06	73	68	—								
14. Rating—military bearing	12	08	10	04	-02	01	02	00	08	-04	64	57	52	—							
15. Rating—core technical	20	24	20	11	-01	29	30	16	15	08	74	81	54	47	—						
16. Rating—other technical	11	18	15	01	00	17	22	08	09	02	66	71	58	40	76	—					
17. Awards/certificates	09	12	06	03	02	10	10	11	-00	-05	17	18	04	11	14	03	—				
18. Physical readiness	01	-10	00	01	-06	-04	-08	04	01	03	11	12	04	34	04	-03	23	—			
19. M-16 qualification	04	05	10	07	05	07	10	08	-04	-06	02	07	-11	-06	05	-03	10	04	—		
20. Disciplinary actions	-09	-03	-07	-12	-03	-16	-09	-13	-20	-10	-31	-31	-32	-25	-16	-17	02	-11	04	—	
21. Promotion rate	08	12	21	09	05	18	17	10	19	13	30	30	26	24	22	22	12	04	03	-34	—

Note: $N = 239$

than 250 entry-level jobs in the U. S. Army. Effort/leadership, personal discipline, and the two technical proficiency constructs appear quite broadly relevant. The military bearing construct seems more specific to a military setting. It would be productive to do more work like this in other job domains to begin to map the performance constructs for a variety of jobs and organizations.

Scientific Implications of Criterion Model Development and Testing

If such models can be confirmed within broad job families, for example, implications for the science of industrial and organizational psychology are considerable. First, the performance requirement constructs of jobs could be more clearly established and delineated by drawing inferences about them from several jobs rather than just one. Second, extensive development and testing of performance models for a variety of jobs might contribute to identification of a way to categorize jobs according to similarities in the performance requirement constructs, leading eventually to a comprehensive mapping of the similarities and differences in these requirements for many kinds of jobs. Third, personnel selection programs could benefit from extended validity generalization efforts in which individual criterion constructs, rather than overall performance, are used within a synthetic validity framework to evaluate the generalizability of test validities. Finally, the reliable and robust representation of performance in multidimensional terms across jobs should considerably improve the understanding of predictor-criterion links by allowing constructive replication of these links in multiple jobs.

Other Observations on Performance Models

Two additional observations should be made concerning the criterion model-building notion. First, criteria for jobs in an organization

necessarily reflect the values of that organization. Thus, differences in values between organizations with respect to degree of emphasis to be placed on particular performance areas will somewhat reduce the generalizability of criterion models across organizations. This factor will certainly affect importance weights placed on performance constructs used to form composites for some personnel research applications. Beyond this, an organization's values may influence even the presence or absence of some criterion constructs considered for a performance model in an organization.

Second, method factors are likely to strongly influence the models. For example, ratings tend to correlate more highly with other ratings than they do with work sample performance or objective measure scores, no matter what the criterion construct. This could make the dimensions and structure of a model quite dependent on the criterion measurement methods employed. The only way to address this potential problem is to include the most conceptually appropriate method or methods to measure each criterion construct.

Overall, however, development and evaluation of criterion models is a promising step toward enhanced scientific understanding of criteria. Valid measurement of multidimensional performance on jobs can only improve the science of industrial and organizational psychology. Further, it should work to enhance personnel research practices, where such a multidimensional depiction of performance is desirable.

Conclusions

The following conclusions can be made about criteria and criterion measurement methods.

Performance Ratings

Ratings have the inherent potential advantage of being sensitive to ratee performance over time and across a variety of job situations.

Ideally, raters can average performance levels observed, sampling performance-relevant behavior broadly over multiple trials. Provided observation and subsequent ratings are made on all important dimensions, ratings can potentially avoid problems of contamination and deficiency. A related advantage of ratings is their flexibility for indexing performance on virtually any dimension. If a definition for a dimension can be articulated, then it can form the basis for a rating scale. For example, performance on task proficiency and job knowledge can be rated, as can such dimensions as interpersonal effectiveness, communication, and organization and planning. A third advantage is that ratings avoid artificiality of work samples and job knowledge tests, in that the latter are simulations of the job, whereas ratings are made using actual job performance as input.

Remember that these are *potential* advantages of the rating method. Rater error, bias, and other inaccuracies, well documented here and elsewhere, must be reduced in order for ratings to realize this potential.

Remember, too, that because ratings are used so often in personnel research, it is doubly important that they reach their potential. Both basic and applied research are needed to learn more about what performance ratings are measuring and how to improve on that measurement. Rater training research appears especially promising for reducing rating errors and enhancing the accuracy of evaluations. Research on the performance rating process has not contributed extensively to improvement in rating procedures, but it may yet do so. Field studies of the actual cues that raters use in making performance evaluations should be especially useful.

Objective Measures

Like other methods of measuring criterion performance, objective measures can be quite useful. However, these measures are almost always deficient, contaminated, or both. Indices such as absences, production rates, sales, and disciplinary cases provide data pertinent to only a portion of a job's performance requirements. In addition, some of these indices, along with job level and salary, are often determined in part by factors beyond the employee's control. The latter problem of contamination can sometimes be alleviated by judicious corrections or norming strategies.

More attention should be paid to the psychology of objective measures to increase our understanding of relationships between objective criteria and other measures and to enhance the usefulness of these criteria. One example is to treat reasons for turnover separately (e.g., leaving to take better job vs. leaving for disciplinary reasons), grouping them together only when they reflect the same or similar underlying behavioral meaning. A second example is to form composites with other criterion measures where conceptual rationale and empirical relationships allow. In the Army enlisted personnel performance model (J. P. Campbell et al., 1990), for example, disciplinary actions taken against ratees and ratings of personal discipline were in the same criterion composite; likewise, number of awards and commendations and ratings of effort and leadership appeared in the same criterion cluster.

Work Sample and Job Knowledge Tests

Work sample performance tests should not in any sense be considered as ultimate or even best criteria. Nonetheless, well-conceived and competently constructed performance tests can be valuable measures of maximum performance. If these tests are focused on a good sampling of the important tasks for a job, then they arguably provide a reasonable index of the "can-do" aspect of performance on the job. However, in keeping with Dunnette's (1963) comments criticizing single, overall criterion measures, a single *method* of measuring performance should be discouraged.

Developers of work sample performance tests should follow the Guion (1978) prescription of attending to the job content universe and domain (i.e., sampling tasks carefully) as well as ensuring a realistic set of test conditions, generalizable to on-the-job settings. Analysis of performance test data should, where technically feasible, employ designs from generalizability theory to help pinpoint sources of measurement error (as in test scorers or testing conditions).

Job knowledge tests are typically most appropriate as training criteria, but also for job performance criteria, especially when considerable knowledge of job content and task procedures is a prerequisite for effective on-the-job performance. Of course, job knowledge test scores usually reflect only a modest portion of the total job performance requirement domain.

Final Remarks

Research studies and everyday organizational experience strongly suggest that job performance is multidimensional. Accordingly, criterion development and measurement should proceed on multiple dimensions of job performance. Because jobs are typically defined by clusters of tasks and activities that require similar knowledge, skills, abilities, and personal characteristics, performance on these dimensions will likely be positively correlated (Cooper, 1981) but sufficiently distinct to warrant a multidimensional treatment. If necessary, criteria for a job can be combined to form an appropriately weighted composite after the multiple dimensions have been identified and measured.

The most rational way to conduct criterion development begins with job analysis. Identifying the conceptual criteria in Astin's (1964) nomenclature should come first. An effective strategy here is to use the critical incidents (Flanagan, 1954) or behaviorally anchored rating scale (BARS; Smith & Kendall, 1963) methodology, because these methods naturally produce samplings of actual job behaviors. The content of categories derived from behavioral examples is thus very likely to reflect important conceptual criteria. After these criteria have been identified, the best possible measure for each conceptual criterion should be selected or developed.

Construct validation methods are preferable in evaluating criterion measures (James, 1973; P. C. Smith, 1976). We should attempt to learn as much as possible about what our criterion measures are actually measuring and thus what the criterion scores mean. A good exemplar in this direction is Hunter's (1983) path analysis work, exploring causal links between performance ratings, task proficiency, job knowledge, and general mental ability.

Multitrait-multimethod approaches are also useful for evaluating construct validity; in particular, confirmatory factor analysis procedures show promise (Schmitt & Stults, 1986). Note, however, that not every criterion measurement method should be considered for measuring every performance construct, as in a completely crossed multitrait-multimethod design. Different measurement methods are more and less appropriate for different sets of criteria. For example, job knowledge tests usually don't—and shouldn't—measure the interpersonal aspects of job performance; supervisory ratings may not be usefully employed in evaluating some kinds of specific task proficiency.

Conceptual advances in criterion development over the years have been impressive, and insights into criteria and ideas about how to measure criterion constructs have often been illuminating. The actual measurement of criterion performance is much more problematic. Raters seem limited in their ability to observe behavior and to provide accurate reports of performance. Objective indices are almost invariably deficient, sometimes overly global, and often contaminated, with differential opportunity to score well on them. Work sample performance tests are expensive and deficient. Job knowledge tests measure only a small proportion of job performance. In some ways, these measurement problems seem insurmountable; for example, the information processing limitations of raters may prove intractable. Yet the effort to improve criterion measurement definitely seems worth it. Criteria provide the foundation for the science of industrial and organizational psychology and the practice of applied personnel research in organizations. Progress is evident, but much more is needed.

Part of this chapter was prepared at the Psychology Department, Ohio State University, while the author was on leave from PDRI. I thank the following Ohio State graduate students for their skilled assistance in reviewing material for the chapter and discussing with me concepts in criterion development during a seminar there: James C. Bassett, Adrienne Colella, Lawrence W. Inks, Laura L. Koppes, Phyllis C. Panzano, and Martha M. Sanders. Thanks also to John P. Campbell, Jeffrey J. McHenry, Lauress L. Wise, and Mike Rumsey for reading and commenting on sections of the chapter, to Marvin D. Dunnette and Patricia C. Smith for providing feedback on an earlier draft, and finally to Kim Downing and John Novak for organizing and typing several versions of this manuscript.

Notes

1   Accuracy of ratings can be distinguished from their validity. *Accuracy* is typically thought to require both the correct rank order of ratees *and* the correct absolute level against some set of target scores. *Validity* is concerned with the correct rank order only. This convention will be followed, although, as we will see, a number of different conceptualizations and operational definitions of accuracy somewhat complicate this depiction of accuracy.

2   There are two comments about this listing. First, to simplify description of the criterion model development analyses, two sets of measures considered in the J. P. Campbell et al. (1990) analyses are not included in the array: (a) experimental combat

performance prediction ratings and (b) training knowledge test measures. Second, the two to six work sample or job knowledge category scores mean that some jobs did not have tasks relevant to some work sample/job knowledge categories. For example, administrative specialists have no communications/radio operation and vehicle maintenance tasks and therefore have missing data for those work sample and job knowledge categories.

References

Abelson, R. P. (1981). Psychological status of the script concept. *American Psychologist, 36,* 715–729.

Ackerman, P. L. (1987). Individual differences in skilled learning: An integration of psychometric and information processing perspectives. *Psychological Bulletin, 102,* 3–27.

Adams-Webber, J. R. (1979). *Personal construct theory.* New York: Wiley.

Althauser, R. P. (1974). Inferring validity from the multitrait-multimethod matrix: Another assessment. In H. L. Costner (Ed.), *Sociological methodology 1973–1974* (pp. 106–107). San Francisco: Jossey-Bass.

Asher, J. J., & Sciarrino, J. A. (1974). Realistic work sample tests: A review. *Personnel Psychology, 27,* 519–533.

Astin, A. W. (1964). Criterion-centered research. *Educational and Psychological Measurement, 24,* 807–822.

Athey, T. R., & McIntyre, R. M. (1987). Effect of rater training on rater accuracy: Levels-of-processing theory and social facilitation theory perspectives. *Journal of Applied Psychology, 72,* 567–572.

Baker, E. M., & Schuck, J. R. (1975). Theoretical note: Use of signal detection theory to clarify problems of evaluating performance in industry. *Organizational Behavior and Human Performance, 13,* 307–317.

Banks, C. G., & Murphy, K. R. (1985). Toward narrowing the research-practice gap in performance appraisal. *Personnel Psychology, 38,* 335–345.

Barrett, G. V., Caldwell, M. S., & Alexander, R. A. (1985). The concept of dynamic criteria: A critical reanalysis. *Personnel Psychology, 38,* 41–56.

Bartlett, C. J. (1983). What's the difference between valid and invalid halo? Forced choice measurement without forcing a choice. *Journal of Applied Psychology, 68,* 218–226.

Becker, B. E., & Cardy, R. L. (1986). Influence of halo error on appraisal effectiveness: A conceptual and empirical reconsideration. *Journal of Applied Psychology, 71,* 662–671.

Bellows, R. M. (1941). Procedures for evaluating vocational criteria. *Journal of Applied Psychology, 25,* 499–513.

Bernardin, H. J. (1977). Behavioral expectation scales versus summated scales: A fairer comparison. *Journal of Applied Psychology, 62,* 422–427.

Bernardin, H. J., Alvares, K. M., & Cranny, C. J. (1976). A recomparison of behavioral expectation scales to summated scales. *Journal of Applied Psychology, 61,* 564–570.

Bernardin, H. J., & Beatty, R. W. (1984). *Performance appraisal: Assessing human behavior at work.* Belmont, CA: Wadsworth.

Bernardin, H. J., & Buckley, M. R. (1981). Strategies in rater training. *Academy of Management Review, 6,* 205–212.

Bernardin, H. J., & Pence, E. C. (1980). Effects of rater training: Creating new response sets and decreasing accuracy. *Journal of Applied Psychology, 65,* 60–66.

Bernardin, H. J., & Smith, P. C. (1981). A clarification of some issues regarding the development and use of behaviorally anchored rating scales (BARS). *Journal of Applied Psychology, 66,* 458–463.

Bernardin, H. J., & Villanova, P. (1986). Performance appraisal. In E. Locke (Ed.), *Generalizing from laboratory to field settings* (pp. 43–62). Lexington, MA: Lexington Books.

Bernstein, V., Hakel, M. D., & Harlan, A. (1975). The college student as interviewer: A threat to generalizability? *Journal of Applied Psychology, 60,* 266–268.

Berry, N. H., Nelson, P. D., & McNally, M. S. (1966). A note on supervisor ratings. *Personnel Psychology, 19,* 423–426.

Billings, R. S., & Wroten, S. P. (1978). Use of path analysis in industrial/organizational psychology: Criticisms and suggestions. *Journal of Applied Psychology, 63,* 677–688.

Blanz, R., & Ghiselli, E. E. (1972). The mixed standard scale: A new rating system. *Personnel Psychology, 25,* 185–200.

Blumberg, H. H., DeSoto, C. B., & Kuethe, J. L. (1966). Evaluations of rating scale formats. *Personnel Psychology, 19,* 243–259.

Borman, W. C. (1974). The rating of individuals in organizations: An alternate approach. *Organizational Behavior and Human Performance, 12,* 105–124.

Borman, W. C. (1975). Effects of instructions to avoid halo error on reliability and validity of performance evaluation ratings. *Journal of Applied Psychology, 60,* 556–560.

Borman, W. C. (1977). Consistency of rating accuracy and rater errors in the judgment of human performance. *Organizational Behavior and Human Performance, 20,* 238–252.

Borman, W. C. (1979a). Format and training effects on rating accuracy and rater errors. *Journal of Applied Psychology, 64,* 410–421.

Borman, W. C. (1979b). Individual difference correlates of accuracy in evaluating performance effectiveness. *Applied Psychological Measurement, 3,* 103–115.

Borman, W. C. (1983). Implications of personality theory and research for the rating of work performance in organizations. In F. Landy, S. Zedeck, & J. Cleveland (Eds.), *Performance measurement and theory.* Hillsdale, NJ: Erlbaum.

Borman, W. C., Motowidlo, S. J., Rose, S. R., & Hanser, L. M. (1987). *Development of a model of soldier effectiveness* (ARI Tech. Rep. No. 741). Alexandria, VA: U.S. Army Research Institute for the Behavioral and Social Sciences.

Borman, W. C., White, L. A., Pulakos, E. D., & Oppler, S. H. *Models of supervisory job performance ratings: Evaluating the effects of ratee ability, technical proficiency, temperament, and problem behavior on supervisor ratings.* Manuscript submitted for publication.

Bosshardt, M. J., Rosse, R. L., & Peterson, N. G. (1984). *Development and validation of an industry-wide electric power plant maintenance selection system* (PDRI Tech. Rep. No. 94). Minneapolis: Personnel Decisions Research Institute.

Brief, A. P., & Motowidlo, S. J. (1986). Prosocial organizational behaviors. *Academy of Management Review, 11,* 710–725.

Brogden, H. E., & Taylor, E. K. (1950). The dollar criterion: Applying the cost accounting concept to criterion construction. *Personnel Psychology, 3,* 133–154.

Campbell, C. H., Campbell, R. C., Rumsey, M. G., & Edwards, D. C. (1986). *Development and field test of task-based MOS-specific criterion measures* (ARI

Tech. Rep. No. 717). Alexandria, VA: U.S. Army Research Institute.

Campbell, J. P. (1986). *Improving the selection, classification, and utilization of Army enlisted personnel: Annual report, 1986 fiscal year* (ARI Tech. Rep. No. 813101). Alexandria, VA: U.S. Army Research Institute.

Campbell, J. P., Dunnette, M. D., Arvey, R. D., & Hellervik, L. V. (1973). The development and evaluation of behaviorally based rating scales. *Journal of Applied Psychology, 57,* 15–22.

Campbell, J. P., Dunnette, M. D., Lawler, E. E., & Weick, K. E. (1970). *Managerial behavior, performance, and effectiveness.* New York: McGraw-Hill.

Campbell, J. P., & Harris, J. H. (1985). *Criterion reduction and combination via a participation decision-making panel.* Paper presented at the 93rd annual meeting of the American Psychological Association, Los Angeles.

Campbell, J. P., McHenry, J. J., & Wise, L. L. (1990). Analyses of criterion measures: The modeling of performance. *Personnel Psychology, 43,* 313–333.

Cantor, N., & Mischel, W. (1977). Traits as prototypes: Effects on recognition memory. *Journal of Personality and Social Psychology, 35,* 38–48.

Cardy, R. L., & Kehoe, J. F. (1984). Rater selective attention ability and appraisal effectiveness: The effect of a cognitive style on the accuracy of differentiation among ratees. *Journal of Applied Psychology, 69,* 589–594.

Cascio, W. F., & Phillips, N. F. (1979). Performance testing: A rose among thorns. *Personnel Psychology, 32,* 751–766.

Christal, R. E. (1968). JAN: A technique for analyzing group judgment. *The Journal of Experimental Education, 36,* 24–27.

Cooper, W. H. (1981). Ubiquitous halo. *Psychological Bulletin, 90,* 218–244.

Cravens, D. W., & Woodruff, R. B. (1973). An approach for determining criteria of sales performance. *Journal of Applied Psychology, 57,* 242–247.

Cronbach, L. J. (1955). Processes affecting scores on understanding of others and assumed "similarity." *Psychological Bulletin, 52,* 177–193.

Cronbach, L. J., & Meehl, P. E. (1955). Construct validity in psychological tests. *Psychological Bulletin, 62,* 281–302.

Cronbach, L. J., Rajaratnam, N., & Gleser, G. C. (1963). Theory of generalizability: A liberalization of reliability theory. *British Journal of Statistical Psychology, 16,* 137–163.

Deaux, K., & Emswiller, T. (1974). Explanations of successful performance on sex-linked tasks: What is skill for the male is luck for the female. *Journal of Personality and Social Psychology, 29,* 80–85.

DeCotiis, T. A. (1977). An analysis of the external validity and applied relevance of three rating formats. *Organizational Behavior and Human Performance, 19,* 247–266.

DeCotiis, T. A., & Petit, A. (1978). The performance appraisal process: A model and some testable propositions. *Academy of Management Review, 3,* 635–646.

De Nisi, A. S., Cafferty, T. P., & Meglino, B. M. (1984). A cognitive view of the appraisal process: A model and research propositions. *Organizational Behavior and Human Performance, 33,* 360–396.

DeVries, D. L., Morrison, A. M., Shullman, S. L., & Gerlach, M. L. (1981). *Performance appraisal on the line.* New York: Wiley.

Dickinson, T. L., & Glebocki, G. G. (in press). Modification in the format of the mixed standard scale. *Organizational Behavior and Human Decision Processes.*

Digman, J. M., & Inouye, J. (1986). Further specification of the five robust factors of personality. *Journal of Personality and Social Psychology, 50,* 116–123.

Downey, R. G., Medland, F. F., & Yates, L. G. (1976). Evaluation of a peer rating system for predicting subsequent promotion of senior military officers. *Journal of Applied Psychology, 61,* 206–209.

Duck, S. (1982). Two individuals in search of agreement: The commonality corollary. In J. Mancuso & J. Adams-Webber (Eds.), *The construing person* (pp. 222–234). New York: Praeger.

Dunnette, M. D. (1963). A note on *the* criterion. *Journal of Applied Psychology, 47,* 251–254.

Dunnette, M. D. (1966). *Personnel selection and placement.* Belmont, CA: Wadsworth.

Eysenck, H. J. (1947). *Dimensions of personality.* London: Routledge, Kegan, & Paul.

Favero, J. L., & Ilgen, D. R. (1989). The effects of ratee prototypicality on rater observation and accuracy. *Journal of Applied Social Psychology, 19,* 932–946.

Feldman, J. M. (1981). Beyond attribution theory: Cognitive processes in performance appraisal. *Journal of Applied Psychology, 66,* 127–148.

Feldman, J. M. (1986). Instrumentation and training for performance appraisal: A perceptual-cognitive viewpoint. In K. M. Rowland & G. Ferris (Eds.), *Research in personnel and human resources management* (Vol. 4). Greenwich, CT: JAI.

Fichman, M. (1989). Attendance makes the heart grow fonder: A hazard rate approach to modeling attendance. *Journal of Applied Psychology, 74,* 325–335.

Fisicaro, S. A. (1988). A re-examination of the relation between halo error and accuracy. *Journal of Applied Psychology, 73,* 239–244.

Fiske, D. W. (1949). Consistency of the factorial structures of personality ratings from different sources. *Journal of Abnormal and Social Psychology, 44,* 329–344.

Fiske, D. W. (1951). Values, theory, and the criterion problem. *Personnel Psychology, 4,* 93–98.

Flanagan, J. C. (1954). The critical incident technique. *Psychological Bulletin, 51,* 327–355.

Fleishman, E. A., & Fruchter, B. (1960). Factor structure and predictability of successive stages of learning Morse code. *Journal of Applied Psychology, 44,* 97–101.

Fleishman, E. A., & Hempel, W. E., Jr. (1954). Changes in factor structure of a complex psychomotor task as a function of practice. *Psychometrika, 19,* 239–252.

Frieze, I. H., & Weiner, B. (1971). Cue utilization and attributional judgments for success and failure. *Journal of Personality, 39,* 591–605.

Funder, D. C. (1987). Errors and mistakes: Evaluating the accuracy of social judgment. *Psychological Bulletin, 101,* 75–90.

Ghiselli, E. E. (1956). Dimensional problems of criteria. *Journal of Applied Psychology, 40,* 1–4.

Ghiselli, E. E., & Brown, C. W. (1955). *Personnel and industrial psychology* (2nd ed.). New York: McGraw-Hill.

Glaser, R., & Klaus, D. J. (1962). Proficiency measurement: Assessing human performance. In R. M. Gagne (Ed.), *Psychological principles in system development.* New York: Holt, Rinehart & Winston.

Glass, G. V., Willson, V. L., & Gottman, J. M. (1975). *Design and analysis of time-series experiments.* Boulder, CO: Colorado Associated University Press.

Gordon, M. E. (1970). The effect of the correctness of the behavior observed on the accuracy of ratings. *Organizational Behavior and Human Performance, 5,* 366–377.

Guilford, J. P. (1954). *Psychometric methods* (2nd ed.). New York: McGraw-Hill.

Guilford, J. P. (1967). *The nature of human intelligence.* New York: McGraw-Hill.

Guion, R. M. (1961). Criterion measurement and personnel judgments. *Personnel Psychology, 14,* 141–149.

Guion, R. M. (1965). *Personnel testing.* New York: McGraw-Hill.

Guion, R. M. (1978). *Principles of work sample testing: III. Construction and evaluation of work sample tests.* Alexandria, VA: U.S. Army Research Institute.

Guion, R. M. (1983). Comments on Hunter. In F. Landy, S. Zedeck, & J. Cleveland (Eds.), *Performance measurement and theory* (pp. 267–275). Hillsdale, NJ: Erlbaum.

Guion, R. M., & Gibson, W. M. (1988). Personnel selection and placement. *Annual Review of Psychology, 39,* 349–374.

Gunderson, E. K. E., & Nelson, P. D. (1966). Criterion measures for extremely isolated groups. *Personnel Psychology, 19,* 67–82.

Hakel, M. D. (1974). Normative personality factors recovered from readings of personality descriptions: The beholder's eye. *Personnel Psychology, 27,* 409–421.

Hakel, M. D. (1986). Personnel selection and placement. *Annual Review of Psychology, 37,* 351–380.

Hamilton, D. L., & Gifford, R. K. (1976). Illusory correlation in interpersonal perception: A cognitive basis of stereotypic judgments. *Journal of Experimental Social Psychology, 12,* 392–407.

Hammer, T. H., & Landau, J. (1981). Methodological issues in the use of absence data. *Journal of Applied Psychology, 66,* 574–581.

Harris, M. M., & Schaubroeck, J. (1988). A meta analysis of self-supervisor, self-peer, and peer-supervisor ratings. *Personnel Psychology, 41,* 43–62.

Harrison, D. A., & Hulin, C. L. (1989). Investigations of absenteeism: Using event history models to study the absence-taking process. *Journal of Applied Psychology, 74,* 300–316.

Harvey, R. J. (1991). Job analysis. In M. D. Dunnette & L. Hough (Eds.), *Handbook of industrial and organizational psychology* (2nd ed., vol. 2). Palo Alto, CA: Consulting Psychologists Press.

Hastie, R. (1981). Schematic principles of human memory. In E. T. Higgins, C. A. Herman, & M. P. Zanna (Eds.), *Social cognition: The Ontario symposium* (Vol. 1). Hillsdale, NJ: Erlbaum.

Hedge, J., & Teachout, M. (1986, April). *Job performance measurement: A systematic program of research and development.* Paper presented at the Conference of the Society for Industrial and Organizational Psychology, Chicago.

Heneman, H. G., III. (1974). Comparisons of self- and superior ratings of managerial performance. *Journal of Applied Psychology, 59,* 638–642.

Hobson, C. J., & Gibson, F. W. (1983). Policy capturing as an approach to understanding and improving performance appraisal: A review of the literature. *Academy of Management Review, 8,* 640–649.

Hobson, C. J., Mendel, R. M., & Gibson, F. W. (1981). Clarifying performance appraisal criteria. *Organizational Behavior and Human Performance, 28,* 164–188.

Hogan, R. (1983). A socioanalytic theory of personality. In M. M. Page (Ed.), *1982 Nebraska symposium on motivation.* Lincoln: University of Nebraska Press.

Hollander, E. P. (1954). Buddy ratings: Military research and industrial implications. *Personnel Psychology, 7,* 385–395.

Hollander, E. P. (1965). Validity of peer nominations in predicting a distant performance criterion. *Journal of Applied Psychology, 49,* 434–438.

Hulin, C. L. (1962). The measurement of executive success. *Journal of Applied Psychology, 46,* 303–306.

Hulin, C. L. (1991). Adaptation, persistence, and commitment in organizations. In M. D. Dunnette & L. Hough (Eds.), *Handbook of industrial and organizational psychology* (2nd ed., vol. 2). Palo Alto, CA: Consulting Psychologists Press.

Hunter, J. E. (1983). A causal analysis of cognitive ability, job knowledge, job performance and supervisory ratings. In F. Landy, S. Zedeck, & J. Cleveland (Eds.), *Performance measurement and theory* (pp. 257–266). Hillsdale, NJ: Erlbaum.

Ilgen, D. R., & Favero, J. L. (1985). Limits in generalization from psychological research to performance appraisal processes. *Academy of Management Review, 10,* 311–321.

Ilgen, D. R., & Feldman, J. M. (1983). Performance appraisal: A process focus. In L. Cummings & B. Staw (Eds.), *Research in organizational behavior* (Vol. 5, pp. 141–197). Greenwich, CT: JAI.

Ilgen, D. R., & Hollenback, J. (1977). The role of job satisfaction in absence behavior. *Organizational Behavior and Human Performance, 19,* 148–161.

James, L. R. (1973). Criterion models and construct validity for criteria. *Psychological Bulletin, 80,* 75–83.

James, L. R., Mulaik, S. A., & Brett, J. M. (1982). *Causal analysis: Assumptions, models, and data.* Beverly Hills, CA: Sage.

Jenkins, J. G. (1946). Validity for what? *Journal of Consulting Psychology, 10,* 93–98.

Joreskog, K. G., & Sorbom, D. (1981). *LISREL VI user's guide.* Moorsville, IN: Scientific Software.

Kane, J. S. (1986). Performance distribution assessment. In R. Berk (Ed.), *Performance assessment: Methods and applications* (pp. 237–273). Baltimore, MD: Johns Hopkins University Press.

Kane, J. S., & Lawler, E. E., III. (1978). Methods of peer assessment. *Psychological Bulletin, 85,* 555–586.

Kavanagh, M. J., MacKinney, A. C., & Wolins, L. (1971). Issues in managerial performance: Multitrait-multimethod analysis of ratings. *Psychological Bulletin, 75,* 34–49.

Kelley, H. H. (1967). Attribution theory in social psychology. In D. Levine (Ed.), *Nebraska symposium on motivation* (Vol. 15, pp. 192–238).

Kelley, H. H., & Michela, J. L. (1980). Attribution theory and research. *Annual Review of Psychology, 31,* 457–501.

Kelly, G. A. (1955). *The psychology of personal constructs.* New York: Norton.

Kenny, D. A. (1979). *Correlation and causality.* New York: Wiley.

King, L., Hunter, J. E., & Schmidt, F. L. (1980). Halo in a multidimensional forced-choice performance evaluation scale. *Journal of Applied Psychology, 65,* 507–516.

Kirchner, W. K. (1965). Relationships between supervisory and subordinate ratings for technical personnel. *Journal of Industrial Psychology, 3,* 57–60.

Klieger, W. A., & Mosel, J. N. (1953). The effect of opportunity to observe and rater status on the reliability of performance ratings. *Personnel Psychology, 6*, 57–64.

Klimoski, R. J., & London, M. (1974). Role of the rater in performance appraisal. *Journal of Applied Psychology, 59*, 445–451.

Komaki, J. (1981, August). *Behavioral measurement: Toward solving the criterion problem.* Paper presented at the annual meeting of the American Psychological Association, Los Angeles.

Komaki, J., Collins, R. L., & Penn, P. (1982). The role of performance antecedents and consequences in work motivation. *Journal of Applied Psychology, 67*, 334–340.

Kozlowski, S. W. J., & Kirsch, M. P. (1987). The systematic distortion hypothesis, halo, and accuracy: An individual-level analysis. *Journal of Applied Psychology, 72*, 252–261.

Kraiger, K., & Ford, J. K. (1985). A meta analysis of ratee race effects in performance ratings. *Journal of Applied Psychology, 70*, 56–65.

Lammlein, S. E. (1986). *Proposal and evaluation of a model for job knowledge testing.* Unpublished doctoral dissertation, University of Minnesota.

Landy, F. J., & Farr, J. L. (1980). Performance rating. *Psychological Bulletin, 87*, 72–107.

Landy, F. J., & Farr, J. L. (1983). *The measurement of work performance: Methods, theory and applications.* New York: Academic Press.

Landy, F. J., Zedeck, S., & Cleveland, J. (1983). *Performance measurement and theory.* Hillsdale, NJ: Erlbaum.

Latham, G. P. (1986). Job performance and appraisal. In C. L. Cooper & I. Robertson (Eds.), *Review of industrial and organizational psychology.* Chichester, England: Wiley.

Latham, G. P., & Pursell, E. D. (1975). Measuring absenteeism from the opposite side of the coin. *Journal of Applied Psychology, 60*, 369–371.

Latham, G. P., & Wexley, K. N. (1981). *Increasing productivity through performance appraisal.* Reading, MA: Addison-Wesley.

Latham, G. P., Wexley, K. N., & Pursell, E. D. (1975). Training managers to minimize rating errors in the observation of behavior. *Journal of Applied Psychology, 60*, 550–555.

Lord, R. G. (1985). Accuracy in behavioral measurement: An alternative definition based on raters'

cognitive schema and signal detection theory. *Journal of Applied Psychology, 70*, 66–71.

Mabe, P. A., & West, S. G. (1982). Validity of self-evaluation of ability: A review and meta analysis. *Journal of Applied Psychology, 67*, 280–296.

Madden, J. M., & Bourdon, R. D. (1964). Effects of variations in rating scale format on judgment. *Journal of Applied Psychology, 48*, 147–151.

Mandell, M. M. (1956). Supervisory characteristics and ratings: A summary of recent research. *Personnel Psychology, 32*, 435–440.

Marks, M. R. (1967). Review of W. W. Ronan & E. P. Prien. Toward a criterion theory: A review and analysis of research and opinion. *Personnel Psychology, 20*, 216–218.

McCain, L. J., & McCleary, R. (1979). The statistical analysis of the simple interrupted time-series quasi-experiment. In T. D. Cook & D. T. Campbell, *Quasi-experimentation:Design and analysis issues for field settings.* Chicago: Rand McNally.

McCormick, E. J. (1976). Job and task analysis. In M. D. Dunnette (Ed.), *Handbook of industrial and organizational psychology* (pp. 651–696). Chicago: Rand McNally.

McIntyre, R. M., Smith, D. E., & Hassett, C. E. (1984). Accuracy of performance ratings as affected by rater training and perceived purpose of rating. *Journal of Applied Psychology, 69*, 147–156.

Murphy, K. R., & Balzer, W. K. (1989). Rater errors and rating accuracy. *Journal of Applied Psychology, 74*, 619–624.

Murphy, K. R., Garcia, M., Kerkar, S., Martin, C., & Balzer, W. K. (1982). Relationship between observational accuracy and accuracy in evaluating performance. *Journal of Applied Psychology, 67*, 562–567.

Murphy, K. R., Herr, B. M., Lockhart, M. C., & Maguire, E. (1986). Evaluating the performance of paper people. *Journal of Applied Psychology, 71*, 654–661.

Nagel, B. F. (1953). Criterion development. *Personnel Psychology, 6*, 271–289.

Norman, W. T. (1963). Toward an adequate taxonomy of personality attributes: Replicated factor structure. *Journal of Abnormal and Social Psychology, 66*, 574–583.

O'Connor, E. J., Peters, L., Rudolf, C. J., & Pooyan, A. (1982). Situational constraints and employee affective reactions: A field replication. *Group and Organization Studies, 7,* 418–428.

Olson, D. M., & Borman, W. C. (1989). More evidence on relationships between the work environment and job performance. *Human Performance, 2,* 113–130.

Organ, D. W. (1988). *Organizational citizenship behavior: The good soldier syndrome.* Lexington, MA: Heath.

Osborn, W. C., & Campbell, R. C. (1976). *Developing skills qualification tests* Paper presented at the annual convention of the Military Testing Association, Gulf State Park, AL.

Osborn, W. C., & Ford, J. P. (1977). *Knowledge tests of manual task procedures.* Paper presented at the annual convention of the Military Testing Association, San Antonio, TX.

Ostrom, T. M., Pryor, J. B., & Simpson, D. D. (1980). The organization of social information. In R. Hastie, T. Ostrom, E. Effesen, R. Wyer, Jr., D. Hamilton, & D. Carston (Eds.), *Person memory: The cognitive basis of social perception.* Hillsdale, NJ: Erlbaum.

Parker, J. W., Taylor, E. K., Barrett, R. S., & Martens, L. (1959). Rating scale content: 3. Relationship between supervisory and self-ratings. *Personnel Psychology, 12,* 49–63.

Passini, F. T., & Norman, W. T. (1966). A universal conception of personality structure? *Journal of Personality and Social Psychology, 4,* 44–49.

Paterson, D. G. (1922–23). The Scott Company graphic rating scale. *Journal of Personnel Research, 1,* 351–376.

Peres, S. H. (1962). Performance dimensions of supervisory positions. *Personnel Psychology, 15,* 405–410.

Peters, L. H., & O'Connor, E. J. (1980). Situational and work outcomes: The influences of a frequently overlooked construct. *Academy of Management Review, 5,* 391–397.

Peters, L. H., O'Connor, E. J., & Rudolf, C. J. (1980). The behavioral and affective consequences of performance-relevant situation variables. *Organizational Behavior and Human Performance, 25,* 79–96.

Peters, L. H., Chassie, M. B., Lindholm, H. R., O'Connor, E. J., & Kline, C. R. (1982). The joint influence of situational constraints and goal setting on performance and affective outcomes. *Journal of Management, 8*(2), 7–20.

Pulakos, E. D. (1984). A comparison of rater training programs: Error training and accuracy training. *Journal of Applied Psychology, 69,* 581–588.

Pulakos, E. D., & Borman, W. C. (1988). *Developing the basic criterion scores for Army-wide and MOS-specific ratings.* Alexandria, VA: U.S. Army Research Institute.

Pulakos, E. D., Borman, W. C., & Hough, L. M. (1988). Test validation for scientific understanding: Two demonstrations of an approach to studying predictor-criterion linkages. *Personnel Psychology, 41,* 703–716.

Pulakos, E. D., Schmitt, N., & Ostroff, C. (1986). A warning about the use of a standard deviation across dimensions within ratees to measure halo. *Journal of Applied Psychology, 71,* 29–32.

Pulakos, E. D., White, L. A., Oppler, S. H., & Borman, W. C. (1989). An examination of race and sex effects on performance ratings. *Journal of Applied Psychology, 74,* 770–780.

Ronan, W. W. (1963). A factor analysis of eight job performance measures. *Journal of Industrial Psychology, 1,* 107–112.

Ross, L. (1977). The intuitive psychologist and his shortcomings. In L. Berkowitz (Ed.), *Advances in experimental social psychology* (Vol. 10). New York: Academic Press.

Rothe, H. F. (1978). Output rates among industrial employees. *Journal of Applied Psychology, 63,* 40–46.

Rounds, J. B., & Dawis, R. V. (1979). Factor analysis of Strong Vocational Interest Blank items. *Journal of Applied Psychology, 64,* 132–143.

Rush, C. H., Jr. (1953). A factorial study of sales criteria. *Personnel Psychology, 6,* 9–24.

Schmidt, F. R., & Kaplan, L. B. (1971). Composite versus multiple criteria: A review and resolution of the controversy. *Personnel Psychology, 24,* 419–434.

Schmitt, N., & Hill, T. (1977). Sex and race composition of assessment center groups as a determinant of peer and assessor ratings. *Journal of Applied Psychology, 62,* 261–264.

Schmitt, N., & Lappin, M. (1980). Race and sex as determinants of the mean and variance of performance ratings. *Journal of Applied Psychology, 65*, 428–435.

Schmitt, N., & Stults, D. M. (1986). Methodology review: Analysis of multitrait-multimethod matrices. *Applied Psychological Measurement, 10,* 1–22.

Schneider, D. J., Hastorf, A. H., & Ellsworth, P. C. (1979). *Person perception.* Reading, MA: Addison-Wesley.

Schneier, C. E., & Beusse, W. E. (1980). The impact of sex and time in grade on management rating in the public sector: Prospects for the Civil Service Reform Act. *Proceedings of the Academy of Management, 40,* 329–333.

Schwab, D. P., Heneman, H. G., III, & DeCotiis, T. (1975). Behaviorally anchored rating scales: A review of the literature. *Personnel Psychology, 28,* 549–562.

Scott, W. E., Jr., & Hamner, W. C. (1975). The influence of variations in performance profiles on the performance evaluation process: An examination of the validity of the criterion. *Organizational Behavior and Human Performance, 14,* 360–370.

Seashore, S. E., Indik, B. P., & Georgopoulos, B. S. (1960). Relationships among criteria of job performance. *Journal of Applied Psychology, 44,* 195–202.

Shweder, R. A. (1975). How relevant is an individual difference theory of personality? *Journal of Personality, 43,* 455–484.

Sisson, E. D. (1948). Forced-choice: The new Army rating. *Personnel Psychology, 1,* 365–381.

Smith, C. A., Organ, D. W., & Near, J. P. (1983). Organizational citizenship behavior: Its nature and antecedents. *Journal of Applied Psychology, 68,* 653–663.

Smith, D. E. (1986). Training programs for performance appraisal: A review. *Academy of Management Review, 11,* 22–40.

Smith, P. C. (1976). Behaviors, results, and organizational effectiveness: The problem of criteria. In M. D. Dunnette (Ed.), *Handbook of industrial and organizational psychology.* Chicago: Rand Nally.

Smith, P. C., & Kendall, L. M. (1963). Retranslation of expectations: An approach to the construction of unambiguous anchors for rating scales. *Journal of Applied Psychology, 47,* 149–155.

Springer, D. (1953). Ratings of candidates for promotion by co-workers and supervisors. *Journal of Applied Psychology, 37,* 347–351.

Taft, R. (1955). The ability to judge people. *Psychological Bulletin, 52,* 1–23.

Taylor, E. K., Parker, J. W., & Ford, G. L. (1959). Rating scale content: IV. Predictability of structured and unstructured scales. *Personal Psychology, 12,* 247–266.

Thorndike, R. L. (1949). *Personnel selection.* New York: Wiley.

Thornton, G. C., & Zorich, S. (1980). Training to improve observer accuracy. *Journal of Applied Psychology, 65,* 351–354.

Thurstone, L. L. (1938). Primary mental abilities. *Psychometric Monograph,* No. 1.

Toops, H. A. (1944). The criterion. *Educational and Psychological Measurement, 4,* 271–297.

Tupes, E. C., & Christal, R. E. (1961). *Recurrent personality factors based on trait ratings* (USAF ASD Tech. Rep. No. 61–67).

Uniform Guidelines on Employee Selection Procedures (1978). *Federal Register, 43,* No. 166, 38290–38304.

Vance, R. J., MacCallum, R. C., Coovert, M. D., & Hedge, J. W. (1988). Construct validity of multiple job performance measures using confirmatory factor analysis. *Journal of Applied Psychology, 73,* 74–80.

Wallace, S. R. (1965). Criteria for what? *American Psychologist, 20,* 411–417.

Waters, L. K., & Waters, C. W. (1970). Peer nominations as predictors of short-term sales performance. *Journal of Applied Psychology, 54,* 42–44.

Weitz, J. (1961). Criteria for criteria. *American Psychologist, 16,* 228–231.

Wherry, R. J., Sr. (1957). The past and future of criterion evaluation. *Personnel Psychology, 10,* 1–5.

Wherry, R. J., Sr., & Bartlett, C. J. (1982). The control of bias in ratings: A theory of rating. *Personnel Psychology, 35,* 521–551.

Whisler, T. L., & Harper, S. F. (1962). *Performance appraisal: Research and practice.* New York: Holt, Rinehart & Winston.

Widaman, K. F. (1985). Hierarchically nested covariance structure models for multitrait-multimethod data. *Applied Psychological Measurement, 9,* 1–26.

Wise, L. L., Campbell, J. P., McHenry, J. J., & Hanser, L. M. (1986). *A latent structure model of job performance factors.* Paper presented at the 94th annual convention of the American Psychological Association, Washington, DC.

Wyer, R. S., Jr., & Srull, T. K. (1980). Category accessibility: Some theoretical and empirical issues concerning the processing of social stimulus information. In E. T. Higgins, C. P. Herman, & M. P. Zanna (Eds.), *Social cognition: The Ontario symposium on personality and social psychology.* Hillsdale, NJ: Erlbaum.

Wyer, R. S., & Srull, T. K. (1986). Human cognition in its social context. *Psychological Review, 93,* 322–359.

Zedeck, S., & Kafry, D. (1977). Capturing rater policies for processing evaluation data. *Organizational Behavior and Human Performance, 18,* 269–294.

Zuckerman, M. (1979). Attribution of success and failure revisited, or: The motivational bias is alive and well in attribution theory. *Journal of Personality, 47,* 245–287.

CHAPTER 6

Personnel Assessment, Selection, and Placement

Robert M. Guion
Bowling Green State University

Central to personnel selection and selection research is the formation of a predictive hypothesis that is based on an understanding of the job for which people are to be selected and on a knowledge of the relevant background research; it consists of a specific, valued aspect of performance or other job behavior to be predicted, with one or more applicant traits hypothesized to predict it. In this chapter, various methods of operationalizing trait constructs are identified. Bivariate criterion-related validation (with some further attention to multivariate prediction) is described as a prototypical method of research for evaluating the predictive hypothesis and its implications in practice. Yet it is not the only method. Other sources of evidence and research designs for the evaluation of tests and their use are also described. A distinction is made between the validity with which a construct is measured and its job relatedness as measured. It is argued that, in many circumstances, criterion-related validation is not sufficient for either. Major themes of the chapter stress the need for scientific foundations and understanding, both for descriptive and relational evaluations of test scores and their uses, and the importance and difficulty of professional judgment throughout the hypothesis-formation, evaluation, and practical-use components of employee selection research and practice.

A YOUNG ENTREPRENEUR has a business in the garage. The business prospers. There is too much work for one person, so the entrepreneur hires an additional person and later another. The business grows into an organization where, instead of a few people who do everything, different people do different things. New people are hired to fill current staffing needs, to fill newly created positions, or to replace employees who have left. From the first person who was hired to the later specialists, each employee of the organization was hired because there was work to do and because the new person was thought to do the work well. Choosing people who are likely to work well at their jobs is the primary purpose of the employment process.

No matter how formally or carefully the employment process is carried out, common elements can be said to characterize the process:

- The need for help is recognized, and potential new employees are recruited.

- The desired characteristics of employees are identified, and candidates are assessed under the assumption that those with the desired characteristics will work out best if hired. There are many chances for mistakes: Irrelevant characteristics may overpower those that are relevant; guesses about what is relevant may be wrong; assessment procedures may be poor or poorly used; and people who do the assessment may not know how. Nevertheless, assessment is the central element in the employment process and is the basis for employment decisions whether poorly or competently done.

- Decisions are made—to hire, to reject, or to decide later—based on well-defined, strictly followed rules or on ad hoc, intuitive judgments. The decisions may turn out to be wise or unfortunate.

- The process, or its key components, may be evaluated. Evaluation ranges from

sophisticated research to simple-minded judgments that the process is (or is not) "getting the people we want."

The specific process differs across organizations and for different jobs. For one organization, recruiting might be a sign in a window and assessment a quick look, the rule being to hire the first acceptable candidate. For another organization, personnel requisitions may be filed, followed by extensive recruiting; assessment may be based on application forms, tests, medical examinations, reference checks, letters of recommendation, and interviews; and for some positions, the decision may be delayed until it is believed the very best candidate has been found. For some jobs, every qualified candidate is offered a job—the definition of "qualified" depending, perhaps, on the number of candidates relative to the number of people needed. For other jobs, no offer is made until a pool of candidates can be ranked according to qualifications.

Choosing those who will be asked to join an organization is a practical problem, not an abstract topic limited to scholars. Yet scientific research and theory are necessary foundations for understanding the practicalities of both the problem and the possible solutions. This chapter is intended to be practical, while recognizing the practicality of theoretical understanding. I will begin with a brief account of the history of relevant research, then turn to the intensely practical question of the influence of Equal Employment Opportunity regulation on hiring practices. With both research and practical issues as the major focus, I will then describe how hypotheses about potential predictors of performance can be developed, examine methods for assessing the traits expected to predict that performance, and then discuss how to evaluate the methods chosen. Brief mention will be made of placement problems.

The Role of Personnel Research

Psychologists began research on personnel selection and placement early in the century (Link,

1919; Munsterberg, 1913; Yerkes, 1921). Most research has concentrated on the evaluation of assessments, mainly tests, or *predictors*. If scores correlate with job behavior of some sort, that is, the *criterion*, then the assessment procedure is considered useful and *valid*, the level of validity being the correlation, or the *validity coefficient*. Little research or research-based theorizing has been devoted to trying to understand the criterion or why predictors work.

Few attempts have been made to develop taxonomies of criteria. In contrast, much factor analytic research has identified and classified personal traits. "Guessing," or more formally hypothesizing, which traits might predict specific job behavior would be helped by taxonomies of both kinds, but there are too many holes in the research literature to date. Peterson and Bownas (1982) summarized efforts made so far but, as matters stand, hypothesizing remains an art based mainly on experience. Over the years, experience has been augmented by research summaries ranging from 426 abstracts compiled by Dorcus and Jones (1950) through tabulations by Ghiselli (1966a) to the techniques of meta-analysis and validity generalization (Hunter, Schmidt, & Jackson, 1982). Such research has been based more heavily on psychometric and statistical research and theory than on research and theory about the nature of work. There has, however, been a widening of the focus of statistical data. For example, early personnel research was considered specific to the jobs and organizations providing the data (Freyd, 1923). Later concerns for smaller organizations (Lawshe, 1952) directed attention to the problem of generalizing research results. The contemporary emphasis is on validity generalization and questioning (even denial) of the *situational specificity hypothesis* (Schmidt & Hunter, 1977).

Since 1954, various joint committees of societies involved in testing have issued various recommendations and standards for the development and use of psychological tests (American Psychological Association [APA], 1954; American Educational Research Association [AERA], American Psychological Association [APA], & National Council on Measurement in Education [NCME], 1985; APA, AERA, & NCME, 1966, 1974). These documents introduced and explicated the concepts of *criterion-related validity*, *content validity*, and *construct validity*. Historically, personnel research emphasized criterion-related validation. The other types of validity have implications as well, but the *logic* of criterion-related validity— that an assessment procedure used in selecting candidates to be hired can predict an important future criterion—remains central to all personnel selection research.

The Role of Equal Employment Opportunity Regulations

Title VII of the Civil Rights Act of 1964 stimulated new developments. It explicitly permitted employment tests, except where used to discriminate on the basis of race, sex, religion, or national origin. However, some early litigation suggested such use. Racial differences were and are often found in mean test performance; some people may have searched for tests or cut scores on tests to magnify the differences. Most personnel researchers, however, endorsed the principle of equal employment opportunity and saw in it researchable questions such as the degree to which test validities were specific to the groups from which validation data were collected. If the data came from white males only, could the results be assumed applicable to blacks or to females of either group? The approach to meta-analysis known as *validity generalization* apparently sprang from research on this question (O'Connor, Wexley, & Alexander, 1975; Schmidt, Berner, & Hunter, 1973).

Federal regulations also led selection test researchers to clarify their concepts of validity, traditionally defined as the correlation of scores and criteria. Concepts of construct validity and content validity were in the psychometric literature, but they did not seem to interest employment testers until the Office of Federal Contract Compliance (OFCC) mentioned them, albeit briefly and confusingly, in its original Testing Order (OFCC, 1968). The OFCC's scientific advisory group, of which I was a member, produced two not-very-helpful sentences about them for that order—after hardly five minutes of discussion. However, subsequent debate over the meaning of these terms and evidence required for establishing them has led to important reconsideration of ideas about assessment procedure evaluation.

Documents issued later did not help; they were influenced little by experts in psychometrics or selection research and were developed more as legal documents than as technical guides. The *Uniform Guidelines on Employee Selection Procedures* (Equal Opportunity Employment Commission [EEOC], Civil Service Commission, Department of Labor, & Department of Justice, 1978) is the most recent, and we shall consider it from time to time. In many respects, however, it perpetuates the outdated thinking of its predecessors.

At times, psychologists have seemed more preoccupied with law and litigation than with psychology and psychometrics. While acknowledging debt to the debates generated by the implementation of the 1964 Civil Rights Act, this chapter will focus primarily on psychological and methodological issues and problems.

The Predictive Hypothesis

The best predictor of future behavior is past behavior; the best predictor of how well a person will perform a job is knowledge of how well that person has previously performed the job. In practical application, that truism is rarely helpful. Even probationary assignments may differ from the later job, and the differences may be crucial. Most employment decisions are likely to be made without knowledge of actual performance on the same or closely related jobs. Whim or simple prejudice aside, options for deciding which candidates to hire in the absence of such knowledge can fit into three categories:

- Option 1 is to select at random. Random selection, or variants of it, may be used for several reasons. It is cheap. Research can be expensive, especially if done only to cover possible lines of future litigation. Perhaps no defensible alternative is known. Most employers do not knowingly use random selection, but the option is a useful point of comparison for evaluating procedures that are used; selection procedures will never be perfect and should not be evaluated against perfection. A selection procedure is useful if the organization can do a better job of hiring people with it than without it.

- Option 2 is to base decisions on assessment procedures shown by research to predict at least one important criterion. One can make sound and defensible employment decisions with good data, but unfortunately, good data are not always available. Option 2 is not universally preferable. Practical research is never flawless; if the data, particularly the criteria, are questionable, the results of research will also be questionable.

- Option 3 is to base selection decisions on assessments hypothesized to be related to important criteria, even if criterion constructs cannot be competently operationalized or if other factors make direct hypothesis-testing research infeasible. In such cases, particularly if the hypothesis is well grounded in careful observation and knowledge of prior research, the assumptions of Option 3 may be better than the findings of Option 2.

The careful formulation of predictive hypotheses is fundamental to both options 2 and 3 because, in either option, the employment decision is based on an implied prediction. The hypothesis should ordinarily be expressed in the form of a functional relationship, $Y = f(X)$, in which Y is the criterion variable to be predicted and X is a variable (or a set of variables) that can be used for prediction at the time of decision. The hypothesis should be based on a clearly arguable reason to believe that the trait identified as X is indeed relevant to that identified as Y. The nature of the functional relationship—linear, parabolic, exponential, or whatever—and of the influences of other variables (e.g., moderators) might also be hypothesized, but the reasoning for predictor choice should be explicit early in the planning process.

A variable can be identified and defined at two levels. One level is the *operational definition:* the test or questions or judgments that result in numbers or scores. The other is the *conceptual definition,* the idea of what the numbers should mean. At the conceptual level, the variable is called a *construct.* In forming the predictive hypothesis, the Y and X variables should ordinarily be defined conceptually, at the construct rather than the operational level.

An unfortunate mystique seems to have developed about the word *construct;* some people insist that an idea of a variable is a construct only if it has been extremely well researched and widely understood. Here, however, we shall think of constructs simply as concepts or ideas, "constructed" in a more or less informed imagination to explain things or events that are or might be observed. In this sense, they may range from those that are well established in the literature to those that are innovative or intuitive inferences drawn from an understanding of the problem at hand. In either extreme, the user of the construct forms a conceptual definition and a further idea of what it might or might not include or be correlated with. Most constructs of interest in selection research are characteristics of people (e.g., intelligence, spatial ability, or sense of responsibility); jobs (e.g., intrinsic feedback, clean vs. dirty, or degree of autonomy); behavior (e.g., attendance, production level, or safe habits); or organizations (e.g., turnover, profitability, or size). They are usually quantitative variables, implying differences in degree, and are usually thought to be fairly stable over time. A construct is not evaluated in terms of some ultimate truth but in terms of its usefulness. Even a construct that is not widely used or researched can be useful if it makes good sense in the context at hand.

The formation of a useful hypothesis requires identification of both a criterion construct and a predictor construct. Empirical research to test the tenability of the hypothesis requires that the constructs be operationalized (i.e., that measurement procedures be available), but I shall discuss other ways to evaluate the usefulness of operationalized predictor constructs, even where criterion constructs remain operationally elusive. The first concern, however, is for hypothesis development; concern for evaluation comes later.

Job and Organizational Information

Informed hypothesis-making requires understanding the jobs for which people are to be hired. Job analysis, a step toward such understanding, is the subject of a later chapter in this *Handbook.* Here, we need only a brief account of its role in hypothesis development.

Analysis involves identifying component parts of a whole; job analysis is any procedure used to develop insights into job components: things people do on a job, resources they draw on in doing them, and organizational implications of doing them well or poorly. A job description is the resulting record of the analysis, perhaps ranging from a casual paragraph to a long research report, depending on the level of detail needed. If the job to be understood does not yet exist, or does not exist in the anticipated form, job analysis is a planning process. The basic job analytic process for an existing job is to observe someone doing the job and ask questions of incumbents, supervisors, or others whose work has some connection to the job being analyzed. Some researchers have tried to determine the relative merits of different methods of job analysis. However, Hakel (1986) found no clear basis for choosing one method over another, which is just as well. The important reason for job analysis is to get enough understanding of the job to move forward with the broader purpose. Since different researchers begin with different levels of understanding, and different purposes call for different kinds and amounts of information, the methods that will provide the needed information are the best in any given situation. These may be idiosyncratic to individual researchers; that is, some people may do better with a survey-type questionnaire, while others may gain more insight from face-to-face meetings with informed people.

Enough detail is needed in identifying the components of a job to enable the researcher to identify important criterion behavior and to develop informed hypotheses about potential predictors. Meta-analyses (specifically, validity generalization studies) of validity coefficients show that they are far more generalizable than previously supposed. Because criteria are not quite the same across studies, one implication is that operational differences in criteria often have trivial effects, if any, on the outcomes of validation studies—that performance measures have a kind of g factor, making analysis of performance into components unnecessary (Schmidt, Hunter, & Pearlman, 1981). Only a general knowledge of the job may be needed; Sackett, Cornelius, and Carron (1981) compared the results of job classification based on detailed task-oriented job analyses with those obtained by asking a group of foremen for paired comparison similarity judgments; the results did not differ.

If there has been little relevant prior research, if one harbors lingering doubts about the verities of validity generalization (cf. Rubin, 1988, pp. 253–256), or if one is interested in aspects of validity not expressible as validity coefficients, then more detail may be needed. One needs enough detail to identify and define an appropriate criterion construct, the possible characteristics most likely to predict it, the most promising assessment methods, and, in some cases, the specifications for developing methods of assessment specific to

the job—all relevant to forming a predictive hypothesis. The level of detail required is a professional judgment influenced in part by the hypothesis-maker's prior experience.

The level of detail *desired* may also be determined by the likelihood of litigation. Prudent personnel researchers these days attend not only to the best wisdom of their profession but to the realities of the court room. In a specific situation, a detailed job analysis may not be necessary technically, but failure to have evidence of an "adequate" job analysis, in the view of a trial judge, may result in an adverse decision in court. Kleiman and Faley (1985) reported that in only 1 of 12 cases did the trial judge consider the job analysis comprehensive enough to assure that the characteristics measured by the test "were critical requirements for successful performance" (p. 807). For many, if not most, selection problems, selection for a broad family of jobs may be a more effective personnel policy than trying to distinguish neatly the prediction of performance in jobs that do not differ much (Pearlman, 1980). The question, then, is how job families should be defined or identified. There is no clear answer. As Ghiselli (1956b) eloquently states:

> It may well be that there is no nice ordering of jobs. The relationships among jobs might be something like the relationships among the stars in the heavens. No clear and distinct groupings occur, but rather there is a continuous distribution with modal regions or constellations. (p. 9)

The grouping of individual positions into jobs or jobs into families is fundamentally a matter of professional judgment made on the basis of job activities, organizational goals, and the objectives to be achieved through improved selection.

An understanding of jobs or job families may be less important to criterion choice than an understanding of the organization's goals and problems. For many, efforts to improve selection may not be as useful as other actions. For example, if the problem is to improve organizational stability by reducing turnover and absenteeism, improving selection may be less fruitful than changing management practices. Similarly, problems of health and safety might or might not be selection problems. High accident rates might be reduced by selecting people with a demonstrable tendency toward safe behavior or, alternatively, by redesigning tools. Health problems might be reduced by physical fitness programs or by choosing people with high stress tolerance. Olian (1984) suggested that genetic screening may become a feasible approach to improving health in high-risk environments by identifying those with especially high probabilities of susceptibility to disorder stemming from, for example, hazardous chemicals, but steps to eliminate chemical spills might be more effective.

The Choice of Dependent Variables

For these behaviors and types of performance, the term *dependent variable* is in a sense preferable to the more common term, *criterion:* It puts the focus on research design. The criterion in validation research is analogous to the dependent variable in an experiment. The analogy, though not perfect, is apt. An experiment's dependent variable is the phenomenon of interest, and attention is focused on it. An independent variable is of interest primarily as a possible cause of the phenomenon. In selection research, the phenomenon of interest is the criterion. An independent variable, a predictor, is of interest not because it might *cause* variation in the criterion, but because the two might vary concomitantly. If so, information available from predictors at the time of decision making can be used to make a reasonably accurate prediction of information not yet available. Moreover, like good experiments, good selection research is often multivariate; that is, there is usually a strong likelihood that criterion or dependent

variable variance is related to more than one predictor.

My continuing disaffection with the word *criterion* stems in part from its semantic ambiguity. Defining a criterion as a standard for judging the excellence of a test (Drever, 1954, p. 54) focuses on the predictor rather than on the phenomenon of interest. In research on the test itself, such focus is proper; such research, also called validation research and perhaps leading to correlation coefficients, may be done with no interest in selection. The word *criterion* is ambiguous, with at least two different meanings. In one, a criterion is a job-related outcome, the phenomenon of interest, and validation research evaluates the accuracy of predictions made of it by one or more potential predictors. In the other, a criterion is one of a set of variables relevant to a theory of the construct being measured; correlations between the measure and the criterion either support or disconfirm that theory. In this second usage of the term, the phenomenon of interest is the measurement of something, and the validation research is intended to evaluate how well that something is being measured by the procedures at hand. How well an attribute is being measured, and how well the measure predicts some other attribute of interest, are different matters.

Job-relevant Criteria. People who are selected for a job are expected to "do better" than others would have done. Job-relevant criteria are the measures of how well people "do," identified and chosen by understanding the organization's needs and the duties and responsibilities of the job. The variety of possible criteria is great, including various production measures, standardized work sample and job knowledge tests, ratings of overall performance or aspects of it, training success, rate of advancement, number of prospects called (or other appropriate activities on the job), and sales records (Society for Industrial and Organizational Psychology [SIOP], 1987). A few basic principles should inform the choice:

- Hypothesis formation begins at the conceptual level and should not get bogged down in operational choices. One may find later that the critical criterion constructs cannot be validly measured, but identifying and clarifying them can be helpful in specifying predictor constructs.

- Criterion constructs are statements of organizational values. If there are several, and practicality dictates studying only a few, then a hierarchy of criterion constructs can be arranged to reflect organizational values. Is speed more important than accuracy? The answer may differ in different organizations; if so, the different organizations must predict different criteria.

- Criterion constructs are not interchangeable. Perhaps supervisory ratings of production can be used in place of production records to measure output, but research carried out to investigate predictions of output will not provide solutions to an attendance problem.

- The critical criterion constructs should be defined conceptually before choosing measurement techniques for operationalizing them. A rush to measure is often ill-advised. Successful prediction of a trivial aspect of performance that happens to be easily measured will effect little improvement in important aspects of performance. Trivial measurement is a likely consequence of trivial thought.

- If one must err, it should be on the side of too much specificity in identifying criterion constructs. Although validity generalization research often suggests a general factor when validities generalize across broad criteria that differ somewhat, it has not invalidated the idea that more specific factors of criterion components require different predictors for optimal prediction (Dunnette, 1963a; Ghiselli,

1956a; Guion, 1961; Linn, 1986). If a general factor accounts for the lion's share of the criterion variance, the fact can be discerned by further research showing high interdependence among the more specific measures. If one starts with the assumption of the general factor and measures only overall performance, one loses any chance of identifying potentially important, differentially predictable components.

Construct-relevant Criteria. Psychometric research may seek to confirm or disconfirm certain inferences about the meaning of scores, that is, to evaluate the validities of inferences about the construct being measured. One of the many approaches to construct validation is to identify expected correlates of the construct, or to identify variables *not* expected to be its correlates, and to collect data to determine whether the scores intended to represent the construct do or do not, in fact, correlate with these other variables. These other variables are criteria, and correlational evaluation of the construct validity of the measurement of interest is therefore criterion-related. In this case, the criterion is chosen because it is relevant to the construct and leads to an understanding of the construct and its measurement.

Because job-relevant and construct-relevant criteria may be different, there may be two similarly distinct uses of the term *criterion-related validity*. The more common use in selection research requires job-relevant criteria, and its purpose is to express and test a predictive hypothesis. The other use, a psychometric use, requires construct-relevant criteria, and its purpose is to evaluate the meaning of measurement (Guion, 1987).

The difference should not be exaggerated. A given criterion may be relevant both to the job and to the construct being measured. Evidence in support of a well-developed predictive hypothesis, indicating that the predictor can appropriately be used in the prediction of future job-related behavior, is also evidence confirming that the predictor scores have the meaning one attributed to them in developing the hypothesis. Moreover, some selection procedures (predictors) are developed to measure the very construct that one wishes to predict (e.g., ability to do the specific job); in such cases the job-relevant criteria are construct-relevant criteria as well.

Neither should the distinction be ignored. Much silliness could be avoided in litigation involving notions of construct validity if (a) supporters of Title VII defendants recognized that part of the defense of a predictor is that its scores correlate well with appropriate criteria and not with criteria suggesting alternative interpretations and if (b) supporters of plaintiffs did not argue that a defense based on the construct validity argument requires an array of job-related criteria. The distinction is important in a more fundamental sense as well. It provides the basis for distinguishing between (a) selection research, statistically testing the predictive hypothesis, and (b) psychometric research, testing whether operational definitions of variables, whether used later as predictors or as criteria, measure the characteristics intended to be measured.

The Choice of Predictors

Three principles for considering possible predictor constructs were given in the earlier edition of the *Handbook*:

(1) Complex behavior cannot be fully predicted by simple means.
(2) Complex behavior is in part a function of the characteristics of the individual, but only in part; it is also a function of the stimulus variables in the situation.
(3) Complex behavior is not likely to be optimally predicted in the same way for all sorts of people. (Guion, 1976, p. 795)

In sequence, these principles imply multiple predictors, situational as well as personal variables as predictors, and concern for possible moderators.

Hypothesizing appropriate predictors is a work of scientific imagination; the hypothesis developer must imagine, perhaps somewhat introspectively, the nature of the personal demands placed on individual workers by the valued criteria and the worker characteristics needed to meet those demands. Hypothesis development should proceed rationally toward the development of a working theory.

Applicant Traits.   Characteristic ways of behaving or thinking, generalizing across situations and enduring for a reasonably long time, can be called *traits, attributes,* or *characteristics.* In this chapter, these terms will be used interchangeably. Distinctions can be made, but they do not seem necessary, and I prefer the simple term *trait* (Guion, 1987, p. 200).

For simple jobs, a simple hypothesis of one trait to predict one criterion may suffice. For more complex jobs, multivariate prediction is often better. Important, well-established constructs for describing applicant characteristics have been summarized by Dunnette (1982), Peterson and Bownas (1982), and in other chapters of this *Handbook* (see the work of J. Hogan, Lubinsky & Dawis, Dawis, R. Hogan, and Mumford & Stokes in this volume and volume 3). Lists of traits, of course, are useful only to the extent that the user understands the literature on which they are based and the nature of the criterion constructs. The greater the knowedge of the hypothesis maker, other things being equal, the more likely that the hypothesis will be supported. Those who are best informed develop the most promising hypotheses. One may become informed by reading, but also by talking with those who know the job and its demands from a day-to-day perspective.

Situational Predictors.   Most literature on situational predictors considers only the tasks to be performed. Task taxonomies are available. One, based on the *Position Analysis Questionnaire* (PAQ; McCormick, Jeanneret, & Mecham, 1972; McCormick, Mecham, &

Jeanneret, 1977), describes 32 job dimensions, two of which are environmental factors. At the other extreme is functional job analysis (FJA; Fine, 1955), which classifies jobs in terms of three categories: responsibilities for people, data, or things.

Task taxonomies neglect other aspects of situations. Experienced industrial and organizational psychologists, if not too narrowly specialized, may consider such intraorganizational variables as patterns of reward and reinforcement, goal-setting opportunities and goal acceptance, incentives, wage patterns, training opportunities, supervisory styles, disciplinary practices, opportunities for leisure or for fulfilling family responsibilities, characteristics of job design, the human-factor quality of machines and equipment, level of computerization or other technology, potential stressors in the work or workplace, work schedules, level of experience or competence of co-workers, and a myriad of other factors that, collectively, define the situation in which a new employee will work. These possibilities are named only because industrial and organizational psychologists have, in other contexts, considered them as possible influences on important work outcomes (cf. Schneider & Schmitt, 1986, p. 67).

Selection researchers have customarily treated situational variables only as potential moderators, but they may be useful predictors in their own right. Vicino and Bass (1978) provided an example using data from the ESSO (later Exxon) Early Identification of Management Potential (EIMP) project (Laurent, 1968). They determined a "success" criterion, a composite of job grade achieved, rated effectiveness, and rated potential. For each manager in the sample, the success score was predicted from the earlier EIMP test battery. *Residuals,* the discrepancies between actual and predicted success, were then predicted by four self-reported situational variables: (a) task challenge on the first job assignment, (b) life stability as measured by the *Schedule of Recent Experiences* requiring coping and adjustment

(Holmes & Rahe, 1967), (c) the match of personality of the manager and the evaluating supervisor, and (d) the success level of the manager's supervisor. These four variables together produced a multiple coefficient of correlation of .60 with the *residuals.* These "life space" variables explained as much variance in managerial success as the original EIMP battery did, even after the possible correlation between the individual characteristics measured in the test battery and the self-reports of the situational variables was reduced to zero.

Selection research has given too little attention to the many intraorganizational variables such as those listed above or those used by Vicino and Bass. To suggest that such variables do not contribute to criterion variance is to suggest that, of all the areas of industrial and organizational research, only selection research has yielded information useful in predicting the phenomena of interest. The suggestion is silly.

Moderator Variables.   The correlation of a predictor with a criterion may be influenced in a number of ways by third variables. A third variable might be another predictor. In effect, it might improve prediction by subtracting unwanted sources of variance from the predictor—a suppressor effect. Or it might influence or moderate accuracy of prediction if the predictor-criterion correlation differs at different levels of the third variable. Suppressor variables may be hypothesized by identifying unwanted sources of variance in predictor variables and ways to measure them. Moderator variables may be hypothesized by identifying variables that might interact with the predictors in predicting criterion levels.

Previously (Guion, 1965, 1976), I confidently cited studies reporting moderator effects. The confidence has waned. Moderators are not widely found nor, if found, replicated. Efforts to place demographic variables such as race, sex, or age in the role have not been successful. The tide of validity generalization has nearly buried the search for moderators to explain differences in validities across situations (cf. Schmidt & Hunter, 1981).

Proponents of validity generalization do not entirely discourage the search for moderators. Although Schmidt, Hunter, and Pearlman (1981) did not find job tasks serving as moderators, they suggested that validities might be moderated by information-processing and problem-solving demands of jobs. Gutenberg, Arvey, Osburn, and Jeanneret (1983) supported the idea, reporting that PAQ scores on decision making and information processing job factors moderated the validities of three of the *General Aptitude Test Battery* (U.S. Department of Labor, 1970) tests.

Abandonment of the search for moderators seems premature. Most moderator searches have relied on serendipity rather than rational thought, so failure is not surprising. A well-developed theory of the criterion (Frederiksen, 1986) is needed to postulate and design research to test for specifically expected moderators; there is no reason to expect vague, unfocused searches to be productive.

A Research Agenda for Hypothesis Formation

Job analysts often convene panels of experts—incumbents, supervisors, psychologists, or others—to develop matrices linking job characteristics to personal traits. The practice has been useful but of limited generality.

Dunnette (1982) proposed a worthy research agenda for developing a job-person characteristics matrix for more general use, an illustrative corner of which is shown in Figure 1. Rows represent performance in classes of job characteristics, and levels of personal characteristics are shown as columns. Cell entries should show how closely row and column variables are related.

Taxonomies are not impervious to change, but after a long history of factor analytic research, general column headings can be

considered fairly well established (perhaps the 51 traits identified by Peterson and Bownas, 1982). Rows are less well fixed. Perhaps more than one matrix is needed. Rows in one matrix might reflect performance in elementary tasks; rows in others might be broader criterion categories for job families or perhaps classes of situations. The research agenda needs taxonomic research on several fronts.

Taxonomies for such a matrix are valuable only if the elements are very nearly orthogonal. Existing research offers little comfort in a search for independent classes of performance, but the criteria in most validation studies are performance ratings. Ratings are somewhat influenced by actual ability to do the work (Guion, 1983; Hunter, 1983; Schmidt, Hunter, & Outerbridge, 1986), but they are also influenced by a variety of rater and process characteristics (Borman, 1983; Feldman, 1981). Examples include rater differences in the personal constructs through which work performance is viewed and evaluated, or in the fidelity of recall for not-very-recent examples of performance or performance-related behavior. Such influences can obscure real performance differences within as well as across jobs. Independence is unlikely, but we should not yet conclude that there are no independent classes of performance. Other taxonomic research is in an even more primitive stage. The research agenda needed to fill the cells of even one such matrix is staggering to contemplate, but the end result is attractive.

Methods of Assessment

Operations for measurement or assessment of candidates and their performance vary greatly. I will use the term *measurement* when systematic psychometric principles have been used to develop internally consistent scales; I will use the term *assessment* in a broader sense to include both measurement and more complex judgments. Classes of constructs and classes

FIGURE 1

A Job-Person Characteristics Matrix

*Classes of
Person Characteristics*

	PC$_1$	PC$_2$	PC$_3$ . . . PC$_k$
JC$_1$	20	70	5
JC$_2$	14	10	61
JC$_3$	82	15	67

Classes of Job Characteristics

JC$_n$

Note: Numbers in the cells of the matrix are shown without designating what they are. They might be validities, estimates of overlap, variance percentages, probabilities, or any other quantitative estimate of the relative usefulness of various classes of personal characteristics for carrying out various classes of job characteristics.

From "Integrating the Organization: A Social Psychological Analysis" (p. 2) by H. L. Fromkin and J. J. Sherwood (Eds.), 1974, New York: Free Press. Copyright 1974 by The Free Press, a division of Macmillan, Inc. Reprinted by permission.

of operations for assessing them are both considered summarily in this section.

Measures of Performance

Whether used as a criterion or a predictor (e.g., in promotion), performance measurement poses severe problems. It may be the most intractable measurement problem of all.

Although it would appear that people who understand a job would easily evaluate performance on it, appearances are deceiving. For some jobs, performance may be measured by counting work products. Only the naive can be wholly satisfied with such measures. One problem is that measures of individual output may be contaminated by factors the individual worker cannot control. For example, shop output may be influenced by the quality of the machinery, equipment, and materials used; consistency of output may depend on motivation, which in turn may depend on pay systems (Rothe & Nye, 1959). A second problem is that maximum output is not necessarily optimum performance (Landy & Farr, 1983); reasons include the possibility of accidents or of excessive fatigue, or a need to emphasize quality or consistency of output. A third problem is that performance may include more than quantity of output; a unified performance measure incorporating various aspects of performance might indeed be one to maximize. A performance domain includes the scope of behaviors relevant to the goals of the organization or organizational unit, not necessarily tied to specific assigned tasks (Murphy, 1987). For example, the best performers may not only do well at their tasks but may also help others, make useful suggestions, and otherwise demonstrate good organizational "citizenship" (C. A. Smith, Organ, & Near, 1983). Even though job descriptions tend to emphasize the duties of a specific job, a total assessment of performance may include such general responsibilities as staying on the job, being there when expected, or working cooperatively with others.

Landy and Farr (1983) included absenteeism, turnover, grievances, and accidents as measures of performance; these certainly deserve a place in a definition of a performance domain. They also point to a confusion of units of analysis: Is performance to be defined at an individual or group level? We usually think first of the individual level because selection generally considers one person at a time. In selecting new people to move into existing work groups, however, one criterion might be the effect of the newcomer on group performance. We do not know much about assessing such effects, and the idea stirs up unpleasant memories in which "fitting in" was used as an excuse for racial or sex discrimination. It is a ripe topic for research.

Styles change. For practical use, the current trend seems to be swinging away from emphasis on component parts of broad constructs to more global measures. For scientific progress, however, research must focus on specific aspects of performance as well as on the overall domain. The measurement of performance by measuring performance-relevant aspects of behavior may lead to a clearer understanding of performance that can be achieved by direct, global measures (cf. Wallace, 1965).

Work Samples and Simulations. In a work sample test, major job tasks, including knowing things or accepting responsibilities, are identified and assembled into a coherent series of tasks or assignments with standard instructions; either the performance itself or the product is scored. The construct assessed by a work sample is the ability to perform these tasks, not actual performance—what one can do (maximum performance) in contrast to what one does do (typical performance). These are not interchangeable constructs (Sackett, Zedeck, & Fogi, 1988).

The construction of work sample tests, whether as criteria or selection tools, uses the logic of content-oriented test development: sampling from a previously defined content domain to choose the content of a test. In general, job content is defined by both task performance (as influenced or shown by actions or physical movements, decisions, plans, knowledge, tools, materials, and other things) and the expected nontask "citizenship" behavior. It is useful to distinguish a content domain from a broader concept of a content universe (Guion, 1978; Lawshe, 1975). A job as a clerk-typist, for example, may consist of filing letters, doing arithmetic, maintaining office schedules, typing letters, typing invoices, typing manuscripts, and related tasks. It may also include activities not usually deemed job-related, such as making coffee or helping others during their peak work periods. The entire set of things a clerk-typist in a given office might do can be called the *job content universe*. To develop a work sample, we might want to consider only a subset of these activities such as filing and typing; the subset can be called a *job content domain*.

It is a more or less carefully defined, non-representative, certainly nonrandom sample of that universe. As illustrated in Figure 2, some of the content universe is discarded, perhaps because it is relatively trivial (e.g., making coffee), is learned on the job (e.g., office schedules), or is assessed better by some other method (e.g., testing arithmetic skill). A work sample test samples the job domain, not the entire job universe.

Test content consists of instructions, standardization rules, stimulus tasks (or items), methods of responding, and methods of scoring. The universe-domain distinction applies also to test content. The *test content universe* consists of *all* ways to present those tasks, procedures that could be established as standard, possible kinds of responses, and alternative ways of scoring the process or product of the task performance. The *test content domain* is the sample of tasks chosen plus the standardization and scoring procedures adopted. These necessary parts of the test are unlikely to be part of the job content domain. Ideally, the work sample will maximize the match of job and test content domains, and will minimize omissions from the defined job domain as well as inclusions of spurious content not in the domain. Essentially, the ideal is to make what Asher (1972) called "point-to-point correspondence" of the two domains.

Good sampling is artful abstraction from the realities of a job. To define a job content domain for a work sample is to abstract from the job content universe those features deemed most important and from the domain those that best reveal ability. Simulations, if distinguished from work samples, are still more abstract—"an imitative representation of one's work" (Howard, 1983, p. 782). Simulations, like literal samples, use tasks like those used on the job, but they do so in artificial circumstances. They vary greatly in their fidelity to the real-world setting. Some, like certain pilot simulations, are so real they produce autonomic reactions not unlike those in the

FIGURE 2

Considerations in the Content-oriented Development of a Work Sample Test

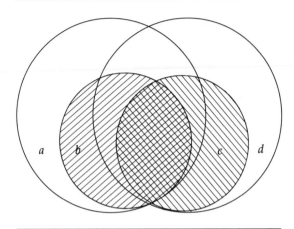

Note: *a* is the job content universe, *b* the job content domain chosen for definition, *c* the actual test content domain, and *d* the potential test content universe. The cross-hatched area represents the degree to which test and job content domains match—the desirable condition—and the diagonal lines represent components of one domain not in the other—the undesirable conditions.

situations being simulated. Others are so far removed from reality that they are like games. Even so, if they elicit behaviors isomorphic to those believed important on the job, they can be useful work samples.

Abstraction from the real job is a virtue, not a flaw, in performance measurement. For many personnel decisions, what people can do may often be a more critical construct than actual job performance; the latter is subject to many influences that, in the abstracted case of a less-than-wholly-faithful work sample, are replaced by standard conditions and, therefore, to more reliable measurement. Moreover, details of jobs and component tasks may change across time or from one incumbent to another, even when the essential character of the job—that which can be caught in an abstract simulation—remains the same.

Abstract simulations can be verbal, even for psychomotor tasks. Job knowledge tests have long been used to identify people who know how to do a job. Early oral trade tests (Osborne, 1940) were intended to contain questions that could be correctly answered only by people with genuine expertise in a given trade; people whose jobs merely brought them into contact with the trade, or people who were just learning the trade, were less likely to know the answers. A different verbal abstraction, interview "walk-through" (Hedge, Lipscomb, & Teachout, 1987), can be adapted for identifying expertise. Such methods do not tie up expensive equipment and personnel for the long time periods that may be required for more literal task performance.

The question, then, is not whether to develop abstract samples of work to be performed but how to develop good ones. Job analysis helps, but it is naive to think that a good simulation or other abstraction of performance requirements will jump magically out of a job description. Good people doing good thinking are more important than specific procedures in developing good performance measures.

Ratings. Most measures of actual performance are supervisory ratings. No other method has been so widely studied; none has more potential flaws. Measurement is no more flawed in performance ratings, however, than in ratings made by interviewers, assessors in assessment centers, or others. Ratings will therefore be considered under the more general heading of judgment as an assessment technique.

Tests and Inventories

Measures of Cognitive Abilities. Cognitive ability tests require responses based on remembering information, producing ideas or solutions to problems, or perceiving, comparing, and evaluating stimuli. Examples include tests of verbal abilities, numerical skills, spatial perception, and perceptual speed; they may be found in general mental ability tests, but they also may be measured independently as specific abilities.

The recent trend in employment testing has been away from highly specific ability tests and toward more general measures; an entire issue of the *Journal of Vocational Behavior* (Gottfredson, 1986) was devoted to the importance of general intelligence, *g*, in employment settings. With a few caveats (see particularly Linn, 1986; Tyler, 1986), the conclusion from that issue is that a general factor of intelligence is quite often a better predictor of success, in training and on a job, than is an "optimally weighted" set of more specific scores. The end of the *g* debate is not at hand, but more attention is now given to what serious employment testers have long recognized: Factorially pure tests will not predict factorially impure criteria as well as more complex predictors will—and intelligence in general is complex indeed.

A different movement in intelligence testing stems from laboratory research in cognitive psychology. The potential relevance of the cognitive sciences to employment testing is promised by such book titles as *Individual Differences in Cognition* (Dillon, 1985; Dillon & Schmeck, 1983) or *The Influence of Cognitive Psychology on Testing* (Ronning, Glover, Conoley, & Witt, 1987). No new employment tests have emerged from such studies, but one application to the selection of military pilots has been reported by H. W. Gordon and Leighty (1988). The cognitive abilities they identified as visuospatial skills, such as visual closure or mental rotation, are associated with the right cerebral hemisphere in laboratory investigations of specialized brain function; corresponding abilities associated with the left hemisphere are known as verbosequential abilities. They found the former, but not the latter, associated with success in aviation training. The verbosequential skills did, however, improve the odds for student pilots with low visuospatial ability but not for those with high ability. Will such research lead to major changes in selection research or practice? It is too soon to know, but maybe interests in individual differences in cognitive information processing will yield other examples, with replications that will be useful in the future.

Sensorimotor and Physical Abilities, Fitness, and Health.   Appropriate motor responses to sensory stimuli are essential for effective performance on many jobs. Rarely, however, are tests of such skills used. Neglecting tests of sensory abilities may be due to forgetting about sensory demands when analyzing jobs (Schneider & Schmitt, 1986, p. 313). That rather begs the question: Why do job analysts ignore them? Maybe such variables are out of fashion; currently, cognition, especially social cognition, attracts more attention among psychologists than do sensorimotor processes. In the jargon of fashion, perception is in, but the sensory bases for perception are out. In any case, I advocate a return to sensory, dexterity, and coordination tests, not only to predict performance but to avoid easily avoided litigation.

In an age of litigation, employing organizations may be legally liable if they have unhealthy or physically inept employees, but they must also guard against liability for discriminating against the handicapped. Employees may sue if they injure themselves or develop health problems as a result of performing physically demanding jobs. Fellow employees or customers or other people may sue because of performance errors or accidents stemming from fatigue or clumsiness. Rejected or underplaced applicants may sue for violation of their civil rights. With these problems added to the usual selection goals, the questions of physical ability are too important to leave to a cursory medical examination. An interdisciplinary approach may be necessary; in fact, "the lines between occupational medicine, kinesiology, engineering psychology, and personnel psychology have become increasingly blurred" (Tenopyr & Oeltjen, 1982, p. 607). Substantive information from other disciplines can inform psychologists, just as the validation strategies of psychometrics and personnel psychology can, in turn, inform them.

Physical standards, when used, are often set arbitrarily, with neither an empirical nor a very rational basis. The ordinary principles of validation and job-relatedness applied to other selection standards apply also to them, yet they present special problems. For example, an infrequently performed but very demanding task may not describe the job on a typical day, but on the day it is performed, it may be the source of injury. Is ability to perform that task an appropriate basis for an employment decision? The task's infrequency may provide the worker with relatively little opportunity to develop the necessary physical skill on the job, but its infrequency provides ample opportunity for rest and recovery between performances; the implications of these opposing consequences may differ. Does either the infrequency of the task or its heavier demand on the worker mean that the problem is better approached by job redesign than by selection? If it is a selection problem, should physical fitness testing look at the job as a whole or at its maximum requirements?

When is a person handicapped? How much musculoskeletal loss of flexibility, or range of motion, or hearing loss, or cardiovascular impairment, or digestive disturbance is really a "handicap," resulting in deterioration of job performance? In routine medical examinations for employment, answers to such questions are left to the judgment of the individual physician—which is rarely evaluated. In a promising approach to systematizing such judgments, Fleishman and his associates (e.g., Myers, Jennings, & Fleishman, 1981) tied an AMA guide to impairment evaluation (American Medical Association [AMA], 1977) to their scales for analyzing physical job demands and developed guides for physicians to use in determining whether particular levels of specific impairments will prevent effective performance on specified job tasks.

Personality, Temperament, and Motivation. Other chapters in this volume describe attributes ordinarily considered under these headings. Here we consider their role in selection.

An attempt to bring the Guion and Gottier (1965) review up to date was abandoned because so few subsequent studies were reported. Contrary to rumor, that review did not conclude that personality tests are not valid; indeed, reported validity coefficients for personality tests were not remarkably different from validity coefficients for other tests (Ghiselli, 1966a). However, much research on the usefulness of personality measures was, and is, seriously flawed: too many concurrent rather than predictive designs and too little replication. The final conclusion is that "it is difficult ... to advocate ... the use of personality measures in most situations ... *as instruments of decision*" (Guion & Gottier, 1965, p. 160, emphasis added). That does not preclude all use. It does not preclude the use of personality measures as sources of questions to be covered in interviewing candidates or calling references, nor in multiple assessment procedures where the final selection decision is based on some redundancy in information about candidates. The conclusion is simply that the evidence does not exist to justify the use of personality measures, without specific research for specific purposes, as the basis for employment decisions.

Most personality inventories are intended to map out "the" dimensions of total personality; each dimension is typically seen as highly generalized, characteristic to some degree of all people in all kinds of situations, even across cultures. A hopeful trend for selection is toward narrower constructs more explicitly defined for special contexts such as work situations (Guion, 1987). Examples are the Service Orientation scale, one of the scales developed for the *Hogan Personnel Selection Series* (J. Hogan, R. Hogan, & Busch, 1984) and the

Orientation Toward Work scale of the *California Psychological Inventory* (Gough, 1985). A third example narrows a construct, the Type A construct, without relating it to a specific kind of situation. Spence, Helmreich, and Pred (1987) used two previously identified components of a Type A scale, achievement striving and impatience-irritability, and found substantially different correlates for them; achievement in school was correlated with the former and health problems with the latter. It remains to be seen whether the findings can generalize to performance and health on a job.

The move to narrower, more situationally explicit personality constructs is the opposite of the apparent trend in the use of cognitive predictors, where g is regaining favor. Narrowing may be a necessary way station on the road to considering broader personality factors analogous to the general factor in intelligence. It remains to be seen—predictive research has not yet been reported—whether narrow, work-related orientation measures will prove more useful than broad, general factors of personality, but the research is worth doing.

A special case of a relatively narrow construct proposed as a predictor in employment settings involves employee theft or other antisocial behavior. Employee theft seems to be an increasing threat that, to many, calls for screening procedures to try to identify potential thieves and substance abusers. Three options seem to be available: (a) polygraph examinations, (b) background investigations, and (c) paper-and-pencil tests. Preemployment use of the polygraph is now illegal, and Sackett and Decker (1979) identified problems both with it and the other options. They were unwilling to endorse paper-and-pencil methods, saying that despite some validity evidence, more evidence is needed, preferably predictive.

I concur. For any personality trait, including the tendency to steal, evaluation for employment testing requires predictive evidence—preferably after a long enough wait for a performance record to be well established.

To illustrate the point, a high correlation between self-confidence and concurrent sales success does not necessarily mean that highly self-confident applicants will subsequently make good salespersons; an equally plausible meaning is that a sales record, sustained over time, influences one's level of self-confidence—or at least responses to a self-confidence inventory. Experience may change people. Adult cognitive characteristics are not immune to change due to training or other experience, including on-the-job experience, and personality characteristics seem more modifiable by experience and, therefore, more in need of validation by predictive designs.

Consider also a genuinely predictive study reported by Helmreich, Sawin, and Carsrud (1986). They studied achievement motivation, conceptualized in terms of (a) "work," motivation to perform job tasks well, (b) "mastery," desire to try new and challenging tasks, and (c) "competitiveness," a desire to do better than others. These are narrower, and more specifically related to work orientations, than the more global notion of achievement motivation. They predicted performance of newly trained airline reservation agents, correlating preemployment scores on the achievement scales with performance at three, six, and eight months after completion of training. No significant correlations were found at the three-month level, but by six months the "work" factor correlated quite well with performance data, the "mastery" less well but significantly, and the "competitive" not significantly better than zero. These are sensible findings; the best predictor is explicitly task oriented, and the six-month criterion allowed time for newness (the honeymoon effect) to wear off and more nearly typical work records to be established.

Background Data. Biographical data offer a good basis for predicting job performance (Cascio, 1982), despite conflicting summaries (Schneider & Schmitt, 1986). Such data work because behavior tends to be consistent. Most new employees lack direct experience on the job at hand; the task is to identify other background experiences consistent with job requirements (Schmitt & Ostroff, 1986).

For most jobs, one useful characteristic is a habit of achievement. Hough (1984) described the development of an *accomplishment record* for selecting or promoting attorneys in a federal agency. She noted that professional people often resist traditional testing, taking the attitude that "my record speaks for itself." The accomplishment record lets those records speak systematically. It probably requires more work than is needed to develop a conventional, job-specific background inventory—which, at least for federal lawyers, proved more valid (Hough, Keyes, & Dunnette, 1983). Nevertheless, the approach deserves attention because of its potential predictive value, obvious relevance, and probable palatability to professional candidates.

A poor but common method of assessing background asks for years of experience. Although experience can be useful, surely quality of background experience is more relevant to quality of future performance than mere duration of exposure. Even in promotion decisions, seniority per se has little predictive value (M. E. Gordon & Fitzgibbons, 1982). Nor is there much reason to expect it.

Computer Testing. Paper-and-pencil tests, apparatus tests, and work sample tests all have common characteristics. In all of them, values are assigned to responses and the values summed to produce scores. All are standardized: Everyone is given the same instructions, tested under the same conditions, and scored by the same formulas. Almost all are scored according to a pre-established key.

Item response theory (see Drasgow & Hulin, 1990) permitted breaking away from so much uniformity. Different sets of items, with different characteristics, could be drawn for different people from a calibrated item pool and scored on a common scale. But item response theory was, for many years, an imponderable, mysterious process known only by a few highly specialized researchers. With the computer age, computerized adaptive testing (CAT) became feasible for large test developers and users; increased use led to more opportunities to understand and use the underlying theory.

In a different, unrelated development, large computers also led to the development of computerized personality test score interpretations. These created some professional issues (e.g., see Eyde & Kowal, 1987; Harris, 1987), but they and CAT are both important advances. Yet, in a sense, they only permitted people to do better or faster what they had already been doing.

The advent of the microcomputer and the concomitant growth in research on individual differences in cognition have made new approaches to measurement, and the measurement of different traits, potentially practical. Pursuit and tracking tasks, tests identifying strategies used by examinees in situations of risk, applications of signal detection theory, tests of abilities to work virtually simultaneously at different tasks—these are examples of microcomputer tests developed for pilot selection in the United Kingdom (Bartram, 1987). In the United States, the Navy Personnel Research and Development Center has developed similarly novel tests, but it has also reported validities for some fairly conventional sorts of test items with latency and speed scores not otherwise available (Wolfe, Alderton, Cory, & Larson, 1987). This is another area where things are beginning to happen that should prove useful for future reported research.

Judgments as Measures

Some selection decisions could perhaps be automatic; for example, everyone above a particular score on a test is offered a job and everyone below that score is rejected. Such procedures, fortunately rare, could be called totally mindless if it were not for the fact that someone would have to make a judgment about what that score should be.

Judgment is an integral part of most selection procedures. If performance evaluations are used for promotion (or as criteria in empirical research on other predictors); if work samples, either the process or results, are rated by observers or inspectors; if history of promotions or salary growth are used or if prior accomplishments are scaled; if interviews or personal appraisals or assessment centers are used; if someone is given the responsibility for considering available evidence and presumably basing a selection decision on the accumulated evidence—if any of these is part of the selection process, then judgment is part of that process. The question is not whether there is subjectivity in selection decisions but whether that subjectivity is recognized, reliable, and understood.

Examples of Rating Scales. Judgments can be quantified using rating scales. In addition to the venerable graphic rating scales, two methods of attitude scale construction, or variants or combinations of them, have been widely used in rating people: (a) them method of *equal appearing intervals* (Thurstone, 1928) and (b) the method of *summated ratings* (Likert, cited in Guilford, 1954). Ratings are most often used to measure employee performance. They may also be used to measure applicant traits; raters may be supervisors, interviewers, assessors, or others.

Either global, overall constructs or more specific aspects of performance or other characteristics can be rated. For more reliability and finer discrimination among candidates, multiple-item scales (for either overall or specific traits) can be developed using Likert's method of summated ratings, even if individual ratings do not follow the usual attitude statement form.

Briefly described are a few of the more interesting examples of rating methods:

- Graphic rating scales are the easiest to devise and use. All that is needed is a straight line, divided into segments. One end of the scale is the positive or favorable end. The division points may have numbers assigned or adjectives or phrases with numerical values. Anchors for scale points need not be haphazard nor merely habitual; adjectives, phrases, sentences, or pictures (e.g., faces; see Kunin, 1955)[1] can be systematically scaled; the scale points can be anchored by those with the closest and least ambiguous scale values. The number of scale points may be even or odd, few or many. The scale itself may be a straight line divided into segments or a discrete series of boxes, one of which is to be checked. In short, the variety of possible forms of graphic rating scales is limited only by the imagination of the people developing them, and there is no reason to say that one form is better than another.

- Checklists are lists of statements, very general or very explicit. Those deemed to describe a ratee are checked; the "rating" is the median scale value of the statements checked. The statements are usually scaled by a variant of the equal-appearing intervals technique. Statements for measuring performance were so scaled by Uhrbrock (1950, 1961); those that seem to fit the situation can be selected for a local form.

- Mixed standard scales (Blanz & Ghiselli, 1972) look like a checklist. The response is either + (the ratee is better than the description in this statement), 0 (the statement describes rather well), or – (the ratee does not do as well as the statement). Statements reflect different levels of performance of the traits they represent, although it is not necessary that they be formally scaled; they are "mixed" in that different statements represent different dimensions to be rated or scored.

- Behaviorally anchored rating scales (BARS; P. C. Smith & Kendall, 1963) and variants of the method (e.g., behavior summary scales [BSS]; behavior observation scales [BOS]) may look like graphic rating scales, one for each dimension to be rated. Behavioral statements are anchors. Behavioral dimensions and illustrative statements are developed by a group of people like those who will eventually use the scales, and the statements are "retranslated" (assigned to the dimensions) by a different group. They are then scaled, essentially by the equal-appearing intervals method. Borman (1986) provided a good discussion of BARS and of behavior assessment methods using a form more like a checklist than a graphic scale. He reported no particular advantage of one method over another.

In their review of the performance rating literature, Landy and Farr (1980) called for a moratorium on studies comparing or developing rating formats. If a rating scale has been carefully developed, they argued, the format matters little. Guion and Gibson (1988), despite general agreement, demurred slightly for two reasons. First, most of the comparative research may have been guilty of what Cooper and Richardson (1986) called "unfair comparisons" in which the procedures being compared lack either procedural or distributional equivalence and are therefore not treated with equal strength. Second, we suspect that format doesn't matter much if the raters are truly experienced or wholly inexperienced in making judgments about people, but in between, it may be possible to match rating formats optimally to rater characteristics and preferences. Note that this suggestion is not made fervently.

Judgment Processes in Rating. To provide valid ratings, raters must have observed ratees at work and then must remember the observations, evaluate them, and record them. Development of the rating forms is arguably the least important and easiest part in setting up rating systems. Other factors to be taken into account are cognitive processes; they have received much attention of late, much of it in so-called laboratory studies.

I remain "unimpressed by [this literature's] relevance to personnel selection" (Guion & Gibson, 1988, p. 362). Much of the research has been done well enough, but it is understandably difficult to compress the confusions, the continuity of observations, the secondary motives and concerns, and the long-range consequences of real-life supervisory rating into the hour or so the college sophomore can devote to an experiment (Bernardin & Villanova, 1986; Campbell, 1986; Ilgen, 1986; Ilgen & Favero, 1985).

Scientifically, the laboratory work is necessary and can be useful. Most hypotheses about cognitive processes cannot be competently tested in the field. Moreover, it may be a useful first step to determine whether a hypothesis can hold up under the more nearly ideal conditions of the experiment before worrying about whether it generally does hold (Mook, 1983). However, if such research is to prove useful for applied purposes, it must lead to implications for practice which can be competently tested in the field; this is the stage to which research on performance rating must now turn.

Interviewers' Judgments. Most reviews of the reliability and validity of interviewers' judgments have ended with the depressing but persistent conclusion that they have neither. Recently, however, Arvey and Campion (1982) held out hope that structured interviews, at least, might predict job behavior. The conclusion will not surprise researchers; there is substantial evidence that well-planned, systematic, job-oriented interviews will be more reliable and lead to better predictions of subsequent performance than will more conversational interviews (Arvey, Miller, Gould, & Burch, 1987; Ghiselli, 1966b; Janz, 1982; Latham & Saari, 1984; Latham, Saari, Pursell, & Campion, 1980; McMurry, 1947; Orpen, 1985).

That hopeful note does not, however, settle questions about interviews. Several issues need to be addressed, both in research and in practice. A reasonable guess is that most interviews are casual conversations, covering different territory according to the whims and immediately preceding experiences of the interviewer. If so, and if such interviews are usually not valid, why are they so typically included in the selection process? And how can they be improved? Answers can be considered in terms of four functions of interviews:

- Interviews serve a public relations role. In making the job and organization attractive, the interviewer may motivate the diffident applicant to present his or her strengths effectively. Organizational interests are best served if the applicant who is rejected or who turns down an offer leaves with, and will convey to others, an impression that the organization is a good one to work for and treats applicants fairly. Good public relations work is also useful if applicants are subsequently hired; the interviewer who shares realistic information with the candidate may reduce the shock sometimes experienced initially on a job. The public relations role may be responsible for much of the mischief spoiling interviews, though. Nice people, aware of their public relations responsibilities, are likely to talk so much they don't find time to listen.

- Information can be gathered about the candidate. Opinions differ about the nature of the information to be collected, that is, in what is considered relevant. Ghiselli (1966b) reported an interviewing success story in which he sought information from prospective stock brokers about school, military, and work history but explicitly *not* about personal information such as family and social relationships. In contrast, an interview form built for prospective life insurance agents (Mayfield, Brown, & Hamstra, 1980) explicitly asked about social life, social conflicts with work, and personal financial affairs, and a situational interview developed by Latham et al. (1980) included a situation involving home and work conflict. Deciding what one should or should not ask about may depend more on personal values than on data or theory.

Many interviewers (e.g., Ghiselli, 1966b) conduct interviews with no prior knowledge about the interviewee. Most, however, will have seen at least some documents ahead of time; all should have prior information about the jobs to be filled. Preliminary information may create an impression of the candidate and of the candidate's suitability. Such impressions should be formalized as hypotheses to be investigated; that is, questions should be planned in advance to elicit information either to confirm or to disconfirm these hypotheses (Sackett, 1982; Snyder & Swann, 1978). Janz (1982) suggested that hypotheses should not focus on broad traits but on behavior patterns that appear relevant to critical incidents discovered in job analysis. Latham and his associates (Latham & Saari, 1984; Latham et al. 1980) also used critical incidents to develop their apparently hypothetical situations.

- Interviewers can be instruments for measuring applicant characteristics that cannot be measured well by other means. They may not be measured well by interviewers, either, but characteristics such as friendliness, ability to make a favorable first impression, or conversational fluency can probably be assessed better by an insightful interviewer than with an inventory. The very nature of interviewing is "sizing up"—assessing candidate characteristics. Can those traits that are measurable be assessed better by interview than by other means? Are some interviewers better measuring instruments than others? What *can* interviewers measure and what should they look for in measuring it? Some attention has been given to nonverbal cues. In a study of questionable generalizability to employment situations, Gifford, Ng, and Wilkinson (1985) found that undergraduates acting as interviewers could use nonverbal cues to measure the social skills of "applicants" (as reported by the applicants themselves) but not work motivation. Because their experiment excluded information about prior work habits and social successes, the nonverbal cues may have received more attention than they deserve, rendering conclusions misleading; at best they are only suggestive. Another experiment (Rasmussen, 1984) found little influence of nonverbal behavior on interviewer judgments when available verbal information was clearly appropriate for the job; that is, if the interviewer was getting a lot of useless information from the content of the interview, then and only then did nonverbal behavior have much effect. Both verbal and nonverbal information might be useful for assessing some characteristics, such as ability to make a good first impression, but if nonverbal behavior is relevant, the interviewer should plan to note it systematically as an integral part of the interview record—not merely as a contaminant interfering with better judgment.

Some research has specified dimensions to be rated by interviewers. Mayfield, Brown, and Hamstra (1980) asked interviewers to rate, on 5-point scales, 39 summary questions about background information (e.g., "In prior jobs, did applicant have to persuade people?") That is, the interviewer, having obtained information about prior work history, must evaluate that history on designated scales or dimensions—a measurement function. In a different example, Zedeck, Tziner, and Middlestadt (1983) asked interviewers to provide ratings on nine dimensions, some of which described behavior in the interview and some of which could be described as relatively general traits. Similarly, Dougherty, Ebert, and Callender (1986) asked interviewers to rate candidates on eight scales. These latter studies, not incidentally, used policy-capturing approaches to study the use of these ratings by individual interviewers. If "sizing up" is an important aspect of an interview, and if the ability to do so is one on which people differ, then attempts to throw the judgments of large numbers of interviewers into one analysis are likely to fail (as shown by Zedeck et al., 1983). The idiographic nature of lens model and policy-capturing research was well demonstrated by Dougherty et al. (1986). They studied three experienced interviewers who rated 120 actual job applicants. Linear regression equations were used as models of their policies, and the policies of each of them were then correlated with supervisory ratings on 10 scales. One of those interviewers made overall judgments that correlated well with nine of the ten criterion scales; judgments of a second interviewer correlated with three of them, and the third interviewer's judgments did not correlate with any. Subsequent training on three of the dimensions resulted in improved predictive validities for all three interviewers, including the one who had done well to begin with. The study should

serve as a model for many more like it. As provocative as these studies are, however, they do not fully come to grips with central questions: How well are the individual dimensions being measured, and what can be done to improve the validity of interviewers' judgments as measures of candidate characteristics? These questions deserve intensive study.

- Interviewers are decision makers. In some circumstances, an interviewer arrives at an overall judgment of applicant suitability, making the recommendation, but not the final decision; someone else may make the final decision. In other circumstances, the interviewer makes an interim decision—for example, whether an applicant will be invited back for further assessment. In still others, the interviewer may be responsible for assembling and considering information from all sources and for making the final decision to hire, to reject, or to hold the decision until other candidates have been seen. In every case, the decision implies a prediction: Candidates who are rated high, sent on to the next step, or hired are those for whom the predicted job behavior and performance is better than for those who are not. We do not know whether different principles operate, or whether different findings of validity can be expected, in these different kinds of decisions and judgments; existing research has not sorted them out. About the only firm statement we can make is that well-planned, clearly structured, behaviorally focused, job-related interviews have better chances of resulting in good predictions than do those that just happen.

Multiple Assessment Procedures

Use of a single test or test battery permits no consideration of other traits assessed in other ways. Personal appraisal or assessment, growing from a vocational counseling perspective, was first studied in the 1950s, mainly in relation to high-level jobs with low hiring rates. Personal appraisals consisted of rather extensive interviews, sometimes done before and after a series of tests, and included large batteries of both group and individual tests to measure many different candidate traits. Test batteries had built-in redundancy to allow assessment of each trait in more than one way. Several such programs were described in Guion (1965, pp. 474–484), and the variety, characteristics, and problems described then are still current. Little, however, is being said or studied about personal appraisals today, despite their bread-and-butter nature for some consulting firms. The reason may be that before the research on personal appraisals had much influence, Bray and Grant (1966) published their report of the first AT&T managerial assessment center and its value in predicting advance through the organizational hierarchy.

Assessment centers caught the imagination because they did all that had been done in personal appraisals with two added features: the appraisal of people in groups so that interpersonal variables could be assessed more directly, and the development of situational exercises designed to elicit behavior deemed relevant to managerial work. Today assessment centers are used extensively for selection into many other kinds of jobs where social skills are important; examples include police work, sales, teaching, and foreign service.

Personal appraisals live on. In a survey of 316 industrial psychologists identified as concerned with employee selection (Ryan & Sackett, 1987), 163 (51.6%) reported doing individual assessments. However, only about a quarter of them do any systematic follow-up of the people they assess.

Evaluation

Despite some notable exceptions, tests and inventories seem to be the only kinds of predictors that people generally insist on being systematically evaluated. This is unfortunate, in part because it places a greater burden on employment tests than on other aspects of the selection process, and in part because nobody knows whether much of the other work done in choosing people is worth doing.

Once upon a time, God told Gideon to use a two-stage personnel selection procedure. And the single-item preliminary screening test used ("Are you scared?") cut 22,000 candidates down to 10,000. And these were put through a single-exercise assessment center (drinking water from a stream), and 300 were chosen. And those who were chosen were good, because the tests were given by God. And, lo, even today many people think their selection instruments are God-given—but they are not, and more than faith is needed in evaluating them.

Criterion-related Validation

The test of a predictive hypothesis has been called validation. Tests of other hypotheses may also be called validation, and the concepts of validity and validation will be examined more closely later.

In any approach to validation, it is important to recognize that validation and validity refer to inferences drawn from data (scores), not to the predictors, except insofar as their nature and use influences the scores. It is not the predictor that is validated in empirical hypothesis testing; if the predictor is a test battery, it is not the battery, either. What is validated is the hypothesis that criterion performance can be inferred from the scores. Levels of one important criterion may be validly inferred from the scores on a given test, but inferences of levels on a different criterion may not be valid.

The researcher who (a) forms rational hypotheses with carefully defined criterion and predictor constructs and (b) has chosen or developed a good way to measure the predictor constructs has a solid foundation for predictive validity. Competent criterion-related research is likely to confirm such a hypothesis. To be sure, a measure that serendipitously but reliably predicts an important criterion is as useful as a measure chosen more rationally. However, a rationally developed hypothesis has a better chance to work, and the selection procedures it produces can be defended more persuasively. If good empirical data give added support, so much the better.

Circumstance may conspire to spoil empirical studies. Results obtained with small samples, low variances, or a criterion that measures nothing of importance (or measures something important but does it poorly) may be worse than no study at all.

The fact that poor studies are misleading does not justify abandoning competent research; even the most carefully developed hypothesis should be tested when feasible. Even the best work in hypothesis formation is not a substitute for good data. But good data are rare, and the point is that a well-developed hypothesis, with well-developed predictors, is more valuable than poor data.

I will begin the discussion of empirical validation with the relatively simple, bivariate case: one criterion and one predictor. The bivariate case not only provides a prototype, it also simplifies subsequent consideration of bias and fairness in employment testing, validity generalization, and utility analyses. Some principles of multivariate validation research and discussion of the use of empirical validation results will follow. The spectre of litigation should be remembered throughout.

Issues in Research Design

Validation uses data collected from a sample of an applicant population. In that sample, both predictor and criterion are known, so the correlation between them is useful only for inferences about the correlation in the population as a whole and therefore in future samples.

Use of a sample statistic to estimate the population parameter is ordinarily accepted if the measurements are reliable, the sample large, and the sample of that population unbiased. These conditions are not routinely found in validation research. Questions of research design are, ultimately, questions of how and whether methods of data collection and data analysis permit inferences from the sample at hand about a larger applicant population.

Data Collection.   Data for validation studies can be collected in several ways. Tiffin (1942) identified two basic methods called the *present employee method* and the *follow-up method*. Using present employees, criterion and performance data are available concurrently; in the follow-up method, applicants are tested, selected on some other basis, and followed over time until they have enough experience to provide stable criterion data.

In a firm if intemperate statement, I wrote, "The present employee method is clearly a violation of scientific principles" (Guion, 1965, p. 20). I argued that applicants and employees come from "decidedly different populations" and were tested under decidedly different circumstances. The view was tempered only slightly for cognitive tests in comparison to personality inventories. Barrett, Phillips, and Alexander (1981) disagreed, arguing, first, that correlation coefficients obtained in concurrent validation are virtually the same as, and provide rather accurate estimates of, those found in predictive validation.[2] They argued, second, that the "missing persons problem" (the concern that a present employee sample is missing those who have failed to get or to keep the job and those who have done so well that they are promoted out of it) is simply a restriction of range problem so that, if they do differ, proper correction formulas can be applied so as to get the two coefficients to agree.

For cognitive tests, evidence supports their first view. Correlation coefficients actually obtained under concurrent and under predictive designs do not differ appreciably (Bemis, 1968; Pearlman, Schmidt, & Hunter, 1980; Schmitt, Gooding, Noe, & Kirsch, 1984). There is less evidence for other kinds of predictors, but reason suggests that differences are plausible. If measures of a trait are likely to be influenced by criterion performance, people with on-the-job experience may provide validity coefficients substantially different from those obtained using applicants. Examples can be drawn from perceptual, personality, and even some cognitive traits. Too little is known about the effect of specific experiences to justify an automatic presumption of no difference.

Nor should it be assumed that method of data collection does not matter in estimating population validity coefficients. Guion and Cranny (1982) described five research designs in which criterion collection follows the collection of predictor data by a nontrivial time interval. Two of these fall within Tiffin's concept of follow-up research; three do not:

1. Applicants are tested, and selection is random; test scores are correlated with subsequently collected criterion data (follow-up, random).
2. Applicants are tested, and selection is based on whatever selection procedures are already in effect; test scores are correlated with subsequently collected criterion data (follow-up, present system).
3. Applicants are tested and selected on the basis of the test scores; test scores are correlated with subsequently collected criterion data (select by test).
4. Applicants are hired and placed on the payroll; they are subsequently tested (e.g., during an orientation or training program), and the scores are correlated with criteria collected at a still later time (hire, then test).
5. Applicants are hired, and their personnel records contain references to test scores (or other predictors), which may or may

not have influenced the hiring decision. At some subsequent time, when criterion data are available, the files are searched for information that might have been used and validated had it occurred to anyone earlier to do so (shelf research). (Guion & Cranny, 1982, p. 240)

To estimate population validity coefficients, correction for the restriction of range is possible for the first three of these. A "correction" can be computed for the fourth, but it cannot be very accurate without knowing the correlation between the predictor being validated and the actual basis for selection. The fifth design, if it can be called such, presents almost impossible obstacles to parameter estimation. With this procedure, predictor data are usually collected over a substantial time period, but the criterion data are obtained all at once; therefore, the time interval and amount of experience vary. The path analysis reported by Schmidt, Hunter, and Outerbridge (1986) found that experience affects job knowledge, which in turn has an impact on both supervisory ratings and work sample performance.[3] If experience varies widely, the bivariate correlation between predictor and criterion is, by itself, virtually meaningless. Other corrections may be needed in these and other designs; if restriction of range, influence of time-related contamination, or third variables cannot be measured, then satisfactory population estimates of validity coefficients cannot be assured. Sussman and Robertson (1986) noted that there are no corrections to apply for some "threats" to external validity; for example, there is no correction for an unrepresentative sample. Different designs pose different threats to the validity of research findings. A fair conclusion is that researchers need to be more explicit in developing and evaluating plans for data collection.

Whatever design is used, data collection should follow some common-sense rules of research procedure:

- Avoid contamination that may spuriously increase or decrease obtained validity coefficients. At the very least, criterion ratings should be made without knowledge of the predictor data.

- Data should be obtained under standard and realistic conditions. Testing, interviewing, and completion of forms should be done with standard provisions for privacy, if only so distractions will not vary widely from one applicant to another. Test time limits, type characteristics and quality of printing, and oral instructions should be the same for all. Content should be pretty well standardized for interviewing procedures. These examples merely illustrate the principle; they are not exhaustive.

- Candidates should be motivated, not to the level of spurious anxiety, but enough to consider the job desirable and worth trying to get.

- Data must be recorded accurately. Scoring, editing, and recording predictor data are usually done carefully; sometimes the work is even double checked and it should always be. Criterion data, however, are too often accepted simply as they come. Computers seem to spawn their own problems when variable names must be compressed to the allowable six- or eight-character neologisms; the code may make perfectly good sense when coined but be totally misinterpreted by a collaborator or clerk or by the original coiner at a future reading.

Such rules are easier to express retrospectively, after something has gone wrong, than in practice. P. C. Smith, Budzeika, Edwards, Johnson, and Bearse (1986) provided 14 rules for clean data and ruefully instructed their readers, "Go forth and do as we say, not as we have done" (p. 460).

Research Sample. The research sample should generally be representative of the population to which findings should generalize. Two points bear repeating. First, if new employees are chosen from inexperienced people, and if experience on the job may lead to changes in predictor scores (which Gulliksen, 1950, indentified as "intrinsic validity"), then the use of existing employees is a poor choice for research. Second, if the sample consists of students pretending to make personnel decisions (e.g., in interviewing), and if those students lack the responsibility for consequences that people in the intended population must accept, then it is drawn from the wrong, or at least a different, population. The importance of such distinguishing factors is an empirical question; if empirical data for answering it are unavailable, then the resulting validity information is potentially flawed to an unknown degree.

A different kind of question centers on size and statistical power. Is the sample large enough to avoid unacceptable likelihood of Type II error? Such a question has importance largely in the practical world of litigation. With an acceptable true validity, finding with perhaps 20 cases a sample *r* not significantly different from zero, one may lose the case and not even know that the predictive inferences are valid. Exceptions occur. Kleiman and Faley (1985) reported on one case (*Cormier v. PPG Industries*, 1981) where, with a sample of 20 cases,

> the judge ruled that the test was valid despite the absence of a statistically significant validity coefficient. The ruling was based on the opinion of the defendant's expert witness that, because of the small sample size, a type II error had occurred. (p. 819)

One can hardly count on a judge declaring a test valid because the contrary evidence might be due to sampling error. Litigation aside, a more useful question is whether the sample is large enough to provide a validity coefficient with an acceptably small margin of error in estimating the population parameter. Even the low end of the confidence interval should be a coefficient high enough to be useful. Much has been written about required sample sizes, and many tables based on varying assumptions have been published for determining adequate samples (Raju, Edwards, & Loverde, 1985; Sackett & Wade, 1983; Schmidt, Hunter, & Urry, 1976). Estimates differ but in any case call for a lot more than the traditional *n* of 30 through 50.

Another way to improve power is to change the significance level sought. Cascio and Zedeck (1983) examined the power question rather thoroughly and suggested weighing the relative merits and costs of Type I and Type II errors and setting levels of significance (probabilities of Type I errors) that will provide a balance. Since the conventional significance level seeks to minimize Type I error, this strategy usually involves an increase in power.

What are we to make of all of this? Primarily that planning for a validation study should consider the power requirements one will accept, the relative dangers, including those of litigation, of Type I and Type II error, and the kinds of assumptions one can realistically make.

Measurement Scale. The prototypical validity discussion generally assumes continuous scales of measurement on both the predictor and the criterion. Continuous measurement is not always possible; ordinal ranking of categories, even dichotomies, may be appropriate.

Even when valid continuous measurement is available, there is often a foolish temptation to set arbitrary dichotomies, in effect changing the measurement scale to one with only two scale points. Perfectly good production data, for example, may be arbitrarily divided into two or three levels of satisfactoriness (e.g., excellent, acceptable, poor) without caring that people at the bottom end of "acceptable"

perform more like those at the top of "poor" than those at the top of their own category. Some people (I am not among them) recommend that predictor score distributions be divided by a pass-fail cut score.

The temptation to dichotomize is foolish because the two-point scale accounts for substantially less criterion variance. If one variable is dichotomized at the mean, the resulting analysis will account for only .647 of the original r^2; dichotomizing both variables at the mean reduces explained variance to only .405r^2 (Cohen, 1983). Losses in explained variance become more pronounced as the point of truncation moves away from the mean on either variable. The effect is, of course, a serious loss of power as well as a loss of information.

When a predictive hypothesis has been validated with fully continuous scales, users will often dichotomize the predictor for actual employment decisions (i.e., set a cutoff score dividing candidates into one group that passes and another that does not). In a predictor distribution spanning perhaps 50 raw score points (e.g., scores of 10 to 60), dichotomizing at a cutoff score (e.g., 30) results in effective scores of either zero or one. That is, people with raw scores of 31 are grouped with people with raw scores of 59 as people who pass and can therefore be selected; people with raw scores of 29 are grouped with people with raw scores of 11 as those who failed and are therefore rejected. This is poor practice. The effective validity of the predictor has been reduced, and predictors usually do not have enough predictive power to justify the loss. For an example, assume $r = .30$ with continuous variables. Then $r^2 = .09$ and, if the cutoff is at the mean, $.647 \times .09 = .05823$. The effective value of r is .24, a 20 percent drop in effective validity. The farther the cutoff score is from the mean, the greater the loss of validity. A highly valid predictor can be rendered virtually useless by dichotomizing at a very high or low cutoff score.

Dichotomizing is usually unnecessary even where a minimum cutoff score is needed.

A "top down" policy (one in which people are hired in a sequence starting with the highest scoring candidate) may set a de facto cutoff score (the score below which no one has in fact been hired) without the validity-destroying effect of an actual dichotomy. A minimum score below which the top-down procedure will not go does not change the fact that selection has proceeded to that point along the continuous distribution. Even such minimums need to be set with some care. As a general rule, most cutoff score decisions turn out to be based (or perhaps violated) on supply and demand; cutoff scores tend to get raised when there are plenty of candidates, and exceptions seem to be permitted when there are not enough. If a minimum score is taken to mean a minimum below which predicted performance is unsatisfactory, based on independent reasoning unrelated to the predictor, then setting such a score makes sense; when selection of people by top-down procedures begins to approach that minimum, more aggressive recruiting is needed, not relaxation of the cutoff score.

Actual dichotomizing may also make sense for predictors used for preliminary screening rather than for selection decisions. Maybe satisfactory performance requires a minimum level of physical fitness, or of typing speed, or of visual acuity, but higher levels hold no special interest or promise; candidates above the minimum are selected on the basis of some other characteristic. In such a situation, validation should be based on the dichotomized pass-fail scores, not on the continuous distribution, if one is to evaluate the validity of the actual use of the predictor.

Figure 3 shows four kinds of relationships. Figure 3, panel (a), shows a positive linear relationship. If it describes the data well, any specified difference along the continuous predictor scale is matched by a constant difference on the criterion scale regardless of score level; in this drawing, for example, a two-point difference in X implies the same difference in criterion performance whether it is at a low, moderate, or high score level.

Figure 3, panel (b), depicts a nonlinear, positive, monotonic relationship. As drawn, a two-point predictor difference in the low end is associated with a large performance difference, but the same predictor difference between high scores is associated with a small performance difference; however, higher scores at any level are associated with better performance. Panels (a) and (b) are situations where top-down selection is the most appropriate policy; in these, if any cutoff score is established at all, it should be based on the predicted level of performance.

Figure 3, panel (c), is positively monotonic up to point X_c, after which there is no relationship. Increases in scores are associated with increased performance only to that point. Figure 3, panel (d), is nonmonotonic; increased scores are associated with increased performance only to a point, after which further score increases are associated with decreased performance.

A cut score can make sense in a situation like in panel (c), and a pair of them (high and low) might make sense where panel (d) describes the data. With a monotonic, including linear, relationship, however, dichotomizing with a cut score simply reduces both information and validity and is not justified.

Data Analysis. Evaluating a validity coefficient is a partly statistical and partly subjective judgment. Factors to consider in evaluative judgments include the logic of the hypothesized relationship; adequacy of criterion, sample, and design; standardization of procedures; and the acceptability of the risks of Type I and Type II errors. For the simple, bivariate case, three kinds of statistical questions need to be considered in evaluating an obtained validity coefficient. First, is it statistically different from zero? Second, does it underestimate the population value because of restriction of range, criterion

FIGURE 3

Kinds of Relationships of Test Scores to Performance

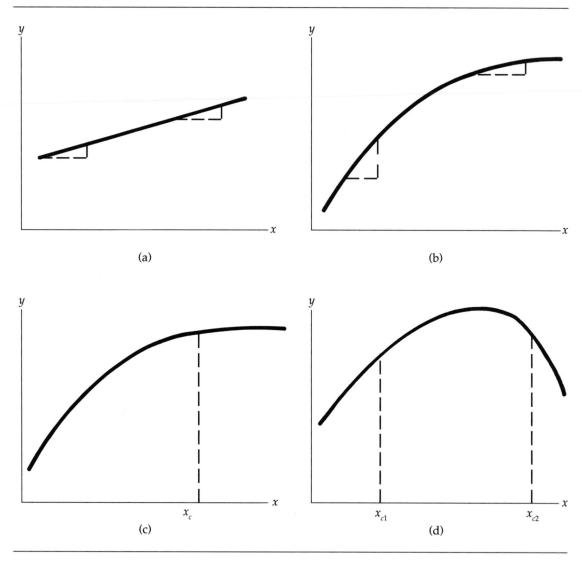

unreliability, or both? Third, is it biased by one or more "third" or unmeasured variables?

The question of significance is routine. It is sometimes forgotten, however, that, if the obtained coefficient is *not* significant, the further questions are moot. The second question is more complex. A simple correction for criterion unreliability (*not* for predictor unreliability) is straightforward, but correction for restriction of range, if needed, poses some problems; choosing the correction formula requires knowledge of the source of curtailment

(Thorndike, 1949; Wells & Fruchter, 1970). The formulas make assumptions (linearity and homoscedasticity) usually not wholly tenable (Lord & Novick, 1968). However, Linn, Harnisch, and Dunbar (1981) studied the effect of violating the assumptions and concluded that violations usually lead to underestimates of population values; even with assumptions violated, population estimates tend to be conservative.

Lee and Foley (1986) found that the conservative effect may not be general; in their data, the effect differed in different score ranges. For low scoring samples, corrections underestimated the population correlation, but for high scoring samples, the corrections were overestimates. Estimates from the midrange were essentially correct. So, if the best scoring people are hired first, leading both to curtailed variance and a high mean, and if the selection ratio is low, the correction is more likely to be an overestimate even though, on the average, the correction may underestimate population validity.

These issues may not be settled, but some guiding generalizations seem appropriate:

- The greater the selectivity (i.e., the more severely range is restricted), the greater the need for correction.

- The higher the correlation in the restricted sample, the lower the bias in the correction and the less the correction is needed.

- The larger the sample, the smaller the bias in corrections because the summary statistics used in the equations will be more reliable.

If the obtained correlation coefficient is itself not error-free, and violations of the assumptions of the correction equations introduce further error, should corrections for both attenuation and restricted variance be made? That is, when one begins with error and then adds the error of one correction to that of another, what happens to the estimate of

FIGURE 4

Representation of Spurious Validity Coefficient Due to Third Variable Contaminant

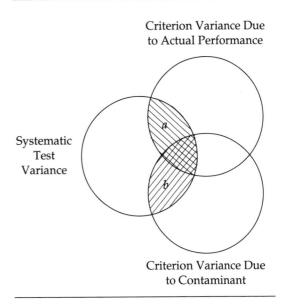

Criterion Variance Due to Actual Performance

Systematic Test Variance

Criterion Variance Due to Contaminant

population validity? A comment in the *Standards for Educational and Psychological Tests* (APA et al., 1974) asserted that the double correction was "unwise." However, Bobko (1983) demonstrated that the double correction is necessarily negatively biased and therefore conservative. The size of the negative bias increases (a) as criterion reliability decreases, (b) as the selection ratio becomes more stringent, and (c) as sample size gets smaller. The assumptions of Bobko's analysis include the assumption of the bivariate normal surface, usually violated, so the generality of the analysis deserves examination; nevertheless, the problem seems not to be severe.

Third variables may be correlated with scores on the predictor, on the criterion, or both, with differing effects. Third-variable contamination of either variable may result in lowered effective variance for correlation with the other and, therefore, a spuriously low coefficient. A third variable correlated with both will ordinarily, but not always, result in a spuriously high correlation (Edwards, 1976) as shown in Figure 4. The example from the earlier edition of the *Handbook* (Guion, 1976) supposed that the criterion was supervisory ratings on a salvage and repair operation, the predictor was a test of arithmetic reasoning, and the third variable was verbal ability. Verbal ability can be an expected correlate of the test, especially with story problems; it may also be a correlate of the ratings if the supervisor is erroneously impressed by subordinates with good verbal skills. If so, the appropriate correlation, represented by area *a*, is spuriously incremented by inappropriate correlation *(b)* attributable to the common third variable.

Clearly, analysis of data in a criterion-related validity study, even the relatively simple bivariate case, is not merely a matter of computing a correlation coefficient. The resulting coefficient itself needs to be examined, corrected, and evaluated for the importance of the deviations from assumptions and for possible spurious effects.

Studying Bias and Fairness

Since 1964, discussions of bias and fairness in tests and test use have been confused with legal issues and governmental regulation of employment practices. The degree to which the legal focus has fostered adversarial attitudes and narrowed the scope of these discussions has been unfortunate. Because of the legal focus and the attending adversarial emotions, some of the relevant language has become confused and charged with unusual meanings. Some definitions are necessary if the problems are to be discussed more broadly.

Bias exists when systematic sources of variance result in different scores for people who are alike in the trait being measured; it is a systematic source of invalidity or contamination in the measurement of a construct. Bias can be discussed at three measurement levels: item responses, overall scores (e.g., test scores or summated ratings), and inferences (e.g., criterion prediction). Sources of bias might be demographic (e.g., race or sex), physical (e.g., sensory acuity, height, or arthritic influences), cognitive (e.g., general intelligence, test wiseness, or knowledge of the language used in measurement), or related to habits and personality (e.g., response biases such as acquiescence or primacy, or habitual methods of task performance such as compulsive attention to detail). A finding that people who differ in these traits have different responses or scores is not evidence of bias; the definition is that bias exists when people who differ in such traits, *but not in the trait being measured*, have different responses or scores. Bias implies nothing about prejudice or intent of either the test developer or test user.

Similarly, *fairness* is defined in the context here as the job relevance of the trait being measured—irrespective of any specific source of bias. In a test of general knowledge, an item asking for the temperature at which one bakes a cake may be statistically biased against males, but it may be a fair question in a job knowledge test for hiring a cook (Ironson & Subkoviak, 1979, p. 22). More precisely, fairness exists when people with equal probabilities of achieving any specified level of success on the job also have equal probabilities of being hired. Readers familiar with the EEO controversies over models of fairness between 1966 and 1976 will recognize that I used similar language before (Guion, 1966). This wording is preferable because it does not imply a dichotomy in the criterion. I have chosen it, rather than "classical" definitions (Cleary, 1968; Humphreys, 1952), to emphasize individual more than group fairness.

These definitions imply knowledge, not likely to be available, of actual levels of predictor traits. Item response theory provides methods for estimating trait levels, but they may be beyond the resources of many employers.

The practical importance of the definitions lies, first, in pointing out that issues of bias or fairness are not settled merely by pointing to the existence or absence of group mean differences[4] and, second, in suggesting that bias and fairness are ultimately to be understood in relation to the systematic forces in an individual decision, not to group membership.

Group Membership. Of course, group membership is not irrelevant to testing or to employment practice. In theory, employment decisions are individual. National policies in countries with fair employment legislation generally hold that discrimination among candidates for employment should be based on merit, not on group membership. Group membership is, however, relevant to many social and political considerations. In America, for example, centuries of slavery and economic deprivation have, for black citizens as a group, had results more serious than mere depression of test scores: poor environmental stimulation, poor education, sense of hopelessness and low motivation, lack of competitive labor market skills, and consequent disadvantage in the job market for disproportionately large numbers of black applicants. To ignore these results is to do nothing to change them. It is in the interests of society to overcome them, in part through increased employment opportunities. It is also in society's interests to increase national productivity, in part through hiring people who perform their jobs very well. These interests may be in conflict, although not as much as suggested by adversarial rhetoric.

Several "fair employment models" have been proposed over the years in which the definitions of fairness have been based on group rather than individual effects, for example, nonzero mean errors of prediction (Cleary, 1968) or representativeness of group proportions selected (Thorndike, 1971). Debate over competing definitions seems to have ended with a special issue of the *Journal of Education Measurement* (Jaeger, 1976). Virtually all contributors emphasized judgment and consensus over psychometric or statistical procedures; insofar as statistical models are helpful, they are based more on utility analyses than on simple prediction, as Dunnette (1974) suggested earlier. The advantage of utility analysis lies in explicitly stating the costs and payoffs of possible decisions and, therefore, in considering outcomes beyond the criterion in regression analysis.

A quota system is anathema to many observers (including courts, except when based on prior findings of discrimination). The attitude deserves reexamination. Two quite different quota procedures might be used. One is to choose, in quota proportions, randomly within each group or by some surrogate for random selection such as first come, first chosen. This procedure has no particular merit since, by definition, it isn't related to anything but the quota. The other is to rank members of each group according to predicted performance and choose the best in each group to fit the preset quota. The mean level of performance of those chosen by this method is higher than it would be with random quotas. To ignore group membership and put all candidates in a single list (i.e., no quotas) would, of course, result in an even higher mean level of performance. However, it would not be appreciably higher according to computer simulations (Jones, 1974) and analytic work (Cronbach, Yalow, & Schaeffer, 1980) on several kinds of distributions and selection problems. A misguided combination uses order-of-merit choice within a majority group but random choice for minorities—a procedure that nearly maximizes group mean performance differences.

Quotas pose other problems. A stringent cut score, in combination with a relatively high minority quota, leads to unintended effects such as vastly increased recruiting (Kroeck, Barrett, & Alexander, 1983), leading in turn to substantial adverse impact.

Adverse Impact. Conceptually, adverse impact exists when members of one group have a reduced likelihood of being accepted for a job. According to the *Uniform Guidelines,* adverse impact means a "substantially different rate of selection in hiring, promotion, or other employment decision which works to the disadvantage of members of a race, sex, or ethnic group" (EEOC et al., 1978, Sec. 16-B). Adverse impact by itself does not necessarily imply discrimination or violation of Title VII of the Civil Rights Act of 1964; it is, however, a first step toward such a determination in court. In litigation, its function is to make a prima facie case of discrimination and transfer the burden of proof to the defendant (employer), who must then demonstrate the job-relatedness of the selection procedures. Many things besides unfair discrimination can produce adverse impact, such as a vigorous affirmative action program that recruits large numbers of a target group without recruiting correspondingly large numbers of well-qualified candidates, or location in a labor market where the qualified members of the target group are disproportionately few. Nevertheless, a determination of adverse impact may be used to trigger the enforcement mechanisms of the *Guidelines,* including the validation requirements. If there is no adverse impact, the regulatory agencies have no interest in the validities or job-relatedness of the selection procedures used; as remarked in the earlier edition of the *Handbook,* the use of the procedure may be fairly stupid if it is stupid fairly (Guion, 1976, p. 818).

The definition of adverse impact has proved difficult to translate into acceptable operations. In general, the *Guidelines* rule most often used in EEO enforcement is that adverse impact for a group of applicants exists when its selection rate is less than 80 percent the rate in the group with the greatest likelihood of selection. Alternatively, where the number of cases is small, or where selection rates are low, adverse impact may be defined as a statistically significant difference in rates. Notice that the base comparison group is the one with the highest proportion of applicants being selected, not necessarily the numerically larger group. Another point to note is that *groups* are differentiated from *subgroups:* Men constitute a group, and black, Hispanic, Asian, or white men are subgroups; black applicants constitute a group, and black men and black women are different subgroups. The *Guidelines* require adverse impact determinations for groups but not ordinarily for subgroups. For the adverse impact provisions to apply to a group, it must make up at least two percent of the labor force in the relevant labor area.

If adverse impact is found, the employer must then not only demonstrate the job-relatedness of the selection procedure but must also show that there is not an alternative that will be equally valid but have less adverse impact. The courts have not been entirely consistent in their treatments of this provision (Day, Erwin, & Koral, 1981, p. 121), but neither have psychologists. The search for alternatives has, for example, included comparisons from tests measuring quite different applicant traits (e.g., Schmidt, Greenthal, Berner, Hunter, & Seaton, 1977), a comparison deemed inappropriate by Ironson, Guion, and Ostrander (1982).

The adverse impact ratio has been criticized. Greenberg (1979) pointed to its vulnerability to Type I and Type II errors, showing circumstances where both errors occurred in excess of the nominally stated probabilities. Such errors may render such comparisons of alternatives questionable. Moreover, Ironson, Guion, and Ostrander (1982), using item response theory (IRT), showed that the differences in shapes of the test characteristic curves (the relation of underlying ability to test scores) could influence the adverse impact ratios. They redefined adverse impact as a distortion of true mean ability differences. Pointing to the fact that mean differences are typically found on ability tests, that to some extent these differences can reflect underlying differences in ability, and that item response theory permits estimates of ability freed from sample characteristics, they argued that item response theory should, if feasible, be used to determine whether obtained score differences reflect or exaggerate IRT-based ability estimates.

Validity Generalization

Traditional wisdom in the field of employee selection said that validity must be determined anew in each situation. Although Lawshe (1952) identified generalized validity as both desirable and occasionally found, his concept of generalization was essentially a subjective judgment based on the frequency of significant findings. My chapter in the first *Handbook* strongly asserted that employee selection was not truly scientific unless validity could be clearly said to generalize across situations (Guion, 1976). Schmidt and Hunter (1977) developed a meta-analysis technique to test a proposition that validity, as expressed by validity coefficients, is indeed generalizable. The technique and underlying logic has become such a powerful force in employment testing that virtually every topic in this chapter has required reference to the method or its findings.

The basic logic begins with the simple idea that, in any single study, the obtained correlation coefficient r consists of a true correlation ρ and error, which may be assumed to be uncorrelated without presenting serious practical problems (Linn & Dunbar, 1986, p. 211). A set of correlation coefficients, all with identical true correlations, would vary because of these errors. Even if true validity coefficients vary, the distribution of obtained coefficients will have somewhat greater variance because of errors. The Schmidt-Hunter method is based on the idea that variability in a distribution of validity coefficients, all testing essentially the same predictive hypothesis across studies within a general job family, is primarily associated with so-called artifactual characteristics of the different studies. Sources of variance, beyond possible variation in true validity coefficients across studies, include (a) sampling

error because of small and varying sample sizes, (b) differences in criterion range restriction, (c) differences in criterion reliability, (d) differences in test reliability, (e) differences in criterion contamination or deficiency, (f) computational or recording errors, and (g) differences in factor structures of tests. Of these, error due to inadequate sample size is said to be the major source of artifactual variance (Schmidt, Hunter, & Pearlman, 1982).

True validity may be viewed in two ways. It might be viewed as a distribution of true validity coefficients, largely at or above a minimally useful level. Considering only sampling error, restriction of range, and criterion unreliability among the artifacts,

> it may become apparent that a very large percentage, say 95%, of all values in the distribution lie above the minimum useful level of validity. In such a case, one could conclude with 95% confidence that true validity was at or above this minimum level in a new situation involving this test type and job. (Schmidt & Hunter, 1977, p. 530)

Such a view makes no estimate of a precise validity coefficient, but it does claim that validity generalizes across situations to a useful degree in each of them, even if there are potential differences of degree. Alternatively, true or population validity might be viewed as a relatively invariant property of the test type and job family combination; hence the mean of the distribution of the corrected validity coefficients is a population estimate.

The two views relate to two distinguishable hypotheses, tested by rule of thumb rather than precise statistical tests. The first is the *validity generalization hypothesis*, demonstrated if the lower bound of the 95 percent credibility interval (a Bayesian term analogous to the confidence interval in conventional statistics) is positive and, I should think, nontrivial. The second is the *situational specificity hypothesis* that validity varies from one situation to another. This is typically examined by comparing the variance of the distribution of obtained coefficients with the estimate of the variance around a true correlation (theoretically zero if true correlations are the same in all situations). One can never correct for all the sources of artifactual variance, so the estimated true variance cannot reduce to zero even if the situational specificity hypothesis is totally false. However, by rule of thumb, it is said that if the three artifacts usually examined—sample size, range restriction, and criterion unreliability—account for at least 75 percent of the obtained variance, the situational specificity hypothesis can be rejected. If it is rejected, the mean of the corrected coefficients is taken as the true validity coefficient regardless of situation; if not, but if the lower bound of the 95 percent credibility interval is positive and nontrivial, validity is still said to generalize across situations, even if not identical in all of them (Schmidt, Hunter, & Pearlman, 1982, pp. 840–841).

Schmidt and Hunter were not alone in their dissatisfaction with traditional narrative methods of summarizing and evaluating prior research. Independently, at about the same time, Glass (Glass, 1976, 1977; Glass, McGaw, & Smith, 1981) coined the term *meta-analysis* to describe his quantitative approach to summarizing research findings; the term has come to include all such methods, including validity generalization. The Glass approach starts with a different assumption—that systematic characteristics of studies (i.e., not mere artifacts) account for much of the variability in their results. Where the Schmidt-Hunter approach would analyze for study characteristics as potential moderators only if the situational specificity hypothesis proves untenable, the Glass approach begins with such a search, correlating study characteristics with effect sizes across studies, and if these do not explain variability in findings, accepts the assumption of generality.

Issues in Validity Generalization. Meta-analytic procedures generally have been subject to criticism. The equations originally used by Schmidt-Hunter have been criticized and subjected to several modifications (described in Linn & Dunbar, 1986), but the resulting differences seem minor. Three other issues seem more important. First is the probability of falsely rejecting the situational specificity hypothesis when it is in fact true. Osburn, Callender, Greener, and Ashworth (1983) examined the statistical power of two methods for testing that hypothesis. One was the 75 percent rule; the other was the Callender–Osburn Monte Carlo method (Callender & Osburn, 1981). For both methods, they found that the statistical power to detect "low-to-moderate true validity variance is inadequate by commonly accepted standards unless truly massive amounts of data are available (i.e., many studies having unusually large sample sizes)" (Osburn, Callender, Greener & Ashworth, 1983, p. 120). Even with substantial true validity variance, power was inadequate with typical sample sizes (100 or less) and with 25 or fewer studies. Of course, for practical purposes, evidence of generalizable validity may be more important than the moderators that might have been found if the situational specificity hypothesis had not been falsely rejected. If selection research is to become firmly scientific, however, differences in validity need to be explored and explained—difficult to do if one has concluded erroneously that there are no such differences. The scientific task is not only to identify permissible generalizations, "but to find and attempt to understand exceptions" (Linn & Dunbar, 1986, p. 232).

A second issue is whether some findings should be omitted from the analysis (cf. Bangert-Drowns, 1986; Linn & Dunbar, 1986). Available studies may include some with multiple findings; if two or more results are reported from the same data set, they are not independent. Statistical analyses assume independent data, so the meta-analysis should not include all findings from the data set—but many do. More controversial is whether every possible study should be located and included. The controversy is not over completeness per se; failure to find a few studies on a topic with many findings reported probably distorts results only slightly. The controversy is over the inclusion of poor research—the argument that garbage in begets garbage out. A few poor studies probably do little damage, but if the research literature being summar-ized is generally poor or shares a common characteristic distorting findings, the results of meta-analysis may be something one would be reluctant to call a "true" validity coefficient.

The third issue, not adequately addressed in the literature, is the degree of precision needed in defining the predictive hypothesis to be generalized. A correlation coefficient shows the relationship of one variable to another; a "true" coefficient must also describe such a relationship, but what are the variables? In the interest of obtaining a large data set, studies of distinguishably different pairs of variables may be included: Criteria may include overall supervisory ratings, ratings on components of performance, production levels, indices of production quality, and others; predictors may include a variety of factorially different tests (interestingly, listed as an artifact in the list of seven artifacts). If the validity generalization hypothesis is well supported and situational specificity rejected, these differences may not be moderating obtained validities, but they obscure the meaning of the "true" validity coefficient.

The meaning of the estimated true or population validity is central to all three issues, and the central issue of meaning is illustrated in an issue of method: Should artifactual corrections include corrections for *test* unreliability as well as criterion unreliability? Conventional wisdom in discussing corrections for attenuation in employment testing has consistently said no. Criterion unreliability should be removed from the estimate of a population validity coefficient because the criterion is not the basis for decisions about people, but unreliability in the predictor is a fact of the decision

situation and must be reckoned with in evaluating the predictor. Conventional wisdom, however, is concerned with the evaluation of a particular predictor in a particular setting; the aim of validity generalization is by definition much broader. Its aim usually is to test the generality of a hypothesis that a general criterion construct such as performance is related to a general predictor construct such as understanding mechanical principles (Schmidt & Hunter, 1977, p. 533).

Differing opinions have been reported even in the Schmidt-Hunter camp. Hunter, Schmidt, and Pearlman (1982) said that the three of them had long debated the "fourth correction" (i.e., for test unreliability). Schmidt and Pearlman took a position consistent with conventional wisdom, or at least recognized the communication problems that would arise from a failure to follow it. Hunter's view was that the validity distribution should represent the trait measured, not specific operations for measuring it. For scientific advance, I side with Hunter; I argue that the practical decision maker using the results of validity generalization has two decisions to make about the choice of a predictor, not one. The first is to decide whether the results support the hypothesis that a particular trait is related to a particular kind of criterion. If so, the second is to decide what to use among the available options for measuring that trait. The work of the decision maker is made easier if scientific foundations for decisions are as clear as possible.

From the scientific perspective, I also advocate (a) the skepticism that persistently looks for exceptions to the general rule in tests of situational specificity, (b) analysis that excludes methodologically poor or biased studies as defined by explicit prior rules, and (c) systematic explication of the hypothesis to be generalized, refusing to throw research on arguably different constructs into the data set. The purpose of validity generalization, for me, is to provide "a tool that may lead to the establishment of general principles about trait-performance relationships in the world of work, thus enabling the field of personnel psychology to move beyond a mere technology to the status of a science" (Schmidt & Hunter, 1977, p. 538). Such principles assure meaning for a corrected mean validity coefficient.

Findings. Validity generalization has broken new ground and challenged old beliefs and fears. It is not flawless, and "there is a danger of overgeneralizing conclusions and carrying the implications of this work too far. Generalizations are important to any scientific area, but so too are the exceptions" (Linn & Dunbar, 1986, p. 232). Despite such caveats, however appropriate, the findings deserve to be considered as the best evidence available at present about the generalizations of employee selection research. The most widely quoted generalization is that "professionally developed cognitive ability tests are valid predictors of performance on the job and in training for all jobs … in all settings" (Schmidt & Hunter, 1981, p. 1128). This generalization does not claim that all cognitive tests are equally valid, that tests of different cognitive constructs are equally valid, or that any test or construct is equally valid for all jobs or in all settings. J. E. Hunter and R. F. Hunter (1984) reported, for example, a range of .27 to .61 in mean validity coefficients for cognitive tests in an unpublished reanalysis of data previously reported by Ghiselli (1973). It may be useful, therefore, to look at some sweeping generalizations:

- Tests of mechanical principles are valid predictors of performance in training in mechanical repair jobs; Schmidt and Hunter (1977) reported a mean validity coefficient, corrected for range restriction and criterion unreliability, of .78.

- The performance of first-line supervisors can be validly predicted by general mental ability tests, tests of mechanical comprehension, and tests of spatial ability

(Schmidt, Hunter, Pearlman, & Shane, 1979).

- General intelligence tests are valid predictors of proficiency criteria for clerks; a corrected mean validity coefficient was .67 (Schmidt & Hunter, 1977). Virtually all of the more specific mental ability tests (e.g., perceptual speed, verbal ability, number skill, reasoning, and memory) used in clerical selection (and many that are relatively rarely used) are valid predictors of both proficiency and training in a wide variety of clerical job families (Pearlman, Schmidt, & Hunter, 1980).

- Finger dexterity tests are valid predictors of proficiency for bench workers, with a mean corrected validity coefficient of .39 (Schmidt & Hunter, 1977).

- The *Programmer Aptitude Test* (McNamara & Hughes, 1961) is a valid predictor of both proficiency and training of programmers (mean corrected validity coefficients of .73 and .91, respectively), although the 90 percent credibility value is trivially negative for Part 1 (Schmidt, Gast-Rosenberg, & Hunter, 1980).

- For operators and maintenance workers in the petroleum industry, tests of job knowledge, general intelligence tests, and (for operators) an arithmetic reasoning test are valid predictors of performance, whether proficiency or training, although the corrected mean validity coefficients are smaller than many reported in other studies, ranging from .25 to .33 (Schmidt, Hunter, & Caplan, 1981).

- *The Aptitude Index Battery* is a valid predictor of sales performance in all 12 insurance companies studied, but validity is moderated by management quality (S. H. Brown, 1981).

- Assessment center performance is a valid predictor of managerial performance and associated criteria, with a mean corrected validity coefficient of .37; it is moderated by type of criterion measure, sex composition of the assessment group, professional background of assessors, use of peer evaluation, and number of kinds of exercises (Gaugler, Rosenthal, Thornton, & Bentson, 1987).

This list is far from exhaustive; very little of the research on moderator variables has been described. But it is an instructive list. One need not be overly perceptive to see that some of these generalizations are also rather sweeping and that exceptions can be plausibly suggested. For example, one may question whether performance of all first-line supervisors can indeed be predicted by spatial ability tests; after all, not all supervisory work, and not all work supervised, requires spatial judgments. But the meta-analysis giving rise to that generalization consisted of far fewer studies than the other generalizations (e.g., mental ability tests) about predicting performance of supervisors. It seems likely that nearly everyone developing a test battery for supervision, regardless of the jobs supervised, would include a mental ability test, but it also seems likely that few people doing validation research would be dim-witted enough to include a spatial relations test for supervisors of general clerks. After all, validation studies are done on tests that the researcher, with some understanding of the job at hand, considered plausible predictors, that is, believed initially to be generally valid for that kind of work. In using generalizations like these, one should avoid being dim-witted. *In short, validity generalization does not eliminate the need for judgment.* Arguments, fine-tuning, Hegelian dialectic, reanalyses, alternative paradigms, and other steps in the march of science will probably modify some of the actual mean validity coefficients reported in these generalizations. Then as well as now, judgments about the

adequacy of the research summarized, the appropriateness of the method used, and the limits and meaning of the results must be made by those who would use the results for their own selection problems. But the results, carefully considered, can be of great help in facing those problems.

For practical selection work, one way to minimize problems of meta-analysis and profit from its contributions is to use the consortium approach to data collection. When large numbers of companies in an industry collaborate, such as has occurred in the petroleum, electric power, and insurance industries, one has a mix of studies from organizations of varying size and policies but otherwise has great control over data collection. That is, the same predictors and criteria are used in the same way and at essentially the same time, and the judgments needed to code data in the literature can be replaced by systematic research procedures. Despite probable objections, I would prefer a validity generalization study based solely on such consortium data to one based on the complete literature with all its uncertainties. Research consortia are not unknown; such studies have been done for the electric power industry under the sponsorship of the Edison Institute (Bosshardt, Rosse, & Peterson, 1984; Dunnette, Houston, Rosse, & Bosshardt, 1982; M. L. Lifter & White, 1984; Personnel Designs, Inc., 1990, in press [b]), for the petroleum industry (personal communications, C. Paul Sparks), insurance industry (Personnel Designs, Inc., in press [a]; Peterson, Houston, & Rosse, 1979, 1981, 1982), protective services (M. Lifter & Jones, 1978)—and perhaps others. However, validity generalization procedures have not been routinely done in all such studies.

Utility Analysis

Utility analysis is discussed elsewhere in the *Handbook* (see the work of Boudreau in this volume), but a few comments may add to the perspective on criterion-related validity. Whether speaking of *utility*, expressed in terms of savings computed mathematically (usually in dollars), or *usefulness*, a nontechnical term, a test has value to the organization in proportion to its validity coefficient, the mean score of the applicants selected, and the initial variability of criterion performance (Jarrett, 1948). These facts can be used either for a general, verbal statement of usefulness or for estimating specific amounts saved.

Dollar estimates of the utility of selection tests have often been staggering. From an estimated true validity coefficient of .76 for the *Programmer Aptitude Test* and a variety of assumptions about validity of previous selection procedures and selection ratios in the selection of computer programmers, Schmidt, Hunter, McKenzie, and Muldrow (1979) estimated that the U.S. government could save at least $5.6 million in a single year, and perhaps as much as $97.2 million, in programmer selection alone. (The latter required such assumptions as no validity in existing selection procedures and a selection ratio of .05, recalling Darlington's, 1976, p. 44, comment, "In many applications, scales of 'utility' are more a pious self-delusion than a practical reality.") Estimates for smaller organizations have been lower, but still suggest that valid selection tests "pay off handsomely" (Boudreau, 1989).

Utility estimates may be used more simply in choosing among options. If a choice is to be made between selection systems A and B, the relative utility estimate may provide a useful decision tool. However, Guion and Gibson (1988, p. 355) suggested that such comparisons, at least as most utility analyses are being done, would merely favor the more valid over the less valid option. The problem is that most utility analyses are based on the model of the prediction of one criterion by a single predictor, although both, of course, may be composite variables. That is, a single outcome is assumed or, if multiple outcomes are assumed, they are assumed to have an overarching general

component. A better model may assume a need for tradeoffs. For example, an increase in mean performance may be accompanied by a corresponding increase in boredom and subsequent turnover; correlations with both are needed for comprehensive estimates of payoffs and costs. A thoroughly developed payoff matrix will predict a variety of outcomes and attempt to determine costs and benefits for the full set if the selection program is put into effect. Decision theory seems to cry out for answers to questions that the ordinary criterion-related validation study has typically ignored—herein lies the future benefit of utility analyses. Future research in utility analysis needs to specify the relevant variables, including "third variables," the valid means of measuring these variables, and the networks of relationships among them.

There are precedents. Dunnette (1974) dealt with varieties of costs, including the costs of undesirable outcomes of decision errors of both types. In addition to recruiting and screening costs, he suggested consideration in an equal employment opportunity context of (a) training costs, (b) remedial training costs for unsatisfactory employees, (c) societal costs for welfare payments, and (d) societal costs for the riots familiar at the time of that paper. In his hypothetical example, use of a valid selection procedure had substantial utility for the organization if only performance benefits and direct costs of recruiting, screening, and training were considered; if the costs of the other two potential outcomes were considered, the least costly decision would be *to hire without regard to the predictor*, despite its substantial validity coefficient for both blacks and whites. The data were, of course, hypothetical, but they illustrated the dilemma one might face if one looks beyond the validity coefficient.

Multivariate Research

Using a battery of predictors, considered either simultaneously or in a sequence, can often improve predictions. The basic principle of test battery development is that criterion-related validity is increased as predictors are added which (a) are themselves valid predictors of criterion performance and (b) are not highly related to other predictors. The usual method of battery building is to identify predictors that meet these requirements, score them, weight the scores according to a specified rule, and sum the weighted scores. Such a procedure simultaneously considers all predictors and yields a linear, additive composite score.

Additive Combinations. Simultaneous least squares regression analysis is the prototypical method of linear, additive data analysis; it results in the prototypical rule for weights to maximize the correlation of the composite with the criterion. If the components are totally uncorrelated, then each component contributes to the explained criterion variance to the extent of its own correlation (squared) with the criterion. Using standard scores, its weight in the linear, additive composite for optimal prediction is its unsquared validity coefficient. Intercorrelations and variances of predictors also influence the optimal weights of predictors in raw score form.

There are two problems with weights from multiple regression. First is the problem of *shrinkage;* the weights derived in one sample capitalize on every chance error in validities and intercorrelations, maximizing the correlation between the weighted composite and the criterion (i.e., the multiple correlation coefficient). In *cross-validation,* when these optimum weights are used to form composite scores in another sample, the correlation is lower; comparison of the correlation in the first sample to that in the second shows the amount of shrinkage. If the sample is quite large, the weights may be fairly stable; in fact, it is not unheard of to find occasionally that the multiple correlation coefficient in a subsequent sample is a bit higher.

Second, many selection situations call for judgments about the relative weights that

should be assigned, perhaps because of the infeasibility of criterion-related validation, or because of expected shrinkage, or because of particular importance of specific components of the composite battery. The question of how components—be they tests in a battery, items in a test, or cues for judgment—should logically be combined to form a composite measure is broader than the single question of finding weights for the maximum multiple correlation. "The general problem of the combination of measures has been obscured by the indiscriminate adoption of the multiple correlation technique as the 'best' solution, *and by the failure to investigate the properties of various weighting systems*" (Richardson, 1941, p. 379, emphasis added). With the advent of computers and the mindless use of software, the problem has become even more obscured than it was when Richardson wrote those words. It is now easy to compute regression weights, whether appropriate or not, if there is any sort of criterion available, and too many researchers become utterly confused if there is not. In their confusion, they may simply assign unit weights, or weight inversely according to standard deviations, with no more thought than they would have given to computing regression weights. These may or may not be appropriate methods of weighting. Again, Richardson (1941) expressed it as clearly as possible:

> It does not follow that test variables with equal linear weights have actually been weighted equally. The mischievous character of arbitrarily assigned weights depends on the fact that the actual or *effective* weights turn out to be quite different from the *nominal* weights originally assigned. (p. 380)

The discussion here of the "mischievous character" will follow Richardson's, limited to linear models with orthogonal or positively correlated variables.

TABLE 1

Data for Hypothetical Three-Variable Composite

Variable	V	s	Correlations		
			A	B	C
A	1	1	1.00	.50	.80
B	3	2		1.00	.60
C	2	3			1.00

Consider a situation with three employment tests, each evaluated in terms of the judged job relevance of the construct measured and the quality of measurement—that is, not in terms of criterion prediction. Or, think of three criterion measures to be combined into a single composite. In such cases, the effective weight of a component is its contribution to the variance of the composite. With the simplifying assumption of perfect reliability, the following general principles can be considered:

- If variances of the component variables are equal (e.g., with standard scores), and if intercorrelations are zero, effective weights are proportional to the *squares* of the nominal weights. If component A is judged twice as important as either components B or C, nominal weights of standard scores may be 2, 1, and 1, but the effective weights would be 4, 1, and 1, respectively.

- If intercorrelations are zero but variances are unequal, the effective weight of a component is proportional to the *product* of the square of its norminal weight and its variance.

- With positively intercorrelated components, unequal variances, and unequal nominal weights, the effective weight of each component is proportional to the product of its nominal weight and the weighted sum of its correlations with other variables. Since reliability is still considered perfect, the self-correlation is treated as 1.00 in these computations:

$$s_t^2 = W_1 \Sigma\ W_i r_{1i} + W_2 \Sigma\ W_i r_{2i} + \ldots + W_n \Sigma\ W_i r_{ni} \quad (1)$$

where s_t^2 is the total variance of the composite, W is the nominal weight assigned to variable i, and the r's are the self-correlations and intercorrelations. Where variances are unequal, the weights W should be identified as influenced by dispersion, so Richardson used V to identify the nominal weight in such cases and rewrote W^2 as V^2s^2; thus, in equation 2, W_i can be written as $V_i s_i$. Equation 2 then becomes:

$$s_t^2 = V_1 s_1 \Sigma V_i r_{1i} s_i + V_2 s_2 \Sigma V_i r_{2i} s_i + \ldots + V_n s_n \Sigma V_i r_{ni} s_i \quad (2)$$

Consider now a situation where variables A, B, and C have nominal weights (V), standard deviations (s), and intercorrelations (r) as in Table 1. The relative nominal weights (summing to 1.00) for component variables A, B, and C are .167, .500, and .333, respectively. The relative *effec-tive* weights, by Equation 2, are substantially different: .067, .458, and .475, respectively.

- To eliminate the remaining simplification, if all other considerations are equal, the effective weight of a component is directly proportional to its reliability. The common practice of weighting by the inverse of the standard deviation is justified only when differences in variances are artifacts of the differences in construction (e.g., when one component has 10 items and another has 100 items). If differences in variances are associated with differences in reliabilities, the practice may give the highest effective weight to the component with the lowest reliability, an anomaly to be avoided.

Several options exist for weighting schemes (Horst, 1966, p. 124). In addition to weighting for best prediction or by arbitrary assignments, whether equal (unit) or differential, one might want to weight components according to their reliability coefficients, that is, to maximize the reliability of the composite (but see Green, 1950). Other goals may be to maximize the variance of the composite or, if intercorrelations are positive and nontrivial, to maximize variance attributable to a common factor. If the number of components in a composite is small, the choice of a weighting scheme may make a substantial difference in effective weights and, therefore, in composite scores; the correlation of composite scores formed by one scheme with those formed by another may be low enough that the researcher will have to choose one method over others. Criterion-related validity coefficients based on composite scores developed by different schemes can be expected to differ. If the number of components is large, however, such as items in a test or in a long set of rating scales, the correlations among composites formed by different weighting schemes will be so high that the easiest, unit weighting, is preferred.

Nonlinear or Nonadditive Models. Critical scores can be assigned to each variable in a battery, just as in the case of cut scores for single predictors; all comments made earlier about cut scores apply also to the components of a battery. Nevertheless, circumstances, such as a need for sequential rather than simultaneous use of predictors, may make the identification and use of such scores necessary. The first hurdle, for example, may be a requirement of relevant formal training. Even if some training programs are better than others, or if more training is better than less, this initial hurdle may be set low enough to disqualify only those with no formal training at all. The next step may be a battery which, among others, includes tests for near-point depth perception and for dexterity. If some minimal level of these traits is deemed essential, then no matter how intelligent, personable, or socially skilled the candidate, those desirable traits cannot compensate for the deficiencies in depth perception or dexterity.

Linear, additive models are compensatory; outstanding performance on one component of a battery can compensate for poor performance on another in forming a composite score. It is a conjunctive noncompensatory model when a candidate who falls below the critical level on any one requirement (e.g., training, depth perception, or dexterity) is eliminated from further consideration; a disjunctive noncompensatory model is one in which a very high score on any one variable is sufficient reason for selection, regardless of scores on others (Einhorn, 1971). Other configural models can be developed heuristically as algorithms for decision.

Noncompensatory models might be wanted, or even may be genuinely superior, in many circumstances. They are often the de facto bases for hiring decisions (e.g., only those with three years experience and a high school diploma need apply). The *Uniform Guidelines* call for cut scores, as contrasted with rank-order decision procedures, if tests are defended solely on the basis of job and test content matching. Dvorak (1956) argued for a multiple cutoff model. Why, then, are non-compensatory models so rarely used?

Perhaps it is because multiple cutoff models can be justified mathematically only if the tests in the battery are perfectly reliable (Lord, 1962, 1963). Or perhaps it is because multiple regression computer programs are ubiquitous. One tends to use the linear additive model because, like Mount Everest, it's there. A more rational reason lies in the "robustness" of the linear model (although, I confess occasional thoughts that robustness means insensitivity). It is undeniably true, surely, that a linear, additive model will account for large portions of variance in virtually any criterion; even clearly curvilinear regressions in bivariate analyses tend to be monotonic with strong linear components.

To argue from the fact that a linear, additive model is good does not logically lead, however, to the argument that it is either good enough or optimal, and researchers in many aspects of selection research need to consider the possibility that employment decisions can be based on still better decision models.

Moderators, Mediators, Suppressors, and Other Complications.   Even with a single predictor, other variables may improve predictions. The truism that a correlation coefficient does not express causation bears repeating as preliminary to an equally true aphorism that one rarely knows what causes a correlation. Bivariate correlation is plagued by unmeasured or unknown third variables causing either inflated or deflated coefficients that are virtually uninterpretable. Selection research that seeks understanding must postulate and explore the influential third variables.

Some of them may be suppressor variables, those that have no predictive validity of their own but are correlated with a valid predictor. In a multiple regression equation, a suppressor will have a negative regression weight if scored positively; its function in the equation

is to suppress variance in the predictor not associated with the criterion. Others may be moderator variables, those that are correlated with the correlation between the predictor and criterion. In the classic example, the correlation between academic achievement and interest was moderated by compulsiveness (Frederiksen & Melville, 1954; Saunders, 1956). Still others may be mediating variables in a causal chain (James & Brett, 1984).

Rarely have suppressor variables been found. Early enthusiasm for moderators has been dampened by findings that critical variables such as sex or ethnic identification have not been found to moderate selection test validities, although both had been highly touted as solutions to the problem of potential discrimination in employment through test use. Other moderators have not held up well in cross validation. It may be, however, that the search for moderators has relied more on searching than on planning, more on serendipity than on thought. There is no clear reason to expect a variable to function as a moderator or to hold up as one under cross validation—if it didn't make much sense in the first place. Moderators, to paraphrase Shaw's comment on Christianity, might be good things if one were to try them sensibly.

Unless a proposed moderator makes sense, the problem of how to find it in data analysis is not very important; if it does make sense, however, the problem is serious. Conventional procedure has moved away from comparisons of validities in artificially formed subgroups toward greater reliance on two-stage moderated regression. In the simple, one predictor case, regression weights are found for both the predictor and the moderator variable in the first stage, and, in the second stage, the regression weight for the interaction term is computed. If the proposed moderator and the predictor are correlated with each other and with the criterion, little unique variance is left for the interaction term to share with the criterion. A suggested solution for this problem

(Morris, Sherman, & Mansfield, 1986) has been attacked as inappropriate by Cronbach (1987), Dunlap and Kemery (1987), and Stone (1988). Both Cronbach and Stone have urged research seeking more powerful means for detecting significant moderators, but both maintain that moderated multiple regression is currently the best available method.

The issue appears to be part of a larger one. Stone (1988) acknowledged what others tiptoe around: that a moderator is a *cause* of changes in the relationships between other variables. If one seriously seeks causal information, a single multiple regression equation is not likely to provide it. Path analysis, causal modeling, structural equations—by whatever title, these are the analytical methods that need to be explored and developed for selection research. I shall use the term *path analysis* as a generic term in identifying some themes in which such analysis integrates other themes of this chapter.

The first such theme is that it is a *confirmatory*, or perhaps disconfirmatory, analysis. One thinks carefully about the literature on a given phenomenon and develops a theory of the nature and actions of the antecedents of the phenomenon; the analysis either does or does not confirm that theory (but see note 3 at the end of this chapter). The overarching theme of this chapter is that the foundation for effective selection is a carefully developed hypothesis that a particular trait that people bring to the employment office is related to performance on the job. We do not often speak of that relationship as causal, but we usually have causation in mind, even if it is not so articulated. If we hypothesize that eye-hand coordination is correlated with job performance, we typically believe that good coordination will help some people (or cause them to) perform well and that poor coordination will cause mistakes and clumsiness and generally poor performance.

The second theme is that a causal model must be self-contained and fully specified (James, Mulaik, & Brett, 1982). That is, all variables influencing the criterion are in the model (it is self-contained) and that the role—direct, mediating, or moderating—of each variable and its direction of influence is fully specified. What are the factors that influence criterion performance? Many have been postulated in this *Handbook*. They include organizational variables and interventions, prior or early on-the-job experiences, and personal traits. Specific findings show that any one of many influences can be shown to be related to job performance. In path analysis, the influence of one correlate among many is seen in clearer perspective; a trait that by itself correlates well with performance may have a trivial path coefficient. If so, then regardless of the size of the validity coefficient, the use of the test will, in fact, have much less utility than a non–self-contained, underspecified regression equation would suggest. In this chapter, much concern has been expressed about the third variable problem; the problem does not exist in a fully identified, fully specified model.

A third theme is that path analyses may consider latent variables as well as manifest ones (i.e., inferred constructs from multiple measures of the constructs) in its theoretical structure. A recurring general theme in this chapter is the call for understanding; if indeed a taxonomy of kinds of performance and kinds of influences on performance can be developed, then latent variable analysis will provide a clearer understanding of the paths to effective performance than can be achieved by using single, error-prone measures. True, the error-prone measures will continue to be necessary operationally, but *understanding* can be enhanced through multiple measures and latent structure analysis.

The Use of Criterion-related Research Results

Procedures that have been developed over the years for evaluating employment tests may show either that a test is useful or that it is not. Ironically, no other part of the employment process has been subjected to similar scrutiny—nor to so much criticism. Another irony is that an empirically evaluated predictor may work well in research but not in practice. It is typically one part, even a small part, of the total employment process, and its use in that process, especially when the decision maker is faced with the need to decide about the individual applicant at hand, may be inconsistent with its use in research.

In practice, applicants present themselves for consideration or are recruited; recruiting may or may not be clearly targeted. For example, campus recruiters may seek applicants among graduates of certain curricula or consider any who apply. Applicants are screened on the basis of common sense using paper credentials or perhaps a preliminary interview. The screening is rarely the subject of research (for an exception, see Pannone, 1984), but it may play an important role in the employment process. It may be strict, resulting in few candidates in later steps in the process, or it may be a mere attempt to remove the "obviously" unqualified from further consideration. The validated predictors may then be administered to the survivors along with intensive but unvalidated interviews, idiosyncratic resume evaluations, and vague reference checks. For each applicant, during or perhaps at the end of the process, a decision is made, based on a priori rules or formal predictions or on information that happens to attract the decision maker's attention at the moment.

One problem with this not atypical process is the third variable problem; a good, well-researched predictor may be inserted into a niche filled with imponderables. Factors in paper credentials or interviews may be correlated with, or interact with, the researched predictor and may therefore affect the correlation between predictor and criterion. The extent and direction of the effect is unknown if the third variables remain unidentified and ignored. When a carefully studied predictor is used along with the many other unevaluated variables or procedures, it is subject to utterly unknown effects. These effects may not be very large, but one does not know.

Another problem is that the use of scores in practice may differ from that in research. The research may have used the full score scale, but real decisions may be based on an effective measurement scale of zero and one. The research would be applied more directly with an empirically determined regression equation, or perhaps a graph of it, to make a point prediction of each candidate's actual position on the criterion used in the research, perhaps embedded in a confidence interval. If each decision maker, at the time each decision is to be made, has available the best possible estimate of probable criterion performance for each candidate, together with knowledge of reasonably expected error around that estimate, choices and decisions will be well informed by the research. Nearly as direct is to select on the basis of relative test scores. The regression line is probably monotonic, so the order of predicted performance matches the order of the scores. At some point, however, the higher-scoring of two candidates may nevertheless have unacceptably low predicted performance, so decision makers still need a fairly good idea of the performance implications of particular score levels.

Expectancy charts or tables (Lawshe, Bolda, Brune, & Auclair, 1958) can show the probability of an identified level of success on the criterion. An expectancy table may divide both predictor and criterion into intervals such as quartiles or quintiles, but the user should be trained to think of the score intervals on both variables as segments of an underlying continuum, not as discrete scores. Such training should help the user treat the expectancy table more as a decision aid than as a decision maker. Ordinarily, the decision maker intends to give preference to candidates who are expected to do better than other available candidates. A score that would be grounds for rejection when candidates are numerous might be quite acceptable when candidates are scarce, or a score that would be good enough for acceptance of most candidates would not be sufficient to override consideration of some out of the ordinary but highly salient characteristic of a specific person.

The easy recital of the principle that people are selected in the order of predicted criterion performance does not quite capture reality. For one thing, it is hard to sell to some organizations, particularly some unions, a plan that is perceived as allowing a change in the cutoff score from time to time. For another, the research criterion rarely includes everything the decision maker wants to consider. One candidate may rank relatively farther down the list than another in predicted performance on the criterion used in research, yet be deemed potentially much better on another criterion that was not studied but is not trivial.

The final decision is rarely based solely on predicted criterion performance; it is rarely purely mathematical. Subjective judgment enters the final decision, based both on validated and unresearched sources of information. Some of that information may be available for all candidates; other information may apply only to the candidate at hand. Much research effort has investigated the criterion-related validities of predictors; little has been devoted to the ways in which that information combines with other information to determine final decisions. At least some of that information may be valid and useful, even if not shown to be so by criterion-related procedures.

Validity and Job Relatedness: A Reexamination

There is more to validity than validity coefficients, and more to evaluation than criterion-related validation. The SIOP *Principles* (SIOP,

1987) refer to various "strategies" for studying validity; the *Standards* (AERA, APA, NCME, 1985) refer to various kinds of "evidence" of validity. I prefer the latter, more general term. "Strategies" seems to fit too well the early concepts of content, construct, and criterion-related validities, treated often as if they represented distinct types of validity. As Dunnette and Borman (1979) pointed out, "the implication that validities come in different types leads to confusion and, in the face of confusion, oversimplification" (p. 483). The notion that one knows all one needs to know to evaluate a test when one has a validity coefficient is the epitome of oversimplification.

The ambiguity of *validity, valid,* and *validation* inhibits recognition of the basic unity in these terms. In their book on validity in research, Brinberg and McGrath (1985), referring to the "heterogeneity" of the use of the word, pointed out that the different uses seem unrelated to each other. In his history of validity discussions, Angoff (1988) quoted definitions ranging from "the extent to which a test measures what it purports to measure" to "a test is valid for anything with which it correlates" (pp. 19–20). These extremes identify two distinctly different ideas: a valid measure of something, and a valid predictor of something else. Stated more formally, one definition is essentially a psychometric question of the meaning or interpretation of a measurement operation, and the other is essentially a question of statistical prediction.

Consider something that "purports" to be a measure of stress tolerance.[5] It is a set of operations; many kinds of operations could be chosen. Paper-and-pencil options could include a conventional inventory or perhaps a set of situations, previously scaled for potential stress, to which people respond on a tolerability scale. It might be psychophysiological responses to scaled stimuli. Whatever the operation, results are numbers; we draw inferences from these numbers, and we want the inferences to be valid. Different kinds of inferences can be drawn from the same set of numbers. One might be an inference about the domain of behavior sampled by the measurement operations; for example, it might be seen as a domain of Type B behavior. It might be an inference of generalized frustration tolerance if stress is seen as a special case of frustration. Or we might infer some future level or condition of health.

The first two inferences share a common characteristic: Both are descriptive inferences about a current trait or construct. The third inference is different in that future health is not the construct measured by the set of operations intended to measure stress tolerance. It is a *different* construct measured by a different set of operations, at a different time, under different conditions, and perhaps evaluated under different standards of evidence. It differs from the other two in that it implies a proposition or a hypothesis *about a relationship between two independently defined and independently measured constructs.* It is a *relational* inference of covariation or predictability.

In contrast, the other two inferences are *measurement* inferences; they are valid to the extent the numbers can be believed to reflect or describe the specified characteristic, that is, to the extent that one can infer different levels of the trait from different numbers or scores.

The investigation of relational hypotheses is necessary—or at least useful—for understanding the constructs measured and, subsequently, for more valid descriptive inferences. The reverse is not necessarily true. Neither the greatest possible clarity of a construct, nor irrefutable evidence that it has been validly measured, necessarily provides acceptable evidence that it can be validly used to draw inferences about another valued variable or construct. In short, the validity of a relational inference is not the same as the validity of a measurement inference. Therefore, to evaluate

a personnel selection procedure, the psychometric validity of an inference it permits about a candidate trait must be distinguished from its job-relatedness as an indicator (a hypothetical if not empirical predictor) of job performance or other important job behavior.

A test can be a marvelous sample of a well-defined content domain (e.g., addition of two- or three-digit numbers with two or three addends) and still not be a useful selection instrument for jobs not requiring a particular skill in that domain (in this case, arithmetic skill); a test can be a major definer of a construct and still be useless unless the validly measured construct predicts something important. Although these truisms now seem obvious, they were once paradoxical to many of us in employment testing; we had treated the words *job relatedness* and *validity* as synonyms because we thought validity meant criterion-related validity with a job-relevant criterion. We thought the Supreme Court in its *Griggs* decision (*Griggs v. Duke Power*, 1971) had called for criterion-related validity when in fact it said only that tests must be job related. There are other ways to determine the job relatedness of valid measures.

Conventionally, whether seeking evidence of psychometric validity or of job relatedness, the process has been called *validation*. The term has come to carry so much excess baggage that from here on I will use the more neutral term *evaluation*. Validation too often implies a stamp of approval, somewhat like a department store "validating" a parking check. Evaluation implies a range of results between unconditional approval and condemnation. It avoids the narrow connotations of post hoc correlations and permits consideration of the possibilities built into a test in the early stages of its construction (Anastasi, 1986). It more clearly implies building an argument for or against a particular inference or use; it cuts more clearly the tie with the old trinitarian concepts of validity—as virtually all test experts insist must be done: "The 30-year-old idea of three types of validity, separate but maybe equal, is an idea whose time has gone" (Cronbach, 1988, p. 4).

Evaluating Psychometric Validity

The basic question of psychometric validity is how well the intended attribute has been measured. More precisely: *With what confidence can numbers resulting from measurement operations be interpreted as representing varying degrees or levels of the intended characteristic?* No single, definitive answer is possible. The answers are judgments, not numbers; evaluations, not coefficients. The evaluation depends on the relative weight of all the available evidence, that is, the weight of accumulated evidence supporting an intended interpretation relative to the weight of accumulated evidence opposing it. If the preponderance of evidence is favorable, it is concluded that the intended inferences from scores are valid.

In the spirit of guidance, not of a checklist, I offer seven broad questions to consider in evaluating psychometric validity. The questions, and the kinds of evidence they imply, are neither complete nor detailed, but they can confuse the bureaucratic "stamp collector" (Landy, 1986) who prefers to match a "kind" of validity and a specific "strategy" for validation. Such people want to know which kinds of evidence are essential in evaluating claims of valid measurement although nothing is universally essential. A variety of evidence is needed, evidence of the sort usually found in psychometrics textbooks in chapters on test construction and reliability as well as in chapters on validity. In some circumstances, information on test construction alone might be enough for a judgment of satisfactory validity, but such circumstances would not be frequent.

Each of these questions implies further questions, so the collection of evidence of validity may never be final. Evaluation of validity

should always be tentative, pending new evidence, even when the evidence available is impressive (Cronbach, 1988). Although the language of testing is used in these questions, they apply to other kinds of measurement, too. "Items," for example, may be test items, points scored on a work sample product, or cycles in psychophysiological tracings.

- *Is the measurement procedure based on a formal theory of measurement?* In formal measurement, numbers are assigned according to rules to represent real relationships (Coombs, Dawes, & Tversky, 1970). One such "real relationship," if the attribute measured is scalable at all, is transitivity. Suppose that oranges really have more of an attribute such as acidity than apples (they can be compared!), and that apples have more of it than bananas. The rule of transitivity says that, therefore, oranges have more of it than bananas, and the rules for assigning numbers must result in numbers that faithfully recreate that transitivity. A given set of numbers—test scores, for example—will always *appear* to be transitive; the issue is whether the numbers match an underlying reality, usually known primarily on the strength of theory. If there is a formal, quantitative theory of the attribute to be measured, and if there is a corresponding mathematical theory of its measurement, and if the assumptions of the two theories are satisfied, then, unless something is dreadfully wrong, the resulting measurement operations can be said to yield scores from which valid inferences about the attribute may be drawn. In most psychological measurement, particularly in most psychological testing, these conditions are rarely if ever met, so, in most measurement problems, the search for evidence of validity goes on. It is certainly useful, however, to have at least   an informal theory of the attribute.

- *Was there a clear idea of the attribute to be measured?* I raise this as a separate question in recognition that "theory of the attribute" can be a daunting term. It can represent ideas ranging from a highly formal quantitative theory through a fairly well-developed and supported verbal theory to a general idea about a potentially useful continuum. The idea might be an abstract construct such as latent anxiety; it might be empirically tangible such as the smoothness of a machined surface; it might be observable such as coordinated motor responses to visual stimuli. These are all abstract attributes—constructs, if you like—of the people or objects being studied. Latent anxiety is an attribute of personality, which itself is an attribute of people; smoothness is an attribute of surfaces; coordination is an attribute of responses. It is a small but positive bit of evidence of psychometric validity if the developer began with a clearly articulated idea of the nature of the attribute to be measured and of what or whom it is an attribute. It is a substantial piece of negative evidence if the developer has neither bothered nor been able to say what attribute is to be measured, how it matches or differs from other attributes under other labels, or whether it is an attribute of people, of groups of people, or of the objects people do something to or with.

- *Are the mechanics of measurement consistent with the concept?* A clear idea of the attribute to be measured should suggest certain kinds of stimuli, rules of procedure, and types of appropriate or inappropriate responses. The idea of the attribute should have governed the development of the measurement operations. For example, the choice of printing the stimulus material on paper, displaying it on a video screen, or recording it on an audio cassette should be consistent with the definition of the attribute. Rules of standardization or control, such as time limits for tests, should be chosen to fit the defined attribute, not for convenience (such as length of a class period) or out of habit. Required responses should be appropriate; it would be silly to define the intended attribute in terms of free recall and then use multiple-choice operations. An excellent troubleshooter may be good because of a systematic diagnostic procedure. Another may be even better because relevant prior problems and their solutions are recalled in detail. If one wants to measure this sort of spontaneous recall, then a test that asks for recognition of a solution that worked embedded in a set of others that did not is simply irrelevant. A parallel testing situation begins with giving examinees time to memorize something, such as paired names and numbers, then having them do something else for an hour or so, and then testing their memory. If one wants to measure memory by free recall, a multiple-choice item that asks only that the matching number be recognized in a set of similar numbers is simply not measuring the intended trait.

- *Is stimulus content appropriate?* The content of the measurement operations should fit the attribute being measured; this is more than so-called content validity. If the attribute implies a specific content domain, such as mastery of skills taught in training, then a content-oriented approach to test development—with its insistence on domain definition and rules for domain sampling—is useful and strong evidence of validity. The principle also holds, however, for more abstract concepts. Consider, for example, the factor generally known as perceptual speed and accuracy. Several kinds of item content have been shown to load heavily on this factor. Measurement operations need not sample all of them, but the item content should either have a good track record for measuring the construct or, if a new item type, should be shown to load well on it.

- *Was the instrument carefully and skillfully developed?* The earlier questions imply that the developer had a clear idea at the beginning and held it long enough to plan the measurement and evaluation operations. One should look for evidence that the plan was carefully and skillfully carried out. Judgments are made (e.g., what kind of equipment to use, or what level of difficulty to build the test on); I am inclined to credit full disclosure of the developer's reasoning as a positive sign of care, and probably of validity. When required judgments are established by consensus in a committee of experts, information about the experts themselves, their qualifications, the reliabilities of their judgments, and procedures used to reconcile any differences should be available for evaluation. Further evaluation can be based on information about the conformity of the end product to the original plan, including whether departures were carefully considered and sensible. Evidence of care can also come from answers to questions like these:

What pilot studies were done to try out ideas about item types, instructions, time limits, ambient conditions, or other standardizing aspects of the instrument?

Were items selected on the basis of item analysis? If so, did the data come from an appropriate sample or from a sample of convenience (less euphemistically, a *scrounge sample*)? Was the sample large enough to yield reliable item statistics? Does the mix of surviving items fit the original plan, or is there some imbalance? Was the item pool big enough to allow stringent criteria for item retention?

Were methods of test construction, particularly if sophisticated methods such as item response theory were used, carried out with full awareness of the assumptions and constraints of the method?

- *Is the internal statistical evidence satisfactory?* It is convenient to use the language of testing in discussing internal statistics, but such analysis is also important in ratings, work samples, interview judgments, and other forms of assessment, even though they may not look like tests. In tests, item statistics or parameters can be examined for spread, averages, appropriateness for measurement purposes, and other factors. Even these hard statistical data need to be evaluated in light of the circumstances that produced them: Sample sizes, populations sampled, or probable distribution of the attribute in the sample should certainly influence the evaluations. No universally "right" statement can be made about the most desirable item characteristics. Ordinarily, one might consider a broad range of item difficulties the mark of a sound test. For a specific purpose, however, a narrow band of difficulties might enhance discriminability in a critical region and be considered better evidence of validity than a broad band.

One might seek evidence of internal consistency in tests and scales. A high alpha coefficient is not direct evidence that the item set as a whole measures what it is intended to measure, but it does offer assurance of some uniformity in the source of response variance. If other information makes it reasonable to assume that most items measure the intended attribute, then a satisfactory alpha is evidence that the scores reflect it without much contamination from irrelevant sources.

There are other inconsistencies to consider. How valid is measurement if it is not consistent over some reasonable period of time, or if fundamentally similar, even parallel, ways of measurement give inconsistent results, or if results are inconsistent across examiners, scorers, or observers? Once again, asking the question does not imply a necessary answer. The question of stability over time, for example, requires judgment about the stability of the attribute before evaluating a low coefficient of stability.

Generalizability theory (Brennan, 1983; Cronbach, Gleser, Nanda, & Rajaratnam, 1972) is an extension of classical reliability theory; some would deny its relevance or that of other reliability data to discussion of validity in any sense other than the traditional limiting sense. Personally, I consider a set of well-placed generalizability coefficients, suggesting that interpretations from scores are consistent over a variety of conditions, as excellent evidence of psychometric validity.

- *How do the scores correlate with other variables?* Here we look to evidence of criterion-related validity where construct-relevant criteria are used. The evidence can come in the form of a validity coefficient, although the term is usually not used in this context. One form of statistical evidence that pleases most observers remarkably well is a nice validity coefficient. Depending on the hypothesis implied by a given construct-relevant criterion, a "nice" coefficient may be high—or it may be near zero. Judgments of validity based on correlations with other variables require two kinds of evidence: (a) evidence that logically expected relatioships with other variables have in fact been empirically shown and (b) evidence that relationships *not* expected are, in fact *not* found—that is, both convergent validity confirming hypotheses about relationships and discriminant validity disconfirming alternative hypotheses.

I refer deliberately to these as *validity coefficients* because the term is increasingly recognized as having caused a lot of mischief. People place too much faith in validity coefficients, usually because they tend to overlook the possibility that a validity coefficient might be high because of common contamination or low because of contaminations or deficiencies in one variable or the other. Validity coefficients are, of course, important evidence in making validity judgments, but one should never confuse a validity coefficient with validity, and one should never base a judgment of psychometric validity on a validity coefficient alone.

This discussion may identify validity of measurement with what has been called *construct validity*, but I intend it to be more inclusive than that. The point is well stated in the *Standards* (AERA et al., 1985):

An ideal validation includes several types of evidence, which span all three of the traditional categories. Other things being equal, more sources of evidence are better than fewer. However, the quality of the evidence is of primary importance, and a single line of solid evidence is preferable to numerous lines of evidence of questionable quality. Professional judgment should guide the decisions regarding the forms of evidence that are most necessary and feasible in light of the intended uses of the test *and any likely alternatives to testing.* (p. 9; emphasis added)

Evaluating Job Relatedness

Tests and other measures are used, among other things, to assess effectiveness of programs or individuals, to classify people or objects, to predict future performance in school or work, or to test hypotheses suggested by one's theories. All such uses imply relational propositions about the attribute measured, expressed as predictive hypotheses. The prototypical test of the hypothesis is the conventional criterion-related validation strategy. If an empirical relationship is indeed found and is reasonably strong, the predictor is said to be a valid predictor, or, in the terms urged here, job related. From a practical point of view, evidence of a predictor's job relatedness is more important than evidence of its psychometric validity. Clear evidence of a substantial and reliable correlation between criterion and predictor is operationally useful even without a clear understanding of what the predictor measures.

Questions to ask about job relatedness can be listed briefly; they have already been discussed in detail:

- *Does the predictive hypothesis make good sense?* Is it based on a genuine understanding of the job or job family or organizational needs? Is it consistent with that understanding? Has it been systematically developed through careful procedures for systematizing and recording judgments?

- *Does the hypothesis include more than one predictor?* If not, is it reasonable to think that a single construct can account adequately for the criterion variance, or is the hypothesis deficient? If deficient, do the omissions make sense, given the circumstances (e.g., are major sources of criterion variance acquired through training or on-the-job experience)? These questions identify a major distinction between concern for psychometric validity, which is an evaluation of one inference from one variable, and job relatedness, which is often multivariate in nature.

- *Does the hypothesis specify functional relationships, or, with multiple predictors, acceptable principles of combination?* If not, does it assume linearity or additivity out of habit, without further examination of data or logic? Are alternatives considered, and accepted or rejected, with clear reasoning? Have the data been plotted?

- *Are the variables, predictors and criteria, validly measured?* This question refers in part to the discussion on psychometric validity, but it also refers to the validities of individual scores obtained under particular circumstances in a particular setting. Were standard procedures followed? For any individual score, is a candidate characteristic—for example, hearing or vision impairment—likely to have had a contaminating and job-irrelevant influence?

- *How accurately is the criterion predicted?* What is the probability of correct predition within acceptable limits of error? How much of the criterion variance has been explained? Does the criterion capture the major aspects of performance, or should several job-relevant criteria have been used in research?

- *Was empirical research conducted with an appropriate sample?* Can the sample reasonably be assumed to represent a realistic view of the applicant population, or is it somehow biased or irrelevant? Is it large enough to minimize risks of Type II as well as Type I error? Is the variance in the sample, for both predictor and criterion variables, like that in the target population?

- *Were research subjects given assurances that would not be given to people in actual decision situations?* Are there other kinds of unusual circumstances for the research subjects that would not be found in conditions of actual use?

Taken as a whole, this list of questions implies criterion-related research. Often, however, the use of tests or other decision-aiding procedures is not based on such research but rests on judgments made by the user. First, the user must decide what kinds of variables—what attributes or constructs—are likely to be useful. This decision constitutes a hypothesis, whether so designated or not, and the first three sets of questions in this list help one evaluate it. Second, the user must choose the measurement operations—the tests, scales, or instruments—for measuring the variables. The fourth question refers to the psychometric validity of the predictors. *If no criterion-related research is done, but the answers to the first four questions are favorable, I would judge the use of the predictor to be shown to be job related.* If so, if empirical data are available, and *if the answers to the last three questions about the data are favorable,* my judgment of job relatedness would be strengthened. For me, the evaluation of job relatedness depends more on the quality of the answers to the first four questions (setting aside the criterion measurement part of the fourth question) than to the last three because of my dimmed confidence in the value of a single empirical study.

Pooled Judgments as Evidence of Job Relatedness

Somebody in an organization must decide whether the evidence of job relatedness is good enough to start using a proposed predictor or battery. If that person has a solid understanding of the job, the criterion construct, the logic of the predictive hypothesis involved, the principles of psychometric validity, and the evidence of the validity of the measurement of the important predictors, that person is qualified to decide, even in the absence of empirical, criterion-related correlation coefficients.

Even though that one person is competent to make the judgment, some circumstances call for pooling the judgments of several people. There are both dangers and benefits from pooled judgments. The principal danger, particularly if some in the pool are not so well qualified, is that quality of judgment may be sacrificed for the sake of consensus; worse, the consensus may be wrong, overriding the better judgment of one really qualified person. The principal benefit of pooling qualified judgments is increased reliability; a secondary but perhaps nontrivial benefit is that no one need go out on a limb alone.

One kind of judgment that might be made in the absence of an empirical study is an estimate of the correlation coefficient that might be obtained if such study were done. Schmidt, Hunter, Croll, and McKenzie (1983) reported research showing that highly trained and experienced employment testing experts (psychologists with excellent national reputations as experts in employee selection) could provide more accurate estimates of the correlation in data from a very large sample than could, on the average, be provided by a single criterion-related coefficient from samples of more conventional sizes. They estimated that, on the average, an empirical study would require a sample of 92 cases to equal the accuracy of the estimate of just 1 of these judges; to equal the accuracy of the pooled judgments of 4 of them, a sample of 326 would be required. To repeat, their judges were extremely well qualified to make such judgments. Subsequently, Hirsh, Schmidt, and Hunter (1986) tried the same research with a panel of well-trained but less experienced judges (i.e., recent doctoral graduates in industrial and organizational psychology with major interests in personnel selection). They did not do as well; the researchers estimated that it would, on average, require pooling judgments from 10 such experts to equal the accuracy achieved by one judge in the earlier pool of experts. Nevertheless, it was possible to get accurate estimates of actual validity in very-large-sample data by even the less expert judgments. The research points both to the value of pooled judgments from experts and, where the pool is small, the need to ensure that panels of judges are indeed experts in employment testing.

Estimation of empirical correlation coefficients is, however, only one way of demonstrating the job relatedness of the predictors, and psychologists provide only one kind of expertise. Another widely used approach calls upon panels of job experts, not necessarily testing experts, to make judgments about the relevance of predictor content to specific aspects of job requirements. In essence, they make judgments of the strengths of relationships in a person-job characteristics matrix (Figure 1), although ordinarily according to some brief scale rather than in correlational terms. To evaluate the judgments of job relatedness obtained from such panels, both the claims of expertise and the clarity and discipline of the procedures used to get the judgments need to be evaluated.

We tend to think of these judgments in terms of the content of tests, but there are other kinds of qualifications as well. Some people (I am one) question the use of tests for promotional decisions where the new job builds on the experience gained in the earlier one. Dunnette (1979) reported such an instance in which job experts (incumbents in supervisory jobs and incumbents in clerical jobs providing the pool from which candidates for promotion were found) completed a qualifications checklist of 162 personal qualifications that would either help or hinder performance on tasks specified in a task checklist; for each of the supervisory or managerial job groups to which people might be promoted, a congruence index was computed to show the degree to which qualifications for certain clerical job groups matched the qualifications for the managerial job groups. The method showed the job relatedness of experience on specific jobs; among the implications is that these jobs identify the pool from which candidates for promotion might be drawn. I would use performance evaluations for choosing among those in the appropriate pool. A similar use of checklist judgments by job incumbents in retail sales resulted in a list of eight kinds of qualifications that could, in different combinations for different jobs, be assessed from resumes, application forms, or interviews. Among other things, these studies demonstrated both (a) that correlation coefficients are not necessary indicators of job relatedness and, in fact, may be misleading, and (b) systematic use of pooled judgments from job experts can be used to develop the predictive hypotheses that are the foundation of evidence of job relatedness of both test and nontest predictors.

Alternative Evaluative Procedures

For almost everything in this chapter, regression and correlational analysis has been a prototype. Alternatives exist and should be considered. The paradigm for selection research has, almost uniformly, been one of testing many people with the same test for the same job, correlating the scores with a criterion, and if the correlation is satisfactory, selecting applicants with the best test scores. That paradigm has worked well, particularly when most nonfarm workers were in large organizations and many people worked at similar jobs. Now, however, only about one-tenth of working Americans are employed in organizations numbering over 1,000 (Hodge & Lagerfeld, 1987), and there is greater job differentiation.

A paradigm shift is needed; it seems to be occurring, and it may require different research designs. The shift is toward an individualized

FIGURE 5

Dunnette's Model of the Personnel Decision Process

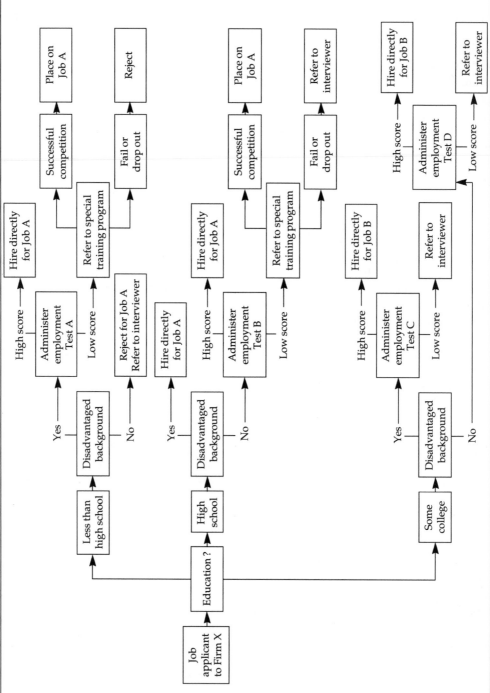

From *Integrating the Organization: A Social Psychological Analysis* (p. 62) by H. L. Fromkin and J. J. Sherwood (Eds.), 1974, New York: Free Press. Copyright 1974 by The Free Press, a division of Macmillan, Inc. Reprinted by permission.

approach to selection decisions with more emphasis on informed judgment, yet with a broader organizational perspective in evaluating the way the decisions are reached. It was presaged by Dunnette (1963b, 1974) in the model presented in Figure 5, although movement toward it was virtually halted by the orthodoxies of federal EEO regulatory documents. In Dunnette's model, different tests may be given to different people, depending on background characteristics and preliminary assessments; and the resulting scores may lead to further assessment, hiring, rejection, or special training.

An Illustrative Program

The model is a program of assessment and seletion decisions, and the idea can be expanded. I will describe a fictional program stemming from dreams about what might be done with some actual programs I have seen.

Consider an organization, perhaps a large one but not highly centralized, in which salaried positions are generally unique and changing as personnel changes lead to changes in the distributions of tasks or responsibilities within specific groups or departments. Background research or planning has provided (a) a specific glossary of terms for position descriptions, each with a fairly precise denotation of tasks or responsibilities defining the position, (b) a glossary of attributes sought for many positions, tightly enough defined that different people within the organization have common understandings of these attributes, (c) specifications of appropriate measurement or assessment methods for these attributes, and (d) results of judgment research linking the attribute list to position descriptors. The employment process in this idealized setting begins with a personnel requisition from the decision maker, the responsible person to whom the selected employee will report. It specifies in standard language the position's major tasks and responsibilities, the attributes to assess and the methods of assessment, and any unique considerations needed. Staff people in human resources management may check both the organization's personnel files and applicant files for people with at least some of the specified attributes. Potential candidates may be queried for their interest in the position. Those interested are referred to the decision maker.

The decision maker identifies those who look good on paper, interviews them using a prepared interview guide based on the information on the requisition, sends some of them for specialized assessment through organizational staff resources, considers the results, and makes a decision. The decision may not be the one that would have been made by personnel specialists or by other managers, but it is the one that sticks. How can selection decisions made in such a program be empirically evaluated for job relevance?

Some Alternative Research Designs

Lens Model and Policy-capturing Analysis. The instrument of decision in the illustrative program is the individual manager. Under the traditional paradigm, the judgments of managers would be correlated with a criterion; the correlation, corrected for restriction of range, would be the basis for evaluating the program. The same correlation can be computed, but with more diagnostic information, using the Brunswikian idea of a lens model, presented in Figure 6 as it relates to selection research. It uses traditional regression methods, so uniformity of data is necessary; each kind of information should be available for each candidate considered. The kinds of information, however, may be classes of assessments or inferences (e.g., ratings of background experiences even though details differ from one person to another or from job to job). The model could be applied to each individual manager, as reported in studies of interviewers (e.g., Dougherty, Ebert, & Callender, 1986; Zedeck, Tziner, &

FIGURE 6

Brunswikian Lens Model for Personnel Selection Research

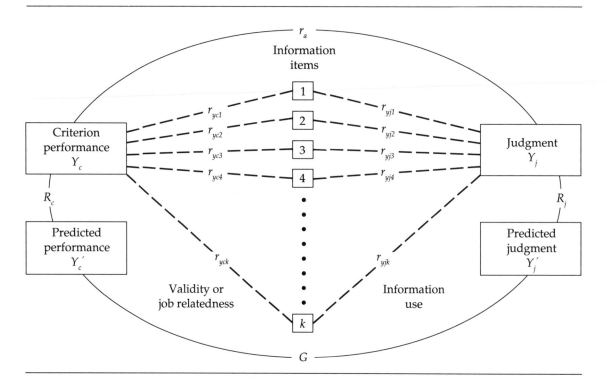

Middlestadt, 1983). On the basis of the accumulated and evaluated information about a set of candidates, the decision maker records his or her judgment about each candidate's probable performance if selected.

In Figure 6, the lines between the judgment and the information categories ("items") represent bivariate correlation coefficients. A multiple regression equation could be developed to predict judgments (Y'_j) from the items and, under some circumstances, can identify those that are heavily weighted, or perhaps not used at all, in a regression model of the judgments. The appropriateness of the weighting can be evaluated by comparing the correlations (or weights in the regression equation) between information items and criterion, that is, the job relatedness (predictive validity) of each item.

The multiple correlations $(R_j$ and $R_c)$ identify, respectively, the predictability of judgments and the criterion, given the available information. The correlation of judgments with subsequent criterion performance (r_a) known in judgment research as the *achievement index,* is a straightforward criterion-related validity coefficient. G is the correlation between predicted judgment and predicted performance, or the *matching index,* and is roughly analogous to the corrected validity coefficient; it indicates the maximum validity (job relatedness) obtainable by linear, additive regression on both sides of the "lens."

The model does more than describe the job relatedness of the judgments. From analysis of their judgment policies, individual decision makers can be trained to be more consistent

FIGURE 7

An Illustrative Model for Path Analysis in Evaluating a Selection Program

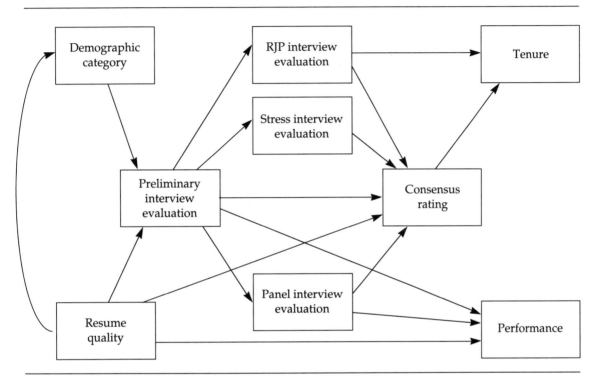

and more effective in their judgment policies; determination of the policies can not only identify people whose judgments are not valid but can identify the changes needed for better judgments (see Dougherty, Ebert, & Callender, 1986).

No one manager is likely to make enough hiring decisions to permit such a personal analysis, but data can be collected from many decisions, all cases can be presented for judgment to each decision maker, and the lens model analyses completed. To evaluate the program as a whole, the collective pool of judgments may be appropriate.

Path Analysis. Path analysis was discussed in the evaluation of bivariate validity coefficients; it can also be an informative tool for evaluating integrated selection systems.

Figure 7 describes a hypothetical college recruiting program in which recruiters examine and evaluate applicant credentials and give preliminary interviews before checking references and evaluating what is learned. In this program, most, but not all, applicants are then invited to the home office for a series of interviews, one with a job specialist giving a realistic job preview (RJP), another with a clinical psychologist giving a mild stress interview, and the third a general session before an interview panel, the members of which have examined all prior information. Interviewers from all three then meet and make a consensus rating of the applicant who, if hired, is evaluated a year later to see if he or she is still with the organization and, if so, to evaluate performance; those who had left had been evaluated at termination. The logic of the program is that the RJP should influence stability but not performance, that the consensus rating should reflect suitability influencing both criteria. It is hypothesized that the basis for the stress interview rating will be useful only in its influence on the consensus evaluation, but that the panel interview may be directly predictive in its own right. In fact, the "theory of the program" includes the possibility that the data alone represent sufficient influence on future performance, that is, that the more elaborate interview procedures may not be needed.

Path analysis provides a means of testing the model as a whole and evaluating component parts of it. As a confirmatory method, it can—if it fits the data—assure the job relatedness of the campus recruiting program. It is also a disconfirmatory method; as such it can identify reasons for changing the program. In more formal language, it provides the basis for a new model to be confirmed or disconfirmed in further research.

Quasi-experimental Designs.   Neither lens model analysis nor path analysis is fully responsive to the needed paradigm shift; both still use the individual case as the unit of analysis, both are regression models, and both require essentially similar data for all cases. In increasing numbers of situations, meeting the latter requirement is simply not possible. More and more, selection programs will require individualization of the kinds of data collected, including information that may be unique for individual positions or candidates.

Another problem is that budget managers have interests different from those of the immediate personnel decision makers. When faced with a personnel decision, the decision maker must make at least an implicit prediction of how well the candidate at hand will do in the prospective position. The budget manager is more removed from the individual decision and wants to know whether the process in general is working

well. To find out, the unit of analysis—and the criterion—is organizational. The method of analysis is likely to be program evaluation (e.g., see Rossi & Williams, 1972; Streuning & Guttentag, 1975) or, to use a more general term, quasi-experimental research (see Cook & Campbell, 1979).

Assume that the organization in the illustrative program has several units and that the program has not been introduced in any of them. It is convenient, but not essential, if two or more such units (different departments, plants, or towns) are similar, producing roughly similar goods and services; they need not be equivalent in any sense. For convenience of illustration, however, assume there are two manufacturing plants, differing somwhat in age and equipment but producing the same product; raw production figures for the two plants would provide an easy dependent variable. Production in such a case could be recorded in each plant for a specified period, say, three months, then the selection program could be introduced in *one* of them for perhaps a year, and production records could be recorded for both during a third time period. No other major programs should be introduced in either plant during these evaluation periods.

The program can be evaluated as useful if production in the plant using it has improved more than in the other plant. This very simple statement might suggest a mere comparison of gain scores; if so, it is masking the much more appropriate and complex analyses required (see Cook & Campbell, 1979, pp. 103–118), but it identifies the basic logic of such research.

I do not know of examples of such evaluative research on such individualized programs, but situations where it could be very useful are not uncommon. Although they did not work with a multifaceted program of personnel decision making, T. S. Brown, Jones, Terris, and Steffy (1987) and Paajanen (1988) used quasi-experimental designs to evaluate inventories designed to predict counterproductive behavior. They used basic pre–post designs in which terminations and inventory shrinkage, used as dependent variables, were recorded before and after introducing the inventories for employee selection in retail stores within large chains. That is, the basic design compared organizational outcomes before the inventory was operational with the outcomes subsequent to its use. In Paajanen's modification, outcomes in 81 stores in which the inventory was developed were compared to those in 207 stores using the inventory as a decision tool the following year. In the Brown et al. design, the same stores were used, and the before and after comparisons involved time series. Both studies reported dramatic differences.

Cook and Campbell (1979) do not consider the simple pretest-posttest design to be one reasonably permitting causal inferences. A more interpretable design, one they call the "untreated control group design with pretest and posttest," would have collected the same data prior to the introduction of the inventories but would have introduced the inventory only in a subset of stores. The changes in the "treated" and "untreated" sets of scores could then be determined, and different patterns of results could have suggested different interpretations. Nevertheless, these studies show that quasi-experimental research for determining the job relatedness of a plan for assessing applicant qualifications is a path worth exploring, whether the plan is based on individual predictors used conventionally or on more integrated selection programs.

Placement

The disparity between the title and the content of this chapter is obvious. Assessment and selection have been explicitly discussed, but considerations of placement have been conspicuously absent. To be sure, they can be inferred when the more general term, *personnel decisions*, has been used, but it requires an inferential stretch.

Despite historical efforts to solve the classification problem, little has happened since the previous edition of the *Handbook* to merit serious discussion. Moreover, most personnel decisions are more job oriented than person oriented; that is, the organization (in the person of a decision maker) is more likely to perceive a vacancy to be filled than to perceive that an applicant not appropriate for that vacancy may nevertheless be immensely valuable to the organization in some other capacity. We ordinarily fill jobs; we do not ordinarily hire people and then decide where to put them.

Exceptions exist. Military organizations are routinely faced with classification decisions for recruits already enlisted. Nonmilitary organizations provide exceptions, I would guess, primarily because of reluctance to fire or demote or change unsatisfactory performers; a search for a place to put them, where they can save face yet not create another problem, seems more likely. This is not the sort of organizational practice that has generated much discussion, let alone research.

For the people-oriented case where serious efforts will be made to find optimal placements for each candidate, or at least for the most promising ones, the typical business organization will find that placement options vary from time to time as much as from person to person. That is, the possible placements for a given candidate appearing on Monday may differ from those if the same candidate appeared on Friday. The lack of standardized options suggests that placement programs need to be devised and evaluated. Perhaps placement, too, needs to try out new research paradigms.

Reprise

Some recurring themes in this chapter merit repetition. The basic theme is that the foundation of useful and defensible personnel selection programs is a competently developed set of hypotheses about the personal traits that make a difference in an organizationally valued criterion. Useful hypotheses begin at the conceptual level, consisting of well-informed, carefully defined, and meticulously articulated criterion and predictor constructs. These major variables are the first of the choices to be made; further decisions are made in choosing or developing the ways these constructs are to be measured, the plans for data collection and analysis, and the relevance of all such plans to the pragmatic needs of the organization. Throughout the development of selection programs, careful planning is crucial; serendipity and milking of data are not as dependable as well-planned procedures that have been thoroughly thought out.

The key theme is the need for scientific understanding. When the hypothesis is being formed, reasons should be collected, examined, and perhaps cataloged as to why the criterion constructs are important, why the predictors should be expected to predict, and why the third variables can be controlled or ignored. Scientific understanding is not an end in itself; it is important because it may lead to better choices. Scientific reasoning always remains skeptical, alert to evidence that will change it; disconfirmation of ideas is as important as confirmation to scientific understanding.

Another central theme woven throughout is that the validation of descriptive inferences—the inferences we make when we try to explain the meaning of a test score or other measure—is not to be confused with the validation of predictive inferences or inferences about proper assignments of people to classifications. I have therefore restricted the word *validity* to the descriptive, psychometric inference and used *job relatedness* for the predictive inference in personnel selection. This is not merely a semantic quibble; it is a recognition of a paradigmatic shift from reliance on numbers narrowly evaluated to broad-based professional judgment as the essential method of evaluating predictor use.

In practice, personnel selection has always been based on judgments. If we develop regression equations or expectancy tables and firm, immutable decision algorithms to govern their use, choices among applicants may appear to be automatic, despite occasional exceptions to the standard rules. That perception overlooks the fact that the foundation for the decision rules rests on judgments about the predictive hypothesis and the evaluative plans.

Emphasizing the role of judgment, particularly in the evaluation of validity and job relatedness, can be dangerous. It opens the door to shoddy practices, trivialities, snap judgments, and a willingness to defend what is easy—all on the grounds of professional judgment; it may permit or even encourage people who are neither well informed nor have much depth of understanding to say, "My judgment is just as good as anyone's." It is therefore vitally important to recognize another recurring theme: *Professional* judgment, unlike hunch or "play- it by ear" decision making, is systematic, informed, and based on understanding and research. The call for professional judgment is neither as difficult as some people may fear nor as easy as others may like. One needs to understand the jobs for which people are selected, not merely how to do an impressive job analysis. One needs to understand the literature on individual differences in abilities, personality, and background, among other considerations, to make judgments wisely about appropriate predictor constructs, not merely how to buy and administer a test. One needs to conduct research or master the relevant research literature to evaluate the psychometric validity of a proposed predictor, not merely to use those that happen to be available. One certainly needs to know the research literature to evaluate probable job relatedness for different categories of predictor-criterion linkages, or to do a logically disciplined study of pooled judgments if the literature does not provide the needed information. Neither meta-analysis nor judgmental approaches to evaluating job relatedness permit personnel selection experts to abandon research; quite the contrary, they call for more research, more competent research, and more varied research. The days of personnel research have not ended.

Notes

1 Note that Ironson and Smith (1981) found that words are more stable in scale value. They also advised that a neutral verbal anchor be somewhere in the central portion of the scale, perhaps displaced from the absolute center to increase sensitivity to one end of the scale. Although it was stated earlier that graphic scales are easy to develop, developing "instant" graphic rating scales without scaling the anchor points is not likely to be very good.

2 With the advent of the Technical Recommendations (APA, 1954), it became common to use the terms of that document instead: *concurrent validity* (or validation) and *predictive validity*, respectively, although these terms were not exact parallels of earlier "present employee" and "follow-up" designations.

3 The language here implies causality. Although path analysis provides a "causal model," it does not *demonstrate* a causal relationship. It tests the plausibility of a set of causal hypotheses; if the fit of model to data is poor, the causal hypotheses are not plausible, i.e., are disconfirmed. If the fit is satisfactory, the causal hypotheses are not fully confirmed, but they remain plausible. I shall undoubtedly use similar language again, but readers should not read into it more confirmation of causality than the method permits.

4 At the item level, some court settlements have shown a remarkable divergence of judicial (or political) and psychometric views by holding that test developers should not use items with even small differences in proportion of right answers (i.e., mean responses) among black and white samples. This suggests that differences in item difficulties are solely due to bias and not at all to genuine mean differences in ability. See Drasgow (1987) for a discussion of two of these cases and their psychometric problems.

5 This view should be recognized as different from other views, notably that of Messick (1988b), whose position is so inclusive that all of construct validity and all consequences of use are included in his unitary concept of validity. I find it more useful for employment practice, however, to make the distinction proposed here.

References

American Educational Research Association, American Psychological Association, & National Council on Measurement in Education. (1985). *Standards for educational and psychological testing*. Washington, DC: American Psychological Association.

American Medical Association. (1977). *Guide to the evaluation of permanent impairment*. Monroe, WI: Author.

American Psychological Association. (1954). Technical recommendations for psychological tests and diagnostic techniques. *Psychological Bulletin, 51*, 201–238.

American Psychological Association, American Educational Research Association, National Council on Measurement in Education. (1966). *Standards for educational and psychological tests and manuals*. Washington, DC: American Psychological Association.

American Psychological Association, American Educational Research Association, National Council on Measurement in Education. (1974). *Standards for educational and psychological tests* Washington, DC: American Psychological Association.

Anastasi, A. (1986). Evolving concepts of test validation. *Annual Review of Psychology, 37*, 1–15.

Angoff, W. H. (1988). Validity: An evolving concept. In H. Wainer & H. I. Braun (Eds.), *Test validity* (pp. 19–32). Hillsdale, NJ: Erlbaum.

Arvey, R. D., & Campion, J. E. (1982). The employment interview: A summary and review of recent research. *Personnel Psychology, 35*, 281–322.

Arvey, R. D., Miller, H. E., Gould, R., & Burch, P. (1987). Interview validity for selecting sales clerks. *Personnel Psychology, 40*, 1–12.

Asher, J. J. (1972). The biographical item: Can it be improved? *Personnel Psychology, 25*, 251–269.

Bangert-Drowns, R. L. (1986). Review of developments in meta-analytic method. *Psychological Bulletin, 99*, 388–399.

Barrett, G. V., Phillips, J. S., & Alexander, R. A. (1981). Concurrent and predictive validity designs: A critical reanalysis. *Journal of Applied Psychology, 66,* 1–6.

Bartram, D. (1987). The development of an automated testing system for pilot selection: The micropat project. *Applied Psychology: An international review, 36,* 279–298.

Bemis, S. E. (1968). Occupational validity of the General Aptitude Test Battery. *Journal of Applied Psychology, 52,* 240–244.

Bernardin, H. J., & Villanova, P. (1986). Performance appraisal. In E. A. Locke (Ed.), *Generalizing from laboratory to field settings* (pp. 43–62). Lexington, MA: Lexington Books.

Blanz, R., & Ghiselli, E. E. (1972). The mixed standard scale: A new rating system. *Personnel Psychology, 25,* 185–200.

Bobko, P. (1983). An analysis of correlation corrected for attenuation and range restriction. *Journal of Applied Psychology, 68,* 584–589.

Borman, W. C. (1983). Implications for personality theory and research for the rating of work performance in organizations. In F. Landy, S. Zedeck, & J. Cleveland (Eds.), *Performance measurement and theory* (pp. 127–165). Hillsdale, NJ: Erlbaum.

Borman, W. C. (1986). Behavior-based rating scales. In R. A. Berk (Ed.), *Performance assessment: Methods and applications* (pp. 100–120). Baltimore: Johns Hopkins University.

Bosshardt, M. J., Rosse, R. L., & Peterson, N. G. (1984). *Development and validation of an industry-wide electric power plant maintenance selection system.* Minneapolis, MN: Personnel Decisions Research Institute.

Boudreau, J. W. (1989). Selection utility analysis: A review and agenda for future research. In M. Smith & I. Robertson (Eds.), *Advances in personnel selection and assessment* (pp. 227–257). Chichester, England: Wiley.

Bray, D. W., & Grant, D. L. (Eds.). (1966). The assessment center in the measurement of potential for business management. *Psychological Monographs, 80* (17, Whole No. 625).

Brennan, R. L. (1983). *Elements of generalizability theory.* Iowa City, IA: American College Testing.

Brinberg, D., & McGrath, J. E. (1985). *Validity and the research process.* Beverly Hills, CA: Sage.

Brown, S. H. (1981). Validity generalization and situational moderation in the life insurance industry. *Journal of Applied Psychology, 66,* 664–670.

Brown, T. S., Jones, J. W., Terris, W., & Steffy, B. D. (1987). The impact of pre-employment integrity testing on employee turnover and inventory shrinkage losses. *Journal of Business and Psychology, 2,* 136–149.

Callender, J. C., & Osburn, H. G. (1981). Testing the constancy of validity with computer-generated sampling distributions of the multiplicative model variance estimate: Results for petroleum industry validation research. *Journal of Applied Psychology, 66,* 274–281.

Campbell, J. P. (1986). Labs, fields, and straw issues. In E. A. Locke (Ed.), *Generalizing from laboratory to field settings* (pp. 269–279). Lexington, MA: Lexington Books.

Cascio, W. F. (1982). *Applied psychology in personnel management* (2nd ed.). Reston, VA: Reston.

Cascio, W. F., & Zedeck, S. (1983). Open a new window in rational research planning. Adjusting alpha to maximize statistical power. *Personnel Psychology, 36,* 517–526.

Cleary, T. A. (1968). Test bias: Prediction of grades for Negro and white students in integrated colleges. *Journal of Educational Measurement, 5,* 115–124.

Cohen, J. (1983). The cost of dichotomization. *Applied Psychological Measurement, 7,* 249–253.

Cook, T. D., & Campbell, D. T. (1979). *Quasi-experimentation: Design and analysis issues for field settings.* Chicago: Rand McNally.

Coombs, C. H., Dawes, R. M., & Tversky, A. (1970). *Mathematical psychology: An elementary introduction.* Englewood Cliffs, NJ: Prentice-Hall.

Cooper, W. H., & Richardson, A. J. (1986). Unfair comparisons. *Journal of Applied Psychology, 71,* 179–184.

Cormier v. PPG Industries, 26 FEP Cases 652 (W.D. Louisiana, 1981).

Cronbach, L. J. (1987). Statistical tests for moderator variables: Flaws in analyses recently proposed. *Psychological Bulletin, 102,* 414–417.

Cronbach, L. J. (1988). Five perspectives on validity argument. In H. Wainer & H. I. Braun (Eds.), *Test validity* (pp. 1–17). Hillsdale, NJ: Erlbaum.

Cronbach, L. J., Gleser, G. C., Nanda, H., & Rajaratnam, N. (1972). *The dependability of behavioral measurements: Theory of generalizability for scores and profiles.* New York: Wiley.

Cronbach, L. J., Yalow, E., & Schaeffer, G. (1980). A mathematical structure for analyzing fairness in selection. *Personnel Psychology, 33,* 693–704.

Darlington, R. B. (1976). A defense of "rational" personnel selection, and two new methods. *Journal of Educational Measurement, 76,* 43–52.

Day, V. B., Erwin, F., & Koral, A. M. (Eds.). (1981). *A professional and legal analysis of the Uniform Guidelines on Employee Selection Procedures.* Berea, OH: American Society for Personnel Administration.

Dillon, R. F. (Ed.). (1985). *Individual differences in cognition* (Vol. 2). Orlando, FL: Academic Press.

Dillon, R. F., & Schmeck, R. R. (Eds.). (1983). *Individual differences in cognition* (Vol. 1). New York: Academic Press.

Dorcus, R. M., & Jones, M. H. (1950). *Handbook of employee selection.* New York: McGraw-Hill.

Dougherty, T. W., Ebert, R. J., & Callender, J. C. (1986). Policy capturing in the employment interview. *Journal of Applied Psychology, 71,* 9–15.

Drasgow, F. (1987). Study of the measurement bias of two standardized psychological tests. *Journal of Applied Psychology, 72,* 19–29.

Drasgow, F., & Hulin, C. (1990). Item response theory. In M. D. Dunnette & L. Hough, *Handbook of industrial and organizational psychology* (2nd ed.). Palo Alto, CA: Consulting Psychologists Press.

Drever, J. (1954). *A dictionary of psychology.* Baltimore: Penguin.

Dunlap, W. P., & Kemery, E. R. (1987). Failure to detect moderating effects: Is multicollinearity the problem? *Psycological Bulletin, 102,* 418–420.

Dunnette, M. D. (1963a). A note on *the* criterion. *Journal of Applied Psychology, 47,* 251-254.

Dunnette, M. D. (1963b). A modified model for test validation and selection research. *Journal of Applied Psychology, 47,* 317–323.

Dunnette, M. D. (1974). Personnel selection and job placement of disadvantaged and minority persons: Problems, issues, and suggestions. In H. L. Fromkin & J. J. Sherwood (Eds.), *Integrating the organization: A social psychological analysis* (pp. 55–74). New York: Free Press.

Dunnette, M. D. (1979, May). *Goodbye r: Strategies for establishing person qualifications–job relatedness linkages.* Paper presented at Second Annual National Conference on EEO Compliance/

Human Resources Utilization, University of Chicago, Chicago.

Dunnette, M. D. (1982). Critical concepts in the assessment of human capabilities. In M. D. Dunnette & E. A. Fleishman (Eds.), *Human performance and productivity: Vol. 1. Human capability assessment* (pp. 1–11). Hillsdale, NJ: Erlbaum.

Dunnette, M. D., & Borman, W. C. (1979). Personnel selection and classification systems. *Annual Review of Psychology, 30,* 477–525.

Dunnette, M. D., Houston, J. S., Rosse, R. L., & Bosshardt, M. J. (1982). *Development and validation of an industry-wide electric power plant operator selection system.* Minneapolis, MN: Personnel Decisions Research Institute.

Dvorak, B. J. (1956). Advantages of the multiple cut-off method. *Personnel Psychology, 9,* 45–47.

Edwards, A. L. (1976). *An introduction to linear regression and correlation.* San Francisco: Freeman.

Einhorn, H. J. (1971). Use of nonlinear, noncompensatory models as a function of task and amount of information. *Organizational Behavior and Human Performance, 6,* 1–27.

Equal Employment Opportunity Commission, Civil Service Commission, Department of Labor, & Department of Justice. (1978). Uniform guidelines on employee selection procedures. *Federal Register,* August 25, *43* (No. 166), 38290–38315.

Eyde, L. D., & Kowal, D. M. (1987). Computerized test interpretation services: Ethical and professional concerns regarding U.S. producers and users. *Applied Psychology: An International Review, 36,* 401–417.

Feldman, J. M. (1981). Beyond attribution theory: Cognitive processes in performance appraisal. *Journal of Applied Psychology, 66,* 127–148.

Fine, S. A. (1955). Functional job analysis. *Journal of Personnel Administration and Industrial Relations, 2,* 1–16.

Frederiksen, N. (1986). Construct validity and construct similarity: Methods for use in test development and test validation. *Multivariate Behavior Research, 21,* 3–28.

Frederiksen, N., & Melville, S. D. (1954). Differential predictability in the use of test scores. *Educational and Psychological Measurement, 14,* 647–656.

Freyd, M. (1923). Measurement in vocational selection: An outline of research procedure. *Journal of Personnel Research, 2,* 215–249, 268–284, 377–385.

Gaugler, B. B., Rosenthal, D. B., Thornton, G. C., III, & Bentson, C. (1987). Meta-analysis of assessment center validity [Monograph]. *Journal of Applied Psychology, 72,* 493–511.

Ghiselli, E. E. (1956a). Dimensional problems of criteria. *Journal of Applied Psychology, 40,* 1–4.

Ghiselli, E. E. (1956b). The placement of workers: Concepts and problems. *Personnel Psychology, 1,* 1–9.

Ghiselli, E. E. (1966a). *The validity of occupational aptitude tests.* New York: Wiley.

Ghiselli, E. E. (1966b). The validity of a personnel interview. *Personnel Psychology, 19,* 389–394.

Ghiselli, E. E. (1973). The validity of aptitude tests in personnel selection. *Personnel Psychology, 26,* 461–477.

Gifford, R., Ng, C. F., & Wilkinson, M. (1985). Nonverbal cues in the employment interview: Links between applicant qualities and interviewer judgments. *Journal of Applied Psychology, 70,* 729–736.

Glass, G. V. (1976). Primary, secondary, and meta-analysis of research. *Educational Researcher, 5,* 3–8.

Glass, G. V. (1977). Integrating findings: The meta-analysis of research. *Review of Research in Education, 5,* 351–379.

Glass, G. V., McGraw, B., & Smith, M. L. (1981). *Meta-analysis in social research.* Beverly Hills, CA: Sage.

Gordon, H. W., & Leighty, R. (1988). Importance of specialized cognitive function in the selection of military pilots. *Journal of Applied Psychology, 73,* 38–45.

Gordon, M. E., & Fitzgibbons, W. J. (1982). Empirical test of the validity of seniority as a factor in staffing decisions. *Journal of Applied Psychology, 67,* 311–319.

Gottfredson, L. S. (Ed.). (1986). The *g* factor in employment. *Journal of Vocational Behavior, 29*(3).

Gough, H. G. (1985). A work orientation scale for the California Psychological Inventory. *Journal of Applied Psychology, 70,* 505–513.

Green, B. F., Jr. (1950). A note on the calculation of weights for maximum battery reliability. *Psychometrika, 15,* 57–61.

Greenberg, I. (1979). An analysis of the EEOC "four-fifths" rule. *Management Science, 25,* 762–776.

Griggs v. Duke Power Company, 401 U.S. 424.

Guilford, J. P. (1954). *Psychometric methods* (2nd ed.). New York: McGraw-Hill.

Guion, R. M. (1961). Criterion measurement and personnel judgments. *Personnel Psychology, 14,* 141–149.

Guion, R. M. (1965). *Personnel testing.* New York: McGraw-Hill.

Guion, R. M. (1966). Employment tests and discriminatory hiring. *Industrial Relations, 5,* 20–37.

Guion, R. M. (1976). Recruiting, selection, and job placement. In M. D. Dunnette (Ed.), *Handbook of industrial and organizational psychology* (pp. 777–828). Chicago: Rand McNally.

Guion, R. M. (1978). Scoring of content domain samples: The problem of fairness. *Journal of Applied Psychology, 63,* 499–506.

Guion, R. M. (1983). Comments on Hunter. In F. Landy, S. Zedeck, & J. Cleveland (Eds.), *Performance measurement and theory* (pp. 267–275). Hillsdale, NJ: Erlbaum.

Guion, R. M. (1987). Changing views for personnel research. *Personnel Psychology, 40,* 199–213.

Guion, R. M., & Cranny, C. J. (1982). A note on concurrent and predictive validity designs: A critical reanalysis. *Journal of Applied Psychology, 67,* 239–244.

Guion, R. M., & Gibson, W. M. (1988). Personnel selection and placement. *Annual Review of Psychology, 39,* 349–374.

Guion, R. M., & Gottier, R. F. (1965). Validity of personality measures in personnel selection. *Personnel Psychology, 18,* 135–164.

Gulliksen, H. (1950). Intrinsic validity. *American Psychologist, 5,* 511–517.

Gutenberg, R. L., Arvey, R. D., Osburn, H. G., & Jeanneret, P. R. (1983). Moderating effects of decision-making/information processing job dimensions on test validities. *Journal of Applied Psychology, 68,* 602–608.

Hakel, M. L. (1986). Personnel selection and placement. *Annual Review of Psychology, 37,* 351–380.

Harris, W. G. (1987). Computer-based test interpretations: Some development and application issues. *Applied Psychology: An International Review, 36,* 237–247.

Hedge, J. W., Lipscomb, M. S., & Teachout, M. S. (1987). Work sample testing in the Air Force job performance measurement project. In H. G. Baker & G. J. Laabs (Eds.), *Proceedings of the Department Defense/Educational Testing Service Conference on Job Performance Measurement Technologies.* Washington, DC: Office of the Assistant Secretary of Defense (Force Management and Personnel).

Helmreich, R. L., Sawin, L. L., & Carsrud, A. L. (1986). The honeymoon effect in job performance: Temporal increases in the predictive power of achievement motivation. *Journal of Applied Psychology, 71,* 185–188.

Hirsh, H. R., Schmidt, F. L., & Hunter, J. E. (1986). Estimation of employment validities by less experienced judges. *Personnel Psychology, 39,* 337–344.

Hodge, R. W., & Lagerfeld, S. (1987). The politics of opportunity. *Wilson Quarterly, 11*(5), 109–127.

Hogan, J., Hogan, R., & Busch, C. M. (1984). How to measure service orientation. *Journal of Applied Psychology, 69,* 167–173.

Holmes, T. H., & Rahe, R. H. (1967). The social readjustment rating scale. *Journal of Psychosomatic Research, 11,* 213–218.

Horst, P. (1966). *Psychological measurement and prediction.* Belmont, CA: Wadsworth.

Hough, L. M. (1984). Development and evaluation of the "accomplishment record" method of selecting and promoting professionals. *Journal of Applied Psychology, 69,* 135–146.

Hough, L. M., Keyes, M. A., & Dunnette, M. D. (1983). An evaluation of three "alternative" selection procedures. *Personnel Psychology, 36,* 261–276.

Howard, A. (1983). Work samples and simulations in competency evaluation. *Professional Psychology: Research and Practice, 14,* 780–796.

Humphreys, L. G. (1952). Individual differences. *Annual Review of Psychology, 3,* 131–150.

Hunter, J. E. (1983). A causal analysis of cognitive ability, job knowledge, job performance, and supervisory ratings. In F. Landy, S. Zedeck, & J. Cleveland (Eds.), *Performance measurement and theory* (pp. 257–266). Hillsdale, NJ: Erlbaum.

Hunter, J. E., & Hunter, R. F. (1984). Validity and utility of alternative predictors of job performance. *Psychological Bulletin, 96,* 72–98.

Hunter, J. E., Schmidt, F. L., & Jackson, G. B. (1982). *Meta-analysis: Cumulating research findings across studies.* Beverly Hills, CA: Sage.

Hunter, J. E., Schmidt, F. L., & Pearlman, K. (1982). History and accuracy of validity generalization equations: A response to the Callender and Osburn reply. *Journal of Applied Psychology, 67,* 853–858.

Ilgen, D. R. (1986). Laboratory research: A question of when, not if. In E. A. Locke (Ed.), *Generalizing from laboratory to field settings* (pp. 257–267). Lexington, MA: Lexington Books.

Ilgen, D. R., & Favero, J. L. (1985). Limits in generalization from psychological research to performance appraisal processes. *Academy of Management Review, 10,* 311–321.

Ironson, G. H., Guion, R. M., & Ostrander, M. (1982). Adverse impact from a psychometric perspective. *Journal of Applied Psychology, 67,* 419–432.

Ironson, G. H., & Smith, P. C. (1981). Anchors away-The stability of meaning of anchors when their location is changed. *Personnel Psychology, 34,* 249–262.

Ironson, G. H., & Subkoviak, M. J. (1979). A comparison of several methods of assessing item bias. *Journal of Educational Measurement, 16,* 209–225.

Jaeger, R. M. (Ed.). (1976). On bias in selection [Special issue]. *Journal of Educational Measurement, 13*(1).

James, L. R., & Brett, J. M. (1984). Mediators, moderators, and tests for mediation. *Journal of Applied Psychology, 69,* 307–321.

James, L. R., Mulaik, S. A., & Brett, J. M. (1982). *Causal analysis: Assumptions, models, and data.* Beverly Hills, CA: Sage.

Janz, T. (1982). Initial comparisons of patterned behavior description interviews versus unstructure interviews. *Journal of Applied Psychology, 67,* 577–580.

Jarrett, R. F. (1948). Percent increase in output of selected personnel as an index of test efficiency. *Journal of Applied Psychology, 32,* 135–145.

Jones, D. P. (1974). *An examination of six fair selection models.* Unpublished master's thesis, Bowling Green State University, Bowling Green, OH.

Klieman, L. S., & Faley, R. H. (1985). The implications of professional and legal guidelines for court decisions involving criterion-related validity: A review and analysis. *Personnel Psychology, 38,* 803–833.

Kroeck, K. G., Barrett, G. V., & Alexander, R. A. (1983). Imposed quotas and personnel selection:

A computer simulation study. *Journal of Applied Psychology, 68,* 123–136.

Kunin, T. (1955). The construction of a new type of attitude measure. *Personnel Psychology, 8,* 65–78.

Landy, F. J. (1986). Stamp collecting versus science: Validation as hypothesis testing. *American Psychologist, 41,* 1183–1192.

Landy, F. J., & Farr, J. L. (1980). Performance rating. *Psychological Bulletin, 87,* 72–107.

Landy, F. J., & Farr, J. L. (1983). *The measurement of work performance: Methods, theory, and applications.* New York: Academic Press.

Latham, G. P., & Saari, L. M. (1984). Do people do what they say? Further studies on the situational interview. *Journal of Applied Psychology, 69,* 569–573.

Latham, G. P., Saari, L. M., Pursell, E. D., & Campion, M. A. (1980). The situational interview. *Journal of Applied Psychology, 65,* 422–427.

Laurent, H. (1968). Research on the identification of management potential. In J. A. Myers (Ed.), *Predicting managerial success.* Ann Arbor, MI: Foundation for Research and Human Behavior.

Lawshe, C. H. (1952). What can industrial psychology do for small business (A symposium). 2. Employee selection. *Personnel Psychology, 5,* 31–34.

Lawshe, C. H. (1975). A quantitative approach to content validity. *Personnel Psychology, 28,* 563–575.

Lawshe, C. H., Bolda, R. A., Brune, R. L., & Auclair, G. (1958). Expectancy charts. II. Their theoretical development. *Personnel Psychology, 11,* 545–560.

Lee, R., & Foley, P. P. (1986). Is the validity of a test constant throughout the test score range? *Journal of Applied Psychology, 71,* 641–644.

Lifter, M., & Jones, D. (1978). *Firefighters selection research project, Vols. I–V.* Detroit, MI: Arthur Young.

Lifter, M. L., & White, M. L. (1984). *Clerical and meter reader testing program: Final report.* Detroit, MI: Arthur Young.

Link, H. C. (1919). *Employment psychology.* New York: Macmillan.

Linn, R. L. (1986). Comments on the *g* factor in employment testing. *Journal of Vocational Behavior, 29,* 438–444.

Linn, R. L., & Dunbar, S. B. (1986). Validity generalization and predictive bias. In R. A. Berk (Ed.), *Performance assessment: Methods and applications* (pp. 203–236). Baltimore, MD: Johns Hopkins.

Linn, R. L., Harisch, D. L., & Dunbar, S. B. (1981).

Corrections for range restriction: An empirical investigation of conditions resulting in conservative corrections. *Journal of Applied Psychology, 66,* 655–663.

Lord, F. M. (1962). Cutting scores and errors of measurement. *Psychometrika, 27,* 19–30.

Lord, F. M. (1963). Cutting scores and errors of measurement: A second case. *Educational and Psychological Measurement, 23,* 63–68.

Lord, F. M., & Novick, M. R. (1968). *Statistical theories of mental test scores* (with contributions by A. Birnbaum). Reading, MA: Addison-Wesley.

Mayfield, E. C., Brown, S. H., & Hamstra, B. W. (1980). Selection interviewing in the life insurance industry: An update of research and practice. *Personnel Psychology, 33,* 725–739.

McCormick, E. J., Jeanneret, P. R., & Mecham, R. C. (1972). A study of job characteristics and job dimensions as based on the Position Analysis Questionnaire (PAQ). *Journal of Applied Psychology, 56,* 347–368.

McCormick, E. J., Mecham, R. C., & Jeanneret, P. R. (1977). *Technical manual for the Position Analysis Questionnaire (PAQ) (System II).* Logan, UT: PAQ Services.

McMurry, R. N. (1947). Validating the patterned interview. *Personnel, 23,* 263–272.

McNamara, W. J., & Hughes, J. L. (1961). A review of research on the selection of computer programmers. *Personnel Psychology, 14,* 39–51.

Messick, S. (1988a). The once and future issues of validity: Assessing the meaning and consequences of measurement. In H. Wainer & H. I. Braun (Eds.), *Test validity* (pp. 33–45). Hillsdale, NJ: Erlbaum.

Messick, S. (1988b). Validity. In R. L. Linn (Ed.), *Educational measurement* (3rd ed. pp. 13–103). New York: Macmillan.

Mook, D. G. (1983). In defense of external invalidity. *American Psychologist, 38,* 379–387.

Morris, J., Sherman, J. D., & Mansfield, E. R. (1986). Failures to detect moderating effects with ordinary least squares—moderated multiple regression: Some reasons and a remedy. *Psychological Bulletin, 99,* 282–288.

Munsterberg, H. (1913). *Psychology and industrial efficiency.* Boston: Houghton Mifflin.

Murphy, K. R. (1987). Are we doing a good job measuring the wrong thing? In H. G. Baker & G. J. Laabs (Eds.), *Proceedings of the Department of Defense/Educational Testing Service Conference on*

Job Performance Measurement Technologies (pp. 49–56). Washington, DC: Office of the Assistant Secretary of Defense (Force Management and Personnel).

Myers, D. C., Jennings, M. C., & Fleishman, E. A. (1981). *Development of job-related medical standards and physical tests for count security officer jobs* (Report R81-3). Washington, DC: Advanced Research Resources Organization.

O'Connor, E. J., Wexley, K. N., & Alexander, R. A. (1975). Single-group validity: Fact or fallacy? *Journal of Applied Psychology, 60,* 352–355.

Office of Federal Contract Compliance. (1968). Validation of tests by contractors and subcontractors subject to the provisions of Executive Order 11246. *Federal Register,* September 24, *33,* (No. 186), 14392–14394.

Olian, J. D. (1984). Genetic screening for employment purposes. *Personnel Psychology, 37,* 423–438.

Orpen, C. (1985). Patterned behavior description interviews versus unstructured interviews: A comparative validity study. *Journal of Applied Psychology, 70,* 774-776.

Osborne, H. F. (1940). Oral trade questions. In W. H. Stead, C. L. Shartle, & Associates (Eds.), *Occupational counseling techniques: Their development and application* (pp. 30–48). New York: America Book.

Osburn, H. G., Callender, J. C., Greener, J. M., & Ashworth, S. (1983). Statistical power of tests of the situational specificity hypothesis in validity generalization studies: A cautionary note. *Journal of Applied Psychology, 68,* 115–122.

Paajanen, G. E. (1988). *The prediction of counterproductive behavior by individual and organizational variables.* Unpublished doctoral dissertation, University of Minnesota, Minneapolis.

Pannone, R. D. (1984). Predicting test performance: A content valid approach to screening applicants. *Personnel Psychology, 37,* 507–514.

Pearlman, K. (1980). Job families: A review and discussion of their implications for personnel selection. *Psychological Bulletin, 87,* 1–28.

Pearlman, K., Schmidt, F. L., & Hunter, J. E. (1980). Validity generalization results for tests used to predict job proficiency and training success in clerical occupations. *Journal of Applied Psychology, 65,* 373–406.

Personnel Designs, Inc. (1990). *The development and validation of selection procedures for construction and skilled trades occupations in the electric utility industry: Final technical report.* Washington, DC: Edison Electric Institute.

Personnel Designs, Inc. (in press [a]). *The development and validation of selection procedures for entry-level supervisory positions in the insurance and financial service industries.* Atlanta, GA: Life Office Management Association.

Personnel Designs, Inc. (in press [b]). *The development and validation of selection procedures for technical occupations in the electric utility industry: Final technical report.* Washington, DC: Edison Electric Institute.

Peterson, N. G., & Bownas, D. A. (1982). Skill, task structure, and performance acquisition. In M. D. Dunnette & E. A. Fleishman (Eds.), *Human performance and productivity. Vol. 1: Human capability assessment* (pp. 49–105). Hillsdale, NJ: Erlbaum.

Peterson, N. G., Houston, J. S., & Rosse, R. L. (1979, 1981, 1982). *The LOMA job effectiveness prediction system: Reports 1, 2, 3, and 4.* Minneapolis, MN: Personnel Decisions Research Institute.

Raju, N. S., Edwards, J. E., & LoVerde, M. A. (1985). Corrected formulas for computing sample sizes under indirect range restriction. *Journal of Applied Psychology, 70,* 565–566.

Rasmussen, K. G., Jr. (1984). Nonverbal behavior, verbal behavior, resume credentials, and selection interview outcomes. *Journal of Applied Psychology, 69,* 551–556.

Richardson, M. W. (1941). The combination of measures. In P. Horst (Ed.), *The prediction of personal adjustment* (pp. 379–401). New York: Social Science Research Council.

Ronning, R. R., Glover, J. A., Conoley, J. C., & Witt, J. C. (Eds.). (1987). *The influence of cognitive psychology on testing.* Hillsdale, NJ: Erlbaum.

Rossi, P. H., & Williams, W. (1972). *Evaluating social programs.* New York: Seminar.

Rothe, H. F., & Nye, C. T. (1959). Output rates among machine operators. II. Consistency related to methods of pay. *Journal of Applied Psychology, 43,* 417–420.

Rubin, D. B. (1988). Discussion. In H. Wainer & H. I. Braun (Eds.), *Test validity* (pp. 241–256). Hillsdale, NJ: Erlbaum.

Ryan, A. M., & Sackett, P. R. (1987). A survey of individual assessment practices by I/O psychologists. *Personnel Psychology, 40,* 455–488.

Sackett, P. R. (1982). The interviewer as hypothesis tester: The effects of impressions of an applicant on interviewer questioning strategy. *Personnel Psychology, 35,* 789–804.

Sackett, P. R., Cornelius, E. T., III, & Carron, T. J. (1981). A comparison of global judgment vs. task-oriented approaches to job classification. *Personnel Psychology, 34,* 791–804.

Sackett, P. R., & Decker, P. J. (1979). Detection of deception in the employment context: A review and critical analysis. *Personnel Psychology, 32,* 487–506.

Sackett, P. R., & Wade, B. E. (1983). On the feasibility of criterion-related validity: The effects of range restriction assumptions on needed sample size. *Journal of Applied Psychology, 68,* 374–381.

Sackett, P. R., Zedeck, S., & Fogli, L. (1988). Relations between measures of typical and maximum job performance. *Journal of Applied Psychology, 73,* 482–486.

Saunders, D. R. (1956). Moderator variables in prediction. *Educational and Psychological Measurement, 16,* 209–222.

Schmidt, F. L., Berner, J. G., & Hunter, J. E. (1973). Racial differences in validity of employment tests: Reality or illusion? *Journal of Applied Psychlogy, 58,* 5–9.

Schmidt, F. L., Gast-Rosenberg, I., & Hunter, J. E. (1980). Validity generalization results for computer programmers. *Journal of Applied Psychology, 65,* 643–661.

Schmidt, F. L., Greenthal, A. L., Berner, J. G., Hunter, J. E., & Seaton, F. W. (1977). Job sample vs. paper-and-pencil trades and technical tests: Adverse impact and examinee attitudes. *Personnel Psychology, 30,* 187–197.

Schmidt, F. L., & Hunter, J. E. (1977). Development of a general solution to the problem of validity generalization. *Journal of Applied Psychology, 62,* 529–540.

Schmidt, F. L., & Hunter, J. E. (1981). Employment testing: Old theories and new research findings. *American Psychologist, 36,* 1128–1137.

Schmidt, F. L., Hunter, J. E., & Caplan, J. R. (1981). Validity generalization results for two job groups in the petroleum industry. *Journal of Applied Psychology, 66,* 261–273.

Schmidt, F. L., Hunter, J. E., Croll, P. R., & McKenzie, R. C. (1983). Estimation of employment test validities by expert judgment. *Journal of Applied Psychology, 68,* 590–601.

Schmidt, F. L., Hunter, J. E., McKenzie, R. C., & Muldrow, T. W. (1979). Impact of valid selection procedures on work force productivity. *Journal of Applied Psychology, 64,* 609–626.

Schmidt, F. L., Hunter, J. E., & Outerbridge, A. N. (1986). Impact of job experience and ability on job knowledge, work sample performance, and supervisory ratings of job performance. *Journal of Applied Psychology, 71,* 434–439.

Schmidt, F. L., Hunter, J. E., & Pearlman, K. (1981). Task differences as moderators of aptitude test validity in selection: A red herring. *Journal of Applied Psychology, 66,* 166–185.

Schmidt, F. L., Hunter, J. E., & Pearlman, K. (1982). Progress in validity generalization: Comments on Callender and Osburn and further developments. *Journal of Applied Psychology, 67,* 835–845.

Schmidt, F. L., Hunter, J. E., Pearlman, K., & Shane, G. S. (1979). Further tests of the Schmidt-Hunter Bayesian validity generalization procedure. *Personnel Psychology, 32,* 257–281.

Schmidt, F. L., Hunter, J. E., & Urry, V. W. (1976). Statistical power in criterion-related validity studies. *Journal of Applied Psychology, 61,* 473–485.

Schmitt, N., Gooding, R. Z., Noe, R. A., & Kirsch, M. (1984). Meta-analysis of validity studies published between 1964 and 1982 and the investigation of study characteristics. *Personnel Psychology, 37,* 407–422.

Schmitt, N., & Ostroff, C. (1986). Operationalizing the "behavioral consistency" approach: Selection test development based on a content-oriented strategy. *Personnel Psychology, 39,* 91–108.

Schneider, B., & Schmitt, N. (1986). *Staffing organizations.* Glenview, IL: Scott, Foresman.

Smith, C. A., Organ, D. W., & Near, J. P. (1983). Organizational citizenship behavior: Its nature and antecedents. *Journal of Applied Psychology, 68,* 653–663.

Smith, P. C., Budzeika, K. A., Edwards, N. A., Johnson, S. M., & Bearse, L. N. (1986). Guidelines for clean data: Detection of common mistakes. *Journal of Applied Psychology, 76,* 457–460.

Smith, P. C., & Kendall, L. M. (1963). Retranslation of expectations: An approach to the construction of unambiguous anchors for rating scales. *Journal of Applied Psychology, 47,* 149–155.

Snyder, M., & Swann, B. M. (1978). Hypothesis-testing processes in social interaction. *Journal of Personality and Social Psychology, 36,* 1202–1212.

Society for Industrial and Organizational Psychology. (1987). *Principles for the validation and use of personnel selection procedures* (3rd ed.). College Park, MD: Author.

Spence, J. T., Helmreich, R. L., & Pred, R. S. (1987). Impatience versus achievement strivings in the Type A pattern: Differential effects on students' health and academic achievement. *Journal of Applied Psychology, 72,* 522–528.

Stone, E. F. (1988). Moderator variables in research: A review and analysis of conceptual and methodological issues. In K. M. Roland & G. R. Ferris (Eds.), *Research in personnel and human resources management* (Vol. 6, pp. 191–229). Greenwich, CT: JAI Press.

Streuning, E. L., & Guttentag, M. (Eds.). (1975). *Handbook of evaluation research* (Vols. 1 & 2). Beverly Hills, CA: Sage.

Sussman, M., & Robertson, D. U. (1986). The validity of validity: An analysis of validation study designs. *Journal of Applied Psychology, 71,* 461–468.

Tenopyr, M. L., & Oeltjen, P. D. (1982). Personnel selection and classification. *Annual Review of Psychology, 33,* 581–618.

Thorndike, R. L. (1949). *Personnel selection: Test and measurement techniques.* New York: Wiley.

Thorndike, R. L. (1971). Concepts of culture fairness. *Journal of Educational Measurement, 8,* 245–251.

Thurstone, L. L. (1928). Attitudes can be measured. *American Journal of Sociology, 33,* 529–554.

Tiffin, J. (1942). *Industrial psychology.* Englewood Cliffs, NJ: Prentice-Hall.

Tyler, L. E. (1986). Back to Spearman? *Journal of Vocational Behavior, 29,* 445–450.

Uhrbrock, R. S. (1950). Standardization of 724 rating scale statements. *Personnel Psychology, 3,* 285–316.

Uhrbrock, R. S. (1961). 2000 scaled items. *Personnel Psychology, 14,* 375–420.

U. S. Department of Labor (1970). *Manual for the U. S. E. S. General Aptitude Test Battery. Section III: Development.* Washington, DC: Manpower Administration, U. S. Department of Labor.

Vicino, F. L., & Bass, B. M. (1978). Lifespace variables and managerial success. *Journal of Applied Psychology, 63,* 81–88.

Wallace, S. R. (1965). Criteria for what? *American Psychologist, 20,* 411–417.

Wells, D. G., & Fruchter, B. (1970). Correcting the correlation coefficient for explicit restriction on both variables. *Educational and Psychological Measurement, 30,* 925–934.

Wolfe, J. H., Alderton, D. L., Cory, C. H., & Larson, G. E. (1987). Reliability and validity of new computerized ability tests. In H. G. Baker & G. J. Laabs (Eds.), *Proceedings of the Department of Defense/Educational Testing Service Conference on Job Performance Measurement Technologies* (pp. 369–382). Washington, DC: Office of the Assistant Secretary of Defense (Force Management and Personnel).

Yerkes, R. R. (Ed.). (1921). *Memoirs of the National Academy of Sciences, Vol. XV: Psychological examining in the United States Army.* Washington, DC: Government Printing Office.

Zedeck, S., Tziner, A., & Middlestadt, S. E. (1983). Interviewer validity and reliability: An individual analysis approach. *Personnel Psychology, 36,* 355–370.

CHAPTER 7

Recruitment, Job Choice, and Post-hire Consequences: A Call for New Research Directions

Sara L. Rynes
University of Iowa

To date, recruitment research has concentrated primarily on three topics: recruiters, recruitment sources, and realistic job previews. Each of these topics has developed in isolation from the others, with the result that there is little basis for integration across the various research streams. For example, research on recruiters tends to use field survey methodologies to explain applicant perceptions of job attractiveness. In contrast, realistic job preview research uses field experiments to explain post-hire attitudes and behaviors, particularly turnover.

This chapter argues that this piecemeal approach to recruitment research leaves unanswered many important questions about attracting applicants to organizations. An alternative framework, incorporating a larger number of contextual, independent, dependent, and process variables, is offered to guide future research. In particular, it is suggested that future research place increased emphasis on the broader context in which recruitment occurs, the interdependencies between different phases of the recruitment process, and the potential trade-offs between quantity and quality in recruiting outcomes.

READERS OF THE first edition of this *Handbook* will probably not remember much about the section on organizational recruiting. In that volume, recruitment received less than one page of coverage in a chapter addressing recruitment, selection, and job placement. The author, Robert Guion (1976), explained the reason this way:

> Technology in employee selection is more highly developed than in recruiting or placement; therefore, the major emphasis is on selection....Recruiting or placement are not less important processes; to the contrary, they probably are more vital and more profitable to the organization. An organization's success in recruiting defines the applicant population with which it will work; selection is more pleasant, if not easier, when any restriction of range or skewness of distribution is attributable to an overabundance of well-qualified applicants....Unfortunately, the contributions and confusions of the literature, the central social pressures, and the facts of contemporary practice conspire to place the emphasis on selection.
> (pp. 777–779)

Despite the brevity of his recruitment discussion, Guion did offer two substantive conclusions: (a) Little recruitment research existed as of 1976 and (b) where it did, it was not characterized by a "search for understanding."

Since that time, the empirical literature on recruitment has expanded considerably. Moreover, there have been a number of important conceptual advances. In particular, researchers have begun to speculate as to how recruitment might influence applicant and employee behaviors. Some theoretical models pertain to recruitment practices in general (e.g., Boudreau & Rynes, 1985; Schwab, Rynes, & Aldag, 1987), while others pertain to specific practices, such as choice of recruitment sources (e.g., Breaugh,

1981; Schwab, 1982) or effects of realistic versus traditional job previews (e.g., Breaugh, 1983; Reilly, Brown, Blood, & Malatesta, 1981; Wanous, 1977, 1980). In addition, a broader range of potential outcomes, such as expectancies of receiving offers or effects of new hires on current employees, have been linked to recruitment (e.g., Boudreau & Rynes, 1985; Schwab, 1982; Sutton & Louis, 1987).

Despite these advances, some of the most central questions about applicant attraction remain almost completely unaddressed. Examples of questions that employers frequently ask, but researchers have not answered, include the following:

- We have a limited amount of money to spend on attracting applicants. What is the most cost-effective way to spend it: on realistic recruitment, on recruitment advertising, on training recruiters, or on improving the characteristics of our vacancies?

- We are willing to train recruiters if we think we can recoup our investment. What are the most essential content areas for recruiters to master? What kinds of improvements can we expect to obtain in terms of applicant acceptance rates or higher acceptee quality?

- Unfortunately, we are constrained to paying below-market wages and salaries. Can we still attract high-quality applicants? If so, how?

- What can we do to really distinguish our organization so that it will be attractive to applicants?

- Dollar for dollar, are we better off recruiting at top-tier or second-tier universities?

- When should we begin campus recruiting to get the greatest number of high-quality applicants? What are the implications of sending (or not sending) recruiters if we might have vacancies but won't know for several months?

- Our recruiters are complaining that we have a poor organizational image on campuses. What are the components of organizational image, and how hard is it to change them?

- We would like to be completely honest with applicants during recruitment, but our line managers argue that we will lose our best candidates because everyone else is "selling" their vacancies. Are they right?

- We spend lots of money on recruiting films and wine and cheese receptions. However, very few applicants bother to attend. What are we doing wrong?

As these questions suggest, recruitment research has advanced in a fragmented fashion. Some topics generate many studies (e.g., recruiters, realistic job previews), while others (e.g., job and organizational attributes, recruitment timing), generate almost none. This chapter will attempt to place recruitment research in a broader context and, in so doing, will direct attention toward new questions that might be of interest to organizational decision makers charged with attracting and retaining a quality work force.

Organization of the Chapter

The chapter is divided into three sections: theory, research, and suggestions for future research. The theory section outlines (a) the major recruitment practices and activities (i.e., independent variables) that have dominated previous speculation and research, (b) the principal outcomes of those practices and activities (i.e., dependent variables), and (c) the process or intervening variables believed to determine

the precise nature of the impact of recruitment activities on outcomes.

The research section reviews previous empirical work in three major categories of recruitment practices and activities. These include (a) recruiters and other organizational representatives, (b) recruitment sources, and (c) administrative policies and procedures, including realistic job previews.

The suggestions for future research section calls for a broader conceptualization of the recruitment function as well as increased variety in future empirical work. Suggestions are made for (a) incorporating additional independent and dependent variables, (b) paying greater attention to the context in which recruitment occurs, and (c) studying the adaptive and interactive features of the recruitment process.

Recruitment Theory

Recruitment theories have focused primarily on *process* variables—that is, on the psychological or environmental mechanisms believed to determine the outcomes of various recruitment practices. However, to discuss these processes, it is first necessary to delineate the major practices (independent variables) and outcomes (dependent variables) that comprise the recruitment domain. We will begin with a discussion of recruitment practices and activities, followed by recruitment outcomes and hypothesized recruitment processes. A summary of these variables and their interrelationships is shown in Figure 1.

Independent Variables

Conceptually, a wide range of policies, practices, and decisions might be regarded as part of organizational recruitment (Rynes & Boudreau, 1986; Taylor & Bergmann, 1987).

FIGURE 1

Summary of Previous Recruitment Theory and Research

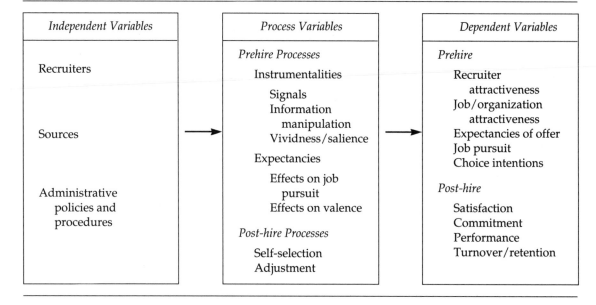

Independent Variables	Process Variables	Dependent Variables

Recruiters
 	
Sources
 	
Administrative
  policies and
  procedures
	Prehire Processes
	Instrumentalities
	  Signals
	  Information
	    manipulation
	  Vividness/salience
	Expectancies
	  Effects on job
	    pursuit
	  Effects on valence
	
	Post-hire Processes
	Self-selection
	Adjustment
		Prehire
		  Recruiter
		    attractiveness
		  Job/organization
		    attractiveness
		  Expectancies of offer
		  Job pursuit
		  Choice intentions
		
		Post-hire
		  Satisfaction
		  Commitment
		  Performance
		  Turnover/retention

However, a review of previous theory (e.g., Schwab, 1982; Wanous, 1977), empirical research (e.g., Alderfer & McCord, 1970; Gannon, 1971; Reilly, Brown, Blood, & Malatesta, 1981), and descriptive research (e.g., Miner, 1979) reveals that recruitment researchers have primarily been concerned with three sets of recruitment variables.

First, research on *recruiters* has focused on the impact of various recruiter characteristics, such as demographics or behaviors, on applicant impressions and decisions. *Recruitment source* research has focused on employer preferences for various sources and on differences in post-hire outcomes among individuals hired through various sources. Finally, research on administrative policies and procedures has examined the roles of realistic previews, recruitment follow-ups, recruiting expenditures, and application processes on job acceptance rates and post-hire outcomes.

Dependent Variables

For the most part, specific recruitment outcomes have been linked rather narrowly to particular recruitment activities. Thus, for example, we have theories of how recruiters influence job choices (e.g., Rynes, Heneman, & Schwab, 1980; Rynes & Miller, 1983) and how recruitment sources influence employee retention (e.g., Breaugh, 1981; Schwab, 1982). In contrast, we have no explicit theories of how sources influence job acceptance or how recruiters influence employee retention.

In an attempt to devise a more general framework for recruitment research, Boudreau and Rynes (1985) integrated recruitment activities into a standard selection utility model. In the process, they identified a variety of potential outcomes that might be affected by recruitment practices. Among these outcomes are variability in qualifications, service costs, and service value. However, only a small subset of the outcome variables suggested by Boudreau and Rynes (1985) have been empirically investigated.

This chapter will focus primarily on outcome variables that have been investigated with some regularity. Generally speaking, these can be classified into two categories: prehire outcomes and post-hire outcomes. *Prehire* outcomes include applicant impressions of recruiters, perceived job or organizational attractiveness, intentions to pursue job offers, expectancies of receiving offers, and actual job choices. *Post-hire* outcomes consist of such variables as satisfaction, commitment, performance, and length of service.

For reasons most likely related to convenience, research on recruiters and recruitment follow-ups has focused almost exclusively on prehire variables. Indeed, with few exceptions (e.g., Taylor & Bergmann, 1987), applicant reactions to recruiters have been obtained immediately following recruitment interviews, but no later. Thus, we have virtually no information about whether or how recruiters influence actual job choices or post-hire adjustment.

In contrast, recruitment source studies and realistic preview research have focused on post-hire outcomes such as satisfaction, performance, and turnover. Again, convenience appears to have played a role: Selectees represent a convenient sample for correlating post-hire effects with prehire variables, both of which can easily be obtained from personnel files. Unfortunately, the practice of studying only selectees introduces competing explanations for observed post-hire phenomena, including potentially serious selection biases (e.g., Lord & Novick, 1968). Equally important, it prohibits investigation of the immediate objective of recruitment—applicant attraction.

Process or Intervening Variables

Increased attention has also been paid to the psychological processes through which recruitment activities and practices translate into applicant decisions and behaviors. However, specific hypotheses vary, depending on whether the concern is with prehire or posthire outcomes. As such, the two are discussed separately.

Prehire Outcomes.   Here, the challenge is to show why recruitment practices should have *any* impact on job choices, over and above characteristics of vacancies per se (see Rynes et al., 1980). After all, the major economic (e.g., Lippman & McCall, 1976; Rottenberg, 1956; Smith, 1976) and psychological models of job choice (e.g., Soelberg, 1967; Vroom, 1964) view those choices as a function of job characteristics rather than recruitment practices.

For example, in expectancy theory, job choices are viewed as a function of the perceived instrumentalities and valences of the characteristics associated with alternative offers (Vroom, 1964). Motivation to pursue alternatives is viewed as a function of the preceding variables (i.e., instrumentalities and valences), multiplied by perceived expectancies of successful pursuit (e.g., probabilities of receiving the various job offers). Thus, the question remains: How might recruitment practices alter applicants' job pursuit strategies or their ultimate job choices?

Rynes et al. (1980) and Schwab (1982) have proposed several ways in which recruitment practices might affect job choices. One set of explanations emphasizes uncertainty in *instrumentality* estimates; the other emphasizes uncertainty regarding *expectancies*.

Instrumentality Effects.   This set of explanations follows from the fact that many important characteristics of vacancies, such as quality of supervision or opportunities for promotion, cannot be determined with certainty before job acceptance. Uncertain instrumentalities would seem to permit at least three possible kinds of recruitment effects.

First, in the absence of perfect information, applicants may interpret recruitment characteristics as *signals* or *cues* concerning unknown organizational attributes (see Einhorn & Hogarth, 1981; Spence, 1973). Thus, recruiter preparedness may become a symbol of general organizational efficiency; dining extravagance may become a signal of the firm's ability to pay.

Second, imperfect attribute information permits recruiters and other organizational representatives to *consciously manipulate* the information they give applicants about job characteristics. Indeed, the entire realistic recruitment literature can be viewed as an attempt to understand the consequences of such manipulations.

The third possibility is that, in contrast to the vague information applicants have about job attributes, recruiter behaviors leave rather *vivid impressions* on applicants. If so, recruitment practices may become highly salient features in applicants' decision models, regardless of whether or not they represent valid bases for making decisions about a job choice (e.g., Behling, Labovitz, & Gainer, 1968).

Expectancy Effects.   At the beginning of a job search, most job seekers are unsure about how well they are likely to do in the job market. More specifically, they are unlikely to know much about the total number of viable alternatives, the number or quality of competing applicants, or how they will be perceived by employers relative to other applicants. Indeed, field research suggests that most applicants approach the job market with considerable apprehension and a feeling of relative disadvantage vis-à-vis employers (e.g., Reynolds, 1951; Sheppard & Belitsky, 1966).

Given this uncertainty, individuals are likely to be on the lookout for any information that might help them estimate their chances of receiving offers. Thus, recruitment experiences may become major sources of expectancy cues: "Did the recruiter look enthusiastic during my interview? Did the recruiter tell me when to expect the next call?"

Expectancy estimates may in turn influence eventual job choices. First, applicants who receive positive expectancy cues may be more motivated to continue *pursuing* a job offer (Schwab, Rynes, & Aldag, 1987; Wanous, 1977). Increased pursuit, in turn, increases the probability of actually receiving an offer, which in turn enhances the probability that the job will ultimately be chosen.

A second possibility is that expectancy perceptions have a direct effect on perceived job *valence* (Rynes & Lawler, 1983). That is, applicants who perceive high probabilities of receiving an offer may cognitively distort their perceptions of its characteristics in a favorable direction (Soelberg, 1967). It should be noted, however, that this hypothesis is inconsistent with expectancy theory, which posits the independence of expectancies and valences.

Post-hire Effects.   Explanations of how recruitment practices influence post-hire outcomes fall into one of two categories: self-selection or adjustment. The *self-selection* hypothesis suggests that variations in recruitment practices create differences in the type of individual who enters the organization in the first place. The best-known articulation of this view comes from the realistic recruitment literature, which hypothesizes that applicants self-select on the basis of "fit" between personal needs and organizational climates (Wanous, 1980).

In contrast, *adjustment* explanations focus on the possibility that some recruitment practices better prepare acceptees for early work experiences than others. Again, the fullest articulation of this explanation is found in the realistic recruitment literature, which posits that realistic information may aid adjustment by reducing new employee expectations, increasing commitment, or triggering anticipatory coping mechanisms (e.g., Reilly et al., 1981).

However, one can think of other recruitment practices that might affect adjustment as well. For example, recruiting from the same sources year after year may create a homogeneous environment to which new entrants quickly adjust (e.g., Louis, 1981; Sutton & Louis, 1987). However, this early adjustment may come at the expense of longer term organizational stagnation and lack of adaptability (e.g., Schneider, 1983, 1987). Alternatively, recruitment from elite sources may facilitate early adjustment (due to high employee ability), but may be associated with early turnover as well (due to high employee marketability).

In summary, previous theoretical work has focused largely on three independent variables: recruiters, recruitment sources, and administrative policies and practices. These variables are presumed to influence both prehire and post-hire outcomes through a variety of intervening process mechanisms as summarized in Figure 1. Empirical research related to each of these independent variables will be summarized in the following discussion.

Previous Research

Recruiters

Overview.   Prior to publication of the first edition of this *Handbook,* most recruitment research focused on applicant likes and dislikes with respect to organizational recruiters (e.g., Downs, 1969). The implicit assumption was that recruiters are capable of affecting applicants' job choice decisions. That assumption was not formally tested, however; impressions of recruiters were not linked empirically to other attitudes or behaviors.

Beginning with Alderfer and McCord (1970), recruiter characteristics began to be treated explicitly as independent variables, potentially capable of influencing a variety of dependent variables. Thus, for the first time,

perceptions of recruiters were empirically linked to choice-related outcomes such as perceived organizational attractiveness and self-reported probabilities of job acceptance.

Table 1 summarizes recruiter research following the publication of Alderfer and McCord's (1970) ground-breaking study. To qualify for inclusion in the table, a study had to (a) present new empirical findings (literature reviews were excluded); (b) address recruiters as central, rather than secondary, issues; (c) be published; and (d) include both independent (recruiter) and dependent (outcome) variables. This last condition disqualified most early recruiter-related research (e.g., Downs, 1969; Driscoll & Hess, 1974; Hilgert & Eason, 1968; for a review, see Rynes et al., 1980).

Before reviewing and evaluating this research, a few general characteristics should be noted. For example, with one exception, subjects have been college students interviewing through campus placement offices. Additionally, field surveys have outnumbered experimental studies by nearly two to one, with most field data collected immediately following initial campus interviews.

In terms of independent variables, three kinds of recruiter characteristics have been examined: (a) recruiter demographics (sex, race, and age), (b) functional area (personnel versus line recruiter, recruiter versus job incumbent), and (c) personality and behavioral traits. Note that these last variables are perceptual in nature and must be inferred by applicants. In field studies, such traits have typically been derived via factor analyses of applicant reactions, a trend begun by Schmitt and Coyle (1976).

Relative to recruitment's implied dependent variable—job choice—operational dependent variables have ranged from distal to proximal criteria, for example, from general impressions of recruiters to stated probabilities of offer acceptance. Generally speaking, previous dependent variables can be grouped into four areas: (a) overall impressions of recruiters, (b)

TABLE 1

Summary of Previous Research Concerning Recruiter Effects on Applicants

Study	Method	Subjects	Independent Variables	Dependent Variables	Results
Alderfer & McCord, 1970	Field survey: postinterview questionnaire	112 MBA students	13 perceptions of recruiter behavior during interview	1. Expectancy of receiving offer 2. Probability of accepting offer	1. *Expectancy of receiving offer* related to recruiter's: willingness to answer questions, interest in applicant, understanding of applicant's perspective, being trustworthy and likable, familiarity with applicant's background, being successful young man, and not making applicant uncomfortable 2. *Probability of accepting offer* related to all of the above, plus recruiter talking about concerns of other MBAs
Wyse, 1972	Field survey: postinterview questionnaire	457 seniors in business	1. Recruiter race 2. Applicant race	1. Attitudes toward recruiters 2. Cynicism toward recruiters	1. Whites were indifferent to recruiter race; blacks preferred black recruiters 2. Black applicants were more cynical about recruiter's truthfulness
Schmitt & Coyle, 1976	Field survey: postinterview questionnaire; factor analysis of applicant impressions	237 undergraduates	Applicant perceptions of: 1. Recruiter warmth 2. Recruiter mannerisms 3. Recruiter aggressiveness 4. Recruiter presentation 5. Extent of job information 6. Recruiter opinions	(Multiple measures of): 1. Impressions of recruiter 2. Impressions of company 3. Likelihood of receiving offer 4. Probability of offer acceptance	1. Recruiter warmth and friendliness predicted all 9 dependent variables 2. Recruiter information about job predicted 7 of 9 dependent variables

TABLE 1

Summary of Previous Research Concerning Recruiter Effects on Applicants (continued)

Study	Method	Subjects	Independent Variables	Dependent Variables	Results
Rogers & Sincoff, 1978	Experiment: audiotaped interviews with questionnaire	312 undergraduates	1. Recruiter age 2. Recruiter title 3. Recruiter presentation	Impression of recruiter	1. Significant main effects for age, title, and presentation 2. Significant age x title interaction 3. Significant age x title x presentation interaction
Fisher, Ilgen, & Hoyer, 1979	Experiment: mailed questionnaire	90 seniors in business	Source of information: recruiter vs. job incumbent	1. Trust in source 2. Expertise of source 3. Affect toward source 4. Interest in company	1. Incumbents were more trusted than recruiters 2. Incumbents were better liked than recruiters 3. Less likely to accept offer if the information source is a recruiter
Herriott & Rothwell, 1981	Field survey: pre- and postinterview questionnaires	72 graduating British students	Applicant perceptions of 7 recruiter behaviors during interview	Intentions to accept offers	No single recruiter behaviors were related to acceptance intentions, but certain combinations of behaviors were related
Rynes & Miller, 1983 (Study 1)	Experiment: videotaped interviews with postviewing questionnaire	133 business undergraduate students	1. Recruiter affect 2. Recruiter knowledge of job	1. Impressions of recruiter 2. Likelihood applicant will receive offer 3. Job attractiveness 4. Pursuit intentions	1. *Recruiter affect* influenced impressions of recruiter, perceived likelihood of receiving offer, perceptions of how company treats employees, and willingness to attend second interview 2. *Recruiter information* influenced impressions of recruiter, expectancies of receiving offer, job attractiveness, and willingness to follow up on job

TABLE 1

Summary of Previous Research Concerning Recruiter Effects on Applicants (continued)

Study	Method	Subjects	Independent Variables	Dependent Variables	Results
Rynes & Miller, 1983 (Study 2)	Experiment: videotaped interviews with postviewing questionnaire	175 business undergraduate students	1. Recruiter affect 2. Job attributes	1. Impression of recruiter 2. Likelihood applicant will receive offer 3. Job attractiveness 4. Pursuit intentions	1. *Recruiter affect* influenced impressions of recruiter and expectancies of offer; no influence on job attractiveness or pursuit intentions 2. *Job attributes* influenced overall job attractiveness, perceptions of how well company treats employees, and willingness to attend second interview and to accept offer
Powell, 1984	Field survey: postinterview questionnaires; factor analysis of applicant impressions	200 graduating college students	1. Perceived recruiter affect 2. Perceived recruiter responsiveness and knowledge 3. Perceived job attributes	Likelihood of job acceptance	Perceptions of recruiters were not significantly associated with acceptance intentions when perceived job attributes were controlled
Harn & Thornton, 1985	Field survey: postinterview questionnaire; factor analysis of applicant impressions	105 graduating college students	Applicant impressions of: 1. Recruiter counseling behaviors 2. Indications that applicant was suitable for job 3. Recruiter informativeness 4. Recruiter interpersonal sensitivity 5. Recruiter listening skills	1. Perceived recruiter warmth and friendliness 2. Willingness to accept offer	1. *Perceived recruiter warmth* was affected by counseling behaviors, indications of suitability, and recruiter listening skills 2. *Willingness to accept offer* was influenced by counseling behaviors and listening skills

TABLE 1

Summary of Previous Research Concerning Recruiter Effects on Applicants (continued)

Study	Method	Subjects	Independent Variables	Dependent Variables	Results
Liden & Parsons, 1986	Field survey: postinterview questionnaire; factor analysis of applicant impressions	422 applicants for seasonal position at amusement park	1. Recruiter sex 2. Applicant impressions of: a. Recruiter competence b. Recruiter personableness c. Recruiter informativeness	1. Affect toward interview 2. Affect toward job 3. Intention to accept offer	1. Affect toward the interview was influenced by recruiter personableness 2. Affect toward the job was influenced by recruiter personableness and informativeness 3. No interview effects on acceptance intentions were found
Harris & Fink, 1987	Field survey: pre- and postinterview questionnaires; factor analysis of applicant impressions	145 graduating college students	Applicant impressions of: 1. Recruiter personableness 2. Recruiter competence 3. Recruiter informativeness 4. Recruiter aggressiveness 5. Recruiter sex 6. Personnel vs. line recruiter	1. Instrumentality of perceived job attributes 2. Expectancy of offer 3. Intention to accept offer 4. Regard for company	1. Perceived recruiter traits influenced all 4 dependent variables 2. No significant effects were found for recruiter sex or recruiter function (personnel vs. line)
Taylor & Bergmann, 1987	Field survey: questionnaires at five stages of recruitment process	1,286 applicants to large manufacturing firm (declining number of subjects at each successive phase)	1. Recruiter demographics 2. Recruiter self-descriptions of interview behavior 3. Applicant description of recruiter interview behavior	1. Company attractiveness 2. Probability of offer acceptance 3. Job offer decision 4. Tenure intentions	1. *Company attractiveness* was lower when the recruiter was older, female, or from the personnel department 2. *Probability of offer acceptance* was lower when the recruiter was female (especially when the applicant was also female), when the recruiter was perceived as cold and unfriendly, and when the recruiter reported a low degree of interview structure

expectancies of receiving offers, (c) perceived job or organizational attractiveness, and (d) probabilities of pursuing or accepting offers.

In the sections that follow, recruiter research will be reviewed in terms of the major independent variable categories of recruiter demographics, functional area, and personality or behavioral traits. The review will be followed by a summary and evaluation.

Recruiter Demographics. Studies of recruiter demographics have rarely presented a theoretical rationale as to why such superficial variables might make a difference in applicants' job choices (e.g., Rogers & Sincoff, 1978). However, a look at the variables that have been investigated suggests at least two implicit theories.

One hypothesis seems to be that *similarity bias* causes applicants to favor recruiters whose demographic characteristics are similar to their own. This is suggested by the fact that several authors have tested for significant recruiter demographic x applicant demographics interactions.

A second hypothesis is that applicants hold *general biases* against certain classes of recruiters, regardless of personal characteristics. This phenomenon would be revealed via main effects favoring certain classes of recruiters over others. It should be noted, however, that the root causes of such biases are not apparent from the existence of main effects per se. For example, applicants might be less favorably disposed to female recruiters either because they do not like them or because femaleness is associated with low power and status. In the latter case, a perceived low recruiter status might unwittingly signal that the vacancy is also low in prestige, thus making it less attractive to applicants.

In regard to recruiter *age*, the possibility of similarity bias has not been tested because subjects have all been homogeneously young. However, Taylor and Bergmann (1987) did find a significant ($p < .01$) negative relationship between recruiter age and perceived company attractiveness at the campus interview stage. Given that the average applicant was 23 years old, this result is consistent with either kind of potential bias.

Rogers and Sincoff (1978) experimentally manipulated recruiter age (20, 30, or 50 years) and then observed the effects on overall impressions of the recruiter. Analyses revealed a positive main effect for age, as well as significant age interactions with recruiter title and verbal fluency. However, closer inspection of the data revealed a curvilinear age effect, with the 30-year-old perceived most positively and the 20-year-old least positively. In retrospect, it appeared that the 20-year-old was not viewed as a credible organizational representative, particularly when introduced as "recruiting director for Sterling Industries."

Thus, ignoring the noncredible manipulation level, Rogers and Sincoff's results also suggest a bias against older recruiters, since the 30-year-old was favored over the 50-year-old. Again, however, it is unclear whether this result is due to similarity or general bias. To distinguish between the two would require a broader distribution of applicant age and explicit tests for applicant age x recruiter age interactions.

Only two studies have examined the effects of recruiter *race*. Wyse (1972) found that black applicants preferred black recruiters, but that race made little difference to white applicants. These results support the presence of similarity or general bias on the part of blacks, but not on the part of whites. On the other hand, Taylor and Bergmann (1987) found that recruiter race made no difference in terms of job attractiveness or probability of accepting an offer. Note, however, that their dependent variables were further removed from recruiter characteristics per se and as such were less likely to yield significant differences.

Three studies examined the effects of recruiter *sex*, with mixed results. Harris and

Fink (1987) found no effects for recruiter sex, applicant sex, or their interaction on any of their dependent variables (perceived job attributes, expectancy of an offer, intention to accept an offer, or general regard for the organization). In contrast, both Liden and Parsons (1986) and Taylor and Bergmann (1987) reported significant sex effects. However, their findings were in opposite directions. Liden and Parsens observed more favorable reactions to female recruiters, particularly among female applicants. In contrast, Taylor and Bergmann (1987) found that female recruiters were associated with lower job attractiveness, as well as with lower probabilities of accepting an offer, among female (but not male) applicants. Although the reasons for these differences are impossible to discern, possible explanations include the higher job levels in Taylor and Bergmann's study or the higher proportion of applicants from male-dominated occupations.

In summarizing the demographic research, it is important to note that with a single exception, the only cases where demographics have had significant impacts involve dependent variables far removed from job acceptance (i.e., overall impressions of the recruiter and/or the interview). Thus, only in Taylor and Bergmann (1987) was any recruiter demographic characteristic associated with perceptions of job attractiveness or intentions to accept an offer. Moreover, even there, effect sizes were very small in comparison with other recruiter characteristics (i.e., empathy and informativeness) and did not maintain significance at later stages of the recruiting process. Thus, although recruiter demographics may influence impressions of recruiters, there is little evidence that they have important effects on job choice.

Recruiter Function. Both Harris and Fink (1987) and Taylor and Bergmann (1987) examined whether line or personnel recruiters create more positive impressions on applicants. Conceptually, personnel recruiters might be expected to excel in terms of general company knowledge and interviewing skills, whereas line recruiters might have advantages in terms of more specific job-related information and (possibly) higher status.

In any event, Harris and Fink (1987) found no differences by recruiter function for any of their dependent variables. In contrast, Taylor and Bergmann (1987) observed lower company attractiveness ratings among applicants interviewed by personnel specialists.

In a tangentially related study, Fisher, Ilgen, and Hoyer (1979) examined the effect of disseminating job information via "formal" organizational recruiters versus job incumbents. Subjects were sent information about a job and were told to assume that it had come from one of four sources: a recruiter, job incumbent, friend, or professor. Results showed that job incumbents, professors, and friends were better liked and more trusted than formal recruiters. Probabilities of accepting an offer were also lowest when the subjects were told that the information had come from a recruiter.

Thus, although job incumbents and recruiters are both presumably organizational representatives, recruiters appear to be regarded with greater skepticism. On a purely speculative basis, perhaps the lower job attractiveness associated with personnel recruiters in Taylor and Bergmann's (1987) study reflects a feeling that personnel representatives are primarily recruiters, while line representatives are primarily co-workers or supervisors (and recruiters only secondarily).

Recruiter Personality and Behavioral Traits. Several field studies have asked applicants to rate recruiters in terms of multiple behaviors exhibited during recruiting interviews (Harn & Thornton, 1985; Harris & Fink, 1987; Herriott & Rothwell, 1981; Liden & Parsons, 1986; Powell, 1984; Schmitt & Coyle, 1976; Taylor & Bergmann, 1987). Responses have then been factor analyzed to produce anywhere from two to six recruiter traits, as summarized in the "Independent Variables" column of Table 1. In addition, one two-part experimental study (Rynes & Miller, 1983) manipulated a videotaped recruiter's behavior to reflect the two traits most commonly derived from such factor analyses: recruiter affect (primarily warmth and supportiveness) and recruiter informativeness about a vacancy.

Although different studies attach different labels to similar factors, in every study the trait that explained the most variance in all dependent variables had something to do with recruiter affect, variously labeled warmth, enthusiasm, counseling, personableness, or empathy. A second factor, reflecting informativeness about the vacancy, also emerged in every study and as a general rule explained the second most variance across dependent variables. Beyond these two factors, however, results diverge across studies. Moreover, other factors have rarely explained much additional variance in dependent variables.

Evaluation. Although a number of studies have established empirical links between perceived recruiter traits and variables related to job choice (e.g., expectancies, instrumentalities, or pursuit intentions), there are reasons to be cautious about concluding that recruiters have important impacts on job choices. One reason is that with the exception of Taylor and Bergmann (1987), subjects were questioned either immediately or very shortly after the initial employment interview. This is when recruiter behaviors are likely to be of greatest salience to applicants, given that other experiences, such as competing interviews or plant visits, are likely to supplant these impressions over time. Indeed, this is precisely what Taylor and Bergmann (1987) found in the only multistage study to date: Recruitment variables had an impact on perceived company attractiveness at the campus interview stage, but not at any of four later stages.

A second reason to be cautious about the impact of recruiters on job choice is that recruiter effect sizes are generally small. This is particularly true (a) as dependent variables get conceptually closer to job choice and (b) when job attributes are also taken into account—in short, precisely under the conditions in which real-world job choices are made.

Regarding point (a), it is instructive to look at explained variance figures from studies that assessed multiple dependent variables with varying degrees of proximity to job choice. For these purposes, it seems reasonable to assume that the least choice-related variables are those that reflect impressions of the recruiter per se, while those closest to choice involve intentions to pursue or accept job offers.

Schmitt and Coyle (1976) reported the following multiple correlations (R, not R^2) between six factor analytically derived recruiter traits and the following dependent variables:

- Overall perception of recruiter
  pleasantness   .68

- Overall perception of recruiter
  competence   .67

- Change in favorableness toward
  interviewer's company   .56

- Likelihood of further exploring a job
  possibility with the company   .48

- Estimate of likelihood of receiving job
  offer immediately after interview   .44

- Estimate of likelihood of job acceptance
  immediately after interview   .33

Similarly, Harn and Thornton (1985) reported that recruiter counseling behaviors explained 47 percent of the variance in perceived recruiter warmth, but only 13 percent of variance in willingness to accept a job offer. Harris and Fink (1987) did not report effects of recruiter behavior on overall impressions of the recruiter, but did report effects on regard for the company (R^2 = .19), the job (R^2 = .09), and job acceptance intentions (R^2 = .10). Taylor and Bergmann (1987) reported significant effects of recruiter empathy on company attractiveness and probability of offer acceptance immediately following the campus interview, but nonsignificant effects thereafter.

In the only experimental study of this kind, Rynes and Miller (1983, Study 1) manipulated recruiter affect and informativeness via videotaped job interviews. Affect accounted for 19 percent of the variance in how well the recruiter represented the company, but only 6 percent in perceived company treatment of employees and 4 percent in whether subjects would accept a second interview.

In general, then, the pattern is clear: Recruiter behaviors have moderate effects on overall impressions of the recruiter, but small or nonsignificant effects on intentions to pursue or accept job offers. Moreover, this is true even at the point at which the recruiter would be expected to have maximal impact—immediately following the recruitment interview.

Growing evidence suggests that once job attributes are taken into account, recruiter traits add little or nothing to explained variance in recruiting outcomes. In fact, Harris and Fink's (1987) study is the only one to report a significant recruiter impact on job choice intentions, controlling for job attributes.

In contrast, Powell (1984) found that perceived recruiter characteristics (path coefficient = .17) did not explain a significant amount of variance in probabilities of offer acceptance, once perceived job attributes (path coefficient = .46) were taken into account. Similarly, in the only experimental study to simultaneously examine recruiters and job attributes, Rynes and Miller (1983) found that recruiter affect influenced job attractiveness and pursuit intentions only when job attributes were held constant (Study 1). When job attributes were also manipulated (Study 2), these recruiter effects were no longer significant.

Taylor and Bergmann (1987) did not collect job attribute information following the campus interview, but collected both recruiter and attribute information at the plant visit stage. Only job attributes had a significant effect on company attractiveness following the plant visit; the change in R^2 due to expected attributes was .29 versus .02 for a set of recruitment variables. In terms of the probability of accepting an offer, only one recruitment variable—discussion of on-site factors—had a significant effect, and that was negative. As a whole, the set of recruitment variables did not explain significant variance in probabilities of offer acceptance.

In sum, previous research suggests that recruiters probably do not have a large impact on actual job choices. Generally speaking, the size of observed recruiter effects (rarely very large to begin with) appears to decrease as (a) dependent variables get conceptually closer to actual job choice, (b) vacancy characteristics are taken into account, and (c) applicants get further along in the recruitment process.

In addition, it should be noted that all previous field studies share a methodological confound that may have caused more variance to be attributed to recruiters than is actually merited. Specifically, applicants have provided data subsequent to recruitment interviews that obviously include both recruiter and job attribute content. Previous researchers have implicitly assumed either that (a) perceptions of job attributes and recruiter behaviors are formulated independently of one another or (b) recruiter behaviors influence perceptions of job attributes; but not vice versa. A third possibility is that impressions of job attributes spill over onto perceptions of the recruiter such that when the vacancy is attractive, applicants may attribute more positive characteristics to the recruiter as well.

Although field research inherently confounds these alternative causal processes, previous researchers have analyzed and interpreted their results as if only the first two are possible.[1] As such, more variance may have been attributed to recruiters than warranted.

Two final comments pertain to future research possibilities. First, the vast majority of what we know about this area comes from campus recruiters and initial screening interviews. Arguably, campus recruiters are less likely than other organizational representatives to have an impact on applicant decisions because (a) they are unlikely to play an important future role in applicants' daily work lives and (b) they are seen at early stages of the job choice process. Thus, organizational representatives involved in second and third interviews (e.g., potential supervisors and co-workers) may have larger impacts than those observed in the research just reviewed.

Of course, it could be argued that potential supervisors and co-workers reflect job attributes rather than recruitment variables. To some extent, this is true. However, at least part of the behavior of potential supervisors and co-workers during a plant visit is properly attributed to recruitment, given that people often act differently during recruitment than they do in daily work life. As such, supervisor and co-worker recruiting behaviors are really only signals—some more accurate than others—of what they will "really be like" to work with.

A second issue that has been neglected is whether improved recruiter selection and training might produce more favorable impacts on job applicants and, if so, what kinds of training are merited. Early research suggested that most recruiters were perceived as ill-prepared and ineffective (e.g., Rynes et al., 1980). More recently, Rynes and Boudreau (1986) documented that most recruiters receive little training, even in large, financially successful organizations. Moreover, where training is provided, it tends to focus on procedural and administrative issues such as filling out records rather than on substantive ones such as what kinds of questions to ask job applicants or what to tell them about the company and job.

It may be, then, that recruiters have had little impact in field research because there are few really good campus recruiters. If so, there may be serious restriction of range in observed recruiter behaviors, centered around a low average level of effectiveness.

It would seem desirable to conduct recruiter training field experiments in much the same manner as realistic preview experiments. Still, extant research suggests that there may be a fairly low limit to what can be accomplished merely by altering the messenger (i.e., recruiter) or the message (realistic preview). Therefore, any such studies should pay careful attention to other variables that might also play a significant role in applicant attraction (e.g., labor market conditions and job attributes).

Recruiting Sources

Overview.   Early studies of recruiting sources focused primarily on differences in employee retention. Based on this criterion, early results suggested that employee referrals were superior to other sources, particularly newspaper advertisements (e.g., Gannon, 1971; Reid, 1972; Ullman, 1966).

Subsequent researchers have broadened the focus of source studies in two ways. First, they have examined a wider variety of dependent variables, including performance, absenteeism, and work attitudes. Second, they have speculated about the processes underlying observed relationships between sources and outcomes.

Table 2 summarizes previous source-related research. Note that although the specific sources examined vary across studies, all have looked at referrals and newspaper advertisements, and nearly all at direct applications and employment agencies. On the dependent variable side, turnover has been most widely studied, although absenteeism, performance, and worker attitudes have also been examined.

The "Other Variables" column reflects the fact that later researchers have sometimes measured additional variables in an attempt to explain the origins of source-related differences. Selection of these variables has largely been governed by the theoretical debate as to whether source-related differences are caused by (a) differences in the type of information conveyed by various sources, or the *realistic information hypothesis* (Breaugh, 1981; Hill, 1970; Ullman, 1966), or (b) differences in the personal characteristics of individuals recruited through various sources, or the *individual differences hypothesis* (Schwab, 1982; Taylor & Schmidt, 1983).

The following review is organized around the following topics: (a) outcome differences by source, (b) attempts to explain outcome differences (i.e., tests of the individual differences versus realistic information hypotheses), and (c) evaluation of the research.

Outcome Differences by Source. The most frequently observed result in source research has been that individuals recruited through employee referrals have lower (or later) *turnover* than other groups (e.g., Conard & Ashworth, 1986; Decker & Cornelius, 1979; Gannon, 1971; Reid, 1972; Ullman, 1966). However, this finding has not been universal. Breaugh and Mann (1984) and Swaroff, Barclay, and Bass (1985) found no turnover differences across sources, whereas Taylor and Schmidt (1983) found the lowest turnover among rehires.

Six studies have examined differences in employee *performance* by source. Three (Hill, 1970; Swaroff et al., 1985; Taylor & Schmidt, 1983) found no significant differences (although in all three of Hill's samples, the direction of performance ratings favored referrals). Breaugh (1981) found that scientists recruited through college placement were rated lower on work quality and dependability than direct applicants and respondents to professional journal advertisements. Those recruited through newspapers were also rated lower than the

other two sources, but only on dependability. Caldwell and Spivey (1983) found that formal advertising was generally more likely to yield successful store clerks, although racial groups varied in terms of specific results. Finally, Breaugh and Mann (1984) reported that social service workers who applied directly had higher performance ratings than other groups. In summary, there has been little consistency in previous findings concerning relationships between source and performance.

Only two studies examined the relationship between source and *absenteeism*, again with varying results. Breaugh (1981) found that research scientists recruited through newspapers were absent twice as often as those recruited through other sources. Taylor and Schmidt (1983) observed significantly lower absenteeism for rehired seasonal packaging employees than for all other sources.

Finally, two studies looked at differences in *worker attitudes* by source. Breaugh (1981) found that scientists recruited through college placement exhibited lower job involvement and lower satisfaction with supervision than did scientists recruited in other ways. Latham and Leddy (1987) reported that referrals had higher organizational commitment and job involvement than did newspaper recruits, and higher job satisfaction than either newspaper recruits or direct applicants.

Attempts to Explain Differences in Source Outcomes. Although the realistic information and individual differences hypotheses are not necessarily mutually exclusive, at least three studies have compared their relative usefulness for explaining source-related differences in work behaviors or attitudes (Breaugh & Mann, 1984; Conard & Ashworth, 1986; Taylor & Schmidt, 1983). Before reviewing them, it should be noted that several other studies have assessed variables pertinent to at least one of the two hypotheses (see Table 2), although they are not examined here.

TABLE 2

Studies of Recruitment Source Effectiveness

Study	Sample	Sources Investigated	Dependent Variables	Other Variables	Results
Ullman, 1966	263 clerical workers in 2 organizations	1. Referrals 2. Newspaper ads 3. Employment agencies	Turnover within 12 months	None	Lower turnover among referrals in both organizations
Hill, 1970	203 clerical workers in 3 insurance firms	1. Referrals 2. Nonreferrals	Performance rating	None	Nonsignificant effect on performance at all 3 firms
Gannon, 1971	6,390 bank employees	1. Referrals 2. Employment agencies 3. Advertisements 4. Direct applications 5. Rehires 6. High school referrals	Quit rates after 12 months	None	Employee referrals had the lowest quit rates
Reid, 1972	876 laid-off engineering & metals trade workers	1. Referrals 2. Direct applications 3. Advertisements 4. Employment services	Turnover within 12 months	None	Referrals stayed on the job longer (significance tests not reported)

TABLE 2

Studies of Recruitment Source Effectiveness (continued)

Study	Sample	Sources Investigated	Dependent Variables	Other Variables	Results
Decker & Cornelius, 1979	2,466 employees in 3 industries; multiple jobs	1. Newspapers 2. Employment agencies 3. Referrals 4. Direct applications	Turnover rates after 12 months	None	Referrals had lowest turnover rates in all 3 organizations; differences were significant in banking and insurance
Breaugh, 1981	112 research scientists	1. Newspapers 2. College placements 3. Journal ads 4. Direct applications	1. Absenteeism 2. Performance ratings 3. Attitudes: work satisfaction; satisfaction with supervisor; job involvement	1. Age 2. Sex 3. Education 4. Years with company 5. Years in present position	1. *Performance*: college placement inferior on rated quality and dependability; newspaper inferior on dependability 2. *Absenteeism*: newspaper inferior 3. *Attitudes*: college placement showed lower job involvement and satisfaction with supervisor 4. *Demographics*: no differences across sources
Quaglieri, 1982	64 recent business school graduates	1. Formal sources 2. Referrals 3. Direct applications	Perceptions of source accuracy and specificity in describing job	None	Formal sources were perceived as less specific and less accurate than other sources
Caldwell & Spivey, 1983	1,400 racially diverse store clerks	1. Referrals 2. In-store notices 3. Employment services 4. Media (mostly newspapers)	1. Performance (rated potential for reemployment) 2. Turnover within 30 days	Race	1. Formal advertising was more likely to produce a successful performer 2. Multiple differences by race

TABLE 2

Studies of Recruitment Source Effectiveness (continued)

Study	Sample	Sources Investigated	Dependent Variables	Other Variables	Results
Taylor & Schmidt, 1983	293 seasonal workers in packaging plant	1. Referrals 2. Newspapers 3. Employment services 4. Radio 5. Rehires 6. TV 7. Direct applications	1. Performance rating 2. Turnover 3. Attendance ratings	1. Height and weight 2. Sex 3. Previous pay 4. Shift preference	1. No differences in performance ratings by source 2. Rehires had longer tenure and less absenteeism 3. Rehires differed in terms of individual differences variate 4. Once individual differences were controlled, no source differences were found for absenteeism and turnover
Breaugh & Mann, 1984	98 social service workers	1. Newspapers 2. Referrals 3. Direct applications	1. Performance ratings 2. Turnover in 12 months	1. Perceived realism of source 2. Demographics 3. Perceived ease of movement at time of hire 4. Retrospective ratings of training and education at hire	1. Performance was highest among direct applicants 2. No source differences were found in overall retention, but there were fewer involuntary terminations among referrals 3. Referrals reported more realistic information 4. Newspaper ads produced more male and older employees

TABLE 2

Studies of Recruitment Source Effectiveness (continued)

Study	Sample	Sources Investigated	Dependent Variables	Other Variables	Results
Swaroff, Barclay, & Bass, 1985	618 technical salespersons	1. Referrals 2. Direct applications 3. Newspapers 4. Employment agencies 5. College recruitment	1. Voluntary turnover in 2 years 2. Performance: rating; percent sales quota in years 1 and 2	1. Age 2. Marital status 3. Number of prior jobs	1. No differences were found in turnover by source 2. No source differences were found in performance 3. Various demographic differences were found by source
Conard & Ashworth, 1986	5,822 life insurance agents	1. Referrals 2. Newspapers	Turnover within 12 months	1. Aptitude index battery 2. Accuracy of job knowledge at hire	1. Differences in aptitude accounted for significant portion of source-turnover relationship; differences in knowledge about the job did not 2. Differences in turnover by source remained even after individual differences were partialed out
Latham & Leddy, 1987	68 employees of auto dealerships; mixed occupations	1. Referrals 2. Direct applications 3. Newspapers	1. Organizational commitment 2. Job satisfaction 3. Job involvement	None	1. Referrals were superior to newspapers in terms of organizational commitment and job involvement 2. Referrals were superior to both newspapers and direct application in terms of job satisfaction

First, in some cases, observed differences in perceived realism were not linked to other dependent variables, but rather were examined as ends in themselves (e.g., Quaglieri, 1982). In other cases, only one of the two hypotheses was specifically addressed. For example, Hill (1970) measured only perceived source accuracy. Breaugh (1981) measured demographic characteristics but did not specifically relate them to the individual differences hypothesis. (Conversely, Breaugh cited the realism hypothesis as a possible explanation for his findings but did not measure realism.) Finally, Swaroff et al. (1985) intended to address both hypotheses but found no significant source-outcome relationships to "explain."

Turning to the studies that addressed both issues simultaneously, Taylor and Schmidt (1983) constructed an individual differences variate composed of personal characteristics that managers believed to be related to performance and tenure. Rehires were found to differ from all other sources in terms of this variate. (Recall that rehires also stayed longer and were absent less frequently than other groups in their study.) Moreover, when individual differences were entered first into a hierarchical regression, source per se no longer accounted for significant variance in either turnover or absenteeism. Consequently, Taylor and Schmidt (1983) interpreted their results as supporting the individual differences hypothesis.

It should be noted that Taylor and Schmidt did not directly measure source realism; rather, they inferred it, based on logic and previous research. Moreover, they conceded that rehires probably had highly realistic information as compared with other applicants. In addition, they acknowledged that one reason for failing to find positive effects for referrals (generally assumed to be a "realistic" source) may have been that the company paid monetary bonuses for successful referrals.

Thus, the positive findings for rehires are, by themselves, consistent with either

hypothesis. However, Taylor and Schmidt's interpretation in favor of individual differences rests on their finding that no source-related absenteeism or turnover differences remained once individual differences were controlled.

In contrast, Breaugh and Mann (1984) reported greater support for the realistic information hypothesis. Specifically, they found significant source-related differences on four of five retrospective measures of perceived source realism. However, they found only two demographic differences (sex and age) by source, no differences in a personnel manager's retrospective ratings of employee qualifications at time of hire, and no differences in employees' (retrospectively recalled) alternative employment opportunities at time of hire. As such, they argued there was little support for the existence of individual differences across sources.

However, Breaugh and Mann did not explicitly analyze the extent to which differences in perceived realism accounted for differences in performance or retention. Rather, the greater number of significant differences in perceived realism (versus individual characteristics) was merely presumed to "explain" differences in performance. (There were no differences in retention.) A more appropriate procedure would have been to determine the extent to which source, perceived realism, and individual differences each accounted for unique variance in performance or retention.

Conard and Ashworth (1986) tested the two hypotheses using a sample of nearly 6,000 life insurance agents. Their study improved on previous research in two ways. First, rather than obtaining retrospective measures of perceived realism, they measured what applicants actually *knew* about the job at the point of application. Second, their individual differences measure (an empirically scored biographical inventory blank [BIB]) came closer than previous measures to assessing the type of individual differences that might have important impacts on post-hire outcomes. That is, the BIB assessed job-related abilities and aptitudes, whereas previous studies focused mainly on applicant demographics (with little theoretical justification).

Using a series of partial and semipartial correlations, Conard and Ashworth found that individual differences in BIB scores accounted for a significant portion of the source-turnover relationship. In contrast, differences in prehire knowledge of the job did not. As such, they obtained more support for the individual differences hypothesis than the realistic information hypothesis. However, significant source effects remained even when individual differences and job knowledge were taken into account, suggesting that additional mechanisms might also be operating.

In summary, attempts to look at the predominant explanations of source-outcome relationships have produced mixed results. Two studies supported the individual differences hypothesis, one the realistic information hypothesis.

These mixed results are probably due in part to the use of weak measures of the hypothesized constructs. With the exception of Conard and Ashworth (1986), source studies have been characterized by superficial individual difference variables, such as demographics or retrospective accounts of alternative opportunities, and by use of contaminated and deficient measures of information accuracy, such as retrospective accounts of perceived realism.

Nevertheless, the causes of inconsistency in previous results probably extend beyond weak measurement. Also implicated are (a) other uncontrolled differences across studies, (b) failure to examine source-related differences prior to hire, and (c) inadequate conceptualization of source-outcome linkages. We turn now to these issues.

Evaluation. The ability to draw conclusions from previous research is hampered by numerous potentially confounding differences across studies. Specifically, studies have varied not only in terms of sources, outcome variables, and operationalizations, but also in terms of statistical power (sample sizes ranged from 68 to more than 6,000), type of subject (e.g., professional versus clerical), whether or not widely varying job types were aggregated into a single analysis, timing of initiation of study (e.g, 6-week post-hire follow-ups vs. cross-sectional surveys of incumbents with varying tenure), and duration of study (6 week- to 2-year follow-ups).

One can easily imagine how some of these variables might affect the conclusions drawn. For example, studies that aggregate widely varying job types inherently confound source explanations of turnover with other explanations (e.g., job attractiveness), given that (a) different sources are used to fill different job types (Schwab, 1982) and (b) different job types have differential turnover rates (see also Swaroff et al., 1985). In addition, studies based on incumbents with widely varying job tenure are less likely to uncover significant turnover differences than are studies that track newly hired cohorts, given that most turnover occurs early in job tenure.

Yet another confound may come from potential correlations between source usage and other variables that affect ease of attraction or retention. For example, newspaper advertisements and other formal sources may be used primarily when less formal methods, such as referrals, prove ineffective, as can be the case with unattractive vacancies or in tight labor markets (Schwab, 1982; Ullman, 1966). If so, advertisements may appear to be inferior sources, when in fact the lower success rates stem from other correlated but unmeasured causes.

Another serious problem with previous research is the failure to examine the impact of recruitment sources during the actual recruitment process. Without exception, source studies have been initiated when recruitment has already been completed—that is, when all organizational selection and applicant self-selection processes have already operated. As a result, there are multiple competing explanations for observed source differences.

For example, if we observe that retention rates for employee-referred selectees are higher than they are for newspaper-generated selectees, we do not know whether the initial pool of referrals was superior to the newspaper recruits in terms of personal characteristics and/or knowledge of the job, whether referrals were treated differently by the employer during the recruitment process (e.g., recruited more vigorously), whether the two groups had different reactions to the recruitment message (e.g., differential self-selection), whether employers treated referred employees more favorably after hire (e.g., paid more attention to them because they had a "sponsor"), or whether referred applicants adjusted better to the job because they had better prehire information (the cause most frequently assumed by previous researchers). Neither theory nor empirical research has pursued these important distinctions.

Source theories and research have also been weak in terms of delineating expected differences across various dependent variables (e.g., job choice, retention, performance). Indeed, turnover is the only outcome variable for which there is any semblance of a source theory. For example, performance has been included in empirical studies with little theoretical justification, a fact that probably accounts for the decidedly mixed results with respect to that outcome.

More importantly, there has been no speculation or research as to how recruitment sources affect job choice, despite the fact that influencing job choice is the immediate objective of the recruitment process. Moreover, one would almost certainly predict differences in job choice processes between, say, Harvard MBAs and MBAs from state universities, or between unemployed and employed job seekers (see Schwab, Rynes, & Aldag, 1987).

Finally, even the two most well-developed hypotheses have been vague as to precisely

what kinds of informational differences (e.g., information about the company? the vacancy? the immediate supervisor?) or individual differences (e.g., aptitudes? abilities? credentials?) are most likely to be observed across sources and to make a difference to recruiting outcomes. In sum, much work remains to be done, conceptually and empirically, before we can offer sound conclusions concerning recruitment sources.

Administrative Policies and Practices

Previous theory and research have not devoted much attention to defining the domain of recruitment policies and practices. However, where such variables have been considered, one or more of the following have generally been included: (a) timing of recruitment follow-ups, (b) policies regarding recruitment expenditures, such as reimbursement policies, (c) nature of the application process, and (d) realism of recruitment messages[2] (e.g., Rynes & Boudreau, 1986; Schwab, 1982; Taylor & Bergmann, 1987).

Only the last topic has generated a substantial body of research. Thus, it will be discussed separately, following a brief review of less well-studied practices.

General Policies and Practices. Administrative practices have been hypothesized to affect job applicants in one of two ways: Either they signal something about the company (e.g., organizational efficiency or ability to pay), or they influence applicants' expectancies of receiving job offers (Rynes et al., 1980).

Other than realistic job previews, the most frequently researched administrative practice has been the promptness of follow-up contacts between various stages of the recruitment process. Two early studies (Arvey, Gordon, Massengill, & Mussio, 1975; Ivancevich & Donnelly, 1971) suggested that dropouts from the applicant pool might be minimized by timely follow-up contacts. However, Taylor and Bergmann (1987) observed no relationship between length of follow-up and perceived company attractiveness. Thus, previous studies again appear to have produced conflicting results.

Although it is risky to speculate from only three studies, the fact that different dependent variables were involved may be of substantive importance. Specifically, the two studies that reported a timing effect (Arvey et al., 1975; Ivancevich & Donnelly, 1971) assessed whether individuals were still part of the applicant pool, whereas the one that did not (Taylor & Bergmann, 1987) assessed perceived job attractiveness among those who remained in their sample at the postcampus interview stage.

Two studies have also examined whether recruiting expenditures on meals, hotels, and the like have any impact on recruitment outcomes. Taylor and Bergmann (1987) examined this question from the perspective of job applicants, Rynes and Boudreau (1986) from that of corporate recruiting directors. Neither study found any evidence of significant relationships between expenditures and outcomes.

Finally, a single study (Gersen, 1976) examined the effects of implementing a more rigorous application process for teacher applicants. There, implementation of a process requiring college transcripts, evidence of teaching certification, and five personal references—in addition to the customary application form—produced only half as many applicants as in previous years. However, contrary to expectations, no detectable differences were observed in applicant quality.

Realistic Job Previews. No recruitment issue has generated more attention than realistic job previews. Indeed, because realistic preview research has already been extensively reviewed (e.g., Breaugh, 1983; McEvoy & Cascio, 1985; Premack & Wanous, 1985; Wanous, 1977; Wanous, 1980; Wanous and Colella, 1988; Wanous & Premack, 1986), the following section will address broad themes

and issues rather than single studies as in previous sections.

Theory. The primary focus of realistic recruitment theory is employee retention rather than applicant attraction. Indeed, realistic recruitment theory hypothesizes that customary strategies for attracting applicants may have detrimental effects on subsequent attempts to retain employees.

The most common hypotheses pertaining to retention involve either applicant self-selection or early work adjustment. *Self-selection* has been conceptualized as the "matching of individual needs and organizational climates" (Wanous, 1980, p. 42). Presumably, this matching leads to lower turnover by producing a better fit between organizational characteristics and characteristics of individuals who remain in the applicant pool.

Empirically, however, the self-selection construct has been operationalized via job acceptance rates. As such, it is impossible to tell whether differences in acceptance rates reflect "matching," in the sense just discussed, or some other phenomenon. For example, an alternative possibility is that realistic job previews (RJPs) cause *adverse* self-selection, whereby the most qualified applicants withdraw from the applicant pool due to the "realistic" (usually more negative) information provided. Because empirical research has failed to distinguish between these two effects (or any other), the self-selection hypothesis will be referred to as the *dropout hypothesis* when reviewing previous research.

Hypotheses pertaining to *early work adjustment* fall into several categories. The most frequently mentioned is the *met expectations hypothesis*, which posits that people are less likely to be dissatisfied, and hence to quit, when early job experiences match pre-employment expectations. The *coping hypothesis* suggests that realistic information allows new hires to devise anticipatory strategies for dealing with problems likely to arise on the job. Finally, the *commitment hypothesis* suggests that people develop stronger commitment to organizations that give them the information they need to make fully informed job choices.

The preceding hypotheses all pertain to the presumed relationship between realism and turnover. However, empirical researchers have also examined the relationship between realistic information and *performance* (Premack & Wanous, 1985).

Despite the growing body of empirical research, theories as to how realistic recruitment might affect job performance are not well developed. Wanous (1978) hypothesized that realistic previews might help new recruits focus their work efforts by removing role ambiguity. Two years later, he cited validation evidence suggesting that performance is affected by the degree of matching between applicant qualifications and job requirements, but he did not link this point explicitly to realistic previews (Wanous, 1980). Moreover, in both discussions, Wanous (1978, 1980) predicted that the RJP-performance relationship was likely to be weak because performance depends on many factors "other than just how well abilities are matched to job requirements" (1980, p. 16).

In summary, theories linking realism to performance are quite general. Moreover, they do not predict strong relationships. Perhaps as a result, empirical research investigating RJP-performance links has been largely atheoretical.

Previous Research.   Three meta-analyses have examined relationships between realistic job previews and turnover. In the first, Reilly et al. (1981) aggregated results from 11 studies and found a significant negative relationship ($Z = 4.33, p < .0001$) between realism and turnover. More specifically, they observed a 5.7 percentage point difference between experimental (19.8%) and control group (25.5%) turnover rates.

In addition, Reilly et al. (1981) found a significant moderator effect for job complexity.

For "simple" jobs (categorized by the authors as telephone operators, telephone service representatives, sewing machine operators, and supermarket clerks), there were no significant turnover differences in any of the individual studies, and only a 1.9 percent overall difference when aggregated across studies. In contrast, studies involving more "complex" jobs (i.e., West Point cadets, Marine Corps recruits, life insurance sales representatives) produced a 9.4 percent difference (14.9% vs. 24.3%). Two other potential moderators were tested (preview medium, length of follow-up), but neither was significant.

Reilly et al. (1981) also concluded that there was little support in previous RJP literature for any of the common process hypotheses (i.e., the dropout, coping, met expectations, or commitment hypotheses). However, process variables were reviewed narratively rather than through meta-analysis.

McEvoy and Cascio (1985) reviewed 15 realistic preview studies and 5 job enrichment studies designed to assess effects on turnover. They obtained an average correlation of .09 between realism and retention and a mean effect size *(d)* of .19; comparable statistics for job enrichment were .17 and .35. On average, those receiving realistic previews had turnover rates of 30 percent, as compared with 40 percent for control groups. Like Reilly et al. (1981), McEvoy and Cascio (1985) also reported a significant moderator effect for job complexity: The average correlation for complex jobs was .12 and for simple jobs was .02.

Given the small size of the correlation between realistic previews and turnover, McEvoy and Cascio concluded that "managers might do well to look elsewhere when seeking turnover reduction strategies" (p. 351). Among the alternatives they suggested were job enrichment, changes in compensation, supervisory training, and application blanks weighted against a turnover criterion.

Premack and Wanous (1985) observed even smaller relationships than did McEvoy and

Cascio (correlation = .06; d = .12), but drew more optimistic conclusions about the usefulness of RJPs for reducing turnover. Specifically, they concluded that "because RJPs are inexpensive to produce, the dollar savings could be substantial for an organization with low job survival among the newly hired" (p. 715).

In addition to turnover, Premack and Wanous (1985) meta-analyzed a variety of other dependent variables, including perceptions of climate, organizational commitment, coping, initial expectations/met expectations (analyzed together), job satisfaction, performance, and prehire dropout rates. The following correlations were obtained: climate (–.01); commitment (.09); coping (–.01); initial and/or met expectations (–.17); job satisfaction (.06); performance (.03); and prehire dropout rates (.00). However, after omitting two "outlier" studies (one with 400 subjects, one with 1,260), the correlation for satisfaction diminished from .06 to .02, while that for prehire dropout rates increased from .00 to .06.

Premack and Wanous' (1985) results differed from the two prior meta-analyses in that they did not find significant residual variance in turnover after correcting for sampling and measurement error. As such, they did not explicitly test for the job complexity–turnover interaction reported in the two previous meta-analyses. Indeed, Premack and Wanous reported only one significant moderator effect across all dependent variables. Specifically, applicants who received audiovisual realistic previews had higher performance than those who received booklets (r = .15 vs. –.02). Two post hoc explanations were offered: Either the videotapes served as role models for applicants, or the results were due to chance. (That particular meta-analysis was based on only seven studies.)

Evaluation.   Before discussing future research needs, two comments are in order about the conclusions drawn from prior meta-analyses. The first such comment involves the potential usefulness of continuing to search for moderator variables in future RJP research. Here, Premack and Wanous conclude:

> Eight criteria were used to assess the effects of RJPs, and for four of these, the variance around the mean effect size can be explained methodologically as a result of sampling error, differences among studies in measurement reliability, or as a result of a single "outlier" study. Only one moderator was found. Considering all eight criteria together, the average amount of variance attributable to sampling error alone is 74.2%. Thus, recent speculation about the possible moderating effects of "personal" or "situational" variables seems unwarranted. (p. 706)

However, a case can be made that Premack and Wanous' data are not compelling enough to preclude future searches for moderator effects. First, for two of the eight dependent variables, findings of low residual variance rest on the arbitrary removal of outlier studies with large sample sizes. That is, Premack and Wanous (1985) merely assumed that the nonconforming results reflected error rather than systematic variance in psychological processes or results. Clearly, the effect of removing outliers is to bias analyses against the likelihood of detecting moderator effects.

Indeed, the rather dramatic changes in effect sizes and residual variability attained by removing single studies points to a second reason for caution in concluding that realistic previews produce only main effects. Specifically, by meta-analytic standards, Premack and Wanous' results were based on a very small number of studies (e.g., eight for job satisfaction, seven for dropout rates, five for commitment, and four each for coping and climate). As a result, they had only low to moderate power for detecting significant moderator effects (Sackett, Harris, & Orr, 1986).

On the issue of sample size, Premack and Wanous (1985) imply that the inclusion of six additional studies makes their conclusions more valid than those of McEvoy and Cascio (1985). In particular, they cite enhanced sample sizes and reduced likelihood of a "file drawer" problem as relative advantages of their study. However, sample size is not the only factor influencing the veracity of meta-analytic conclusions. Rather, the relative quality of the studies included is also at issue (e.g., Cotton & Cook, 1982).

In the present case, 38 percent (8 of 21) of Premack and Wanous' (1985) studies were unpublished (and in five cases, had remained so for five years or more). The most common assumption about unpublished (or "file drawer") studies is that they remain unpublished due to negative results. However, in the area of realistic recruitment, negative results have been regarded as substantively interesting and certainly have not prevented publication of studies that failed to disprove the null hypothesis (e.g., Dugoni & Ilgen, 1981; Reilly, Tenopyr, & Sperling, 1979; Wanous, 1973; Zaharia & Baumeister, 1981).

An alternative possibility, then, is that unpublished RJP studies suffer from design or other methodological problems rather than from nonsignificant results. To the extent that methodological difficulties characterize unpublished research, their inclusion in a meta-analysis may obscure, rather than clarify, true relationships. Unfortunately, Premack and Wanous (1985) did not provide any information—sample sizes, variables investigated, results, potential confounds—that might help the reader judge the likely merits of their unpublished sources.

Finally, despite the large number of subjects in Premack and Wanous' analysis (6,088 for turnover; fewer for other dependent variables), close scrutiny of the job types involved suggests very narrow occupational representation. Specifically, the vast majority of subjects came from four occupations: bank tellers (N = approximately 400), insurance agents (N = 900), low-level clerical workers in phone companies (N = 2,200), and military recruits (N = 2,400). Needless to say, these samples hardly tap the full diversity of occupational labor markets. Again, probabilities of finding significant moderator variables are correspondingly reduced.

A second conclusion from the Premack and Wanous meta-analysis also merits closer scrutiny, namely, that "the question of why RJPs reduce turnover...is of greater scientific than applied interest" (p. 717). As the following examples illustrate, employers and "applied" human resource professionals might well care a great deal about the mechanisms responsible for lower turnover.

Researchers have not yet assessed whether those who drop out of the applicant pool following realistic previews are different in any substantive way from those who remain or from those who do not receive previews[3]. However, given that realistic previews tend to increase the amount of negative information provided, one might reasonably hypothesize that applicants who drop out prior to hire are likely to be those with more attractive employment alternatives. If so, lower subsequent turnover among selectees might reflect their lower employability rather than better "fit" between selectee values and organizational climates.

A second possibility, consistent with findings from several empirical studies, is that the *level* of initial expectations has a greater influence on job satisfaction and turnover than does the *discrepancy* between initial and realized expectations (e.g., Dugoni & Ilgen, 1981; Meglino, DeNisi, Youngblood, & Williams, 1988; Miceli, 1986). In the words of Dugoni and Ilgen:

> Wanous (1980) points out that RJPs are no substitute for good working conditions. [We] strongly concur. Telling prospective employees about unpleasant

working conditions may improve the probability that they will remain on the job in comparison to those who are not told about the conditions. However, the data in this study imply that those who are told about less pleasant conditions will be no more satisfied with them once they are experienced than will those who are not told. To improve satisfaction and the quality of work, ultimately some changes must be made in those aspects of the work environment with which employees are dissatisfied. (p. 590)

Indeed, several studies that have examined both initial expectations and met expectations have shown stronger support for the former, and occasionally disconfirming evidence for the latter (see Miceli, 1986).

The point of the preceding examples is not to argue that realistic previews actually cause adverse self-selection or that expectation levels are truly more important than expectational discrepancies. In both cases, evidence is insufficient to draw firm conclusions. Rather, the point is that some of the processes that have been hypothetically linked to realistic recruitment are of considerable "applied" interest to organizations.

Looking ahead, numerous authors have suggested future directions for RJP research (e.g., Breaugh, 1983; Miceli, 1983, 1986; Premack & Wanous, 1985; Reilly et al., 1981). In general, their suggestions fall into one of two categories: (a) examination of realistic recruitment processes or (b) searches for potential moderator variables.

Attempts to better understand the processes associated with realistic recruitment have been hindered by a variety of factors. One of these is that *realistic* and *traditional* recruitment have rarely been defined in explicit operational terms. Rather, most researchers have been vague about the content of both the realistic and traditional messages provided through

previews. Thus, we do not really know which aspects of realistic recruitment messages—job information, organizational information, or suggestions on how to cope—are associated with differences in recruiting outcomes. Nor do we know the extent to which so-called traditional recruitment messages were "unrealistic" to begin with across the various studies.

In 1981, Reilly et al. argued, "While it may not be feasible to operationally define realism in most field studies, it should be possible to use consistent guidelines in developing RJPs....It would seem that, at a minimum, RJP development should include steps parallel to those involved in content validation" (p. 832). Unfortunately, there has been little more attention paid to this issue subsequent to 1981 than before.

The ability to draw process-related conclusions has also been hampered by weak definitions of constructs, inconsistent measurement, and confusing terminology. For example, the following constructs have commonly been interchanged in the literature: (a) realistic, balanced, and accurate recruiting messages; (b) realistic, reduced, and met expectations; (c) initial expectations and anticipated satisfaction; (d) early satisfaction and early value attainment; (e) job, organizational, and occupational information; (f) self-selection and matching; and (g) realistic previews versus realistic socialization.

Finally, process research has been hampered by designs that do not examine applicants' decisions as *processes*. For example, many RJP studies have not assessed applicant perceptions prior to, or immediately following, realistic versus traditional presentations. Only half the studies have examined whether realistic previews cause differential dropout rates. Even then, none have pursued information about the kinds of individuals who left or stayed,[4] or their reasons for doing so. Similarly, few researchers have studied the coping hypothesis; when they have, they have typically done so via cross-sectional responses to a single scale item. In other words, realistic recruitment processes have been *inferred* far more often than they have actually been studied.

Previous research has also been poorly designed for revealing moderator variables or boundary conditions (Breaugh, 1983). Despite only limited previous findings of moderator effects, logical arguments continue to suggest that realistic previews are likely to have different impacts under different conditions (e.g., Breaugh, 1983; Meglino et al., 1988; Miceli, 1983, 1986). Unfortunately, some of the most likely moderator variables have either been inappropriately operationalized (e.g., alternative employment opportunities; see Breaugh, 1983) or ignored (e.g., actual vacancy characteristics). Moreover, insufficient attention has been paid to generating wide variance across studies in terms of theoretically interesting variables (e.g., type of work or typical job acceptance rates). As such, it seems premature to rule out the possibility of important moderator variables.

The preceding research suggestions notwithstanding, a case can be made that the amount of attention focused on realistic job previews has been out of proportion to their probable importance in actual recruiting. First, as Wanous (1980) and others (Krett & Stright, 1985; Stoops, 1984) have noted, the vast majority of organizations and organizational representatives still use marketing strategies (rather than realism) to recruit job applicants. One obvious reason they do so is from fear that if they are the only ones to "tell the truth, the whole truth, and nothing but the truth," candidates—perhaps the best ones—will be lost to other organizations.

Realistic recruitment research has not assuaged their fears. Indeed, the one meta-analysis to address the question reported (after removing an outlier study) that dropout rates *were* higher for realistic preview recipients (Premack & Wanous, 1985). Similarly, Meglino et al. (1988) reported higher turnover among military recruits who were shown a realistic "reduction" preview (one focusing on negative aspects) subsequent to entry into the organization. Although realistic recruitment theory optimistically hypothesizes that dropouts are probably not well matched anyway, this has not been empirically demonstrated. As such, the possibility of adverse self-selection, or losing the best candidates, remains.

Second, the vast majority of job applicants get most of their prehire information through sources other than formally designed booklets, films, or recruiter presentations. Moreover, previous research has shown that the typical recruiter receives almost no training concering how to describe vacancies to potential recruits (Rynes & Boudreau, 1986). Thus, in studying realistic recruitment as transmitted through booklets, films, or rehearsed recruiter presentations, we are studying a phenomenon that probably occurs in a very small percentage of recruitment efforts. In contrast, other recruitment variables, such as recruitment sources or characteristics of the jobs themselves, are present in nearly all recruitment situations. Thus, one might argue that they should receive proportionately more research attention.

Third, common sense suggests that actual characteristics of the job and organization probaly swamp the effects of realism manipulations. Indeed, the content of both realistic and traditional previews must be designed around the constraints of actual job and organizational characteristics. Nevertheless, researchers continue to study the effects of realism, while ignoring the job characteristics on which realistic presentations are based. Indeed, because job characteristics (e.g., relative and absolute pay levels or benefits) have not been recorded, they cannot even be investigated via meta-analyses. As a result, we know nothing about whether realistic previews work better, or differently, with "bad" jobs than with "good" ones.

Finally, it seems somehow puzzling that the dominant issue in recruitment theory and research should be employee retention rather than applicant attraction. Although it is certainly legitimate to question what happens after people are attracted to organizations, it seems rather curious to pay so little attention to the implications of realistic recruiting for attraction per se. Moreover, the effect sizes observed with respect to post-hire behaviors such as turnover and performance are hardly large enough to render prehire outcomes uninteresting or unimportant.

Does realistic recruitment cause the best candidates to turn elsewhere? If so, does this effect occur consistently, or only under certain conditions, for example, with "bad" jobs or with low unemployment? To date, RJP studies have not provided the data necessary to answer these and other crucial questions. In short, it is time for *recruitment* to play a more prominent role in recruitment research.

Theory and Research Needs

Overview

As the preceding review illustrates, recruitment theory and research have broadened considerably since Guion (1976) wrote his chapter for the first edition of this *Handbook*. Nevertheless, there are still major gaps in theory and research, particularly with respect to applicant attraction.

The remainder of this chapter addresses future research needs. In so doing, the following conceptualization of recruitment is used: *Recruitment encompasses all organizational practices and decisions that affect either the number, or types, of individuals who are willing to apply for, or to accept, a given vacancy.* As will be seen, this conceptualization leads to a broader view of recruitment activities, processes, and outcomes than has typically been considered.

The structure for the remainder of this chapter is illustrated in Figure 2. Note that in comparison with Figure 1, Figure 2 contains a new category, recruitment context, and adds a number of independent, dependent, and process variables to the model.

Recruitment Context

Recruitment practices, processes, and outcomes do not occur in isolation from broader contextual factors. Rather, they are affected by (a) environmental factors, (b) organizational characteristics, and (c) institutional norms.

As suggested in Figure 2, contextual factors may have both direct and indirect effects on recruiting outcomes. For example, labor markets, an external factor, have a direct effect on recruiting outcomes: All else being equal, employers will attract fewer and/or less qualified employees when applicants are scarce. However, the very fact that external conditions are unfavorable for attraction may cause employers to change their recruitment practices, for example, by using different sources or increasing advertising expenditures, which in turn should improve recruitment outcomes (an indirect effect). Similar logic applies to the other contextual variables, each of which is discussed below.

External Characteristics. All recruitment takes place within the context of at least two important external variables: labor markets and the legal environment. These variables are external in the sense that in the short run, any particular organization has little, if any, control over them.

Labor Market Characteristics. Previous research suggests that employers modify their recruiting behaviors in response to changes in market conditions. For example, as labor becomes increasingly scarce, employers have been observed to (a) improve vacancy characteristics by, among other steps, raising salaries or increasing training and educational benefits (Hanssens & Levien, 1983; Lakhani, 1988; Merrill, 1987; Tannen, 1987), (b) reduce hiring

FIGURE 2

Model for Future Recruitment Research

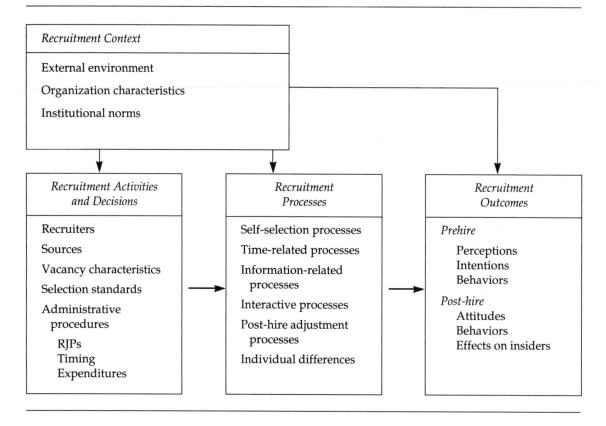

standards (Kerr & Fisher, 1950; Lewin, 1987; Malm, 1955; Thurow, 1975), (c) use more (and more expensive) recruiting methods (Hanssens & Levien, 1983; Malm, 1954), and (d) extend searches over a wider geographic area (Kerr & Fisher, 1950; Malm, 1954).

By modifying these recruitment practices, employers attempt to counter the difficulties posed by unfavorable market conditions. Thus, one important direction for future research would be to examine the extent to which changes in various recruitment practices are capable of overcoming adverse market conditions or enhancing favorable ones (e.g., see

Altman & Barro, 1971; Hanssens & Levien, 1983). At a minimum, the importance of market characteristics to both recruitment practices and outcomes should be acknowledged through more careful reporting (e.g., of unemployment rates) and, wherever possible, explicit statistical control.

Legal Requirements. Employment law and litigation are similarly assumed to affect both recruitment practices and outcomes (Cascio, 1982; Rosen & Mericle, 1979; Schwab, 1982). In terms of practice, equal employment regulations have been linked to broader use of recruitment sources (Miner, 1979), shifts in screening procedures (Tenopyr, 1981), and lower minimal position requirements (Dreher & Sackett, 1982). In terms of outcomes, the latter two practices have been linked with decreases in average applicant and selectee qualifications (Dreher & Sackett, 1982; Tenopyr, 1981). However, almost no empirical research has been conducted that establishes links between legislative requirements, recruitment practices, and recruiting outcomes, perhaps because of the sensitive nature of such data.

Organizational Characteristics.   At present, we have little information about the impact of organizational characteristics on recruiting. In part, this is because most recruitment research has focused on job seekers rather than employing organizations. Moreover, those studies that have examined employer practices have typically done so within single organizations (Arvey et al., 1975; Taylor & Bergmann, 1987). Neither of these methodologies permits examination of organizational differences in recruiting practices or outcomes.

Nevertheless, it is clear that different organizations recruit differently (Miner, 1979; Schwab, 1982). Moreover, it seems intuitively likely that a company like IBM would recruit differently from smaller, lesser known computer firms or from firms in very different industries. However, there exists no overall conceptual scheme for thinking about which organizational characteristics are likely to produce differences in recruiting practices, processes, or outcomes.

One broad category of relevant variables would seem to be those that are both (a) readily observable (e.g., industry, size, profitability, recent growth and financial trends) and (b) likely to affect applicants' general impressions of organizations. In the short run, most of these variables are largely fixed for recruitment purposes; nevertheless, they almost certainly have an impact on the size and composition of appli-

cant and acceptee pools. Moreover, they are also likely to affect the recruitment strategies used (e.g., sources used or salaries offered) and hence to have indirect effects on recruiting outcomes.

Therefore, such organizational characteristics should be attended to in future recruitment research. In single-organization studies, this can be done by more thoroughly describing the organizational context in which the research takes place (e.g., declining vs. growing organization and industry, profitability relative to industry competitors, etc.) for the benefit of future meta-analyses. In multiorganization research, such characteristics can be incorporated as substantive or control variables.

Business strategies (e.g., Miles & Snow, 1978; Porter, 1985) and general human resource strategies (e.g., Schuler & Jackson, 1987; Snow & Miles, 1986) have also been hypothesized to affect recruitment practices. For example, using Miles and Snow's (1978) typology, Olian and Rynes (1984) developed a set of normative propositions as to how various business strategies might be reflected in recruitment practices. For example, they proposed that prospector and defender organizations would vary with respect to relative emphasis on internal versus external applicant pools, the mix of recruitment sources, the formality of selection criteria, and the extent to which prescreening services are required from recruitment sources.

Empirical research on these or similar propositions is highly desirable, particularly since recruitment strategies are more readily manipulated than the broader organizational characteristics mentioned earlier. Moreover, organizations with similar characteristics have been found to vary widely in terms of such things as general human resource strategies, organization of internal labor markets, and internal versus external recruitment emphases (e.g., Miles & Snow, 1978; Osterman, 1987).

Institutional Norms. In many occupations and industries, traditions have developed with respect to typical or accepted means of recruiting. For example, in executive recruitment, large sums of money are expended on consultants or search firms to determine the suitability of candidates for a given vacancy (Ryan & Sackett, 1987). Executive recruitment has also evolved a series of elaborate norms regarding such sensitive issues as the acceptability of "pirating," possible violations of trade secrets legislation, conflicts of interest in raiding client organizations, and whether search firms should accept retainers to "feel out" executives from the client's own firm (as a way of determining the executive's "loyalty"). In contrast, such issues are nonexistent in recruiting for the typical production or service worker.

Thus, in a descriptive sense, we know that recruitment is conducted very differently for different occupations. In addition, we know that the kinds of information available about prospective employees differ across occupations as well—performance is more visible for executives than, say, for human resource specialists or secretaries. Finally, there are reasons to suspect that the effectiveness of various inducements such as pay, scheduling, or career ladders differs across occupations (e.g., nursing vs. law; Lawler, 1971; Rynes et al., 1983).

The major implication of these differences is that findings from one type of occupational or industrial market may be ungeneralizable to others. This is particularly important given that only one market has been studied with any frequency over the past quarter century—college graduates for entry-level business and engineering positions. In contrast, virtually nothing is known (except anecdotally) about how to improve recruiting effectiveness for low-level, low-paying positions—precisely the areas where the greatest long-term labor shortages are predicted.

Summary. Future research should examine the impact of contextual factors on recruitment practices and recruitment outcomes. In cross-sectional, single-organization research, studies should more fully describe the context in which the research is conducted, given that such information may be critical for interpreting differential results across studies. In designs that permit temporal or cross-organizational comparisons, contextual variables should be included as controls wherever possible. In this way, we can begin to determine the incremental contribution of recruitment practices, over and above the context in which recruitment is conducted (e.g., Hanssens & Levien, 1983).

Independent Variables

As mentioned earlier, previous research has focused on a rather narrow range of recruitment practices—primarily recruiters, recruitment sources, and realistic job previews. Clearly, other employer practices and decisions also affect employment matches and hence should receive increased attention. Three are suggested here: (a) vacancy characteristics, (b) employer selectivity, and (c) recruitment timing.

Vacancy Characteristics. One set of employer decisions that merits closer scrutiny concerns the determination of vacancy characteristics such as pay, hours, working conditions, benefits, and perquisites. Applicants' job choices are obviously affected by these variables; yet there has been little speculation about how vacancy characteristics might be modified in the service of attracting applicants.

Limited field evidence suggests that vacancy characteristics indeed swamp other variables as influences on job choice and retention. For example, Tannen (1987) studied the impact of a pilot program to improve educational benefits for Army applicants meeting certain aptitude requirements. Results revealed a dramatic increase in both the quantity and quality of Army applicants. Indeed, the increase was so dramatic that other branches of the service began to lobby Congress about "unfair" Army recruitment practices.

Similarly, Lakhani (1988) studied the effects of salary increases and retention bonuses on the reenlistment behaviors of soldiers whom the Army wished to retain. Although both forms of compensation were found to increase retention, bonuses were more effective than equivalent increases in salaries. This is a potentially important finding for employers, in that bonuses are not "rolled into" base pay and hence may be a more cost-effective means of attracting and retaining labor.

Given the obvious importance of vacancy characteristics to applicant attraction, it is strongly recommended that a variety of methodologies (e.g., field and laboratory experiments in addition to field surveys) be used to investigate the role of job and organizational attributes in job pursuit and choice behaviors. One potential objection to this suggestion, raised consistently in the realistic recruitment literature, is that employers must be concerned not only with attracting applicants but also with retaining them. However, in contrast to "unrealistic" recruitment, modifying actual vacancy characteristics in order to make them more attractive to applicants is likely to have beneficial effects on satisfaction and retention as well (e.g., McEvoy & Cascio, 1985; Miceli, 1986; Reilly et al., 1981).

A second potential objection follows from the belief that vacancy characteristics are impossible, or prohibitively expensive, to modify. For example, Wanous and Colella (1988) argue that it is "of limited usefulness" to determine the relative effect sizes for recruiters versus job attributes in various contexts because it is easier to "manipulate recruiter behavior via selection and training than it would be to try to change the entire organization (or at least its image)" (pp. 44–45).

Although it is unarguably easier to manipulate recruiters and recruiting brochures than to change entire organizations, it is not obvious that entire organizations must be changed in order to attract more or better applicants. Second, not all vacancy characteristics are equally expensive to modify. For example, provision of flextime or on-site daycare—even at the employee's expense—might yield high returns in terms of attraction and retention, because such nonstandard benefits more clearly distinguish an employer from its competitors (Rynes et al., 1983; Schwab et al., 1987). Similarly, there are several benefits that might be used only by a subset of the employee population (and hence be relatively inexpensive), but that might have substantial effects on an organization's image as a "good place to work" (e.g., educational benefits or sick child daycare).

Moreover, even in the case of the most "expensive" vacancy characteristic—salary—it is *unit* labor costs, that is, productivity-adjusted costs, that determine firm competitiveness (e.g., Weiss, 1980). Thus, organizations can afford to pay higher wages if other personnel policies, such as selection practices, job design, career paths, or performance standards, are structured to obtain greater employee effort, higher ability, or broader skill bases in return.

In the end, it is an empirical question whether investments in modifying various job characteristics are compensated by higher job acceptance rates, higher quality workers, or improved employee retention. In the meantime, the failure to even consider the question has contributed to an erroneous tendency in the recruitment literature to regard vacancy characteristics as fixed, rather than as managerial decision points subject to strategic manipulation and evaluation.

Because job and organizational characteristics are the dominant factors in applicant attraction, they cannot be ignored—even in studies of other recruitment variables—without serious risk of omitted variable bias (James, Mulaik, & Brett, 1982). As such, greater attention must be paid to vacancy characteristics, both as direct objects of study and as potentially relevant contextual or control variables in studies of other recruitment variables.

Employer Selectivity.   Although the issue has not been addressed in previous research, it also seems likely that recruitment outcomes are affected by the selectivity of employers in targeting their recruitment activities. That is, all else being equal, it should be easier to attract applicants if one is willing to recruit less-qualified individuals or those considered somehow less desirable by other employers.[5]

Thurow (1975) has gone furthest toward formalizing a theory of how vacancy characteristics and applicant qualifications interact to produce employment matches. He suggests that both jobs and job seekers can be arrayed in hierarchies from most to least desirable. Employers at the top of the organizational hierarchy are able to attract workers from the top of the applicant hierarchy, while less attractive employers have to settle for less marketable applicants. Should employers experience labor shortages, they need only to move down the job seeker queue to attract the necessary work force (as long as there is some positive level of unemployment). Any selectee deficiencies resulting from this approach are remedied via enhanced training and socialization procedures.

Economists have documented that employers shift hiring standards (both work-related qualifications and demographic characteristics) in response to recruiting difficulties (Kerr & Fisher, 1950; Malm, 1955; Thurow, 1975). For example, employers faced with labor shortages in World War II turned to women to fill jobs for which they would not previously have been considered. More recently, foreign immigrants have been recruited for jobs deemed unacceptable by native-born citizens.

Thus, in the typical case, employers are likely to be able to fill most of their vacancies with *somebody* (see also Rynes & Boudreau, 1986). As such, the most critical measures of attraction success are not whether vacancies

are filled, but rather with whom they are filled and at what costs. Thus, there is a need to move beyond purely quantitative assessments of attraction success (e.g., percent of vacancies filled or job acceptance ratios) to assessments of the productivity- and cost-related characteristics of those attracted. To date, few studies have reported even job acceptance rates, let alone specific acceptee characteristics.

Finally, an often discussed but little researched question involves the relationship between applicant pool characteristics and posthire outcomes. Despite common assertions that hiring overqualified applicants leads to subsequent dissatisfaction and turnover (e.g., Lindquist & Endicott, 1984), there is little research documenting this proposition. Indeed, meta-analytic findings that turnover is generally higher among poor performers (McEvoy & Cascio, 1987) would appear to indirectly challenge this assumption. (Overqualified individuals should not, on average, be poorer performers.)

Recruitment Timing.   To date, the only research on recruitment timing has addressed the length of delay between various recruiting stages. However, other timing issues may also be important. For example, there is some reason to believe that job seekers develop subconscious preferences for early job offers due to job search anxiety and uncertainty about other offers (Reynolds, 1951; Schwab et al., 1987; Soelberg, 1967). If so, companies that enter the market early in the recruiting season or that begin pursuing individuals even before they are "in the market" may have a competitive advantage in terms of securing job acceptances. Indeed, internship, co-op, and early enlistment programs are predicated on this assumption. However, if Thurow (1975) is correct, early recruiting advantages may accrue only to the most desirable employers.

A second, and more speculative, possibility is that early entry into the market affects applicant *quality* as well as quantity. Presumably, highly qualified candidates generate offers more quickly and easily than the less qualified. If so, firms that delay recruitment may find only less-qualified individuals still available. Indeed, indirect evidence of a negative relationship between worker quality (proxied by re-employment wages) and length of unemployment has been reported in the economic job search literature (see Schwab et al., 1987).

Finally, because job search and choice are longitudinal processes, applicants may be subject to primacy, recency, contrast, and other time-based effects. Such effects have been ignored in the recruitment literature; applicant reactions to one vacancy have been assumed independent of reactions to other vacancies. However, evidence from the selection literature (e.g., Hakel, 1982) suggests that such an assumption is probably untenable.

Dependent Variables

Overview. Since the mid-1970s, the dominant dependent variables in recruitment research have shifted away from applicant attraction and toward turnover and other post-hire outcomes. This development, along with the increasing tendency to study selectees rather than job applicants, is problematic from a number of perspectives. Two particularly important ones are that (a) multiple explanations exist for most reported post-hire results (e.g., self-selection vs. post-hire adjustment hypotheses) and (b) very little has been learned about applicant attraction.

Thus, the principal recommendation with respect to dependent variables would be to accord the immediate objective of recruitment—applicant attraction—higher priority in future research. Although turnover and other post-hire variables are of obvious importance to overall recruitment utility, the nature of their relationship to recruitment should be kept in perspective.

First, recruitment is *not* the primary management technique for influencing post-hire outcomes such as turnover or performance. However, it *is* a major technique for influencing applicants' job choices.

Second, it is quite true that attempts to attract high-quality applicants through "marketing" tactics might prove counterproductive if such practices merely lead to earlier, or more frequent, turnover. However, observed effect sizes for the post-hire behavioral outcomes of performance and turnover have been very modest. Recall, for example, that Premack and Wanous (1985) reported mean correlations of .03 between RJPs and performance, and .06 between RJPs and job survival. These correlations are hardly so large that they render pre-hire processes and outcomes unimportant or uninteresting.

Prehire Dependent Variables. As the literature review demonstrated, a variety of dependent variables have been used as indicants of applicant attraction (see also Figure 1). However, nearly all previous research has examined either applicant perceptions or behavioral intentions. As such, very little is known about the dependent variables of greatest interest to employers: (a) decisions to apply for vacancies and (b) actual job choices.

Job Application Decisions. Application decisions are critical to organizations; if individuals do not apply, there will be little opportunity to influence their choices through recruitment activities. However, most recruitment research has been conducted subsequent to the first employment interview. As such, little is known about the determinants of job application behaviors.

Given applicants' limited information early in the job search process, it seems likely that application decisions are based heavily on general impressions of organizational attractiveness. As such, one useful direction for future research would be to determine the major components of organizational image, and whether any of them can be cost-effectively modified or communicated to improve applicant attraction.

Other influences on application behaviors have been proposed as well. These include social influences (Granovetter, 1974; Kilduff, 1988), convenience (Reynolds, 1951), timing (Soelberg, 1967), self-esteem (Ellis & Taylor, 1983), job search anxiety (Sheppard & Belitsky, 1966), and costs of search (Lippman & McCall, 1976). At least some of these are potentially manipulable by employers and as such are worthy of research attention. For example, employers might build stronger informal social networks with favored recruitment sources, or they might schedule interviews at more convenient times or locations to reduce the costs of search.

Job Choice. The other pre-employment behavior that has been underresearched is job choice. To date, researchers have implicitly assumed that conclusions about job choice can be drawn on the basis of information about applicants' perceptions and intentions. However, perceptions and intentions are actually quite different from choices (Rynes et al., 1983). For example, stating one's perceptions or intentions is a completely "costless" exercise. In contrast, real job choices involve serious opportunity costs: Accepting one offer precludes accepting others. Unfortunately, we have virtually no information about how preferences and intentions are converted into actual job choices.[6]

Post-hire Dependent Variables. Much of this chapter has argued that greater relative attention should be focused on prehire rather than post-hire outcomes. Nevertheless, it is recognized that the overall utility of recruitment practices is dependent upon *both*. Thus, continued study of post-hire outcomes is necessary for a complete understanding of recruitment processes and outcomes.

However, future research on post-hire outcomes might be made more useful in a number of ways. First, there is a need to obtain prehire data from job applicants as well as post-hire information from acceptees. Without such data, selection biases will always represent alternative explanations for observed results (e.g., Lord & Novick, 1968). Of course, incorporating both pre- and post-hire outcomes in single studies will necessitate a corresponding shift from one-shot to longitudinal designs.

Second, there is a greater need to focus on qualitative as well as quantitative aspects of post-hire outcomes. Given that dissatisfaction and turnover are more dysfunctional among certain employees than others, it is important to assess the productivity-related characteristics of those who leave versus those who stay. Again, similar information is required concerning pre-employment applicant dropouts.

Finally, there are a number of additional post-hire variables that might profitably be examined. For example, Schneider (1983, 1987) and Sutton and Louis (1987) have argued that recruitment processes can have important effects on organizational insiders. For example, new recruits bring up-to-date information about the external labor market and as such may influence the satisfaction levels of current employees. Similarly, job applicants are a source of clues about an employer's image and market competitiveness, which in turn may cause a rethinking of recruitment strategies or practices.

To date, speculation in this area has not been very explicit about the possible implications for recruitment. However, because of the importance of new entrants to organizational vitality and adaptability, future work in this area is worth pursuing.

Process Variables

Overview. The vast majority of recruitment research has been justified on the basis of one or more process hypotheses. For example, studies of recruiters have generally been based on the premise that recruiters somehow influence applicants' instrumentality and valence perceptions (i.e., perceived job attractiveness). Similarly, realistic recruitment studies have been pursued on the assumption that RJPs affect either self-selection or post-hire adjustment processes.

Despite the widespread use of process hypotheses as justifications for recruitment research, few process-related conclusions can be drawn from extant research. In some areas, hypothesized processes have gone largely untested (e.g., recruiter signaling hypotheses or RJP coping hypotheses). In other areas, weak measures have been used to test hypothesized constructs (e.g., retrospective recall of prehire information). In still others, the research designs do not rule out alternative explanations for the conclusions drawn (e.g., RJP-turnover relationships).

Indeed, a case can be made that the recruitment literature has more than enough studies demonstrating that recruiters, sources, or realistic previews are sometimes related to both pre- and post-hire outcomes. What is missing is a clear understanding of why, and under what conditions, such relationships are likely to emerge. Thus, the time has come to pay closer attention to the design and measurement issues necessary to isolate recruitment processes.

Research suggestions pertaining to recruiter, source, and realistic preview processes were addressed in earlier sections and so will not be repeated here. Rather, additional ideas will be offered concerning less commonly researched processes.

Time-related Processes. Recruitment and job choice occur over time. Thus, many of the sequencing and order effects that have been observed with respect to other decision makers (e.g., primacy, recency, contrast effects; Hakel, 1982) are likely to apply to job applicants as well. Also, as mentioned previously, early job offers may receive more favorable evaluations

from applicants due to the security-enhancing effects of having a firm offer in hand versus uncertain future alternatives (Reynolds, 1951; Soelberg, 1967).

Additionally, the passage of time per se may modify individuals' decision processes. As the duration of unemployment increases, perceptions of employability decrease, while psychological and financial difficulties increase (e.g., Arvey et al., 1975; Lippman & McCall, 1976; Sheppard & Belitsky, 1966). In response, applicants may use different job search methods, search more extensively, become more flexible in their aspiration levels, or apply to organizations believed to have less selective hiring standards. Thus, the ease of attracting individuals would appear to be partly a function of their prior experiences in the job search process.

To the extent that longitudinal and sequence effects influence job choices, they would appear to have important implications for recruitment timing and for recruitment strategies vis-à-vis individual applicants (e.g., inducement levels or time permitted to consider an offer). However, the existence of such processes cannot be detected through the usual recruitment research methodologies of one-shot field surveys or measures of preferences rather than choices. Rather, experimental simulations or longitudinal field studies will be necessary to investigate time-based dynamics.

Information-related Processes. Other potentially important processes may arise because job seekers are forced to make choices based on imperfect information about job attributes. Some implications of this fact were discussed earlier in this chapter, such as the possibility that recruiters might explicitly manipulate informational presentations to produce particular beliefs among uninformed applicants (see Figure 1).

Other hypotheses suggest that imperfect information may influence the relative importance of various job attributes. These hypotheses follow from the fact that (a) some information is acquired earlier than others and that (b) some attributes—for example, starting salary or location—are known with greater certainty than others—e.g., opportunities for promotion or level of autonomy.

These factors suggest that certain vacancy characteristics may acquire greater (or lesser) importance in job choice than they would under perfect information. For example, early information may take on greater importance if applicants "anchor" their initial impressions on this information and then make smaller-than-appropriate adjustments when subsequent information is acquired (Tversky & Kahneman, 1974). Similarly, known job characteristics may take on greater importance via their role as signals of unknown characteristics (e.g., Einhorn & Hogarth, 1981; Spence, 1973).

To the extent that such phenomena exist, decisions about how to present information to applicants become more critical. Moreover, they extend well beyond previously raised questions of realism to such issues as information vividness and order of informational presentation.

To date, such questions have not been explored. This is because typical methodologies have either (a) presented subjects with hypothetical job descriptions in which all attributes are presented simultaneously and defined with certainty or (b) asked subjects to provide instrumentality or valence estimates for researcher-generated attributes, regardless of whether subjects have specific information upon which to do so. Thus, the study of signaling, anchoring, and other time- and uncertainty-related processes will require new methodological approaches.

Interactive Processes.   A third set of processes that merits future attention comprises those arising from the interactions between employers and prospective employees. Dipboye (1982) has discussed such processes in the context of the employment interview. How-

ever, interactive effects are possible during virtually any phase of the recruitment process.

For example, applicants may be discouraged by seeming employer indifference (e.g., failure to provide requested information) either before or after employment interviews. Although one might suppose that these effects would become irrelevant if an offer were eventually made, this may not be the case. First, the employer's lack of attention may signal something negative about the organization and thus permanently affect perceived organizational attractiveness. Second, apparent disinterest may cause applicants to turn their attention to other organizations and to accept offers that are more readily forthcoming.

Other kinds of interactive processes also merit future attention. For example, holding "true" job attributes constant, certain recruitment messages may trigger particular kinds of behaviors on the part of applicants, while alternative messages may trigger other behaviors. Thus, if a recruiter discusses high salaries and high performance standards in the first interview, applicants may adjust their behaviors by (a) trying to sell themselves as highly competent, energetic, and assertive (i.e., impression management) or by (b) seeking employment in a less demanding environment. In contrast, different applicant behaviors might emerge if the initial interview stresses organizational commitment to quality and service, or if salaries and performance standards are not discussed until later in the process (when the applicant has escalated his or her commitment level).

Again, because little research has been done (a) across time or (b) on the *types* of applicants attracted by different organizational characteristics, such interactive effects are at present largely speculative.

Individual Differences.   Although individual differences are not processes, they are discussed here because individuals appear to differ widely in both job search and choice processes. For example, even individuals in the same occupation have been found to differ widely as to (a) the number of alternatives examined, (b) the intensity with which each is examined, (c) the length of delay prior to beginning the search (e.g., after layoff or graduation), (d) whether or not searches are instituted even where no known vacancies exist, (e) whether applicants set minimal standards of acceptability on such attriutes as pay, benefits, or location, and (f) whether individuals are deterred by low expectancies of receiving job offers (e.g., Dyer, 1971; Glueck, 1974; Rynes et al., 1983; Rynes & Lawler, 1983; Sheppard & Belitsky, 1966; Ullman & Gutteridge, 1973).

More importantly, at least some of the variables just listed have been correlated with job search success (e.g., duration of unemployment or starting salary) and post-hire outcomes (e.g., career satisfaction or subsequent earnings). Although previous research of this type has been designed from the applicant's perspective, the significant findings suggest that individuals' search and choice processes may also be relevant to organizational outcomes.

For example, it would be interesting to determine whether more intensive search strategies are accurate signals of employee motivation, or whether delays in job search signal potentially troublesome personal characteristics such as procrastination, low self-esteem, or low work centrality. Similarly, it would be interesting to know whether individuals who search in different ways also tend to evaluate job offers differently. Finally, from the applicant's perspective, if differences in search strategies are associated with differences in search outcomes, can successful strategies be induced through counseling or training? Or do previously discovered relationships merely reflect underlying personality or motivational differences across applicants?

Summary. Many interesting job search and choice processes have received little research attention. Two factors probably account for the relative paucity of true process investigations: (a) Methodological requirements for studying processes are generally more elaborate than those typically pursued in recruitment research and (b) researchers may be unaware of many process issues due to the fragmented nature of previous theory and research.

Regarding the latter point, at present we have separate subtheories and empirical research streams for recruiters, recruitment sources, and realistic previews. For example, the commitment hypothesis has been tested only in the context of realistic previews, even though one might speculate that certain sources (e.g., employee referrals) or recruiters (e.g., high-level managers) are likely to engender higher commitment as well. Similarly, signaling has been regarded as potentially relevant to recruiters and vacancy characteristics (Rynes et al., 1980; Schwab et al., 1987), but not to recruitment sources.

Thus, most of the theoretical foundations for previous recruitment research have been too narrow to illuminate general process questions. Regardless of how narrow the research question, the tendency to ignore critical issues or variables should be lessened when research is designed with the entire recruitment process in mind. It is hoped that the present chapter provides a useful model of that process for future research design (see also Figure 2).

Future Prospects

Throughout most of the 1970s and 1980s, recruitment has not been perceived as a burning issue by either human resource practitioners or researchers. On the practitioner side, descriptive research has revealed that recruiters are largely untrained, recruitment sources largely unevaluated, and costs and benefits of recruitment practices largely unknown (Miner, 1979; Rynes & Boudreau, 1986). On the research side, Campbell, Daft, and Hulin's (1982) survey of perceived research needs in industrial and organizational psychology revealed that only one of 105 respondents noted a need for additional recruitment research (i.e., "Must study the effects of baby boom demographics," p. 65).

However, the times are clearly changing. Whereas long-standing labor surpluses previously enabled employers to "sift and winnow" applicants rather than attract them, long-term labor shortages are now predicted in major segments of the economy (e.g., Bernstein, 1987; Hanigan, 1987; Johnston, 1987; Merrill, 1987).

As such, the importance of recruitment is bound to increase, regardless of what we do as researchers. However, recruitment research might become a more integral factor in shaping recruitment practices if it were to ask more critical questions, if it were to be designed in ways that are capable of answering those questions, and if it were to frame questions and results, no matter how specific, in relation to the broader recruitment context and environment. It is hoped that the present chapter provides useful guidelines for broadening and improving research on this increasingly critical human resource function.

This research was carried out with support from the U.S. Army Research Institute, Contract SRFC MDA903–87–K–001. The views, opinions, and findings reported in this chapter are those of the author and should not be construed as an official Department of the Army policy or decision.

The author wishes to thank Marvin Dunnette, Lee Dyer, Barry Gerhart, Marcia Miceli, Howard Miller, Susan Taylor, Caroline Weber, and especially Judy Olian and Donald Schwab for critical comments on earlier versions of this manuscript.

Notes

1 Harris and Fink (1987) attempted to eliminate the problem by controlling for applicants' preinterview perceptions of job attributes and then looking only at incremental recruiter effects on postinterview attribute perceptions. However, adding a preinterview control does not change the fact that interviewer and attribute information were still acquired simultaneously during the interview, but then causally analyzed and interpreted (i.e., with perceived recruiter characteristics as independent variables and perceived job attributes as dependent variables).

2 Few previous reviews have categorized realistic job previews as administrative practices (Schwab, 1982, is an exception). However, they are similar to the other practices discussed here in that when a decision is made to be more "realistic," active changes are necessitated in administrative procedures (e.g., recruiter training or design of recruitment advertising).

3 By substantive differences, I mean differences in attributes that might reasonably be expected to affect worker quality, such as qualifications or aspiration levels. Neither substantive nor superficial (race, sex) differences between dropouts and other groups have been investigated in the RJP literature; however, future research should clearly address the former rather than the latter.

4 Meglino et al. (1988) did examine differences in personal characteristics of stayers and leavers, once on the job. However, the realistic previews in their study were presented subsequent to organizational entry, and as such are more appropriately regarded as socialization than recruitment practices.

5 Arrow (1972) and others have shown how characteristics that are not necessarily productivity-related, such as race, sex, or age, can come to be regarded as signals of potential productivity, and thus influence employers' judgments of applicant quality. To the extent that some demographic groups are favored over others, they will also be more difficult (or expensive) to attract, regardless of true productivity characteristics.

6 This issue has been addressed in previous expectancy theory research, but methodological difficulties (e.g., ambiguous causality or demand characteristics) preclude conclusions about actual choice processes; see Schwab et al., 1987.

References

Alderfer, C. P., & McCord, C. G. (1970). Personal and situational factors in the recruitment interview. *Journal of Applied Psychology, 54,* 377–385.

Altman, S. H., & Barro, J. (1971). Officer supply—the impact of pay, the draft, and the Vietnam war. *American Economic Review, 61,* 649–664.

Arrow, K. J. (1972). Models of discrimination. In A. H. Pascal (Ed.), *Racial discrimination in economic life.* Lexington, MA: Lexington Books.

Arvey, R. D., Gordon, M., Massengill, D., & Mussio, S. (1975). Differential dropout rates of minority and majority job candidates due to 'time lags' between selection procedures. *Personnel Psychology, 38,* 175–180.

Behling, O., Labovitz, G., & Gainer, M. (1968). College recruiting: A theoretical base. *Personnel Journal, 47,* 13–19.

Bernstein, A. (1987, October 19). Dispelling the myths about a higher minimum wage. *Business Week,* p. 146.

Boudreau, J. W., & Rynes, S. L. (1985). Role of recruitment in staffing utility analysis. *Journal of Applied Psychology, 70,* 354–366.

Breaugh, J. A. (1981). Relationships between recruiting sources and employee performance, absenteeism, and work attitudes. *Academy of Management Journal, 24,* 142, 147–148.

Breaugh, J. A. (1983). Realistic job previews: A critical appraisal and future research directions. *Academy of Management Review, 8,* 612–619.

Breaugh, J. A., & Mann, R. B. (1984). Recruiting source effects: A test of two alternative explanations. *Journal of Occupational Psychology, 57,* 261–267.

Caldwell, D. F., & Spivey, W. A. (1983). The relationship between recruiting source and employee success: An analysis by race. *Personnel Psychology, 36,* 67–72.

Campbell, J. P., Daft, R. L., & Hulin, C. L. (1982). *What to study: Generating and developing research questions.* Beverly Hills, CA: Sage.

Cascio, W. F. (1982). *Applied psychology in personnel management* (2d ed.). Reston, VA: Reston.

Conard, M. A., & Ashworth, S. D. (1986, April). *Recruiting source effectiveness: A meta-analysis and re-examination of two rival hypotheses.* Paper presented at the annual meeting of the Society for Industrial and Organizational Psychology, Chicago, IL.

Cotton, J. L., & Cook, M. S. (1982). Meta-analyses and the effects of various reward systems: Some different conclusions from Johnson et al. *Psychological Bulletin, 92,* 176–183.

Decker, P. J., & Cornelius, E. T., III. (1979). A note on recruiting sources and job survival rates. *Journal of Applied Psychology, 64,* 463–464.

Dipboye, R. L. (1982). Self-fulfilling prophecies in the selection-recruitment interview. *Academy of Management Review, 7,* 579–586.

Downs, C. W. (1969). Perceptions of the selection interview. *Personnel Administration, 32,* 8–23.

Dreher, G. F., & Sackett, P. R. (1982). *Perspectives on employee staffing and selection.* Homewood, IL: Irwin.

Driscoll, J., & Hess, H. R. (1974). The recruiter: Women's friend or foe? *Journal of College Placement, 34,* 42–48.

Dugoni, B. L., & Ilgen, D. R. (1981). Realistic job previews and the adjustment of new employees. *Academy of Management Journal, 24,* 579–591.

Dyer, L. D. (1971). *An analysis of the job search behavior patterns and re-employment experiences of middle-aged managers.* Unpublished doctoral dissertation, University of Wisconsin, Madison.

Einhorn, H. J., & Hogarth, R. M. (1981). Behavioral decision theory: Processes of judgment and choice. *Annual Review of Psychology, 32,* 53–88.

Ellis, R. A., & Taylor, M. S. (1983). Role of self-esteem within the job search process. *Journal of Applied Psychology, 68,* 632–640.

Fisher, C. D., Ilgen, D. R., & Hoyer, W. D. (1979). Source credibility, information favorability, and job offer acceptance. *Academy of Management Journal, 22,* 94–103.

Gannon, M. J. (1971). Sources of referral and employee turnover. *Journal of Applied Psychology, 55,* 226–228.

Gersen, W. F. (1976). The effects of a demanding application process on the applicant pool for teaching positions (Doctoral dissertation, University of Pennsylvania, 1975). *Dissertation Abstracts International, 36,* 7773A.

Glueck, W. F. (1974). Decision making: Organizational choice. *Personnel Psychology, 27,* 77–93.

Granovetter, M. S. (1974). *Getting a job: A study of contacts and careers.* Cambridge, MA: Harvard University Press.

Guion, R. M. (1976). Recruiting, selection, and job placement. In M. D. Dunnette (Ed.), *Handbook of industrial and organizational psychology* (pp. 777–828). Chicago: Rand McNally.

Hakel, M. D. (1982). Employment interviewing. In K. M. Rowland & G. R. Ferris (Eds.), *Personnel management.* Boston: Allyn & Bacon.

Hanigan, M. (1987). Campus recruiters upgrade their pitch. *Personnel Administrator, 32,* 55–58.

Hanssens, D. M., & Levien, H. A. (1983). An econometric study of recruitment marketing in the U.S. Navy. *Management Science, 29,* 1167–1184.

Harn, T. J., & Thornton, G. C., III. (1985). Recruiter counseling behaviours and applicant impressions. *Journal of Occupational Psychology, 58,* 57–65.

Harris, M. M., & Fink, L. S. (1987). A field study of employment opportunities: Does the recruiter make a difference? *Personnel Psychology, 40,* 765–784.

Herriott, P., & Rothwell, C. (1981). Organizational characteristics and decision theory: Effects of employers' literature and selection interview. *Journal of Occupational Psychology, 54,* 17–31.

Hilgert, R., & Eason, L. (1968). How students weigh recruiters. *Journal of College Placement, 28,* 99–102.

Hill, R. E. (1970). New look at employee referrals as a recruitment channel. *Personnel Journal, 49,* 144–148.

Ivancevich, J. M., & Donnelly, J. H. (1971). Job offer acceptance behavior and reinforcement. *Journal of Applied Psychology, 67,* 577–580.

James, L. R., Mulaik, S. A., & Brett, J. M. (1982). *Causal analysis: Assumptions, models and data.* Beverly Hills, CA: Sage.

Johnston, W. B. (1987). *Workforce 2000: Work and workers for the 21st century.* Indianapolis, IN: Hudson Institute.

Kerr, C., & Fisher, L. H. (1950). Effect of environment and administration on job evaluation. *Harvard Business Review, 28,* 77–96.

Kilduff, M. J. (1988). *Decision making in context: Social and personality correlates of choices of organizations.* Unpublished doctoral dissertation, Cornell University, Ithaca, NY.

Krett, K., & Stright, J. F. (1985). Using market research as a recruitment strategy. *Personnel, 62,* 32–36.

Lakhani, H. (1988). The effect of pay and retention bonuses on quit rates in the U.S. Army. *Industrial and Labor Relations Review, 41,* 430–438.

Latham, V. M., & Leddy, P. M. (1987). Source of recruitment and employee attitudes: An analysis of job involvement, organizational commitment, and job satisfaction. *Journal of Business and Psychology, 1,* 230–235.

Lawler, E. E., III. (1971). *Pay and organizational effectiveness.* New York: McGraw-Hill.

Lewin, T. (1987, March 11). Law firms add second tier. *New York Times.*

Liden, R. C., & Parsons, C. K. (1986). A field study of job applicant interview perceptions, alternative opportunities, and demographic characteristics. *Personnel Psychology, 39,* 109–122.

Lindquist, V. R., & Endicott, F. S. (1984). *Trends in the employment of college and university graduates in business and industry* (38th annual report). Evanston, IL: Northwestern University.

Lippman, S., & McCall, J. (1976). The economics of job search: A survey. Part 1. *Economic Inquiry, 14,* 155–190.

Lord, S. M., & Novick, M. R. (1968). *Statistical theories of mental test scores.* Reading, MA: Addison-Wesley.

Louis, M. R. (1981). Surprise and sense-making: What newcomers experience in entering unfamiliar organizational settings. *Administrative Science Quarterly, 25,* 226–251.

Malm, F. T. (1954). Recruiting patterns and the functioning of labor markets. *Industrial and Labor Relations Review, 7,* 507–525.

Malm, F. T. (1955). Hiring procedures and selection standards in the San Francisco Bay Area. *Industrial and Labor Relations Review, 8,* 231–252.

McEvoy, G. M., & Cascio, W. F. (1985). Strategies for reducing employee turnover: A meta-analysis. *Journal of Applied Psychology, 70,* 342–353.

McEvoy, G. M., & Cascio, W. F. (1987). Do good or poor performers leave? A meta-analysis of the relationship between performance and turnover. *Academy of Management Journal, 30,* 744–762.

Meglino, B. M., DeNisi, A. S., Youngblood, S. A., & Williams, K. J. (1988). Effects of realistic job previews: A comparison using an enhancement and a reduction preview. *Journal of Applied Psychology, 73,* 259–266.

Merrill, P. (1987). Sign of the times. *Personnel Administrator, 32,* 62–65.

Miceli, M. P. (1983). Why realistic job previews cannot meet our unrealistically high expectations. *Academy of Management Proceedings,* 282–286.

Miceli, M. P. (1986). Effects of realistic job previews on newcomer affect and behavior: An operant perspective. *Journal of Organizational Behavior Management, 8,* 73–88.

Miles, R. E., & Snow, C. C. (1978). *Organizational strategy, structure, and process.* New York: McGraw-Hill.

Miner, M. G. (1979). *Recruiting policies and practices.* Washington, DC: Bureau of National Affairs.

Olian, J. D., & Rynes, S. L. (1984). Organizational staffing: Integrating practice with strategy. *Industrial Relations, 23,* 170–183.

Osterman, P. (1987). Choice of employment systems in internal labor markets. *Industrial Relations, 26,* 46–67.

Porter, M. E. (1985). *Competitive advantage: Creating and sustaining superior performance.* New York: Free Press.

Powell, G. N. (1984). Effects of job attributes and recruiting practices on applicant decisions: A comparison. *Personnel Psychology, 37,* 721–732.

Premack, S. L., & Wanous, J. P. (1985). A meta-analysis of realistic job preview experiments. *Journal of Applied Psychology, 70,* 706–719.

Quaglieri, P. L. (1982). A note on variations in recruiting information obtained through different sources. *Journal of Occupational Psychology, 55,* 53–55.

Reid, G. L. (1972). Job search and the effectiveness of job-finding methods. *Industrial and Labor Relations Review, 25,* 479–495.

Reilly, R. R., Brown, B., Blood, M. R., & Malatesta, C. Z. (1981). The effects of realistic previews: A study and discussion of the literature. *Personnel Psychology, 34,* 823–834.

Reilly, R. R., Tenopyr, M. L., & Sperling, S. M. (1979). Effects of job previews on job acceptance and survival of telephone operator candidates. *Journal of Applied Psychology, 64,* 218–220.

Reynolds, L. G. (1951). *The structure of labor markets.* New York: Harper & Row.

Rogers, D. P., & Sincoff, M. Z. (1978). Favorable impression characteristics of the recruitment interviewer. *Personnel Psychology, 31,* 495–504.

Rosen, B., & Mericle, M. F. (1979). Influence of strong versus weak fair employment practices and applicant's sex on selection decisions and salary recommendations in a management simulation. *Journal of Applied Psychology, 64,* 435–439.

Rottenberg, S. (1956). On choice in labor markets. *Industrial and Labor Relations Review, 9,* 183–199.

Ryan, A. M., & Sackett, P. R. (1987). A survey of individual assessment practices by industrial/ organizational psychologists. *Personnel Psychology, 40,* 455–489.

Rynes, S. L., & Boudreau, J. W. (1986). College recruiting in large organizations: Practice, evaluation, and research implications. *Personnel Psychology, 39,* 729–757.

Rynes, S. L., Heneman, H. G., III, & Schwab, D. P. (1980). Individual reactions to organizational recruiting: A review. *Personnel Psychology, 33,* 529–542.

Rynes, S. L., & Lawler, J. (1983). A policy-capturing investigation of the role of expectancies in decisions to pursue job alternatives. *Journal of Applied Psychology, 68,* 620–632.

Rynes, S. L., & Miller, H. E. (1983). Recruiter and job influences on candidates for employment. *Journal of Applied Psychology, 68,* 147–154.

Rynes, S. L., Schwab, D. P., & Heneman, H. G., III. (1983). The role of pay and market pay variability in job application decisions. *Organizational Behavior and Human Performance, 31,* 353–364.

Sackett, P. R., Harris, M. M., & Orr, J. M. (1986). On seeking moderator variables in meta-analysis of correlational data: A Monte Carlo investigation of statistical power and resistance to Type I error. *Journal of Applied Psychology, 71,* 302–310.

Schmitt, N., & Coyle, B. W. (1976). Applicant decisions in the employment interview. *Journal of Applied Psychology, 61,* 184–192.

Schneider, B. (1983). Interactional psychology and organizational behavior. In L. L. Cummings & B. M. Staw (Eds.), *Research in organizational behavior, V* (pp. 1–31). Greenwich, CT: JAI Press.

Schneider, B. (1987). The people make the place. *Personnel Psychology, 40,* 437–454.

Schuler, R. S., & Jackson, S. E. (1987). Linking competitive strategies with human resource management practices. *Academy of Management Executive, 1,* 207–219.

Schwab, D. P. (1982). Recruiting and organizational participation. In K. Rowland & G. Ferris (Eds.), *Personnel management* (pp. 103–128). Boston: Allyn & Bacon.

Schwab, D. P., Rynes, S. L., & Aldag, R. J. (1987). Theories and research on job search and choice. In K. Rowland & G. Ferris (Eds.), *Research in personnel and human resources management* (Vol. 5, pp. 129–166). Greenwich, CT: JAI Press.

Sheppard, H., & Belitsky, A. H. (1966). *The job hunt.* Baltimore: Johns Hopkins Press.

Smith, A. (1976). *An inquiry into the nature and causes of the wealth of nations.* Dunwoody, GA: Norman S. Berg.

Snow, C. C., & Miles, R. E. (1986). Organizational strategy, design, and human resources management. In S. L. Rynes & G. T. Milkovich (Eds.), *Current issues in human resource management: Commentary and readings* (pp. 60–69). Plano, TX: Business Publications.

Soelberg, P. O. (1967). Unprogrammed decision making. *Industrial Management Review, 8,* 19–29.

Spence, M. (1973). Job market signaling. *Quarterly Journal of Economics, 87,* 355–374.

Stoops, R. (1984). Reader survey supports market approach to recruitment. *Personnel Journal, 63,* 22–24.

Sutton, R. I., & Louis, M. R. (1987). How selecting and socializing newcomers influences insiders. *Human Resource Management, 26,* 347–361.

Swaroff, P. G., Barclay, L. A., & Bass, A. R. (1985). Recruiting sources: Another look. *Journal of Applied Psychology, 70,* 720–728.

Tannen, M. B. (1987). Is the Army college fund meeting its objectives? *Industrial and Labor Relations Review, 41,* 50–62.

Taylor, M. S., & Bergmann, T. J. (1987). Organizational recruitment activities and applicants' reactions at different stages of the recruitment process. *Personnel Psychology, 40,* 261–285.

Taylor, M. S., & Schmidt, D. W. (1983). A process-oriented investigation of recruitment source effectiveness. *Personnel Psychology, 36,* 343–354.

Tenopyr, M. (1981). The realities of employment testing. *American Psychologist, 36,* 1120–1127.

Thurow, L. (1975). *Generating inequality.* New York: Basic Books.

Tversky, A., & Kahneman, D. (1974). Judgment under uncertainty: Heuristics and biases. *Science, 185,* 1124–1131.

Ullman, J. C. (1966). Employee referrals: Prime tool for recruiting workers. *Personnel, 43,* 30–35.

Ullman, J. C., & Gutteridge, T. G. (1973). The job search. *Journal of College Placement, 33,* 67–72.

Vroom, V. H. (1964). *Work and motivation.* New York: Wiley.

Wanous, J. P. (1973). Effects of a realistic job preview on job acceptance, job attitudes, and job survival. *Journal of Applied Psychology, 58,* 327–332.

Wanous, J. P. (1977). Organizational entry: Newcomers moving from outside to inside. *Psychological Bulletin, 84,* 601–618.

Wanous, J. P. (1978). Realistic job previews: Can a procedure to reduce turnover also influence the relationship between abilities and performance? *Personnel Psychology, 31,* 249–258.

Wanous, J. P. (1980). *Organizational entry: Recruitment, selection, and socialization of newcomers.* Reading, MA: Addison-Wesley.

Wanous, J. P., & Colella, A. (1988). *Organizational entry research: Current status and future directions* (Working paper series 88–57). Columbus: Ohio State University, College of Business.

Wanous, J. P., & Premack, S. L. (1986). *The effects of met expectations* (Working paper series 87–67). Columbus: Ohio State University, College of Business.

Weiss, A. (1980). Job queues and layoffs in labor markets with flexible wages. *Journal of Political Economy, 88,* 526–538.

Wyse, R. E. (1972). Attitudes of selected black and white college business administration seniors toward recruiters and the recruitment process. (Doctoral dissertation, Ohio State University, 1972). *Dissertation Abstracts International, 33,* 1269–1270A.

Zaharia, E. S., & Baumeister, A. A. (1981). Job preview effects during the critical initial employment period. *Journal of Applied Psychology, 66,* 19–22.

CHAPTER 8

Adaptation, Persistence, and Commitment in Organizations

Charles Hulin
University of Illinois, Champaign-Urbana

This chapter attempts to integrate attitude-behavior models and organizational adaptation, persistence, and commitment. Work role attitudes include employee job satisfaction and form the basis for persistence in and commitment to an organization. Work role attitudes arise from individuals' evaluation of their work role outcomes as influenced and moderated by their frames of reference, personal utilities of direct and indirect costs of work role membership, and individual dispositional factors. If their evaluations of job outcomes are discrepant from their work role membership costs, job dissatisfaction is likely to result. Job dissatisfaction is assumed to be stressful and unpleasant. Individuals experiencing such stress are hypothesized to select individual behaviors from behavioral families that increase job outcomes or decrease job costs related to those job facets with which they are dissatisfied. Both theoretical analyses and empirical studies suggest patterns of work role behaviors that reflect general positive or negative orientations toward the work role, predictable from a knowledge of work role attitudes. These behavioral patterns include many ways of decreasing job inputs, increasing job outcomes, changing the work role, or decreasing involvement in a work role; they form the appropriate dependent variables in our studies of organizational withdrawal, persistence, and adaptation.

Introduction

ORGANIZATIONAL PERSISTENCE, commitment, and withdrawal are hypothesized as attitudinal and behavioral responses comprised by what is referred to as *organizational adaptation*. Different manifestations of the adaptation construct, both behavioral and attitudinal, have been intensively researched by organizational researchers for the past three decades. The focus of much of this research has been on isolated responses without considering whether specific responses represent a more general domain.[1]

Models have been developed to explain organizational turnover (March & Simon, 1958; Mobley, 1977), absenteeism (Steers & Rhodes, 1978, 1984), attitudinal commitment (Mowday, Porter, & Steers, 1982; Porter & Steers, 1973), behavioral commitment (Salancik, 1977), socialization (Premack & Wanous, 1985; Van Maanen, 1973; Wanous, 1977), satisfaction (March & Simon, 1958; Smith, Kendall, & Hulin, 1969; Vroom, 1964), and other responses to work environments. These models, although limited in scope, have provided theoretical explanations of different phenomena, and tests of the models have generated much empirical data that address the antecedents and correlates of these responses.

Models that specifically attempt to relate job affect and other psychological responses to a multivariate set of behavioral responses are rare. Rosse and Miller (1984) offer an exception, although their model is limited to job affect and responses assumed to reflect job adaptation and withdrawal. Rosse (1983, 1988) and Rosse and Hulin (1985) examined relations within a limited set of withdrawal and adaptive responses. Hulin, Roznowski, and Hachiya (1985) presented a heuristic model derived from previous conceptual developments that similarly addressed questions of job affect and different families of responses to job dissatisfaction.

Two characteristics of the empirical and theoretical work in this area raise questions about what general and theoretical knowledge can be gained from it. Empirically, the research is limited by its focus on individual, isolated responses often characterized by low base rates and skewed distributions. Although the empirical relations from many of these studies provide insight into the antecedents or correlates of absenteeism or turnover in organizations, they provide little information about the antecedents and correlates of any theoretical construct that may have generated the observed responses. As shown later in the chapter, relations based on events that have low base rates are often badly biased estimates of relations between underlying theoretical constructs. In addition, all of the developments in this area should be integrated with basic theoretical developments in the areas of attitude formation, attitude-behavior consistencies, and decision making, all of which are basic theoretical research areas contributing to our understanding of relevant phenomena.

Finally, behavior families, behavioral switching among competing behavior families (Atkinson & Birch, 1970; Fichman, 1984; Rosse & Miller, 1984), and relations among different withdrawal behaviors (Beehr & Gupta, 1978; Hill & Trist, 1955; Porter & Steers, 1973; Rosse, 1988) all suggest a degree of complexity of responses that must be matched by a researcher's choice of dependent variables.

In spite of the concentration of research efforts on the prediction of specific, isolated behavioral responses from behavioral intentions and attitudes toward these same acts, there is little scientific merit in the practice—nor are the conceptual bases of this focus at all compelling. A congruence between the generality and psychological function of the behavioral dependent measures and the attitudinal predictors is required if we want empirical research efforts to make conceptual sense and achieve high degrees of predictive validity; it is not required that we achieve these goals by making our attitude measures and criteria as narrow and as specific as they have been.

Thurstone (1931), Doob (1947), Fishbein and Ajzen (1974), and others have made a strong case against the wisdom of expecting general social or organizational attitudes to predict specific behaviors. However, congruence of attitudes and behaviors can be achieved either by (a) constructing measures of attitudes toward specific acts and behavioral intentions to engage in those acts as predictors of specific acts or by (b) constructing general behavioral measures to match the generality of the attitudes being considered. As a field, we have embraced the former and have achieved impressive predictive validities for individual specific behaviors. The price we have paid for these impressive empirical validities seems to have been in terms of knowledge about general constructs that comprise many manifest behaviors. Such general behavioral constructs would provide both empirical data and conceptual bases for integrating many manifest behaviors into fewer, more general constructs with better scientific bases. Continued focus on these specific behaviors seems unlikely to provide a sound basis for general statements about scientifically important behavioral propensities in organizations.

The purposes of this chapter are to review and integrate contemporary models of organizational withdrawal into basic developments in attitude-behavior theory and applied motivation theory. Empirical data are reviewed to the extent that they contribute directly to the validity of these theoretical models. The empirical data reported in the many studies of absenteeism, tardiness, turnover, satisfaction, and related responses said to comprise the construct of organizational withdrawal will be reviewed briefly. These data often provide estimates of underlying theoretical relations but are biased to such an extent that their theoretical meaningfulness is questionable.

Caution is therefore required in interpreting much of the empirical data.

Specifically, this chapter presents a brief review of selected conceptual models of attitude formation, including theoretical models of attitude-behavior consistencies as well as selected empirical findings specifically relevant to job affect and job withdrawal. I also develop the concept of job withdrawal as a multifaceted response family and discuss the psychological functions of job withdrawal responses within a general model of job affect and job adaptation. Finally, I consider the influence of alternative job opportunities on job affect and job behaviors as well as the moderating effect.

Theoretical and Conceptual Background

Models of Job Attitude Formation

This section provides a summary of some important models of job attitude formation. The first four models addressed below consider attitude-affect formation as a function of contributions to and outcomes of a role or relationship, stressing both the direct and indirect impact of comparison levels on evaluations of (work) roles. All of the models assume role incumbents act on, respond to, and enact information and environments in ways consistent with their past experiences. Although the models each use different constructs, use different terms for similar constructs, and emphasize different elements of the environment and the role being evaluated, their similarities will be emphasized. The goal is to provide a description of the state of conceptual development and empirical data in this research area rather than to focus on minor discrepancies and differences.

Thibaut and Kelley's Model. Thibaut and Kelley (1959) developed a conceptual model of attractions of individuals to dyadic and group relationships and roles. They introduce two concepts to account for individuals' role affect and attractions as well as their behavioral tendencies to leave—or persist in—a specific role. Thibaut and Kelley hypothesized that individuals evaluate a particular role on the basis of past experience with similar relationships or roles. This standard for evaluation is called the *comparison level*, denoted CL. Judgments and evaluations about roles and relationships are assumed to generate affect toward roles: Roles with outcomes that surpass the CL are likely to be satisfying; roles with outcomes below the CL are likely to be dissatisfying. CL represents an attempt to define a psychological midpoint of a scale used to evaluate outcomes. The affect, positive or negative, experienced as a result of a given role or relationship is indicated by the location—above or below the CL—of the associated outcomes.

CL is the modal or average value of all outcomes known or experienced by the person, each outcome weighted by its salience to the person. Thibaut and Kelley do not specifically address the role of the variance of these outcomes in determining affect. Individuals can know about and experience outcomes through a number of mechanisms other than firsthand experience. Information from others, vicarious experience, and observations of role models are all sources of information about role outcomes.

A second standard for comparison introduced by Thibaut and Kelley is the *comparison level for alternatives*, denoted CL_{ALT}. CL_{ALT} represents all of the outcomes associated with the best of the alternative roles available to the person. CL_{ALT}'s that are greater, more positive or less negative, than the outcomes experienced by the person in his or her current role are likely to cause withdrawal from the present role and entrance into an alternative role that has better outcomes. On the other hand, if the CL_{ALT} is below the person's current role

outcomes, there should be no tendency for the person to leave his or her current role—the role outcomes are already better than those obtainable in any other role. Neither CL nor CL_{ALT} is fixed for an individual. Both are expected to vary as a function of environmental events and individuals' interpretations of these events.

These two conceptually independent comparison standards are used to account for individuals' affect levels and behavior relative to their role memberships. Two independent comparison standards used by incumbents to evaluate and make decisions about their role behaviors introduce discordances between role affect and role behaviors. Role incumbents who are satisfied with the outcomes of a given role may leave that role to obtain even better outcomes in another role; dissatisfied individuals may remain in a given role for a long time because the best of the available alternative roles is worse than their current role.

Table 1 depicts four combinations of current role outcomes, role affect, and behavior. The first row, for example, depicts a situation in which the current role outcomes are greater than (>) both CL and CL_{ALT}. The second row depicts a situation in which the outcomes are greater than CL but less than CL_{ALT}. Corresponding differences in affect and withdrawal behavior are noted.

The behavior of individuals in situations A and D is consistent with their role affect; the behavior of individuals in situations B and C, however, provides interesting sources of information. For example, what attributions do managers make about the motivations of satisfied employees who leave an organization? Do they assume these employees were in reality dissatisfied and therefore left, or that they were lured away by offers of greater outcomes and generally higher pay? If turnover in certain organizations is low because of a poor job market for its employees, putting many workers into situation C, do managers or other

TABLE 1

Relations Among Current Role Outcomes,
CL, CL_{ALT}, Affect, and Role Withdrawal Behavior

		CL	CL_{ALT}	*Affect*	*Behavior*
Current	Situation A	>	>	Satisfied	Stay
Role	Situation B	>	<	Satisfied	Leave
Outcomes	Situation C	<	>	Dissatisfied	Stay
	Situation D	<	<	Dissatisfied	Leave

employees attribute their staying to satisfaction or to lack of opportunities? What attributions do the employees make about their own behavior?

The discordance illustrated in Table 1 arises because, in Thibaut and Kelley's model, the events and processes that generate CL's and CL_{ALT}'s are independent. CL is determined by past experienced role outcomes; CL_{ALT} is determined by alternative roles known to be available to the role incumbent. Conceptually, there is little reason to expect any necessary relation between these two comparison standards. The relative frequencies of concordances and discordances between attitudes and behavior are a function of the extent to which CL and CL_{ALT} are determined by covarying sets of events.

Questions arise about how dissatisfied individuals will behave while in a role that, in spite of its dissatisfying outcomes, is better than any other role currently available to them. Other models, considered below, offer a variety of withdrawal and adaptive behaviors. For instance, an individual may reevaluate role outcomes, comparison levels, and outcomes of alternative roles. Distortion of dissatisfaction, resignation to one's fate, and other Panglossian response tendencies need to be considered. The Thibaut and Kelley model is mute with respect to these questions.

Consider also the role of CL_{ALT} on both present (or immediately future) job moves and

job moves in the more distant future. Individuals who behave according to Thibaut and Kelley's model and leave their current work role for another with greater outcomes may continue to change jobs frequently because each job may provide them with more direct information about alternative jobs and with a wider network of contacts who provide information about still other jobs. They may be satisfied in each succeeding work role; however, because of their increased knowledge and social networks, they are more likely to learn about jobs with better outcomes and move again. Thus, job-hopping, or the *Hobo syndrome* (Ghiselli, 1974), may in part be explained by rational job choices driven by CL_{ALT} rather than by perpetual dissatisfaction, instability, or lack of commitment.

Generalizing Thibaut and Kelley's model from dyadic and group roles to work roles and work role outcomes does not appear to involve unsupported inductive leaps of faith. The roles involved, dyadic and group roles on one hand and work roles on the other, differ in their formality, the explicitness of the role behavior prescriptions, the range of outcomes provided, and perhaps in the importance of role memberships to the individuals involved. These differences, however, do not appear to define substantially different concepts. Extending Thibaut and Kelley's model to work roles also addresses important questions about relations between work role attitudes and specific withdrawal, persistence, and commitment responses. Much evidence from research on the role of alternatives on job affect and job turnover supports, in part, the Thibaut and Kelley model. Katz and Kahn's (1978) role treatment of organizational behavior also presents evidence relevant to the validity of the Thibaut and Kelley model. This model of work role attachment assumes a calculative or an instrumental basis for the attachment. That is, individuals' work role attachments serve instrumental functions and are predicated on the results of hedonic calculus in which contributions to work roles are compared to the extrinsic rewards offered by the organization for work role membership. Generalizations of this basic model to include identification and internalizations of organizations' dominant values may be necessary to account for noninstrumental work role attachments (Clark, Mills, & Powell, 1986; Clark & Waddell, 1985; Kelman, 1958).

March and Simon's Model.   A model of organizational participation developed by March and Simon (1958) provides hypotheses about individual differences in affective responses to work roles and differences in individuals' responses to job affect with a specific work role. The March and Simon model of organizational participation defines affective responses as the result of the ratio of inputs to outcomes, the ratio of contributions to inducements. This view of affect formation is part of a general model of organizational participation that is reviewed in detail below. External economic conditions are hypothesized to influence job affect through their influences on the subjective utility of job contributions, or *job inputs*. Utility of contributions is measured by the utility of foregone opportunities, or *opportunity costs*.

The market values of a person's time, effort, skills, and formal training are assumed to fluctuate with local, regional, and national unemployment rates as well as specific occupational unemployment rates. The value of one's contributions would be substantially lower during periods of relatively high levels of relevant unemployment; they would be substantially higher during periods of relatively low levels of relevant unemployment. For example, during periods when alternative work roles are plentiful, organizations are likely to offer better work role outcomes as inducements to members to stay. These increases in work role outcomes, driven by labor markets, increase the opportunity costs for the member of any specific work role. However, during times of surplus labor, most individual employees do not have a wide range of alternative work roles from which to choose. Fewer organizations buying labor leads to a reduction in the subjective value of the job contributions of any employee because of reduced opportunity costs. There are also likely to be more individuals in the labor market who are attempting to sell their time and services to organizations. These individuals will require fewer inducements to assume a specific work role. Competition from others in the surplus labor market as well as a reduced market in the form of fewer organizations willing to hire employees should act together to reduce the value and subjective utility of any given set of work role contributions by individuals.

A graphic representation of this model of work role affect is presented in Figure 1. This model contains direct influences of contributions (inputs) and inducements (outcomes) on work role affect as well as an indirect influence of labor markets through their effects on the utility of direct and opportunity costs of contributions.

The differences between Thibaut and Kelley's model and March and Simon's model are important. Thibaut and Kelley hypothesize an effect of comparison levels on evaluations of *outcomes* (or inducements, in March and Simon's model). March and Simon hypothesize an effect of market conditions (a candidate for an index of CL_{ALT} in Thibaut

FIGURE 1

**Outcome/Input Model of Work Role Satisfaction With Moderating Influences
of Economic Conditions on the Subjective Utility of Contributions to a Work Role**

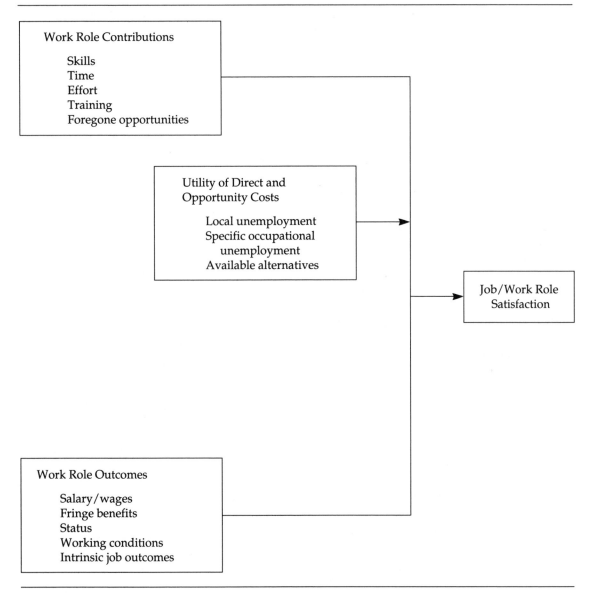

From "Alternative Opportunities and Withdrawal Decisions" by C. Hulin, M. Roznowski, and D. Hachiya, 1985, *Psychological Bulletin, 97*, pp. 233–250.
Copyright 1985 by the American Psychological Association. Adapted by permission.

and Kelley's model) on the utility of *inputs* (contributions). Whatever the target of the influence of economic conditions, inputs, or outcomes, the two models make consistent predictions about the resulting effects on job affect. There is no construct in the March and Simon model to parallel the CL_{ALT} construct in Thibaut and Kelley.

The Cornell Model. The Cornell model of job satisfaction (Smith, Kendall, & Hulin, 1969) is also similar to Thibaut and Kelley's model. The similarity is in terms of the hypothesized influence of comparison standards, or *frames of reference* (Helson, 1964a, 1964b), that individuals use to evaluate their current work role outcomes. The Cornell model conceptualizes job satisfaction as a function of what individuals receive from their work roles in relation to what they expect to receive, judged in terms of their frames of reference for evaluating such outcomes. Role expectations are determined by what the individuals bring to the job in terms of skills, education, experience, and so on, as well as their specific contributions of time and effort, for instance. Frames of reference for evaluating outcomes are determined by past experience with outcomes from other jobs or work roles as well as what other individuals are concurrently receiving from work roles. Such frames of reference are a function of the central tendency of the distribution of weighted outcomes experienced in the past by the individual, as well as the outcomes others are concurrently experiencing. The weights are a function of the recency of the exposure to the outcome. In tests of this model, local economic conditions have been used to index frames of reference individuals are likely to use to judge their outcomes (Hulin, 1966b; Kendall, 1963).

A graphic representation of the Cornell model of job satisfaction is shown in Figure 2. This model is similar to March and Simon's except that the influence of local economic conditions and past experience is assumed to be through the mechanism of

frames of reference for evaluating job outcomes rather than influencing the utility of job contributions. The model is also similar to Thibaut and Kelley's except it provides for only one standard of comparison (analogous to CL) rather than two independent standards (CL and CL_{ALT}).

Hulin, Roznowski, and Hachiya's Combined Model. Hulin, Roznowski, and Hachiya (1985) attempted to synthesize and combine elements of the three models just described, integrating general findings from the empirical literature. A graphic representation of their model is shown in Figure 3. This model provides for two related processes that influence the value of work role contributions and work role inducements in opposite directions with a resulting consistent effect on their ratio and on job affect.

Poor economic conditions marked by high unemployment should decrease both the subjective utility of work role contributions and individuals' frames of reference for evaluating work role outcomes. The subjective utility of work role contributions is defined in this model as their value in terms of anticipated affect as influenced by the local labor market. Other things being equal, decreased frames of reference for evaluating any given work role outcome will increase work role affect; decreased utility of contributions will increase the ratio of outcomes to contributions and should have a positive effect on work role affect. For example, high unemployment decreases the opportunity costs of work role memberships; there are few alternatives and the utility of contributions should decrease. Frames of reference for evaluating outcomes are decreased, and evaluations of the work role are increased because an employed individual is relatively well off during periods of high unemployment. Decreased utilities of contributions and increased evaluations of outcomes both act consistently to increase satisfaction. The effects of local economic conditions on subjective utilities of role contributions and on frames of reference for

FIGURE 2

_____

**Graphic Representation of the Cornell Model of Job Satisfaction With Moderating
Effects of Frames of Reference on Judgments of Quality of Work Role Outcomes**

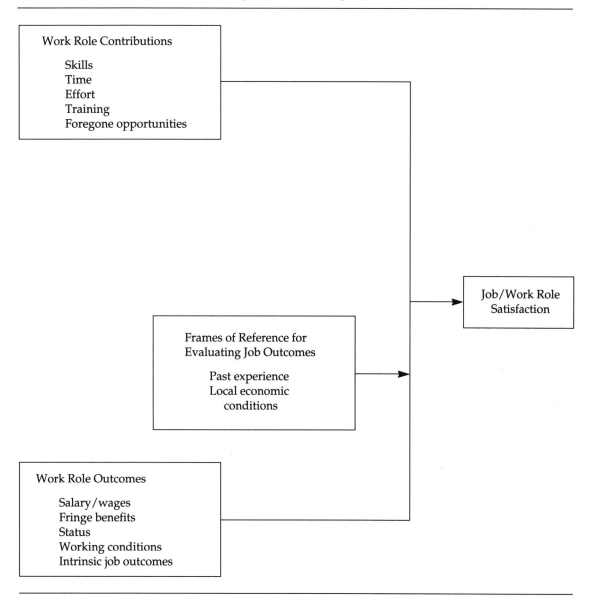

FIGURE 3

Graphic Representation of a Model of Work Role Satisfaction With Influences on Subjective Utilities of Role Contributions and on Evaluation of Role Outcomes

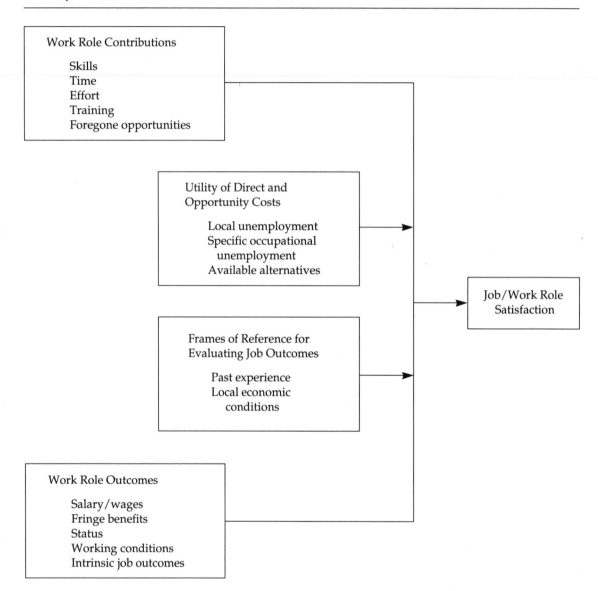

From "Alternative Opportunities and Withdrawal Decisions" by C. Hulin, M. Roznowski, and D. Hachiya, 1985, *Psychological Bulletin, 97*, pp. 233–250. Copyright 1985 by the American Psychological Association. Adapted by permission.

judging role outcomes are hypothesized to be additive.

The nature of these interrelated processes as they influence individuals' work role affect can be illustrated by considering four individuals who work in jobs that provide objectively identical outcomes for work role membership. The subjective utility of these outcomes will be influenced by the frames of reference individuals have for evaluating such work role outcomes. Person A, who in the past has worked in high-income jobs with good working conditions and good fringe benefits, will likely perceive these outcomes as having less utility than Person B, who in the past has worked only in part-time or minimum wage jobs. If Person C lives in a community where there is significant unemployment, he or she is likely to perceive the utility of his or her opportunity costs to be significantly less than Person D, who lives in an area with a shortage of labor in his or her occupational specialty. Other influences on both the utility of work role contributions and the evaluations of work role outcomes will operate analogously (Hulin, 1966; Kendall, 1963; Smith, Kendall, & Hulin, 1969).

Frames of reference for evaluating work role outcomes are a joint function of local economic conditions and individuals' past experiences. The common element in the two sources of influence on work role affect, local economic conditions, should create a relation between the two influences across time within individuals and across situations within time. Indeed, local economic conditions, indexed by such factors as unemployment rates, per capita income, housing, and cost of living (Hulin, 1966b; Kendall, 1963; Smith, Kendall, & Hulin, 1969), may overwhelm other influences on frames of reference and on subjective utilities of direct and opportunity costs.

The Hulin, Roznowski, and Hachiya model of work role satisfaction is similar to March and Simon's model. Work role satisfaction is hypothesized to be a joint function of work role contributions and work role outcomes.

Decreases in contributions relative to inducements or increases in inducements relative to contributions should increase an individual's work role satisfaction. Similarly, decreases in inducements or increases in contributions should decrease satisfaction. These effects, in part controllable by the role incumbent, are important for conceptual developments in the models of work role withdrawal and adaptation discussed below.

In contrast to the models of role affect and attitudes outlined above, in which the relationship between work role involvements and work role contributions are interpreted by the incumbent and lead to feelings of satisfaction and dissatisfaction, a relatively recent approach stresses the cognitive interpretation of social events and behaviors—including especially the incumbents' own behaviors—as the precursors to affect. This general approach is the cognitive social information processing model of affect.

The Social Information Processing Model. Social information processing approaches to work role affect represent an extreme emphasis on social influences and information—including the observers' own behaviors—on the salience and meaning of different contributions, outcomes, and comparison levels for evaluating work role outcomes (Salancik & Pfeffer, 1977, 1978; Weick, 1977). Essentially, this approach assumes that job affect is influenced by individuals' interpretations of their own behaviors or by the information they receive about their behavior from co-workers or other sources.

An extreme version of this approach argues that individuals experience little affect about their job satisfaction until they are *asked* (usually by social scientists). This view argues that social attitudes and affect are latent and unrecognized until some event triggers an evaluation. The nature of the triggering event (e.g., an attitude survey) may influence the resulting expressed and experienced attitude as much as the events that presumably formed the latent attitudes. If asked, the respondents will produce an answer *because they are expected to;* they will then search their environments for information to justify their response—they enact subjective environments that provide a justification for their response. However, the concerns of workers as expressed in songs within the oral tradition of the labor movement belie the idea that social scientists, with their ubiquitous questionnaires and interview forms, are the source of workers' dissatisfaction and their behavioral reactions to their jobs. This oral tradition antedates social scientists' concerns with workers' job affect by a century or so.

The first four models reviewed above are traditional in their approach. They all stress judgments and evaluations of dimensions of job contributions and inducements as if the dimensions had a fundamental existence and generality beyond the instruments used to assess work role affect. This assumption raises an epistemological question that most likely cannot be answered with complete certainty. However, evidence on item bias and item relevance obtained in cross-cultural studies of work affect and motivation (Candell & Hulin, 1986; Candell & Roznowski, 1984; DeVera, 1985; Drasgow & Hulin, 1987; Hulin, 1987; Hulin, Drasgow, & Komocar, 1982; Hulin & Mayer, 1986) from western and nonwestern cultures and industrialized and nonindustrialized nations suggests that the assumed cultural universality is at least a good working hypothesis. In essence, these studies report that job characteristics considered satisfying in one culture are generally considered satisfying across a variety of cultures, often to the same degree based on results of instruments translated into the appropriate languages. The similarity of items' characteristic curves across cultures suggests a striking degree of convergence across dissimilar cultures—a degree of convergence that strains the credibility of an explanation based on cross-cultural social information.

A social information processing interpretation would stress that levels of job satisfaction associated with different jobs (e.g., garbage collector vs. archaeologist) simply reflect general social information shared among individuals, between and within cultures, about which jobs are satisfying and which dissatisfying. The shared social information would be viewed as the proximal cause of the different levels of affect associated with different jobs, rather than characteristics of the jobs themselves.

This argument seems strained. As an experiment, consider the following: A researcher constructs two job descriptions. One describes the tasks of an archaeologist; the other describes the tasks of a garbage collector. One job requires work with ancient garbage, the other with newer garbage. One requires a Ph.D.; the other requires an 8th-grade education. One has relatively high prestige, the other very low prestige. One occasionally requires excavations in exotic foreign locales; the other requires driving a truck through neighborhoods of the same city year after year. One has relatively high income, the other low income. One job involves recovering and classifying artifacts to provide clues of previous civilizations; the other involves removing the trash of the present civilization. The characteristics of the proposed jobs could be expanded to include provisions for co-workers, supervision, environmental factors, and so on. The point is that if these descriptions were presented to individuals who were then asked to rate (a) the degree of affect they might experience if working on these jobs, (b) the amount of satisfaction they would expect others on the job to experience, (c) how long they might stay on such a job even if better-paying jobs became available, the results would show a marked preference for the archaeologist's job. If the appropriate job labels of garbage collector and archaeologist were attached to the descriptions and the study repeated with an independent sample, the results might accentuate the differences between the jobs, but they would probably not change the results significantly.

Such an experiment does not prove that the proximal stimuli for job affect lie largely in the job characteristics rather than in social information. It does suggest that significant differences in job satisfaction among a sample of job incumbents in terms of work role affect may be carried in the job characteristics, even cross-culturally; social information may merely reinforce positive and negative interpretations of events and characteristics already found to be satisfying or dissatisfying by job incumbents.

Several additional points should be considered when evaluating the scientific basis, contributions, and empirical support for the social information processing models of job attitudes. Effects of social information on attitudes can be documented in highly controlled settings. The external validity of these findings for work roles and work role outcomes commonly encountered in organizations has not been established generally.

The results of many studies of the relative amounts of variance in work role affect accounted for by different factors may be generalizable to no known populations of work roles within organizational environments. Investigators use fixed-effects designs to answer what is inherently a random-effects question. We lack knowledge of the naturally occurring distributions of levels of social information that are encountered in work roles in nonsimulated organizations. Because of our limited knowledge of these ecological distributions, investigators must arbitrarily create different levels of positive or negative social information about a task. This information is conveyed to subjects in the studies with little knowledge about the variance represented by such a set of statements relative to the variance of the naturally occurring distribution of social information encountered by organizational members.

The variance represented by other outcomes with which social information effects are being compared, such as manipulated or naturally occurring task characteristics, is another source of concern. How, for example, would we scale "This is the most boring job I have ever had" as a statement conveying social information about the interest of a job? How negative is this as a statement about the interest of a job? How would we scale an increase from five minutes to eight hours in the time a worker could spend on a job without supervisory review of his or her work? A more difficult question involves comparisons of the stimulus values of the statement and the manipulation. Does the statement about the boringness of a job represent social information as negative as the time span of discretion manipulation represents a change in the positive direction? Such basic scaling work has not been done. Fixed-effects designs can tell us which sources of information, social or otherwise, influence incumbents' affective responses to work roles and work role outcomes. They cannot tell us about the relative potency of the different sources of influence on affect levels unless we have obtained scale values of the statements used as sources of social information and the manipulations along a common metric.

There is also a degree of looseness in the social information processing models that allows much post hoc explaining of data. For instance, Zalesny and Farace (1985) argued that social influences are more likely to have effects on the variance of work attitudes within naturally occurring groups, departments, or organizations than on the mean levels of these work attitudes. These effects on variances, coupled with small mean changes, can yield "significant" effects that are interpreted as support for the hypotheses. Zalesny and Farace tested this hypothesis in a longitudinal field study of the effects of a move from one office building to another. Manipulations of the salience of characteristics as well as the characteristics themselves provided a test of the derivations. The data supported the hypothesized effects on variances rather than mean levels of affect.

An integration of social information models with the more traditional models would acknowledge the role of social information as an influence on subjective utilities of role contributions and on frames of reference for evaluating role outcomes. These influences are recognized as potentially powerful—particularly in situations where the individuals have had little a priori information or experience. The *realized* impact of such influences in organizations, relative to the impact of economic conditions and past experience in similar roles with similar outcomes, is a matter of conjecture at this time. Rather than main effects, social influences perhaps should be treated as moderators similar to frames of reference (Smith et al., 1969), comparison standards (Thibaut & Kelley, 1959), or subjective utilities (March & Simon, 1958) that influence judgments of work contributions and outcomes.

Dispositional Approaches. An additional theoretical approach in the study of job attitude formation, formulated originally by Weitz (1952) and rearticulated recently by Staw, Bell, and Clausen (1986), suggests that the general affective disposition of individuals to be happy or satisfied with life's everyday events is a significant correlate of the satisfaction they report with their job. The two studies, done more than 30 years apart using different methods on strikingly different samples and for different purposes, produced highly similar findings.

Weitz was concerned about the predictions of turnover on the basis of job satisfaction. He argued that employees' dissatisfactions would be more meaningful and predictive of subsequent behaviors if these affect levels were contrasted with their reported satisfactions with a wide variety of events that everybody experiences, some with more equanimity than others. Employees whose dissatisfaction with their jobs was no more extreme than their general "gripe index" about everyday events would be less likely to quit their jobs, for example, than

employees who were equally dissatisfied with their jobs but were substantially more satisfied with daily life events. Similarly, employees who were satisfied with their jobs but were also generally satisfied with everything might behave differently than those who were equally satisfied with their jobs but were generally dissatisfied with everything else.

In a preliminary report summarizing the efforts to develop a general "gripe scale," referred to by Weitz as a test of general satisfaction, he described a checklist of 44 items common to everyday life. The respondents reported whether they were satisfied, neutral, or dissatisfied with each of the items. The items included such things as U.S. foreign policy, local newspapers, one's first name, people's driving habits, one's telephone number, and (my all-time favorite) $8\frac{1}{2}$-by-11-inch paper. The scale had a split-half reliability of .75 and was correlated .39 with job satisfaction.

After a gap of nearly 35 years following Weitz's (1952) seminal work on the topic, six empirical studies have appeared that address a number of interrelated issues pertaining to dispositional and genetic influences on job satisfaction and the implications of dispositions and genetics for behaviors and organizational interventions. These studies by Staw and Ross (1985), Staw, Bell, and Clausen (1986), Gerhart (1987), Arvey, Bouchard, Segal, and Abraham (1989), Levin and Stokes (1989), and Judge (1990) represent the foundations of a data base that will permit empirically based statements about alternative sources of influence, other than environmental and organizational influences, on job satisfactions. To summarize these recent studies briefly, it appears that dispositions influence job satisfaction (Judge 1990; Levin & Stokes, 1989) that are reported by individuals both across time (Staw, Bell, & Clausen, 1986; Gerhart, 1987) and across jobs (Staw & Ross, 1985).

Individuals who are satisfied in one time period, and on one job, are likely to be satisfied in another time period in spite of intervening job changes that may have occurred. The correlations between reported satisfactions across time periods are modest, around .35, and any straightforward interpretation of the data is complicated because of the underlying process that governs job changes. Competing hypotheses would suggest that well-educated or highly skilled, intelligent individuals are likely to have jobs that provide many desired job outcomes; these same individuals are likely to work on similar "desirable" jobs even after job changes. Individuals occupying such jobs are likely to report relatively high satisfaction levels across time and on different jobs they might hold. Less well-trained individuals with less education and ability are likely to occupy jobs with lower pay, poorer working conditions, less security, and more routine work. These individuals, even following job change (to similar jobs because of their training and education), are likely to report lower levels of job satisfaction than those on jobs with objectively better outcomes. Thus, the evidence that relies on stability across time and jobs is not definitive with respect to the source of the reported job affect, individuals' disposition, or job outcomes. A causal model of job affect that was intended to account for its multiple sources of influence would need to include ability as an exogenous variable that influenced job outcomes independently of job changes. An additional barrier to simple interpretations of consistencies in satisfaction across time and job changes is that few of the studies (Judge, 1990, and Levin & Stokes, 1989, are exceptions) report independent assessments of individual dispositions; Staw, Bell, and Clausen (1986) have an indirect assessment of individual dispositions.

Arvey et al. (1989) take the development of the disposition approach one step further. They report intraclass correlations between measures of job satisfaction reported by monozygotic twins reared apart. Their results were based on a sample of 34 pairs of twins, or 21 twin pairs after removing all pairs involving at least one housewife. The intraclass correlation

between pairs of twins' reports of general job satisfaction, one of four job satisfaction measures analyzed, was .308 (ns, $p > .05$); the correlation based on the full sample of 34 twin pairs was .309 ($p < .05$). These results, in spite of the marginal level of significance, suggest a genetic basis that leads individuals to be satisfied with jobs, and perhaps with other quotidian events and characteristics in their lives (Weitz, 1952). Thus, Arvey et al. may have provided evidence for the theoretical basis and etiology of dispositions for individuals to be satisfied or dissatisfied.

Judge (1990) reported a LISREL analysis of links between individuals' dispositions, subjective well-being, and job satisfaction. His analyses suggest a causal link between dispositions to be satisfied and reports of subjective well-being. There were reciprocal causal links between subjective well-being and job satisfaction. This latter finding of reciprocal causal links between job satisfaction and subjective well-being may reflect the overall importance of jobs to the professional sample of employees (nurses) he studied. His design also included data from the significant others of his sample members. Analyses of their data indicated that the previously described causal links cannot be attributed to response sets.

Staw, Bell, and Clausen argue that their results suggest the field has erred too far on the side of situational determinism of job affect; we may have thrown away valuable dispositional predictors of affect. Whether the theoretical explanations of job affect stress situational determinism to such an extent is debatable. Certainly the theoretical explanations of the formation of job attitudes reviewed in this chapter stress the influences of both situational and individual differences. Job inputs, job outcomes, individual frames of reference for evaluating job outcomes, situational influences on the utility of job inputs, past experiences with role outcomes, and other concepts offered as explanations for individual differences in job satisfaction span the range from individual to situational determinants. These theoretical factors may be independent of, or substantially correlated with, individuals' dispositions.

The arguments offered by Weitz and by Staw, Bell, and Clausen for the importance of dispositional influences on job affect are well taken. Correlations of approximately .35, however, suggest that Staw, Bell, and Clausen's conclusions about the importance of individual dispositional factors relative to the importance of other variables may be overstated.

It would be a mistake at this point to conclude that job satisfaction and its correlates were due to differences in job characteristics *or* to individuals' dispositions. Any complete model of the antecedents of job satisfaction will need to take dispositional differences into account either directly or indirectly through their effects on related theoretical constructs. Complete models of job satisfaction, however, cannot ignore the significant and often apparently sizable influence of job characteristics on job satisfaction.

Summary. The models of work role affect discussed above represent process rather than content models of attitude formation (Campbell & Pritchard, 1976). They do not specifically address the roles of values and needs that were an important part of Locke's concerns in the chapter on job satisfaction in the first edition of this *Handbook* (Locke, 1976). Only the Cornell model raises the issue of expectations and met expectations as influences on job affect. Questions about how and why different dimensions of work role outcomes become differentially valued are not addressed here, nor are debates about what individual workers want or do not want from their jobs.

All of the models discussed are sufficiently general to permit individual differences in preferences for different work role outcomes. The models make no assumptions about the bases of individual differences in preferences. Needs (Alderfer, 1972; Maslow, 1943; Porter, 1964), work values (Hulin & Blood, 1968;

Wollack, Goodale, Wijting, & Smith, 1971), social information cues (Salancik & Pfeffer, 1977, 1978), and values (Locke, 1976) are all potential antecedents of the observed differences in outcome preferences. A major source of variance in individuals' preferences for different job outcomes may simply be experience with past job outcomes and what they provide in the way of satisfactions and dissatisfactions. Jobs that provide good income may be satisfying to some because of the many desirable things that money can buy; others, with fewer material desires, may not find money particularly satisfying. Jobs that provide status may be satisfying to some because high-status individuals are treated differently than low-status individuals; others, with less desire for deferential treatment, may find status outcomes a matter of indifference. Jobs with responsibility may be dissatisfying to some because of the stress and problems that covary with responsibility; others may find responsibility a source of positive affect. Challenging jobs may be satisfying to some because of how they feel about themselves after completing difficult job assignments; others may find such self-administered rewards irrelevant.

Experience and learning what job or role outcomes are satisfying as an explanation for individual differences in preferences for job outcomes have the advantage of avoiding references to needs and related psychological terms with problematic theoretical status. Such an explanation, however, leaves open the question of how some individuals come to value material goods or deferential treatment or self-reward while others do not. Explanations for acquired preferences for classes of outcomes that depend on developmental experiences, without reference to questionable theoretical constructs, may, in the long run, have an advantage. For the industrial and organizational psychologist, the question can be finessed by assuming the existence of individual differences in preferences for classes of job outcomes and ignoring, for the moment, the specific source of these individual differences.

It would be disingenuous to pretend that the six models of job affect discussed above can be integrated to produce one, verifiable, wieldy model of job affect. The Hulin, Roznowski, and Hachiya model is an attempt to combine elements of the Thibaut and Kelley, March and Simon, and Cornell models, possible in part because they all assume that expectations and frames of reference (differently operationalized) influence role incumbents' judgments of inputs and outcomes to produce role affect. The social information processing approaches are outliers in terms of these assumptions unless social information is interpreted as specifying moderating influences on evaluations of inputs and outcomes rather than true main effects. A strict social information processing model in which the "givens" in a situation are the role incumbents' own behavior makes these models much less interpretable within the framework established above. A general affective dispositional approach suggests an explanation for individual differences in job affect not accounted for by the other models.

The purpose of explicating these models of attitudes and affect is to develop a general theoretical framework to be used in the discussion and evaluation of conceptual models of behavioral persistence and commitment in organizations. Models purporting to explain job attitudes and certain kinds of job behaviors should take into account these basic models so as to make use of existing theoretical developments and empirical work. Further inventions of the wheel are redundant. A second kind of theoretical work directly relevant to this area, valence models of work role affect and motivation, is reviewed below.

Valence Models

The models of work role affect presented above account for variance in current affect levels in terms of past and present job contributions, outcomes, and standards for evaluating them. In most models of organizational adaptation and withdrawal, work role dissatisfaction serves as an impetus to behavioral intentions to change dissatisfying elements of the work role. Valence models are explicitly future oriented. They account for individuals' choices to commit time and effort to different behaviors in terms of subjective *expected* utilities. Expectations about future rather than current affect are assumed to be the impetus for behaviors and behavioral choices.

Valence theory was popularized in the industrial and organizational psychology literature by Vroom (1964) and received its most complete explication and development by Naylor, Pritchard, and Ilgen (1980), who built on and extended the earlier contributions of Tolman (1932), Peak (1955), Rosenberg (1956), Vroom (1964), and others. Its historical roots can be traced to Epicurus, who argued that virtue was represented by the wise management of pleasure. Valence, defined as anticipated satisfaction or pleasure in these models, represents the link to Epicurus.

Only the elements of Naylor, Pritchard, and Ilgen's detailed theory of behavior in organizations that are related to the formation of subjective expected utilities are considered in this section. Relations between affect and valence theories of behavior are also addressed.

Naylor, Pritchard, and Ilgen conceptualize the process by which individuals generate subjective expected utility estimates as a result of multiple-contingency learning. The relevant contingencies in this process are subjective conditional probabilities between *acts* or *behaviors* and *products* ($C_{A \rightarrow P}$), between products and *perceived products* ($C_{P \rightarrow P'}$), between perceived products and *evaluations* ($C_{P \rightarrow E}$), and between evaluations and *outcomes* ($C_{E \rightarrow O}$). A final relationship between outcomes and *utility* allows individual differences in preferences for dif-ferent outcomes. This last link is not a contingency; it reflects individual differences in

FIGURE 4

Graphic Representation of the Major Components and Contingencies Among the Components in Naylor, Pritchard, and Ilgen's Valence Model

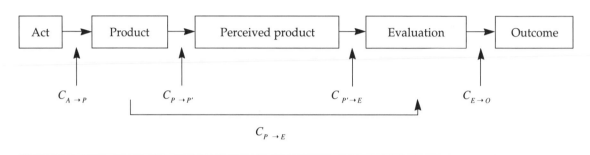

From *A Theory of Behavior in Organizations* (chap. 1, Figure 1.2) by J. C. Naylor, R. D. Pritchard, and D. I. Ilgen, 1980. New York: Academic Press. Copyright 1980 by Academic Press, Inc. Adapted by permission.

preferences for outcomes. The contingencies that constitute the core of the valence portion of the model are assumed to reflect experience and learning in organizations. These contingencies and the relation between outcomes and utilities establish an expected utility for the behaviors individuals enact. The utility of act A results from contingencies between the act and all possible products of the act, the contingencies between each possible product of the act and evaluations of those products, the contingencies between the evaluations and outcomes, and the relations between each possible outcome of the different evaluations of the products and the valence of each outcome.

According to Naylor, Pritchard, and Ilgen, individuals make choices to commit resources to acts or behaviors that will generate the greatest valence when evaluated across the multiple products, evaluations, outcomes, and utilities associated with each act. Obviously, heuristics and shortcuts are used by most individuals to approximate the full cognitive model. Figure 4 shows the components of the model and the contingencies that lead to work role valence.

If this model were used to explain commitment or persistence of membership in an organization, individuals would be expected to engage in persistence behaviors, such as arriving at work regularly and on time, not quitting, and not retiring early, as long as the expected utilities for these behaviors were greater than the utilities of the alternative or competing acts of absenteeism, tardiness, turnover, and retirement. Whenever the utility of absenteeism or quitting is greater than the utility of attendance or remaining in an organization, the individual is expected to be absent or to quit.

One important aspect of this valence model of role behavior is that it emphasizes that individuals make choices among alternative behaviors rather than deciding to engage in act A as an isolated act divorced from other choices. Thus, absence behavior is not determined solely by the valence of absenteeism. The relative valences of absence on a specified day and of attendance at work on that day are the determining factors.

Individuals in an organization learn the contingencies that transform today's acts into valences—tomorrow's satisfactions. The valence of various outcomes is determined by the extent to which each outcome satisfies the individual's needs. Thus, Naylor, Pritchard, and Ilgen's model represents a model of valence-determined behavioral choice in which individuals are assumed to make decisions about time and effort commitments to acts in terms of need fulfillment. In this model, satisfaction is an epiphenomenon, a by-product of behavior in a role, with no direct implications for persistence, commitment, or other organizationally relevant behaviors.

Integration of Valence and Affect Models. Valence and affect models of behavioral choices made by work role incumbents are competing explanations of organizational behaviors, the valence model emphasizing anticipated satisfaction from behaviors and the affect model emphasizing the role of past experience in determining behaviors. These models can be integrated, however, to some degree. Such an integration stresses learning the outcomes of past work role behaviors as well as distinctions between *impetus* to action, a concept not well handled within a strict valence model, and *choice* or *direction* of acts.

Through firsthand and vicarious experience, individuals become aware of the direct and indirect effects of different outcomes on their satisfactions. As noted above, if they found money satisfying in the past, they will more likely commit time and effort to acts in current work roles that have in the past led to acquisition of money. If they found responsibility dissatisfying, they are unlikely to commit time and effort to today's acts that will lead to increased responsibility in the future. Other individuals, because of experienced satisfaction from responsibility and the attendant outcomes, might invite increased responsibility through their choice of behaviors.

Current affect levels with job outcomes provide information to job incumbents about the outcomes and affect levels they can expect if they continue their current behaviors in their current work roles. Dissatisfied individuals might be expected to change their behavior patterns in their work roles, or even change their work roles, under the assumption that current affect levels are the best predictor of future affect; if nothing is done to change the situation, they will continue to be dissatisfied. Satisfied individuals might be expected to make behavioral choices in the future, including choices of work roles, that are similar to those made in the past that led to their current situation.

In a hybrid model combining affect and valence concepts, relative dissatisfaction is the impetus to action that is missing from a strict valence model. Many work role behaviors, particularly those that involve change, need a mechanism that stimulates *action*. This is in addition to mental calculus or cognitive activity that generates estimates of valence or utility of the possible actions. The stress or discomfort that accompanies job dissatisfaction is such a stimulus, triggered by an event, act, or experience in the work environment (Rosse & Miller, 1984). The specific action taken or the act to which time and effort are committed is likely determined by anticipated satisfaction with the outcomes of the chosen acts. Knowledge about the anticipated satisfactions or valences of the outcomes comes from experienced satisfaction from similar acts in the past.

Employees are aware of the possible behavioral choices and the consequences of these choices, although newer employees are probably less aware of them than the longer tenured employees. They evaluate possible acts on the basis of experience with similar classes or families of acts and their associated outcomes. In highly constrained choice situations, employees choose, from among the possible acts, those acts or behaviors that they learned are more likely to be the most satisfying, or the least dissatisfying or stressful. If an act or behavior has produced satisfying or valued outcomes in the past, it is likely to be repeated. If the act has produced dissatisfying outcomes, it is unlikely to be repeated.

This integration of valence and affect models of behavioral choice in work roles has the advantage over valence models of providing a trigger mechanism for behavior and behavioral change. The employee is no longer left, like a rat in the start box of a maze, evaluating the utility of acts without a mechanism to incite action. It also provides for affect models a psychological process by which the employee can extrapolate from outcomes of past behaviors to anticipated satisfaction with outcomes of similar behaviors in the future via a feedforward loop. Such a feedforward loop can act as a guide for employees' choice of behaviors.

The integration also provides a different interpretation of the roots of individual differences in utilities of outcomes. This is more than a cosmetic change in wording for the sake of an integration of models. That is, individuals are expected to learn what outcomes are satisfying to them in the same way that they learn which acts lead to positively evaluated products and which to negatively evaluated products. The change removes the emphasis on needs with their questionable theoretical basis (Campbell & Pritchard, 1976; Ebel, 1974) and substitutes an emphasis on learning, by means of direct or vicarious experience, which outcomes are satisfying. Individuals are assumed to be more aware of their satisfactions from outcomes than they are of the links between commitment of resources and satisfactions of abstract needs.

Models of Organizational Role Withdrawal

The models reviewed in this section explain individuals' decisions to leave an organization. Models of organizational adaptation in which turnover is but one of many possible responses, and not necessarily the most theoretically interesting response at that, are considered in the next section.

This distinction in terms of the complexity of the dependent variable is important. It has an impact on the theoretical status and testability of the models. At one extreme, the dependent variable is a binary representation of remaining in an organizational role versus leaving the role during a specified period. Alternatives to this binary, and often low-frequency, variable (Hulin & Rousseau, 1980) include a continuously distributed, latent propensity to leave a role or an organization as well as a multivariate set of dependent variables representing different forms of organizational adaptation and role withdrawal (Hanisch & Hulin, 1990; Harrison & Hulin, 1989; Hulin, Roznowski, & Hachiya, 1985; Rosse & Hulin, 1985; Rosse & Miller, 1984).

The choice of our dependent variables— binary measures of specific organizational behavior versus continuously distributed composites of behavioral propensities, intentions, predispositions, and component acts— often determines the apparent empirical validity of our models. Organizational turnover rates are rarely above 20 percent per year and often as low as 2 or 3 percent per year (Porter & Steers, 1973). Absenteeism has a similar range across industries and time (Steers & Rhodes, 1984). Low base rate, binary variables impose a severe ceiling on the empirical validities of a model developed to account for variance in infrequent events because of the effects of base rates on empirical correlations (Hulin, 1984; Olsson, Drasgow, & Dorans, 1982; Wiggins, 1973). Thus, models that are valid representations of the events and processes leading to turnover or absenteeism may often appear invalid because of artifactually low empirical correlations.

Thibaut and Kelley's Model.   The role withdrawal model presented by Thibaut and Kelley (1959) represents a bridge between the organizational turnover models and basic developments in attitude theory. The central concepts of Thibaut and Kelley's model have already been discussed and are represented in Table 1. The important elements of this model for role withdrawal behaviors are the independent influences on role attitudes and role withdrawal. For example, labor market conditions, as a determinant of the number and range of jobs available, should affect job termination decisions. Low levels of unemployment mean more alternative jobs are available, with the increased likelihood that they will offer better role outcomes than those associated with an incumbent's present job. Thus, CL_{ALT}, the best alternative role available, would most likely be more positive than the outcomes associated with the current work role during times of low unemployment or expanding labor markets. Individuals would consequently be expected to quit their jobs more frequently during times of better economic conditions.

At the macrolevel of labor market analyses, this prediction is clearly supported (Eagley, 1965). However, unless assumptions are made about the relationship between role affect and labor market information or about the relationship between CL and CL_{ALT} (e.g., both being influenced by related events and processes in the labor market), there should be no necessary empirical relationship and no direct causal connection between work role affect and work role withdrawal in the Thibaut and Kelley model. The consistent and often strong negative correlation between job satisfaction and likelihood of role withdrawal frequently reported in the empirical literature (Hom & Hulin, 1981; Hom, Katerberg, & Hulin, 1979; Hulin, 1966a; Michaels & Spector, 1982; Porter & Steers, 1973) may be a problem for the Thibaut and Kelley model as originally stated. Given the negative bias that probably exists in the empirical relationships between job satisfaction and turnover as estimators of the underlying theoretical relationship between job attitudes and latent propensity to quit, the underlying relationship is probably strong and negative. Additional assumptions about common antecedents between CL and CL_{ALT} are required before the Thibaut and Kelley model should be generalized to organizational turnover. The hypothesized role of labor markets is a factor of this model that requires consideration.

March and Simon's Model. March and Simon (1958) hypothesize that organizational participation and its obverse, turnover, are a function of individuals' perceptions of the desirability and ease of job movement. Desirability of job movement, defined as leaving an organization, is determined largely by level of job satisfaction and to a lesser extent by perceptions of the possibility of intraorganizational transfer. Perceptions of the ease of job movement are related to the number of extraorganizational alternative positions, which in turn is a function of the business activity level, number of other visible organizations, and personal characteristics related to marketable job skills.

According to the March and Simon model, imbalances in an individual's present work role contributions and inducements lead to dissatisfaction (March & Simon, 1958, pp. 84–85). Dissatisfaction triggers a job search as an attempt to reestablish the balance. Initial searches for alternative jobs are normally internal to the organization in which the person works. Failure to find acceptable alternatives within the organization leads to job searches outside the organization. Failure to find a suitable external job usually leads to a reduction in the individual's level of aspiration. Such a reduction will have the effect of redressing the imbalance in contributions and inducements by either reducing the utility of contributions or increasing the utility of inducements. Inducements and contributions are the two theoretical components of job satisfaction; in March and Simon's model, changes in job satisfaction, absent changes in objective conditions of the job, must be through these two components.

In one interpretation, March and Simon's model proposes two independent and additive effects, ease and desirability of movement, on job turnover. Their verbal description of the model suggests, however, that when some level of negative job affect triggers a job search, there should be an interaction between job satisfaction and alternative positions available that plays a part in organizational turnover.

Dissatisfaction should lead to organizational turnover only if the dissatisfied individual perceives there are better alternative positions available. March and Simon contend that very few individuals who are satisfied leave an organization, contrary to the predictions of Thibaut and Kelly's model, and some who are dissatisfied do not leave because of a lack of alternative employment opportunities.

The model has received few empirical tests in which causal or path coefficients from assumed antecedents of turnover decisions were estimated. In spite of this, the model has been influential in shaping the thinking of researchers who have done both conceptual work (e.g., Mobley, 1977; Mobley, Horner, & Hollingsworth, 1978) and empirical research (e.g., Carsten & Spector, 1987; Dansereau, Cashman, & Graen, 1974; Jackofsky & Peters, 1983; Miller, 1981; Miller, Katerberg, & Hulin, 1979; Rosse, 1983; Shikiar & Freudenberg, 1982; Steers & Rhodes, 1978). Indeed, the impact of March and Simon's model is more extensive than its empirically verified hypotheses suggest is justified. Mobley's process model of organizational turnover (1977), developed nearly 20 years after March and Simon's, is similar to the model just presented. Rosse and Miller's adaptation model (1984), although more complex in its specifications of the possible responses to job dissatisfaction and emphasizing adaptive response cycles, is also a direct descendant of the March and Simon model. Unfortunately, the March and Simon model's rich description of the job search process is not matched by its description of the antecedents and process leading to job satisfaction.

Mobley's Process Model.   Mobley (1977; Mobley, Horner, & Hollingsworth, 1978) developed a multistep process model of organizational turnover that begins with an evaluation of one's current job and, given that the evaluation results in dissatisfaction, proceeds step by step through thinking of quitting, intentions to search for alternative positions, intentions to

quit or stay, and eventually to quitting or staying. A graphic representation of this process model is shown in Figure 5.

Mobley's work is an extensive elaboration of March and Simon's (1958) model of organizational participation. Mobley has included steps involving behavioral intentions as the proximal causes of behaviors (steps E and I). The model explicitly includes considerations of labor markets (steps D, F, G, and H) and evaluations of one's current position against unspecified but presumably internal standards and against standards established by available alternative positions (steps A and H). Inclusions of intentions, labor market considerations, and comparison standards to evaluate one's current job establish connections between Mobley's process model and the models developed by Fishbein and Ajzen (1975), Fishbein (1979), March and Simon (1958), Thibaut and Kelley (1959), and, to a lesser degree, the Cornell model (Smith et al., 1969).

The linear, step-by-step, causal nature of the model also allows it to be interpreted as a simplex model of behavior with every step in the model mediating the effects of all previous steps, from the first mild feelings of dissatisfaction to quitting. This is equivalent to hypothesizing that $r_{ik.j} = 0$ for all $i < j < k$ where i, j, and k are ordered steps in the cognitive and behavioral process. Joreskog and Sorbom (1983) discuss testing such simplex models in LISREL-VI.

Miller, Katerberg, and Hulin (1979) exploited the simplex aspect of Mobley's model and carried out an informal linear structural relations analysis. Their results generally supported the validity of a simplified version of Mobley's model at the construct level, although several individual variables that were used to index different constructs did not operate as predicted by the model. Perceptions of alternative jobs, however, did not yield results that supported the model even at the construct level.[2] Hulin et al. (1985) discuss the implications of failures to find supporting evidence of the

FIGURE 5

Graphic Representation of Mobley's (1977) Process Model of Organizational Turnover

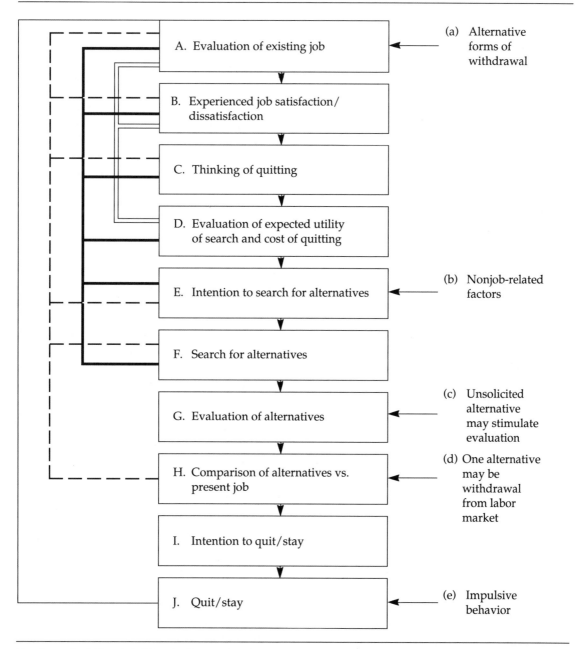

hypothesized operation of perceptions of the labor market for this model.

Carsten and Spector (1987) carried out a meta-analysis of approximately 50 studies of the satisfaction-turnover relationship. They reported an average correlation of −.23 (−.26 corrected for attenuation) between satisfaction and turnover. The analogous coefficients between intentions to quit and turnover were +.38 and +.47. Of particular interest to this discussion are the correlations intended to test the hypothesized interaction effects of alternative job opportunities on turnover contained in Mobley's model (1977) and in Muchinsky and Morrow's derivative model of turnover (1980). These correlations between unemployment rates and the satisfaction-turnover association ranged from −.18 (using state unemployment rates, $N = 16$ studies) to −.52 (using occupational unemployment rates, $N = 15$ studies). Carsten and Spector argue that these results support the hypothesis that the job satisfaction-turnover relationship becomes weaker as the number of available alternatives decreases. That is, adverse labor market conditions prevent individuals from translating their dissatisfaction into termination decisions. This is the effect hypothesized by Mobley, Muchinsky and Morrow, March and Simon, and others and is opposite the labor market effect reported by Shikiar and Freudenberg (1982) in a review of empirical studies in this area.

Unfortunately, the design used by Carsten and Spector is not adequate to test the hypothesized effect of unemployment (available alternative employment) on turnover and relations involving turnover. Quit rates are directly related to unemployment rates (Eagley, 1965). Quit rates are generally low and severely attenuate any correlations involving them that assume bivariate normality for their evaluation. If unemployment rates have an artifactual, statistical effect on satisfaction-turnover correlations because of their effects on the base rate for turnover, then correlations between employment rates and such correlations cannot be

relied on to test either the simple conceptual hypotheses or the complete turnover models that generated the hypothesis. Correlations involving turnover must be corrected by the attenuation factors discussed by Olsson, Drasgow, and Dorans (1982) to estimate the theoretical correlation between continuously distributed measures of turnover propensity and satisfaction. Otherwise, the empirical correlations are likely to be badly biased underestimates of the theoretical relations. In this case, labor market effects are directly related to the amount of attenuation in the correlations involving turnover. Thus, labor markets have a hypothesized model-based effect and an artifactual effect that are confounded. These artifactual effects must be removed before any substantive interpretations are made of the labor market effects on correlations between job satisfaction and turnover. The log transformation carried out by Carsten and Spector will not adequately correct for the attenuating effect of low turnover rates on the correlations. As a test of the complete turnover models of Mobley, March and Simon, Hulin et al., and others, the procedure is also inadequate.

Ambiguities in Mobley's model should not be overlooked. It is not clear, for example, what effect alternate forms of withdrawal noted by Mobley (see [a] in Figure 5) will have on the subsequent psychological process. Are these alternative forms of withdrawal psychologically and functionally equivalent to turnover? If so, will they reduce job dissatisfaction, precluding the necessity for quitting (assuming, of course, that reduction of dissatisfaction is the psychological function of turnover)?

Note also the feedback loop from H to A in Figure 5. This feedback loop, from comparisons of alternatives against one's present job, allows individuals to reevaluate their present job in terms of what alternatives are available in the labor market. This loop, although a potentially important element of the model, is a source of ambiguity. What are the expected actions of a dissatisfied employee who finds no better alternative positions? (This is analogous to the situation depicted in row C of Table 1, where a person experiencing a given set of outcomes is dissatisfied because they are below *CL*, but will not quit because the current role outcomes are above CL_{ALT}.) Will such employees reevaluate their job and experience less dissatisfaction because it is better than anything else obtainable, or will they continue to be dissatisfied but do nothing about it, or will they engage in alternative forms of withdrawal? What are the psychological consequences of being dissatisfied but having no alternatives to the current work role? Most turnover models are mute with respect to this question; Mobley's model is no exception.

Fishbein and Ajzen's Model.   The Fishbein and Ajzen attitude–behavioral intention model is a general theoretical statement about relations between antecedents of attitudes, attitudes, behavioral intentions, and behaviors (Ajzen & Fishbein, 1977; Fishbein, 1967; Fishbein & Ajzen, 1975). The most complete statement of the model as a theory of reasoned action is found in Fishbein (1979). The model is not restricted to any specific behavior or set of behaviors except that they should be unconstrained choice behaviors. Habitual, reflexive, constrained, and phobic behaviors would normally be beyond the range of this model. To the extent that role persistence behaviors have elements of constraint, habituation, or impulsiveness, the behavioral intention model would be less than perfectly applicable.

The model proposes that behavior is a consequence of behavioral intentions, which, in turn, are a linear function of attitudes toward the act *(Aact)* and subjective norms *(SN)*. *Aact* is defined as the sum of the beliefs (b_i) about the consequences of performing the behavior, weighted by the evaluations (valences) of those consequences $(Aact = \Sigma b_i e_i)$. *SN* is the general perception about whether important referents expect the subject to perform the act. *SN* is equated with the sum of the normative beliefs *(NB)* that specific significant others think the subject should perform the behavior, weighted by the motivation to comply *(Mc)* with these referent others $(SN = \Sigma NB_i \, Mc_i)$. Rather than attitudes toward objects as the determining factor in behavior with respect to that object, the model proposes that attitudes toward the act and subjective norms about the act are the major determinants of behavioral intentions; behavioral intentions are sufficient predictors of the behavior.

Algebraically, the model can be expressed as follows:

$$\text{Behavior} \approx BI = (Aact)W_1 + (SN)W_2$$

where *BI*, *Aact*, and *SN* have been previously defined and W_1 and W_2 are theoretical weights reflecting the importance of the components to individuals in the determination of *BI*.[3]

The general validity of the Fishbein and Ajzen intention model has been well established across a broad range of behaviors, including organizational turnover (Hom & Hulin, 1981; Hom, Katerberg, & Hulin, 1979). Most of the turnover models discussed in this chapter have adopted one or more of the elements from the behavioral intention model, especially the role of behavioral intentions as the proximal cause of behavior rather than hypothesizing a relation between attitudes and behavior absent the formation of behavioral intentions.

Fishbein and Ajzen also argue that the attitudes and intentions must be congruent with the behavior being predicted. Thus, if we are predicting decisions by individuals to leave their present job and organization within a specified time period, our assessments of behavioral intentions must match the criterion; that is, we must ask work role incumbents about the probability that they will quit their job and their current organization within the specified time period. We must also assess attitudes toward the act of quitting rather than attitudes toward the job. If, on the other hand, we are interested in predicting an individual's standing along a general dimension that reflects engaging in multiple acts that form a general response syndrome within a work role, then general attitudes toward the object (the job) should suffice to predict this general behavioral criterion; the attitude and the behavioral criterion are congruent.

There is little question about the predictive validity of behavioral intention models. Their conceptual and empirical history (Dulany, 1968; Fishbein & Ajzen, 1975; Locke, Shaw, Saari, & Latham, 1981; Ryan, 1970; Triandis, 1979) is impressive. Such models, and particularly the behavioral intentions variable, do what they are intended to do so well they have been referred to as the "idiots savants" of industrial and organizational psychology: They do one thing extremely well, but that is the extent of their usefulness.[4]

A final crucial element in the Fishbein and Ajzen model is that the relevant antecedents of *BIs* are attitudes toward the *act* (persistence or quitting), not attitudes toward the object (the job or work role). *Aacts* share many of the characteristics of *BIs*. Researchers gain precision and predictability of a specific behavior at the expense of general information, predictability of a general behavioral syndrome, and generalizability across behaviors when they assess *Aact*. Perhaps for these reasons, many investigators have not adopted the specificity of the Fishbein and Ajzen model. They use attitudes toward a job, a work role, or even an entire organization in place of specific *Aacts*. The loss of predictive validity for specific acts may be compensated for by the information contained in the more general affective responses that are often related to a number of different acts and predict multiple-act criteria better.

Summary.   The four models of role withdrawal or role behavior just discussed are important for their relations to attitude theory and to a general theory of organizational behavior. Thibaut and Kelley's model, as generalized to withdrawal from work roles, seems unable to

account for empirical results showing a strong relationship between role affect and role withdrawal unless certain assumptions are made about the relation between CL and CL_{ALT}. However, this model does emphasize the theoretical role of labor markets on role withdrawal that has been confirmed empirically in many studies (Carsten & Spector, 1987).

March and Simon's model also includes a provision for influences from labor market conditions; in this model, the influences are assumed to be on the utility of job contributions, assessed in the metric of opportunity costs, and indirectly on work role affect or satisfaction. Thus, the influence of labor markets on turnover involves a three-step sequence.

Both the Thibaut and Kelley and March and Simon models of affect and role behavior appear to be single behavior models. That is, in the former, the hypothesized response by a role incumbent to a CL_{ALT} greater than the current role is to leave the current role. March and Simon similarly focus on role withdrawal as a response to negative role affect, although their model does include a provision for alternative forms of role withdrawal; "internal bargaining as an alternative to movement is a factor in several types of organizational participation" (1958, p. 111).

Mobley's model is similar in many respects to March and Simon's. Its main emphasis is on turnover as a response to dissatisfaction; provisions for alternate withdrawal behaviors are included, but their role is not spelled out in any specificity. It includes influences from the outcomes of a job search and from labor market conditions. The precise impact of such influences is not given in detail, except as moderating effects on the relations between satisfaction and turnover.

The Fishbein and Ajzen model establishes the framework within which specific turnover and role withdrawal models can be evaluated. It also seems to establish the ceiling against which predictive validities of role withdrawal models can be compared. The impressive single behavior validities of the Fishbein and Ajzen model in many different areas and its comparative validity in predicting organizational turnover make this use of the model compelling if one is interested in predicting single behavior, specific responses within a specified time period.

Job Adaptation

The first part of this section contains a methodological discussion of expected relations between different kinds of withdrawal behaviors, the purpose of which will be to highlight some of the problems inherent in studying low base rate events in isolation or as single outcroppings of an assumed underlying theoretical construct. Serious mischief is done to empirical results by studying these infrequent events in isolation from the other variables with which they may combine to compose a general theoretical construct. The concept of *job adaptation* as a construct encompassing job withdrawal is also introduced to provide an alternative to continued analyses of the antecedents and correlates of absences, turnover, and tardiness as isolated variables.

Methodological Considerations

Several factors that were relevant in evaluating the results reported by Carsten and Spector (1987) are relevant to evaluations of all relations involving absence, turnover, or other low base rate behaviors. One is the limitation on the values of Pearson product-moment correlations involving low base rate variables with badly skewed distributions. Among others, Wiggins (1973), Hulin (1984), and Olsson, Drasgow, and Dorans (1982) have discussed the problems inherent in interpreting these correlations.

A second factor is the time period over which the behaviors—say, absences or terminations—are aggregated. Two contradictory goals are at work in choosing the time interval.

The first is to keep the interval short so that the assessment of the predictor variable—say, work role job satisfaction—is still relevant to the affect levels being experienced by employees as they decide whether to attend or to be absent or quit. The longer the period over which absences are aggregated, however, the greater the base rate of absences, the greater the variance of the distribution of absences, the greater the maximum observable correlation between satisfaction and absences, and the better the estimate the empirical correlation is of the population theoretical correlation. But we need short time intervals to maximize the relevance of our predictor assessments to the behaviors being predicted.

Unfortunately, there is no adequate theory of organizational time that guides our choice of optimal time intervals in such studies. We could select time periods for aggregating our observations that were long enough to provide substantial correlations between time periods under the assumption that these correlations indicated reliability of the aggregated measures. This decision rule only substitutes psychometric theory that is of questionable applicability in this specific instance for relevant organizational theory. Treating correlations between absences in two time periods as reliability estimates requires, for example, that we be able to define *parallel* time periods (as analogous to parallel measures of a trait) or assume that two arbitrary periods are parallel. This requires a theory of organizational time to define parallel periods (Hulin, 1984). Carsten and Spector (1987) attempted to test a hypothesis about the length of the time period of the study (across which turnover decisions were aggregated) as a moderator of the size of the correlation between affect and subsequent turnover. This test involved the use of correlations as the dependent variable; these correlations may be biased estimates of the underlying relationship, as demonstrated below.

To appreciate the magnitude of these effects, consider the following model of three behavioral propensities that partially define a latent withdrawal construct:

Absence propensity = $X = a_1\theta + s_1(S_x) + E_x$

Tardiness propensity = $Y = a_2\theta + s_2(S_y) + E_y$

Turnover propensity = $Z = a_3\theta + s_3(S_z) + E_z$

where θ represents a general withdrawal factor; S_X, S_Y, and S_Z represent specific, nonerror factors that are not common to the other behavioral propensities in the model; a_i and s_i represent the loadings of the behavioral propensities on the common and specific factors, respectively; and E_X, E_Y, and E_Z represent random errors. For convenience, θ and S are scaled to have unit variance. X, Y, and Z represent continuous, normally distributed action tendencies (behavioral propensities) that underlie the observed manifestations of absence, x, tardiness, y, and turnover, z. Under assumptions of uncorrelated errors and specific factors, it can be shown that:

S^2 (Absence Propensity) = $S_X^2 = a_1^2 + s_1^2 + S_{E_x}^2$

S^2 (Tardiness Propensity) = $S_Y^2 = a_2^2 + s_2^2 + S_{E_y}^2$

S^2 (Turnover Propensity) = $S_Z^2 = a_3^2 + s_3^2 + S_{E_z}^2$

where a_i is the loading of the behavioral propensity on the general withdrawal factor θ, s_i is the loading on the specific factor, and S_E^2 is error variance.

The correlations between the behavioral propensities can be shown to be:

$\rho_{XY} = a_1 a_2$

$\rho_{XZ} = a_1 a_3$

$\rho_{YZ} = a_2 a_3$

Assume that there exist three threshold cut scores, γ_i, along the absence continuum such that if an individual's propensity to be absent, X_i, is less than the lowest threshold, γ_1, the individual is not absent during that quarter and therefore $x_i = 0$. If $\gamma_1 < X_i < \gamma_2$, the individual will be absent once, $x_i = 1$. If $\gamma_2 < X_i < \gamma_3$, the

individual will be absent twice, $x_i = 2$. If $X_i > \gamma_3$, the individual will be absent three or more times, $x_i = 3$. The use of three threshold cut scores to generate observed absences, x, from the underlying behavioral propensity, X, is arbitrary; three cut scores were chosen to represent a distribution of observed absences that could reasonably be expected within a group of employees. During any given quarter, a range of absences from 0 to 3 would be expected to cover the absences taken by the overwhelming majority of the employees (Harrison & Hulin, 1989; see Steers and Rhodes, 1984, for a discussion of absence rates in organizations in the United States). Such an underlying distribution, the cut scores, and the observed values of x are depicted in Figure 6.

Similarly, we can hypothesize five threshold cut scores, $\tau_1, \tau_2 \ldots \tau_5$, that divide the tardiness propensity continuum into six different observed values of Y, $y = 0, 1, \ldots, 5$. Five cut scores were chosen to generate a range of tardinesses that should cover the majority of individuals in an organization during a quarter.

The turnover propensity continuum Z has one threshold cut score, ζ. Individuals with $Z \geq \zeta$ will quit during the quarter, $z = 1$. Otherwise, they will not quit, $z = 0$.

These assumptions define a simple model in which three behaviors are manifestations of a single, common underlying latent withdrawal construct, θ. The continuous and normally distributed underlying propensities generate observed polytomous manifestations through the operation of thresholds. The thresholds are assumed to be generated by organizational and social factors in the situation. The individuals' locations along the propensity continuum reflect individual differences and person-situation interactions. By specifying loadings of the behavioral propensities on the underlying withdrawal factor, θ, and different thresholds on the three propensities, we can derive the population Pearson product-moment correlations among the three observable

FIGURE 6

**Relationship Between Assumed Underlying Distribution of
Absence Propensity, X, Threshold Scores, γ, and Observed Values of Absences, x**

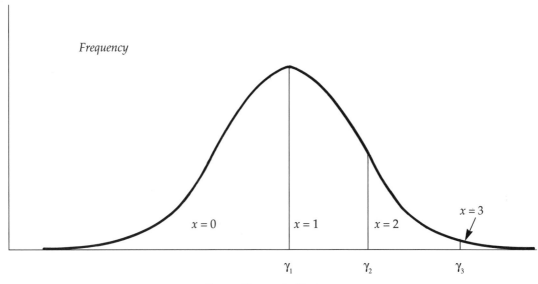

Absence Propensity X →

behaviors. The reasonableness of these derivations depends on the loadings of the behavioral propensities on θ and on the threshold cut scores that generate observable values of $x, y,$ or z from the underlying propensities, $X, Y,$ or Z. The other assumptions (e.g., pairwise bivariate normality) needed to derive expected relations among observed variables are standard in this area.

Assume the loadings of the behavioral propensities on θ are .5, .4, and .6, respectively, for absence, tardiness, and turnover. Thus, $\rho_{XY} = .20, \rho_{XZ} = .30,$ and $\rho_{YZ} = .24$. The important question is what are the expected values of the observed empirical correlations between $x, y,$ and $z,$ the observed manifestations of the latent propensities—if we have probability density distributions of $x, y,$ and z as follows:

Absence		Lateness		Turnover	
x	Prob.	y	Prob.	z	Prob.
0	.50	0	.40	0	.98
1	.30	1	.20	1	.02
2	.15	2	.15		
3	.05	3	.10		
		4	.10		
		5	.05		

The correlations between the observed behavioral manifestations of withdrawal as described by the above model are $\rho_{xy} = .04, \rho_{xz} = .08,$ and $\rho_{yz} = .08$. With unrealistic loadings of each of the three behavioral propensities of .80 on the common factor, the expected Pearson correlations are $\rho_{xy} = .38, \rho_{xz} = .21,$ and $\rho_{yz} = .23$.

Although these latter correlations are marginally large enough to be interesting, they have not been attenuated by the effects of unreliability in the assessments of both variables. Sampling fluctuations will generate sampling distributions of observed values such that about half of the observed correlations would be less than these theoretical values. *Empirical correlations among this sample of infrequent withdrawal behaviors with badly skewed distributions provide little information about the underlying relations.* Research methods based on normal curve statistics and assumptions do not provide the power necessary to address important questions in this area.

We can also derive what the expected Pearson correlations would be between a continuously distributed measure of satisfaction and each of these behaviors assuming satisfaction has a specified loading on the common withdrawal factor, θ. If the loading of satisfaction on the common withdrawal factor were $-.60$, then $\rho_{sx} = -.30$, $\rho_{sy} = -.24$, and $\rho_{sz} = -.36$. The expected values of the Pearson correlations between satisfaction and the observed behaviors would be $-.23$ for absence, $-.22$ for lateness, and $-.12$ for turnover. These expected correlations would probably not be interpreted as strong empirical support for a common factor withdrawal model, even though the underlying bivariate distributions that generated the observed correlations are consistent with such a single common factor model. [5]

The point of this methodological note is that meta-analyses or any other reviews of accumulated empirical correlations between satisfaction and polytomous behaviors cannot be relied on to estimate population correlations *if the empirical correlations themselves are biased estimates of the underlying relationships.* Empirical correlations involving absence, turnover, and tardiness measures will nearly always be biased estimates of the underlying relationship. Removing artifactual sources of variance from a distribution of biased estimates of a population value only produces a biased estimate free of influences of unreliability, sampling fluctuations, and some other statistical artifacts. The specter of bias in the empirical estimators of population correlations cannot be avoided even following meta-analyses of empirical results unless extraordinary steps are taken to correct all observed correlations for bias caused by distributional properties of the behavior.

Adaptation as a Theoretical Construct

A limiting factor on much research done in the area of job withdrawal, quite apart from the problems caused by low base rates, is the focus on single behaviors in isolation (Rosse & Hulin, 1985; Roznowski & Hanisch, 1990). This focus ignores the possibility that the behaviors may represent outcroppings of an underlying construct. Manifest behaviors should be judged and studied according to their scientific merit as indicators of an underlying construct rather than according to whether they are noticeable or costly.

In addition to the questionable scientific merit of predicting specific individual behaviors, another effect on empirical results should be noted. In the above example, the expected correlation between job affect and a composite behavioral criterion, an unweighted sum of the three withdrawal behaviors of tardiness, absenteeism, and turnover, is $-.32$. The increase in the expected correlation with the composite withdrawal criterion represents a doubling of the variance accounted for over that represented by the maximum correlation between job satisfaction and any one of the specific behaviors. This increase is not due to increased reliability of the composite criterion over the reliability of any one specific behavior; for this example, no reliability attenuation effects were included. Less-than-perfect reliabilities for each of the behavioral criteria would only accentuate the advantages of using composite criteria.

Job adaptation is an abstract construct hypothesized to underlie a number of diverse behavioral responses and can be inferred only from manifest data. It is defined in terms of covariances among relevant observable variables; its meaning resides in these covariances. One should be able to argue conceptually and demonstrate empirically that a specified set of psychological and behavioral responses is functionally similar, or at least partially substitutable, and is theoretically as well as empirically related to the same job adaptation construct. We should also define the expected manifestations of the latent variable of adaptation—without resorting to the laundry list approach to domain specification. We need some degree of theoretical rigor in the specifications of the domain as well as the psychological functions of the responses within the domain of job adaptation.

In this section, the psychological functions of the responses to job dissatisfaction will be considered within the context of the models of job affect reviewed above. A model describing responses to job dissatisfaction by Hulin, Roznowski, and Hachiya (1985) will be used in conjunction with Rosse and Miller's (1984) developments to specify the content of behaviors that fall within the definition of organizational adaptation.

In the Rosse and Miller (1984) organizational adaptation model and the Hulin et al. (1985) model, individuals are hypothesized to enact a few of the many possible responses to job dissatisfaction. The responses they select to alleviate job dissatisfaction are likely to be targeted to the specific sources or causes (e.g., pay, working conditions, supervision) of their dissatisfaction. Stealing supplies or moonlighting at work by doing outside work on the job might be reasonable responses to dissatisfaction with pay, for example, but not to dissatisfaction with one's supervision. Voting in favor of union representation also may alleviate blue collar workers' dissatisfaction with pay but not dissatisfaction with the work itself or with co-workers. The assumed function of the enacted behaviors is for individuals to reduce the specific dissatisfaction they

experience. Rosse and Miller (1984) define the precipitating event that triggers an adaptation cycle as any stimulus that induces individuals to realize that they could be better off (in a subjective sense) than they currently are.

On the basis of an evaluation of possible responses, reinforcement history, and opportunity constraints, individuals enact a behavior, the intended function of which is to reduce relative dissatisfaction. Behaviors that were found to be effective in the past in reducing dissatisfaction and behaviors that are relatively unconstrained by the situation might be repeated if dissatisfaction continues or reoccurs. Secretaries, for example, have access to the telephone for personal calls or the word-processing system for outside moonlighting assignments while at work; production employees generally do not have access to this equipment. Managers may easily spend large portions of Mondays talking about the weekend sports scores, office politics, or other trivia; secretaries, because of physical office constraints, may not be able to do so. Air traffic controllers in the United States are unlikely in the near future to turn to an organized work stoppage (or perhaps even a strong union) as a way of increasing their job outcomes. The strike of the Professional Air Traffic Controllers Organization (PATCO) in 1982, which was disastrous for the union and many air traffic controllers, makes that course of action unlikely to be seen as effective in reducing dissatisfaction with work outcomes. Teachers, on the other hand, are finding work stoppages and unionization an increasingly frequent response to job dissatisfaction. Rosse and Miller's (1984) model is shown in Figure 7.

The dissatisfaction-adaptation behavior cycle shown in Figure 7 is repeated until dissatisfaction is reduced to tolerable levels. The specific adaptive behaviors selected are assumed to be a function of individuals' reinforcement histories interacting with their opportunity constraints. The range of behaviors that could be selected is potentially broad but

FIGURE 7

Rosse and Miller's Adaptation Cycle Model

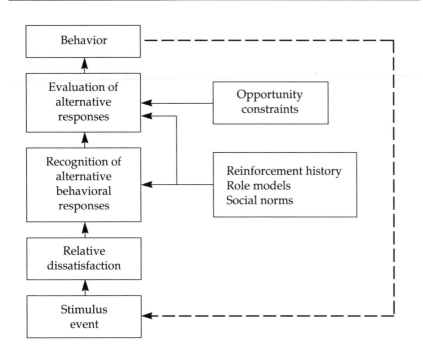

From "Relationship Between Absenteeism and Other Employee Behaviors (p. 208) by J. G. Rosse and H. E. Miller, 1984. In P. S. Goodman, R. S. Atkin, and Associates, *Absenteeism*, San Francisco: Jossey-Bass. Copyright 1984 by Jossey-Bass. Adapted by permission.

is limited by the function of the behavior (to reduce specific relative dissatisfaction), reinforcement history of the individual, and opportunity constraints. This adaptation model is not being offered as a complete and testable model that explains the variance in adaptive organizational responses made by individuals; it is intended as a summary heuristic model that can be used to derive hypotheses about the frequencies with which individuals—in different organizational situations with different reinforcement histories—enact behaviors composed of different families of adaptive responses. These specific hypotheses can be tested to provide evidence of the overall value of the model.

Job Withdrawal as a Set of Adaptive Behaviors

Job withdrawal comprises the set of behaviors that dissatisfied individuals enact to avoid the work situation; they are behaviors designed to allow avoidance of participation in dissatisfying work situations. Circularity in the definition can be broken by defining avoidance on the basis of a consensus among informed researchers working in the field. Specification of avoidance behaviors as behaviors that reduce the inclusion of the individual in the work role or increase the independence of the worker from the work role is one conceptual approach offered by Katz and Kahn (1966, 1978). Some degree of empirical covariation among indicators of the construct is required. Correlations of these behavioral responses with assumed common causes of avoidance or withdrawal are also expected. Agreement among informed researchers in this area—that the behaviors reflect avoidance or withdrawal—is desirable and reflects consensual validation.

Four acts that can be viewed as possible job withdrawal tendencies, within the broader set of adaptation responses, are voluntary absenteeism, lateness, voluntary turnover, and retirement—all acts that can be considered attempts to put physical and psychological distance between a dissatisfied worker and the work environment. Because the behaviors reduce the time individuals must spend in a dissatisfying environment, they decrease their inclusion in the work role and are hypothesized to decrease relative dissatisfaction. They also serve as stimuli that role incumbents can use to interpret their own internal states. However, even with this small sample of four behaviors, there is a considerable amount of controversy (Hackett & Guion, 1985; Rosse & Hulin, 1985; Rosse & Miller, 1984; Scott & Taylor, 1985) about the meaning of the empirical relations. The inclusion of retirement within this set of withdrawals is reasonable because of the changes in age discrimination laws in the United States (Hanisch & Hulin, 1990).

Consistent correlations with a common antecedent, although not conclusive, increase our confidence that the behaviors may reflect the same latent trait or construct. In reviews of the empirical literature, Rosse and Hulin (1985) and Rosse and Miller (1984) report consistent negative empirical relations between overall job satisfaction and absenteeism, turnover, and tardiness. The conclusions of Rosse and Hulin and Rosse and Miller are contradicted in part by Hackett and Guion (1985), who report an average empirical correlation of only −.09 between satisfaction and all forms of absenteeism based on a meta-analysis of the published empirical literature as well as unpublished data.

The conclusions of Hackett and Guion are in turn contradicted by yet another meta-analytic review based on a somewhat narrower set of studies by Scott and Taylor (1985). In this latter review, Scott and Taylor report an average correlation of −.15 between satisfaction and absence frequency. The correlation becomes −.29 when corrected for unreliability in both measures.

These reported average correlations, −.09 and −.15, are in striking agreement with the correlation of −.12 derived from a simple unifactor model of absence propensity and job satisfaction described above. The similarity between the average empirical findings and the expected correlation derived from the simple unifactor model does *not* demonstrate that the process suggested by the hypothetical model generated the absence frequencies that resulted in the empirical correlations. It *does* indicate that the obtained empirical correlations do not disconfirm the existence of this simple model in which absences, tardiness, turnover, and job affect all have moderate loadings on a common, single factor. It also suggests that Hackett and Guion (1985) erred in their interpretation of the average correlation. They concluded the correlation indicated that work absences do not fit within a syndrome of behaviors composing a latent withdrawal propensity. The average correlation they report cannot be used to reject this hypothesis.

Neither the meta-analysis by Hackett and Guion (1985) nor the meta-analysis by Scott and Taylor (1985) correct the observed correlations to reflect the negative biasing effects of base rates on empirical correlations. Although the evidence is not completely consistent, the best conclusion is that overall job satisfaction has a strong negative relation to turnover propensity, a moderately negative relation to absence propensity, and a weakly negative relation to tardiness propensity. The relation between satisfaction and tardiness is less consistent than the relations involving turnover and absenteeism. It has also been less studied.

How retirement decisions, as enacted job withdrawals, fit within a simple unifactor model is yet to be determined. One empirical study by Hanisch and Hulin (1990) provides evidence that individuals' retirement intentions are consistent with the hypothesis that such decisions represent job withdrawal behavior whose psychological function is similar to other such withdrawal behavior. Hanisch and Hulin also found that retirement intentions are related in much the same way to measures of job affect as are behavioral scales representing reported withdrawal and work avoidance behaviors. However, their two samples of university employees appeared to differentiate between work withdrawal behaviors on one hand and job withdrawal behaviors on the other. These results indicate that employees are quite selective in their adaptation behaviors. Further research on the full range of retirement decisions is needed before this response can be argued to be part of a general withdrawal propensity; the only empirical data available are consistent with such a hypothesis.

In addition to the empirical evidence suggesting the common antecedent of tardiness, absenteeism, and turnover, the structure of the relations among the three variables is another important consideration. Rosse and Miller (1984) identified at least six different models that were developed to account for the expected relations among the three behaviors.

The Independent Forms of Withdrawal Model. This model was described by Porter and Steers (1973) and March and Simon (1958), who argue that absence and turnover should be unrelated to each other and studied separately because they have different functions and consequences. March and Simon's advocacy of this model should perhaps be regarded as tentative. They note that absences and turnover are different not because of "differences in the factors inducing the initial impulse but primarily...[because of]...differences in the consequences of the alternative forms of withdrawal" (p. 93). They

also state that "the satisfaction (or motivation to withdraw) is a general one that holds for both absences and voluntary turnover" (p. 93). Thus, they suggest that absence and voluntary turnover are alternate forms of withdrawal behavior with different consequences but a common antecedent.

Empirical support for this model is problematic. Rosse and Miller (1984) and Rosse and Hulin (1985), on the bases of literature reviews, report that weak but positive empirical correlations are generally found between measures of absenteeism, turnover, and tardiness and conclude that these three potential withdrawal behaviors are positively related to each other and appear to be manifestations of a general latent trait of withdrawal. The empirical evidence presented by Hanisch and Hulin (1990), which indicates that reported work avoidance behaviors (including lateness, absenteeism, and quitting) are significantly related to retirement intentions, is also relevant.

The Spillover Model.   The spillover model was articulated by Beehr and Gupta (1978), who argued that withdrawal behaviors should have positive intercorrelations—there should be a "nucleus of withdrawal events that occur in concert" (p. 77). Aversive work situations should generate nonspecific avoidance tendencies. There should be relations among behavioral responses such that the conditional probability of one response, given that another has occurred, is greater than its unconditional probability. There should be relatively large differences between the unconditional probabilities of responses and the conditional probability of the response, given that another response within a family of withdrawal behaviors has occurred. The differences between conditional and unconditional probabilities of responses across families would be expected to be smaller.

The empirical literature cited earlier (Hackett & Guion, 1985; Rosse & Hulin, 1985; Rosse & Miller, 1984; Scott & Taylor, 1985) regarding the relations among withdrawal behaviors and between withdrawal behaviors and satisfaction, appears to support the spillover model. The psychological basis for this model suggests any response that increases the psychological distance between the employee and a dissatisfying work situation is likely to be enacted. Therefore, the conditional probability of a response, given that another withdrawal response has occurred, should be higher than the unconditional probability of the response. Correlations among continuously distributed response propensities would also support the spillover model of the structure among these behaviors.

The spillover model, however, may be too simple an interpretation of organizational withdrawal. The systematic effects of external variables on withdrawal responses suggest modifications are required. For instance, the model does not address how the relations among withdrawal behaviors vary with respect to changes in the local labor market. Eagley (1965) has demonstrated that high unemployment rates are strongly related to lower levels of voluntary job terminations. Very high unemployment rates may rule out voluntary turnover as a reasonable response to dissatisfaction. What effect does this suppression of turnover have on other responses? According to the spillover hypothesis, such behaviors should be positively related. However, if environmental factors suppress quitting as a possible response to job dissatisfaction, is it reasonable to expect the probabilities of other responses will also be reduced? Would it be more reasonable to expect an *increase* in the probabilities of other adaptive or withdrawal responses? An increase in some adaptive responses following a suppression of one response would suggest that relations among these behaviors follow an alternate forms model or a compensatory model.

The Alternate Forms Model. The alternate forms model hypothesizes that withdrawal behaviors can be substituted (Mobley, 1977;

Rice & Trist, 1952; Rosse & Miller, 1984). Thresholds for different behaviors are in large part situationally determined. When constraints are placed on one form of withdrawal, the probability of an alternate form of withdrawal behavior will increase. If turnover is prevented because of labor market conditions, absence or tardiness should *increase*. Where frequent absences or tardiness is precluded by legal or situational constraints, the frequency of alternate forms of withdrawal, such as turnover, should increase. This process is suggested in Figure 5 from Mobley (1977).

The psychological basis of this model is that dissatisfaction caused by the work situation will be relieved by *any* avoidance behavior that reduces the individual's inclusion in the work role or increases the psychological distance between the employee and the work situation. The alternate forms model is not well articulated in the articles that discuss it as a possible description of the expected relations among withdrawal behaviors. Although psychological bases are different for the independent forms model and the alternate forms model, the statistical evidence supporting the independent forms model may be indistinguishable from that supporting the alternate forms model under certain environmental conditions. If there are no external environmental constraints related to labor market conditions on quitting or if there are few organizational contingencies between absenteeism or tardiness and negative outcomes that constrain absence and lateness, then the two models may be indistinguishable in terms of the between-subject statistical evidence. In situations where there are environmental constraints on certain forms of withdrawal, the alternate forms model would predict negative correlations among some of the possible withdrawal behaviors; if one form of withdrawal is blocked, the probability of other forms of withdrawal should increase.

The alternate forms model may be contradicted by the evidence reviewed in conjunction with the independent forms model

(Rosse & Hulin, 1985; Rosse & Miller, 1984). This model is obviously closely related to the compensatory behaviors model, although the psychological mechanism underlying the selection of withdrawal behaviors is different.

The Compensatory Behaviors Model. According to the compensatory behaviors model, one form of avoidance, in varying amounts for different situations, may be sufficient for individuals who find themselves in dissatisfying work situations (Hill & Trist, 1955). They note that absences are a characteristic of "stayers" rather than "leavers." This does not, however, preclude the possibility of using lesser amounts of two or more forms of withdrawal; the total amount of withdrawal represented by all withdrawal behaviors enacted is the important consideration in this model. All withdrawal behaviors are assumed to have the same function: relieving work role dissatisfaction and psychological distress. One form of withdrawal behavior compensates for another. All withdrawal behaviors allow workers to avoid dissatisfying and stressful work environments. *Avoidance behaviors that successfully disengage an employee from the work environment should be negatively correlated among employees with a constant level of work withdrawal propensity caused by work dissatisfaction.* If the psychological distance or withdrawal created by the enacted behaviors is sufficient, they should compensate for the dissatisfaction and make other withdrawal or adaptive responses unnecessary, thereby reducing the probability other responses will occur.

Unfortunately, Hill and Trist (1955) muddy the already unclear waters by noting that sanctioned forms of absences are substituted for unsanctioned forms. This introduces elements of the alternate forms model into the compensatory model as well as suggests that employees gradually learn what they can get away with to relieve job dissatisfaction. Thus, the pure form of the compensatory behaviors model may represent the withdrawal process in only a few situations.

The generally positive correlations among different withdrawal behaviors cannot be used as evidence that this hypothesized model is invalid. One needs to examine partial correlations among withdrawal behaviors when the level of job satisfaction is held constant. Negative partial correlations among different forms of withdrawal would support the compensatory model.

The Progression-of-Withdrawal Model. Baruch (1944), Herzberg, Mausner, Peterson, and Capwell (1957), Melbin (1961), Lyons (1972), Rosse (1988), and Rosse and Miller (1984) have described a somewhat more complex model of the relations among withdrawal behaviors. Baruch (1944) described absences from work as short-term "quits." Herzberg et al. (1957) argued that the problems of absenteeism and turnover should be considered together because "the small decision which is taken when the worker absents himself is a miniature version of the important decision he makes when he quits his job" (p. 103). Melbin (1961) colorfully argues:

> We generally assume that leaving a job is the outcome of a chain of experiences building up to the final break....The same events on a "smaller" scale may be such signs.... High absenteeism (lateness and absence) appear to be an earlier sign, and turnover (quitting and being fired) the dying stage of a long and lively process of leaving. (p. 15)

The progression-of-withdrawal model specifies that individuals should enact an ordered sequence of withdrawal responses, ranging from (a) minor acts, such as daydreaming or frequent trips to water fountains and restrooms, to (b) absence from meetings, lateness, and leaving work early, to (c) abuse of sick and personal leave, and finally to (d) absenteeism and eventual quitting. Rosse and Miller's (1984) account argues that when work conditions worsen or when mild forms of withdrawal are ineffectual, progressively more extreme forms of avoidance are needed. Daydreaming, for example, may not be sufficient to relieve moderate distress, even though such mild responses may provide adequate distance from mildly bad working conditions. An alternative explanation is that employees gradually become aware of the lack of fit between themselves and some elements of their work role, leading to behaviors reflective of this and to increasing dissatisfaction and expectations of leaving the organization.

Another factor, according to Rosse and Miller (1984), is an iterative adaptive process in which dissatisfied individuals experiment with avoidance responses with the fewest negative consequences. If individuals' mild behaviors are not adaptive, then they will try more extreme behaviors with potentially greater negative consequences. The advantage of the rewards over the costs reinforces the behaviors and encourages individuals to engage in even stronger forms of avoidance with progressively greater rewards (e.g., an entire day off is more rewarding than a long coffee break if avoidance or reduction of work role inclusion is the psychological function of the behavior).

There is little research testing this model of organizational withdrawal. Most studies investigate only one or two withdrawal behaviors; the studies of Clegg (1983) and Rosse (1983, 1988) are exceptions. Positive correlations among different withdrawal behaviors do not necessarily support this model because such results do not distinguish the progression-of-withdrawal model from the spillover model. In general, the evidence is mixed. Burke and Wilcox (1972) and Waters and Roach (1979) found an increase in the number of absences taken just prior to quitting. Miller (1981) failed to replicate this finding. The finding

itself, it should be noted, is equivocal support at best for the progression-of-withdrawal model. The increase in absences may reflect an already-made decision to quit in the immediate future rather than a true progression of adaptive behaviors. The evidence reported by Rosse (1988), however, supports a progression-of-withdrawal hypothesis among newly hired employees.

The progression-of-withdrawal hypothesis requires a specific structure among the behaviors enacted by individuals; it also requires a specific structure between each behavior and the underlying construct. The structure among the behaviors is relatively simple; the behaviors should form a Guttman scale (Guttman, 1944). Individuals reporting relatively strong avoidance or withdrawal responses as ways of adapting to their jobs should also report having engaged in milder forms of withdrawal. Knowing the most extreme form of avoidance behavior the individual has enacted should be sufficient to scale him or her along the job-avoidance continuum.

Longitudinal analyses should also reveal a specific pattern of behaviors *and* behavioral changes across time. If the reports of avoidance behaviors by individuals during two contiguous time periods are arranged as shown in Figure 8, a definite pattern should be evident if the progression-of-withdrawal hypothesis is valid. Individuals can be scaled according to their most extreme form of withdrawal behavior in two adjacent time periods. Individuals may continue to enact the same avoidance behaviors in both time periods if they were sufficient to reduce their dissatisfaction to tolerable levels. Thus, they would repeat avoidance behaviors and would be scaled as exhibiting the same strength of avoidance in both time periods. If the behavior in Time 1 was not sufficient to reduce dissatisfaction, then individuals should *increase* the strength of their avoidance behaviors. On the other hand, changes from relatively strong avoidance behaviors to milder forms should be infrequently observed. Thus, we should observe relatively large frequencies in cells along the main diagonal (cells 1,1; 2,2;...; k,k) or in cells defined by stronger avoidance behaviors in Time 2 than in Time 1 (cells 1,2; 1,3; 2,3; $i, i + k$; etc.). Cells below the main diagonal (e.g., $i, i-k$) should be empty. Absorbing states (leaving the organization) can be included in such transition matrices.

A transition analysis as depicted in Figure 8 requires that the strength of avoidance behaviors be scaled so that individuals can be scaled to reflect the strength of their work-avoidance tendencies. Such scaling is an integral part of the progression-of-withdrawal hypothesis and could be done by rating the strength of the avoidance behaviors or by noting the frequencies of the behaviors within a sample of individuals.

Summary. The six models of organizational withdrawal behaviors reviewed above were presented only to describe expected relations among three potentially relevant behaviors under certain assumptions. To too great an extent and for far too long, researchers have been preoccupied with these three specific behaviors. To some, the three behaviors have perhaps come to represent the underlying construct of organizational withdrawal. This assumption is rejected in this chapter. Withdrawal should be considered as a general construct encompassing many different behaviors, such as turnover, absenteeism, or tardiness, as well as less obvious manifestations of withdrawal. Both conceptual and empirical efforts devoted to specifying and studying multiple manifestations of organizational withdrawal might prove very fruitful. However, if researchers are going to concentrate on easily observed behavioral manifestations of the hypothesized construct, then the expected relations among the behaviors under different assumptions should be spelled out in detail at the same time that the fit of the

FIGURE 8

Transition Matrix of Avoidance Behaviors During Time 1 and Time 2

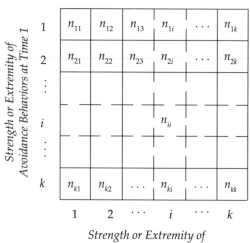

Strength or Extremity of Avoidance Behaviors at Time 2

hypothesized structure to the data should be assessed.

An Adaptation and Withdrawal Model

A model somewhat closely related to Rosse and Miller's (1984) adaptation cycle model is the model of Hulin, Roznowski, and Hachiya (1985), presented as a steady-state model rather than the dynamic, cyclical model of Rosse and Miller. It specifies in some detail behaviors, roughly classified by the target of the act, that may be expected as a result of work role dissatisfaction. A graphic representation of this model, slightly modified from the original, is shown in Figure 9. The model is offered here as a possible synthesis of adaptation and withdrawal models.

This model integrates previous theoretical work of March and Simon (1958), Mobley (1977), and Rosse and Miller (1984) in the turnover area and incorporates elements from

FIGURE 9

Modified Organizational Adaptation/Withdrawal Model

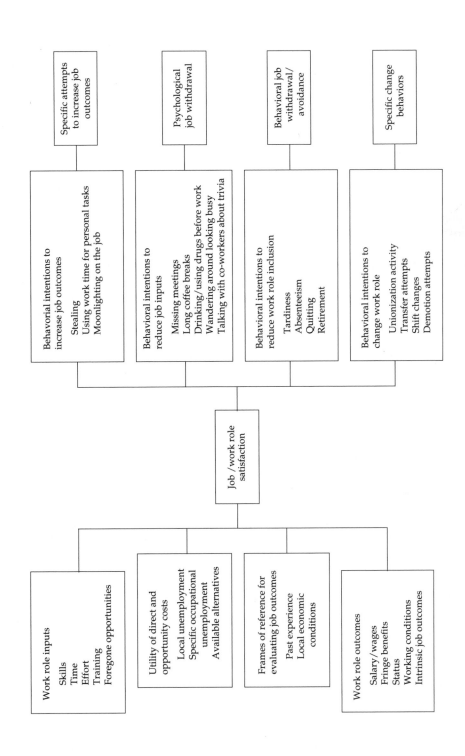

From "Alternative Opportunities and Withdrawal Decisions" by C. Hulin, M. Roznowski, and D. Hachiya, 1985, *Psychological Bulletin, 97*, pp. 233–250. Copyright 1985 by the American Psychological Association. Adapted by permission.

theoretical models in attitude formation by Thibaut and Kelley (1959), March and Simon, and Smith et al. (1969). It represents a synthesis of the existing theoretical and empirical literature, rather than a unique theoretical perspective or development, and recognizes the many possible responses to dissatisfaction. These include attempts to increase job outcomes, decrease job inputs, reduce work role inclusion, and alter specific characteristics of the work role.

These four hypothesized behavioral families illustrate some of the expected behaviors employees might enact as adaptations to dissatisfying work roles. The targets of the acts are those characteristics of work roles that are modifiable—characteristics that workers may expect to change, as a result of their behaviors, to decrease job dissatisfaction.

Some behaviors are ambiguous in terms of these job families. Drinking before work or on the job may represent an attempt to decrease job inputs or to reduce work role inclusion; tardiness may represent a reduction of work role inclusion or a reduction in job inputs if no penalties are assessed; demotion attempts may be attempts to reduce job inputs or to change the work situation; promotion could represent an attempt to increase job outcomes or to change important characteristics of the work role.

It is tempting to suggest that these are empirical questions; specific behaviors can be classified or clustered by reference to the other behaviors with which they covary or in terms of common causes or common targets. However, as noted above, it is difficult to interpret empirical relations among behaviors with low base rates. Classification into families on the basis of the relative strengths of covariation of such behaviors can generate artifactual taxonomies. Behaviors may be classed together because of the artifactual effects of base rates on covariances and correlations. This is analogous to "difficulty" factors in factor analyses (Hulin, Drasgow, & Parsons, 1983) of binary items. There are a number of statistical procedures that may solve some of these base rate problems without creating additional problems, for example, through use of latent class models (Traub & Lam, 1985), log-linear models (Feinberg, 1977), clustering models (Anderberg, 1973), and discriminant function analyses (Klecka, 1980; Tatsuoka & Tiedeman, 1954). The procedure used will depend on how the substantive questions are conceptualized and how much a priori knowledge is assumed about the number and sizes of the clusters. These analytic models are not interchangeable.

Another basis for categorizing behaviors into families could be their perceived causes and effects. Cause maps (Bougon, Weick, & Binkhorst, 1977; Komocar, 1985) have not been used for this purpose, but similarities between individual behaviors expressed in terms of the cognitive maps of the individual employees can be derived and used as input into classification routines.

The model outlined in Figure 9 predicts that enacting any of the adaptive or withdrawal behaviors contained in one or more of the families is negatively related to job satisfaction. However, it is also possible that withdrawal and some change behaviors are stimulated by negative job affect; other change behaviors are more likely to be displayed by those who are satisfied. It takes effort to change a situation. Very dissatisfied individuals may not be willing to make an effort to change what they see as a totally negative situation. Satisfied employees may be the only ones willing to make some specific changes because they see long-term positive utilities. Rosse and Hulin (1985), for example, found withdrawal behaviors to be negatively related to job satisfaction, but some change attempts were positively related to job affect within a sample of newly hired hospital employees. Alterations in the basic model shown in Figure 9 will undoubtedly be made on the basis of empirical findings.

Another complicating feature is added by the behavioral switching of individuals across time. Under the assumption that individuals choose behaviors to maximize subjective expected utility (Atkinson & Birch, 1970; Naylor, Pritchard, & Ilgen, 1980; Vroom, 1964) but that the marginal utility of individual acts is a negatively accelerated positive function, or even a nonmonotonic function with a downturn with respect to the number of repetitions of the act, then we can expect a great deal of behavioral switching to occur within the families of acts. This assumes the behaviors identified in each of the boxes are functionally equivalent, or at least similar, and relatively homogeneous within families.

In summary, the model depicted in Figure 9 attempts to go beyond the work of Rosse and Miller (1984) in job adaptation and to incorporate elements of attitude formation (Fishbein & Ajzen 1974; Smith, Kendall, & Hulin, 1969; Thibaut & Kelley, 1959) as well as elements of conceptual models of turnover. The model takes advantage of the different targets of adaptive and avoidance behaviors—increases in outcomes, decreases in inputs, decreases in work role inclusion, leaving the work role entirely, and changing the characteristics of the work role through formal change processes. The dimensionality of the behavioral response space has not been explored thoroughly. Predicting which of these behaviors or clusters of behaviors will be selected requires (a) a knowledge of situational constraints, (b) organizational, departmental, or work group climates (defined as perceptions of behavior-outcome contingencies), and (c) individuals' reinforcement histories.

Both the adaptation model of Rosse and Miller (1984) and the withdrawal-adaptation model of Hulin et al. (1985) have the unfortunate characteristic of concentrating largely on what are often regarded as negative behaviors. First, note that classifying any adaptive behavior as a negative behavior assumes a particular perspective—that of the organization or organizational manager. To the worker, they are adaptive. Second, both models assume that feelings of dissatisfaction or relative discontent

(e.g., the feeling that you could be better off doing something different for a different organization or that you are not very happy with what you're doing for a living and where you're doing it) are the major impetus for many of these work role adaptation behaviors. The models assume that in-role, productive, conforming behaviors are prompted by role requirements and the acceptance of the work role by the incumbent. Without dissatisfaction or discontent, there is little impetus for change; role incumbents should feel little need for adaptation or withdrawal. Their in-role behaviors should be understandable from the contingencies between acts, products, evaluations, and outcomes established to regulate their on-the-job behaviors (Lawler, 1976; Naylor, Pritchard, & Ilgen, 1980). Thus, the models of adaptation and withdrawal are attempts to understand and predict behaviors when the outcomes provided by the role behaviors are not sufficiently rewarding to the role incumbents.

For these reasons, the preceding discussion has focused on behavioral responses to work role dissatisfaction. This emphasis on behavioral responses is in keeping with much of the research on job affect and the attitude-behavior models that are a significant part of the foundations of research in this area.

Caveat.   Affect is an individual's psychological response to characteristics of his or her work role. Dissatisfaction as an instantiation of affect need not obey the principles of formal logic. The idiosyncratic basis of the affective response means that individuals in given work roles who experience great dissatisfaction may, after the fact, alleviate their dissatisfaction by cognitive rather than behavioral responses. These individuals can (a) deemphasize the importance of dissatisfying outcomes, (b) reevaluate the utility of their job inputs, (c) decide that the alternative jobs available are not that great after all, or (d) decide that their job is not too important a part of their lives and downgrade job dissatisfaction to a minor annoyance rather than something to be redressed by effortful or risky behaviors.

This caveat suggests that individuals can make cognitive adjustments in any of the antecedents of work role affect specified in Figure 9—work role inputs, utility of inputs, work role outcomes, or frames of reference for evaluating such outcomes—without tight coupling between their cognitions and external reality. If successful, these cognitive adjustments may preclude the necessity of behavioral responses to bring about changes in contributions, outcomes, or any of the other antecedents of role affect.

This expansion in the response repertoire of individuals to work role dissatisfaction should not be regarded as an alternative to the behavioral models discussed above. Rather, the changes are more in the nature of an expansion of the range of possible responses to dissatisfying roles; the basic model is unchanged. One problem is that the expansion of the model to include such responses makes it nearly untestable. Cognitive and behavioral responses to dissatisfaction are likely made simultaneously or nearly so. For some, cognitive responses may be sufficient to solve the problem. For others, these responses only suffice until such time as they take action against their troubles and end them. These cognitive responses were referred to by Hamlet when he noted that:

> ...the native hue of resolution
> Is sicklied o'er with the pale cast of
>   thought,
> And enterprises of great pitch and
>   moment
> With this regard their currents turn
>   awry
> And lose the name of action.
> (*Hamlet*, III, i)

We need independent means of identifying the Hamlets in our work populations.

Selectivity of Adaptive Behaviors

We should expect different affective and behavioral responses to different precipitating events (Rosse & Miller, 1984) or different perceived sources of dissatisfaction. Differential relations between affect with different kinds of work role outcomes and the behaviors considered above are suggestive of the discriminations employees make among the sources of dissatisfaction and their potential responses. Evidence of selective responses to dissatisfaction is found in the literature on satisfaction and voting in favor of union representation in National Labor Relations Board-sanctioned elections (Getman, Goldberg, & Herman, 1976; Schriesheim, 1978). Satisfaction with job characteristics, such as pay and supervision, most likely to be changed by union representation was most strongly related to probability of voting in favor of union representation in the study of 33 union representation elections by Getman et al. Satisfaction with those work role elements unlikely to be changed by unionization, such as work content and co-workers, was less strongly related to union voting.

Schriesheim (1978) found that the highest bivariate correlations (−.76) with prounion voting involved satisfaction with economic factors of the job. The correlation involving noneconomic factors and union voting was significantly lower (−.38).

Hamner and Smith (1978) found that an index developed to predict the unionization activity (e.g., card signing campaigns) that precedes NLRB-sanctioned elections in bargaining units of an organization contained 13 items from an initial pool of 42 items. Eight of these 13 items were related to satisfaction with supervision, physical working conditions, and amount of work—characteristics that could be altered by unionization. The remaining five items were scattered across four different aspects of the work role. Note that the original 42 satisfaction items have been subjected to extensive validity studies (Dunham & Smith, 1979).

The areas of dissatisfaction that predict prounion voting or unionization activity can be expected to change with the nature of the sample and jobs involved. Zalesny (1985), for example, found noneconomic factors more predictive of union voting than economic factors in a study of a union campaign at a large midwestern state university. More generally perhaps, she found that the perceived instrumentality of the union for redressing specific areas of dissatisfaction was an important factor in a model of union voting that she developed. A knowledge of areas of dissatisfaction and the perceived instrumentality of the union for addressing these issues is crucial in testing this selectivity-of-behaviors hypothesis. In general, employees would be expected to vote for union representation if they were dissatisfied with elements of their job they perceived the union to be instrumental in improving.

Other relations between measures of affect with different job characteristics and specific behaviors are harder to interpret in terms of the selectivity-of-behaviors hypothesis; the specific target of the action is often difficult to determine. Satisfaction with the work itself seems to be one of the better predictors of turnover; overall satisfaction or satisfaction with the work itself appears to be a better attitudinal predictor of absenteeism (Scott & Taylor, 1985). The available data are scarce and difficult to interpret in terms of the specific targets of the adaptive behaviors.

Summary.   Individuals appear to respond selectively to dissatisfaction. When there is a perceived connection between the source of dissatisfaction and the target of a behavior (e.g., dissatisfaction with pay and voting for union representation), the set of behaviors enacted by workers should be selectively directed toward the *source* of their dissatisfaction or toward acts that are instrumental in alleviating

their discomfort through changes in the environment. In many instances, the source of the dissatisfaction is nonspecific—for example, the company as a whole or co-workers in general—and behaviors cannot be specifically targeted. The specificity of the relations reported by Getman et al. (1976), Schriesheim (1978), Hamner and Smith (1978), and the model developed by Zalesny (1985) argue there is specificity in the selection of behavioral responses to negative job affect.

There is no intent here to make any general statements about relations between attitudes towards objects (a work role is analogous to an object in this case) and general behaviors toward that object. Some empirical evidence reviewed above suggests that this is the case in the specific instance of work roles, work role attitudes, and adaptive behaviors. A conceptual analysis presented later in this chapter suggests this indeed should be the case.

Work roles in the United States are frequently salient aspects of individuals' lives. For many, there is much truth to the expressions, "You are what you do; to do nothing is to be nothing," and "The American dream begins and ends with a job." Most individuals spend a substantial portion of their adult lives embedded in their work roles, although exceptions certainly may be found (see Hulin et al., 1985, for examples). If individuals perceive themselves to be substantially rather than marginally included in their work roles and if they spend a significant portion of their adult lives at work, then we should expect them to regard dissatisfactions with work role characteristics as more than petty annoyances. They will respond if they perceive their behaviors will change the source of their dissatisfactions. They may reduce their inclusion or participation in the work role to reduce its salience, or they may leave the work role altogether.

We might hypothesize stronger and more general relations between attitudes toward work roles or jobs, considered as objects, and general behavior patterns toward those objects in the area of job attitudes and job affect than with attitudes and behaviors toward other objects. This is because work roles are generally very important to individuals and because there may be stronger contingencies between some work role behaviors that directly and indirectly influence job attitudes.

Employees are likely to perceive the contingencies between their own acts and changes in work role outcomes. Although our attitudes toward the church, for example, may be positive, we may see little connection between our behaviors toward it and our expected utilities. We may be altruistic in general, but may see little effect in donating blood on our own utilities or our own happiness. In the case of work roles, the contingencies between behaviors and utility are stronger and should be veridically perceived. Thus, we should generally expect consistent relations among job dissatisfaction, behavioral intentions, and adaptive or withdrawal behaviors when individuals perceive that their behaviors will have a positive impact on characteristics of their work roles and on their satisfaction.

Organizational Commitment

Commitment is a construct invoked to explain consistent sequences of behavior or courses of action. These consistencies are usually seen by both *focal* persons and observers as behavioral choices dedicated to the pursuit of a common goal. Commitment involves behavioral choices and implies a rejection of feasible, alternative courses of action. Consistency in the face of no alternatives does not reflect so much commitment as it does forced compliance, a series of Hobson's choices. In this regard, commitment is obviously related to withdrawal and adaptation.

Paradoxically, commitment may also lead to shifting or changing courses of action. If, for example, we are strongly committed to an organization's claims that what it does is best for its clients, then when the organization changes its course, so will we. We may commit ourselves to the claims that our political organization possesses the truth, not that we know what the truth is. Therefore, we follow the organization's dogma as it bobs and weaves through an entanglement of conflicting actions and changing values and remain secure in our beliefs that we are consistent and committed to our behaviors. The line between fanaticism and commitment may be blurred at times.

Commitment cannot be judged from behaviors alone. Just as consistent behaviors may reflect a lack of choice rather than commitment, changing courses of action may reflect commitment to a consistent goal that can be reached by multiple paths. Interpretation of their behaviors by the individuals involved as well as their attitudes and cognitions are important parts of the concept.

Research on organizational commitment seems to have been unnecessarily imprecise in both the conceptual developments and their operationalization. Morrow (1983), for example, noted that there are more than 25 commitment-related concepts and measures. O'Reilly and Chatman (1986) attempted to provide some structure to this literature by noting theoretical and empirical distinctions in the attitude-change and development literature—distinctions that are also relevant to research on organizational commitment. Specifically, they delineate (a) exchange (also referred to as compliance or instrumentality), (b) identification, and (c) internalization as three bases for individuals' commitment to an organization. Commitment based on an exchange relationship occurs when the individuals expect to gain rewards in exchange for specified acts. Identification-based commitment occurs when individuals feel a certain pride in association with membership in the organization, perhaps because of what the organization represents, or because of what it has accomplished or is attempting to accomplish. Commitment based on internalization implies a congruence of the organizational values with those of the individual. This differentiation scheme is both conceptually and empirically helpful. The distinctions still leave room for improvement. The referent of organizational values, for example, is not clear—organizations do not have values; individuals do. Commitment based on internalization of values, therefore, must refer to agreements between the focal individual's values and those of some subset of the organization's members. Which subset should be selected to represent the organization's values?

These three bases of organizational commitment delineated by O'Reilly and Chatman (1986) are taken from Kelman's (1958) work on attitude change. O'Reilly and Chatman note that previous measures of commitment have typically not distinguished the different antecedents, or bases, of such commitment for purposes of questionnaire development or assessment. They further note that commitment based on different antecedents may have different behavioral consequences. Stated differently, different types of commitment—based on exchange, identification, or internalization—may be differentially related to behavioral responses to the job or organization.

The current discussion on organizational commitment emphasizes consistency in behavioral choices regarding organizational membership, rather than changing courses of action that reflect a consistent set of beliefs in an organization or set of scriptures. For our purposes, we shall define organizational commitment as follows: *Organizational commitment refers to an attitude-like attraction to an organization. The attitude object is the overall organization rather than specific work role characteristics. The utility or value associated with role or organizational membership is contingent on remaining in an organization; it is not contingent on any specific work role behaviors other than not quitting or retiring.* The bases or antecedents of the commitment of individuals to an organization may be in the exchange relationship between the individual and the organization or may go beyond such exchange/calculative bases and involve identification or internalization of values.

Attitudinal Commitment

The attitudinal approach to organizational commitment derives from the role-attitude models discussed in detail above. The distinction between the attitudinal-commitment model and the general role-attitude model is the conceptualization of the target of the attitudes—the attitude object—rather than a significant change in conceptual or theoretical approaches as to why individuals remain in organizational roles.

Most attitude or role-attitude models conceptualize attitude formation as directed toward different, specific work role characteristics or outcomes, such as pay, the work itself, or supervision. Overall role attitudes are occasionally part of these developments. They are either the result of a weighted and combined series of affective responses to different role characteristics or role outcomes, or they may represent a general, undifferentiated response to the total organizational role. Hulin, Drasgow, and Parsons (1983) and Parsons and Hulin (1982) have argued that empirical results consistently suggest a hierarchical model of job affect characterized by an overall affect dimension and a small number of oblique dimensions representing affect with different job characteristics or outcomes. Conceptually, however, overall job affect is different from organizational commitment as it is normally defined.

Mowday, Porter, and Steers' (1982) definition of organizational commitment stresses identification with and involvement in a particular organization. They characterize commitment as involving belief in and acceptance of an organization's goals and values, willingness to exert considerable effort on behalf of the organization, and a strong desire to maintain a membership in the organization. Conceptually

FIGURE 10

Simplified Behavioral Commitment Model:
Hypothesized Process by Which Individuals Become Committed to Their Acts

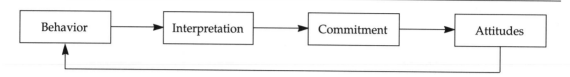

this definition is problematic; it emphasizes behavioral intention-like elements on behalf of the organization, not just intentions to remain in the organization. This emphasis generates such statements as "we would expect commitment to influence the amount of effort an employee puts forth on the job and this effort should have some influence on actual performance" (Mowday, Porter, & Steers, 1982, p. 36). Or, "highly committed employees would be more motivated to attend *so they could facilitate organizational goal attainment*" [italics added] (p. 36). The first statement resurrects the often studied but rarely confirmed relationship between job attitudes and job performance. The second seems to overlook the conceptual and theoretical parsimony of assuming that individuals may attend work frequently because they perceive positive utility *for them* for remaining a member of an organization or because they perceive positive utility from many on-the-job behaviors. It is neither necessary to assume committed individuals want to facilitate the goals of an organization nor desirable to hypothesize a general attitude-productive behavior relationship. The empirical results of O'Reilly and Chatman (1986) also suggest that it is useful empirically to separate the bases or antecedents of commitment. They found differential relationships between independent operationalizations of commitment that stressed different antecedents and relevant behaviors.

Empirical support for the usefulness of the organizational commitment construct comes from empirical studies testing models of organizational turnover. In some of these studies, different models were compared to determine the extent to which each could account for variance in termination decisions. Hom, Katerberg, and Hulin (1979), for example, compared the relative effectiveness of a weighted satisfaction model, the Fishbein-Ajzen attitude-intention-behavior model, and an organizational commitment model (among others). They found the satisfaction model had a predictive validity for reenlistment decisions of Illinois National Guardsmen (across six months) of .55, the Fishbein-Ajzen model had a predictive validity of .65, and organizational commitment, assessed using the Porter, Crampon, and Smith (1976) scale, had a predictive validity of .58. The differences between the three validities were statistically significant ($p \leq .05$), although of limited practical significance. Hom et al. concluded that the modest predictive advantage of the organizational commitment model was due to the inclusion of items measuring withdrawal intentions in the operationalizations of commitment. Organizational commitment is also a more general construct than role affect. If turnover represents a general rejection of the organization, then the correspondence between a nonspecific behavioral rejection and the general attitude toward the organization may account for the results. These studies do suggest the theoretical advantage of an organizational commitment model for predicting the specific behavior of organizational withdrawal.

Other studies have found significant correlations between organizational commitment and turnover (Angle & Perry, 1981; Koch & Steers, 1978; Mowday, Steers, & Porter, 1979; Porter, Crampon, & Smith, 1976). The correlations of organizational commitment with turnover are typically statistically significant, negative, and range from −.02 to −.48. Most of these studies, however, do not test competing models; the advantage of a commitment model over the Fishbein-Ajzen model or a satisfaction model is unknown.

Relations between organizational commitment and absenteeism are mixed. Mowday et al. (1979) and Steers (1977) report significant correlations (−.13, −.28) among samples of public employees, scientists, and engineers, but Angle and Perry (1981) and Steers report nonsignificant positive correlations between commitment and absenteeism (.05 and .08, respectively). The problems discussed above with interpreting correlations involving a low-frequency, binary, individual behavior apply also to these data.

Commitment to Past Behaviors

Consider a model of work role attitudes that argues the proximal cause of such attitudes is the processing of social information by the work role incumbent and is not associated with the objective environment, work role characteristics, needs, or other enduring individual difference factors. Social information processing interpretations of work-attitude formation derive from basic conceptual work by Festinger (1957) and Bem (1965) and applications of this work by Berger and Luckmann(1967), Salancik (1977) Salancik and Pfeffer (1978), and Weick (1977). The raw data for these social information processing models are past and present behaviors that are interpreted by the incumbents, as observers of their own responses, to provide information that becomes the proximal cause of their present and future attitudes. Social

environments provide cues that both allow the construction of reality—enactments of environments—and determine the salience of certain cues and information by focusing attention on these cues (Salancik & Pfeffer). Zalesny and Farace (1985) argue that the focusing effect on the salience of cues is the more expected of the two effects and has predictable effects on the *variance* of job attitudes rather than on mean levels of job or role attitudes. Characteristics of work roles are not "given" in this approach. They are constructed by work role incumbents.

This theoretical approach to social attitudes hypothesizes that the process begins as individuals behave. Their behaviors become stimuli to interpret. Their behaviors and subsequent interpretations generate attitudinal responses that are consistent with their interpretations of their past and ongoing behaviors. The hypothesized causal sequence progresses from behaviors to attitudes and commitment rather than the reverse as hypothesized by most traditional models in this area.[6] This hypothesized sequence is shown in Figure 10.

This framework for studying and explaining organizational commitment emphasizes a process by which individuals become bound by their own actions. Kiesler and Sakamura (1966) and Salancik (1977) have identified characteristics of behaviors that increase the likelihood of individuals becoming committed to behaviors. These characteristics include the number of similar acts or behaviors, the degree of choice (volition) of the acts, the revocability of the acts, and the explicitness of the acts. Essentially, if, in the absence of other information, individuals see themselves as having freely and repeatedly engaged in an act or a series of acts that cannot be denied and whose consequences are irrevocable, they conclude that the actor (*person* in this case rather than *other*) enjoys the acts or their consequences. The observers develop attitudes that are consistent with this positive interpretation of acts.

Within this general theoretical framework, a number of hypotheses have been developed that specify in more detail the process that generates positive attitudes of commitment or negative attitudes towards the acts. The under-justification and overjustification effects are of particular importance to this chapter; they are hypothesized to be relevant to motivation, attitudes, and behaviors in organizations.

Overjustification Effect. Empirical research that has generated support for this effect has followed a somewhat standard set of procedures. Individuals are asked to do things in an experiment that are intrinsically interesting enough that most subjects do them without any external rewards (e.g., soma puzzles, chess end-game problems, male subjects assembling *Playboy* centerfold puzzles). Following the manipulation (contingent payment for assembling the puzzles vs. no payment or noncontingent pay for *time* spent in the experiment), subjects characteristically show less persistence in the activity if they receive contingent pay than if they are not paid contingently (Deci, 1971, 1972; Kruglanski, Riter, Amitai, Margolin, Shabtai, & Zaksh, 1975; Pritchard, Campbell, & Campbell, 1977; Scott, 1976). This reduction in the amount of time spent on intrinsically interesting tasks as a result of receiving performance-contingent pay has been interpreted as due in part to the individuals observing their own behaviors. Their behaviors in the experiment are justified on the basis of either an internal (intrinsic interest) or an external (contingent pay) source of reward. Rewards are interpreted as controls of individuals' behaviors. If a behavior is justifiable on the basis of either internal or external control, the attribution of the cause of the behavior is unstable. In such situations, the argument continues, individuals will attribute the causes of their behaviors to the external (contingent pay) control rather than to the internal (intrinsic interest in the task) control. Following the administration of contingent pay for

performing intrinsically interesting tasks, we should observe decreases in the intrinsic motivations and commitment to the acts. Future behaviors, consistent with individuals' interpretations of their decreased intrinsic motivation and the presence of external control, should be observed.

The findings generated by the overjustification paradigm are interpreted as having implications for motivation in organizations; adding extrinsic motivation to intrinsically motivating tasks should decrease rather than increase the overall motivation of individuals to perform their required work role behaviors. Pritchard et al. (1977) and Scott (1976) have raised a number of questions about the manipulations and assessment procedures in this research paradigm (e.g., behavior during a free period equated with motivation) and the interpretations. However, the *results*, if not their interpretations, are consistent: Subjects who engage in the behaviors during periods when contingent payments are in effect are more likely to show a decrease in task persistence when these external factors are removed than are individuals who have not received contingent payments.

Although these effects have been frequently observed in a variety of experimental laboratory studies using populations of children and college students as subjects, generalizability of the results to organizational behaviors as well as the ecological validity of the studies can be questioned. These issues are addressed below, after a discussion of research on the obverse of the overjustification effect.

Underjustification Effect. Research conducted on this effect has been directed toward understanding how individuals interpret their actions when they find themselves engaging in or committed to behaviors for which there is underjustification in the environment or the task for their actions. What are the attitudinal and behavioral consequences of the resulting interpretations of the behaviors for the individuals and organizations involved?

Research on the underjustification effect has typically involved either neutral or unpleasant tasks (e.g., eating dead worms, being a reluctant member of the ROTC, and generating and recording random numbers only to see the work thrown away without being used). Individuals who can find no justification in the environment for engaging in these behaviors observe themselves behaving inconsistently. They see themselves performing disgusting, boring, or useless tasks for no external rewards. To avoid seeing themselves as irrational, they interpret their behaviors as being caused by the intrinsic interests or importance of the tasks. They justify their behavior by expressing greater interest in the task and reporting it as more rewarding or important in some fashion than individuals who are able to find some source of external, task-exogenous justification (Comer & Laird, 1975; Pallak, Sogin, & Van Zante, 1974; Pfeffer & Lawler, 1980; Staw, 1974).

As in the interpretation of overjustification effects, observers' own behaviors become the source of their information about their attitudes and motivational states. Attitudes are formed that are consistent with the cognitive interpretations of the behaviors. These should lead to future behaviors that are consistent with past behaviors and current attitudes.

Discussion of Social Information Processing Effects

Individuals' own behaviors are a significant part of the social and organizational environment. The more restricted the amount of information about the meanings of events, roles, and behaviors, the more individuals rely on the little information that remains. Often what remains in new, ambiguous, and information-impoverished situations are observers' own responses—both physiological and behav-ioral—and little else. Ultimately, we are always a part of the situation in which we are trying to understand our own behaviors. Our own behaviors and responses may be the only element common to all situations in which we behave.

The ideas behind social information processing approaches are not new. Interpretations of our internal states, on the basis of observations of our own behaviors, are a vital part of a theory of emotion formulated over 100 years ago (James, 1890). A more recent interpretation of this theory is that we interpret our physiological responses as indicating arousal, searching our environments to find the source of the stimulation causing the arousal (Schachter & Singer, 1962). The environmental events we identify as causes determine the content of the emotion—anger, aggressiveness, fear, and so on.

Two important points should be noted regarding generalizations of social information processing theories to job affect and organizational commitment. Few individuals are likely to find themselves in work roles in which they do not have multiple sources of converging information. Except for new employees on an unfamiliar job or subjects in a controlled study in which sources of information are controlled by the experimenters after commitment or compliance has been subtly obtained, most individuals encounter such situations only rarely. The experimental situations typically studied represent a biased sample from the population of situations normally found in organizations.

The limiting factors that are necessary before the overjustification effect can be successfully induced speak eloquently and suggest a lack of ecological validity and serious limitations on generalizations regarding individuals in organizations. A number of factors are necessary before the effect is reliably observed: External rewards must be present, the external rewards must be contingent on task performance, participants must expect a reward for task participation (Lepper & Greene, 1975; Lepper, Greene, & Nisbett, 1973), the reward for task participation must be salient (Ross, 1975), it must be task exogenous or an incidental consequence of task participation (Kruglanski et al., 1975), no norms for payment can exist in the situation (Staw & Calder, 1980), and there must be a choice to engage in the task (Folger, Rosenfield, & Hays, 1978). With these factors present, the overjustification effect can be readily observed. Without them, the effect is unlikely. The problem for those who would generalize to organizations and organizational members is that the simultaneous occurrence of all of these factors defines a nearly empty set of *organizational situations*. This has not prevented the generalizations of the effect as an explanation of organizational phenomena, however.

Research pinpointing limitations on the ecological validity of the underjustification effect is less readily available. It is instructive to note, however, that Staw's (1974) study of ROTC members is the only study conducted in a realistic organizational setting with organizational members in which the underjustification effect was unequivocally supported. Staw's study was conducted during a time when ROTC membership was to some an attractive alternative to being drafted into the armed forces of the United States. Many individuals signed contracts committing themselves to three years of service in the Army following completion of college and ROTC training. Some of these individuals, following their contractual commitment to the ROTC, received a high number in the draft lottery. High numbers effectively meant they would not have been drafted even without the protection of their ROTC membership. As predicted by the social information processing theory, individuals who were committed to the ROTC but who would not have been drafted by reason of their high lottery number justified their ROTC commitments by reporting that ROTC activities were more interesting and important than did those with low draft numbers. The latter group had sufficient external justification—legally avoiding the draft—for their ROTC commitment.

Members of formal work organizations, no less than anybody else, are social animals. They respond to social information, make sense of their behaviors and responses, and attend to information from their own behaviors and from the statements and behaviors of others. However, they are also more or less rational in their belief systems. When the only information subjects have about a situation is highly restricted by an experimenter, they will very likely believe what the experimenter is attempting to induce. If they find themselves about to do something truly bizarre, such as eating a dead worm as part of a psychology experiment because they have been subtly coerced into committing themselves to doing such a thing (Comer & Laird, 1975), they will very likely search the environment for ways to interpret the act such that it will not do too much damage to their egos or self-beliefs. When they have other information, they will use it also.

The effects of social or organizational roles on behavior also need to be considered in evaluating these models. Behaviors consistent with social and organizational roles into which individuals have been placed (roles can be conceptualized as a set of behavioral expectations) have long been observed and considered a part of general social science as well as organizational research (Graen, 1976; Landsberger & Hulin, 1961; Mead, 1934; Sarbin, 1954). Role theory suggests that if you want to know how people will behave, examine the requirements or behavioral expectations of their role. They will behave and respond attitudinally in ways that are consonant with expectations others have of people in their role. Lieberman (1956) demonstrated the effects of this principle in organizations by assessments of attitudes and motivations of rank-and-file workers who were promoted to the position of foreman and later returned into the rank and file because of labor cutbacks. The results indicated shifts of attitudes in the promanagement direction following promotion and shifts in the prounion direction following demotion.

These role expectations of behavior hypothesize that the social and organizational roles create expectations about incumbents' behaviors, beliefs, and attitudes. If people are placed in these roles, they respond according to the role expectations. Anything that is done to make one of the multiple potential roles more salient than others accentuates the tendencies to behave according to the salient role. Catholic women, for example, express stronger agreement with the established dogma of the Catholic church when their Catholicism, and hence their role as Catholics, is pointed out to them prior to responding to belief questionnaires (Kelley, 1955).

One can readily agree that the basic psychological process of sense making, distortion, rationalizing, biased recalling, and justifying are real phenomena. The questions for this chapter are the degree to which these principles apply to the behaviors and other responses of work role incumbents in formal work organizations. Basically, three questions about these effects should be addressed before they are generalized to explain questions about organizational commitment:

- What are the time periods across which effects such as those observed in the underjustification and overjustification paradigms can be expected?

- To what extent can these effects be generalized to individuals in complex, information-rich environments?

- Can these results be understood within the framework of established conceptual models of organizational attitudes and behaviors?

Conclusion

This chapter has addressed a series of interrelated questions concerned with responses—attitudes and behaviors—of individuals in formal organizations. These responses are important because they are manifestations of underlying, general constructs and not because turnover represents a problem in need of a solution or because it is an indication of the operation of free market forces that are so vital "for the flexibility with which millions of people and an amazing variety of jobs have been matched ... and for the self-development and acquisition of skills which contribute greatly to our economic development" (Bakke, 1954, p. 3). Such assumptions about the meanings of turnover, as either a problem to be controlled or as a vital part of the free enterprise system, obscure the theoretical importance of turnover and related responses that define a construct, or constructs, important to the general study of behavior in complex organizations. They direct researchers' energies into the study of turnover isolated from other construct-relevant variables. Both assumptions about turnover are well represented in the literature. To be sure, interventions aimed at changing the probability or frequency of a behavior or set of behaviors represent a rigorous test of a theory purporting to explain the behavior. Organizational interventions designed to decrease turnover or the frequency of absence or other withdrawal behaviors may, if successful, gladden the hearts of managers and practitioners. The view advocated in this chapter is that successful interventions are important because they reflect the validity of the model of organizational withdrawal from which they were derived or developed.

An attitude-behavior framework consistent with the tradition of attitude-behavior models described by theorists from Likert to Fishbein and Ajzen has been assumed. This attitude-behavior framework, discussed by Thurstone (1931), Doob (1947), and Fishbein and Ajzen (1974), argues that social attitudes reflect general orientations toward an attitude object or role. As such, when we identify individuals' attitudes, we have only identified their general tendency to behave for or against the object. On the basis of their general attitudes toward an object, we cannot predict the likelihood of their engaging in any specific behavior. However, we can predict their general behavioral tendencies—their standing along a behavioral continuum described by a combination of many specific behaviors that have a general favorableness-unfavorableness toward the attitude object in common. This general favorable-unfavorable orientation can take many forms in the area of organizational research. The common elements emphasized in this chapter are the behavioral tendencies to withdraw from an organization or organizational role. Attitudes toward organizational roles or work roles are integral to all of the models discussed. Dissatisfactions with different, specific aspects of one's work role are assumed to trigger a sequence of behavioral and cognitive responses that lead to what are termed adaptive behaviors; withdrawal behaviors represent a subset of these adaptive behaviors. Adaptive responses by dissatisfied individuals are not limited to attempts to reduce work role inclusion. Any behavior perceived by a work role incumbent to alter his or her work role characteristics and to lessen dissatisfaction could be enacted. The specific behaviors chosen are likely to be a function of situational constraints, personal constraints, and past (rewarded and punished) behaviors.

Job attitudes have been shown to be consistent predictors of turnover decisions. Using different measures of job attitudes in a variety of organizations with turnover decisions aggregated across varying time periods, Carsten and Spector (1987) found correlations that range from −.59 to +.10 (corrected for attenuation due to unreliability); the average corrected correlation is −.26 across 40 studies. Correlations between intentions and turnover range from −.02 to +.88 (corrected for attenuation due to unreliability), with an average corrected correlation of +.28 across 29 studies (Carsten & Spector). Both sets of correlations are almost surely influenced by labor market conditions and the length of time across which the studies were conducted. Statistical artifacts related to low base rates and skewed distributions of turnover have very likely attenuated these correlations below their expected theoretical values. Carsten and Spector address some of these substantive and statistical issues. It is not clear that their analyses have successfully removed these sources of bias or solved the statistical problems in this area; that was not the intent of their review. Their study is an important contribution, however.

The expected relationship between attitudes and absence is more controversial; two meta-analytic reviews (Hackett & Guion, 1985; Scott & Taylor, 1985) came to opposite conclusions on the basis of partially overlapping sets of studies. It seems likely the theoretical correlation between absence propensity and attitudes is less than that between turnover propensity and attitudes. The statistical and methodological artifacts discussed above suggest that empirical correlations as normally computed and reported may be poor guides to the theoretical, model-based correlations. The average correlation of −.09 between satisfaction and absence reported by Hackett and Guion (1985) is consistent with a simple unifactor model of absence propensity and affect in which the theoretical correlation between satisfaction and a continuously distributed latent propensity to be absent is −.36.

Although the precise structure of the different behavioral measures of withdrawal is not clear, most of the empirical evidence reviewed by Rosse and Miller (1984) and here suggests that some form of dependence among different behaviors should be expected. An alternate-forms model or a compensatory-forms-of-withdrawal model may be the best summary of the expected structure among the different behavioral measures. A progression-of-withdrawal model also needs to be tested across time following the scaling of behaviors and individuals. Evidence testing these models is equivocal at this time.

The volitional control of the behaviors in this area has been established by independent but converging evidence. The relations between attitudes and withdrawal behaviors reported above provide correlational evidence. Successful interventions to reduce turnover (Hackman, Oldham, Janson, & Purdy, 1975; Hulin, 1968; Labovitz & Orth, 1972; Pritchard, Dunnette, & Jorgenson, 1972) provide evidence supporting the volitional nature of turnover and the direct impact of affect on quitting. Note that such studies also support the validity of the basic attitude → behavior model and raise questions about behavior → commitment → attitude models stressing interpretations of our own behaviors as the influences on commitment and attitudes. That is, the studies attempted to manipulate or influence employees' attitudes toward attendance and not, for example, influence behavior directly by coercion. Following these attitude changes, changes in behavior were observed.

Interventions intended to reduce absences (Latham & Napier, 1984; Pedalino & Gamboa, 1974; Schlotzhauer & Rosse, 1985; Stephens & Burroughs, 1978) by means of influences on job affect and incentives for attendance support the hypothesis that absences are influenced by attitudes and motivation. An analysis of a naturally occurring event by Smith (1977) provides further converging evidence about this hypothesis. In this study, employees had been informed that their attendance at work was optional because of a severe late-season blizzard. Job attitudes in departments were related to departmental attendance rates.

Studies of antecedents of tardiness and interventions intended to reduce the occurrence of tardiness are less consistent and less frequent than similar studies of absence and turnover. Tardiness may be more casual and more influenced by environmental events such as weather, traffic, car problems, babysitter illness, and similar random events. Although the evidence is not sufficient to reach a firm conclusion about tardiness in relation to absence and turnover, Rosse and Miller (1984) tentatively conclude that it should be considered a withdrawal or adaptive behavior similar to absence and turnover.

Dissatisfied individuals whose possible responses to job dissatisfaction are severely constrained by environmental, organizational, or personal factors are still assumed to respond according to the model outlined in Figure 9. However, these individuals are expected to select their responses from different families of responses than do individuals whose choice of responses is not so constrained. For example, dissatisfied individuals constrained from quitting because their age or training makes it difficult for them to obtain another job may still behave in accordance with the model. They should select only those responses that are personally acceptable, however. They may select responses that deal with their dissatisfaction by reducing job inputs (missing meetings, occasional tardiness, or absenteeism) or increasing outcomes (stealing supplies) or they might change their work situation by working second or third shifts (when a disliked supervisor is not working or so that they can engage in other desirable activities, such as trout fishing during the day) or choose other responses that stop short of permanent behavioral withdrawal from their work role. Their responses should also depend on the source of their negative affect—pay, supervision, the work itself. From a manager's perspective, they may be judged to be passive and their behavior to be maladaptive; apparent passivity or maladaptiveness may, however, be effective when judged against the goal of reducing job dissatisfaction.

The model outlined in Figure 9 is intended as a heuristic framework summarizing many hypothesized and obtained results in this area. The portions of the model most likely to be controversial are the specific influences that job market factors have on the turnover process. This model hypothesizes a direct labor market effect on affect rather than a moderating effect on the relation between affect and decisions to quit. The model also assumes theoretical families of job withdrawal/adaptation behaviors that underlie observed behavioral manifestations in this area. The evidence for these families is still tentative. This, however, may be more due to the complex nature of the possible structures among the data and problems caused by the empirical manifestations of different possible structures than any lack of validity. Hanisch and Hulin (1990) have reported data that support an interpretation of multiple withdrawal families.

Distinctions between work role affect and organizational commitment models of job withdrawal were discussed. The evidence suggests, although not conclusively, that if researchers want to predict a single behavior such as turnover, then commitment models may have higher validities than more traditional work role affect models. Of course if this is the criterion by which models are judged, then the Fishbein-Ajzen attitude-toward-the-act → intention → behavior model will usually have a higher validity than either a work role affect model or an organizational commitment model. If scientific criteria, such as generalizability to similar, unstudied behaviors, are used to judge the value of different withdrawal models, then single behavior models may be judged to be less valuable than more general multiple behavior models.

Social information processing models of job attitudes and withdrawal behaviors were also discussed. This discussion concentrated on the assumed generalizability and ecological validity of the underjustification and overjustification effects. More specifically, the discussion was concentrated on the apparent lack of ecological validity of the social information processing paradigms. The generalizability of the model to unconstrained organizational behavior was questioned.

Finally, the rationality of employees and their response selectivity in the face of experienced job dissatisfaction was discussed. Accumulated empirical data and conceptual analyses of specific job attitudes and behaviors suggest that employees select behaviors with high perceived instrumentality for reducing their specific job dissatisfaction. Examples ranging from absenteeism to union voting in NLRB elections were discussed.

Throughout this chapter, the underlying integrity and meaning of different adaptive and withdrawal behaviors was stressed. A basic assumption was that individuals in complex organizations do not enact isolated behaviors. Their behaviors are patterned. Fundamental research on applied organizational problems seems necessary at this stage of development in knowledge of organizational withdrawal and adaptation. We learn about important underlying theoretical constructs when we study patterns of behaviors of employees in organizations. Antecedents and correlates of frequencies of multiple behaviors chosen from different families of behaviors representing manifestations of theoretical constructs are more informative than even the most dramatic empirical findings of the antecedents of a specific behavior. The accumulation of evidence about antecedents and structures among the behaviors composing hypothesized behavioral families could be accelerated by theoretical and conceptual developments that stress the role of enacted behaviors in terms of the antecedents of organizational attitudes. Studies of organizational behaviors conducted within such theoretical antecedent-attitude-behavior frameworks should do much to advance our theoretical and practical knowledge of organizational withdrawal, persistence, and commitment.

Notes

1 Discussions with Mary Roznowski during the writing of this chapter and our joint efforts in this and related areas have improved the clarity of the concepts discussed. Fritz Drasgow, David Harrison, and Lloyd Humphreys contributed greatly to the conceptual developments and statistical models discussed in the section on job adaptation. Joe Rosse, James Austin, and Kathy Hanisch read and commented extensively on a earlier draft of the chapter. Their comments materially improved the clarity of the ideas and expression.

2 A unified test of this model, in which a measurement model and the causal model are tested simultaneously by exploiting the simplex structure of the model and latent structure models relating manifest observations to latent constructs, is clearly needed.

3 Logically it would seem that these weights should reflect the idiosyncratic importance of *Aact* and *SN* for each individual. Thus W_1 and W_2 should vary from individual to individual to reflect the weight individuals place on each factor. An individual who was more of a social animal and sensitive to social pressures and expectations of others but relatively sanguine about maximizing more objective outcomes should have a large weight on *SN*. Other individuals, more inner- than other-directed, might be expected to place a large weight on *Aact* and a smaller weight on *SN*. Whyte (1955), for example, provided a description of the behaviors of individuals with differing sensitivities to social expectations within the context of incentive pay systems. However, in empirical tests of the model, W_1 and W_2 are estimated as multiple regression constants and are used for the entire sample. The applicability of sample weights to individuals remains, except by implication, an unexplored issue.

4 M. Roznowski, personal communication.

5 The contributions of David Harrison for his invaluable programming and computer analyses are greatly appreciated.

6 Note that active participation by observers in the interpretations and perceptions of the environment can be acknowledged without abandoning the assumption that knowing and learning about our environments requires that we attend to the consistencies of characteristics of the external environment. Selection, recall, reconstruction, and storage of social and physical cues and information probably *end* the perception process (Garner, Hake, & Eriksen, 1956); they do not initiate it. A lack of complete consensus and agreement among independent observers of the same environment does not invalidate an interpretation of the process of attitude formation and attitude-behavior consistencies as presented in the opening sections of this chapter.

References

Ajzen, I., & Fishbein, M. (1977). *Understanding attitudes and predicting social behavior.* Englewood Cliffs, NJ: Prentice-Hall.

Alderfer, C. P. (1972). *Existence, relatedness, and growth: Human needs in organizational settings.* New York: Free Press.

Anderberg, M. (1973). *Cluster analysis for applications.* New York: Academic Press.

Angle, H. L., & Perry, J. L. (1981). An empirical assessment of organizational commitment and organizational effectiveness. *Administrative Science Quarterly, 26,* 1–14.

Arvey, R. D., Bouchard, T. J., Jr., Segal, N. L., & Abraham, L. M. (1989). Job satisfaction: Environmental and genetic components. *Journal of Applied Psychology, 74,* 187–192.

Atkinson, J. W., & Birch, D. (1970). *The dynamics of action.* New York: Wiley.

Bakke, E. W. (1954). *Labor mobility and economic opportunity.* Cambridge, MA: The Technology Press of M.I.T.

Baruch, D. W. (1944). Why they terminate. *Journal of Consulting Psychology, 8,* 35–46.

Beehr, T. A., & Gupta, N. (1978). A note on the structure of employee withdrawal. *Organizational Behavior and Human Performance, 21,* 73–79.

Bem, D. J. (1965). An experimental analysis of self-persuasion. *Journal of Experimental Social Psychology, 1,* 199–218.

Berger, P. L., & Luckmann, T. (1967). *The social construction of reality.* London: Penguin Books.

Bougon, M. E., Weick, K. E., & Binkhorst, D. (1977). Cognition in organizations: An analysis of the

Utrecht Jazz Orchestra. *Administrative Science Quarterly, 22,* 606–639.

Burke, R., & Wilcox, D. (1972). Absenteeism and turnover among telephone operators. *Personnel Psychology, 25,* 639–648.

Campbell, J. P., & Prichard, R. D. (1976). Motivation theory in industrial and organizational psychology. In M. D. Dunnette (Ed.), *Handbook of industrial and organizational psychology* (pp. 63–130). Chicago: Rand McNally.

Candell, G. L., & Hulin, C. L. (1986). Cross-language and cross-cultural comparisons in scale translations. *Journal of Cross-Cultural Psychology, 17,* 417–440.

Candell, G. L., & Roznowski, M. (1984). *Application of IRT to the assessment of measurement equivalence across United States and Canadian subpopulations.* Paper presented at the meeting of the American Psychological Association, Toronto, Canada.

Carsten, J. M., & Spector, P. E. (1987). Unemployment, job satisfaction and employee turnover: A meta-analytic test of the Muchinsky model. *Journal of Applied Psychology, 72,* 374–381.

Clark, M. S., Mills, J., & Powell, M. C. (1986). Keeping track of needs in communal and exchange relationships. *Journal of Personality and Social Psychology, 51,* 333–338.

Clark, M. S., & Waddell, B. (1985). Perceptions of exploitation in communal and exchange relationships. *Journal of Social and Personal Relationships, 2,* 403–418.

Clegg, C. (1983). Psychology of employee lateness, absence, and turnover: A methodological critique and an empirical study. *Journal of Applied Psychology, 68,* 88–101.

Comer, R., & Laird, J. D. (1975). Choosing to suffer as a consequence of expecting to suffer: Why do people do it? *Journal of Personality and Social Psychology, 32,* 92–101.

Dansereau, F., Jr., Cashman, J., & Graen, G. (1974). Expectancy as a moderator of the relationship between job attitudes and turnover. *Journal of Applied Psychology, 59,* 228–229.

Deci, E. L. (1971). The effects of externally mediated rewards on intrinsic motivation. *Journal of Personality and Social Psychology, 8,* 217–229.

Deci, E. L. (1972). The effects of contingent and non-contingent rewards and controls on intrinsic motivation. *Organizational Behavior and Human Performance, 8,* 217–229.

DeVera, M. V. M. (1985). *Establishing cultural relevance and measurement equivalence using emic and etic items.* Unpublished doctoral dissertation, University of Illinois at Urbana-Champaign.

Doob, L. W. (1947). The behavior of attitudes. *Psychological Review, 54,* 135–156.

Drasgow, F., & Hulin, C. L. (1987). Assessing the equivalence of measurement of attitudes across heterogeneous subpopulations. *Interamerican Journal of Psychology, 21,* 1–24.

Dulany, D. E. (1968). Awareness, rules, and propositional control: A confrontation with behavior S-R theory. In D. Horton & T. Dixon (Eds.), *Verbal behavior and S-R theory* (pp. 340–387). New York: Prentice-Hall.

Dunham, R. B., & Smith, F. S. (1979). *Organizational surveys: An internal assessment of organizational health.* Glenview, IL: Scott, Foresman.

Eagley, R. V. (1965). Market power as an intervening mechanism in Phillips Curve analysis. *Economics, 32,* 48–64.

Ebel, R. L. (1974). And still the dryads linger. *American Psychologist, 29,* 485–492.

Feinberg, S. E. (1977). *The analysis of cross-classified data.* Cambridge, MA: MIT Press.

Festinger, L. (1957). *A theory of cognitive dissonance.* Stanford, CA: Stanford University Press.

Fichman, M. (1984). A theoretical approach to understanding employee absence. In P. S. Goodman & R. S. Atkin (Eds.), *Absenteeism: New approaches to understanding, measuring, and managing employee absence* (pp. 1–46). San Francisco: Jossey-Bass.

Fishbein, M. (1967). Attitude and the prediction of behavior. In M. Fishbein (Ed.), *Readings in attitude theory and measurement* (pp. 477–492). New York: Wiley.

Fishbein, M. (1979). A theory of reasoned action: Some applications and implications. In H. Howe & M. Page (Eds.), *Nebraska symposium on motivation* (pp. 65–116). Lincoln: University of Nebraska Press.

Fishbein, M., & Ajzen, I. (1974). Attitudes toward objects as predictors of single and multiple behavioral criteria. *Psychology Review, 81,* 59–74.

Fishbein, M., & Ajzen, I. (1975). *Beliefs, attitudes, intention, and behavior.* Reading, MA: Addison-Wesley.

Folger, R., Rosenfield, D., & Hays, R. P. (1978). Equity and intrinsic motivation: The role of choice. *Journal of Personality and Social Psychology, 36*, 557–564.

Garner, W. R., Hake, H. W., & Eriksen, C. W. (1956). Operationism and the concept of perception. *Psychological Review, 63*, 149–159.

Gerhart, B. (1987). How important are dispositional factors as determinants of job satisfaction? Implications for job design and other personnel programs. *Journal of Applied Psychology, 72*, 366–373.

Getman, J. G., Goldberg, S. B., & Herman, J. B. (1976). *Union representation elections: Law and reality.* New York: Russell Sage.

Ghiselli, E. E. (1974). Some perspectives for industrial psychology. *American Psychologist, 80*, 80–87.

Graen, G. B. (1976). Role-making processes within complex organizations. In M. D. Dunnette (Ed.), *Handbook of industrial and organizational psychology.* Chicago: Rand McNally.

Guttman, L. L. (1944). A basis for scaling qualitative data. *American Sociological Review, 9*, 139–150.

Hackett, R. D., & Guion, R. M. (1985). A reevaluation of the absenteeism-job satisfaction relationship. *Organizational Behavior and Human Decision Processes, 35*, 340–381.

Hackman, J., Oldham, G., Janson, R., & Purdy, K. (1975). A new strategy for job enrichment. *California Management Review, 17*, 57–71.

Hamner, W., & Smith, F. (1978). Work attitudes as predictors of unionization activity. *Journal of Applied Psychology, 63*, 415–421.

Hanisch, K. A., & Hulin, C. L. (1990). Job attitudes and employee withdrawal: An examination of retirement and other voluntary organizational behaviors. *Journal of Vocational Behavior, 36*.

Harrison, D., & Hulin, C. L. (1989). Investigations of absence-taking using Cox regression. *Journal of Applied Psychology, 74*, 300–316.

Helson, H. (1964a). *Adaptation-level theory.* New York: Harper.

Helson, H. (1964b). Current trends and issues in adaptation-level theory. *American Psychologist, 19*, 26–38.

Herzberg, F., Mausner, B., Peterson, R., & Capwell, D. (1957). *Job attitudes: Review of research and opinion.* Pittsburgh: Psychological Service of Pittsburgh.

Herzberg, F., Mausner, B., & Snyderman, B. S. (1959). *The motivation to work.* New York: Wiley.

Hill, J. M., & Trist, E. L. (1955). Changes in accidents and other absences with length of service: A further study of their incidence and relation to each other in an iron and steel works. *Human Relations, 8*, 121–152.

Hom, P. W., & Hulin, C. L. (1981). A competitive test of prediction of reenlistment by several models. *Journal of Applied Psychology, 66*, 23–39.

Hom, P. W., Katerberg, R., Jr., & Hulin, C. L. (1979). Comparative examination of three approaches to the prediction of turnover. *Journal of Applied Psychology, 64*, 280–290.

Hulin, C. L. (1966a). Job satisfaction and turnover in a female clerical population. *Journal of Applied Psychology, 50*, 185–192.

Hulin, C. L. (1966b). Effects of community characteristics on measures of job satisfaction. *Journal of Applied Psychology, 50*, 185–192.

Hulin, C. L. (1968). Effects of changes in job satisfaction levels on employee turnover. *Journal of Applied Psychology, 52*, 122–126.

Hulin, C. L. (1984). Suggested directions for defining, measuring, and controlling absenteeism. In P. S. Goodman & R. S. Atkin (Eds.), *Absenteeism: New approaches to understanding, measuring and managing employee absence* (pp. 391–420). San Francisco: Jossey-Bass.

Hulin, C. L. (1987). Psychometric theory of item and scale translations: Equivalence across languages. *Journal of Cross-Cultural Psychology, 8*, 115–142.

Hulin, C. L., & Blood, M. R. (1968). Job enlargement, individual differences, and worker responses. *Psychological Bulletin, 69*, 41–55.

Hulin, C. L., Drasgow, F., & Komocar, J. (1982). Applications of item response theory to analysis of attitude scale translations. *Journal of Applied Psychology, 67*, 818–825.

Hulin, C. L., Drasgow, F., & Parsons, C. K. (1983). *Item response theory: Application to psychological measurement.* Homewood, IL: Dow Jones-Irwin.

Hulin, C. L., & Mayer, L. J. (1986). Psychometric equivalence of a translation of the JDI into Hebrew. *Journal of Applied Psychology, 71*, 83–94.

Hulin, C. L., & Rousseau, D. M. (1980). Analyzing infrequent events: Once you find them your troubles begin. In K. H. Roberts & L. Burstein (Eds.), *Issues in aggregation: New directions for methodology of social and behavioral science, 6.* San Francisco: Jossey-Bass.

Hulin, C. L., Roznowski, M., & Hachiya, D. (1985). Alternative opportunities and withdrawal decisions: Empirical and theoretical discrepancies and an integration. *Psychological Bulletin, 97,* 233–250.

Humphreys, L. G. (1960). Investigations of the simplex. *Psychometrika, 25,* 313–323.

Jackofsky, E. F., & Peters, L. H. (1983). Job turnover versus company turnover: Reassessment of the March and Simon participation hypothesis. *Journal of Applied Psychology, 68,* 490–495.

James, L. R., Mulaik, S. A., & Brett, J. M. (1982). *Causal analysis: Assumptions, models, and data.* Beverly Hills, CA: Sage.

James, W. (1890). *Principles of psychology.* New York: Holt.

Joreskog, K. G., & Sorbom, D. (1983). *LISREL VI user's guide.* Uppsala, Sweden: Department of Statistics, University of Uppsala.

Judge, T. (1990). *Job satisfaction as a reflection of disposition: Investigating the relationships and its effect on employee adaptive behaviors.* Unpublished doctoral dissertation, University of Illinois at Urbana-Champaign.

Kanfer, R. (1990). Motivation theory in industrial and organizational psychology. In M. D. Dunnette & L. Hough (Eds.), *Handbook of industrial and organizational psychology* (2nd ed., Vol. 1). Palo Alto, CA: Consulting Psychologists Press.

Katz, D., & Kahn, R. (1966). *The social psychology of organizations.* New York: Wiley.

Katz, D., & Kahn, R. L. (1978). *The social psychology of organizations* (2nd ed.). New York: Wiley.

Kelley, H. H. (1955). Salience of membership and resistance to change of group anchored attitudes. *Human Relations, 8,* 275–290.

Kelman, H. C. (1958). Compliance, identification, and internalization: Three processes of attitude change. *Journal of Conflict Resolution, 2,* 51–60.

Kendall, L. M. (1963). *Canonical analysis of job satisfaction and behavioral, personal background, and situational data.* Unpublished doctoral dissertation, Cornell University, Ithaca, NY.

Kiesler, C. A., & Sakamura, J. (1966). A test of a model for commitment. *Journal of Personality and Social Psychology, 3,* 349–353.

Klecka, W. R. (1980). *Discriminant analysis.* Beverly Hills, CA: Sage.

Koch, J., & Steers, R. M. (1978). Job attachment, satisfaction and turnover among public sector employees. *Journal of Vocational Behavior, 12,* 119–129.

Komocar, J. M. (1985). *Cause maps.* Unpublished doctoral dissertation, University of Illinois at Urbana-Champaign.

Kruglanski, A. W., Riter, A., Amitai, A., Margolin, B. S., Shabtai, L., & Zaksh, D. (1975). Can money enhance intrinsic motivation? A test of the content-consequence hypothesis. *Journal of Personality and Social Psychology, 31,* 744–750.

Labovitz, G., & Orth III, C. D. (1972). Work conditions and personality characteristics affecting job satisfaction of student interns in extended health care. *Journal of Applied Psychology, 56,* 434–435.

Landsberger, H. A., & Hulin, C. L. (1961). A problem for union democracy: Officers' attitudes toward union members. *Industrial and Labor Relations Review, 14,* 419–431.

Latham, G., & Napier, N. (1984). Practical ways to increase employee attendance. In P. S. Goodman & R. S. Atkin (Eds.), *Absenteeism: New approaches to understanding, measuring and managing absence.* San Francisco: Jossey-Bass.

Lawler, E. E. (1976). Control systems in organizations. In M. D. Dunnette (Ed.), *Handbook of industrial and organizational psychology* (pp. 1247–1291). Chicago: Rand McNally.

Lepper, M. R., & Greene, D. (1975). Turning play into work: Effects of adult surveillance and extrinsic rewards on children's intrinsic motivation. *Journal of Personality and Social Psychology, 31,* 479–486.

Lepper, M. R., Greene, D., & Nisbett, R. E. (1973). Undermining children's intrinsic interest with extrinsic reward: A test of the oversufficient justification hypothesis. *Journal of Personality and Social Psychology, 28,* 129–137.

Levin, I., & Stokes, J. P. (1989). Dispositional approach to job satisfaction: Role of negative affectivity. *Journal of Applied Psychology, 74,* 752–758.

Lieberman, S. (1956). The relationship between attitudes and roles: A natural field experiment. *Dissertation Abstracts International, 15,* 636–637.

Locke, E. A. (1976). The nature and causes of job satisfaction. In M. D. Dunnette (Ed.), *Handbook of industrial and organizational psychology* (pp. 1297–1350). Chicago: Rand McNally.

Locke, E. A., Shaw, K. N., Saari, L. M., & Latham, G. P. (1981). Goal setting and task performance: 1969–1980. *Psychological Bulletin, 90,* 125–152.

Ludwig, T. (1985). *A multivariate approach in the analysis and interpretation of withdrawal behaviors.* Unpublished bachelor's thesis, University of Illinois at Urbana-Champaign.

Lyons, T. F. (1972). Turnover and absenteeism: A review of relationships and shared correlates. *Personnel Psychology, 25,* 271–181.

March, J. G., & Simon, H. A. (1958). *Organizations.* New York: Wiley.

Maslow, A. H. (1943). A theory of human motivation. *Psychological Review, 50,* 370–396.

Mayer, L. (1985). *A study of the relationship between job satisfaction and employees' perceptions of a variety of job behaviors.* Unpublished tutorial, Institute of Labor and Industrial Relations, University of Illinois at Urbana-Champaign.

Mead, M. (1934). The use of primitive material in the study of personality. *Character and Personality, 3,* 1–16.

Melbin, M. (1961). Organizational practice and individual behavior: Absenteeism among psychiatric aides. *American Sociological Review, 26,* 14–23.

Michaels, C. E., & Spector, P. E. (1982). Causes of employee turnover: A test of the Mobley, Griffeth, Hand, and Meglino model. *Journal of Applied Psychology, 67,* 53–59.

Miller, H. E. (1981). *Withdrawal behaviors among hospital employees.* Unpublished doctoral dissertation, University of Illinois at Urbana-Champaign.

Miller, H. E., Katerberg, R., & Hulin, C. L. (1979). Evaluation of the Mobley, Horner, and Hollingsworth model of employee turnover. *Journal of Applied Psychology, 64,* 509–517.

Miller, H. E., Rosse, J. R., Rozonowski, M., & Hulin, C. L. *Behavioral symptoms of job withdrawal.* Manuscript in preparation.

Mobley, W. H. (1977). Intermediate linkages in the relationship between job satisfaction and employee turnover. *Journal of Applied Psychology, 62,* 237–240.

Mobley, W. H., Horner, S. O., & Hollingsworth, A. T. (1978). An evaluation of precursors of hospital employee turnover. *Journal of Applied Psychology, 63,* 408–414.

Morrow, P. (1983). Concept redundancy in organizational research: The case of work commitment. *Academy of Management Review, 8,* 486–500.

Mowday, R. T., Porter, L. W., & Steers, R. S. (1982). *Employee-organization linkages: The psychology of commitment, absenteeism, and turnover.* New York: Academic Press.

Mowday, R. T., Steers, R. M., & Porter, L. W. (1979). The measurement of organizational commitment. *Journal of Vocational Behavior, 14,* 224–247.

Muchinsky, P. M., & Morrow, P. C. (1980). A multidisciplinary model of voluntary employee turnover. *Journal of Vocational Behavior, 14,* 43–77.

Naylor, J. C., Pritchard, R. D., & Ilgen, D. R. (1980). *A theory of behavior in organizations.* New York: Academic Press.

Olsson, U., Drasgow, F., & Dorans, N. J. (1982). The polyserial correlation coefficient. *Psychometrika, 41,* 337–347.

O'Reilly III, C., & Chatman, J. (1986). Organizational commitment and psychological attachment: The effects of compliance, identification, and internalization of prosocial behavior. *Journal of Applied Psychology, 71,* 492–499.

Pallak, M. S., Sogin, S. R., & Van Zante, A. (1974). Bad decisions: Effects of volition, locus of causality, and negative consequences on attitude change. *Journal of Personality and Social Psychology, 30,* 217–227.

Parsons, C. K., & Hulin, C. L. (1982). An empirical comparison of item response theory and hierarchical factor analysis in applications to the measure. *Journal of Applied Psychology, 67,* 826–834.

Peak, H. (1955). Attitude and motivation. In M. R. Jones (Ed.), *Nebraska symposium on motivation* (pp. 149–188). Lincoln: University of Nebraska Press.

Pedalino, E., & Gamboa, V. (1974). Behavior modification and absenteeism: Intervention in one industrial setting. *Journal of Applied Psychology, 59,* 694–698.

Pfeffer, J., & Lawler, J. (1980). Effects of job alternatives, extrinsic rewards, and behavioral commitment on attitude to the organization: A. *Administrative Sciences Quarterly, 25,* 38–56.

Porter, L. W. (1964). *Organizational patterns of managerial job attitudes.* New York: American Foundation for Management Research.

Porter, L. W., Crampon, W. J., & Smith, F. J. (1976). Organizational commitment and managerial turnover: A longitudinal study. *Organizational Behavior and Human Performance, 15,* 87–98.

Porter, L. W., & Steers, R. M. (1973). Organizational, work and personal factors in employee turnover and absenteeism. *Psychological Bulletin, 80,* 151–176.

Premack, S. L., & Wanous, J. P. (1985). A meta-analysis of realistic job previews. *Journal of Applied Psychology, 70,* 706–719.

Pritchard, R. D., Campbell, K. M., & Campbell, D. J. (1977). Effects of extrinsic financial rewards on intrinsic motivation. *Journal of Applied Psychology, 62,* 9–15.

Pritchard, R. D., Dunnette, M. D., & Jorgenson, D. O. (1972). Effects of perceptions of equity and inequity on worker performance and satisfaction. *Journal of Applied Psychology, 56,* 75–94.

Rice, A. K., & Trist, E. L. (1952). Institutional and subinstitutional determinants of change in labor turnover. *Human Relations, 5,* 347–372.

Rosenberg, M. J. (1956). Cognitive structure and attitudinal affect. *Journal of Abnormal and Social Psychology, 53,* 367–372.

Ross, M. (1975). Salience of reward and intrinsic motivation. *Journal of Personality and Social Psychology, 32,* 245–254.

Rosse, J. G. (1983). *Employee withdrawal and adaptation: An expanded framework.* Unpublished doctoral dissertation, University of Illinois at Urbana-Champaign.

Rosse, J. G. (1988). Relations among lateness, absence, and turnover: Is there a progression of withdrawal? *Human Relations, 41,* 517–531.

Rosse, J. G., & Hulin, C. L. (1985). Adaptation to work: An analysis of employee health, withdrawal, and change. *Organizational Behavior and Human Decision Processes, 36,* 324–347.

Rosse, J. G., & Miller, H. E. (1984). Relationship between absenteeism and other employee behaviors. In P. S. Goodman & R. S. Atkin (Eds.), *Absenteeism: New approaches to understanding, measuring, and managing employee absence.* San Francisco: Jossey-Bass.

Rotter, J. B. (1966). Generalized expectancies for internal and external control of reinforcement. *Psychological Monographs, 80,* 609.

Roznowski, M. A., & Hanisch, K. A. (1990). Building systematic heterogeneity into work attitudes and behavior measures. *Journal of Vocational Behaviors, 36,* 361–375.

Ryan, T. A. (1970). *Intentional behavior: An approach to human motivation.* New York: Ronald Press.

Salancik, G. R. (1977). Commitment and the control of organizational behavior and belief. In B. M. Staw & G. R. Salancik (Eds.), *New directions in organizational behavior* (pp. 1–54). Chicago: St. Clair Press.

Salancik, G. R., & Pfeffer, J. (1977). An examination of need-satisfaction models of job attitudes. *Administrative Science Quarterly, 22,* 427–456.

Salancik, G. R., & Pfeffer, J. (1978). A social information processing approach to job attitudes and task design. *Administrative Science Quarterly, 23,* 224–251.

Sarbin, T. R. (1954). Role theory. In G. Lindzey (Ed.), *Handbook of social psychology, I.* Cambridge, MA: Addison-Wesley.

Schachter, S., & Singer, J. E. (1962). Cognitive, social, and physiological determinants of emotional state. *Psychological Review, 69,* 379–399.

Schlotzhauer, D., & Rosse, J. (1985). A five year study of a positive incentive absence control program. *Personnel Psychology, 38,* 575–585.

Schriesheim, C. (1978). Job satisfaction, attitudes toward unions, and voting in a union representation election. *Journal of Applied Psychology, 63,* 548–552.

Scott, K. D., & Taylor, G. S. (1985). An examination of conflicting findings on the relationship between job satisfaction and absenteeism: A meta-analysis. *Academy of Management Journal, 28,* 599–612.

Scott, W. E. (1976). The effects of extrinsic rewards on "intrinsic motivation." *Organizational Behavior and Human Performance, 15,* 845–856.

Seligman, M. E. P. (1975). *Helplessness.* San Francisco: Freeman.

Shikiar, R., & Freudenberg, R. (1982). Unemployment rates as a moderator of the job dissatisfaction-turnover relation. *Human Relations, 35,* 845–856.

Smith, F. (1977). Work attitudes as predictors of attendance on a specific day. *Journal of Applied Psychology, 62,* 16–19.

Smith, P. C., Kendall, L., & Hulin, C. L. (1969). *The measurement of satisfaction in work and retirement.* Chicago: Rand McNally.

Staw, B. M. (1974). Attitudinal and behavioral consequences of changing a major organizational reward: A natural field experiment. *Journal of Personality and Social Psychology, 29*, 742–751.

Staw, B. M., Bell, N. E, & Clausen, J. A. (1986). The dispositional approach to job attitudes: A lifetime longitudinal test. *Administrative Science Quarterly, 31*, 56–77.

Staw, B. M., & Calder, B. J. (1980). Intrinsic motivation and norms about payment. *Journal of Personality, 48*, 1–14.

Staw, B. M., & Ross, J. (1985). Stability in the midst of change: A dispositional approach to job attitudes. *Journal of Applied Psychology, 70*, 469–480.

Steers, R. M. (1977). Antecedents and outcomes of organizational commitment. *Administrative Science Quarterly, 22*, 46–56.

Steers, R. M., & Rhodes, S. R. (1978). Major influences on employee attendance: A process model. *Journal of Applied Psychology, 63*, 391–407.

Steers, R. M., & Rhodes, S. R. (1984). Knowledge and speculation about absenteeism. In P. S. Goodman & R. S. Atkin (Eds.), *Absenteeism: New approaches to understanding, managing, and measuring employee absence*. San Francisco: Jossey-Bass.

Stephens, T., & Burroughs, W. (1978). An application of operant conditioning to absenteeism in a hospital setting. *Journal of Applied Psychology, 63*, 518–521.

Tatsuoka, M. M. (1970). *Discriminant analysis: The study of group differences*. Champaign, IL: Institute for Personality and Ability Testing.

Tatsuoka, M. M. (1971). *Multivariate analysis*. New York: Wiley.

Tatsuoka, M. M., & Tiedeman, D. V. (1954). Discriminant analysis. *Review of Educational Research, 24*, 402–420.

Thibaut, J. W., & Kelley, H. H. (1959). *The social psychology of groups*. New York: Wiley.

Thurstone, L. L. (1931). The measurement of social attitudes. *Journal of Abnormal and Social Psychology, 26*, 249–269.

Tolman, E. C. (1932). *Purposive behavior in animals and men*. New York: Appleton-Century-Crofts.

Traub, R. E., & Lam, Y. R. (1985). Latent structure and item sampling models for testing. *Annual Review of Psychology, 36*, 19–48.

Triandis, H. C. (1979). Values, attitudes, and interpersonal behavior. In H. E. Howe, Jr. (Ed.), *Nebraska symposium on motivation* (pp. 159–259). Lincoln: University of Nebraska Press.

Triandis, H. C. (in press). Cross-cultural research in organizations. In M. D. Dunnette & L. Hough (Eds.), *Handbook of industrial and organizational psychology* (2nd ed., Vol. 3). Palo Alto, CA: Consulting Psychologists Press.

Van Maanen, J. (1973). Observations on the making of a policeman. *Human Organization, 32*, 407–418.

Vroom, V. (1964). *Work and motivation*. New York: Wiley.

Wanous, J. P. (1977). Organizational entry: The individual's viewpoint. In E. E. Lawler, III & L. W. Porter (Eds.), *Perspectives on behavior in organizations*. New York: McGraw-Hill.

Waters, L. K., & Roach, D. (1979). Job satisfaction, behavioral intention, and absenteeism as predictors of turnover. *Personnel Psychology, 32*, 393–397.

Weick, K. E. (1977). *The social psychology of organizing* (2nd ed.). Reading, MA: Addison-Wesley.

Weitz, J. (1952). A neglected concept in the study of job satisfaction. *Personnel Psychology, 5*, 201–205.

Whyte, W. F. (Ed.) (1955). *Money and motivation*. New York: Harper.

Wiggins, J. S. (1973). *Personality and prediction: Principles of personality assessment*. Reading, MA: Addison-Wesley.

Wollack, S., Goodale, J. G., Wijting, J. P., & Smith, P. C. (1971). Development of the survey of work values. *Journal of Applied Psychology, 56*, 331–338.

Zalesny, M. D. (1985). Comparison of economic and noneconomic factors in predicting faculty vote preference in a union representation election. *Journal of Applied Psychology, 70*, 243–256.

Zalesny, M. D., & Farace, R. V. (1986). A field study of social information processing: Mean differences and variance differences. *Human Communication Research*.

CHAPTER 9

Training in Work Organizations

Irwin L. Goldstein
University of Maryland, College Park

Training represents a positive hope both for those first entering the work world and for those changing their work environment. In the next decade, emphasis on training systems is likely to grow, as fewer persons enter the work force and increasingly sophisticated technology makes it even more important that everyone have the opportunity to reach his or her potential. For those involved in the research and design of training, the future presents a great opportunity and challenge. Only in the last decade has there been much research and theory development involving training systems. This chapter focuses on these developments in the hope of stimulating further research.

The first sections of this chapter discuss assessment of needs, with a particular focus on recent developments, including systems that not only permit the establishment of KSA–task linkages as a basis for developing training programs but also help specify organizational analysis parameters that determine whether training will actually transfer to the job. The next sections focus on recent research in the areas of cognitive and instructional psychology and trainee readiness and motivation, all of which are important in determining whether trainees will learn. The chapter's material on evaluation models focuses both on criterion development and on the specification of alternative evaluation models useful for research in complex organizational settings. A further section of the chapter presents a sample of recent training techniques, such as rater training and management training that uses behavioral role modeling, and self-management techniques. The final section of the chapter discusses important social system issues associated with training, such as fair employment practices, aging, international training questions, career change, and technical obsolescence.

Introduction

LEARNING OPPORTUNITIES IMPINGE on humans every day of their lives. In many instances, these opportunities are not planned and the degree of learning is a function of a whole series of events, ranging from whether the experience is at an appropriate level for their prior state of knowledge, to whether the experience appears useful for the situation, to many other such factors. Usually, when learning events are systematically planned and related to the work environment they are called *training programs*. From this viewpoint, the training process is defined as the systematic acquisition of attitudes, concepts, knowledge, rules, or skills that result in improved performance at work. Thus, training programs can be planned to produce a more considerate supervisor or a more consistent technician. In some cases, such as on-the-job training, the instructional environment is almost identical to the actual job environment. In other instances, such as a classroom lecture on electronics theory for technicians, the learning environment is far removed from the job situation. However, in both situations, effective training stems from a systematically designed learning atmosphere based on a careful needs assessment of job requirements and the capabilities of the trainees.

From this perspective, training represents a positive hope for persons such as those who are either first entering the work world or are changing their work environment. When training is designed well and implemented properly, it provides opportunities for people to enter the job market with needed skills, perform in new functions, and be promoted into new situations. It should not be a surprise, then, that labor unions often include training opportunities as a part of contract negotiations or that companies are designing new multimillion-dollar facilities to annually train individuals in new technological innovations.

This chapter explores the interacting components of training systems, including information related to training needs assessment, instructional design, and training evaluation. The chapter also presents information about different types of training programs and issues that involve both training and social concerns, such as the relationship between training and fair employment practices.

Training Today

Almost more than any other intervention, training has been dominated by concerns about its faddish nature, the design of training systems without appropriate needs assessment, and the failure to adequately evaluate training systems. These concerns present a limited reflection of the state of the art. From the perspective of the entrepreneur, it is true that profits are made not by assessing needs or evaluating training but by selling an organization a training system, such as films for a behavioral role-modeling program. Indeed, a training evaluation might show that the expensive training program does not work. Also, the organization's internal consultant often finds it difficult to convince the organization that time should be spent on needs assessment and evaluation rather than providing stand-up training to overcome the latest management crisis.

However, some fine work is being done in training needs assessment, development, and evaluation. I am not sure what has spurred these developments. Perhaps the answer lies in recent research efforts or in the pressures of other concerns, such as fair employment practices lawsuits, that demand better data to support the implementation of training techniques. This chapter will acknowledge the poor state of the art at appropriate places, but it will concentrate most on the important developments that now dominate the field.

First, it must be acknowledged that training programs are big business, both in terms of the amount of effort expended and in money spent. For example, a report by the Carnegie Foundation (Eurich, 1985) indicated that education and training has become a booming business, with industrial corporations spending more than $40 billion a year on programs ranging from those addressing such basic skills as reading to those that develop managers and executives. Another illustration is the FAA's decision to let business jet pilots use a simulator to meet many of their training requirements without the use of actual flying time in the plane because flight simulators have become so sophisticated (Caro, 1984). The *Training and Development Journal* (Ralphs & Stephan, 1986) explored these developments by surveying the human resources area in Fortune 500 firms. They found the following:

- Ninety-one percent of the firms provided training for middle management, 75 percent for sales training, 56 percent for secretarial or clerical training, 51 percent for executive development, and 44 percent for technical training.

- For all these types of training, the most frequently used approach was in-house seminars or other internal programs.

- As presented in Table 1, the most popular approach to training was the conference method, but other techniques, including role playing, films, and business games, are frequently used.

- Unfortunately, evaluation approaches are still an area of concern. As presented in Table 2, most evaluations (86%) consist of trainee reactions to be written up at the end of the course. Relatively few efforts are made to collect information by means of follow-up on the job, which is when both trainee and organization usually discover whether anything has been learned. Similarly, survey questions about needs assessment revealed that the most common method for evaluation was informal discussion—a sad commentary,

given the needs assessment techniques developed in the last decade.

In another analysis of survey results (Clement, Walker, & Pinto, 1979), data were reported about the most important skill or knowledge requirement for the training practitioner. In this instance, members of the American Society for Training and Development were asked, What is the most important skill or knowledge requirement for success as a training and development professional? Table 3 reports the results of this question. The largest number of respondents affirmed that human relations skills, including the ability to develop mutual trust and effective interpersonal relationships, were most important. Their responses focused especially on relationships between managers and the trainees with whom they must work when designing training programs. The next largest group of respondents affirmed the importance of communications skills needed in the training process. The next largest set of respondents emphasized knowledge of the training field, including recent developments and understanding of new training technology and the adult learning process. The fourth group of respondents emphasized analytical skill, related to such abilities as analyzing performance deficiencies and assessing training needs. The responses concerning management skill referred mainly to items related to managing the training department. The final set of responses referred to the organizational knowledge necessary for anticipating training needs and understanding organizational goals. The activities presented in Table 1 and the knowledge and skill responses in Table 3 present a good illustration of the complex role of the training practitioner.

Training Tomorrow

Technological Advances. A significant portion of our lives is already spent in

TABLE 1

How Often Are the Following Training Methods Used in Your Organization?

	Almost Always 5	4	3	2	Almost Never 1
				5 Only	4 and 5
A. Case study				9%	33%
B. Conference method (discussion)				27%	62%
C. Lecture with questions				18%	40%
D. Business games				7%	22%
E. Films/videos				31%	35%
F. Programmed instruction (books)				4%	14%
G. Role plays				16%	44%
H. Computer-assisted instruction (CAI)				1%	4%
I. Audiocassettes				2%	7%
J. Interactive video				1%	7%

From "HRD in the Fortune 500" by L. T. Ralphs and E. Stephan, 1986, *Training and Development Journal, 40,* pp. 69–76. Copyright 1986 by the American Society for Training and Development, Inc. Reprinted by permission.

TABLE 2

How Often Are the Following Evaluation Methods Used in Your Organization?

	Almost Always 5	4	3	2	Almost Never 1
				5 Only	4 and 5
A. Course evaluation form filled out by learner at end of course				73%	86%
B. Course evaluation form filled out by instructor at end of course				12%	23%
C. Evaluation by boss, peers, or subordinate				8%	23%
D. Follow-up evaluation by participants				7%	16%
E. Follow-up questionnaire by participants				5%	14%
F. Use of pre- or post-tests				6%	15%
G. Use of business data records				5%	12%

From "HRD in the Fortune 500" by L. T. Ralphs and E. Stephan, 1986, *Training and Development Journal, 40,* pp. 69–76. Copyright 1986 by the American Society for Training and Development, Inc. Reprinted by permission.

TABLE 3

Most Important Skill or Knowledge Requirements

Response Category	Responses	Percentage
Human relations skill	698	35.1%
Communications skill	506	25.4%
Knowledge of training and development field	277	13.9%
Analytical skill	203	10.2%
Management skill	136	6.8%
Knowledge of the organization	95	4.8%
Other	74	3.7%
Total	1989	100.0%

From "Changing Demands on the Training Professional" by R. W. Clement, J. W. Walker, and P. R. Pinto, 1979, *Training and Development Journal, 29*, pp. 3–7. Copyright 1979 by the American Society for Training and Development, Inc. Reprinted by permission.

educational and training programs. Some people feel that instructional technology is likely to have an even greater impact. There are a number of reasons for such a prediction. One reason is certainly the increasing demand for a more sophisticated management work force in order to compete in worldwide markets. Another reason is the startling effects of technological developments. There is a clear trend toward more highly automated systems; Klein and Hall (1988) point to technological developments such as programmable automation, which includes the use of reprogrammable robots, multifunctional machines that manipulate materials, and various forms of computer-assisted design and computer-assisted manufacturing. Some authors (e.g., Cascio & Zammuto, 1987) point to the hope that automation will result in increased productivity and product quality, permitting the United States to regain a competitive edge in global markets. Howell and Cooke (1989) note that the demands of operating extremely sophisticated computer systems require the human operator to become an even more sophisticated information processor and decision maker. Such developments in automation and computer technology place greater demands on training systems to produce a highly sophisticated work force.

An illustration of increased training demands can be found in the development of General Electric's multimillion-dollar training facility, used annually to train 3,000 craftspeople in new technological innovations (*Training and Development Journal*, 1980). Some of the training includes instruction in safe handling of radioactive materials, maintenance of solid-state data communications equipment, use of sensors to detect hot spots in equipment and buildings, and computerized failure analysis of construction equipment. The effects of failing to provide adequate training was sadly demonstrated in the nuclear power plant accident at Three Mile Island. A major finding of that investigation (United States President's Commission on the Accident at Three Mile Island, 1979) was that key maintenance personnel did not have adequate training for their jobs. The training demands likely to affect the future of organizations are clearly stated by Vobejda's (1987) description of the expectations of executives at the new Mazda plant in Michigan:

They want employees to be able to work in teams, to rotate through various jobs, to understand how their tasks fit into the entire process, to spot problems in production, to troubleshoot, articulate the problems to others, suggest improvements, and write detailed charts and memos that serve as a road map in the assembly of the car. (p. A14)

Shifts in Economy.   Another important aspect of future changes in the work force is the shift in our economy from a manufacturing to a service orientation. The manufacturing share of our economy has decreased from 33.7 percent in 1950 to 22.4 percent in 1980 (Cascio & Zammuto, 1987). Many service jobs are labor intensive and not particularly amenable to automation. This probably implies even more competition for entry-level workers and increased stress on training programs to prepare the work force. Interestingly, advances in technology are also having an impact on service-oriented jobs (e.g., witness the use of automated banking services). Analysts have just begun to explore the implications of such factors on future system training needs (Goldstein & Gilliam, 1990).

Equal Opportunity Issues.   Training programs also offer a possible solution to the problem of equal opportunities. All segments of our society, from the federal government to local school systems, have begun to offer programs that give previously unemployed individuals an opportunity to obtain the skills necessary for future employment. These programs include basic language skills, job skills, consumer information, and counseling. The design and implementation of these programs require a special sensitivity to the needs of the applicant population and the job requirements. As difficult as the initiation of these programs may be, there is little dispute that the need for such efforts will greatly increase in the next decade.

Minority groups have faced problems of substantial unemployment as well as discrimination related to job promotion. Previously, the Equal Employment Opportunities Commission (EEOC) focused on those firms that unfairly discriminated against minority employees in hiring. Now the focus is increasingly on firms that fail to provide opportunities to move up the corporate ladder or that deny persons jobs in occupations that were previously the province of one select group.

With this focus, the question of training programs and their fairness to minority groups (particularly those related to sex, race, and age) has become a serious issue. Training techniques that have not been validated and that are discriminatory relevant to promotion and job opportunities are being struck down by the courts. It is also not unusual to find legal actions charging that little or no training was offered to employees seeking technical or professional jobs or that announcements of vacancies were not posted. Settlements often result in millions of dollars in back pay to current employees, as well as require ments that training be given to enable employees to qualify for better jobs. Many of these issues involve complex questions about needs assessment and evaluation that are presented and discussed later in this chapter.

Changes in Demographics.   Based on past trends of labor force activity, it is possible to project, with relative accuracy, future trends in labor force participation (Fullerton, 1985). Individuals entering the labor force in the year 2000 have already been born. Projections clearly indicate that the work force is changing, and this will dramatically affect human resource management. These data (Cascio & Zammuto, 1987; Fullerton, 1985) clearly indicate that the rate of work force increase will slow down significantly in the upcoming decades and that the number of new entrants—primarily between the ages of 16 and 24—will decrease substantially. Also, the composition of the work force will change, especially at the entry level: It is estimated that minorities will represent an increasingly high proportion of the reduced entry pool. This means that increased attention will be given to the utilization of available workers, including older individuals, minorities, and women. Unfortunately, as discussed earlier and detailed by Goldstein and Gilliam (1990), these are the very groups that historically have suffered from discrimination and misguided training efforts. In addition, demographics also indicate that a large number of the individuals available for entry into the work force will be undereducated youth, significant numbers of whom will be members of culturally diverse groups that have not been completely integrated into the work force (Goldstein, 1986). Although many members of minority groups have successfully entered professional and technical careers, a disproportionately large number are among the hard-core unemployed. Many undereducated youth lack basic literacy skills. Emphasis by organizations on the type of training needed to educate individuals for entering working roles is likely to be a very high priority. One successful military program, known as Project 100,000 (Sticht, Armstrong, Hickey, & Caylor, 1987), reached the conclusion that reading, writing, and arithmetic were best learned by having practice material coordinated with relevant information from the intended job field. It is likely that training issues regarding these culturally diverse and undereducated populations will be a major focus of attention.

Emphasis on Utility. Competitive organizational environments have increased the number of questions concerning the utility of training programs and what an organization gains from its investment. For example, it is not unusual for organizations to accept contracts with school systems whereby payment is directly related to the degree of improvement by students on nationally standardized achievement tests. In management circles, it is becoming more conventional to question the effects of expensive training and development programs. This is a healthy trend that will test the ingenuity of training analysts in determining the effectiveness of their programs in terms of performance improvements, costs, and other subsidiary benefits by establishing systematic evaluation programs. Important work on this topic by researchers such as Arvey and Cole (1989) and Cascio (1989) is discussed in the section of this chapter on evaluation models.

Training as a Subsystem

A chapter that considers only the technical aspects of needs assessment and evaluation design misses out on most of the dynamics concerning training systems. Training programs exist within organizations, not in a vacuum. Many investigators have been disappointed with the results of their training programs because they assumed success would always follow the implementation of a well-conceived program. In some instances, supervisors do not permit employees to use new skills obtained in the training program; in other cases, train-ing is not the answer. For example, Sheridan (1975) describes with pointed clarity AT&T's attempt to comply with a consent decree to place 19 percent women in outside craft jobs. Despite rigorous recruiting and training efforts, the women they did manage to recruit dropped from training at an average rate of 50 percent. The women who completed training usually did not last a full year. Later analysis determined that the physical differences between men and women made the job extremely difficult to perform. Some of the most serious problems centered on use of long and heavy ladders which exceeded the physical skills of most women. Using the basic principles of human factors, the job was redesigned so that it could be better performed by women. Interestingly, the changes also made the job easier to perform by men, and the number of back injuries suffered on the job declined.

In other instances, training analysts have thoughtfully considered their organizational environment when determining what type of program might work. For example, Thayer and McGehee (1977) describe a case where the motivation among foremen to attend a formal training program was so low that any such program was doomed to failure. Instead of developing a training program, they developed a difficult open-book test on the topic (which in this case was the terms of the union contract). As an incentive to do well on the test, they offered a steak dinner to the foreman who submitted the most correct answers. McGehee encouraged plant managers to wager with each other as to whose foreman would do best on the test, and managers began to encourage their foremen to organize group study sessions. As soon as the very difficult exam was distributed, the test designer was besieged by phone calls for an entire week; callers argued that there were two or more correct answers to almost every question. By the end of the week, all the exams had been turned in and were perfect or near-perfect. Faced with such performance, the company president decided to host a steak dinner for all the foremen and their managers. Interestingly, the exam was the most popular topic during the dinner.

Certainly, most implementers of training programs would have been delighted with the degree of involvement with this "non-training" approach. The point is that organizations are complex systems and that training programs are but one subsystem. Thus, changes in the selection system that result in the selection of persons with higher or lower job-relevant skills and abilities will have a dramatic effect on the level of training required, and changes in jobs as new technologies develop can have similar effects. Also, of course, more effective training programs can affect all the other systems in the work organization.

The dynamics of training systems must include the realization that one of the first places to which many new employees in an organization are sent is a training program. Even when individuals change positions as a result of a career change or promotion, many enter a training program. It is as important to understand the socialization process that occurs in this way as it is to evaluate specific training outcomes. This chapter will attempt to provide some understanding of these dynamics as well as explain the systematic development and evaluation process of training programs.

The next section of this chapter presents an instructional model that outlines the factors to be considered in the design of systematic programs. The description of these interacting components should clearly indicate that there is no easy technique or gadget that can be used to develop a well-conceived program.

Training as an Instructional System

One useful model in conceptualizing training systems is the instructional technology model that emphasizes careful needs assessment, precisely controlled learning experiences designed to achieve instructional objectives, and use of performance criteria and evaluation information. Other characteristics of instructional systems include the use of feedback to continually modify the instructional process. In addition, the instructional systems view is just one of a whole set of interacting systems. Training programs interact with and are directly affected by a larger system involving corporate policies (for example, selection and management philosophy).

Figure 1 presents one model of an instructional system. The initial components of the model refer to the needs assessment process necessary to establish both the training program and the evaluation model. One aspect of the needs assessment process is an organizational analysis, used to assess the systemwide components of the organization (including

FIGURE 1

An Instructional System

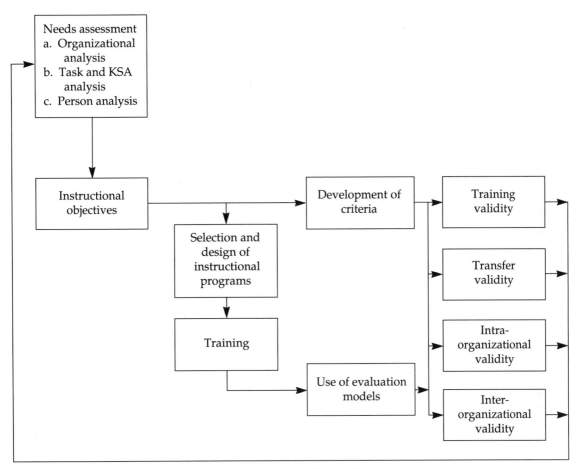

From *Training and Organizations: Needs Assessment, Development and Evaluation* by I. L. Goldstein, 1986, Monterey, CA: Brooks/Cole.
Copyright 1986 by Brooks/Cole Publishing Company. Reprinted by permission.

whether training is even needed) and also whether what is learned in training will be supported in the training environment. In addition to the organizational analysis, it is necessary to assess to determine what tasks are required on the job and which knowledge, skills, and abilities (KSAs) are necessary to perform those tasks.

From information obtained in the assessment of instructional needs, a blueprint emerges that describes the KSAs to be achieved upon completion of the training program. This provides input for the design of the training program as well as for the criteria for success that will be used to judge the program's adequacy. Thus, objectives communicate the goals of the program to both the learner and the training designer. Once the tasks, KSAs, and objectives have been specified, the next step is designing the environment to achieve the objectives. This is a delicate process that requires a blend of learning principle and media selection, based on the tasks that the trainee is eventually expected to perform. Gilbert (1960) describes the temptations that often lead to a poor environment:

> If you don't have a gadget called a teaching machine, don't get one. Don't buy one; don't borrow one; don't steal one. If you have such a gadget, get rid of it. Don't give it away, for someone else might use it. This is a most practical rule, based on empirical facts from considerable observation. If you begin with a device of any kind, you will try to develop the teaching program to fit that device. (p. 478)

This recommendation is especially interesting because Gilbert has devoted much of his research to the study and use of teaching machines. Trainers choose airline simulators that reproduce the characteristics of flight in order to teach pilots; however, a simulator is not usually considered an appropriate tool with which to teach an adult a foreign language. The analysis of job tasks and required KSAs, and the design of a training environment to match, are at this point as much an art as a technology.

Another aspect of the design of instructional environments is the consideration of learning principles to support the acquisition and transfer of the learned behavior. Unfortunately, a definite list of principles from the learning environment that could be adapted to the training setting has not completely emerged. However, cognitive and instructional theorists have progressed to a stage of development at which it is evident that there are now clear choices that need to be considered when designing the learning environment (J. P. Campbell, 1988; Howell & Cooke, 1989).

Since developing a training program involves an assessment of needs and a careful design of the training environment, trainers sometimes assume the trainees will perform their job at acceptable criterion levels. Unfortunately, such faith may be far from justified. Careful examinations of the instructional process disclose numerous pitfalls resulting from mistakes or deficiencies in our present state of knowledge. For example, the assessment of an instructional need might have changed since the program was designed, or there may be uncertainties about which training technique is most appropriate to establish the required behaviors. Thus, the third column in the model refers to evaluation components.

The evaluation process revolves around two procedures—establishing measures of success (criteria) and using research designs to determine what changes have occurred during the training and transfer process. Criteria must be established both to evaluate trainees at the conclusion of the training program and to evaluate on-the-job performance (referred to as transfer validity in the model). There are serious issues pertaining to the integration of the large number of criteria often needed to evaluate a program and to the difficulties, such as biased estimates of performance, associated with collecting criterion information. These issues are discussed later in this chapter.

In addition to criterion development, the evaluation phase must also focus on the design necessary to assess the training program. As indicated in Figure 1, a number of different designs can be used to evaluate training programs, and to some extent the choices depend on what information is desired and what constraints are operating to affect evaluation. The following questions are related to the potential goals listed in the last column of Figure 1:

- *Training validity.* Do the trainees learn during training?

- *Transfer validity.* Does what has been learned in training transfer on the job as enhanced performance in the work organization?

- *Intraorganizational validity.* Is the performance for a new group of trainees in the organization for which the training program was developed consistent with the performance of the original training group?

- *Interorganizational validity.* Can a training program validated in one organization be used successfully in another organization?

These questions often result in different evaluation models or, at the very least, different forms of the same evaluation model. For example, the experimental design model is based on the creative use of various combinations of pre- and posttests as well as control groups to assess the effectiveness of the training efforts. In addition to experimental designs, there are other approaches to evaluation that provide varying degrees of information. For example, individual differences designs relate individual performance in training to individual performance on the job to determine whether those who tend to perform better in training also perform better on the job. If so, the training score can be used to select the better job performers. However, such a model does not prove very informative about the actual quality of the training program: Individuals who do well in training may also do well in the job even when the training program does not teach as much as it should. Another model, also represented in Figure 1, is content validity, which refers to whether the KSAs determined in the needs assessment are emphasized in the training program. Such emphasis does not guarantee that the material will be learned, but if critical KSAs are not included in the training program there is not much hope for the effort.

Finally, the model in Figure 1 stresses the idea that a training program should be a closed-loop system in which the evaluation process provides for continual modification of the program. The information may become available at many different stages in the evaluation process. For example, an effective monitoring program might show that the training program has not been implemented as originally planned. In other instances, different conclusions might be supported by comparing data obtained from the training evaluation or transfer evaluation. Furthermore, even when the training program achieves its stated objectives, there are always developments that can affect the program, including the addition of new training techniques and changes in the characteristics of trainees. In this sense, the development of training programs must be viewed as a continually evolving process.

One purpose of this overview of the instructional process is to provide a model that can be used to organize the material in the following sections. A more comprehensive discussion of the components of instructional programs begins in the next section by examining the assessment of training needs.

The Importance of Needs Assessment

Training programs are designed to achieve goals that meet instructional needs. There is always the temptation to begin training without a thorough analysis of these needs; however, a reexamination of the instructional model just discussed will show the danger of beginning any program without a complete assessment of tasks, behaviors, and environment. The model shows that the objectives, criteria, and design of the program all stem from these analyses.

In their classic text, McGehee and Thayer (1961) describe three basic components of needs assessment: *organizational analysis, task analysis,* and *person analysis.* Years later, Moore and Dutton (1978) found that these three organizing categories were still being used. Unfortunately, research on alternate systems does not exist for comparison, and authors such as Levine and his colleagues (Levine, Ash, Hall, &

Sistrunk, 1983) have been forced to compare job analysis methodologies by asking experts which method they favor. In addition, training researchers face another problem. That is, considerable information is still needed concerning the design of effective systems to obtain the KSAs required for both training program design and program evaluation. Thus, McCormick (1976), who developed a major job analytic technique in the *Position Analysis Questionnaire* (PAQ), previously despaired that there was little progress toward a task analytic system necessary for designing training procedures. Actually, in the last ten years, considerable progress has been made in this area, although much research is still needed. Before beginning a discussion of the various components of needs assessment, I shall first focus on some general concerns about the collection of job analysis information.

Job Analysis Information

Although many different methods exist for collecting information about the task and the organizations, all these methods attempt to provide valid and reliable information. However, it is important to make sure an individual method does not bias the quality of the information. Unfortunately, this is more easily said than done. Each method has unique characteristics that can affect both the kind and quality of information obtained. An interview depends on the interviewer's skills and biases, while a mail questionnaire is subject to the sampling biases that occur when a substantial number of participants do not return the survey.

A summary of the advantages and disadvantages of the various techniques offered by Steadham (1980) is presented in Table 4. To be aware of these difficulties and to arrive at methodologies that avoid potential sources of bias involves several steps:

- Potential problems in each of the methods should be spotted and the needs assess-

ment designed accordingly. Interviewers should be trained and questionnaire systems designed to achieve maximum rates of return.

- More than one type of methodology should be used. Each method is likely to produce information sources with particular biases. One way to avoid this difficulty, for example, is to use interviews, job observations, and questionnaire methods together; or, when interviews are being used, to conduct both individual and group interviews with more than one interviewer.

- Respondents should represent cross-sections of the organization who have relevant information about the job. Thus, in the organizational analysis where the concerns are issues such as unspecified organizational goals or organizational conflict, it is critical to involve top-level management as well as direct supervisors of the trainees.

- All relevant members of the work organization, including union representatives, personnel representatives, and training representatives, for example, should be involved in the job analysis process.

- Tasks, KSAs, and judgments (such as task criticality) about these components should be collected from experienced job incumbents as well as direct supervisors. If the information collected is inconsistent, the best approach is that the training analyst first determine why, rather than simply designing a training program. O'Reilly (1973) reported a study in which supervisors and subordinates strongly disagreed about which tasks were performed at all. In this study, the analysts concluded that the supervisors were frequently misreporting what their subordinates were actually required to do in their jobs. Whether those tasks should

TABLE 4

Advantages and Disadvantages of Nine Basic Needs Assessment Techniques

Techniques	Advantages	Disadvantages
Observation		
Can be as technical as time-motion studies or as functionally or behaviorally specific as observing a new board or staff member interacting during a meeting	Minimizes interruption of routine work flow or group activity	Requires a highly skilled observer with both process and content knowledge (unlike an interviewer who needs, for the most part, only process skill)
May be as unstructured as walking through an agency's offices on the lookout for evidence of communication barriers	Generates in situ data, highly relevant to the situation where response to identified training needs/interests will impact	Carries limitations that derive from being able to collect data only within the work setting (the other side of the first advantage listed in the preceding column)
Can be used normatively to distinguish between effective and ineffective behaviors, organizational structures, and/or process	(When combined with a feedback step) provides for important comparison checks between inferences of the observer and the respondent	Holds potential for respondents to perceive the observation activity as "spying"
Questionnaires		
May be in the form of surveys or polls of a random or stratified sample of respondents, or an enumeration of an entire "population" ranking	Can reach a large number of people in a short time	Make little provision for free expression of unanticipated responses
Can use a variety of question formats: open-ended, projective, forced-choice, priority-ranking	Are relatively inexpensive	Require substantial time (and technical skills, especially in survey model) for development of effective instruments
Can take alternative forms such as Q-sorts, or slip shorts, rating scales, either pre-designed or self-generated by respondents	Give opportunity of expression without fear or embarrassment	Are of limited utility in getting at causes of problems or possible solutions
	Yield data easily summarized and reported	Suffer low return rates (mailed), grudging responses, or unintended and/or inappropriate respondents
May be self-administered (by mail) under controlled or uncontrolled conditions, or may require the presence of an interpreter or assistant		

TABLE 4

Advantages and Disadvantages of Nine Basic Needs Assessment Techniques (continued)

Techniques	Advantages	Disadvantages
Key Consultation Secures information from those persons who, by virtue of their formal or informal standing, are in a good position to know what the training needs of a particular group are: a. Board chairman b. Related service providers c. Members of professional associations d. Individuals from the service population Once identified, data can be gathered from these consultants by using techniques such as interviews, group discussions, questionnaires	Is relatively simple and inexpensive to conduct Permits input and interaction of a number of individuals, each with his or her own perspectives of the needs of the area, discipline, group, etc. Establishes and strengthens lines of communication between participants in the process	Carries a built-in bias, since it is based on views of those who tend to see training needs from their own individual or organizational perspective May result in only a partial picture of training needs due to the typically nonrepresentative nature (in a statistical sense) of a key informant group
Print Media Can include professional journals, legislative news/ notes, industry "rags," trade magazines, in-house publications	Are an excellent source of information for uncovering and clarifying normative needs Provide information that is current, if not forward looking Are readily available and are apt to have already been reviewed by the client group	Can be a problem when it comes to the data analysis and synthesis into a usable form (use of clipping service or key consultants can make this type of data usable)

TABLE 4
_____

Advantages and Disadvantages of Nine Basic Needs Assessment Techniques (continued)

Techniques	Advantages	Disadvantages
Interviews		
Can be formal or casual, structured or unstructured, or somewhere in between	Are adept at revealing feelings, causes of and possible solutions to problems which the client is facing (or anticipates); provide maximum opportunity for the client to represent himself or herself spontaneously on his or her own terms (especially when conducted in an open-ended nondirective manner)	Are usually time consuming
		Can be difficult to analyze and quantify results (especially from unstructured formats)
May be used with a sample of a particular group (board, staff, committee) or conducted with everyone concerned		Unless the interviewer is skilled, the client(s) can easily be made to feel self-conscious
		Rely for success on a skillful interviewer who can generate data without making client(s) feel self-conscious, suspicious, etc.
Can be done in person, by phone, at the work site, or away from it		
Group Discussion		
Resembles face-to-face interview technique, e.g., structured or unstructured, formal or informal, or somewhere in between	Permits on-the-spot synthesis of different viewpoints	Is time consuming (therefore initially expensive) both for the consultant and the agency
Can be focused on job (role) analysis, group problem analysis, group goal setting, or any number of group tasks or themes (e.g., "leadership training needs of the board")	Builds support for the particular service response that is ultimately decided on	Can produce data that are difficult to synthesize and quantify (more a problem with the less structured techniques)
	Decreases client's "dependence response" toward the service provider since data analysis is (or can be) a shared function	
Uses one or several of the familiar group facilitating techniques: brainstorming, nominal group process, force fields, consensus ranking, organizational mirroring, simulation, and sculpting	Helps participants to become better problem analysts, better listeners, etc.	

TABLE 4

Advantages and Disadvantages of Nine Basic Needs Assessment Techniques (continued)

Techniques	Advantages	Disadvantages
Tests		
Are a hybridized form of questionnaire	Can be especially helpful in determining whether the cause of a recognized problem is a deficiency in knowledge or skill or, by elimination, attitude	The availability of a relatively small number of tests that are validated for a specific situation
Can be very functionally oriented (like observations) to test a board, staff, or committee member's proficiency		Do not indicate if measured knowledge and skills are actually being used in the on-the-job or "back home group" situation
May be used to sample learned ideas and facts	Results are easily quantifiable and comparable	
Can be administered with or without the presence of an assistant		
Records, reports		
Can consist of organizational charts, planning documents, policy manuals, audits, and budget reports	Provide excellent clues to trouble spots	Cause of problems or possible solutions often do not show up
Includes employee records (grievance, turnover, accidents, etc.)	Provide objective evidence of the results of problems within the agency or group	Carry perspective that generally reflects the past situation rather than the current one (or recent changes)
Includes minutes of meetings, weekly and monthly program reports, memoranda, agency service records, program evaluation studies	Can be collected with a minimum of effort and interruption of work flow since it already exists at the work site	Need a skilled data analyst if clear patterns and trends are to emerge from such technical and diffuse raw data

TABLE 4

Advantages and Disadvantages of Nine Basic Needs Assessment Techniques (continued)

Techniques	Advantages	Disadvantages
Work samples		
Are similar to observation but in written form	Carry most of the advantages of records and report data	Case study method will take time away from actual work of the organization
Can be products generated in the course of the organization's work (e.g., ad layouts, program proposals, market analyses, letters, training designs)	Are the organization's data (its own output)	Need specialized content analysis
		Analyst's assessment of strengths/weaknesses by samples can be challenged as "too subjective"
Written responses to a hypothetical but relevant case study provided by the consultant		

From "Learning to Select a Needs Assessment Strategy" by S. V. Steadham, 1980, *Training and Development Journal, 30*, pp. 56–61. Copyright 1980 by the American Society for Training and Development, Inc. Reprinted by permission.

have been part of the job was not determined in the study; however, it was clear that more information was needed before an effective training program could be designed.

In addition to these points, Steadham (1980) suggests several additional guidelines:

- *Methods Potpourri, or Never Use One When Two Will Do:* Select two or more methods in such a way that the advantages of one offset the disadvantages of another. There is strength in a good blend; improved reliability of the needs data is the result.

- *Freedom to Respond:* Each assessment method exerts a degree of control on its subject (your client). Reduce the control and increase the methods flexibility to allow the client to respond in the way he or she considers important.

- *Having Something Happen:* Needs assessment efforts that never lead to a relevant response are useless. Be clear with the client system's decision makers that you expect an appropriate response to the assessment data. Reach an understanding before you begin the data collection and then stick to it. (p. 60)

Organizational Analysis

Considerable change has occurred in the conception of what constitutes organizational analysis. Originally, organizational analysis as conceptualized by McGehee and Thayer (1961) focused on factors that provided information about where and when training could be used in an organization. Thus, the analysis focused on variables such as manpower and skill inventories. More recently, Goldstein (1978b, 1986) reconceptualized organizational analysis into an examination of systemwide components that determine whether the training program can produce behavior that will transfer into the organization. Goldstein also noted that persons who participate in training are faced with a problem: They are required to learn something in one environment—the training situation—and to use it in another—on the job. He suggested that this requires an examination of the systemwide components of the organization that may affect a trainee arriving with newly learned skills. Thus, training programs are often judged to have failed because of organizational constraints that they were not intended even to address. For example, a trainee will find it difficult to overcome a situation in which he or she arrives with a set of behaviors that are inconsistent with the way the manager prefers to have the job performed. Also, training programs are not likely to be successful when managers are forced to maintain production standards while employees are being trained.

Other authors have also focused on similar concerns. Michalak (1981) warns us that trainers overemphasize the portion of training that deals with acquisition of skill and place little emphasis on what happens afterward. Similarly, Marx (1982) stressed the identification of high-risk situations faced by trainees and the need for coping skills in those situations. Baumgartel and his associates (Baumgartel & Jeanpierre, 1972; Baumgartel, Sullivan, & Dunn, 1978) found that training is more effective when management provides a supportive climate that encourages trainees to explore new ideas and use their training knowledge. In their research, Baumgartel and his associates studied 240 managers who attended programs in India designed to promote the introduction of advanced technology. They found that once returned, managers only used the skills they had gained when the organizational climate was favorable. This was especially true for low-status managers. In the study, what most affected the transfer of learning to the home organizational setting were (a) the degree to which the organization stimulated and approved of innovation and technology, (b) the degree to which the management was willing to spend money for training, (c) the degree of free and open communication among the management group, and (d) the degree to which organizations expressed their desire for managers to use the knowledge gained in management courses.

Another recent study also stressed the importance of a supportive organizational climate. Russell, Terborg, and Powers (1985) evaluated co-worker and supervisory practices to determine whether these personnel were using methods similar to those taught in training. The belief was that if these co-workers and supervisors behaved in a manner consistent with the training, then trainees would be "reminded" to use such behavior on the job. The results of the study indicated that organizational support was significantly related to the application of training to organizational performance.

A recent experience of mine concerning these issues was especially illuminating because everyone I told about the incident recalled similar experiences. I was invited by an organization's top management team to design a needs assessment package that would be used to establish rating scales for performance appraisal. As part of that process, I requested that the first meeting be with a union-management committee I had heard about from top management. The committee had representatives from all parts of the organization.

The hostility of the atmosphere at the meeting was made quite apparent by some of the questions: "What are you trying to sell us?" "Did you ever do this type of work before?" "Are you trying to stick us with a system you developed for someone else?" Finally, after several hours of such conversation, I learned that this committee had, at the request of top management, developed an earlier plan for the project. After countless hours of volunteer time, they had submitted a report. On the same day their report was submitted, they were informed that an outside consultant had been asked to perform the same activity. Unfortunately for me, I was the chosen consultant.

I decided not to even try to begin the project right away. Rather, my research team and I arranged for meetings between top management, the committee, and ourselves to work out everyone's feelings and to establish appropriate roles for each group. Eventually we proceeded with the project with everyone's cooperation. Months later, members of the committee noted that if we had not met with them or if we had not resolved those difficulties, no one in the organization would have cooperated during the needs assessment. They had intended instead to subvert the assessment process. I have no doubt they would have accomplished their purpose.

Some Organizational Analysis Indicators. The issues just discussed specify the importance of organizational climate issues in transfer of training. However, compared to task and KSA analysis, work in this area is at an early stage. As noted by Goldstein and Thayer (1987), a conceptual model that specifies the type of concerns that should be examined is sorely lacking. Recently, Rouillier and Goldstein (1990) have worked on the development of a conceptual model and indicators for various aspects of the model that could reflect the degree of positive organizational climate for transfer. Their research identified transfer climate components and classified them based on an organizational behavior model developed by Luthans and Kreitner (1985). Two major components of transfer climate—situational cues and consequences—were predicted to influence the extent to which transfer would occur. Some of the types of items included in each of these categories are presented in Table 5.

Rouillier and Goldstein conducted the first study investigating their model with a large franchise that owned and operated over 100 fast-food restaurants. Surveys were developed to measure the transfer climate (situational cues and consequences) of each of the 100 organizational units and the transfer behavior of trainees assigned to each. The trainees were assistant managers who completed a week-long training program and then were randomly assigned to one of the 100 organizational units. They found that in units that had a more positive transfer climate in that trainees were influenced to use what they had learned (situational cues) and were rewarded for doing so (consequences), trainees demonstrated more transfer behavior. As expected, trainees who had learned more in training also performed better on the job, but the interaction between transfer climate and learning was not significant. This provided evidence that the degree of positive transfer climate affected the degree to which learned behavior was transferred onto the job—independent of the degree to which the trainees had learned in the training program. The investigators concluded that transfer climate was a potentially powerful tool that organizations should consider in order to facilitate training transfer. Certainly, the extent to which the training analyst is left with a feeling of uncertainty about the transfer climate suggests that considerable preliminary work may be needed before it even makes sense to begin training.

Task Analysis

Since the mid-1970s, there have been several steps forward in the use of task analysis as input for the design of training systems. This has resulted in the specification of a number of steps as input for the training procedure. They are presented in Table 6.

This section will describe each of these steps, beginning with the determination of the task analysis. Just as an organizational analysis is necessary to determine the organizational objectives, a task analysis is used to determine the instructional objectives that will be related to the performance of particular activities or job operations. The task analysis results in a statement of the activities or work operations

TABLE 5

Some Examples of Organizational Items for the Assessment of Transfer Climate

Situational Cues	*Consequences*
Existing managers make sure that new managers have the opportunity to use their training immediately	Existing managers let new managers know they are doing a good job when they use their training
Existing managers have new managers share their training experience and learning with co-workers on the job	Existing managers refuse to accept statements or actions from new managers that are different from those learned in training
The equipment used in training is similar to the equipment found on the job	More experienced workers ridicule the use of techniques taught in training (reverse scored)
Existing managers assign an experienced co-worker to help trainees as needed back on the job	Existing managers do not notice new managers who are using their training (reverse scored)
Existing managers ease the pressure of work for a short time so new managers have a chance to practice new skills	New managers who successfully use their training are likely to receive a salary increase
Training aids are available on the job to support what new managers have learned in training	New managers who use their training are given preference for new assignments

From *The Determination of Positive Transfer of Training Climate Through Organizational Analysis* by J. Z. Rouillier and I. L. Goldstein, 1990, unpublished manuscript. Copyright 1990 by J. Z. Rouillier and I. L. Goldstein. Reprinted by permission.

TABLE 6

Task and KSA Development Steps as Input for the Design of Training Systems

Development of task statements
↓
Development of task clusters
↓
Development of KSAs
↓
Determination of relevant tasks and KSAs
↓
Linkage of relevant KSAs to tasks
↓
Design of the training environment from the KSA–task links
↓
Content validation of KSAs in the training environment
to the relevant KSAs from the job analysis

FIGURE 2

Examples of Different Types of Job Groupings at Different Levels of Analysis

Level of Analysis	Composition of Group

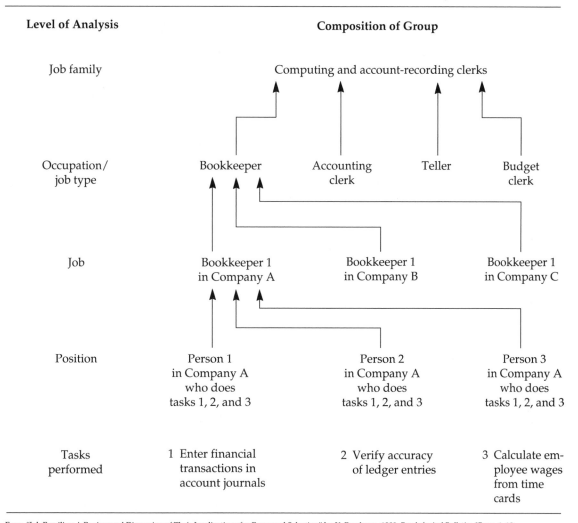

From "Job Families: A Review and Discussion of Their Implications for Personnel Selection" by K. Pearlman, 1980, *Psychological Bulletin, 87*, pp. 1–18. Copyright 1980 by the American Psychological Association. Reprinted by permission.

performed on the job and the conditions under which the job is performed. It is not a description of the worker, but rather a description of the job.

As presented in Figure 2, Pearlman (1980) shows the various levels of analysis in looking at a job. In this example, the tasks performed are the fundamental units of analysis. They determine the groupings at each of the levels in the diagram. Thus, Pearlman identifies three of the many tasks performed by persons in Company A who hold the job of Bookkeeper l.

He also labels four of the occupation/job types (bookkeeper, accounting clerk, teller, and budget clerk) that constitute the job family of computer and account-recording clerks.

As noted earlier and as listed in Table 6, advances have been made in the use of task and KSA analysis as input for the design of training systems. Some of the important early work was conducted by Ammerman and his colleagues (Ammerman & Pratzner, 1974, 1975, 1977). These authors described, for the design of tasks, rules and procedures that removed much of the ambiguity concerning the descriptive nature of tasks. They also developed methodology for collecting information relevant to task dimensions such as importance and frequency. Their findings enabled them to decipher clues that indicated the need for training. Christal (1974) developed similar procedures for the military and in a system named CODAP developed computer routines for analyzing job inventory data.

Another group of researchers (Goldstein, 1986; Goldstein, Macey, & Prien, 1981; Goldstein & Wexley, 1983; Prien, Goldstein, & Macey, 1987) joined to broaden the needs assessment data base for training systems. They argued that while task analysis provides a critical foundation for any training job analysis, a task-based system could not provide the entire foundation for a training system. Basically, Goldstein argued that using task analyses was the same thing as having *physical fidelity*. The goal in training system design is usually not perfect physical fidelity, however, because the reason most training systems exist is that you cannot train an individual on the exact tasks that constitute the job. In some cases, such as flying an airplane, it is simply too dangerous, while in other cases, the representation of the exact task is too overwhelming for the trainee to learn. In almost all situations the task is some simulation of the actual job. This includes simulations for learning management techniques, such as role

playing, or learning to fly an airplane in a simulator. In these situations, the goal is to choose simulated tasks that call forth the KSAs that need to be learned. This type of training environment is typically known as one that has *psychological* fidelity in the sense that it sets the stage for the behavioral processes or KSAs that need to be learned.

Recently, Goldstein and his colleagues designed procedures to obtain specific KSAs that needed to be learned to perform specific tasks and used scaling systems to obtain information on the importance of the KSAs, the difficulty of learning them, and where they were needed on the job. In addition, they designed procedures to link KSAs to specific tasks so that training developers could design programs teaching particular KSAs with certain simulated tasks. While these procedures are still being designed and implemented, there have been some unexpected benefits, one of which is providing the job analytic base for content validation of training programs. This is discussed further in the section of this chapter on evaluation.

The following material outlines the techniques and procedures developed by Goldstein and his colleagues as listed in Table 6.

Development of Task Statements. The first phase in the task analysis is to completely specify the tasks performed. Collecting such information involves a number of techniques, including interviewing panels of job experts and observing the job being performed. The rules for the specification of tasks have been evolving for a number of years. The following summary is a synthesis of the work of a number of individuals (Ammerman & Pratzner, 1977; Prien, Goldstein, & Macey, 1987):

- Use a terse, direct style, avoiding long, involved sentences that can confuse the organization. The present tense should be used. Avoid words that do not give necessary information. Examples of task statements from studies of several different job analyses of the job of police radio operator are presented in Table 7. It should be noted that police operators are the vital link for state police who patrol the nation's roads and highways. Communication depends on them, and they provide information and backup aid as required.

- Each sentence should begin with a functional verb that identifies the primary job operation. It is important for the word to specifically describe the work to be accomplished.

- The statement should describe *what* the worker does, *how* the worker does it, *to whom* or *what*, and *why* the worker does it. The following illustration stems from the job of a secretary:

What?	*To Whom/What?*
Sorts	Correspondence, forms, and reports
Why?	*How?*
To facilitate filing them	Alphabetically

The next example comes from the job of a supervisor:

What?	*To Whom/What?*
Informs	Next shift supervisor of departmental status
How?	*Why?*
Through written reports	So that the number of employees needed at each workstation can be determined

Note that by examining the tasks just illustrated and the tasks listed in Table 7, the development of task statements is possible for different types of jobs, ranging from craft to managerial.

- The tasks should be stated completely, but they should not be so detailed that it becomes a time and motion study. For example, a task could be "slides fingertips over machine edges to detect ragged edges and burrs." However, it would not be useful for the identification of tasks to say, for example, that the worker raises his or her hand to table, places fingers on part, presses fingers on part, or moves fingers to the right six inches. Rather, each statement should refer to what makes sense as a whole task. Usually the breaking down of the tasks into a sequence of activities is useful when the task is being taught in the training program. However, that step doesn't occur until the total task domain has been identified and it is determined which tasks should be taught in the training program. Similarly, trivial tasks like unlocking the file cabinet or turning out the light when leaving the office should usually be avoided.

Development of Task Clusters.   As noted in Table 6, after a full task set is developed from the job analysis, task clusters can then be developed. An example of a task cluster title and definition of the cluster for the job of police radio operator is also presented in Table 7.

Clustering is done to help organize the task information and to help in the editing of tasks. As such, clustering usually takes place after the collection of the complete task set from the job observations, panels, and interviews. It usually involves the following steps:

- First, definitions of task clusters are developed that describe job functions. In the case of the police radio operator job, the cluster and definition presented in Table 8 are for providing information to the public. Some other potential clusters for that job might include maintaining

TABLE 7

Examples of Tasks From the Job of Police Radio Operator

Working With the Public: Providing Information

This category includes providing information to the public and other non–law-enforcement personnel or agencies which are concerned with weather, road conditions, accidents, and public safety.

Provides directions to citizens concerning various geographical areas of landmarks as a public service

Provides emergency information, such as weather and road hazards, to the public and other non–law-enforcement agencies in order to provide for public safety

Interprets letters from the highway department concerning drivers license revocation in order to advise citizens on the appropriate course of action

Provides information concerning the state traffic code in order to help the public understand the rules and regulations governing traffic regulations in the state

From *Training in Organizations: Needs Assessment, Development, and Evaluation* (2nd ed.) by I. L. Goldstein, 1986, Monterey, CA: Brooks/Cole. Copyright 1986 by Brooks/Cole. Reprinted by permission.

records and logs or providing information to law enforcement personnel.

- Once a set of task cluster definitions has been developed, a group of subject matter experts (SMEs) should independently sort each of the tasks into one of the clusters.

- Next, a rule that defines whether there is agreement on whether a task is successfully clustered is usually employed. For example, if ten persons are performing the clustering, a rule might be that eight of ten persons need to agree on where the task should be clustered.

- Disagreement about the placement of tasks indicates a need for further work on either the task or the cluster. Usually, disagreement occurs for the following reasons:

  —The task has more than one work component in it, and different judges focus on different parts of the task.

  —The task is ambiguous, so different judges interpret the task differently.

  —The purpose of the task is not clear, so different judges place the task in different clusters.

  —The clusters themselves are so broad or so poorly defined that it is not possible to cluster the tasks.

The clustering process usually leads to very useful re-editing of the tasks and the cluster definitions. This typically results in tasks becoming much clearer. If the tasks are modified by this procedure, it is usually necessary to recluster to ensure that the changes have achieved their purpose. When the changes have been minimal, such as rewording a few tasks, then it is usually possible just to recluster those few tasks. If the changes have been extensive, such as changing many tasks or changing the cluster definitions, it becomes necessary to repeat the entire clustering procedure. This procedure for organizing clusters is often called a *rational clustering exercise.*

There are other procedures for clustering, such as factor analytic techniques. If these procedures are used, it is necessary to collect scaled judgments, such as the importance of the tasks, and then apply factor analytic techniques to those judgments. However, there seems to be some question as to whether factor analytic techniques lead to useful task clusters. Cranny and Doherty (1988) have argued that factors emerging from such analyses are frequently not interpretable as important job dimensions. More seriously, they note that SMEs have often found that the job dimensions they deem important may not emerge as factors. At this point, there are no definitive answers to questions posed by these issues, leading many researchers (e.g., Schmitt, 1987) to suggest that research on them is badly needed. In any case, while there may still be some question about which techniques are appropriate for developing clusters, most researchers agree that developing clusters is a useful procedure, not only for the reasons specified earlier but because the clusters can then be used to provide input (see Table 6) for the development of KSAs.

The organizational analysis and task analysis provide a picture of the task and its environmental setting. However, the task analysis provides a specification of the required job operations regardless of the individual performing the task. Yet a very critical part of the total process—the human being—remains. Two populations must be considered: The first comprises those persons who are already performing the job, while the second comprises those persons who will be trained. Sometimes, these are the same individuals, but they may be new trainees. Since new individuals differ from those already performing the task, this second population must be examined. The key issue is, What are the capabilities necessary to effectively perform the job? After these capabilities are specified, then it is possible to analyze the performance of the target population to determine whether training is necessary.

Knowledge, Skill, and Ability Analysis

There are several different systems for specifying human capabilities. One system, advocated by Goldstein and Prien (e.g., Goldstein, Macey, & Prien, 1981; Prien, 1977; Prien, Goldstein, & Macey 1987) emphasizes the KSAs necessary to effectively perform the tasks developed in the task analysis. Prien defines these categories as follows:

- *Knowledge* (K) is the foundation upon which skills and abilities are built. Knowledge refers to an organized body of knowledge, usually of a factual or procedural nature, which if applied makes adequate job performance possible. It should be noted that possession of knowledge does not ensure that it will be used. Examples of KSA characteristics are presented in Table 8.

- *Skill* (S) refers to the capability to perform job operations with ease and precision. Most often, skills refer to psychomotor activities. The specification of a skill usually implies a performance standard required for effective job operations.

- *Ability* (A) usually refers to cognitive capabilities necessary to perform a job function. Most often, abilities require the application of some knowledge base.

Prien recommends the use of interview procedures with panels of job supervisors, personnel specialists, or experienced successful incumbents to develop the KSA information. Often the best procedure is to use panels of five to eight knowledgeable persons. It should be noted that the description of KSAs involves

TABLE 8

Examples of Knowledge, Skills, and Abilities for the Job of Police Radio Operator

Knowledge of radio codes and call signs of law enforcement agencies in the area

Knowledge of department rules regarding radio communication

Ability to organize incoming information for verbal transmission on the radio or telephone

Ability to speak over the radio and telephone in a way that is understood by others

Ability to recognize relevant voices and numbers in radio communications that are the radio operators' responsibility

Ability to remain attentive to radio traffic throughout the shift

Ability to keep track of geographical location of law enforcement personnel

From *Training in Organizations: Needs Assessment, Development, and Evaluation* (2nd ed.) by I. L. Goldstein, 1986, Monterey, CA: Brooks/Cole. Copyright 1986 by Brooks/Cole. Reprinted by permission.

inferences about what KSAs are needed to perform particular tasks. Often persons who directly supervise the job being analyzed serve as effective SMEs to provide this information because they often think about what a job incumbent needs to know or what skills and abilities the incumbent needs in order to perform the tasks. In contrast, when collecting task information the job incumbents themselves often know exactly what tasks they perform on the job.

Thus, one procedure used to collect KSA information is to present one of the task clusters, such as that shown in Table 7, and ask members of the SME panel to give the following kinds of information:

- Describe the characteristics of good and poor employees on [*tasks in cluster*].

- Think of someone you know who is better than anyone else at [*tasks in cluster*]. What is the reason they do it so well?

- What does a person need to know in order to [*tasks in cluster*]?

- Recall concrete examples of effective or ineffective performance. Why did they occur?

- If you are going to hire a person to perform [*tasks in cluster*], what kind of KSAs would you want to have? What do you expect a person to learn in training that would make him or her effective at [*tasks in cluster*]?

On the basis of this input, the job analyst would obtain the information necessary to write KSA statements. The KSAs shown in Table 8 are a sample of some KSAs that might come from a panel working with the task cluster shown in Table 7 for the job of police radio operator. Some of the guidelines for developing such statements include:

- Maintain a reasonable balance between generality and specificity. Exactly how general or specific the KSAs should be will depend on this information's intended use. When the information is being used to design a training program, it must be specific enough to suggest what must be learned in training.

- Avoid simply restating a task or duty statement. Such an approach provides little or no new information about the job. It is necessary to ask what KSAs are necessary to perform the task. For example, a task might be to "Analyze hiring patterns to determine whether company practices are consistent with fair employment practices guidelines." Clearly, one of the knowledge components for this task will involve "Knowledge concerning federal, state, and local guidelines on fair employment practices." Another component might involve "Ability to use statistical procedures appropriate to perform these analyses." Both the knowledge and ability components would have implications for the design of any training program to teach individuals to perform the required task.

- Avoid the error of including trivial information when writing KSAs. For example, for a supervisor's job, "Knowledge of how to order personal office supplies" might be trivial. Usually, it is possible to avoid most trivial items by emphasizing the development of KSAs only for those tasks that have been identified in the task analysis as important for job performance. However, because the omission of key KSAs is a serious error, borderline examples should be included. At later stages inthe process, these KSAs will be eliminated if SMES judge them as unimportant.

It should be noted that asking for KSAs in this exercise is helpful in getting all of the pieces of information. It is clear that having knowledge—for example, knowledge about how to hit a golf ball—is very important in performing tasks. Yet we are all familiar with persons (such as this author's colleague, Ben Schneider) who certainly have the required knowledge but, to continue our golfing example, show very limited ability to hit the ball. Thus, it pays to attempt to delineate the various KSAs, although at times it may

become difficult to decide what might be a K, an S, or an A.

Determination of Relevant Dimensions. Once the tasks and KSAs are specified, it is necessary to collect judgments concerning their relevance for the design of training programs. In part, this means having an understanding of which KSAs are important for which tasks. However, as shown in Table 6, it is first important to obtain further information about the relevance of both the tasks and KSAs. For example, it is typically necessary to know which tasks are important and which are frequently performed. Similarly, it is necessary to determine which KSAs are important and which are difficult to learn. It would not make much sense to design a training program around KSAs that are unimportant, unnecessary for the job, or simple to learn. Similarly, it would not make much sense to design a simulation for the learning of the KSAs around tasks that don't relate easily to those KSAs or around tasks so difficult to perform that it is impossible for a trainee to learn the KSAs.

Determining the importance and difficulty usually starts with judgments concerning the relevance of the tasks and KSAs. Typically, these judgments are collected in a survey form from groups of SMEs, such as experienced job incumbents and supervisors. This survey format permits the collection of greater amounts of information than can occur in the job observations, interviews, and panels that led to the original collection of tasks and KSAs. Thus, it permits the analyst to involve more of the organization. It also makes it possible to collect data across large enough samples to ensure confidence in indicators such as the importance of the task. Also, by checking items such as different geographical locations or different units in the organization, it is possible to determine whether the job is viewed the same way across the organization.

The specific questions of the survey depend very much on the purpose of the analysis. If the purpose is training design, the analyst probably wants information on the difficulty of learning the KSA. If the purpose is selection, the analyst probably wants to know the likelihood of the employee needing those KSAs at entry. Similarly, if the purpose of the analysis is to determine which tasks should be learned on the job and which should be learned in training, then answers to questions about how difficult it is to learn the KSAs associated with the task and where they should be learned need to be included. Some examples of the dimensions for which scales can be designed for the assessment of tasks include:

- Is the task performed?

- How frequently is the task performed compared to other tasks?

- How important is the task for effective performance on the job?

Here are some of the dimensions that might be used for KSAs:

- How important is the KSA for performing the job?

- How difficult is it to learn the KSA?

- Where do you expect the KSA to be acquired—before selection, in training, or on the job?

- Do you need the KSA the first day on the job?

An example of an importance scale for tasks is presented in Table 9. An example of a recall level required on day one for knowledge is presented in Table 10. This scale would be used when the level of knowledge required on day one is especially important. If certain knowledge is critical and required on day one and individuals are not required to have it when selected, then this becomes a serious training issue. In such an instance, it is important in the design of training to know whether general familiarity or full recall is required.

Response scales similar to those in Table 9 and 10 can be built for each of the questions about the tasks and KSAs. The data collected are analyzed to determine such information as average responses, variability, and degree of agreement between different judges. It is also possible to include some form of carelessness index that can identify respondents who are not really responding to each item but instead are giving each item the same value or giving patterned responses such as 1, 2, 3, 4, 5, 5, 4, 3, 2, 1.

Sometimes, in the analyses of these data, researchers discover that different groups of judges, such as supervisors and employees, don't agree on what tasks are required to perform the job. In such instances it is important to resolve the disagreement before designing training programs. Obviously, the type of information collected in these analyses is useful for decisions that extend beyond the training program, for example, by developing questions related to what KSAs individuals need for selection into a job.

Linking of KSAs to Tasks. Once it is determined which KSAs and tasks are needed for the job and which are important, it is then necessary to determine, as shown in Table 6, which KSAs are important for which tasks. An example of a set of instructions for obtaining these data is presented in Table 11.

This step links KSAs to tasks so that training design can teach those KSAs using either the actual tasks on which they are needed or simulations of them. For example, the entry "Ability to keep track of geographical location of law enforcement personnel" found in Table 8 might be linked to several tasks in

TABLE 9

Example of Importance Scale for Tasks

Importance	How important is this task to effective performance in your position?
1 =	Not important (Improper task performance results in *no* error or consequences for people, things, or places.)
2 =	Slightly important (Improper task performance may result in *slightly serious* consequences for people or *slightly serious* damages to things and places.)
3 =	Important (Improper task performance may result in *moderate* consequences for people or *moderate* damages to things and places.)
4 =	Very important (Improper task performance may result in *serious* consequences for people or *extensive* damages to things and places.)
5 =	Crucial (Improper task performance may result in *very serious* consequences for people or *very extensive* damages to things and places.)

Indicate how important this task is to effective job performance in your assignment. Write the appropriate number from the Importance scale in the second space opposite each task.

This table reflects results of a research project involving many authors and researchers. See the acknowledgment section at the end of this chapter for listings.

TABLE 10

Example of Recall Level Scale for Knowledge

Recall Level Required Day 1	What level of recall do you need at the time of appointment to apply this knowledge on the job?
1 = General familiarity	A person must be aware of general principles and be able to efficiently locate pertinent details in source documents and/or seek guidance from others.
2 = Working knowledge	A person must be able to apply general principles and specific details from memory in typically encountered occurrences, but refer to source documents or seek guidance from others for applying specifics in unusual occurrences.
3 = Full recall	A person must be able to apply both general principles and specific details in a wide variety of occurrences from memory without referring to source documents or seeking guidance from others.

This table reflects results of a research project involving many authors and researchers. See the acknowledgment section at the end of this chapter for listings.

TABLE 11

KSA–Task Rating Scale

You will be rating the relationship of every task to every KSA using the scale below.

How important is this KSA in the performance of this task?

NA = This task or KSA is *not* part of the job as it is performed.

1 = Not at all important
2 = Of minor importance
3 = Important
4 = Of major importance
5 = Critically important

Please rate each Task–KSA pair separately. Note that the question asks how important a particular KSA is to the performance of a specific task. That is, *regardless of the KSA's overall importance to the job, you are rating the KSA's importance only to the performance of a specific task.*

This table reflects results of a research project involving many authors and researchers. See the acknowledgment section at the end of this chapter for listings.

Table 7. Let us assume that this ability is linked to tasks such as "Receive information by radio on the status of law enforcement personnel who are on stops in order to ensure the safety of the officer." If so, the trainee would be trained on how to keep track of the geographical location of officers while they are on stops. This makes it much more likely that training is job relevant.

Some other examples of links that have been established in a variety of jobs are presented in Table 12. In the first example, the job of state trooper radio operator, the link refers to the knowledge of map formats and is tied to a variety of tasks, including "Searches maps for geographical information in order to respond to requests from the general public." From this type of link, the actual specifications of training become quite clear. Here, the trainer would be designing activities that provide enough physical fidelity in searching maps to call forth the psychological fidelity necessary to gain the knowledge of map formats and symbols.

In the second example in Table 12, the job of customer service representative, it is necessary for the trainee to learn to explain technical information, and the job involves tasks like providing basic self-checks. It is obvious that a customer service representative who does not know what the self-checks are or what services are available will have difficulty explaining technical information to a customer. With these links, it is even possible to imagine what types of criteria need to be developed to assess the ability to explain technical information in a way the customer might understand. Also, since the only tasks and KSAs involved in this step are those that in the survey have been found to meet certain criteria, such as being important, the training not only ties KSAs to tasks but also ties only important KSAs to important tasks. Using the survey results, training might focus on the KSA–task links to other paraeters, such as what trainees need to know immediately as well as what is most important. In any case, the careful design of this needs assessment can trans late directly into training input.

TABLE 12

Examples of KSA–Task Linkages

Job of State Trooper Radio Operator		*Job of Customer Service Representative*	
KSA	Knowledge of map formats and symbols used in reading maps	KSA	Ability to explain technical information to the customer in a way that he or she understands
Task links	Searches maps for geographical information in order to respond to requests from the general public	Task links	Provides instructions to the customer concerning basic self-checks that can be used to resolve the customer's difficulty
	Receives information from troopers by phone, such as requests for assistance to relay to the closest available trooper		Provides information to the customer about services that are available to resolve the customer's difficulty
	Receives information from the public by telephone, concerning such items as speeders or accidents to relay to the trooper responsible for that geographical area		

This table reflects results of a research project involving many authors and researchers. See the acknowledgment section at the end of this chapter for listings.

Person Analysis

As stated by McGehee and Thayer (1961), the final step in determining training needs focuses on whether the individual employees need training and on exactly what training is required. At this stage, the needs assessment has already accomplished an organizational analysis that permits understanding of where the training system fits in the work environment and what facilitators and inhibitors exist. Also, the task analysis has determined what important tasks are performed, and the KSA analysis has provided considerable information for the person analysis, including data such as those indicating whether the KSA should be learned before entering the job, on the job, or during training.

Person analysis asks two questions: Who within the organization needs training, and what kind of instruction do they need? This analysis can be directed at a specific training effort, such as training for advancement in the organization. It might even be possible to ask, from a career development point of view, what KSAs need to be learned at various times to reach the next level of the organization; this information can then be used to design the appropriate systems. While there may be such systems in place, it is not very obvious from the literature. An exception is a study by Klimoski (1982), which examined self-assessments as well as assessments by subordinates and peers of managers in city government for a personalized training development program.

Most of the assessment questions for person analysis require consideration of all the issues facing organizations in the use of performance appraisal systems because it is necessary to appraise employees to determine their training needs. Some observers might think there would be less resistance to this type of performance appraisal because it is intended to be used as a basis for providing learning experiences helpful to the employee, but that is likely to depend on how the whole process is viewed and managed by the organization. There is no research to date on this issue. Another way of approaching the problem is to have the employee perform an assessment of his or her own abilities for training purposes. Unfortunately, a review of 55 studies (Mabe & West, 1982) in which self-evaluation of ability was compared with measures of performance found a low mean validity coefficient of 0.29 with very high variability of $SD = 0.25$. Interestingly enough, Mabe and West did find some conditions that maximize the validity, such as when employees expected the self-evaluations to be compared with other evaluations, when employees had previous experience performing self-evaluations, and when there were guarantees of anonymity.

A recent study (Noe & Schmitt, 1986), which involves educators participating in an assessment center for high school principals, adds some important information to the consideration of assessment of training skills. In this study, one variable of interest was employees' acceptance of assessment of their skill. Noe and Schmitt found that trainees who reacted positively when the needs assessment procedure indicated their skill needs were being met were more likely to be satisfied with the training program content. Such consideration is important because it asks not only whether we can assess trainee skills in order to determine appropriate training placement, but also whether it is possible to determine which variables affect the trainees' willingness to participate in and learn from training. In this regard, Noe and Schmitt found that trainees who had the strongest commitment to job involvement were also more likely to acquire the key behaviors in the training program. In addition, those employees committed to career planning were more likely to apply training content to

their work behavior, resulting in actual on-the-job improvement.

A clear warning of the difficulties researchers are likely to encounter in the use of self-assessments is provided by the work of McEnery and McEnery (1987). McEnery and McEnery found that self and supervisory needs assessments performed by hospital employees were not related. They also discovered that supervisors tended to project their own needs when asked to identify the needs of their subordinates. Clearly, more work in these areas is needed.

Another area of growing concern is the question of future objectives. As technology continues to change the workplace, training programs are actually being considered for jobs that may not exist. Thus, Hall (1986) described the importance of establishing a relationship between the future strategic objectives of the organization and the future requirements for its executives. To accomplish this, techniques will need to be developed that permit SMEs to explicitly describe future requirements for their organization. A person analysis of future job requirements is needed. Although this work is still in developmental stages, Schneider and Konz (1989) have described such a possible strategy. Their procedure uses strategies similar to those described earlier to obtain tasks and linked KSAs. Then they use SME expert panels, such as trainers or upper-level management, to develop information about how the job will change and how that will affect the KSAs required.

In summary, the results of task, person, and performance analysis can provide critical information about such items as present level of performance, criticality of tasks and KSAs, frequency of occurrence, opportunity to learn, and difficulty in learning on the job. These responses can be organized into composite indices that reflect the different judgments. For example, the content to be included in the training curriculum can be identified with reference to a composite index identifying the

KSAs important for full job performance and for which there is minimal opportunity to learn them on the job. The indices thus provide information about the content and priorities of the training curriculum.

In addition to providing input for the design of new instructional programs, the thoughtful application of job analysis procedures can provide input relevant to a variety of training development and evaluation questions. Some examples of other potential applications include the following:

- *Examination of previously designed training programs.* It is possible to compare the emphasis of training programs presently being used with the needs assessment information. This type of comparison could determine whether the emphasis in training is being placed on tasks and KSAs that are important and that are not easily learned on the job.

- *Design of trainee assessment instruments.* Needs assessment information provides valuable information about the capabilities of trainees to perform a job appropriately. As such, the needs assessment procedures can help in the design of performance appraisal instruments that assess the capabilities of trainees at the end of training and on the job. It is also possible to design performance appraisal instruments to determine which employees presently occupying jobs might need further training.

- *Input to the interaction between selection systems and training systems.* Determination of the task and person elements domains can provide input into the selection system by specifying the KSAs required to perform the various job tasks. The degree to which the selection system is able to identify and hire persons with various KSAs affects the design of the training system. For example, training

programs should not emphasize those KSAs already in the repertoire of the trainee. Often this consideration results in a training program that is not only more interesting but also less time-consuming.

It is important to re-emphasize that the choice of particular methodology should be based on an analysis of the particular application requiring job information. Even the choice of questions within a particular method depends on the application. The critical point is that thoughtful planning that considers the variety of methods and applications must precede any needs assessment effort. It is a terrible waste of valuable resources to conduct a needs assessment effort only to discover the wrong questions have been asked. It is amazing to me how much time and effort are put into sophisticated statistical analyses of job analysis results that are ultimately meaningless because the questions and scales being used were not designed properly.

A final point is the importance of maintaining a systems perspective during the needs assessment process. The design of instructional programs is affected by legal, social, economic, and political factors. Interrelationships among these variables should be carefully considered during needs assessment. Discrimination suits based on failure to provide training and promotional opportunities have important implications for factors such as the evaluation of programs, the selection of participants, and even the type of records that must be maintained. It should be noted that the requirements stemming from fair employment legislation are only one illustration of the large number of factors that must be considered. In other cases, it might be new federal or state safety or environmental requirements that affect the objectives of training programs. Again, the solution to some of these problems does not involve design of training programs; instead, it might require organizational responses such as the resolution of conflicts or job redesign.

Thus, one other aspect of the organizational analysis is to determine what problems actually exist and what interventions are necessary. It is not unusual for an organization to believe it has a "simple training problem" when the difficulties are actually related to other organizational issues, such as a poor selection system, management conflict, or poor job design.

In any case, by the end of the needs assessment process the objectives of training should be apparent. The next step should be the choice of a learning environment that matches the media and technique with the kind of learning necessary to achieve those objectives. This process is discussed next.

The Training Environment

The training environment discussed in this section refers to the dynamics of the instructional setting, with particular emphasis on those components that support learning in the training setting.

The establishment of instructional procedures is based on the belief that it is possible to design an environment in which learning can take place that can later be transferred to another setting. It might seem that to apply traditional learning principles to modern training or institutional settings would be effective so that the rest of this section would simply list the strategies that should be used. Unfortunately, that is not the case. The gulf between learning theory and its application to instructional methodology has led many researchers to believe that a link must be developed between the theorist in the laboratory and the practitioner in the applied setting. A statement concerning this goal and its associated problems was made by Bruner (1963):

> A theory of instruction must concern itself with the relationship between how things are presented and how they are learned. Though I myself have worked hard and long in the vineyard of learning theory, I can do no better than to start by warning the reader away from it. Learning theory is not a theory of instruction. It describes what happened. A theory of instruction is a guide to what to do in order to achieve certain objectives. Unfortunately, we shall have to start pretty nearly at the beginning for there is very little to guide us in this subtle enterprise. (p. 524)

Twenty years later, a cognitive revolution appears ready to occur. A number of researchers (Christensen, 1987) have noted that advances in robotics and artificial intelligence are forcing a redefinition of the work load; machines are beginning to assume many of the roles we considered unique human intellectual functions requiring cognition and thought. As discussed by Howell and Cooke (1989), increasing the scope of machine responsibility paradoxically increases the demands on the human being. It gives the individual responsibility for an increasingly smart machine, thereby also increasing the cognitive demands on the human being. Instead of simple procedural and predictable tasks, the human becomes responsible for inferences, diagnosis, judgment, and decision making, often under severe time pressure. This has forced a marriage between recent developments in cognitive psychology and their application to humans at work in complex settings. As Howell and Cooke (1989) note, traditional learning principles and prescriptions have little to say about "how to make people better diagnosticians, how to increase their available attentional capacity, or how to help them create appropriate mental models for the complex processes under their control" (p. 125).

Essentially, Howell and Cooke are saying that the kinds of task and KSA analyses described in the needs assessment section of this chapter are a nice beginning but are not enough. These researchers feel that needs assessment information gathering requires a further step: determination of the types of cognitive processing and learning that are required to perform the tasks in question. Thus, Glaser (1984) asks what kinds of knowledge are necessary to learn to read an instructional manual or to learn a new language (including a computer language), and Gagné and his colleagues (e.g., Gagné & Briggs, 1979) classified learning in categories such as cognitive strategies, information attainment, and motor skills. Theories are being developed to indicate how the learner organizes and integrates information as well as how information is stored. In addition, research is attempting to discover what learning and training strategies can be used to enhance performance, such as information concerning how learners can store more information as well as exploring the differences between naive learners and experts whom may very well provide information about the differences between trainee and job-experienced persons.

It would be wonderful if at this point we could toss out old information from the history of learning theory and adopt new cognitive models. Unfortunately, as noted in a very important chapter by Howell and Cooke (1989), that cannot happen yet. However, it is possible to begin to note some of the principles developing from cognitive psychology. This section on instruction thus attempts to blend some of the new and the old.

To do so, I shall begin this section with a discussion of trainee readiness, continue with material on learning conditions, and follow with an analysis of transfer issues. I shall also present material on positive qualities of training environments and trainers. I hope to clarify the following goal stated by me in another article (Goldstein, 1980):

> It should be possible on the basis of need assessment techniques to determine what tasks are performed, what behaviors are essential to the performance of these tasks, and what type of instructional content is best suited to accomplish that type of learning. (p. 262)

The goal, while still elusive, has become the focus of instructional theory efforts. Thus, a final section of this chapter discusses such an approach as developed by Gagné and Briggs (1979) and complemented by Howell and Cooke's (1989) material on cognitive instructional variables.

Preconditions of Training

Before trainees can benefit from any form of training, they must be ready to learn; that is, (a) they must have the particular background experience necessary for the training program and (b) they must be motivated. There is a tendency to believe that some individuals perform poorly in training because they were either ill-prepared to enter the program or unwilling to learn. If these reasons are valid and the cause is not an ill-conceived program, the implementer must be certain that the preconditions for learning are satisfied.

Previously, when discussing needs assessment, the point stressed was that assessment provided the information necessary for designing the instructional program. A related point is that this same information provides the training analyst with information on the characteristics of the trainees. If the trainees are measured on what they know before entering training, this will indicate which trainees may already know the material, which may require remedial work, and which are ready for training. Too often, training analysts think the only purpose of a pretest before training is to compare the results to a posttest after training in order to evaluate the instructional program. Pretests also provide information about trainee readiness.

In addition to having the requisite KSAs, the trainee must also be motivated to learn.

Most researchers agree that motivational level affects performance through an energizing function. As will be indicated in the next section on conditions of training, it is important to use as many motivational variables in the instructional setting as possible in order to enhance learning. However, it is also clear that individuals who are motivated upon entry to the training program have an advantage from the very beginning. Some interesting data concerning motivation of trainees upon entry were collected in a study of the Navy School for Divers (Ryman & Biersner, 1975). The investigators had trainees fill out a training confidence scale before training. Some of the motivational items on the scale were:

> If I have trouble during training,
> I will try harder.
>
> I will get more from this training than most people.
>
> I volunteered for this training as soon as I could.
>
> Even if I fail, this training will be a valuable experience.

The trainees rated these items on a five-point scale from "Disagree Strongly" to "Agree Strongly." The investigators discovered that scores on these items predicted eventual graduation from the program: The more the pretrainees agreed with items like these, the more likely they were to graduate.

Sanders and Vanouzas (1983) further developed these ideas in terms of the trainers' ability to socialize trainees to the learning environment. They note that trainees come to the learning environment with certain attitudes and expectations that may or may not be helpful in the learning process. Table 13 lists a number of items about the role of a student in the class. Trainees with expectations that are positive and supportive of activities like this are more likely to be ready for training. If attitudes are generally negative, then it is necessary to determine why and correct problems before training begins. Without such intervention, learning is unlikely to occur.

Motivation as a Condition of Training

Industrial psychologists examining the effects of motivational states on performance have directed their attention to two sets of theories. *Process theories* seek an explanation of how behavior is energized, directed, sustained, and stopped, and *content theories* consider what specific things motivate people. (For a review of these theories and the empirical research, see Steers & Porter, 1983.) Most of this research is related to performance on the job rather than to learning in the training environment. However, the role of motivational performance on the job can provide important insights into performance in a training environment. Also, if the motivational level in the transfer setting is extremely poor, learning in the instructional setting becomes an academic exercise.

Goldstein (1986) presented an analysis of the various motivation theories and how they apply to the design of training environments. A summary of those principles as they relate to training follows.

Goal Setting and Motivation.   Locke, Latham, and their colleagues (e.g., Latham & Locke, 1979; Locke, Shaw, Saari, & Latham, 1981) conducted and reviewed an extensive set of studies describing the behavioral effects of setting goals. In their 1981 review, they found that in 90 percent of the laboratory and field studies, specific and challenging goals led to higher performance than easy goals, do-your-best goals, or no goals. These authors postulate that goals affect task performance by "directing energy and attention, mobilizing energy expenditure

TABLE 13

Indicators of Trainee Readiness

	SD	D	N	A	SA
As a student in this class, my role is to:					

1. Accept personal responsibility for becoming involved in learning experiences
2. Be willing to participate actively in classroom analysis of learning activities
3. Be willing to engage in self-assessment
4. Be willing to learn from classmates
5. Believe that information learned will be useful in the future
6. Complete assignments and readings prior to class

SD Strongly disagree
D   Disagree
N   Neutral
A   Agree
SA Strongly agree

From "Socialization to Learning" by P. Sanders and J. N. Yanouzas, 1983, *Training and Development Journal, 37*, pp. 14–21. Copyright 1983 by the American Society for Training and Development, Inc. Adapted by permission.

or effort over time (persistence), and motivating the individual to develop relevant strategies for goal attainment" (Locke et al., 1981, p. 145). These authors also specified a number of the conditions that affect performance. They include the following points:

- Individuals who are given specific, hard, or challenging goals perform better than those given specific, easy goals, do-your-best goals, or no goals at all.

- Goals appear to have more predictable effects when given in specific terms rather than as a vague set of intentions.

- Goals must be matched to individuals' ability levels in such a way that each person is likely to be able to achieve the goal.

- Feedback concerning the degree to which the goal is being achieved is necessary for goal setting to have an effect.

- The individual has to accept the goal that is assigned or set. Often, such acceptance is related to the degree of support or commitment of the organization to the goal-setting program.

These points, based on extensive research studies, suggest a number of ways that training programs can be more effective. The setting of specific, challenging goals, matched to individual ability and followed by feedback on degree of goal achievement, provides a solid foundation for the design of an instructional program. Recent research by R. Kanfer and Ackerman (1989) provides important indications about the need for examining this interaction between motivational and ability constructs. Their work indicates that interventions such as early goal setting may impede the learning of simulated air traffic control tasks, especially when it occurs before trainees understand what the task is all about. On the other hand, the same type of intervention, coming at a later stage when the trainee understands the tasks, is very helpful. In addition, their work suggests an intriguing notion that low-ability trainees were helped even more than high-ability trainees when the intervention was presented after the trainees had learned what the tasks were about. These researchers have systematically developed a model of the interactions between motivation and cognitive learning strategies which should prove fruitful for the testing of a number of these interactions.

Instrumentality Theory and Motivation. Vroom (1964) developed a process theory of motivation related to the question of how behavior is energized and sustained. The theory is based on cognitive expectancies concerning outcomes that are likely to occur as a result of the participant's behavior and individual preferences among those outcomes. The expectancy can vary, as can the valence, or strength, of an individual's preference for an outcome. Vroom states that outcomes have a particular valence value because they are *instrumental* in achieving other outcomes. For instance, money and promotion have potential valence value because they are instrumental in allowing an individual to achieve other outcomes, like an expensive home or a college education for his or her children. The motivational level is based on a combination of the individual's belief that he or she can achieve outcomes from acts and the value he or she has placed on those outcomes.

Training programs have a valence value for individuals if they permit individual achievement of other outcomes. Thus, training becomes a low-level outcome in that it permits the achievement of other more valuable higher-level outcomes, such as a job, a promotion, or a raise, which in turn might lead to further outcomes. The instrumentality theory implies that it is necessary to show individuals the value of the instructional program in order to properly motivate them. Programs that

appear unrelated to future outcomes will probably not meet the desired objectives.

Need Theory and Motivation.   A number of content theories emphasize learned needs that are to be satisfied and do not attempt to specify the exact processes by which these needs motivate behavior. These theories suggest to the training researcher that his or her programs must meet particular needs in order to motivate learners.

One need theory that has been given considerable attention involves the need for achievement motivation (nAch), which is defined by Atkinson and Feather (1966) as a behavioral tendency to strive for success. It is assumed to operate when the environment signals to the individual that certain acts will lead to need achievement. An illustration of this approach can be found in the studies of McClelland and Winter (1969), which were designed to instill achievement motivation through training programs. In a number of studies (Miron & McClelland, 1979), limited evidence was found that indicated participants in their training program were successful in later economic ventures. A series of studies (Raynor, 1970; Raynor & Rubin, 1971) combining the approaches of the need and instrumentality theories indicated that persons capable of high achievement do not necessarily perform well unless their behavior is viewed as being instrumental for later success. Thus, students with high achievement motivation received superior grades when they were regarded as important for career success.

Need theory emphasizes the importance of learning as much as possible about the various needs and viewpoints of trainees. An illustration of such an approach is a study that examines the work goals of engineers and scientists (Ritti, 1968). Ritti found that the goals of the scientists were largely related to academic achievement (like publication of data and professional autonomy), while the goals of the engineers were related to advancement and decision making. The organization's attempts to increase the professional aspects of the engineering positions were viewed as inconsistent with the goals of the engineer and as motivationally ineffective.

Suggestions include stressing the future utility or value of the activity, providing feedback that shows the degree of accomplishment attained, relating that material to meaningful activity outside the instructional setting, finding tasks that are interesting because they are challenging, and enlarging the job to make it more interesting and to provide greater degrees of responsibility (which usually means enlarging the training program, too).

Self-efficacy as a Motivational Construct.
In recent years, an intriguing idea has emerged: Trainees will achieve to a greater extent if they believe they can learn the materials. Or, as stated in psychological terms, they will achieve to the degree to which they have high self-efficacy. The theoretical development of this hypothesis stems from Bandura (1979) and F. H. Kanfer and Gaelick (1986). As interpreted by J. P. Campbell (1988), the process as related to a training program is as follows: First, trainees end up in a program because someone assessed their capabilities and decided they should attend that program. If the trainees think this assessment is valid, there will be greater achievement that relates at least partially to their assessment of themselves (or their self-efficacy). Dunnette (1989) offers the notion that if the assessment is valid, we might expect trainees to have high self-efficacy because they have had a history of past successes. In that case, selection to attend training is a confirmation of previous success, not necessarily the primary event leading to increased self-efficacy. In either case, a critical aspect is that the trainees must view the training program as responsive to their own efforts; as Campbell puts it, the training program

must be viewed as instrumental for achieving success. Finally, the conditions of training must be seen as instrumental to job performance, and increased job performance must be viewed as instrumental for the trainees. Campbell further stresses that if there is no self-efficacy for the activity, then there is a rejection of the choice to perform. While this work is at a very early stage of development, it appears clear to me that research on self-cognitions such as self-efficacy will be very important in the next decade. An example of this type of formulation and its implication for training is the work on self-regulation by Latham and Frayne (Frayne & Latham, 1987; Latham & Frayne, 1989), which is described in this chapter in a later section on training techniques.

Conditions of Learning and Transfer

There is a long history of basic learning variables documented in many training texts, beginning with McGehee and Thayer (1961), continuing with Bass and Vaughan (1966), Goldstein (1974), Wexley and Latham (1981), and concluding most recently with Goldstein (1986) detailing basic learning and transfer variables. These texts all include discussions of such issues as spaced versus massed practice, whole versus part learning, the importance of overlearning, identical elements and transfer theory, and positive versus negative reinforcement. Almost all of the data underlying these constructs stem from basic learning situations, with limited data from training situations. Most recently, Baldwin and Ford (1988) in a monumental effort detailed all of the learning variables actually studied in a training context. Their review provides a badly needed update on training design, trainee characteristics, and environmental conditions. Unfortunately they also found that the literature was limited and fragmented and that "the samples, tasks, designs, and criteria used limit even further our ability to understand the transfer process" (p. 86). Even given their conclusion, it may be encouraging that they were able to find so many studies that actually examined these types of variables in training settings. It is likely that developments will result from work in cognitive and instructional psychology, discussed in a later section of this chapter. However, in the meantime, the person concerned with the basic design of learning environments should be forewarned to consult the references cited here for a discussion of basic learning variables and their relationship to training system design.

Climate for Transfer.   It is also crucial to remember that transfer of training from an instructional setting (such as an organization's training program) to a work environment involves all the issues related to the necessity of having a positive transfer climate in the work organization. These concerns were previously discussed in this chapter as part of the organizational analysis section in needs assessment. Table 5 presents some of the positive transfer climate indicators that Rouillier and Goldstein have found make a difference in whether learning that occurred in training will transfer to the work organization. It is important to realize that situations that should result in positive transfer have at best resulted in zero transfer because of a failure to consider issues related to the work organization. Based on the research of Rouillier and Goldstein and other investigators (e.g., Baumgartel & Jeanpierre, 1972; Leifer & Newstrom, 1980; Michalak, 1981), the following points seem especially salient:

- We must have a system that unites the trainer, trainee, and manager in the transfer process.

- Before training, the expectations for the trainee and manager must be clear.

- We must identify obstacles to transfer and provide strategies to overcome these problems.

- We must work with managers to provide opportunities for the maintenance of trainees' learned behavior in the work organization.

The importance of maintaining behavior and overcoming obstacles is clearly detailed in a model developed by Marx (1982). His model is based on another model originally designed to examine relapse problems in addictive behavior such as smoking and alcoholism. The model, as shown in Figure 3, outlines the importance of having coping responses in the repertoire of managers to prevent relapses in their learned behavior. Thus, as part of his training program, Marx made managers aware of the relapse process. He also had them diagnose situations likely to sabotage their efforts at maintaining the new learning. For example, he notes in the model that if one problem is increased stress resulting from time pressure, then a coping skill such as time management techniques would be taught. As described in the model, these coping responses result in increased self-efficacy and decreased probability of relapse. The model also describes the situations that occur when no coping response is available. In this situation, the results can lead to a giving up of attempts to incorporate new learning. Then, opportunities for positive transfer disappear regardless of what has been learned in training. While many of the ideas in the model remain to be tested, it is clear that researchers are beginning to recognize the important issues concerning a positive climate for transfer.

The Role of Cognitive and Instructional Psychology

Gagné's Instructional Theory.   In the preceding sections there is a discussion of the development of a new approach to the study of learning environments known as *instructional theory.* As defined by Gagné and Dick (1983), "theories of instruction attempt to relate

FIGURE 3

Cognitive-Behavior Model of the Relapse Process

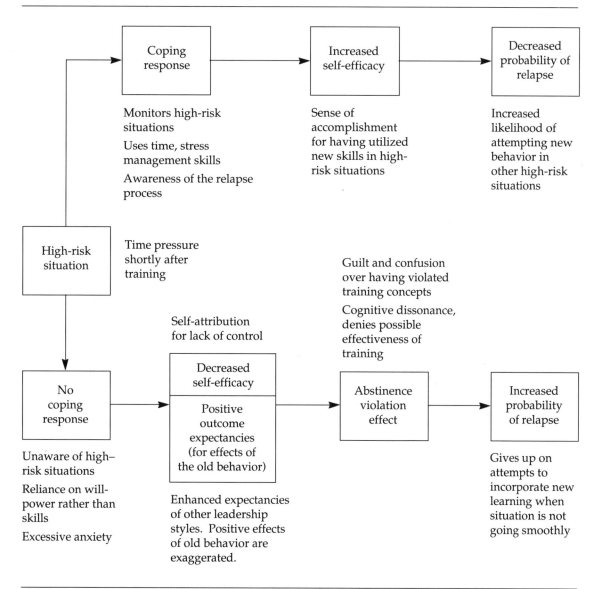

specified events comprising instruction to learning processes and learning outcomes, drawing upon knowledge generated by learning research and theory" (p. 264). They also note that these theories are often prescriptive in that they identify conditions of instruction that will optimize learning, retention, and transfer. Such instructional theories often become the underlying foundation for instructional design procedures that will support the learning activities. One of the better-developed theories in the area has also been formulated by Gagné and his colleagues (Gagné, 1974, 1984; Gagné & Briggs, 1979; Gagné & Dick, 1983). His model describes a set of categories of learning outcomes to organize human performance. Then he relates these learning outcomes to the conditions necessary to support learning performance. Gagné's learning outcomes are as follows:

- *Intellectual skills*. These skills include concepts, rules, and procedures. Sometimes this is referred to as *procedural knowledge*. Some of the best examples of intellectual skills are found in mathematics, such as the rules for computations. Some further examples of types of intellectual skills and the tasks they are associated with can be found in Table 14.

- *Verbal information*. This category, also sometimes referred to as *declarative information*, refers to the ability of an individual to declare or state something. In Table 14, the relevant example given is to state the main kinds of fire extinguishers and their uses.

- *Cognitive strategies*. This refers to the idea that learners bring to a new task not only intellectual skills and verbal information but also a knowledge of how and when to use this information. The cognitive strategies form a type of strategic knowledge that enables learners to know when

and how to choose which intellectual skills and verbal information they will use.

- *Motor skills*. This category refers to one of the more obvious examples of human performance. Examples of motor skills include writing, swimming, and using tools.

- *Attitudes*. Gagné notes that student preferences for particular activities often reflect differences in attitudes. He points out that persons learn to have these preferences and notes that the number of commercial messages we are bombarded with are evidence of the common belief that attitudes are learned.

One of the interesting questions concerning the categories just listed is what constitutes a category and why there are five rather than, say, seven categories. Gagné's (1984) rules for the establishment of categories are as follows:

- Each category should be distinguishable in terms of a formal definition of human performance.

- The category should include a broad variety of activities that do not depend on such characteristics as intelligence, age, or race. Gagné excludes (although recognizing their existence) special categories such as musical virtuosity or wine tasting.

- Each category should differ in terms of the basic learning processes, such as information processing demands.

- The learning principles should be similar for tasks within a learning outcome category, but it should not be possible to generalize the principles across tasks from different categories.

Thus, Gagné and his colleagues developed a set of learning categories that permits them to

TABLE 14

Examples of Tasks Reflected in Target Objectives and the Learning Categories They Represent

Task	Learning Category
Discriminates printed letters *g* and *p*	*Intellectual skill* (discrimination)—perceiving objects as same or different
Identifies *ovate* shape of tree leaves	*Intellectual skill* (concrete concept)—identifying an object property
Classifies *citizens* of a nation, by definition	*Intellectual skill* (defined concept)—using a definition to identify a class
Demonstrates instances of the rule relating pressure and volume of a gas at constant temperature	*Intellectual skill* (rule)—applying a rule to one or more concrete examples
Generates a rule predicting the inflationary effect of decreasing value of currency in international exchange	*Intellectual skill* (higher-order rule)—generating a more complex rule by combining simpler rules
Originates a written composition on the cybernetic features of a bureaucracy	*Cognitive strategy*—inventing a novel approach to a problem
States the main kinds of fire extinguishers and their uses	*Information*—communicating organized knowledge in a way that preserves meaning
Chooses reading novels as a leisure-time activity	*Attitude*—choosing a course of personal action toward a class of events
Executes the tightening of a lag screw with a socket wrench	*Motor skill*—carrying out a smoothly timed motor performance

From *Principles of Instructional Design* by R. M. Gagné and L. J. Briggs, 1979, New York: Holt, Rinehart & Winston. Copyright 1979 by CBS College Publishing Company, Inc. Reprinted by permission.

analyze tasks and code the behaviors into one of the learning outcomes. The most fascinating part of the system is that Gagné and Briggs (1979) have begun to examine the learning outcomes to determine the conditions of learning and instructional events that best support each. This system is presented in Table 15. In that table, the behavioral learning outcomes (e.g., intellectual skill or cognitive strategy) are presented across the top of the table. Down the left side of the table, Gagné and Briggs present a series of events considered important to the instructional system, such as gaining the learner's attention or providing feedback. The body of the table indicates how each instructional event would be manipulated for each learning outcome. For example, when presenting stimulus material, you would present examples of concepts or rules for intellectual skill development, and you would present novel problems for the development of cognitive strategies. As more and more is learned about various ways to support learning performance, it is clear that such systems

TABLE 15

Instructional Events and the Conditions of Learning They Imply for Five Types of Learned Capabilities

Instructional Event	Type of Capability				
	Intellectual Skill	Cognitive Strategy	Information	Attitude	Motor Skill
1. Gaining attention	Introduce stimulus change; variations in sensory mode				
2. Informing learner of objective	Provide description and example of the performance to be expected	Clarify the general nature of the solution expected	Indicate the kind of verbal question to be answered	Provide example of the kind of action choice aimed for	Provide a demonstration of the performance to be expected
3. Stimulating recall of prerequisites	Stimulate recall of subordinate concepts and rules	Stimulate recall of task strategies and associated intellectual skills	Stimulate recall of context of organized information	Stimulate recall of relevant information, skills, and human model identification	Stimulate recall of executive subroutine and part-skills
4. Presenting the stimulus material	Present examples of concept or rule	Present novel problems	Present information in propositional form	Present human model, demonstrating choice of personal action	Provide external stimuli for performance, including tools or implements
5. Providing learning guidance	Provide verbal cues to proper combining sequence	Provide prompts and hints to novel solution	Provide verbal links to a larger meaningful context	Provide for observation of model's choice of action, and of reinforcement received by model	Provide practice with feedback of performance achievement
6. Eliciting the performance	Ask learner to apply rule or concept to new examples	Ask for problem solution	Ask for information in paraphrase, or in learner's own words	Ask learner to indicate choices of action in real or simulated situations	Ask for execution of the performance

TABLE 15

Instructional Events and the Conditions of Learning They Imply for Five Types of Learned Capabilities (continued)

Instructional Event	Type of Capability				
	Intellectual Skill	Cognitive Strategy	Information	Attitude	Motor Skill
7. Providing feedback	Confirm correctness of rule or concept application	Confirm originality of problem solution	Confirm correctness of statement of information	Provide direct or vicarious reinforcement of action choice	Provide feedback on degree of accuracy and timing of performance
8. Assessing performance	Learner demonstrates application of concept or rule	Learner originates a novel solution	Learner restates information in paraphrased form	Learner makes desired choice of personal action in real or simulated situation	Learner executes performance of total skill
9. Enhancing retention and transfer	Provide spaced reviews including a variety of examples	Provide occasions for a variety of novel problem solutions	Provide verbal links to additional complexes of information	Provice additional varied situations for selected choice of action	Learner continues skill practice

From *Principles of Instructional Design* by R. M. Gagné and L. J. Briggs, 1979. New York: Holt, Rinehart & Winston. Copyright 1979 by CBS College Publishing Company, Inc. Reprinted by permission.

will be very important in helping us design effective training environments.

Certainly one of the points that instructional theorists are trying to make is that our traditional learning models do not provide enough information for the design of instructional environments. They are not saying that feedback is unimportant or that massed versus spaced learning does not make any difference; they are saying that it is necessary to understand the type of learning involved and the instructional event being considered before it is possible to choose the most effective learning procedures.

Cognitive Principles of Instruction.   It is clear from Howell and Cooke's (1989) analyses that research developments exploring cognitive principles of instruction are at a delicate stage. At this point, there is not an extensive list of instructional support systems that fit Gagné's taxonomy—or any other. Yet some general ideas are developing, and the interested reader should consult Howell and Cooke (1989) for an exploration of these possibilities. It is important to realize that most of the work of cognitive psychologists in this area is heavily influenced by advances in technology, giving rise to concerns about the human beings who will be depending on computer input to operate very sophisticated machines. In this environment, the emphasis is on making people better diagnosticians, increasing their available attentional capacity, and creating mental models for the complex processes under their control.

A few of the ideas covered by Howell and Cooke that show particular promise and deserve increased research emphasis by individuals interested in training systems are outlined below.

Automatic Processing.   When it is possible to identify consistent stimulus elements and appropriate responses to those elements, overlearning through intensive practice dramatically improves performance. It is necessary for the trainee to practice each element actively and repeatedly in a situation where correct responding is ensured. In these conditions, the learner eventually shifts to automated processing, which dramatically enhances performance and permits the conservation of remaining mental capacity to be used on other activities, such as planning and decision making, which cannot be so easily automated. Perhaps the most dramatic example of the use of automated processing as a training procedure involves the *vigilance decrement*. As most readers probably know, the vigilance decrement refers to the problem of decline in performance over time during a watchkeeping period when the number of signals to be detected are infrequent. Thousands of studies have been devoted to this problem because of its implications for areas of work such as radar signal detection, monitoring of warning signals indicating machine malfunctions (including those in nuclear power plants), and detection involving product quality control on the assembly line. In a dramatic study, Fisk and Schneider (1981) were able to eliminate this decrement by automatizing the activity through a training program that emphasized stimulus-response pairing over 4,000 training trials. When the trainees performed the real task with only 18 targets presented over 6,000 presentations, there was virtually no decrement over time.

The Use of Mental Models as Training Systems. Another emphasis in the cognitive approach is to understand the mental models that individuals use in performing a task. In part, this involves verbal protocols where individuals actually talk through their thought processes while performing a task. Another aspect of this procedure involves the comparison of novices with experts. Thus, a study of computer programmers (Cooke & Schavnelt, 1988) resulted in being able to distinguish experts from novices and revealed the misconceptions in novice knowledge. Possibilities here for use in the design of training systems, based on expert models and the differences between experts and novices, make this an important area for future training research. Of course, this also depends on the development of taxonomic systems permitting the reliable identification and use of these cognitive strategies.

The Use of Organizing Structures to Enhance Working Memory.　Another area of emphasis for cognitive psychologists is the use of strategies to organize and retain information. Many situations involving complex cognitive tasks place a high demand on memory systems. Yet a learner in a short-term memory situation will find it difficult to temporally retain more than seven items of information. The emphasis here has been on exploration of various cognitive schemes to enhance memory systems, such as organizing the material into chunks through mnemonic schemes or analogy systems. Similar principles are being developed and studied (see Howell & Cooke, 1989) for use in storing information for the purposes of long-term memory.

In addition, organizer schemes based on learners' existing knowledge are being used in the design of instructional systems themselves. An *organizer* can be any type of cue—including verbal, quantitative, or graphic—that identifies the learner's present knowledge, to which the new material is related. It is called an *advanced organizer* if the material is presented before training and a *comparative organizer* if it is used later in training to clarify further distinctions. In an important series of studies, Mayer and his colleagues (Mayer, 1975; Mayer & Bromage, 1980) showed that a simplified diagram of the functional structure of a computer greatly enhanced learning of some of the more technical terms and rules in a college course on computer programming. The organizer employed familiar examples, such as shopping lists and ticket windows, in the diagrams. So far, there is limited research on this in actual training systems, but the potential seems apparent.

Metacognition and Learning Systems.　Another area of emphasis in cognitive instructional research is the design of systems to help learners understand what they do and do not know at any given point in time. This self-monitoring capability has been named *metacognition*. The purpose of this research area is to teach learners how to test themselves so that they might try a problem and receive diagnostic feedback that includes what they tried, why it did or did not work, and what could have been done instead. Much of this work is combined with ideas concerning the learner's level of development, with the possibility that different types of information and probes may be more worthwhile than others at different points in the learning process.

In addition to the work mentioned so far, developments in cognitive psychology are also stimulating other work that has direct relevance to training systems. One example is the development of an instructional quality inventory, which is presented next.

Instructional Quality.　A group of researchers (Wulfeck, Ellis, Richards, Merrill, & Wood, 1978) at the Navy Personnel Research and Development Center concentrated on indicators of instructional quality. Using information gained from research in cognitive and instructional theory, they specified conditions concerning the adequacy of the course objectives, the test consistency, and the presentation consistency. Their work was based on the idea that there is a task dimension and a content dimension to training. The *task dimension* refers to tasks a trainee can perform; the trainee can either remember information or use it to do something. The trainee who so uses information can either do it unaided, where there are no aids available except memory, or aided, where some form of support is provided. The *content dimension* is divided into five types of content that can be provided in a training program—facts, concepts, procedures, rules, and principles.

A matrix showing the task and content dimensions (with definitions) is shown in Table 16.

Wulfeck et al. then use the dimensions to analyze the objectives, presentation, and tests used in a training program in order to establish the instructional quality. An example of their system for analyzing training presentations is shown in Table 17.

Across the top of the table are the content dimensions, such as facts and concepts. Along the left side are various types of presentation components, such as statements or examples. The body of the table gives the appropriate presentation procedure. Thus, when presenting statements in a training program for a concept, all critical characteristics and their combinations are given. Similarly, when presenting statements for a procedure, all steps are given in the correct order. Wulfeck and his associates present similar rules for analyzing training objectives and training tests. For example, they ask questions concerning the conditions under which student performance is expected for each of the following:

- *Environment*
  Physical—weather, time of day, lighting
  Social—isolation, individual, team, audience
  Psychological—fatigue, stress, relaxed

- *Information*
  Given information—scenario, formula, values
  Cues—signals for starting or stopping
  Special instructions

- *Resources*
  Job aids—cards, charts, graphs, checklists
  Equipment, tools
  Technical manuals

Similarly, the *Instructional Quality Inventory* offers rules for test items. For example, all tests are judged according to the following criteria:

- Determine whether each item is clear and unambiguous.

- Determine whether each item is well constructed. For this criterion, separate instructions are given for different types of test items. For example, the following are criteria for tests that require trainees to list something:

  —Specify the number of things to be listed (if appropriate and if the number of things is not a hint).
  —Specify whether or not order is important. If so, the scoring key should score sequence separately.
  —Identify in the scoring key allowable synonyms or alternatives and specify different weights, if appropriate.
  —Ensure that each item is free from hints.
  —Ensure that items permit no common errors to be made.
  —Ensure that there are enough items to test objectives adequately and that they reflect the full range of performance expected on the job.

The development of test items reflects the use of criteria to measure training performance. This is a very important topic that must examine a number of issues, such as the relevance and type of criteria.

In addition to developing the inventory and handbooks describing its use, these researchers have also begun to conduct research studies. They have generally found that when instructional materials have been modified according to the principles stated in the inventory, increases in trainee performance result.

Instruction and Interventions

There are many other instructional considerations that designers and trainers must attend to when designing training programs. Probably one of the most important items is the role of the trainer, who often makes the difference between a successful or unsuccessful learning experience. The potency of the trainer's role

TABLE 16

The Task–Content Matrix of the *Instructional Quality Inventory*

	Fact—Recall or recognize names, parts, dates, places, etc.	*Concept*—Remember characteristics, or classify objects, events, or ideas according to characteristics	*Procedure*—Sequence of steps remembered or used in a single situation or on a single piece of equipment	*Rule*—Remember or use a sequence of steps which apply across situations or across equipments	*Principle*—Remember, or interpret or predict why or how things happen, or cause–effect relationships
Remember—Recall or recognize facts, concept definitions, steps of procedures or rules, statements of principle					
Use-Unaided—Tasks which require classifying, performing a procedure, using a rule, explaining, or predicting with no aids except memory					
Use-Aided—Same as Use-Unaided, except job aids are available					

From Wulfeck, W. H. , II, Ellis, J. A., Richards, R. E., Wood, N. D., and Merrill, M. D. *The Instructional Quality Inventory: I. Introduction and Overview* (NPRDC SR 79–3). Navy Personnel Research and Development Center.

TABLE 17

Presentation Consistency

Presentation Component	Content Type of the Objective				
	Fact	*Concept*	*Procedure*	*Rule*	*Principle*
Statement	Complete fact presented	All critical characteristics and their combinations are given	All steps are given in the correct order	All steps and branching decisions are given in the correct order	All causes, effects, and relationships are given
Practice Remembering	Recall or recognition required	Recall of concept definition required	Recall of all steps in correct order required	Recall of all steps and branch decisions in correct order required	Recall of all causes, effects, and relationships required
For all content types:	Practice Remembering items must be the same as the test item. They must be the same format as the test item. All practice items must include feedback.				
Examples	Not applicable	Examples show all critical characteristics required for classification, nonexamples show absence of critical characteristics	Application of the procedure must be shown and steps must be shown in the correct order	Application of each step or branching decision must be shown in the correct order	Interpretation or prediction based on causes, effects, and relationships must be shown
Practice Using	Not applicable	Classification of both examples and nonexamples is required	All steps must be performed in the correct order	All steps and branching decisions must be performed in the correct order	Explanation or prediction based on the principle is required
For all content types:	Practice Using items must reflect what is to be done on the job or in later training. The task/content level, conditions, and standards must match the test item and objective. The practice item format must be the same as the test item format. All practice items must include feedback.				
For concepts, rules, and principles:	Some practice items should be different than either the test items or the examples. (Common error items might be the same.)				

From Wulfeck, W. H. , II, Ellis, J. A., Richards, R. E., Wood, N. D., and Merrill, M. D. *The Instructional Quality Inventory: I. Introduction and Overview* (NPRDC SR 79–3). Navy Personnel Research and Development Center.

has been demonstrated in some important research conducted by Eden and his colleagues (Eden & Ravid, 1982; Eden & Shani, 1982). In these studies, trainers were informed that they had trainees with very high success potential attending their course. Learning performance, as measured by both weekly performance measures and instructor ratings, was significantly higher for these trainers' classes compared to control groups. Interestingly, the control groups in these cases consisted of trainees with the same ability levels as the persons in the high success groups; the only difference was that the trainers were informed that only certain groups had high success potential.

Eden's analyses, which included reports from trainees, indicated that inducing high expectations in trainers similarly enhanced trainee performance. He feels that the high expectations communicated by trainers or immediate superiors lead trainees to expect more of themselves and to perform better. An interesting facet of Eden's data is that although several instructors were replaced in the middle of the training program, the performance differentials continued unabated. Eden believes that by this time the induction of high expectancy effects had occurred so the trainees continued to perform at a high level. The researchers dubbed this the *Pygmalion effect* in honor of George Bernard Shaw's literary work, in which the central theme is the powerful effect our expectations have on us. Certainly this research demonstrates the powerful role instructors can have on our learning performance.

Training Evaluation and Criterion Issues

Evaluation is the systematic collection of descriptive and judgmental information necessary to make effective training decisions related to the selection, adoption, value, and modification of various instructional activities. The objectives of instructional programs reflect numerous goals, ranging from trainee progress to organizational goals. From this perspective, evaluation is an information-gathering technique that cannot possibly result in decisions that categorize programs as good or bad. Rather, evaluation should capture the dynamic flavor of the training program. Then necessary information will be available to revise instructional programs to achieve multiple instructional objectives. The key construct in the development of criteria is criterion relevancy.

Criterion Relevancy

One of the purposes of a needs assessment is to determine the KSAs required for successful job performance. As shown in the instructional model presented in Figure 1, this information must provide direct input into the training program to determine the actual content of the instructional material. The same information concerning the KSAs necessary for successful job performance should also provide input for establishing measures of training success.

Logically, trainers should want their training program to consist of materials that develop the KSAs needed to perform successfully on the job. Just as logically, it should be possible to determine the success of a training program by developing measures (or criteria) that tell the training evaluator how well the training program works in teaching trainees the same KSAs necessary for job success. Trainers would likely use these criteria at the end of the training program to determine how well their program is working; they might also want to use these criteria later when the trainee is on the job to determine how much of the KSAs learned in training transferred to the actual job.

The chosen criteria are judged relevant to the degree that the KSAs required to succeed in the training program are the same as those required to succeed at the ultimate task

FIGURE 4

The Constructs of Criterion Deficiency, Relevance, and Contamination

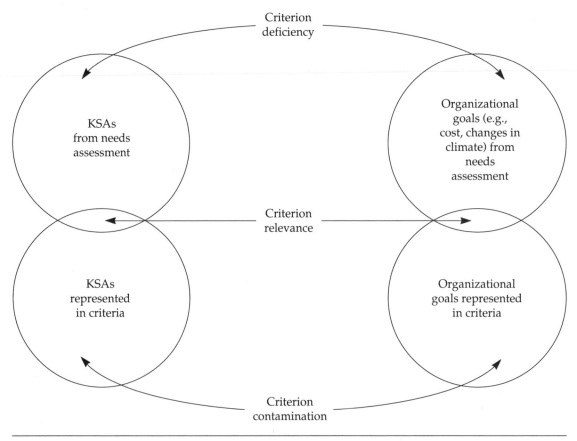

(Thorndike, 1949). Evaluators often choose a criterion because of its immediate availability, so it must be examined for relevance—the fundamental requirement that transcends all other considerations related to criterion development. Accurate job analysis and the ensuing behavioral objectives suggest more clearly the actual criteria to be employed in achieving the behavioral objectives. This relationship between the objectives and the criteria is an exercise in determining relevance.

Figure 4 presents the relationship that can exist between items established by needs assessment and items represented in the criteria chosen to assess the training program. The degree of overlap between these two sets establishes the relevance of the criteria. Another way of expressing this point is that the degree of relevance is an indicator of the content validity of the criterion measure. The term *criteria* refers to the many measures of success that must be used to evaluate instructional programs and their numerous objectives. Those shown on the left side in Figure 4 refer to characteristics of individual achievement for trainees as represented by the KSAs. However, it is just as possible to conceive of organizational goals established from the needs assessment and the degree to which these organizational goals are reflected in the criteria. The degree to which they overlap would determine the relevance of the criterion set. These relationships are represented on the right side of Figure 4.

It is interesting to note that historically (Blum & Naylor, 1968) this relationship used to be presented as the overlap between actual and ultimate criteria. In the Blum and Naylor presentation, the actual criteria duplicated the circle described as the KSAs represented in the criteria. The ultimate criteria duplicated the circle described in Figure 4 as KSAs from needs assessment. The rationale for this approach was that psychologists struggle to measure ultimate criteria that define success but can never be perfectly captured. The degree to which our actual criteria reflect such ultimate criteria is defined as *relevance*.

The present approach (Goldstein, 1986) presents the idea somewhat differently, stating instead that however we define success, it is determined by the needs assessment. The degree to which it is possible to design actual criteria that capture success as defined in the needs assessment determines the extent of relevance or content validity. The present approach also recognizes that some criteria can be considered more "ultimate" than others and suggests that criteria measuring the success of trainees on the job are more "ultimate" than measures of training success. However, it is still possible to question the degree of relevance for both the training measure and the on-the-job measure by relating the KSAs from the needs assessment to the KSAs measured by the criterion measure. Actually, this approach suggests some measurement possibilities for determining the degree of relevance

or content validity of the criterion measure. This will be discussed further in this chapter in a later section on the measurement of content validity of training programs.

Another way of conceptualizing these relationships is presented in Figure 5. To simplify the diagram, the relationships are just presented for KSAs. Note, however, that the diagram could be redrawn to show the same relationships for organizational goals such as cost. In this diagram, the horizontal axis across the top of the figure represents KSAs determined by the needs assessment. As indicated below that title, there are two possibilities: The KSAs are either represented or not. Similarly, along the vertical axis, the KSAs are shown as either represented or not in the criteria. The result is the fourfold figure labeled A, B, C, and D in Figure 5.

Using this method of conceptualizing criterion relevance, both Boxes A and D are labeled *relevance*. Box D identifies a situation where the KSAs are represented in the needs assessment and the criteria. Box A represents a situation where the KSAs are not identified by the needs assessment as being part of the situation being studied, so the criteria are appropriately designed not to represent them. Essentially, this point of view says that relevance is determined by making sure the criteria not only contain the components identified as needed for job success, but also leave out those components determined irrelevant for job success. Of course, even though this diagram is drawn as a fourfold figure, there is actually a continuum. Particular KSAs may be identified by the needs assessment, for example, as very important, slightly important, or not at all important. Nevertheless, the essential idea is that the criteria should measure only those KSAs determined relevant.

The same point can be made about the content of the training program. It also should be composed of materials related to the relevant component and should not contain materials that are judged irrelevant by the

FIGURE 5

The Relationship Between Criteria and Needs Assessment

KSAs determined
by the needs assessment

	− Not represented	+ Represented
− Not represented	Criterion relevance A	Criterion deficiency B
KSA represented in the criteria		
+ Represented	C Criterion contamination	D Criterion relevance

From *Training and Organizations: Needs Assessment, Development and Evaluation* by I. L. Goldstein, 1986, Monterey, CA: Brooks/Cole. Copyright 1986 by Brooks/Cole Publishing Company. Reprinted by permission.

needs assessment. The kinds of errors that can occur in this process are discussed in the next section.

Criterion Deficiency

Criterion deficiency is the degree to which components identified in the needs assessment are not present in the actual criteria. This situation is represented in the fourfold Figure 5 as Box B. It is also represented in the upper part of the circles in Figure 4. In many cases, it is necessary to make careful judgments about the relationship expected between the KSA components established in the needs assessment and the criteria used in the training program.

Actually, there are several kinds of deficiency. The most obvious kind is the type represented in Figures 4 and 5: That is, an important KSA is identified but left out of the criterion constructs. It may also be left out of the training program itself. For example, an organization may expect all middle-level managers to be able to appraise the performance of their employees and provide them feedback so that they can improve their level of performance. However, as most managers have found out, training courses often present only general information about human relations without providing any instructional material on the complex process of appraising the performance of employees. Sometimes the material is included in the training program but criteria are still not developed to measure the manager's performance either in training or on the job. This also represents a deficiency; the organization does not even know if a manager cannot perform. Even though the organization provided training materials, it has no idea whether the manager has learned the material because no criteria are available to measure the performance. The only solution is to determine, through the methodology of needs assessment, the most appropriate multiple criteria to measure success. The complexity of these criteria should be represented in those criteria chosen to judge the initial success of individuals in the training program and on the job. Of course, depending on the level of expertise expected by the organization, the trainee may often be unable to perform with the same skill as an experienced worker. The criteria must be able to reflect such differences.

A systems perspective that treats training as one part of an organizational system suggests there are probably other forms of deficiency. The needs assessment might indicate that particular KSAs are required for the job, but there is no intention to teach them in training. For example, a salesperson could be hired with the understanding that he or she will already know the advantages and disadvantages of various advertising media. In this case, even though this knowledge is identified as critical for job success, it is not to be learned in the training program. Thus, criteria developed for evaluating the training program for salespersons would not be deficient if they excluded measures of this knowledge component, even though this component should be represented in the selection system.

The issues related to deficient criteria are just as important to the measurement of organizational objectives, thereby adding a degree of complexity that some evaluators would prefer to avoid. It is one matter to specify all the components that determine the success of an individual on required tasks, but it is another to insist that all the components that determine the success of an entire training program be specified in criteria that can be measured and evaluated. However, criteria representing organizational objectives should provide information critical for the feedback and decision processes; it is necessary to make the effort to ensure that these factors are considered.

Criterion Contamination

Box C in Figure 5 and the lower part of the circles in Figure 4 show a third construct, *criterion contamination:* This construct pertains to extraneous elements present in the criteria that result in the measure not appropriately representing the construct identified in the needs assessment. The existence of criterion contamination can lead to incorrect conclusions about the validity of a training program. For example, a supervisor may give better work stations to those who have participated in the new training program on the assumption that they are better equipped to handle the assignment than those who have simply been placed on the job. In this case, the training program may demonstrate its validity because the participants have better assignments, but it is just as easy to imagine situations in which the opposite occurs. It is important to be aware of these factors because many of them can be avoided. During the evaluation process, for example, training designers can keep the scores of trainees confidential and can control for factors like work assignments.

Multiple Criteria

In almost all instances, it is necessary to consider the use of multiple criteria to adequately assess most training efforts. It is often useful to have measures that, say, assess trainees' reactions, the amount of learning they do, their eventual performance on the job, and the cost of the program. The collection of different criteria reflecting the multiple objectives of an organization leads to a more difficult decision process than the collection of a single criterion of performance. Yet judgment and feedback processes depend on the availability of *all* sources of information. For instance, a particular training program might lead to increased achievement but dissatisfied participants. It is important to find out why the program is not viewed favorably so changes that might improve the reactions may be considered. If decision makers are more concerned with achievement than reaction, they might not be willing to institute changes. However, at least the decision makers do have the information available to make the choice and can consider the possible consequences.

An illustration of the thoughtful development of multiple criteria is offered by Freeberg's (1976) study of work training programs for youths. He investigated training projects of the Out-of-School Program of the Neighborhood Youth Corps located in thirteen different cities. Freeberg noted the importance of developing criteria based on constructs chosen rationally from the stated objectives of the program. In this case, the youth training programs had goals related to trainees' social, community, and occupational adjustments and attitudinal perceptions. Freeberg examined the original manpower legislation and the standards of the sponsoring federal agency. He also interviewed the professionals running the training programs and directly observed operational practices. Based on this work, Freeberg established a number of measures for both short-term program criteria and post-program criteria. He also used a number of measures for each of the short-term and long-term criteria. An example of a short-term criterion was work motivation (based on willingness to train

full-time or part-time and to accept jobs under specified adverse conditions). A long-term criterion was job performance and adjustment (e.g., salary raises, employee proficiency ratings, and number of jobs held).

An example of the careful tracing-out process for each of these criteria is made obvious by the measures chosen. For example, measures chosen for the construct of job motivation include number of jobs interviewed for, number of applications filed, number of sources used to find a first job, and number of visits to the state employment service. Freeberg studied the relationships between his short- and long-term criteria and found a number of strong relationships. For example, trainees who assessed themselves as higher on the necessity of keeping out of trouble tended to have higher ratings from their employer, had less actual police contacts, and found their families had more positive feelings about them after training. Similar relationships were found for trainees who had positive self-perceptions of employment capability, high proficiency ratings by counselors and peers, and a positive attitude toward further training.

As is made obvious by Freeberg's study, there are many different dimensions by which criteria can vary, including the time they are collected and the type of criteria data collected. These dimensions are not independent; for example, learning criteria and behavior on the job not only are different types of criteria but also vary according to the time of collection. Some of the more important dimensions that should be considered are discussed in the following sections.

Multiple Levels of Training Criteria

The most popular classification of training criteria was developed by Kirkpatrick (1959), who suggested that evaluation procedures should consider four levels of criteria: reaction, learning, behavior, and results. Kirkpatrick defined *reaction* as what the trainees thought of the particular program. Most trainers believe that initial receptivity provides a good atmosphere for learning in the instructional program but does not necessarily cause high levels of learning. It is important to realize that reaction measures, like any other criteria, should be related to the needs assessment. Thus, it makes no sense to use reaction measures that ask if the trainee is happy (from "Agree" to "Disagree") unless there is some relationship between happiness and the course objectives as established by the needs assessment. In case anyone still needs a reminder that reaction measures by themselves may not indicate very much, a study by Campion and Campion (1987) makes the point. These researchers conducted a very carefully designed interviewer training program to teach employees interviewing skills to help them obtain jobs. Despite positive indicants of trainee reactions and learning, the study did not find any differences between the trained group and nonparticipants in terms of actual interview behavior and job offers. This result confirms recent analysis (Alliger & Janak, 1989), which found that reaction data tend to correlate only slightly with other levels of criteria. Interestingly, the levels of criteria discussed next (e.g., learning, behavior, and results) tend to correlate higher. However, as described by Alliger and Janak, these data must be treated with caution because there are few studies that report such data.

The second level of criteria suggested by Kirkpatrick, *learning*, refers to learning performance that occurs in the training program. The training analyst is concerned with measuring the learning of principles, facts, techniques, and attitudes that were specified as training objectives. The measures must be objective and quantifiable indicants of the learning that has taken place in the training program. They are not measures of performance on the job. Again, the objectives determined from the needs assessment must be the most important

determinant of the measure to be used. An illustration of the importance of developing good proficiency measures for training is demonstrated by the work of Gordon and Isenberg (1975). These investigators noted that the growing concern in a program for machinist training was that passing or failing began to depend on which particular trainer was grading. These researchers developed standardized exercises based on the goals of the training program. They developed a criterion based on the difficulty of the machine operation, tolerance requirements, and finish specifications. For example, they developed a point system whereby the smoother the finish required for the part, the higher the points earned by the trainee for completing the work within the specified standards. As a result of this work, the investigators were able to develop a reliable system whereby judges strongly agreed on the scores earned by individual trainees.

There are many other imaginative examples of the development of relevant criteria. One of these examples is the measure used by the Army to assess the performance of trainees involved in a two-sided exercise under simulated battlefield conditions. As described by Uhlaner and Drucker (1980), "each soldier's weapon is equipped with a 6x telescope, and all participants wear black, three inch, two digit numbers on their helmets. Opponents try to read each other's numbers using the telescopes" (p. 134). This system is portrayed in Figure 6. When opponents can identify the number, they fire a blank shot and radio a report to the controller, causing the observed person or equipment to be removed from the exercise.

Another illustration is offered by Goldstein and Bartlett (1977) and involves peer evaluations of police trainees at the end of an 11-week training program. In this study, trainees were asked to rate each other based on who they wanted to have as a backup officer in an armed robbery call, a high-speed chase, or a domestic dispute.

564   *Goldstein*

FIGURE 6

Realtrain Simulation Identification

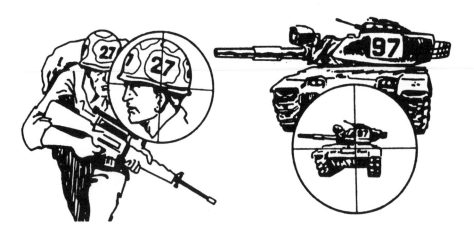

From "Military Research on Performance Criteria: A Change of Emphasis," by J. E. Uhlaner and A. J. Drucker, 1980, *Human Factors*, 22, pp. 131–139. Copyright 1980 by the Human Factors Society, Inc. Reprinted by permission..

They found that these paper nominations did not correlate with grades and other learning measures at the end of academy training. However, the peer nominations at the end of field training correlated −.43 with the number of days a trainee spent in field training—that is, the more positive the peer nominations, the fewer days spent in field training. Evidently, the trainee's peers saw something in the performance of their fellow trainees that was not reflected in their grades in the police academy. It is important to remember the results of the Campion and Campion (1987) study discussed earlier: Positive learning indicants do not guarantee changes in behavior on the job. On the other hand, job behavior changes are not very likely without some learning occurring, especially if the learning criteria measures behavior relevant to job success.

The third level of criteria in Kirkpatrick's classification, *behavior*, refers to measures of performance on the job. Just as favorable reaction does not necessarily mean learning

will occur in the training program, superior training performance does not always result in similar behavior in the transfer setting. The significance of this point was emphasized by a review that examined research studies from 1906 to 1952. In this investigation, Severin (1952) found that the median correlation between production records and training grades was .11. He concluded that training records did not always accurately represent performance on the job and should not be substituted for studies of on-the-job behavior without first determining that a strong relationship exists.

There are a large number of measures that can be used to assess on-the-job performance. Many times, measures employed during training can also be useful in measuring job performance. For example, the illustration offered by Gordon and Isenberg (1975) for machinist training including finish specifications and tolerance requirements is just as useful on the job as in training. In other cases, measures might be needed that reflect other skills that are expected to be developed on the job as a result of initial learning in training. Again, it is particularly important to make sure the criteria fit the objectives of the training program as established by the needs assessment. Latham and Wexley (1981) offer a large number of behavioral rating item examples for a number of different jobs based on careful needs assessment. For example, managers who had been trained in these areas could be rated from "Almost Never" to "Almost Always" on the following types of items based on job performance:

- Establishes mechanisms for spotting trends/patterns on key departmental/ functional areas

- Clearly defines the role responsibilities of key managers.

A mechanic in a bowling alley might be rated on the following items:

- Asks the mechanic leaving the shift what machines need watching

- Checks the tension of chains weekly and keeps them oiled

Kirkpatrick's fourth level of criteria, *results*, refers to the achievement of organizational objectives. Some results that could be examined include costs, turnover, absenteeism, grievances, and morale. The earlier section in this chapter on needs assessment described the various components of organizational analyses, including goals and objectives, which in turn should suggest relevant organizational criteria. Again, it is important to emphasize the tracing-out process so that relevant criteria stemming from the needs assessment are developed. One criterion that has received increasing attention over the last several years is cost. Many organizations have designed instructional programs in the hope that it will reduce other costs. Thus, an entry-level sales training course is used in the hope that the trainee, if upon beginning on the job,

can produce at a higher rate than might otherwise be expected. Obviously such analyses require very careful detailing of all the costs and gains associated with training. Mirabal (1978) has outlined the costs associated with the actual instructional program. Table 18 illustrates a chart designed to show some of these costs as related to the trainee, the instructor, and the facilities. Other charts developed by Mirabal address items such as the development costs of training.

An important addition to the concept of cost in evaluating training programs is the idea of utility. Most of the work involving utility has been applied to the usefulness of selection programs (Cascio, 1989), but it is just as possible to apply the concepts to training programs. The basic idea is that the utility of a training program is the translation of validity information into cost figures that permit comparisons between different types of programs. A more complete description of Cascio's approach is presented later in this chapter with the material on evaluation models.

The use of such concepts considerably broadens the number of ways to measure the success of a training program. For example, it is possible to ask what the training program will add to other interventions, such as a selection system that itself has varying degrees of success. It is also possible to ask what the utility of a formal training program is compared to placing the trainees on the job and expecting them to learn from other more experienced employees. Here, it would be necessary to ask what differences in productivity for the new employee result from the two approaches, what is the loss in productivity from people on the job who have to teach the employee (as compared to the cost of the formal training program), and what is the dollar payoff to the organization. If the cost of formal training is very high, the production return is very little, and the employee moves on to other jobs in a short time, a formal training program may not be worth it.

TABLE 18

Charts for Specifying Training Costs

Date:

Chart I. Trainee Costs

Course Title	Trainees and hours				Salary		Travel and per diem	Materials and supplies	Total trainee costs	
	Number of trainees	Level and step	Curriculum hours	Trainee hours	Hourly salary plus benefits	Total salary	Annual travel and per diem	Annual cost	Total trainee cost	Trainee cost per trainee hour
	1	2	3	4	5	6	7	8	9	10

Chart II. Instructor Costs

Course Title	Agency/Instructors							Nonorganizational Instructors			Travel and per diem		Total instructor costs	
	Number of instructors and level	Salary per hour	Overhead per hour	Salary plus overhead	Hours per year	Annual salary plus overhead cost	Annual salary plus overhead cost per trainee hour	Number of instructors fee	Annual salary or fee	Annual salary per trainee hour	Annual travel and per diem	Annual travel and per diem per trainee hour	Total annual instructor cost	Annual instructor costs per trainee hour
	1	2	3	4	5	6	7	8	9	10	11	12	13	14

TABLE 18

Charts for Specifying Training Costs (continued)

Chart III. Facilities Costs

Course Title	Nonorganization owned space			Cost per trainee hour	Improvement to space		Equipment and furnishings			Total facilities costs	
	Annual cost of required space	% of time used for course	Annual cost of space for course		Cost per year	Annual cost per trainee hour	Total cost of items	Annual cost of items for course	Annual cost of items per trainee hour	Total annual facilities cost	Annual facilities cost per trainee hour
	1	2	3	4	5	6	7	8	9	10	11

From "Forecasting Future Training Costs" by T. E. Mirabal. In *Training and Development Journal*, 1978, 32, pp. 78–87. Copyright 1978 by the American Society for Training and Development, Inc. Adapted by permission.

Process and Outcome Measures

Outcome measures refer to criteria, such as learning and performance, that represent various levels of achievement. While these measures are critical in determining the viability of instructional programs, strict reliance on outcome measures often makes it difficult to determine why the criteria were achieved. Thus, I have stressed the importance of process measures that examine what happens during instruction (Goldstein, 1978b). This emphasis is illustrated in the training instructional model in Figure 1 by the arrow between training and use of evaluation models.

It is not unusual for a training program to bear little relationship to the originally conceived format. Evaluation designs and specification of outcome criteria have often been based on a product or outcome view of training validity. Researchers have collected pre- and postcriterion measures, compared them with control groups, and discovered that they did not understand the results they had obtained. This problem was especially apparent when the collectors of these data were outside consultants who appeared only to collect pre- and postdata but had no conception of what had occurred in training between pre- and postmeasurement.

The following example illustrates this issue. In a study of computer-assisted instruction in a school setting (Rosenberg, 1972), two teachers each agreed to instruct a geometry class by traditional methods and by computer-assisted instruction (CAI). Thus, each teacher taught one traditional and one CAI class. Further, the teachers agreed to work together to design an exam that would cover material presented in each of the classes. At the end of the first testing period, the traditional classes taught by each teacher significantly outperformed the CAI groups taught by these same teachers. However, at a later testing, one of the CAI groups improved so that it was now equivalent to the two traditional groups; the other CAI group performed significantly worse than the other three instructional groups. One reasonable conclusion is that one of the teachers learned to instruct a CAI group so that it was now equivalent to the two traditional groups but that the other teacher had not been able to do so with the other CAI group. Indeed, if the investigators had only collected the outcome measures, this or other similar erroneous conclusions would probably have been offered as explanations for the data. In this case, the investigators also observed the instructional process to provide information about the program. They learned that the instructor for the CAI group that eventually improved had become disturbed over the performance of his students and offered remedial tutoring, essentially turning the CAI class into a traditional group.

The use of process measures may provide all sorts of unanticipated dividends. I will never forget the look of astonishment on the faces of a number of high-level executives who had just discovered that the reason entry-level grocery clerks could not operate their cash registers was because that instructional sequence was no longer part of their carefully designed instructional program. Another perspective on such events is that unintended as well as intended outcomes result from our programs. For example, criteria might be established to measure the side effects of a training program for hard-core unemployed workers. Since such a program would place more minority group workers on the job, it might have the unintended and unwanted effect of increasing racial tensions by introducing workers with different sets of personal and social values. By carefully considering these possibilities, criteria could be established to measure these unintended outcomes in order to deal effectively with them. Thus, with the appropriate information, it might be possible in our illustration concerning hard-core unemployed workers to design programs to ease the entry of workers with different values into the organization. This again reinforces the belief that criterion development should be approached with thoughtful emphasis on relevant criteria.

Criterion- and Norm-referenced Measures

Criterion-referenced measures depend on an absolute standard of quality, while norm-referenced measures depend on a relative standard. Criterion-referenced measures provide a standard for the achievement of trainees as compared with specific behavioral objectives and thereby indicate the degree of competence attained by a trainee. Norm-referenced measures, because they compare the capabilities of an individual to those of other trainees, are not especially useful for the evaluation of training programs, unless such measures also provide information about the degree of proficiency in relationship to the tasks involved. Data merely indicating that the trainee is equal to or above 60 percent of the population provide little information about specific capabilities, making it difficult to help the individual or redesign the program to make improvements.

Those interested in the procedures necessary to develop criterion-referenced measures should consult Swezey's (1981) excellent book. One recent example of the development of such measures in a training situation is offered in a study by Panell and Laabs (1979). These investigators were interested in using criterion-referenced measures for a training program for Navy boiler technicians. They designed a set of 186 items by setting up hypothetical job situations that required the knowledge and skills contained in each of the training modules. Then they had job experts check the items to determine the correspondence between the job situations and the KSAs and to ensure adequate question representation for each module. The hypothetical job situations were also checked to make sure that each situation was based on known job requirements and that each situation used job materials such as maintenance requirement cards, charts describing maintenance actions, and illustrations of tools and equipment.

Pannel and Laabs followed these procedures with empirical methods to establish the reliability of the items and cut scores for passing and failing, which resulted in 127 usable items. The investigators administered the test to 75 trainees who were about to enter the training course and another 75 trainees who had just completed it. They then compared the results of the performance of the two groups on the test items. The test items did differentiate between the two groups. For example, 88 percent of the individuals who were in either the group entering training or who had completed training were identified correctly by their test score performance—that is, persons who had completed training knew the test items stemming from the needs assessment while persons entering training did not. Four percent of the preinstruction group did well enough on the test that they were identified as not needing training, and 8 percent of the group that had completed training was still identified as needing training. Of course, there could be many reasons why some persons were misidentified. If that happened with large numbers of persons, it is possible that the test items were not very well constructed or that the training course was not doing its job. As Swezey (1981) points out, the criteria must be developed with an emphasis on criterion relevance; otherwise, no judgments can be made about the training program or the knowledge level of the trainees. As Swezey (1981) states:

> First, it must be determined that objectives have been properly derived from adequate task analyses that prescribe clearly what an examinee must do or must know in order to perform the task under examination.
>
> Second, each item must be carefully evaluated against its associated objective

to ensure that the performances, conditions, and standards specified in the item are the same as those required by the objective. (p. 151)

In summary, note that a large number of general criterion issues have not been treated in this section, for example, issues related to so-called objective versus subjective criteria or the reliability of the criteria. However, those issues are related to all the uses of criteria, including, for example, performance appraisal in the organization and evaluation of selection programs. In this section I tried to emphasize criterion issues specifically important to training constructs. Even there, most of these concepts, such as relevancy, are recognizably related to the use of criterion measures for all situations.

In concluding this section, I want to emphasize two important ideas. First, the greatest degree of effort should be placed on developing relevant criteria, where relevance is conceptualized as a relationship between the operation measures (criteria) and the KSAs determined from the needs assessment. Emphasis on measurement issues such as reliability will not help if the criterion is measuring the wrong thing. While this seems self-evident, it is bewildering to note the amount of time and effort frequently spent on data crunching to establish the reliability of ludicrous criterion measures. The second point is that because of the complexity of most training programs and the corresponding evaluation efforts, criterion selection must reflect the breadth of the objectives. For example, it makes no sense to have measures of various types of performance without considering cost or utility factors that provide information about whether training offers more than other interventions. Also, criteria must reflect the organizational objectives as determined by the organizational analysis. Otherwise, no matter how successful individual performance is, the organization might judge the training intervention as a failure.

Traditional Training Evaluation Models

As stated earlier in the section on criterion measures, evaluation is the systematic collection of descriptive and judgmental information necessary to make effective training decisions related to the selection, adoption, value, and modification of various instructional activities. Instructional programs reflect numerous objectives, ranging from trainee progress to organizational goals. From this perspective, evaluation is an information-gathering technique that makes possible the revision of instructional programs to achieve multiple instructional objectives.

It is interesting to categorize the questions that are asked about training programs. I have indicated some of the concerns that evaluators are asked to respond to by trainees, trainers, and organizational executives (Goldstein, 1978). A close examination of these complaints reveals certain underlying evaluation questions that have to be asked in order to respond. The complaints are as follows:

- *The trainee complaint.* There is a conspiracy. I just finished my training program. I even completed a pretest and a posttest. My posttest score was significantly better than the scores of my friends in the on-the-job control group. However, I just lost my job because I couldn't perform the work.

- *The trainer complaint.* There is a conspiracy. Everyone praised our training program. They said it was the best program they ever attended. The trainees even had a chance to laugh a little. Now, the trainees tell me that management won't let them perform the job the way we trained them.

- *The organization's complaint.* There is a conspiracy. My competition used the training program, and it worked for them. They saved a million. I took it straight from their manuals, and my employees still can't do the job. (1978, p. 131)

The dimensions of particular concern for this chapter are the evaluation questions that must be asked and answered in order to respond to these complaints. Rational decisions related to the selection, adoption, support, and worth of the various training activities require some basis for determining that the instructional program was responsible for whatever changes occurred. Instructional analysts should be able to respond to the following questions:

- Does an examination of the various criteria indicate that a change has occurred?

- Can the changes be attributed to the instructional program?

- Is it likely that similar changes will occur for new participants in the same program?

- Is it likely that similar changes will occur for new participants in the same program in a different organization?

These questions could be asked about measures at each criterion level (e.g., reaction, learning, behavior, results). Evaluations of training programs are not likely to produce dichotomous answers. Training analysts who expect results to lead to a yes or no value judgment are unrealistically imposing a simplistic structure and raising false expectations among both recipients and sponsors of training programs.

While the answers to these questions provide information about the accomplishments of training programs and the revisions that may be required, it is also important to realize that there are other types of questions that investigators may be interested in asking. They may be interested in the relative accomplishments of two different training approaches or in discovering which training approach works best with what types of training participants or in what type of organization. Researchers may also be interested in testing the various theoretical hypotheses that provided the foundation for the design of a new training approach. In this instance, researchers will still want to know if a change has occurred and whether it can be attributed to the training program. However, they may also want to know what the effects are of the training program on trainees with varying characteristics such as high and low verbal ability.

Values and the Evaluation Process

Before beginning a discussion of evaluation models and strategies, it is important to consider the context in which evaluation occurs. The evaluator, the trainees, the decision makers in the organization, the trainers, and everyone else involved bring their own sets of values and attitudes to the training process. It would be naive to suggest that these values and attitudes don't affect many of the decisions involving both the evaluation and the resulting data interpretations. Some of the more obvious factors can be controlled by the evaluation design; medical researchers, for example, use designs that assure that the investigator does not know which subjects received the experimental drug and which subjects received a placebo. However, it is useless to pretend that all values and attitudes affecting our research are controlled, much less recognized. Researchers are now beginning to acknowledge these variables and to design research to study the outcomes occurring when these variables are manipulated.

J. P. Campbell (1978) warns us that the choice of criteria is a value judgment that all concerned parties should examine and discuss; if not, when the results are in, there is likely to be widespread disagreement about the outcomes. In this regard, Weiss (1975) notes that decision maker values often determine how data are interpreted. For example, if the decision maker is concerned about trainees holding on to skilled jobs, then negative evaluations about the impact of instructions are treated with alarm. Yet if the training organization is interested in the number of people who attend training because that is the basis for their contract payment, then negative evaluations of the training outcomes might be ignored or treated as irrelevant. At the very least, the organizational analysis stage of the needs assessment should provide the opportunity for these value systems to be made public so that their potential interaction with the evaluation can be explored.

In addition to the realization that values affect evaluation efforts, recognition is growing that all decisions made in conducting research affect the study itself. This point of view is often described as the *philosophy of intervention:* It recognizes that even the decision to evaluate affects the data collected. Cochran (1978) pointed out that the use of criterion data changes when organizations discover these data are being used in an evaluation study. For example, when there are programs to lower crime, the criterion data often consist of the number of larcenies of $50 or more, which are counted in the Uniform Crime Act. One result of programs to lower crime is that the statistics give the appearance of a decrease in crime when none actually exists. In some cases, this comes about because of outright falsification of data; in other cases, it is more subtle. These larceny figures are based on stolen goods— which are used items. Thus, there is some value judgment in setting the actual cost of the item. Many psychological studies indicate that the criteria used in making these judgments are often altered by the context and purposes of the study.

An important warning about the consequences of conducting research is provided by

Argyris (1968a) in an article with the very descriptive name "Some Unintended Consequences of Rigorous Research." Argyris points out that our empirical-appearing research tends to treat research subjects in an authoritarian manner as passive, predictable creatures. He feels that subjects do not simply accept deception research and less than meaningful control procedures. Instead, they may try to second-guess the research design or circumvent the study in some other fashion. The result of these well-controlled studies may be behavior unrepresentative of what happens in that organizational situation. For example, in a training study by Pfister (1975), the researcher's procedure of assigning 24 of 78 officer volunteers to a control condition resulted in officers becoming angry, withdrawing, and making unpublishable comments regarding the research investigators. The most important aspect of the issue is to understand that the development of a training program or its evaluation is an intervention in the trainees' lives. Researchers who ignore such concerns are likely to suffer the consequences.

Basic Principles of Experimental Design

Each research design has different assets and liabilities in controlling extraneous factors that might threaten the evaluator's ability to determine (a) if a real change has occurred, (b) whether the changes are attributable to the training program, and (c) whether the change is likely to occur again with a new sample of trainees. The kind of threats that will challenge the evaluator trying to answer such questions will soon be listed. However, before discussing these threats, it is important to describe a few considerations of experimental design, because often the ingenious use of design can help the evaluator respond positively to these problems.

Pre- and Posttesting.   The first question is whether the participants, after exposure to the training program, change their performance in a significant way. In order to respond to this question, it is necessary to administer a pretest before training and a posttest after training. Several important issues are masked by the simplicity of this statement. First, there is the question of whether a posttest only will suffice. The problem here is that without the pretest, there is little information available to determine whether changes have occurred. Even worse, it is difficult to make more subtle adjustments in the training program based on information that might suggest there are positive changes in learning some KSAs but no changes in learning others.

Second, there is the question of the content of the tests. Obviously, criterion relevance is critical; the tests must measure the outcome and objectives to be achieved as a result of the training program. All the concepts of criterion relevance discussed in the previous section are relevant here. It must also be recognized that criterion relevance for a measure of training performance may differ from what is expected on the job as a result of both training and on-the-job practice. This raises the third issue of when the tests are to be administered—a more complicated question for the posttest. In this instance, the timing usually involves both testing at the end of training and later posttesting for relevant changes expected on the job.

Control Groups. The specification of changes indicated by pre- and postmeasurement is only one consideration. It must be determined whether the changes occurred as a result of the training intervention. To help eliminate the possibility of other explanations for changes between pre- and posttesting, a control group can be used (treated like the experimental group on all variables that might contribute to pre–post differences except the actual training program). While this is a basic and fundamental concept, it is amazing how many problems related to threats to validity that are discussed next can be avoided by

creative use of control groups. For example, Latham and Saari (1979) examined the effects of a training technique for supervisors known as *behavioral role modeling*. The use of a formal control group that was never trained would have created serious problems for the organization. However, the researchers solved this problem by randomly assigning supervisors either to training or to a group to be trained later but which in the meantime served as a control group. The researchers not only demonstrated the positive effects of their training program by comparing the training group to the control group, but they were also able to show how these differences disappeared later after the control group was also trained.

Threats to the Interpretation of Interventions

Experimental research design, including the creative use of pre- and posttesting and control groups, is a topic that deserves extensive consideration; fortunately, such a treatment does exist. In a classic text, D. T. Campbell and J. C. Stanley (1963) presented and organized the research on experimental design. Cook and D. T. Campbell (1976, 1979) updated this text, and Cook, Campbell, and Peracchio (1990) have further updated this work for this edition of the *Handbook*. Their work includes discussions of many of the intervention threats stemming from a growing appreciation of the values of trainees, trainers, evaluators, and organizational sponsors. The material presented in this chapter on experimental design is for the most part devoted to particular adaptations of their work that are most relevant to the discussion for the evaluation of training programs.

Threats to Internal Validity. *Internal validity* asks the basic question, Did the treatment make a difference in this particular situation? Unless internal validity has been established, it is not possible to interpret the effects of any intervention, training or otherwise. Threats to internal validity are variables other than the training program that can affect its results. The solution to this difficulty is to control these variables so that they may be discounted as competing explanations for the experimental effect. A number of internal validity threats of particular relevance to the evaluation of training programs are listed below.

History.   In this sense, *history* refers to specific events, other than the experimental treatment, occurring between the first and second measurement that could provide alternative explanations for the results. For instance, an instructional program designed to produce positive attitudes toward safe practices in coal mines may find significant differences that have no relationship to the material presented if a coal mine disaster occurs between pre- and posttesting.

Testing.   This variable refers to the influence of the pretest on the scores of the posttest. This is a serious problem for training programs in which the pretest can sensitize the participant to search for materials or to ask friends for information that provides correct answers on the posttest. Thus, improved performance could occur simply by taking the pre- and posttests without any intervening instructional program.

Statistical Regression.   Participants in training research are often chosen on the basis of extreme scores. Thus, trainees with extremely low or high scores on a pretest measure may be selected for training because the organization believes either they need training the most or can benefit from it the most. In this situation, a phenomenon known as *statistical regression* can occur: On the posttesting, the scores regress toward the mean, with the trainees with high scores tending toward lower scores and the trainees with low scores tending toward higher scores. Thus, if you had all lower-score

trainees, you might believe that your training program had achieved something, when in reality the scores had only regressed toward the mean. This regression occurs because tests are not perfect measures; some changes from the first to second testing will occur simply because of measurement error. If you have chosen persons whose scores tend toward the extreme ends of the continuum, the variability often moves toward the center or mean of the group.

Differential Selection of Participants.   This effect stems from biases in choosing comparison groups. One of the more obvious differences would occur if volunteers are used in the training group and randomly chosen participants are used in the control group. In these cases, differences occur simply because the groups are different. The degree to which the evaluator would even be aware of the problem depends on whether pretest information is collected. This variable is best controlled by random assignment to experimental and control groups.

Experimental Mortality.   This threat refers to the differential loss of participants from the treatment or control group. Sometimes members who score poorly on a pretest drop out of the control group. Then the experimental group as a whole may appear to score higher on the posttest simply because the lower-scoring members have dropped out.

In addition to the threats to internal validity listed so far, others that can be labeled intervention threats to internal validity result mainly from the decision to evaluate a program. Interestingly, many of the internal threats to validity discussed so far can be constrained by the use of experimental design procedures. For example, the internal threat of history effects can often be contained by having both experimental and control groups so that whatever the historical occurrence, it happens to both groups. However, most of the following set of threats cannot be contained by experimental methodology. Rather, as discussed in the section on values and evaluation, the solution will require other approaches, such as working with the participants as part of the evaluation model so that they do not feel threatened by such events as being assigned to a control group. Since many persons in organizations are success oriented, it should be no surprise that a mysterious announcement from a training analyst assigning only certain individuals to a training program might be viewed by the controls as a message that they are not held in favor by the organization. Also, as will be described, some organizations tend to interfere with group assignment because they are so sure that training will work, they want the control group to also have the benefit of the effect—even while evaluation is proceeding. Such threats to validity (adapted from Cook & D. T. Campbell, 1976, 1979, and Cook, Campbell, & Peracchio, 1990) include those listed below.

Diffusion of Imitation of Treatments. In organizations where members of the experimental and control groups know each other, information passed on to the control group members by members of the training group can diffuse the effects of training. As a result, some of the differences between the two groups based on the training treatment could disappear, and the evaluator would not learn whether the program accomplished its goals.

Compensatory Equalization of Treatments. When the training treatment is perceived to produce positive benefits, there is often a reluctance to permit perceived inequalities to exist. Administrators or trainers may provide control subjects with similar or other benefits that wipe out any measured differences between the control and experimental groups in the evaluation. Cook and Campbell (1979) note that in several national educational experiments, so-called control schools tended to be given other federal funds by well-meaning administrators. This, of course, resulted in these control schools actually being another form of experimental condition. Unfortunately, as later analyses indicated, the differences between the experimental and control treatments were wiped out, leaving many individuals thoroughly confused as to why their training treatments had no effect.

Compensatory Rivalry by Respondents Receiving Less Desirable Treatments. In some situations, competition between the experimental and control group may be generated. This is more likely to occur when the assignments are made public or when intact units (like whole departments or work crews) are assigned to a particular group. This special effort may wipe out the differences between the training group and the control group yet may not be a reflection of how control subjects would ordinarily perform. This kind of effect would also be possible in a situation where the control condition is the old training procedure. In this case, the control subjects might work extra hard so that their performance would be equivalent to the persons assigned to the new treatment condition. Saretsky (1972) labels this type of effort the *John Henry effect.* As memorialized in the folk song, John Henry was being compared to a steam drill. He worked so hard that he outperformed the drill and died of overexertion.

Resentful Demoralization of Respondents Receiving Less Desirable Treatments. In some instances, persons selected for a control condition can become resentful or demoralized, especially when they believe their assignment to be a message that they are not as highly valued by management. This can result in control subjects' not performing as capably as possible, and their drop in performance may result in differences between the treatment and control that lead to an incorrect conclusion that the training program has been successful.

Threats to External Validity.   *External validity* refers to the generalizability or representativeness of the data to other groups and situations. The evaluator is concerned with the generalizability of the results to other populations, settings, and treatment variables. External validity is always a matter of inference and thus can never be specified with complete confidence. Internal validity is a prerequisite for external validity, since the results for the study must be valid for the group being examined before there can be concern over wider validity. The representativeness of the investigation determines the degree of generalizability. For example, when the data are initially collected in a low socioeconomic setting, it is unreasonable to claim that the instructional program will work equally well for a high socioeconomic area. The following external validity threats that are potentially relevant to the evaluation of training programs are adapted from the original text by D. T. Campbell and Stanley (1963), the Cook and Campbell (1976) chapter in the first edition of this *Handbook,* and the Cook, Campbell, and Peracchio (1990) chapter in volume 1 of this edition of the *Handbook.*

Reactive Effect of Pretesting.   The effects of pretests often lead to increased sensitivity to the instructional procedure. The participants' responses to the training program might be different from the responses of individuals who are exposed to an established program without the pretest; the pretested participants might pay attention to certain material in the training program only because they know it is covered in test items. Often, it is speculated that pretest exposure improves performance; however, Bunker and Cohen (1978) discovered that the posttest scores of persons low in numerical ability were hindered by exposure to the pretest. They offer several reasons why this may have occurred. The trainees may have mistakenly attended only to the limited sample of material appearing on the pretest, for example. Or those with low numerical ability,

made anxious by the pretest, may have had difficulty with later learning. Further research is needed to explore these suggestions. However, generalizations to later training populations not exposed to a pretest would be in error. Interestingly, the problem occurred only for low-ability students, not high-ability students; thus, the external validity threat of pretesting interacted with the selection of the participating group. This kind of threat is discussed next.

Interaction of Selection and Experimental Treatment.   In this case, the characteristics of the group selected for experimental treatment determine the generalizability of the findings. The characteristics of employees from one division of the firm, for example, may result in the treatment's being more effective for them than for employees from another division with different characteristics. Similarly, characteristics such as low numerical ability may make trainees more or less receptive to particular instructional programs.

Reactive Effects of Experimental Settings.   The procedures used in the experimental setting may limit the generalizability of the study. Observers and experimental equipment often make the participants aware of their participation in an experiment. This can lead to changes in behavior that cannot be generalized to those individuals who will participate in instructional treatment that is not the focus of research. The Hawthorne studies have become the standard illustration for the "I'm a guinea pig" effect: This research shows that a group of employees continued to increase production regardless of the changes in working conditions designed to produce both increases and decreases in production. Interpreters believe that the experimental conditions resulted in the workers' behaving differently. Explanations for the Hawthorne effect include (a) novelty, (b) awareness of being a participant in an experiment, (c) changes in the environment due to observers, enthusiasm of the instructor, recording conditions, and social interaction, and (d) daily feedback on production figures. The important point is that since the factors affecting the treatment group will not be present in future training sessions, the performance obtained is not representative of that of future participants.

The potency of such variables was demonstrated by Eden and Shani (1982) in their study of military combat training. Instructors had been led to expect that some of these trainees were better students than others, although actually ability differences were negligible. Where the trainers had high expectancies for the trainees, the trainees scored significantly higher on objective achievement tests, exhibited more positive attitudes toward the course, and had more positive perceptions of instructor leadership. Variables like this become a threat to external validity because there is often more enthusiasm when a course is first being offered (and evaluated) than when the course becomes more routine. To the extent that the training effect is due to enthusiasm, it disappears with routine. However, if organizations can learn to use and maintain the factors underlying such enthusiasm, there are indications training performance will improve, hopefully enabling positive attitudes and performances like those generated in the Eden and Shani study to continue on the job. Further study, however, is required to establish this.

Multiple-Treatment Interference.   Because effects of previous treatments are not erasable, threats to external validity occur whenever there is an attempt to establish the effects of a single treatment from studies that actually examined multiple treatments. Trainees exposed to role playing, films, and lectures may perform best during the lectures, but this does not mean they would perform similarly if they were exposed to lectures all day long without the other techniques.

An Example of Experimental Design

As noted, Cook and Campbell (1976, 1979) and Cook, Campbell, and Peracchio (1990) have presented an extensive array of creative designs that can be used in a variety of organizational settings. The sections in this chapter on internal and external validity discussed some of the factors that make it difficult to determine whether a treatment has produced the hypothesized results. These threats are controlled better by some designs than others. Often, the main difficulty in choosing the correct design has been the failure to plan for evaluation before the program was implemented; in these instances, the utilization of a few procedures— for example, pre- and posttesting and control groups—could dramatically improve the quality of information. Before concluding this section, it seems worthwhile to give at least one good example of the use of creative designs and to show how alternative threats to validity can be considered in light of the design used.

The research of Komaki, Heinzmann, and Lawson (1980) serves as a good example. These investigators were studying safety problems in the vehicle maintenance division of a city's department of public works. The department being studied had one of the highest accident rates in the city. Komaki and her colleagues performed a needs assessment, including an analysis of the factors that led to unsafe practices and hindered safe acts. They examined safety logs for the previous five years to determine what types of accidents occurred, then wrote down safety behaviors that would have prevented those accidents. Throughout this procedure they worked with supervisors and workers to specifiy and develop safety procedures. The following are some examples of safety items generated for the vehicle maintenance department:

- *Proper use of equipment and tools.* When reaching upward for an item more than 30 cm (1 ft.) away from extended arms, use steps, stepladder, or solid part of vehicle. Do not stand on jacks or jack stands.

- *Use of safety equipment.* When using brake machine, wear full face shield or goggles. When arcing brake shoes, respirator should also be worn.

- *Housekeeping.* Any oil/grease spill larger than 8 x 8 cm (3 x 3 in.) in an interior walking area (defined as any area at least 30 cm [1 ft.] from a wall or a solid standing object) or an exterior walking area (designated standing object) or an exterior walking area (designated by outer white lines parallel to the wall and at least 30 cm [1 ft.] from the wall) should be soaked up with rice hull or grease compound.

- *General safety procedures.* When any type of jack other than an air jack is in use (i.e., vehicle is supported by jack or off the ground), at least one jack stand should also be used. (pp. 262–263)

Komaki and her colleagues designed a training program that used slides to depict the unsafe practices used in the department. They examined the trainees on their knowledge of appropriate safe behaviors, discussed correct safety behaviors, and then showed the same slides but this time demonstrated safe practices. Also, the employees were given copies of the appropriate safety rules to take with them. Later, in addition to the training given earlier, the employees were informed about realistic safety goals that were set on the basis of their previous performance. Randomly timed daily safety observations were then made and the results posted on a graph so that employees could see their progress toward their goals.

The design of this study is called a *time series*, which uses at least four to five observations for each of the first three phases of the study and an average of three observations for each of

the last two phases. The phases are depicted in Figure 7. The first phase, referred to as *baseline*, consisted of the collection of data before any training or feedback. It essentially consists of multiple pretests. The second phase was the training program; the third phase added feedback to the already trained employees. The fourth phase went back to training but without feedback, and the final phase renewed feedback to the already trained employees. Note that all persons proceeded through the entire sequence of five phases and that there were multiple data collection points in each phase. The data collected in this study consisted of the number of incidents performed safely. It was collected by trained observers, and there was high agreement among them. In the data shown in the graph for two departments (preventive maintenance and light equipment repair), performance improved from baseline to after-training and then improved more when feedback was added. When feedback was taken away, performance went down, but it improved when feedback was resumed in the last phase of the study. Komaki's point is that feedback on employee performance is a critical component of training programs. In two other departments, Komaki obtained similar data for the first four phases, but improvement did not occur again as a result of the fifth phase. The investigators in this study considered the various threats to validity and how their quasi-experimental design accounted for these factors. They noted:

Plausible alternative hypotheses (history,…statistical regression) were ruled out because the two phases were introduced to the sections at different points in time and improvements occurred after, and not prior to, the introduction of these phases. History was ruled out as a source of internal invalidity because it is not likely that an extraneous event would have the same impact in

FIGURE 7

Percentage of Incidents Performed Safely by Employees in Vehicle Maintenance Under Five Experimental Conditions

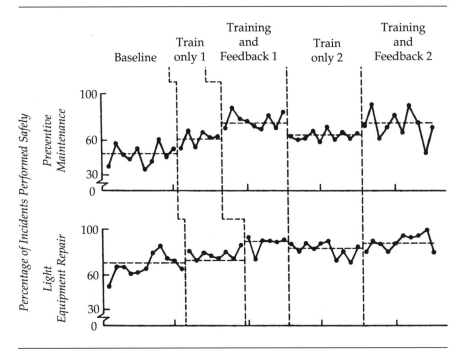

From "Effect of Training and Feedback: Component Analysis of a Behavioral Safety Program" by J. Komaki, A. T. Heinzmann, and L. Lawson, 1980, *Journal of Applied Psychology, 65*, pp. 261–270. Copyright 1980 by the American Psychological Association. Reprinted by permission.

separate sections at different times. If maturations were responsible, performance would be expected to improve as a function of the passage of time; however, improvements occurred, with few exceptions, after the introduction of Phase 3. The effects of statistical regression were ruled out because regression effects would be seen in any series of repeated measurements and not just after the introduction of the two phases.

Reactivity of measurement was also not likely to be a plausible explanation for the improvements obtained because the observers were present during all phases.

Therefore, improvements in performance during any one phase could not be due to the reactivity of the measure per se. Questions concerning reactivity and external validity, however, were not so straightforward. Although the issue of the generality of improvements was not addressed directly in the present study, support was provided by accident records, which showed that injuries were reduced by a factor of seven from the preceding year. Since the observers were present during a relatively small percentage of working hours, it is unlikely that improvements were confined to these times. (Komaki et al., 1980, p. 267)

Statistical Considerations in Evaluating Change Due to Training

Statistical considerations as well as the choice of design are important. For example, there is a long history on the best methods to control differences in pretest scores between training and control groups. While these measurement considerations are beyond the scope of this chapter, it is clear that statistical sophistication is a necessary prerequisite. This has been made more obvious in a very important article by Arvey and Cole (1989). One factor these authors explore is the likelihood of detecting a difference when it is really there (otherwise known as statistical power). They note that when they compared different designs, they were not all comparable in detecting differences that really existed. The designs compared were a posttest-only design that ignored pretest information completely, a gain score design that analyzed the differences between pretest and posttest, and an analysis of covariance (ANCOVA) design that treated the pretest as a covariate in a between-group design. In general, they found that the ANCOVA was more powerful; yet the extent of these power differences between designs was dramatically affected by a host of other factors, including the sample sizes and the degree of correlation between the pre- and posttests. For example, in the gain score and ANCOVA designs, power always increased as the correlation between pre- and posttest increased.

Alternatively, when the correlation was very small, the advantage of ANCOVA over the gain score approach was substantial and any advantages for the posttest-only design became nonexistent. The effect of greater score reliability increased the power of all three designs, but the benefits were more substantial in the gain score and ANCOVA designs than in the posttest-only design. Most importantly, in all the work described in this article, the assumption was made that the

pretest scores were equivalent. The effect of nonequivalent groups at the pretest phase was crushing on the power of all of these designs. It is clear that evaluators should pay careful attention to statistical power considerations before choosing experimental designs and procedures.

Utility Considerations

The other side of the coin is whether a statistical effect really means anything. As mentioned in the section on criterion issues, an important consideration in the evaluation of a training program is the concept of *utility*. As noted by Schneider and Schmitt (1986) in their discussion of utility and selection procedures, psychologists act as if a significant statistical effect relating a test and criterion measure proved the test's usefulness. Management personnel, however, usually find financial considerations more meaningful. They note, for instance, that when a production manager requests a new piece of machinery, it is usually supported by projected increases in productivity and resulting decreases in unit cost of production. Maintenance managers support hiring requests with figures showing decreases in down time due to equipment problems and the resulting savings.

Again, this is an area where there have been important recent developments. Cascio (1989) developed methodology to apply utility analysis to the assessment of training outcomes. Several steps are involved. First, Cascio introduces the use of capital budget methodology to analyze the minimum annual benefits in dollars required from any program. This phase of the analysis requires specifying the cost of the program, the increased benefits expected for any given period, the duration of the benefits, and the discount rate to determine the firm's minimum expected return on investment. The acceptance ratio that Cascio uses for a training program based on these figures is that the net present value of the program must be greater than zero. Second, Cascio details the use of a break-even analysis originally introduced by Boudreau (1984) to estimate the minimum effect size for a program to produce the required benefits. Basically, this operates on the premise that if the training program has any effect, the mean job performance of the trained group should exceed that of the untrained group. The difference between the trained and untrained group, expressed in standard deviation units, represents the effect size. Once the effect size is corrected for unreliability of the criterion, it is an estimate of the true differences between the trained and untrained groups. As a third step, Cascio uses meta-analysis data across multiple studies to estimate the expected actual payoff from the program. Cascio also provides information on the effects of the outcome when other factors are considered, such as an enhancement or decay of the size of the training effect. As a result of Cascio's work, it is now possible to express the gains resulting from effective training in terms of a number of outcomes, such as dollar costs, percentage increases in output, or reductions in the size of the work force required to accomplish the same work. It is likely that Cascio's work will have ramifications for many years to come as managers attempt to assess the utility of their interventions.

An important point raised by Cascio is that these analyses depend on a careful tracing out of the costs of training. An examination of such costs and issues in structured versus unstructured training for a production worker is presented in the work of Cullen, Sawzin, Sisson, and Swanson (1978), illustrated in Figure 8. Training costs here would include training development, training materials, training time, and production losses. Each of these variables would be detailed. For example, "time" would involve trainee time, including total hours and resulting salary for the trainee to reach competency, as well as the total hours and resulting salary for the

trainer until the trainee reached competency. The complexity of the cost analyses for specifying training costs is illustrated in Table 14 referred to earlier in this chapter. Such analyses may be difficult to perform, but the failure to analyze our programs in dollars makes it more likely that training will be viewed as a cost rather than as a benefit to the organization.

Other Training Evaluation Models

The experimental models of evaluation that center on issues such as pre- and posttests, control groups, and threats to validity represent the traditional models used to assess the effects of training programs. A number of other models are particularly relevant to training evaluation.

Individual Differences and Trainability Models

Many industrial and organizational psychologists have emphasized the use of training scores as a way to predict the future success of potential employees. For example, Kraut (1975) found that peer ratings obtained from managers attending a month-long training course predicted several criteria, including future promotion and performance appraisal ratings of job performance. Other investigators have used early training performance to predict performance in later, more advanced training. An example of this approach is offered by Gordon and Cohen (1973), whose study involved a welding program that was part of a larger manpower development project aimed at training unemployed and underemployed individuals from the east Tennessee area. The program consisted of 14 different tasks that fell into 4 categories and ranged in difficulty from simple to complex. Advancement from one task to the next depended on successful

FIGURE 8

Industrial Training Cost-Effectiveness Model

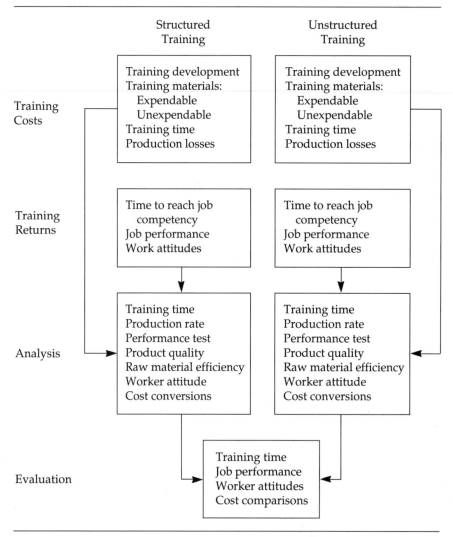

From *Cost Effectiveness: A Model for Assessing the Training Investment* by J. G. Cullen, S. A. Sawzin, G. R. Sisson, and R. A. Swanson, 1978, *Training and Development Journal, 32,* pp. 24-29. Copyright 1978 by the American Society for Training and Development, Inc. Reprinted by permission.

completion of all previous tasks, so trainees progressed at a rate commensurate with their ability to master the material. For each trainee, data were collected on the amount of time spent on each task. The correlations between the completion times for the four categories of tasks and total time to complete the plate welding course indicated that early performance in the lab is generally an excellent predictor of final performance. These investigators understood that they were predicting the performance of individuals on a later task (e.g., on the job or later in training) based on performance in the training program. As a matter of fact, once these relationships have been established in an appropriately designed study, it is possible to select individuals for a job or for later training based on their training scores. As stated by these authors, "It is possible, therefore, to identify those trainees who will take longer than average to complete the plate welding course by simply examining their performance on the first few tasks" (p. 286). In other words, the training score serves as a validated predictor of future performance.

Studies such as Gordon and Cohen's have led some researchers to consider another use for the type of learning that occurs in training situations. Investigators (Robertson & Downs, 1979, 1989; Siegel, 1983) interested in predicting job performance have suggested that a person who is able to demonstrate proficiency in learning to perform on a job sample will also be able to learn and perform on the job itself, assuming appropriate training. Thus, the measure consists of a trainability test that is used to predict later performance. Note that the trainability test is not the entire training program, but rather a sample of the tasks that reflects some of the KSAs needed for job performance. This sample must naturally be based on a careful needs assessment, and the sample should not serve in lieu of a training program. Rather, the purpose is to use a learning measure based on performance on a relevant sample of tasks to predict later performance either in the full training program or actually on the job. In other words, the trainability test becomes a selection measure, and all the cautions involving the validation of selection measures apply.

Most of the trainability test work involves psychomotor performance. Robertson and Downs (1979) have reported on over 20 years of a variety of research using trainability tests to predict later performance. They found it possible to predict training success in a large number of jobs, including carpentry, welding, sewing, fork truck operating, dentistry, and bricklaying. They even found in some studies that persons who performed poorly on the training tests were less likely to turn up for training and more likely to leave in the first month, suggesting that the trainability test might have communicated some realistic expectations about what the training and job would be like. Robertson and Downs (1989) have also distinguished between normal work sample tests and trainability tests. The work sample is for trained people, while the trainability test is specifically for untrained people and incorporates a learning period. A meta-analysis conducted by these authors lends support for trainability tests as predictors of both training performance and later job performance, although the evidence supporting the former is considerably stronger. However, the number of studies where job performance is predicted is quite small, so more research is needed on this interesting technique.

An important note of caution should be considered when this technique is used to evaluate a training program. The relationship between training performance and on-the-job performance means that persons who perform best on the training test also perform well on the job. This does not necessarily mean that the training program is properly designed or that persons learned enough in training to perform well on the job. It is entirely possible that the training program did not teach anything or that the trainees did not learn anything. In other words, the training program might not have achieved anything except to maintain the individual differences between trainees that might have existed before they entered training. There are two solutions to this problem. First, the use of appropriate pretests and control groups would establish whether learning had occurred and whether it was likely to be a result of the training program. Even when the purpose is to use the training scores as a predictive device, experimental methodology evaluation is useful to ensure that the training program had actually accomplished its learning objectives. A second solution is to demonstrate that the training program and the criteria used to evaluate training are based on a thorough needs assessment so that the training program really does reflect the job's required KSAs. This procedure introduces another evaluation methodology, content validity.

Content Validity Models

If the needs assessment is appropriately carried out and the training program is designed to reflect the KSAs, then the program should be judged as having content validity. An interesting question is whether it is possible *after* the design of the training program to determine if it indeed does have content validity. Another question is whether it is possible to determine if a training program designed several years ago is content valid in the sense that it reflects the content established by a recently completed needs assessment.

Goldstein's (1986) conception of a training program's content validity is presented in Figure 9. The horizontal axis across the top of the figure represents the dimension of the importance or criticality of the KSAs as determined by the needs assessment. While the diagram only presents KSAs as being important or not important, note that this is an oversimplification of a dimension with many points. The vertical dimension represents the degree of emphasis on the KSAs in training, simplified to indicate that the KSA either is or is not emphasized in the training program. This results in a fourfold figure. Using this approach, both boxes A and D provide support for the content validity of the training program. KSAs that fall into Box D are judged as important for the job and emphasized in training; items in Box A are judged as not important for the job and not emphasized in training. Conceptually, to the degree to which KSAs fall into categories A and

D, it is possible to think about the training program as being content valid. Of course, this is an oversimplification; there will be KSAs that are judged as moderately important for the job and KSAs that are moderately emphasized in training. However, it is possible to conceive of this type of relationship and to actually measure the degree to which those KSAs judged as important are emphasized (and hopefully learned) in training.

Box B represents a potential error that could affect the degree to which a program is judged content valid: KSAs in this category are judged as important for the job but are not emphasized in training. From a systems perspective, these KSAs must be analyzed to determine whether the organization intends for them to be gained through training. If that is the case, then there is a problem; however, it is also possible that individuals are expected to be selected with that particular KSA or to learn it on the job. To that extent, the training program should not be expected to emphasize the item and its content validity would not be questioned. Nevertheless, it would still be important to determine that such KSAs are indeed covered in the ways expected. If not, then the organization must decide whether revision of the training program is necessary or whether some other system can cover that material.

Box C represents KSAs emphasized in training but judged as unimportant for the job. A common criticism of training programs is that they emphasize non–job-related material. Most analysts agree that when needs assessment procedures are used and training content is examined, the amount of training time necessary to complete the training program decreases. This usually is accomplished by eliminating items like those represented in Box C. Interestingly, a systems view of this process might even suggest a reduction of items represented in Box D. Selection experts like Bartlett (1982) might suggest that sometimes KSAs represented in Box D are unnecessary because they have already been used as a basis for

FIGURE 9

A Conceptual Diagram of Content Validity of Training Programs

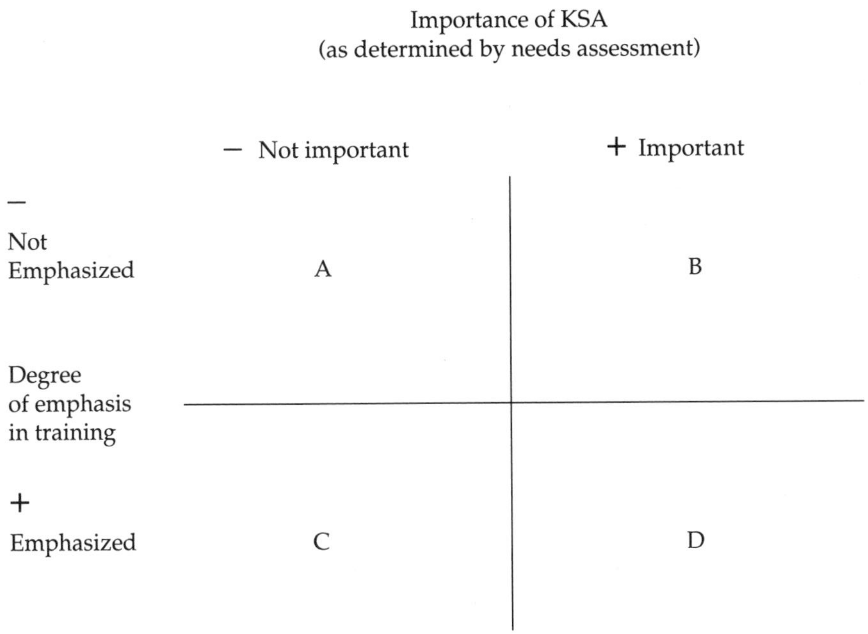

Importance of KSA
(as determined by needs assessment)

	− Not important	+ Important
− Not Emphasized	A	B
Degree of emphasis in training		
+ Emphasized	C	D

From *Training and Organizations: Needs Assessment, Development and Evaluation* by I. L. Goldstein, 1986, Monterey, CA: Brooks/Cole. Copyright 1986 by Brooks/Cole Publishing Company. Reprinted by permission.

selection. Thus, if such materials are included in the training program, trainees are again subjected to materials on KSAs that are already in their repertoire.

As noted in the introduction to this section, very few of the analyses in the research literature are based on this type of content validity strategy. Ford and Wroten (1984) did explore some of these strategies in an examination of police officer training programs. On the basis of needs assessment procedures, these investigators identified 383 KSAOs. (The "O" stands for other personal characteristics, such as attitudes.) Then they had 114 experts independently rate the importance of each item for job performance. They discovered that 237, or 62 percent, of the KSAOs met the criteria they

specified as important for job performance. In another analysis, they found 57 items that were rated as important for job performance but were not included in the training program. A few of those items were judged as KSAs that were trainable and important and thus were added to the program.

As part of our own research program attempting to develop content validity models to understand training, Newman (1985) researched the implications of the diagram in Figure 9. His study was conducted on the job of cook foreman for the Federal Bureau of Prisons. A needs assessment was conducted to determine the KSAs needed for the job. Since the training program already existed, a separate needs assessment was conducted to determine the KSAs taught in the training program. The training program is a two-week course covering the basics of institutional cooking and baking for cook foremen who supervise inmates in the preparation of meals in federal prisons. Trainees come from 45 institutions across the country. A KSA analysis was done for the training program as well as the job because this provided for the possibility that there would be KSAs emphasized in training that were not important on the job (Box C in Figure 9).

Both sets of KSAs were combined into an inventory. Then Newman had 87 SMEs rate the KSAs in terms of their importance on the job, difficulty of learning, and where best acquired. The same KSAs were also rated by two training SMEs—the training director and the course instructor—on importance on the job, difficulty in learning it, and time spent teaching the KSA.

As an indicator of content validity, Newman correlated the KSA job importance ratings and the training emphasis ratings (as reflected by time spent). For the cooking and baking KSAs, the correlation was .52. For a set of KSAs related to supervision and administration, the correlation was .55. These data provided some evidence that KSAs judged as higher in job importance were the KSAs most emphasized in training. Interestingly, the trainer SMEs and the job SMEs also agreed on what was important, with a correlation of .59 for cooking and baking KSAs and .76 for supervision and administration KSAs. Newman also collected other quantitative and qualitative data about the program. For example, he found improvement from pretraining to posttraining based on test scores and found that trainees as compared to a control group received higher performance ratings on training-relevant dimensions.

In a recently completed study, we (Goldstein, Schneider, Katzman, & Braverman, 1989) extended this methodology to investigate three different phases of a training program. The data indicated that the degree of content validity of the training program varied between the three phases. We determined the correlation between importance ratings for

KSAs from the job analysis and for ratings of degree of emphasis in training for a pretraining phase designed to prepare the job incumbents for a formal training program. The ratings for the job analysis came from managers who had participated in it, and the ratings for the training program came from trainees as they completed each phase of the training program. The pretraining program had a formal curriculum, and we found that the correlation between the job analysis importance ratings and degree of emphasis in pretraining was .41. For the actual on-site training program where instruction was given, the correlation went up to .61. For the posttraining program, however, which allowed individual managers across the country to institute what was learned in the formal training program on the job, the correlation was only .21. In addition, we were able to provide information concerning which important or unimportant KSAs were included or not in each of the three different phases of the training program. As a result of this study, it was possible to do an analysis of where KSAs should be learned and which KSAs fell into the four boxes diagramed in Figure 9.

Two other approaches that are variants of the previously described methods for examining content validity have been published. In one effort, Bownas, Bosshardt, and Donnelly (1985) developed an approach to test the degree of fit between training curriculum content and job task performance requirements. In another study, Faley and Sundstrom (1985) presented a procedure using the *Position Analysis Questionnaire* to compare a training program and its profile match with the job.

A final word of caution should be added to any conclusion about the use of content validity of training programs. Obviously, content validity is very important and all training programs should be content valid; it makes no sense to have training programs that do not cover the KSAs necessary for the job. However, using the concept of content validity as the only evaluation of a training program is problematic. The program may very well be content valid, but that does not guarantee that the trainees learned the material in the training program and that they were able to transfer that knowledge to the job. Some of the additional data that Newman collected about pre–post differences allow stronger inferences about training program effects than content validity information by itself could permit. Exploring this issue requires the use of principles of experimental and quasi-experimental design to ensure that learning occurred and that it transferred to the job.

For these reasons, some researchers (e.g. Guion, 1977) have argued that the term *content validity* not be used. They prefer that a term be used that indicates that the important domains are present in the instrument or program but that assumptions about validity are weak. This view makes sense, and the term *content relevance* might be more satisfactory. In any case, the important point is not the words used but an understanding of the strength of the inference concerning the validity of the training program that can be made based on the procedures used.

It is possible to consider training evaluation as a succession of steps that provide better and better quality information. Thus, as a next step following content validation, it is possible to add a pre- and posttest on relevant criteria. Then, it is possible to be more certain about training validity because there would be information that there were changes in trainee performance from before to after training. If in addition a control group were added, there would be more information ruling out other possible reasons for the changes from pre- to posttest. Establishing the validity of training programs involves building a network to give more and more information with better and better controls so that the evaluator has more faith in the information. In some cases, it may only be possible to start with an individual differences methodology as discussed earlier (see "Individual Differences and Trainability Models" in this chapter). On that basis, the

investigator will know whether persons who perform well on training test measures also perform well on the job. Then, it might be possible to obtain a pretest, then content validity, and so on. As I have previously stated (Goldstein, 1980):

> In order to gain an appreciation for the degree to which training programs achieve their objectives, it is necessary to consider the creative development of evaluation models. The models should permit the extraction of the greatest amount of information within the constraint of the environment.... Researchers cannot afford to be frozen into inactivity by the spectra of threats to validity. (p. 262)

From Needs Assessment to Training Validity— Concluding Words

Earlier I listed a number of complaints concerning training made by trainees, trainers, and organizations. In answering these complaints, the analyst must examine various components of the training systems approach, including needs assessment, criterion development, and evaluation models. One way to conceptualize responses to these complaints is to ask what the actual purpose of the instructional system is. Is there interest in having a program where trainees simply perform better at the end of the training program, or is there interest in trainees who both perform better at the end of the training program *and* perform better on the job? An additional goal might be knowledge about how another group of trainees (after the program has been developed and evaluated) performs, or in how the program would work in another organization with other trainees. To address these concerns, the analyst must consider what system training issues are involved. One might characterize instructional design as an attempt to achieve one of the following types of validity (Goldstein, 1978):

- *Training validity.* This refers only to the validity of the training program itself. Validity is determined by the performance of trainees on criteria established for the program.

- *Transfer validity.* This refers to the validity of the training program as measured by performance in the transfer or on-the-job setting. Ordinarily, training and transfer validity are both considered indicators of internal validity—that is, they indicate whether the treatment made a difference in a very specific situation. Here, performance validity is considered an external validity concept, because training programs are typically developed in a particular environment different from the organizational settings in which the trainee will eventually be expected to perform.

- *Intraorganizational validity.* This refers to the performance for a new group of trainees within the organization that developed the original training program. In this instance, the analyst is attempting to predict the performance of new trainees based on the evaluated performance of a previous group.

- *Interorganizational validity.* This refers to whether a training program validated in one organization can be used in another organization.

The first two stages, training validity and transfer validity, have been the major focus of the chapter thus far. Thus, training validity begins with needs assessment and continues with criterion development, evaluation, and feedback necessary to revise the program. Transfer validity requires attention to all aspects of training validity but also must consider the idea that the trainee must perform on the job. Considering the needs assessment and

evaluation procedures necessary to establish training validity, it would seem that there is little to add to a discussion of transfer validity. However, that is not true. In a sense, this is now a discussion of external validity operations that involve the transfer of performance in one environment (training) to another (on the job). As noted earlier, the tracing process from needs assessment to criterion development must now be concerned with relevant on-the-job criteria while avoiding deficiency and contamination. Transfer validity is further affected by the fact that the trainee will enter a new environment, one affected by all the interacting components that represent organizations today. Certainly some aspects of the environment that may determine the success or failure of training programs lie beyond the attributes the trainee must gain as a result of attending the program. For example, as described in the section of this chapter on organizational analysis, the training program and the organization often specify different performance objectives, and trainees are caught in a conflict that can sometimes result in failure. Both the trainee and the training program may be declared inadequate because the training analyst did not consider the relevant variables that determine success or failure at each of the four stages of validity. I have become convinced that many training programs are judged failures because of organizational systems constraints. Transfer validity thus requires the use of organizational analysis as a critical component of program development. Most of these concepts have been discussed in the preceding section of this chapter; however, the concepts of intraorganizational validity and interorganizational validity prompt several new considerations, which I will now discuss.

Intraorganizational Validity

Intraorganizational validity assumes that the trainer has established training and performance validity and is now concerned with the performance of a new group of trainees. Just as performance validity assumes the consideration of the points established for training validity, intraorganizational validity assumes that the points discussed for training and transfer validity have been established.

Earlier I discussed evaluation as an information-gathering process that provides feedback about the multiple objectives of most training programs. Evaluation should be a continual process that provides data as a basis for revisions of the program. New data should be collected based on the performance of a new group of trainees to provide further understanding about the achievement of objectives and the variables that affect such achievement. That does not mean that each effort must start anew from the very beginning, but it should be possible to collect further new information about the effects of revisions and to collect data that can be checked against previously collected information to make sure that the instructional program is having the same effect.

Given this philosophy, how dangerous is it to generalize results from the previous training program to a new group of trainees in the same organization? The answer to that question stems from consideration of many of the factors already discussed. First, consider the components of the needs assessment process, including tasks, person, and organizational aspects: If the job tasks and resulting KSAs have been revised, or if their frequency, importance, or degree of difficulty have changed, then the training program requires revisions. In these cases, generalizations based on the old program are speculative at best. Such task changes can occur for a variety of reasons, including technological developments or revisions in jobs at other levels in the organization. Similarly, if the kinds of persons entering the organization are different, then it is difficult to generalize from the old program. Reasons for these changes may vary—for example, an organization's move to an urban from a suburban environment or market and career shifts that change the KSAs of individuals desiring certain jobs. Also, of course, modifications in the organization or constraints that affect it also affect the degree to which generalizations are safe. While time itself would not ordinarily be considered a variable, changes eventually occur in all organizations, making long-term generalization of training results to new populations suspect. A good procedure might be to recheck the needs assessment for applicability before attempting to generalize to new trainee populations. If needs assessment procedures were not carried out, the original program is questionable and generalizations are treacherous.

A second factor to consider before generalizing is how well the evaluation was performed in the first place. If the only data on which generalizations will be based are the reactions of the trainees to the instructional program, then the original evaluation is suspect and so are any future generalizations. Similarly, properly evaluated instructional programs will provide a variety of information about the achievement of multiple goals. It is necessary to assess what has been achieved and what remains questionable before deciding whether to generalize to new trainees.

A third factor to consider is whether the training program will be the same. This idea sounds misleadingly simple. Most everyone would agree that it is dangerous to generalize to new trainee populations when they are not being instructed in the same training program. Yet most training analysts fail to realize how different established training programs tend to be from the original program from which evaluation data were collected. Some of these difficulties can generally be labeled problems of reactivity: Observers, experimental equipment, and questions asked often result in changes in behavior that are not a result of the actual training program. To the extent that these variables are a source of the training results, and to the extent that they are not present the next time training is offered, it is difficult to generalize. There is a certain aura of excitement surrounding new instructional treatments or training programs that may simply disappear over time. Researchers (R. Rosenthal, 1966) have described how the expectations of the experimenters, trainers, or teachers themselves can affect an individual's performance. To the extent that these factors change over time, the training program has changed, and it is difficult to generalize. Also, programs tend to change over time as trainers and managers add to and delete from the originally designed program. Sometimes changes in carefully designed programs radically alter the training system. One of the most compelling reasons for the use of process criteria is in an attempt to specify these variables and their effect. When process criteria indicate that the training programs have not changed, then it is obviously safer to generalize.

From a consideration of the needs assessment component, the quality of the evaluation, and the similarity of the training program, the decision about whether to generalize becomes easier. The greater the confidence in the training and transfer validity, the easier it is to generalize. Even so, my personal choice will always be to collect evaluative information to ensure that the program continues to work.

Interorganizational Validity

In this instance, the analyst attempts to determine whether a training program validated in one organization can be implemented in another organization. All the factors discussed in connection with training validity, performance validity, and intraorganizational validity affect this decision. As indicated in the section on intraorganizational validity, when the needs assessment shows differences (e.g., in the task, person, or organizational components), or the evaluation is questionable, or the training program will differ, then generalization is dangerous. In interorganizational validity, however, the needs assessment and evaluation have not

been performed for the organization that desires to use the training program. Clearly, the more similar the organizations as shown by a needs assessment, the more likely similar results will occur, and in that sense, the easier it is to borrow meta-analysis results indicating the potency of a particular training method. Still, considering the number of ways organizations differ, it remains dangerous to generalize the training results from one organization to another. Yet it is entirely appropriate to borrow needs assessment methodologies, evaluation strategies, and training techniques. Through these procedures, organizations can establish techniques that work, and perhaps it will be possible to begin to understand what variables affect the success of programs across organizations. However, given the present state of knowledge, simply borrowing results from another organization as a shortcut in the training process is asking for trouble.

A Limited Sample of Training Techniques

An effort to cover all of the training techniques used in organizations would fill several chapters in this volume. Thus, some techniques are included because they were developed recently and seem to have drawn the attention of both researchers and implementers in organizations. They are behavioral role modeling, Leader Match, rater training, and simulations. In addition, self-management training is likely to receive attention in the future, so as a gamble, I've included that technique in this discussion.

Most of these techniques are focused on managers and interpersonal skill training, but that does not mean that they could not be used for other populations. Behavioral role modelling is potentially useful for many types of personal interactions, ranging from teaching a store clerk how to respond to customer complaints to teaching a member of the hard-core unemployed how to respond in a job interview. Unfortunately, research on uses outside of direct management training is rather limited.

A few other techniques that don't seem particularly focused on management training, such as machine simulations and computer-assisted instruction, are also included in this section. Readers interested in the many other techniques being used are advised to consult texts such as those written by me (Goldstein, 1986) and by Wexley and Latham (1981). This discussion will begin with to pics focusing on management training and development.

Management Training and Development

Management training and development programs have become a fact of life for most organizations. The purpose of these programs is to teach and develop managerial skills that will increase managerial effectiveness. Perhaps one of the most severe problems in management development programs, one not often explicitly addressed in the training literature, is conceptual in nature. Within the field of management, there appears to be little agreement about the nature of the construct itself, much less a consensus about which skills are necessary or relevant. This lack of consensus makes the task of developing effective training programs problematic and that of creating programs that would be generalizable across organizations even more difficult.

Techniques associated with management training and development include achievement motivation training, behavioral role modeling, business games, case studies, encounter groups, problem-solving/decision-making training, and self-awareness programs (Burke & Day, 1986). Wexley (1984) reached the conclusion that most of the literature was neither empirical nor theoretical, but rather was prone to anecdotal reports—any review of the literature would be hard-pressed to reach any other conclusion.

However, studies have been conducted on a number of these techniques, such as achievement motivation, behavioral role modeling, Fiedler's Leader Match, and rater training. A meta-analysis of some of these techniques has been conducted by Burke and Day (1986). These researchers examined 70 managerial training studies, both published and unpublished, including six training content areas, seven training methods, and four types of criteria (subjective learning, objective learning, subjective behavior, and objective results). In general, management training, as measured by objective criteria, was found to be effective in improving performance; however, in many instances the meta-analysis was based on a small number of studies and the authors warn the readers that more research is necessary to reach firmer conclusions. They note also that the number of studies using objective results criteria are few, thus further limiting interpretations. Finally, they indicate that a more thorough reporting of methodology and analysis is crucial when describing evaluations of training techniques in order to facilitate further efforts at comparison. While Burke and Day's analyses include research conducted over a period of years, an examination of the most recent literature indicates other interesting trends. The following section describes some of these developments.

Behavioral Role Modeling and Other Behavioral Interventions

Latham (1989) recently analyzed the positive contributions of behavioral approaches to the training literature. In his review, he notes that the roots of these programs stem from both a behavioral tradition and a strong theoretical tie to social learning theory. He notes also that the methodology employed has been made explicit as a result of its reliance on operant techniques and that its application has been subjected to systematic and carefully controlled research and evaluation. The reliance on theoretical insight and the focus on careful evaluation has resulted in some important developments.

In the past decade, the approach that has generated the most excitement is *behavioral role modeling*. This approach is based on Bandura's (1969, 1977) social learning theory, which stresses the use of observation, modeling, and vicarious reinforcement as steps for modifying human behavior. Bandura's theory focuses on the acquisition of novel responses through observational learning. He notes that evidence for this form of imitative learning consists of persons exhibiting novel responses which have been demonstrated by observers and which are not likely to have occurred without such a demonstration. Also, the responses of the observers should be highly similar in form to the response of the model. Bandura obtained these effects in a number of studies, many of which focused on children demonstrating highly novel responses.

In 1974, A. P. Goldstein and Sorcher published a book called *Changing Supervisory Behavior*, which adapted many of the principles of Bandura's social learning theory into a training approach, the goal being to improve interpersonal and related supervisory skills. These authors criticized other approaches to training managers as focusing on attitudes rather than the behaviors necessary to carry out the work. Thus, they argue, training programs typically tell managers that it is important to be good communicators—with which few would disagree, and which most managers already know before training—yet the programs do not teach managers what to do in order to be good communicators or motivators. Also, as pointed out by Moses (1978), most training programs don't appear to have any usefulness for later job performance, and the adult learner tends to be put off by the artificial atmosphere. In contrast, A. P. Goldstein and Sorcher's (1974) approach consists of

> providing the trainee with numerous vivid, detailed displays (on film, video-tape or live) of a manager-actor (the

model) performing the specific behaviors and skills we wish the viewer to learn (i.e., modeling); giving the trainee considerable guidance in and opportunity and encouragement for behavioral rehearsing or practicing the behaviors he has seen the model perform (i.e., role playing); providing him with positive feedback, approval or reward as his role playing enactments increasingly approximate the behavior of the model (i.e., social reinforcement). (p. 37)

The use of behavioral role modeling in indutrial and organizational settings was pioneered by Sorcher (1971) in a study at General Electric, and a number of pilot studies were reported in the 1970s (e.g., Burnaska, 1976). These studies were preliminary, with little confirmed information available about effective changes in the work setting. After several years passed without further studies being reported, McGehee and Tullar (1978) published an article commending the original researchers but noting the lack of further work. They cautioned against taking the reported results as ironclad evidence of the effectiveness of behavioral modeling.

Interestingly, at the time of the McGehee and Tullar critique, a major study by Latham and Saari (1979) was being completed, and since their study a number of carefully carried out empirical research efforts have been reported. The Latham and Saari study set an excellent standard for the conduct of training research. They randomly selected 40 supervisors from a total group of 100, and then randomly assigned 20 of them to a training condition and the other 20 to a control group. The control group was informed that they would be trained at a later date, but in the interim served as a control condition for the study. Each of the group's training sessions followed the same procedure:

> (a) Introduction of the topic by two trainers (attentional processes); (b)

presentation of a film that depicts a supervisor model effectively handling a situation by following a set of 3 to 6 learning points that were shown in the film immediately before and after the model was presented (retention processes); (c) group discussion of the effectiveness of the model in demonstrating the desired behaviors (retention processes); (d) practice in role playing the desired behaviors in front of the entire class (retention processes; motor reproduction processes); and (e) feedback from the class on the effectiveness of each trainee in demonstrating the desired behaviors (motivational processes). (p. 241)

During the practice sessions involving role-playing, one of the trainees took the role of the supervisor and another trainee the role of the employee. The trainees did not use prepared scripts. Rather, they were asked to recreate an incident that occurred during the past year that was relevant to the training topic for that week. During the session, the learning points emphasized in the film were posted so that the person role-playing the supervisor could make use of the principles.

At the end of each session, the trainees received printed versions of the learning points and were sent back to their jobs with instructions to use the supervisory skills they had gained. The purpose here was to facilitate transfer of the learned skills back to the job. At the next session, the trainees reported their experiences. In situations where the supervisors had difficulty, they were asked to report it back to the class. Then they role-played the situation, with the class providing feedback on the desired behaviors and the supervisor again practicing the appropriate behaviors. Latham and Saari also noted that some of the learning points for some of the programs did not fit their specific situation, so the points were revised by the

trainees and the investigators. Latham and Saari also provided training for the supervisors of the trainees to ensure that the trainees would be rewarded for their on-the-job behavior.

In addition to carefully designing a training program, Latham and Saari also evaluated the results using reaction measures, learning measures, behavioral measures, and job performance measures and found strong evidence supporting the training program. For example, they used job performance indicators that consisted of ratings made by the supervisors of the trainees on rating scales based on a job analysis that produced critical incidents depicting effective and ineffective supervisory behavior. The investigators found no difference between pretest measures of the training and control groups. Posttest measures indicated that the training group performed significantly better than the control group.

As a final step, Latham and Saari trained the control group. After training was complete, the differences between the now-trained control group and the original training group on all four measures disappeared. This kind of careful implementation and evaluation in a real work environment should serve as a model for what can be accomplished with thoughtful effort.

There have been a number of studies (e.g., Meyer & Raich, 1983) that have produced similar positive results. However, the dangers of simply assuming a technique will work and skipping the evaluation step is made obvious in a study by Russell, Wexley, and Hunter (1984), which produced less favorable results. The results of this study indicate that although the modeling elicited favorable reactions and showed an increase in learning, it did not appear to produce changes on the job or improved performance results. The authors suggested that the posttraining environment did not permit adequate reinforcement of the learned behaviors.

In addition to the evaluation research, some recent research on behavioral role modeling has explored questions as to what components of the program make it effective. A series of studies by Decker (1980, 1982, 1983, 1984) is particularly noteworthy because of his efforts to explore various means of enhancing the behavioral rehearsal and social reinforcement components of behavioral modeling training. For example, Decker (1983) explored two issues affecting learning in a typical role modeling workshop. His results indicate that small groups of observers (one or two) should be present during a behavioral rehearsal and that videotaped feedback presented with the trainer's critique is more effective than the trainer's critique without videotape. Other studies have focused on issues of symbolic coding. A field study by Hogan, Hakel, and Decker (1986) compared trainee-generated coding to trainer-provided coding for generalization purposes. The underlying rationale was that allowing individuals to generate their own codes would facilitate the integration of the information in each one's cognitive framework. Trainee-generated codes were found to result in significantly superior performance, although it is not clear that all trainees are capable of producing their own codes.

All these lines of research should be applauded. It is uncommon enough to have solid evaluation research; to also have research that seeks to understand why techniques work is delightful. It should be noted that behavior-based models have produced other important lines of research. For example, the research by Komaki, Heinzmann, and Lawson (1980) discussed in the evaluation section of this chapter offers an important example of the use of feedback as a training procedure.

The most recent example of behavior-based training models comes from Latham and his colleagues (Frayne & Latham, 1987; Latham & Frayne, 1989) and relates to self-management skills. In one study (Frayne & Latham, 1987),

training in self-management was given to unionized government employees, with the goal of increasing their attendance at work. The training in self-regulatory skills was based on F. H. Kanfer and Gaelick's (1986) work on self-management that teaches individuals to assess their problems, set goals, monitor their behaviors, and identify and administer reinforcers for working toward goal attainment. The researchers administered the program to employees who had used more than 50 percent of their sick leave. Within the Kanfer framework, employees were taught how to manage personal and social obstacles to job attendance. Employing experimental and control groups, the data indicated that the trained groups did learn the self-management skills, resulting in raising their perception that they could influence their own behavior. As a result, employee attendance was significantly higher in the training group; the higher the perceived self-efficacy, the better the attendance performance.

In their next study, Latham and Frayne (1989) conducted a follow-up at the six-month and nine-month marks. Their data revealed that the enhanced self-efficacy and improved job attendance was maintained and that the degree of self-efficacy still predicted the degree of subsequent job attendance. Also, in this study, the control group from the previous study was given the same self-management training by a different trainer. Three months following their training, this group showed the same positive improvement as the original group concerning both their increased self-efficacy and increased job attendance. These studies provide another important example of the combination of thoughtful theory-driven training development followed by empirical research.

Leader Match Training

Leader Match training is based on a contingency model of leadership developed by Fiedler and his associates (Fiedler, 1964, 1967; Fiedler

& Chemers, 1984; Fiedler & Mahar, 1979). The theory states that effective leadership depends on a proper match between the leader's style and situational characteristics—that is, in certain situations, one style of leadership might be most effective while other situations might require other styles. Fiedler defined the leadership situation according to three major dimensions:

- *Leader-member relations.* This dimension refers to whether group members like, trust, or are loyal to the leader. Leader-member relations measures the manager's perceptions of the amount of loyalty and support the leader expects to receive from the groups.

- *Task structure.* This dimension measures how clearly items such as goals, procedures, and task requirements are specified for the manager.

- *Position power.* This refers to how much authority the manager perceives the organization has given him or her in terms of control for dispensing rewards and punishment.

Fiedler dichotomized each of these dimensions so that leader-member relations could be considered good or bad, task structure high or low, and position power strong or weak. To the extent that a leader has good member relations, high task structure, and high position power, the situation is considered highly favorable. If there are poor leader-member relations, the task is unstructured, and if there is limited control or authority, the situation is considered unfavorable.

The second aspect of the match between a leader's style and the situational characteristics refers to the leader characteristics. This is measured on a scale known as the Least Preferred Co-worker (LPC) scale, an index requiring a leader to rate the very worst person he or she has ever worked with on a number of traits. The traits include dimensions on a scale such as

pleasant versus unpleasant, sincere versus insincere, nice versus nasty, and cheerful versus gloomy. In Fiedler's terms, if you are a high-LPC leader, you would have values toward the positive end of the scale and would describe your least preferred co-worker in terms such as sincere, nice, and cheerful. On the other hand, the low-LPC leader would have negative scale values and would describe the least preferred co-worker in terms such as insincere, uncooperative, or nasty.

On the basis of his research, Fiedler maintains that low-LPC leaders, who are characterized as having a nonparticipative, direct, structured style, perform well in situations that are either highly favorable or highly unfavorable. High-LPC leaders, who are characterized as participative, democratic, and relationship-oriented, tend to perform well in situations of moderate control.

Since there are two aspects of the match, the leader's style and the situational characteristics, any attempt at change related to this model would have the option of either changing the leader's personality to better match the situation or changing the situation to better match the leader's style. Fiedler and his associates maintain that changing the leader's basic style is very difficult and demanding. Essentially, he argues that organizational engineering that changes the nature of the situation to better match the style of the particular leader is a more fruitful approach. Thus, he has designed a training program showing the prospective leader how to increase or decrease the closeness of his or her interpersonal relations with subordinates, how to structure tasks, and how to change the various aspects of position power. This approach forms the foundation for Fiedler's training program known as *Leader Match* (Fiedler, Chemers, & Mahar, 1976).

The training program itself consists of a self-administered programmed workbook that trainees can complete on their own and that can be augmented by lectures, discussions, or films. The program takes anywhere from 4 to 12 hours and is best completed over several days to obtain maximum benefit. The first part of the program is designed to enable trainees to identify their own leadership style by completing the LPC scale and interpreting their own scores. The second part of the program asks participants to determine their own situational aspects by filling out scales and measuring their perceptions of leader-member relations, task structure, and position power. Participants are given information on how to change or modify situational factors in order to match the situation to their leadership styles. For example, depending on the situation most desirable for the style, changes could consist of requests for more routine assignments or less structured assignments, or could consist of the leader developing either more or less formal relationships.

Each chapter of the program's workbook consists of a short presentation that explains the basic aspects of the contingency model and how it can be applied. This material is followed by several short problems consisting of leadership episodes. These are known as *probes*, and the trainees are asked to select the best answer for each probe. Then they are given feedback on the correct response. If the participant makes an incorrect response, he or she is required to review the material to make sure that the chapter is understood. Each chapter closes with a summary. Throughout the program, there are several short tests and a final exam.

In evaluating the training program, it is possible to make the following points:

- Fiedler and his associates have conducted more extensive research and more evaluation studies than almost anyone else. Also, the studies tend toward collecting multiple criteria from different sources; some of the studies have designs that include pre- and posttest measurement as well as control groups. Indeed, Fiedler correctly notes that many of his studies have employed rigorous procedures, including random assignment of participants to training and control groups, that are not typical in complex environments. These studies were included in Burke and Day's (1986) meta-analysis, which supported management training.

- The results of the studies present a somewhat mixed picture. For example, Fiedler and Mahar (1979) reviewed 12 validation studies they had conducted. Five of the studies examined participants in civilian occupations such as police sergeants, managers in county government, public service workers, and public health workers. In 3 of the studies, serious attrition problems made the results difficult to interpret; in the police study, for example, only 7 of the 15 sergeants completed the training book. In most of the studies, rating scores were in the predicted direction but were often not statistically significant. Thus, in the study of middle managers in county government, two superiors rated each manager on the organization's 16-item rating scale three months after training. Eleven of the 16 items were in the predicted direction, but only two of the scales (cost consciousness and dependability-reliability) were statistically significant. In the study on public works supervisors, 14 of 16 were in the predicted direction, but only two were significant (makes decisions within the scope of the job and oral communication). The other studies were conducted in miliary settings involving either active-duty personnel, military college students, or ROTC students. There were fewer problems with the conduct of these studies, and the data were more consistent in supporting training program effects.

- While Fiedler and Mahar strongly believe that these data support the viability of their training program, they do share concerns about threats to viability that might lead some readers to be less certain. The first serious issue is the problem of attrition. Of course, one concern about attrition is that it is not random, so it is possible that those persons who did not feel they were getting much from training dropped out. Not only subjects, but data sometimes also disappeared: In one study of volunteer public health personnel in South and Central American villages, only 11 of 25 persons completed the program, and some performance evaluations were lost in transit from Central America. Another issue of concern is rater bias; that is, raters tended to know who did and did not participate in training, and that could have affected their ratings. Fiedler and Mahar argue that they tried to check that point in some of their studies. In one study involving 6-month follow-ups, supervisors could not remember who did or did not complete training. Since training in these studies often consisted of reading the programmed manual on site, it is entirely possible that they in fact could not have remembered who participated this way.

Another very interesting question is, What is the source of the effect—is it Leader Match that made the difference, or would any special treatment produce similar effects? Fiedler did an analysis that indicated that those who showed on a test that they knew more about the program tended to perform better. Cadets who reported that they applied the principles more often also had higher performance ratings. However, Fiedler also reported that 36 cadets stated they did not use the program on any occasion—and this group also performed significantly better than the control group.

It is hard to reach a final conclusion regarding this training program, although the degree of effort must certainly be applauded. The difficulties of the environment also must be recognized: No investigator wants data to disappear or subjects who drop out. Some data do support the efficacy of the training. Given the threats to validity, however, such data must be treated with caution. Certainly more research carefully specifying exactly how a leader changed the environment to match his or her leadership style would be extremely helpful. Specific hypotheses concerning these situational changes and how leadership effectiveness is changed are important. Otherwise, questions remain as to what is happening in training to produce these effects.

Rater Training

Rater training refers to the instructional programs designed to teach managers how to appraise employees' performance. Such training programs are intertwined with the research on the development of appropriate performance appraisal instruments. Research in this area of training, and to some extent in the development of appraisal instruments, is marked by considerable controversy. In part, these controversies reflect a growing frustration among industrial and organizational psychologists that they have been unable to design research to capture the flavor of the dynamic interactions involved in performance appraisal situations.

Most early studies focused on how to reduce errors made by managers in the rating process. Some errors that research found were:

- *Halo error,* or a tendency to rate a person high or low on all dimensions because of a global impression. A rater's impression that an employee is an effective performer may cause the individual to be rated highly on all performance dimensions regardless of actual performance. Similarly, a person considered an ineffective performer might be rated low on all of these dimensions, even when he or she performs some aspects of the job well.

- *Leniency error,* or a tendency to give all ratees higher ratings than warranted. The opposite dimension is a *severity error,* or a tendency to give lower ratings than warranted.

- *Central tendency,* or a tendency to give all ratees scores in the middle of the scale and to avoid extreme ratings. This can occur across dimensions for the single individual, across individuals for all dimensions, or both.

- *Contrast effects,* or a tendency to let the rating of an extremely effective or ineffective individual influence the rating of the next individual to be rated.

An illustration of the type of training program developed to reduce rater error is provided by the work of Latham, Wexley, and Pursell (1975). These authors noted that earlier work indicated that lectures on the problems of rating errors did not seem to have much effect on reducing the problem. They concluded that an intensive workshop that would give subjects a chance to practice observing and rating actual videotaped candidates along with immediate feedback regarding the accuracy of the ratings might be more effective. In order to study this problem, the authors randomly assigned sixty managers in a large corporation to one of three conditions: a workshop, a group discussion, or a control group that did not receive any training. The workshop group viewed videotapes of hypothetical job candidates being appraised by a manager. The trainees then gave a rating indicating how they thought the manager would have rated the candidate and how they themselves would have rated the candidate. Group discussion concerning the ratings followed. As the authors noted, this gave the trainees the opportunity to observe videotaped managers making observational errors, find out how frequently they themselves made such errors, receive feedback on their own behavioral observations, and practice ways to reduce their own errors. The workshop group worked on a variety of rater errors, including contrast effects, halo error, and other errors such as first impressions where judgments are made based on initial observations rather than the behavior that follows.

In the group discussion format, trainers first defined various types of errors and presented examples of each. Then trainees generated personal examples involving each kind of error. They also divided into subgroups so they could share examples, discuss them, and generate solutions to each of the rating problems. The control group did not have any form of training.

Testing of the effects of the various forms of training was conducted six months later by giving members of the workshop group, the discussion group, and the control group videotapes to observe. They also were given detailed job descriptions and lists of requirements for the job, then were asked to rate the individuals in the videotape in terms of the degree of job acceptability based on the job descriptions and requirements provided. The results showed that the workshop group was no longer prone to any of the types of rater error examined in the study. The group discussion trainees also performed well, exhibiting only a tendency toward last-impression error, or error that results from evaluating someone on previous behaviors based on the impression of that person. The control group made a number of errors, including halo errors and contrast effects. The authors also collected data related to trainees' reactions to the training and found that trainees reacted more favorably toward the workshop program than toward the group discussion. Trainees reported that the structured workshop format including the videotapes made them feel their time away from the job was being used wisely. The only disadvantage the authors noted for the workshop procedure was that it is costly and time consuming to develop. They indicated that where cost is an important factor, the discussion group technique could be used because it also worked quite well.

Interestingly, even though the study by Latham, Wexley, and Pursell (1975) was well done, controversy still surrounds the rater training literature. Researchers cannot even agree on the criterion measure that should be used to judge the effectiveness of training programs. An excellent review of this problem is provided by Zedeck and Cascio (1984), who note that "we have developed procedures and conducted comparative studies of appraisal methods using indices as criteria that are unclear, ambiguous, and in part, wrong" (p. 471). Some of these comments are related to the idea of having true scores, where *truth* is defined on the basis of using expert raters who typically constitute a sample from the population eventually asked to complete the rating. Zedeck and Cascio question how viewers of such tapes can be experts when they typically have not ever performed the job in question. After reviewing 34 rater training studies, Bernardin and Villanova (1986) make the same points concerning true scores and then wonder why research has focused almost exclusively on psychometric characteristics such as halo, leniency, and accuracy, while ignoring the idea that the true goal is accuracy in observing. Bernardin and Beatty (1984) further argue that training programs that focus on minimizing rating errors such as halo or leniency simply exchange one response set for another and thus may substitute one set of errors for another without improving the accuracy of observations. The significance of this problem is made clear by Borman's (1979) research. He found that a rater training program did reduce halo somewhat but did not improve accuracy.

Another serious problem noted by a number of authors (e.g., Bernardin & Villanova, 1986; Goldstein & Musicante, 1986) is that the vast majority of rater training studies involve student raters in an experimental context, often rating paper people. As noted by Goldstein and Musicante, even the few field studies often involve managers rating hypothetical persons. Also, very few studies examine the effects of rater training over any reasonable time period in order to determine whether training has any lasting effects. All of these issues make generalizing to real work situations tenuous at best. The dangers here are amply noted by Murphy, Herr, Lockhart, and Maguire (1986), who evaluated research involving the performance of paper people and found that results for such studies led to systematically different outcomes from studies in which ratings were based on direct or indirect (e.g., videotape) observations of behavior. Basically, the point is that we have failed to understand the dynamics of organizations and thus our research seems unable to focus on the issues that make a difference. This point is made particularly well by Ilgen and Favaro (1985), who note, for example, that rater behavior is likely to be influenced by the fact that in an organization the appraisal of the ratee will affect his or her future. As nearly as we are able to determine, no training efforts have even begun to explore these types of intervention issues. It seems sad that considerable training research is being conducted while the relevance of the effort is questionable.

Machine Simulators

Training simulators are designed to replicate the essential characteristics of the real world necessary to produce learning and transfer. These efforts can vary from flight simulators, which have a substantial degree of *physical fidelity*—that is, accurate representation of the real world of operational equipment—

to methods such as behavioral role modeling, in which the degree of physical simulation is minimal. In any case, the purpose of the simulation is to produce *psychological fidelity*—that is, to reproduce in the training tasks those KSAs necessary to perform the job. This last point is sometimes lost in the development of management simulations, resulting in poor training efforts. Obviously, recent techniques such as behavioral role modeling have been very concerned with psychological fidelity and have benefited from that consideration. Rater training may benefit from similar emphases. However, in this discussion, the emphasis is on machine simulations that often focus on skills such as flying an airplane or even performing medical surgery.

One important aspect of these simulators is that they permit the environment to be reproduced under the control of the training analyst. By careful design and planning, environments are created that supply variation in the essential characteristics of the real situation. In addition, simulation permits the trainer to expand, compress, or repeat time, depending on the needs of the trainees.

Often the required final behavior is too complex to be safely handled by a trainee in a real-life situation. The simulator permits the learner to be slowly introduced to the essential task characteristics without danger to the learner, his or her co-workers, or expensive equipment. Simulations also permit the trainee to practice emergency techniques before being exposed to hazardous situations in real settings. The focus of safety should not be narrowed to skills development; consider, for example, the psychological safety in training of a manager required to face racial strife on the job. Role-playing several solutions to such situations in the comparative safety of a training environment could have some benefits.

Another issue is cost. While most simulation efforts are expensive, they are often an economical alternative to using high-priced on-the-job equipment. Quite probably, the be-havior of a beginning trainee handling a multimillion-dollar jet airplane might quickly convince passengers to make donations to simulation training programs.

All of these reasons for simulation have prompted the development of skill simulators. These simulators are used when the required skills are quite explicit and the behavior can be objectively measured. Frequently these simulations have extensive physical fidelity and can represent a large num ber of potential environmental situations. Flight simulators are so complex that nearly all flight training can be accomplished on them. For example, the Navy's primary jet trainer, simulated for research purposes at the Naval Training Equipment Center in Orlando, Florida, reproduces all normal carrier operations, including provisions for ship pitch, roll, and heave, as well as variations in sea conditions, wind conditions, and turbulence. I have used the simulator and can attest to the complexities of landing a plane on an aircraft carrier: In numerous tries I never even hit the carrier, but rather managed to continually land in the ocean.

The design of machine simulators need not be limited to expensive large-scale operations. Many efforts are part-simulations, which replicate a critical or difficult portion of the task without attempting to provide a complete environment. A good example of the use of simulation is provided in a study by Salvendy and Pilitsis (1980), which investigated its use in teaching medical students suturing techniques needed in surgical operations. The traditional method consisted of a lecture-slide and videotape describing the technique. Included in the instructions were materials related to the general geometry of the suture path, descriptions of the instruments and their functions, and general guidelines on what to do. The student then practiced on pigs' feet until the instructor decided that the student was performing the task appropriately. One of the simulators used as an alternative to this procedure is known as the "inwound" procedure simulator. A description of this device and its characteristics follows:

> The "inwound" procedure simulator... assists the student in acquiring the manipulative motor skills during the inwound procedure phase by puncturing a simulated tissue with an electrically activated needle holder.... The simulated tissue contains related wound path geometry such as "entry"and "exit" points. The overall unit is mounted on a revolving fixture located in a manequin-type arm. The student is able to monitor his/her progress by gaining information as to correctness of motions through the student feedback console. This console consists of 11 clearly marked amber and red lights that correpond to correct and incorrect motions. Both audio and visual channels are activated by the suture needle as the needle is guided by the student through the "wound." If the various phases (entry, depth, exit) are performed correctly, the amber lights are activated.... An incorrect needle motion while the needle is in the wound causes a corresponding red light and tone generator to be activated momentarily. When the needle is corrected in its path, the related visual and auditory feedback is discontinued. Number of errors, time in the wound, and number of cycles performed for each of the procedure phases are recorded individually on the monitoring console. (p. 155–156)

These investigators also designed a knot-tying simulator for surgery. In addition to the simulators, another training condition in this study consisted of a perceptual training method where students observed filmed performance of both experienced surgeons and inexperienced medical students.

Generally, the investigators found that simulation training and perceptual training improved the performance of the medical students beyond the traditional training methods. In addition, the investigators collected psycho-physiological measures of stress such as heart rate variance and muscle tension. These data tended to confirm that students trained by simulation showed less stress when they were required to perform new suturing tasks.

Another interesting and more amusing study of part-simulators is a laboratory study designed by Rubinsky and Smith (1973). They examined simulated accident occurrence in the use of a grinding wheel. Traditionally, teaching the operation of power tools relies on written or verbal instructions, with an occasional demonstration. These authors devised a task that exposed operators (college students) to a simulated accident (a jet of water). The "accident" was designed to occur when the operator stood in front of the grinding wheel during the starting operation—that is, the time when there is the greatest danger of the wheel exploding. The investigators found that those subjects who experienced a simulated accident as part of their training program were less likely to repeat the hazardous behavior than those who were given written instructions or demonstrations of safe procedures. The results were maintained over a series of retention tests. The authors suggest that simulated accidents might be effective in reducing power tool accidents. Certainly this procedure provides an interesting form of feedback for incorrect responses.

Other Types of Simulations

In addition to machine simulations, there are similar efforts involving the teaching of inter-personal skills. As noted earlier, behavioral role modeling is also a simulation, and clearly one goal of researchers studying such techniques is to produce as much psychological fidelity as possible. The use of complex simulations involving role playing and assessment elements appears to have become more widespread in industry although there are no actual statistics concerning their use. One of the more interesting efforts is a simulation exercise known as Looking Glass, Inc. (McCall & Lombardo, 1982) whose purpose is to develop both a management team and the individuals on it. In this six-hour program, participants are assigned management roles in a fictitious glass manufacturing company. On the basis of the information they receive in an in-basket, they are asked to interact with each other as if in a typical working day. Their behavior and interactions in the recognition and solution of complex problems involving the daily running of this organization are carefully assessed. The participants then receive intensive feedback for their performances both as a team and as individuals. Research has been conducted to demonstrate the content validity of this simulation (McCall & Lombardo, 1979). In another study, Kaplan, Lombardo, and Mazique (1983) describe the use of this program with a 17-member management team from a public service agency. Several follow-up studies were conducted examining both qualitative interview data and survey questionnaires of the managers. The originally positive results showed some decay over time, but were still reasonably stable given various shifts in the organization. Their evaluation supports the use of Looking Glass, Inc., as a valuable learning device for organizational interaction process, although more evaluations should be encouraged.

Computer-assisted Instruction

One of the more recent innovations in instructional technology is computer-assisted instruction (CAI). With the advent of microcomputers, there is clearly a revolution in progress, exemplified by the number of primary schools teaching computer programming as well as by the move toward office automation systems. Computer-assisted instruction is growing with this revolution. It is not unusual to use CAI to educate students on the use of the computer and employees on the use of office automation systems. In CAI systems, the student interacts directly with the computer, which has stored information and instructional materials necessary for the program. The degree of computer interaction with the student varies with the system.

The excitement about CAI is based on the storage and memory capabilities of the computer, which in turn provide the potential for true interaction with the student. The proponents of this system believe that it provides the ultimate in branching programs. The computer records the individual's previous response, analyzes its characteristics, and determines the next presentation on the basis of the student's needs. The most creative work involving CAI involves tutorial systems, which may be complete course sequences or special supplementary units. These programs have the capability for real-time decisions, with branching contingent on the student's previous responses or set of responses. The numerous branching patterns often result in students' following diverse paths.

The most creative work involving CAI stems from researchers investigating the possibilities of tutorial instruction. Collins (1977) has been exploring the Socratic method of teaching as a way to understand the dialogue between teachers and students in learning situations. Collins and his colleagues have analyzed dialogues between tutors teaching different subjects, such as medicine and geography. The strategies involve determining the types of mistake made by a student and confronting him or her with examples that show the error. In this system, the student is required to derive general principles from specific cases, then learn to use these principles to make predictions about new cases.

The flexibility of such programs was demonstrated by the work of Collins, Adams, and Pew (1978) in a program called

Map-SCHOLAR. In the program, a system was developed to permit the integration of graphic information with verbal information. The graphic information consisted of map capability so that the student could refer to the display by either names of geographic areas or by pointing to the areas.

Unfortunately, the work of persons such as Collins appears to represent the exception rather than the rule. CAI was hailed as the hot technique, first in the 1970s by Goldstein (1974) and later by Wexley and Latham (1981). Yet Wexley's annual review chapter in 1984 cites only six references to recent research, four of which are technical reports, and Goldstein (1986) noted a continuing lack of progress. However, the promise of such work is indicated by one of the few studies published in this period.

Dossett and Hulvershorn (1983) conducted two studies of peer training using CAI in technical training of electronics in a military setting. In the first study, they compared three groups—a peer-trained CAI group, an individually trained CAI group, and a conventionally trained group. No differences in mean level of achievement were found; however, significant differences in training time were found between all three groups. Peer-trained CAI groups were trained in less time than the individually trained CAI groups, who in turn were trained faster than the conventionally trained group. This study has important implications for the use of CAI as a cost-effective training technique. Two people can be trained using a single terminal more quickly than one person can be trained. In other words, more people can be trained in less time using fewer terminals, which greatly increases the training capabilities of facilities with limited resources.

Even though there are few research efforts, there are still many believers. Hassett and Dukes (1986) assert that computer-based training (CBT) software is becoming increasingly popular in both private industry and government. They discuss programs currently in use teaching a diverse range of topics from managerial skills to medical diagnosis. A similar revolution in training is being predicted because of the use of compact discs (e.g., Zygmont, 1988). It is important to avoid being a cynic, but virtually the same forecasts have occurred for many decades for the use of television, cable television, programmed instruction, and CAI. Successful learning in training systems is not guaranteed by the advent of a new, revolutionary technique alone. It requires careful needs assessment, careful design of training based on those needs, and evaluation efforts to fine-tune the program; theory-driven training techniques are even better. Behavioral role modeling is a good example of a technique that can serve as a model for training development as well as a modeling technique for teaching managers interpersonal effectiveness. Unfortunately, both the video and computer industries have extolled promises but have limited research ascertaining effectiveness. Future research should concentrate on how to use techniques most appropriately, efficiently, and creatively.

Training Issues

This section focuses on issues where training often intersects with societal concerns. The first topic addresses issues pertaining to fair employment practices, including a discussion of why training has become an important issue in civil rights litigation. The next topic focuses on training and the hard-core unemployed. Training programs for these people must consider many aspects of a complex system, including the support services (for example, counseling and job placement) necessary for individuals who have never been employed. It is also clear in a systems sense that training programs are only part of an answer to a complex problem. The final topic examines retraining for second careers and presents material concerning individuals who have been forced out of work by technological changes and others who have decided that they are no longer interested in their first career. Many of these potential employees face the additional hurdle of age discrimination.

Training and Fair Employment Practices

In 1964, President Johnson signed the Civil Rights Act. One section of that act, Title VII, has had a dramatic effect on employers, employees, job applicants, labor unions, lawyers, and industrial and organizational psychologists. Title VII makes it illegal for employers to discriminate on the basis of race, color, religion, sex, or national origin. The categories of the aged and handicapped were not included in this particular act, but were added later on the basis of other legislative action. The 1964 Act resulted in the establishment of the Equal Employment Opportunities Commission (EEOC) as an enforcement agency for fair employment practices. Since that time, numerous events have affected practices in this area. In 1972 an amendment to Title VII broadened it from essentially covering private employers with 15 employees or more to include state and governmental agencies as well as educational institutions. The amendment also extended the authority of the EEOC to bring court actions against organizations. In addition, the EEOC published a set of guidelines in 1970. Eight years later, the EEOC, the Civil Service Commission, the Department of Labor, and the Department of Justice published a new set of guidelines. Also, the Society for Industrial and Organizational Psychology published the *Principles for the Validation and Use of Personnel Selection Procedures* (Society for Industrial and Organizational Psychology, 1986) as a way of providing guidelines for the field. Various court actions ranging from decisions in district courts to the United States Supreme Court have added to the complexity. A review of all this material is beyond the scope of this chapter; however, an excellent summary of the basic issues is provided by Arvey and Faley (1979).

In order to understand the issues concerning training and fair employment practices, it is important to understand several basic ideas. First, there is the principle of discrimination. As noted by Arvey and Faley (1979), the basic objective of selection research is to develop valid instruments for use in helping to make selection decisions among applicants for employment. Persons might be selected for promotion to a new job on the basis of their training scores, but there are concerns that unfair discrimination or bias may enter into the situation. While such situations are complex and subject to many interpretations, Arvey's definition makes the basic point clear:

> Unfair discrimination or bias is said to exist when members of a minority class have lower probabilities of being selected for a job when, in fact, if they had been selected, their probabilities of performing successfully in a job would have been equal to those of nonminority group members. (p. 7)

Most of the original controversy involved entry or selection of persons into work organizations. So what does this have to do with training issues? In addressing the issue of testing in Title VII of the 1964 Civil Rights Act, the EEOC guidelines (1970) define a test as "any paper-and-pencil or performance measure used as a basis for employment decision." This means that if adverse impact is established, it would also be necessary to establish the job relatedness of any instrument used in the personnel decision. Almost all of the original legal decisions in the short history of fair employment practices involved persons attempting to enter the job market. Thus, the cases concerned the job relatedness of selection tests such as paper-and-pencil tests, application blanks, and interviews. Goldstein and Gilliam (1990) have detailed the degree to which discrimination in the workplace still affects persons in protected classes, such as minorities, women, and the elderly. Gilliam (1988) even reports on a training study of the hard-core unemployed where all of the individuals in the training programs were minorities who had college degrees. Recently, as more persons from protected classes have successfully entered the job market, the issues have shifted to concerns about opportunities to move up the corporate ladder. As a result, cases concerning opportunities for promotion have become more frequent. This often involves opportunities for entry into training and career development programs because the completion of such training is often viewed as a requirement before consideration for promotion.

Bartlett (1978), in a perceptive analysis, listed some of the kinds of decisions involving training programs that were likely to be involved in litigation:

- Use of training as a job prerequisite

- Use of instruments to select persons for training

- Use of training performance, retention, or graduation as a criteria for another job or for entry into another training program

- Use of training as a basis for advancement or increased compensation

This chapter emphasizes the point that it is critical to demonstrate job relevancy regardless of whether there is adverse impact because there is no other way of determining whether the training program is accomplishing its purpose. However, the courts' actions, in support of Title VII of the 1964 Civil Rights Act and other similar provisions involving handicapped individuals and older individuals, are prompted by the evidence of adverse impact. As a result, the courts' actions have led some individuals who might not otherwise understand the importance of evaluation to become interested in the topic.

As noted earlier, a variety of models, such as experimental designs and content validity, can be used to make inferences about the job relevancy of the training program. The models can, to varying degrees, permit inferences to be made about validity. Also, of course, the procedures used to carry out each of the evaluation models affect the strength of the inferences. Thus, content validity with a poor needs assessment weakens the inference.

In addition to questions about the use of training evaluation models to establish inferences about the validity of the training program, training scores can sometimes be used in a manner similar to a selection test. In this situation, the question is whether training performance can predict job performance. As described in the training evaluation section, this type of inference relates to the use of the training technique as a selection instrument so all of the guidelines in the *Principles for the Validation and Use of Personnel Selection Procedures* (Society for Industrial and Organizational Psychology, 1986) apply.

One other way training scores are used in fair employment practices cases is as a criterion measure—for example, when a selection test or an interview score is used to predict training performance. Again, the question becomes what inferences can be made. It is clear that this model is being used to predict, based on the selection test, which persons will perform well in training. Actually, it is extremely difficult to draw inferences about job performance on this basis. Some persons assume that if a selection test predicts training performance, it is possible to draw inferences about job performance. But everything discussed in this chapter about whether training performance necessarily translates into job performance should warn the reader to be extremely conservative in making that assumption. If there is a strong relationship between selection and training and the training program is content valid, that permits stronger inferences than would otherwise be possible.

In summary, note that training is now in the middle of fair employment practices issues, many of which will be in the public eye during the next decade. Readers interested in a further analysis of training and fair employment practices should read an excellent review by Russell (1984). In addition, Goldstein and Gilliam (1990) have traced the problems of employment discrimination and issues involving training and fair employment practices for many affected classes, including the elderly, minorities, and women.

Training for the Hard-core Unemployed

The civil disorders of the 1960s prompted a reconsideration of our poverty-ridden communities. In the cities alone, there were 500,000 unemployed persons (Report of the National Advisory Commission on Civil Disorders, 1968). These unemployed individuals resulted in the introduction of a new term, the *hard-core unemployed* (HCU). This group is characterized as not being regular members of the work force who, in many cases, have been without employment for more than six months. Further, the HCU are usually young, are members of a minority group, and lack a high school education. In addition, they are below the poverty level specified by the Department of Labor (Goodman, Salipante, & Paransky, 1973). One would hope that this problem, which has now been pressing for decades, could have been resolved and thus no longer discussed in chapters like this one. Sadly, recent estimates show the fact that the HCU remain a serious problem. For the last decade, the jobless rate for black teenagers seeking employment has been two and three times the national unemployment rate (Berlin, 1983). In addition, Gilliam (1988) has been involved in training research where the groups are hard-core unemployed in the sense that they have been without employment for periods of more than a year, and yet all the members of her training groups were college graduates!

The importance of this problem is likely to become magnified in coming years as a result of the declining number of individuals available for entry-level jobs. As discussed in the early part of this chapter, many of the persons who will become available will lack many basic skills. This might result in the replacement of the term *hard-core unemployed* with the term *undereducated youth*. In this regard, the reports of Sticht and his colleagues (Sticht, Armstrong, Hickey, & Caylor, 1987) on experiences in the military with "low-aptitude youth" training programs are quite relevant. The authors present data describing the success of these groups on measures as varied as retention rates, numbers of persons completing high school equivalency degrees, performance in the military, and other assorted indicators. The training is based on a functional literacy approach, which focuses on the development of basic skills within the context of the job. In addition, the authors report on other training support schemes, including revision of training materials to match trainee aptitudes.

Most of the early research on hard-core unemployed youth is available from a variety of sources (e.g., Goodman, Salipante, & Paransky, 1973) and thus will not be repeated here. However, it is critical to note an important common theme identified in most HCU research because it has implications for future research on all training systems: Training systems must be examined from a broader perspective than just the trainee, the trainer, and the necessary job skills. In one of the earliest studies, Friedlander and Greenberg (1971) found that supportive behavior by the supervisor was the key to HCU success. Research by Miller and Zeller in 1967 indicated that "it might have been helpful to have included, within the training experience itself, practice in job hunting, assistance in contacting employees before the end of training, followup counseling, and job-placement help" (p. 31). More than thirty years after that experience, an editorial titled "How Not to Retrain Workers" (see Table 19), based on an analysis of training efforts in the 1980s, repeats all the same lessons.

International Training Issues

It is expected that more and more organizations will continue to cross international lines, where training issues are likely to become serious concerns. Interestingly, Wexley (1984) describes a survey of 105 American companies with overseas branches in which 68 percent have no training programs to prepare individuals for work abroad. The absence of such programs has been discussed as one possible reason for the high rate of failure of Americans abroad. One of the major issues in this research is where and how training should be conducted. Eden (1989) describes a study by the International Labor Office which reached the conclusion that most of the multinational enterprises' training programs in host countries were modeled after the training programs of the parent organization, a practice that may be dysfunctional. Mitchell (1981) points out that many American organizations often automatically use their domestic training programs overseas without consideration of the appropriateness to the needs of the international setting. Eden suggests that while technology can be imported, training cannot (Eden, 1989). It certainly seems that needs assessment techniques focusing on organizational analysis should be useful here. The complexity of these issues is brought home by Alromaithy and Reynolds (1981), who note that training programs that focus on job skills and ignore the entire experience of shifting cultures are likely to fail. These authors also note the concern for the attitudes and training of nonemployees such as spouses and families. One can't help but feel that many of the lessons of working with the hard-core unemployed may apply here. Unfortunately, there has not been much thought or research concerning international

issues in training. One exception is Ronen (1989), who examines the theoretical and available research literature concerning training and the international assignee. For example, Ronen asks whether managers educated in one culture are equipped to make attributions about emotional, cognitive, and value sets that may affect a host-country manager's behavior. In discussing the enormous training implications, Ronen notes that the manager given an assignment in a foreign country must possess the "patience of a diplomat, the zeal of a missionary, and the linguistic skill of a U.N. interpreter" (p. 418). He sets out an agenda for interested researchers that should keep everyone busy for some time to come.

Career Change and Training

There are a number of interesting issues related to training and career change. Large numbers of individuals, for one reason or another, find themselves seeking retraining for new jobs or careers. In some cases, jobs have been lost because rapidly changing technologies made them obsolete; in other cases, a formal or informal age limit (say, for athletes, airline pilots, or firefighters) has prompted the career change. In still other cases, the first career offers little opportunity for advancement or the jobholder wishes to pursue other interests.

Such concerns involve a whole set of individual, organizational, and societal issues. One set of issues relates to the needs of the future labor force. Vobejda (1987) describes the executives of the new Madza plant in Michigan as having very clear future objectives for their work force. "They want their new employees to be able to work in teams, to rotate through various jobs, to understand how their tasks fit into the entire process, to spot problems in production, to troubleshoot, articulate the problems to others, suggest improvements and write detailed charts and memos that serve as a road map in the assembly of the car" (p. A14).

TABLE 19

How Not to Retrain Workers

When General Motors laid off 3,800 assembly line workers in Southgate, California, a federal "trade-adjustment" grant enabled 30 of them to enroll in a specially created electronics training course. *Washington Post* reporter Jay Mathews spent eight months following the experience of the first enrollees. His observations—set forth in a four-part series in this newspaper last week—provide a handy guide for anyone who wants to run an unsuccessful training program.

The first requirement is to make sure the workers are unsuited to the training. You can administer a placement test just to make sure that you're on the wrong track, but be sure that the trainees are already enrolled and enthusiastic about their prospects so that there is no chance to replace them with a more suitable group. The Southgate program accomplished this mismatching so deftly that only two members of the class were able to pass a basic math test. Many couldn't use a simple calculator.

Run the class at breakneck speed. Many of the students will be highly motivated and will try to keep up by studying through the night even while holding evening jobs. But if you go fast enough—the Southgate course crammed a year of instruction into 20 weeks—you can quickly build up the frustration level so that even the best-prepared will fall behind. But don't flunk anyone. String the trainees along with inflated grades or they might drop out and cost you your training fee.

Of course, a little basic review could refresh the memories of the average trainee, who has, typically, been out of school for some years. And a few months of remedial education might help others to prepare for more suitable employment or training. But given the pace that you have set for the class, you won't have to worry that your trainees will be able to do any catch-up preparation.

You'll probably have to order some training equipment for appearance's sake. But make sure that it doesn't arrive on time and that certain key items are missing.

Create unrealistic expectations. You're dealing with longtime assembly line workers who have been earning as much as $12 an hour for what is basically unskilled work. They don't yet realize that most job openings for which they are qualified—including those in the electronics field—pay much less. Or that the higher-paying jobs in electronics—which are relatively few in number compared with the old-line manufacturing jobs—require substantially more training and experience than they are likely to get in your course. Tell them they are almost sure to find lucrative employment if they stick with the course so that they'll be especially embittered when they end up sweeping floors.

It's helpful to add to the stresses that the trainees and their families are already undergoing as a result of their prolonged—in this case more than six months—unemployment. That was accomplished by a two-month delay in paying continued unemployment benefits so that some of the trainees had to work at night in addition to their 12 hours of course work. (The administration's new job-training program has improved upon this technique by eliminating training stipends entirely.) General Motors also helped out in mid-course by ordering half the class to report to an assembly line in Oklahoma and terminating unemployment benefits for those who refused.

You can count on the fact that, once they have graduated, few of your trainees will have the foggiest idea how to find a job. Most of them went right from school to the assembly line, and they can't even write a resumé much less sell themselves to an employer. Keep them away from "job clubs" and other successful placement programs. If you want to look as if you're doing something to help, offer employes special bonuses to hire and retrain your graduates—that's usually a sure-fire turn-off.

These lessons aren't new—ineffective training programs have flourished for years. But successful job programs keep cropping up, and their example poses a threat to training industry standards. That's why reporter Mathews' careful documentation of the necessary ingredients for failure is must reading for anyone concerned about the future of this country's training establishment.

Complicating this issue is rapid technical obsolescence of individuals who previously had very advanced training. It is estimated that an engineer's education has a half-life of five years—half of what has been learned in school is obsolete five years after graduation. Fleishman and Mumford (1989) ask a series of very important questions about these issues. Is it possible to develop training programs focusing on KSAs that influence performance in a variety of task domains? Is it possible to determine how different abilities are acquired at different points in the training process? Given the rapid shifts in technology, it may become necessary to rethink what we mean by training for specific and general skills.

An important article by Fossum and his colleagues (Fossum, Arvey, Paradise, & Robbins, 1986) presents a model of the skills obsolescence process and describes factors contributing to job and personal changes. It also considers job and organizational influences associated with obsolescence. London and Bassman (1989) indicate that midcareer shifts will further complicate the training scene during the next several decades. These authors predict these shifts will occur more frequently because of changes in job requirements brought about in response to technological shifts. In addition, they note that there are health and economic factors beyond an individual's control that will result in job shifts. Intriguingly, they also predict that as people live longer, individuals may discover forty years is a long time to devote to a single career and therefore may develop different careers for the latter portion of their lives. I cannot help but wonder if individuals with relatively secure retirement benefits may feel even freer to explore such alternatives than persons have in the past.

Such issues present quite a menu of challenges for training. Some predict that the declining number of persons in a number of industrialized societies will make every worker a very valuable resource, so training and retraining will become increasingly important.

As discussed in the section on the HCU, there is a strong belief that decreasing proportions of entry-level workers will eventually affect all sectors of the work economy. As we approach the year 2000, there will be an increasing demand for workers, especially in service industries. Some analysts (e.g., Goldstein & Gilliam, 1990) believe that society will need to become concerned about keeping everyone in the work force. The effects of such views on employment of minorities, the elderly, and women should be quite dramatic.

Odiorne (1980) suggests that strategic planning should be an integral part of the jobs of industrial trainers. He feels that trainers must assume part of the responsibility of determining the needs of future labor forces and must start developing programs now to meet those needs. It is worth noting that this kind of planning is not just necessary for jobs that are being changed because of technology; Zenger (1981) points out, for instance, that career planning is an overlooked skill in management training. In his view, one responsibility of organizations should be to ensure that employees have qualified people with whom to discuss their future career goals and how to attain them. A serious issue in the realm of training and retraining is that the individuals involved are often entering nontraditional careers, such as women entering management. In other cases, the individuals changing careers are older than those traditionally entering the work force. As indicated earlier, both groups have been subjected to discrimination in employment situations and the issues involved are quite emotional. In the case of the older worker, most discrimination cases are based on the premise that older workers cannot perform as well on the job and cannot acquire new skills.

Rhodes' (1983) review of studies conducted over the last 30 years does not support such a premise. While a few studies have found relationships between age and performance, these relationships tend to disappear when the effects of experience are considered. Those few studies where relationships between age and performance remain tend to be where there is high demand for speed and accuracy of movement. For the most part, however, the requirements of the jobs were not extreme enough for these differences to show up, and in those cases where there were high-demand jobs, the older persons remaining were individuals who could perform the job. These issues become even more complicated when measures other than turnover are used. Rhodes' analysis found evidence for a negative relationship—that is, the higher the age, the less the turnover. Unfortunately, the entire literature is marked by problems, including failing to conduct longitudinal rather than cross-sectional studies. There is also a tendency to make unjustified linear assumptions, for example, that if 30- to 40-year-olds have lower morale than 20- to 30-year-olds, then 40- to 50-year-olds must have still lower morale.

Another problem is the lack of literature regarding analysis of training and retraining data to help us understand issues concerning older workers. An excellent article by Sterns and Doverspike (1989) summarizes what we presently know about training for older workers. Two aspects are particularly relevant. First, there is the question of training program design and whether particular techniques of training are more supportive for one age group than another. Sterns and Doverspike's review of the literature about effective training systems for older persons reveals many aspects that are consistent with what we already know about training systems for all workers. Thus, these authors point to the importance of careful task analysis in making training programs particularly job relevant. They also note the importance of slowing the pace of training and avoiding early errors so as not to discourage the trainees. At this point, it is hard to tell whether there are specific aspects of training design for older workers that wouldn't be just as helpful for workers of all ages. A second question is whether older workers perform differently in training programs than do younger workers. The answer to this question is also unclear. A number of studies indicate that older workers take a longer period of time to learn. For example, Hartley, Hartley, and Johnson (1984) found that older workers took longer and required more assistance than younger workers in word processing training. It is not obvious whether this will be a consistent finding and whether, given enough time and support, older persons would perform as well at the end of training and on the job. Clearly, considerable research is needed on these issues.

Several training issues concern individuals entering careers that previously were not considered traditional for those people, for example, women entering work organizations as managers. An article by White, Crino, and DeSanctis (1981) discusses many of these issues, including the problem of barriers to women entering such careers. One serious issue is whether persons entering nontraditional fields require some sort of special training program. I have not seen any evidence from needs assessment that indicates that the job of manager for a woman is different from the job of manager for a man. Also, there is no clear-cut evidence from person analysis that women need special training on particular KSAs that are not needed by men. At this time, therefore, it is difficult to support the need for special training programs. As noted by White, Crino, and DeSanctis (1981), that has not prevented the development of a large number of special training programs for women. However, also as noted by White et al., data supporting any accomplishments by these programs is virtually nonexistent. My conclusion about these efforts is similar to the thoughts I offered about programs like those for the hard-core unemployed: It makes more sense to train people in the organization to work with individuals who might have different ethnic and cultural values.

It probably also makes sense to help people enter an organization by making the socialization process a part of training and entry. Wanous (1980) noted that one of the most important aspects of entry into organizations is the socialization process and that one of the first ways a person is socialized is through the training process. While the evidence is limited, one might speculate that inaccurate or limited socialization in training may very well create unrealistic expectations about the work environment, which in turn make the adjustment to work more difficult. Feldman (1989) explores the idea of "multiple socialization processes," which suggests that it is necessary to explain the interactions among learning work tasks and other types of learning during socialization. In that paper, Feldman explores in-depth issues integrating socialization and training research and sets a research agenda for years to come. Perhaps, in closing this discussion, it makes sense to again offer the idea that success depends on both the trainee and the organization. It is just as important for organizations to remove the in-place stereotyped behavior that result in blocks to the careers of the elderly, minorities, and women as it is for the trainee to have realistic expectations about the world of work.

Conclusion

For the individual, training opportunities are very important because they are instrumental in earning entry into and enjoying the satisfactions and rewards associated with work. Training represents a positive hope both for persons first entering the work force and for individuals changing their work environment. Individuals expect that training will give them the opportunities to enter the job market with needed skills, to perform in new functions, and to be promoted into new situations. This emphasis on training opportunities is consistent with the concept of work and the value it has as an activity in the daily lives of those within society.

Presently, employees, managers, and organizations are turning more frequently to training as a solution to work issues. This increased emphasis is reflected in a variety of ways. For example, as noted in the beginning of this chapter, labor unions insist that new contracts must include opportunities for training to meet technological changes in the workplace, and training programs are frequently offered as a court-imposed solution to give individuals who have been victims of discrimination an opportunity for equal employment. Well-designed training programs are more likely to accomplish these goals, but the point is that there are positive expectations that training should be able to accomplish these purposes. One goal of this chapter has been to present the knowledge base stemming from our research literature, which if utilized makes it more likely that training will have positive outcomes. To the degree that training is based on careful needs assessment, well-designed instructional strategies, and a research strategy that permits the collection of data providing feedback on where revisions are necessary, training is more likely to meet everyone's expectations.

While many of these same expectations concerning the positive value of training existed many years ago, theory and research lagged far behind. It has only been in the last decade that there has been considerable research and theory development in this area. Now even more researchers are refocusing their attention on training issues. Thus, another goal of this chapter is to help stimulate a future research agenda. There are many challenges facing training research in the next several decades. As discussed in this chapter, demographic trends make it clear that the rate of growth in the work force will seriously decline during the next decade, making it increasingly important for each individual to have the opportunity to reach his or her maximum potential, and resulting in increased emphasis on the use of training programs for both entry-level and experienced workers. In addition, jobs are likely to become more technologically complex, resulting in increased cognitive demands on the individual worker. This situation is likely to result in further demands on the use of training programs to prepare the individual for jobs in the workplace.

For persons involved in training research and design, these events present both a great opportunity and a great challenge. While it is clear that there is a growing knowledge base, many issues remain unresolved. For example, we are just beginning to understand the factors involved in establishing a positive training transfer climate and to determine the cognitive component of instructional program design.

The demands of society and the increasing number of researchers interested in training make for exciting possibilities that should keep interested researchers busy for decades to come. I hope this chapter provides some stimulation for those efforts.

I wish to thank and acknowledge the help of my frields and colleagues. In particular, Wiley Boyles, Joyce Hogan, Wayne Cascio, Doris Maye, Jim Outtz, Erich Prien, Paul Sackett, Ben Schneider, Joe Schneider, Neal Schmitt, and Shelly Zedeck. Many of the ideas concerning needs assessment were generated in projects that we worked on together. I gratefully acknowledge their friendship and their contributions. I also want to thank Brooks/Cole Publishing Company for permission to use materials from my training book (Goldstein, 1986), which will soon enter its third edition.

I especially want to thank my wife, Micki, for her constant care and support. I want to sincerely express my appreciation to my friend, Ben Schneider, for providing psychological support that goes far beyond that of a colleague.

My sincere thanks go to Marv Dunnette for giving me this opportunity. His thoughtfulness and kindness in working with all of us are traits worth copying many times over.

References

Alliger, G. M., & Janak, E. A. (1989). Kirkpatrick's levels of training criteria: Thirty years later. *Personnel Psychology, 42,* 331–341.

Alromaithy, A., & Reynolds, A. (1981). A new model for international training. *Training and Development Journal, 35*(10), 63–69.

Ammerman, H. L., & Pratzner, C. (1974). *Occupational survey report on business data programmers: Task data from workers and supervisors indicating job relevance and training criticalness* (R & D Serial No. 108). Columbus, OH: Center for Vocational Education.

Ammerman, H. L., & Pratzner, F. C. (1975). *Occupational survey report on automotive mechanics: Task data from workers and supervisors indicating job relevance and training criticalness* (R & D Serial No. 110). Columbus, OH: Center for Vocational Education.

Ammerman, H. L., & Pratzner, F. C. (1977). *Performance content for job training* (R & D Serial No. 121–125, vols. 1–5). Columbus, OH: Center for Vocational Education.

Argyris, C. (1968a). Issues in evaluating laboratory education. *Industrial Relations, 8,* 28–40, 45.

Argyris, C. (1968b). Some unintended consequences of rigorous research. *Psychological Bulletin, 70,* 185–197.

Arvey, R. D., & Cole, D. A. (1989). Evaluation change due to training. In I. Goldstein (Ed.), *Training and development in work organizations: Frontiers of industrial and organizational psychology.* San Francisco: Jossey-Bass.

Arvey, R. D., & Foley, R. H. (1988). *Fairness in selecting employees* (2nd ed.). Reading, MA: Addison-Wesley.

Atkinson, J. W., & Feather, N. T. (1966). *A theory of achievement motivation.* New York: Wiley.

Baldwin, T. T., & Ford, J. K. (1988). Transfer of training: A review and directions for future research. *Personnel Psychology, 41,* 63–105.

Bandura, A. (1969). *Principles of behavior modification.* New York: Holt, Rinehart & Winston.

Bandura, A. (1977). *Social learning theory.* Englewood Cliffs, NJ: Prentice-Hall.

Barbee, J. R., & Keil, E. C. (1973). Experimental techniques of job interview training for the disadvantaged: Videotape feedback, behavior modification, and microcounseling. *Journal of Applied Psychology, 58,* 209–213.

Bartlett, C. J. (1978). Equal employment opportunity issues in training. *Human Factors, 20,* 179–188.

Bass, B. M., & Vaughan, J. A. (1966). *Training in industry: The management of learning.* Belmont, CA: Wadsworth.

Baumgartel, H., & Jeanpierre, F. (1972). Applying new knowledge in the back-home setting: A study of Indian managers' adoptive efforts. *Journal of Applied Behavioral Science, 8* (6), 674–694.

Baumgartel, H., Sullivan, G. J., & Dunn, L. E. (1978). How organizational climate and personality affect the pay-off from advanced management training sessions. *Kansas Business Review, 5,* 1–10.

Berlin, G. B. (1983). *Not working: Unskilled youth and displaced adults.* New York: Ford Foundation.

Bernardin, H. J., & Beatty, R. W. (1984). *Performance appraisal: Assessing human behavior at work.* Boston: Kent.

Bernardin, H. J., & Villanova, P. (1986). Performance appraisal. In E. A. Locke (Ed.), *Generalizing from laboratory to field settings.* Lexington, MA: Lexington Books.

Blum, M. L., & Naylor, J. C. (1968). *Industrial psychology.* New York: Harper & Row.

Borman, W. C. (1979). Format and training effects on rating accuracy and rater errors. *Journal of Applied Psychology, 64,* 410–421.

Bownas, D. A., Bosshardt, M. J., & Donnelly, L. F. (1985). A quantitative approach to evaluating training curriculum content sampling adequacy. *Personnel Psychology, 38,* 117–131.

Bruner, J. S. (1963). A theory of instruction. *Educational Leadership, 20,* 523–532.

Bunker, K. A., & Cohen, S. L. (1978). Evaluating organizational training efforts: Is ignorance really bliss? *Training Developmental Journal, 32,* 4–11.

Burke, M. J., & Day, R. R. (1986). A cumulative study of the effectiveness of managerial training. *Journal of Applied Psychology, 71,* 232–245.

Burnaska, R. F. (1976). The effects of behavior modeling training upon managers' behaviors and employees' perceptions. *Personnel Psychology, 29,* 235–328.

Campbell, D. T., & Stanley, J. C. (1963). *Experimental and quasi-experimental designs for research.* Chicago: Rand McNally.

Campbell, J. P. (1978). *What we are about: An inquiry into the self-concept of industrial and organizational psychology.* Presidential address to the Division of Industrial and Organizational Psychology, 86th annual meeting of the American Psychological Association, Toronto.

Campbell, J. P. (1988). Training design for performance improvement. In J. P. Campbell & R. J. Campbell (Eds.), *Productivity in organizations: Frontiers of industrial and organizational psychology.* San Francisco: Jossey-Bass.

Campion, M. A., & Campion, J. E. (1987). Evaluation of an interview skills training program in a natural field experiment. *Personnel Psychology, 40,* 675–691.

Caro, P. W. (1984). ISD-CAI technology applications to pilot training. *Training Technical Group Newsletter of the Human Factors Society, 10,* 3–4.

Cascio, W. F. (1982). *Costing human resources: The financial impact of behavior in organizations.* Boston: Kent.

Cascio, W. F. (1989). Using utility analysis to assess training outcomes. In I. Goldstein (Ed.), *Training and development in work organizations: Frontiers of industrial and organizational psychology.* San Francisco: Jossey-Bass.

Cascio, W. F., & Zammuto, R. F. (1987). *Societal trends and staffing policies.* Denver: University of Colorado Press.

Christal, R. E. (1974). The United States Air Force occupational research project (AFHRL Tech. Rep. No. 77-34). TX: Brooks Air Force Base.

Christensen, J. M. (1987). The human factors profession. In G. Salvendy (Ed.), *Handbook of human factors.* New York: Wiley.

Clement, R. W., Walker, J. W., & Pinto, P. R. (1979, March). Changing demands on the training professional. *Training and Development Journal, 29,* 3–7.

Cochran, N. (1978). Grandma Moses and the corruption of data. *Evaluation Quarterly, 2,* 363–375.

Collins, A. M. (1977). Processes in acquiring knowledge. In R. C. Anderson, R. J. Spiro, & W. E. Montague (Eds.), *Schooling and the acquisition of knowledge.* Hillsdale, NJ: Erlbaum.

Collins, A., Adams, M. J., & Pew, R. W. (1978). Effectiveness of an interactive map display in tutoring geography. *Journal of Educational Psychology, 70,* 1–7.

Cook, T. D., & Campbell, D. T. (1976). The design and conduct of quasi-experiments and true experiments in field settings. In M. D. Dunnette (Ed.), *Handbook of industrial and organizational psychology.* Chicago: Rand McNally.

Cook, T. D., & Campbell, D. T. (1979). *Quasi experimentation. Design and analysis issues for field settings.* Chicago: Rand McNally.

Cook, T. D., Campbell, D., & Peracchio, L. (1990). Quasi experiments. In M. D. Dunnette & L. Hough (Eds.), *Handbook of industrial and organizational psychology* (2nd ed., vol. 1). Palo Alto, CA: Consulting Psychologists Press.

Cooke, N. M., & Schvaneveldt, R. W. (1986). *The evolution of cognitive networks with computer programming experience.* Paper presented at the workshop on empirical studies of programmers, Washington, DC.

Cranny, C. J., & Doherty, M. E. (1988). Importance ratings in job analysis: Notes on the misinterpretation of factor analysis. *Journal of Applied Psychology, 73,* 320–322.

Cullen, J. G., Sawzin, S. A., Sisson, G. R., & Swanson, R. A. (1978). Cost effectiveness: A model for assessing training investment. *Training and Development Journal, 32,* 24–29.

Decker, P. J. (1980). Effects of symbolic coding and rehearsal in behavior modeling training. *Journal of Applied Psychology, 65,* 627–634.

Decker, P. J. (1982). The enhancement of behavior modeling training of supervisory skills by the inclusion of retention processes. *Personnel Psychology, 35,* 323–335.

Decker, P. J. (1983). The effects of rehearsal group size and video feedback in behavior modeling training. *Personnel Psychology, 36,* 763–773.

Decker, P. J. (1984). Effects of different symbolic coding stimuli in behavior modeling training. *Personnel Psychology, 37,* 711–720.

Dossett, D. L., & Hulvershorn, P. (1983). Increasing technical training efficiency: Peer training via computer-assisted instruction. *Journal of Applied Psychology, 68,* 552–558.

Eden, D. (1989). Training. In B. Bass, P. Drenth, & P. Weissenberg (Eds.), *Advances in organizational psychology: An international review.* Beverly Hills, CA: Sage.

Eden, D., & Ravid, G. (1982). Pygmalion versus self-expectancy: Effects of instructor and self-expectancy on trainee performance. *Organizational Behavior and Human Performance, 30,* 351–364.

Eden, D., & Shani, A. B. (1982). Pygmalion goes to boot camp: Expectancy, leadership and trainee performance. *Journal of Applied Psychology, 67,* 194–199.

Eurich, N. P. (1985). *Corporate classrooms.* Princeton, NJ: Carnegie Foundation.

Faley, R. H., & Sundstrom, E. (1985). Content representativeness: An empirical method of evaluation. *Journal of Applied Psychology, 70,* 567–571.

Feldman, D. C. (1989). Socialization, resocialization, and training: Reframing the research agenda. In I. Goldstein (Ed.), *Training and development in work organizations: Frontiers of industrial and organizational psychology* (pp. 121–182). San Francisco: Jossey-Bass.

Fiedler, F. E. (1964). A contingency model of leadership effectiveness. In L. Berkowitz (Ed.), *Advances in experimental social psychology.* New York: Academic Press.

Fiedler, F. E. (1967). *A theory of leadership effectiveness.* New York: McGraw-Hill.

Fiedler, F. E., & Chemers, M. M. (1984). *Improving leadership effectiveness: The Leader Match concept* (rev. ed.). New York: Wiley.

Fiedler, F. E., Chemers, M. M., & Mahar, L. (1976). *Improving leadership effectiveness: The Leader Match concept.* New York: Wiley.

Fiedler, F. E., & Mahar, L. (1979). The effectiveness of contingency model training: A review of the validation of LEADER MATCH. *Personnel Psychology, 32,* 45–62.

Fisk, A. D., & Schneider, W. (1981). Controlled and automatic processing during tasks requiring sustained attention: A new approach to vigilance. *Human Factors, 23,* 737–750.

Fleishman, E. A., & Mumford, M. D. (1989) Individual attributes and training performance. In I. Goldstein (Ed.), *Training and development in work organizations: Frontiers of industrial and organizational psychology* (pp. 121–182). San Francisco: Jossey-Bass.

Ford, J. K., & Wroten, S. P. (1984). Introducing new methods for conducting training evaluation and for linking training evaluation to program redesign. *Personnel Psychology, 37,* 651–655.

Fossum, J. A., Arvey, R. D., Paradise, C. A., & Robbins, N. W. (1986). Modeling the skills/obsolescence process: A psychological/economic integration. *Academy of Management Review, 11,* 362–374.

Frayne, C. A., & Latham, G. P. (1987). The application of social learning theory to employee self-management of attendance. *Journal of Applied Psychology, 72,* 387–392.

Freeberg, N. E. (1976). Criterion measures for youth-work training programs: The development of relevant performance dimensions. *Journal of Applied Psychology, 61*(5), 537–545.

Friedlander, F., & Greenberg, S. (1971). Effect of job attitudes, training, and organizational climate on performance of the hard-core unemployed. *Journal of Applied Psychology, 55,* 287–295.

Fullerton, H. N., Jr. (1985). The 1995 labor force: BLS' latest projections. *Monthly Labor Review, 117,* 17–25.

Gagné, R. M. (1974). *Essentials of learning for instruction.* Hinsdale, IL: Dryden Press.

Gagné, R. M. (1984). Learning outcomes and their effects: Useful categories of human performance. *American Psychologist, 39,* 377–385.

Gagné, R. M., & Briggs, L. J. (1979). *Principles of instructional design.* New York: Holt, Rinehart & Winston.

Gagné, R. M., & Dick, W. (1983). Instructional psychology. In *Annual review of psychology* (pp. 261–295). Palo Alto, CA: Annual Reviews.

Gilbert, T. F. (1960). On the relevance of laboratory investigation of learning to self-instructional programming. In A. A. Lumsdaine & R. Glaser (Eds.), *Teaching machines and programmed instruction.* Washington, DC: National Education Association.

Gilliam, P. (1988). *The effects of a job acquisition training program on the attitudes, behaviors, and knowledge of black educated adults.* Unpublished doctoral dissertation, University of Maryland, College Park.

Glaser, R. (1984). Education and thinking: The role of knowledge. *American Psychologist, 39,* 93–104.

Goldstein, A. P., & Sorcher, M. (1974). *Changing supervisor behavior.* New York: Pergamon.

Goldstein, I. L. (1980). Training in work organizations. In *Annual review of psychology.* Palo Alto, CA: Annual Reviews.

Goldstein, I. L. (1986). *Training in organizations: Needs assessment, development and evaluation* (2nd ed.). Monterey, CA: Brooks/Cole.

Goldstein, I. L., & Bartlett, C. J. (1977). [Validation of a training program for police officers]. Unpublished raw data.

Goldstein, I. L., & Gilliam, P. (1990). Training system issues in the year 2000. *American Psychologist, 45,* 134–143.

Goldstein, I. L., Macey, W. H., & Prien, E. P. (1981). Needs assessment approaches for training development. In H. Meltzer & W. R. Hord (Eds.), *Making organizations humane and productive.* New York: Wiley.

Goldstein, I. L., & Musicante, G. R. (1986). The applicability of a training transfer model to issues concerning rater training. In E. A. Locke (Ed.), *Generalizing from laboratory to field settings.* Lexington, MA: Lexington Books.

Goldstein, I. L., Schneider, B., Katzman, L., & Braverman, E. P. (1989). *A content validity approach to analyzing training systems.* Unpublished manuscript.

Goldstein, I. L., & Thayer, P. W. (1987). *Inhibitors and facilitators for effective transfer of training into the work organization.* Discussion conducted at the conference for the Society for Industrial and Organizational Psychology, Atlanta.

Goldstein, I. L., & Wexley, K. N. (1983). *Needs assessment approaches in the design of training systems.* Workshop presented at the annual meeting of the American Psychological Association, Los Angeles.

Goodman, P. S., Salipante, P., & Paransky, H. (1973). Hiring, training, and retraining the hard-core unemployed: A selected review. *Journal of Applied Psychology, 58,* 23–33.

Gordon, M. E., & Cohen, S. L. (1973). Training behavior as a predictor of trainability. *Personnel Psychology, 26,* 261–272.

Gordon, M. W., & Isenberg, J. F. (1975). Validation of an experimental training criterion for machinists. *Journal of Industrial Teacher Education, 12,* 72–78.

Guion, R. M. (1977). Content validity—the source of my discontent. *Applied Psychological Measurement, 1,* 1–10.

Hall, D. T. (1986). Dilemmas in linking succession planning to individual executive learning. *Human Resources Management, 25,* 235–265.

Hartley, A. A., Hartley, J. T., & Johnson, S. A. (1984). The older adult as computer user. In P. K. Robinson, J. Livingston, & J. E. Birren (Eds.), *Aging and technological advances* (pp. 347–348). New York: Plenum Press.

Hassett, J., & Dukes, S. (1986). The new employee trainer: A floppy disk. *Psychology Today, 20* (9), 30–36.

Hogan, P. M., Hakel, M. D., & Decker, P. D. (1986). Effects of trainee-generated versus trainer-provided rule codes on generalization in behavior modeling training. *Journal of Applied Psychology, 71,* 469–473.

Howell, W. C., & Cooke, N. J. (1989). Training the human information processor: A review of cognitive models. In I. Goldstein (Ed.), *Training and development in work organizations: Frontiers of industrial and organizational psychology.* San Francisco: Jossey-Bass.

Ilgen, D. R., & Favero, J. L. (1985). Limits in generalizing from psychological research to performance appraisal processes. *Academy of Management Review, 10,* 311–321.

Kanfer, F. H., & Gaelick, L. (1986) Self-management methods. In F. H. Kanfer & A. P. Goldstein (Eds.), *Helping people change: A textbook of methods* (3rd ed.). Elmsford, NY: Pergamon.

Kanfer, R., & Ackerman, P. L. (1989). Motivation and cognitive abilities: An integrative / aptitude-treatment interaction approach to skill acquisition. *Journal of Applied Psychology, 74,* 657–690.

Kaplan, R. E., Lombardo, M. M., & Mazique, M. S. (1983). *A mirror for managers: Using simulation to develop management teams* (Tech. Rep. No. 13). Greensboro, NC: Center for Creative Leadership.

Klimoski, R. J. (1982). *Needs assessments for management development.* Paper presented at the annual meeting of the American Psychological Association, Washington, DC.

Kirkpatrick, D. L. (1959, 1960). Techniques for evaluating training programs. *Journal of the American Society of Training Directors, 13,* 21–26, and *14,* 13–18, 28–32.

Komaki, J., Heinzmann, A. T., & Lawson, L. (1980). Effect of training and feedback: Component analysis of a behavioral safety program. *Journal of Applied Psychology, 65,* 261–270.

Komaki, J., Wadell, W. M., & Pearce, M. G. (1977). The applied behavior analysis approach and individual employees: Improving performance in two small businesses. *Organizational Behavioral Human Performance, 19,* 337–352.

Kraut, A. I. (1975). Prediction of managerial success by peer and training-staff ratings. *Journal of Applied Psychology, 60,* 14–19.

Latham, G. P. (1989) Behavioral approaches to the training and learning process. In I. Goldstein (Ed.), *Training and development in work organizations: Frontiers of industrial and organizational psychology.* San Francisco: Jossey-Bass.

Latham, G. P., & Frayne, C. A. (1989). Self-management training for increased job attendance: A follow-up and a replication. *Journal of Applied Psychology, 74,* 411–416.

Latham, G. P., & Locke, E. A. (1979). Goal setting: A motivational technique that works. *Organizational Dynamics, 8,* 68–80.

Latham, G. P., & Saari, L. M. (1979). Application of social learning theory to training supervisors through behavior modeling. *Journal of Applied Psychology, 64,* 239–246.

Latham, G. P., & Wexley, K. N. (1981). *Increasing productivity through performance appraisal.* Reading, MA: Addison-Wesley.

Latham, G. P., Wexley, K. N., & Pursell, E. D. (1975). Training managers to minimize rating errors in the observation of behavior. *Journal of Applied Psychology, 60,* 550–555.

Leifer, M. S., & Newstrom, J. W. (1980). Solving the transfer of training problems. *Training and Development Journal, 34,* 42–46.

Levine, E. L., Ash, R. A., Hall, H., & Sistrunk, F. (1983). Evaluation of job analysis methods by experienced job analysts. *Academy of Management Journal, 26,* 339–348.

Locke, E. A., Shaw, K. N., Saari, L. M., & Latham, G. P. (1981). Goal setting and task performance. *Psychological Bulletin, 90,* 125–152.

London, M., & Bassman, E. (1989). Retraining midcareer workers for the future workplace. In I. Goldstein (Ed.), *Training and development in work organizations: Frontiers of industrial and organizational psychology.* San Francisco: Jossey-Bass.

Mabe, P. A., III, & West, S. G. (1982). Validity of self-evaluation of ability: A review and meta-analysis. *Journal of Applied Psychology, 67,* 280–296.

Marx, R. D. (1982). Relapse prevention for managerial training: A model for maintenance of behavior change. *Academy of Management Review, 7,* 433–441.

McCall, M. W., Jr., & Lombardo, M. M. (1979). *Looking Glass Inc.: The first three years* (Vol. 8, Tech. Rep. No. 13). Greensboro, NC: Center for Creative Leadership.

McCall, M. W., Jr., & Lombardo, M. M. (1982). Using simulation for leadership and management research: Through the looking glass. *Management Science, 28,* 533–549.

McClelland, D. C., & Winter, D. C. (1969). *Motivating economic achievement.* New York: Free Press.

McCormick, E. J. (1976). Job and task analysis. In M. D. Dunnette (Ed.), *Handbook of industrial and organizational psychology* (pp. 651–696). Chicago: Rand McNally.

McEnery, J., & McEnery, J. M. (1987). Self-rating in management training need assessment: A neglected opportunity. *Journal of Occupational Psychology, 60,* 49–60.

McGehee, W., & Thayer, P. W. (1961). *Training in business and industry.* New York: Wiley.

McGehee, W., & Tullar, W. L. (1978). A note on evaluating behavior modification and behavior modeling as industrial training techniques. *Personnel Psychology, 31,* 477–484.

Meyer, H. H., & Raich, M. S. (1983). An objective evaluation of a behavior modeling training program. *Personnel Psychology, 36,* 755–761.

Michalak, D. F. (1981). The neglected half of training. *Training and Development Journal, 35,* 22–28.

Miller, R. W., & Zeller, F. A. (1967). *Social psychological factors association with responses to retraining* (Final Report, Research Grant No. 91–52–66–56). Washington, DC: U.S. Department of Labor.

Mirabal, T. E. (1978). Forecasting future training costs. *Training Developmental Journal, 32* (7), 78–87.

Miron, D., & McClelland, D. C. (1979). The impact of achievement motivation training on small business. *California Management Review, 21,* 13–28.

Mitchell, F. G. (1981). Developing an international marketing training approach. *Training and Development Journal, 35* (11), 48–51.

Moore, M. L., & Dutton, P. (1978). Training needs analysis: Review and critique. *Academic Management Revision, 3* (3), 532–545.

Moses, J. L. (1978). Behavior modeling for managers. *Human Factors, 20,* 225–232.

Murphy, K. R., Herr, B. M., Lockhart, M. C., & Maguir, E. (1986). Evaluating the performance of paper people. *Journal of Applied Psychology, 71,* 654–661.

Newman, D. (1985). *The pursuit of validity in training: An application.* Unpublished doctoral dissertation, University of Maryland, College Park.

Noe, R. A., & Schmitt, N. (1986). The influence of trainee attitudes on training effectiveness: Test of a model. *Personnel Psychology, 39,* 497–523.

O'Brien, G. E., & Plooij, D. (1977). Comparison of programmed and prose culture training upon attitudes and knowledge. *Journal of Applied Psychology, 62,* 499–505.

Odiorne, G. S. (1980). Training to be ready for the 90's. *Training and Development Journal, 34,* 12–20.

O'Reilly, A. P. (1973). Skills requirements: Supervisor-subordinate conflict. *Personnel Psychology, 26,* 75–80.

Panell, R. C., & Laabs, G. J. (1979). Construction of a criterion-referenced, diagnostic test for an individual instruction course. *Journal of Applied Psychology, 64,* 255–261.

Pearlman, K. (1980). Job families: A review and discussion of their importance for personnel selection. *Psychological Bulletin, 87,* 1–28.

Pfister, G. (1975). Outcomes of laboratory training for police officers. *Journal of Social Issues, 31,* 115–121.

Prien, E. P. (1977). The function of job analysis in content validation. *Personnel Psychology, 30,* 167–174.

Prien, E. P., Goldstein, I. L., & Macey, W. H. (1987). Multidomain job analysis: Procedures and applications in human resource management and development. *Training and Development Journal, 41,* 68–72.

Raynor, J. O. (1970). Relationships between achievement-related motives, future orientation, and academic performance. *Journal of Personality and Social Psychology, 15,* 28–33.

Raynor, J. O., & Rubin, I. S. (1971). Effects of achievement motivation and future orientation on level of performance. *Journal of Personality and Social Psychology, 17,* 36–41.

Report of the National Advisory Commission on Civil Disorder. New York: Bantam.

Rhodes, S. (1983). Age-related differences in work attitudes and behavior: A review and conceptual analysis. *Psychological Bulletin, 93,* 328–367.

Ritti, R. R. (1968). Work goals of scientists and engineers. *Industrial Relations, 7,* 118–131.

Robertson, I., & Downs, S. (1979). Learning and the prediction of performance: Development of trainability testing in the United Kingdom. *Journal of Applied Psychology, 64,* 42–50.

Robertson, I. T., & Downs, S. (1989). Work-sample tests of trainability: A meta-analysis. *Journal of Applied Psychology, 74,* 402–410.

Ronen, S. (1989). Training the international assignee. In I. Goldstein (Ed.), *Training and development in work organizations: Frontiers of industrial and organizational psychology.* San Francisco: Jossey-Bass.

Rosenthal, R. (1966). *Experimenter effects in behavioral research.* New York: Appleton-Century-Crofts.

Rosenthal, B. D. (1978). *An evaluation of computer-assisted instruction in the Anne Arundel Country school system.* Unpublished master's thesis, University of Maryland, College Park.

Rouillier, J. Z., & Goldstein, I. L. (1990). *The determination of positive transfer of training climate through organizational analysis.* Unpublished manuscript.

Rubinsky, S., & Smith, N. (1973). Safety training by accident simulation. *Journal of Applied Psychology, 57,* 68–73.

Russell, J. S. (1984). A review of fair employment cases in the field of training. *Personnel Psychology, 37,* 261–276.

Russell, J. S., Terborg, J. R., & Powers, M. L. (1985). Organizational performance and organizational level training and support. *Personnel Psychology, 38,* 849–863.

Russell, J. S., Wexley, K. N., & Hunter, J. E. (1984). Questioning the effectiveness of behavior modeling training in an industrial setting. *Personnel Psychology, 37,* 465–481.

Ryman, D. H., & Biersner, R. J. (1975). Attitudes predictive of diving training success. *Personnel Psychology, 28,* 181–188.

Salvendy, G., & Pilitsis, J. (1980). The development and validation of an analytical training program for medical suturing. *Human Factors, 22,* 153–170.

Sanders, P., & Vanouzas, J. N. (1983). Socialization to learning. *Training and Development Journal, 37,* 14–21.

Severin, D. (1952). The predictability of various kinds of criteria. *Personal Psychology, 5,* 93–104.

Schmitt, N. (1987, April). Principles III: Research issues. In N. Schmitt (Chair), *Areas of continued debate in personnel selection: Principles III.* Symposium conducted at the conference of the Society for Industrial and Organizational Psychology, Atlanta.

Schneider, B., & Konz, A. (1989). Strategic job analysis. *Human Resource Management, 28,* 51–63.

Schneider, B., & Schmitt, N. W. (1986). *Staffing organizations.* Glenview, IL: Scott, Foresman.

Sheridan, J. A. (1975). *Designing the work environment.* Paper presented at the annual meeting of the American Psychological Association, Chicago.

Siegel, A. I. (1983). The miniature job training and evaluation approach: Additional findings. *Personnel Psychology, 36,* 41–56.

Society for Industrial and Organizational Psychology (1986). *Principles for the validation and use of personnel selection procedures* (3rd ed.). College Park, MD: Author.

Sorcher, M. (1971). A behavior modification approach to supervisory training. *Professional Psychology, 2,* 401–402.

Steadham, S. V. (1980, January). Learning to select a needs assessment strategy. *Training and Development Journal, 30,* 55–61.

Steers, R. M., & Porter, L. W. (1983). *Motivation and work behavior.* New York: McGraw-Hill.

Sterns, H. L., & Doverspike, D. (1989). Aging and the training and learning process. In I. Goldstein (Ed.), *Training and development in work organizations: Frontiers of industrial and organizational psychology.* San Francisco: Jossey-Bass.

Sticht, T. G., Armstrong, W. B., Hickey, D. T., & Caylor, J. S. (1987). *Cast-off youth.* New York: Praeger.

Swezey, R. W. (1981). *Individual performance assessment: An approach to criterion-referenced test development.* Reston, VA: Reston Publishing.

Thayer, P. W., & McGehee, W. (1977). On the effectiveness of not holding a formal training course. *Personnel Psychology, 30,* 455–456.

Thorndike, R. L. (1949). *Personnel selection.* New York: Wiley.

Uhlaner, J. E., & Drucker, A. J. (1980). Military research on performance criteria: A change of emphasis. *Human Factors, 22,* 131–139.

United States President's Commission on the Accident at Three-Mile Island. (1979). *Report of the President's commission on the accident at Three-Mile Island.* Washington, DC: U.S. Government Printing Office.

Vobejda, B. (1987, April 14). The new cutting edge in factories. *Washington Post*, p. A14.

Vroom, V. H. (1964). *Work and motivation.* New York: Wiley.

Wanous, J. P. (1980). *Organizational entry: Recruitment, selection and socialization of newcomers.* Reading, MA: Addison-Wesley.

Weiss, E. C. (1975). Evaluation research in the political context. In E. L. Streuning & M. Guttentag (Eds.), *Handbook of evaluation research.* Beverly Hills, CA: Sage.

Wexley, K. N. (1984). Personnel training. In *Annual review of psychology.* Palo Alto, CA: Annual Reviews.

Wexley, K. N., & Latham, G. P. (1981). *Developing and training human resources in organizations.* Glenview, IL: Scott, Foresman.

White, M. C., Crino, M. D., & DeSanctis, G. L. (1981). A critical review of female performance, performance training and organizational initiatives designed to aid women in the workrole environment. *Personnel Psychology, 34,* 227–248.

Wilson, W. J. (1979). *The declining significance of race.* Chicago: University of Chicago Press.

Wulfeck, W. H., Ellis, J. A., Richards, R. E., Merrill, M. D., & Wood, N. D. (1978). *The instructional quality inventory: Introduction and overview* (NPRDC Tech. Rep. No. 79-3). San Diego: Navy Personnel Research and Development Center.

Zedeck, S., & Cascio, W. F. (1984). Psychological issues in personnel decisions. In *Annual review of psychology.* Palo Alto, CA: Annual Reviews.

Zenger, J. H. (1981). Career planning: Coming in from the cold. *Training and Development Journal, 35*(7), 47–52.

Zygmont, J. (1988, February). Compact-disc companies test new frontiers. *High Technology Business*, pp. 18–23.

CHAPTER 10

Utility Analysis for Decisions in Human Resource Management

John W. Boudreau
Cornell University

This chapter presents utility analysis, *a family of theories and measures designed to describe, predict, and/or explain what determines the usefulness or desirability of decision options (e.g., improved selection, training, performance appraisal, internal staffing, and compensation) and to examine how information affects decisions. Utility analysis has been proposed as a way to help managers better understand the substantial value organizations can gain by using information from industrial and organizational psychology, economics, and information theory to make better choices regarding human resource management activities. This chapter shows how utility analysis requires an expansive view of the decision tasks and environments faced by human resource managers, recognizing contributions beyond industrial and organizational psychology in areas such as labor economics and information theory.*

This chapter proceeds through nine sections: (a) introducing and establishing utility analysis as a component of decision models; (b) historical review of utility model development and summary of the fundamental assumptions underlying utility analysis models; (c) review and summary of studies measuring the utility of industrial and organizational psychology intervention on work force consequences; (d) critical review of research measuring the dollar value of variability in employee performance; (e) risk and uncertainty in utility analysis estimates; (f) enhancements to traditional selection utility models, including financial and economic considerations, equal employment opportunity, and constituencies; (g) application of utility analysis to programs affecting an existing "stock" of employees; (h) application of utility analysis to programs affecting the "flow" of employees into, through, and out of the organization; and (i) thoughts on future utility analysis research to produce a broader understanding of managerial decisions about human resource management activities.

Introduction

THE QUESTIONS STUDIED by industrial and organizational psychologists are closely linked to the decisions facing managers of people in organizations, decisions about issues affecting the employment relationship—hiring, training, compensation, performance appraisal, and so on—that draw on theories of human work behavior. Analogously, industrial and organizational psychologists, as well as other social scientists, find the organizational environment a rich source of information for advancing knowledge and testing employment-related theories. Both scientists and managers benefit from the knowledge gained about the behaviors of individuals in the workplace, who can then search for ways to apply that knowledge to achieve individual and organizational outcomes of efficiency and equitable employment.

The similarity of interests between industrial and organizational psychologists and human resource management (HRM) professionals has produced some close collaborative relationships—for example, the many psychologists who consult for industry, conduct studies designed to support HRM decisions, or, through their work, influence the direction of employment policies. Still, the HRM teams of organizations typically lack the influence and visibility of other management teams such as marketing, finance, and operations. The literature for HRM professionals routinely laments the slow implementation of HRM programs in organizations, even though these programs have gained wide acceptance by scientists (cf. Jain & Murray, 1984), and admonishes and instructs these professionals to "sell" their

programs by emphasizing their effects on attainment of organizational goals (Bolda, 1985b; Fitz-Enz, 1984; Gow, 1985; Jain & Murray, 1984; Sheppeck & Cohen, 1985). With increased competition and evidence from the United States and abroad that competitive organizations are likely to manage their people differently, HRM personnel are more frequently expected to justify their contributions to the employer and to account for their existence.

One must question whether the lack of influence and slow implementation of HRM programs is a rational response by organizations. Could it be that behavioral theories and findings are relevant only to the scientific community and have such little relevance to organizational decisions and outcomes that they can be ignored by successful organizations? If the theories and findings are relevant, then how should they be communicated to decision makers? Do decisions that consider social science evidence produce greater organizational success, and, if so, are the successes great enough to justify the resources necessary to generate and apply the evidence?

This chapter will discuss utility analysis (UA), which attempts to answer such questions by focusing on decisions about human resources. *Utility analysis* refers to the process that describes, predicts, and/or explains what determines the usefulness or desirability of decision options and examines how that information affects decisions. In HRM and industrial and organizational psychology, the focus lies on decisions involving employment relationships and employee behaviors. Thus, industrial and organizational psychologists use the term *utility analysis* to refer to a specific set of models that reflect the consequences, usually performance-related, of programs designed to enhance the value of the work force to the employing organization.

Utility analysis offers great potential for enhancing the link between the theories and findings of industrial and organizational psychological research and the human resource decisions of organizational managers. To achieve this potential, however, UA research and applications must proceed from a framework that recognizes the broad effects of such decisions on the work force and the organization. Such a framework requires an expansive view of the decision tasks facing managers of people in organizations, a view that recognizes the contributions, limits, and implicit assumptions not only of psychological models, but also of models from other social sciences. The UA framework provides both a rationale and a significant new direction for an integration between the science and practice of industrial and organizational psychology and other scientific disciplines relevant to organizational employment decisions.

This chapter is intended as a step toward such an integrative framework. Thus, it will not only review and describe UA theories and applications but will propose new and integrative directions that have received little attention. UA research must certainly acknowledge the considerations of related disciplines such as economics, management, and sociology. But as a true theory of organizational decision making, it must go beyond simple acknowledgment so as to produce a mechanism for truly interdisciplinary approaches to employment decisions.

Chapter Outline

This chapter comprises ten sections. The first section introduces and establishes some fundamental concepts, including the nature of utility models, decision options, attributes, and payoff functions, and shows where UA models fit within the broader domain of decision models. It further establishes some ground rules guiding subsequent sections.

The second section outlines the historical development of concepts integral to utility analysis, the roots of which can be traced to the earliest stages of industrial and organizational psychological research. Not only does this historical outline provide some basic concepts for those not familiar with UA research, it also identifies certain fundamental concepts and assumptions essential to understanding utility analysis, which are sometimes ignored or forgotten in more recent theoretical developments.

The third section summarizes findings from previous studies revealing the effect of industrial and organizational psychological interventions on work force consequences. The fourth section critically reviews the research topic commanding the greatest attention to date—measuring the dollar value of performance variability.

The fifth section examines UA research from the perspective of information theory by examining the role of risk and uncertainty in decision making. Such a perspective suggests that UA models can improve decisions even when information is severely lacking. Methods for identifying risk and uncertainty are described, as well as a technique for identifying when additional information is valuable. The role of UA research in defining statistical and substantive significance is also discussed.

The sixth section presents enhancements to the traditional selection utility models. These include the roles of financial and economic considerations, "intangible" factors such as equal employment opportunity and affirmative action, and "constituencies" (Tsui, 1984, 1987; Tsui & Gomez-Mejia, 1988) in evaluating the usefulness of HRM programs. This section also shows how UA research can link industrial and organizational psychology and labor economics. It suggests that utility analysis offers a mechanism for truly interdisciplinary approaches to employment issues as long as UA models reflect economic considerations, stocks, and flows.

The seventh section discusses the role of utility analysis in describing consequences of programs that affect the "stock" of existing employees by altering the characteristics of the work force or work situation. Recent research is reviewed, suggesting implications for extending UA research to important new areas.

The eighth section presents a unified utility model reflecting outcomes of HRM decisions that affect the composition of the work force by changing the flow of employees into, through, and out of organizations—an employee-movement utility model. Important links are proposed between recruitment, selection, turnover, and internal staffing. Empirical simulation analyses are described that suggest that the actual consequences of HRM decisions are likely to reach beyond those reflected in current models addressing only the consequences of selection. It demonstrates the need for a fully integrated framework for considering the consequences of changing both the stocks and flows of employees, which can lead to greater synergy in planning and implementing employment programs.

Finally, the ninth section presents a matrix to guide future UA research, emphasizing the need to move beyond selection models and measurement issues and toward a broader understanding of HRM program decision making.

Concepts and Definitions

Utility Analysis as a Subclass of Multiattribute Utility Analysis

Multiattribute utility (MAU) models are "decision aids" (Edwards, 1977; Einhorn, Kleinmuntz, & Kleinmuntz, 1979; Einhorn & McCoach, 1977; Fischer, 1976; Huber, 1980;

Keeney & Raiffa, 1976) that provide tools for describing, predicting, and explaining decisions. MAU models share certain characteristics and requirements. To apply such models, one must:

- Identify a set of *decision options* that represent the alternative programs or courses of action under consideration

- Identify a set of *attributes* that reflect the characteristics of the options that are important because they represent the things that matter to the decision makers and/or the relevant constituents

- Measure the level of each attribute produced by each option using a *utility scale* for each attribute

- Combine the attribute values for each option using a *payoff function* reflecting the weight given each attribute and combination rules for deriving an overall total utility value for each option

Table 1 illustrates an extremely simple application of MAU analysis. Suppose productivity is below desired levels among salespeople. Two *decision options* might be identified, involving two different training programs, Program A and Program B. Three *attributes* are of interest: (a) effects on sales levels, (b) resources required to develop and implement the program, and (c) effects on salesperson job satisfaction. Attributes (a) and (b) use a *utility scale* of dollars, while attribute (c) uses a rating scale from 1 to 7. The *payoff function* consists of multiplying the level of attribute (a) by 1, multiplying the level of attribute (b) by –1, multiplying the level of attribute (c) by 3,000, and adding the results to produce a total utility value. We could construct a multiattribute utility matrix like that shown in Table 1, with the cells of the matrix containing the expected level of each attribute for each option, and the total utility values below each option computed using the payoff function. Although

TABLE 1

Example of a Multiattribute Utility Matrix for a Training Decision

| | Decision Options | | |
Attributes	Program A	Program B	Attribute Weights
(a) Sales levels (Dollars per year)	$100,000	$130,000	1
(b) Required resources (Total dollar value)	$10,000	$30,000	−1
(c) Job satisfaction (1=low, 7=high)	6.0	2.0	3,000
Total utility value =	$108,000	$106,000	

Program B has the higher first-year dollar payoff, the high weight given to attribute (c), Job Satisfaction, combined with Program B's lower Job Satisfaction, cause it to attain a lower utility value than Program A; thus, it is less preferred. Obviously, MAU models can encompass a variety of decision options, numerous and diverse sets of attributes reflecting many different constituents, and very complex payoff functions, but they generally share the characteristics shown in the simple example of Table 1.

MAU models can assist decision makers in overcoming "limits on rationality" (March & Simon, 1958) by providing a simplified, structured framework within which to consider a number of decision options. Huber (1980, pp. 61–62) identifies five advantages of MAU models over less systematic and structured decision systems:

- Because they make explicit a view of the decision situation, they help to identify the inadequacies of the corresponding implicit, mental model.

- The attributes contained in such models serve as reminders of the information needed for consideration of each alternative.

- The informational displays and models used in the mathematical model serve to organize external memories.

- They allow the aggregation of large amounts of information in a prescribed and systematic manner.

- They facilitate communication and support to be gained from constituencies.

As a subclass of MAU models, UA models also serve as decision aids and can provide the advantages listed above. Unfortunately, little theoretical or empirical research has approached utility analysis from this decision-making perspective. Nonetheless, a keen appreciation of the role of UA models in the decision process suggests some very different research questions and directions, which will be emphasized throughout. Unlike the generic MAU model described in Table 1, UA models focus on a particular type of decision option, a restricted set of attributes, and a defined mathematical formula for attribute weights and combination rules. The next sections examine these MAU components and how they apply to UA models.

The Decision Options: HRM Productivity-Enhancement Programs

Any MAU model requires a focus of analysis—the decision options considered. For example, an MAU model for deciding where to build a new hospital might focus on options reflecting different types of facilities, combined with different locations, combined with different service offerings. Each combination would constitute a decision option. Utility analysis has focused on HRM programs designed to enhance work force productivity. Such programs include selection testing, recruitment, training, and compensation—all of which affect the organizational value of the work force, whether they are explicitly chosen using decision models or evolve implicitly over time (Milkovich & Boudreau, 1991). Utility analysis involves describing, predicting, and explaining the consequences of such program options, their desirability, and the decision processes leading to choices among them. Thus, while the focus of utility analysis is more specific than generic MAU models, it covers a wide array of options relevant to organizational goals. As we shall see, the majority of UA research has focused only on selection prgrams, but we now have the theoretical models to apply to virtually any HRM program.

Decisions About Individuals Versus Decisions About Programs. Utility analysis models might seem to focus on decisions about individuals rather than programs. For example, Cascio (1980) stated that "all personnel decisions can be characterized identically. In the first place there is an individual about

whom a decision is required. Based on certain information about the individual (e.g., performance appraisals, assessment center ratings, or a disciplinary report), decision makers may elect to pursue various alternative courses of action" (p. 128). In MAU terms, the decision options comprise different courses of action for each individual.

However, closer examination shows that UA models are intended to apply to decisions about the *programs* that guide the countless decisions about individuals made by human resource managers. The options under consideration are the procedures, rules, or "strategies" (Cronbach & Gleser, 1965, p. 9) meant to be used with many individuals and evaluated by their "total contribution when applied to a large number of decisions" (p. 23). Decisions about whom to hire depend on what programs of recruitment and testing have been chosen to generate applicants and information about them. Decisions about how much to pay individuals depend on what compensation programs and rules have been chosen for that work force. Decisions about assigning individuals to new jobs depend on what career development and training programs have been chosen to generate skills and forecast future needs. Thus, UA models focus on strategic and tactical decisions about programs rather than on the operational decisions about each individual.

Because program decisions affect many individuals throughout their tenure with the organization, the impact of even a single program decision on future work force consequences can be quite large. A selection program that affects the hiring decisions for 1,000 people, people, each of whom stays for 5 years, affects 5,000 person-years of organizational behavior. If a more correct program decision produces even a modest work force quality increase of $10 per person-year, its impact can be $50,000. Of course, this also suggests that the consequences of wrong decisions have large potential negative effects. Utility analysis uses information from social and behavioral sciences to attempt to improve such important decisions.

Two Types of Programs Addressed by UA Models. It is useful to group the variety of HRM programs that can be addressed by UA models according to whether they affect *employee flows* or *employee stocks*. First, programs affecting employee *flows* change the composition or membership of the work force through employee movement (Boudreau, 1991; Boudreau & Berger, 1985a, 1985b; Milkovich & Boudreau, 1991). For example, *selection programs* allow additions to be made to the work force, *retention programs* determine which employees are retained when separations take place, and *internal staffing programs* determine which employees move between positions within an organization (Milkovich & Boudreau, 1991, chap. 10–13). UA models applied to such programs focus on the process used to determine which individuals are chosen to move or to remain, and the program's consequences reflect the effects of having a different set of employees in the work force. UA models are typically applied to decisions about this type of program, with external selection programs receiving the greatest attention.

Second, programs affecting the employee *stock* change the characteristics of the existing set of employees in their current positions. For example, *training programs* operate by altering knowledge, skills, attitudes, or other employee characteristics, *compensation and reward programs* operate by altering the relationship between behaviors/outcomes and rewards, and *performance feedback and goal-setting programs* operate by altering employee perceptions of the consequences of their behaviors. Such programs work to the extent that they lead to different behaviors by existing employees, in turn leading to more valuable organizational outcomes. UA models address decisions about such programs by focusing on options representing different kinds of programs affecting the stock of existing employees.

The Attributes of Programs in UA Models

Once a set of decision options is defined, MAU models specify the set of attributes reflecting the outcomes of concern to the decision makers and relevant constituents, and the level of each attribute achieved by each decision option. For example, the decision about where to build a hospital might include attributes as diverse as the environmental impact of the facility, speed of treatment in emergencies, and impact on local property values, reflecting the concerns of constituents as diverse as community planners, potential patients, nearby property owners, and the future medical staff.

UA models focus on decisions about HRM programs so the attribute set is more focused but still quite broad. Cronbach and Gleser (1965) defined the attribute domain as "all the consequences of a given decision that concern the person making the decision (or the institution he represents)" (p. 22). HRM program attributes may be placed in two categories—efficiency and equity (Milkovich & Boudreau, 1991). *Efficiency* attributes reflect the organization's ability to "maximize outputs while minimizing inputs," such as labor costs, job performance, sales volumes, revenues, profits, market share, and various financial and economic indicators of organizational strength. *Effectiveness* attributes reflect the "perceived fairness" of organizational procedures and outcomes, such as employee attitudes, labor relations, minority and female representation, compliance with legal requirements, and community relations.

To date, most UA research and applications have focused on a very small set of efficiency-related attributes reflecting the productivity consequences of HRM program decisions. Although UA models can become mathematically complex, all existing UA models reflect just three basic attributes (Boudreau, 1984c, 1986a, 1986b, 1988; Boudreau & Berger, 1985a, 1985b; Milkovich & Boudreau, 1991):

- *Quantity*—the number of employees and time periods affected by the consequences of program options

- *Quality*—the average effect of the program options on work force value, on a per-person, per-time-period basis

- *Cost*—the resources required to implement and maintain the program option

The program options addressed by UA models encompass a potentially large set of attributes reflecting both efficiency and equity, but existing model development has focused on a subset of the efficiency-related attributes reflecting program costs and employee productivity. Thus, like all models, UA models simplify reality by omitting or ignoring some factors. Models, by definition, are deficient because it is impossible to accurately reflect all the potential attributes affected by decisions. As we shall see, examining the nature of the attributes that are and should be included in utility models is one of the most critical issues facing UA research. Defining the domain of appropriate attributes offers fruitful opportunities for further debate and development. We shall discuss these opportunities in some detail as we review existing research.

The Utility Scale for Attributes in UA Models

With the attributes identified, an MAU model must assign a value for each attribute in each decision option. This requires establishing a utility scale for each attribute as well as determining the particular level of each attribute associated with each decision option. For example, in deciding where to locate a new hospital, the attributes are quite diverse (e.g., environmental impact, speed of treatment, facility cost, and community satisfaction) and might be measured in units as diverse as dollars, time, number of complaints, ratings, or rankings.

UA models focus on HRM programs and therefore face a more limited set of attributes. Yet even the relatively simple example in Table 1 had attributes measured in dollars (costs and productivity) as well as ratings (job satisfaction). UA models can potentially include a variety of efficiency and equity-related attributes, requiring diverse payoff scales. However, most UA models have focused primarily on productivity-related outcomes, striving to measure them in units relevant to managerial decisions. Attributes reflecting quantity are usually measured in person-years, and those reflecting cost are usually measured in dollars. The appropriate scale for the quality attributes has been subject to some debate, as we shall see, but the majority of research has been devoted to scaling quality in dollars per person-year.

Attaching a level of each attribute to each option often reflects a process using both subjective and objective information. When evaluating past programs, it may be possible to determine the actual levels of each attribute achieved by different options. But UA models are planning tools used to anticipate future consequences and support current decisions, so attaching attribute levels involves predictions and forecasts. Indeed, one major motivation for UA models was to better express statistical forecasts in terms understandable to managers. The predictive nature of attribute measurement means that utility estimates possess uncertainty and risk. While uncertainty and risk take prominence in general MAU research, UA research has largely ignored them. As we shall see, mechanisms exist to promote further research in this important area.

The choice of attribute utility scales and derivation of attribute levels is important and has received too little attention in UA research. Throughout this chapter we will highlight controversies where additional debate and research attention can be fruitful.

Combining Attributes Using a Payoff Function for UA Models

The fourth component of an MAU model is the payoff function, which specifies how the attribute levels are to be combined into an overall utility value. Deciding where to locate a new hospital might produce very diverse attributes measured on very different scales, such as dollars, time, ratings, or rankings. Payoff functions for such decisions must specify both the weights attached to each attribute level and the rules for combining the weighted attribute levels to produce an overall utility value. Such rules might range from a simple numerical weighting and addition of the weighted values, to more complex nonlinear weighting schemes and quadratic combination rules.

Because UA models focus on decisions about HRM programs, their attributes and payoff scales are more limited and the payoff functions are often simpler. Still, any payoff function must reflect both the importance of each attribute and its underlying scale. The example in Table 1 adopted a relatively simple combination rule that takes the difference between increased productivity and costs, then adds the job satisfaction level multiplied by 3,000. Obviously, the choice of weights and combination rules can have large effects on resulting utility values and should reflect the values of the decision makers and relevant constituencies.

UA research has usually focused on productivity-related outcomes and thus has adopted payoff functions reflecting dollar-valued productivity and program costs. The payoff function may be considered a variant of the cost-volume-profit models used in other managerial decisions to invest resources. The utility of an HRM program option is derived by subtracting cost from the product of quantity times quality, with the program exhibiting the largest positive difference being preferred.

It is typical to refer to UA models as cost-benefit analysis models and to categorize attributes as either costs or benefits. Simply put,

costs represent attributes that reduce overall utility values, while *benefits* represent attributes that increase overall utility values. Depending on the decision, a given attribute (e.g., reduced employee separations) may represent either a cost or a benefit. Rather than attempt a classification, this chapter will proceed from the more general position that costs and benefits are defined by the attributes, their utility scales, and the payoff functions used to combine them. It is appropriate to question whether such a payoff function is adequate or even appropriate to UA research, and we will explore this issue at length.

Summary

UA research is a subclass of more general MAU research, and the structure of MAU models provides a useful framework for organizing and understanding UA models. As we have seen, UA models reflect a set of decision options, attributes, utility scales, and payoff functions, just as any MAU model does. UA models have historically focused on a particular set of options (usually selection programs), attributes (quality, quantity, and cost), utility scales (dollars), and payoff functions (quantity times quality, minus cost). Measuring the payoff in UA research has been characterized as the Achilles' heel of UA research (Cronbach & Gleser, 1965, p. 121). As we have seen, such measurement reflects three MAU components. The attributes included the utility scale used to measure them and to attach a value to each option, with the payoff function specifying the combination rules across attributes. These components reflect implicit and explicit assumptions about the appropriate decision makers, constituents, and consequences to be considered. Throughout the chapter, we will use these MAU concepts to organize and analyze existing and needed future UA research.

We have also seen that UA models, like all models, strike a balance between simplicity and realism. All UA models are deficient by definition, and much research debate has centered on whether and how to reduce that deficiency. But we will never develop a UA model that completely reflects all relevant attributes with perfect accuracy. Does this mean that UA research is unlikely to provide any real information about the effects of HRM program decisions on organizations? If the ultimate objective of UA is to *measure the impact* of program decisions on organizations, then the answer might be yes, and we could declare a moratorium on UA research. However, like all MAU models, UA models are decision aids, not just measurement tools. A decision aid's usefulness lies in *its ability to describe, predict, explain, and improve decisions.* Such value is assessed by asking whether the model allows the best decision to be made with the given body of information, whether it helps to determine if gathering more information would permit better decisions, and whether it helps to determine how much different decision procedures contribute to decision quality (Cronbach & Gleser, 1965, p. 21). Depending on the cost and value of the next best alternative decision aid, even a very deficient or inaccurate UA model might prove effective in improving decision processes or outcomes. Thus, this chapter will approach UA research less from a measurement perspective and more from a decision-making perspective.

Historical Development of Utility Analysis Models

Though utility analysis is applicable to virtually every HRM program decision, present models resulted from a concern with selection (and later, placement or classification) decisions. Indeed, as Cronbach and Gleser (1965) point out, UA models can be characterized as responses to the inadequacies of traditional measurement and test theory in expressing the usefulness of tests:

The traditional theory views the test as a measuring instrument intended to assign accurate numerical values to some quantitative attribute of the individual. It therefore stresses, as the prime value, precision of measurement and estimation. The roots of this theory lie in surveying and astronomy, where quantitative determinations are the chief aim. In pure science it is reasonable to regard the value of a measurement as proportional to its ability to reduce uncertainty about the true value of some quantity. The mean square error is a useful index of measuring power. There is little basis for contending that one error is more serious than another of equal magnitude when locating stars or determining melting points: measurement theory is unobjectionable when applied to such appropriate situations.

In practical testing, however, a quantitative estimate is not the real desideratum. A choice between two or more discrete treatments must be made. The tester is to allocate each person to the proper category, and accuracy of measurement is valuable only insofar as it aids in this qualitative decision.... Measurement theory appears suitable without modification when the scale is considered in the abstract, without reference to any particular application. As soon as the scale is intended for use in a restricted context, that context influences our evaluation of the scale. (pp. 135–136)

Therefore, the history of UA will be discussed from a decision-making perspective, focusing on the contributions and implications of UA developments for describing, predicting, explaining, and enhancing decision processes and outcomes. Because the vast majority of research has emphasized the selection utility model, this will be the focus of the discussion.[1] In this model, the option set involves using a test versus random selection (or choosing between two selection tests), and the utility value reflects only the effects of selection on the first job to which one group of selectees is assigned. Later sections will describe more recent developments that extend utility analysis beyond selection.

Defining the Payoff Based on the Validity Coefficient

Description of the Model. The attribute of selection tests that has the longest history is the *validity coefficient*, or correlation between a predictor measure and some criterion measure of subsequent behavior, usually expressed as $r_{x,y}$. Classical measurement theory suggested this concept as a measure of the "goodness" of a test in predicting subsequent behavior. In addition to the validity coefficient, two translations are most commonly cited (e.g., Cronbach & Gleser, 1965, chap. 4; Hunter & Schmidt, 1982); both lead to the conclusion that only relatively large differences in the validity coefficient produce important differences in the value of a test. First, one can translate the validity coefficient into the *index of forecasting efficiency* (symbolized as E) using Equation 1:

$$E = 1 - (1 - r^2_{x,y})^{1/2} \qquad (1)$$

This index, emphasized by early statistical texts (e.g., Hull, 1928; Kelley, 1923), indicates the proportionate reduction in the standard error of criterion scores predicted by the test compared to the standard error of criterion scores predicted using only the group mean. Second, the *coefficient of determination*, or the squared validity coefficient, appeared as early as 1928 in Hull's text and reflects the proportion of variance shared by the predictor and the criterion.

Obviously, very large increases in validity are required to substantially increase these indices. As Cronbach and Gleser (1965) noted, "The index of forecasting efficiency describes a test correlating .50 with the criterion as

predicting only 13 percent better than chance; the coefficient of determination describes the same test as accounting for 25 percent of the variance in outcome" (p. 31). Yet correlations as high as .50 may be rare. In short, using these indices, it appeared that very great improvements in testing would be necessary to have any substantial effect on organizational outcomes.

Evaluation From a Decision-Theory Perspective. As MAU models of a test's usefulness for decisions, such formulas are deficient. Only one attribute of the selection system is considered—the accuracy of prediction, expressed as the shared variance between two normally distributed variables. From a decision-making perspective, the usefulness of a selection system depends on its ability to provide information that will improve decisions, where decision improvements are measured in terms of valued decision outcomes. Therefore, this model omits selection system attributes such as the quality of the existing selection system, the effect of the proposed selection system information on actual decisions, and the impact of those effects on valued consequences.

The utility scale for attaching attribute values to each option is a statistic that measures squared deviations from a predicted linear function. Thus, both positive and negative prediction deviations from the linear function are equally undesirable. This implies that a decision maker would consider overpredicting a qualified candidate's future performance just as costly as underpredicting it. In fact, of course, the important deviations from predictions are the ones that result in selection errors (i.e., selecting a candidate who should not have been hired and/or failing to select a candidate who should have been hired). These models adopt an implicit payoff function that assigns equal value or loss to inaccurate predictions at all points in the predictor-criterion space (Wesman, 1953). Because there is only one attribute, there is no payoff function for combining different attributes. The statistic serves as the sole utility value.

These models fail to reflect most of the three basic program attributes (i.e., quantity, quality, and cost). They reflect neither the quantity of time periods affected by the selection decisions nor the quantity of employees affected in each time period. Though these models reflect one statistical quality of the predictor, this is only indirect evidence of that predictor's effect on work force quality. Finally, they fail to acknowledge the costs to develop and apply tests. Though the deficiencies inherent in these formulas are apparent when viewed from a decision-making perspective, the fundamental notion of expressing the relationship between a predictor and a criterion in terms of the correlation coefficient remains a basic building block of UA models. Later models began to explore ways to embed the correlation coefficient within a set of decision attributes that made it easier to interpret.

Defining Payoff Based on the Success Ratio

Description of the UA Model.   These utility models reflected a new utility concept—the *success ratio*, or proportion of selected employees who subsequently succeed. Taylor and Russell (1939) proposed a UA model designed to reflect the fact that the usefulness of a test depends on the situation in which it is used. Unlike models based solely on the validity coefficient, the *Taylor-Russell model* reflects three attributes of the decision situation: (a) the *validity coefficient*, (b) the *base rate*, scaled as the proportion of applicants who would be successful if selection were made without the proposed predictor, and (c) the *selection ratio*, scaled as the proportion of applicants falling above the hiring cutoff on the predictor.

The payoff function combining these attributes assumes a linear, homoskedastic, and bivariate normal relationship between the predictor (or predictor composite) and the criterion, and uses formulas for the area

under a normal curve to derive the success ratio. The Taylor-Russell model assumes fixed-treatment selection (i.e., each applicant will either be hired or rejected) and a dichotomous criterion (i.e., selectee value is classified as either successful or unsuccessful). Total utility under the Taylor-Russell approach is the difference between the success ratio predicted for a specific combination of validity, selection ratio, and base rate, minus the success ratio that would result without using the proposed predictor (i.e., the base rate). The combination producing the greatest improvement is the preferred option. Taylor and Russell derived extensive tables indicating the predicted success ratio for various combinations of base rates, validity coefficients, and selection ratios (Cascio, 1987, reprints these tables).

To apply the model, a decision maker would choose the criterion (e.g., job performance) and determine the level of criterion performance that represents the dividing line between acceptable and unacceptable (or successful and unsuccessful) selectees. Then, he or she would estimate the current base rate implied by this criterion level in the population of individuals on which the proposed predictor would be applied, perhaps by examining the current success rate, if the predictor is to be added to those already in use. Finally, he or she would use the Taylor-Russell tables to determine the expected change in the success ratio under various assumptions about validity and selection ratios.

Detailed summaries of the Taylor-Russell model are provided elsewhere (Cascio, 1980, 1987, chap. 7; Taylor & Russell, 1939). According to the Taylor-Russell tables, when other parameters are held constant, (a) higher validities produce more improved success ratios (because the more linear the relationship, the smaller the area of the distribution lying in the false-positive or false-negative region); (b) lower selection ratios produce more improved success ratios (because lower selection ratios mean more "choosy" selection decisions, and the predictor scores of selectees lie closer to the upper tail of the predictor distribution); and (c) base rates closer to .50 produce more improved success ratios (because as one approaches a base rate of zero, none of the applicants can succeed, thus, selection has less value; as one approaches a base rate of 1.0, all applicants can succeed even without selection, so again, selection has less value).

Evaluation From a Decision-making Perspective. The Taylor-Russell model reflects three attributes, rather than only the validity coefficient, but it still provides a limited description of selection program utility. Like its predecessors, this model ignores both the number of employees affected and the number of time periods during which that effect will last. The model's measure of quality (proportion successful) is also troublesome because it does not reflect the natural units of value such as sales, productivity, or reduced errors. Finally, the model excludes attributes reflecting program costs (Cascio, 1980, 1987), but cost differences will occur, especially as the selection ratio is changed by screening more or fewer applicants.

Scaling the base rate as a dichotomous criterion (i.e., success/failure) will often lose information because the value of performance is not equal at all points above the satisfactory level; nor is it equal at all points below the unsatisfactory level (Cascio, 1982, p. 135; Cronbach & Gleser, 1965, pp. 123–124, 138; Hunter & Schmidt, 1982, p. 235). More typically, performance differences exist within the two groups, so a continuous criterion scale could be more appropriate. Cascio (1982, 1987) suggests it may be more appropriate for truly dichotomous criteria (e.g., turnover occurrences), or where output differences above the acceptable level do not change benefits (e.g., clerical or technician's tasks), or where such differences are unmeasurable (e.g., nursing, teaching, or credit counseling). Combining the attributes by assuming bivariate normality and linearity

implied in the payoff function may also be unrealistic in some selection situations.

Some have proposed that the choice of the criterion cutoff is arbitrary (Cascio, 1982, p. 133; Hunter & Schmidt, 1982, p. 235; Schmidt, Hunter, McKenzie, & Muldrow, 1979) because it is set by management consensus or because objective information on which to base such a decision is rarely available, and that changing this "arbitrary" cutoff will change the base rate and thus substantially alter the conclusions from the model. If indeed there is no objective method of setting the performance cutoff, then the Taylor-Russell utility model is inappropriate. However, the concept of a criterion cutoff is not arbitrary, nor does the Taylor-Russell model imply that arbitrary changes in that cutoff are to be regarded as legitimate methods of enhancing the success ratio. Rather, the criterion cutoff and the base rate it implies should be based on the relationship between the selection situation (i.e., the level of minimally acceptable criterion levels) and the applicant population (i.e., the proportion of the population that would exceed that level if hired). This concept is essential to evaluating the effects of recruitment on staffing utility and should not be abandoned by labeling it "arbitrary."

Variations on the Taylor-Russell Model. The models discussed next add program costs to the model and/or redefine the attribute utility scales to include dollar-scaled consequences of different selection mistakes. Cascio (1980, p. 35) noted that Smith (1948) provides a method of adjusting the Taylor-Russell results to reflect preexisting selection ratios and validities. Technically, if characteristics of current employees are used as inputs to the model, this assumes that current employees are similar to the applicant population to which the new predictor system will be applied. This is appropriate if one is adding the new predictor to an existing set of predictors and if the base rate, selection ratio, and validity coefficient reflect this situation. However, if the predictor will replace a previous predictor, then one should use the table corresponding to the observed success ratio given current selection ratios and validities.

Sands (1973) proposed the *CAPER model* (Cost of Attaining Personnel Requirements). Its payoff objective is a recruiting and selection strategy that minimizes total costs of recruiting, inducting, selecting, and training enough new hires to meet a set quota of satisfactory employees. This model adds the notion of the costs involved in hiring and recruiting, but it suffers from the same weaknesses in the payoff function as the Taylor-Russell model.

Mahoney and England (1965) noted that success and failure probabilities on a new predictor are conditional on the success and failure probabilities existing in the applicant population after previous methods have been employed. They proposed that previous decision rules (Meehl & Rosen, 1955; Stone & Kendall, 1956) implicitly assumed that these probabilities are .50. They defined the cost of selection mistakes to include not only false positives (hires who do not succeed) as in the Taylor-Russell model, but also false negatives (rejected applicants who would have succeeded), which could be important where high-quality rejected applicants are hired by competitors and reduce the organization's competitive advantage (Guttman & Raju, 1965). Mahoney and England simulated various values for the selection ratio on the proposed predictor, the selection ratio on previous predictors, the existing failure probability, the failure probability under the new system, the ratio of recruitment costs to selection mistakes (i.e., 05, .10, .30, and .50), and the ratio of predictor costs to selection mistakes (i.e., .05, .10, and .30). They concluded that a new predictor's value exceeds its cost only when the probability of selection mistakes is quite low (i.e., less than .30), and that "the opportunities for developing and installing predictive measures that are worth the additional cost appear relatively restricted" (p. 375). This conclusion conflicts with

more recent evidence based on newer UA models. One explanation is that their ratios of costs to mistakes were really quite large. Because selection mistakes may reduce performance for many years and predictors can cost less than a few hundred dollars, it is difficult to imagine situations where the ratio would exceed .10, and it would probably frequently fall below .01.

Hunter and Schmidt (1982) also note a number of studies based on the notion of a dichotomous criterion (Alf & Dorfman, 1967; Curtis, 1967; Darlington & Stauffer, 1967; Schmidt, 1974). While obviously deficient, if the dichotomous-criterion model is easier to implement, then a more complex model, such as one of those to be discussed subsequently, must prove its value based on its ability to improve decisions over the simpler model.

Defining Payoff Based on the Standardized Criterion Level

Description of the Utility Model. The major criticism of the Taylor-Russell model was that it used a dichotomous notion of total utility (i.e., success/failure) that failed to reflect the true range of variation in selectee performance. The next version of the selection utility model attempted to remedy this by scaling total utility on a continuous scale. Brogden (1946a, 1946b) showed that the correlation coefficient is the proportion of maximum predictive value obtained using a predictor, where maximum predictive value is what would hypothetically be obtained if the criterion itself were used to select employees. Moreover, he used the principles of linear regression to demonstrate the relationship between the correlation coefficient and increases in a criterion (measured on a continuous scale). Brogden's logic serves as the basic building block for virtually all subsequent UA research.

Assuming a linear relationship between criterion scores (y) and predictor scores (x), the best linear unbiased estimate of the criterion score associated with a predictor score is:

$$E(y) = A + B(x) \tag{2}$$

The intercept (*A*) and the slope (*B*) of this line reflect the linear relationship between *x* and *y* as well as the units in which each was originally scaled. However, because predictor and criterion scales vary from study to study, it is difficult to compare these parameters or to use them in a general model. However, if we transform both the *y* and *x* variables into standardized (*Z*-score) units (i.e., Z_x and Z_y), we can write Equation 2 as follows:

$$Z_y = (r_{x,y})(Z_x) \tag{3}$$

Therefore, if we knew the average standardized predictor score of a selected group of applicants (i.e., $\overline{Z}_x$), our best prediction of the average standardized criterion score of the selected group (i.e., $\overline{Z}_y$) would be the product of the validity coefficient and the standardized predictor score, as shown in Equation 4:

$$\overline{Z}_y = (r_{x,y})(\overline{Z}_x) \tag{4}$$

The validity coefficient was well established. One way to estimate the average standardized test score of the selected group would be to actually observe the value after applying a selection device. However, Kelley (1923) suggested that if one assumes that the predictor scores are normally distributed and that one ranks applicants by test score and selects from the top down, then the average standardized predictor score is a function of the proportion of the applicant population falling above the predictor cutoff score (i.e., the selection ratio). However, if one assumes the predictor is normally distributed, then Equation 4 holds only if one also assumes normally distributed criterion scores as well.

Brogden (1949, Equation 6) and Cronbach and Gleser (1965, p. 309) make use of this approach to derive their models. If we

symbolize the *ordinate of the normal distribution* corresponding to the standardized predictor cutoff score as lambda (i.e., λ), and the selection ratio corresponding to the standardized predictor cutoff as *SR* (also symbolized by ø), then Equation 3 can be rewritten as shown:

$$\overline{Z}_y = (r_{x,y})(\lambda / SR) \tag{5}$$

The ordinate of the normal distribution is an important variable, multiplicatively related to the average standardized predictor score, and a statistically sophisticated concept. It is sufficient, however, to understand that the ordinate is simply a mathematical value that is completely determined by the selection ratio, and, when divided by the selection ratio, can be used to compute the expected average standardized predictor score of those selected using that selection ratio. Computing the relationship between the selection ratio and the average standardized predictor score of the selected group was made even easier by Naylor and Shine (1965), who computed extensive tables showing, for each selection ratio, the corresponding standardized predictor cutoff score, the corresponding ordinate of the normal distribution, and the corresponding average standardized predictor score under the assumptions noted above.

Evaluation From a Decision-making Perspective. The attributes of the *Naylor-Shine utility model* still include the validity coefficient and the selection ratio, but their contributions appear through a different payoff function. The validity coefficient now has a constant multiplicative effect on expected standardized criterion levels at all selection ratios. The selection ratio still reflects the "choosiness" of the selection program but is now used to derive a new attribute—the standardized predictor score of selectees (Z_x). The lower the selection ratio, the greater the predictor score required to meet selection standards and the greater the resulting standardized predictor score of those meeting the selection standard. Unlike the Taylor-Russell model, the base rate no longer appears as an attribute because the standardization used to go from Equation 2 to Equation 3 defines the average value of the applicant pool as zero.

The utility model of Equations 3, 4, and 5 addresses one shortcoming of the Taylor-Russell model by using a total utility concept based on a continuous scale. Utility is defined as the difference in average standardized criterion score between those selected using a test and those selected without it. The translation from Equation 2 to Equation 3 requires that the utility concept be expressed in standardized units, which are difficult to interpret in units more natural to the decision process (e.g., performance ratings, dollars, units produced, or reduced costs). Also, this utility concept reflects only the difference between the average standardized criterion score of those selected using the predictor and the average standardized criterion score that would be obtained through selection without the predictor. The absolute utility from the program is not computed, only the increment over not using the predictor. Finally, the model assumes that selection occurs as if applicants were ranked based on their predictor scores and then hired from the top down until the desired selection ratio is reached, which may or may not describe a realistic selection approach.

Considering the three basic utility model concepts (i.e., quantity, quality, and cost), the Naylor-Shine utility model reflects the effects of selection on per-person, per-time-period quality on a continuous criterion. The quantity of employees and the number of time periods affected are not explicitly reflected, nor are program costs. However, the next section will demonstrate that they can be easily added.

Defining Payoff in Terms of Dollar-valued Criterion Levels

Description of the Utility Model. The most obvious drawback of the Naylor-Shine model is that standardized criterion levels are difficult to interpret in "real" units. Correlation-based statistics are useful when predictor and criterion scales vary from study to study (as in selection research) because the standardized scale underlying the correlation coefficient allows direct comparison between studies. However, when one wishes to evaluate utility in units relevant to a particular situation, such standardized scales create problems.

Actual selection makers usually face choices among selection strategies. Each strategy carries with it a set of activities required for development and implementation as well as the possibility of various outcomes resulting from more accurate selection. The development and implementation activities are often expressed as costs (i.e., the value of required resources) usually scaled in dollars. Therefore, the question becomes whether it is worthwhile to spend that dollar amount to produce the selection consequences. With a standardized criterion scale, one must ask questions such as, Is it worth spending $10,000 to select 50 people per year in order to obtain a criterion level 0.5 standard deviations greater than what would be obtained without the predictor? Many HRM managers may not even be familiar with the concept of a standard deviation and would therefore find it difficult to attach a dollar value to a 0.5 standard deviation increase in the criterion, particularly because the decision makers may never actually observe the population of applicants to which the predictor would be applied.

These limitations suggest modifying the UA model for selection so it is expressed in dollar terms. Both Brogden (1946a, 1946b, 1949) and Cronbach and Gleser (1965, pp. 308–309) eventually derived their utility formulas in terms of payoff, often expressed in dollars, rather than standardized criterion scores. Also, they both included the concept of costs. In fact, Brogden's (1949) treatment explicitly computed utility values in dollar terms and attempted to derive guidelines for testing costs. Brogden and Taylor's (1950) formula introduced a scaling factor to translate standardized criterion levels into dollar terms. The scaling factor is the dollar value of a one-standard-deviation difference in criterion level (e.g., σ_y, σ_e, and SD_y). The cost attribute is usually expressed as the cost to administer the predictor to a single applicant (usually symbolized as C). Finally, the utility value is symbolized as $\Delta \bar{U}$ to indicate that it represents the *difference* between the dollar payoff from selection without the predictor and the dollar payoff from selection with the predictor—usually termed the *incremental utility of the predictor*. The resulting utility equation may be written as shown in Equation 6:

$$\Delta \bar{U} = (SD_y)(r_{x,y})(\bar{Z}_x) - C/SR \qquad (6)$$

The per-applicant cost (C) is divided by the selection ratio (SR) to reflect total cost of obtaining each applicant (e.g., if the selection ratio is .50, then one must test two applicants to find each selectee, and the testing cost per selectee is two times the cost per applicant). Sometimes, the entire formula is simply written in terms of per-selectee outcomes, and the symbol C is used to denote the cost per selectee. Equation 6 depicts the incremental dollar value ($\bar{U}$) produced by using a predictor (x) in a population of applicants where the validity coefficient is $r_{x,y}$; a one-standard-deviation difference in dollar valued criterion levels equals SD_y; the average standardized predictor score of those selected is $\bar{Z}_x$; and the per-selectee cost of using the predictor equals C/SR.

To express the total gain from using the predictor to select N_s selectees, we simply multiply by the number selected, change the symbol for incremental utility from $\Delta \bar{U}$ to ΔU, and multiply the per-applicant cost by the number of applicants (N_{app}) as shown in Equation 7:

$$\Delta U = (N_s)(SD_y)(r_{x,y})(\bar{Z}_x) - (C)(N_{app}) \qquad (7)$$

This formula is stated in terms of the per-selectee incremental criterion level multiplied by the number selected (Brogden, 1949), but Cronbach and Gleser (1957, 1965) derived their formulas in terms of the per-applicant incremental criterion level, which can be derived by dividing the total utility by the number of applicants, as expressed in Equation 8:

$$\Delta U / \text{applicant} = (N_s / N_{app})(SD_y)(r_{x,y})(\lambda / SR) - C \qquad (8)$$

In Equation 8, the term (λ / SR) has been substituted for the average standardized test score.

If we note that the term N_s / N_{app} equals the selection ratio SR, we can cancel terms and produce the Cronbach and Gleser equation for per-applicant incremental dollar-valued utility, as shown in Equation 9:

$$\Delta U / \text{applicant} = (SD_y)(r_{x,y})(\lambda) - C \qquad (9)$$

Cronbach and Gleser (1965, p. 39) also developed a utility formula for comparing the usefulness of two tests, one producing lower validity and lower costs, the other producing higher validity with higher costs. They recommended computing the difference in utility between the two tests, which simply involves substituting the difference in validities for $r_{x,y}$ and the difference in costs for C in Equations 6 through 9.

Recent embellishments of these models have explicitly incorporated the duration of the events of better-selecting one group by multiplying the value component (i.e., the

TABLE 2

One-Cohort Entry-level Selection Utility Decision

Cost-Benefit Information	Entry-level Computer Programmers
Current employment	4,404
Number separating	618
Number selected (N_s)	618
Average tenure in years (T)	9.69
Test Information	
Number of applicants (N_{app})	1,236
Testing cost/applicant	$10
Total test cost (C)	$12,360
Average test score ($\bar{Z}_x$)	.80 *SD*
Validity ($r_{x,y}$)	.76
SD_y (per person-year)	$10,413

Utility Computation

Quantity	=	Average tenture x applicants selected
	=	9.69 years x 618 applicants
	=	5,988 person-years
Quality	=	Average test score x test validity x SD_y
	=	.80 x .76 x $10,413
	=	$6,331 per person-year
Utility	=	(Quantity x quality) – cost
	=	(5,988 person-years x $6,331 per person-year) – $12,360
	=	$37.9 million

From "Utility Analysis" by John W. Boudreau, 1988. In Lee Dyer (Ed.), *Human Resource Management: Evolving Roles and Responsibilities.*Washington, DC: The Bureau of National Affairs, Inc. Copyright 1988 by the Bureau of National Affairs, Inc. Reprinted by permission.

component containing $r_{x,y}$) by the expected average tenure of the hired group (i.e., *T*). These equations have come to be known as the *Brogden-Cronbach-Gleser* (B-C-G) *selection utility model.*

Evaluation From a Decision-making Perspective. The B-C-G selection utility model reflects the same attributes as Naylor-Shine, but adds the attribute of dollar-valued criterion standard deviation (i.e., SD_y). It also adds attributes reflecting the duration of selection effects (i.e., *T*) and program costs (i.e., *C*). In terms of the overall utility concept, scaling the per-person,

per-time-period incremental criterion level in dollars seems more in keeping with organizational objectives evaluated in dollars. The model continues to focus on the incremental utility added by using the predictor versus not using it. Thus, all utility values are scaled as differences from an unknown utility level that would be attained without the predictor.

Table 2 summarizes the results of the Schmidt, Hunter, McKenzie, & Muldrow (1979) application of the B-C-G model for entry-level computer programmers in the U.S.

government. The application reflects the consequences of hiring one group of 618 computer programmers, assumed to stay for 9.69 years and then leave. The utility computation is organized according to the quantity, quality, and cost components developed earlier. Unlike earlier models, the B-C-G model incorporates all three concepts. Although modifications to this basic model have recently been proposed, the B-C-G model has been the dominant framework for studying HRM program utility.

Assumptions of the B-C-G Selection Utility Model. The payoff function translating the attributes into utility values reflects certain assumptions (Cronbach & Gleser, 1965, p. 307):

- Decisions focus on an indefinitely large population of "all applicants after screening by any procedure which is presently in use and will continue to be used." Thus, the appropriate population for deriving the validity coefficient, SD_y, and the selection ratio depends on the decision situation. If one is contemplating adding a new procedure to a group of previously used procedures, then it is the "incremental" validity coefficient and the prescreened population SD_y and selection ratio that count. If, however, one contemplates replacing an old procedure with a new one, then the parameters should reflect the unscreened population.

- Regarding any person, one can decide only to accept or reject them. Thus, no adaptive decisions can be made to reflect different predictor scores (e.g., training those who achieve a moderately high score in order to bring them to minimally qualified levels).

- Predictor (or "test") scores are standardized to zero mean and unit standard deviation.

- The "payoff" resulting from accepting a person has a linear regression on predictor score, and the predictor is scored so that validity is positive.

- The payoff resulting from rejecting a person is unrelated to predictor score, and is set to zero. Thus, it is assumed that the organization is indifferent to the consequences of rejection, regardless of the qualification level of those rejected.

- The average cost of administering the predictor ("testing") a person is C, and C is greater than zero. In practice, it is often easier to separate this cost into its fixed components (i.e., one-time development costs) and its variable components (i.e., ongoing per-applicant administration costs). Also, if the decision options include the possibility of testing more or fewer applicants, then the differences in recruiting costs necessary to provide different quantities of applicants should be included (Boudreau & Rynes, 1985; Hunter & Schmidt, 1982, p. 241).

- The strategy for selection is to set a predictor cutoff score so that the desired proportion (selection ratio) of the applicant group falls above it. All applicants scoring above that level are accepted, those below it are rejected. This is equivalent to ranking applicants from the top down on predictor score, and then hiring by rank order until the established quota of new hires is met (assuming there are no rejected offers). When such hiring does not take place, the effective selection ratio is different.

Validity for the Dollar-valued Criterion Versus Proxy Criteria. Adopting the SD_y scaling factor carries with it some assumptions about observed and implied correlations. There is no clear consensus regarding the meaning of *y* (we will discuss this after reviewing empirical attempts to estimate SD_y), but it undoubtedly reflects a wide variety of employee behaviors and attributes that affect dollar-valued organizational outcomes. If it were possible to measure such a criterion, the best utility model would simply reflect the regression equation of *y* on the predictor score (similar to Equation 2). In reality, however, predictors are not validated on such a dollar-valued criterion because it cannot be directly measured. Thus, UA models substitute a validity coefficient ($r_{x,y}$) that reflects the regression of one or more proxy criteria (e.g., performance ratings, tenure, or sales) on the predictor, with all variables standardized to *Z*-scores. This substitution not only assumes that dollar-valued criterion levels are linearly related to predictor scores but that the proxy criterion and unobserved dollar-valued productivity are also linearly related.

Hunter and Schmidt (1982) and Schmidt, Hunter, McKenzie, and Muldrow (1979) proposed that many mistakenly believe that utility equations are of no value unless the data exactly fit the linear homoskedastic model and all marginal distributions are normal. They state that the B-C-G model only introduces the normality assumption for "derivational convenience" (Hunter & Schmidt, p. 243) because it provides an exact relationship between the selection ratio and the average standard test score of selectees. They further state that the only critical assumption is a linear homoskedastic relationship between predictor and criterion, and they present evidence in support of this relationship using observable proxy criteria. They argue (Schmidt et al., 1979, p. 613) that the relationship between the proxy and employee dollar value will be linear or that ceiling effects on proxy measures will make the correlation between the proxy and the predictor underestimate the correlation between the dollar value and the predictor. Raju, Burke, and Normand (1987) note that equality between these correlations implies a correlation close to unity between the proxy and dollar value.

Evidence of low correlations between typical and maximum performance (Sackett, Zedeck, & Fogli, 1988) suggests that validity might differ depending on whether dollar value reflects typical or maximum performance. Evidence that test validity may be higher at higher predictor score ranges (Lee & Foley, 1986) suggests that the level of test scores in the applicant population may also moderate incremental utility values. We have no direct evidence regarding the correlation between predictors and dollar-valued utility, but small estimation errors may not seriously reduce the utility model's ability to improve decisions compared to less sophisticated decision models.

Hunter and Schmidt (1982) and Schmidt et al. (1979) also state it is a mistake to believe that test validities are situationally specific, making application of utility analysis possible only when a criterion-related validity study has been performed in the particular situation. *Validity generalization research* (Hunter, Schmidt, & Jackson, 1982), which allows data from many studies to be analyzed together, strongly suggests that much of the variability in validity coefficients observed across studies is due to artifacts of the studies (e.g., different sample sizes, different criterion reliabilities, or different range restrictions) rather than to real differences in the predictor-criterion relationship. Moreover, the variability that does remain after correcting for these artifacts may be so small that it does not seriously reduce the utility model's ability to enhance decisions. Indeed, it has been suggested that selection validities might usefully be estimated by experts or even less experienced judges (Hirsh, Schmidt, & Hunter, 1986; Schmidt, Hunter, Croll, & McKenzie, 1983).

The Role of Testing Costs.   Both Brogden (1949) and Cronbach and Gleser (1965) portrayed testing costs as a fundamental characteristic of their UA models. The cost attribute recognizes that improvements in validity and/or reductions in selection ratios are not infinitely desirable. At some point, additional costs will offset gains from improved employee quality. At the extreme, it seems unlikely that pursuit of selection systems with validities close to unity would be cost effective. Cronbach and Gleser (1965) discussed the importance of the cost of testing in deciding between competing predictors (p. 39), in determining optimum test length (p. 323–324) and in determining the optimum predictor cutoff score (p. 308). Brogden (1949) noted that considering the cost of testing can show that higher selection ratios (i.e., testing fewer applicants and being less choosy) can be preferable to low ones if the testing cost is high. He concluded that "the ratio of cost of testing to the product of the validity coefficient and SD_y (in dollar units) should not exceed .10. It would be desirable to hold it below .05" (p. 177). Below .05, lower selection ratios contribute to higher utility. Brogden presented an example for hosiery loopers and used a one-year payoff duration. His analysis indicated that testing costs above $5.00 per person decreased utility at low selection ratios. As we shall see, in actual applications SD_y (per person, per year) is usually fairly large compared to testing costs. Moreover, testing costs occur once, but benefits usually accrue over the selected group's tenure. Thus, the value of SD_y when considered over the group's tenure is larger, and testing costs become less likely to detract from utility except at very low selection ratios (Hunter & Schmidt, 1982, p. 240).

However, omitting such costs from the UA model or assuming they equal zero removes much of the justification for dollar-valued utility estimates. Faced with a costless selection procedure, any nonnegative validity coefficient must produce positive utility because N_s, SD_y, and $\bar{Z}_x$ must always be positive (see Equation 7); therefore, a utility model based solely on the sign of the validity coefficient would suffice. In reality, implementing employee selection programs may require time, energy, and other resources that could be used to implement other managerial programs. If so, the lost value of the foregone programs represents a legitimate cost of the selection program, so that actual costs (i.e., the true investment necessary to implement the selection program) may be much higher than testing costs alone.

The Appropriate Applicant Population. Cronbach and Gleser (1965) stated, "We use 'validity' subsequently to refer to a correlation computed on men who have been screened on whatever *a priori* information is in use and will continue to be available" (pp. 34–35) and that the appropriate utility calculation depends on the situation in which the selection program will be used. They noted three possible situations:

- All prior information will continue to be used and the new system added to it.

- The new system will be substituted for some of the prior information.

- A composite of previous and new information will be used.

Each has different implications for the UA model. The *incremental* program contribution is key. Moreover, any new program should be compared to the efficient use of information already available. Some have concluded that the B-C-G model presumes concurrent validity (e.g., Cascio, 1980, p. 39), but the precise assumption is that selection devices be evaluated in light of the conditions under which they will actually be applied. In fact, such conditions may indicate a population less restricted than current applicants (e.g., if the predictor is to be substituted for an existing predictor and applied to unscreened applicants) or it may imply a more restricted population (e.g., if the new predictor is not only going to be added to an existing screening system, but the existing system will be improved before adding it).

Mueser and Maloney (1987) argue that validity coefficients used in utility analysis may be severely overstated if test validation data arise from situations where composite predictors are already in use, and validity estimates fail to correct for multivariate restriction in range on those composites versus test scores. Applicant population characteristics also affect the selection ratio and SD_y (Boudreau & Rynes, 1985). Determining the appropriate population requires assumptions that have important implications for integrating additional staffing processes (e.g., recruitment or turnover) into the selection utility model, as discussed subsequently.

Several enhancements to the B-C-G model have been proposed and applied, but the vast majority of empirical UA research has focused on selection systems using the B-C-G model. Therefore, we will now review empirical research based on the B-C-G model and discuss the enhancements and empirical findings. Existing UA applications have produced two kinds of findings: (a) evidence of the utility values from selection programs and (b) evidence of differences in SD_y.

Utility Values for Selection Programs

Appendix A summarizes the utility values reported in existing literature. Twenty-one empirical studies were located, with utility values for 48 interventions. Two of these studies reported results for nonselection activities (Florin-Thuma & Boudreau, 1987; Mathieu & Leonard, 1987), but the utility model used by these studies is sufficiently similar to include their results here; the utility model for nonselection programs will be discussed subsequently. Several studies used enhanced utility models incorporating additional attributes (Burke & Frederick, 1986; Cronshaw, Alexander, Wiesner, & Barrick, 1987; Florin-Thuma & Boudreau, 1987; Mathieu & Leonard, 1987; Rich & Boudreau, 1987). The symbols at the top of the table stand for the parameters of the utility model. N_s is the number selected or

treated; T is the tenure of the selectees, or F is the analysis period; SR is the selection ratio; $\bar{Z}_x$ is the estimated average standardized predictor score of selectees; $r_{x,y}$ is the validity coefficient; SD_y is the dollar-valued standard deviation of performance among the applicant population (or the untreated group for nonselection programs); $Cost$ is the total program cost; and ΔU is the total utility of the program over all treated employees and all time periods. The last two columns contain an equation expressing total utility as a function of SD_y, as well as the "break-even" (B-E) SD_y value necessary for the program's total returns to equal its costs (Boudreau, 1984a, and as discussed subsequently).

The overwhelming conclusion from Appendix A is that selection programs pay off handsomely. Virtually every study has produced dollar-valued payoffs that clearly exceeded costs. (Van Naersson, 1963, did report that improved selection to reduce accidents did not pay off because accident frequency and damages were already quite low.) Even the earliest studies that reported utility per person (or per person, per hour in the case of Roche, 1961) found that the payoff exceeded costs. In studies dealing with more employees, multiple-year tenure, and more recent studies that take into account the effects of inflation, the utility estimates are always positive and have ranged into the millions (e.g., Cascio & Ramos, 1986; Cronshaw, Alexander, Wiesner, & Barrick, 1986; Rich & Boudreau, 1987; Schmidt et al., 1979; Schmidt, Hunter, Outerbridge, & Trattner, 1986). The clear positive payoff from selection programs remains evident in studies with both small and large SD_y values and with selection ratios as high as 81 percent (Van Naersson, 1963). The largest utility values occur where large numbers of individuals are affected by the program and N_s is large.

Many of the studies were designed to examine whether substituting a more valid selection method for a less valid one, usually an interview, produced greater dollar-valued payoff

(Burke & Frederick, 1986; Cascio & Ramos, 1986; Cascio & Silbey, 1979; Ledvinka, Simonet, Neiner, & Kruse, 1983; Rich & Boudreau, 1987; Schmidt et al., 1979, 1984). In these cases, Appendix A reports a utility value for each selection method separately and a utility value for the difference between them. As shown, in every case the more valid, and usually more costly, selection procedure produced the greater estimated utility. However, even the interview produced positive utility despite its cost and low validity. This is not an argument in favor of less valid selection, but it does illustrate that even modestly valid selection programs may produce substantial utility values.

The utility values measured by the B-C-G model appear to be quite high. Moreover, the estimated costs of improved selection are often minuscule compared to the benefits. A $10 per-applicant testing cost might produce over five times greater validity if the *Programmer Aptitude Test* is substituted for the interview (Schmidt et al., 1979). As noted earlier, testing costs are unlikely to reflect the full range of resources required to implement top-down selection based on more valid predictors, but even inflating costs by a factor of 10 or 100 often would not change the positive utility values. According to these findings, the economic impact of improved selection might well surpass many more traditional investment opportunities such as in plant and equipment purchases, marketing, or in the financial arena. Such a conclusion seems at odds with the observations reported earlier, and verified by many HR managers, that human resource management's contribution is often ignored, that HR issues are not considered in organizational planning, and that debate continues over whether HR activities are really an appropriate use for organizational resources. This suggests several important research issues regarding the decision processes of managers and the way in which payoff information about HRM programs is interpreted and evaluated. However, only one research issue has received substantial attention in the industrial and organizational psychology literature—the accuracy, psychometric quality, and proper measurement method for SD_y.

Research Measuring SD_y

The standard deviation of dollar-valued job performance in the applicant population (SD_y) was characterized as the Achilles' heel of utility analysis by Cronbach and Gleser (1965, p. 121). The amount of recent research aimed at estimating this elusive concept suggests that many of today's UA researchers agree. Moreover, researchers often regard accurate SD_y measurement as fundamental to useful UA research (Burke & Frederick, 1984, 1986; DeSimone, Alexander, & Cronshaw, 1986; Greer & Cascio, 1988; Weekley, O'Connor, Frank, & Peters, 1985). This section reviews this research from a decision-theory perspective, focusing its contribution toward better describing, predicting, explaining, and enhancing HRM program decisions. The review will focus on four decisions that must be made in measuring SD_y:

- The definition of utility (i.e., y)

- The focus population

- The setting of the study

- The operational measurement method used

From a decision-making perspective, these decisions should be guided by how well the analysis will describe, explain, predict, or enhance HRM program decisions. SD_y measurement is fundamentally linked to the decision context in which the measure is applied. However, existing research seldom explores whether utility analysis and SD_y measures affect decisions or reflect decision maker objectives and values. Instead, research tends to pit one measure against others, often advocating a particular measure, with quality usually defined psychometrically (e.g., in terms of consistency with other measures, reliability across estimators, or consistency with distributional assumptions). Such research provides interesting tests of measurement principles. However, its value in describing, predicting, explaining, and enhancing decision processes is difficult to determine because most SD_y studies don't reflect actual decisions.

UA models were spawned by the limitations of measurement theory and correlational statistics to fully capture the decision processes and consequences of selection programs (see Cronbach & Gleser, 1965, pp. 135–137). It is ironic that with the resurgence of UA research the focus is once again on measurement issues. UA research (including SD_y measurement research) should focus clearly on the ultimate purpose of UA models to describe, predict, explain, and enhance decision processes. This focus is frequently absent in the rush to develop and test each new SD_y measure.

Appendix B summarizes existing SD_y measurement research. The studies are arranged chronologically, with each study described in terms of its setting and sample, utility scale, estimation method, and research findings. The research findings are described in terms of the mean SD_y estimate derived (i.e., *MEAN*), the standard deviation of the SD_y estimate in the sample (i.e., *SD*), the standard error of the mean SD_y estimate (*SE*), the percent of average salary represented by average SD_y, and the percent of the mean payoff estimate represented by average SD_y. In studies estimating dollar-valued payoff (y) directly (e.g., Day & Edwards, 1987; DeSimone et al., 1986; Edwards, Frederick, & Burke, 1988; Greer & Cascio, 1987), Appendix B reports the actual average payoff estimate (Mean y) as well as the estimate of the standard deviation (SD_y). Thirty-four studies were located, producing over 100 individual SD_y estimates (the results shown in Appendix B sometimes represent averages of groups of estimates derived by the authors). The trend in research activity is clearly evident, with only five studies between 1953 and 1978, but with 29 studies between 1979 and 1988.

The Utility Scale

Viewing UA models as special cases of MAU models suggests that utility will be largely in the eye of the beholder. Generic MAU models often rely on subjectively scaled payoff functions, measured by having decision makers indicate their preferences for different levels of certain attributes on a scale of zero to 100 (see Huber, 1980, for examples). The decision makers and the nature of the decision situation determine the payoff function, and the MAU model makes explicit the values, assumptions, and priorities.

Because UA models serve, in part, to translate HRM program consequences into units that managers understand (usually dollars), UA research has used more focused utility scales. Equations 6 through 9 clearly indicate that the utility scale reflects the expected average increase in employee dollar value due to the selection program on a per-person, per-year basis. Little consensus exists regarding the meaning of dollar value. The variety of criteria available for evaluating HRM decisions (see Milkovich & Boudreau, 1991; Smith, 1976; or other introductory textbooks) virtually guarantees that different researchers will adopt diverse definitions of the payoff scale. Still, a broad concept of the utility scale must be maintained to avoid basing decisions on a dangerously narrow perspective.

Defining the meaning and scale of the criterion is important to advancing UA research and applications (Day & Edwards, 1987; DeSimone et al., 1986; Steffy & Maurer, 1988). While a single definition will not apply in all situations, this section will attempt to develop a framework for categorizing existing definitions and developing new ones. At the very least, such a framework will allow researchers to clearly identify the objectives and assumptions underlying various studies. Eventually, it may aid understanding of the appropriate utility scales for different situations.

The Utility Concept. A general definition of payoff for utility analysis is *"all consequences of a given decision that concern the person making the decision (or the institution he represents)"* (Boudreau, 1987, 1989; Cronbach & Gleser, 1965, p. 22). Some of these consequences may be positively valued—often referred to as *benefits*—and some may be negatively valued—often referred to as *costs*. This definition has several implications:

- Utility may reflect different outcomes (e.g., productivity increases, labor cost reductions, affirmative action goal attainment, improved organization image, consistency with fundamental organizational beliefs, or high levels of financial return) consistent with the desires and objectives of decision makers and the constituents they serve (see Cronbach & Gleser, 1965, p. 23).

- Utility measures should reflect the decision context. Work force quality improvements will have different value depending on how they are used by the organization. For example, improved work force quality may be used to increase the number of units produced, to increase their average quality, or to reduce costs. The dollar implications of these strategies are quite different.

- Increased measurement precision will not always improve decision quality. For example, if a simple (and inexpensive) payoff measure implies positive program utility but a more accurate (though more expensive) measure leads to the same decision, then the more accurate measure does not improve decision quality.

A Framework for the Payoff Scale Defining SD_y. The payoff scales in UA research usually focus on the economic consequences of programs that increase quality of the labor force. Yet there are many ways an organization might employ a higher quality work force (Cronbach & Gleser, 1965, p. 23), and the payoff from HRM programs depends on how the organization uses the quality enhancements they produce. The quantity, quality, and cost concepts introduced earlier provide a useful framework. Among other objectives, organizations aim to increase economic value. They can do this through some combination of: (a) producing high *quality* per unit of product sold in order to generate high prices/revenue from selling each product unit, (b) producing and selling a large *quantity* of units, and (c) producing units at low *cost* (i.e., the value of resources in their next best alternative use; Levin, 1983). This framework applies even to nonprofit organizations, whose objective is to provide the maximum quantity of service at the minimum cost, with a target profit of zero. This implies three general uses for improved labor force quality: (a) increasing the quantity of production, (b) increasing the quality of production, and (c) reducing production costs. Managers may choose to use labor force quality increases in any combination of ways. A payoff scale defined in terms of economic profit can reflect any or all of these uses. A payoff scale defined in terms of quantity will be sufficient to reflect uses affecting product quantity, but it will fail to reflect the other two, and so on. Payoff scales reflecting revenue enhancements (through higher quality or quantity) and cost reductions dominate the UA literature, though profit-based scales are emerging.

Payoff as Cost Reduction. Most of the earliest UA applications focused on cost reduction from improved selection. Doppelt and Bennett (1953) focused on reductions in training costs. Van Naersson (1963) focused on reductions in driving accident and training costs. Lee and Booth (1974) and Schmidt and Hoffman (1973) focused on reduced costs of replacement (e.g., recruitment, selection, and hiring costs) when turnover is reduced. More recently, Eaton, Wing, and Mitchell (1985) and Mitchell, Eaton, and Wing (1985) measured payoff in terms of the avoided costs of additional tanks to achieve a given military objective. Boudreau (1983a, p. 555) noted that utility models including variable costs applied to situations where cost reduction is an important selection outcome. Schmidt and Hunter (1983, p. 413) noted that increases in work force productivity might be used to reduce payroll costs by producing the same amount of output with a smaller number of employees. Arnold, Rauschenberger, Soubel, and Guion (1982), DeSimone et al. (1986), and Schmidt et al. (1986) emphasized cost reduction from hiring fewer employees to do the same amount of work. These payoff functions are also consistent with the behavioral costing approach to HRM program analysis described by Cascio (1982, 1987) in which HRM program effects are evaluated according to their ability to reduce costs associated with undesirable employee behaviors. A few authors (Mahoney & England, 1965; Sands, 1973) have incorporated not only the costs of replacing employees, but also the costs of false negatives (i.e., costs of mistakenly rejecting applicants who would have been successful if hired).

Cost-based payoff functions reflect an important element of economic payoff, but they can be misleading in those situations where programs that reduce costs also reduce revenue. For example, improved selection may identify employees who stay longer and reduce separation expenses, but if they stay because they are mediocre performers and have few employment opportunities, the reduction in replacement costs may be offset by a reduction in productivity. Although this danger is less apparent with a payoff scale reflecting reduced training time costs, because training success is likely to positively relate to subsequent job performance, training cost reductions may understate selection utility. Where cost reduction is the dominant consideration, cost reduction alone may represent a useful payoff scale. However, its deficiencies have led researchers to explore further options.

Payoff as the Value of Output as Sold. Schmidt et al. (1979) proposed an SD_y measure that asked estimators to consider the "yearly value of products and services" and the "cost of having an outside firm provide these products." This payoff scale reflects the product of price and quantity sold, or the sales value (Boudreau, 1983a) of productivity. Hunter and Schmidt (1982, pp. 268–269) interpreted the payoff function as the value of "output as sold," or what the employer "charges the customer." As Appendix B indicates, much research has focused on similar payoff scales (Bobko, Karren, & Parkington, 1983; Bolda, 1985b; Burke, 1985; Burke & Frederick, 1984; Burke & Frederick, 1986; Cascio & Ramos, 1986; Cascio & Silbey, 1979; Cronshaw et al., 1986; Day & Edwards, 1987; DeSimone et al., 1986; Eaton, Wing, & Lau, 1985; Eaton, Wing, & Mitchell, 1985; Edwards, Frederick, & Burke, 1988; Eulberg, O'Connor, & Peters, 1985; Greer & Cascio, 1987; Ledvinka et al., 1983; Mathieu & Leonard, 1987; Mitchell, Eaton, & Wing, 1985; Reilly & Smither, 1985; Rich & Boudreau, 1987; Schmidt et al., 1984, 1986; Weekley et al., 1985; Wroten, 1984).

The *sales value payoff scale* implies that the appropriate benefit from improved HRM programs is the increased revenue generated by higher quality employees. Its widespread adoption reflects, in part, the strong endorsement it originally received. For example, Hunter and Schmidt (1982) characterized Roche's payoff definition (contribution to company profits) as "deficient on a logical basis" because it subtracted costs of production from the value of output as sold. This view is difficult to reconcile with the general payoff definition originally proposed by Brogden and Taylor (1950) and Cronbach and Gleser (1965), both of whom included the notion of revenue minus costs, or simply cost reduction, as part of the payoff function.

Boudreau (1983a) and Reilly and Smither (1985) proposed that the practice of asking estimators to consider both the value of products and services and the cost of having an outside firm provide these products may be confusing in an economic sense because a firm will pay an outsider a maximum of the *internal costs* of providing a service, not their value. Day and Edwards (1987) found that when the latter instruction was dropped, SD_y values were slightly higher for account executives, and much higher for mechanical foremen, though the interrater variability of the estimates was also higher.

As Boudreau (1983a, p. 553, 1983b, 1987, 1989) noted, the value of output as sold produced by employees can be a deficient payoff definition for organizations using traditional financial investment decision models. When other organizational invest-ments are being evaluated based on profit contribution, evaluating HRM investments based on revenue contribution, without considering associated costs of production, can cause HRM program value to be relatively inflated. Hunter, Schmidt, and Coggin(1988) adopted a similar position, stating that "increase in the dollar value of output as sold is the most relevant index when the concern is with sales figures, total firm income, market share and so forth" (p. 526), noting that this is a different payoff definition from profits.

Payoff as Increased Profits. The initial attention to the payoff function for utility analysis proceeded from the notion that the payoff scale should be applicable to business decisions and should be generalizable across business organizations. Brogden and Taylor (1950) proposed the *dollar criterion*, providing a number of computations for dollar-valued criterion measures. All of them share the notion that each unit produced (e.g., square feet of flooring laid) represents some value to the organization. That value reflects the sales revenue generated when the unit is sold, less any costs involved in producing that unit. Brogden and Taylor list a number of elements to be considered in such a criterion, including:

- Average value of production or service units

- Quality of objects produced or service accomplished

- Overhead—including rent, light, heat, cost depreciation, and rental of machines and equipment

- Errors, accidents, spoilage, waste, and damage to machines or equipment due to unusual wear and tear

- Such factors as appearance, friendliness, poise, and general social effectiveness where public relations are involved

- The cost of time of other personnel consumed

Roche (1961) explicitly followed Brogden and Taylor (1950) in developing a dollar criterion that would convert "production units, errors, time or other personnel consumed, etc. into dollar units" (p. 255).

Cronbach and Gleser (1965) provided a very general payoff concept, including all consequences important to decision makers. Thus, their payoff concept is consistent with a profit definition, though it can encompass even broader definitions. Cronbach's comments on Roche's dissertation (Cronbach & Gleser, 1965, p. 266) seem to suggest that the concept of profit, that is, revenue less costs, fits their definition. Indeed, Cronbach suggested a formula for hourly profit that reflected revenue less variable and fixed costs.

More recently, Cascio and Ramos (1986) discussed the concept of "the difference between benefits and costs" (p. 20) as their payoff function, and Greer and Cascio (1987) used *contribution margin* to reflect a similar concept. Hunter et al. (1988) also endorse the profit concept, noting that "when the focus of concern is with pretax profits, that would be the most relevant index" (p. 526).

Reilly and Smither (1985) compared several different payoff definitions for SD_y, including profits. Their results suggest that the graduate students in their simulation differed most in their SD_y estimates when they were asked to consider net revenue rather than new sales or overall worth. The results of Bobko et al. (1983) may reflect a similar phenomenon in that their sales counselor supervisors exhibited much greater variability in their SD_y estimates when attempting to estimate yearly value to the company rather than total yearly dollar sales. Greer and Cascio (1987) estimated SD_y based on contribution margin, the revenue generated by better quality workers less the costs associated with them, and found that the average value of y and SD_y were both higher than SD_y estimates derived by scaling average salary levels (Cascio-Ramos estimate of performance in dollars [CREPID]) but were only slightly higher than those based on revenue (Schmidt et al., 1979).

Summary.   Although costs, sales, and profits have enjoyed some attention as payoff functions, the usefulness of any payoff function should be judged in terms of its ability to better describe, predict, explain, and enhance decisions. Because UA models focus on the consequences of improving the quality of an organization's labor force, a fundamental consideration is how the organization uses quality improvements. In some organizations, improved work force quality may reduce costs (e.g., through reduced staffing levels), but maintain the same quantity, quality, and price of output. In other applications, the quantity of output may be increased while maintaining the quality and price. A revenue-based utility scale (e.g., output as sold) will reflect the objectives in the latter situation but not in the former (because revenue doesn't change in the former), and vice versa for a cost-based utility scale. A profit-based utility concept encompasses the objectives of both, because quantity, quality, and cost are included, though they

may not vary in every decision. One can use a revenue-based payoff function in estimating SD_y and add other parameters to the UA model so that overall utility values reflect a profit focus. In Appendix A, several studies have adopted a total utility function reflecting profit contribution (Burke & Frederick, 1986; Mathieu & Leonard, 1987; Rich & Boudreau, 1987), though their SD_y measures reflected revenue increases. This financial/economic approach (Boudreau, 1983a) will be discussed subsequently.

Comparing the psychometric characteristics of SD_y estimates resulting from different payoff functions can provide interesting insights about measurement, but research addressing decision processes and outcomes efforts should place the estimates within a decision context and apply them to actual decisions. All existing payoff scales reflect a concern with productivity-based outcomes, virtually ignoring other factors that might be affected by selection decisions, such as community relations, work force attitudes, and adherence to a code of ethics. Thus, every payoff function is deficient in some way. While deficiency is a characteristic of all models because models simplify reality, research should address the effects of incorporating these broader outcomes into actual decisions.

Effects of Jobs Studied

A variety of occupations has been examined, with the occupation usually determined by the research setting presented to the researchers; SD_y studies often occur within a validation study. Different occupations should exhibit different SD_y values. Jobs in which workers exercise more discretion regarding production and/or where variation in production has large implications for organizational goals should exhibit higher SD_y values than jobs without these characteristics. However, this effect may be reduced if variability in skills and motivation among applicants is negatively related to discretion and variation in productivity. Even jobs with high discretion and variability may emerge with lower SD_y values when their employees/applicants have low ranges of skill and motivation. Most SD_y studies examine only one job, making across-job comparisons difficult because jobs, measurement methods, settings, and time periods are confounded. Five studies employed more than one job (Day & Edwards, 1987; Eaton, Wing, & Lau, 1985; Mathieu & Leonard, 1987; Mitchell, Eaton, & Wing, 1985; Wroten, 1984). Wroten (1984) did not statistically test the effect of jobs on SD_y estimates, but his results indicate different rankings of jobs based on SD_y level for each estimation method. Similarly, although Eaton, Wing, and Lau (1985) found a significant effect of MOS (job type) for their GLOBAL estimation technique, they found no such significant effect for the EQV technique. Nor did they find that military rank or the interaction between rank and MOS were significantly related to SD_y. Mitchell, Eaton, and Wing (1985) found very similar results for crewman and transport operators. Day and Edwards (1987) found higher SD_y values for account executives than for mechanical foremen, with the differences more pronounced for more subjective and global estimation methods. Mathieu and Leonard (1987) found similar SD_y levels for head tellers and operations managers at banks, but substantially higher values for branch managers. Thus, in studies estimating SD_y in different jobs, there is mixed evidence of across-job variation in SD_y.

Hunter, Schmidt, and Judiesch (1988) studied the effects of occupational complexity, defined using Hunter's (1980) system, on performance variability. Instead of examining SD_y estimates, however, they examined the ratio of the standard deviation of output to mean output (SD_p). Across many studies, they used the actual reported ratio of the standard deviation to the mean. For low or medium complexity jobs that reported only the ratio of highest performer output to lowest performer output,

they used a formula that assumed normality (Schmidt & Hunter, 1983, p. 408). For some highly complex jobs, such as those of attorneys, physicians, and dentists, they used the mean and standard deviation of income. They corrected observed distributions to reflect a constant time period. They conclude that for incumbents in routine clerical or blue-collar work, SD_p is about 15 percent; in moderately complex jobs it is 25 percent; and in highly complex jobs it is 48 percent. For life insurance sales it was 97 percent, and for other sales it was 42 percent. After correcting for selective hiring (assuming applicants were hired using general mental ability), they estimate that the progression from low- to medium- to high-complexity jobs is 20 to 30 to 50 percent. For life insurance sales it is 123.8 percent and for other sales it is 54.2 percent. To the extent that dollar-valued productivity is linearly related to these productivity measures, one could expect SD_y to rise with job complexity as well.

Pitfalls of Job Descriptions as Group Identifiers. Every study used job titles to distinguish the group for analysis. By using job titles to identify employees holding similar job duties and tasks, existing research may be inadvertently including across-job differences in the SD_y measure. For example, although computer programmers may all hold the same job title, certain programming jobs may involve primarily transcribing flowcharts into computer code, while other programming jobs may involve designing the logic of the program (Rich & Boudreau, 1987). Clearly the latter jobs have more potential for both valuable positive contributions and/or costly mistakes. Yet existing SD_y measurement methods would include both groups in the SD_y estimate. If the selection test will primarily be used to select programmers assigned as coders, this will overstate SD_y (and vice versa). Still, the Hunter et al. (1988) study suggests that even job titles may be sufficient to detect consistent differences in SD_y according to job complexity.

The Focus Population

The focus population is the population of individuals over which variability occurs. Virtually all SD_y measurement methods focus on job incumbents. The incumbent population is most familiar to job supervisors who provide the SD_y estimates, and it is the only population on which actual output information exists. However, the incumbent population is not strictly the appropriate population of interest for most utility models.

For selection utility models, the appropriate population is the applicant population to which the selection procedures will be applied. This population may differ from the incumbent population for a number of reasons.

- First, certain procedures may operate to make the incumbent population a restricted sample of applicant job performance (e.g., promoting the best performers and dismissing the worst performers), as discussed by Hunter et al. (1988) and Schmidt et al. (1979). Such a situation would make SD_y estimated on job incumbents a downward-biased estimate of the applicant population.

- Second, the applicant population may change over time due to different recruitment procedures or labor market influences (Becker, 1988; Boudreau & Rynes, 1985). Such influences may operate either to increase or decrease performance variability among applicants and may produce applicant SD_y levels either higher or lower than the variability among job incumbents.

- Third, SD_y estimates based on job incumbents encourage estimators to consider all of the incumbents in their experience. This group includes incumbents with very different tenure levels. If performance varies with tenure, then job incumbent variability will reflect this. However,

each cohort of hired applicants will have equal tenure throughout employment, removing this source of variability of selectees within cohorts.

Thus, where job tenure and performance are related, SD_y estimates based on job incumbents will include variability not present in applicants and will tend to overestimate. However, Greer and Cascio (1987) examined this possibility in a sample of beverage salespersons and found that though wide variations in tenure existed, tenure was not significantly correlated ($r = 0.118$) with dollar-valued output estimates.

- Fourth, as noted earlier, UA studies have grouped employees with similar job titles to form the focus population. If task assignments or work environments, differ within the same job, the variability of performance may differ as well. This is not a problem if selected individuals are assigned to tasks and environments in the same proportion as the incumbent group. If, however, entering employees tend to be assigned to specific tasks or environments, perhaps with less chance for error, then SD_y estimates based on incumbent populations may be inaccurate reflections of the actual SD_y in the selection system (Bobko et al., 1983; Rich & Boudreau, 1987). Most authors argue that incumbent-based SD_y estimates are conservative due to restricted range. However, there is no evidence regarding the possible biasing effects of different recruiting approaches or different labor market conditions.

Measurement Techniques

Without doubt, the research question most addressed by existing UA research is whether using different SD_y measures produces different SD_y values. Appendix B attests to this fact, indicating that the vast majority of studies compare one SD_y estimation method to another. Authors customarily argue that because SD_y was characterized as the Achilles' heel of utility analysis by Cronbach and Gleser (1965) and because differences in SD_y can cause such large differences in total utility estimates (because SD_y is multiplied by many other factors in the selection utility formula), it is important to develop better SD_y measures.

SD_y measurement methods fall into four categories:

- *Cost accounting,* which refers to methods in which accounting principles are used to attach a value to units of performance or output for each individual, with the standard deviation of these individual performance values representing SD_y (e.g., Greer & Cascio, 1987; Lee & Booth, 1974; Roche, 1961; Schmidt & Hoffman, 1973; Van Naersson, 1963)

- *Global estimation,* where experts are asked to provide estimates of the total yearly dollar valued performance at two, three, or four percentiles of a hypothetical performance distribution, and average differences between these percentile estimates represent SD_y (e.g., Bobko et al., 1983; Bolda, 1985b; Burke, 1985; Burke & Frederick, 1984, 1986; Cascio & Silbey, 1979; Eaton, Wing, & Lau, 1985; Eaton, Wing, & Mitchell, 1985; Hunter & Schmidt, 1982; Mathieu & Leonard, 1987; Mitchell, Eaton, & Wing, 1985; Rich & Boudreau, 1987; Schmidt et al., 1979; Schmidt, Mack, & Hunter, 1984; Weekley et al., 1985; Wroten, 1984)

- *Individualized estimation,* which refers to methods in which some measurable characteristic of each individual in the sample (e.g., pay, sales activity, or performance ratings) is translated into dollars using some scaling factor, such as average salary or average sales, with the standard deviation of these values representing SD_y (e.g., Arnold et al., 1982;

Bobko et al., 1983; Burke & Frederick, 1984; Cascio, 1980; Cascio & Ramos, 1986; Dunnette et al., 1982; Eulberg, O'Connor, & Peters, 1985; Greer & Cascio, 1987; Janz & Dunnette, 1977; Ledvinka et al., 1983; Reilly & Smither, 1985)

- *Proportional rules,* which involve multiplying the value of some available productivity-related variable (e.g., average wage, average sales, or average productivity value) by a proportion to arrive at an SD_y estimate (e.g., Cascio & Ramos, 1986; Eaton, Wing, & Lau, 1985; Eulberg et al., 1985; Hunter & Schmidt, 1982; Mathieu & Leonard, 1987; Schmidt et al., 1986; Schmidt & Hunter, 1983; Weekley et al., 1985)

Cost Accounting. As noted above, the initial concept of a payoff function measured in dollars (Brogden & Taylor, 1950) proposed using cost accounting to attach a dollar value to production units based on their contribution to organizational profit. Then, the number of units produced by each individual in a sample over a constant period of time is recorded, and each unit produced is multiplied by its profit contribution, producing a dollar-valued productivity level for each individual. The standard deviation of these values is used as SD_y.

One early study attempted this technique (Roche, 1961, in Cronbach & Gleser, 1965). In summarizing the method, Roche notes that "many estimates and arbitrary allocations entered into the cost accounting" (Cronbach & Gleser, 1965, p. 263), and Cronbach's comments note that it is possible the accountants did not fully understand the utility estimation problem (pp. 266–267). Cascio and Ramos (1986, p. 20) also discuss the difficulties they encountered in applying a cost-accounting approach to SD_y estimation for telephone company managers. Greer and Cascio (1987) applied cost accounting to estimate productivity of route salespersons in a midwestern U.S. soft drink bottling company. Their method involved estimating the contribution margin (revenue less variable costs) associated with selling cases of different sizes and types, multiplying that by the number of cases sold by each salesperson, and then multiplying that by the percentage of sales attributable to salesperson effort on each route. This produced an estimate of the contribution margin for each route salesperson, and the standard deviation of these values represented SD_y. The difficulty and arbitrariness of the cost-accounting method has frequently been cited as arguing in favor of simpler methods (e.g., Cascio, 1980; Cascio & Ramos, 1986; Hunter & Schmidt, 1982; Schmidt et al., 1979), because although cost accounting methods are complex, costly, and time consuming, they are still prone to arbitrary estimation and subjectivity, especially in jobs for which there is no identifiable production unit, such as managerial jobs.

Global Estimation. This SD_y measurement method, first proposed by Schmidt et al. (1979), involves having experts estimate the dollar value of several points on a hypothetical distribution of performance (usually the 15th percentile, the 50th percentiles, and the 85th percentile). If the average difference between the 15th and 50th percentiles is not significantly different from the difference between the 85th and 50th percentiles, the presumption of normally distributed payoff levels is accepted, and the average of the two differences is used as the SD_y estimate. This procedure has the advantage of being relatively simple and straightforward (Cascio, 1980; Schmidt et al., 1979). Schmidt et al. (1979) proposed that obtaining estimates from a sample of experts would cancel any individual biases. Studies using such global SD_y estimates have generally produced large SD_y values and resulting large utility values, so the global estimation procedure has been the subject of substantial study by researchers interested in testing its reliability and construct validity, producing several controversies.

First, subjects frequently find the task of estimating the dollar value of performance distribution percentiles somewhat difficult. Some respondents gave inconsistent percentile estimates, found the task difficult, refused to do the task, or provided percentile estimates extremely different from the other respondents' estimates (e.g., Bobko et al., 1983; Mathieu & Leonard, 1987; Mitchell, Eaton, & Wing, 1985; Reilly & Smither, 1985; Rich & Boudreau, 1987). In these cases, and even where authors do not report subject difficulty, the interrater variability in SD_y estimates is usually as large or larger than the mean SD_y estimate. The SD_y Values column of Appendix B indicates the within-sample standard deviation of SD_y estimates (abbreviated SD), where reported. Such high interrater variability is disturbing, of course, because it suggests that the measures may be capturing bias or error. DeSimone et al. (1986) explicitly examined the interrater and temporal stability of their SD_y estimates and found both to be low. Weekley and Gier (1986) also noted inconsistencies in Global estimates across a three-month period. This has led some researchers to suggest new measurement methods; others have suggested or investigated variations on the global estimation method designed to improve consensus. The most frequently used tactic is to provide an anchor for the 50th percentile (e.g., Bobko et al., 1983; Burke, 1985; Burke & Frederick, 1984, 1986; Eaton, Wing, & Mitchell, 1985; Wroten, 1984), which is supported by evidence of a high correlation between 50th percentiles and SD_y (e.g., Bobko et al., 1983; Edwards et al., 1988; Schmidt et al., 1984; Wroten, 1984). Research comparing the anchored method to the unanchored method generally suggests that providing anchors reduces interrater variability (e.g., Burke & Frederick, 1984; Wroten, 1984), but that the value for the anchor is positively related to the SD_y values that result. Another frequently used tactic is to have groups of raters provide consensus judgments of different percentiles (e.g., Burke & Frederick, 1984;

Wroten, 1984). Some researchers (e.g., Burke & Frederick, 1984; Mathieu & Leonard, 1987) simply drop inconsistent or outlier values on the assumption that they represent error, though there is no theory or empirical data to suggest how inconsistent or unusual an estimate must be to qualify for deletion as an outlier.

A second controversy involves the underlying assumption of normality inherent in the global estimation approach. Averaging the differences between the 15th and 50th percentiles with the differences between the 85th and 50th percentiles presumes a normally distributed dollar-valued performance distribution. This assumption is often justified by failing to reject the hypothesis that the means of the two differences are significantly different, but this amounts to accepting a null hypothesis. In view of the large interrater variability associated with these measures, it seems possible that failure to reject this hypothesis may be due to unreliability of the measure rather than to an underlying normal distribution. Some studies have suggested nonnormal performance distributions or significantly different percentile estimates (e.g., Bobko et al., 1983; Burke, 1985; Burke & Frederick, 1984; Rich & Boudreau, 1987; Schmidt et al., 1984). However, other studies found no significant differences, and there is evidence that actual performance distributions follow a normal distribution (Hunter & Schmidt, 1982). Some researchers examined this issue by including an additional percentile estimate, the 97th percentile, which would be expected to be as different from the 85th percentile as the 85th and 15th percentiles are different from the 50th. Bobko et al. (1983) and Burke and Frederick (1984) found the difference between the 97th and 85th percentiles significantly smaller than the other two, suggesting either a nonnormal underlying distribution or that estimating the 97th percentile taps a different estimation process than that tapped in estimating the other three percentiles.

A third controversy arises because the initial research on the global estimation method provided no information to indicate what processes are used in arriving at the SD_y estimates (e.g., what anchors respondents use, what performance attributes they consider, and whether similar anchors and attributes are considered by different experts). This has prompted a few researchers to investigate the judgment processes underlying SD_y. Bobko et al. (1983) noted that sales managers reported using pay as an anchor for their estimates of overall worth. Burke and Frederick (1984) gathered anecdotal data following their main study and found that supervisors of sales managers reported using five dimensions: (a) management of recruiting, training and motivating personnel, (b) amount of dollar sales achieved, (c) management of sales coverage, (d) administration of performance appraisal, and (e) forecasting and analyzing sales trends. Burke (1985) found that supervisors of clerical workers followed job evaluation dimensions in their judgments, with salary-related factors most frequently used.

How accurate is the global estimation technique? Only limited evidence exists, usually based on arguably deficient objective performance measures (sales performance). Bobko et al. (1983) found that the actual distribution of sales revenue (number of policies sold times average policy value) for sales counselors was normally distributed and that the SD_y estimate based on the average of the 85th minus 50th percentile and the 50th minus 15th percentile was not significantly different from SD_y based on the actual sales distribution, although the percentile estimates were quite different. DeSimone et al. (1986) found the opposite results. However, when respondents in the Bobko et al. (1983) study were asked to consider the "overall worth of products and services" and "what you would pay an outside organization to provide them," the values were only about one-tenth the actual sales standard deviation, and apparently anchored on pay levels rather than sales. Burke and Frederick (1984) also found SD_y estimates of overall worth were lower, about 1 percent of the actual sales standard deviations, and anchored on various activities including sales. Reilly and Smither (1985) found that graduate students participating in a business simulation, who had been provided with data to estimate actual standard deviations, produced global SD_y estimates slightly higher than the simulation information for repeat sales and new sales, and much higher than the simulation for net revenue. The SD_y estimate of overall worth was 49 percent of actual repeat sales, 3.45 times actual new sales, and 1.92 times actual net revenue. DeSimone et al. (1986) found that the global SD_y estimate for medical claims approvers was 19 percent of the compensation-weighted standard deviation of actual claims approved. Greer and Cascio (1987) found no significant differences between the global SD_y measure and their cost accounting estimate. Thus, the research comparing global SD_y estimates to objective performance is sparse, and the results are mixed.

Individualized Estimation.   This is similar to the cost accounting method in that it attempts to attach a dollar value to the output of each individual in a sample, the standard deviation of those dollar values becoming the SD_y estimate. However, more recent versions of this approach have forgone the complex and costly cost accounting approach in favor of approaches derived from industrial psychology and HR management practices.

Cascio (1982, 1987) and Cascio and Ramos (1986) have developed the *Cascio-Ramos estimate of performance in dollars* (CREPID) method. This method breaks a job into important *principal activities*. Then, each activity is rated on two dimensions—time/frequency and importance (originally, difficulty and consequence of error were also included)—and the ratings multiplied to give an overall weight to the activity. The proportion of total weights becomes the final importance weight assigned to each activity. To assign a dollar value to each

activity, average salary for the job is divided among the activities according to the proportional importance weights. After this phase, supervisors are asked to rate a sample of employees in terms of their performance on each principal activity, using a 0 to 200 scale,

> with a value of 100 points indicating average performance ("This employee is better than 50% of those I've seen do this activity"). A value of 200 indicated that the employee was better than 99% of those the supervisor had seen do the activity, and a value of 50 indicated that the employee was better than 25% of those he or she had seen do the activity. A value of zero indicated that the employee was the worst the supervisor had seen do the activity. (Cascio & Ramos, 1986, p. 22)

Then, to translate these ratings into dollars, the ratings are divided by 100 (to produce a 0 to 2.0 scale) and multiplied by the dollar value assigned to that activity. Finally, after each employee has been assigned a dollar value for each activity, these values are summed over activities to provide the total dollar value of yearly performance for that employee. Thus, a person performing better than 50 percent of the incumbents the supervisor has experienced on all dimensions will receive a dollar value equal to the average yearly salary for that job. A person performing better than 99 percent of all incumbents will receive a dollar value equal to twice the average salary, and the worst performer each supervisors has experienced will receive a dollar value of zero.

Edwards et al. (1988) modified the basic CREPID procedure applied to district sales managers by substituting archival data for either performance ratings, job analysis ratings, or both. They found that SD_y levels were similar for the original procedure and when substituting either performance or job analysis archival information, but were much smaller when using archival data for both performance and job analysis (see Appendix B).

Janz and Dunnette (1977) also proposed identifying critical job activities. However, rather than allocating salary to each activity based on its time/frequency and importance, the *Janz and Dunnette procedure* requires job experts to estimate the "relative dollar costs associated with different levels of effectiveness on each of the various job performance dimensions" (p. 120). This requires tracing the consequences of the various levels of effectiveness to determine their impact on activities to which costs and/or value can be attached. For example, different levels of equipment maintenance effectiveness might be traced to breakdowns, which in turn can be traced to repairs, which in turn can be traced to dollar losses due to repair costs and/or lost productivity during repair. Different levels of effectiveness would produce different levels of breakdowns, repair costs, and lost productivity. This method was applied to power plant operators by Dunnette et al. (1982), producing results that supported the high SD_y values derived using the Schmidt et al. (1979) global estimation method for the same jobs (see Appendix B).

Another individualized estimation approach involves having experts directly assign dollar values to individual employees. Bobko et al. (1983) used this method to derive an SD_y estimate based on sales (sales volume times average policy value) levels, with each person's yearly sales representing the individual value estimate. Burke and Frederick (1984) also used individual sales levels. Wroten (1984) adopted a similar approach, but did not have sales data available. He simply asked his supervisors to provide a direct estimate of the yearly dollar value of each employee's performance. Ledvinka et al. (1983) and DeSimone et al. (1986) used total payroll plus benefits divided by the number of insurance claims as the value per claim and then multiplied this value by the actual standard deviation of claims processed. Greer and Cascio (1987), as noted, multiplied the quantity of cases sold by an estimate of the contribution margin per case. Day and

Edwards (1987) proposed a return on investment (ROI) approach that calculated average annualized investments for a job as total compensation plus benefits plus 40 percent overhead. Supervisors estimated the percentage return on this investment represented by each of the seven points on their existing performance appraisal form, with the product of this percentage and the average annualized investment representing the value of that performance rating. Each person's value was estimated according to the ROI value of their performance rating.

Individualized estimation has the advantage of assigning a specific value to each employee that can be explicitly examined and analyzed for its appropriateness. Such analysis might be useful in determining which individual attributes contribute to differences in payoff values. It may provide a more understandable or credible estimate to be communicated to those familiar with the job. The very limited evidence on this issue is mixed. Greer and Cascio (1988, p. 594) stated that four top managers and an accountant preferred CREPID. Day and Edwards (1987) found no significant differences in managerial confidence ratings for different estimation methods. Edwards et al. (1988) found supervisors perceived their CREPID job analysis ratings as more accurate than their global utility value estimates, but found the CREPID less feasible than Procedure B. These tests do not directly examine the effects of SD_y estimation methods on confidence or accuracy of decisions.

Each method makes certain basic assumptions regarding the nature of payoff. CREPID is based on the assumption that the average wage equals average productivity, a condition that may be violated if each employee's wage is not equal to the value of his or her productivity (Becker, 1975; Bishop, 1987; Frank, 1984; Rynes & Milkovich, 1986), as may occur in organizations with tenure-based pay systems, rank-based pay systems, hourly-based pay systems, and where training may have different value to different organizations. Sales-based measures assume that sales captures sufficient performance differences to be useful, an assumption that may omit important job tasks, such as training, that reduce an individual's sales but increase the group's sales; and the Janz-Dunnette measure assumes that job behaviors' effects on costs and revenues can be accurately traced by managers. Such estimation methods are usually more complex, costly, and time-consuming than the direct estimation methods, which may provide perfectly adequate SD_y values for many decisions.

Proportional Rules. The final SD_y measurement method emerged from observations concerning the relationship between SD_y estimates and average salary levels and from the desire to provide a straightforward SD_y measurement method. The method involves multiplying average salary in a job by some proportion (e.g., between 40 and 70 percent) to derive the SD_y estimate for the incumbent employee group.

Hunter and Schmidt (1982, pp. 257–258) reviewed empirical studies for which an SD_y estimate was reported or could be derived. They compared the SD_y estimates to reported average salary levels (or made assumptions about average salary levels) and discovered that on average SD_y was about 16 percent of average salary in previous studies. They observed that these values "refer to only partial measures of value to the organization" (p. 257) because they generally relied on partial job performance measures (e.g., tenure or reduced training costs). The authors also reviewed two of their own studies employing the global estimation procedure, where SD_y was 60 percent of annual salary in one study of budget analysts and 55 percent of annual salary in another study of computer programmers. They estimated that "the true average for SD_y falls somewhere in the range of 40 to 70% [of average salary]" (p. 258). In a follow-up investigation, Schmidt and Hunter (1983) proposed the following logic: In the United States economy

(based on National Income Accounting methods), wages and salaries make up approximately 57 percent of the total value of goods and services produced. Therefore, if we knew the ratio of SD_y to mean *salary*, we could multiply that ratio by .57 to obtain a predicted ratio of SD_y to mean *output* value. Thus, if the ratio of SD_y to salary ranges between 42 and 60 percent, the ratio of SD_y to output value should fall between 23 and 34 percent. To test this logic, the authors reviewed studies reporting empirical data on productivity levels measured in units of output. Their review indicated that for studies examining non–piece-rate situations the average ratio of SD to the mean was .185 (standard deviation of .052), for studies examining piece-rate situations, the average ratio was .150 (standard deviation of .044), and for studies with uncertain compensation systems, the average ratio was .215 (standard deviation of .067). Though all three average ratios fell below the predicted lower bound of 23 percent (the values for both the nonincentive and incentive conditions were statistically significantly lower), Hunter and Schmidt made five post hoc observations: (a) that their method was "intended to apply to jobs without incentive-based compensation systems" (p. 409); (b) that though the lowest mean values were statistically significantly different from the predicted value, the lowest value was "still 77 percent as large as the predicted lower bound value" (p. 409); (c) that the studies reviewed "reflect primarily quantity of output: quality of output is probably reflected only crudely in these figures" (p. 411); (d) that SD of output value would be higher "if quality and quantity are uncorrelated or positively correlated" (p. 411–412); and (e) that the reviewed studies were conducted on "blue collar skilled and semiskilled jobs and lower level white collar jobs," while the Schmidt et al. studies were conducted on middle-level jobs which may "often allow for more expensive errors" (p. 412). These observations led them to conclude that "researchers examining the utility of personnel programs such as selection and training can estimate the standard deviation of employee output at 20% of mean output without fear of overstatement," and that "the findings of this study provide support for the practice that we have recommended of estimating SD_y as 40% of mean salary" (p. 412). Schmidt et al. (1986) state "the standard deviation of employee output can safely (if conservatively) be estimated as 20% of mean output, or alternatively, 40% of mean salary" (p. 5).

Hunter et al. (1988) extended this research by analyzing the ratio of output standard deviation to mean output (SD_p) in a larger sample of jobs, including highly complex jobs and sales jobs as well as those analyzed earlier. They employed new corrections for unreliability that reduced observed SD_p, corrected for restricted range assuming selection on general mental ability, and used variability in salary levels as a proxy for output variability in professional jobs (see the earlier section on focus population). Their findings suggest that as one moves from routine to medium complexity to professional work, the SD_p values progress from 20 to 30 to 50 percent.

The proportional rules proposed by Schmidt and Hunter are intriguing because they suggest that SD_p estimation may be quite feasible in many applications where job complexity can be estimated, removing a major stumbling block to widespread utility measurement. However, knowing SD_p allows one to estimate only the percentage increase in productivity likely from HRM programs. Determining whether such increases offset dollar costs or whether to invest program resources in different jobs requires assumptions or estimates of the dollar value of this percentage. The assumption that average salary is equal to about half the average value of products "as sold" may be violated in tenure-based pay systems, negotiated pay systems, or due to labor market conditions such as unemployment and internal labor markets, (e.g., Becker, 1975). Indeed, National Income accounting used to generate the national GNP and labor cost figures used by Schmidt and Hunter (1983) assigns the same value to both output and wages for jobs where output is not readily measurable (e.g., government services), producing a ratio of output to wage of 1.0, not .57. Thus, the .57 figure represents an average around which specific jobs may vary.

Existing research provides limited support for the proportional rules applied to output, and less for proportional rules applied to salary. Appendix B shows that of the 44 SD_y values from studies reporting mean productivity values, only two SD_y values fell below 20 percent of mean productivity, with 13 falling in the predicted 20 to 35 percent range, and 29 falling above 35 percent. However, of 66 values in studies reporting salaries, 24 fell below 40 percent, 18 within the predicted 40 to 70 percent range, and 22 above 70 percent. The values falling above the ranges may reflect highly complex jobs. In fact, Eaton, Wing, and Lau (1985) conclude that 125 percent of base pay would be a conservative estimate of SD_y for military personnel. Using 40 percent of salary may overestimate the SD_y value that would result from other methods, but using 20 percent of mean output seems to be conservative compared to other measurement methods. Still, overly conservative SD_y estimates may produce severely understated utility estimates and possible rejection of potentially useful HRM programs. Clearly, the impact depends on the decision situation.

Evidence Directly Comparing Measurement Techniques. Wroten (1984) compared the Schmidt et al. method, individual subjective payoff estimates, and group consensus percentile estimates for six jobs, with either no anchor, high, low, or "accurate" anchors. The means for the six unanchored methods and for each of the three anchors are shown in Appendix B for each job. He found that unanchored SD_y estimates had higher variance, that the mean unanchored SD_y estimate was not significantly different from the actual anchored condition, but that it did differ significantly from both the high and low anchored conditions. He also found that individualized estimation usually produced less SD_y variation than the global method.

Eaton, Wing, and Lau (1985) compared the Schmidt et al. (GLOBAL) technique to a variant of the proportional technique called *superior equivalents* (EQV) in which experts estimated the number of 85th and 15th percentile performers it takes to equal the work of 17 average performers (the value of an average performer anchored by either average compensation or the subjective estimate of the 50th percentile). They also used a new *system effectiveness technique* (EFF) in which the standard deviation of payoff is expressed as a proportion of mean payoff (in units of the cost of a tank). The underlying payoff scale of these latter techniques is cost savings, either in terms of payroll or tank costs. Results indicated that as a percent of the GLOBAL value, the EQV salary anchor technique was 66.7 percent, the EQV global anchor technique was 72 percent, and the EFF technique was 150 percent.

Eaton, Wing, and Mitchell (1985) compared the GLOBAL technique (using only the 85th and 50th percentiles), the EQV technique, and the 40 to 70 percent of salary rule, producing SD_y estimates for five military occupations (MOS). Over all five MOS, the average SD_y of the GLOBAL technique was \$9,387, and for the EQV technique it was \$14,990. As shown in Appendix B, the EQV values were higher for every MOS. The GLOBAL estimates always fell within the 40 to 70 percent range of salary (though they always fell above 35 percent of the mean y estimate), while the EQV estimates were always higher than 70 percent of salary. The EQV technique produced a larger range but a lower between-subject dispersion in SD_y values compared to GLOBAL. The EQV produced no significant differences by MOS, rank, or their interaction. The GLOBAL technique also produced no significant differences by rank or by the interaction of rank and MOS, but

it did produce significant MOS differences, with armor crewmen having a lower SD_y than vehicle mechanics, medical specialists, and radio operators.

Mitchell, Eaton, and Wing (1985) explored whether job incumbents could provide usable SD_y estimates, and studied the jobs of motor transport operator and cannon crewman in the U.S. Army. They used the GLOBAL technique, the EQV technique, and then the GLOBAL technique after feedback of dollar values for soldiers in other specialties. For both jobs, EQV produced highest SD_y values, GLOBAL next, and feedback lowest, as Appendix B shows. The authors also reported that they had respondents delineate job tasks before making estimates and this "seemed to reduce extreme values." Eulberg, O'Connor, and Peters (1985) explicitly compared the SD_y estimates provided by supervisors and job incumbents of medical technicians in the U.S. Air Force. They used the CREPID method, applying the same performance ratings on each job dimension and the same average salary value for both group's estimates. Each group provided its own set of importance ratings for the job dimensions. As Appendix B shows, the SD_y values were quite similar (approximately \$3,300 per year) for both methods and for the 40 percent of salary rule. The authors find this convergence "remarkable," but it reflects only similar rankings of job task importance between both groups because the same pay levels and performance ratings were used, and the mathematical properties of CREPID suggest it will produce values approximately 40 percent of pay (Raju, Burke, & Normand, 1987; Reilly & Smither, 1985).

Reilly and Smither (1985) provided graduate students taking part in a management simulation with sales data on 10 employees, based on three job components: selling established products, selling new products, and cost control. They used CREPID methods to obtain importance ratings on the three job dimensions and then compared these to the actual simulated data provided. They also obtained SD_y

estimates for each job component using Schmidt et al. (1979) techniques. Both methods caused some confusion among subjects, and there were no order effects. The Schmidt et al. SD_y values for established sales, new product sales, and cost control were significantly correlated ($r > .68$), but none of these were correlated with the SD_y for overall worth. The Schmidt et al. (1979) estimates were slightly higher than actual for repeat sales, 13 percent higher than actual for new product sales, and 51 percent higher for revenue less costs. The CREPID SD_y estimate was below all the Schmidt et al. (1979) estimates, slightly higher than the actual SD_y of new sales, and far lower than the actual SD_y for repeat sales and net revenue. These inconsistencies are interesting because subjects had the information necessary to make exact calculations of the dollar-valued performance for each employee, but apparently failed to use it in their estimates, even under such "ideal" conditions.

Weekley et al. (1985) compared CREPID to the Schmidt et al. technique and the 40 percent of salary rule for convenience store managers. They discovered very high variability in using the Schmidt et al. method, and this method produced a value almost twice as high as CREPID. The CREPID value was 36 percent of average salary, and the Schmidt et al. value was 66 percent of average salary. Cascio and Ramos (1986) also applied the CREPID technique to telephone company managers and found that it produced an SD_y value roughly 35 percent of salary.

DeSimone et al. (1986) found that GLOBAL SD_y estimates were much lower than compensation-weighted deviations in the number of processed claims. Similarly, Greer and Cascio (1987) found cost accounting SD_y estimates to be slightly higher than GLOBAL estimates for soft drink route salespersons. Greer and Cascio (1987) also found the CREPID method produced the lowest SD_y estimate. Day and Edwards (1987) found that SD_y values were highest for the GLOBAL and modified GLOBAL method,

followed by the percent ROI, and lowest for the 40 percent of salary and CREPID methods for account executives and mechanical foremen. Finally, Edwards et al. (1988) found that the GLOBAL method with feedback (Burke & Frederick's, 1984, Procedure B) produced the highest SD_y values, followed by various forms of the CREPID method.

CREPID estimates frequently fall near 40 percent of salary and below GLOBAL estimates, prompting the argument that because the CREPID scale is based on salary, it "considers only the contribution of labor not the combined contribution of labor, equipment, capital, overhead and profit, as does a standard based on the value of output as sold" (Greer & Cascio, 1987, p. 593). Edwards et al. (1988) also argue that average salary cost should be increased by the amount of benefits and "overhead" before scaling, to better reflect the "value of the total cost of services" (p. 533). The ROI method (Day & Edwards, 1987) proposes a similar scaling approach. It is undoubtedly true that larger scaling factors would increase CREPID estimates, but it is not clear that such adjustments are justified. As noted earlier, salary, or salary plus benefits, will not necessarily reflect the average value of employees, and may overstate it. Selecting higher quality employees often has little effect on expenditures for equipment, capital, and overhead, so including these factors as potential cost reductions seems inappropriate. Moreover, while all of these factors moderate the contribution of higher quality labor to organizational goals, the SD_y concept always reflects such contributions because it is estimated across employees within a particular mix of capital, equipment, and overhead. Salary-scaled estimates may or may not reflect this quality, but the concept is no different whether scaled using salary or some other method. As noted in the discussion of payoff scales, the key question is how the high-quality labor will be used to enhance organizational goals, and this is likely to be situationally specific. SD_y measures and post hoc adjustments should make their assumptions explicit. Simple proportional rules or compensation-based scaling factors may not generalize to every situation. Yet where do such questions fit the decision-theory perspective on utility analysis?

Summary and Conclusion: The Need to Look Beyond SD_y

Differences between SD_y estimates using different methods are often less than 50 percent and may be less than \$5,000 in many cases. Still, these differences may be multiplied by factors of hundreds or thousands, depending on the number of employees selected, the validity of the device, and the selection ratio (as shown in Appendix A) in deriving the final total utility value. Even a small SD_y difference multiplied by such large values implies vast total utility differences. The tempting conclusion is that we need substantially more research on SD_y measurement to whittle down such differences and provide more precise total utility estimates.

This conclusion is not encouraging. The unfortunate fact is that industrial and organizational psychology and human resource management have produced no well-accepted measure of job performance differences on any scale, let alone dollars. The task of estimating dollar-valued performance variability has proven confusing and difficult for some subjects and virtually always produces substantial disagreement among raters. When SD_y estimates can be verified against an objective criterion (e.g., sales or units produced), the criterion is arguably deficient, leading to the conclusion that any observed differences in SD_y estimation methods cannot serve as justification for using one measure over another (Burke & Frederick, 1984; Day & Edwards, 1987; Weekley et al., 1985). Thus, measured against the accuracy of SD_y estimates, the contribution of this research must await development of an acceptable dollar-valued performance measure. Greer and Cascio (1987) state, "Researchers within the accounting profession must develop an objective, verifiable, and reliable method for estimating the standard deviation of job performance in dollars" (p. 594), but accounting systems are neither designed nor intended to reflect this variable. Of course, if a measure of y existed, we could derive SD_y directly, making estimation unnecessary. Indeed, even the SD_y concept would have little value because one could use the slope of the regression line in Equation 2 to predict selection utility. Thus, while SD_y measurement research produces information on the variability across raters, methods, or jobs, it is unlikely to provide information on measurement accuracy, nor is it likely to allow us to substantially reduce the uncertainty associated with total utility values.

SD_y estimation research can advance measurement theory. Here, the value of the research rests not on its ability to better describe, predict, explain, or enhance decisions, but rather to illuminate new aspects of measurement. This may be a quite useful and legitimate application of the SD_y concept. However, it is very different from utility analysis, and this difference should be made clear by those researchers pursuing measurement theory.

If SD_y research is unlikely to produce the most accurate measure and unlikely to alleviate uncertainty in utility estimates, then what is the role of SD_y measurement research in advancing UA knowledge? The B-C-G utility model emerged from traditional psychological measurement theory, which focused only on standardized error terms but provided no context within which to evaluate them. UA models were formulated to better account for the decision context facing selection program managers. It seems ironic that after over 30 years, the major research efforts remain focused on measurement, taking little notice of the decision context in which such measures will be used. We have evolved from focusing only on the correlation coefficient to focusing only on the SD_y value. We must return to describing, predicting, explaining, and improving *decisions,* taking into account the context within which those decisions must be made. This suggests several research issues which have been all but ignored in the rush to develop new SD_y measures.

First, the effects of SD_y measures on the perceived quality of the utility analysis should be examined. Though virtually every new measure is justified by proponents because it may produce more credible, understandable, or easily communicated utility values, not one study has directly addressed these issues. If decision makers find the utility values resulting from a relatively simple proportional rule just as credible as complex job-analysis-based methods (e.g., CREPID and Janz-Dunnette) or GLOBAL estimation (Schmidt et al., 1979), they may have little motivation to pursue the latter to increase decision credibility. Of course, even decision-maker preferences are not the real issue. Research (e.g., Kahneman & Tversky, 1972, 1973) shows that decision makers frequently prefer and use heuristics that are detrimental to decision quality. UA research must focus on the quality of decisions as well as on decision maker preferences.

Second, and related to the first issue, we have little information on the relative effort and cost required to implement the different SD_y measurement procedures. On their face, the proportional rules seem least complex, followed by the GLOBAL estimation methods, followed by individual estimation methods, followed by the job-analysis-based methods. In a sense, the burden of proof rests with those who would advocate more complex and costly measures to demonstrate that the improvement in decision quality or our ability to understand the decision process justifies the additional resources necessary to gather the information. The costs of the different SD_y estimation methods have not been computed, though Cascio and Ramos (1986) noted that CREPID ratings took 15 minutes per employee and Edwards et al. (1988) noted that their managers felt the CREPID procedure took too long.

Third, and most important, comparative SD_y studies seldom estimate overall utility values for actual decisions, producing results that are completely devoid of any decision context. It is often impossible to tell whether the measurement differences detected would have made any difference to actual decisions. Yet, as Appendix A demonstrates, virtually every study that has accounted for the decision context (by computing a utility value) has produced extremely high utility values regardless of the SD_y level. Weekley et al. (1985) proposed that while break-even SD_y values are low when comparing implementing an HRM program to doing nothing (with zero cost and zero benefits), comparing HRM programs to other organizational investments might produce decision situations where differences in SD_y estimates indeed affect the ultimate decision. Research incorporating such contextual variables could prove quite fruitful. Still, in the absence of any criterion against which to verify SD_y values, one would still be left with little basis for choosing one over another. Further SD_y measurement research seems unlikely to explain how apparently high HRM program payoffs can exist while the HRM function holds low status and importance in organizational decision making. Answering that question, and developing decision models to alleviate the situation, requires that UA research explicitly recognize organizational decision contexts. The next sections discuss how utility models can better reflect such contextual factors and link UA research to other fruitful research.

The Role of Uncertainty and Risk in Utility Analysis

How is it that UA research can simultaneously produce such clear evidence of HRM program payoff and such a raging debate on the proper measurement method for one utility parameter, SD_y? Although the expected utility values are quite high, if substantial uncertainty is associated with these utility estimates, and if that uncertainty results from uncertain SD_y values, then reducing SD_y measure uncertainty will improve decisions. However, uncertainty affects all UA parameters, not just SD_y. Just as all models are deficient, all predictions contain uncertainty. UA research cannot ignore this fact, but must instead embrace its implications for advancing understanding of decisions and decision processes.

Frameworks incorporating uncertainty (Alexander & Barrick, 1987; Boudreau 1984a, 1987, 1988, 1989; Cronshaw, Alexander, Wiesner, & Barrick, 1987; Milkovich & Boudreau, 1991; Rich, 1986; Rich & Boudreau, 1987) change the focus of utility analysis from estimating the expected utility value to estimating both the expected value and the distribution of values. Measurement issues become relevant as they affect uncertainty in the decision situation. This framework emphasizes the role of utility value variability in changing decisions, rather than simply measuring the sources of that variability (e.g., SD_y measurement error) in the absence of a decision context. It is surprising that the issue of uncertainty and risk in utility analysis received little attention for so long because decision theory has traditionally been concerned with decision making under uncertainty and has recognized that the riskiness of alternatives plays a role in decision making. This emphasis has been especially evident in the literature on financial investment decision making (e.g., Bierman & Smidt, 1975; Hertz, 1964; Hillier, 1963; Hull, 1980; Wagle, 1967). If two alternative resource investments offer the same expected value, but offer substantially different risks of large losses (below the expected value) or large gains (above the expected value), rational decision makers should take such risks into account.

Four Alternative Approaches for Estimating Uncertainty

Rich and Boudreau (1987) provided an initial conceptual framework for uncertainty in UA and empirically compared four alternative methods addressing uncertainty: (a) sensitivity analysis, (b) break-even analysis, (c) algebraic derivation of utility value distributions, and (d) Monte Carlo simulation analysis.

Sensitivity Analysis. Though existing utility models contain no parameters reflecting variability in utility value, the notion that utility values represent estimates made under uncertainty has not been completely overlooked. Several previous UA applications and demonstrations (e.g., Boudreau, 1983a, 1983b; Boudreau & Berger, 1985a; Cascio & Silbey, 1979; Cronshaw et al., 1987; Florin-Thuma & Boudreau, 1987; Schmidt et al., 1979, 1984) have addressed possible variability in utility parameters through sensitivity analysis. In such an analysis, each of the utility parameters is varied from its low value to its high value while holding other parameter values constant. The utility estimates resulting from each combination of parameter values are examined to determine which parameters' variability has the greatest effect on the total utility estimate. These sensitivity analyses virtually always indicate that utility parameters reflecting changes in employee quality caused by improved selection (i.e., $r_{x,y}$, Z_x, SD_y) and the quantity of employees affected (i.e., N_s) have substantial effects on resulting utility values. A variant of sensitivity analysis involves attempting to be as conservative as possible in making utility estimates. This approach has led researchers to produce clearly understated SD_y values (Arnold et al., 1982), or to estimate the 95 percent confidence interval surrounding the mean SD_y value and use the value at the bottom of this interval in the utility computations (e.g., Cronshaw et al.,

1987; Hunter & Schmidt, 1982; Schmidt et al., 1979, 1984). If estimated utility values remain positive despite such conservatism, it is presumed they will be positive in the actual application.

Though valuable in assessing the effects of individual parameter changes, sensitivity analyses provide no information about the effects of simultaneous changes in more than one utility parameter, though Boudreau and Berger (1985a) and Boudreau (1986b) expressed utility as a function of changes in several parameter levels, to present the effects of simultaneous changes in utility parameters more concisely. They also provide no information regarding the utility value distribution nor the probabilities associated with particular parameter value combinations (Hillier, 1963, p. 444). Moreover, when all parameters are estimated at their most conservative levels, a statistically unlikely event, one runs the danger of incorrectly concluding that some programs will not pay off.

Break-even Analysis. Boudreau (1984a) proposed that a relatively simple and straightforward uncertainty analysis could be carried out by calculating the lowest value of any individual utility parameter, or parameter combination, that would still yield a positive total utility value. These parameter values were termed *break-even* values because they represent the values at which the HRM program's benefits are equal ("even with") the program's costs. Any parameter value exceeding the break-even value would produce positive total utility values, and vice versa. Such logic is well known in microeconomic theory and financial management (i.e., Bierman, Bonini, & Hausman, 1981). Boudreau showed how to apply break-even analysis not only when considering one program option (i.e., where the alternative is to do nothing, incur no costs, but receive no benefits), but also when multiple alternatives are involved (with more expensive alternatives offering greater potential payoffs). With multiple alternatives, one computes a series of decision rules specifying the range of parameter values that would justify choosing that alternative over the others (e.g., Boudreau, 1988; Milkovich & Boudreau, 1991). The break-even approach is simple and focuses on the decision context. Boudreau proposed that break-even analysis allows decision makers to maximize the value of existing information, determine the critical values for the unknown parameters that could change the decision, and determine whether further measurement effort is warranted. Because controversy surrounded the accuracy and validity of SD_y estimates, Boudreau (1984a) concentrated his analysis on that utility parameter, demonstrating that the break-even SD_y values for the studies by Cascio and Silbey (1979) and Schmidt et al. (1979) were substantially lower than the expected SD_y value they derived.

Appendix A updates Boudreau's analysis to incorporate additional and more recent utility analyses. The column labeled "Utility Formula" presents incremental utility as a function of SD_y. These payoff functions were derived for each study and each selection device. The coefficient multiplied by SD_y in each equation was derived by dividing the total program payoff (before subtracting program costs) by the SD_y value. The number subtracted from this product is the reported total cost. All equations express payoff in terms of total utility, but for studies that reported only per-person utility values, the payoff function reflects the utility of selecting one individual. The last column of Appendix A computes the break-even SD_y value based on the payoff equation. This is simply the cost figure divided by the coefficient on SD_y. For studies reporting no incremental cost for more valid selection, the implied break-even SD_y value is also zero because any positive return justifies a costless program, so SD_y becomes irrelevant.

The equations and break-even values not only verify the earlier conclusion that HRM program utility is uniformly high, but also shed some light on the SD_y controversy. Compare the reported SD_y values (in the column labeled "SD_y") to the break-even values for each study. Without exception, the break-even SD_y values fall at or below 60 percent of the estimated SD_y value. In many cases, the value necessary to break even is less than 1 percent of the estimated value. The break-even SD_y value exceeds 20 percent of the estimated value in only 6 of the 42 analyses. In three of these six cases (Burke & Frederick, 1986; Rich & Boudreau, 1987; Schmidt et al., 1984), this reflects an interview with low validity. The break-even value determining whether to replace the interview with a more valid predictor was much smaller in the latter two studies.

In short, the vast majority of UA applications conclude that the selection device that is more valid is worth its extra costs. This conclusion would probably have been apparent without ever actually measuring SD_y, or by measuring it in the simplest manner possible, because the break-even SD_y values are so low that they often fall several standard deviations below the expected value. Rich and Boudreau (1987) found that the break-even SD_y value fell below the lowest value estimated by any of the subjects.

Boudreau's (1984a, 1987, 1988, 1989) findings produced a similar conclusion, leading him to propose that future UA research should use break-even analysis to put parameter measurement controversies into perspective. He speculated that many UA applications do not require costly and complex SD_y measurement but could simply present decision makers with the break-even SD_y values and ensure that there is consensus that it would be exceeded. Moreover, he proposed that such an approach may prove much less confusing and difficult for decision makers than attempting to estimate an exact point estimate. In other words, the break-even approach suggests a mechanism for concisely summarizing the potential impact of uncertainty in one or more utility parameters. It shifts emphasis away from estimating a utility value toward making a decision using imperfect information. It pinpoints areas where controversy is important to decision making (i.e., where there is some doubt whether the break-even value is exceeded) versus areas where controversy has little impact (i.e., where disagreements about SD_y do not indicate a serious risk of values below break-even). Thus, break-even analysis provides a simple expedient allowing UA models to assist in decision making even when some utility parameters are unknown or uncertain. Measurement research (on SD_y or other utility parameters) is not always unnecessary, but such research must consider the decision context, and report not only the magnitude of the uncertainty but also its likely effect.

Recent research incorporating Boudreau's break-even analysis approach has reached similar conclusions (e.g., Burke & Frederick, 1986; Cascio, 1987; Cascio & Ramos, 1986; Florin-Thuma & Boudreau, 1987; Karren, NKomo, & Ramirez, 1985; Mathieu & Leonard, 1987). Eaton, Wing, and Lau (1985) also concluded that HRM program decisions in the military seldom hinge on differences of 10 or 20 percent of testing costs, so a rough estimate of SD_y may often be sufficient for decision making.

Although relatively simple, break-even analysis is not without limitations. It is more difficult, but quite possible, to conduct break-even analysis when more than two or three utility parameters vary. Moreover, the distribution of utility values is not estimated, so two programs could have similar break-even values and similar expected utility values, but one might be preferable because its distribution may be more positively skewed. Neither traditional utility analysis, sensitivity analysis, break-even analysis, nor algebraic derivation, discussed next, adequately reflect such situations.

Algebraic Derivation of Utility Value Variability. Goodman's (1960) equations for the variance of the product of three or more random variables under conditions of independence were adapted by Alexander and Barrick (1987) to produce a formula for the standard error of utility values associated with a one-cohort selection utility model. They demonstrated this derivation using data from the Schmidt et al. (1979) study, as well as variance estimates for employee tenure, SD_y, validity, and the number selected. Their standard deviations, estimated for various selection ratios, were about 50 percent of the expected utility values. By assuming a normal distribution of utility values, determining the utility value at the lower end of a 90 percent confidence interval, and using break-even analysis, the authors concluded that the selection program had a very high probability of producing benefits exceeding costs.

Algebraic derivation reflects simultaneous variability in several utility parameters and can be useful in estimating the risk associated with utility values. However, it is more complicated than break-even analysis and has limitations. First, the formula can incorporate dependencies between variables, but doing so produces very complex estimation equations and requires information on covariances that is seldom available. Variance estimates become especially difficult when programs can be expanded or abandoned during the project's life, or when variables are related in a nonlinear fashion, as the selection ratio and the average standardized predictor score are related in utility formulas. Alexander and Barrick (1987) surmounted this difficulty by holding the selection ratio and average predictor score constant for each variance estimate. Second, algebraic derivation provides a variance estimate, but it requires assumptions about the distribution shape (e.g., normality) to make strong probabilistic inferences. Existing literature provides no empirical information supporting or refuting the assumption of normality, but Hull

(1980) noted that nonnormal distributions are likely when (a) programs can be abandoned or expanded during their life, (b) nonnormal components heavily influence the distribution, and (c) there is only a small number of variables. Each of these conditions may characterize utility analysis, as discussed below.

Monte Carlo Simulation of Utility Value Variability. Monte Carlo simulation attempts to address limitations of the three previous methods. Simulation describes each utility model parameter in terms of its expected value and distribution shape. In each simulated trial, a value for each utility parameter is "chosen" from the distribution for that parameter, and the combination of chosen parameter values is used to calculate total utility for that trial. Repeated application of this choosing and calculating procedure, using a computer, produces a sample of trials from which to describe the distribution properties of utility values. Thus, unlike the other three methods, simulations can vary many parameters at once, reflect dependencies among the parameters, acknowledge possible program expansion or abandonment, and reflect nonnormal distribution assumptions.

Rich and Boudreau (1987) applied Monte Carlo simulation and the other three uncertainty estimation methods to a decision to use the *Programmer Aptitude Test* (PAT) to select computer programmers in a midsize computer manufacturer. They used a utility model enhanced to reflect financial and economic factors and employee flows through the work force, and discovered that all of the utility parameters were subject to some degree of uncertainty or variability over time. They also discovered that SD_y variability heavily influenced the utility value distribution and that the distribution of SD_y values was positively skewed, as in other studies (e.g., Bobko et al., 1983; Burke, 1985; Burke & Frederick, 1984; Mathieu & Leonard, 1987; Schmidt et al., 1984). The simulation suggested greater risk (variability) in utility values than the algebraic derivation because the simulation better reflected dependencies among utility parameters and parameter relationships over time. However, break-even analysis, algebraic derivation, and Monte Carlo simulation all led to the same conclusion: The selection program had a very small probability of negative payoff.

Cronshaw et al. (1987) also simulated utility values, but their analysis held validity, costs, and SD_y constant and used subjective estimates of optimistic, likely, and pessimistic parameter levels rather than observed distributions. Their analysis also focused only on effects for the first cohort of selectees hired, while Rich and Boudreau (1987b) incorporated effects of subsequent program application and employee turnover. Still, Cronshaw et al. (1987) reached a similar conclusion: The selection program had a very small probability of negative payoff.

Thus, Monte Carlo simulation better reflects factors affecting utility value variability and indeed suggests that substantial variability existed due to both measurement error and uncertainty regarding future conditions (Rich and Boudreau, 1987). This methodology may prove very useful in describing the behavior of utility value variability in future research. However, existing research also suggests that the simpler break-even analysis procedure may describe the decision situation adequately enough to reveal the correct decision. We should also note that all selection utility models and all of the variability estimation procedures except Monte Carlo analysis presume a linear and constant relationship between utility and the parameters reflecting employee quantity and quality (i.e., N_s, $\bar{Z}_x$, SD_y, and $r_{x,y}$). Economic theory suggests this assumption may be questionable in certain situations. Therefore, Monte Carlo simulation may have an advantage over the other three methods when such nonlinearities are important enough to alter decisions and when they can be quantified sufficiently to be incorporated into a simulation algorithm.

Statistical Hypothesis Testing and Uncertainty in Utility Analysis

The Inferential Statistics Approach. Researchers are familiar with the classic statistical tools of confidence intervals, hypothesis tests, and probability statements. Such tools usually emphasize the probability of Type I error (accepting an alternative hypothesis that is false) by specifying the significance level of the statistical test. A statistical approach uses sample information to estimate the variability of the sampling distribution in a statistic (e.g., t, F, etc.). Then, assuming that the null hypothesis (usually a hypothesis of zero effect) is the mean of the sampling distribution, a decision rule for the statistic is established such that the null hypothesis is rejected in favor of the alternative hypothesis only if the observed effect in the sample is large enough to fall near the tail of the assumed distribution (i.e., in the highest 5 or 1 percent of the distribution). Of course, this ignores the probability of Type II error (incorrectly failing to reject the null hypothesis when it is false). Although some methods for reducing Type I error (e.g., increasing sample size and measurement reliability) reduce both errors by producing a smaller variance in the sampling distribution, other mechanisms for reducing Type I error (e.g., requiring larger effects before rejecting the null hypothesis) actually increase the probability of Type II error.

Utility models are intimately connected to both statistical inference and to decision making. UA models make use of statistics (e.g., the correlation coefficient) that summarize sample information. However, they also can illuminate the limitations of statistical analysis in a decision-making context and suggest a more complete approach to using statistical evidence in decision making. Several authors have argued for increased emphasis upon substantive significance as opposed to statistical significance (e.g., Campbell, 1982; Rosenthal & Rubin, 1985). With its emphasis on decision making,

UA research can contribute to formalizing and quantifying this more substantive emphasis. It is beyond the scope of this chapter to fully debate the philosophical and practical issues surrounding the question of substantive and statistical inference. However, it is important to delineate some important roles for utility analysis in such a debate.

The Role of Utility Analysis in Defining Substantive Significance. Statistical inference emphasizes extreme conservatism in the interest of maximizing confidence in reported findings. Specifically, it sets very stringent standards for new research results to replace previously accepted findings. Consider validation studies, where the correlation coefficient is tested for statistical significance using the inferential model specified above. Assuming the true distribution of correlation coefficients has a mean of zero and a variance determined by the sample size, the reliability of the measures, and other factors, the observed correlation must be large enough that the probability of its occurrence in such a distribution is below 5 percent before rejecting the null hypothesis of zero correlation. Such an approach amounts to an extremely conservative decision rule, especially because practical *sample sizes and measure reliabilities* often require quite large sample correlation coefficients to reach statistical significance (Schmidt, Hunter, & Urry, 1976). Meta-analysis techniques can help to place the results of many small-sample studies in perspective and provide a truer picture of the correlation coefficient mean and variability.

The inferential statistical model is usually applied outside of a decision-making context. No costs or benefits are attached to the two types of error, and the implied value judgments inherent in statistical testing are accepted implicitly. But suppose the study described above were being conducted in an actual organization, where managers must decide whether to adopt a particular selection device. Costs associated with Type I error—that is,

adopting the selection device when it should have been rejected—include test development, test administration and scoring, and possible productivity reductions from using the test instead of, or in addition to, the existing selection system. Adopting a decision rule that rejects the selection device unless the observed correlation is large enough to reach statistical significance "protects" the organization from needlessly incurring these costs. However, Type II error—failing to adopt the selection device when it should have been adopted—also brings costs such as the lost productivity enhancements or cost reductions from improved person-job matching. The B-C-G utility model suggests that productivity enhancements and cost reductions are often quite sizable even with very modest correlation coefficients and performance variability. Thus, improved selection systems may often be worth the risk, because the costs of Type I errors are fairly small, the costs of Type II errors are relatively large, and only a modest validity level is required to produce benefits from the improved selection system. Classical statistics attempts to minimize Type I error even at substantial risk of Type II error, reflecting values that are virtually opposite to these characteristics.

Several authors have made a similar argument, though the link to utility analysis has not been as clear. Rosenthal and Rubin (1985) take issue with the notion that statistical inference is designed to establish facts, proposing that the purpose is to summarize information efficiently. They make three important points: (a) that "when the dependent variable is of some importance and where obtaining additional data is difficult, expensive or unlikely" (p. 528), even nonsignificant results can contribute to scientific understanding; (b) that by taking the ratio of the probability of Type I error to Type II error, we obtain an index of the "perceived relative seriousness" of the two errors, which indicates that in most studies Type I errors were implicitly "from 5 to 95 times more serious than Type II errors" (pp. 528–529); and

(c) that the notion of value-free scientific inference is usually inaccurate because investigators use their own values in choosing what statistical tests and contrasts to investigate. Cascio and Zedeck (1983) also suggested computing the ratio of Type I to Type II errors as a measure of the relative importance of decision consequences. Using UA formulas, they demonstrated that less stringent decision rules increase power (the ability to detect nonzero effect sizes), but also increase Type I error. They suggested that researchers adjust alpha levels (i.e., acceptable Type I error levels) downward to increase statistical power.

Fowler (1985) noted Campbell's (1982) lament that statistical significance is often incorrectly taken as substantive significance and his admonition that researchers argue for the substantive as well as the statistical significance of their findings. Using a definition of substantive significance derived from Cohen's (1977) signal to noise ratio and Lykken's (1968) observations concerning common variance in psychological variables, Fowler reviewed *Journal of Applied Psychology* articles from 1975 and 1980, finding that 75 percent of the 1975 effect sizes and 69 percent of the 1980 effect sizes were "below Cohen's large effect" (p. 217), though they reached statistical significance. Abelson (1985) described the paradox whereby baseball batting skill explains less than 1 percent of the variance in single at-bat performance but is regarded with extreme importance by decision makers in selecting baseball players and assigning them positions (batting opportunities in games). Abelson pointed out that decision makers must consider the season-long performance of a team, not the single at-bat performance. Because any player may have 1,000 at bats in a season, and because scoring rallies are more likely when groups of skilled batters build on each other's skills, even the "modest" explanatory power of batting skill has important implications for team performance compared to other alternative selection and assignment schemes.

These observations suggest an important role for UA research in explicating the debate on substantive versus statistical significance. Rosenthal and Rubin's first observation supports the earlier conclusion that the potential effect of HRM programs on productivity is important enough that even imperfect information about utility parameters may be quite valuable, because further data gathering may be difficult or expensive. Their second observation, as well as the Cascio and Zedeck observations, suggests that HRM program decision rules should be adjusted so that the ratio of Type I to Type II error probabilities is consistent with the costs and benefits of both types of errors. Rosenthal and Rubin's third observation suggests that both the organizational implications and scientific value judgments should be considered when interpreting statistical tests, and UA models can provide valuable information describing organizational implications. Fowler's observation that a majority of research studies may produce statistically significant findings that have low substantive importance is not unlike our earlier observation that although many of the discrepancies between SD_y measurement methods are quite large in absolute terms, break-even analysis reveals that the discrepancies appear to have little bearing on the quality of HRM program decisions. Fowler's findings also reinforce our conclusion that such research should report the decision context in which SD_y information will be used. Finally, Abelson's (1985) explanation for the variance explanation paradox parallels the break-even analysis of Appendix A, suggesting that most organizations, like baseball teams, are more concerned with productivity outcomes reflecting multiple employees and time periods than with the behaviors of one employee.

Incorporating the Value of Information

The issues of necessary precision, statistical versus substantive significance, and uncertainty regarding utility analysis for HRM programs are analogous to similar issues for other organizational investment decisions. Decision makers must implicitly or explicitly assess the value of additional information and the cost of acting with uncertainty in light of the particular decision context they face, and several models for quantifying these issues are available (cf. Bierman et al., 1981). Yet these well-known models are not usually applied to HRM decisions, at least partly because of the widespread failure even to attempt to quantify the effects of HRM interventions. Utility analysis allows quantification and thus offers one link to decision models that more explicitly incorporate the value of information. Although it is not possible to fully develop the mathematical and logical arguments inherent in such an information model, we can briefly summarize how UA models can be used for this purpose and the implications of viewing utility analysis as a component of the larger task of making decisions under uncertainty.

The Basic Information Value Model Incorporating Utility Analysis. Information has value when it reduces uncertainty in a way that produces better decisions. Gathering information such as utility model parameter measurement is a decision in itself, subject to both desirable and undesirable consequences. In simplest terms, the value of additional information depends upon (a) the probability that the information's results can change decisions, (b) the consequences of the changed decisions, and (c) the cost of gathering the additional information. The value of additional information may be considered as the product of (a) and (b), less (c). Additional information has greatest value when the probability that the additional information will change the decision is very great, the consequences of changed decisions are very large, and the information can be gathered at low cost. Additional information has less value under the opposite conditions.

Evaluating information requires: (a) an explicit decision (i.e., the alternatives, their attributes, and the value of the differences in their consequences), (b) a decision rule for using the additional information to alter decisions, (c) assumptions or data regarding the results likely to be revealed by the information, and (d) the cost of the additional information. Two models for evaluating information value are commonly discussed (cf. Bierman et al., 1981)—*perfect information* and *imperfect information*. The two models differ primarily in the way they treat the third factor listed above (i.e., the probable results of the additional information).

Suppose an organization is considering two selection devices. One device is more valid but is also more costly to develop, administer, and evaluate. The decision maker realizes that selection utility consequences will be quite different if future conditions produce very large applicant pools, allowing the organization to be very choosy and to achieve a high average selectee test score, as opposed to very small applicant pools, providing less choice and thus less payoff to improved validity. Suppose it has been determined that two selection ratios are possible (i.e., .30 or .70). Utility analysis reveals that if the selection ratio is .30, then the more expensive device offers a utility of $500,000, and the less expensive device offers a utility of $300,000. If the selection ratio is .70, then the more expensive device offers a utility of $50,000 and the less expensive device offers a utility of $200,000. Should the decision maker gather additional information (e.g., labor market forecasts or strategic forecasts of labor demand) to attempt to predict the selection ratio more precisely? Without further information, the decision maker attaches a 20 percent probability to the .30 selection ratio, and an 80 percent probability to the .70 selection ratio. Thus, with no additional information the expected values are $140,000 and $220,000 for the more and less expensive alternatives, respectively, and the less valid and less expensive alternative is preferred. The expected value of this decision is $220,000.

In the perfect information model, one assumes that a perfect predictor would foretell the actual selection ratio in advance, and calculates the additional decision value that could be derived from that information. In the example, if the decision maker had perfect information, then there is a 20 percent chance that the information would foretell a low selection ratio. With this information, the decision maker would switch to the more expensive alternative and enjoy the $500,000 utility instead of the $300,000 utility of the less expensive selection device. However, there is an 80 percent chance the perfect information will reveal a high selection ratio, in which case the original decision was correct anyway. Thus, the value of perfect information is equal to 20 percent times the utility difference under the high-selection-ratio condition (i.e., .20 times $200,000), or $40,000. Under these assumptions, this is the upper limit of the value of any information that improves the ability to predict the actual selection ratio. The information value is realized only under the conditions where it changes the decision and depends on the consequences as well as the probability of that change. Even in the absence of selection ratio information, it is possible to compute the value for the two probabilities that would change the decision. The more expensive option is preferred if the probability of the low selection ratio exceeds 43 percent, and the probability of the high selection ratio does not exceed 57 percent.

In the imperfect information model, one uses Bayesian probability relationships to determine how imperfect information changes the a priori probability estimates, the decisions implied by these changes, and the expected consequences of the decisions under all future conditions and information outcomes. Frequently, decision trees can represent the decision situation. However, the main objective is similar—to determine the economic value of information designed to reduce uncertainty.

Moreover, the same three factors determine the economic value of additional information.

Variations on these models can be developed that reflect continuous as well as discrete distributions of future conditions, information outcomes, and probabilities. Indeed if the distribution of information outcomes is assumed to be normal, it is possible to evaluate the consequences of various statistical decision rules (e.g., setting Type I error at 5 percent) in light of alternative future conditions (e.g., decision consequences, true values for utility parameters) and determine the economically optimum decision rule and/or the economically optimum sample size for a future study. Moreover, such methods can be applied not just to uncertainty regarding future selection ratios, but to uncertainty regarding any of the utility parameters. Such a framework makes it possible to explicitly consider not only expected utility values, but uncertainty and risk inherent in those values, as well as the implications of decision rules derived from inferential statistics or other methods.

Linking the Information Value Model and Emerging UA Research. Recall the three determinants of information value: (a) the probability that the additional information will change decisions, (b) the consequences of the changed decisions, and (c) the cost of gathering the additional information. Despite research on SD_y variability, actual selection device decisions are unlikely to be altered by different SD_y measures because (a) different SD_y measures have low probabilities of producing SD_y values below break-even, (b) even crude SD_y estimates will often lead to a decision favoring improved selection, and (c) refined SD_y measures may be complex and costly. Boudreau (1984a) developed this point in detail using the perfect information model.

When the costs of implementing improved selection are modest compared to the potential benefits, relying on decision rules based on statistical significance may be overly conservative. Failure to adopt improved selection devices because validities do not reach statistical significance may imply a belief that the consequences of erroneous implementation are tens, or hundreds, of times as great as the consequences of erroneous failure to implement. Existing evidence suggests that implementation costs are low and potential productivity benefits are very large, so *HR managers often cannot afford the risk of not trying improved selection devices*. Still, the B-C-G model reflects only a portion of relevant decision factors, and we have no research to suggest what other factors decision makers may consider.

Conclusion

In view of the high variability associated with utility parameter estimates (especially SD_y), it seems plausible that perceived uncertainty and risk associated with utility estimates may explain why HRM programs do not enjoy widespread acceptance and why the utility values may appear larger than many researchers would have expected (Hunter & Schmidt, 1982; Schmidt et al., 1979). However, this view may also reflect ignorance of the capacity for improved HRM to affect organizational goals. As the illustration in Table 2 and the break-even analysis of Appendix A vividly illustrate, the *leverage* or quantity of person-years affected by HRM programs can be quite large. Thus, the coefficient on SD_y is often quite large, and even modest levels of performance variability offer substantial opportunities for highly valuable HRM program effects. Schmidt et al. (1986, 1984) have expressed utility values as a percentage of output and wages, suggesting that if decision makers or researchers find utility values implausible, it may reflect the fact that they do not appreciate the magnitude of their human resource investment.

Uncertainty about SD_y would not have been an important factor in any published UA applications. Further research on the cognitive processes affecting SD_y estimation and further efforts to develop new and more reliable SD_y estimation methods may provide more information on the nature and magnitude of this uncertainty (Bobko, Karren, & Kerkar, 1987). Such research should reflect the decision context so that the implications of these findings can be meaningfully interpreted. The information value model suggests that valuable future UA research will address issues likely to alter decisions in contexts where such alterations carry large consequences.

Recognizing the decision context reveals that UA models reflect an organizational process, not merely the single application of a particular program. The next sections review enhancements to the B-C-G utility model designed to better reflect such organizational processes. Such enhancements can have at least three purposes: (a) to provide more accurate and realistic utility values, (b) to improve the usefulness of UA models in enhancing decisions, and (c) to allow UA research to encompass a broader theoretical domain that advances scientific understanding of decisions about HRM programs. The first objective must be measured against actual or presumed objective values which may not be available. The second objective can be measured against the information value principles noted above. The third objective may be the most important for research and can be measured against the ability of enhancements to incorporate and integrate fruitful new directions for scientific inquiry.

Expanding the Domain of Attributes in Selection Utility Analysis

UA models are special cases of MAU models, representing some but certainly not all factors affected by HRM decisions. All MAU models, including UA models, are undoubtedly deficient. This deficiency offers another possible explanation for utility values that may be higher than expected or for the lack or wide-spread application of the models. The UA model may be missing important variables that are relevant to decision makers. Such deficiencies would be especially troubling if the omitted variables tend to argue against interventions, because UA models could produce positive utility values, suggesting program implementation, while a more complete UA model might reveal reasons against implementation. Moreover, because UA models focus on decisions to invest organizational resources in HRM programs, they implicitly draw on assumptions regarding both financial decision processes and labor market phenomena that interact with such decisions. We now explore how attributes from each of these related domains affect the B-C-G selection utility model.

Financial and Economic Considerations

The dollar-valued payoff function in UA models has led to speculation that UA models can provide a link between personnel/HRM research and more traditional management functions (e.g., marketing, finance, accounting, or operations). For example, Landy, Farr, and Jacobs (1982, p. 38) suggested that utility analysis models may be capable of "providing the science of personnel research with a more traditional 'bottom line' interpretation," Cascio and Silbey (1979) called for a closer liaison between personnel researchers and cost accountants, and Greer and Cascio (1987) proposed that cost accounting should contribute to defining the criterion in utility analysis. Even the original treatments of Brogden and Taylor (1950) and Cronbach and Gleser (1965) reflected a concern with the profit contribution of enhanced work force quality. Recently, researchers have suggested enhancements to the B-C-G selection utility model designed to incorporate financial and economic considerations.

Variable Costs, Taxes, and Discounting. Boudreau (1983a) recognized that UA models

addressed economic and financial consequences of HRM decisions, but failed to incorporate certain financial and economic considerations. He suggested that measuring utility with a payoff function reflecting sales revenue or "the value of output as sold" would probably overstate HRM program effects on discounted after-tax profit, the payoff scale used for financial investments. He showed how the utility formulas could easily be altered to account for three basic financial and economic concepts: variable costs, taxes, and discounting.

First, Boudreau noted the difference between *sales* (or service) *value* (i.e., the value of the increase in sales revenue or output as sold), *service cost* (i.e., the change in organizational costs associated with the increased revenue), and *net benefits* (i.e., the difference between service value and service costs) produced by an HRM intervention. He suggested that productivity enhancements through improved HRM programs may require additional support costs (e.g., increased inventories to support higher sales, increased raw materials used to support higher output volumes, or increased salaries and benefits as incentives for improved performance). Moreover, many interventions operate not by increasing sales revenue or output levels but by reducing costs (e.g., Florin-Thuma & Boudreau, 1987; Schmidt et al., 1986). He suggested including the effects of HRM programs on service costs in the model in either of two ways: (a) by reflecting the change in costs through a correlation coefficient (between the predictor and service costs) and the dollar-valued standard deviation of service costs among applicants or (b) by assuming service costs are proportional to service value increases and simply multiplying the incremental service value increase by a proportion $(1-V)$ reflecting the change in net benefits. Greer and Cascio (1987) derived variable costs more precisely using accounting conventions for soft-drink route salesmen. Boudreau (1983a) showed how incorporating such considerations could increase utility values (if costs fall when productivity increases) or decrease utility values (if costs rise when productivity increases).

Second, Boudreau noted that most organizations do not keep the full value of increases in net benefits. Rather, they must pay taxes on increased income to federal, state, and local governments. Thus, adjusting utility values from the B-C-G model to reflect increases in net benefits may still overstate the organizational payoff by failing to account for increased taxes. Boudreau proposed multiplying both the net benefits and the implementation costs (C) by one minus the applicable tax rate (i.e., $1 - TAX$) to reflect after-tax effects. He speculated that TAX levels might be as low as zero for organizations reporting losses and as high as .55 for organizations subject to multiple income tax obligations.

Third, Boudreau observed that UA models typically focused upon benefits from interventions lasting into future time periods; the second column of Appendix A indicates the number of future time periods analyzed in empirical applications. UA models had treated such year-to-year effects as equivalent to each other. Returns derived in future years were simply added to the returns from initial years. He noted that such treatment ignored a fundamental fact of organizational management—money can be invested to earn interest. When interest can be earned, accelerated program returns and postponed program costs can be invested to earn interest for a longer time period. Therefore, financial analysis "discounts" future earnings and costs to reflect these potential investment returns. Boudreau demonstrated how the interest rate earned on program returns *(i)* could be incorporated into the UA model, producing a *discount f factor* (i.e., *DF*, the summed effects of discounting over a number of future periods). He demonstrated that discounting reduced utility value levels, with the most substantial reductions occurring when program returns occur farther into the future and when the discount rate is high.

Boudreau (1983a) incorporated these factors into the selection utility formula and derived the combined effects of hypothetical levels of the parameters on reported utility values. His derivations suggested that when HRM programs face zero tax and interest rates, and variable costs are reduced with productivity increases, B-C-G utility values might understate actual discounted, after-tax net benefits by as much as 33 percent. However, when HRM programs face positive tax and interest rates and costs rise with productivity, reported values might be overstated by as much as 84 percent. Studies applying financial and economic considerations suggest that unadjusted utility values commonly exceed adjusted values. As shown in Appendix A, Mathieu and Leonard (1987) found $TAX = .46$, $i = .15$, and $V = .07$; Burke and Frederick (1986) found $TAX = .49$, $i = .18$, and $V = .05$; Rich and Boudreau (1987) found $TAX = .39$, $i = .15$, and $V = 0$.

Table 3 extends the example begun in Table 2, incorporating the financial and economic considerations noted by Boudreau (1983b), assuming the variable cost proportion equals 5 percent, the tax rate equals 45 percent, and the interest rate equals 10 percent. Program costs are assumed to occur at the beginning of the analysis, so they are not discounted but are adjusted only for their effect on taxes. Assuming a 10-year analysis period, unadjusted quantity equals 6,180 person-years. Unadjusted quality per person-year is $6,331 per person-year. Thus, the unadjusted product of quantity and quality is $39.125 million. This is adjusted to reflect the 5 percent variable costs and 45 percent taxes. Finally, to reflect discounting at a 10 percent rate, the 10-year quality effect is multiplied by .614, producing an after-cost, after-tax discounted net program benefit of $12.5519 million as shown in Table 3. Subtracting the after-tax testing cost of $6,798 produces the after-cost, after-tax, discounted net utility of $12.55 million as shown. Though

TABLE 3

Financial One-Cohort Entry-level Selection Utility Model

Cost-Benefit Information	*Entry-level Computer Programmers*
Current employment	4,404
Number separating	618
Number selected (N_s)	618
Average tenure in years (T)	10
Test Information	
Number of applicants (N_{app})	1,236
Testing cost/applicant	$10
Total test cost (C)	$12,360
Average test score ($\bar{Z}_x$)	.80 SD
Validity ($r_{x,y}$)	.76
SD_y (per person-year)	$10,413
Financial Information	
Variable costs (V)	5%
Tax rate (TAX)	45%
Interest rate (i)	10%

Utility Computation

Unadjusted quantity	=	Average tenture x applicants selected
	=	10 years x 618 applicants
	=	6,180 person-years
Unadjusted quality	=	Average test score x test validity x SD_y
	=	.80 x .76 x $10,413
	=	$6,331 per person-year
Adjusted costs	=	Tests costs – tax savings
(after taxes)	=	$12,360 – (.45 x $12,360), or .55 x $12,360
	=	$6,798

Utility	=	Unadjusted quantity	x	Unadjusted quality	x	Variable cost adjustment	x	Tax cost adjustment	x	Discount rate adjustment	−	Adjusted costs
	=	[6,180	x	$6,331	x	.95	x	.55	x	.614]	−	$6,798
	=	$12.55 million										

From "Utility Analysis" by John W. Boudreau, 1988. In Lee Dyer (Ed.), *Human Resource Management: Evolving Roles and Responsibilities.*Washington, DC: The Bureau of National Affairs, Inc. Copyright 1988 by the Bureau of National Affairs, Inc. Reprinted by permission.

substantially smaller than the $37.9 million reported by Schmidt et al. (1979), derived in Table 2, this return remains substantial.

Boudreau (1983a) stated that utility values incorporating these financial and economic considerations would better reflect the decision context of organizations that compute such investment values for programs in other management functions and might be more credible to managers accustomed to working with financial analysis. He also noted a number of theoretical implications. First, employee wages and salaries are a different concept from their productive value, with wages and salaries reflecting resource costs, while productive value reflects the output of applying human resources to a production process. Equating compensation with productive value will usually understate value, but in some cases will overstate it because wages may exceed production value for some jobs or individuals. As we shall see, the relationship between improved labor quality and compensation is central to labor economic theory, and this model provides a framework in which to integrate them. Second, utility analysis reflects temporal effects that may not remain constant over time, as the B-C-G model assumes, and might lead to biased utility value estimates. Although Schmidt, Hunter, Outerbridge, and Goff (1988) found that validities and performance differences remained constant over time, temporal instability has been incorporated into utility models for training (Mathieu & Leonard, 1987; Schmidt et al., 1982). Third, the enhanced financial and economic utility model might partially explain the unreliability observed in managerial SD_y estimates when managers are asked to use two conceptually different anchors—the value of output and the cost of contracting for that output—to derive one value (Day & Edwards, 1987; Reilly & Smither, 1985).

Applying Capital Budgeting Indices to Utility Analysis. Cronshaw and Alexander (1985) suggested that "a major reason for the differential success of human resource and financial managers in implementing their respective evaluation models is the greater rapprochement of capital budgeting with the everyday language of line managers and with the financial planning needs of the organization" (p. 102). They speculated that by integrating UA results into the financial decision-making context, personnel managers would better communicate the impact of their programs on the value of the firm as opposed to increased productivity or operating costs.

Cronshaw and Alexander (1985) separated the cost component of the selection utility model into two components, C_o, the original one-time costs of developing and validating a selection instrument, and C_i, the implementation costs incurred each time the instrument is used. The *return* (i.e, R) of the program was the one-year, one-cohort productivity increase from a selection device (i.e., the product of N_s, SD_y, $r_{x,y}$, and Z_x). They also explained the analogies between the selection utility model and five standard capital budgeting indices often discussed in financial investment textbooks. First, the *payback period* (PP), or the number of years a firm requires to recover its original investment from net returns, was formulated as the sum of C_i and C_o divided by R. (A more consistent formulation would be C_o divided by the difference between R and C_i.) The authors note that this index is deficient because it ignores interest earned on returns over time, and it ignores returns that occur subsequent to the payback period.

Second, they defined *return on investment* (ROI) as the ratio of annual cash returns to original cost and formulated it as the ratio of R to the sum of C_i plus C_o. (A more consistent formula might be the difference between R and C_i divided by C_o.) They noted that this index ignores interest returns, but it also ignores any multiple-year returns because it reflects only the one-year return from selection divided by the entire implementation cost.

Third, they defined *net present value* (NPV) as the difference between the discounted sum of returns over time (where the discount rate is the expected rate of return earned by the firm on contributed capital) and the original and implementation costs. This formulation is virtually identical to Boudreau's (1983a) formula, but Cronshaw and Alexander do not account for variable production costs, multiyear implementation costs, and taxes.

Fourth, they defined the *profitability index* (PI) as the ratio of the present value of net cash inflows to cash outflows and formulated it as the discounted sum of returns (R) divided by the sum of implementation and original costs. (A more consistent formulation might be the discounted sum of R minus C_i divided by the original costs.) The authors note that a PI greater than 1.0 suggests a payoff exceeding costs as well as meeting the discount rate. They note that such an index fails to take into account the relative size of investments.

Fifth, they defined the *internal rate of return* (IRR) as the rate which equates the NPV of cash inflows with cash outflows and formulated it as the value of the discount rate that equates the discounted sum of the returns with the sum of the one-year implementation costs and the original costs. (A more correct formulation might equate original costs with the discounted sum of the difference between the returns and implementation costs.) The authors noted that the derived rate of return is then compared to the organization's required rate of return to determine project acceptability. An additional important limitation to this index is its assumption that each project's returns would earn interest at that project's IRR, thus incorrectly implying different interest rates on the returns from different projects.

Cronshaw and Alexander (1985) briefly discuss the issues of taxation, application to nonselection programs, multiyear benefits, and the flow of employees through the work force over time, which would make their financial models more compatible with Boudreau's

(1983a, 1983b) derivations and could address some of the inconsistencies noted above. They also provide a useful distinction between viewing HRM program expenditures as *operating costs* written off in the current period, presumably implying that program returns occur only in that period, and as *capital investments*, presumably implying multiyear future returns. They speculate that the reason for the low credibility and the presumed expendability of HRM programs may be that HRM managers fail to adequately communicate the multiyear benefits accruing from such programs. This point is analogous to an earlier observation made by Boudreau (1984a), which showed that break-even values suggested high HRM payoffs and suggested that even large cost outlays were justified by HRM program returns. However, two of Cronshaw and Alexander's financial indices (payback period and one-year return on investment) will also understate multiyear benefits.

In fact, only two indices (net present value and profitability index) accurately reflect the relative discounted multiyear payoffs from competing financial investments. The profitability index is especially intriguing because it suggests considering payoff in terms of the benefits *per dollar expended*, rather than the benefits *minus dollars expended*, as is the traditional utility focus. It is straightforward to reformulate utility equations to reflect this alternative perspective. It would be interesting to learn whether such reformulations would affect decision processes.

Limitations in Using Financial and Economic Considerations.   Hunter, Schmidt, and Coggin (1988) proposed that financial accounting methods are "frequently inapplicable to human resource programs and, in addition, may sometimes have negative consequences even when they are applicable on a purely logical basis" (p. 522). First, they noted that except for discounted present value, the financial indexes discussed by Cronshaw and Alexander (1985) require that a portion of the costs be designated as the *investment* (e.g., *Co*), and they speculate that many improved selection systems may actually involve no original costs and/or may actually reduce ongoing testing costs. They correctly note that under such conditions, one can compute discounted net present value (as described by Boudreau, 1983a), but not the other indices. However, to assume costless HRM programs reduces the justification for *any* dollar-valued utility analysis because any nonnegative change in validity must produce increased value for the organization, as we have seen. Thus, this argument is less an indictment of capital budgeting than a recognition that UA models are best applied to decisions where programs compete for resources and those resources are obtained at some cost.

Second, Hunter et al. (1988) argued that "discounting is meaningful only if there is in fact a delay in receiving the benefit" (p. 524). They correctly recognize that the B-C-G model reflects hiring only one cohort of employees, but when HRM programs are applied repeatedly their effects build as the work force becomes progressively more saturated with better selected individuals (Boudreau, 1983b, 1987, 1988, 1989; Boudreau & Berger, 1985a). They observed that once the saturation point is reached (after year 4 in their example), better selected new hires simply replace departing better selected employees, so the total work force value remains the same as long as the program is reapplied (we will discuss employee flows subsequently). They stated that "there is no such time delay in receiving the utility benefits once the program attains its equilibrium utility level" (p. 524) and that "if the program were used indefinitely, as is typically the case" the equilibrium value is constant for every future year. Technically, discounted and undiscounted utility values are equal for infinitely long investments with constant returns. However, the investment *decision* must be made at the *beginning* of the program, not in the middle after it has reached equilibrium.

Thus, the time delay *is* relevant. Moreover, the typical decision involves not one, but two or more competing alternatives, and different programs often reach equilibrium at different times, so that utility differences between programs will be affected by discounting. Hunter, Schmidt, and Coggin (1988, p. 523, note 1) also noted that when businesses typically omit discounting from their investment evaluation methods, they may find that discounted utility values do not enhance credibility. This remains an empirical question, but considering the logically sound basis for discounting, it seems unlikely that discounting will actually detract from credibility.

Hunter et al. (1988) further proposed that even when programs involve investments, "return on investment and other capital budgeting figures for personnel programs, even when correctly calculated, will often appear to be extreme compared to other investment opportunities, and that, as a result, they could appear to management as lacking credibility" (p. 524). Their example, like the results in Appendix A, demonstrates that the return on investment, payback period, profitability index, and internal rate of return calculated for many HRM programs will be quite high. Yet the adjustments to compute after-tax, discounted net benefits will frequently produce *lower* utility values than those derived from simpler models. For example, Boudreau (1983a, p. 569) noted that such adjustments would produce values that were 33 percent as large as the original values reported by Schmidt et al. (1979), as demonstrated in Table 3. Thus, rather than threatening credibility, financial and economic factors can reduce utility values to potentially more credible levels when compared to other financial investments. If they remain extreme after such adjustments, it is difficult to see how the unadjusted (i.e., more extreme) values are more credible than adjusted values.

As noted earlier in discussing the payoff function for SD_y, Hunter et al. (1988, p. 526) correctly noted that adjustments for variable costs are often appropriate and consistent with utility definitions that emphasize cost reduction or profit contribution and that the value of output as sold is appropriate only when concern focuses on increases in revenue. They also acknowledged that "contribution to after tax profits...might also have informational value for some purposes" (p. 527).

Financial accounting methods are not frequently inapplicable to utility analysis. The discounted present value model (Boudreau, 1983a) is inapplicable only for costless investments and/or investments with an infinite time horizon and equal temporal returns. Under such conditions, any dollar-valued utility model is of little value, and programs could be chosen based on their effect size alone. However, where programs require investments and where competing investments may produce different temporal returns (i.e., where dollar-valued utility analysis is applicable), the financial and economic utility model (Boudreau, 1983a, 1983b) integrates potentially important factors so that they can be explicitly considered.

Hunter et al. (1988) correctly concluded that "there is no single correct index of utility" and that "industrial and organizational psychologists and other human resource specialists should maintain the flexibility to match the information presented with the information needed for the purposes at hand" (p. 527), a position completely consistent with the arguments presented here and elsewhere (Boudreau, 1983a, 1983b, 1984a, 1987, 1988, 1989; Boudreau & Berger, 1985a; Boudreau & Rynes, 1985; Florin-Thuma & Boudreau, 1987; Rich & Boudreau, 1987). As we have seen, every utility model is deficient, including models that fail to adjust for financial and economic factors. However, this is not synonymous with saying that the financially or economically adjusted model is "the only legitimate definition of utility" (Hunter et al., 1988, p. 526). Indeed, as we have seen, the model proposed by Boudreau (1983a, 1983b) encompasses both the unadjusted and adjusted utility values.

As Boudreau (1983a) and Table 3 demonstrated, by setting the tax rate, discount rate, and variable cost proportion to zero, one obtains utility values identical to those of the unadjusted B-C-G model. Explicitly recognizing such factors encourages and enables managers and researchers to consider each factor's relevance to their decision, and then, if appropriate, to focus on those that are most important. Hunter et al. (1988) argued that such a general model would produce an equation that is "so long and complex as to be daunting...and as such is very difficult for personnel psychologists and human resource managers to understand" (p. 527). They claimed that "most managers and human resource personnel would rather deal with different models and different computational procedures for different cases." Research has demonstrated the financial and economic model's appropriateness (Boudreau, 1983b; Boudreau & Berger, 1985a; Boudreau & Rynes, 1985; Burke & Frederick, 1986; Cronshaw et al., 1987; Florin-Thuma & Boudreau, 1987; Mathieu & Leonard, 1987; Rich & Boudreau, 1987). Managerial preferences for using general models versus inventing new models for every situation remain an empirical question, but this question can only be tested if such general models exist. Rauschenberger and Schmidt (1987) correctly noted that it would be "presumptuous" to contend that research building such models should be "scaled down in lieu of an emphasis on better communicating existing utility methods to organizational decision makers" (p. 57).

Human Resource Accounting. *Human resource accounting* (HRA) *models* enjoyed substantial attention during the 1960s and early 1970s. These models were derived by researchers with accounting expertise who were concerned with the fact that standard accounting reports provided no explicit mechanism for recognizing the contributions of human resources in the same manner as capital or land resources. Flamholtz (1974, 1985) provided the most widely cited treatment of the HRA model. HRA models arose out of a desire to provide accounting data for managers to use in HRM decisions. They were motivated by desires to put people on the balance sheet, to measure the value of human resources as assets to the organization, and to better reflect the accounting consequences of managerial decisions, such as the possibility that a manager might achieve apparent short-term salary savings at the expense of hidden long-term productivity detriments by allowing high turnover to "liquidate" human assets.

HRA models address the value of human resources in two ways. First, the *cost method* (embodied in Flamholtz's original cost and replacement cost notions) measures or estimates what the cost would be of replacing a person or group of persons with another group capable of rendering the same value to the organization. This approach provides methods for measuring costs of separation, hiring, and development, under the notion that these costs represent investments that should not be charged as expenses in the year they are incurred, but rather should be allocated over the tenure of individuals. Individuals have value to the extent that their investment has not been "amortized" (Flamholtz, 1974, p. 20). Such an approach has some merit as a mechanism for helping managers appreciate the magnitude of the costs associated with human resources. In situations where managers are inclined to allow excessive turnover because they do not appreciate its effect on costs, such a model might help decision makers realize that keeping experienced individuals has value. However, such a model ignores individual differences because it uses "typical" hiring, separation, and development costs. Moreover, it fails to recognize job performance, implicitly equating the costs of replacing an individual with their value, and could lead managers to incorrectly attempt to reduce replacement costs by reducing turnover when in fact the opposite strategy might better enhance productivity.

Second, the *asset method* (embodied in Flamholtz's human resource asset value) measures or estimates "the present worth of the set of future services the person is expected to provide during the period he or she is expected to remain in the organization" (Flamholtz, 1985, p. 173). Such a model considers the discounted stream of productive value and the costs incurred to maintain and improve that productive value over an individual's useful life with the organization. The aggregate value of human resources is the total productive value generated by the employee group over time. Such a concept is logically consistent with the notion of human resources as assets, and it effectively focuses attention away from acquisition costs and toward net productive value. Such a model rapidly becomes highly complex (requiring estimates of future productivity, future career progressions, probabilities of turnover, probabilities of dismissal, probabilities of death, and so on). Like the cost approach, it assumes all job incumbents achieve typical or average productivity in a job, ignoring individual differences.

Both the cost and asset models focus on measurement rather than decision making. Neither model explicitly proposes how HRA information should be used to make decisions concerning HRM programs. Conceivably, one could compute the replacement cost consequences of different managerial decisions causing different levels of turnover, and could use that information to compare the decision options. One could also conceivably compute the asset value of a work force likely to result from different HRM program decisions to determine the program producing the greatest asset value. However, both methods imply ongoing, detailed, and complex measurement tasks and do not emphasize individual responses to HRM programs. Thus, they fail to address the program decisions fundamental to HR management.

Traditional investment decisions for new plant and equipment must translate the values on a balance sheet or income statement to reflect the discounted cash inflows and outflows of that particular investment decision. Similarly, even if HRA data were available, specific HRM program decisions must focus on the relative investment value of different options, so the ongoing and detailed measurement tasks implied by HRA models may not be necessary for many HRM decisions.

Still, HRA research provides extremely useful measures for HRM program costs. Also, HRA models focus attention on the long-term impact of HRM decisions on work force productivity, suggesting that HR managers avoid considering programs in isolation or considering only the short-term impact of HRM programs. As will be discussed subsequently, it is possible for UA models to incorporate this focus in a manner that emphasizes decision making as opposed to measurement.

Behavioral Costing. Recently, Cascio (1982, 1987) proposed integrating the cost focus of HRA with behaviors. His behavioral costing approach consists of the "quantification in financial terms of a set of common behavioral and performance outcomes. Standard cost accounting procedures are applied to employee behavior" (Cascio, 1987, p. 7). This approach measures the cost consequences of behaviors such as turnover, absenteeism, and smoking to quantify the effects of HRM programs reducing those behaviors. While such an approach links the costing methodology of HRA with a more behavioral focus, it may also cause decision makers to overemphasize cost reduction as opposed to performance enhancement. This can lead to incorrect decisions when cost reductions are gained at the expense of performance (e.g., where banning smoking causes better performers to leave or be absent, or where reductions in turnover reduce opportunities to replace poor performers with better performers). Cascio (1987) discusses some of these limitations but does not integrate these behavioral costing methodologies with selection

utility. Moreover, the behavioral costing methodology suggests ongoing behavioral measurement which may not be necessary for all HRM program decisions. Still, Cascio's (1987) behavioral costing treatment provides several costing systems for employee behaviors and suggests one link between HRA costing procedures and HRM decisions.

Equal Employment Opportunity

Equal employment opportunity (EEO) and affirmative action (AA) programs are often adopted or mandated by courts. In the United States, discrimination against protected groups is illegal, and organizations are held responsible for guarding against such discrimination. All HRM programs are subject to examination for their discriminatory effects, though most attention has centered on staffing decisions, usually on the use of selection predictors. Unlike the factors discussed earlier, EEO and AA reflect *equity* rather than *efficiency* (Milkovich & Boudreau, 1991). However, in view of the importance of these issues to organizations, it seems quite likely that decision makers take them into account when considering HRM programs, especially selection. Such equity considerations may help to explain decisions that appear at variance with the UA model prescriptions. For example, simple top-down hiring may produce the highest utility, but if minorities score lower, the test can reject a substantially higher proportion of minority group members (Wigdor & Hartigan, 1988). Such selection devices are likely to be more closely scrutinized by government agencies, so decision makers may reject them in favor of methods presumed to be legally safer, such as setting low cutoff scores or using less valid procedures that produce less adverse impact. Utility analysis can help to quantify the economic impact of such decisions. Although existing legislation appears to allow more valid selection devices even if they reject more minority applicants, it is up to the organization to demonstrate that there is clear justification for the devices—that the devices are a "business necessity." Dunnette et al. (1982, p. 26) noted that UA models can provide evidence of business necessity, defined as the need for improved selection so as to reduce instances of ineffective and costly job performance.

No research has examined whether EEO considerations explain the failure to adopt selection devices that are more valid, or to adopt other HRM programs to enhance productivity. However, several authors have recognized EEO in their utility analyses, providing mechanisms for computing the effects of different EEO or AA strategies on selection utility. Kroeck, Barrett, and Alexander (1983) developed a simulation depicting the effects of different affirmative action policies on minority hiring and performance levels. Schmidt et al. (1984) used utility data for U.S. park rangers to examine the effects of setting minimum cutoff scores at different points in the applicant population distribution; such minimum cutoffs might be adopted in an effort to allow less qualified minorities to meet hiring standards. They found that setting the cutoff at the mean reduced utility values to 45 percent of the utility of top-down hiring, and setting the cutoff one standard deviation below the mean reduced them to 16 percent of top-down hiring. Finally, Steffy and Ledvinka (1989) developed a simulation designed to examine the utility consequences of selection strategies based on three different definitions of fairness. As Schmidt et al. (1984) conclude, "The question can be raised whether those employers currently using the low cutoff method of employment test use are aware of the large price in productivity that they are paying" (p. 496). Wigdor and Hartigan (1988) also showed how alternative race-conscious scoring systems can enhance minority representation with smaller reductions in the standardized productivity level of selectees. It remains for future research to determine whether such estimates actually affect decisions.

Integrating Labor Economics and Industrial and Organizational Psychology Through Utility Analysis

The hypotheses and findings of labor economics seem well suited to provide insight into future UA research. Moreover, the UA framework suggests that theories of labor economics can be tested more rigorously at the level of individual decisions, in contrast with the more traditional focus of labor economics at the level of the firm or the economy. We can identify a number of issues suggesting a bridge between labor economics, personnel management, and industrial and organizational psychology.

Labor economics has traditionally dealt with the implications of economic theory for the behavior of organizations and individuals in a labor market. A labor market is the arena in which individuals provide a *supply* of limited labor resources to organizations, with the characteristics of the labor resources depending on individual/organizational characteristics and decisions regarding the "human capital" investments they make (e.g., education, training, willingness to relocate, and so on). Organizations *demand* labor resources from individuals, depending on the needs of the organization's services or production processes. Thus, a market of labor supply and demand exists, with both parties bargaining to identify the prices at which certain labor resources will be supplied to fill demand. Labor economic investigations often focus on the behavior of wages and the quantity of labor employed as a function of various individual and organizational characteristics to determine whether such behavior can be explained using the labor market model.

Although several industrial and organizational psychology research areas are related to labor market behavior (e.g., motivation theory is often studied within the context of organizational reward systems), seldom are the two disciplines explicitly related. Labor economics tends to presume a market-based pattern of choices and behaviors at the individual or firm level, or at least presumes that useful predictions can be made by assuming such patterns, and focuses on national or industry-wide trends. Industrial and organizational psychology often focuses on the individual behaviors and choices related to organizational attributes (e.g., predicting the likelihood of separation as a function of satisfaction with various organizational attributes), but devotes less attention to the implications for aggregate behavior among those supplying and demanding labor resources. Clearly both perspectives are important to fully understand the implications of HRM program decisions. UA research will inevitably lead to greater concern with labor-market-related issues and implications, because it inevitably directs attention to the dollar-valued market performance of the organization (Boudreau, 1988).

Labor Markets Require a Price for Labor Force Quality.   UA models generally ignore labor market reactions to improved selection (or other HRM programs), reflecting an assumption that an organization adopting more valid selection is the only firm affected by that decision. However, if other firms become aware of the more valid procedure, competitive pressures can provide an incentive for them to adopt it as well, increasing competition for higher quality applicants and initiating bidding for these applicants through increased wages or other incentives (Boudreau, 1983b, p. 404). Becker (1989) noted that this can occur even if firms are unaware of their competitors' improved selection, because those without such selection will observe the decrease in applicant quality as their competitors pull the best qualified applicants out of their applicant pool. Such effects become more likely as the duration of the selection program increases and under conditions where organizations adopt selection procedures with unequal validities. Bishop's (1987, p. 239) analysis of the U.S. Bureau of Labor Statistics data also suggests that

"workers' background characteristics have large and significant effects on both starting and latest relative wage rates" and "realized productivity has almost no effect on the starting wage when background is controlled but large and significant effects on wage rates after a year or so at the firm." Thus, firms apparently pay more for better qualified workers, both initially and throughout their employment. As the financial and economic model showed, higher wages represent variable costs that rise with productivity, so realized utility values are likely to be lower than those computed using a simple revenue-focused model.

Recognizing that compensation responds to labor quality leads to concern with the "incentive effects of screening" (Bishop, 1988; Mueser & Maloney, 1987). Mueser and Maloney (1987) argue that if more valid selection devices measure stable abilities that are unaffected by individuals' efforts to become more productive, then using such devices may be unwise because they reduce the incentive for applicants to invest in self-improvement. Why should applicants work hard in school or take technical training if their job prospects depend on an innate general trait that cannot be affected by such activities? However, Bishop (1988) argues that "greater use by employers of tests measuring competence in reading, writing, mathematics and problem solving will increase the supply of these competencies" (p. 2). He presents secular, cross-sectional, and longitudinal data on IQ-type tests, suggesting that traits measured by these tests are indeed malleable. Thus, increased test use associated with greater incentives (e.g., wages) for better qualified workers may increase the average quality of applicants, though utility will reflect not only greater productivity but higher variable costs as well.

Raising wages is only one of many ways to improve applicant inducements (others include more intensive recruiting, job redesign, and improved career opportunities), but virtually all inducement improvements are likely to increase variable costs in utility estimates. UA models that systematically incorporate this variable offer opportunities for needed integration between industrial and organizational psychology and labor economic theories.

Labor Markets Determine Applicant Population Characteristics.   Incentive effects are one example of how selection programs affect not only the incremental value compared to random selection, but the average and distribution of value in the applicant population itself. For example, it is widely recognized that higher selection ratios (less choosiness) will lower selection utility levels. As labor demand rises and unemployment falls, the number of job applicants may also fall, leading to higher selection ratios.

Labor economic theory offers additional insights about how changing labor market conditions determine characteristics of the applicant population even if firms endeavor to maintain the same number of applicants through increased recruiting efforts. We have seen how firms demanding highly qualified workers pay higher rewards to attract them, producing a hierarchy of firms with applicant pools that reflect the average and variability in qualifications available at each firm's pay level. Becker (1989) noted that increased labor demand (i.e., lower unemployment) can reduce the supply of higher qualified candidates for lower paying jobs. Highly qualified applicants, who originally represented the upper tail of the applicant distribution for lower paying jobs, now can qualify for higher paying jobs and are scarcer in the pool for lower paying jobs. Fewer better qualified applicants suggests a lower average applicant qualification level.

Becker (1989) suggests that this may also lower the effective validity coefficient in the new applicant pool, due to truncation at the upper end of the predictor-criterion distribution. However, it seems possible that validity may not fall if the bottom tail of the distribution is increased as recruiting efforts

are stepped up. Thus, incremental utility (i.e., the difference between random and more valid selection) may not fall as much, but the value of selectees will fall because the average applicant value is lower. Utility estimates originally made under conditions of high unemployment and plentiful labor supplies will overstate actual utility values when the opposite conditions occur. While the opposite phenomenon is likely to occur in times of rising unemployment (i.e., more highly qualified applicants will be forced to enter the pool for lower paying jobs), the short-run hiring advantages may be subsequently negated because these individuals may leave the organization to take jobs in higher paying organizations when labor demand increases again (Becker, 1989).

Thus, labor economics predicts that selection decisions are affected by the quality of the applicant pool, which may change with changing market conditions. Moreover, these changes are not only reflected in the parameters of the B-C-G selection utility model, but also through variable costs, average applicant value/costs, and future separation rates and patterns.

Labor Markets Determine Training Consequences.   The B-C-G utility model has been extended beyond selection to training activities (Schmidt, Hunter, & Pearlman, 1982). As with selection, however, labor economic theory demands that utility models acknowledge the effects of such programs on service costs and separation patterns. Becker (1975) distinguishes between general versus specific training. *General training* refers to training that can be readily used by competing firms (e.g., word processing or computer programming). *Specific training* refers to training that is useful only to the organization providing it (e.g., operating a patented production process unique to the organization). Becker (1989) proposes that if training is general, other organizations will be willing to pay the firm's trained employees to leave and work for them, essentially buying the value of training by paying higher wages, rather than provide the training themselves. Thus, general training will either increase employee separations among the most valuable trained employees or increase variable costs of wages or other rewards to induce trained employees to stay. In the case of specific training, employers can profit from training if the wages they pay following training are below the increase in productivity but are still high enough to induce trained employees to stay, because no competing employer has an incentive to pay more, or if employees are willing to accept lower wages during training but not so low that the entire training cost is paid by the individual because then the firm could lay off the employee and train someone else at no loss. Specific training costs are predicted to be "shared" through some combination of lower wages during training and higher, but below-productivity, wages after training. Thus, with both specific and general training, labor economic theory would predict that variable costs and separation patterns are likely to substantially affect training utility and that omitting such factors may lead to overstated training effects.

Summary.   Labor economic theory, proceeding from a basic premise of competitive labor markets and price-based decisions and behaviors, suggests several intriguing integrative research issues. Investigating these issues requires utility models incorporating recruitment, variable costs, employee separations, and internal employee movement in the form of promotions, transfers, and demotions. Moreover, the models demand explicit recognition that programs such as selection, affecting the flow of employees into, through, and out of the work force, interact with HRM programs such as training, affecting the existing stock of employees.

Utility models recognizing these issues would permit integrative research drawing on insights from both industrial and organizational psychology about the actual behaviors and decisions of employers and employees

and labor economics about market-based predictions concerning labor supply and demand. UA models offer a bridge that can help integrate the two disciplines. We currently have little information on whether HRM programs truly produce the turnover and reward consequences suggested by labor economic theory. At the same time, most industrial and organizational psychology research is notably deficient in addressing individual behaviors within the context of alternative opportunities and labor market variables.

As shown in Appendix A, the vast majority of UA research focuses on employee selection. The B-C-G utility model emphasizes translating validity coefficients into terms more relevant to organizational decisions. However, as we have seen, HRM program consequences are certainly not limited to selection programs. UA models have the potential to integrate virtually all HRM program decisions, but that requires a UA theory encompassing HRM program consequences that affect employee flow as well as the existing stock of employees (Boudreau, 1987, 1988, 1989). We now develop such a framework, categorizing HRM program decisions and their consequences into two types: (a) programs/consequences affecting employee "stocks" by changing characteristics of the existing work force or work situation (e.g., through training, performance feedback, or compensation) and (b) programs affecting employee "flow" by changing the composition of the work force by adding, removing, or reassigning employees (e.g., through recruitment, selection, turnover, or internal staffing).

Changing the Characteristics of the "Stock" of Employees

Programs affecting employee stocks (such as training, compensation, performance feedback and employee involvement) aim to increase valuable characteristics (such as skills, abilities, or motivation) among existing employees to improve their current job performance. In terms of quantity, quality, and cost, decisions affecting employee stocks enhance productivity more when they affect a broad range of employees and time periods, cause large average increases in the value of employee job behaviors, and achieve both effects at minimum cost. Thus, decisions affecting employee stocks "work" by improving employee behaviors in their existing assignments. (Boudreau, 1988, p. 1–134)

The Characteristic-changing Utility Model

Landy et al. (1982) and Schmidt et al. (1982) first applied UA concepts to employee stocks. Both studies reformulated the utility model, with Schmidt et al. (1982) focusing on training programs and Landy et al. (1982) focusing on performance appraisal and feedback programs. They recognized that in the B-C-G utility model, the product of the validity coefficient and the standardized predictor score of selectees represented the estimated difference between the average standardized criterion score of randomly selected applicants and the average standardized criterion score of better selected applicants. One could consider this standardized difference the effect of selecting *treated* (i.e., better selected) applicants as opposed to *untreated* (i.e., randomly selected) applicants. Other HRM programs could also be considered *treatments* (i.e., training, compensation, or performance feedback), so it was logical to extend the utility concept to encompass them. The problem with a direct extension, however, is that characteristic-changing programs do not operate by choosing which employees to add to (or remove from) the work force. There is no predictor score, so there is no validity coefficient, no selection ratio, and no estimate of the average standardized predictor score of selectees.

However, characteristic-changing program effects are often reported in statistical terms, just as selection program effects are often reported in terms of validity coefficients. Landy et al. (1982) and Schmidt et al. (1982) noted the direct relationship between standard effect size measures (i.e., t and F statistics) and the correlation coefficient, and proposed transforming such statistics into d_t, the true difference in job performance between the treated and untreated groups, in standard deviation units. This concept is similar to the product of the validity coefficient and the standardized predictor score of selectees in the selection utility model. Thus, just as the B-C-G selection utility model provided a framework for placing the correlation coefficient into a more managerial perspective, so the Landy et al. (1982) and Schmidt et al. (1982) enhancements of the utility model place statistical findings from other personnel program interventions into a managerial perspective. Moreover, as is true for the validity coefficient, recent advances in cumulating findings from many studies to better identify generalizable effects (i.e., meta-analysis, Hunter et al., 1982), can also be used to examine studies of characteristic-changing programs (e.g., Burke & Frederick, 1986; Hunter & Hunter, 1984; Locke, Farren, McCaleb, Shaw, & Denny, 1980), producing d_t estimates even when experimental study is inappropriate or impossible in the decision situation.

The *characteristic-changing model* is analogous to the selection utility model in that it also reflects the three fundamental utility variables—quantity, quality, and cost. The quantity is the number of person-years affected by the program; the quality change is the product of the effect size (i.e., d_t) and a scaling factor translating this standardized value into dollars (usually SD_y); the costs of developing, implementing, and maintaining the program are defined similarly to the costs of employee movement programs, though the actual cost components will differ.

The employee stock utility model can be reformulated to reflect financial and economic considerations (Boudreau, 1983a) and repeated program applications over time (Boudreau, 1983b), and can be analyzed using a break-even framework (Boudreau, 1984a, 1988). Expressed in terms of quantity, quality, and cost, the employee stock utility model can be integrated with utility models for employee flows (see the next section in this chapter for a discussion). In addition to the Schmidt et al. (1982) and Landy et al. (1982) treatments, Mathieu and Leonard (1987) and Florin-Thuma and Boudreau (1987) applied utility analysis to a training program and performance feedback program, respectively. As noted in Appendix A, both studies' findings suggested substantial program benefits and low break-even values.

The Scaling Factor

In selection utility, there is a conceptually clear population upon which the utility parameters are based—the applicant population. While identifying characteristics of this population may be difficult, the model is nonetheless internally consistent in that all utility parameters refer to this population. However, in the characteristic-changing model the focus population is not as clearly defined. The treatment is given to the entire employee group, so two populations exist during the intervention—the pretreatment population and the posttreatment population. Consistency would suggest that all utility parameters be based upon the same population, but applications of the model generally derive the d_t statistic from t or F statistics based upon the estimated standard deviation of the *pooled* samples, and derive the scaling factor (i.e., SD_y) based upon the pretreatment group (Landy et al., 1982; Schmidt et al., 1982) because organizational experts can seldom estimate SD_y among the pooled group. Yet the pretreatment and pooled SD_y values may differ if

the program alters within-group performance. For example, if training alleviates severe performance problems by moving the low performers closer to the mean, then the pretreatment standard deviation will exceed the pooled standard deviation, biasing utility estimates upward.

At least two approaches might resolve this dilemma. First, when estimating d_t, researchers might rescale it in terms of the pretreatment group variability. Second, researchers might focus on the performance difference induced by the program *in actual production units*. Florin-Thuma and Boudreau (1987) found that a high-quality measure of employee performance consequences (i.e., the level of inventory needed to support production) demonstrated substantial change associated with a performance feedback program. This production measure reflected the total group's performance in each period rather than individual performance differences. Thus, it was not necessary to measure the program's effect on a per-person, per-period basis because the performance measure already reflected the per-period effect for the entire treated group. Moreover, this performance index was easily translated into dollars using standard inventory cost figures, thus circumventing the need to measure SD_y or to express the experimental results in standardized form. This second strategy focuses the utility analysis more directly on the program's consequences and their value to the organization, rather than on deriving a scaling factor (i.e., SD_y) to translate program effects into dollars. However, this process is very situation-specific and is unlikely to produce results that are as easily cumulated across studies as d_t values. Measuring performance effects for entire employee groups might appear to move away from "psychological" variables because it moves away from measuring individual behaviors, but such an approach is necessary to reflect the concept of program utility and may often be a more accurate representation of decision maker's objectives for HRM programs.

Conclusion

Extending utility analysis to encompass characteristic-changing programs allows increased application of UA models, as well as integration between HRM program planning in different functional areas. So far, this UA model has been applied only to decisions concerning whether to adopt a program or not, similar to selection utility applications focusing on whether to replace a relatively low-validity predictor with a highly valid one, but the potential exists for a much broader integrative perspective. HRM decision makers need not consider their programs as competitors when program combinations may produce higher productivity enhancements than individually designed and evaluated programs. A program to enhance performance feedback and a program to improve training could be addressed separately by estimating which program provides the highest utility if used individually, but such a strategy ignores the fact that there are actually four options: (a) Do neither program, (b) do training alone, (c) do performance feedback alone, and (d) do both programs. UA models can be applied to all four options and may demonstrate that a version of the fourth option is superior to the others (Boudreau, 1984a, p. 213). Thus, this UA model provides the potential for integrative HRM strategies that draw on program interactions. This potential for integration is even more apparent when one realizes that UA models can apply not only to characteristic-changing programs and selection programs, but also to virtually any HRM program whose consequences alter the pattern of employee movement into, out of, and through the organization. The next section develops such an employee movement utility model—the utility model for employee flows.

Changing the "Flow" of Employees

Employee flows occur when employees move into, through, and out of an organization through selection, promotion, demotion, transfer and separation. In terms of quantity, quality and cost, decisions affecting employee flows enhance productivity more when they impact large numbers of employee flows and time periods, greatly increase the value of job behaviors through better person-job matches, and achieve these goals at minimum cost.... Programs affecting employee flows "work" by improving the pattern of movements into, through, and out of the organization so that more valuable employees are placed in jobs or work roles.
(Boudreau, 1988, p. 1–134)

The B-C-G selection utility model reflects the consequences of HRM programs that add one group of better selected employees to the work force. However, actual managerial decisions seldom hinge on the consequences of hiring only one cohort of new employees. The selection program decision usually occurs in an environment where employees are dismissed or choose to leave, where they are selected or choose to move to other positions within the organization, and where new groups of employees will flow into, through, and out of the organization over time. Decision makers will often wish to consider the effects of different selection systems on these other movement patterns. A selection program could appear to produce high utility values when considering only its effects on the first cohort hired, but may produce changes in other movement patterns over time that might negate such high utility values (e.g., where turnover is increased because better qualified employees have more external opportunities). Moreover, HRM decisions contain opportunities for substantial synergy between programs affecting employee movement. For example, the benefits of improved selection may be enhanced by retaining the best performing employees or moving them into higher level jobs. The one-cohort selection utility model can be enhanced to reflect HRM decisions and consequences affecting employee movements between positions.

A Definition of Employee Movement

Employee movement may be defined as "the establishment, alteration, or termination of the employment contract between an individual and an organization" (Boudreau & Berger, 1985b, p. 33). Jacques (1961) defined the employment contract as "an implicit or explicit agreement between employees and employers in which the employee carries out designated tasks or objectives in return for payments over a specified or (usually) unspecified time period" (Boudreau & Berger, 1985b, p. 34). This definition is consistent with previous employee movement definitions and taxonomies, though previous research had focused on one type of movement at a time, usually turnover.

Boudreau and Berger (1985b) proposed a taxonomy of employee movement in which each movement type could be characterized by four attributes: (a) whether the employee was previously a member of the organization, (b) whether the direction of movement was inward, outward, upward, downward, or lateral, (c) whether the duration of the movement was specified in advance and the degree to which it is permanent, and (d) whether the decision maker was the employee, the employer, or both. They demonstrated how this taxonomy distinguished employee movements based on the degree of discretion allowed the decision maker, the types of information available, and the certainty with which outcomes can be predicted, among other variables. They distinguished between external employee movement that involves crossing the organizational boundary by initiating or terminating an employment contract, and internal employee movement that involves altering an employment contract but not terminating it.

Like other UA models, movement utility models focus on three variables: (a) the quantity of movers, (b) the quality of the movers, and (c) the costs incurred to produce the movement (Boudreau, 1984c, 1987, 1988, 1989; Boudreau & Berger, 1985a, 1985b). Because these three basic variables are common to all employee movements, we can derive an extended utility model that simultaneously encompasses the consequences of decisions affecting not only selection, but decisions affecting other types of external employee movement and internal movement as well.

The Employee Flows Utility Model

Organizations seldom invest in a selection program to use it once and then stop, but continuously reapply the program as new members enter the work force. To analyze only the first-cohort effects is tantamount to a financial analyst attempting to analyze an investment in new manufacturing facilities by assuming the facilities will only be used for one production run. Clearly, such a focus omits a large part of the decision's effects. Boudreau (1983b) redefined the one-cohort selection utility model to encompass the flow of employees into and out of the work force over time.

Boudreau's (1983b) *employee flows utility model* was derived by changing the quantity of employee-years of production to reflect employee inflows and outflows over a given evaluation period. Previous models reflected the quantity of employment-years as the product of the number hired times average tenure. Boudreau's model used the number of treated (i.e., better selected) employees entering the work force in each future period (i.e., N_{a_t}) and the number of treated employees separating from the work force in each future period (i.e., N_{s_t}) to compute the number of treated employees in the work force in each future time period

TABLE 4

Entry-level Selection Utility Decision With Financial/Economic Consideration and Employee Flows

Cost-Benefit Information	Entry-level Computer Programmers
Current employment	4,404
Number separating (N_{s_t})	618
Number selected (N_{a_t})	618
Average tenure in years (T)	10
Test Information	
Number of applicants (N_{app})	1,236
Testing cost/applicant	$10
Total test cost (C)	$12,360
Average test score ($\bar{Z}_x$)	.80 SD
Validity ($r_{x,y}$)	.76
SD_y (per person-year)	$10,413
Financial Information	
Variable costs (V)	5%
Tax rate (TAX)	45%
Interest rate (i)	10%
Flow Information	
Analysis period (years)	10
Test application period (years)	7
Person-years affected	31,282
After-cost, after-tax, discounted utility increase over random selection (millions)	Benefit – cost $54.32 – $0.04 = $54.28

From "Utility Analysis" by John W. Boudreau, 1988. In Lee Dyer (Ed.), *Human Resource Management: Evolving Roles and Responsibilities*. Washington, DC: The Bureau of National Affairs, Inc. Copyright 1988 by the Bureau of National Affairs, Inc. Reprinted by permission.

(i.e., N_k). The utility in each future period was the product of N_k times the incremental quality per person-year (i.e., the product of $r_{x,y}$, $\bar{Z}_x$, and SD_y), minus the costs incurred to select the employees joining the work force in that future time period (i.e., C_k). Summing these values over all future time periods of analysis ($k = 1...F$) produced the total utility of the selection program. Boudreau also incorporated the effects of discounting, variable costs, and taxes into his formulation (Boudreau, 1983b, p. 399,

Equation 6). Though this formula reflected constant utility parameters over time, Boudreau showed how to incorporate temporal changes.

Table 4 continues the earlier example of entry-level computer programmers, incorporating the effects of selecting multiple cohorts over time. The number of incumbents, separations and acquisitions, test information, and financial information remain the same. New parameters now reflect the analysis period and test application period, which combine to produce the leverage, or number of person-years affected by the selection program: The analysis period is 10 years by convention (Boudreau & Berger, 1985a), and the test is assumed to be reapplied for seven years.

In each of the first seven years, 618 better selected new hires are added to the work force, replacing 618 employees selected without the PAT. Because each cohort stays for 10 years, the number of better selected programmers in the work force steadily increases by 618 employees in each of the seven years until, in Year 7, the work force is virtually saturated with better selected workers. In Year 7, 4,326 (i.e., 7 x 618) out of 4,404 programmers have been selected using the PAT. All 4,326 programmers stay for the remaining 3 years of the 10-year analysis. Thus, the total leverage is 31,282 person-years (618 + 1,236 + 1,854, and so on).[2]

The calculation at the bottom of Table 4 reveals the effects of multiple-cohort selection. After-tax, discounted selection costs increase substantially (from $6,798 in Table 3 to $0.04 million in Table 4), but selection program returns also increase substantially (from $12.55 million to $54.32 million), producing a total multiple-cohort utility value of $54.28 million. Repeatedly applying improved selection programs can have massive potential productivity effects because of their huge leverage. Just as one would not attempt to justify a million-dollar investment in a new manufacturing plant based only on the first production run, HRM decision makers should not evaluate HRM programs based only on the first cohort affected.

Mathieu and Leonard (1987) and Rich and Boudreau (1987) incorporated the concept of cohort flows through the work force into their analyses. Rich and Boudreau employed a methodology that incorporated period-to-period differences in turnover due to group tenure. Mathieu and Leonard (1987) incorporated period-to-period differences due to training effect dissipation.

Integrating Recruitment Into Selection Utility Analysis

Boudreau and Rynes (1985) noted that while the early Taylor-Russell selection utility model explicitly included the base rate (i.e., the proportion of applicants whose performance would exceed minimally acceptable levels if randomly selected), subsequent utility models did not reflect this factor. Indeed, the majority of selection utility research was conducted under the implicit or explicit assumption that all selection options would be implemented within the same applicant population. Such assumptions probably simplify organizational reality. We have already discussed how labor economic theory suggests that applicant populations change both independently and as a result of selection decisions. Boudreau and Rynes (1985) noted the common belief that more rigorous or intrusive selection methods may affect the size and/or characteristics of applicant pools and that recruitment strategies (e.g., personalized follow-ups, realistic job previews, or choices of recruitment sources) are explicitly designed to alter applicant population characteristics, presumably to enhance organizational outcomes. Boudreau and Rynes (1985) derived a selection utility model that can explicitly incorporate the effects of recruitment, reflecting financial and economic factors and employee flows.

Every parameter of the B-C-G selection utility model could be affected by applicant reactions to recruitment and selection strategies. For example, applicant populations might become more homogeneous, reducing both SD_y and the correlation coefficient, if more stringent recruitment standards were used. Or higher salary offers might increase the size and perhaps the qualifications of the applicant pool, affecting both the selection ratio and the average qualification level of the population.

Although the Taylor-Russell model had explicitly incorporated a variable reflecting the average level of applicant qualifications (e.g., the base rate), this variable was removed from later utility models, which adopted an incremental focus, computing utility values by comparing selection strategies to random selection. In the Boudreau-Rynes model, utility values are represented on an absolute scale, reflecting both the average and the incremental value of the selectees. The Boudreau-Rynes model encompassed the observation by Alexander, Barrett, and Doverspike (1983) that self-selection and initial organizational screening might cause "examinees" to be a nonrandom sample from the applicant population, and reflected the observations by Hogarth and Einhorn (1976) and Murphy (1986) that job offer rejections can affect selection utility.

Boudreau and Rynes showed how recruitment effects might alter the conclusions of utility models reflecting only selection. Improved selection may offer less incremental utility (compared to random selection) when recruitment practices produce a more qualified but less diverse applicant pool. However, an integrated recruitment-selection strategy applied to such an applicant pool can produce the greatest total value despite reducing incremental selection utility. The key is whether the increased average applicant value is great enough to offset the reduction in incremental selection utility, so that the combined strategy becomes more economically attractive. Utility models reflecting only incremental selection utility cannot reflect this possibility because they assume constant applicant population parameters and they omit the average applicant qualifications.

Table 5 continues the running example of computer programmer selection, integrating recruitment strategy options. It estimates the returns from selection when combined with two competing recruitment strategies—recruitment advertising or use of a recruitment agency. Recruitment advertising produces an applicant pool with diverse qualifications but a moderate average applicant value, because advertising reaches a wide audience but provides little prescreening. The recruitment agency generates a less diverse applicant pool with a higher average applicant value due to the agency's screening of applicants before referral. The upper part of Table 5 shows the variables that are assumed not to change as a result of recruitment. Utility is assessed using the same 7-year application of the staffing program and 10-year analysis period.

The variables assumed changed by recruitment are shown at the bottom of Table 5. Recruitment advertising costs $2,500 per hire, while the recruitment agency costs $4,450 per hire (American Management Association, 1986). Recruitment advertising is expected to produce an applicant pool similar to the present one, so validity is .76 and SD_y is $10,413 as before. Through prescreening, the recruitment agency generates applicants with less variability, reducing validity to .60 and SD_y to $8,500 per person-year. Net applicant value for advertising-recruited applicants is $15,620, reflecting an average service value of $52,065 and average service costs of $36,445 per person-year. Agency prescreening is presumed to identify higher quality applicants, with a net value of $20,000, reflecting higher average service value of $60,000 per person-year, partially offset by higher service costs of $40,000 per person-year, including higher salaries and benefits to attract and retain these applicants.

The expected value of each new hire is the sum of two values: the value produced by random selection—hiring average-value applicants from a particular applicant pool—plus the incremental value produced by systematic selection from that applicant pool. Thus, the expected value of those hired from the advertising-generated pool is the average value of the pool (i.e., $20,000) plus the incremental value added by selection (i.e., .60 x .80 x $8,500, or $4,080) or $24,080 per person-year. Similarly, the expected value of those hired from the agency-generated pool is $15,620

TABLE 5

**Entry-level Recruitment/Selection Utility Decision With
Financial and Economic Consideration and Employee Flows**

Cost-Benefit Information	Entry-level Computer Programmers
Current employment	4,404
Number separating (N_s)$_t$	618
Number selected (N_a)$_t$	618
Average tenure in years (T)	10
Test Information	
Number of applicants (N_{app})	1,236
Average test score ($\bar{Z}_x$)	.80 SD
Financial Information	
Variable costs (V)	5%
Tax rate (TAX)	45%
Interest rate (i)	10%
Flow Information	
Analysis period (years)	10
Test application period (years)	7
Person-years affected	31,282

Staffing Variable	Work Force Utility Results	
	Recruitment Advertising	Recruitment Agency
Test validity ($r_{x,y}$)	.76	.60
Testing cost (C_s)/applicant	$10	$10
Recruitment cost (C_r)/selectee	$1,250	$2,225
Average applicant service value	$52,065	$60,000
Average applicant service cost	$36,445	$40,000
SD of applicant value (SD_y)	$10,413	$ 8,500
Value of random selection (millions)	$141.04	$180.50
Cost of random selection (millions)	–$ 4.55	–$ 8.10
Value added by testing (millions)	$54.32	$35.00
Cost added by testing (millions)	–$ 0.04	–$ 0.04
Total after-tax, after-cost discounted work force value (millions)	$190.76	$207.45

From "Utility Analysis" by John W. Boudreau, 1988. In Lee Dyer (Ed.), *Human Resource Management: Evolving Roles and Responsibilities*. Washington, DC: The Bureau of National Affairs, Inc. Copyright 1988 by the Bureau of National Affairs, Inc. Reprinted by permission.

plus $6,331, or $21,951 per person-year. As before, these quality levels are multiplied by the quantity of person-years affected by the selection program (i.e., 31,282) and adjusted to reflect financial and economic considerations, recruitment costs, and selection costs. The lower section of Table 5 shows the total, after-tax, discounted value of the employee flows. It separates the effects into the work force value and movement costs if only random selection were used (i.e., the only quality difference is created by recruitment), and the incremental work force value and movement costs added by testing.

If only selection utility is considered, the testing pays off under either recruiting strategy, although its payoff is smaller when applied to agency-generated applicants rather than advertising-generated applicants ($34.96 million versus $54.28 million). However, the agency-generated applicant pool produces a much higher average value than the advertising-generated pool ($180.5 million versus $141.04 million). Integrating the effects of recruitment and testing demonstrates the advantage of combining agency recruiting with testing (i.e., $207.45 million versus $190.76 million). Sacrificing some testing effectiveness for an increase in average applicant quality makes sense.

HRM decision makers may often face opportunities to integrate recruitment with selection. A recruitment-selection utility model is necessary to accurately reflect such situations and to provide a framework for explaining and enhancing managerial decisions. For example, in spite of its low validity, the recruitment interview still enjoys widespread application while more valid cognitive ability tests do not. One explanation for such decisions may be that decision makers feel accurate selection is not necessary because their recruitment activities have already identified such a well-qualified pool of applicants. Decision makers may feel that virtually any applicant from such a pool will be an acceptable

performer, and thus use the interview primarily to attract enough applicants to fill existing job openings. Indeed, subsequent research (Rynes & Boudreau, 1986) found that filling job openings was the primary measure of recruitment effectiveness and that variables related to subsequent job performance (i.e., performance ratings or turnover) were seldom even recorded. Thus, the enhanced recruitment-selection utility integrates two highly complementary organizational processes and encourages future recruitment and selection research.

The External Employee Movement Utility Model

Drawing on the substantial similarities between employee acquisitions and employee separations in their effects on work force value (Boudreau, 1983b, 1984b, 1984c, 1987, 1988, 1989; Boudreau & Berger 1985a, 1985b; Milkovich & Boudreau, 1991), Boudreau and Berger (1985b) developed a utility model that could encompass not only the effects of employee acquisitions but also of employee separations. UA research typically ignores the potential effects of HRM programs on the quantity and pattern of employee separations (e.g., quits, layoffs, and dismissals). Similarly, employee turnover research usually focuses on describing the cognitive processes leading to turnover, but not on the cost and benefit consequences of turnover. Boudreau and Berger (1985b) proposed to integrate and enhance both utility analysis and turnover research with a utility reflecting employee acquisitions and separations. Because both acquisitions and separations involve crossing the organizational boundary by initiating or terminating an employment contract, this is an external employee movement model.

The external movement utility model was developed to encompass three related phenomena: (a) repeated acquisitions without separations over time (where the work force is increased through selection), (b) repeated unreplaced separations over time (where the work force is reduced in future time periods), and (c) repeated separations over time that are replaced with acquisitions. The first case reflects the focus of most selection utility models; the second case reflects decisions about using layoffs, attrition, or dismissals to reduce a work force; and the third situation is the most general case, capable of encompassing both of the other two. Figure 1 depicts the concepts underlying the Boudreau-Berger external movement utility model. Each box describes a component of the utility model. Figure 1 presents two periods of employee acquisitions and separations with the work force value in each prior time period serving as the starting point for the utility effects on the subsequent time period. Box A represents the work force utility at the beginning of the analysis (i.e., in the period prior to implementing programs to change the quantity or quality of employee movement). Box C represents the work force utility at the end of the first period, serving as the starting point for the next period (Box E), as indicated by the arrow from Box C to Box E.

In each time period, two processes may occur to change work force utility. First, employees may be added. The utility of acquisitions in the first time period ($t = 1$) is represented by Box B. The utility of the acquisitions becomes part of the utility of the work force following acquisitions, as indicated by the arrow from Box B to Box C, and by the description within Box C. Second, employees may separate. In the first period, this is shown in Box D. These separations will affect the quantity and/or quality of those retained from the beginning work force, as indicated by the arrow between Boxes A and C and by the description within Box C. In the second period (shown in Boxes E through H), the same process occurs, but the beginning work force utility reflects the work force at the end of the first time period, so the quantity, quality, and costs of acquisitions and retentions may differ from the first period.

Finally, as indicated at the bottom of Figure 1, the process is assumed to continue for the duration of the utility analysis (time periods 3 through F). The utility values produced by this model reflect the sum of the discounted, after-tax net benefits of the work force in each period of analysis (e.g., the sum of Boxes A, C and E for the two-period illustration in Figure 1).

Figure 1 demonstrates the close analogies between selection and retention utility. Selection utility involves choosing a subset of employees to join the work force from a pool of applicants. Retention utility involves a subset of the previous period's incumbent work force choosing or being chosen to remain with the organization. Though retentions are somewhat more bilaterally chosen than acquisitions (Boudreau & Berger, 1985a, 1985b), the analogy is still correct. The utility of both acquisitions and retentions depends on the quantity, or number of employees hired and retained; the quality, or per-person, per-time period effects of selection and retention patterns; and the costs incurred to implement or accommodate the movements, such as selection device development/implementation, severance pay, and relocation assistance (Boudreau, 1987, 1988, 1989; Boudreau & Berger, 1985a, 1985b; Milkovich & Boudreau, 1991).

Building on these analogies, Boudreau and Berger (1985a) derived an algebraic utility model encompassing both acquisitions and retentions. This utility model represented a multiple-cohort acquisition and retention utility model and was capable of reflecting the effects of both types of movement on organizational outcomes. Boudreau and Berger summarized the derivation as both a formula (Equation 14, p. 594) and as shown in Figure 1. The Boudreau-Berger model is expressed in terms of the absolute value of the work force, rather than the incremental value added by improved selection.

Boudreau and Berger (1985a, pp. 598–599) demonstrated that their model was a more general case of both the one-cohort selection

FIGURE 1

Diagram of External Movement Utility Model Concepts

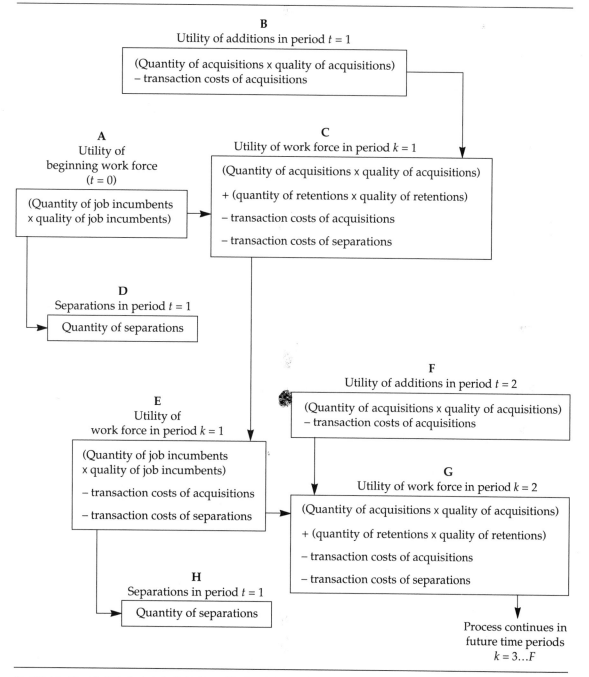

B
Utility of additions in period $t = 1$

(Quantity of acquisitions x quality of acquisitions) − transaction costs of acquisitions

A
Utility of beginning work force $(t = 0)$

(Quantity of job incumbents x quality of job incumbents)

C
Utility of work force in period $k = 1$

(Quantity of acquisitions x quality of acquisitions)

+ (quantity of retentions x quality of retentions)

− transaction costs of acquisitions

− transaction costs of separations

D
Separations in period $t = 1$

Quantity of separations

E
Utility of work force in period $k = 1$

(Quantity of job incumbents x quality of job incumbents)

− transaction costs of acquisitions

− transaction costs of separations

F
Utility of additions in period $t = 2$

(Quantity of acquisitions x quality of acquisitions) − transaction costs of acquisitions

G
Utility of work force in period $k = 2$

(Quantity of acquisitions x quality of acquisitions)

+ (quantity of retentions x quality of retentions)

− transaction costs of acquisitions

− transaction costs of separations

H
Separations in period $t = 1$

Quantity of separations

Process continues in future time periods $k = 3...F$

utility model and the employee flows utility model. They described the assumptions necessary to produce the two previous models from the more general external movement utility model and discussed conditions under which such assumptions might be appropriate, concluding that a utility analysis based only upon selection consequences often risks producing not only deficient utility values but values that could lead to faulty decision making.

Table 6 continues the example of computer programmer selection using the external movement utility model. The size, number selected and number separating per year, financial and economic considerations, and 10-year analysis period are all the same as before. We assume recruitment through advertising, so the selection and recruitment parameters correspond to the "Recruitment Advertising" portion of Table 5. The test validity, number of applicants, standard test score, testing cost, average applicant service value, average applicant service cost, and SD_y remain the same as before, with each group of 618 acquisitions producing an average value of $21,951 per person-year.

Each acquisition is assumed to carry costs of $7,000 per year, reflecting the $2,500 recruitment cost, relocation, orientation, and other administrative activity. Each separation likewise carries a cost of $7,000, reflecting administrative activity, outplacement assistance exit interviews, severance pay, and other activities undertaken when separations occur (Boudreau & Berger, 1985a). Such costs are incurred regardless of the quality of the person joining or leaving. Because the external movement utility model does not assume hired cohorts stay intact for the duration of average tenure, we can now drop the assumption of a 7-year test application period and adopt the more realistic assumption that the test is applied throughout the 10-year analysis.

Because the analysis now focuses on the total work force value rather than on simply the value of those added and retained, we assume that at the beginning of the analysis the work force resembles the average of the applicant population. Average incumbent service value per person-year is $52,065, and average incumbent service cost per person-year is $36,445, for a net value of $15,620 per person-year.

The "Work Force Utility Results" reflect two levels of test validity—random selection and validity of .76, contrasted with three separation pattern effects. The separation effect reflects whether the organization retains its better or poorer performers and is the average performance difference between those retained and the preseparation work force. Boudreau and Berger (1985a) noted that this parameter would usually be directly observed, but estimated it as the product of the standard deviation of service value in the preseparation work force and the standardized difference in average service value between the retained and preseparation work force (i.e., $d_{sv_{r_t}}$). Under assumptions similar to those used to estimate the average standardized test score from the selection ratio, $d_{sv_{r_t}}$ can be estimated from the retention ratio—proportion of the work force retained. Boudreau and Berger (1985a) assumed values for $d_{sv_{r_t}}$ ranging from -0.26 to $+0.26$ and an incumbent service value standard deviation of $10,413, producing a range of separation effects from $-$2,707 to $0, to $2,707 per person-year. The negative value reflects the assumption that the organization retains its worst employees, with those retained producing an average service value $2,707 less per person-year than the preseparation work force. Zero assumes retentions are random with respect to service value, so those retained produce an average service value equal to the preseparation work force. The positive value reflects the assumption that the organization retains its best employees, with those retained producing an average service value $2,707 more per person-year than the preseparation work force.

A specially designed LOTUS 1-2-3 ® personal computer program (Boudreau, 1984b)

TABLE 6

**Entry-level Recruitment/Selection/Retention Utility Model
With Financial/Economic Consideration**

Cost-Benefit Information	Entry-level Computer Programmers
Current employment	4,404
Beginning average service value	$52,065
Beginning average service cost	$36,445
SD of incumbent service value (SD_y)/person-year	$10,413
Number of separating (N_{s_t})	618
Number selected (N_{a_t})	618
Acquisition cost/hire	$7,000
Separation cost/separation	$7,000
Number of applicants (N_{app})	1,236
Average applicant service value/year	$52,065
Average applicant service cost/year	$36,445
Average test score ($\bar{Z}_x$)	.80 SD
SD of applicant service value (SD_y)/person-year	$10,413
Testing cost/applicant	$10
Variable costs (*V*)	5%
Tax rate (*TAX*)	45%
Interest rate (*i*)	10%
Analysis period (years)	10

Staffing Variable	Work Force Utility Results			
	Option 1	Option 2	Option 3	Option 4
Test validity ($r_{x,y}$)	0.00	0.76	0.76	0.76
Separation effect	$0	$0	$2,707	–$2,707
After-tax, after-cost discounted work force value (millions)	$200.31	$242.10	$351.69	$132.50

From "Utility Analysis" by John W. Boudreau, 1988. In Lee Dyer (Ed.), *Human Resource Management: Evolving Roles and Responsibilities*.Washington, DC: The Bureau of National Affairs, Inc. Copyright 1988 by the Bureau of National Affairs, Inc. Reprinted by permission.

simulated various acquisition and retention strategies (Boudreau & Berger, 1985a). The results of four of the strategies are shown in Table 6. Under Option 1, the organization selects and retains randomly, attaining a 10-year work force value of $200.31 million. Under Option 2, valid selection is introduced, but retentions remain random, increasing the work force value to $242.10 million. Option 3 illustrates the best of worlds—highly valid selection combined with retaining the best employees, producing the highest work force value of $351.69 million. Option 4 acknowledges that better performing employees may have more opportunities and separate more often, in this case causing the worst employees to be retained, producing a total work force value of $132.50 million.

The interaction between separation and selection patterns is obvious. Considering only the incremental value of improved selection suggests a $41.79 million increase in work force value (i.e., $242.10 million–$200.31 million). However, combining improved selection with improved retention can provide an additional $109.59 million (i.e., $351.69 million–$242.10 million). Conversely, dysfunctional retention patterns can disrupt the effects of improved selection, as illustrated by Option 4, where the work force value is $67.81 million lower than even random selection and retention. If more valid selection acquires high-quality employees who leave in response to better opportunities, projected selection utility can be substantially reduced. While these effects are based on a specific set of assumptions, the model allows them to be explicitly manipulated to examine their relative effects (Boudreau, 1988).

Though the simulation was intricate, the results could be expressed as a linear equation (Boudreau & Berger, 1985a, Table 30), as shown in Equation 11, with dollar values expressed in millions:

$$U_w = \$200.31 + \$54.95\,(r_{x,sv_{a_t}}) + \$421.53\,(d_{sv_{r_t}})\ (11)$$

Where:

U_w = the total discounted, after-tax, after-cost work force utility summed over 10 future analysis periods

$r_{x,sv_{a_t}}$ = the correlation between the selection device score and service value among job applicants in future time period t

$d_{sv_{r_t}}$ = the standardized service-value difference between those retained and the preretention work force in future time period t

The substantially larger coefficient on the retention utility parameter (i.e., $d_{sv_{r_t}}$) relative to the correlation coefficient suggested that the utility effects of HRM decisions on retention patterns could be substantial, and that models failing to acknowledge these retention effects risk ignoring important organizational outcomes. Omitting retention considerations can severely bias selection utility estimates when either (a) improved selection causes the retention pattern to become less optimal or (b) the retention pattern causes the value of improved selection to be quickly lost. Turnover and selection research can be better integrated, with both areas attending to the effects of the other.

The Boudreau-Berger model demonstrates the danger in focusing only on the separation, or turnover, *rate*. HRM program utility should reflect not just the quantity of employee acquisitions and separations, but also the pattern of separations or retentions relative to employee value. The costs of separations or the characteristics of those who leave and stay (e.g., Cascio & McEvoy, 1985; Dalton, Krackhardt, & Porter, 1981; McEvoy & Cascio, 1985) must be considered in light of the effects of those acquired to replace the separations. Thus, the external employee movement utility model integrates and expands employee movement research. Moreover, such a model encourages integration between industrial and organizational psychological theory and labor economic theory, where employee mobility is a central concept (Bishop, 1987, p. 240; Gerhart, 1987). Still, even this integrated model focuses only on the utility consequences for one job in the organization. A more complete perspective would encompass movement between jobs within the organization as well (Boudreau & Berger, 1985a, 1985b).

Integrating Internal and External Employee Movement Utility

Boudreau and Berger (1985b) described similarities and distinctions between *internal employee movement* that alters an employment contract but does not involve crossing the organizational boundary (such as promotions, demotions, and transfers) and *external employee movement* that does involve crossing the organizational boundary. Internal staffing research usually describes internal movement patterns or examines the effects of career processes on individuals, but less frequently addresses the effects of career systems on organizational performance and the reasons for using different internal staffing arrangements in organizing the employment relationship (cf. Milkovich & Andersen, 1982, p. 382; Pfeffer & Cohen, 1984, p. 550). The effects of *external* movement on organizational performance have received more attention, but such effects interact with internal employee movement so a full analysis demands an integrated framework.

Selection and retention programs that appear optimum for a single job may have substantial consequences for internal movement. For example, if improved selection for lower level jobs also identifies skills and abilities useful in upper level jobs, then more valid external acquisition strategies may produce substantially higher benefits than the simple selection utility model, or even the external movement utility model, can recognize. Conversely, selection devices targeted exclusively to skills applicable only in the entry-level job may appear valuable in a single-job model, but if employees routinely move from that job to upper level jobs using other skills, then maximizing entry-level selection utility may simultaneously reduce utility in the upper level job.

Finally, evaluating internal selection devices based only on their validity for jobs receiving employees (e.g., Cascio & Silbey, 1979) may miss important negative consequences for the lower level jobs that lose the internal movement candidates. High-performing engineers are commonly promoted from technical engineering positions into managerial positions. Such a strategy may produce acceptable managerial job performance but, if it removes the best engineering talent from the technical

jobs, may actually decrease organizational effectiveness. All of these phenomena require integrating the consequences of internal and external employee movement and identifying variables likely to determine the utility of such movements—an integrated *internal/external movement utility model.*

Boudreau's (1986b) utility model draws upon the analogies between internal and external employee movement, proposing that each internal employee movement involves a separation from one organizational job and an acquisition by another. Thus, the pattern of internal employee movement can be analyzed using the concepts of selection and retention utility but it must be recognized that both types of utility are affected by the same movement (Milkovich & Boudreau, 1991, chap. 10).

Boudreau (1986b) proposed that modeling the relationships between internal and external employee movement would reveal substantial opportunities for optimizing employee movement decisions. Therefore, the internal/external employee movement utility model encompasses the Boudreau-Berger (1985a) external employee movement utility model while recognizing internal movement utility consequences. Boudreau (1986b) illustrated the internal/external movement utility model using the simplified hypothetical external and internal movement system depicted in Figure 2.

In this movement system, external selections and internal movements fill vacancies created by external separations. Job B represents an upper level job that experiences *external separations,* those that leave the organization. To fill these vacancies, individuals are moved through *internal selection* from a lower-level position (Job A) to Job B through a promotion-from-within policy. Job A also experiences external separations. Thus, the organization must make *external acquisitions* into Job A to fill the vacancies created by both internal and external separations. It is the quality, quantity, and cost of these four movement types that determine total work force utility over the analysis period. In each analysis period, the total work force utility is the sum of the work force value in the two jobs, minus the costs of accommodating internal/external movements occurring during that period. Figure 2 depicts the work force value in the two jobs initially (Boxes A and B), and following the movements occurring in the first analysis period (Boxes G and H). The full utility model tracks these effects and calculates the discounted, after-tax, net work force value in the two jobs over the period of analysis $(t = 1...F)$.

Three types of movement affect Job A. First, employees separate from Job A and leave the organization (depicted in Box C of Figure 2), so the utility of job A's work force (Box G) reflects the quality and quantity of employees retained after these *external separations*. Second, employees move from Job A to Job B (depicted in Box E of Figure 2), so the utility of Job A's work force (Box G) also reflects the quality and quantity of employees retained in Job A after these *internal separations*. Third, after external and internal separations have reduced Job A's work force, *external acquisitions* occur to bring the work force back to its original level (depicted in Box F of Figure 2), so Box G reflects the quality and quantity of these external acquisitions.

Two types of movement affect Job B in Figure 2. First, employees separate from Job B and leave the organization (depicted in Box D), so the utility of Job B's work force (Box H) reflects the quality and quantity of the employees retained as a result of these *external separations*. Second, to fill the vacancies, employees move to Job B from Job A (depicted in Box E), so the utility of Job B's work force (Box H) reflects the quality and quantity of the employees acquired through these *internal acquisitions*.

The total utility value is the discounted, after-tax, after-cost sum of the work force utilities in Jobs A and B over the period of analysis. In Figure 2, this sum would include the work force values represented by Boxes G and H (for

Time Period $t = 1$), plus any subsequent work force values affected by movement in Future Time Periods 2 through F. Though this movement system is simplified, the concepts of internal and external separations and acquisitions apply generally, even to more complex systems. The jobs serving as sources of employees represent applicant populations for internal acquisitions, just as external applicant populations are the source of external acquisitions. The model analyzes internal separations similarly to external separations by focusing on the quality and quantity of those retained, recognizing that the pattern of internal separations (i.e., promotions or transfers out of a job) will probably differ from the pattern of external separations (i.e., separations from the organization).

The sequence of employee movements is important when considering internal and external movement utility (Boudreau, 1986b). If external separations occurred from Job A before internal promotion decisions were made, then the internal applicant pool for promotion into Job B would not include those who externally separated from Job A, and vice versa. In reality, internal/external movements do not all occur in a group but occur throughout each time period. This model can encompass such phenomena simply by choosing time periods for analysis that are short enough to meaningfully capture the movement pattern, as has often been done in Markov analysis, or to adjust the initial value of employee movements to reflect that the movers only occupy the job for a partial period (see Rich & Boudreau, 1987).

This model reflects the effects of employee characteristics for both their current job and for jobs representing potential destinations of internal movement. Selection utility models recognize that skill and ability differences between job incumbents imply performance differences (e.g., SD_y) for their current job. The internal and external movement utility model recognizes that the same skill and ability differences may also affect performance differences

FIGURE 2

Diagram of Internal-External Movement Utility Model Concepts

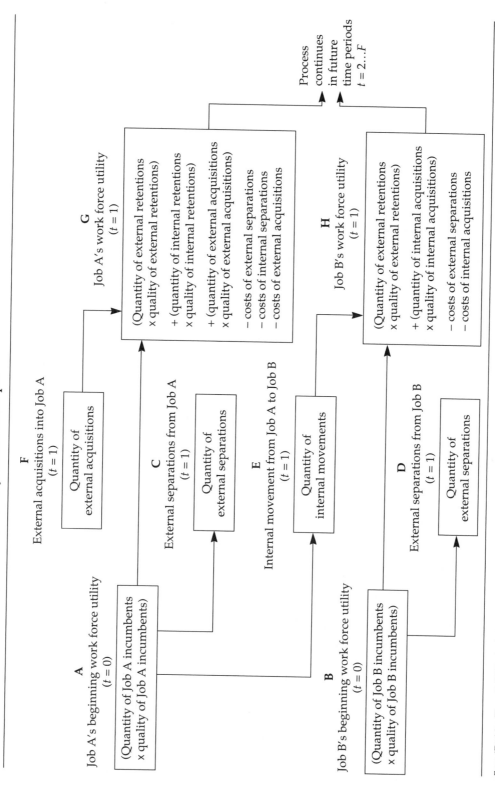

From "Decision-Theoretic Utility Analysis Applied to External Employee Movement" by J. Boudreau and C. Berger, 1985, *Journal of Applied Psychology, 70*, pp. 581–612. Copyright 1985 by the American Psychological Association. Adapted by permission.

in internal destination jobs. If the destination job is a higher level job allowing more discretion, SD_y among job incumbents in their *current* job can be lower than the SD_y of the same employees when considered as the applicant pool for the destination job. Thus, the ability of promotion to enhance incumbent job performance differences is explicitly modeled. Similar relationships exist for other utility parameters, such as the validity, selection ratio, and average predictor score.

The internal/external employee movement utility model encompasses the one-cohort selection utility model, the employee flows model, and the external employee movement model. Internal movements have measurable consequences not only for the jobs that internally acquire employees, but for the jobs that internally separate employees as well. Such implications are seldom discussed, with virtually all research preferring to focus on the consequences of internal movements for the receiving job. However, whenever an internal acquisition takes place, it is associated with an internal separation that has consequences for the jobs that lose employees.

Table 7 extends the computer programmer staffing example to encompass internal employee movement consequences. The example now encompasses an upper level job (Job B in Figure 2) of data system manager, presumed to serve as a destination for promotions among computer programmers (Job A in Figure 2). Internal selection is assumed to occur through an assessment center, and all separations among data system managers are assumed to be filled from the computer programmer job.

The internal staffing variables for the programmer job are the same as before, except that instead of 618 new hires to replace external separations, this example requires 718 new hires to replace both the 618 external separations and the 100 promotions out of the programmer job. The financial and economic considerations and 10-year analysis period are the same for both jobs.

One hundred external separations occur from the manager job, replaced by 100 internal acquisitions. Each separation from the manager job costs $8,000, slightly higher than the $7,000 cost for programmers, and these costs are incurred regardless of the quality of retentions. Each promotion from programmer to manager also costs $8,000 (including relocation, orientation, administration, and so on) regardless of promotion quality. Moreover, internal selection uses an assessment center which, at an average cost of $380 per tested applicant (Cascio & Silbey, 1979), produces a total cost of $1.44 million per year to assess all 3,786 promotion candidates.

Because the managerial job involves more discretion and responsibility, average applicant service value among programmers when considered as promotion candidates is assumed to be 10 percent higher than the average value of the same employees serving as programmers. The ratio of average applicant service value for the manager job divided by average incumbent service value in the programmer job is 1.10. Average service costs are also 10 percent higher when programmers are promoted to managers, reflecting higher average salaries, benefits, and other employment costs. As the value of the programmer work force changes as a result of external selection and retention, programmers' value as promotion candidates also changes. Decisions that improve the programmer work force produce an added benefit by improving promotion candidates for manager jobs even when promotion candidates are selected randomly, and vice versa for decisions that worsen the quality of programmers. Stronger or weaker relationships between individual differences among programmers and managers could be modeled by changing this parameter.

The internal staffing variables affecting the manager job are analogous to the external staffing variables affecting the programmer job. The applicant pool for promotions is the group of 3,786 programmers (4,404 incumbents

TABLE 7

Internal/External Recruitment/Selection/Retention
Utility Decision With Financial and Economic Consideration

Cost-Benefit Information	Entry-level Computer Programmers	Upper-level Data System Manager
Current employment	4,404	1,000
Beginnng average service value	$52,065	$57,272
Beginning average service cost	$36,445	$40,000
Number separating	618	100
Number selected	718	0
Number promoted	100	100
Acquisition cost	$7.000	NA
Separation cost	$7,000	$8,000
Promotion cost	NA	$8,000
Number of applicants	1,436	3,786
Average applicant service value/year	$52,065	1.10 times average programmer value
Average applicant service cost/year	$36,445	1.10 times average programmer value
Average test score	.80 *SD*	2.32 *SD*
SD of applicant value (SD_y)/year	$10,413	$11,454
Testing cost/applicant	$10	NA
Assessment center cost/year in millions	NA	$1.44
Variable costs	5%	5%
Corporate tax rate	45%	45%
Corporate interest rate	10%	10%
Analysis period (years)	10	10

Staffing Variable	Total Work Force Utility Results			
	Option 1	Option 2	Option 3	Option 4
Programmer selection validity	0.00	0.76	0.76	0.76
Programmer promotion effect	$0	$0	$0	−$625
Manager promotion validity	0.00	0.00	0.35	0.35
After-cost, after-tax, discounted total work force value (millions)	$249.86	$296.90	$302.51	$278.68

From "Utility Analysis" by John W. Boudreau, 1988. In Lee Dyer (Ed.), *Human Resource Management: Evolving Roles and Responsibilities*. Washington, DC: The Bureau of National Affairs, Inc. Copyright 1988 by the Bureau of National Affairs, Inc. Reprinted by permission.

minus 618 separations) available each year. This assumes that all programmers are promotion candidates, but it could easily be adjusted for situations where only a limited number of programmers are eligible or tested. With 3,786 applicants for 100 job openings, the organization can be quite choosy, so the average standard assessment center score of those promoted is 2.32 standard deviations above average (using the Naylor-Shine table with a selection ratio of 100/3,786). Performance differences among programmers considered as managerial candidates are presumed to be about 10 percent larger (SD_y = $11,454) than among applicants for programmer jobs (SD_y = $10,413).

Although the algebraic model is intricate, its explicitness permitted simulation using a LOTUS 1-2-3® personal computer program (Boudreau, 1986a) that greatly simplified the analysis. The bottom of Table 7 shows the effects of four different internal/external staffing patterns, representing the after-tax, after-cost, discounted work force value in both jobs, summed over the 10-year analysis period. Option 1 depicts random external and internal staffing. Under such a system, the average value of each job's work force remains constant as internal and external movements occur, producing a total 10-year value of $249.86 million. Option 2 introduces valid external selection using the selection test with a validity of .76. This enhances the value of programmers, which in turn augments the value of the managerial work force when programmers are promoted, producing a total work force value of $296.90 million. Option 3 analyzes internal staffing in the typical manner, acknowledging the validity of the assessment center (presumed to equal .35; Cascio & Silbey, 1979) for internal acquisitions but still assuming that promoting highly qualified programmers has no effect on the quality of the programmer work force. Total work force value increases to $302.51 million. Finally, Option 4 considers the possibility that internal promotions will pull high performers from the programmer work force, reducing the

average value of the retained programmers by $625 per person-year.[3] This produces a total work force utility of $278.68 million. Although the assessment center validly predicts future job performance for managers, its negative impact on the programmer work force costs the organization $12.22 million compared to random internal staffing (Option 4 minus Option 2).

It would be inappropriate to conclude from this hypothetical analysis that assessmen centers always represent poor investments, but it illustrates that internal selection programs which pull the best employees from lower level jobs can have serious organizational consequences—consequences that are virtually ignored by simple selection utility models. Typical internal staffing analyses that consider only the quantities or rates of movement between jobs will also omit the effects of such movements on the quality of the work forces in the internal staffing system. Substantial work force quality differences emerged in Table 7, despite the fact that the quantity of movements was held constant.

Modifying the model parameters allows extending these concepts to encompass other decisions affecting internal/external employee movements such as "make-or-buy" decisions between internal and external selection, reductions in work force size, and internal staffing systems involving more than two jobs. Of course, such extensions require considering a larger number of parameters, and these parameters are likely to represent estimates under uncertainty. Computer-based analysis permits sensitivity analysis to explore the implications of such uncertainty. Boudreau (1986b) simulated combinations of different parameter values for seven effects, producing a linear equation showing the relative impact of seven model parameters. Boudreau (1988) demonstrated how break-even analysis could also be applied to the integrated internal/external movement utility model.

Summary. The actual decision situations facing human resource managers and program planners are seldom as simple as the choice between two selection devices, evaluated based upon the productivity of the first cohort selected. HRM decisions, even if they only involve new selection devices, are likely to affect employee separations and employee internal movement patterns (Boudreau, 1987, 1988, 1989; Ledvinka, Archer, & Ladd, 1990). The effects of these phenomena may act to enhance or reduce selection utility. Moreover, HR managers frequently face situations in which it is possible to optimize decisions affecting employee movement. Investments in improved selection may be combined with investments designed to improve recruitment, separation patterns, or internal movement patterns. In situations where resources are limited, it may not be optimal to devote all resources to one task (e.g., improved selection); it may be better to combine programs, producing synergistic effects that surpass those achievable by only one employee movement program. An employee movement utility model that encompasses both external and internal movement can accommodate such decision situations. Moreover, such a model extends the theoretical domain of utility analysis because the internal movement responses of individuals and organizations are often studied in sociology and labor economics. Integrating these theories with industrial and organizational psychology research can produce a broader understanding of the implications of HRM program decisions.

Is the Complexity Really Worth It?

A common reaction from reviewers and commentators on the movement utility models is that they are complex and detailed. Rauschenberger and Schmidt (1987) point out that such enhancements might be

> expanding the models to a point where their practical application may be

jeopardized. The complexity of these new and expanded models will make it very difficult for researchers, let alone practicing industrial psychologists, to fully comprehend their implications and communicate the models and their findings to organizational decision makers. (pp. 56–57)

From the standpoint of communicating and improving decisions, UA model enhancements should be evaluated according to the value of the information they add, as noted in earlier sections of this chapter and elsewhere (Boudreau, 1984a, 1987, 1988, 1989; Boudreau & Berger, 1985a; Boudreau & Rynes, 1985; Florin-Thuma & Boudreau, 1987; Rich & Boudreau, 1987). The value of the added considerations for enhancing particular decisions will be situationally specific, depending on the probability that it would change decisions in important ways, and on the costs of incorporating it into the decision process (Boudreau, 1984a). *Measuring* the entire movement utility model will prove unnecessary when the enhanced model is unlikely to improve decisions based on a simpler framework. Simple one-cohort selection utility models derived from Equation 7 have proved quite popular with researchers (see Appendix A) and have produced useful insights. Still, without enhanced models reflecting variables such as discount rates, variable costs, recruitment, turnover, and internal movement, it becomes much more difficult to explicitly distinguish situations where simple models are sufficient from those where added complexity adds value. More complex models help explicitly identify when additional measurement is unnecessary, rather than simply ignoring these considerations. Moreover, when simple one-cohort selection models produce biased or misleading results by omitting these variables (Boudreau, 1983a, 1983b, 1984a, 1986, 1988; Boudreau & Berger, 1985a; Boudreau & Rynes, 1985), these enhanced models allow measuring variables that can enhance decisions (see Tables 3 through 7).

The employee movement utility model, integrated with the utility model for effects on employee stocks and reflecting financial and economic considerations, represents progress toward a more general utility model. With such a model, UA research can include or exclude variables as appropriate, acknowledging such practices explicitly. Hunter et al. (1988) speculated that "the resulting equation is so long and complex as to be daunting. Furthermore, for any particular application, it contains numerous irrelevant terms and as such is very difficult for personnel psychologists and human resource managers to understand"(p. 527). The accuracy of these speculations remains an empirical question, but simulation results (Boudreau, 1986; Boudreau & Berger, 1985a; Boudreau & Rynes, 1985) suggest that recruitment, separation, and internal movement will often be relevant, and personnel psychologists and HR managers have long recognized interactions between these phenomena but have had few integrative models to describe them. Moreover, with increasing computational power, such integrative models offer frameworks for developing computer-based models that greatly ease managerial effort required to apply them (Boudreau, 1984b, 1986a, 1988; Ledvinka, Archer, & Ladd, 1990).

Aside from their practical ability to enhance decisions, integrated utility models bridge research topics in industrial and organizational psychology (e.g., test development and validation, career effects on individual behaviors and attitudes, or cognitive processes affecting turnover) with topics often considered by other behavioral sciences such as sociology (e.g., the demographic patterns and causes of internal movement) and economics (e.g., the effect of HRM programs on employee qualifications, internal and external labor market behavior, and wages). The integrated UA perspective offers a step toward forging an interdisciplinary approach to such important topics—an approach necessitated by the myriad of organizational consequences affected by HRM programs and decisions. Lacking such integrated frameworks, future research risks becoming parochial, vastly limiting its potential for describing, predicting, and explaining decision processes. "It would be presumptuous, of course, to contend that research in utility analysis should be halted or scaled down in lieu of an emphasis on better communicating existing utility methods to organizational decision makers" (Rauschenberger & Schmidt, 1987, p. 57). In fact, research that extends utility analysis to encompass and integrate such important variables should be encouraged.

Future Applications and Research

Although the UA models were initially developed to address selection decisions, we have seen that the UA framework is really a special case of multiattribute utility models applied to HRM program decisions. Viewed in this way, the model has great potential for studying HRM program decisions in virtually every functional area of personnel management. Our review of empirical research suggests that UA applications are embryonic, with selection utility demonstrations dominating reported utility values. Moreover, existing research seems fixated upon the measurement properties of one particular selection utility parameter (SD_y). While this state of affairs should not be surprising in view of the fairly recent resurgence of attention to UA issues, the potential integrative role of UA models remains untapped.

A Framework for UA Research

Figure 3 depicts a matrix of future UA research directions. The rows (A through J) of the matrix represent specific content areas of HR management that can serve as the focus of UA research. Except for the top and bottom rows, these areas fall generally into the categories used to describe HRM activities (Milkovich & Boudreau, 1991), but they could be expanded to include several additional research areas from organizational behavior or industrial and organizational psychology. For example, Row D includes issues of test theory and job analysis (Burke & Pearlman, 1988). Row A refers to research that develops general models or frameworks applicable across functional areas, such as financial and breakeven utility models. Row J refers to research that examines decision-making processes, also spanning one or several functional areas.

The columns of Figure 3 represent types of research activity that can contribute to each area identified by a row. These research types progress from developing a conceptual framework that includes the row's content (Column V), to simulation analyses demonstrating the potential effects of the concepts on organizational outcomes (Column W), to empirical demonstrations actually measuring UA parameters and deriving utility estimates for different functional programs in different settings (Column X). With sufficient simulation and empirical application, it becomes possible to infer the behavior and boundary conditions of UA results across settings and applications (Column Y). Finally, with well-developed and widely applied utility models, it is possible to test general theories regarding those models (Column Z).

Existing Research

The asterisks in the cells of Figure 3 represent an admittedly crude index of existing research activity. Cells with asterisks have received attention, while those without have not. As we have seen, substantial progress has been made in the first columns, across several functional areas. Concepts extending outcome evaluation (Cell A-V) have been developed to include

financial and economic considerations, equal employment opportunity, affirmative action, risk, and uncertainty. Simulations (Cell A-W) have demonstrated substantial potential effects of these variables, and extended models have been applied to actual program decisions (Cell A-X). Future valuable research could incorporate less quantitative HRM program consequences. Tsui (1984, 1987) and Tsui and Gomez-Mejia (1988) proposed a measure of personnel department effectiveness based upon the reputation of the department among its "important" constituencies. Tsui's unit of analysis is the personnel department, while UA focuses on HRM program decisions, but HRM program consequences will be evaluated by a wide group of constituents on nonfinancial as well as financial attributes. Factors outside the UA model, such as labor union pressures, public opinion, and organizational tradition, may well determine program decisions in actual organizations. Can a personnel department increase its reputation for effectiveness if it communicates the consequences of its decisions using UA models? If UA models reveal suboptimal organizational traditions, such as selecting employees through unstructured interviews, would they actually be changed? UA research should examine these questions.

As in Row A of Figure 3, the functional areas of recruitment, selection, training, internal movement, and turnover/layoff analysis (Rows C, D, E, G, H, and I) also exhibit concept development, simulations, and empirical demonstrations (Columns V, W, and X).

In data-based inference (Column Y), meta-analysis and validity generalization are producing findings about the distributions of program effects across settings and studies. Cell D-Y reflects substantial evidence of selection procedure validity generalization (e.g., Hunter & Hunter, 1984; Schmidt et al., 1982). Indeed, Appendix A suggests tentative conclusions about boundary conditions on selection utility, such as that

FIGURE 3

Matrix of Research Issues in Utility Analysis

	Type of Research Study				
Research Content	**V** Conceptual framework	**W** Simulation analysis	**X** Empirical demonstration	**Y** Data base inference	**Z** Theory testing
A Outcome evaluation	∗	∗	∗		
B Human resource planning					
C Recruiting	∗	∗			
D Selection	∗	∗	∗	∗	
E Training	∗	∗	∗	∗	
F Compensation					
G Internal movement	∗	∗			
H Turnover and layoffs	∗	∗	∗	∗	
I Performance assessment	∗		∗	∗	
J HRM decision processes	∗		∗		

substituting highly valid predictors for much less valid ones apparently pays off unless the costs are extremely high (Burke & Pearlman, 1988, p. 125). Others have conducted meta-analyses on training programs (Burke & Frederick, 1986), turnover programs (Cascio & McEvoy, 1985), and other HRM programs (Locke et al., 1980) as reflected in Cells E-Y, H-Y, and I-Y. Valuable future research will link these effect-size estimates into a decision context.

Developing Utility Models for Other HRM Functions

An obvious gap in Figure 3 is the absence of UA concepts in several functional and theoretical areas. Little research addresses how existing UA models apply to compensation decisions (Row F) such as pay policies, reward structures, and benefits (Milkovich & Newman, 1990). Yet substantial and identifiable organizational resources are constantly being invested here. It seems likely that UA concepts reflecting characteristic-changing consequences on employee stocks can encompass compensation decisions. In this regard, compensation is similar to training or performance feedback. As Figure 3 illustrates, fruitful future research will identify the concepts and simulate and apply them, paving the way for inferences and theory testing (Row F).

Similarly, human resource planning (Row B) has not been well addressed by UA research. This is surprising because the conceptual link between the two areas is so clear. Human resource planning ensures that the human resource decisions that managers make are integrated and directed toward achieving objectives (Milkovich & Boudreau, 1991). The integrated movement utility model can reflect the productivity implications of human resource planning and the synergy between human resource programs (Boudreau, 1986b), as illustrated in

Tables 3 through 7. Future research should apply the integrated utility model to examine the implications of various HR planning systems and decisions. It is necessary, but not sufficient, to "fill in" the matrix by developing models and demonstrations for each different type of HRM program. The ultimate contribution will be derived by adopting a synergistic and integrative perspective on UA research. Research might begin with the planning process, where strategic program decisions are made. Little information exists on how decision makers decide what program combinations to implement, whether they consider the interactions between programs in different functional areas and their effects on organizational outcomes. Simulations reflecting such an integrative model (Boudreau, 1986b; Ledvinka, Archer, & Ladd, 1990) represent a start (Cell B-W). Demonstrations including programs from several functional areas (Cell B-X), such as training and selection, are also promising. It seems likely that the classification and variable-treatment selection models developed by Cronbach and Gleser (1965) will be relevant here (Human Resources Research Organization and others, 1984).

Column Z of Figure 3 suggests theory-testing research addressing the functional issues in each row. This type of research is the logical step that can integrate the demonstrations and parameter-focused research of Columns X and Y. Undoubtedly these decision theories will have unique attributes depending on the functional area they address; it is certainly not currently possible to outline theoretical frameworks for each cell of Column Z. However, it is important to recall the links between industrial and organizational psychology and labor economic theory discussed earlier and the potential for enhanced UA models to support an integration between these social sciences. It seems likely that future research addressing Column Z will draw upon this and other related social science theories.

Decision Processes and Contexts

The bottom row (Row J) of Figure 3 reflects HRM decision processes, perhaps the most fundamental, important, and complex issue facing future UA research. This chapter has noted that while UA results are often presumed to influence decisions, enhance credibility, and encourage a broader decision focus, existing research has not empirically investigated these phenomena. Future research must examine whether the UA results affect managerial decisions, whether decision makers' reactions to UA results are affected by different parameter estimation techniques, and whether UA models accurately reflect decision makers' concerns. UA models serve to describe, predict, explain, and enhance decision making, which requires attention to actual decision processes.

For some time, researchers (Boudreau, 1984a, 1984b, 1987, 1988, 1989; Boudreau & Berger, 1985a, 1985b; Florin-Thuma & Boudreau, 1987; Rich & Boudreau, 1987) have called for studies linking UA models and actual managerial decision processes. More recent appeals for greater attention to better communication of UA results to organizational decision makers also reflect this concern (Burke & Pearlman, 1988; Rauschenberger & Schmidt, 1987). Such research must transcend simply persuading decision makers to provide more resources and status to industrial and organizational psychology and HRM programs and exploit the full potential of UA research.

Florin-Thuma and Boudreau (1987) assessed performance feedback utility in a small organization that had decided against implementing a performance feedback intervention. The authors asked decision makers to explicate their own decision models and had them estimate the parameters of the normative utility model. Though only three decision makers were available, making the results exploratory, the authors found that decision makers under-estimated the magnitude of the performance problem and the intervention's effect. They considered factors not included in the UA model, and these factors worked against the intervention. Yet when dollar values were attached to these factors and when the decision makers' assumptions were incorporated into the UA model, the results still suggested substantial payoffs. Informal discussions with the decision makers indicated that they had failed to implement the performance feedback intervention because they simply had never considered the problem serious enough to warrant systematic consideration. No one believed that altering employee performance could have such a profound effect. Notably, the entire study was conducted without measuring SD_y. These results suggest research questions and methodologies to be replicated in other settings to explore how UA information affects decisions.

Future research should draw on the substantial body of knowledge regarding irrationality in decision making (e.g., Kahneman & Tversky, 1972, 1973; March & Simon, 1958). Bobko, Karren, and Kerkar (1987) suggested such research was directed at estimating SD_y, but the broader focus of such research is the entire process of HRM decision making. UA models offer detailed, normative theories about the factors decision makers *should* consider in making HRM decisions, but actual decisions probably depart from UA prescriptions. Etzioni (1986) has suggested that rational decision making must be induced because it is contrary to natural inclinations. For UA models to serve as one such inducement, we must first understand how actual decisions depart from UA prescriptions and focus our efforts to induce more rational decision making. In exchange, such research will probably discover how to enhance UA models by better reflecting actual organizational decisions.

Utility analysis offers vast research potential. Moreover, the results of such research are likely to have important implications for the ways HR managers and those who assist them apply findings from industrial and organizational psychology and other social sciences. With attention to the research questions discussed in this chapter, it seems likely that researchers and decision makers will soon have decision tools that truly reflect a partnership between applied social science research and managerial decisions regarding human work behavior.

Thanks to Joan Chang, Tom Friedrich, Cathy Smith, and Ljubomir Stambuk for their assistance in preparing this chapter.

Notes

1 This section emphasizes developments that set the stage for more recent research and future research directions. Much of this material is drawn from Boudreau (1987, 1989). Other historical summaries can be found in Cronbach and Gleser (1965, chap. 4), Hunter and Schmidt (1982), and Cascio (1982, 1987).

2 Boudreau (1983b) assumed the PAT would be reapplied for 15 years, that 6,180 job vacancies existed, and analyzed effects for 25 years. The effect of these assumptions was that the number of better selected employees in the work force steadily rose (by 618 per year) during the first 10 years until it reached 6,180. Then, in years 11 through 15, vacancies were filled with better selected employees, so the number of treated employees in the work force remained at 6,180. When the program was terminated, the number of treated employees in the work force slowly diminished (by 618 each year) until it reached zero in year 25. This produced higher costs, leverage, and utility values. Table 4 adopts assumptions more consistent with financial convention and the size of the reported computer programmer work force.

3 The $625 value was derived based on the retention ratio for promotions (i.e., 3,686/3,786),

the Naylor-Shine tables, and the presumed incumbent programmer standard deviation of $10,413 (Boudreau, 1986b; Boudreau & Berger, 1985a). In actual applications, this parameter could be estimated directly based on differences between the retained and prepromotion work force.

References

Abelson, R. P. (1985). A variance explanation paradox: When a little is a lot. *Psychological Bulletin, 97*, 129–133.

Alexander, R. A., Barrett, G. U., & Doverspike, D. (1983). An explication of the selection ratio and its relationship to hiring rate. *Journal of Applied Psychology, 68*, 342–344.

Alexander, R. A., & Barrick, M. R. (1987). Estimating the standard error of projected dollar gains in utility analysis. *Journal of Applied Psychology, 72*, 475–479.

Alf, E. F., & Dorfman, D. D. (1967). The classification of individuals into two criterion groups on the basis of a discontinuous payoff function. *Psychometrika, 32*, 115–123.

American Management Association. (1986). *Hiring strategies and costs: The AMA report*. New York: Author.

Arnold, J. D., Rauschenberger, J. M., Soubel, W., & Guion, R. M. (1982). Validation and utility of a strength test for selecting steel workers. *Journal of Applied Psychology, 67*, 588–604.

Becker, B. (1989). The influence of labor markets on human resources 'utility' estimates. *Personnel Psychology, 42* (3), 531–546.

Becker, G. (1975). *Human capital* (2nd ed.). New York: National Bureau of Economic Research.

Bierman, H., Jr., Bonini, C. P., & Hausman, W. H. (1981). *Quantitative analysis for business decisions*. Homewood, IL: Irwin.

Bierman, H., Jr., & Smidt, S. (1975). *The capital budgeting decision*. New York: Macmillan.

Bishop, J. (1987). The recognition and reward of employee performance. *Journal of Labor Economics, 5*, 536–556.

Bishop, J. (1988). *The economics of employee testing* (Working paper No. 88–14). Ithaca, NY: Cornell

University, Center for Advanced Human Resource Studies.

Bobko, P., Karren, R., & Kerkar, S. P. (1987). Systematic research needs for undestanding supervisory-based estimates of SD_y in utility analysis. *Organizational Behavior and Human Decision Processes, 40,* 69–95.

Bobko, P., Karren, R., & Parkington, J. J. (1983). Estimation of standard deviations in utility analysis: An empirical test. *Journal of Applied Psychology, 68,* 170–176.

Bolda, R. A. (1985a). *Individual productivity: A sourcing analysis.* Unpublished manuscript.

Bolda, R. A. (1985b). Utility: A productivity planning tool. *Human Resource Planning, 8* (3), 111–132.

Boudreau, J. W. (1983a). Economic considerations in estimating the utility of human resource productivity improvement programs. *Personnel Psychology, 36,* 551–557.

Boudreau, J. W. (1983b). Effects of employee flows on utility analysis of human resource productivity improvement programs. *Journal of Applied Psychology, 68,* 396–407.

Boudreau, J. W. (1984a). Decision theory contributions to HRM research and practice. *Industrial Relations, 23,* 198–217.

Boudreau, J. W. (1984b). *EXTMOV: A spreadsheet program for quantifying external employee movement decisions.* Ithaca, NY: Author.

Boudreau, J. W. (1984c, August). *Utility analysis for productivity improvement programs affecting work group composition.* Paper presented at the annual meeting of the American Psychological Association, Toronto (ERIC Document Reproduction Service temporary accession number CG 017 713).

Boudreau, J. W. (1986a). *MOVUTIL: A spreadsheet program for analyzing the utility of internal and external employee movement.* Ithaca, NY: Author.

Boudreau, J. W. (1986b). *Utility analysis applied to internal and external employee movement: An integrated theoretical perspective.* Ithaca, NY: Author.

Boudreau, J. W. (1987, May). *Utility analysis: A review and agenda for future research.* Paper presented at the International Conference on Advances in Selection and Assessment, University of Manchester Institute of Science and Technology, Buxton, UK.

Boudreau, J. W. (1988). Utility analysis. In L. D. Dyer (Ed.), *Human resource management: Evolving roles and responsibilities,* 1–125—1–186. Washington, DC: Bureau of National Affairs.

Boudreau, J. W. (1989). Utility analysis: A review and agenda for future research. In M. Smith & I. Robertson (Eds.), *Advances in personnel selection and assessment* (pp. 227–258). London: Wiley.

Boudreau, J. W., & Berger, C. J. (1985a). Decision-theoretic utility analysis applied to external employee movement [Monograph]. *Journal of Applied Psychology, 70,* 581–612.

Boudreau, J. W., & Berger, C. J. (1985b). Toward a model of employee movement utility. In K. M. Rowland & G. R. Ferris (Eds.), *Research in personnel and human resource management* (pp. 31–53). Greenwich, CT: JAI Press.

Boudreau, J. W., & Rynes, S. L. (1985). The role of recruitment in staffing utility analysis. *Journal of Applied Psychology, 70,* 354–366.

Brogden, H. E. (1946a). On the interpretation of the correlation coefficient as a measure of predictive efficiency. *Journal of Educational Psychology, 37,* 65–76.

Brogden, H. E. (1946b). An approach to the problem of differential prediction. *Psychometrika, 14,* 169–182.

Brogden, H. E. (1949). When testing pays off. *Personnel Psychology, 2,* 171–183.

Brogden, H. E., & Taylor, E. K. (1950). The dollar criterion—Applying the cost accounting concept to criterion construction. *Personnel Psychology, 3,* 133–154.

Burke, M. J. (1985). *An investigation of dimensions employed and percentile ordering effects in estimating performance standard deviations in dollars for clerical occupations.* Unpublished manuscript.

Burke, M. J., & Frederick, J. T. (1984). Two modified procedures for estimating standard deviations in utility analyses. *Journal of Applied Psychology, 69,* 482–489.

Burke, M. J., & Frederick, J. T. (1986). A comparison of economic utility estimates for alternative rational SD_y estimation procedures. *Journal of Applied Psychology, 71,* 334–339.

Burke, M. J., & Pearlman, K. (1988). Recruiting, selecting, and matching people to jobs. In

J. P. Campbell, & R. J. Campbell (Eds.), *Productivity in organizations*. San Francisco: Jossey-Bass.

Campbell, J. P. (1982). Editorial: Some remarks from the outgoing editor. *Journal of Applied Psychology, 67,* 691–700.

Cascio, W. F. (1980). Responding to the demand for accountability: A critical analysis of three utility models. *Organizational Behavior and Human Performance, 25,* 32–45.

Cascio, W. F. (1982). *Costing human resources: The financial impact of behavior in organizations.* Boston: Kent.

Cascio, W. F. (1987). *Costing human resources: The financial impact of behavior in organizations* (2nd ed.). Boston: Kent.

Cascio, W. F., & McEvoy, G. M. (1985). Strategies for reducing employee turnover: A meta-analysis. *Journal of Applied Psychology, 70,* 342–353.

Cascio, W. F., & Ramos, R. (1986). Development and application of a new method for assessing job performance in behavioral/economic terms. *Journal of Applied Psychology, 1,* 20–28.

Cascio, W. F., & Silbey, V. (1979). Utility of the assessment center as a selection device. *Journal of Applied Psychology, 64,* 107–118.

Cascio, W. F., & Zedeck, S. (1983). Open a new window in rational research planning: Adjust alpha to maximize statistical power. *Personnel Psychology, 36,* 517–526.

Cohen, J. (1977). *Statistical power analysis for the behavioral sciences* (rev. ed.). New York: Academic Press.

Cronbach, L. J., & Gleser, G. C. (1957). *Psychological tests and personnel decisions.* Urbana: University of Illinois Press.

Cronbach, L. J., & Gleser, G. C. (1965). *Psychological tests and personnel decisions* (2nd ed.). Urbana: University of Illinois Press.

Cronshaw, S. F., & Alexander, R. A. (1985). One answer to the demand for accountability: Selection utility as an investment decision. *Organizational Behavior and Human Decision Processes, 35,* 102–118.

Cronshaw, S. F., Alexander, R. A., Wiesner, W. H., & Barrick, M. R. (1987). Incorporating risk into selection utility: Two models for sensitivity

analysis and risk simulation. *Organizational Behavior and Human Decision Processes, 40,* 270–286.

Curtis, E. W. (1967, February). *The application of decision theory and scaling methods to a selection test evaluation.* Technical Bulletin, STB 67–18. San Diego, CA: U.S. Naval Personnel Research Activity.

Dalton, D. R., Krackhardt, D. M., & Porter, L. W. (1981). Functional turnover: An empirical assessment. *Journal of Applied Psychology, 66,* 716–721.

Darlington, R. B., & Stauffer, G. F. (1966). Use and evaluation of discrete test information in decision making. *Journal of Applied Psychology, 50,* 125–129.

Day, R. D., & Edwards, J. E. (1987, August). *A comparative study of multiple SD_y estimation procedures.* Paper presented at the national meeting of the Academy of Management, New Orleans.

DeSimone, R. L., Alexander, R. A., & Cronshaw, S. F. (1986). Accuracy and reliability of SD_y estimates in utility analysis. *Journal of Occupational Psychology, 59,* 93–102.

Doppelt, J. E., & Bennett, G. K. (1953). Reducing the cost of training satisfactory workers by using tests. *Personnel Psychology, 6,* 1–8.

Dunnette, M. D., Rosse, R. L., Houston, J. S., Hough, L. M., Toquam, J., Lammlein, S., King, K. W., Bosshardt, M. J., & Keyes, M. (1982). *Development and validation of an industry-wide electric power plant operator selection system.* Edison Electric Institute.

Eaton, N. K., Wing, H., & Lau, A. (1985). *Utility estimation in five enlisted occupations.* Paper presented at the meeting of the Military Testing Association (MTA), San Diego, CA.

Eaton, N. K., Wing, H., & Mitchell, K. J. (1985). Alternate methods of estimating the dollar value of performance. *Personnel Psychology, 38,* 27–40.

Edwards, J. E., Frederick, J. T., & Burke, M. J. (1988). Efficacy of modified CREPID, SD_y's on the basis of archival organizational data. *Journal of Applied Psychology, 73,* 529–535.

Edwards, W. (1977). Use of multiattribute utility measurement for social decision making. In

D. E. Bell, R. L. Keeney, & H. Raiffa (Eds.), *Conflicting objectives in decisions*. New York: Wiley.

Einhorn, H. J., Kleinmuntz, D. N., & Kleinmuntz, B. (1979). Linear regression and process-tracing models of judgment. *Psychological Review, 86*, 465–485.

Einhorn, H. J., & McCoach, W. P. (1977). A simple multiattribute utility procedure for evaluation. *Behavioral Science, 22*, 270–282.

Etzioni, A. (1986). Rationality is anti-entropic. *Journal of Economic Psychology, 7*, 17–36.

Eulberg, J. R., O'Connor, E. J., & Peters, L. H. (1985). *Estimates of the standard deviation of performance in dollars: An investigation of the influence of alternative sources of information*. Paper presented at the annual meeting of the Academy of Management, San Diego, CA.

Fischer, G. W. (1976). Multidimensional utility models for risky and riskless choice. *Organizational Behavior and Human Performance, 17*, 127–146.

Fitz-Enz, J. (1984). *How to measure human resources management*. New York: McGraw-Hill.

Flamholtz, E. G. (1974). *Human resource accounting*. Encino, CA: Dickenson.

Flamholtz, E. G. (1985). *Human resource accounting* (2nd ed.). San Francisco: Jossey-Bass.

Florin-Thuma, B. C., & Boudreau, J. W. (1987). Performance feedback utility in a small organization: Effects on organizational outcomes and managerial decision processes. *Personnel Psychology, 40*, 693–713.

Fowler, R. L. (1985). Testing for substantive significance in applied research by specifying nonzero effect null hypotheses. *Journal of Applied Psychology, 70*, 215–218.

Frank, R. H. (1984). Are workers paid their marginal products? *The American Economic Review, 74*, 549–571.

Gerhart, B. (1987). How important are dispositional factors as determinants of job satisfaction? Implications for job design and other personnel programs. *Journal of Applied Psychology, 72*, 366–373.

Goodman, L. A. (1960). On the exact variance of products. *Journal of the American Statistical Association, 55*, 708–713.

Gow, J. F. (1985, April). Human resource managers must remember the bottom line. *Personnel Journal*, 30–32.

Greer, O. L., & Cascio, W. F. (1987). Is cost accounting the answer? Comparison of two behaviorally based methods for estimating the standard deviation of job performance in dollars with a cost-accounting-based approach. *Journal of Applied Psychlology, 72*, 588–595.

Guttman, I., & Raju, N. S. (1965). A minimum loss function as determiner of optimal cutting scores. *Personnel Psychology, 18*, 179–185.

Hertz, D. B. (1964, Jan-Feb). Risk analysis in capital investment. *Harvard Business Review*, pp. 95–106.

Hillier, F. S. (1963). The derivation of probabilistic information for the evaluation of risky investments. *Management Science, 9*, 443–457.

Hirsh, H. R., Schmidt, F. L., & Hunter, J. E. (1986). Estimation of employment validities by less experienced judges. *Personnel Psychology, 39*, 337–344.

Hogarth, R. M., & Einhorn, H. J. (1976). Optimal strategies for personnel selection when candidates can reject offers. *Journal of Business, 49*, 478–495.

Huber, G. P. (1980). *Managerial decision making*. Glenview, IL: Scott, Foresman.

Hull, C. L. (1928). *Aptitude testing*. Yonkers, NY: World Book.

Hull, J. C. (1980). *The evaluation of risk in business investment*. Oxford: Pergamon Press.

Hunter, J. E. (1980). *Test validation for 12,000 jobs: An application of synthetic validity and validity generalization to the General Aptitude Test Battery (GATB)*. Washington, DC: U.S. Employment Service.

Hunter, J. E., & Hunter, R. F. (1984). The validity and utility of alternative predictors of job performance. *Psychological Bulletin, 96*, 72–98.

Hunter, J. E., & Schmidt, F. L. (1982). Fitting people to jobs: The impact of personnel selection on national productivity. In M. D. Dunnette & E. A. Fleishman (Eds.), *Human performance and productivity* (Vol. 1, pp. 233–284). Hillsdale, NJ: Erlbaum.

Hunter, J. E., Schmidt, F. L., & Coggin, T. D. (1988). Problems and pitfalls in using capital budgeting and financial accounting techniques in assessing the utility of personnel programs. *Journal of Applied Psychology, 73*, 522–528.

Hunter, J. E., Schmidt, F. L., & Jackson, G. B. (1982). *Metaanalysis: Cumulating research findings across studies*. Beverly Hills, CA: Sage.

Hunter, J. E., Schmidt, F. L., & Judiesch, M. K. (1988). *Individual differences in output as a function of job complexity.* Working paper.

Jain, H., & Murray, V. (1984). Why the human resources management function fails. *California Management Review, 26,* 95–110.

Janz, J. T., & Dunnette, M. D. (1977). An approach to selection decisions: Dollars and sense. In J. R. Hackman, E. E. Lawler, III, & L. W. Porter (Eds.), *Perspectives on behavior in organizations* (pp. 119–126). New York: McGraw-Hill.

Kahneman, D., & Tversky, A. (1972). Subjective probability: A judgment of representativeness. *Cognitive Psychology, 3,* 430–454.

Kahneman, D., & Tversky, A. (1973). On the psychology of prediction. *Psychological Review, 80,* 237–251.

Karren, R. J., NKomo, S., & Ramirez, D. (1985). *Improving personnel selection decisions: A field survey using decision theory and utility analysis.* Paper presented at the annual meeting of the Academy of Management, San Diego, CA.

Keeney, R. L., & Raiffa, H. (1976). *Decisions with multiple objectives: Preferences and value tradeoffs.* New York: Wiley.

Kelley, T. L. (1923). *Statistical method.* New York: Macmillan.

Kroeck, G., Barrett, G. V., & Alexander, R. A. (1983). Imposed quotas and personnel selection: A computer simulation study. *Journal of Applied Psychology, 68,* 123–136.

Landy, F. J., Farr, J. L., & Jacobs, R. R. (1982). Utility concepts in performance measurement. *Organizational Behavior and Human Performance, 30,* 15–40.

Ledvinka, J., Archer, R. W., & Ladd, R. T. (1990). *Utility analysis of internal selection.* Paper presented at the national meeting of the Adademy of Management, San Francisco.

Ledvinka, J., Simonet, J. K., Neiner, A. G., & Kruse, B. (1983). *The dollar value of JEPS at Life of Georgia.* Unpublished technical report.

Lee, R., & Booth, J. M. (1974). A utility analysis of a weighted application blank designed to predict turnover for clerical employees. *Journal of Applied Psychology, 59,* 516–518.

Lee, R., & Foley, P. P. (1986). Is the validity of a test constant throughout the test score range? *Journal of Applied Psychology, 71,* 641–644.

Levin, H. (1983). *Cost-effectiveness: A primer.* Beverly Hills, CA: Sage.

Locke, E. S., Farren, D. B., McCaleb, V. M., Shaw, K. N., & Denny, A. T. (1980). The relative effectiveness of four methods of motivating employee performance. In K. Duncan, M. Gruneberg, & D. Wallis (Eds.), *Changes in working life.* New York: Wiley.

Lykken, D. T. (1968). Statistical significance in psychological research. *Psychological Bulletin, 70,* 151–159.

Mahoney, T. A., & England, G. W. (1965). Efficiency and accuracy of employee selection decision rules. *Personnel Psychology, 18,* 361–377.

March, J. G., & Simon, H. G. (1958). *Organizations.* New York: Wiley.

Mathieu, J. E., & Leonard, R. L., Jr. (1987). An application of utility concepts to a supervisor skills training program: A time-based approach. *Academy of Management Journal, 30,* 316–335.

McEvoy, G. M., & Cascio, W. F. (1985, August). *Turnover and employee performance: A meta-analytic review.* Paper presented at the annual meeting of the National Academy of Management, San Diego, CA.

Meehl, P. E., & Rosen, A. (1955). Antecedent probability and the efficiency of psychometric signs, patterns, or cutting scores. *Psychological Bulletin, 52,* 194–216.

Milkovich, G. T., & Andersen, J. C. (1982). Career planning and development systems. In K. M. Rowland & G. R. Ferris (Eds.), *Personnel management* (pp. 364–388). Boston: Allyn & Bacon.

Milkovich, G. T., & Boudreau, J. W. (1991). *Human resource management.* Homewood, IL: Irwin.

Milkovich, G. T., & Newman, J. M. (1990). *Compensation* (3rd ed.). Chicago: Irwin.

Mitchell, K. J., Eaton, N. K., & Wing, H. (1985). *Putting the "dollars" into utility analyses: More findings with the superior equivalents technique.* Paper presented at the national meeting of the American Psychological Association, Los Angeles.

Mueser, P., & Maloney, T. (1987). *Ability, human capital and employer screening: Reconciling labor market behavior with studies of employee productivity.* Unpublished manuscript.

Murphy, K. M. (1986). When your top choice turns you down: The effect of rejected offers on the utility of selection tests. *Psychological Bulletin, 99,* 133–138.

Naylor, J. C., & Shine, L. C. (1965). A table for determining the increase in mean criterion score obtained by using a selection device. *Journal of Industrial Psychology, 3,* 33–42.

Pfeffer, J., & Cohen, Y. (1984). Determinants of internal labor markets in organizations. *Administrative Science Quarterly, 29,* 550–572.

Raju, N. S., Burke, M. J., & Normand, J. (1987). *A new model for utility analysis* (Working paper). Chicago: Illinois Institute of Technology, Department of Psychology.

Rauschenberger, J. M., & Schmidt, F. L. (1987). Measuring the economic impact of human resource programs. *Journal of Business and Psychology, 2,* 50–59.

Reilly, R. R., & Smither, J. W. (1985). An examination of two alternative techniques to estimate the standard deviation of job performance in dollars. *Journal of Applied Psychology, 70,* 651–661.

Rich, J. R. (1986). *Variance and risk in utility analysis: A case study.* Unpublished master's thesis, Cornell University, Ithaca, NY.

Rich, J. R., & Boudreau, J. W. (1987). The effects of variability and risk on selection utility analysis: An empirical simulation and comparison. *Personnel Psychology, 40,* 55–84.

Roche, U. F. (1961). *The Cronbach-Gleser utility function in fixed treatment employee selection.* Unpublished doctoral dissertation, Southern Illinois University, Carbondale. Portions reproduced in L. J. Cronbach & G. C. Gleser (Eds.). (1965). *Psychological tests and personnel decisions* (pp. 254–266). Urbana: University of Illinois Press.

Rosenthal, R., & Rubin, D. B. (1985). Statistical analysis: Summarizing evidence versus establishing facts. *Psychological Bulletin, 97,* 527–529.

Rusmore, T. T., & Toorenaar, G. J. (1956). Reducing training costs by employment testing. *Personnel Psychology, 9,* 39–44.

Rynes, S. L., & Milkovich, G. T. (1986). Wage surveys: Dispelling some myths about the 'market wage.' *Personnel Psychology, 39,* 71–90.

Sackett, P. R., Zedeck, S., & Fogli, L. (1988). Relations between measures of typical and maximum job performance. *Journal of Applied Psychology, 73,* 482–486.

Sands, W. A. (1973). A method for evaluating alternative recruiting-selection strategies: The CA-

PER model. *Journal of Applied Psychology, 57,* 222–227.

Schmidt, F. L. (1974). Probability and utility assumptions underlying use of the Strong Vocational Interest Blank. *Journal of Applied Psychology, 59,* 456–464.

Schmidt, F. L., & Hoffman, B. (1973). Empirical comparison of three methods of assessing utility of a selection device. *Journal of Industrial and Organizational Psychology, 1,* 13–22.

Schmidt, F. L., & Hunter, J. E. (1983). Individual differences in productivity: An empirical test of estimates derived from studies of selection procedure utility. *Journal of Applied Psychology, 68,* 407–414.

Schmidt, F. L., Hunter, J. E., Croll, P. R., & McKenzie, R. C. (1983). Estimation of employment test validities by expert judgment. *Journal of Applied Psychology, 68,* 590–601.

Schmidt, F. L., Hunter, J. E., McKenzie, R. C., & Muldrow, T. W. (1979). Impact of valid selection procedures on work-force productivity. *Journal of Applied Psychology, 64,* 609–626.

Schmidt, F. L., Hunter, J. E., Outerbridge, A. N., & Goff, S. (1988). Joint relation of experience and ability with job performance: Test of three hypotheses. *Journal of Applied Psychology, 73,* 46–57.

Schmidt, F. L., Hunter, J. E., Outerbridge, A. N., & Trattner, M. H. (1986). The economic impact of job selection methods on size, productivity, and payroll costs of the federal work force: An empirically based demonstration. *Personnel Psychology, 39,* 1–29.

Schmidt, F. L., Hunter, J. E., & Pearlman, K. (1982). Assessing the economic impact of personnel programs on work-force productivity. *Personnel Psychology, 35,* 333–347.

Schmidt, F. L., Hunter, J. E., & Urry, V. W. (1976). Statistical power in criterion-related validity studies. *Journal of Applied Psychology, 61,* 473–485.

Schmidt, F. L., Mack, M. J., & Hunter, J. E. (1984). Selection utility in the occupation of U.S. park ranger for three modes of test use. *Journal of Applied Psychology, 69,* 490–497.

Sheppeck, M. A., & Cohen, S. L. (1985, November). Put a dollar value on your training programs. *Training and Development Journal, 39,* 59–62.

Smith, M. (1948). Cautions concerning the use of the Taylor-Russell tables in employee selection. *Journal of Applied Psychology, 32,* 595–600.

Smith, P. C. (1976). Behaviors, results and organizational effectiveness: The problem of criteria. In M. D. Dunnette (Ed.), *Handbook of industrial and organizational psychology.* Chicago: Rand McNally.

Steffy, B. D., & Ledvinka, J. (1989). The long-range impact of five definitions of "fair" employee selection on black employment and employee productivity. *Organizational Behavior and Human Decision Processes, 44,* 297–324.

Stone, C. H., & Kendall, W. E. (1956). *Effective personnel selection procedures.* Englewood Cliffs, NJ: Prentice-Hall.

Taylor, H. C., & Russell, J. T. (1939). The relationship of validity coefficients to the practical effectiveness of tests in selection: Discussion and tables. *Journal of Applied Psychology, 23,* 565–578.

Tsui, A. S. (1984). Personnel department effectivness: A tripartite approach. *Industrial Relations, 23,* 184–197.

Tsui, A. S. (1987). Defining the activities and effectiveness of the human resource department: A multiple-constituency approach. *Human Resource Management, 26,* 35–69.

Tsui, A. S., & Gomez-Mejia, L. R. (1988). Evaluating human resource effectiveness. In L. D. Dyer (Ed.), *Human resource management: Evolving roles & responsibilities,* 1–187—1–227. Washington, DC: Bureau of National Affairs.

Van Naersson, R. F. (1963). *Selectie van chauffers.* Groningen, The Netherlands: Wolters-Noordhoff. Portions reproduced in L. J. Cronbach & G. C. Gleser (Eds.). (1965). *Psychological tests and personnel decisions.* Urbana: University of Illinois Press.

Wagle, B. (1967). A statistical analysis of risk in investment decisions. *Operational Research Quarterly, 18,* 13–33.

Weekley, J. A., & Gier, J. A. (1986, August). *An examination of the temporal consistency of rational SD_y estimates.* Paper presented at the annual meeting of the Academy of Management, Chicago.

Weekley, J. A., O'Connor, E. J., Frank, B., & Peters, L. W. (1985). A comparison of three methods of estimating the standard deviation of performance in dollars. *Journal of Applied Psychology, 79,* 122–126.

Wesman, A. G. (1953). Better than chance. *Test Service Bulletin, 45,* 1–67.

Wigdor, A. K., & Hartigan, J. A. (1988). *Interim report: Within-group scoring of the General Aptitude Test Battery.* Washington, DC: National Academy Press.

Wroten, S. P. (1984, August). *Overcoming the futilities of utility applications: Measures, models, and management.* Paper presented at the annual meeting of the American Psychological Association, Toronto.

APPENDIX A

Results of Studies Deriving Actual Program Utility Values

Reference	Setting	N_s	T or F	SR	$\bar{Z}_x$	$r_{x,y}$	SD_y	Cost	ΔU	Utility Formula	B-E SD_y
Doppelt & Bennett (1953)[a]	Examined selection utility for predicting training success of grocery clerks	1		.10			$308		$197		
Doppelt & Bennett (1953)[a]	Examined selection utility for predicting training success of adding machine operators	1		.13			$214		$180		
Doppelt & Bennett (1953)[a]	Examined selection utility for predicting training success of produce workers	1		.07			$179		$116		
Rusmore & Toorenaar (1956)[a]	Examined selection utility for predicting training success of telephone operators	1						$28,000			
Roche (1961)	Examined selection utility of a test battery for predicting radial drill operators' overall performance per hour	1	1 hr.	.33	1.11	.313	$0.585	$0.0006 /hr.	$0.203 /hr.	$\Delta U = (.348\,SD_y) - \$0.0006$	$0.0017
Van Naersson (1963)	Examined selection utility of a driving experience questionnaire for reducing training time for drivers in the Dutch Army	4,392	1 yr.	.81	.334	.66	$77.00	$1,627	$73,049	$\Delta U = (970\,SD_y) - \$1,627$	$1.68

APPENDIX A

Results of Studies Deriving Actual Program Utility Values (continued)

Reference	Setting	N_s	T or F	SR	$\bar{Z}_x$	$r_{x,y}$	SD_y	Cost	ΔU	Utility Formula	B-E SD_y
Schmidt & Hoffman (1973)	Examined weighted application blank selection utility for reducing separations among nurse's aides	308	2 yrs.	.302	NR	.47	$1,652	$628 per separation	$161,243	NA	NA
Lee & Booth (1974)[a]	Examined selection utility of a weighted application blank for predicting turnover among clerical employees	245	25 mos.	.17	1.47	.56	$1,238	$0	$249,900	$\Delta U = (202\ SD_y) - \$0$	$0
Cascio & Silbey (1979)	Examined assessment center selection utility for food and beverage sales managers	50	5 yrs.	.50	.80	.35	$9,500	$73,928	$504,211	$\Delta U = (61.04\ SD_y) - \$40,328$	$660.70
Cascio & Silbey (1979)	Examined interview selection utility for food and beverage sales managers	50	5 yrs.	.50	.80	.25	$9,500	$62,600	$350,357	$\Delta U = (43.59\ SD_y) - \$29,000$	$665.29
Cascio & Silbey (1979)	Examined assessment center selection utility minus interview selection utility for food and beverage sales managers	50	5 yrs.	.50	.80	.10	$9,500	$11,328	$350,357	$\Delta U = (17.45\ SD_y) - \$11,328$	$649.16
Schmidt et al. (1979)	Examined interview selection utility for U.S. government computer programmers	618	10 yrs.	.50	.80	$.14^b$	$10,413	$358,440^c$	$6,849,022	$\Delta U = (692\ SD_y) - \$358,440$	$517.85

APPENDIX A

Results of Studies Deriving Actual Program Utility Values (continued)

Reference	Setting	N_s	T or F	SR	$\bar{Z}_x$	$r_{x,y}$	SD_y	Cost	ΔU	Utility Formula	B-E SD_y
Schmidt et al. (1979)	Examined PAT selection utility for U.S. government computer programmers	618	10 yrs.	.50	.80	.76	$10,413	$370,800[d]	$38,755,422	$\Delta U = (3{,}757\ SD_y) - \$370{,}800$	$98.70
Schmidt et al. (1979)	Examined PAT selection utility minus interview selection utility for U.S. government computer programmers	618	10 yrs.	.50	.80	.76	$10,413	$12,360	$31,906,400	$\Delta U = (3{,}065\ SD_y) - \$12{,}360$	$4.03
Arnold et al. (1982)	Examined selection utility of a strength test to select steel-workers	1,853	1 yr.	.06	1.97	.84	$3,000	$0	$9,199,033	$\Delta U = (3{,}066\ SD_y) - \$0$	$0
Dunnette et al. (1982)	Examined selection utility of a test battery to select hydroelectric power plant operators	1	1 yr.	.50	.80	.28	$15,600[e]	$100	$3,295	$\Delta U = (.216\ SD_y) - \$100$	$46.30
Dunnette et al. (1982)	Examined selection utility of a test battery to select fossil power plant operators	1	1 yr.	.50	.80	.44	$21,400[e]	$100	$7,335	$\Delta U = (.347\ SD_y) - \$100$	$288.18
Dunnette et al. (1982)	Examined selection utility of a test battery to select fossil power plant control room operators (CRO)	1	1 yr.	.50	.80	.44	$72,400[e]	$100	$25,285	$\Delta U = (.351\ SD_y) - \$100$	$284.90

APPENDIX A

Results of Studies Deriving Actual Program Utility Values (continued)

Reference	Setting	N_s	T or F	SR	$\bar{Z}_x$	$r_{x,y}$	SD_y	Cost	ΔU	Utility Formula	B-E SD_y
Dunnette et al. (1982)	Examined selection utility of a test battery to select nuclear power plant operators	1	1 yr.	.50	.80	.30	$23,500[e]	$100	$5,440	$\Delta U=(.236\ SD_y) - \$100$	$424
Dunnette et al. (1982)	Examined selection utility of a test battery to select nuclear power plant control room operators	1	1 yr.	.50	.80	.30	$134,800[e]	$100	$32,150	$\Delta U=(.239 SD_y) - \$100$	$418
Ledvinka et al. (1983)	Examined selection utility of the JEPS test for life insurance claim approvers	10	1 yr.	.07	1.918	.36	$5,542	$1,104	$37,162	$\Delta U=(6.90\ SD_y) - \$1,104$	$160
Ledvinka et al. (1983)	Examined selection utility of the interview for life insurance claim approvers	10	1 yr.	.07	1.918	.14	$5,542	$0	$14,881	$\Delta U=(2.68\ SD_y) - \$0$	$0
Ledvinka et al. (1983)	Examined selection utility of the JEPS test minus the selection utility of the interview for life insurance claim approvers	10	1 yr.	.07	1.918	.22	$5,542	$1,104	$22,281	$\Delta U=(4.22\ SD_y) - \$1,104$	$262
Schmidt, Mack, & Hunter (1984)	Examined selection utility of using the interview to select U.S. park rangers	80	10 yrs.	.10	1.758	.14	$4,451	$232,000[e]	$644,384	$\Delta U=(197\ SD_y) - \$232,000$	$1,178
Schmidt, Mack, & Hunter (1984)	Examined selection utility of using the PACE test to select U.S. park rangers	80	10 yrs.	.10	1.758	.51	$4,451	$232,000[f]	$2,960,542	$\Delta U=(717\ SD_y) - \$232,000$	$323.57

APPENDIX A

Results of Studies Deriving Actual Program Utility Values (continued)

Reference	Setting	N_s	T or F	SR	$\bar{Z}_x$	$r_{x,y}$	SD_y	Cost	ΔU	Utility Formula	B-E SD_y
Schmidt, Mack, & Hunter (1984)	Examined selection utility of the PACE test minus the selection utility of the interview to select U.S. park rangers	80	10 yrs.	.10	1.758	.37	$4,451	$0	$2,316,482	$\Delta U=(520\ SD_y) - \$0$	$0
Wroten (1984)	Calculated selection utility of using various selection tests compared to random selection for head operators	1	10 yrs.	.15	1.55	.30	$29,472[g]	$1,000	$136,045	$\Delta U=(4.65\ SD_y) - \$1,000$	$216.00
Wroten (1984)	Calculated selection utility of using various selection tests compared to random selection for outside operators	1	5 yrs.	.15	1.55	.30	$21,591[g]	$1,000	$49,199	$\Delta U=(2.33\ SD_y) - \$1,000$	$429.18
Wroten (1984)	Calculated selection utility of using various selection tests compared to random selection for pump operators	1	3 yrs.	.15	1.55	.30	$14,205[g]	$1,000	$18,816	$\Delta U=(1.40\ SD_y) - \$1,000$	$714.28
Wroten (1984)	Calculated selection utility of using various selection tests compared to random selection for instrument technicians	1	15 yrs.	.15	1.55	.30	$46,396[g]	$1,000	$322,612	$\Delta U=(6.97\ SD_y) - \$1,000$	$143.47
Wroten (1984)	Calculated selection utility of using various selection tests compared to random selection for outside mechanics	1	8 yrs.	.15	1.55	.30	$26,438[g]	$1,000	$97,349	$\Delta U=(3.72\ SD_y) - \$1,000$	$268.82

APPENDIX A

Results of Studies Deriving Actual Program Utility Values (continued)

Reference	Setting	N_s	T or F	SR	$\bar{Z}_x$	$r_{x.y}$	SD_y	Cost	ΔU	Utility Formula	B-E SD_y
Wroten (1984)	Calculated selection utility of using various selection tests compared to random selection for welders	1	17 yrs.	.15	1.55	.30	$18,291[g]	$1,000	$143,590	$\Delta U=(7.90\ SD_y)-\$1,000$	$126.58
Weekley et al. (1985)	Examined selection utility of a test battery for convenience store managers	1,000	1 yr.	.33	1.102	.45	$7,701[h]	$30,000	$3,788.926	$\Delta U=(495.9\ SD_y)-\$30,000$	$60.49
Burke & Frederick (1986)[j]	Examined selection utility of an assessment center to select mid-level sales managers (TAX = .49, i = .18, V = .048)	29	4.2 yrs.	.22	.872	.59	$12,789[i]	$134,454[k]	$115,727	$\Delta U=(19.56\ SD_y)-\$134,454$	$6,874
Burke & Frederick (1986)[j]	Examined selection utility of an interview to select midlevel sales managers (TAX = .49, i = .18, V = .048)	29	4.2 yrs.	.22	.872	.16	$12,789[i]	$25,747[k]	$42,098	$\Delta U=(5.30\ SD_y)-\$25,747$	$4,858
Burke & Frederick (1986)[j]	Examined selection utility of an assessment center minus interview selection utility to select midlevel sales managers (TAX = .49, i = .18, V = .048)	29	4.2 yrs.	.22	.872	.43	$12,789[i]	$108,707[k]	$73,629	$\Delta U=(14.26\ SD_y)-\$108,707$	$7,625
Cascio & Ramos (1986)	Examined selection utility of an assessment center for promoting telephone company office managers	1,116	4.4 yrs.	.32	1.17	.388	$10,421	$2,399,400	$20,830,312	$\Delta U=(2,229\ SD_y)-\$2,399,400$	$1,076

APPENDIX A

Results of Studies Deriving Actual Program Utility Values (continued)

Reference	Setting	N_s	T or F	SR	$\bar{Z}_x$	r_{xy}	SD_y	Cost	ΔU	Utility Formula	B-E SD_y
Cascio & Ramos (1986)	Examined selection utility of an inteview for promoting telephone company office managers	1,116	4.4 yrs.	.32	1.17	.14	$10,421	$1,046,250	$7,335,605	$\Delta U = (804\ SD_y) - \$1,046,250$	$1,301
Cascio & Ramos (1986)	Examined selection utility of an assessment center versus interview for promoting telephone company office managers	1,116	4.4 yrs.	.32	1.17	.248	$10,421	$1,353,150	$13,494,707	$\Delta U = (1,425\ SD_y) - \$1,353,150$	$950
Cronshaw et al. (1987)	Examined selection utility of a cognitive ability test to select one group of clerical/administrative employees for the Canadian military ($i = .1125$)	470	18 yrs.	.333	1.09	.52	$10,680[i]	$159,900	$21,738,270	$\Delta U = (2,020\ SD_y) - \$159,900$	$79.16
Schmidt et al. (1986)	Examined selection utility of selecting one cohort of U.S. government employees with a test of cognitive abilities versus nontest methods ($d_t = .487$)	225,731	13 yrs.	.15[l]	1.55[l]	.31[l]	$5,429	Assume zero	$7.87 billion[m]	$\Delta U = (1.43\ \text{million} \times SD_y)$	$0
Florin-Thuma & Boudreau (1987)	Examined the one-year utility of performance feedback for yogurt shop counter workers	15	1 yr.			utility of production units (no SD_y)		$409.75	$11,719	—	—

APPENDIX A

Results of Studies Deriving Actual Program Utility Values (continued)

Reference	Setting	N_s	T or F	SR	$\bar{Z}_x$	$r_{x,y}$	SD_y	Cost	ΔU	Utility Formula	B-E SD_y
Mathieu & Leonard (1987)[n]	Examined training program utility for head tellers in the Bank of Virginia. Utility calculated based on training 10 head tellers, who remain a maximum of 18 yrs (TAX = .46, i = .15, V = .0668)	10	18 yrs.	Calculated d_t of .3146			$2,369	$3,089[o]	$9,790	$\Delta U = (5.44\ SD_y) - \$3,089$	$568
Mathieu & Leonard (1987)[n]	Examined training program utility for operations managers in the Bank of Virginia. Utility calculated based on training 10 operations managers who remain a maximum of 20 yrs (TAX = .46, i = .15, V = .0729)	19	20 yrs.	Calculated d_t of .3146			$3,123	$5,830[o]	$28,694	$\Delta U = (11.05\ SD_y) - \$5,830$	$527
Mathieu & Leonard (1987)[n]	Examined training program utility for branch managers in the Bank of Virginia. Utility calculated based on training 36 branch managers who remain a maximum of 19 yrs (TAX = .46, i = .15, V = .0287)	36	19 yrs.	Calculated d_t of .3146			$10,064	$14,814[o]	$156,400	$\Delta U = (17.01\ SD_y) - \$14,814$	$871
Rich & Boudreau (1987)[p]	Examined the selection utility of the PAT for computer programmers (TAX = .39, i = .15, V = 0.0)	flows	11 yrs.	.398	.73	.73	$15,888	$229,101[k]	$3,198,258	$\Delta U = (216\ SD_y) - 229,101$	$1,062

APPENDIX A

Results of Studies Deriving Actual Program Utility Values (continued)

Reference	Setting	N_s	T or F	SR	$\bar{Z}_x$	$r_{x,y}$	SD_y	Cost	ΔU	Utility Formula	B-E SD_y
Rich & Boudreau (1987)[p]	Examined the selection utility of the interview for computer programmers (TAX = .39, i = .15, V = 0.0)	flows	11 yrs.	.398	.73	.14	$15,888	$225,543[k]	$431,744	$\Delta U = (41.4\ SD_y) - \$225{,}543$	$5,452
Rich & Boudreau (1987)[p]	Examined the selection utility of the PAT minus the utility of the interview for computer programmers (TAX = .39, i = .15, V = 0.0)	flows	11 yrs.	.398	.73	.59	$15,888	$3,557[k]	$2,775,889	$\Delta U = (174\ SD_y) - \$3{,}557$	$20.44

[a] As reported in Hunter & Schmidt (1982)
[b] Interview validity based on subsequent estimates by these authors (e.g., Schmidt et al., 1984)
[c] Cost per interview estimated as $290, following Cascio & Silbey (1979) (authors provided no cost information)
[d] Cost per test estimated as $300, following the author's statement that the cost of testing would be an additional $10 per applicant
[e] Conservatively estimated at the bottom of the 95 percent confidence interval
[f] Cost per test estimated at $290, based on the authors' statement that "it is unlikely to be greater than the cost per interview" (p. 493)
[g] SD_y estimates based on the average of the Schmidt et al. (1979) estimation method and the realistically anchored estimation method
[h] SD_y estimates based on CREPID estimation method (40% of salary produced $8,489; Schmidt et al. produced $13,968)
[i] Adjusted for financial/economic factors
[j] SD_y estimate based on 40 percent of salary
[k] After-tax cost
[l] Derived from previous studies (reported utility value based on the empirically observed d, value of .487)
[m] Value differs slightly from the reported utility value ($7.84 billion), which was based on an average across positions
[n] Adjusted for financial/economic considerations and employee turnover over time
[o] After-tax, discounted cost (includes $12,800 fixed program development cost allocated according to the number trained in each job)
[p] Adjusted for financial/economic factors as well as employee flows over time

Note: N_s = number selected or treated; T = tenure; F = analysis period; SR = selection ratio; Z_x = estimated average standardized predictor score; r_{xy} = validity coefficient; SD_y = dollar-value standard deviation of performance; Cost = total program cost; ΔU = total program utility

APPENDIX B

Results of Studies Estimating SD_y Values

Reference	Setting	Utility Scale	Estimation Method	SD_y Values
Doppelt & Bennett (1953)[a]	Estimated savings in training costs			Grocery clerks: Mean = \$ 308/year SE = SD = % salary = 15% % mean y = NR Adding machine operators: Mean = \$214/year SE = SD = % salary = 10% % mean y = NR Produce workers: Mean = \$179 SE = SD = % salary = 10% % mean y = NR
Roche (1961); reported in Cronbach & Gleser (1965)	Estimated the value of production units of radial drill operators ($N = 291$) in a manufacturing organization by attaching value to each unit	"The dollar profit which accrues to the company as a result of an individual's work"	Used cost accounting to attach standard costs (materials, labor, and facility usage) and prices to units. Price less cost was value per unit, and SD_y was based on individual output quantities.	Mean = \$1,217 (\$.585/hour) SE = NA SD = NA % salary = 25%[a] % mean y = NR
Van Naersson (1963); reported in Cronbach & Gleser (1965)	Used training time data to estimate the SD of training time costs across military driver trainees in the Dutch Army	Reduction in training time costs	Used training time data to estimate SD training hours (12.9), and then multiplied by average training cost/hour (\$6.00) to produce SD of cost equal to \$77.00	Mean = \$77 SE = NA SD = NA % salary = 4% % mean y = NR

[a] As reported by Hunter & Schmidt (1982).

APPENDIX B

Results of Studies Estimating SD_y Values (continued)

Reference	Setting	Utility Scale	Estimation Method	SD_y Values	
Schmidt & Hoffman (1973)	Estimated savings from reducing turnover costs (hiring, training, administration, and overhead)	Reduction in recruitment, hiring, and training costs due to longer tenure and fewer replacements among nurse's aides in a hospital	No SD_y calculated, but an SD_y estimate can be derived by working backward from the known $\bar{Z}$, $r_{x,y}$, and ΔU/selectee	Mean SE SD % salary % mean y	= $624/year = NA = NA = 15% = NR
Lee & Booth (1974)[a]	Estimated the clerical employees' tenure, and calculated the cost savings due to reduced recruiting, hiring, and training costs	Reduction in recruitment, hiring, and training costs due to longer tenure and fewer replacements	No SD_y measurement per se, but an SD_y measure can be derived by working backward from the known $\bar{Z}$, $r_{x,y}$, and ΔU/selectee	Mean SE SD % salary % mean y	= $1,238 = NA = NA = 20% = NR
Cascio & Silbey (1979)	Third-level food and beverage sales managers ($N = 4$) estimated yearly sales levels for incumbent second-level sales managers	Yearly value of sales	Global estimation of 15th, 50th, and 95th percentiles (average difference between two endpoints equals SD_y estimate)	Mean SE SD % salary	= $9,500 = NA = NA = 42.2%
Schmidt et al. (1979)	Supervisors ($N = 105$) estimated "yearly value of products and services" and "cost of having an outside firm provide these products" for incumbent federal government (GS 9–11) computer programmers.	Value of products and services and/or cost of having an outside contractor provide them	Global estimation of 15th, 50th, and 95th percentiles (average difference between two endpoints equals SD_y estimate)	Mean SE SD % salary % mean y	= $10,413 = $1,354 = $13,874 = 55% = 31.6%
Arnold et al. (1982)	Examined the amount shoveled by steelworkers	The amount of work accomplished	Attempted to provide a highly conservative SD_y estimate: (1) Evidence indicated that top 10% did 8–9 times as much as the bottom 10%, so the ratio of the top 1% to the bottom 1% was estimated to be 2 to 1. (2) A conservative estimate of yearly salary plus benefits was $18,000 per year. (3) Deduced a savings of $18,000 from hiring one top 1% worker instead of a bottom 1% worker. (4) Assumed top 1% and bottom 1% were 6 SD's apart.	Mean % salary	= $3,000 = 17%

APPENDIX B

Results of Studies Estimating SD_y Values (continued)

Reference	Setting	Utility Scale	Estimation Method	SD_y Values
Dunnette et al. (1982)	Power industry experts participated in a workshop in which they discussed critical incidents of effective and ineffective power plant operator performance, were presented with 8 previously derived performance dimensions, retranslated 667 performance examples into the dimensions, and then made dollar contribution judgments for five jobs: (1) Hydroelectric plant operator ($N = 31$); (2) fossil fuel plant operator ($N = 20$); (3) fossil fuel plant control room operator (CRO; $N = 48$). ($N = 48$); nuclear plant operator and (5) nuclear plant CRO ($N = 34$).	Dollar value contribution of operator performance	Schmidt et al. (1979) method	*Hydro Operator* Mean = $20,790 SD = $14,110 SE = $2,530 *Fossil Operator* Mean = $30,350 SD = $19,120 SE = $4,280 *Fossil CRO* Mean = $88,720 SD = $56,210 SE = $8,110 *Nuclear Operator* Mean = $74,900 SD = $107,150 SE = $24,580 *Nuclear CRO* Mean = $213,730 SD = $226,600 SE = $38,860
Hunter & Schmidt (1982)	Supervisors ($N = 62$) of budget analysts estimated values similar to those of Schmidt et al. (1979).	Value of products and services and/or cost of having an outside contractor provide them	Global estimation of 15th, 50th, and 95th percentiles (average difference between two endpoints equals SD_y estimate)	Mean = $11,327 SE = $1,120 SD = $8,818 % salary = 60% % mean y = NR

APPENDIX B

Results of Studies Estimating SD_y Values (continued)

Reference	Setting	Utility Scale	Estimation Method	SD_y Values
Bobko, Karren, & Parkington (1983)	Sales counselor supervisors ($N = 17$) estimated SD_y for counselor sales and performance levels (also performance data obtained for 92 actual insurance counselors).	"Total Yearly Dollar Sales" versus "Yearly value to the company of the overall products and services produced (considering the cost of having an outside contractor provide them)"	Global estimation of the 15th, 50th, 85th, and 97th percentiles of both sales and value (also gathered empirical sales data, computed by taking the number of policies sold and multiplying by the average policy value in his or her area)	*Sales, 4 distribution points* Mean = \$47,967 SE = \$9,969 SD = \$34,533 % salary = 352% % mean y = 50% *Value, 4 distribution points* Mean = \$4,967 SE = \$2,089 SD = \$7,533 % salary = 37% % mean y = 31% *Sales, 3 distribution points* Mean = \$56,950 SE = \$15,365 SD = \$55,400 % salary = 419% % mean y = 59% *Value, 3 distribution points* Mean = \$5,550 SE = \$2,413 SD = \$8,700 % salary = 41% % mean y = 35% *Actual Sales Data* Mean = \$124,882 SD = \$52,308 % salary = 384% % mean y = 42%

APPENDIX B

Results of Studies Estimating SD_y Values (continued)

Reference	Setting	Utility Scale	Estimation Method	SD_y Values		
Ledvinka, Simonet, Neiner, & Kruse (1983)	Claims processed per day for 15 insurance claims approvers were recorded for 2 months.	Dollar value to the company of claims processed per year	Average dollar value of a processed claim was estimated by dividing total payroll plus benefits per year by the average number of processed claims per year. Assumption was that the wages and benefits paid to the average employee equals his or her value to the organization. Then the standard deviation of claims processed per year (1679.29, as corrected for range restriction) times the average value/claim ($3.30) became the SD_y estimate.	Mean	=	$ 5,542
				SD	=	NA
				SE	=	NA
				% salary	=	42.6%
				% mean y	=	31.4%
Burke & Frederick (1984)	Regional manufacturing sales managers ($N = 26$) provided global ratings for SD_y regarding their subordinate district sales managers ($N = 69$). They estimated four percentiles (15th, 50th, 85th, and 97th).	Used actual yearly sales revenue, plus estimates of "total yearly value of services," considering the cost of "having an outside firm provide these services" (p. 484)	Yearly sales volume for the 69 sales managers in 1982 was one estimate of SD_y. 1982 annual salaries for these managers was another distribution. Three distributions were derived from estimates of the 4 percentiles. Standard procedure simply gathered individual estimates for each percentile and calculated the mean differences between them. Procedure A fed back the 50th percentile to 4 managers and had them reach consensus on the other 3. Procedure B fed back the 50th percentile estimate to 18 managers and had them reestimate the other 3 percentiles.	*Standard*		
				Mean	=	$32,284
				SE	=	$9,199
				SD	=	$45,996
				% salary	=	105%
				% mean y	=	32%
				Procedure A		
				Mean	=	$38,333
				SE	=	NA
				SD	=	NA
				% salary	=	124%
				% mean y	=	51%
				Procedure B		
				Mean	=	$32,323
				SE	=	$1,797
				SD	=	$8,983
				% salary	=	104%
				% mean y	=	43%
				Actual Sales Revenue		
				Mean	=	$ 6.02 M
				SD	=	$ 2,634 M
				Actual Salary		
				Mean	=	$30,900
				SD	=	$4,600

APPENDIX B

Results of Studies Estimating SD_y Values (continued)

Reference	Setting	Utility Scale	Estimation Method	SD_y Values
Schmidt, Mack, & Hunter (1984)	Park ranger supervisors ($N = 114$) provided data for Schmidt et al. SD_y estimates by considering the park rangers they supervised. Only two supervisors could not estimate the 15th percentile.	Not reported, but assumed to follow the Schmidt et al. method of "value of goods and services." Authors note subjects were asked to "consider what the cost would be of having an outside firm provide the products or services to them." (p. 492)	Standard Schmidt et al. method of surveying respondents	*85th – 50th* Mean = \$3,801 SE = \$239 SD = \$2,546 % salary = 36% % mean y = 28% *50th – 15th* Mean = \$5,101 SE = \$357 SD = \$3,813 % salary = 49% % mean y = 38%
Wroten (1984)	Groups of supervisors ($N = 3$ to 4) of petroleum workers in 7 different organizations and 16 different locations provided SD_y estimates for 6 refinery jobs using 6 different methods.	Not reported, but probably similar to Schmidt et al. (1979) because all measures were described as variants of this method	12 estimation methods were used for each of 6 jobs: (1) head operator, (2) outside operator, (3) pump operator, (4) instrument technician, (5) outside mechanic, (6) welder. The 12 estimation methods were of 4 types: (1) direct estimates (including the Schmidt et al. method, obtaining y estimates for individuals and calculating SD_y from them, and obtaining percentile estimates by group consensus); (2) actual anchored estimates (which replicated the first three methods, but provided accurate 50th percentile estimates first); (3) high anchored estimates (which replicated the first three methods, but provided a high 50th percentile estimate first); and (4) low anchored estimates (which replicated the first three methods, but provided a low 50th percentile estimate first). Accurate anchor was derived from "cost accounting" and unanchored group's 50th percentile estimate. High anchor was twice actual, and low anchor was half of actual.	*Direct, Head Operator* Mean = \$31,423 SD = \$26,663 SE - \$ 6,383 *Direct, Outside Operator* Mean = \$20,468 SD = \$16,041 SE = \$ 3,638 *Direct, Pump Operator* Mean = \$13,950 SD = \$9,532 SE = \$2,124 *Direct, Instrument Technician* Mean = \$35,037 SD = \$25,004 SE = \$6,266 *Direct, Outside Mechanic* Mean = \$25,297 SD = \$19,310 SE = \$4,776

APPENDIX B

Results of Studies Estimating SD_y Values (continued)

Reference	Setting	Utility Scale	Estimation Method	SD_y Values
Wroten (1984) (continued)				*Direct, Welder* Mean = $19,708 SD = $13,430 SE = $3,235 *Actual, Head Operator* Mean = $27,521 SD = $17,795 SE = $8,227 *Actual, Outside Operator* Mean = $22,714 SD = $13,877 SE = $3,942 *Actual, Pump Operator* Mean = $14,461 SD = $8,969 SE = $2,516 *Actual, Instrument Technician* Mean = $57,754 SD = $50,419 SE = $20,046 *Actual, Outside Mechanic* Mean = $27,579 SD = $12,202 SE = $3,884 *Actual, Welder* Mean = $16,874 SD = $8,306 SE = $3,592 *High, Head Operator* Mean = $50,714 SD = $20,835 SE = $5,241

APPENDIX B

Results of Studies Estimating *SD*_y Values (continued)

Reference	Setting	Utility Scale	Estimation Method	SD_y Values
Wroten (1984) (continued)				*High, Outside Operator* Mean = $38,626 SD = $17,995 SE = $4,672
				High, Pump Operator Mean = $27,368 SD = $14,174 SE = $3,848
				High, Instrument Technician Mean = $96,554 SD = $48,360 SE = $15,248
				High, Outside Mechanic Mean = $79,789 SD = $36,766 SE = $24,344
				High, Welder Mean = $60,356 SD = $29,735 SE = $11,432
				Low, Head Operator Mean = $27,294 SD = $27,163 SE = $9,617
				Low, Outside Operator Mean = $20,571 SD = $18,353 SE = $6,263
				Low, Pump Operator Mean = $10,358 SD = $8,868 SE = $2,863

APPENDIX B

Results of Studies Estimating SD_y Values (continued)

Reference	Setting	Utility Scale	Estimation Method	SD_y Values
Wroten (1984) (continued)				*Low, Instrument Technician* Mean = $17,501 SD = $10,307 SE = $3,574 *Low, Outside Mechanic* Mean = $12,752 SD = $7,287 SE = $2,514 *Low, Welder* Mean = $10,718 SD = $5,761 SE = $792
Bolda (1985)	Estimated the job performance value for employees in maintenance and toolroom jobs in a manufacturing operation	The dollars-per-hour value of the employee's performance	Gathered estimates of the 15th, 50th, and 84th percentiles, and used the average difference as SD_y	Mean = $6.00/hr. SE = NR SD = NR % salary = 46% % mean y = 46%
Burke (1985)	Supervisors of clerical workers made global y ratings for one of the three job classes they supervised. 132 gave estimates of the 50th percentile (mean = $22,045). This mean was fed back to two groups.	Used the Schmidt et al. (1979) function of the "total yearly value of services" considering how performance contributes to the "sales value of products sold"	After making the global estimate, the 50th percentile was fed back to two groups of supervisors. The first group ($N = 50$) estimated the 15th before the 85th percentile, while the second group ($N = 41$) did the opposite. They also provided self-reported dimensions used in the estimates. Sixteen of the original 118 surveys produced inconsistent estimates. Dimensions used tended to follow job evaluation.	Mean = $5,529 SE = $400 SD = $3,800 % salary = NR % mean y = 25%

APPENDIX B

Results of Studies Estimating *SD*_{*y*} Values (continued)

Reference	Setting	Utility Scale	Estimation Method	SD_y Values
Eaton, Wing, & Lau (1985)	Supervisors of soldiers in 5 military occupations (MOS) provided data estimating the value of first-term soldiers operating at different performance levels. The 5 MOS's were identified as: infantryman (11B), armor crewman (19E), vehicle mechanic (63B), medical specialist (91B), radio operator (05C). Total number of supervisors was 270. Computed equivalent civilian salary levels to be approximately $16,000/yr.	Used questionnaires similar to Eaton et al. (1985a,1985b). The payoff scale was the "worth to the Army" of the soldiers, considering "such factors as salary, output, responsibility, and equipment." (p. 4)	Used the GLOBAL technique of Schmidt et al. (1979), the superior equivalents technique (EQV), and examined the 40–70% Rule. Only the 85th and the 50th percentiles were estimated.	*11B EQV* Mean = $12,881 SD = NR SE = NR % salary = 81% % mean y = 81% *11B GLOBAL* Mean = $9,774 SD = NR SE = NR % salary = 61% % mean y = 51% *19E EQV* Mean = $13,630 SD = NR SE = NR % salary = 84% % mean y = 84% *19E GLOBAL* Mean = $6,254 SD = NR SE = NR % salary = 39% % mean y = 45% *91B EQV* Mean = $16,720 % salary = 105% % mean y = 105% *91B GLOBAL* Mean = $9,132 % salary = 57% % mean y = 51%

APPENDIX B

Results of Studies Estimating SD_y Values (continued)

Reference	Setting	Utility Scale	Estimation Method	SD_y Values
Eaton, Wing, & Lau (1985) (continued)				*63B EQV* Mean = \$15,068 % salary = 94% % mean y = 94% *63B GLOBAL* Mean = \$10,625 % salary = 66% % mean y = 68% *05C EQV* Mean = \$16,653 % salary = 104% % mean y = 104% *05C GLOBAL* Mean = \$11,150 % salary = 70% % mean y = 61%
Eaton, Wing, & Mitchell (1985)	Trainers/supervisors of U.S. Army tank commanders (N = 40 and 48) estimated the value of different levels of tank commander (TC) performance. Dollar-valued anchors were the average yearly compensation of TCs (\$30,000), a subjective estimate of average value, and the average tank cost.	The superior equivalents technique (EQV) derives the number of 85th and 15th percentile performers it takes to equal 17 average performers. The system effectiveness technique (EFF) derives the ratio of SD_y to standard y (where y is expressed in natural production units per tank), indicating how much a standard unit (tank) can be "saved" for each SD productivity increase.	The difference between the medium supervisor 85th and 50th percentile dollar-valued performance global subjective estimate was called SD\$. Average compensation and the 50th percentile global estimate formed the anchor for the EQV technique. The value for the EFF estimate of the ratio of SD_y to standard y (i.e., .2) was from previous validation studies. The cost of a tank was estimated at \$300,000 per year.	*GLOBAL (SD\$) Method* Mean = \$40,000 SD = \$235,000 (3rd – 1st quartile) SE = NR % salary = 133% % mean y = 123% *EQV, Salary Anchor* Mean = \$26,700 SD = \$21,857 (3rd – 1st quartile) SE = NR % salary = 89% % mean y = 89%

APPENDIX B

Results of Studies Estimating SD_y Values (continued)

Reference	Setting	Utility Scale	Estimation Method	SD_y Values
Eaton, Wing & Mitchell (1985) (continued)				*EQV, GLOBAL Anchor* Mean = $28,900 SD = $23,678 (3rd – 1st quartile) SE = NR % salary = 96% % mean y = 89% *EFF* Mean = $60,000 SD = NR SE = NR % salary = 200% % mean y = 185%
Eulberg, O'Connor, & Peters (1985)	Air Force supervisors ($N = 69$) and job incumbents ($N = 113$) from the medical technician speciality provided ratings necessary for CREPID estimates. These ratings were then combined with actual performance ratings and average salary for 95 technicians to derive a CREPID SD_y estimate, which was compared to 40% of salary.	Not reported, but the authors note that in this job, pay is "strictly a function of rank and years of service" (p. 7), which makes it unlikely that average pay is equal to average service value or net benefits	CREPID estimates were derived using task importance ratings from either supervisors or incumbents, combined with the same performance ratings and average salary levels. 40% estimates were derived by multiplying average salary by .40.	*Supervisors* Mean = $3,336 % salary = 37% % mean y = NR *Incumbents* Mean = $3,307 % salary = 37% % mean y = NR *40% rule* Mean = $3,581
Mitchell, Eaton, & Wing (1985)	Collected ratings from cannon crewmen ($N = 35$) and motor transport operators ($N = 26$) job incumbents in the U.S. Army	(1) "Yearly value to the Army of the average entry-level soldier in their field" (also an 85th percentile performer) GLOBAL. (2) "Number of superior performers needed to obtain the output of 10 (cont. on next page)	See Payoff Scale section	*GLOBAL, Crewman* Mean = $6,000 SD = $10,000 (3rd – 1st quartile) SE = NR % salary = NR % mean y = 40%

APPENDIX B

Results of Studies Estimating SD_y Values (continued)

Reference	Setting	Utility Scale	Estimation Method	SD_y Values
Mitchell, Eaton, & Wing (1985) (continued)		average producers working for an equivalent amount of time" (EQV). (3) "Re-estimate dollar values for average and superior performers in light of dollar values cited for soldiers in other specialties" (FEEDBACK)		*FEEDBACK, Crewman* Mean = $4,000 SD = $0 (3rd – 1st quartile) SE = NR % salary = NR % mean y = 25% *EQV, Crewman* Mean = $9,600 SD = NR SE = NR % salary = NR % mean y = NR *GLOBAL, Transport* Mean = $7,000 SD = $7,000 (3rd – 1st quartile) SE = NR % salary = NR % mean y = 47% *FEEDBACK, Transport* Mean = $6,000 SD = $12,000 (3rd – 1st quartile) SE = NR % salary = NR % mean y = 40% *EQV, Transport* Mean = $10,000

APPENDIX B

Results of Studies Estimating SD_y Values (continued)

Reference	Setting	Utility Scale	Estimation Method	SD_y Values
Reilly & Smither (1985)	Graduate students ($N = 16$) with prior management experience played a computerized management simulation. They were provided sales data on 10 representatives, based on 3 job components.	Job performance was measured through 3 job components: (1) selling established products, (2) selling new products, (3) expense control. The first and third were reported in dollars, and the second could be computed in dollars using a formula. In addition, information on variable cost levels was provided.	Used CREPID to obtain ratings of performance dimensions that could be compared to actual performance. Used the Schmidt et al. method to obtain SD_y estimates of established product sales, new product sales, net sales less expenses, and value of "overall products and services produced."	*Simulated Repeat Sales* Mean = $1,093,641 SD = $170,119 *Simulated New Sales* Mean = $156,225 SD = $24,302 *Simulated Net Revenue* Mean = $175,600 SD = $43,639 *Schmidt et al. Repeat Sales* Mean = $178,725 SE = $13,651 SD = $54,604 % salary = 357% *Schmidt et al. New Sales* Mean = $29,477 SE = $3,374 SD = $13,496 % salary = 60% *Schmidt et al. Net Revenue* Mean = $119,605 SE = $57,773 SD = $231,092 % salary = 242% *Schmidt et al. Overall Worth* Mean = $83,994 SE = $25,247 SD = $100,988 % salary = 170% *CREPID $ Performance* Mean = $26,485 SE = $1,381 SD = $5,524 % salary = 54% % mean y = 49%

APPENDIX B

Results of Studies Estimating SD_y Values (continued)

Reference	Setting	Utility Scale	Estimation Method	SD_y Values
Weekley et al. (1985)	Supervisors of store managers ($N = 110$) provided global SD_y estimates as well as ratings for CREPID. Subjects worked for a convenience store chain. CREPID ratings were obtained for 805 store managers.	Global estimation was based on subjects' estimates of the "yearly value of the output produced" to the company. No reference to subcontracting was made.	Schmidt et al. (1979) estimation was used for the global method. Standard CREPID method was also used, and both were compared to 40% of salary.	*CREPID* Mean = $7,701 % salary = 36% *Schmidt et al.* Mean = $13,968 % salary = 66% % mean y = 51% *40% of Salary* Mean = $8,850
Burke & Frederick (1986)	Same as Burke & Frederick (1984)	Same as Burke & Frederick (1984)	Same as Burke & Frederick (1984), except that estimates were made that omitted the 97th percentile	*Standard (3 Point Estimate)* Mean = $35,192 *Proced. A (3 Point Estimate)* Mean = $27,500 *Proced. B (3 Point Estimate)* Mean = $28,151
Cascio & Ramos (1986)	Second-level managers provided CREPID ratings for 602 first-level managers in a telephone operating company.	Not reported, but assumed to be the standard CREPID notion of payoff to the organization, based on salary. These were combined with salary data to derive CREPID estimates and then were compared to 40% of salary.	Standard CREPID method, but the originally derived estimate of $10,081 was adjusted for restricted range because this sample of managers was composed of job incumbents, not applicants. The authors report (p. 28) that SD_y varied between 40% and 60% of annual wage across job classes.	*CREPID* Mean = $10,081 SE = NR SD = NR % salary = 35% % mean y = 34%
Cronshaw et al. (1987)	Clerical/administrative employees in the Canadian military	Similar to Schmidt et al. (1979)	40% of average salary	Mean = $10,680
DeSimone et al. (1986)	Surveyed supervisors ($N = 27$) of medical claim approvers in a large financial service company	Similar to Schmidt et al. (1979)	Similar to Schmidt et al. (1979)	Mean = $3,871 SD = $1,765 SE = $334 % salary = 25%

APPENDIX B

Results of Studies Estimating SD_y Values (continued)

Reference	Setting	Utility Scale	Estimation Method	SD_y Values
DeSimone et al. (1986) (continued)	Actual medical claims approver performance in a large financial services company	Payroll cost reductions that could be achieved by having fewer approvers process a similar number of claims per claim were $1.79.	Used 12 monthly averages of claims processed per day for 176 approvers. Mean was 47, SD was 11.54, extrapolated to yearly mean and SD of 11,139 and 2,735.	Mean y = $19,939 SD_y = $4,896 % Salary = 31%
Schmidt et al. (1986)	U.S. government employees across levels GS-1 to GS-18	Value of output as sold	40% of lowest 1984 salary level in each grade, averaged by weighting according to the number hired at each GS level	Mean = $5,429 SD = $2,251
Day & Edwards (1987)	Estimated utility for 43 account executives using ratings from 34 supervisors in a midwestern U.S. transportation company	Similar to Schmidt et al. (1979) (N = 17) supervisors	Same as Schmidt et al. (1979)	Mean = $161,471 SD = $252,639 SE = $61,274 % salary = 471% % mean y = 80%
		Similar to Schmidt et al. (1979)	Modified Schmidt et al. (1979) by omitting the instruction, "In placing an overall dollar value on this output, it may help to consider what the cost would be of having an outside firm provide these products and services" (N = 17 supervisors)	Mean = $180,382 SD = $248,153 SE = $60,186 % salary = 526% % mean y = 80%
		"Worth in dollars of an employee's overall job performance"	% ROI method: (1) calculated the "average annual investments" (sum of salary plus incentive pay plus benefits, plus 40% "overhead," which equaled $65,280 per position (2) Had N = 34 supervisors estimate the percent return on this investment (ROI) corresponding to each of the 7 performance appraisal scale points (3) Applied these figures to each account executive based on their actual appraisal	Mean y = $180,920 SD_y = $34,103 % salary = 99% % mean y = 19%
		Similar to Cascio (1982)	CREPID method as described in Cascio (1982)	Mean y = $45,320 SD_y = $13,392 % salary = 39% % mean y = 30%

APPENDIX B

Results of Studies Estimating SD_y Values (continued)

Reference	Setting	Utility Scale	Estimation Method	SD_y Values		
Day & Edwards (1987) (continued)		Similar to Schmidt et al. (1979)	40% of average salary	SD_y	=	$13,723
	Estimated utility for 107 mechanical foremen using ratings from 28 supervisors in a midwestern U.S. transportation company	Similar to Schmidt et al. (1979)	Same as Schmidt et al. (1979) (N = 13 supervisors)	Mean	=	$41,423
				SD	=	$38,698
				SE	=	$10,733
				% salary	=	129%
				% mean y	=	54%
		Similar to Schmidt et al. (1979)	Modified Schmidt et al. (1979) (N = 15 supervisors)	Mean	=	$134,335
				SD	=	$258,618
				SE	=	$66,775
				% salary	=	417%
				% mean y	=	65% –
		"Worth in dollars of an employee's overall job performance"	% ROI	Mean y	=	$95,744
				SD_y	=	$14,440
				% salary	=	45%
				% mean y	=	15%
		Same as Cascio (1982)	CREPID	Mean y	=	$43,237
				SD_y	=	$11,988
				% salary	=	37%
				% mean y	=	28%
		Same as Schmidt et al. (1979)	40% of salary	SD_y	=	$12,881
Greer & Cascio (1987)	Estimated the performance value of route salesmen (N = 62) for a midwestern U.S. soft drink company	Value of output as sold, similar to Schmidt et al. (1979)	Global estimation model using the questionnaire-based procedure of Schmidt et al. (1979), completed by supervisors (N = 29)	Mean y	=	$31,979
				SD_y	=	$14,636
				% salary	=	55%
				% mean y	=	46%
		"Contribution of labor"	CREPID method (Cascio & Ramos, 1986)	Mean y	=	$38,435
				SD_y	=	$8,988
				% salary	=	34%
				% mean y	=	23%

APPENDIX B

Results of Studies Estimating SD_y Values (continued)

Reference	Setting	Utility Scale	Estimation Method	SD_y Values
Greer & Cascio (1087) (continued)		"Contribution margin of salesmen" defined as revenue less variable costs	"Cost-accounting" method that calculated the revenue less cost per unit sold, and multiplied by the quantity of units sold by each salesman	Mean y = $44,985 SD_y = $15,864 % salary = 60% % mean y = 35%
Mathieu & Leonard (1987)	Supervisors of bank employees (head tellers, operations managers, and branch managers) responded to a questionnaire similar to that used by Schmidt et al. (1979)	Similar to Schmidt et al. (1979)	The original distribution of SD_y estimates was examined for nonnormality, which was assumed to result from "systematic error." The 50–15 SD_y estimates (SD_y 1) differed from normal for branch managers and operations managers and marginally for head tellers. The 85–50 distribution (SD_y 2) differed from normality for operations managers. So the authors trimmed a number of "outliers" from each distribution, which normalized them. The average SD_y was used.	*Head Tellers, Trimmed* Mean = $2,369 SD = NR SE = NR % salary = 19% % mean y = NR *Operations Mgr., Trimmed* Mean = $3,123 SD = NR SE = NR % salary = 17% % mean y = NR *Branch Manager, Trimmed* Mean = $10,064 SD = NR SE = NR % salary = 44% % mean y = NR *Head Teller, Untrim* Median = $2,150 % salary = 17% *Operations Manager, Untrim* Median = $3,250 % salary = 18% *Branch Manager, Untrim* Median = $10,000 % salary = 44%

APPENDIX B

Results of Studies Estimating SD_y Values (continued)

Reference	Setting	Utility Scale	Estimation Method	SD_y Values		
Rich & Boudreau (1987)	Supervisors of computer programmers ($N = 29$) in a computer manufacturing organization estimated the value of performance for computer programmers.	Similar to Schmidt et al. (1979)	Gathered estimates of the 15th, 50th, and 85th percentiles and used the average difference as SD_y	Mean SD SE % salary % mean y	= = = = =	$15,888 $14,617 $2,761 60% 47%
Edwards et al. (1988)	Directors of sales, regional managers, and field personnel managers ($N = 33$) in a national manufacturing company estimated performance value for the job of district sales managers.	See description for Burke & Frederick (1984), Procedure B.	Burke & Frederick (1984), Procedure B	Mean SD SE % salary % mean y	= = = = =	$63,326 $16,177 $2,816 174% 72%
			CREPID-O, followed CREPID using job components from Burke & Frederick (1984), applied to 33 district sales managers	Mean y SD_y % salary % mean y	= = = =	$42,002 $12,170 33% 29%
			CREPID-AP, followed CREPID using job components from Burke & Frederick (1984), applied to 33 district sales managers, but used archival job analysis data on performance	Mean y SD_y % salary % mean y	= = = =	$33,475 $11,342 31% 34%
			CREPID-AJ, followed CREPID using job components from Burke & Frederick (1984), applied to 33 district sales managers, but used archival job analysis data on activity frequency and importance	Mean y SD_y % salary % mean y	= = = =	$42,318 $11,160 31% 26%
			CREPID-AA, followed CREPID using job components from Burke & Frederick (1984), applied to 33 district sales managers, but used archival data on performance and job analysis	Mean y SD_y % salary % mean y	= = = =	$38,293 $7,890 22% 21%

Attributes of Individuals in Organizations

Industrial and organizational psychology grew out of psychology's early success in measuring differences between people. Large numbers of academic psychologists were first thrust into the "real world" in response to this country's need for rapid mobilization and utilization of human resources during the first World War. I noted earlier in Volume 1 of this *Handbook* (Dunnette, 1990) that times of national challenge have almost always been accompanied by applied psychology's most significant advances. Among examples of such advances are the great expansion of psychological testing during World War I, the flowering of vocational guidance and employment counseling during the years of the Great Depression, the development of psychomotor and physical ability measures and multiple assessment procedures during and immediately after World War II, and advances in concepts, methods, and ways of thinking about personnel selection theory in response to civil rights legislation and court decisions during the 1960s, 1970s, and 1980s.

Such advances have as a common theme the fact that persons differ from each other, in reasonably stable ways, on some finite number of attributes. Moreover, particular patterns of individual attributes are more or less suited to particular patterns of job requirements. The idea that reasoned or rationally determined person job assignments yield more productive outcomes than random assignments is fundamental to practices of vocational guidance, counseling, and personnel selection and placement. Measurement of human attributes is the first step in programs having anything to do with human resources utilization.

The following three chapters give systematic attention to what is currently known about three of the primary groupings of measurable human attributes relevant to what people can and will do in work settings.

J. Hogan in Chapter 11 [Physical Abilities] draws on knowledge from many disciplines—differential psychology, industrial engineering, biomechanics, work physiology, and case law—to describe and evaluate methods, research, and strategies for implementing physical ability tests in personnel selection programs. She identifies and discusses critical factors such as work load, adequacy of training, physiology, and nature of injury information that are fundamental considerations in designing and evaluating selection systems for physically demanding jobs. Central to these factors in the design and evaluation of such systems are the physical ability content of job analyses, job criteria, and physical testing practices. She summarizes legislative and case law doctrine and its implications for physical ability assessment in relation to the employment of women, handicapped persons, and older workers. J. Hogan also has provided an exceptionally useful and interesting account of the history of physical ability testing from the early years of this century to the present. Finally, she discusses fundamental issues related to problems of employment discrimination and outlines future concerns bearing on the need for continued methodological and empirical advances in knowledge about physical abilities and workplace requirements.

R. V. Dawis in Chapter 12 [Vocational Interests, Values, and Preferences] defines interests, values, and preferences as consisting of the distillation of the affective evaluations of countless life experiences to form stable human dispositions. Dawis summarizes evidence demonstrating that these dispositions have been shown empirically to be reasonably powerful predictors of occupational persistence and/or change, job and career satisfaction, and performance effectiveness (though secondary to abilities). The chapter presents a brief historical account, highlighting milestones in the development of interests, values, and preferences measures. Dawis also provides a comprehensive review of research results that pinpoint similarities and differences between various instruments driven initially by contrasting conceptualizations, using different methods of item development, and employing a variety of criteria for validating and elaborating on the constructs being measured. The chapter is especially valuable in that it provides a succinct summary of what is known about major findings from a vast literature that contains many small and poorly integrated studies. Accordingly, this chapter contains much that will be of immediate use to vocational psychologists in their work with counselees or to industrial and organizational psychologists in their work on matters of job placement, job satisfaction, and job and organizational commitment. In concluding this chapter, Dawis comments that if people do indeed "make the place," as has been suggested by Schneider (1987), then measures of individuals' vocational interests, values, and preferences can contribute substantially to a better understanding of work motivation and work performance.

R. Hogan in Chapter 13 [Personality and Personality Measurement] argues that recent developments in personality measurement and in understanding the applied usefulness of personality constructs have been impressive. He hastens to add that such advances were blocked for some time due to the influence of a behaviorist perspective of personality psychology. This perspective had been eloquently presented by Mischel (1968), which held that differences in behavior resided primarily in differential patterns of *situational* stimuli, which in turn evoked differential human responses. Hogan states that significant advances in personality measurement for applied purposes were dependent on the successful repudiation of the situationist perspective; repudiation of this perspective occurred slowly, fueled at first by Bowers (1973), Hogan, De Soto, and Solano (1975), then by Epstein and his colleagues (see references for Chapter 13), and was finally laid to rest permanently by the review of research and theory published in 1985 (Epstein & O'Brien, 1985).

Hogan defines personality as referring both to a person's social reputation and to his or her inner nature. He presents a historical perspective and a review of how personality concepts and measurement evolved since the time of Allport and Odbert's (1936) seminal taxonomic effort that eventuated in their trait lexicon. The bulk of Chapter 13 is then devoted to a summary of positive results, most of which has been accumulated recently (during the years since 1980) demonstrating the usefulness of personality theory and personality measurement for purposes of personnel selection. Hogan emphasizes that the field of industrial and organizational psychology has come only recently to be more conversant with and more accepting of personality measures as comprising potentially useful predictors of job performance, though Ghiselli's (1966) work was an early precursor of such findings for a subset of occupations. Hogan's evidence is convincing in showing that substantial progress has, in fact, been made in developing and understanding such measures. He predicts that a rapid expansion in the use of personality assessment instruments is in the offing.

Two additional chapters describing the measurement of human attributes are included in the forthcoming Volume 3 of the *Handbook of Industrial and Organizational Psychology*. Chapter 1 of Volume 3 [Aptitudes, Skills, and Proficiencies] by D. Lubinski and R. Dawis presents what is known about the measurement of human cognitive abilities as determinants of work behavior. Central to the authors' treatment of cognitive abilities is the criterion of scientific significance. Lubinski and Dawis accept the robustness of general intelligence while also arguing —convincingly—that multiple ability dimensions are worthy of continued attention, especially in the context of increased research attention being given to multiple measures in assessing performance.

M. D. Mumford and G. S. Stokes in Chapter 2 of Volume 3 describe theory and practice in the development and application of background information as a basis for measuring individual attributes. They point out that patterns of individuals' past behaviors as reflected in biodata measures may be interpreted according to empirically based predictions of future behavioral outcomes.

These five chapters—the three in this volume and the first two in Volume 3—describe the many measures that may be used to aid both individuals and institutions in making more informed and more accurate job or career decisions and institutional selection or placement decisions. Information about these individual attributes is also of critical importance to organizations as they undertake any of a number of other human resources programs for the purpose of enhancing the quality of their human capital investments. Such programs will typically include job redesign, changes driven by human factors protocols, changing organizational structures, designing or modifying training programs, or any number of other changes designed to enhance organizational effectiveness.

Changes such as these can be made even more effective by taking account of the status of employees on the measures of individual attributes that are described in these chapters.

–Marvin D. Dunnette

References

Allport, G. W., & Odbert, H. S. (1936). Trait-names: A psycholexical study. *Psychological Monographs, 47*, 171–220 (1, Whole No. 211).

Bowers, K. S. (1973). Situationism in psychology: An analysis and a critique. *Psychological Review, 80*, 307–336.

Campbell, J. P. (1990). Modeling the performance prediction problem in industrial and organizational psychology. In M. D. Dunnette & L. M. Hough (Eds.), *Handbook of industrial and organizational psychology* (2nd ed., vol. 1, pp. 687–732). Palo Alto, CA: Consulting Psychologists Press.

Dunnette, M. D. (1990). Blending the science and practice of industrial and organizational psychology: Where are we and where are we going? In M. D. Dunnette & L. M. Hough (Eds.), *Handbook of industrial and organizational psychology* (2nd ed., vol. 1). Palo Alto, CA: Consulting Psychologists Press.

Epstein, S., & O'Brien, E. J. (1985). The person-situation debate in historical and current perspective. *Psychological Bulletin, 98*, 513–537.

Ghiselli, E. E. (1966). *The validity of occupational aptitude tests*. New York: Wiley.

Hogan, R., De Soto, C. B., & Solano, C. (1975). Traits, tests, and personality research. *American Psychologist, 6*, 255–264.

Mischel, W. (1968). *Personality and assessment*. New York: Wiley.

Schneider, B. (1987). The people make the place. *Personnel Psychology, 40*, 437–454.

CHAPTER 11

Physical Abilities

Joyce C. Hogan
University of Tulsa

Industrial psychologists bear the professional responsibility to develop, monitor, and evaluate research leading to the implementation of physical ability tests for personnel selection. This responsibility is a recent one and to fulfill it requires interdisciplinary knowledge beyond the standard psychological principles for selection. It requires knowledge from a variety of fields—individual differences psychology, work physiology, industrial engineering, biomechanics, and law. This chapter identifies factors that affect the ability to perform in the workplace including physiological responses, training, ability and injury, and work load. The chapter also reviews procedures and methods for designing personnel selection systems for physically demanding jobs and emphasizes the unique physical ability content of job analyses, criteria, and tests. In addition, the chapter summarizes legislative decisions designed to protect women, handicapped persons, and older workers in light of their implications for physical ability assessments by employers. Finally, the chapter argues that the need to improve development and implementation of fair physical ability selection procedures and the need to understand the relationship between physical performance and other organizational effectiveness outcomes are important issues for future research.

Introduction

HISTORICALLY, THE MEASUREMENT of individual differences in physical abilities parallels the development of other human attribute assessments. World Wars I and II created a manpower requirement for soldiers who could perform successfully under combat conditions and underscored the importance of reliable and valid physical measurements. Shockingly low levels of physical capability heightened interest in both selection and training for combat performance. In part, measures used to evaluate fitness for military duty form the basis for today's assessments, and in some cases they have not changed dramatically. Public interest in physical ability surged again in response to national preparedness implications of the Soviet Union's 1957 Sputnik launches. International comparisons showed the fitness levels of American youth to be substantially below those of foreign peers. There followed a program of national physical ability assessment that goes on today under the auspices of the president of the United States.

More recently, the response to the requirement for equal opportunities in employment has introduced new interest in demographic differences and physical abilities. Although there may be gender and race differences in some physical abilities, these differences do not provide a rational basis for excluding entire classes of individuals from employment in physically demanding jobs. Yet prior to the 1972 amendment of the Civil Rights Act of 1964, class exclusions were common among American industries as well as federal, state, and local governments. The Equal Employment Opportunity Commission's (EEOC) enforcement of Title VII of the Civil Rights Act sent a message to employers that presumptive exclusion of individual classes from employment in any job, including jobs with physical demands, is prohibited. The lesson for employers who have physically demanding jobs to fill is to assess each person appropriately for the job using standardized and valid measures.

What, then, is the domain of physical abilities that persists over time and across work requirements? Distinguishing concepts that are clearly outside the domain of physical abilities from those that are within it is a good place to start. Physical abilities do not include body size, physical attractiveness, psychophysical perceptions of body structure, physiognomy, body image, or somatotype (Sheldon, 1940). Physical abilities are concerned with maximum gross muscular performances as objectively measured. Fleishman (1964, p. 12) defines abilities as relatively "enduring traits" that are unlikely to change once the individual reaches adulthood. This may be less true of physical abilities than cognitive abilities. It is clear that some parameters of abilities are biologically determined and, therefore, will not markedly change. However, physical performances are highly susceptible to training, although the degree of improvement may ultimately depend on basic ability. Physical abilities might be best understood using Cronbach's (1970, p. 35) distinction between maximum performance and typical performance. He suggests that aptitudes, skills, and abilities fall in the category of *maximum performance* because we measure these to assess an individual's best effort. In contrast, *typical performance* refers to measures that reflect the average response. Dunnette (1976, p. 475) concludes that aptitudes, abilities, and skills are not mutually exclusive; thus, attempts at precise definitions have not been overwhelmingly successful. He goes on to suggest that the subtle differences between them are less important than the fact that they all lie within the domain of maximum performance.

The fundamental question concerns how many and what kinds of abilities are necessary for an adequate taxonomy of physical performance. As an outgrowth of his work on human perceptual–motor abilities, skill learning, and test development, Fleishman (1964) conducted the first systematic research to provide an answer. This pioneering effort identified nine basic physical abilities.[*] We currently believe that these nine, in addition to some psychomotor factors, form three classes of physical abilities important for understanding occupational performance: (a) muscular strength, (b) cardiovascular endurance, and (c) factors affecting movement quality. The abilities that fall into the movement quality class tend to blur the distinction between physical and psychomotor abilities because they involve coordinated muscular responses. Such constructs as neuromuscular coordination, joint flexibility, and static and dynamic balance are fundamental for performance in both domains. Although definitional lines are not as vivid as they might be, they will become clearer in subsequent discussion of physiology and work performance. Nevertheless, it should be noted that only a few taxonomic efforts have been undertaken in this area since Fleishman's original work, and their contributions are in refining the definitions and conceptualizing more parsimoniously the structure of physical abilities.

---

[*] Fleishman (1972) identifies the factors as follows: (a) static strength: maximum force that can be exerted against external objects (e.g., lifting weights or dynamometer tests); (b) dynamic strength: muscular endurance in exerting force continuously or repeatedly; power of the muscles to propel, support, or move one's body over time (e.g., pull-ups); (c) explosive strength: ability to mobilize energy effectively for bursts of muscular effort (e.g., sprints or jumps); (d) trunk strength: limited dynamic strength specific to trunk muscles (e.g., leg lifts or sit-ups); (e) extent flexibility: ability to flex or stretch trunk and back muscles (e.g., twist and touch test); (f) dynamic flexibility: ability to make repeated, rapid, flexing trunk movements; resistance of muscles in recovery from strain (e.g., rapid repeated bending over and floor touching test); (g) gross body coordination: ability to coordinate the movement of the arms, legs, and torso together in activities where the whole body is in motion (e.g., cable jump); (h) gross body equilibrium: ability to maintain balance with nonvisual cues (e.g., rail walk test); (i) stamina: capacity to sustain maximum effort requiring cardiovascular exertion (e.g., 600-yard run-walk).

Historical Perspective

We have no formal history from which current efforts in physical abilities research evolved. Like the field of industrial psychology, roots can be traced to aspects of industrial engineering, applied psychology, and individual differences measurement. The common theme among these otherwise diverse fields is that of measurement, and this influence is discussed historically from the perspective of each contributing field.

Industrial Engineering

In the summer of 1910, the Interstate Commerce Commission received a petition from northeastern United States railroads calling for increases in freight rates. Hearings were held to present the issues, and vehement debates between shippers and railroad management ensued. The railroad managers argued that rate increases were essential to cover wage increments; shippers argued that greater efficiency in the workplace could prevent such hikes. Louis D. Brandeis, unpaid counsel for the shippers and later U.S. Supreme Court justice, introduced a group of engineers and industrial managers who testified that railroads could reduce costs and increase wages simultaneously if they adopted the practice of *scientific management*. The press popularized the idea as the panacea for problems in industry and commerce. In January 1912, Frederick W. Taylor, author of the scientific management philosophy (Taylor, 1923), testified before the Special Investigating Committee of the House of Representatives to explain the theory and application of his scientific management principles (see Copley, 1923, for annotation and discussion of Taylor's testimony). Taylor achieved immediate national recognition for his methods which during the preceding thirty years had remained unnoticed by the scientific community.

The methodology of choice for Taylor's scientific management was *time study*. In 1881, Taylor introduced these procedures to the Midvale Steel Company, and the methodology remains a major tool for practicing industrial engineers. Taylor's first investigations sought to define what constituted a day's work for a "first class man." Taylor (1923) summarized his inquiry as follows:

> Our first step was to employ a young college graduate to look up all that had been written on the subject in English, German, and French. Two classes of experiments had been made: one by physiologists who were studying the endurance of the human animal, and the other by engineers who wished to determine what fraction of a horse-power a manpower was. These experiments had been made largely upon men who were lifting loads by means of turning the crank of a winch from which weights were suspended, and others who were engaged in walking, running, and lifting weights in various ways. However, the records of these investigations were so meager that no law of any value could be deduced from them. We therefore started a series of experiments of our own. (p. 54)

In a series of investigations, Taylor used the time study method to answer his question and to determine a lawful relationship between work and rest. He designed experiments to time each element of motion required to perform a task. Using a stopwatch to evaluate motions made by various known "first-class workers," he translated the work accomplished into foot-pounds or fractions of horsepower. Although a large amount of time study data accumulated, Taylor could find no consistent relationship between horsepower exerted and daily fatigue. Reanalyzing the data so that each measured time element was graphically displayed, Taylor (1923) discovered a relationship between time spent under load and time spent at rest:

> And the law is that for each given pull or push on the man's arms it is possible for the workman to be under load for only a definite percentage of the day. For example, when pig iron is being handled (each pig weighing 92 pounds), a first-class workman can only be under load 43 per cent of the day, and as the load becomes lighter, the percentage of the day under which the man can remain under load increases. So that if the workman is handling a half-pig, weighing 46 pounds, he can then be under load 58 percent. As the weight grows lighter the man can remain under load during a larger and larger percentage of the day, until finally a load is reached which he can carry in his hands all day long without being tired out. When that point has been arrived at this law ceases to be useful as a guide to a laborer's endurance, and some other law must be found which indicates the man's capacity for work.

> When a laborer is carrying a piece of pig iron weighing 92 pounds in his hands, it tires him about as much to stand still under the load as it does to walk with it, since his arm muscles are under the same severe tension whether he is moving or not. A man, however, who stands still under a load is exerting no horse-power whatever, and this accounts for the fact that no constant relation could be traced in various kinds of heavy laboring work between the foot-pounds of energy exerted and the tiring effect of the work on the man. It will also be clear that in all work of this kind it is necessary for the arms of the workman to be completely free from load (that is, for the workman to rest) at frequent intervals. Throughout the time that the man is under a heavy load the tissues of his arm muscles are in process of degeneration, and frequent periods of rest are required in order that

the blood may have a chance to restore these tissues to their normal condition. (pp. 57–58)

Although the overriding contribution of Taylor's work was his scientific method and its introduction into every facet of work performance, time study is the fundamental element of his theory and one still used today, particularly in relation to establishing performance standards. Taylor's method required exact information regarding time to perform each of the smallest task elements, identification of the quickest and most efficient motions to complete the operation, and computation of actual rest each kind of work necessitated. The standard, best method of performance was created from integrating the information. Once standard performance times (and elements) were established, they became the basis for worker training, performance measurement, incentives, and compensation.

Taylor's philosophy was not without its critics (cf. Hoxie, 1915); however his influence on work performance measurement has transcended many of these skeptics. For example, consider the joint automobile manufacturing venture of Toyota and General Motors, New United Motors Manufacturing, Inc. (NUMMI), which is the model for the American auto industry. Parker and Slaughter (1988) describe the production philosophy as intensifying Taylorism by specifying every move a worker makes in greater detail than ever before. Fortunately, Taylor was not alone in his pursuit of worker proficiency. Frank and Lillian Gilbreth confronted the same problems, but instead applied the tools of *motion study*.

Motion study developed under industrial conditions similar to those that led Taylor to develop and use time study. In 1885, Frank Gilbreth entered the building contracting business employed as a bricklayer. There was no standard method for doing the job; workers each used their own technique for laying bricks, and these techniques changed as the work pace

changed. Convinced that there must be a best method for performing the tasks, Gilbreth noted that the number and type of motions used by the workers were associated with their output. His ideas for analyzing the movements of workers were quite successful, and eventually Gilbreth gave up his contracting business to pursue the development and application of motion study.

Gilbreth defined motion study as "the science of eliminating wastefulness from using unnecessary, ill-directed, and inefficient motions" (Spriegel & Myers, 1953, p. 74). The first stage of motion study involved identifying the best work practice. As reported by Spriegel and Myers (1953, p. 152), Gilbreth used six steps for this analysis:

1. Reduce *present* practice to writing.
2. Enumerate motions used.
3. Enumerate variables that affect each motion.
4. Reduce *best* practice to writing.
5. Enumerate motions used.
6. Enumerate variables that affect each motion.

Gilbreth listed three categories of variables that affect worker output, each considered in turn for its relevance. For example, when evaluating the "weight of the unit moved," one must consider (a) weight of the body part moved, (b) weight of the tool used, and (c) weight of the material used. Gilbreth's principle here was that, other things being equal, the less body movement, the less fatigue. In his classic study of bricklaying (Gilbreth, 1909), Gilbreth applied motion study to achieve astonishing gains in productivity and efficiency. These gains were due to the introduction of a new scaffold that could be easily raised to convenient working level and held bricks and mortar at a height that eliminated stooping. He also devised wooden frames to hold bricks prearranged so that the bricklayer could work with both hands simultaneously. Improving the consistency of mortar eliminated the necessity of tapping down each brick after it was placed. Gilbreth (1911) reported that in using the "pick and dip" bricklaying method the number of motions required to lay a single brick was reduced from 18 to $4^1/_2$. Figure 1 shows Gilbreth's analysis. As Konz (1983) pointed out, Gilbreth's method represented the first real advance in 3,000 years of bricklaying.

Gilbreth was philosophically committed to the principles of scientific management and regarded his work in motion study as consistent with Taylor's position. Gilbreth also made use of time study in his own work, which became fundamental to the methodological development of motion study. Gilbreth and his wife Lillian, a psychologist, made their greatest contribution to motion study through use of photography. In Gilbreth's early studies of bricklaying, he used photographs of individual workers in various steps of the task. However, this documentation had only limited value for understanding and evaluating the path and length of motions. Time measurements without a visual record of movements were deficient in information as well as measurement accuracy. The Gilbreths' use of the motion picture camera in conjunction with a speed clock was the technique that solved this problem. It was this invention, the microchronometer, that laid the foundation for *micromotion*, or motion study.

Gilbreth (1912) explained the concept of micromotion at a meeting of the American Society of Mechanical Engineers as the study of fundamental elements of an operation using a motion picture camera and a timing device. Although this initial methodology provided intermittent records of movement paths, lengths, directions, speeds, and time, it was still difficult to measure exact path and length of motions and to recapture all the motions of a movement cycle. The Gilbreths developed a series of instruments and procedures to counter these limitations. The *cyclegraph* method of capturing motions with photography made use of a small electric light attached to moving body parts. Although this two-dimensional record provided accurate data, the *stereocyclegraph* showed motion in three dimensions—length, breadth, and depth. This procedure excluded the time element; however, when an interrupter was placed in the electric circuit with the bulb, the flashing light produced a time line in the photographic record. The final instrument, the *stereochronocyclegraph*, showed three-dimensional direction of motion by manipulation of volts, amperes, and the filament in the light source. Gilbreth then used the data to construct wire models of the motion paths for instruction and demonstration as an aid to employee performance.

The principles of time and motion study largely remain unchanged since their original development by Taylor and Gilbreth. Today's practicing industrial engineers receive training in time and motion methods, and Taylor and Gilbreth's procedures form the basis of task analysis and personnel training for jobs that require skilled motor performance. In addition, substantial research and application has led to the successful adoption of industrial performance standards. Using time and motion analyses, standard performance times are adopted for performance of tasks within a system. Although performance standards serve many purposes, including performance appraisal, the standards provide an answer to the original and fundamental question of what constitutes a day's work.

Applied Scientific Psychology

Over a century ago, Francis Galton, keenly interested in measurement and the development of statistical procedures, established an anthropometric laboratory at the International Health Exhibition in South Kensington, London. After the exhibition's closing, Galton developed another laboratory in the Science Galleries of the South Kensington Museum, now the Victoria and Albert Museum. The purpose of the laboratories was, in part, "for anthropometric experiment and research, and for obtaining data for statistical discussion" (Pearson, 1924, p. 358). The overriding purpose of Galton's work during this time grew out of a concern for the properties of measurement and only secondarily was it directed toward the study of physical characteristics. Obviously, the measurement of characteristics possessed by all people using easily administered procedures yielded large data sets. Johnson et al. (1985) reported that approximately 17,000 individuals were assessed in the anthropometric laboratories during the 1880s and 1890s. Galton's assessments led to the introduction of the science of *psychometrics,* which was later extended by Galton's followers, Karl Pearson and Charles Spearman.

Galton collected data on two classes of measures. The first class was physical measures of body dimensions, including length of head, breadth of head, height, weight, sitting height, height of knee, arm span, length of lower arm, and length of middle finger. Beyond these physical characteristics, however, he searched for ways to investigate psychological differences between individuals and included a second class of measures that could be described as behavioral. Sensory measures included visual acuity or keenness, auditory acuity, and auditory upper threshold. Performance measures such as grip strength, speed of blow (revised from a push to a pull motion), and breathing or vital capacity were assessed using the dynamometer and spirometer or laboratory devices designed by Galton (Galton, 1885). In addition, he included measures of simple reaction time which, according to Jenson (1980), he believed might be associated with intelligence. Figure 2 presents a typical data sheet from the Galton laboratory that summarizes measures from James McKeen Cattell, the American psychologist who attempted to extend Galton's notion that measures of motor performance could be used to reflect mental abilities.

Several interesting psychometric findings appear in analyses of Galton's data. Both Macey,

Plomin, and McClearn (1979) and Johnson et al. (1985) report test-retest reliabilities to be generally high. The exceptions appear to be greatest with the reaction time measures and speed of blow. Johnson et al. (1985) report intercorrelations and found a general and significant relationship between the performance measures and all others in the matrix, with the best pattern of association achieved using breathing capacity and grip strength. They further suggest that although Galton's data bank was not maintained over the years, it still provides valuable individual differences data that are simply unavailable elsewhere.

Heavily influenced by Galton's work and referring to him as "the greatest man I have ever known," Cattell visited the International Health Exhibition at the South Kensington Museum in October of 1884. Cattell's initial interests were in Galton's research methods investigating psychological individual differences. Cattell's experimental techniques consisted of those developed at G. Stanley Hall's psychological laboratory at Johns Hopkins University and those he developed while studying with Wilhelm Wundt at the University of Leipzig. Interestingly, historians believe that his ideas about the mind led him to Wundt's laboratory and to what became known as *differential psychology* (Boring, 1950).

Galton encouraged Cattell to develop his interest in individual differences through the framework of physical and physiological anthropometry (Sokal, 1981, p. 223); however, this interest was actively discouraged in Wundt's laboratory. By 1890, Cattell began writing about physical anthropometry and mental tests. Collection of test statistics was encouraged by both the American Psychological Association (APA) and the American Association for the Advancement of Science (Cattell & Farrand, 1896), which led Cattell to establish an ambitious testing program first at the University of Pennsylvania and later at Columbia College's School of Arts and School of Mines.

FIGURE 1

Gilbreth's Pick and Dip Method for Bricklaying: An Analysis

Operation Number	Wrong Way Motions per Brick $^1/_4$ $^1/_2$ $^3/_4$ $^4/_4$	Right Way Motions per Brick $^1/_4$ $^1/_2$ $^3/_4$ $^4/_4$	Pick and Dip Method. The Exterior 4 Inches (Laying to the Line)
1	Step for Mortar	Omit	On the scaffold the inside edge of mortar box should be plumb with inside edge of stock platform. On floor the inside edge of mortar box should be 21 inches from wall. Mortar boxes never over 4 feet apart.
2	Reaching for Mortar	$^4/_4$	Do not bend any more than absolutely necessary to reach mortar with a straight arm.
3	Working up Mortar	Omit	Provide mortar of right consistency. Examine sand screen and keep in repair so that no pebbles can get through. Keep tender on scaffold to temper up and keep mortar worked up right.
4	Step for Brick	Omit	If tubs are kept 4 feet apart no stepping for brick will be necessary on scaffold. On floor keep brick in a pile not nearer than 1 foot nor more than 4 feet 6 inches from wall.
5	Reach for Brick	Included in 2	Brick must be reached for at the same time that the mortar is reached for, and picked up at exactly the same time the mortar is picked up. If it is not picked up at the same time, allowance must be made for operation.
6	Pick up Right Brick	Omit	Train the leader of the tenders to vary the kind of brick used as much as possible to suit the conditions; that is, to bring the best brick when the men are working on the line.
7	Mortar Box to Wall	$^4/_4$	Carry stock from the staging to the wall in the straightest possible line and with an even speed, without pause or hitch. It is important to move the stock with an even speed and not by quick jerks.
8	Brick Pile to Wall	Included in 7	Brick must be carried from pile to wall at exactly same time as the mortar is carried to the wall, without pause or jerk.
9	Deposit Mortar on Wall	Included in 7	If a pause is made, this space must be filled out. If no pause is made it is included in No. 7.
10	Spreading Mortar	Omit	The mortar must be thrown so as to require no additional spreading and so that the mortar runs up on the end of the previous brick laid, or else the next two spaces must be filled out.

FIGURE 1

Gilbreth's Pick and Dip Method for Bricklaying: An Analysis (continued)

Operation Number	Wrong Way	Right Way	Pick and Dip Method. *The Exterior 4 Inches (Laying to the Line)*
	Motions per Brick $^1/_4$ $^1/_2$ $^3/_4$ $^4/_4$	*Motions per Brick* $^1/_4$ $^1/_2$ $^3/_4$ $^4/_4$	
11	Cutting off Mortar	Omit	If the mortar is thrown from the trowel properly no spreading and no cutting is necesary.
12	Disposing of Mortar	Omit	If mortar is not cut off, this space is not filled out. If mortar is cut off keep it on trowel and carry back on trowel to box, or else butter on end of brick. Do not throw it on mortar box.
13	Laying Brick on Mortar	$^4/_4$	Fill out this space if brick is held still while mortar is thrown on wall. When brick is laid on mortar it presses mortar out of joints; cut this off only at every second brick. It takes no longer to cut mortar off two bricks than one.
14	Cutting off Mortar	Every $^1/_2$ 2nd brick	
15	Disposing of Mortar	Butter $^4/_4$ End Joint	When this mortar is cut off it can be used to butter that end of the last previous brick laid or it can be carried on the trowel back to the box.
16	Tapping Down Brick	Omit	If the mortar is the right consistency, with no lumps in it, and the right amount is used, the bricks are wet as possible without having them run, no tapping with the trowel will be necessary.
17	Cutting off Mortar	Omit	If the brick must be tapped, hit it once hard enough to hammer it down where it belongs. Do not hit the brick several light taps when one hard tap will do.
18	Disposing of Mortar	Omit	Do not cut off the mortar oftener than every second brick, and when you do cut it off do not let fall to the ground; save it; keep it on the trowel, and do not make another motion by throwing it at the box. Carrying it to the box does not count another motion.
	18	$4^1/_2$	Total number of motions per brick.

From Spriegel & Myers, 1953, pp. 56–57. Originally published in 1909 by Myron C. Clark Publishing.

FIGURE 2

Cattell's Record at Galton's Anthropometric Laboratory

Date of Measurement.	Initials.	Birthday. Day. Month.	Eye Color.	Sex.	Single, Married, or Widowed ?	Page of Register.
11 Augst 88	J McK	25 · 5 · 60	Grey	M	Single	626

Head length, maximum from root of nose.	Head breadth maximum.	Height standing, less heels of shoes.	Span of arms from opposite finger tips.	Weight in ordinary clothing.	Strength of squeeze. Right hand. / Left hand.	Breathing capacity.	Keenness of Eyesight. Distance of reading diamond numerals. Right eye. Left eye. / Snellen's type read at 20 feet.		Color Sense.
Inch. Tenths.	Inch. Tenths.	Inch. Tenths.	Inch. Tenths.	lbs.	lbs. / lbs.	Cubic inches.	Inches.	Inches. / No. of Type	? Normal.
7 7	5 8½	66 · 7	68 · 9	144	89 / 82	238	16	12 D18	Yes

Height sitting above seat of chair.	Height of top of knee, when sitting, less heels.	Length of elbow to finger tip left arm.	Length of middle finger of left hand.	Keenness of hearing.	Highest audible note.	Reaction time. To sight. / To sound.		Judgment of Eye. Error in dividing a line of 10 inches in half / in thrds	Error in degrees, estimating an angle of	
Inch. Tenths.	Inch. Tenths.	Inch. Tenths.	Inch. Tenths.	? Normal.	Vibrations per second.	Hundredths of a second.	Hundredths of a second.	Per cent. / Per cent.	90°	60°
34 8	21 1	17 · 7	4 · 3	Yes	19,000	30	20	0 3	1	10

Note: Figure reproduced from Cattell papers, Library of Congress

He assembled a one-hour test battery that included physical characteristics, hearing, dermal and muscular sensations, reaction time, space and time perception, memory, afterimages and imagery, and background information—perhaps the first use of biodata in the United States. Physical performance measures of breathing capacity were evaluated using a fluid spirometer, reaction time was measured using a .01 second chronoscope, and hand strength was measured using a dynamometer. An additional test of movement and fatigue was planned for future testing, which would use ergographic instrumentation described first by the Italian physiologist Angelo Mosso (1883). Cattell also proposed plans for "validating" these tests using performance in college courses and criteria regarding class standing (Cattell & Farrand, 1896).

Cattell firmly believed that no problem was more important than the study of human development. His quest, much like Galton's, concerned the demonstration that assessment of individual traits could serve educational and vocational purposes. If differences among individuals could be demonstrated and if these differences were important, then the source of such variation in differences would be an important topic. To the degree that performance differences could be attributed to acquired characteristics as opposed to inherited predispositions, managers could influence workers through training programs. Although it appears that his overall goal was to understand developmental influences of heredity and environment, the questions of immediate importance concerned interrelations between measured traits, prediction of one variable from knowledge of another, and the relationship between descriptive characteristics and higher intellectual performance. Cattell referenced arguments by Hugo Munsterburg and Alfred Binet who suggested that the tests be made strictly psychological, but he countered with the theory that the anthropometric and sensory measures were as important to the scope of his work as were measures of higher mental processes. The same criticism arose from within the APA's Committee on Physical and Mental Tests, as James Mark Baldwin urged that the tests take on a psychological character. Prior to this, however, there were no data to support the preference for anthropometric measures over mental process tests.

Two research investigations effectively ended both Cattell's testing program and his career as an experimental psychologist. In 1898, Stella Emily Sharp, a student under the direction of Edward Titchener, compared mental tests developed by Binet with Cattell's tests and argued that Cattell's tests were highly specific and useless in the study of mental traits (Sharp, 1898). One of Cattell's students, Clark Wissler (1901), applied Galton's correlation techniques to the results of Cattell's "physical and mental tests" and found no relationship between academic performance and test scores; moreover, performance in any one academic class predicted class standing better than any of the Cattell tests.

Experimental psychologists' interest in anthropometric and physical performance measures effectively ceased except for the use of such tests as reference or marker tests for the study of other phenomena. However, individual difference assessments in physical work performances and psychological fitness of soldiers were about to emerge as national research problems (Driskell & Olmstead, 1989).

Individual Differences

Anthropometric data collected on college students was not the unique domain of Cattell. Dudley Sargent, a physician who developed a system of physical measures and equipment, such as the chest expander, might be considered the father of modern strength testing. In 1880, Sargent was appointed director of the new Hemenway Gymnasium at Harvard with the responsibility for medical and physical examinations of entering freshman students. The health of university students during the nineteenth century was of heightened concern to

physicians and administrators because they believed students were subject to significant nervous strain as a result of college study. Sargent collected data consisting of anthropometric measures, strength tests, and personal histories. As the number of gymnasiums at colleges and universities grew prior to 1900, so did programs using measures and testing equipment similar to those developed by Sargent (Hartwell, 1885). Until 1908, 41 percent of university gymnasium directors held medical degrees, and their major responsibilities were student physical assessments and health instruction. However, the appearance of a study on medical education conducted for the Carnegie Foundation by Abraham Flexner led to the immediate upgrading of medical training and a decrease of medically trained physical education directors (Hackensmith, 1966, pp. 396–397).

When the United States entered World War I, the medical examiner's report indicated a need for physical training to improve the fitness of draftees between the ages of 21 and 35; consequently, the Commission on Training Camp Activities of the War Department was created to develop the physical capacities of recruits. Nevertheless, the postwar medical examiner's report indicated that of the 3 million men called to military service, one-third were physically unfit for duty. Moreover, in 1918, a government study of health conditions among industrial employees revealed that 270 million workdays were lost annually due to "loss of health and physical vigor" (Hackensmith, 1966, p. 412). The deplorable state of the nation's health led to legislation for health and physical education instruction in the public schools.

The 1920s brought about an interest in using tests and measurements for scientific and instructional applications. Following the lead of Thorndike, Terman, and others, David K. Brace (1927) developed a group of motor tests that would serve to measure, classify, and evaluate the motor ability of individuals. Frederick Rand Rogers, who proposed a physical fitness index, emphasized strength measurement and large muscle capacity. Tests and measurements were also influenced by Clifford Lee Brownell (1928), Harvey Lehman, and Paul Andrew Witty (1927), although Brace was actually the first to propose a scientific approach to assessment in the profession of physical education. Drawing on this foundation, the decade following 1930 produced an era of scientific investigation resulting in an extensive literature and new research tools.

The conceptual base for performance measurement that developed during this pre–World War II era underlies many measurement procedures used today. The objectives of most research efforts were directed toward improving assessment technology as well as the psychometric properties of the measures themselves. This research advanced due to recurring pressure associated with national defense. For example, Bucher (1968) cites health statistics from selective service for U.S. military recruits entering military duty during World War I, indicating that "...one third of our men were found physically unfit for armed service, and that many more were physically inept" (p. 347). Because of World War I experience with poor physical conditioning among recruits, the Navy and the Army Air Force set up physical training programs under Gene Tunney and Hank Greenburg, respectively. Again, selective service examinations indicated the need for formal programs to condition soldiers in the service of national defense, and as a result, agencies to carry out such an agenda were created. In 1942, the Office of Defense, Health, and Welfare Services developed a separate Division of Physical Fitness; a year later the Federal Security Agency established a committee on physical fitness with John B. Kelly as chairman. Kelly also served as President Roosevelt's National Director of Physical Training.

Also, consider World War II medical statistics indicating that 900,000 of 2 million volunteers for military service were rejected due to mental or physical defects. President Roosevelt responded by establishing a division of physical fitness within the Office of Defense, Health, and Welfare Services to promote physical fitness within all age groups. The lack of personnel readiness evident in two national emergencies signaled the need for more formalized physical conditioning programs for America's youth. Democratic nations' real and potential conflicts with communist countries heightened the U.S. concern for defense preparedness. Such articles as "Minimum Muscular Fitness Test in School Children" (Kraus & Hirschland, 1954) that found American youth physically deficient when compared to European children highlighted the inadequacies of American youth who potentially were the next generation of soldiers. It was this publication that attracted the attention of President Eisenhower, and at his request the President's Conference on Fitness of American Youth was convened in 1955, followed by an Executive Order to establish a President's Council on Youth Fitness—a program that continues today.

Public reactions to the military action in Korea, the national comparisons kindled by the Cold War, and the Soviet Union's *Sputnik* launches in 1957 culminated in the mobilization of education for national defense. Hans Kraus, who formulated six "minimum muscular fitness tests" (Kraus & Hirschland, 1953) to diagnose muscular fitness and low back pain, was appointed chair of a committee to develop a program of national fitness under Eisenhower. National fitness among schoolchildren was assessed in 1958 using measures still used today—American Association of Health, Physical Education, and Recreation (AAHPER) National Fitness Tests (Hunsicker, 1958). President Kennedy expanded this assessment program into a fitness development program administered under the auspices of the President's Council on Youth Fitness and the AAHPER. Much of the political concerns of the 1950s and 1960s about the country's ability to respond to a national crisis is captured in Kennedy's statements:

> The strength of our democracy is no better than the collective well-being of our people. The vigor of our country is no stronger than the vitality and will of our countrymen. The level of physical, mental, moral, and spiritual fitness of every American citizen must be our constant concern.

Perhaps the only applied psychologist to become interested in individual differences in physical fitness during this time was Edwin Fleishman. Fleishman's research in human abilities and performance taxonomies led him to evaluate a range of physical fitness tests used commonly in military and educational settings. Findings from this programmatic effort were published in *Structure and Measurement of Physical Fitness* (Fleishman, 1964), and these contributed to the understanding of assessments for evaluating the domain of physical fitness. Given the investment the physical education profession had made in the AAHPER youth fitness tests and program, it is surprising that Fleishman's fitness research recommendations had only minor influence on the work of practicing physical educators. On the other hand, Fleishman's work provided the foundation for the study of individual differences and taxonomic issues of physical performance in the workplace. Psychologists interested in physical performance measurement must begin with Fleishman's seminal work, which is the single most influential contemporary reference for physical abilities assessment.

Because Fleishman's (1964) analyses of physical fitness dimensions serve as the foundation for much of his subsequent work, it is useful to review briefly the studies he completed. The project, which gained the interest and support of the Office of Naval Research, sought to provide guidance for the assessment of physical proficiency to those who engage in fitness evaluation and direct fitness programs. The research included two phases of fitness testing using Navy personnel in their sixth week of basic training. In the first study, 30 tests designed to assess strength were administered to male recruits ($N = 201$) and the scores intercorrelated and factor analyzed. The factor analysis yielded three general strength factors and a fourth derivative one. These factors (defined in the introduction of this chapter) and the test with the loading highest on each are (a) Dynamic Strength—pull-ups to limit; (b) Static Strength—hand grip; (c) Explosive Strength—shuttle run; and (d) Trunk Strength—leg lifts. In the second study, the strength factors were minimized and 30 tests of speed, flexibility, balance, and coordination were administered to Navy recruits ($N = 204$). Factor analysis of the test score correlation matrix revealed six factors; the factor names and highest loading test for each are: (a) Explosive Strength—dodge run; (b) Gross Body Equilibrium—one foot lengthwise balance with eyes closed; (c) Dynamic Flexibility—lateral bend and one foot tapping; (d) Balance with Visual Cues—one foot lengthwise balance with eyes open; (e) Extent Flexibility—abdominal stretch; and (f) Speed of Limb Movement—ball balance. Fleishman's recommendations for basic fitness tests included tests representing these factors as well as a Stamina or Cardiovascular Endurance factor, tests that had not been included in previous analyses (Fleishman, 1964, p. 104).

Because Fleishman's recommendations are compiled from results of two factor analyses plus the stamina factor, a conceptual addition, Hogan (1989) analyzed the structure of physical fitness using Fleishman's reference tests for the nine factors. Scores from tests administered to Navy enlisted men ($N = 97$) were intercorrelated and the resulting matrix factor analyzed. Table 1 presents the rotated factor matrix for the nine basic fitness tests; this three-factor solution accounted for 56 percent of the total

TABLE 1

Factor Analysis of Fleishman's Basic Fitness Tests

	Varimax rotation		
Test	Factor 1	Factor 2	Factor 3
Grip strength	.8506	−.0584	−.0662
Medicine ball	.8089	.1965	.0091
Balance rail	.4174	.3058	−.1009
1.5-mile run	−.0659	−.7976	−.0532
Pull-ups	.1391	.7477	.1284
Sit-ups	.0182	.5548	.1567
Bend, twist, & touch	−.0986	.1911	.8007
Cable jump	−.1453	.2382	.6492
Twist & touch	.4595	−.1932	.5876

From "Personality Correlates of Physical Fitness" by J. Hogan, 1989, *Journal of Personality and Social Psychology, 56*, pp. 284–288. Copyright 1989 by the American Psychological Association. Adapted by permission.

variance in the matrix. Factor 1 is a muscular strength dimension defined by the factor loadings for grip strength and medicine ball throw, Factor 2 is a general endurance factor encompassing both muscular and cardiovascular activities, and Factor 3 reflects coordination or movement quality. These three general factors provide an organizing structure for Fleishman's more specific fitness dimensions, and together, although with modifications, they form a basis for the study of work requirements and occupational performances.

Factors Affecting Ability to Work

In an age of information and high technology, one assumes the need for physical performances in the workplace has long passed. However, manual labor still exists in all countries and will probably be with us, though perhaps to a lesser extent, in the future. Moreover, and aside from the real possibilities and eventualities of near total workplace automation, some individuals prefer and enjoy work of an active nature.

Holland (1985) refers to such individuals as *realistic* types—those who prefer to work with their hands and are well coordinated and more interested in things than people. Industrial psychologists can expect to confront problems of physical performance in the workplace because unsophisticated manual tasks will not be totally engineered out of operations and because some portion of the work force will enjoy performing them.

Knowledge of job requirements provides roughly half of the information necessary to make informed personnel decisions about this kind of work; the remaining information must address the physical work capacity of the individual. Work physiologists confront problems associated with assessing the physical capacity of individuals under varying work conditions. This research is important for industrial and organizational psychologists because they assume responsibility for assessment, selection, placement, training, and appraisal of individuals for physically demanding jobs. Due to the interdisciplinary nature of physical ability personnel considerations, it is appropriate to review physiological factors essential to performance in the workplace.

Physiological Responses

The body's response to the demands of physical work is accomplished through a complex series of interactions involving nearly all body systems. The nervous system initiates and controls muscles responsible for movement. The major contributor to physical work is *skeletal muscle,* and its capacity is completely dependent on the activity of body systems, particularly circulatory and respiratory functions that service the muscle. The respiratory system provides air to the lungs and is responsible for the exchange of oxygen and carbon dioxide between the air and the blood. While the muscular system performs the work, the heart and the vascular system deliver the oxygen and nutrients to the active tissues and remove the metabolic waste products. The blood and body fluids transport materials between cells and tissues. Energy for the body's cells is provided through the process of metabolism, which increases directly with work intensity until exhaustion is reached.

The muscles, pistons of the human engine, depend on (a) stimulation from the nervous system for initiation and maintenance of muscular contraction and (b) energy delivery and by-product removal from the circulatory system. Movement is initiated, either consciously or automatically, by nervous impulses that stimulate the appropriate motor units. Although three types of muscle tissue exist, skeletal muscles are perhaps the most relevant here. Each muscle group (e.g., biceps brachialis) is composed of *bundles,* which in turn are composed of thousands of *fibers.* Muscle fibers are the functional group within the muscle bundle, and groups of these fibers are innervated by a single *motor neuron.* The number of muscle fibers within the muscle bundle remains constant after the human embryo reaches four to five months of development. Recent physio-

logical investigations have focused on a functional distinction between muscle fibers that depend on oxygen for contraction and those that do not. *Fast-twitch fibers,* which do not depend on oxygen, are thought to be important for rapid speed and power activities, whereas *slow-twitch fibers* rely on a supply of oxygen and are associated with sustained muscular work. A higher maximal tension can be achieved by fast-twitch fibers than by aerobic, energy-yielding slow-twitch fibers.

The anatomy and function of the muscle is well understood (e.g., see Bourne, 1973), including the structure and physiology of contraction (the interested reader is referred to A. F. Huxley, 1974, and H. E. Huxley, 1965, 1969). The muscle fiber is composed of *myofibrils,* and each myofibril is structured with the sarcomeres arranged next to each other, end to end. The *sarcomere* is the functioning unit of the myofibril and contains parallel filaments of actin and myosin. The action of these filaments is primarily for muscular contraction because the length of the sarcomere shortens, and even overlaps, when the filaments slide toward one another during the contraction process.

Muscles communicate with the brain through *efferent* or motor nerves and *afferent* or sensory nerves. Motor nerves carry information from the brain to instruct muscular contraction, thereby controlling muscular activity. The contraction is controlled through the nervous impulses received by the muscle fiber from the motor neuron. A single motor neuron terminating within the muscle innervates a number of muscle fibers. That number appears to be a function of movement-output precision, with fewer muscle fibers (three to six) controlled by a single motor neuron during finer movements. Sensory nerves forward impulses from the muscles to either the spinal cord or the brain. The impulses are a source of information or feedback and help to direct or remember movement.

Coordinated movement depends not only on muscular response to stimulation but on

FIGURE 3

Nervous Control of Skilled Performance

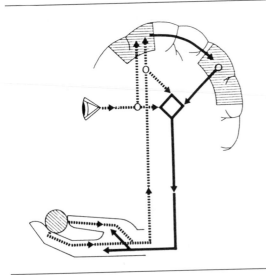

From *Fitting the Task to the Man* (p. 22) by E. Grandjean, 1982, London: Taylor & Francis. Copyright 1982 by Taylor & Francis, Ltd. Reprinted by permission.

integration of sensory information as well. Special sensory organs called *proprioceptors* are located within the muscle bundles, muscle tendons and sheaths, joint capsules, and surrounding tissues. These proprioceptors provide information regarding stretch, pressure, and position. This continuous feedback, along with sensory information provided though vision, vestibular function, and hearing, is vital for coordination and skillful muscular performance.

Figure 3 presents Grandjean's (1982, p. 220) illustration of nervous control during skilled work. Here, information from the eye travels along the optic nerve in the form of nervous impulses. Once in the brain, the information is integrated into an image of the hand and the object to be grasped. Impulses pass to the medulla and the cerebellum, which control motor activity through motor and sensory impulses. These impulses direct and control movement of the hand in grasping the object. Proprioceptors transmit sensory impulses to the cerebral

cortex where they are translated into sensation experienced. These sensations provide the feedback for hand adjustments in the grasping action. The activity associated with muscular contractions of the grasping hand can be determined using a technique called *electromyography*, which indicates the amount of muscular force developed.

Muscular activity depends on circulation of the blood to deliver energy and remove waste products from cell metabolism. The heart serves as a pump for the blood, which travels through a system of vessels. Blood vessels (the vascular system) are a network of channels responsible for transporting blood from the heart to the tissues, including the muscles, and back again. The blood travels from the heart through the arteries and into the progressively smaller arterioles. Next, oxygen and nutrients from the blood are exchanged for carbon dioxide and waste products at the intermediary site of the capillaries. The blood begins its return to the heart by entering the venules and finally completes the cycle at the right atrium of the heart.

If the muscles are the pistons of the human engine, then respiration provides the fuel for the engine's combustion. The respiratory system involves the gaseous exchange between ambient air and the blood. *Respiration* is the exchange process by which (a) air is brought into the lungs and exchanged for carbon dioxide in the alveoli and (b) gases are exchanged between blood and tissue in order to replenish oxygen and remove carbon dioxide. This system provides for the oxygenation of blood, which in turn provides for the oxygenation of tissues. In exchange for this oxygen, carbon dioxide is removed. Gas exchange is a function of the pressure gradient between two involved areas and the distance the gas molecules must travel. Breathing involves the active process of inspiration and the passive process of expiration. However, during vigorous physical work, expiration will become more active as the abdominal muscles contract, increasing intraabdominal and intrathoracic pressure. Both the inspiratory and expiratory muscles are activated and function reciprocally. Muscular contraction will expand the chest cavity during inspiration. The effect of physical activity is to increase the tidal volume of air (usually ranging from 0.5 liters to 2.5 liters) to accommodate the increased rate of gas exchange.

The *tidal volume* is the volume of gas moved during one respiratory cycle. Total lung capacity is a function of air volume left in the lungs after expiration (functional residual capacity) and the volume achieved from a maximum inspiration. Following this maximum inspiration, a maximal expiration of gas defines *vital capacity*. P. O. Astrand (1952) proposed vital capacity as a measure of physical work capacity since it is significantly related to *maximal oxygen uptake* (VO₂ max)—a measure considered by physiologists to be the best laboratory assessment of physical work capacity. Although vital capacity reflects a static volume, a dynamic volume can also be measured through spirometry.

Muscular work depends on transforming chemical energy into mechanical energy, in the same way that transforming air and gasoline into power moves the pistons of an internal combustion engine. *Metabolism* is the process by which energy is provided to the body's cells. Although energy production serves many biological functions (e.g., maintenance of body temperature), satisfying the energy demands associated with the mechanical work of contracting muscles is essential. Food taken in from the normal diet is transformed into glucose, fatty acids, and amino acids; these are further transformed within the cell by the *mitochondria*, and this energy is stored in the form of *adenosine triphosphate* (ATP) and *creatine phosphate* (CP). A muscle cell involved in muscle fiber contraction receives its energy from ATP or CP. This can be the result of either *aerobic* (with oxygen) or *anaerobic* (without oxygen) metabolism. Astrand and Rodahl (1977) liken the process of energy liberation and transfer to that of a battery pack. ATP, the charged battery,

donates its energy (phosphate bond) to support functions of the cell. Once this transfer takes place, ATP becomes a discharged battery, and *adenosine diphosphate* (ADP) is the result. The ADP battery, in order to be used, must be recharged. The energy store CP is responsible for this recharging; aerobic metabolism provides for the resynthesis of CP. Although the biochemistry of anaerobic and aerobic metabolism is beyond the scope of this chapter, the breakdown and resynthesis of ATP and CP are fundamental to muscular work. Figure 4 displays the steps in the metabolic process (Wilmore, 1977, p. 21).

During work, the amount of oxygen present in a cell determines the degree to which metabolism will proceed anaerobically and aerobically. At the start of muscular work, while oxygen is being transported to the working muscles, the body relies on anaerobic metabolism for its energy yield. When the oxygen supply is sufficient, and under conditions of moderate physical work, energy metabolism is aerobic. ADP and lactic acid (a waste product) accumulate over conditions of intense and prolonged activity; anaerobic metabolism assists to some extent in regenerating ATP but is an inefficient energy source. When work exceeds full oxygen uptake capacity, work will continue only for a short period by anaerobic metabolism. Similarly, in performance where oxygen is unavailable, the source of energy comes solely through anaerobic metabolism. The percentage of ATP molecules that can be produced under these conditions is approximately one-thirteenth as much as can be produced aerobically and, therefore, muscular work performance is curtailed severely.

Static and Dynamic Muscle Contraction

Two types of muscular activity or mechanical work can be distinguished, defined, and measured; these are termed *dynamic* and *static* muscular contractions. Virtually all researchers in the area of human physical performance

FIGURE 4

Anaerobic and Aerobic Metabolism

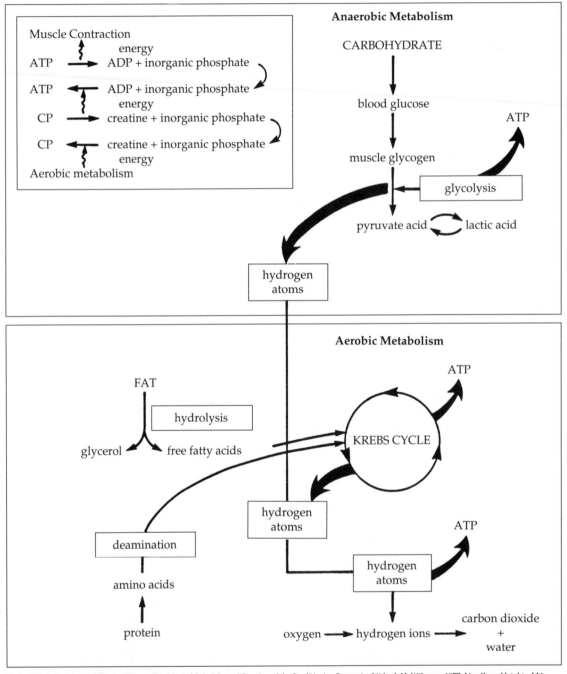

From *Athletic Training and Physical Fitness: Physiological Principles and Practices of the Conditioning Process* (p. 21) by J. H. Wilmore, 1977, Needham Heights, MA: Allyn and Bacon. Copyright 1977 by Allyn and Bacon. Reprinted by permission.

agree on these categories and definitions. Dynamic, or isotonic, contractions involve a change in muscle length as a result of nervous activation. Under this condition, the muscular effort can be characterized by a rhythmic change of contraction and relaxation of the muscles (Grandjean & Hunting, 1977). When the muscle shortens, the work is termed *positive* or *concentric;* when the muscle lengthens, the work is termed *negative* or *eccentric.* External work results, as indicated by a change in angle of the affected joint, and work can be calculated from the weight lifted times the distance traveled.

Static, or isometric, contraction results in no observable change in muscle length or joint angle. During static contraction, the muscle stays in a constant state of tension, during which force is maintained over time. As Kroemer (1970) points out, no mechanical work is performed using static effort because without joint movement the distance component of the work equation is zero. Grandjean (1982, p. 7) likens the muscle under isometric tension to an electromagnet—it has a steady consumption of energy while supporting a given weight, but does not appear to be involved in positive work. The physiology of static work is quite different from that of dynamic work, and this has important implications for understanding fatigue and performance of industrial tasks.

Training

Hickey (1983) reviewed 46 studies of physical training effects and summarized the results for anthropometry, cardiovascular endurance, and strength changes. The studies that were analyzed varied in terms of participants and parameters of training, and the results were collapsed into broad categories. Anthropometric changes were evaluated in terms of component body fat and lean body weight as well as total body weight measures. Generally, total body weight remained unchanged by training; however, women responded to training with a slightly greater increase in lean body weight than men. Total increases for both groups ranged from 0 to 6 percent. Men responded to training with greater decreases in body fat (10% to 22%) than women (0% to 14%). Training can increase cardiovascular endurance as measured by VO_2 max by as much as 14 percent, and it appears that men and women respond to training with similar relative increments. Some investigations provided evidence for even greater training effects for women; however, such effects could be the result of their initial low levels of fitness. Hickey reviewed research indicating male and female training effects of up to 30 percent using measures of static strength and up to 36 percent using calisthenic exercises (dynamic strength). Percentage increments were slightly lower for women across both types. However, Robertson (1982) reported a 205 percent increment in push-up performance by women over a seven-week military training program. This is not surprising, because many women cannot perform a single push-up. Strength training evaluated using a maximum single isotonic repetition indicated increments for men and women up to approximately 30 percent of their baseline capability.

Results of studies reviewed by Hickey vary considerably. Much of this variability can be attributed to differences in training parameters and assessment procedures. Nevertheless, if initial levels of physical performance are known, the general findings provide useful guidelines for identifying probabilities associated with obtaining a particular job-related employment requirement.

Physical Ability and Injury

Statistics compiled by the U.S. Department of Health and Human Services (National Institute for Occupational Safety and Health, 1981) and the U. S. Department of Labor (1982) indicate that musculoskeletal disorders, including back pain, (a) constitute the second most common occupational problem in the United States, (b) affect over 1 million workers annually, and (c) account for approximately $14 billion in costs (Taber, 1982). Given these facts and other indicators, employers are extremely concerned with the integrity of employees' musculoskeletal systems and the maintenance of worker health. Low back problems are not exclusive to older workers; symptoms appear also in workers who are relatively young. Although there may be many causes of low back pain and disability, the incidence and severity of injury increases for those workers engaged in heavy lifting of materials (Chaffin & Park, 1973a, 1973b).

Any movement that produces a force—or, in biomechanical terms, a *moment*—on the spinal column is classified as a lifting task. Tichauer (1978) evaluates the mechanical stress imposed on the worker through a systematic analysis of the lift. This analysis serves as a basis for understanding and minimizing disabling injuries related to handling objects. The severity of manual materials handling and lifting can be evaluated through an analysis of moments, gravitational components, and inertial forces (Tichauer, 1978, p. 47). In the case of lifting, moments are forces acting on the lumbar spine calculated from the product of mass (including those of body segments) and the distance from the point of application; these moments are summed and that figure becomes the biomechanical lifting equivalent. These biomechanical computations are useful for analyzing comparative effects of work postures, work methods, and gender differences. For example, consider the individual who must lift a standard weight from either a standing or seated position. If the body segments involved are identical in both postures, the distance between the lumbosacral joint and the center of the whole body's mass is considerably greater when seated than when standing. This is a result of the increase in distance from the lumbosacral joint caused by the extension of the trunk and arm reach while seated. Therefore, the torque exerted on the

lumbar spine is significantly greater than the torque generated from lifting in the standing position. The analysis confirms the wisdom of locating the object to be lifted close to the worker. Performing a lifting task while seated can undermine this work strategy. Also, consider Tichauer's (1978) analysis of gender differences in Figure 5. Holding height approximately constant, body segment distance differences can interact with work surface height to create different and greater stresses for women than for men. Although women are at a disadvantage in lifting objects from the floor (see Figure 5), these lifting stress differences are virtually eliminated by placing the load on a pallet 12 to 14 inches high.

Further understanding of the lifting task should take into account both gravitational components and inertial forces in conjunction with static moments. Gravitational components include calculations of work (force x distance) whose nature is either dynamic (e.g., lift load), negative (e.g., lower load), or isometric (e.g., maintain load). Severe stress can also be placed on the body either through acquiring or releasing a load. Because the center of mass is displaced, the posture must readjust to maintain equilibrium. The postural adjustments necessary when a load is released are achieved in a shorter period of time than when the load is lifted, which contributes to greater musculoskeletal stress. Such stresses can be minimized by training workers and, possibly, by elevating the release location.

Frequency of lift is the final element of the lifting task. When multiple objects are to be handled, one must factor in the requirement to move the entire body mass along with the item to be transported. The work stress associated with handling multiple items simultaneously is considerably less than when handling them one at a time. This is one of the principles realized by Gilbreth (1909) in his study of techniques and motions associated with efficient bricklaying. Teeple (1957) estimates maximum efficiency for carrying loads as 35

FIGURE 5

Effects of Gender and Load Location on Lumbosacral Joint Stress in Lifting

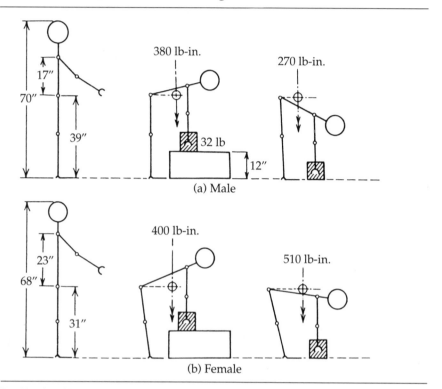

(a) Male

(b) Female

From *Biomechanical Basis of Ergonomics* (p. 50) by E. R. Tichauer, 1978, New York: Wiley. Copyright 1978 by John Wiley & Sons, Inc. Reprinted by permission.

percent of one's body weight at a speed of 4.5 to 5 kilometers per hour.

Across American industry, approximately one-third of the disabling injuries suffered by workers are related to manual materials handling tasks. The disability rate increases when lifting is a frequent and substantial part of the job. Back injuries, the most highly visible of these permanent and temporary injuries, usually occur under conditions in which, from a biomechanical analysis, the sum of all static moments acting on the lumbosacral spine is located at a point either in front of or behind the base of support in the feet. This condition causes postural instability and increased lower back

pressure; the musculature must be adjusted quickly in order to prevent a fall and to accommodate the load.

Williams (1974) presents a clear analysis of the lower back injury and its associated pain. The crushed intervertebral disc in the lumbar spine is the most frequent cause of low back injury and low back and leg pain. Williams likens the anatomy of the spine to a stack of alternating hockey pucks (vertebrae) cushioned by firm doughnuts (discs). There are five of these vertebrae and discs in the low back or lumbar spine; mechanical stressors produced from loads lifted affect this area. Processes which form joints and to which muscles attach protrude from the rear of each vertebra. These processes align vertically to create a canal through which the spinal cord and nerves pass.

Because of the S-shape of the spine and our upright posture, the upper body weight is not distributed evenly across the vertebrae, but exerts pressure on the back edges of the lumbar and cervical (neck) vertebrae in particular. This added pressure is transferred to the intervertebral discs, which rupture over time. The nuclear material of the disc ruptures into the spinal canal producing pressure on the spinal nerves; the rate at which the nuclear material is absorbed by the system is quite slow. The ruptured disc produces structural effects of (a) reduced cushioning for the vertebra and (b) settling of the upper vertebra on the one below it. As illustrated in Figure 6, bone comes into direct contact with bone, the openings through which nerves emerge are reduced, and nerve pressure and irritation result. This occurs almost exclusively at the fifth lumbar vertebra (L_5/S_1), and if the opening is sufficiently reduced, the nerve may become pinched, causing extreme back and leg pain. Williams (1974, p. 19) emphasizes the seriousness of the problem by pointing out that by the age of 20, the lower lumbar disc has ruptured in most individuals. Although they may not have experienced discomfort, they are in fact at risk for pain in the future.

Consider the structural consequences of lifting materials. Forces or moments created in the lifting phase act directly on the lumbosacral spine, and specifically the L_5/S_1 vertebra and the disc below it. These forces are substantially greater than those currently imposed to maintain an erect body posture. The worker shifts the body weight forward to acquire the load, and then in lifting the load, the back muscles must contract forcefully to lift the load and maintain balance while the weight shifts backward. When a ruptured disc is present, which is likely, the lift produces a stress causing the lumbar vertebrae to move together.

FIGURE 6

Upper Vertebra Settling on Vertebra Below

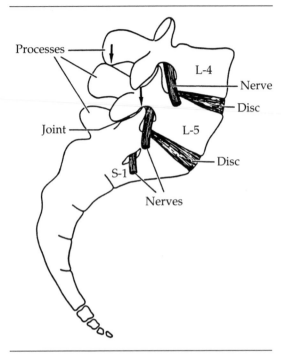

From *Low Back and Neck Pain* (p. 19) by P. C. Williams, 1974, Springfield, IL: Charles C. Thomas, Publisher. Copyright 1974 by Charles C. Thomas, Publisher. Reprinted by permission.

This results in nerve compression and bone-on-bone contact between the vertebrae. The contact between the fourth and fifth vertebral processes creates a false weight-bearing joint due to the structural dislocation. Continued and repeated lifting will increase lower back pressure, increase dislocation, and cause the joint processes to lose their ability to function appropriately, resulting in possible pain, spasms, and disability.

Correct postures for handling loads are essential to minimize low back pain and disability. For the lifting task, the classic principle of "knees bent—back straight—head up" has biomechanical advantages over postures where the legs are straight and the trunk is inclined forward (Tichauer, 1978, p. 52). This is because the distance between the center of mass of the load and the lumbosacral joint (L_5/S_1) is minimized. Williams' (1974) anatomical analysis provides a similar principle but with the emphasis on reducing "the hollow in the back" (p. 20). Muscles in the back and abdomen work in opposition; back muscles increase the hollow or arch of the low back, while abdominal muscles reduce this hollow. In addition, muscles of the buttocks serve to draw the back of the pelvis down, and with the contraction of the abdominal muscles the front of the pelvis is drawn up. When used in conjunction, these two sets of muscles will reduce the hollow and thus the pressure on the low back. Most daily activities require extensive use of the low back muscles; over time, the strength of these muscles is substantially developed and the muscles tend to shorten. This increases pressure on the back edges of the lumbar vertebrae and their associated discs.

Weakened abdominal and buttocks muscles can be strengthened through exercise; this is an effective treatment for low back pain and can also be used as a preventive strategy. Training industrial workers in proper lifting technique is essential. Such training requires the worker to squat next to the load with one or both feet flat on the floor. Then, using the legs to lift the load, the abdominals contract and round out the lower back. The load should be held as close to the center of gravity of the body as possible for both lifting and carrying. The knees and hips remain slightly flexed for balance, efficiency of movement, and reduction of pressure on the low back. Williams (1974, p. 34) cautions that loads below waist level should always be lifted with the hips and knees bent; loads should never be lifted above the waist. Although general laws tend to blur individual differences, researchers who specialize in the evaluation of low back pain and lifting capacity indicate that recommendations for bent-leg

lifting procedures need to be evaluated on a case-by-case basis (Garg & Herrin, 1979; NIOSH, 1981).

Evaluation and Classification of Work

The direct and indirect costs of injuries, which include medical treatment, worker compensation, and lost productivity, are of considerable concern to individual employers as well as to state and federal agencies. Many of these injuries are attributed to the overexertion that results from handling materials manually. The hazards associated with materials handling have been recognized since the early 1900s, when protective laws were enacted to limit the physical loads handled by women and children. Although Title VII of the Civil Rights Act supersedes these laws, agencies such as the National Institute for Occupational Safety and Health (NIOSH) conduct research programs to establish guidelines for manual materials handling (MMH). Considering that (a) approximately 30 percent of the total work force is exposed to hazardous manual materials handling (NIOSH, 1981), (b) overexertion accounts for 27 percent of all compensated injury claims (National Safety Council, 1975) and (c) about two-thirds of overexertion incidents involve lifting (Bureau of Labor Statistics, 1978), we must conclude that the MMH problem is of national importance, affecting the health of both industries and workers. Generally, two strategies are available to deal with MMH overexertion: evaluating and establishing safe work loads, and implementing valid personnel selection procedures. Evaluation and classification of work loads will be discussed in this section.

Criteria for determining safe work loads for MMH jobs can be developed using several different approaches. Although experts in the hazards area identify five or six methodologies for investigation, three approaches are common to most reviews. These are biomechanical, physiological, and psychophysical techniques for assessing job demands and related capacities in workers. *Biomechanical models* evaluate the strain capabilities of the musculoskeletal structure, particularly the spinal column and its discs, during an act of materials handling. Of particular concern is the effect of body segment position on muscular strength; this model uses mechanical properties to identify conditions producing muscle strain and sprain. *Physiological models* evaluate the metabolic and circulatory responses to work loads. Using such indexes as oxygen consumption, metabolic rate, and heart rate, maximum work intensity and physical fatigue can be identified and predicted. Measures recorded are typically reflections of systemic responses, and therefore localized muscular activity such as that involved in a single lift task may not be reflected. *Psychophysical models* quantify individuals' subjective reports of perceived physical exertion or fatigue; results from these models can reflect evaluations of both single and multiple repetitions of tasks as well as of discrete adjustments of task parameters (e.g., weight, size, and distance). Contributions of each model are discussed next, as are safe work load guidelines suggested from cumulative research results.

Biomechanical Approaches to Work Load Criteria.   The biomechanical approach attempts to predict muscle strain and sprain from forces acting in the musculoskeletal system. A biomechanical analysis typically entails (a) a simulation of the lifting task, (b) computation of forces and moments for joints of interest (usually at the L_5/S_1 disc), and (c) comparison of these forces and moments with population data indicating percentage of the population that could be expected to perform under these conditions without risk (Garg, Sharma, Chaffin, & Schmidler, 1983).

Simulation of the lifting task can involve specification of task parameters so that the task can be performed by a subject or modeled mathematically. The two major influences on task simulation are *task characteristics* and *con-*

tainer characteristics. Herrin, Chaffin, and Mach (1974) specified five parameters of each that can affect task simulation. The parameters within task characteristics are:

- Workplace geometry (movement distance, direction and extent of path, etc.)

- Frequency, duration, and pace of task

- Complexity

- Environment (vibration, foot traction)

- Movement through a progression of postures while lifting the body and load

The parameters within container characteristics are:

- Load

- Dimensions of load

- Distribution of load

- Couplings (devices to aid grasping)

- Stability of load

These parameters can be used to enhance physical fidelity of the task simulation. The real issue for task simulation is not only fidelity, however, but correct functional task performance either by subjects or by statistical modeling.

After the parameters of the tasks are specified, the posture for handling the load is then analyzed. When a load is lifted, both the body mass and load induce torques at joints of the body. These forces are counterbalanced by the skeletal muscles which act in an equal and opposite direction at the specific joints; the function of the skeletal muscles during the lift task is that of a reactive torque. Task torques are, therefore, offset by reactive torques, and reactive torques required to perform a given lifting task can be computed through biomechanical models. Perhaps the most extensive work in this area has been completed by Chaffin and his associates. Chaffin developed and validated a biomechanical model that conceptualizes man as a system of seven solid links

FIGURE 7

Chaffin's Seven Solid Links in Biomechanical Analyses of Lifting

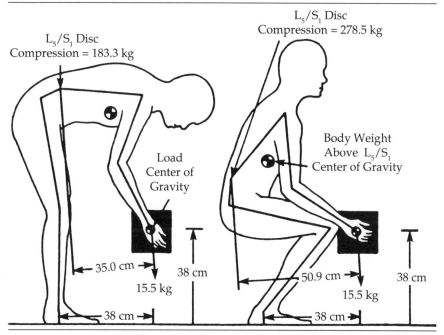

From "Biomechanical Evaluation of Two Methods of Manual Load Lift" by K. S. Parks and D. B. Chaffin, 1974, *Transactions of the American Institute of Industrial Engineers, 6*, pp. 105–113. Copyright 1974 by the Institute of Industrial Engineers. Reprinted by permission.

(see Figure 7; Chaffin, 1969, 1975; Chaffin & Baker, 1970). Traditional methodology in biomechanics analyzes the human skeleton using a link-joint system. The links are long bones between articulations; the number of link-joints specified in an analysis is a function of the need for accuracy and reality of the model (Kroemer, 1986, p. 171). As seen in Figure 7, the links in Chaffin's model are articulated at the balls of the feet, ankles, knees, hips, L_5/S_1 disc, shoulders, elbows, and hands. Each link can be quantified in terms of length, mass, and center of gravity. Data from Dempster (1955) can be used to estimate mass distribution of each link, and Contini, Drillis, and Bluestein (1963) provide measures of limb length. Independent variables for biomechanical computations include body-joint angles, hand coordinates relative to the gross body posture, and direction

and magnitude of the hand forces. The model simulates the body posture specified, and such dependent variables as resultant moments at each joint center, back muscle tension (erector spinal), and compressive force at L_5/S_1 can be computed.

When these results are compared to normative data for men and women, muscle strengths by joint reflect probabilities of overexertion. Although only limited validation research has been conducted, the results of Garg and Chaffin (1975) are promising and suggest that the relationship between predicted and actual hand force capabilities using biomechanical models is quite high ($r \geq .85$). Tests on cadaver columns provide a second type of biomechanical validation research. Compression investigations by Evans and Lissner (1959) and Sonoda (1962) indicate not only substantial variability in the

L_5/S_1 disc's ability to withstand stress, but that such tolerance differs by age and gender. In general, male cadavers under 40 years withstood an average of 675 kilograms of compressive force at L_5/S_1 before cartilage end plates began to suffer microfractures. Due to the smaller force-bearing area, Sonoda (1962) estimated the spinal compression tolerance of women to be about 17 percent less than that of men of the same age. Based on these data and observed incident rates for low back pain relative to predicted compressive forces in L_5/S_1 (Chaffin & Park, 1973a), NIOSH (1981) concluded that

> jobs which place more than 650 kg compressive force in the low-back are hazardous to all but the healthiest of workers. In terms of a specification for design a much lower level of 350 kg or lower should be viewed as an upper limit. (p. 36)

Using this recommendation in conjunction with the biomechanical model developed by Chaffin, Herrin, and Keyserling (1978), Figure 8 presents the tradeoffs between task load variables of weight, horizontal location, and vertical location that produce 350 kilograms of compressive force on the L_5/S_1 disc of the average woman and 650 kilogram of compressive force on the L_5/S_1 disc of the average man. Although in each example the compressive forces remain constant, there is an inverse relation between combinations of weight and horizontal location of the load.

Additional MMH recommendations from NIOSH (1981, p. 40) based on biomechanical research can be summarized in six points:

- Older workers are at risk for L_5/S_1 damage when lifting loads in excess of 5 kilograms with the center of gravity of the load within 50 centimeters of the ankles.

- Even light loads should be handled close to the body; as the load moves away from the body, compressive forces on the low back increase proportionally.

- Loads should not be stored on the floor but at least at knuckle height (minimum 50 centimeters); as loads approach the floor, the body weight moment increases, thereby increasing low back stress.

- Lifting loads with one hand or lifting at the side of the body can impart hazardous stress to the lumbar column, so the workplace design should permit the worker to address the load symmetrically.

- Rapid or jerking dynamic force can multiply stress; even light loads should be handled smoothly.

- When a load is lifted from the floor, NIOSH recommends that no instructions to workers for "proper" lifting postures be given. The rationale is that "specific instructions as to the safe posture to use will be necessarily complex, reflecting such factors as leg strengths, load and load size. Until such complexities are better researched, it is recommended that instructions as to lifting postures be avoided" (NIOSH, 1981, p. 40).

Standards and recommendations of the workplace are established through biomechanical analyses of infrequently occurring physical actions of short duration. Models constructed from a mechanical analog of the human body use body segments with their associated lengths and masses as links. The resulting forces created by manipulating linkages are of particular interest to designers and safety engineers as well as to those responsible for the human factor in the workplace. Substantial research exists on the act of lifting, and attention is now focused on models for dynamic lifting (Ayoub & El-Bassoussi, 1978), lifting angle and technique (Garg, Sharma, Chaffin, & Schmidler, 1983), and analyses of effective push/pull postures (Chaffin, Andres, & Garg, 1983). With more recent research on analysis of lifting motion, Ayoub, Selan, and Jiang (1986) differentiate between static and dynamic

FIGURE 8

Task Variables Producing Compression

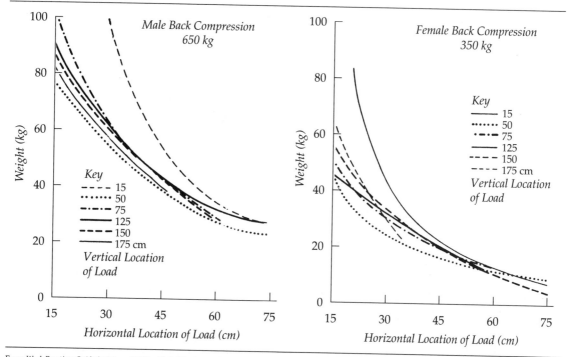

biomechanical models to determine physical stresses imposed on the musculoskeletal system during lifting. They explain that static models, such as those used by Chaffin and his associates, assume that forces due to acceleration need not be considered because the lifting action is slow, smooth, and controlled. Conversely, the dynamic model, such as that described by Ayoub and El-Bassoussi (1976), accounts for the time, force, and torque involved in motion through kinematic and kinetic analyses.

Given the amount of research dedicated to the act of lifting and the direction of future research, it seems odd that NIOSH is unwilling or unable to specify guidelines for lifting techniques. The NIOSH (1981, pp. 100–101) position that workers' literal application of rules can

lead to unsafe lifting practices is understandable; however, proposed training strategies that involve teaching workers where "their strengths and weaknesses lie" and basic principles of physics are not very explicit or helpful instructional guidelines. It appears that a major application of biomechanical analyses is to inform safe and effective procedures for handling materials. To the degree that in the workplace we are unable to translate established empirical biomechanical principles into practice, injury rates among MMH workers will not decline.

Physiological Approaches to Work Load Criteria. The physiological approach to assessments of work load is most useful for evaluating prolonged or intermittent physical work. Metabolic and heart rate measures are most frequently used to indicate capacity for continued muscular performance. Both static and dynamic muscular contractions are involved in lifting and other MMH tasks, and these are used to maintain and overcome the inertia of the load. With repetitive tasks, these contractions are required over time, making possible physiological measurements of work intensity.

As discussed, increases in physical activity require increases in oxygen supplied to the tissues. At the beginning of activity, respiration and circulation adjust to the demands of contracting muscles. When oxygen uptake (VO_2) equals the oxygen requirements of the tissues, a steady state exists, indicating a linear relation between oxygen used and external work accomplished by the muscles. Astrand and Rodahl (1977) estimate that for every liter of oxygen consumed, about 5 kilocalories of energy output can be expected. Maximal oxygen uptake (VO_2 max; often referred to as maximum aerobic power) is defined as the upper limit of aerobic metabolism and represents the highest oxygen consumption value in exhaustive activity. During short, intense activity, energy is provided almost exclusively from high-energy phosphates ATP and CP. With heavier work loads, anaerobic processes are used to deliver part of the energy during early phases of activity and lactic acid is produced. The heavier the work load, the greater the anaerobic contribution and thus the greater the blood lactate concentration. Under these conditions, the work becomes more subjectively strenuous and fatiguing; the accumulation of waste products triggers the need for work cessation. During heavy work, both VO_2 max and maximal heart rate may be reached within one minute.

Under conditions of prolonged heavy work, the individual's VO_2 max is perhaps the most significant factor influencing work capacity. Well-trained individuals can work for hours at an elevated VO_2 max percentage; Costill (1970) reports this may be as high as 70 to 80 percent of maximum, with little increase in lactate

accumulation. However, I. Astrand (1960) found that for subjects working continuously over seven 50-minute periods with 10-minute rest intervals, a 50 percent rate of aerobic capacity was too high even for the most fit subjects. Based on studies by Lehmann (1953), Bink (1962, 1964), Ekblom, Astrand, Saltin, Stenberg, and Wallstrom (1968), and Rodgers (1978), NIOSH (1981) proposed that prolonged physical effort over an eight-hour workday not exceed 33 percent of an individual's aerobic capacity. These recommendations are based on an average aerobic capacity of 15 kilocalories per minute for men and a 10.5 kilocalories per minute for women.

Most muscular work required in industry is not maintained for an eight-hour period, and therefore much of the physical work that currently takes place can be considered intermittent. The primary key to work output under intermittent conditions appears to be the nature of the work-rest cycle. This limitation is well illustrated in an experiment by I. Astrand, P. Astrand, Christensen, and Hedman (1960). By varying the duration of the work-rest cycle while maintaining the ratio between the two and holding constant the total work-period time, they found that shorter work-rest cycles produced less fatigue than cycles of longer duration (see Figure 9). The 1:2 ratio 30-second cycles resulted in virtually no increase in blood lactate concentration over 30 minutes. Further investigations suggest, however, that the critical variable for work output without fatigue is the length of the work period, with less importance attributed to length of rest pauses. P. Astrand and Rodahl (1977) explain that under relatively short work periods the muscles first use oxygen stores available in the tissues; circulation and respiration provide replacements for depleted stores during the rest cycles. With optimal spacing and duration of work-rest cycles, anaerobic lactic acid production is minimal. Two important considerations follow. First, the heavier the work load, the shorter the work periods should be. Rest periods should be proportional, but not so long as to negate the

FIGURE 9

Effects of Work-Rest Cycle on Blood Lactate Concentration

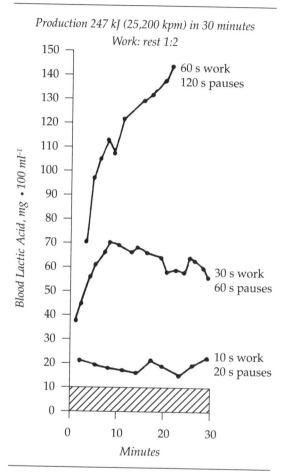

Production 247 kJ (25,200 kpm) in 30 minutes
Work: rest 1:2

60 s work
120 s pauses

30 s work
60 s pauses

10 s work
20 s pauses

Blood Lactic Acid, $mg \cdot 100\ ml^{-1}$

Minutes

From "Myohemoglobin as an Oxygen-Store in Man" by P. O. Astrand, 1960, *Acta Psychiatrica Scandinavica, 8,* p. 454. Copyright 1960 by Munksgaard International Publishing, Ltd. Reprinted by permission.

Although physiological assessments of individuals' work capacities over both prolonged and intermittent activities are basic to work criteria, work physiologists devote considerable effort to the assessment of specific physiological task requirements. These evaluations are useful for determining an individual's suitability for work, the design of task duration and sequence within a job, possible work and tool redesign, and forecasts for work output, health, and productivity. Energy requirements of tasks can be determined either through direct measurements of incumbents' oxygen utilization and/or heart rate or through indirect estimates from regression models predicting metabolic energy expenditure.

Perhaps the earliest evaluations of physical effort required for classifying industrial tasks were conducted by Christensen (1953) in Sweden's steel industry. More recently, however, many studies reporting energy expenditure of task performance have become available, including comprehensive listings compiled by Durnin and Passmore (1967) and Karvonen (1974). These listings indicate substantial variations in energy expended at work, which range from 1,000 kilocalories for men performing eight hours of office work to 5,000 kilocalories for men performing a day of heavy labor (e.g., harvesting and forestry). Evidence suggests that (a) worker variables such as gender, body weight, and technique and (b) task variables such as load, frequency, vertical travel distance and origin, and temperature and humidity affect metabolic energy expenditure rate (NIOSH, 1981). Studies of energy expenditure required for task performance have led to work load severity classifications. Several of these are compiled in Table 2.

A basic problem for work physiologists is to evaluate work rates and assess the capacities of individuals to perform given quantities of work. Productivity and safety are primary concerns; these are influenced by physical and psychological fatigue. The physiological approach to the study of work load is concerned with physiological fatigue insofar as it disturbs homeo-

beneficial effects or decrease total work output. Second, when the work pace is machine driven (e.g., as with conveyors), long work periods will outstrip the physical capacity of the human elements in the system. Banister and Brown (1968) found that in cases of intermittent, repetitive muscular work where the work-rest cycle is 1:2, the worker should apply less than the 40 percent maximal muscular strength during each cycle.

TABLE 2

Classification of Industrial Work by Physiological Indices

	Oxygen Uptake[a] Liter/Min^{-1}	Heart Rate[a] Beats/Min^{-1}	Energy Expenditure[a] kcal/Min/55kg (Women)
Light work	0.0–0.5	0–90	1.5–3.4
Moderate work	0.5–1.0	90–110	3.5–5.4
Heavy work	1.0–1.5	110–130	5.5–7.4
Very heavy work	1.5–2.0	130–150	7.5–9.4
Extremely heavy work	2.0–	150–170	9.5
	Energy Expenditure[b] kcal Min/65kg (Men)	Heart Rate[b] Beats/Min^{-1}	Body Temperature[b] Degrees Centigrade
Light work	2.0–4.9	75	37.0
Moderate work	5.0–7.4	100	37.5
Heavy work	7.5–9.9	125	38.0
Very heavy work	10.0–12.4	150	38.5
Extremely heavy work	12.5	175	39.0

Note: Entries represent general guidelines for average individuals.

[a] Astrand & Rodahl, 1977
[b] Christensen, 1953
[c] Durnin & Passmore, 1967

stasis. However, subjective symptoms of fatigue are extremely important because they too are warning mechanisms that serve to prevent strain and overexertion. The next section presents the methodology for linking subjective evaluations of fatigue to physical work load.

Psychophysical Approaches to Work Load Criteria. The psychophysical approach to the study of work load criteria entails the interaction of objective performance requirements with subjective evaluations of those demands. Psychophysical methodologies are appropriate to evaluate both frequent and infrequent work tasks. The approach depends on a worker's ability to evaluate and regulate physical work performed to determine acceptable work loads and work rates and avoid fatigue. Although biomechanics is concerned with the strain capabilities of musculoskeletal components and

work physiology is concerned with the biological limitations of physical tissue systems, psychophysics, as applied to the study of work capacity, is concerned with perceived levels of exertion or physical discomfort. *Psychophysics* —that area of psychology which examines the relationship between physical stimuli and human sensation—is an extremely useful methodology for the study of work capacity and physical exertion. Modern psychophysical theory, which introduced new techniques for scaling sensory magnitude, proposes that the strength of a sensation is directly related to physical stimulus intensity and can be described mathematically in terms of a power function (Stevens, 1960). Under different sensory modalities and conditions, the size of the exponent of the power function changes; for example, researchers have derived exponents for taste (1.3; salt), loudness (0.6; binaural), and heaviness (1.45; lifted weights). Psychophysical laws are relevant for the study of perceived muscular effort and force. These investigations also conform to the power law (Borg, 1962; Stevens & Cain, 1970). Psychophysical investigations of work performance fall into two general categories: (a) investigations of the relationship between cardiovascular endurance and perceived physical exertion and (b) examinations of the relationship between strength/capacity and fatigue.

Cardiovascular Endurance and Perceived Exertion. The work of Borg and his associates provides a substantial research base for investigating the relationship between metabolic energy expenditure and perceived physical exertion. Currently, much of what we know is summarized in Borg (1977); most subsequent studies are extensions of Borg's paradigm for ratings of perceived exertion. Originally, Borg set out to investigate and quantify subjective intensity of exertion. Using the "new psychophysics" (Stevens, 1956, 1958), which replaced the logarithmic function of stimulus intensity (Fechner, 1966), studies of heavy muscular work indicated that subjective intensity of exertion increases as a power function of work with an exponent of about 1.6 (Borg, 1962; Borg & Dahlstrom, 1960). Because of interindividual differences, difficulties in comparing results from ratio scaling methods (Borg, 1972), and possible interactions between memory span and perceptual recognition (Borg & Lindblad, 1976), Borg developed a category rating scale to elicit ratings of perceived exertion (RPE) during work. The RPE scale, or *Borg scale*, is a 15-point graded scale with values from 6 to 20 which correspond to variations in heart rate from 60 to 200 beats per minute. The scale was formulated on the basis that heart rate increases linearly with work load (i.e., performed on a bicycle ergometer). Scale anchors range from "very, very light" to "very, very hard" (Borg, 1970). Research using the RPE scale involves: (a) either training subjects in the content of the scale or making it available to them, (b) engag-

ing subjects in prolonged submaximal work, (c) collecting physiological data (e.g., heart rate and VO_2 max) over the work cycle, and (d) collecting subjects' verbal reports of RPE over successive time periods of the work cycle. A major finding across research studies is that when subjects are instructed to verbally rate the degree of exertion they feel while actually performing work, their ratings are systematically correlated with physiological indexes such as metabolic costs (Borg & Dahlstrom, 1959), heart rate (Arstila, Wendelin, Vuori, & Valimaki, 1974; Borg, 1977), blood lactate (Gamberale, 1972), and oxygen consumption (Gamerale, 1972; Noble & Borg, 1972; Skinner, Hutsler, Bergsteinova, & Buskirk, 1973a, 1973b). In addition, Arstila et al. (1974) report high test-retest reliabilities using the RPE scale.

Borg's methodology and other rating procedures are central to the study of effort, fatigue, exertion, and strain. Borg (1977, p. 5) points out that it is naive to think the physical effort required for different tasks or for the same task by different individuals is the same; rather, the "costs" of activities are a function of perceptual, performance, and physiological variables. Psychophysics research attempts to determine functions that describe variations in subjective intensities with stimulus intensities. Although absolute and discrimination thresholds had been studied, systematic investigation of thresholds or levels of work preference, work adaptation, and work stress were not quantified until Borg introduced his methods. For determining workplace criteria, the RPE methodology or its variations will continue to be useful for the study of work performance under adverse physical conditions (e.g., heat/cold stress or high altitudes; Gamberale & Holmer, 1977) and for the study of individuals with physical impairments and handicaps (e.g., cardiac abnormalities or partial curarization of muscles; Jones, 1986).

Strength/Capacity and Perceived Exertion. Psychophysics is an equally useful approach for determining capacities for handling tasks involving both frequent and infrequent manipulation of loads. Snook and Irvine (1969) distinguish between strength and capacity, indicating that *strength* determines the amount that can be lifted at infrequent intervals whereas *capacity* implies work performed over an extended time. Regardless of task frequency, three classes of variables influence sensations associated with exertion; these are (a) worker characteristics, such as gender, training, aerobic power, or attitude, (b) task variables, such as load, task complexity, or work space, and (c) environmental variables, such as heat, vibration, and work surface. Due to the influence of these variables and their interactions, it might appear that the possibilities for any psychophysical regularities or consistencies are limited. Although this may be true, interesting research has been done using consistent experimental procedures and that attempts to overcome the infinite situational constraints.

A pioneering series of studies by Snook and associates at Liberty Mutual Research Center focused on determining MMH tasks, maximum weights, forces, and rates acceptable to male and female populations (cf. Ciriello & Snook, 1983; Snook & Ciriello, 1974; Snook, Irvine, & Bass, 1970). The psychophysical methodology used to establish these strengths and capacities required subjects to manipulate loads according to their own perceptions of muscular effort. Snook and his associates evaluated six basic MMH tasks—lifting, lowering, pushing, pulling, carrying, and walking—because these activities, singly or in combination, constitute an adequate taxonomy of industrial MMH tasks. Task parameters varied by height, distance, and rate of work, with more recent work extending the basic paradigm to variations in hand placement (Drury & Pizatella, 1983) and posture (Chaffin, Andres & Garg, 1983). During the lifting, lowering, and carrying tasks, subjects were required to handle an industrial tote box using two handles. Subjects varied the weight of the box by adding or taking away loose lead shot; cues concerning total amount of shot contained within the box

were concealed from the subject. Pushing, pulling, and walking tasks were simulated using a treadmill, and subjects controlled the resistance of the treadmill belt, thereby controlling the force necessary to perform the task. Subjects were instructed to adjust their work load to the maximum amount they could perform without straining or becoming tired, weak, overheated, or out of breath. Typical dependent variables studied included force exerted and heart rate; the independent variables manipulated were usually load height, distance traveled, and rate of work performed.

Results for maximum weights and acceptable work loads are contained within a set of reference tables categorized by gender, task type, and task parameter (Ciriello & Snook, 1983; Snook, 1978). These results indicate that material handling task variables of size, distance, height, and frequency are important and different for male and female workers. For female workers, maximum acceptable task weights and forces are significantly and proportionally less than those for male workers.

The goal of Snook and others is to develop a normative data base for evaluation of population percentages capable of performing a task without overexertion or excessive fatigue. The implications for task evaluation, task design, and worker assessment are apparent. Obviously, the higher the population percentage who find a weight or work load acceptable, the lower the risk of injury; conversely, the lower the population percentage expected to perform the task, the greater the probability of injury. Samples of these data with population percentages of acceptable weights and rates are presented in Table 3 (Snook & Ciriello, 1974, p. 530). Other important results from this work indicate that (a) housewives handled less weight than either men or women in industry; (b) performance differences between men and women were greater at slow work rates (70%) than at fast work rates (85%); (c) gender differences were more pronounced for lifting, lowering, and carrying tasks than for pushing and pulling tasks—a finding consistent with

TABLE 3

**Maximum Weights Acceptable to Various Percentages
of the Male and Female Populations While Lifting a Tote Box**

		90%	*75%*	*50%*	*25%*	*10%*
Shoulder height to arm reach	Industrial men	29	39	49	59	68
	Industrial women	24	26	29	32	35
	Housewives	13	15	18	21	23
Knuckle height to shoulder height	Industrial men	14	43	53	62	71
	Industrial women	25	29	34	38	42
	Housewives	16	18	21	23	26
Floor level to knuckle height	Industrial men	17	45	54	63	70
	Industrial women	28	33	37	42	47
	Housewives	14	17	21	24	27

From: "Maximum Weights and Work Loads Acceptable to Female Workers" by S. H. Snook and B. M. Ciriello, 1974, *Journal of Occupational Medicine*, *16*, p. 530. Copyright 1974 by The American Occupational Medical Association. Adapted by permission.

Laubach's (1976) review indicating that gender differences in muscle strength are more pronounced in the upper extremities than in the lower extremities; and (d) gender differences in body size are not as great as gender differences in maximum acceptable weights and work loads, a finding consistent with that of Nordgren (1972).

A great deal of research exists that uses psychophysical methodology to determine guidelines for work practices. Ayoub, Mital, Bakken, Asfour, and Bethea (1980) reviewed the literature related to MMH activities to develop norms for strength and capacity activities. Their findings are limited to weight-lifting activities and are based on research by Snook and his associates and a NIOSH-supported study of lifting capacity (Ayoub et al., 1978). Generally, women's strength in lifting is about 65 percent that of men's, with comparative modal values of 11.77 kilograms versus 18.12 kilograms, respectively (Chaffin, 1974). With regard to lifting capacity, Ayoub et al. (1978) found that lifting capacity diminishes linearly with increases in box volume and performance frequency; they also concluded that lifting capacity diminishes with increases in height of

lift and with lowering of the lifting task's point of origin. Studies of push/pull activities indicate that force capabilities augment with increases in foot traction. Contrary to popular stereotypes, Kroemer (1974) found that body weight and body size are inaccurate predictors of force output. Both initial and sustained push forces acceptable to male and female workers diminish with distance moved, and this trend is identical for carrying tasks (Snook & Ciriello, 1974).

Ayoub, Selan, and Jiang (1986) reviewed biomechanical, physiological, and psychophysical criteria used to determine lifting capacity and compared the recommendations emerging from the use of these procedures. In some cases, recommendations from the use of biomechanical and physiological models conflict; this is especially the case where the load to be lifted, though neither heavy nor lifted frequently, is sufficiently far from the spine that the compressive forces are substantial. Ayoub et al. suggest that the general MMH recommendations based on biomechanical models specifying lifting light loads at higher frequencies of lift and those based on physiological models specifying lifting heavier loads at lower frequencies of lift are oversimplifications of the complex nature of the lifting task. They correctly point out that biomechanical and physiological stresses are present in every lifting task; however, these need to be evaluated in light of psychophysical perceptions in order to determine lifting capacity.

The *Work Practices Guide for Manual Lifting* (NIOSH, 1981) summarizes weight-lifting recommendations in tabular form. These guidelines are based in part on the psychophysical studies discussed as well as on regression models for predicting lifting capacity. Generally, these regression models have two independent variables in common—the first is a measure of isometric back strength, and the second is gender. Although the inclusion of gender may contribute to the mathematical prediction of acceptable lifting load, the usefulness of such models for personnel decisions will no doubt be questioned under federal law. Nevertheless, the NIOSH guide provides an excellent summary of materials handling strength and capacity data that are unavailable in any other single source.

Personnel Selection Methodology in Physically Demanding Jobs

The study of physical requirements of jobs from an individual differences perspective falls into the methodological tradition of industrial psychology. Although the issue of greatest interest is personnel selection, the research base on individual differences in physical work performance is substantially underdeveloped. For example, consider that the first APA publication on physical abilities personnel selection research appeared as recently as 1979 (cf. Reilly, Zedeck, & Tenopyr, 1979) and that only four additional studies have appeared subsequently in APA journals (cf. Arnold, Rauchenberger, Soubel, & Guion, 1982; Hogan, 1985, in press; Hogan & Quigley, 1986). Nevertheless, there is considerable interest in such research because incorrect personnel decisions can result in lost

productivity, increased medical and insurance costs due to job injuries, and possible legal challenges of unfair employment practices.

Over the past decade, industry has relied on physical performance research to provide assessments of job requirements and applicant capabilities for purposes of personnel selection. These efforts have been carried out by a handful of researchers, and in many cases, their results are guarded closely by the sponsoring organizations. Methods for developing and validating physical ability tests have not achieved the visibility of methods used in other selection research. Therefore, this section focuses on alternative methods and procedures useful for establishing fair physical ability selection tests. Areas considered include job analysis, criterion development, and physical ability tests.

Job Analysis

Personnel selection, placement, and performance appraisal decisions that address physical ability to perform a job are subject to the same conceptual considerations and professional guidelines as other personnel decisions. Complete job analysis information enumerates in detail the tasks to be performed and the knowledge, skill, and ability requirements to perform them. As the most important step in the development of any assessment procedure, it provides the foundation of evidence upon which all subsequent decisions regarding the form, content, administration, and scoring of assessment procedures are based. Professional guidelines, as reflected in the *Standards for Educational and Psychological Testing* issued by the APA (1985), the American Educational Research Association, and the National Council on Measurement in Education, and the *Principles for the Validation and Use of Personnel Selection Procedures* (3rd ed.), issued by the Society for Industrial and Organizational Psychology (SIOP; 1987) of the APA, stress the importance of job analysis. The *Standards* notes: "Job analyses provide the primary basis for defining the content domain of a job." In addition, the U.S. Supreme Court ruled in *Albemarle Paper Company v. Moody* (1975) that job analysis must be an integral part of any validation study that claims to demonstrate a relationship between a selection device and job performance. Likewise, the federal *Uniform Guidelines on Employee Selection Procedures* (EEOC, 1978) requires that job analyses be performed for all jobs on which any validation studies are conducted.

As with other requirements, the evaluation of physical ability requirements of jobs attempts to identify component requirements, such as tasks, through the application of a formalized systematic process for data collection, analysis, and interpretation (Sparks, 1982). Job analyses documenting physical requirements are conducted almost exclusively for test validation purposes, which extend to personnel selection, placement, and performance appraisal. Job analysis information serves to identify important/critical tasks and physical behaviors, and performance-related costs associated with varying degrees of ability. Although job analysis information may be developed in many ways, identification of the physical requirements of a job typically relies on multiple methods and procedures.

Interestingly, early modern job analytic procedures were used to identify, describe, and evaluate physical actions. Taylor's scientific management evaluations, as well as the Gilbreths' motion studies, are the essence of job analysis used for these purposes. Although we have probably not improved on the task inventory methodology important for time and motion studies, other methodologies are available—some of which are only moderately appropriate for personnel selection. Our focus here is the use of job analysis for personnel selection in physically demanding jobs.

In their evaluation of job analysis methodologies, Levine, Ash, Hall, and Sistrunk (1981, 1983) note that methodologies differ in terms of descriptors used (e.g., tasks, activities, or elements), sources consulted, and methods of data collection. They also suggest that methodologies can be evaluated in terms of their orientation—either microscopic or macroscopic. *Microscopic* orientations focus on the functional outcome of descriptor types, whereas *macroscopic* orientations consider the job analysis as a gestalt and ask if different methods will result in different outcomes. Although methodologies to assess the physical requirements of jobs differ in the ways suggested by Levine et al., little or no research has evaluated the benefits or shortcomings of either microscopic or macroscopic orientations. Within the larger scope of job analysis evaluations, research by Pearlman (1980) suggests that fine-grained descriptors, such as tasks or activities, are not as useful for personnel selection as broader descriptors, such as functions or duties; further, it is clear from the Levine et al. evaluation that job analyses vary enormously in their organizational purposes and outcomes. Because these results are drawn from a variety of methods and occupational settings, we would expect similar trends from evaluations of methods to analyze physical requirements of jobs.

Eight methods are widely used by job analysts to assess the physical requirements of work and represent very different approaches to the study of work requirements. Seven of these methods were reviewed by Levine et al. (1981, 1983); those data provide additional evaluative criteria not covered in this discussion.

Personnel selection research whose primary focus is physical abilities relies heavily on job analytic procedures developed by Fleishman and his associates. These procedures focus on systematic identification and scaling of human abilities required for either job or task performance. Although several forms of Fleishman's instrument exist, the most comprehensive appears in the *Manual of Ability Requirement Scales* (MARS; Fleishman, 1975, in press; Fleishman & Quaintance, 1984, pp. 461–464). Within MARS is a set of nine physical ability rating scales (Physical Abilities Analysis; PAA), which correspond to the factor structure of physical fitness tests identified by Fleishman (1964).

Fleishman (1964) defines abilities as general traits, which are to be contrasted with skill—proficiency at a single task. Because the scales are derived from a taxonomy, they are appropriate for evaluating any task and identifying individual differences in task and performance requirements. The physical abilities for which rating procedures are available include: static strength, dynamic strength, explosive strength, trunk strength, dynamic flexibility, extent flexibility, stamina, balance, and gross body coordination. Each ability is defined and examples presented that distinguish it from other conceptually similar abilities. Five- or seven-point rating scales are provided with generic task examples. Anchor examples were chosen empirically, based on their rated means and standard deviations, to ensure clarity and agreement on the amount of ability required. Raters, who may be job analysts or subject-matter experts, are given a list of tasks along with the PAA scales and independently rate each task on each ability scale. The result is a physical ability profile by task and, through desired analyses, by job and by job family. A sample rating scale is presented in Figure 10.

The PAA is most useful for specifying abilities appropriate for measurement in either criterion-related or construct validation research. Use of this method alone is not appropriate for justification of employment tests based on a content validity rationale. The method identifies abilities important for job performance and uses task behavior insofar as it permits analysis of abilities. In fact, a task inventory is a prerequisite for PAA use. Although task inventories differ from job to job, the PAA rating process is standardized (Fleishman, 1979) and is sufficiently powerful to differentiate abilities required among jobs (Hogan, Ogden, & Fleishman, 1979); further, its results tend to be reliable across rating groups (Hogan, Ogden, & Fleishman, 1979).

A second job analysis procedure, developed exclusively for the evaluation of physically demanding jobs, is the *Index of Perceived Effort* (IPE; Hogan & Fleishman, 1979). The IPE is a rating scale developed using psychophysical procedures; it was designed to estimate the work costs associated with task performance. The seven-point scale includes a definition of perceived effort and uses either generic anchors (very, very easy to very, very hard) or task anchors whose psychometric characteristics are known (Hogan & Fleishman, 1979). The index differentiates reliably among tasks and can be used reliably across rating groups (Hogan, Ogden, Gebhardt, & Fleishman, 1980). Validity evidence for the IPE exists using both metabolic and ergonomic work costs (Hogan & Fleishman, 1979; Hogan, Ogden, Gebhardt, & Fleishman, 1980). The strengths of the IPE for the study of physical demands include demonstrated reliability and validity, developmental background of psychophysics, and prediction of both metabolic rates and forces required to perform physically demanding tasks.

Supervisors and job analysts use the IPE to evaluate individual tasks identified as part of a job. The IPE means and standard deviations are calculated for each task, and on this basis decisions can be made to identify critical, physically demanding tasks. Mean ratings calculated for numerous tasks within individual job inventories are available as are grand means across jobs and job families (Hogan & Arneson, 1988; Hogan & Bane, 1982; Hogan, Jennings, Ogden, & Fleishman, 1980; Hogan, Ogden, & Fleishman, 1979; Hogan, Pederson, & Zonderman, 1981). This allows the researcher to make mean comparisons across jobs, job families, and industries in order to evaluate and justify a task as critical for job performance.

Other than the PAA and IPE, no job analysis procedure is dedicated exclusively to the study of physically demanding work. However, three well-known methods could be applied in personnel research about specific physical demands. First, an approach such as *Task Inventory with the Comprehensive Occupational Data Analysis Program* (TI/CODAP; Christal, 1974)

FIGURE 10

Physical Ability Analysis Rating Scale for Static Strength

Static Strength: This is the ability to use muscle force to lift, push, pull, or carry objects. This ability can involve the hand, arm, back, shoulder, or leg.

How Static Strength Is Different From Other Abilities

Use muscle to exert force against *objects*.	vs.	**Dynamic Strength and Trunk Strength:** Use muscle power repeatedly to hold or move the body's own weight.
Use continuous muscle force, without stopping, up to the amount needed to lift, push, pull, or carry an object.	vs.	**Explosive Strength:** Gather energy to move one's own body to propel some t object with *short bursts* of muscle force.
Does not involve the use of muscle force over a *long* time.	vs.	**Stamina:** *Does* involve physical exertion over a long time.

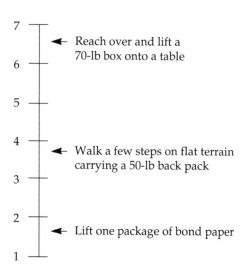

Requires use of all the muscle force possible to lift, carry, push, or pull a very heavy object.

7 — Reach over and lift a 70-lb box onto a table

6

5

4 — Walk a few steps on flat terrain carrying a 50-lb back pack

3

2 — Lift one package of bond paper

1

Requires use of little muscle force to lift, carry, push, or pull a light object.

From "Ability Requirement Scales" by E. A. Fleishman and M. D. Mumford. In *Job Analysis Handbook* (p. 923) by S. Gael (Ed.), 1988, New York: Wiley. Copyright © 1988 by John Wiley & Sons, Inc. Reprinted by permission.

is fundamental for identification of required job behaviors. A task inventory lists tasks performed by workers in a way that is meaningful to the incumbent. The inventory format then requires some type of task evaluation by the incumbent or rater. This might be an estimate of relative time spent, importance, difficulty, consequence of performance error, or frequency. Although TI/CODAP procedures can serve several distinct purposes, particularly those of a large military system, the general procedures for developing task statements and task inventories are useful as a first step in a systematic study of physical requirements.

Second, the *Critical Incident Technique* (Flanagan, 1954) is an invaluable tool for criterion development in empirical validation studies. From incumbents or supervisors, incidents are gathered that represent outstanding job performance and inferior or unacceptable performance. Both the actions and the consequences of the incidents are fully described; the researcher then investigates and attempts to gather as many viable incidents as possible. Incidents take the form of recorded scenarios that describe (a) what led up to the incident, (b) what the employee did that was so effective or ineffective, and (c) what the consequences of the behavior were. After the incidents are collected, they are analyzed and interpreted. The outcome of the analysis is a set of attributes, categories, or dimensions that underlie successful performance; the quality of this outcome depends entirely on the richness of the incidents and the "clinical" judgment of the analysts. Under the best of circumstances, this method yields excellent dimensions for performance-rating criteria in physically demanding jobs.

Third, *Functional Job Analysis* (FJA; Fine & Wiley, 1971) can be extremely helpful for the development of physical tests. Because of their complexity, the procedures for use are not described here; however, features that are relevant for physical ability testing are mentioned briefly. FJA requires the development of a *task bank*—a detailed account of what the worker does, the sequence in which the work is performed, and the immediate result expected from the worker's action. Each task is rated using seven different scales and placed in a context that details the organization's goals and objectives, training needed, and performance standards. The advantage of this information for test development is that (a) the worker actions are explicit, (b) the sequence for task performance is documented, and (c) the evaluation or scoring system is built into the performance standards. Two weaknesses are in translating task content to test content and in operationalizing scoring procedures from task standards. However, these problems may be more appropriately solved by the test developer than the job analyst.

The remaining three job analysis methods in which the physical requirements of jobs receive some attention are the *Job Element Method* (Primoff, 1971), the *Position Analysis Questionnaire* (McCormick, Jeanneret, & Mecham, 1972; Mecham, 1977), and *threshold traits analysis* (Lopez, Kesselman, & Lopez, 1981). The goal of each method is to describe a job in terms of rated elements or functions representing a broad range of worker requirements. Although each method has definite strengths (Levine et al., 1981, 1983), it would be difficult to rely solely on any one of them to develop tests for assessing physical job requirements. Two major limitations are that the methods are not sufficiently comprehensive and that they do not provide adequate detail for assessment purposes. This is not to suggest that these methods are inappropriate for evaluating physical requirements of jobs; however, it would be necessary to augment the results with information specific to the physical domain.

Finally, Zedeck et al. (1988) applied a job analysis linkage model developed by Zedeck and Goldstein (1988) to the analysis of physical tasks performed by entry-level firefighters. The model, developed originally to evaluate the knowledge, nonphysical abilities, and skills used in job performance, required (a) identifying tasks performed on the job, (b) identifying physical abilities and skills required to do the tasks effectively, (c) eliminating tasks and abilities that were unimportant and unnecessary the first day on the job, and (d) linking the remaining abilities to task clusters and tasks that require them. The process yields a pool of critical tasks and abilities from which an appropriate and comprehensive battery of assessment procedures can be developed. This linkage model depends on a number of job analysis procedures, including observations, interviews, panel discussions, and questionnaires; these procedures require the participation of incumbents, their supervisors, and job analysts. Because the analysis uses detailed and sequential evaluations, the results lead to clear test development information about content, administration, scoring, and test weights. In addition, the link between the job task and the ability required to perform it is clear and defensible; moreover, this linkage procedure provides documentation that is acceptable under the federal *Uniform Guidelines* for demonstrating the relationship between work behavior and abilities necessary in studies reporting the content validity evidence for selection procedures.

Criterion Development

In any empirical validation study, job analysis results are fundamental for the development of criterion measures. Two of the three types of criteria used in past research rely heavily on job analysis information for development. A third criterion type, archival data, may be the most heavily influenced by the physical abilities of personnel. These data are usually maintained in employees' service records.

Job Performance Ratings.   Rating instruments that evaluate individual and overall aspects of job performance are perhaps the most commonly used means of gathering criterion data. Performance dimensions can be derived from the task or ability analysis or from critical incidents (Flanagan, 1954). Three themes that

repeatedly emerge from critical incidents of physical performance concern the ability to perform strenuous work, the ability to perform prolonged physical work, and the use of proper physical technique. Critical incident examples can not only be used to identify criterion rating categories, but can also be scaled and subsequently used for scale anchors. Regardless of how these rating categories are developed and scaled, they should reflect the degree to which incumbents perform critical tasks properly and effectively.

Although supervisory ratings of incumbents' performance are typically used as criterion data, at least two other rater groups should be considered. First, self-ratings using an identical appraisal instrument can be a useful check on the accuracy of supervisory ratings. Denning (1984) collected both supervisory and self-ratings on 12 dimensions of performance developed from a task analysis and an ability analysis and found that incumbent ($N = 1,100$) self-ratings correlated significantly with supervisory ratings as well as with most of the physical ability test predictors in the experimental battery. The information was useful in evaluating the possibility of so-called supervisor bias in ratings of women and minority group members. Denning's study suggests that, when properly trained, supervisors should not provide evaluations that are inherently biased and that the typical validities achieved for physical tests using supervisory ratings are not gender-biased ratings, but are in fact a function of job performance. Self-ratings are therefore a useful check on the validity of other criterion ratings. Although traditionally the accuracy of self-assessments has been questionable (cf. Anderson, Warner, & Spencer, 1984), Denning's results are corroborated by more recent research by Farh, Werbel, and Bedeian (1988), who found congruency between self- and supervisor ratings as well as criterion-related validity using both types of ratings.

Second, peer ratings can be extremely useful in situations where incumbents cannot be supervised closely and where the work is performed by teams or crews. Established crews are quite capable of evaluating their members' performance; in some situations (e.g., remote work sites), peer ratings may be of higher quality than supervisory ratings. Obviously, however, the more sources of rating data available, the greater the possibility for evaluating their reliability and validity. A word of advice for obtaining performance ratings in concurrent validation research might be appropriate: The collection of criterion data prior to administration of the predictor battery will reduce the "contamination" effect that occurs when prior knowledge of test performance influences the subsequent rating given to an incumbent.

Job Domain or Job Sample Measures. Through the task analysis inventory results, IPE ratings, and/or ability analysis, it is possible to identify critical physically demanding tasks that may constitute a large portion of the physical requirements of a single job. It may also be the case that satisfactory performance of a critical task would ensure satisfactory job performance of all or most physical requirements. If so, requirements of this critical task could be constructed into a job sample criterion measure where task characteristics are simulated. Although the degree of similarity between the job task and the criterion measure can vary, performance fidelity is more important than physical fidelity. A job sample criterion usually involves either measuring or rating the performance of a simulated task required on the job. Physical ability job samples are developmentally and methodologically identical to job samples in other domains; they enjoy the same advantages and are handicapped by the same weaknesses (e.g., see Guion, 1977, 1978; Tenopyr, 1977). Therefore, there are only a few points that might be raised about them, three of which will be mentioned here.

First, concurrent validation studies, the most frequently used empirical strategy, are conducted using predictor and criterion scores from the current incumbent research sample. For jobs with physical demands, employees who are unable to perform are frequently transferred to other less demanding jobs. As a result, some individuals who are physically incapable of performing adequately are excluded from the research sample, with the effect of restricting the range of criterion scores and quite possibly the range of predictor scores as well. Use of a job sample criterion measure would permit testing of individuals previously found to be unacceptable performers and would provide important information otherwise unobtainable on the abilities of low-rated employees.

Second, because the content of the job sample is explicit, criterion measurement is clear. This is not always the case with rating criteria even after all precautions are taken to ensure standardization and reliability. Therefore, interpretation of predictor-criterion relationships is made easier and more explicit when the criterion measure is a job sample.

Third (and this point may be of concern to only a few researchers), this measure, if properly developed, can satisfy the provisions of the *Uniform Guidelines* as well as the peer review process for research within the psychology profession (cf. Arnold, Rauschenberger, Soubel, & Guion, 1982). However, the job sample measures are test behaviors. The measure is constructed specifically for the purpose of gathering research data; it is standardized with regard to instructions, scoring, starting point, and ending point. The performance of a work sample typically takes place independent of job performance and is often administered along with the battery of predictor tests. Although a job sample can be considered a criterion measure, it is also in the domain of test behavior. Results of predictor-criterion relationships reflect this status, with correlations substantially higher than those obtained between test-nontest performance. In fact, within the assessment of strength capabilities, test–job sample correlations begin to approach the results obtained when two measures of strength are correlated. The point is not to suggest that job sample measures are inappropriate as criteria; rather, it appears that they are conceptually and procedurally different from nontest criteria. Nevertheless, we need to consider carefully the meaning of strong relationships between maximum performance on physical ability tests and on job sample measures when the relationship between physical ability and on-the-job performance is unknown (e.g., see Campion, 1983).

Archival Data. The incumbent's service record may provide an excellent source of criterion data that reflect a relatively uncontaminated view of physical ability to perform. Such objective criteria as accidents, work-related injuries, absences, assignment to light or special duty, job transfer, and so on may indicate insufficient physical capabilities. Unfortunately, data to support this assumption are often not available or have not been gathered and analyzed in the most appropriate manner. Reports by Chaffin (1974), Keyserling (1979), Pederson (1984), Laughery and Schmidt (1984), and Hogan and Arneson (1990) suggest that even with conservative evaluations there is a reliable association between physical ability and industrial incidents. Chaffin's (1974; Chaffin, Herrin, & Keyserling, 1978) work linking biomechanical strength assessments with incident rates of low back injuries indicates that low back injuries increase as employees approach or exceed their capabilities while working on the job. Keyserling (1979) found that employees hired and placed on jobs according to results of strength tests had fewer medical incidents than a group hired without such standards. Using a retrospective analysis, Laughery and Schmidt (1984) analyzed 229 back injuries that occurred over a two-year period among petrochemical workers in a large manufacturing complex. Their results indicated that most injuries were due to overexertion and occurred in tasks requiring manual materials handling, valve operation, and equipment assembly/disassembly.

Although most of these investigations deal with jobs held almost exclusively by men,

analysis of jobs with physical demands and performed largely by women shows similar results. For example, Hogan and Arneson (1990) found that the lift strength of female therapists who provide direct care for profoundly retarded residents of care facilities was predictive not only of supervisor ratings but also of injuries. Compared to the total group ($N = 167$), therapists scoring below the strength mean for the group suffered twice as many on-the-job injuries, each of which required twice the recovery time and twice the amount of insurance compensation as injuries sustained by others.

Methodological constraints prevail for obtaining and using archival data in validation research. The primary concern is for accurate, reliable, and systematic record keeping. Errors are difficult to detect and often go unnoticed; the result is an attenuated relationship between predictors and criteria. Causal interpretations of criteria are also of concern. Numerous studies confirm the association between physical inability and injuries. However, the psychological correlates of these incidents should not be dismissed or overlooked. Conventional wisdom among employers is that some injuries and workers' compensation claims are bogus and that a small number of individuals in the work force accounts for a disproportionate number of incidents. This syndrome is called *malingering*, a form of organizational delinquency associated with a stable set of personality characteristics (Hogan & Arneson, 1990). This possible explanation for injuries in the workplace should be recognized and not confounded with physical inability to perform the job.

Physical Ability Tests

Predictor development or specification usually requires merging several sources of job information to provide comprehensive coverage of the job domain. If one chooses to develop content-oriented tests, the tests represent a sample of the content of the job and are thus capable of providing a description of performance. The validity of these tests comes not from empirical prediction and inferences made from test scores, but from the knowledge that an applicant's performance on the test will most likely resemble performance on the job domains sampled. It is difficult to draw conclusions about the potential usefulness of content-oriented tests across situations because of their inherent specificity. However, considerations for using these types of tests and rules for constructing test content are examined in detail by Guion (1978). Content-oriented tests are used widely by state and local police and fire organizations, and although they tend to differ across organizations, they typically sample critical activities associated with subduing and rescuing victims, gaining access, and handling equipment. Tests of this type are developed and evaluated on a case-by-case basis; as a result, the knowledge base for "content valid" physical tests has not accumulated systematically.

On the other hand, the knowledge base for physical ability tests used as predictors in empirical validation studies has grown steadily since the late 1970s. The strategy for developing and specifying predictors is to represent and measure physical ability constructs identified as important in the job analysis phase and to design test properties and procedures that permit empirical validation. In addition, researchers who develop tests often attempt to include content activities that simulate or require actions common to large numbers of tasks across job categories (e.g., lifting action). Test development that results in an adequate experimental battery must take into account construct definitions of the relevant ability domain, as well as the behavioral definitions of these abilities, in order to ensure a reasonable degree of physical fidelity to actual job operations. Selection of experimental predictors should also be based on evidence of validity, adverse impact, and administrative feasibility and reliability.

As emphasized in Fleishman's (1964) factor analyses, numerous physical fitness and ability tests exist. The problem is to evaluate them for usefulness in making employment decisions. Since the appearance of the *Uniform Guidelines,* research to determine the validity of physical tests for personnel selection has been conducted in many employment settings. These investigations are concerned exclusively with the prediction of physically demanding work performance, and the data are provided by male and female incumbents whose abilities approximate normally trained rather than highly trained subjects.

A sample of these studies shall now be presented to provide structure and measurement information for evaluating alternative predictors (see Tables 4, 5, and 6). Although the studies covered a wide range of jobs across a variety of industries, the measures generally included were based on job analysis results and therefore represented an attempt to match job requirements to abilities measured by the test. That is, the predictors are ability tests hypothesized to be important for performance in the jobs under evaluation. The studies included were construct and criterion-related investigations using either a concurrent or predictive strategy; content-oriented tests were not analyzed. The research samples included both male and female employed adults in private and public sector organizations.

Classification of Predictors. The tests were classified in two separate steps. First, they were categorized according to seven physical performance constructs. Although any number of constructs and taxonomies could be used for classification (e.g., see Fleishman, 1964; Fleishman & Quaintance, 1984; Hogan, 1989), the seven constructs chosen provided a parsimonious yet sufficient model for conceptualizing the physical performance test under review (see Hogan, 1985, in press). Second, within each physical construct, tests were grouped according to criteria used for validation. These criteria

TABLE 4

Descriptive Statistics and Correlations for Physical Performance Tests: Empirical Validation Studies Using Objective Criteria

Physical Dimension	Ref. No.[a]	Test	Criterion	Males Females			Males			Females			Percent Overlap
				r	r	r	M	SD	n	M	SD	n	
Muscular tension	4	Grip-dominant	Production units	.30**	-.09	-.11	115.4	18.4	108	69.4	13.5	21	15
	4	Grip-dominant	Production units	.34**	.14	-.15	108.3	17.7	108	65.6	14.8	21	19
	5	Pull (isometric)	No. medical days off	-.15*	-.06	-.07	18.2	8.0	127	10.2	5.6	25	57
	7	Static push	Employed vs. transferred	.75**	—	—	709.4	142.7	41	451.6	121.4	22	33
	7	Static pull	Employed vs. transferred	.67**	—	—	563.3	100.0	41	382.1	83.3	22	32
	11	Grip strength	Training completion time	-.11	-.25	-.14	58.4	16.2	132	38.9	15.9	78	34
	11	Cable pull	Training completion time	.24**	.20*	.06	60.6	13.4	132	40.2	8.2	78	34
Muscular power	5	Power	No. medical days off	.07	.12	.59**	319.1	112.5	127	34.7	10.7	25	56
Muscular endurance	4	Push-ups	Production units	.20*	-.03	-.33	14.2	3.9	108	4.0	3.5	21	17
	4	Leg lifts	Production units	.06	-.07	-.33	13.0	2.1	108	10.5	1.9	21	53
	5	Ratchet	No. medical days off	.19*	-.06	-.12	45.2	8.8	127	34.7	10.7	25	60

TABLE 4

Descriptive Statistics and Correlations for Physical Performance Tests: Empirical Validation Studies Using Objective Criteria (continued)

Physical Dimension	Ref. No.[a]	Test	Criterion	Males Females			Males			Females			Percent Overlap
				r	r	r	M	SD	n	M	SD	n	
Muscular endurance (continued)	7	Dynamic arm strength (ergometer)	Employed vs. transferred	.54**	—	—	166.3	36.1	41	123.8	24.2	22	48
	11	Dynamic leg strength (ergometer)	Training completion time	.03	-.07	.12	82.0	20.7	83	61.7	14.7	54	47
	11	Dynamic arm strength (ergometer)	Training completion time	.06	.06	-.12	61.9	14.7	132	33.9	11.2	78	29
	11	Sit-ups	Training completion time	.02	-.15	-.18	15.4	4.2	132	10.1	3.9	78	51
Cardio-vascular endurance	11	Step-up time	Training completion time	.26**	.24**	.32*	137.7	57.9	132	85.5	47.4	78	62
	11	Body density	Training completion time	.40**	.31**	.54**	106.5	2.0	132	105.0	1.4	78	66
Flexibility	4	Sit & reach	Production units	.10	.03	.05	15.4	3.1	108	14.0	3.1	21	82
	4	Bend, twist & touch	Production units	.22*	.17	.04	13.1	2.5	108	11.1	2.8	21	71
	5	Flexibility course	No. medical days off	.08	-.03	-.16	19.1	5.2	127	24.0	6.3	25	67
	7	Flexibility course time	Employed vs. transferred	-.60**	—	—	86.5	23.2	41	105.2	22.3	22	68

TABLE 4

Descriptive Statistics and Correlations for Physical Performance Tests: Empirical Validation Studies Using Objective Criteria (continued)

Physical Dimension	Ref. No.[a]	Test	Criterion	Males Females			Males			Females			Percent Overlap
				r	r	r	M	SD	n	M	SD	n	
Flexibility (continued)	7	Flexibility course faults	Employed vs. transferred	-.41**	—		1.2	1.5	41	1.8	1.9	22	85
	11	Twist & touch	Training completion time	-.20	-.31	-.22	15.2	8.5	132	14.5	7.7	78	97
Balance	7	Balance against resistance	Employed vs. transferred	.72**	—		350.2	79.5	41	198.6	74.1	22	32
	11	Static rail balance ($^3/_4$-inch beam)	Training completion time	.29**	.27**	.45**	5.3	2.0	132	4.4	1.8	78	81
Neuro-muscular coordination	4	Order picker simulation	Production units	.47**	.37**	.25	108.7	30.3	108	161.5	33.9	21	41
	7	Minnesota Rate Manipulation	Employed vs. transferred	-.38**	—		89.3	14.5	41	90.8	11.7	22	96

*p ≤ .05 **p ≤ .01

[a]Validation Study References
1. Arnold, Rauschenberger, Soubel, & Guion, 1982 (site b)
2. Denning, 1984 (Production)
3. Denning, 1984 (Maintenance)
4. Hogan, Ogden, & Fleishman, 1979
5. Hogan & Pederson, 1984
6. Hogan, Arneson, Hogan, & Jones, 1986
7. Hogan & Arneson, 1988
8. Jackson & Osburn, 1983
9. Myers, Gebhardt, Crump, & Fleishman, 1984
10. Reilly, Zedeck, & Tenopyr, 1979 (Exp. 1)
11. Reilly, Zedeck, & Tenopyr, 1979 (Exp.2)
12 Robertson & Trent, 1983
13. Wilmore & Davis, 1979
14. Wunder, 1981

TABLE 5

Descriptive Statistics and Correlations for Physical Performance Tests: Empirical Validation Studies Using Subjective Criteria

Physical Dimension	Ref. No.[a]	Test	Criterion	Males Females			Males			Females			Percent Overlap
				r	r	r	M	SD	n	M	SD	n	
Muscular tension	2	Push (isometric)	Overall job performance	.18**	.05	.08	283.2	69.6	630	186.1	42.5	187	38
	2	Pull (isometric)	Overall job performance	.11**	−.03	.02	224.2	50.2	630	160.0	37.2	187	46
	2	Cable pull	Overall job performance	.19**	.04	.07	163.7	38.3	630	100.0	24.8	187	31
	3	Push (isometric)	Overall job performance	.12**	.04	−.23	287.2	61.8	221	216.8	46.1	16	51
	3	Pull (isometric)	Overall job performance	.12**	.05	−.28	233.3	49.9	221	178.6	38.2	16	53
	3	Cable pull	Overall job performance	.25**	.02	.24	172.9	42.8	221	106.2	29.3	16	35
	5	Static lift	Related job performance	.25**	.15	.09	47.3	12.7	127	32.9	12.7	25	57
	6	Static lift	Ratings of physical activity	.49**	.27*	.24**	8.7	.9	38	3.3	1.0	113	0
	10	Grip strength	Overall training performance	.24**	−.04	.34*	60.3	8.1	83	40.6	5.4	45	14
	11	Cable pull	Overall training performance	.29**	.17	.19	52.9	10.2	83	35.8	7.0	45	32
	12	Valve turn (progressive)	Summary physical performance rating	.43*	—	—	—	—	—	—	—	—	—
	12	Static push	Summary physical performance rating	.54**	—	—	—	—	—	—	—	—	—

TABLE 5

Descriptive Statistics and Correlations for Physical Performance Tests: Empirical Validation Studies Using Subjective Criteria (continued)

Physical Dimension	Ref. No.[a]	Test	Criterion	Males Females			Males			Females			Percent Overlap
				r	r	r	M	SD	n	M	SD	n	
Muscular tension (continued)	12	Static lift	Summary physical performance rating	.56**	—	—	—	—	—	—	—	—	—
Muscular power	2	Medicine ball put	Overall job performance	.26**	.12**	.06	39.1	8.3	630	18.5	5.3	187	13
	3	Medicine ball put	Overall job performance	.20**	.03	.26	39.3	8.5	221	19.7	4.6	16	13
	5	Torque	Related job performance	.13*	.05	-.16	314.2	118.2	127	203.5	84.1	25	56
	14	Leverage	Summary physical performance rating	.41**	—	—	—	—	—	—	—	—	—
Muscular endurance	2	Arm ergometer	Overall job performance	.16**	.00	.23**	194.8	52.6	630	126.1	34.0	187	43
	3	Arm ergometer	Overall job performance	.11	.14*	.43	197.9	53.8	221	120.8	46.7	16	44
	5	Endurance (ergometer)	Related job performance	.10	.01	.17	45.2	8.8	127	34.7	10.7	25	58
Cardio-vascular endurance	2	Skinfold	Overall job performance	-.17**	.00	-.06	27.0	10.6	630	47.4	14.1	187	41
	3	Skinfold	Overall job performance	-.27*	-.10	-.46	24.1	9.8	221	52.1	11.6	16	24
	9	Body density	Overall training performance	.16*	-.03	.15	106.6	1.4	83	105.0	1.2	45	54

TABLE 5

Descriptive Statistics and Correlations for Physical Performance Tests: Empirical Validation Studies Using Subjective Criteria (continued)

Physical Dimension	Ref. No.[a]	Test	Criterion	Males	Females		Males			Females			Percent Overlap
				r	r	r	M	SD	n	M	SD	n	
Cardiovascular endurance (continued)	9	Step-up time	Overall training performance	-.01	.20*	-.17	127.8	74.2	83	77.5	35.8	45	65
	9	Harvard step index	Overall training performance	-.02	.20*	-.17	32.0	19.1	83	22.8	12.2	45	76
Flexibility	2	Sit & reach	Overall job performance	.04	.10**	.01	53.1	16.5	630	59.4	14.5	187	84
	3	Sit & reach	Overall job performance	-.12	.09	.47	49.7	17.8	221	64.2	13.5	16	64
	5	Flexibility course	Rated job performance	.22**	-.11	-.21	19.1	5.2	127	24.0	6.3	25	67
	10	Twist & touch	Overall training performance	-.03	-.02	.02	21.0	11.2	83	23.6	9.7	45	90
	14	Twist & touch	Summary performance rating	-.14	—	—	—	—	—	—	—	—	—
	14	Flexibility course	Summary performance rating	-.20	—	—	—	—	—	—	—	—	—
Balance	2	Static rail balance (3/4-inch beam)	Overall job performance	.05	.02	.01	11.0	13.0	630	7.9	6.4	187	85

TABLE 5

Descriptive Statistics and Correlations for Physical Performance Tests: Empirical Validation Studies Using Subjective Criteria (continued)

Physical Dimension	Ref. No.[a]	Test	Criterion	Males Females r	Males r	Females r	Males M	Males SD	Males n	Females M	Females SD	Females n	Percent Overlap
Balance (continued)	3	Static rail balance (³/₄-inch beam)	Overall job performance	.03	.02	.20	10.7	10.0	221	10.6	9.7	16	100
	10	Static rail balance (³/₄-inch beam)	Overall training performance	.19*	.14	.21	20.3	23.3	83	14.4	14.5	45	79
	14	Static rail balance	Summary performance rating	.16	—	—	—	—	—	—	—	—	—
	14	Pipe walk	Summary performance rating	.11	—	—	—	—	—	—	—	—	—
Neuromuscular coordination	2	Minnesota rate manipulation	Overall job performance	−.13**	−.14**	−.18**	66.5	9.4	630	65.5	8.7	187	96
	3	Minnesota rate manipulation	Overall job performance	.00	−.07**	−.24	68.0	10.5	221	59.1	5.2	16	57

*$p \leq .05$ **$p \leq .01$

[a]Validation Study References

1. Arnold, Rauschenberger, Soubel, & Guion, 1982 (site b)
2. Denning, 1984 (Production)
3. Denning, 1984 (Maintenance)
4. Hogan, Ogden, & Fleishman, 1979
5. Hogan & Pederson, 1984
6. Hogan, Arneson, Hogan, & Jones, 1986
7. Hogan & Arneson, 1988
8. Jackson & Osburn, 1983
9. Myers, Gebhardt, Crump, & Fleishman, 1984
10. Reilly, Zedeck, & Tenopyr, 1979 (Exp. 1)
11. Reilly, Zedeck, & Tenopyr, 1979 (Exp.2)
12. Robertson & Trent, 1983
13. Wilmore & Davis, 1979
14. Wunder, 1981

TABLE 6

Descriptive Statistics and Correlations for Physical Performance Tests: Empirical Validation Studies Using Work Sample Criteria

Physical Dimension	Ref. No.[a]	Test	Criterion	Males	Females		Males			Females			Percent Overlap
				r	r	r	M	SD	n	M	SD	n	
Muscular tension	1	Leg dynamometer	Work sample composite	.73**	—	—	132.3	36.9	168	76.9	26.2	81	38
	1	Arm dynamometer	Work sample composite	.85**	—	—	21.8	3.8	168	12.1	2.9	81	15
	1	Back dynamometer	Work sample composite	.78**	—	—	58.8	11.4	168	34.8	6.8	81	19
	7	Static push	Tube lance cleaning	.82**	.61**	.71**	709.4	142.7	41	451.6	121.4	22	33
	7	Static pull	Crawler hose removal	.87**	.79**	.88**	563.3	100.0	41	382.1	83.3	22	32
	7	Total isometric strength	Roof bolting task	.91**	.77**	.74**	417.5	77.3	25	242.6	46.8	25	16
	7	Isokinetic bench press	Roof bolting task	.90**	.78**	.59**	471.0	117.8	25	205.3	80.4	25	18
	8	Handgrip	Lift task	.68**	.29**	.21**	47.4	7.3	976	30.2	5.5	999	64
	8	Lift 60 kg.	Lift task	.77**	.43**	.35**	60.6	10.7	969	29.8	5.4	986	45
	8	Lift 72 kg.	Lift task	.76**	.42**	.33**	56.7	10.5	969	25.6	4.7	986	45
	8	Upright pull	Lift task	.71**	.35**	.26**	124.8	21.2	974	77.1	13.5	1000	62
	11	Arm lift	Torque bolt	.82**	.54**	.46**	104.8	17.5	350	60.9	11.4	269	13
	11	Arm pull	Torque bolt	.91**	.78**	.68**	147.5	26.1	350	79.4	17.6	269	12
	12	Handgrip	Rescue simulation	—	-.29*	—	53.7	7.7	412	36.1	4.8	16	16

TABLE 6

Descriptive Statistics and Correlations for Physical Performance Tests: Empirical Validation Studies Using Work Sample Criteria (continued)

Physical Dimension	Ref. No.[a]	Test	Criterion	Males Females			Males			Females			Percent Overlap
				r	r	r	M	SD	n	M	SD	n	
Muscular tension (continued)	12	Bench press	Rescue simulation	—	-.35*	—	70.7	13.8	412	48.1	6.4	16	26
Muscular power	11	Ergometer	Torque bolt	.82**	.55**	.49**	58.4	9.4	350	35.0	8.5	269	19
	12	Vertical jump	Arrest simulation	—	.50*	—	20.1	2.6	412	16.9	2.8	15	56
Muscular endurance	1	Leg lifts	Work sample composite	.30**	—	—	16.4	3.2	168	11.4	4.7	81	53
	1	Push-ups	Work sample composite	.66**	—	—	26.5	11.9	168	5.5	5.4	81	77
	1	Pull-ups	Work sample composite	.59**	—	—	6.5	3.8	168	0.5	0.8	81	19
	1	Squat thrusts	Work sample composite	.35**	—	—	16.6	3.8	168	12.1	4.1	81	57
	7	Dynamic arm strength (ergometer)	Employed vs. transferred	.54**	—	—	166.3	36.1	41	123.8	24.2	22	48
Cardiovascular endurance	1	Step test	Work sample composite	.30**	—	—	40.2	22.7	168	25.5	11.7	81	67
	8	Lean body mass	Lift task	.74**	.38**	.28**	60.7	6.8	980	43.7	4.2	1003	72
	8	Maximum VO_2	Lift task	.40**	-.08	-.06	46.8	7.3	715	36.5	6.8	659	78

TABLE 6

Descriptive Statistics and Correlations for Physical Performance Tests: Empirical Validation Studies Using Work Sample Criteria (continued)

Physical Dimension	Ref. No.[a]	Test	Criterion	Males Females r	Males Females r	r	Males M	Males SD	Males n	Females M	Females SD	Females n	Percent Overlap
Cardiovascular endurance (continued)	11	Step test	Work sample composite	.37**	—		40.2	22.7	168	25.5	11.7	81	67
	12	1.5 mile run	Arrest simulation	—	.39*		13.1	2.4	412	13.9	1.9	15	85
Flexibility	1	Twist & touch	Work sample composite	.15	—		11.1	2.2	168	10.3	1.8	81	84
	7	Flexibility course time	Tube lance cleaning	-.60**	—		86.5	23.2	41	105.2	22.3	22	68
Balance	1	Static rail balance (1-inch beam)	Work sample composite	.17	—		.05	.06	168	.04	.01	81	89
	7	Balance against resistance	Tube lance cleaning	.77**	.44**	.66**	350.2	79.5	41	198.6	74.1	22	32
Neuromuscular coordination	7	Minnesota rate manipulation	Free-held lance cleaning	-.30**	.34**	.09	89.3	14.5	41	90.8	11.7	22	96

$*p \leq .05$ $**p \leq .01$

[a] Validation Study References

1. Arnold, Rauschenberger, Soubel, & Guion, 1982 (site b)
2. Denning, 1984 (Production)
3. Denning, 1984 (Maintenance)
4. Hogan, Ogden, & Fleishman, 1979
5. Hogan & Pederson, 1984
6. Hogan, Arneson, Hogan, & Jones, 1986
7. Hogan & Arneson, 1988
8. Jackson & Osburn, 1983
9. Myers, Gebhardt, Crump, & Fleishman, 1984
10. Reilly, Zedeck, & Tenopyr, 1979 (Exp. 1)
11. Reilly, Zedeck, & Tenopyr, 1979 (Exp.2)
12. Robertson & Trent, 1983
13. Wilmore & Davis, 1979
14. Wunder, 1981

included objective (archival) data, subjective (ratings) data, and job sample performance; their distinctions follow the rationale outlined in the previous section.

It was possible to classify most test results using the construct/criterion scheme, and these are displayed by criterion in Tables 4, 5, and 6. In cases where the authors specified the construct measured by the test and the nature of the criteria used, classification followed the authors' intentions. When information for test classification was incomplete, the nature of the performance construct was deduced from the test content and the criterion. When the authors used multiple criteria, the criterion appearing most relevant for validation purposes was reported. Note that the classification of predictors (and, perhaps for some readers, criteria) is not as distinct and precise as it might otherwise be. Some tests require multiple abilities for performance; moreover, some researchers argue for further categorizing of tests into those of upper body and lower body strength. The problem occurs in classifying a frequently used test, such as an isometric lifting test, which requires use of major muscle groups from both extremities.

A number of test validation studies were not included in the tables because they lack data for evaluating sex differences in performance or subgroup validity. Predictors from the following studies were not classified because of one or more of the following reasons:

- Single-sex samples were used (Davis, 1976; Hogan, 1985; Hogan & Hogan, 1989; Laughery, Jackson, Osburn, Hogan, & Hayes, 1986).

- Descriptive statistics were not reported by sex (Cooper & Schemmer, 1983; Jones & Prien, 1978).

- The criterion data were insufficient to demonstrate criterion-related or construct validity (Keyserling, Herrin, Chaffin, Armstrong, & Foss, 1980; Laubach, 1976;

Laughery, Jackson, Sanborn, & Davis, 1981; Massciotte, Avon, & Corriveau, 1979; Montoye & Lamphiear, 1977; Osburn, 1977; Snook & Ciriello, 1974).

For each test, the tables show raw score means and standard deviations by subgroup; Tilton's (1937) O statistic is also presented as a measure of overlapping test score distributions. Validities for each test are shown by criterion for the total group and for male and female subgroups. Due to the small numbers of tests in any one category, no validity generalization methods were used to correct variance across studies for the effects of measurement error, range restrictions, or sampling error on tests, scores, and samples. Therefore, the true validities of the tests reviewed may be somewhat higher than those reported in the original sources.

Muscular Tension Tests. Job tasks requiring muscular tension for performance are typically single events of MMH activities such as pushing, pulling, lifting, lowering, or carrying heavy objects. Tests of muscular tension are measures of force exerted either by means of isometric tension or by a single repetition of motion (Clarke, 1966). These tests typically require maximal exertion of force for a brief time period. Instruments such as tensiometers, dynamometers, and load cells are used to measure force, and scores are reported in units such as kilograms or pounds.

In the studies using objective criteria, two predictors were significant (see Table 4). The cable pull, which measures force generated using a static arm pull across the chest, and grip strength are both isometric tests of upper body strength. Individually, neither measure was significantly related to performance for female subgroups. Male and female score distributions overlapped minimally for both tests. All muscular tension measures significantly predicted rated performance (see Table 5). Although it is difficult to compare tests across studies, distribution overlaps were greater for tests involving lower extremity strength (viz., lift, pull, and leg dynamometer tests) than for those involving upper extremity strength. Muscular tension tests correlated significantly with work sample performance in both the total group and the male and female subgroups (see Table 6). In general, muscular tension measures correlated more highly with work sample performance than with either objective or subjective criteria. Also, dynamic tests used by Wilmore and Davis (1979) showed higher correlations than static tests within the same study.

Trends for muscular tension tests indicate that the highest test validities were found with either subjective or work sample criteria. It is worth noting the significant subgroup validities for tests correlated with work sample criteria as well as for studies conducted with an adequate female sample size. The potential adverse impact of these tests, in general, is quite substantial—approximately two-thirds of all males scored above the highest-scoring female.

Muscular Power Tests.   Many tasks where muscular power is used require the worker to overcome some initial resistance, such as in loosening a nut on a bolt or raising a section of ladder using a halyard. Job tasks requiring muscular power may involve the use of either hand tools, such as wrenches, hammers, and mauls, or direct forces applied to objects through arm/hand action. Tests reflecting muscular power require rapid use of dynamic force (Wilmore, 1977). The muscular power dimension adds speed to muscular tension and is defined as the rate of performing work (O'Connell & Gardner, 1972, p. 83). All power tests used in these studies are dynamic and most require equipment. Either commercial or custom-designed ergometers were used to measure power. The instrumentation registered force generated by means of a lever arm against a fixed resistance. Scores are reported in foot-pounds or watt conversions.

Only one study using objective criteria included a measure of muscular power; however, the correlation was unexpectedly negative. Two studies using subjective criteria and two using work sample criteria included power measures in the predictor battery. For subjective criteria, both the leverage test and the torque test required transmitting force from the arms, trunk, and legs using a speeded motion, and both significantly correlated with rated job performance. However, higher correlations were obtained using the ergometer and vertical jump tests with work sample criteria. The ergometer test involved upper body power while the vertical jump involved lower body power. Subgroup validities, where available, were generally significant, but lower than total group validities.

Although muscular power tests are rarely used in test validation, their relationship to job performance evaluations tends to be positive. These tests also show substantial potential adverse impact. Tests that require lower extremity power tend to produce greater distribution overlap between male and female scores than those requiring upper extremity power.

Muscular Endurance Tests.   Tasks where muscular endurance is crucial for job performance usually involve repetitions of tool use or MMH activities over time, such as in loading materials onto pallets or in removing conveyed objects from moving belts—all tasks performed repetitively for continuous time periods and involving localized muscular activity. Tests classified under this dimension require ongoing muscular work at either a maximum or submaximum level of effort. Shephard (1969, p. 3) maintains that "endurance fitness is the main determinant of heavy work that can be performed in the factory" or other industrial setting. He also defines muscular endurance as the ability to maintain processes associated with metabolic exchange as close to resting state as possible during strenuous performance.

Test conditions for muscular endurance involve continual or repeated applications of muscular tension. Test equipment consists either of ergometers or custom-designed devices similar to those described earlier. Some tests require no equipment because work consists of moving and/or supporting one's body weight. Test scores are the number of repetitions completed within a unit of time.

Studies in which muscular endurance tests were correlated with objective criteria revealed two significant predictors—push-ups and a ratchet test. No subgroup validities were significant. These two tests yielded both the least amount (17%) and greatest amount (60%) of score distribution overlaps for tests of this type. Using subjective criteria, the arm ergometer cranking test was a significant predictor in two separate studies, although the correlations were modest. Arnold, Rauschenberger, Soubel, and Guion (1982) reported substantial correlations for muscular endurance tests with work sample composite criteria. Tests requiring almost exclusively upper body muscular endurance (e.g., push-ups, pull-ups) resulted in even less score overlap than other tests.

Like the findings for the other muscular construct measures, tests of muscular endurance yielded higher validity coefficients with work sample criteria. Subgroup validities were largely unavailable. On the whole, male and female score distributions overlapped to a greater extent than with other muscular measures. Again, tests of lower extremity endurance produced greater distribution overlap than those of upper extremity endurance.

Cardiovascular Endurance Tests. Cardiovascular endurance is required to perform job tasks where gross body muscular activities must be sustained over time. Although tasks performed by protective service employees (e.g., search and rescue of victims by firefighters) readily come to mind, industrial tasks such as those requiring prolonged stair climbing or wearing of protective equipment also increase the demands for cardiovascular endurance. Tests of cardiovascular endurance assess aerobic capacity and are concerned with general systemic fitness as opposed to localized muscular capacity (deVries, 1980, pp. 418–421). In gross body activity, as opposed to localized movement, "it is the central systems of respiration, circulation and heat dissipation, and the nervous system and the homeostatic mechanisms, in addition to peripheral muscle function, that are likely to establish the outer limits of performance" (deVries, 1980, p. 419). Cardiovascular endurance tests measure the individual's capacity to sustain gross body muscular activity. Both direct and indirect assessments of the metabolic costs of performance can be obtained; however, direct assessments that involve analysis of expired air are typically carried out in the laboratory. Indirect assessments of metabolic work load consist either of heart rate measures during work or heart rate recovery times at the conclusion of a work interval. Heart rate is a reasonably good indirect measure of cardiovascular endurance because of its linear relationship with VO_2 max. Although sophisticated laboratory equipment is necessary for direct metabolic assessments, little or no equipment is required for indirect assessments. Measures such as completion time for a demanding event are also used as indirect assessments of cardiovascular endurance. Each of these measures reflects systemic responses to work accomplished.

Investigations that include cardiovascular assessments all report significant validity coefficients regardless of the criterion used. The test most frequently chosen is the step test, which requires stepping up and down on a bench to a cadence. Results tend to follow the pattern noted previously; that is, validity coefficients increase from objective to work sample criteria. Subgroup correlations are also significant with large samples and tests validated against objective criteria. Measures of body density, validated against direct physiological indicators of cardiovascular fitness, also appear to be useful predictors of training performance.

These results indicate the general construct validity of cardiovascular measures for training and job performance and, where sample sizes are sufficient, validity for both male and female subgroups. The potential adverse impact of these tests is less than that for strength tests—the average score for women is about two-thirds that for men.

Flexibility Tests.   Job tasks where flexibility of a body segment or limb segment occurs require the worker to bend, twist, stretch, and/or reach to execute the task. When work is performed in confined areas or requires awkward positions, flexibility is important. Examples include gaining access to vessels through manways (openings of minimally 18-inch clearance), performing underground mining operations in a narrow seam, and installing lighting fixtures. Flexibility tests measure the range of motion through which a limb can rotate (Wilmore, 1977, p. 88) and include both single displacements or rotations (e.g., twist and touch) and multiple sequences of movements requiring flexion (e.g., flexibility course). Fleishman (1964) makes a distinction between extent and dynamic flexibility that appears to differentiate single, unspeeded movements (extent) from those actions requiring repetition and speed (dynamic). Both types of flexibility tests appear in the studies reviewed.

All tests included in Tables 4 through 6 are considered field measures of flexibility and require no laboratory instrumentation such as goniometers or flexometers. Scores from these tests are either direct measures of limb displacement in inches or centimeters or indirect measures such as repetitions or time to complete a movement sequence. As a group, these measures are only moderately successful predictors of job performance. Of the different tests included in experimental batteries, four achieved total group validities, but in three

cases these validities were not maintained when the analyses were computed by subgroup. In general, these predictors may result in greater score distribution and overlap and therefore less potential adverse impact than measures assessing the other constructs presented thus far.

Balance Tests.   Tasks that require workers to use balance are those where stability of body position is difficult to maintain. This may be due to a reduced base of support for the foot (e.g., rungs of a ladder or painter's stilts), awkward body position, or impaired floor conditions. Tests of balance measure the capacity to maintain body stability under conditions where the base of support changes or is reduced (O'Connell & Gardner, 1972). The tests included in Tables 4 through 6 measure either static or dynamic balance. The equipment used in all the tests is characterized by a raised surface, the width of which is less than that of an individual's foot. Scores are reported as either time elapsed or distance traveled while maintaining one's stability.

Empirical validation of balance measures has not been very successful except in two cases. For pole-climbing jobs, the rail balance test was validated for both objective and subjective criteria, and for high-pressure cleaning jobs, a test that required balancing against a resistance was a significant predictor of two different criterion types. Other experimental predictors have not been found useful for personnel selection in the jobs for which they were intended.

Neuromuscular Coordination.   Tasks that require neuromuscular coordination are almost exclusively those for which movement sequencing and response timing are crucial. In tasks that necessitate the skillful use of tools or machines, both temporal and spatial organization of movement are primary. Representative examples include operating a dragline, intercepting an object, and accessing an offshore platform from a swinging rope. Tests of neuromuscular coordination require the subject to organize movements in sequence within temporal and spatial limits in response to either internal or external stimuli. Schmidt (1982, p. 157) suggests that skilled performance cannot occur without accurate anticipation of environmental events followed by the initiation of a motor program or "coordinative structure" (Bernstein, 1967; Turvey, 1977) that will achieve the performer's movement goal. Tests of neuromuscular coordination typically require multiple limb sequencing, quality movement, and accuracy. The tests are normally custom-designed; the test scores are either lapsed time or measures of target error.

Although only two types of tests are classified under this dimension, both have empirical support as valid predictors of job performance criteria. Such tests are valid for male subgroups and marginally so for female subgroups, but these findings are limited by small samples. The overlap in the distribution of scores for men and women is also high. If one considers the bend, twist, and touch test to be a measure of neuromuscular coordination, the validity and score distribution overlap indicates its promise for use in experimental batteries. Although few studies include tests of this type, the data suggest that they are potentially useful predictors of job performance.

Tests, Validation, and Concerns for Implementation.   For each core dimension of physical performance presented in Tables 4 through 6, one or more tests of that dimension are significantly related to the criterion measured. Therefore, each of these physical constructs has some usefulness for the assessment of general work performance. The most successful predictors seem to be those that are (a) sensitive to individual differences and (b) correlated with work sample criteria. Unfortunately, such sensitive measures are also those with the greatest potential adverse impact, and measures that correlate with work sample

criteria provide only limited prediction of total job performance. Concerning the latter point, one might question the external validity of a study where predictors are correlated with other tests—in this case, work sample measures—rather than with nontest behaviors. Nevertheless, these relationships are consistent with those found by Nathan and Alexander (1988), who analyzed validity coefficients from clerical tests for five criteria. Test validities resulting from work sample criteria were, on average, higher than those from ratings and quantity of production. There may be some generality of this test-criterion relationship across predictor types (e.g., see Lewis, 1989).

Some conclusions can be drawn about the best set of predictors—where *best* is defined in terms of validity and minimal potential adverse impact. First, no strength test reviewed is free from adverse impact unless, of course, applicant selectivity is substantially reduced by lowering cutoff scores. Given this and the obtained validity coefficients, the best muscular strength tests are those that require lower body strength. Such tests either assess lower body strength directly (e.g., leg dynamometer) or use MMH postures (e.g., isometric pull or static lift). The same conclusion holds for tests of muscular power and endurance, where vertical jump and sit-ups show both validity and relatively less potential adverse impact than other tests. These results are not surprising given that most jobs included in this analysis involve materials handling requiring lower body strength. The arm ergometer, when used as a measure of both muscular power and muscular endurance, has substantial empirical support; however, only about 20 percent of women score higher than the lowest-scoring men. Cardiovascular endurance measures are moderately successful predictors of criterion performance, and the mean scores for women are approximately two-thirds those for men. Gender differences almost always occur with body density assessments because they reflect fat composition differences between men and

TABLE 7

Predictors With Highest Mean Validity Coefficients by Criterion

	Criterion								
	Work Sample			Supervisor Rating			Training Criteria		
Predictor	rho	N	K	rho	N	K	rho	N	K
Muscular strength	.816	2,064	10	—	—	—	.23	396	3
Anthropometric	.49	2,176	12	.255	1,426	6	.23	396	3
Muscular endurance	.367	1,740	6	.23	2,022	9	.30	750	5
Muscular power	—	—	—	.26	1,699	5	—	—	—

Note: *rho* = corrected mean validity; *N* = number of subjects; *K* = number of samples

women (Behnke, 1969; Wilmore & Behnke, 1969, 1970). Performance-based measures, therefore, could result in less adverse impact than measures of physical characteristics because they capitalize to a lesser extent on physical sex differences. There is also the concern that because measures of body density are nonperformance assessments, they may be considered physical characteristics similar to height and weight by a court of law. If so, this would suggest that more direct performance assessments of cardiovascular endurance are preferable to anthropometric measures (*Dothard v. Rawlinson*, 1977).

Focusing on strength and endurance constructs, Lewis (1989) computed a meta-analysis of 24 physical ability selection samples and classified tests and criteria using a scheme similar to the one described here; Table 7 presents those results. Muscular strength, muscular endurance, and anthropometric measures reliably predicted the performance of job applicants and incumbents using supervisor rating, work sample, and training-related criteria. Because of low statistical power, Lewis recommends caution in interpreting the validity of muscular power tests. He concluded that gender does not moderate the physical ability–job performance relationship and did not pursue other moderators because insufficient variance remained after the correction for sampling error, measurement error, and criterion unreliability.

Tests of the remaining three dimensions—which concern movement quality—tend to have little or no potential adverse impact as defined in terms of score distribution overlap. For the flexibility construct, the most predictive tests are the bend, twist and touch test and the flexibility course. Although used in several studies, the twist and touch test yielded no significant validity coefficients. Static rail balance appears to be a useful measure of balance, particularly when evaluated in terms of the specific performance required by the job—in this case, telephone pole climbing. Most studies, however, have not included balance measures in the predictor battery. Similarly, tests of coordination have not often been used, but the task performance simulation nature of these tests makes them seem promising.

A striking feature of Tables 4 through 6 is the shrinkage of validities when the group is split into male and female subgroups. The issue most investigators raise is whether, in these cases, job performance is being predicted on the basis of test performance or gender (e.g., see Arnold, Rauschenberger, Soubel, & Guion, 1982, p. 600). To demonstrate that test performance rather than gender is responsible for the correlation, validities must be established within single-sex subgroups. When one tries to do this, however, the variability of predictor and criterion scores is restricted and validities shrink. This problem is compounded in studies using concurrent strategies because a substantial amount of screening has taken place before the research sample is composed. There is evidence elsewhere showing that single-group validity is an artifact of small samples (Boehm, 1977). Nevertheless, we need to recognize that the reason for subgroup mean differences in physical test performance is not as mysterious as gender differences in manual dexterity or race differences in cognitive test scores. Factors associated with gender differences in strength and endurance are understood (Astrand & Rodahl, 1977; Hogan, 1980). Gender will inevitably be correlated with strength in a representative sample of the population, and women as a group will score lower than men on muscular strength and endurance measures (Arnold et al., 1982, p. 595). The point is that gender and muscular test performance are predictably related, their relationship can be explained, and the within-gender validities obtained will be lower than total group validities due to score range restriction and other artifacts.

Although the discussion focuses on gender differences in physical test performance, it should be emphasized that these studies show the tests to be fair; they indicate that as a group women score lower than men on strength and endurance tests and that women also score correspondingly lower on measures of job performance. These subgroup predictor/criterion differences are obviously the key issue for analysis of test fairness—that is, evaluating the degree to which differences in subgroup test scores correspond to differences in job performance. Several of the studies reviewed use the Cleary (1968) method to evaluate test fairness. The general finding is that although predictor and criterion mean differences by subgroup exist, regression line slope differences are not significant (e.g., see Arnold et al., 1982, site a & site c; Hogan, Ogden, & Fleishman, 1979; Jackson & Osburn, 1983). Moreover, as Ruch (1972) and Cleary, Humphreys, Kendrick, and Wesman (1975) found using cognitive tests with minorities, when differences in regression line intercepts exist, the common regression line will overpredict the physical performance of women (Arnold et al., 1982; Myers, Gebhardt, Crump, & Fleishman, 1984). The results reviewed here for strength and endurance tests suggest that they are predictably related to job performance and are fair; however, their potential for adverse impact increases as cutoff scores rise. Or, as a careful observer once remarked: "If physically demanding jobs require greater strength and endurance than many women possess, the adverse impact may reside in the jobs, not in the tests."

The final determinant of adverse impact is the cutoff score. Adverse impact may be evaluated several ways (e.g., see Ironson, Guion, & Ostrander, 1982); the *Uniform Guidelines* defines adverse impact by an 80 percent rule, calculated from the proportion of applicants with the highest selection rate and the selection rate of any other subgroup. Lawshe (1979) referred to this proportion as the *adverse impact ratio;* adverse impact exists for a subgroup when this ratio is below .80. Two questions are relevant: (a) What is the adverse impact of a test in use? and (b) What is the adverse impact of an experimental predictor? A single example provides a way to examine both questions.

Consider source data from a physical performance test validation study based on production and maintenance jobs in a petrochemical plant (Hogan & Pederson, 1984). Using construct validation strategy, seven experimental predictors were administered to an incumbent sample of men ($N = 127$) and women

TABLE 8

Adverse Impact Ratios for Sample Distribution Cutoffs

Test (Construct)	r	O	Upper 25%	Upper 50%	Upper 75%
Static lift test (muscular strength)	.25	57%	.13	.35	.38
Flexibility course (flexibility)	.22	67%	.28	.44	.61
Coordination course (neuromuscular coordination)	.22	73%	.59	.52	.54

($N = 25$), and job performance ratings were obtained from their supervisors. These criterion ratings were measures of overall job performance. Table 8 presents correlation coefficients, O statistics, and adverse impact ratios for each test by criterion cutoff. These tests were chosen as examples because their validities are similar and they represent a range of overlap in score distributions in the sample. As can be seen by comparing the test results, the adverse impact ratio is different when one selects the top 25 percent of candidates versus the top 50 or 75 percent. This is more than a matter of mean group differences, because although women have lower mean scores on each test, the variance at certain selection percentiles can minimize adverse impact. This type of analysis can answer the question of the adverse impact of a test in use. However, results associated with the O statistic also provide estimates of potential adverse impact. Although there is a definite and expected linear relationship between the O statistic and the impact ratio, the actual impact will depend on the score distributions of the subgroups and the selection cutoff used. It seems, however, that the O statistic could also be used to compare experimental predictors for on-the-average potential adverse impact. This may provide some guideline for answering the second question.

Cascio, Alexander, and Barrett (1988) reviewed considerations for setting cutoff scores from legal, psychometric, and professional guideline interpretations. They recommend seven guidelines to aid professional judgment in determining cutoff scores. Although all their suggestions are useful, the two most important for physical ability testing results are: (a) "The process of setting a cutoff score (or a critical score) should begin with a job analysis that identifies relative levels of proficiency on critical knowledge, skills, abilities, or other characteristics" and (b) "How a test is used (criterion-referenced or norm-referenced) affects the selection and meaning of a cutoff score" (p. 21).

Campion and Pursell (1980) correctly point out that test scores are used ultimately to make dichotomous personnel decisions—to accept or to reject. They argue that selection of candidates with the top scores is identical to rank ordering and that this maximizes adverse impact. Also, the *Principles for the Validation and Use of Personnel Selection Procedures* (SIOP, 1987) refer to the use of cutoff scores for personnel selection:

> Cutoff or other critical scores may be set as high or as low as the purposes of the organization require, if they are based on valid predictors.... Consequently,

selecting from the top scores on down is almost always the most beneficial procedure from the standpoint of an organization if there is an appropriate amount of variance in the predictor.... In some circumstances, such as those where a production line limits the speed at which a worker can produce, a critical score may be in order. (p. 32)

An alternative method, a critical or cutoff score, identifies a group of "qualified" applicants and results in less adverse impact than ranking. Both professional standards (American Psychological Association, American Educational Research Association, & National Council on Measurement in Education, 1985) and the federal *Uniform Guidelines* require that the rationale for a cutoff score be documented. The overriding consideration is that this score be consistent with "acceptable proficiency within the workforce" (Equal Employment Opportunity Commission, 1978, p. 38298). The method proposed by Campion and Pursell for setting cutoff scores includes an analysis of adverse impact, validity, and expected levels of job performance at each potential cutoff score. This method holds much promise for maximizing validity while minimizing the adverse impact of physical tests. Although validity and utility argue strongly for top-down hiring, employers responsible for such decisions must live with their social and regulatory consequences. On this issue, the view from the ivory tower is hazy.

Employment Discrimination

Employers with physically demanding jobs to fill are concerned with legislative decisions designed to protect three classes of individuals—women, handicapped persons, and older workers. The protective laws enacted during the early part of the century in an attempt to improve working conditions have been superseded by Title VII of the Civil Rights

Act of 1964. Title VII prohibits employment discrimination against individuals on the basis of race, color, religion, national origin, and sex. Although some might argue that turn-of-the-century protective legislation was a pretense for discrimination against women, the overall result was protection for men as well as women and children and a general improvement in working conditions for all employees (e.g., see *Muller v. Oregon*, 1908). Some use of differential employment standards persisted after the passage of the Civil Rights Act. In those instances that were litigated where classes of individuals were treated differently in the employment process, differential standards and both intentional and unintentional discrimination were prohibited (e.g., *Weeks v. Southern Bell Telephone & Telegraph Co.*, 1969). The Equal Employment Opportunity Act of 1972 amended the Civil Rights Act (42 U.S.C. § 2000c–1 to 2000c–17 [1964]) and gave the Equal Employment Opportunity Commission the power to enforce Title VII. Perhaps the major impact of this amendment was to require federal, state, and local governments to comply with Title VII. Employment decisions that result in identification of differences or distinctions between individuals or groups are not prohibited by Title VII; however, there is a distinction between employment practices that discriminate unlawfully and those that discriminate lawfully (Arvey & Faley, 1988). Our focus will be on unlawful discrimination.

Sex Discrimination

The courts have addressed three types of employment policies or standards applying to physically demanding jobs (Hogan & Quigley, 1986). The first type was addressed shortly after the passage of the Civil Rights Act and concerned differential weight lifting restrictions. Although the court has handed down a number of decisions on this subject, two cases in particular provide insight into the legal interpretation of weight standards for employment. The first major decision involving weight lifting criteria set a precedent for interpreting both Bona Fide Occupational Qualification (BFOQ) and state restrictions law defenses (*Weeks v. Southern Bell*, 1969). Southern Bell, the defendant, had refused a female employee's bid for a switchman job vacancy—a position with a 30-pound lifting requirement—claiming sex as a BFOQ. Southern Bell relied on the Georgia state protective legislation prohibiting women from lifting 30 pounds as its BFOQ defense. However, it was unable to show that the requirements of the switchman's job exceeded most women's strength capabilities, and it introduced no data regarding the strength characteristics of women that could be used to support its position. The court concluded that Southern Bell's lifting requirement was based on a "stereotyped characterization" and that:

> Title VII rejects just this type of romantic paternalism as unduly Victorian and instead vests individual women with the power to decide whether or not to take on unromantic tasks. Men have always had the right to determine whether the incremental increase in remuneration for strenuous, dangerous, obnoxious, boring or unromantic tasks is worth the candle. The promise of Title VII is that women are now to be on equal footing. We cannot conclude that by including the bona fide occupational qualification exception Congress intended to renege on that promise. (*Weeks v. Southern Bell & Telegraph Co.*, 1969)

In a second case involving weight lifting restrictions and sex as a BFOQ for employment, Southern Pacific, the defendant, excluded women from certain jobs because of possible violations of California's statute prohibiting women from lifting more than 25 pounds (*Rosenfeld v. Southern Pacific*, 1971). Southern Pacific produced no job analyses supporting its BFOQ contention and failed to show that the

sexual characteristics of employees were crucial to the successful performance of the job. The court held, on the contrary, that Southern Pacific's BFOQ claim was based on an assumption regarding the physical capabilities of women that characterized women as the "weaker sex." The court ruled that where state labor laws were inconsistent with the objectives of the Civil Rights Act, the laws must be disregarded (*Rosenfeld v. Southern Pacific*, 1971).

Height and weight standards have been widely used as selection criteria, particularly for public sector positions such as firefighter and police, security, or corrections officer. Height and weight standards are alleged to be disguised forms of sex discrimination (Callis, 1974) and to result in adverse impact against women and some minorities (e.g., Hispanics) unless selection cutoff scores are set extremely low. The position taken by the EEOC and the courts on issues of both weight lifting restrictions and minimum height/weight requirements is that such policies effectively create "conclusive presumptions" about individual applicants' abilities to perform. Reliance on such standards does not take into account the individual's unique capacities and abilities; hence, the courts will generally overturn height and weight requirements. The case law accumulated in this area is rather substantial (cf. Hogan & Quigley, 1986).

Today, it comes as no surprise that employment decisions based on physical stature standards are difficult to defend. First, data for demonstrating adverse impact are relatively easy to gather; generally, any height standard above five feet one inch will result in adverse impact. And second, the defendant's burden to justify the job-relatedness of physical stature standards is a heavy one, particularly when faced with rebuttal of the "conclusive presumptions" argument (Stillman & Polk, 1981). The most important and instructive judicial decision involving height and weight standards for employment ultimately reached the U.S. Supreme Court and was handed down in

Dothard v. Rawlinson (1977). Challenged were Alabama's height and weight standards for state trooper and correctional counselor positions for violation of Title VII and the Fourteenth Amendment of the U.S. Constitution. Although the plaintiffs had gathered no local data on applicants' height and weight, the Court accepted general population data and upheld the prima facie finding of sex discrimination. In determining the issue of job-relatedness of these standards, the Supreme Court affirmed the district court's finding that rejected the use of these selection procedures, stating that "if the job related quality that the applicants identify is indeed *bona fide,* their purpose could be achieved by adopting and validating a test for applicants that measures strength directly" (*Dothard v. Rawlinson,* 1977, 433 U.S. at 322).

Employment decisions based on content-oriented selection test results have also been challenged by women seeking employment in physically demanding jobs. Court decisions where validation, especially content validation, is used to justify the job-relatedness of an employment practice are more recent than litigation involving weight lifting standards or height/weight requirements. These decisions focus increasingly on review of the technical merits for the justification of test use. Presently, litigation surrounding the use of physical ability tests is confined to the district court and appellate levels; the Supreme Court has not ruled on employment decisions based on physical ability tests. However, the Supreme Court's decision in *Dothard* invited the use of strength tests instead of height and weight standards and concluded that "such a test, fairly administered, would fully satisfy the standards of Title VII because it would be one that 'measures the persons for the job and not the person in the abstract'" (*Dothard v. Rawlinson,* 1977, 433 U.S. at 322).

The majority of cases decided have involved physical tests administered by state and local public employers for hiring police officer and firefighter personnel. Although decisions depend on the persuasiveness of the evidence, the use of preplacement physical ability tests has been upheld when the employer can demonstrate that the tests are nondiscriminately administered and are valid, job-related, or truly representative of critical job requirements. On the other hand, courts have struck down or prohibited further use of physical ability tests with demonstrated adverse impact and without adequate validation. Such decisions turn almost exclusively on the adequacy and accuracy of the job analysis information used to support the selection procedure.

Three decisions stand out as illustrations of the problems encountered when the job analysis is inappropriate or insufficient for the selection tests implemented. In *United States v. New York* (1979), where the job analysis specified knowledge, skills, abilities, or other characteristics necessary for successful performance as a state trooper, the court found the analysis to be deficient in supporting content valid tests because "to the extent that the job analysis for position of trooper did not study the tasks and duties associated with the job of trooper and did not study the frequency, importance and skill level of such tasks and duties, it was a departure from professional standards and federal guidelines dealing with content validity" (*United States v. New York,* 1979). In the second important decision, *Berkman v. City of New York* (1982), the job analysis leading to test specification identified physical abilities necessary to perform firefighter tasks. The court clearly rejected this analysis as a basis for supporting tests alleged to be content valid, stating "that the 9 categories of physical ability constitute anything other than constructs would seem beyond debate by almost any definition" (*Berkman v. City of New York,* 1982, 536 F. Supp. 206).

Finally, when the job analysis does not provide evidence that can be used to justify the way in which a test is scored, the court may reject the validity of the test. In *Brunet v. Columbus* (1986), the court ruled that in developing tests for city firefighter jobs, "anecdotal evidence regarding the speed at which fire-fighters must work is not sufficient to justify a timed, competitive examination. There must be systematic evidence based on a job analysis" (*Brunet v. Columbus*, 1986, 42 FEP cases 1875). This issue of developing job analysis evidence to justify a physical test performed at maximum speed is not a new one. In fact, in *Berkman* (1982) the court objected to the premium placed on maximum speed and all-out effort because such tests failed to reflect the demands of actual firefighter jobs. Again, this issue was significant in the court's evaluation of New York City's new entry-level physical firefighter examination, administered in 1982 (*Berkman v. City of New York*, 1985). In *Berkman* (1985) the court ruled that, because of an inadequate job analysis, the firefighting test's emphasis on speed and anaerobic energy could not be defended. The court cited deficiencies in the job analysis that precluded resolution of the speeded versus pacing nature of the job. Such deficiencies included the following:

> Rather than ask the respondents to describe the pace (or even speed) at which various firefighting tasks are performed, the questionnaire describes the proposed new physical test for entry-level firefighters and then baldly asks whether firefighters performing those tasks should complete them in the "fastest possible time," assuming only that they are not hindered by smoke or obstructions.... Among the responses from incumbent firefighters (on a questionnaire which did not even leave space for comments) were the following: What is considered maximum possible speed? On the fire scene most is done walking, not running, for safety reasons; Hose-stretching at fire operations is never performed at maximum speed (or to the point of exhaustion) because the truly arduous task begins at the apartment door. (*Berkman*, 1985, 43 FEP cases 312)

Some who specialize in employment discrimination law regard the prospects of successfully defending the job-relatedness of validated tests as improbable (cf. Koral, 1980; Scott, 1977). The merit of this pessimistic view will be evaluated in upcoming decisions; however, decisions such as those in *Berkman v. City of New York* (1987) and *Zamlen v. City of Cleveland* (1988), where the plaintiffs failed to prove that physical tests discriminated unfairly, suggest that carefully constructed and properly validated tests will withstand scrutiny. Nevertheless, it is clear that employment testing issues addressed by the court in the future will be technically and conceptually complex. Issues likely to receive attention include technical adequacy of empirical test validity—particularly construct validity—transportability and validity generalization, affirmative action, and challenges to the "bottom line" guideline in cases where multiple selection procedures are used.

Handicapped Workers

The Rehabilitation Act of 1973 prohibits discrimination on the basis of disability and requires employers to take affirmative action to hire and advance the handicapped. Employers' obligations under the Act require that employment decisions (e.g., recruitment, hiring, fringe benefits, and discharge) not be based on the existence of a handicap if the person is able to perform the essential job requirements with a "reasonable accommodation." The definitional sections of the Act have not provided employers the degree of clarity they desire for unambiguous decisions, and some litigation has arisen out of this confusion alone. The handicapped individual is defined as:

> any person who (i) has a physical or mental impairment which substantially limits one or more of such person's major life activities, (ii) has a record of such an impairment, or (iii) is regarded as having an impairment. (29 U.S.C. § 706 [7] [B])

Amendments to the Act in 1978 omitted current alcohol and drug abuse from the definition of "handicapped person" on the grounds that such behaviors constitute a threat to the property and safety of others. With regard to employment in physically demanding jobs, persons who are obese, recovered from a previous handicap such as a heart attack, or impaired in their ability to move about are considered handicapped.

Most recent litigation involving provisions of the Rehabilitation Act has involved substantive rather than procedural disputes; these tend to fall into the areas of reasonable accommodation, risk of future injury, and categorical exclusions. The regulations surrounding the concept of reasonable accommodation are somewhat vague, and the courts have not issued any clear guidance to elucidate its meaning or implementation. Section 504 of the Act states that recipients of federal financial assistance should make "reasonable accommodation to the known physical and mental limitations of an otherwise qualified handicapped applicant or employee unless the recipient can demonstrate that the accommodation would impose an undue hardship on the operation of its program" (45 CFR § 84.12[a]). According to this definition the word *qualified* means, with respect to hiring, an individual with a handicap who can perform the essential or critical functions of the job with reasonable accommodation to the handicap. Although financial costs and safety are factors to be considered in determining the feasibility of accommodation, the Act does not require employers to hire individuals who are incapable of performing critical requirements of the job sought.

Although the statutes do not distinguish between applicants and employees who are returning to work after having sustained a handicapping condition, it would appear that the courts may be more demanding about reasonable accommodation for the long-time employee than for the new job applicant. Three separate cases illustrate this point (*Holland v.*

Boeing Co., 1978; *Simon v. St. Louis County, Mo.*, 1981; *Manso v. Jacobs Rubber Division*, 1975). Generally, the former employer has the responsibility of finding a place for the disabled former employee, if such a place exists and if it can be done without an unreasonable burden on the employer. The courts appear to favor continued employment of long-term employees who have sustained a disability while meeting the requirements of the original job competently. For example, in *Holland v. Boeing Co.* (1978), the court ruled that the plaintiff could have used certain procedures to accommodate the disabled plaintiff—a 20-year employee suffering from cerebral palsy. Some speculation exists that in the future the court may use a double standard to evaluate the equity of accommodating applicant versus long-term employee handicaps.

Perhaps the most frequently encountered obligation an employer faces from the Rehabilitation Act is that of offering or denying employment to applicants whose physical qualifications pose future risks. An exemplary case in this area is *E. E. Black, Ltd. v. Marshall* (1980) in which an applicant was rejected for a job as apprentice carpenter due to a back condition detected during the preemployment medical examination. The job of apprentice carpenter is considered heavy labor, requiring bending, twisting, and heavy lifting. After the plaintiff, Crosby, was rejected for employment, he was examined by an orthopedist who concluded that his back condition did not prevent him from performing the job. Crosby filed a complaint charging the employer with failing and refusing to hire a qualified handicapped individual, failing and refusing to take affirmative action, and violating the Act through use of his medical examination results.

The practical issue was whether potential future risks associated with employing an individual of Crosby's condition were a valid reason for rejecting his application. The court ruled that Crosby was impaired and that impairment constituted a substantial handicap to his employment. The court found that Crosby could perform the apprentice carpenter job at the time he was denied employment, which affirmed his status as a qualified handicapped individual. On the future risk disqualifier, Donald Elisburg, Assistant Secretary of Labor, rejected the employer's argument that not

> hiring someone with a great risk of future back injury was justified by business necessity because of the very high potential workers' compensation costs. "A policy of excluding potential employees to reduce an employer's costs shifts the financial burden to the rejected handicapped individual. This is contrary to the intent of protective statutes such as the Act." (*E. E. Black, Ltd. v. Marshall*, 1980)

However, the court ruled that the risk of future injury might under some circumstances be the basis for rejecting an otherwise qualified applicant in light of business necessity and safe performance of the job. Nevertheless, the court was clear in its intention not to formulate a legal standard.

Some employment law specialists believe that the courts' analyses of physical qualifications under the Rehabilitation Act will be more rigorous than those challenged under Title VII (cf. Marr, 1982). However, it may be some time before sufficient case law accumulates. Although the issues in *E. E. Black* are complex, defendants who attempt a business necessity defense for rejection of applicants based on risk of future injury may face considerable difficulty. This will be especially true if the success of this type of justification in Title VII cases is any indication.

The concept of categorical exclusion in litigation regarding handicapped workers is analogous to the concept of conclusive presumptions regarding sex discrimination: An employer cannot exclude individuals from certain jobs due to specific disabilities because the employer presumes the applicant is unable to perform adequately and safely. The employer's obligation is to evaluate the disabled person's

ability to do the job or perform critical job tasks regardless of the nature of the disability. In two separate cases where amputees were excluded categorically from jobs as vehicle operators, the court concluded, on the basis of ability to perform driving job requirements, that the plaintiffs were qualified handicapped individuals (*Coleman v. Casey County Board of Education*, 1980; *Boynton Cab Co. v. Dept. of Industry, Labor, & Human Relations*, 1978). On the other hand, when the applicant's disability was evaluated on the basis of legitimate job requirements, the court upheld the employer's rejection of the handicapped individual (*Coleman v. Darden*, 1979). The court also indicated that the handicapped individual must be given the opportunity to demonstrate how an accommodation in job requirements could be made (*Gurmankin v. Costanzo*, 1977).

Although the employer who wishes to use medical standards and other criteria faces numerous problems, the most significant of these may be establishing the job-relatedness of the selected criteria. At least two approaches have been proposed. Hogan and Bernacki (1981) suggest that with a thorough analysis of the critical requirements of a job, physical abnormalities and disease states can be identified which, based on epidemiologic data, indicate inability to perform tasks adequately and safely. With knowledge of the job requirements, the occupational physician evaluates each applicant using the appropriate medical categories and makes a recommendation for employment or for reasonable accommodation. Nylander and Nelson (1982) have proposed and used a system of medical standards also based on job analysis information: Incumbents provide information about the physical demands of their jobs using physical abilities analysis procedures (Fleishman, 1975); then the occupational physician performs a routine physical examination. If abnormalities are discovered, the physician consults a volume of medical standards. The standards were developed with the use of experts in various areas of occupational medicine and consist of some 400 medical conditions organized by 12 body systems. The standards indicate the degree to which the abnormalities and disease states may be incompatible with job requirements and working conditions. If the applicant's condition does not exceed exclusionary criteria for the standard, then he or she is accepted.

As competition in the personnel marketplace increases both for job candidates and employers, issues of valid medical standards could become as problematic as the issues already faced about valid selection tests. Before the County of San Bernardino, California, undertook a five-year project to develop valid medical standards, it faced a dramatic rise in workers' compensation claims and disability retirements; at the same time, the county was rejecting job applicants based on its medical examination at three times the rate of the state average (Nylander & Nelson, 1982). It believed that this possible rejection of qualified applicants could lead to future litigation in which its practice could not be defended. The concerns addressed by the County of San Bernardino are the same concerns faced by others. The decision to develop medical standards meeting the same legal tests required for other employment practices is a timely one.

Older Workers

The desires of older workers to seek employment and remain in the work force are protected by the federal Age Discrimination in Employment Act of 1967 (Age Act; 29 U.S.C. § 621 et seq., as amended). The Age Act prohibits discrimination against employees and applicants for employment who are between the ages of 40 and 70. For physically demanding jobs (or any other job), an employer cannot reject an applicant on the assumption that the candidate is too old to perform effectively and safely; the determination of suitability must be made on the basis of ability to meet job-related criteria. On the other hand, an employer is not required to employ older workers (or anyone else) who cannot perform the critical physical requirements of the job. The prohibition against presumptive conclusions is as applicable to issues of age discrimination as it is to issues of sex or handicap discrimination.

Employers should face few problems with charges of age discrimination in the hiring process if all applicants are treated identically. However, different decisions must be made when employed older workers can no longer perform the critical job duties safely or effectively. This issue may become increasingly important where jobs have specialized physical, dexterity, or sensory demands, in which case it is quite possible that these employees will be considered "handicapped" by developmental processes attributable to age and will then be afforded protection by the Rehabilitation Act of 1973. The reasonable accommodation obligation would require employers to transfer the older worker to a job where the demands can be met adequately or to modify the duties of the existing job.

A more probable strategy that employers will adopt for deciding issues of job performance affected by increasing age is the adoption of a BFOQ. Perhaps the most visible of these policies exists in the commercial airline industry. In 1959, the Federal Aviation Administration prohibited carriers from employing pilots for commercial flights who had reached 60 years of age, and some airlines have expanded this BFOQ to exclude all persons over 60 from any flight duty. Some judicial support has accrued for this position since the court in *Aldendifer v. Continental Air Lines, Inc.* (1978) upheld Continental's refusal to allow pilots who had reached 60 years of age to transfer to the position of third-cockpit-seat flight engineers.

Mandatory retirements have been successfully upheld for bus drivers, state troopers, and foreign service employees; however, these actions were brought under the equal protection provision of the U.S. Constitution. Actions litigated under the Age Act are reviewed under stricter standards, so it is possible that some mandatory retirement decisions upheld previously would have been decided differently had the action been brought under federal age legislation. The EEOC—the agency responsible for enforcement of the Age Act—has adopted a narrow interpretation of age as a BFOQ. Stillman and Polk (1981) conclude that enforcement agencies have taken the position that employers cannot presume that older workers are more subject to injury in physically demanding jobs than younger workers, nor can they presume that younger workers will be more productive than their older co-workers.

Future Concerns

Although numerous physical ability issues require additional research, two overriding concerns illustrate the breadth and diversity of future investigations. For the industrial psychologist, there is a continued concern for defensible decisions about individuals' physical abilities and workplace requirements. Advances in this area of employment testing have not achieved the same methodological or empirical sophistication as those achieved, for example, with cognitive abilities (Hunter & Hunter, 1984). On the other hand, organizational psychologists may be asked increasingly about the effects of physical performance and health on organizational effectiveness. We can anticipate some specific topics and questions to guide research in each area.

Industrial psychologists responsible for employment decisions in physically demanding jobs face at least four job analysis issues. First, it is insufficient to presume that a job is physically demanding and to simply adopt testing procedures on the basis of that judgment. Most physical tests will result in adverse impact, making it essential to fully document the physical requirements of work and to link tests explicitly to assessments of those

requirements. As we witnessed in *Berkman* (1982), performing a job analysis per se does not ensure this link. Second, links between job requirements and cutoff scores should be explicit, and these should be developed from analyses of such job criteria as performance evaluations, production rates, and injury rates. In addition, we should attempt to evaluate the economic utility of performance at various criterion levels. This will both contribute documentation for defending the criterion cutoffs chosen and provide input data for calculating the economic impact of valid selection procedures. Consider, for example, the effects of a recommended cutoff score for rehabilitation therapists working at a state hospital housing the profoundly retarded; those who scored below the cutoff suffered twice as many on-the-job accidents as those who scored above the cutoff, with each accident resulting in twice the number of days off and twice the cost of the above-the-cutoff employees' accidents. Had these screening procedures been implemented five years earlier, the employer would have saved more than $1.75 million in insurance costs alone (Hogan, Arneson, Hogan, & Jones, 1986).

Third, content-oriented procedures developed from job analysis information should be sampled carefully in order to justify representativeness and functional fidelity. The accuracy with which these content-oriented measures are constructed affects the quality of inferences made about test behavior. Because of this, it is expected that increasing emphasis will be placed on methods that link physical abilities with job tasks requiring them (e.g., see Zedeck & Goldstein, 1988) as well as on methods that determine critical cutoff scores (Cascio, Alexander, & Barrett, 1988). Without empirical support, decisions made from measurements of maximum physical performance can lead to incorrect inferences about job behavior if the actual job requires submaximal performance. Campion (1983) makes this point quite well in his excellent review of personnel selection for physically demanding jobs: For example, maximum performance on a one-mile-run test may reveal little about successful performance of a two-block police chase.

Finally, job analysis methodologies for construct-oriented validation strategies need to advance. This requires both conceptual and empirical developments in order to understand what dimensions we should measure and how they can best be used to evaluate observable-reportable, simple-complex, and concrete-abstract job requirements (Landy, 1986; Lawshe, 1985). Such new methodologies should take into account the value of constructs (i.e., strength) in psychological measurement. Job analysis must ultimately lead to measurements that permit correct inferences about attributes of people taking employment tests. For personnel selection, this is the unique purpose of the job analysis.

Industrial psychologists must also be concerned about advancing the knowledge we have about physical abilities and workplace requirements. Two steps can now be taken to deepen understanding of these human performances. First, we need to cumulate validity results across studies to establish facts. This is particularly relevant in the area of human strength assessment, where there are numerous validation studies that measure the extent to which performance in physically demanding jobs can be predicted from strength tests. As seen in Tables 4 through 6, the number of studies evaluating the validity of measures other than strength are not extensive, although these tables are by no means exhaustive. Nevertheless, data reported within these investigations are sufficient for meta-analytic procedures. Although sample sizes tend to be small, making sampling error the most obvious problem, these errors—as well as errors of measurement and range variation—can be corrected. Further, the alleged bias arising from the use of convenience samples drawn from referred published research is also avoided since all but two test validation studies are either unpublished or

contained in technical reports. Unlike other well-studied relationships, such as that between IQ and training performance, there is still a need for more empirical studies examining the relationship between nonstrength physical ability measures and work performance. Such meta-analyses will assist in integrating our findings and help us understand the contribution of physical ability dimensions to successful work performance.

These empirical facts—products of meta-analysis in general and validity generalization more specifically—will provide substance to construct a physical performance model of occupational tasks. Fleishman's original taxonomic work (1964) and the job analysis methods associated with it (Fleishman, 1975, in press; Fleishman & Mumford, 1988) have resulted in physical testing procedures with substantial validities for a wide variety of physically demanding jobs in many different work situations (e.g., electric power company workers, firefighters and police, telephone line workers, tire manufacturing workers, gas pipeline workers, court security personnel, refinery workers, maintenance personnel, paramedical personnel, and grocery warehouse workers). A recent review of this work appears in Fleishman (1988). Since Fleishman's original analyses of physical performance tests, additional large-scale confirmatory and exploratory factor analyses with a wide range of tests, including cardiovascular tests, and in samples of men and women, support findings for strength and cardiovascular endurance factors (Myers, Gebhardt, Crump, & Fleishman, 1984). The degree to which we have been able to borrow successfully from aspects of the structure of physical fitness attests to the overlap in the domains of physical fitness and occupational task performance. There is currently a need for concerted efforts to develop a theory of occupational task performance, although some attempts have been made (Hogan, 1984, in press). However, it is clear that the measurement base is well advanced of the conceptual base.

Progress on the conceptual base may come less from additional factor analyses than from aligning the empirical facts within the context of applied work physiology. Substantial work is needed in this area.

Organizational psychologists will be increasingly concerned about physical performance as it affects health at the workplace. Although this is a new area of inquiry and research for industrial and organizational psychologists, there is growing interest in employee health and health costs. In addition, we have a real scientific finding to report which could dramatically shift the way we view physical activity in the workplace. Let us first examine a summary of this finding, then speculate about its organizational implications.

The *New England Journal of Medicine* published the definitive longitudinal investigation by Paffenbarger, Hyde, Wing, and Hsieh (1986), which concludes that moderate physical exercise significantly increases life expectancy. Physical activity and other lifestyle characteristics of approximately 17,000 male Harvard alumni were examined for link to mortality rates. Men who participated in activities such as walking, stair climbing, and sports that used 2,000 calories per week had death rates one-quarter to one-third lower than those studied who were least active. Exercise was inversely related to total mortality, due primarily to cardiovascular and respiratory causes. Regardless of tobacco use, hypertension, extreme body weight, gains in body weight, or early parental death history, mortality rates were significantly lower for the physically active. This study is identified as one of the most detailed in the history of public health research and indicates that exercise in and of itself is protective.

The implication of this research for industry is that although there is a well-established dark side to physically demanding work, performance of some physical work may increase the health and longevity of the work force. In addition to job requirements, physical activity is now regarded as a central component of recently developed employee health, fitness, and wellness programs. Workplace health promotion programs are designed for healthy individuals to enhance personal practices associated with fitness, health, and wellness (Davis, 1984; Gebhardt & Crump, 1990). Organizational psychologists need to evaluate the effects of such programs on organizational productivity and employee costs. In addition to the impact these programs have on health and health care costs, they may also be associated with recruitment, absenteeism, turnover, satisfaction, and performance. Most reports of health promotion programs at the workplace are optimistic about their effects. For example, consider the following:

- Participants in Mesa Petroleum's fitness program averaged $173 in medical costs and 27 hours of sick leave compared to nonparticipants' $434 in medical costs and 44 hours of sick leave in 1982 (Hartman & Cozzetto, 1984).

- Of the 100 Pillsbury employees whose health care claims were tracked before and after participation in a fitness program, both the number and cost of claims decreased, yielding the company a $3.63 return for every dollar spent on the program (Damberg, 1984).

- The fitness program at Canada Life Assurance is credited with reducing employee turnover costs by an estimated $231,000 (Jacobs, 1983).

- Implementation of the "Healthy Back" exercise program at Burlington Industries is associated with an absenteeism reduction from 400 to 19 days over the same time period (Hartman & Cozzetto, 1984).

Unfortunately, most reports from health promotion programs at the workplace are anecdotal rather than empirical (e.g., see Bernacki & Baun, 1984). However, Terborg's (1986) excellent review and the more recent analysis of Gebhardt and Crump (1990) suggest that evidence, though fragmentary, is accumulating to support the value of health and fitness promotion activities. Morbidity and mortality rates can be altered through changes in lifestyle and moderate physical activity; these behavior patterns substantially affect organizational health care costs. Terborg (l986) contends that the efficacy of many health promotion programs has been demonstrated, but he considers program effectiveness to be a premature question. What is *not* premature is a plan to improve the organization's productivity, broadly defined, while simultaneously emphasizing the health, safety, and fitness of the employees who work there. Benefits to the individual, the organization, and society could be substantial, but industrial and organizational psychologists must help with the research effort.

References

Age Discrimination in Employment Act of 1967, 29 U.S.C. § 621 et seq.

Albemarle Paper Co. v. Moody, 422 U.S. 405, (1975). 10 Fair Empl. Prac. Cas. (BNA) 1181.

Aldendifer v. Continental Air Lines, Inc. 18 Empl. Prac. Dec. (CCH) 8874 (C.D. Cal. 1978).

American Psychological Association, American Educational Research Association, & National Council on Measurement in Education. (1985). *Standards for educational and psychological testing.* Washington, DC: Author.

Anderson, C. D., Warner, J. L., & Spencer, C. C. (1984). Inflation bias in self-assessment examinations: Implications for valid employee selection. *Journal of Applied Psychology, 69,* 574–580.

Arnold, J. D., Rauschenberger, J. N., Soubel, W. G., & Guion, R. M. (1982). Validation and utility of a strength test for selecting steelworkers. *Journal of Applied Psychology, 67,* 588–604.

Arstila, M., Wendelin, H., Vuori, I., & Valimaki, I. (1974). Comparison of two rating scales in the estimation of perceived exertion in a pulse-conducted exercise test. *Ergonomics, 17,* 577–584.

Arvey, R. D., & Faley, R. H. (1988). *Fairness in selecting employees* (2nd ed.). Reading, MA: Addison-Wesley.

Astrand, I. (1960). Aerobic work capacity in men and women with special reference to age. *Acta Physiologica Scandinavica, 49* (Suppl. 169).

Astrand, I., Astrand, P. O., Christensen, E. H., & Hedman, R. (1960). Intermittent muscular work. *Acta Physiologica Scandinavica, 48,* 443.

Astrand, P. O. (1952). *Experimental studies of working capacity in relation to sex and age.* Copenhagen: Ejnar Munksgaard.

Astrand, P. O., & Rodahl, K. (1977). *Textbook of work physiology* (2nd ed.). New York: McGraw-Hill.

Ayoub, M. M., Bethea, N. J., Deivanayagam, S., Asfour, S. S., Bakken, G. M., Liles, D., Mital, A., & Sherif, M. (1978). *Determination and modeling of lifting capacity.* Final Report, DHEW (NIOSH). (Grant No. 5 RO1 OH–00545–02). Washington, DC: U.S. Government Printing Office.

Ayoub, M. M., & El-Bassoussi, M. M. (1976). Dynamic biomechanical model for sagittal plane lifting activities. *Proceedings of the 6th Congress of International Ergonomics Association* (pp. 355–359).

Ayoub, M. M., & El-Bassoussi, M. M. (1978). Dynamic biomechanical model for sagittal plane lifting activities. In G. G. Drury (Ed.), *Safety in manual materials handling* (DHEW [NIOSH]: Publication No. 78–185). Washington, DC: U.S. Government Printing Office.

Ayoub, M. M., Mital, A., Bakken, G. M., Asfour, S. S., & Bethea, N. (1980). Development of strength and capacity norms for manual materials handling activities: The state of the art. *Human Factors, 22,* 271–283.

Ayoub, M. M., Selan, J. L., & Jiang, B. C. (1986). Manual materials handling. In G. Salvendy (Ed.), *Handbook of human factors* (pp. 790–818). New York: Wiley.

Banister, E. W., & Brown, S. R. (1968). The relative energy requirements of physical activity. In H. B. Falls (Ed.), *Exercise physiology* (chap. 10). New York: Academic Press.

Behnke, A. R. (1969). New concepts in height-weight relationships. In N. Wilson (Ed.), *Obesity.* Philadelphia: Davis.

Berkman v. City of New York, 1982, 536 F. Supp. 177, 30 Empl. Prac. Dec. (CCH) ¶ 33320 (E.D. N.Y.).

Berkman v. City of New York, 1985, 43 Fair Empl. Prac. Cas. (BNA) 305, 312.

Berkman v. City of New York, 1987, 43 Fair Empl. Prac. Cas. (BNA) 318.

Bernacki, E. J., & Baun, W. B. (1984). The relationship of job performance to exercise adherence in a corporate fitness program. *Journal of Occupational Medicine, 26*, 529–531.

Bernstein, N. (1967). *The co-ordination and regulation of movements.* Oxford: Pergamon Press.

Bink, B. (1962). The physical working capacity in relation to working time and age. *Ergonomics, 5*, 25–38.

Bink, B. (1964). Additional studies on physical working capacity in relation to working time and age. *Proceedings of the 2nd International Congress of Ergonomics.* Dortmund, West Germany.

Boehm, V. R. (1977). Differential prediction: A methodological artifact? *Journal of Applied Psychology, 62*, 146–154.

Borg, G. (1962). *Physical performance and perceived exertion.* Lund, Sweden: Gleerup.

Borg, G. (1970). *Relative response and stimulus scales* (Report No. 1). University of Stockholm, Institute of Applied Psychology.

Borg, G. (1972). *A ratio scaling method for interindividual comparisons* (Report No. 27). University of Stockholm, Institute of Applied Psychology.

Borg, G. (Ed.). (1977). *Physical work and effort.* Oxford: Pergamon Press.

Borg, G., & Dahlstrom, H. (1959). Psykofysisk undersokning av arbete pa cykelergometer. *Nordisk Medicin, 62*, 1383–1386.

Borg, G., & Dahlstrom, H. (1960). The perception of muscular work. *Umea Vetenskapliga Bibliotek Scriftserie, 5*, 1–26.

Borg, G., & Lindblad, I. (1976). *The determination of subjective intensities in verbal descriptions of symptoms* (Report No. 75). University of Stockholm, Institute of Applied Psychology.

Boring, E. G. (1950). *A history of experimental psychology.* New York: Appleton-Century-Crofts.

Bourne, G. H. (Ed.). (1973). *The structure and function of muscle* (Vols. 1–2). New York: Academic Press.

Boynton Cab Co. v. Dept. of Industry, Labor, & Human Relations, 18 Fair Empl. Prac. Cas. (BNA) 841 (Wis. Ct. App. 1978).

Brace, D. K. (1927). *Measuring motor ability.* New York: Barnes.

Brownell, C. L. (1928). *Scale for measuring antero-posterior posture of ninth grade boys.* New York: Columbia University, Bureau of Publications.

Brunet v. Columbus, 1986, 42 Fair Empl. Prac. Cas. (BNA) (1975).

Bucher, C. A. (1968). *Foundations of physical education.* St. Louis: Mosby.

Bureau of Labor Statistics. (1978). *1976 SDS Report for Arkansas.* Little Rock: Arkansas Department of Labor, Research and Statistics Division.

Callis, P. E. (1974). Minimum height and weight requirements as a form of sex discrimination. *Labor Law Journal, 25*, 736–745.

Campion, M. A. (1983). Personnel selection for physically demanding jobs: Review and recommendations. *Personnel Psychology, 36*, 527–550.

Campion, M. A., & Pursell, E. D. (1980, August). *Adverse impact, validity, expected job performance, and determination of cut scores.* Paper presented at the 88th meeting of the American Psychological Association, Montreal, Canada.

Cascio, W. F., Alexander, R. A., & Barrett, G. V. (1988). Setting cutoff scores: Legal, psychometric, and professional issues and guidelines. *Personnel Psychology, 41*, 1–24.

Cattell, J. M. (1981). *An education in psychology.* Cambridge, MA: MIT Press.

Cattell, J. M., & Farrand, L. (1896). Physical and mental measurements of the students of Columbia University. *Psychological Review, 3*, 618–648.

Chaffin, D. B. (1969). Computerized biomechanical model: Development of and use in studying gross body action. *Journal of Biomechanics, 2*, 429–441.

Chaffin, D. B. (1974). Human strength capability and low back pain. *Journal of Occupational Medicine, 16*, 248–254.

Chaffin, D. B. (1975). *On the validity of biomechanical models of the low-back for weight lifting analysis* (Tech. Rep. No. 75–WA/BIO–1). New York: American Society of Mechanical Engineers.

Chaffin, D. B., Andres, R. O., & Garg, A. (1983). Volitional postures during maximal push/pull exertions in the sagittal plane. *Human Factors, 25*, 541–550.

Chaffin, D. B., & Baker, W. H. (1970). Biomechanical model for analysis of symmetric sagittal plane lifting. *American Institute of Industrial Engineers Transactions, 2*, 1.

Chaffin, D. B., Herrin, G. D., & Keyserling, W. M. (1978). Pre-employment strength testing—An updated position. *Journal of Occupational Medicine, 20*, 403–408.

Chaffin, D. B., & Park, K. S. (1973a). Longitudinal study of low back pain and its relation to occupational weight lifting factors. *American Industrial Hygiene Association Journal, 30,* 12.

Chaffin, D. B., & Park, K. S. (1973b). A longitudinal study of low-back pain as associated with occupational lifting factors. *American Industrial Hygiene Association Journal, 34,* 513–525.

Christal, R. E. (1974). The United States Air Force occupational research project. *Journal Supplement Abstract Service Catalog of Selected Documents in Psychology, 4,* 61 (Ms. No. 651).

Christensen, E. H. (1953). Physiological valuation of work in the Nykoppa Iron Works. In W. F. Floyd & A. T. Welford (Eds.), *Ergonomic society symposium on fatigue.* London: Lewis.

Ciriello, V. M., & Snook, S. H. (1983). A study of size, distance, height, and frequency effects on manual handling tasks. *Human Factors, 25,* 473–483.

Civil Rights Act of 1964, as amended, 42 U.S.C. § 2000e et seq. March 24, 1972.

Clarke, H. H. (1966). *Muscular strength and endurance in man.* Englewood Cliffs, NJ: Prentice-Hall.

Cleary, T. A. (1968). Test bias: Prediction of grades of Negro and white students in integrated colleges. *Journal of Educational Measurement, 5,* 115–124.

Cleary, T. A., Humphreys, L. G., Kendrick, J. A., & Wesman, A. (1975). Educational uses of tests with disadvantaged students. *American Psychologist, 30,* 15–41.

Coleman v. Casey County Board of Education, 510 F. Supp. 301, 26 Fair Empl. Prac. Cas. 357 (W.D. Ky. 1980).

Coleman v. Darden, 595 F. 2d 533, 20 Fair Empl. Prac. Cas. 137 (10th Cir. 1979).

Contini, R., Drillis, R. J., & Bluestein, M. (1963). Determination of body segment parameters. *Human Factors, 5,* 493–504.

Cooper, M. A., & Schemmer, F. M. (1983, August). *The development of physical abilities tests for industry-wide use.* Paper presented at the annual meeting of the American Psychological Association, Anaheim, CA.

Copley, F. B. (1923). *Frederick W. Taylor, Vol. 1.* New York: Harper.

Costill, D. L. (1970). Metabolic responses during distance running. *Journal of Applied Psychology, 28,* 251.

Cronbach, L. J. (1970). *Essentials of psychological testing* (3rd ed.). New York: Harper & Row.

Damberg, C. (1984). *Worksite health promotion: Examples of programs that work.* Washington, DC: U.S. Department of Health and Human Services.

Davis, M. F. (1984). Worksite health promotion. *Personnel Administrator, 29,* 45–50.

Davis, P. O. (1976). Relationship between simulated firefighting tasks and physical performance measures. *University Microfilms International,* 77–16, 365.

Dempster, W. T. (1955). *Space requirements of the seated operator* (WADC Tech. Rep. 55–159). Wright Patterson Air Force Base, OH: Wright Air Development Center.

Denning, D. L. (1984, August). *Applying the Hogan model of physical performance of occupational tasks.* Paper presented at the American Psychological Association convention symposium, Toronto, Canada.

deVries, H. (1980). *Physiology of exercise for physical education and athletics.* Dubuque, IA: Brown.

Dothard v. Rawlinson, 433 U.S. 321, 97 S. Ct. 2720, 53 L. Ed. 2d 786 (1977).

Driskell, J. E., & Olmstead, B. (1989). Psychology and the military. *American Psychologist, 44,* 43–54.

Drury, G. G., & Pizatella, T. (1983). Hand placement in manual materials handling. *Human Factors, 25,* 551–562.

Dunnette, M. D. (1976). Aptitudes, abilities, and skills. In M. D. Dunnette (Ed.), *Handbook of industrial and organizational psychology* (pp. 473–520). Chicago: Rand McNally.

Durnin, J. V., & Passmore, R. (1967). *Energy, work and leisure.* London: Heinemann.

E. E. Black, Ltd. v. Marshall, 24 Empl. Prac. Dec. (CCH) 31260 (D. Haw. 1980).

Ekblom, B., Astrand, P. O., Saltin, B., Stenberg, J., & Wallstrom, B. (1968). Effects of training on circulatory response to exercise. *Journal of Applied Physiology, 24,* 518–527.

Equal Employment Opportunity Commission, Civil Service Commission, Department of Labor, & Department of Justice. (1978). Uniform guidelines on employee selection procedures. *Federal Register, 43,* 38289–28309.

Evans, F. G., & Lissner, H. R. (1959). Biomechanical studies on the lumbar spine and pelvis. *Journal of Bone Joint Surgery, 41A,* 218–290.

Farh, J., Werbel, J. D., & Bedeian, A. G. (1988). An empirical investigation of self-appraisal-based performance evaluation. *Personnel Psychology, 41,*

141–156.

Fechner, G. T. (1966). *Elements of psychophysics*. D. H. Howes & E. G. Boring, Eds. (H. E. Adler, Trans.). New York: Holt, Rinehart & Winston. (Original work published 1860)

Fine, S. A., & Wiley, W. W. (1971). *An introduction to functional job analysis: Methods for manpower analysis* (Monograph No. 4). Kalamazoo, MI: Upjohn Institute for Employment Research.

Flanagan, J. C. (1954). The critical incident technique. *Psychological Bulletin, 51*, 327–358.

Fleishman, E. A. (1964). *Structure and measurement of physical fitness*. Englewood Cliffs, NJ: Prentice-Hall.

Fleishman, E. A. (1972). On the relation between abilities, learning, and human performance. *American Psychologist, 27*, 1017–1032.

Fleishman, E. A. (1975). *Development of ability requirements scales for the analysis of Bell System jobs*. Bethesda, MD: Management Research Institute.

Fleishman, E. A. (1979). Evaluating physical abilities required by jobs. *Personnel Administrator, 24*, 82–91.

Fleishman, E. A. (1988). Some new frontiers in personnel selection research. *Personnel Psychology, 41*, 679–701.

Fleishman, E. A. (in press). Physical abilities analysis manual (rev. ed.). Palo Alto, CA: Consulting Psychologists Press.

Fleishman, E. A., & Mumford, M. D. (1988). Ability requirement scales. In S. Gael (Ed.), *Job analysis handbook for business, industry, and government* (Vol. 2, p. 923). New York: Wiley.

Fleishman, E. A., & Quaintance, M. K. (1984). *Taxonomies of human performance*. New York: Academic Press.

Galton, F. (1885). On the anthropometric laboratory at the late International Health Exhibition. *Journal of the Anthropological Institute, 14*, 205–219.

Gamberale, F. (1972). Perceived exertion, heart rate, oxygen uptake and blood lactate in different work operations. *Ergonomics, 15*, 545–554.

Gamberale, F., & Holmer, I. (1977). Heart rate and perceived exertion in simulated work with high heat stress. In G. Borg (Ed.), *Physical work and effort* (pp. 323–332). Oxford: Pergamon Press.

Garg, A., & Chaffin, D. B. (1975). Biomechanical computerized simulation of hand strength. *American Institute of Industrial Engineers Transactions, 7*, 1–15.

Garg, A., & Herrin, G. D. (1979). Stoop or squat: A biomechanical and metabolic evaluation. *American Institute of Industrial Engineers Transactions, 11*, 293–302.

Garg, A., Sharma, D., Chaffin, D. B., & Schmidler, J. M. (1983). Biomechanical stresses as related to motion trajectory lifting. *Human Factors, 25*, 527–539.

Gebhardt, D. L., & Crump, C. E. (1990). Employee fitness and wellness programs in the workplace. *American Psychologist, 45*, 262–272.

Gilbreth, F. B. (1909). *Bricklaying system*. New York: Clark.

Gilbreth, F. B. (1911). *Motion study*. Princeton, NJ: Van Nostrand.

Gilbreth, F. B. (1912). Present state of the art of industrial management. *Transactions of the American Society of Mechanical Engineers, 34*, 1224–1226.

Grandjean, E. (1982). *Fitting the task to the man*. London: Taylor & Francis.

Grandjean, E., & Hunting, W. (1977). Ergonomics of posture—Review of various problems of standing and sitting posture. *Applied Ergonomics, 8.3*, 135–140.

Guion, R. M. (1977). Content validity—The source of my discontent. *Applied Psychological Measurement, 1*, 1–10.

Guion, R. M. (1978). Scoring of content domain samples: The problem of fairness. *Journal of Applied Psychology, 63*, 499–506.

Gurmankin v. Costanzo, 411 F. Supp. 982 (E.D. Pa. 1976), aff'd. 556 F. 2d 184 (3d Cir. 1977).

Hackensmith, C. W. (1966). *History of physical education*. New York: Harper & Row.

Hartman, S., & Cozzetto, J. (1984). Wellness in the workplace. *Personnel Administrator, 29*, 108–117.

Hartwell, E. M. (1885). *Physical training in American colleges and universities* (Circular of Information No. 5, 59–92). Washington, DC: Bureau of Education.

Herrin, G. D., Chaffin, D. B., & Mach, R. S. (1974). *Criteria for research on the hazards of manual materials handling* (DHEW [NIOSH]). Washington, DC: U.S. Government Printing Office.

Hickey, D. T. (1983). *Evaluation of physical training effects in the development of occupational physical selection standards* (Defense Technical Information Center, Tech. Rep. ADB 074–408). Washington, DC: U.S. Government Printing Office.

Hogan, J. (1980). The state of the art of strength testing. In D. C. Walsh & R. H. Egdahl (Eds.), *Women, work and health: Challenges to corporate policy.* New York: Springer-Verlag.

Hogan, J. (1984). *A model of physical performance for occupational tasks.* Paper presented at the 92nd annual meeting of the American Psychological Association, Toronto, Canada.

Hogan, J. (1985). Tests for success in diver training. *Journal of Applied Psychology, 70,* 219–224.

Hogan, J. (1989). Personality correlates of physical fitness. *Journal of Personality and Social Psychology, 56,* 284–288.

Hogan, J. (in press). The structure of physical performance for occupational tasks. *Journal of Applied Psychology.*

Hogan, J., & Arneson, S. (1988). *Development and validation of physical ability tests for high pressure cleaning worker jobs.* Tulsa, OK: University of Tulsa.

Hogan, J., & Arneson, S. (1990). Physical and psychological assessments to reduce worker compensation claims. In J. W. Jones, B. D. Steffy, & D. W. Bray (Eds.), *Applying psychology in business: The handbook for managers and human resource professionals.* Lexington, MA: Lexington.

Hogan, J., Arneson, S., Hogan, R., & Jones, S. (1986). *Development and validation of personnel selection tests for the habilitation therapist job.* Tulsa, OK: Hogan Assessment Systems.

Hogan, J., & Bane, A. (1982). *Job analyses of physical requirements of Carter Mining Company jobs.* Tulsa, OK: University of Tulsa.

Hogan, J., & Bernacki, E. J. (1981). Developing job-related preplacement medical examinations. *Journal of Occupational Medicine, 23,* 469–475.

Hogan, J., & Fleishman, E. A. (1979). An index of physical effort required in human task performance. *Journal of Applied Psychology, 64,* 197–204.

Hogan, J., & Hogan, R. (1989). Psychological and physical performance factors associated with attrition in explosive ordnance disposal training. *Journal of Military Psychology, 3,* 117–133.

Hogan, J., Jennings, M. C., Ogden, G. D., & Fleishman, E. A. (1980). *Determining the physical requirements of Exxon apprentice jobs: Job analyses and test development.* Washington, DC: Advanced Research Resources Organization.

Hogan, J., Ogden, G. D., & Fleishman, E. A. (1979). *The development and validation of tests for the order selector job at Certified Grocers of California, Ltd.* Washington, DC: Advanced Research Resources Organization.

Hogan, J., Ogden, G. D., Gebhardt, D. L., & Fleishman, E. A. (1980). Reliability and validity of methods for evaluating perceived physical effort. *Journal of Applied Psychology, 65,* 672–679.

Hogan, J., & Pederson, K. (1984). *Validity of physical tests for selecting petrochemical workers.* Unpublished manuscript.

Hogan, J., Pederson, K. R., & Zonderman, A. B. (1981). *Job analysis and test development for physically demanding Dow Chemical jobs.* Baltimore, MD: The Johns Hopkins University.

Hogan, J., & Quigley, A. M. (1986). Physical standards for employment and the courts. *American Psychologist, 41,* 1193–1217.

Holland, J. L. (1985). *Making vocational choices: A theory of vocational personalities and work environments* (2nd ed.). Englewood Cliffs, NJ: Prentice-Hall.

Holland v. Boeing, Co., 90 Wash. 3d 324, 523 P.2d 621, 18 Fair Empl. Prac. Cas. (BNA) 37 (1978).

Hoxie, R. F. (1915). *Scientific management and labor.* New York: Appleton.

Hunsicker, P. A. (1958). *A.A.H.P.E.R. youth fitness manual.* Washington, DC: A.A.H.P.E.R., Youth Fitness Project.

Hunter, J. E., & Hunter, R. F. (1984). Validity and utility of alternative predictors of job performance. *Psychological Bulletin, 96,* 72–98.

Huxley, A. F. (1974). Muscular contraction. *Journal of Physiology, 243,* 1–43.

Huxley, H. E. (1965). Mechanism of muscular contraction. *Scientific American, 213,* 18–27.

Huxley, H. E. (1969). Mechanism of muscular contraction. *Science, 164,* 1356–1366.

Ironson, G. H., Guion, R. M., & Ostander, M. (1982). Adverse impact from a psychometric perspective. *Journal of Applied Psychology, 67,* 419–432.

Jackson, A. S., & Osburn, H. G. (1983). *Validity of isometric strength tests for predicting performance in underground coal mining tasks.* Houston: Shell Oil, Employment Services.

Jacobs, B. A. (1983). Sound minds, bodies…and savings. *Industry Week, 216,* 67–68.

Jensen, A. R. (1980). *Bias in mental testing.* New York: Free Press.

Johnson, R. C., McClearn, G. E., Yuen, S., Nagoshi, C. T., Ahern, F. M., & Cole, R. E. (1985). Galton's data a century later. *American Psychologist, 40,* 875–892.

Jones, L. A. (1986). Perception of force and weight: Theory and research. *Psychological Bulletin, 100,* 29–42.

Jones, M. A., & Prien, E. P. (1978). A valid procedure for testing the physical abilities of job applicants. *Personnel Administrator, 23,* 33–38.

Karvonen, M. J. (1974). Work and activity classification. In L. A. Larson (Ed.), *Fitness, health, and work capacity.* New York: Macmillan.

Keyserling, M. D. (1979). Women's stake in full employment: Their disadvantaged role in the economy—challenges to action. In A.F. Cahn (Ed.), *Women in the U.S. labor force.* New York: Praeger.

Keyserling, W. M., Herrin, G. D., Chaffin, D. B., Armstrong, T. J., & Foss, M. L. (1980). Establishing an industrial strength testing program. *American Industrial Hygiene Association Journal, 41,* 230–236.

Konz, S. (1983). *Work design: Industrial ergonomics.* Columbus, OH: Grid Publishing.

Koral, A. M. (1980). Practical application of the Uniform Guidelines: What to do till the agency comes. *Employee Relations Law Journal, 5,* 473–491.

Kraus, H., & Hirschland, R. P. (1953). Muscular fitness and health. *Journal of Health, Physical Education and Recreation, 24,* 17–18.

Kraus, H., & Hirschland, R. P. (1954). Minimum muscular fitness test in school children. *Research Quarterly, 25,* 177–188.

Kroemer, K. H. (1970). *Human strength: Terminology, measurement, and interpretation of data.* Wright Patterson Air Force Base, OH: Aerospace Medical Research Laboratory.

Kroemer, K. H. (1974). Horizontal push and pull forces. *Applied Ergonomics, 5,* 94–102.

Kroemer, K. H. (1986). Biomechanics of the human body. In G. Salvendy (Ed.), *Handbook of human factors* (pp. 169–181). New York: Wiley.

Landy, F. (1986). Stamp collecting versus science: Validation as hypothesis testing. *American Psychologist, 41,* 1183–1192.

Laubach, L. L. (1976). Comparative muscular strength of men and women: A review of the literature. *Aviation, Space, and Environmental Medicine, 47,* 534–552.

Laughery, K. R., Jackson, A. S., Osburn, H., Hogan, J., & Hayes, T. (1986). *Development and validation*

of physical ability tests for underground miners. Houston: Rice University, Department of Psychology.

Laughery, K. R., Jackson, A. S., Sanborn, L., & Davis, G. (1981). *Pre-employment physical test development for offshore drilling and production environments.* Houston: Shell Oil Company.

Laughery, K. R., & Schmidt, J. K. (1984). *Scenario analysis of back injuries in industrial accidents.* Paper presented at the 28th annual meeting of the Human Factors Society, San Antonio, TX.

Lawshe, C. H. (1979, June). Shrinking the cosmos: A practitioner's thoughts on alternative procedures. In P. Griffin (Chair), *Proceedings from the search for alternative selection procedures: Developing a professional standard.* Symposium presented at the meeting of the Personnel Testing Council of Southern California.

Lawshe, C. L. (1985). Inferences from personnel tests and their validities. *Journal of Applied Psychology, 70,* 237–238.

Lehman, H. C., & Witty, P. A. (1927). *Psychology of play activities.* New York: Barnes.

Lehmann, G. (1953). *Praktische arbeitsphysiologie.* Stuttgart, West Germany: Verlag.

Levine, E. L., Ash, R. A., Hall, H., & Sistrunk, F. (1981). *Evaluation of seven job analysis methods by experimental job analysts.* Tampa: University of South Florida, Department of Psychology.

Levine, E. L., Ash, R. A., Hall, H., & Sistrunk, F. (1983). Evaluation of job analysis methods by experienced job analysts. *Academy of Management Journal, 26,* 339–348.

Lewis, R. E. (1989). *Physical ability tests as predictors of job-related criteria: A meta-analysis.* Unpublished manuscript.

Lopez, F. M., Kesselman, G. A., & Lopez, F. E. (1981). An empirical test of a trait-oriented job analysis technique. *Personnel Psychology, 34,* 479–503.

Macey, T., Plomin, R., & McClearn, G. (1979, June). *Evidence for the reliability of data from Galton's anthropometric laboratory.* Paper presented at the meeting of the Behavior Genetics Association, Middletown, CT.

Manso v. Jacobs Rubber Division, Case No. Fair Empl. Prac. (PD) 2–4, Conn. Comm. on Human Rights (June 30, 1975).

Marr, C. (1982). Primer on case interpretation and legal update: Handicap discrimination case law in the 1980s. In S. W. Nylander & M. E. Nelson

(Eds.), *Medical standards project final report*. San Bernardino, CA: County of San Bernardino.

Masciotte, D. R., Avon, G., & Corriveau, G. (1979). Comparative effects of aerobic training on men and women. *Journal of Sports Medicine, 19*, 23–32.

McCormick, E. J., Jeanneret, P. R., & Mecham, R. C. (1972). A study of job characteristics and job dimensions as based on the Position Analysis Questionnaire (PAQ). *Journal of Applied Psychology, 56*, 347–368.

Mecham, R.C. (1977). *Technical manual for the Position Analysis Questionnaire*. Palo Alto, CA: Consulting Psychologists Press.

Myers, D. C., Gebhardt, D. L., Crump, C. E., & Fleishman, E. A. (1984). *Validation of the military entrance physical strength capacity test* (Tech. Rep. No. 610). Alexandria, VA: U.S. Army Research Institute for the Behavioral and Social Sciences.

Montoye, H. J., & Lamphiear, D. E. (1977). Grip and arm strength in males and females, age 10 to 69. *Research Quarterly, 48*, 109–120.

Mosso, A. (1883). Ricerche sulla fisiologiz della fatica. *Rendiconti dell'Accademia de medicina Torino, 31*, p. 667 ff.

Muller v. Oregon, 208 U.S. 412, 52 L. Ed. 557 (1908).

Nathan, B. R., & Alexander, R. A. (1988). A comparison of criteria for test validation: A meta-analytic investigation. *Personnel Psychology, 41*, 517–535.

National Institute for Occupational Safety and Health [NIOSH], U.S. Department of Health and Human Services (1981). *Work practices guide for manual lifting* (DHHS [NIOSH] Publication No. 81–122). Cincinnati, OH: NIOSH.

National Safety Council. (1975). *Accident facts*. Chicago: Author.

Noble, B. J., & Borg, G. (1972). Perceived exertion during walking and running. In R. Piret (Ed.), *Proceedings of the 17th International Congress of Applied Psychology* (pp. 387–392). Brussels.

Nordgren, B. (1972). Anthropometric measures and muscle strength in young women. *Scandinavian Journal of Rehabilitation Medicine, 4*, 165–169.

Nylander, S. W., & Nelson, M. E. (Eds.). (1982). *Medical standards project final report*. San Bernardino, CA: County of San Bernardino.

O'Connell, A. L., & Gardner, E. B. (1972). *Understanding the scientific basis of human movement*. Baltimore: Williams & Wilkins.

Osburn, H. G. (1977). *An investigation of applicant physical qualifications in relation to operator tasks at the Deer Park Manufacturing Complex*. Houston: Shell Oil Company.

Paffenbarger, R. S., Jr., Hyde, R. T., Wing, A. L., & Hsieh, C. (1986). Physical activity, all-cause mortality, and longevity of college alumni. *The New England Journal of Medicine, 314*, 605–613.

Park, K. S., & Chaffin, D. B. (1974). Biomechanical evaluation of two methods of manual load lifting. *Transactions of the American Institute of Industrial Engineers, 6*, 105–113.

Parker, M., & Slaughter, J. (1988). Management by stress. *Technology Review, 91*, 37–44.

Pearlman, K. (1980). Job families: A review and discussion of their implications for personnel selection. *Psychological Bulletin, 87*, 1–27.

Pearson, K. (1924). *The life, letters, and labours of Francis Galton: Vol 2. Researches of middle life*. London: Cambridge University Press.

Pederson, K. R. (1984). *Medical and safety data: Critical criteria for physical ability testing*. Paper presented at the 92nd annual meeting of the American Psychological Association, Toronto, Canada.

Primoff, E. S. (1971). *Summary of job-element principles: Preparing a job-element standard*. Washington, DC: Personnel Measurement and Development Center, U.S. Civil Service Commission.

Rehabilitation Act of 1973, 29 U.S.C. § 701 et seq.

Reilly, R. R., Zedeck, S., & Tenopyr, M. L. (1979). Validity and fairness of physical ability tests for predicting craft jobs. *Journal of Applied Psychology, 64*, 262–274.

Robertson, D. (1982). *Development of an occupational strength test battery (STB)* (Report No. NPRDC TR 82-42). San Diego, CA: Navy Personnel Research and Development Center.

Robertson, D. W., & Trent, T. T. (1983, August). *Predicting muscularly demanding job performance in Navy occupations*. Paper presented at the 91st annual meeting of the American Psychological Association, Anaheim, CA.

Rodgers, S. H. (1978). Metabolic indices in materials handling tasks. In C. G. Drury (Ed.), *Safety in manual materials handling* (DHEW [NIOSH] Publication No. 78–185). Washington, DC: U.S. Govenment Printing Office.

Rosenfeld v. Southern Pacific Co., 444 F. 2d 1219, 3 Empl. Prac. Dec. (CCH) ¶ 8247 (9th Cir. 1971).

Ruch, W. W. (1972, September). *A re-analysis of published differential validity studies*. Symposium paper presented at the annual meeting of the

American Psychological Association, Honolulu, HI.

Schmidt, R. A. (1982). *Motor control and learning.* Champaign, IL: Human Kinetics.

Sharp, S. E. (1898). Individual psychology: A study in psychological method. *American Journal of Psychology, 10*, 329–391.

Sheldon, W. H. (1940). *The varieties of human physique: An introduction to constitutional psychology.* New York: Harper.

Shephard, R. J. (1969). *Endurance fitness.* Toronto: University of Toronto Press.

Simon v. St. Louis County, Mo., 497 F. Supp. 141, 23 Fair Empl. Prac. Cas. (BNA) 1315 (E.D. Mo. 1980) reversed in part 656 F2d 316, 26 Fair Empl. Prac. Cas (BNA) 1003 (8th Cir. 1981).

Skinner, J. S., Hutster, R., Bergsteinova, V., & Buskirk, E. R. (1973a). Perception of effort during different types of exercise and under different environmental conditions. *Medicine and Science in Sports, 5*, 110–115.

Skinner, J., Hutster, R., Bergsteinova, V., & Buskirk, E. R. (1973b). The validity and reliability of a rating scale of perceived exertion. *Medicine and Science in Sports, 5*, 94.

Snook, S. H. (1978). The design of manual handling tasks. *Ergonomics, 21*, 963–985.

Snook, S. H., & Ciriello, V. M. (1974). Maximum weights and work loads acceptable to female workers. *Journal of Occupational Medicine, 16*, 527–534.

Snook, S. H., & Irvine, C. H. (1969). Psychophysical studies of physiological fatigue criteria. *Human Factors, 11*, 291–299.

Snook, S. H., Irvine, C. H., & Bass, S. F. (1970). Maximum weights and work loads acceptable to male industrial workers. *American Industrial Hygiene Association Journal, 31*, 579–586.

Society for Industrial and Organizational Psychology. (1987). *Principles for the validation and use of personnel selection procedures* (3rd ed.). College Park, MD: Author.

Sokal, M. M. (1981). *An education in psychology: James McKeen Cattell's journal and letters from Germany and England 1880–1888.* Cambridge, MA: MIT Press.

Sonoda, T. (1962). Studies on the compression, tension, and tension strength of the human vertebral column. *Journal Kyoto Prefectural Medical University, 71*, 659–702.

Sparks, C. P. (1982). Job analysis. In G. R. Ferris (Ed.), *Personnel management: New perspectives.* Boston: Allyn & Bacon.

Spriegel, W. R., & Myers, C. E. (Eds.). (1953). *Writings of the Gilbreths.* Homewood, IL: Irwin.

Stevens, J. C., & Cain, W. S. (1970). Effort in muscular contractions related to force level and duration. *Perception Psychophysics, 8*, 240–244.

Stevens, S. S. (1956). The direct estimation of sensory magnitude-loudness. *American Journal of Psychology, 69*, 1–25.

Stevens, S. S. (1958). Problems and methods of psychophysics. *Psychological Bulletin, 55*, 177–196.

Stevens, S. S. (1960). The psychophysics of sensory function. *American Scientist, 48*, 226–253.

Stillman, N. A., & Polk, D. J. (1981). Employment discrimination. In J. La-Dou (Ed.), *Occupational health law: A guide for industry* (pp. 179–206). New York: Marcel Dekker.

Taber, M. (1982). Reconstructing the scene. Back injury. *Occupational and Health Safety, 51*, 16–22.

Taylor, F. W. (1923). *Principles of scientific management.* New York: Harper.

Teeple, J. B. (1957). Work of carrying loads. *Journal of Perceptual and Motor Skills, 7*, 60–68.

Tenopyr, M. L. (1977). Content-construct confusion. *Personnel Psychology, 30*, 47–54.

Terborg, J. R. (1986). Health promotion at the worksite. In K. M. Rowland & G. R. Ferris (Eds.), *Research in personnel and human resources management* (Vol. 4, pp. 225–267). Greenwich, CN: JAI Press.

Tichauer, E. R. (1978). *Biomechanical basis of ergonomics.* New York: Wiley.

Tilton, J. W. (1937). The measurement of overlapping. *Journal of Educational Psychology, 28*, 656–662.

Turvey, M. T. (1977). Preliminaries to a theory of action with reference to vision. In R. Shaw & J. Bransford (Eds.), *Perceiving, acting, and knowing.* Hillsdale, NJ: Erlbaum.

U.S. Department of Labor. (1982). *Back injuries associated with lifting.* Washington, DC: Author.

United States v. New York, 21 Empl. Prac. Dec. (CCH) 30314 (N.D.N.Y. 1979).

Weeks v. Southern Bell Telephone & Telegraph Co., 408 F.2d 228, 1 Empl. Prac. Dec. (CCH) ¶ 9970 (5th Cir. 1969).

Williams, P. C. (1974). *Low back and neck pain.* Springfield, IL: Charles C. Thomas.

Wilmore, J. H. (1977). *Athletic training and physical fitness: Physiological principles and practices of the conditioning process.* Boston: Allyn & Bacon.

Wilmore, J., & Behnke, A. R. (1969). An anthropometric estimation of body density and lean body weight in young men. *Journal of Applied Physiology, 27,* 25–31.

Wilmore, J., & Behnke, A. R. (1970). An anthropometric estimation of body density and lean body weight in young women. *American Journal of Clinical Nutrition, 23,* 267–274.

Wilmore, J. H., & Davis, J. A. (1979). Validation of a physical abilities field test for the selection of state traffic officers. *Journal of Occupational Medicine, 21,* 33–40.

Wissler, C. (1901). Correlation of mental and physical tests. *Psychological Monographs,* No. 16.

Wunder, R. S. (1981). *Predictive validity of a physical abilities testing program for process apprentices.* Houston: Personnel Research, Employee Relations Department, Exxon, U.S.A.

Zamlen v. City of Cleveland (1988). U.S. District Lexis 5420.

Zedeck, S., & Goldstein, I. L. (1988, July). *Linking tasks and KSAs: A job analysis procedure.* Paper presented at the meeting of the Personnel Testing Council of Southern California, Los Angeles.

Zedeck, S., Hogan, J., Cascio, W. F., Goldstein, I. L., Barrett, R. S., & Outtz, J. (1988). *Development of tests for entry level firefighters.* Pleasant Hill, CA: CORE Corporation.

CHAPTER 12

Vocational Interests, Values, and Preferences

René V. Dawis
University of Minnesota

Interests, values, and preferences are stable dispositions distilled from affective evaluations of numberless life experiences. As such, they are thought to be good indicators of motives, and therefore, when combined with abilities, good predictors of performance. Lacking well-articulated theoretical foundation, they nevertheless are well operationalized in self-report instruments that have proven their worth in predicting (a) occupational membership, tenure, and change, (b) job and career satisfaction, and (c) worker satisfactoriness, though secondary to abilities in this regard. This chapter reviews how applied psychologists became interested in interests, values, and preferences, how they conceptualized and operationalized these constructs, and what successes and/or problems they had in the use of these instruments. If "people make the place"(Schneider, 1987), then consideration of people's vocational interests, values, and preferences can contribute to the industrial and organizational psychologist's better understanding of work motivation and work performance.

THIS CHAPTER IS about human motives as reflected in measures of interests, values, and preferences and about the use of such measures in industrial and organizational psychology. The topic of motivation has been a central concern in psychology and has given rise to much theorizing. However, applied psychologists have traditionally been wary of theorizing and have not entertained much discussion of motivation theory in their literature until the 1960s. This atheoretical stance was engendered in part by the notorious unreliability and invalidity—with some notable exceptions—of instruments purporting to measure motives. This is ironic, because one of the most enduring formulations in industrial and organizational psychology is the proposition that performance is a function of ability and motivation, or $P = A \times M$. Whereas ability measurement has become the foundation for the subfield of personnel selection, motivation measurement appears to have led only to controversy.

In recent times, the formula $P = A \times M$ has been criticized as being overly simplistic (Hakel, 1986). In addition, to be useful, each of its terms requires elaboration and specification, the motivation term more so than the ability term. From one viewpoint, to specify motivation is to specify motives, and among these are interests, values, and preferences.

This chapter builds on the solid foundation provided by Holland's chapter in this *Handbook's* first edition (Holland, 1976). In that chapter, Holland reviewed the major research findings about vocational interests and vocational preferences and made a persuasive case for classifying occupations and occupational membership according to his six-category hexagonal model known by its acronym, RIASEC. Much of the material covered by Holland will not be reexamined in this chapter, except as it pertains to a particular discussion.

The objectives of this chapter are (a) to examine the concepts of interest, value, and preference in some detail, (b) to review the measures by which they have been operationalized, (c) to survey the research findings resulting from their use and the problems that have appeared as a result, and (d) to chart the implications of this knowledge for practice and theory.

We shall begin with a brief historical account of the origins of the field.

Historical Background

Modern applied psychology can be said to have begun with Alfred Binet. The Binet test was the prototypic data-collection device that—coupled with *correlation*, the new data analytic method invented by Galton and developed by Pearson and Spearman—was to give rise to one of psychology's two disciplines (Cronbach, 1957): the psychology of individual differences. Applied psychology in the beginning was almost exclusively the application of the psychology of individual differences, which, in the beginning, was almost exclusively the assessment of human ability, intelligence in particular (Anastasi, 1949; Tyler, 1947; Viteles, 1932).

The Binet test was a breakthrough that led to a flood of developments in what came to be called *psychological testing* (DuBois, 1970). Binet succeeded where many others failed because of his discovery that an aggregation of fallible indicators could yield a global index that was both reliable and valid, much more so than any of the indicators taken singly—provided that the indicators were selected against a sound and relevant criterion. With these beginnings, the evolution of test construction technology was set into motion.

By the 1920s, the objective psychological test had gained such acceptance that industry, schools, and government were using ability tests for selection, classification, and evaluation. Even then, however, psychologists were aware that ability was only part of the picture. Conventional wisdom identified motivation as the needed complement to ability. Whereas experimental psychologists focused on *drive* as the significant construct in motivation (Woodworth, 1918), correlational psychologists looked toward *interests, values,* and *preferences* in their search for some objective measure of this factor.

The Carnegie Institute of Technology (now Carnegie-Mellon University) was the first academic institution to establish an applied psychology unit. Under the leadership of W. V. Bingham, it became a center for the study of work motivation. Much of the activity issued from the famous seminar conducted by C. S.

Yoakum on the measurement of interests. The *Carnegie Interest Inventory*, a product of the seminar, incorporated the features that later were to characterize successful interest measurement: the variety of items, the rating-scale format, and, most importantly, the empirical key—the scoring of only those items that differentiated between criterion groups (Dubois, 1970).

E. K. Strong, Jr., stood out as the most eminent figure in interest measurement. At Carnegie during the Yoakum years, he was later appointed to Stanford University where he embarked on his life's work of measuring vocational interests. One of Strong's students had demonstrated that different professional groups—engineers, lawyers, and physicians—could be differentiated on the basis of their responses to a modified *Carnegie Interest Inventory*. Intrigued, Strong began to study other occupations, revising and expanding the inventory, simplifying the complicated scoring system, enlarging the occupational samples, and developing a procedure using letter grades for reporting results in terms understandable to the layperson. Publication in 1927 of the *Strong Vocational Interest Blank* (SVIB) was welcomed by practitioners and researchers alike. Thus began one of the most successful and widely studied measures in the modern history of psychology.

The 1930s saw two other measures of motives that were to become prominent in their genre. In 1931, G. W. Allport and P. E. Vernon published the *Study of Values*, and in 1934, G. F. Kuder published the *Kuder Preference Record.*

Allport was, of course, the well-known student and theorist of personality whose investigations into the development of personality led him to examine what the mature personality should be. Among the criteria he identified was the formation of a unifying philosophy of life, and among the approaches he considered for ascertaining such formation was the study of values.

Allport's concern for individuality and its expression can be seen in his approach to the measurement of values. The *Study of Values* was one of the earliest instruments to use forced choice and paired comparison items, producing scores to reflect *intraindividual*, rather than *interindividual*, differences. Such ipsative scores were more compatible with the idiographic approach to personality description that Allport favored, in contrast to normative scores that remain in common use with most psychological tests.

Kuder was not a personality theorist but rather a psychometrics theorist best known for his contributions to reliability theory. Early in his career, Kuder became concerned that too many young people did not know what kind of work they should be doing. Consequently, he developed the *Kuder Preference Record* to follow through on his idea that through the systematic examination of preferences for common, everyday activities, young people could discover the kind of work suitable for them.

Like the *Study of Values*, the *Kuder Preference Record* made use of the forced-choice item, although with three rather than two response choices. Like the *Study of Values*, the *Kuder* was scored on a rational, or planned, basis in contrast to the *Strong's* empirical, or data-derived, basis. Like the *Study of Values*, the *Kuder* produced ipsative scores rather than normative scores as in the *Strong*. What all three instruments had in common, however, was that they far outstripped their competitors in the field of motive measurement through structured self-report.

All three instruments were used extensively in research that involved high school and college students, the population in our society most immediately confronted with having to choose careers or life work. It is not surprising, therefore, that the research findings based on these instruments suggested prompt application in vocational guidance and career planning, causing vocational and counseling psychologists to become more and more interested in such measures. At the same time, however, the generally disappointing performance of these measures in personnel selection led industrial and organizational psychologists to become less and less interested. By the late 1950s and early 1960s, industrial and organizational psychologists were looking at other ways of viewing work motivation (e.g., Herzberg, Mausner, & Snyderman, 1959; Vroom, 1964), and the study of interests, values, and preferences became by default almost exclusively the province of vocational and counseling psychologists.

There are, however, signs of change. For a number of reasons, including the renewed interest in job satisfaction, the challenge of Japanese management methods, the influx of counseling psychologists into industry, and the advent of employee-assistance programs, fostering careers in organizations has once again become an important concern of industrial and organizational psychologists (Hall, 1976; Schein, 1978). This, in turn, has rekindled and refocused attention on the concepts and measures of interests, values, and preferences.

Attention in industrial and organizational psychology may also be shifting from emphasis on organizational structure and process as explanations for organizational behavior toward a renewed consideration of the types of people who inhabit organizations. Schneider (1987), for one, has argued that organizational structure and process are determined by the people who are attracted to, selected by, and remain in the organization. This view suggests that measures of interests, values, and preferences can become more useful in the study of behavior in organizations.

Before we can consider how interests, values, and preferences might be used in studying organizational behavior, we must first examine how these concepts are defined and operationalized.

Conceptual Definition

From the earliest years, applied psychologists have preferred to define their concepts by constructing measures of the concepts and studying the measurements and their correlates. In Carter's (1944) words:

> [We are] not concerned with verbal distinctions…[We are] interested in the dynamics of behavior rather than in logical classification…[Our] main concern is with what is measured by the standardized instrument, and what can be done with the results of such measurement. (p. 9)

One could say that applied psychologists have preferred *operational* definition to *conceptual* definition.

The problem with conceptual definition—in which a concept is defined in terms of lower-level, more fundamental, previously defined, or more familiar concepts—is that eventually one is reduced to having to specify the operations that denote the final defining concepts. On the other hand, the problem with operational definition—in which a concept is defined in terms of the operations used to measure the concept—is that one has to begin somewhere when developing the item pool used to construct the instruments. It is safe to say that no psychological test has been constructed that did not begin with some concept of what the test was to measure. The test constructor's concept very likely was modified as the test was used, revised, and validated. Obviously, conceptual definition and operational definition are complementary, and each is incomplete without the other.

With these considerations in mind, we will next explore the various conceptual definitions of interests, values, and preferences.

Definitions of Interests

"What are interests?" asked E. K. Strong, Jr. (1960).

> Let me say that they are activities that are liked or disliked. Each person engages in thousands of activities, or habits, if you prefer that term, and attached to each is a liking-disliking affective tone. They remind me of tropisms. We go toward liked activities, go away from disliked activities. (p. 12)

Like Strong, Kuder (1977) saw interests as being manifested in preferences for activities. Other researchers, including Berdie (1944) and Cole and Hanson (1978), saw interests simply as constellations of likes and dislikes leading to consistent patterns of behavior. However, Carter (1944) believed that interests are based on evaluative attitudes and as such are stable personality traits, a position also held by Darley (1941) and Holland (1973).

Most authors agree that the relationship of interests to satisfaction is pivotal. For Strong (1943), interests are reflections of what the individual considers satisfying. For Kuder (1977), the purpose of an interest inventory is to help people discover the occupations they will find most satisfying. For Carter (1944), interests relate specifically to satisfaction. However, as Cole and Hanson (1978) note, the various conceptualizations of interest lack clear explication of the link between interests and satisfaction.

Perhaps the most comprehensive, and in some ways the most contemporaneous, conceptual definition of interest was one of the earliest. According to Bingham (1937):

> An interest is a tendency to become absorbed in an experience and to continue in it...[Interests are defined] not only in terms of the objects and activities which get attention and yield satisfaction, but also in terms of the strength of the tendencies to give attention to and seek satisfaction in these competing objects of interest. (p. 62)

On analysis, Bingham's definition consists of the following elements: An interest (a) is a dispositional variable (tendency); (b) has cognitive (attention), behavioral (experience), and affective (satisfaction) components; and (c) has dimensions of intensity (strength of tendency) and duration (continuation in experience).

Yet some time ago, Crites (1969) observed:

> Conceptual definitions of interests have lagged considerably behind operational definitions and have not been necessarily (logically or theoretically) related to them. ....No measure of interests...has as yet been constructed to define operationally the variables in an explicit theory of interests so that hypotheses deduced from it might be tested. (p. 678)

As we shall see, Crites' observation still holds.

Definitions of Values

Rokeach (1973) believed that the concept of values, more than any other concept, showed promise of being able to unify the various sciences concerned with human behavior. Unfortunately, as Tyler (1978) observed, the concept of values may be the most comprehensive, but it is also the least understood. Values have been viewed as equivalent to beliefs (Allport, 1961; Rokeach, 1973), attitudes (Campbell, 1963), needs (Maslow, 1954), interests (Allport, 1961; Perry, 1954), preferences (Katzell, 1964; Rokeach, 1973), standards or criteria (Rokeach, 1973; Rosenberg, 1957; Smith, 1969), and the conception of the desirable (Dewey, 1939; Kluckhohn, 1951; Rosenberg, 1957; Smith, 1969). Obviously, values comprise a complex variable that has to be described in terms of several dimensions, such as modality, content, generality, and intensity (Kluckhohn, 1951).

One such description and definition is Rokeach's (1973): "A value is an enduring belief that a specific mode of conduct or end-state of existence is personally or socially preferable to an opposite or converse mode of conduct or end-state of existence" (p. 5). Thus, for Rokeach, there are different kind of values: *instrumental* (modes of conduct) versus *terminal* (end-states of existence), or personal versus social. Values are cognitive representations and transformations of needs; they are enduring, although they are not traits. Manifested in interests but broader and more basic, values are standards that determine behavior.

Allport (1961) conceptualized values as beliefs upon which a person acts by preference. For Allport, values, together with interests, are *propriate motives*, a kind of trait more general than attitudes, although Allport, Vernon, and Lindzey (1970) described values as *evaluative attitudes*.

For Smith (1969), values are a special kind of attitude, functioning as standards by which choices are evaluated. For England (1967; England & Lee, 1974), values are similar to attitudes but more ingrained, permanent, and stable, more general and less tied to any specific referent, and provide a perceptual framework that shapes and influences behavior.

Super (1973) differentiated among traits, values, and interests, all seen as derived from needs. Traits are ways of acting to meet needs; values are objectives sought to satisfy needs; and interests are specific activities and objects through which to attain values and meet needs.

Katz (1963) saw values as characteristic outer expressions and culturally influenced manifestations of needs. Dawis and Lofquist (1984) defined values as "second-order needs." Needs are reinforcer requirements described in terms of the relative importance of particular reinforcers. Values represent common elements in need dimensions and are construed, in the factor analysis sense, as reference dimensions for the description of needs. But Locke (1976) distinguished further between values, or what a person consciously or subconsciously desires, wants, or seeks to attain, and needs, the conditions required to sustain the life and well-being of a living organism. For Locke, values are subjective and acquired or learned, whereas needs are objective and innate or inborn.

It is obvious that defining values is as inconclusive an enterprise as defining interests, and also that distinguishing interests from values can be problematic. However, there is agreement of sorts that values function as the standards, or criteria, by which persons evaluate things and that such evaluation is on the basis of the relative importance of things to the person. Values, then, can at least be differentiated from interests in that the latter refer to liking/disliking, whereas the former refer to importance/unimportance. As Carter (1944) put it, "Some things may be regarded as interesting but not important, and vice versa" (p. 9).

Definitions of Preferences

The term *preference* has been used in connection with interests (Holland, 1973; Kuder, 1977) and values (Lofquist & Dawis, 1978; Rokeach, 1973), suggesting a broader range of referent meaning. Preference has also been used synonymously with *choice*, especially in psychophysics (Bock & Jones, 1968). In psychophysics, choice is used when personal preference is involved, as opposed to *judgment*, when personal preference is not involved.

Preference is one of the most basic of psychological terms and refers to a choice among alternatives. The alternatives in psychophysical studies typically are narrowly defined experimental stimuli or stimulus objects. In more naturalistic studies, they include a wide range of psychological objects, such as friends, jobs, school subjects, and hobbies. The behavioral operation in preference is one of rank-ordering the alternatives, whether these be two, as in paired comparisons, or more than two. The evaluative basis for the expression of preference may be one or many—liking/disliking and important/unimportant are examples— all of which reflect what Thurstone (1931b) called *affective value*. Affective value may be unidimensional, in which case expressed preferences can be expected to show transitivity; in other words, if *A* is preferred over *B*, and *B* over *C*, then *A* should be preferred over *C*. But affective value can also be complex and multidimensional, hence showing intransitivity (Tversky, 1969).

In vocational psychology, a distinction between preference and choice has gained currency. Following Super's (1957) lead, preference (as in "vocational preference") is limited to the verbal expression of choice, whereas choice (as in "vocational choice") is the behavioral manifestation. High school students who have not yet entered the work world can only express a vocational preference; when they enroll for particular programs of vocational study or take other steps to enter an occupation, they are expressing a vocational choice. Following Super's distinctions, then, typical self-report inventories or questionnaires designed to measure interests or values are best described as measures of vocational preferences.

From this discussion of conceptual definition, we can perhaps appreciate why applied psychologists have preferred operational definition. The variety of conceptual definitions shows that these concepts are still very much in the early stages of evolution. What has emerged is that interests, values, and preferences have to do with the affective evaluation of cognitive representations of reality with some link to satisfaction/dissatisfaction. This point will become more evident as we survey the different approaches to the measurement of these concepts and the findings resulting from the use of such measures.

Operational Definition

As we have seen, *preference* is used as a more basic term in defining interests and values. Furthermore, extensive and largely separate literatures have developed in applied psychology for interests and values but not for preference. For these reasons, the following discussion focuses only on instruments designed to measure interests and values in the vocational or occupational domain.

Measures of Interests

The distinction between behavioral and verbal manifestation of interests is of particular pertinence to its operational definition. As shown in Table 1, however, it is only the first of several distinctions needed to classify the procedures devised to assess interests. Table 1 shows the distinctions as paired contrasts, each pair being nested within the preceding one. These distinctions may be described as follows.

Interests are manifested behaviorally through voluntary participation in particular activities, sustained attention in and enjoyment of the activities, and subsequent persistence in them. Interests have been assessed through behavioral manifestation in studies of small children (e.g., Harris, 1950) but typically not in studies of adults. Although behavioral manifestation is observed most feasibly in the laboratory, it may be too expensive and too circumscribed. In the field, observation is usually complicated by too many confounding factors and is too much a function of opportunity, which can be unevenly distributed at best. As a consequence, nearly all assessment of adult interests—in particular, vocational interests— has been based on verbal manifestation.

Assessing interests through verbal manifestation can be structured or unstructured in form. Unstructured approaches are those used in conversation or in open-ended interviews using such questions as, "What are your

TABLE 1

Distinctions Used to Classify Procedures in the Assessment of Interests

I. Behavioral manifestation

II. Verbal manifestation

    A. Unstructured

    B. Structured

        1. Test

        2. Self-report

            a. Rational scale

            b. Empirical scale

                (1) Internal criterion

                (2) External criterion

                    (a) Group differences approach

                    (b) Group similarity approach

                        i. Activity similarity

                      ii. People similarity

                          [a] Item pattern similarity

                          [b] Scale pattern similarity

interests?" and "What do you like to do when you're not at work?" In unstructured approaches, the kind and form of questions are not prescribed, and constraints are not placed on the response choices of the respondent. As a result, the data are often difficult to scale, quantify, or use in comparisons with other data.

In contrast, structured approaches require response within well-defined limits in which both the questions and response choices are specified. This permits the construction of instruments based on psychometric principles. Two kinds of structured instruments can be built: the test, which probes for "maximum performance" (Cronbach, 1970), and the self-report instrument, either a questionnaire or an inventory, which asks for expressions of preferences.

Attempts to develop objective tests of interests (Super & Crites, 1962) typically have been limited to development of information or vocabulary tests, based on the rationale that superior information or vocabulary in an occupational area is indicative of interest in that area. A good example of such a test is the *Michigan Vocabulary Profile Test* (Greene, 1951). Unfortunately, these tests have not prospered.

In contrast, the assessment of interests through the use of structured self-report instruments has flourished. Those currently in most use are the *Strong Interest Inventory* (SII; formerly the *Strong-Campbell Interest Inventory*) and the *Kuder Occupational Interest Survey* (KOIS). Such measures typically yield a number of scale scores to indicate the respondent's interest in a number of occupations or other fields of activity. Scales comprise groups of items that have been selected in some manner. Responses to these items are scored according to some rule, and the item scores are aggregated to produce the scale score.

Scales can be constructed by either the rational or empirical method. If by the rational method, items are written, selected or evaluated, and scored in accordance with theory. Items and their response choices are then judged as to how well they embody or represent theory. From this point on, the scale may be subjected to data-based scale development procedures. The General Occupational Themes of the SII are examples of scales constructed, at least initially, by the rational method.

Scales developed by the empirical method are data-based; that is, item selection and item scoring are based on the analysis of response data. The items may or may not have been written in accordance with some theory. Regardless of the source of the items, the responses to the items of empirically derived scales are the bases for both the selection of items to constitute the scales and the scoring of these items to produce the scale scores.

Item selection and scoring by the empirical method can be done according to an (a) internal or (b) external criterion. The internal criterion typically used is the *total score* on the try-out pool of items, the premise being that total score best represents the construct the item pool in the aggregate is designed to represent. This premise requires that (a) each of the items tap into the construct, that is, have content validity and (b) scoring weights be assigned to the response choices in a manner that best reflects the construct. The items and response choices most representative of the construct are those that have the highest correlation with the total score. An earlier method for selecting such items involved the contrasting of extreme groups based on total score—for example, the top 25 percent versus the bottom 25 percent—and the calculation of the groups' mean difference on each item. The items that best differentiated between the groups were the ones retained as a scale. This was the method introduced by Likert (1932) to measure attitudes. Likert used a 5-point rating scale for the

response choices, hence the common misuse of the term *Likert scale* to refer to any scale that uses 5-point ratings, whether the scale was developed by Likert's method or not (see Triandis, 1971).

A more sophisticated method of item selection according to an internal criterion makes use of the *principal component.* According to factor theory, the principal component, or factor, is the representation of the underlying construct. Items that tap into the construct are identified by their high correlation with the principal component, or, in factor analysis, by their *high factor loading.* Because such items tend to correlate highly with one another, the principal component can also be isolated by identifying items that intercorrelate highly among themselves. *Cluster analysis* is often used to accomplish this task. The Basic Interest Scales of the SII, produced by cluster analysis, are examples of scales developed largely by an internal criterion method.

Selecting and scoring items according to an internal criterion tends to produce scales that are relatively homogeneous in content. For a given pool of items, only as many scales can be developed as there are homogeneous content groups of items in the pool. That is, the number of scales that can be developed from a given item pool by internal criterion methods is limited—a characteristic that contrasts with scale development using an external criterion (see Clark, 1961).

The empirical method with the use of an external criterion, the method pioneered by Strong (1943), came to be known as *the* empirical method. Strong's basic discovery, with far-reaching implications for applied psychology, was that samples from different occupations could be differentiated dependably—reliably and validly—on the basis of their responses to a structured questionnaire. Strong's method was simple but effective: Identify and score only those items on which the occupational samples differed markedly in response. In other words, use (a) occupational membership as the criterion for item selection and (b) the response differences between samples as the basis for the scoring key.

In the beginning, Strong compared each occupational sample with all other occupational samples in his studies, but this quickly became impractical as more occupational samples were added. Strong then invented the idea of a *reference sample* against which to compare each of the occupational samples. This became the Men-in-General and Women-in-General samples. For each occupational sample, an Occupational Scale could be developed by identifying the items on which the occupational sample's preferences differed greatly from those of the reference sample. The particular response choices on which the two samples differed could then be assigned scoring weights for use in a scoring key. Strong's further discovery that scores obtained on his empirical scales were not only reliable and valid but remarkably stable over time, making them useful in predicting subsequent occupational membership—at least for college-educated men—brought the empirical method into prominence and ushered in a period in which the empirical approach predominated in applied psychology.

Selecting and scoring items on the basis of external criteria tends to produce scales that are heterogeneous in content for the simple reason that most external criteria are heterogeneous in content also. For such scales, internal consistency reliability does not apply, and reliability has to be assessed by the test-retest method. Also, unlike scale development by the internal criterion method, there is practically no limit to the number of scales that can be developed from a given item pool. Strong developed more than fifty Occupational Scales from his pool of 400 items, enhancing the practical usefulness of the instrument. From the present SII pool of 325 items, 207 Occupational Scales have been developed.

Strong's group difference method results in the scoring of only the subset of items that differentiates the occupational sample from the reference sample. In this respect, Strong's method is a primitive form of *discriminant function analysis*. Strong's scoring weights for the keyed response choices are analogous to the weights for the optimal linear combination of predictors in the discriminant function. The score on a *Strong* Occupational Scale is therefore best interpreted as indicating the *probability* of group membership, as in discriminant function analysis. Furthermore, the Occupational Scale score on the *Strong* cannot be interpreted as indicating magnitude of interest in the occupation. It also cannot, strictly speaking, be said to indicate similarity of interests with the occupational sample because only a subset of the items (typically 10–20%) is scored. In effect, the Occupational Scale score captures only the unique interests of the occupational sample.

Similarity of interests can be operationalized in two ways (Cole & Hanson, 1978). The first is based on the "activity similarity" rationale—that persons who enjoy activities similar to activities required in a given occupation will be satisfied with the occupation if they enter it. The *Ohio Vocational Interest Survey* (D'Costa, Winefordner, Odgers, & Koons, 1970) and the *ACT Interest Inventory* (American College Testing Program, 1981) were constructed on this basis. The second way is based on the "people similarity" rationale—that persons with interests similar to members of a given occupation will be satisfied with the occupation if they enter it. Both the SII and the KOIS are based on this rationale.

Kuder (1977) uses a scoring method that, unlike Strong's, does indicate how similar a respondent's interests are to those of the criterion sample. The ingenious approach, developed by Clemans (1968), entails using the respondent's responses to "score" the responses of the members of a given criterion sample.

This scoring procedure yields a *proportion score,* Σp, that represents the average similarity of the criterion sample members' responses to the respondent's responses. A coefficient, *lambda,* is then calculated as follows (Kuder, 1977, p. 42):

$$\lambda = \frac{\Sigma p - 66.67}{HPPS - 66.67}$$

where Σp is the respondent's proportion score, *HPPS* is the highest possible proportion score for the criterion sample, and 66.67 is the chance proportion score. Besides being an actual index of similarity, lambda has the additional advantage over the *Strong* Occupational Scale score of not requiring a reference sample, the composition of which may be subject to argument.

Jackson (1977) uses a somewhat different version of the similarity approach in his scoring method for the *Jackson Vocational Interest Survey* (JVIS). This method entails constructing the respondent's profile of scale scores on the instrument's 34 homogeneous scales and comparing the profile with (a) modal profiles obtained for the criterion groups, such as samples of students in different academic programs, and (b) estimated modal profiles for 32 occupational clusters obtained by estimating JVIS scale scores from SVIB data. Thus, Jackson's method uses patterns of scale scores, whereas Kuder's method uses patterns of item scores.

The nested structure of the distinctions presented above may serve the purposes of presentation, but the reader is not supposed to get the idea that the categories are air-tight and the hierarchical arrangement is logically unassailable. Nature delights in confounding logic, and in the actual world there is much more blurring of boundaries and cutting up of categories.

The several methods of assessing interests described above all presume the use of a structured self-report instrument, typically a questionnaire or inventory. Choosing which method to use does not address the matter of what the

item content of such an instrument should be. Indeed, as was pointed out earlier, the problem with operational definition is that it does not resolve the question of content domain.

At least two approaches could be taken in generating items for an interest inventory. One could start with a plan of what the item content should be, for example, as given by theory or by some proposed taxonomy of interests or other a priori mapping of the content domain. This was the approach that both Kuder (1939) and Jackson (1977) used for their interest measures. The other approach is what Strong (1943) used: trying out a variety of items and using empirical results to modify and improve the item pool. In practice, item pools generated by either method can be modified further on the basis of empirical results. Hence, the question of defining the content domain of interests remains conceptually unresolved.

Factor analysis provides an after-the-fact answer to questions about the content domain, not by pointing out what the domain should be but by describing what the domain in a given item pool has been. Thurstone's (1931a) early factor analysis of 18 SVIB Occupational Scales yielded four factors: Science, People, Language, and Business. Strong's (1943) own factor analysis of 36 SVIB Occupational Scales identified five factors: Thurstone's four, plus Things vs. People.

Guilford, Christensen, Bond, and Sutton (1954) conducted the most definitive factor analytic study to date of the interest content domain. Starting with 33 postulated factors, they were able to represent 19 of these with at least three measures each, 9 factors with two measures each, and 4 factors with one measure only; they failed to find a measure for one postulated factor. Factor analysis confirmed 14 of the 19 three-measure factors and 4 of the 9 two-measure factors. Of these 18 confirmed factors, 7 were thought to be distinctively vocational interest factors and 11 similar to what are ordinarily considered personality factors. The

TABLE 2

Interest Factors Identified in Five Factor Analytic Studies

Guilford et al. (1954)	Lorr & Suziedelis (1973)	Rounds & Dawis (1979)	Kuder (1977)	Zytowski (1976a)
Mechanical	Mechanical Activities	Mechanical Activity	Mechanical	Skilled Trades
Scientific	Quantitative Science	Science Mathematics	Science-Mathematics	Mathematic-Numeric
		Medical Science	Medical Engineering	Medical Service
	High-status Professional		Dietetics	
Social Welfare	Social Welfare Activities	Social Service Public Service	Social Welfare	Helping
Aesthetic Expression	Art Activities	Aesthetics	Artistic Literary Musical	Art
Clerical		Clerical Activity	Accounting-Clerical	
Business	Sales & Business Management	Business Contact	Persuasive	Business vs. Physical Science
	Leading & Directing	Meeting & Directing People	Political	
Outdoor Work	Outdoor Work	Nature	Outdoor	Agriculture
	Military Activities	Military Activity		
Physical Drive	Outdoor Sports Extrovertive-Competitive Games	Athletics-Adventure	Drive, Aggressiveness Physical Education	Active vs. Sedentary
Adventure vs. Security	Risk & Change	Security vs. Adventure		
	Religious Activities	Religion	Religious	
		Teaching Domestic Arts	Library Science Femininity-Masculinity	Homemaking

(continued)

TABLE 2

Interest Factors Identified in Five Factor Analytic Studies (continued)

Guilford et al. (1954)	Lorr & Suziedelis (1973)	Rounds & Dawis (1979)	Kuder (1977)	Zytowski (1976a)
Aesthetic Appreciation		Aesthetic Appreciation Fashionable Appearance		
Cultural Conformity Diversion Attention Aggression Thinking Orderliness Sociability Precision	Liberal Non-conformist	Nonconformity		

vocational interest factors are shown as the first seven Guilford et al. factors named in Table 2.

Also shown in Table 2 are factor names from two factor analyses of the SVIB items (Lorr & Suziedelis, 1973; Rounds & Dawis, 1979) and from two factor analyses of the KOIS (Kuder, 1977; Zytowski, 1976a). Taking into account the differences in samples and factor analytic methodologies among the five studies, two conclusions stand out: (a) A large number of factors (14–20) is required to describe the interest content domain represented in the two most frequently used instruments and (b) at least half of these factors are given the same or similar names across the studies. To the extent that factor names accurately reflect item content, these factors may be said to be *constructively replicated* (Lykken, 1968). Among the "replicated" factors are the seven that Guilford et al. (1954) designated as vocational interests: Mechanical, Scientific, Social Welfare, Aesthetic Expression, Clerical, Business, and Outdoor Work. Note that if Mechanical and Outdoor

Work are combined to constitute the Realistic category, these factors correspond to Holland's six personality types.

Brief descriptions of some of the more prominent interest measures are given in an appendix at the end of the chapter.

Measures of Values

Instruments purporting to measure values have often been categorized as interest measures in the vocational psychology literature (Super & Crites, 1962; Zytowski, 1973). Like measures of interests, measures of values are likely to be verbal measures rather than behavioral, structured rather than unstructured, and in a self-report format rather than a test. Indeed, measures of values can be classified according to the distinctions listed in Table 1, making it easy to confuse or commingle the two types of instruments.

In terms of measurement operations, there seems to be little that differentiates between the two types of instruments. The two basic psychometric operations of judgment and magnitude estimation have both been used in developing measures of values as well as interests. However, developers of value measures have tended to use judgment methods, which involve the ranking of stimuli, whereas developers of interest measures are better known for their use of magnitude estimation methods, which involve the rating of stimuli. This preference for judgment methods in value measurement goes back to the classic work of Thurstone (1927) on the law of comparative judgment. The *Allport-Vernon-Lindzey Study of Values*, the *Rokeach Value Survey*, the *Minnesota Importance Questionnaire* (MIQ), Gordon's *Survey of Interpersonal Values*, the *Occupational Values Inventory*, and an earlier version of Super's *Work Values Inventory* are all examples of value measures that use judgment methods.

Judgment methodology appears to fit in well with the various conceptual definitions of values. According to these definitions, value measures should focus on stimulus differences; hence, they should emphasize *intra*individual differences. In contrast, interest measures have tended to focus on respondent differences and have emphasized *inter*individual differences. However, this contrast may have to do more with the practical purposes for which interest measures have been constructed than with the conceptual definition of interest. From a conceptual viewpoint, one could convincingly argue that interest measures, like value measures, should stress stimulus differences and intraindividual differences. From a practical standpoint, however, one could just as convincingly argue that value measures should emphasize respondent differences and interindividual differences.

Although judgment methodology and the statistics associated with it have an extensive literature beyond our purview, we will discuss the three basic, most frequently used formats for rank ordering that are seen with value measures—(a) paired comparisons, (b) multiple rank orders, and (c) ranking.

In rank order methodology, one typically starts with a set of *stimuli*, or, in the case of value measurement, statements about values. In the paired comparisons method, each stimulus is paired with every other stimulus, and the respondent chooses one stimulus in each pair, effectively rank ordering the pair. The proportion of times a stimulus is chosen can be converted to a corresponding scale value that locates the stimulus, with respect to other stimuli, on the same preference continuum—a scale of importance in the case of value measurement. The distances between stimuli reflect the differences in importance between the values. The *Study of Values* and the MIQ use the paired comparison format.

In the method of multiple rank orders, the stimuli are presented in subsets of more than two: triads, tetrads, pentads, and so on. Designs are available to enable the pairing of each stimulus just once with every other stimulus (Gulliksen & Tucker, 1961). In effect, paired comparisons are implicit in the multiple rank order subsets. The respondent rank orders the stimuli in each subset and from these multiple rankings a paired comparison matrix can be constructed. *Scaling,* the assignment of scale values to stimuli, then proceeds as in the paired comparison method. The ranked form of the MIQ uses the multiple rank orders format.

When the total set of stimuli is presented all together, as one set to be rank ordered, the method is simply called *ranking*. The respondent assigns a rank to each stimulus according to some rule—according to importance in value measurement. The ranking can be made more reliable by alternating between the two ends of the rank order, or between most and least important in value measurement. Ranking judgments tend to be most reliable at the extremes of the distribution and least reliable in the middle of the distribution. The *Rokeach Value Survey* uses the ranking format.

All three rank order formats yield a simple ranking of stimuli. The scores for all three formats—scale values for paired comparisons and for multiple rank orders, ranks for ranking—can be converted to interval-scale scores by transformation to normal deviate scores, and even to ratio-scale scores by the addition of an absolute judgment procedure to the instrument (Guilford, 1954).

Value measures have tended to be rational rather than empirical in origin. The number and composition of value statements used in a measure have typically been dictated either by theory or by some a priori procedure for selecting stimuli, such as a proposed taxonomy of values or a review of value "coverage" in other instruments. Subsequent instrument development may involve empirical procedures, for example, the use of internal or external criteria for item selection. Nonetheless, because of their origins, value measures have often been labeled rational instruments, with the accompanying negative connotations.

Value measures appear to differ from interest measures in at least two respects. First, values are scaled on the importance dimension, whereas interests are scaled on the liking dimension. Second, value measures usually have ends, such as goals or standards, for item content, whereas interest measures generally have means, such as activities or instrumentalities. Even these apparent differences break down upon further analysis. Judgments of value statements in terms of importance might include considerations of liking or disliking; likewise, evaluations of liking/disliking might include considerations of importance. Also, distinguishing between ends and means can be problematic because some ends can serve or be viewed as means, and vice versa. Values can be reflected in means as well as ends (Rokeach, 1973).

Furthermore, item content may, in part, be a function of questionnaire instructions in the sense that certain items may fit the instruction about importance better than that about liking,

and vice versa. For example, it seems more appropriate to speak about the importance of truth, harmony, peace, and justice than to speak about liking or disliking them. Likewise, liking/disliking seems more appropriate than importance for evaluating different kinds of hobbies or leisure activities.

Whatever the content and scaling differences between value and interest measures, the available data have consistently shown that the two domains are distinct, if overlapping. Cross-correlations between value and interest scales are typically significant but low. For instance, the *Study of Values* scales rarely correlate higher than .35 with the *Strong* scales (Ferguson, Humphreys, & Strong, 1941; Sarbin & Berdie, 1940). Studies correlating the MIQ with the *Strong* (Kohlan, 1968; Thorndike, Weiss, & Dawis, 1968a, 1968b), with Holland's *Vocational Preference Inventory* (Salomone & Muthard, 1972), and with the JVIS (Kulakowski, 1986) report similarly low scale cross-correlations, multiple R's in the .30s to .60s, canonical R's in the .70s, and separate value and interest factors upon factor analysis. Similar findings are reported for Super's *Work Values Inventory* with the *Strong* (Kinnane & Suziedelis, 1962; Super, 1962) and with the *Kuder* (Ivey, 1963). The low value/interest cross-correlations are easy to attribute to differences in item content. What needs to be done is to compare importance and liking ratings on the same set of items.

With respect to item content, existing measures of values can be grouped in two categories: (a) general measures that are broad in scope and apply to the totality of human living, such as the *Study of Values* and the *Rokeach Value Survey*, and (b) work-related, vocational, or occupational measures that are intended to apply only to the work setting, such as the *Work Values Inventory* and the MIQ. An idea of the content domain coverage of work-related value measures can be obtained from Table 3, which lists scale names for five well-established instruments.

TABLE 3

Names of Scales From Five Work-Related Value Measures

Minnesota Importance Questionnaire	Work Values Inventory	Occupational Values	Job Values and Desires Questionnaire	Occupational Values Inventory
Ability Utilization Achievement Activity	Achievement	Use special abilities		Preparation and ability
Advancement				Advancement
Authority		Exercise leadership	Leadership power	
Company Policies and Practices Compensation	Management Economic Returns	Earn good money	Profit	Salary
Co-Workers	Associates	Work with people		
Creativity	Creativity	Creative, original	Self-expression	
Independence[a] Moral Values Recognition	Way of Life		Fame	Personal goal
Responsibility[a] Security Social Service	Independence Security Altruism	Free of supervision Secure future Helpful to others	Independence Social service	Security
Social Status	Prestige	Social status, prestige	Status, esteem	Prestige
Supervision, Human Relations Supervision, Technical	Supervisory Relations			
Variety	Variety			
Working Conditions	Surroundings Intellectual Stimulation Esthetics	Provide adventure	Interesting experience	Interest and satisfaction

[a] Independence for the MIQ is "I could work alone on the job," whereas Responsibility is "I could make decisions on my own."

TABLE 4
___

Factors in the Factor Analysis of the MIQ

Factor	Description	Defining MIQ Scales
Achievement	The importance of an environment that encourages accomplishment	Ability Utilization Achievement
Comfort	The importance of an environment that is comfortable and not stressful	Activity Independence Variety Compensation Security Working Conditions
Status	The importance of an environment that provides recognition and prestige	Advancement Recognition Authority Social Status
Altruism	The importance of an environment that fosters harmony and service to others	Co-Workers Social Service Moral Values
Safety	The importance of an environment that is predictable and stable	Company Policies and Practices Supervision, Human Relations Supervision, Technical
Autonomy	The importance of an environment that stimulates initiative	Creativity Responsibility Autonomy

Factor analysis of the MIQ provides some insight into the dimensional structure of the domain of work values. The same six-factor structure was obtained for each of eight large samples representing a sex-by-age (four age groups) cross-classification (Seaburg, Rounds, Dawis, & Loquist, 1976). Similar structures were obtained in studies by Elizur (1984) and Pryor (1982). The MIQ scales, factors, and factor descriptions are shown in Table 4.

An interesting aspect of this structure is revealed by an unpublished multidimensional scaling study conducted by Rounds and Dawis (see Dawis & Lofquist, 1984). Scoring only the defining MIQ scales to provide six factor-based scores, or MIQ value scores, Rounds and Dawis found the scores to fit best in a three-dimensional space, with each dimension being anchored at each pole by one of the values. The bipolar pairings were Achievement versus

Comfort, Altruism versus Status, and Safety versus Autonomy. Furthermore, note that the Achievement and Autonomy values refer to *self* reinforcers, the Altruism and Status values to *social* reinforcers, and the Safety and Comfort values to other *environmental* reinforcers. The structure, therefore, identifies three major classes of work reinforcers and opposing sets of values as well.

Brief descriptions of some of the better known value measures are included in the Appendix.

Having seen how interests and values are operationalized, we next examine the important applied research findings obtained with the use of these measures.

Selected Findings

Much, if not most, of the applied psychology research literature on interests, values, and preferences concerns vocational interests. For that reason, the following discussion is directed largely toward vocational interests. The literature on vocational interests—on the *Strong* alone—is vast, so we focus on the findings that have made measures of interests, values, and preferences important in vocational and occupational psychology.

Predicting Later Occupational Membership

The validity of the *Strong* was initially based on its ability, on cross-validation, to differentiate occupational samples from one another and from the reference group. This is known as *concurrent validity*. But it was the results of Strong's 5- and 10-year follow-up studies (Strong, 1935, 1943) that established the SVIB as the foremost instrument of its kind. In these studies, Strong found that a large majority of his subjects, 78 percent, had scored A's on relevant occupational scales, whereas only a small fraction, 17 percent, had scored C's.

In 1954, McArthur reported on a 14-year follow-up of 60 subjects. Using a system for assessing "hits" and "misses" that became standard usage for such studies, McArthur (1954) estimated that the *Strong* provided "good hits" (A's on relevant occupational scales) for 45 percent of his subjects, "poor hits" (B+'s) for 20 percent, and "clean misses" (anything lower) for 35 percent. The following year, Strong (1955) published the results of his 18-year follow-up of over 600 Stanford students, reporting 48 percent good hits, 18 percent poor hits, and 34 percent clean misses.

Over the years, other investigators (e.g., Bartling & Hood, 1981; Brandt & Hood, 1968; Cairo, 1982; Campbell, 1966; Dolliver, Irvin, & Bigley, 1972; Dolliver & Will, 1977; Worthington & Dolliver, 1977) have reported on follow-up studies of 3- to 21-year intervals for which findings were similar: 45 to 50 percent good hits, 15 to 20 percent poor hits, and 30 to 40 percent clean misses. Few findings in applied psychology can claim this record of replication, which is all the more remarkable when one considers the variability in samples and methodology, particularly in occupational categorization. Similar results have been obtained for the *Kuder* (Zytowski, 1976b) and for the Navy version of the *Minnesota Vocational Interest Inventory* (Lau & Abrahams, 1972).

From these studies, one can conclude that, at least for college students, the degree to which interests expressed at about age 20 are similar to those of members of an occupation is significantly associated with later membership in the occupation. That is, one is more likely to be found later in an occupation for which one's interests were more similar (to those of members of the occupation) than in an occupation for which one's interests were less similar. This conclusion can be explained if interests expressed at age 20 remain relatively the same over the person's work life and if the interests of occupational members are likewise relatively stable. That is, predicting later occupational membership from interests at an earlier age has to be predicated on the stability of vocational interest scores. The data (Johansson & Campbell, 1971; Strong, 1955) show that SVIB occupational scale scores are quite stable from age 25 on, with test-retest correlations of .80 or higher for intervals of up to 20 years; somewhat stable from age 22 to 25, with correlations in the .70s; and less stable for age 21 and below, with correlations below .70. Few data are available that bear directly on the stability of interests of occupational members, although there is indirect evidence (e.g., similarity of interests of cross-generational occupational samples as reported in Hansen & Campbell, 1985). The questions about interest stability raised by these data shall be treated later in this chapter.

As with interests, one type of evidence for the validity of value measures has consisted of demonstrating the ability of such measures to differentiate among occupational groups (e.g., England, 1967; Gay, Weiss, Hendel, Dawis, & Lofquist, 1971; Munson & Posner, 1980). For instance, professional occupational groups tend to rank the Autonomy value over the Comfort value, but the reverse is true for nonprofessional occupational groups (Gay et al., 1971).

That occupational groups differ in levels and patterns of interests and values can be regarded as an established finding. Such a finding can plausibly be attributed to selection pressures originating from both self-selection and organizational selection. If this is so, one might infer that among the bases used for career choice and personnel selection are interests and values. Note, however, that asking people which interests and values served as the bases for their choice is not the same as discovering which interests and values differentiate among occupational groups. There are *effective* bases, as opposed to *expressed* bases, for choice and selection, analogous to *captured* versus *professed* policy in organizations.

With respect to predicting later occupational membership, no data have been compiled for values that can compare with the vocational interest data. Until recently, researchers on values have not been interested in predicting later membership in occupations. Rather than using values as a predictor variable, value researchers have been more interested in values as a criterion variable, preferring to examine occupational and other group differences in values. Also, the stability of values has, for the most part, been taken for granted, and only a few longitudinal studies have been undertaken (e.g., Kapes & Strickler, 1975); results have been promising, though not definitive.

Predicting Job Satisfaction

In discussing conceptual definition, we established that both interests and values are linked conceptually to job satisfaction. Surprisingly, the empirical exploration of this link has not attracted as much attention as its theoretical importance warrants. Current evidence for the link is, at best, modest. For example, Bartling and Hood (1981), Cairo (1982), Dolliver, Irvin, and Bigley (1972), McArthur (1954), and Schletzer (1966) failed to find any relationship between vocational interests (more accurately, similarity of subjects' vocational interests to those of occupational members) and subsequent job satisfaction on follow-up. However, Barak and Meir (1974), Klein and Wiener (1977), and Worthington and Dolliver (1977) did report finding such a relationship. The situation with values is less mixed. Aldag and Brief (1975), Betz (1969), Blood (1969), Butler (1983), Elizur and Tziner (1977), Kazanas (1978), Lichter (1980), Rounds (1981), Rounds, Dawis, and Lofquist (1987), Salazar (1981), and Wood (1971), among others, found relationships between vocational values and job satisfaction.

A number of explanations can be advanced to account for the mixed results found for interests. If, as previously hypothesized, the subjects of follow-up studies were the survivors of a selection process, one might infer that in this process, the dissatisfied would have tended to leave, whereas the satisfied—and satisfactory— would have tended to remain. The restriction of range that would result could contribute to the lowering of the "true" correlations. Unfortunately, the means and standard deviations of variables frequently go unreported so that a straightforward check of this simple explanation is often thwarted.

Another explanation for the mixed results has to do with the empirical keys used with the *Strong* Occupational Scales. The empirical key is constructed to maximize the prediction of the criterion, which, in this case, is occupational membership. Unless job satisfaction were highly correlated with occupational membership, the empirically keyed Occupational Scale cannot be expected to predict it. With the base rate of job satisfaction at 80 to 85 percent, correlation of job satisfaction with occupational membership is bound to be low, which would make its prediction problematic.

In contrast, value scales have not usually been constructed with the intention of predicting to some criterion. The fact that relationships with job satisfaction have usually been found speaks to the relevance of the importance dimension to satisfaction. As an illustration, the MIQ was designed to present 20 outcomes of work, or work reinforcers, that different groups of workers considered important to their job satisfaction and which respondents are to rank in terms of their relative importance for "an ideal job." The MIQ scales were not developed empirically, that is, to maximize prediction to a criterion such as job satisfaction. Instead, MIQ scores are compared with *occupational reinforcer patterns*, which are independently obtained ratings of the presence or absence of work reinforcers in specific occupations, to ascertain the *correspondence*, or similarity, of the individual to an occupation on the basis of preference and presence of work reinforcers. A *correspondence score* is then calculated, which is used to predict job satisfaction. Rounds, Dawis, and Lofquist (1987) found that

predictive accuracy does depend on scoring methodology, but it is also clear from their results and others (e.g., see Lichter, 1980; Rounds, 1981; Salazar, 1981) that job satisfaction can be predicted from correspondence scores at the .30 to .50 level.

The accuracy of predicting job satisfaction from interests and values is affected also by the almost universal use of overall, total, or global satisfaction scores. Job satisfaction is known to consist of several components, the two major ones being *intrinsic satisfaction*, or satisfaction with the work itself (type of work), and *extrinsic satisfaction*, or satisfaction with the conditions of work (Campbell & Pritchard, 1976; Locke, 1976). The use of overall satisfaction scores masks differences in the component scores. If interests reflect liking or disliking for activities, they should be related more to intrinsic than extrinsic job satisfaction. If values reflect what is important to people, their relation to intrinsic and extrinsic job satisfaction would depend on which was held by the respondents to be important or more important—type of work or working conditions. Differing levels of correlation with intrinsic and extrinsic satisfaction would be averaged out in the correlation with overall job satisfaction, resulting in a lower correlation. Unfortunately, the use of overall satisfaction prevents these suppositions from being subjected to more serious scrutiny.

Korman (1967) proposed a different explanation for the low relationship between interests and satisfaction. Korman believed that the relationship holds true only for individuals whose self-esteem is high, not for those whose self-esteem is low. Korman's studies (1966, 1967) show self-esteem as functioning as a moderator variable, but results from other investigators (e.g., Dipboye, Zultowski, Dewhirst, & Arvey, 1978) do not support this conclusion.

Predicting Worker Satisfactoriness

The term *worker satisfactoriness* is used here instead of the more commonly used term *job performance* to underscore the author's conviction that the distinction between behavior, or actual performance of a job, and the evaluation of behavior by the employee or by others is not trivial. Examination of most studies reporting on job performance shows that the data were actually ratings of job performance. Much of the literature on personnel selection is, therefore, about the prediction of job performance ratings. There is also a sizable literature in personnel psychology about rating methodology and the factors that affect ratings, which warrants the assertion that only part—and not always the major part—of the variance of performance ratings does correspond to performance behavior. Hence the author's preference for the term *satisfactoriness*, that is, the rater's satisfaction with the employee.

Interests have been reported to correlate significantly, if at a low level, with satisfactoriness ratings (Ghiselli, 1966; Strong, 1943; Super & Crites, 1962). However, they take a backseat to abilities, which are still the best predictors of satisfactoriness. Interests contribute only small amounts of predicted variance over and above that contributed by abilities (e.g., Kaufman, 1972). Interests have also been reported to correlate with actual performance (behavior) measures (e.g., see Ghiselli, 1966, and Strong's, 1943, data on insurance agents). Even correlations with accident rate have been reported (Kunce, 1967).

Values have also been reported to correlate, at a significant but low level, with satisfactoriness (England & Lee, 1974; Kazanas, 1978; Munson & Posner, 1980; Watson & Williams, 1977). Many of these studies have been about managers, with pay as the measure of satisfactoriness.

Of the several values postulated, achievement is the one most frequently linked conceptually to performance. However, it is the achievement *motive* about which there is an extensive literature (e.g., see McClelland, 1961). Whether motive is equivalent to value is unclear, and the claims for the achievement

motive cannot automatically be conferred on the achievement value. Nevertheless, the achievement value itself has been reported to correlate significantly, if at a low level, with satisfactoriness (Cole & Miller, 1967).

The lower correlation of satisfactoriness with interests and values, in comparison with abilities, can be explained at two levels. At the methodological level, one might observe that interest and value measures have more measurement error than ability measures. Furthermore, because variance analysis is relative, that is, given in terms of proportions, the variable with the relatively greater variance has the better chance of showing up as the more important in the analysis, and abilities may have the greater variance. At the conceptual level, one might argue that particular abilities are necessary, though not sufficient, for satisfactory performance, but not particular motives (interests and values). That is, with the same abilities, different individuals can work equally satisfactorily for different motives. But with the same level of motivation, performance, and therefore satisfactoriness, will vary with different abilities. Hence the lower correlation with interests and values.

Predicting Occupational Change

Strong (1943) proposed four tests to evaluate the validity of vocational interest measures. Persons who continue in an occupation should obtain higher scores in the occupation (a) than they obtain in any other occupation, (b) than persons entering other occupations, and (c) than persons changing from the occupation to another. Further, persons who change from one occupation to another should, before the change, (d) score higher in the second occupation than they score in any other occupation, including the first. The first, second, and third tests pertain to occupational tenure, or continuing in an occupation; the third test pertains also to occupational turnover, or change in occupation, as does the fourth. Tenure and turnover are mirror images so that the data on one include or imply data on the other. Since Strong proposed his tests, follow-up studies (referred to earlier) have typically involved the collection of data on both occupational membership and occupational change. These studies have consistently found support for the second and third tests, which are interindividually based, but mixed results for the first and fourth tests, which are intraindividually based. The first and fourth tests require one to have the highest score in the occupation in which one continues or to which one changes. What the studies have found is that it is possible to have a high score in the occupation in which one continues or to which one changes and to have still *higher* scores in other occupations—although, in most cases, not the occupation from which one has changed.

Relation to Ability

That interests reflect abilities is a belief that strongly persists in everyday thinking. Career counseling services often foster this belief by basing their counsel solely on interests and avoiding discussion of abilities. The data, however, invalidate this belief. The correlation between interests and abilities is low, the common variance between these two classes of variables being reported to range typically between 0 and 4 percent, rarely exceeding 10 percent (Barak, 1981; Dawis & Sung, 1984; Keierleber, 1981; Lee & Thorpe, 1956; Lowman, Williams, & Leeman, 1985; Strong, 1943; Super & Crites, 1962; U.S. Department of Labor, 1970). The data are limited, but what data there are show that the correlation between values and abilities is no higher than that between interests and abilities (e.g., see Dawis & Lofquist, 1984).

This low correlation with abilities may be due in part to the difference in method of assessment: Abilities are assessed through tests, that is, through performance or behavior tests, whereas interests and values are assessed

through self-report instruments. Cronbach's (1970) distinction between measures of maximum performance and measures of typical performance appears to be well taken, inasmuch as, random error aside, ability test scores can be biased only in terms of underestimation, whereas self-reported interest and value scores can be biased in terms of overestimation as well. When both abilities and interests were assessed by self-report, the correlation was higher (Fryer, 1927; McCall & Moore, 1965; Thorndike, 1917); no comparable data have been reported for values. One suspects that behavioral assessments of interests and values might be more highly related to tested abilities, but no reports exploring this possibility have appeared.

The relation of interests and values to abilities is probably more complex than can be revealed in ordinary linear correlation. For instance, Wesley, Corey, and Stewart (1950) obtained intraindividual correlations between interests and abilities ranging from -.57 to +1.00. Furthermore, studies of group differences (Loehlin, Lindzey, & Spuhler, 1975; Maccoby & Jacklin, 1974) have indicated that ability test performance might be moderated by interest in the content of the test items. For example, in Shimberg's (Loehlin et al., 1975, pp. 67–68) pioneering 1929 study, urban and rural children differed strikingly—and predictably— on two information tests, one composed of urban-interest content and the other of rural-interest content. Likewise, male superiority in mathematical and quantitative ability during the high school years, but not during the elementary school years, is associated with a divergence between the sexes in their interest in science and other activities requiring quantitative ability (Maccoby & Jacklin, pp. 85–91).

If interests and values function as moderator variables, the low correlation with abilities should work to advantage in prediction. If interests and values are used along with abilities as predictors in multiple regression, the low correlation should again be advantageous. In other words, the low correlation of interests and values with abilities is desirable from both the conceptual and methodological point of view. The low correlation affirms the distinction between the concepts, enhancing their utility as separate concepts. It also guarantees that prediction will be maximized, given the linear methods of data analysis that are currently our best methodological tools.

Relation to Other Personality Variables

The material on this topic is extensive and diffuse, with much of it being adjunctive to other topics or peripheral with respect to the present topic. Few studies focus primarily on our topic; illustrative of these few are Costa, McCrae, and Holland (1984), Dunnette, Kirchner, and DeGidio (1958), Siess and Jackson (1970), Sloan (1979), and Stewart (1971). The overriding impression that one gets from these and other studies is the low level of correlation that interests and values have with other personality variables. For the most part, these personality variables are measured—like interests and values—through the use of structured self-report instruments. The level of correlation of scales *between* self-report instruments is not much different from that of scales *within* such instruments. One suspects that the content domain of structured self-report instruments is so heterogeneous, dimensionally speaking, that many more new scales can be constructed that would correlate with existing scales at the current low level.

There also remains a strong suspicion that a significant amount of the common variance among self-report scales should be attributed to rating bias, especially that caused by "acquiescence" (Bentler, Jackson, & Messick, 1971; but see Block, 1971). One way of circumventing this problem would be through the use of some form of hierarchical analysis to define higher-order variables, as Elizur (1984) and Costa, Fozard, and McCrae (1977) have done. Even then, the relationship of higher-order interests

and values with other personality variables is not high.

Relation to Biodata

Interests, values, and preferences, even as measured via structured self-report instruments, are thought to be the products of life-history experiences. Accordingly, correlation with biodata variables is expected. This expectation is borne out in several studies that also use self-report instruments to collect information on biodata variables (Chaney & Owens, 1964; Eberhardt & Muchinsky, 1982; Eberly, 1980; Engdahl, 1980; Kuhlberg & Owens, 1960; Meresman, 1975; Rounds, Dawis, & Lofquist, 1979). These studies uniformly report significant but low correlations between interests or values and biodata variables, the r's rarely exceeding .40. Many cross-validated relationships have been reported; however, these findings concern *inter*individual differences and involve linear, or compensatory, models. Work remains to be done to uncover *intra*individual patterns of life-history experiences related to specific interests and values.

Conclusions

Five conclusions are drawn from this selective survey of significant findings:

- Interests—and to a lesser extent, values—are predictive of occupational membership, occupational tenure, and occupational change.

- Values—and to a lesser extent, interests—are predictive of job satisfaction.

- Interests and values are secondary to abilities as factors in predicting worker satisfactoriness.

- Interests, values, and preferences—as manifestations or expressions of personality—are distinct from conventional personality traits.

- Interests, values, and preferences are associated with life-history variables.

These conclusions are bounded by the current levels of instrumentation technology, data collection methodology, and data analysis technique.

Some Problems of Validity

The question of validity lies at the heart of both the scientific and practical usefulness of interest, value, and preference measures. No attempt will be made to summarize the voluminous literature on the validity of these measures; the respective technical manuals typically contain such summaries. Rather, because over the years a number of questions relating to validity have surfaced, particularly in connection with interest measurement, several of these questions will be addressed around a discussion of three types of validity, namely, convergent, predictive, and construct validity.

Convergent Validity

Expressed Versus Inventoried Preferences. Inventories of interests and values have been constructed to help respondents think about their preferences more systematically. The assumption was that if people failed to consider a wide range of alternatives, their expressions of preference may not be valid. With the development of the *Strong*, the robust validity of the empirically keyed Occupational Scales and the relatively low correlation (about .50) between "measured" and "expressed" interests (Berdie, 1950) contributed to a widespread belief that measured interests were superior to expressed interests. Dolliver (1969a) challenged this belief, finding that in the few studies where expressed and inventoried interests were directly compared, inventoried interests were not superior in predictive accuracy, although they were more reliable. Several studies since then (e.g., Bartling & Hood, 1981; Borgen & Seling, 1978; Cairo, 1982; Dolliver & Will, 1977; Holcomb & Anderson, 1978) have confirmed Dolliver's conclusions and have shown that, if anything, expressed interests were superior in predictive accuracy. Also, predictive accuracy was found to be greatest when expressed and inventoried interests agreed. When they disagreed, expressed interests proved a better predictor than inventoried interests (Bartling & Hood, 1981; Borgen & Seling, 1978). Furthermore, convergence of expressed and inventoried interests was found to be related to persistence in college major or occupation (Laing, Swaney, & Prediger, 1984).

This focus on the relative merits of expressed versus inventoried interests masks a more difficult problem for vocational counselors: What about those persons *without* any expressed interests? Presumably they would be the ones whom the inventories should be able to help. Unfortunately, clinical experience suggests that they tend also to be the ones who show no salient interests on the inventories (Darley & Hagenah, 1955). There have been studies of the vocationally undecided; for example, Bartling and Hood (1981) report that the *Strong* is just as accurate for the undecided as for the decided. But then, even the undecided in these studies were not without expressed interests; they just had not made a choice. There have also been studies of flat profiles, that is, of individuals without any high Occupational Scale scores (e.g., Frantz, 1972; Murray, 1981), with the unsurprising finding that such individuals are most like the reference samples (the Men- or Women-In-General groups) in their interests. But even they have interests. No one, however, has studied flat profiles on the Basic Interest Scales.

No comparable studies of expressed versus inventoried values nor of flat value profiles have come to my attention. When expressed values have been studied, only one or at most a few values typically have been involved, as in the study of the Protestant ethic. When several values have been studied, inventories invariably have been used. In these studies, inventoried values have been treated as expressed values. Empirical keying has not been used much in the study of values, although see England and Lee (1974) for an exception.

Intrainstrument Consistency. This problem is specific to the *Strong* because it is scored on several different kinds of scales, thereby raising the possibility of inconsistency, lack of agreement, or even contradiction in the inferences derived from them. Two comparisons in particular have been examined: (a) the Basic Interest Scales versus the Occupational Scales and (b) the two sex forms of the Occupational Scales.

Johnson (1972a, 1972b) tabulated the items common to the Basic Interest Scales and the Occupational Scales of the men's form of the *Strong* and found them to range from 41 percent to 77 percent, with a median of 59 percent. In spite of this, he found the median correlation between matched Basic Interest and Occupational Scales—for example, Art versus Artist, Mathematics versus Mathematician—to be only .32 for a diverse sample of college men. Johnson also found the inconsistent combination of a high Basic Interest Scale score occurring with a low Occupational Scale score appearing on at least one pair of matched scales for 21 percent of his sample, and the combination of low Basic Interest and high Occupational Scale scores for 14 percent of the sample.

The Basic Interest Scales, constructed to be homogeneous in content, obviously yield different, if overlapping, information from that given by the Occupational Scales, constructed by the empirical method and heterogeneous in content. Because Basic Interest Scales are scored only in the direction of "Likes," interpretation of the scores is relatively straightforward. In contrast, with its mixture of "Likes," "Dislikes," and occasional "Indifferents," the Occupational key produces a score that is difficult to interpret except in terms of similarity to the unique interests of the Occupational criterion group.

Reconciling disparate Basic Interest and Occupational Scale scores can become an exercise in ingenuity on the part of the vocational counselor. Interestingly enough, Borgen (1972) and Dolliver (1975) found that the Basic Interest Scales did as well as the Occupational Scales in predictive accuracy.

With respect to the two sex forms, we shall arbitrarily separate the issue of bias (to be discussed later) from the issue of convergent validity, although recognizing that they are linked. Regarding the convergence of the two sex forms, Dolliver's (1981) review of relevant research showed that both female and male subjects tended to score higher on the other-sex scale than on their own-sex scale; nevertheless, for some scales, the higher scores were generally obtained on the male scale, and for others, on the female scale, regardless of sex of respondent. Generally, for occupations stereotyped as female occupations, the higher scores were obtained on the male scale, and vice versa, although there were some exceptions. Higher scores mean more similarity to, or less differentiation from, the criterion sample, hence—paradoxically—they indicate poorer validity. These findings notwithstanding, Dolliver and Worthington (1981) found that the other-sex scale was just as predictive as the own-sex scale and that prediction was best when both sex scale scores were high.

Interinstrument Consistency. When scales purporting to measure interests in the same occupation are found in different instruments, they can be a source of confusion for client and counselor alike when they yield different, especially conflicting, implications. Several studies of so-called same-named scales have borne out the actuality of this concern. Median correlations between same-named *Strong* and *Kuder* occupational scales were reported to be between .25 and .40 (Carek, 1972; Johnson, 1971; King, Norrell, & Powers, 1963; O'Shea & Harrington, 1971; Wilson & Kaiser, 1968; Zytowski, 1968, 1972). Correlating profiles of same-named scales increased the median correlations to the level of .55 to .70 (Johnson, 1971; Zytowski, 1972), but factor analysis showed separate instrument factors, indicating that factor overlap between scales of the two instruments was low (Harrington, Lynch, & O'Shea, 1971). Layton and Borgen (1972) and Lefkowitz (1970) have pointed out that because different scoring methods, norm groups, and item formats are used, correlations between *Strong* and *Kuder* scales cannot be expected to be high. That, of course, is an explanation that laypersons, and even some counselors, may find hard to accept. As with the other problems of convergent validity discussed, the vocational counselor is still left with the task of reconciling or rationalizing apparently conflicting psychometric information.

Predictive Validity

Stability. This topic is ordinarily discussed in connection with reliability, but it is discussed here because predictive validity, often called predictive accuracy, is premised on stability. More precisely, *predictive validity* is premised on (a) no significant change in either the predictor or the criterion or (b) predictable or lawful change, such as in biological development. *Stability*, in turn, has many meanings (Pryor, 1980). In addition to individual versus group stability, there is item response stability, scale score stability, higher-order (e.g., factor) score stability, and profile stability. Finally, there is stability of the mean, the variance or standard deviation, the covariance, and the covariance structure.

In general, stability is lower for individuals and higher for groups, reflecting in part the statistical effect of sample size. Stability tends to be lowest at the item level, higher at the scale level, and highest at the profile level. The paradox of low stability at the item level but high stability at the scale level is due to the fact that the scale score is a linear function of the mean of the item scores, and the mean

increases in stability with increasing N. Very high stability is observed at the profile level because the components of the profile—the scale scores—are themselves highly stable, and furthermore, profile correlation, the usual index of stability, takes account only of rank order and not of level. Stability of group profiles is especially high when group profiles are constituted from scale means, because the correlation of means is statistically spuriously high. Note that the profile of means is not the same as the mean or average profile (Sidman, 1952). Any account of stability, therefore, can be a complicated affair.

Much of the empirical evidence for the stability of interests, values, and preferences is reported as test-retest correlations of scale scores. As previously noted, one of the best-documented findings in interest research, and a major reason for the preeminence of the *Strong*, is the high test-retest reliability of the empirically keyed Occupation Scale scores (Johansson & Campbell, 1971; Strong, 1955). Median correlations were in the .90s for a 2-week interval; in the .80s and high .70s for respondents 25 years and older, for intervals of from 5 to 18 years; in the high .70s for all age groups, 17 years and older, for intervals of up to 5 years; and in the low .70s and high .60s for respondents 17 to 25 years, for intervals of from 8 to 23 years. In general, the older the age at first testing and the shorter the retest interval, the higher the test-retest correlation. Similar data, but for much shorter time periods, have been reported for values (e.g., see Gay et al., 1971). Stability also differs from occupation to occupation. Three-year retest correlations on the *Strong*, for example, range from .73 (for Food Service Manager) to .95 (for Mathematician).

As noted, test-retest correlation as the index of stability refers mainly to the stability of the rank order of the respondents and only partly to score stability. Another way to show score stability is through a distribution of difference scores, the standard deviation of which is estimated by the standard error of measurement

(*SEM*). For a scale that has a standard deviation of, say, 10 points, the *SEM* would be 3 points when test-retest *r* is .90, 4.5 points when the test-retest *r* is .80, and 5.5 points when the test-retest *r* is .70. Viewed from this perspective, a test-retest *r* of .80 or even .90 does not reflect much stability. Nonetheless, the question of how much stability is required or even desired depends on the purpose of use and on the comparison with available alternative means.

The preceding has referred to stability at the predictor end of the equation. Evidence for stability at the criterion end has also been shown in the form of equivalent scores (item and scale means) for cross-generational occupational criterion groups (Campbell, 1971; Strong, 1955). However, not all occupations and not all items, even for stable occupations, have proved to be stable. For example, to the item "Farmer," the "Like" response by the male Farmer occupational sample was 88 percent in the 1930–40s and 100 percent in the 1970–80s, but for the male Forester sample, it was 47 percent in the 1930s–40s and 73 percent in the 1970s–80s, and for the female Physical Education Teacher sample, it was 21 percent in the 1930s–40s versus 51 percent in the 1970s–80s (Hansen & Campbell, 1985, p. 23). This has meant that the empirical keys of the Occupational Scales have needed revision and recalculation from time to time and on more current criterion groups—an extremely expensive and time-consuming proposition!

Assuming that interests and values are stable, one might ask why they are stable. Conceptually speaking, such stability could result from one of three conditions: (a) both individuals and environments are stable, (b) individuals are stable and relatively uninfluenced by changes in the environment, or (c) environments are stable and exert strong influence on individuals. Individual stability refers to stability of the internal environment, that is, stability of cognitive, affective, and behavioral predispositions largely as a result of genetic inheritance. Some investigators look to

heritability studies for evidence of such genetic inheritance. Indeed, there are some data that indicate a significant heritability for interests (e.g., Carter, 1932; Grotevant, Scarr, & Weinberg, 1977; Nichols, 1978; Vandenberg & Stafford, 1967). However, the heritability index, being a proportion index, may reflect limited variability in environments as much as strong genetic influence in individuals.

Why should we expect interests and values to be stable? Most of us would assume that interests and values are influenced by environmental events such as schooling, change in socioeconomic status, change in marital status, even change in occupation. There are, however, few studies about the influence of specific external environmental factors on the stability of interests and values, if one discounts correlational and group difference studies. Taylor and Hanson (1972) examined interest stability and change in students who stayed in their engineering major versus those who transferred out. Hazer and Alvares (1981) observed value stability and change among police officers as a result of organizational entry and assimilation. But these studies are in the distinct minority. No studies have, for instance, reported on individual as opposed to group changes on specific interest or value items as a function of environmental factors. The question of what accounts for stability and change in interests, values, and preferences is empirically unexplored territory.

Base Rate. One of Strong's (1955) most quoted conclusions from his famous 18-year follow-up study was that individuals were three-and-a-half times as likely to be in an occupation for which they scored an A than in one for which they scored a C. Brown (1961), Dolliver (1969b), and Schmidt (1974) pointed out that such a conclusion can be erroneous and misleading. What users of empirically keyed scales did not realize was that the scale score indicated the probability of the score given group membership—not the probability of group membership given the score, which was what the user needed. The two probabilities are related in Bayes' theorem as follows:

$$P(G|S) = \frac{P(S|G) \times P(G)}{P(S)}$$

where $P(G|S)$ = probability of group membership G, given score S

$P(S|G)$ = probability of score S, given group membership G

$P(G)$ = probability of the group G, or the base rate

$P(S)$ = probability of score S, or, in a selection situation, the selection ratio

From the theorem, it can be seen that $P(G|S)$ will equal $P(S|G)$ only when $P(G)$ equals $P(S)$, that is, when the base rate equals the selection ratio—an unlikely event in most applied situations. Thus, as Schmidt (1974) has pointed out, when more realistic assumptions about the base rate are made for the *Strong* scales, the hit rate for some scales can drop toward the level of the base rate. Users of any prediction instrument would be served best if they had tables of expected hit rates that take account of these considerations.

Bias.   To begin with, *bias* is a statistical term that denotes systematic over- or underestimation of a population parameter. In applied psychology, bias and its companion term *unfairness* have been used in connection with group differences in scores on psychometric instruments. A widely accepted distinction between the two terms is that *bias* refers to attributes of the instrument itself, whereas *unfairness* refers to the use of the instrument (Shepard, 1982).

In the field of vocational preference, bias and unfairness have been much discussed with respect to interest measurement, but not as much with respect to value measurement. This could be because interest measures have been used for predictive purposes and validated in predictive studies, whereas value measures have been used largely for descriptive pur-

poses and required only concurrent validation. In any event, only a few value measures such as the MIQ, which have been used for predictive purposes, have been scrutinized for bias and unfairness.

In interest measurement, the issue was joined with respect to sex differences (Diamond, 1975; Tittle & Zytowski, 1978). Established instruments were criticized for (a) using sex-specific language, (b) using items with differing response rates for the sexes (biased or "unbalanced" items), (c) having separate forms and norms for the sexes, including having different item pools, (d) developing fewer occupational scales for women, and (e) in general, adhering to a system that tended to maintain the status quo. The use of sex-specific language was easiest to correct, although psychometrically it did not seem to make much difference (Boyd, 1978; Gottfredson & Holland, 1978). The other issues required more study.

Researchers have generally agreed that there are significant sex differences in interests. On the *Strong*, for example, differences between the sexes (between Women- and Men-in-General samples) of 16 percent or more have been observed on a third of the items (109 of 325). Furthermore, differences for many of these items were just as large for men and women in the same occupation as in the general samples, and were just as large in the 1970s and 1980s as they were in the 1930s and 1940s (Hansen & Campbell, 1985). There are, of course, items on which little difference has been observed, but also items for which the size of the difference as well as the response proportions have been changing over the years.

Developers of interest measures quickly agreed on the need to use one item pool for both sexes; what they disagreed on was what kind of items to include. One group (Hanson & Rayman, 1976; Rayman, 1976) advocated the use of only "sex-balanced" items, those where the sexes do not differ in response by more than 10 percent. Another group (Campbell, 1977;

Hansen & Campbell, 1985) would eliminate sex-role bias from the items, but not limit the item pool to sex-balanced items. The first group produced a unisex interest inventory with common scales for both women and men. The second group also produced a single form, or a single item pool to use with both men and women, but developed separate-sex scales for each occupation.

The problem with the sex-balanced items approach is the same as the problem of post hoc matching in quasi-experimental studies. Having succeeded in balancing on sex, do you not have to go on and balance on race, age, socioeconomic status, geographic location, and so forth? Unfortunately, it is highly likely that balancing items on one variable will result in unbalancing on another variable (Meehl, 1970).

The problem with the separate-sex scales approach is one of logistics. The more an occupation is dominated by one sex, as, for example, nursing or coal mining, the more difficult it is to implement the goal of constructing a separate scale for each sex.

The problem with any study of group differences is sampling. Only when we have been able to sample *randomly* from precisely defined populations can we confidently make inferences about population differences. With opportunity or convenience samples, as is almost universally the case in this type of research, there is no good way of telling if the observed group difference is sample-specific or is generalizable—except through extensive replication. One or two replications will not be enough; there should be enough replications to produce a relatively stable frequency distribution of group differences.

In actuality, there have been no technical studies of test bias or item bias in interest, value, or preference measures, as such studies are defined by psychometricians; that is, there have been no reports of intercept, slope, or standard error bias, and no reports of significant item-by-group interaction. There are, of course, many reports on mean differences between groups,

but mean differences by themselves are not evidence of bias.

There is yet one other problem of bias associated with empirically keyed scales. Scores on such scales reflect similarity to the criterion group. When such scale scores are used in making career or personnel decisions, choice or selection is effectively based on similarity to the criterion group. Therefore, persons from groups not represented in the criterion group, such as minorities or women, would be at a distinct disadvantage. Basing decisions on similarity to the criterion group will tend to perpetuate the likes of the criterion group. Furthermore, in occupations that are changing, for example, from being an outdoor occupation to being an indoor one, or vice versa, use of a static criterion group would contribute to invalidity.

Construct Validity

Rothney (1967) questioned the construct validity of the *Strong* and the *Minnesota Vocational Interest Inventory* (MVII), calling their validity "validity by fiat." He complained that group differences and test-retest data were not sufficient evidence of validity. Furthermore, he faulted the lack of true, multipoint longitudinal studies and, at that time, studies comparing measured interests with results from other assessment approaches. He pointed out that inventories were not tests but rather self-report instruments that should be studied as such, with investigations into important variables that might affect self-report, such as reading comprehension, fakeability, level of motivation, and social desirability. To use Embretson's (1983) terms, the *Strong* and MVII may have data bearing on nomothetic span, but they lack data on construct representation. The same might be said of every other interest and value measure.

Especially lacking are experimental studies with actual manipulations that would show change in interests or values in either level or pattern. For example, would exposure of a certain kind change interests from "Indifferent" to "Like" or "Dislike," or change values from "Unimportant" to "Important"? It is true that numerous laboratory experiments on attitude change have been conducted in social psychology, but not in connection with the construct validation of work-related interest or value measures. Furthermore, the external validity, or validity in the field, of such laboratory results has yet to be demonstrated.

Occasional validity-related experiments have appeared in the applied psychology literature (e.g., Heilman, 1979; Stulman & Dawis, 1976). Unfortunately, these are the exception, not the rule.

Before such experiments can be carried out, what may be needed is a conceptual analysis of the behavior of actually filling out a structured self-report questionnaire, describing the cognitive-affective mechanisms involved and identifying the variables that affect the behavior as well as maintain its stability. Perhaps what may be needed is analysis of the kind described by Ericsson and Simon (1980), who used the theoretical framework of human information processing to explicate the cognitive mechanisms that generate verbal report.

Perhaps what we have here is yet another parallel to the attenuation paradox (Loevinger, 1954). This time the classic tradeoff between reliability and validity might be mimicked in a tradeoff between theory and practice. In applied psychology's past, concentration on theory has appeared to yield little of value to professional practice. Concentration on practice, on the other hand, has effectively kept practice away from the mainstream of psychological theory, or at least has not promoted the use of psychological theory in professional practice.

Conclusions

Multiple measurement, if not multimethod measurement, is not just desirable—at our current level of measurement technology, we cannot afford *not* to require it. The large errors of measurement with which we work require a correspondingly large measure of built-in redundancy. Information must be obtained from more than one source. Multiple measurement must be mandated for all measurement of interests, values, and preferences.

In this respect, the *Strong* again emerges as the leading and pioneering instrument. The Basic Interest Scales, scaled at the predictor end, and the Occupational Scales, scaled at the criterion end, as well as the two sex forms of the Occupational Scales, when used together, provide redundant information that has proved to be more predictively ac-curate than that provided by a single scale or form. Such or similar redundancy might   well be made a standard feature of self-report instruments.

Scaling at the criterion end—empirical keying, or scale construction by the empirical method—arguably may produce the most useful scales for the purposes of professional practice. However, associated with such scaling are two intractable problems. First, scales produced in this manner are highly specific to the criterion, or, more precisely, to the criterion group. Scores of such scales function more as indicators pointed at the target criterion group than as measurements of the predictor (Dawes, 1972). Such scores can, in principle, indicate any characteristic on which the criterion group differs from the reference group; the larger the difference, the more likely the indication. Differentiating characteristics may produce effects that are irrelevant or, worse, inimical to the measurement purposes for which the scales are being used.

Second, scales produced empirically have to take special account of base rates. Scores of such scales index the probability of a score given group membership, rather than the probability of group membership given a score. The latter is what practitioners require, and it is affected by the base rate, or the proportion of group members among the population. Not even replication can rescue the empirically keyed score from this intrinsic fault.

We still need a theory of interests, values, and preferences that encompasses the behavior of responding to the instrument and that links this behavior to the individual's experience and history. In other words, we need to explain why we get the results we get when we use these instruments, and the explanation has to be psychological as well as psychometric.

Final Comments

We can summarize our discussion as follows:

- Interests, values, and preferences, as measured by self-report inventories, are stable dispositions of most adult individuals.

- Self-report measures of interests, values, and preferences are useful predictors of occupational or job tenure and occupational or job satisfaction and can contribute significantly, if modestly, to the prediction of worker satisfactoriness.

These are hard-won conclusions and will not easily wash away with the changing waters of theoretical predilection. In a science of cyclically shifting enthusiasms, these are dependable foundations on which to base sound professional practice. Paradoxically, to reinforce these foundations, a foremost need is a "theory of the test" that would explicate the behavior of responding to the self-report instrument and explain such behavior in the context of the main body of psychological knowledge.

About the first conclusion: We return to the theme that interests, values, and preferences have to do with cognitive representations of reality, that they are reflections of our constructions of reality. Interests, following Strong (1960), are manifested in attraction toward or repulsion by objects, situations, or events, and thereby provide clues about the affect associated with these stimuli. Values, following Skinner (1971), reflect the reinforcement effects of experience with various stimuli—objects, situations, events—and therefore are manifested in the standards or criteria by which such stimuli are evaluated. Both interests and values are refined distillations from numerous and successive experiences; hence, they become manifested in enduring preferences. Interests, values, and preferences thus may be best construed as stable dispositions.

About the second conclusion: We return also to the theme that interests, values, and preferences have to do with motives and motivation. Interests, values, and preferences have proved to be important individual differences variables that can and should be incorporated into the industrial and organizational psychologist's models of work motivation. A long and productive history of development and use, especially in the case of interests, has generated a sound and extensive knowledge base on which research as well as professional practice can be founded. To understand how "people make the place" (Schneider, 1987), an excellent starting point is a cogent consideration of people's interests, values, and preferences.

My thanks to the Department of Applied Psychology, University of Wales Institute of Science and Technology, and its head, Professor Keith Duncan; to the secretarial staff and library personnel; and especially to my UWIST collaborator and friend, Dr. Charles Jackson, for their help during the writing of this chapter. My stay at UWIST was made possible by a sabbatical leave from the Department of Psychology, University of Minnesota. Special thanks to Betty Adams for preparing the manuscript.

Appendix: Representative Measures of Interests and Values

Interests

Strong Interest Inventory (SII): 325 items listing a variety of occupations (sample item: "Actor/ Actress"), school subjects ("Agriculture"), activities ("Making a speech"), types of people ("Emotional people"), and personal characteristics ("Usually start activities of my group"). A person responds by indicating "Like," "Indifferent," or "Dislike," or, for some items, a preference. Scored for 6 General Occupational Themes, 23 Basic Interest Scales, and 207 Occupational Scales (with separate female and male scales for 101 occupations). Time: About 30 minutes. Distributed by Consulting Psychologists Press, 577 College Avenue, Palo Alto, CA 94306.

Kuder DD Occupational Interest Survey (KOIS): 100 items, each consisting of three activities known to sixth graders (e.g., "Introduce a stranger to people at a large party"). A person responds by indicating the most and least preferred of the three activities. Scored for 40 female and 79 male occupations, and 19 female and 29 male college majors. Time: About 30 minutes. Published by Science Research Associates, 155 N. Wacker Drive, Chicago, IL 60606.

Vocational Preference Inventory (VPI: also the Occupations section of the *Self Directed Search*, or SDS): 160 items (84 items in the SDS), consisting of occupational titles (sample item: "Criminologist"). A person responds by indicating those occupations that are interesting or appealing and those that are disliked or found uninteresting. Scored on six Holland personality types. Time: 5 to 10 minutes. Published by Psychological Assessment Resources, P.O. Box 998, Odessa, FL 33556.

ACT Interest Inventory, Unisex Edition (UNIACT): 90 items, each describing a work-related activity (sample item: "Play jazz in a combo"). A person responds by indicating "Dislike," "Indifferent," or "Like." Scored on six comprehensive career areas that correspond to Holland's personality types. Time: 5 to 10 minutes. Published by American College Testing Program, P.O. Box 168, Iowa City, IA 52243.

Jackson Vocational Interest Survey (JVIS): 289 items, each consisting of pairs of statements describing occupational activities (sample item: "Making unusual glass vases"). A person responds by choosing which statement of each pair is preferred or more characteristic of the person. Scored on 27 work roles (work content areas) and 7 work styles. A profile of these 34 scores can then be compared with profiles identifying 32 occupational clusters (representing 278 occupations). Time: 45 to 60 minutes. Published by Research Psychologists Press, P.O. Box 3292, Station A, London, Ontario, Canada, N6A 4K3.

Values

Study of Values: 45 items, 30 items being two-choice statements or questions on controversial subjects (sample item: "The main object of scientific research should be the discovery of truth rather than its practical applications—Yes or No") and the remaining 15 items being 4-choice questions ("At an evening discussion…, are you more interested when you talk about: a. the meaning of life b. developments in science c. literature d. socialism and social amelioration"). A person responds by rating or ranking the choices. Scored on six values. Time: About 20 minutes. Published by Riverside Publishing Co., 1919 Highland Avenue, Lombard, IL 60025.

Rokeach Value Survey (RVS): Two sets of 18 items, each of which describes a value (sample items: "A Comfortable Life," "Ambitious"). A person responds by rank ordering the items within a set. Time: 10 to 20 minutes. Published by Consulting Psychologists Press.

The Values Scale (VS): 105 items that describe values people consider important in their work (sample item: "It is…important for me to use all my skills and knowledge"). A person responds by rating the importance of the value on a 4-point scale. Scored on 21 values. Time: 30 to 45 minutes. Published by Consulting Psychologists Press.

Minnesota Importance Questionnaire (MIQ, Paired Form): 210 items, the first 190 of which are pairings of 20 statements describing work reinforcers—conditions that make work satisfying (sample item: "The job would provide an opportunity for advancement"). A person responds by indicating the work reinforcer in each pair that is more important in an ideal job. The last 20 items (the same 20 statements) are rated in terms of importance/unimportance. Scored on 20 work needs and 6 work values. A profile of work needs can be compared with profiles for 185 occupations, and a profile of work values can be compared with profiles for 1,769 occupations as categorized in the *Minnesota Occupational Classification System III* (MOCS III). Time: 30 to 40 minutes. The MIQ is also available in Ranked Form (time: 15 minutes), Triad Form (time: 20 minutes), and Adapted Form for the Hearing Impaired (time: 30 to 40 minutes). Published by Vocational Psychology Research, University of Minnesota, 75 E. River Road, Minneapolis, MN 55455.

References

Aldag, R. J., & Brief, A. P. (1975). Some correlates of work values. *Journal of Applied Psychology, 60,* 757–760.

Allport, G. W. (1961). *Pattern and growth in personality.* New York: Holt, Rinehart & Winston.

Allport, G. W., Vernon, P. E., & Lindzey, G. (1970). *Manual: Study of Values.* Boston: Houghton Mifflin.

American College Testing Program. (1981). *Technical report for the unisex edition of the ACT Interest Inventory.* Iowa City: Author.

Anastasi, A. (1949). *Differential psychology.* New York: Macmillan.

Barak, A. (1981). Vocational interests: A cognitive view. *Journal of Vocational Behavior, 19,* 1–14.

Barak, A., & Meir, E. I. (1974). The predictive validity of a vocational interest inventory—"Ramak": Seven year follow-up. *Journal of Vocational Behavior, 4,* 377–387.

Bartling, H. C., & Hood, A. B. (1981). An 11-year follow-up of measured interest and vocational choice. *Journal of Counseling Psychology, 28,* 27–35.

Bentler, P. M., Jackson, D. N., & Messick, S. (1971). Identification of content and style: A two-dimensional interpretation of acquiescence. *Psychological Bulletin, 76,* 186–204.

Berdie, R. F. (1944). Factors related to vocational interests. *Psychological Bulletin, 41,* 137–157.

Berdie, R. F. (1950). Scores on the Strong Vocational Interest Blank and the Kuder Preference Record in relation to self ratings. *Journal of Applied Psychology, 34,* 42–49.

Betz, E. L. (1969). Need-reinforcer correspondence as a predictor of job satisfaction. *Personnel and Guidance Journal, 47,* 878–883.

Bingham, W. V. (1937). *Aptitudes and aptitude testing.* New York: Harper.

Block, J. (1971). On further conjectures regarding acquiescence. *Psychological Bulletin, 76,* 205–210.

Blood, M. R. (1969). Work values and job satisfaction. *Journal of Applied Psychology, 53,* 456–459.

Bock, R. D., & Jones, L. V. (1968). *The measurement and prediction of judgment and choice.* San Francisco: Holden-Day.

Borgen, F. H. (1972). Predicting career choices of able college men from Occupational and Basic Interest scales of the Strong Vocational Interest Blank. *Journal of Counseling Psychology, 19,* 202–211.

Borgen, F. H., & Seling, M. J. (1978). Expressed and inventoried interests revisited: Perspicacity in the person. *Journal of Counseling Psychology, 25,* 536–543.

Boyd, V. S. (1978). Neutralizing sexist titles in Holland's Self-Directed Search: What difference does it make? In C. K. Tittle & D. G. Zytowski (Eds.), *Sex-fair interest measurement: Research and implications.* Washington, DC: National Institute of Education.

Brandt, J. E., & Hood, A. B. (1968). Effect of personality adjustment on the predictive validity of the Strong Vocational Interest Blank. *Journal of Counseling Psychology, 15,* 547–551.

Brown, F. (1961). A note on expectancy ratios, base rates, and the SVIB. *Journal of Counseling Psychology, 8,* 368–369.

Butler, J. K., Jr. (1983). Value importance as a moderator of the value fulfillment-job satisfaction relationship: Group differences. *Journal of Applied Psychology, 68,* 420–428.

Cairo, P. C. (1982). Measured interests versus expressed interests as predictors of long-term occupational membership. *Journal of Vocational Behavior, 20,* 343–353.

Campbell, D. T. (1963). Social attitudes and other acquired behavioral dispositions. In S. Koch (Ed.), *Psychology: A study of a science.* New York: McGraw-Hill.

Campbell, D. P. (1966). Occupations ten years later of high school seniors with high scores on the SVIB Life Insurance Salesman scale. *Journal of Applied Psychology, 50,* 51–56.

Campbell, D. P. (1971). *Handbook for the Strong Vocational Interest Blank.* Stanford, CA: Stanford University Press.

Campbell, J. P., & Pritchard, R. D. (1976). Motivation theory in industrial and organizational psychology. In M. D. Dunnette (Ed.), *Handbook of industrial and organizational psychology.* Chicago: Rand McNally.

Carek, R. (1972). Another look at the relationships between similar scales in the Strong Vocational Interest Blank and the Kuder Occupational Interest Survey. *Journal of Counseling Psychology, 19,* 218–223.

Carter, H. D. (1932). Twin similarities in occupational interests. *Journal of Educational Psychology, 23,* 641–655.

Carter, H. D. (1944). Vocational interests and job orientation: A ten-year review. *Applied Psychology Monographs,* No. 2.

Chaney, F. B., & Owens, W. A. (1964). Life history antecedents of sales, research and general engineering interests. *Journal of Applied Psychology, 48,* 101–105.

Clark, K. E. (1961). *The vocational interests of nonprofessional men.* Minneapolis: University of Minnesota Press.

Clemans, W. V. (1968). Interest measurement and the concept of ipsativity. *Measurement and Evaluation in Guidance, 1,* 50–55.

Cole, C. W., & Miller, C. D. (1967). Relevance of expressed values to academic performance. *Journal of Counseling Psychology, 14,* 272–276.

Cole, N. S., & Hanson, G. R. (1978). Impact of interest inventories on career choice. In E. E. Diamond (Ed.), *Issues of sex bias and sex fairness in career interest measurement.* Washington, DC: National Institute of Education.

Costa, P. T., Jr., Fozard, J. L., & McCrae, R. R. (1977). Personological interpretation of factors from the Strong Vocational Interest Blank scales. *Journal of Vocational Behavior, 10,* 231–243.

Costa, P. T., Jr., McCrae, R. R., & Holland, J. L. (1984). Personality and vocational interests in an adult sample. *Journal of Applied Psychology, 69,* 390–400.

Crites, J. O. (1969). Interests. In R. E. Ebel (Ed.), *Encyclopedia of educational research.* New York: Macmillan.

Cronbach, L. J. (1957). The two disciplines of scientific psychology. *American Psychology, 12,* 671–684.

Cronbach, L. J. (1970). *Essentials of psychological testing.* New York: Harper & Row.

Darley, J. G. (1941). *Clinical aspects and interpretation of the Strong Vocational Interest Blank.* New York: Psychological Corporation.

Darley, J. G., & Hagenah, T. (1955). *Vocational interest measurement: Theory and practice.* Minneapolis: University of Minnesota Press.

Dawes, R. M. (1972). *Fundamentals of attitude measurement.* New York: Wiley.

Dawis, R. V., & Lofquist, L. H. (1984). *A psychological theory of work adjustment.* Minneapolis: University of Minnesota Press.

Dawis, R. V., & Sung, Y. H. (1984). The relationship of participation in school activities to abilities and interests in a high school student sample. *Journal of Vocational Behavior, 24,* 159–168.

D'Costa, A. G., Winefordner, D. W., Odgers, J. G., & Koons, P. B., Jr. (1970). *Ohio Vocational Interest Survey.* New York: Harcourt Brace Jovanovich.

Dewey, J. (1939). *Theory of valuation.* Chicago: University of Chicago Press.

Diamond, E. E. (Ed.). (1975). *Issues of sex bias and sex fairness in career interest measurement.* Washington, DC: National Institute of Education.

Dipboye, R. L., Zultowski, W. H., Dewhirst, H. D., & Arvey, R. D. (1978). Self-esteem as a moderator of the relationship between science interests and the job satisfaction of physicians and engineers. *Journal of Applied Psychology, 63,* 289–294.

Dolliver, R. H. (1969a). Strong Vocational Interest Blank versus expressed vocational interests: A review. *Psychological Bulletin, 72,* 95–107.

Dolliver, R. H. (1969b). "3.5 to 1" on the Strong Vocational Interest Blank as a pseudo-event.

Journal of Counseling Psychology, 16, 172–174.

Dolliver, R. H. (1975). Concurrent prediction from the Strong Vocational Interest Blank. *Journal of Counseling Psychology, 22,* 199–203.

Dolliver, R. H. (1981). A review of female-male score differences on the Strong-Campbell twin occupational scales. *Journal of Counseling Psychology, 28,* 334–341.

Dolliver, R. H., Irvin, J. A., & Bigley, S. S. (1972). Twelve-year follow-up of the Strong Vocational Interest Blank. *Journal of Counseling Psychology, 19,* 212–217.

Dolliver, R. H., & Will, J. A. (1977). Ten-year follow-up of the Tyler Vocational Card Sort and the Strong Vocational Interest Blank. *Journal of Counseling Psychology, 24,* 48–54.

Dolliver, R. H., & Worthington, E. L. (1981). Concurrent validity of other-sex and same-sex twin Strong-Campbell Interest Inventory occupational scales. *Journal of Counseling Psychology, 28,* 126–134.

DuBois, P. H. (1970). *A history of psychological testing.* Boston: Allyn & Bacon.

Dunnette, M. D., Kirchner, W. K., & DeGidio, J. (1958). Relations among scores on Edwards Personal Preference Schedule, California Psychological Inventory, and Strong Vocational Interest Blank for an industrial sample. *Journal of Applied Psychology, 42,* 178–181.

Eberhardt, B. J., & Muchinsky, P. M. (1982). Biodata determinants of vocational typology: An integration of two paradigms. *Journal of Applied Psychology, 67,* 714–727.

Eberly, R. E. (1980). *Biographical determinants of vocational values.* Unpublished doctoral dissertation, University of Minnesota.

Elizur, D. (1984). Facets of work values: A structural analysis of work outcomes. *Journal of Applied Psychology, 69,* 379–389.

Elizur, D., & Tziner, A. (1977). Vocational needs, job rewards, and job satisfaction: A canonical analysis. *Journal of Vocational Behavior, 10,* 205–211.

Embretson, S. (1983). Construct validity: Construct representation versus nomothetic span. *Psychological Bulletin, 93,* 179–197.

Engdahl, B. E. (1980). *The structure of biographical data and its relationship to vocational needs and values.* Unpublished doctoral dissertation, University of Minnesota.

England, G. W. (1967). Personal value systems of American managers. *Academy of Management Journal, 10,* 53–68.

England, G. W., & Lee, R. (1974). The relationship between managerial values and managerial success in the United States, Japan, India, and Australia. *Journal of Applied Psychology, 59,* 411–419.

Ericsson, K. A., & Simon, H. A. (1980). Verbal reports as data. *Psychological Review, 87,* 215–251.

Ferguson, L. W., Humphreys, L. G., & Strong, F. W. (1941). A factorial analysis of interests and values. *Journal of Educational Psychology, 32,* 197–204.

Frantz, T. T. (1972). Reinterpretation of flat SVIB profiles. *Journal of Vocational Behavior, 2,* 201–207.

Fryer, D. H. (1927). Interest and ability in educational guidance. *Journal of Educational Research, 16,* 27–39.

Gay, E. G., Weiss, D. H., Hendel, D. D., Dawis, R. V., & Lofquist, L. H. (1971). Manual for the Minnesota Importance Questionnaire. *Minnesota Studies in Vocational Rehabilitation,* No. 28.

Ghiselli, E. E. (1966). *The validity of occupational aptitude tests.* New York: Wiley.

Gottfredson, G. D., & Holland, J. L. (1978). Toward beneficial resolution of the interest inventory controversy. In C. K. Tittle & D. G. Zytowski (Eds.), *Sex-fair interest measurement: Research and applications.* Washington, DC: National Institute of Education.

Greene, E. B. (1951). The Michigan Vocabulary Profile Test after ten years. *Educational and Psychological Measurement, 11,* 208–211.

Grotevant, H. D., Scarr, S., & Weinberg, R. K. (1977). Patterns of interest similarity in adoptive and biological families. *Journal of Personality and Social Psychology, 35,* 667–676.

Guilford, J. P. (1954). *Psychometric methods.* New York: McGraw Hill.

Guilford, J. P., Christensen, P. R., Bond, N. A., Jr., & Sutton, M. A. (1954). A factor analysis study of human interests. *Psychological Monographs: General and Applied, 68* (Whole No. 375).

Gulliksen, H., & Tucker, L. R. (1961). A general procedure for obtaining paired comparisons from multiple rank orders. *Psychometrika, 26,* 173–183.

Hakel, M. D. (1986). Personnel selection and placement. *Annual Review of Psychology, 37,* 351–380.

Hall, D. T. (1976). *Careers in organizations.* Santa Monica, CA: Goodyear.

Hansen, J. C., & Campbell, D. P. (1985). *Manual for the SVIB-SCII*. Palo Alto, CA: Consulting Psychologists Press.

Hanson, G. R., & Rayman, J. (1976). Validity of sex-balanced interest inventory scales. *Journal of Vocational Behavior, 9,* 279–291.

Harrington, T. F., Lynch, M. D., & O'Shea, A. J. (1971). Factor analysis of 27 similarly named scales of the Strong Vocational Interest Blank and the Kuder Occupational Interest Survey, Form DD. *Journal of Counseling Psychology, 18,* 229–233.

Harris, D. B. (1950). How children learn interests, motives, and attitudes. *National Society for the Study of Education, Forty-Ninth Yearbook, Part I. Learning and Instruction* (pp. 129–155).

Hazer, J. T., & Alvares, K. M. (1981). Police work values during organizational entry and assimilation. *Journal of Applied Psychology, 66,* 12–18.

Heilman, M. E. (1979). High school students' occupational interests as a function of projected sex ratios in male-dominated occupations. *Journal of Applied Psychology, 64,* 275–279.

Herzberg, F., Mausner, B., & Snyderman, B. B. (1959). *The motivation to work.* New York: Wiley.

Holcomb, W. R., & Anderson, W. P. (1978). Expressed and inventoried vocational interests as predictors of college graduation and vocational choice. *Journal of Vocational Behavior, 12,* 290–296.

Holland, J. L. (1973). *Making vocational choices: A theory of careers.* Englewood Cliffs, NJ: Prentice-Hall.

Holland, J. L. (1976). Vocational preferences. In M. D. Dunnette (Ed.), *Handbook of industrial and organizational psychology.* Chicago: Rand McNally.

Ivey, A. E. (1963). Interests and work values. *Vocational Guidance Quarterly, 11,* 121–124.

Jackson, D. N. (1977). *Jackson Vocational Interest Survey Manual.* London, Ontario: Research Psychologists Press.

Johansson, C. B., & Campbell, D. P. (1971). Stability of the Strong Vocational Interest Blank for men. *Journal of Applied Psychology, 55,* 34–36.

Johnson, R. W. (1971). Congruence of Strong and Kuder interest profiles. *Journal of Counseling Psychology, 18,* 450–455.

Johnson, R. W. (1972a). Content analysis of the Strong Vocational Interest Blank for men. *Journal of Counseling Psychology, 19,* 479–486.

Johnson, R. W. (1972b). Contradictory scores of the SVIB. *Journal of Counseling Psychology, 19,* 487–490.

Kapes, J. T., & Strickler, R. E. (1975). A longitudinal study of change in work values between ninth and twelfth grades as related to high school curriculum. *Journal of Vocational Behavior, 6,* 81–93.

Katz, M. R. (1963). *Decisions and values.* New York: College Entrance Examination Board.

Katzell, R. A. (1964). Personal values, job satisfaction, and job behavior. In H. Borow (Ed.), *Man in a world at work.* Boston: Houghton Mifflin.

Kaufman, H. G. (1972). Relations of ability and interest to currency of professional knowledge among engineers. *Journal of Applied Psychology, 56,* 495–499.

Kazanas, H. C. (1978). Relationship of job satisfaction and productivity to work values of vocational education graduates. *Journal of Vocational Behavior, 12,* 155–164.

Keierleber, D. L. (1981). *The relationship of measured vocational abilities and interests: A reassessment.* Unpublished doctoral dissertation, University of Minnesota.

King, P., Norrell, G., & Powers, P. G. (1963). Relationships between twin scales on the SVIB and the Kuder. *Journal of Counseling Psychology, 10,* 395–401.

Kinnane, J. F., & Suziedelis, A. (1962). Work value orientation and inventoried interests. *Journal of Counseling Psychology, 9,* 144–148.

Klein, K. L., & Wiener, Y. (1977). Interest congruency as a moderator of the relationships between job tenure and job satisfaction and mental health. *Journal of Vocational Behavior, 10,* 92–98.

Kluckhohn, C. (1951). Values and value orientation in the theory of action: An exploration in definition and classification. In T. Parsons & E. A. Shils (Eds.), *Toward a general theory of action.* Cambridge, MA: Harvard University Press.

Kohlan, R. G. (1968). Relationships between inventoried interests and inventoried needs. *Personnel and Guidance Journal, 46,* 592–598.

Korman, A. K. (1966). Self-esteem variable in vocational choice. *Journal of Applied Psychology, 50,* 479–486.

Korman, A. K. (1967). Relevance of personal need satisfaction for overall satisfaction as a function of self-esteem. *Journal of Applied Psychology, 51,* 533–538.

Kuder, G. F. (1939). *Kuder Preference Record.* Chicago:

Science Research Associates.

Kuder, G. F. (1977). *Activity interests and occupational choice.* Chicago: Science Research Associates.

Kuhlberg, G. E., & Owens, W. A. (1960). Some life history antecedents of engineering interests. *Journal of Educational Psychology, 51,* 26–31.

Kulakowski, D. M. (1986). *Life history correlates of vocational interests and vocational needs.* Unpublished doctoral dissertation, University of Minnesota.

Kunce, J. T. (1967). Vocational interests and accident proneness. *Journal of Applied Psychology, 51,* 223–225.

Laing, J., Swaney, K., & Prediger, D. J. (1984). Integrating vocational interest inventory results and expressed choices. *Journal of Vocational Behavior, 25,* 304–315.

Lau, A. W., & Abrahams, N. M. (1972). Predictive validity of vocational interests within nonprofessional occupations. *Journal of Applied Psychology, 56,* 181–183.

Layton, W. L., & Borgen, F. H. (1972). Comment. *Journal of Counseling Psychology, 19,* 461–462.

Lee, E. A., & Thorpe, L. P. (1956). *Manual for the Occupational Interest Inventory.* Monterey, CA: California Test Bureau.

Lefkowitz, D. M. (1970). Comparison of the Strong Vocational Interest Blank and Kuder Occupational Interest Survey scoring procedures. *Journal of Counseling Psychology, 17,* 357–363.

Lichter, D. J. (1980). *The prediction of job satisfaction as an outcome of career counseling.* Unpublished doctoral dissertation, University of Minnesota.

Likert, R. (1932). A technique for the measurement of attitudes. *Archives of Psychology,* No. 140, 5–53.

Locke, E. A. (1976). The nature and causes of job satisfaction. In M. D. Dunnette (Ed.), *Handbook of industrial and organizational psychology.* Chicago: Rand McNally.

Loehlin, J. C., Lindzey, G., & Spuhler, J. N. (1975). *Race differences in intelligence.* San Francisco: W. H. Freeman.

Loevinger, J. (1954). The attenuation paradox in test theory. *Psychological Bulletin, 51,* 493–504.

Lofquist, L. H., & Dawis, R. V. (1978). Values as second-order needs in the theory of work adjustment. *Journal of Vocational Behavior, 12,* 12–19.

Lorr, M., & Suziedelis, A. (1973). A dimensional approach to the interests measured by the SVIB.

Journal of Counseling Psychology, 20, 113–119.

Lowman, R. L., Williams, R. E., & Leeman, G. E. (1985). The structure and relationship of college women's primary abilities and vocational interests. *Journal of Vocational Behavior, 27,* 298–335.

Lykken, D. T. (1968). Statistical significance in psychological research. *Psychological Bulletin, 70,* 151–159.

Maccoby, E. E., & Jacklin, C. N. (1974). *The psychology of sex differences.* Stanford, CA: Stanford University Press.

Maslow, A. H. (1954). *Motivation and personality.* New York: Harper.

McArthur, C. (1954). Long term validity of the Strong Interest Test in two subcultures. *Journal of Applied Psychology, 38,* 346–353.

McCall, J. N., & Moore, G. D. (1965). Do interest inventories measure estimated abilities? *Personnel and Guidance Journal, 43,* 1034–1047.

McClelland, D. C. (1961). *The achieving society.* New York: Free Press.

Meehl, P. E. (1970). Nuisance variables and the ex post facto design. In M. Radner & S. Winokur (Eds.), *Minnesota studies in the philosophy of science* (Vol. 4). Minneapolis: University of Minnesota Press.

Meresman, J. F. (1975). *Biographical correlates of vocational needs.* Unpublished doctoral dissertation, University of Minnesota.

Munson, J. M., & Posner, B. Z. (1980). Concurrent validation of two value inventories in predicting job classification and success for organizational personnel. *Journal of Applied Psychology, 65,* 536–542.

Murray, S. G. (1981). Personality characteristics of adult women with low and high profiles on the SCII or SVIB occupational scales. *Journal of Applied Psychology, 66,* 422–430.

Nichols, R. C. (1978). Twin studies of ability, personality, and interest. *Homo, 29,* 158–173.

O'Shea, A. J., & Harrington, T. F., Jr. (1971). Using the Strong Vocational Interest Blank and the Kuder Occupational Interest Survey, Form DD, with the same clients. *Journal of Counseling Psychology, 18,* 44–50.

Perry, R. B. (1954). *Realms of value: A critique of human civilization.* Cambridge, MA: Harvard University Press.

Pryor, R. G. L. (1980). Some types of stability in the

study of students' work values. *Journal of Vocational Behavior, 16,* 146–157.

Pryor, R. (1982). Values, preferences, needs, work ethics, and orientations to work: Toward a conceptual and empirical integration. *Journal of Vocational Behavior, 20,* 40–52.

Rayman, J. (1976). Sex and the single interest inventory: The empirical validation of sex-balanced interest inventory items. *Journal of Counseling Psychology, 23,* 239–246.

Rokeach, M. (1973). *The nature of human values.* New York: Free Press.

Rosenberg, M. (1957). *Occupations and values.* Glencoe, IL: Free Press.

Rothney, W. M. (1967). Test reviews. *Journal of Counseling Psychology, 14,* 187–191.

Rounds, J. B., Jr. (1981). *The comparative and combined utility of need and interest data in the prediction of job satisfaction.* Unpublished doctoral dissertation, University of Minnesota.

Rounds, J. B., Jr., & Dawis, R. V. (1979). Factor analysis of Strong Vocational Interest Blank items. *Journal of Applied Psychology, 64,* 132–143.

Rounds, J. B., Jr., Dawis, R. V., & Lofquist, L. H. (1979). Life history correlates of vocational needs for a female adult sample. *Journal of Counseling Psychology, 26,* 487–496.

Rounds, J. B., Jr., Dawis, R. V., & Lofquist, L. H. (1987). Measurement of person-environment fit and prediction of job satisfaction in the theory of work adjustment. *Journal of Vocational Behavior, 31,* 297–318.

Salazar, R. C. (1981). *The prediction of satisfaction and satisfactoriness for counselor training graduates.* Unpublished doctoral dissertation, University of Minnesota.

Salomone, P. R., & Muthard, J. E. (1972). Canonical correlation of vocational needs and vocational style. *Journal of Vocational Behavior, 2,* 163–171.

Sarbin, T. R., & Berdie, R. F. (1940). Relation of measured interests to the Allport-Vernon Study of Values. *Journal of Applied Psychology, 24,* 287–296.

Schein, E. H. (1978). *Career dynamics: Matching individual and organizational needs.* Reading, MA: Addison-Wesley.

Schletzer, V. M. (1966). SVIB as a predictor of job satisfaction. *Journal of Applied Psychology, 50,* 5–8.

Schmidt, F. L. (1974). Probability and utility assump-

tions underlying use of the Strong Vocational Interest Blank. *Journal of Applied Psychology, 59,* 456–464.

Schneider, B. (1987). The people make the place. *Personnel Psychology, 40,* 437–454.

Seaburg, D. J., Rounds, R. B., Jr., Dawis, R. V., & Lofquist, L. H. (1976). *Values as second-order needs.* Paper presented at the 84th convention of the American Psychological Association, Washington, DC.

Shepard, L. A. (1982). Definition of bias. In R. A. Berk (Ed.), *Handbook of methods for detecting test bias.* Baltimore: Johns Hopkins University Press.

Sidman, M. (1952). A note on functional relations obtained from group data. *Psychological Bulletin, 49,* 236–269.

Siess, T. F., & Jackson, D. N. (1970). Vocational interests and personality: An empirical integration. *Journal of Counseling Psychology, 17,* 27–35.

Skinner, B. F. (1971). *Beyond freedom and dignity.* New York: Knopf.

Sloan, E. B. (1979). *An investigation of the relationships between vocational needs and personality.* Unpublished doctoral dissertation, University of Minnesota.

Smith, M. B. (1969). *Social psychology and human values.* Chicago: Aldine.

Stewart, L. H. (1971). Relationships between interests and personality scores of occupation-oriented students. *Journal of Counseling Psychology, 18,* 31–38.

Strong, E. K., Jr. (1935). Predictive value of the Vocational Interest Test. *Journal of Educational Psychology, 26,* 332.

Strong, E. K., Jr. (1943). *Vocational interests of men and women.* Stanford, CA: Stanford University Press.

Strong, E. K., Jr. (1955). *Vocational interests 18 years after college.* Minneapolis: University of Minnesota Press.

Strong, E. K., Jr. (1960). An 18-year longitudinal report on interests. In W. L. Layton (Ed.), *The Strong Vocational Interest Blank: Research and uses.* Minneapolis: University of Minnesota Press.

Stulman, D. A., & Dawis, R. V. (1976). Experimental validation of two MIQ scales. *Journal of Vocational Behavior, 9,* 161–167.

Super, D. E. (1957). *The psychology of careers.* New York: Harper.

Super, D. E. (1962). The structure of work values in

relation to status, achievement, interest, and adjustment. *Journal of Applied Psychology, 46,* 234–239.

Super, D. E. (1973). The Work Values Inventory. In D. G. Zytowski (Ed.), *Contemporary approaches to interest measurement.* Minneapolis: University of Minnesota Press.

Super, D. E., & Crites, J. O. (1962). *Appraising vocational fitness.* New York: Harper & Row.

Taylor, R. G., & Hanson, G. R. (1972). Interest change as a function of persistence and transfer from an engineering major. *Journal of Counseling Psychology, 19,* 130–135.

Thorndike, E. L. (1917). Early interests: Their permanence and relation to abilities. *School and Society, 5,* 178–179.

Thorndike, R. M., Weiss, D. J., & Dawis, R. V. (1968a). Canonical correlation of vocational interests and vocational needs. *Journal of Counseling Psychology, 15,* 101–106.

Thorndike, R. M., Weiss, D. J., & Dawis, R. V. (1968b). Multivariate relationships between a measure of vocational interests and a measure of vocational needs. *Journal of Applied Psychology, 52,* 491–496.

Thurstone, L. L. (1927). A law of comparative judgment. *Psychological Review, 34,* 273–286.

Thurstone, L. L. (1931a). A multiple factor study of vocational interests. *Personnel Journal, 10,* 198–205.

Thurstone, L. L. (1931b). The measurement of social attitudes. *Journal of Abnormal and Social Psychology, 26,* 249–269.

Tittle, C. K., & Zytowski, D. G. (Eds.). (1978). *Sex-fair interest measurement: Research and implications.* Washington, DC: National Institute of Education.

Triandis, H. C. (1971). *Attitude and attitude change.* New York: Wiley.

Tversky, A. (1969). Intransitivity of preferences. *Psychological Review, 76,* 31–48.

Tyler, L. E. (1947). *The psychology of human differences.* New York: Appleton-Century-Crofts.

Tyler, L. E. (1978). *Individuality.* San Francisco: Jossey-Bass.

U.S. Department of Labor (1970). *Manual for the USTES General Aptitude Test Battery, Section III. Development.* Washington, DC: U.S. Government Printing Office.

Vandenberg, S. G., & Stafford, R. E. (1967). Hereditary influences on vocational preferences as shown by scores of twins on the Minnesota Vocational Interest Inventory. *Journal of Applied Psychology, 51,* 17–19.

Viteles, M. S. (1932). *Industrial psychology.* New York: Norton.

Vroom, V. H. (1964). *Work and motivation.* New York: Wiley.

Watson, J., & Williams, J. (1977). Relationship between managerial values and managerial success of black and white managers. *Journal of Applied Psychology, 62,* 203–207.

Wesley, S. M., Corey, D. Q., & Stewart, B. M. (1950). The intra-individual relationship between interest and ability. *Journal of Applied Psychology, 34,* 193–197.

Wilson, R. N., & Kaiser, H. E. (1968). A comparison of similar scales on the SVIB and the Kuder, Form DD. *Journal of Counseling Psychology, 15,* 468–470.

Wood, D. A. (1971). Background characteristics of work values distinguishing satisfaction levels among engineers. *Journal of Applied Psychology, 55,* 537–542.

Woodworth, R. S. (1918). *Dynamic psychology.* New York: Columbia University Press.

Worthington, E. L., Jr., & Dolliver, R. H. (1977). Validity studies of the Strong Vocational Interest Inventories. *Journal of Counseling Psychology, 24,* 208–216.

Zytowski, D. G. (1968). Relationships of equivalent scales on three interest inventories. *Personnel and Guidance Journal, 47,* 44–49.

Zytowski, D. G. (1972). Equivalence of the Kuder Occupational Interest Survey and the Strong Vocational Interest Blank revisited. *Journal of Applied Psychology, 56,* 184–185.

Zytowski, D. G. (Ed.). (1973). *Contemporary approaches to interest measurement.* Minneapolis: University of Minnesota Press.

Zytowski, D. G. (1976a). Factor analysis of the Kuder Occupational Interest Survey. *Measurement and Evaluation in Guidance, 9,* 120–123.

Zytowski, D. G. (1976b). Predictive validity of the Kuder Occupational Interest Survey: A 12- to 19-year follow-up. *Journal of Counseling Psychology, 23,* 221–233.

CHAPTER 13

Personality and Personality Measurement

Robert T. Hogan
University of Tulsa

*Implicit in most traditional problems in industrial and organizational psychology
are assumptions about human nature. Because personality psychology concerns
human nature, a natural affinity would appear to exist between personality and
industrial and organizational psychology. Recent textbooks, however, present an
image of personality psychology that is inconsistent with modern work in the
field. In response to that image, this chapter tries to make five general points.
First, the behaviorist critique of personality psychology that was popular in the
early 1970s has been largely repudiated. Some of the criticisms (e.g., that validity
coefficients for personality measures rarely exceed .30) are empirically false;
others (e.g., that behavior is unstable across "situations") were supported by
research based on faulty methodology. The "person-situation" debate is now seen
in historical terms. Second, traditional personality psychology was rooted in
clinical practice and intended to explain disordered behavior; its models are not
particularly relevant to much of industrial and organizational psychology.
Modern personality psychology, however, is concerned with the dynamics of
everyday behavior and is thus more relevant to industrial and organizational
psychology. Third, research since the early 1960s converges on the conclusion
that people can be and are described in terms of about five broad dimensions.
Assessments of personality should include these five at a minimum; it is insufficient to define personality in terms of single dimensions (e.g., locus of control,
self-esteem, or self-monitoring). Fourth, the processes by which we evaluate
others—that is, our social perception—is a research topic common to both
personality and industrial and organizational psychology, one that is enjoying*

renewed interest. Finally, personality assessments are a useful addition to selection batteries because they are blind to race and gender and faking does not seem to be a problem.

Introduction

PERSONALITY THEORY IS the subdiscipline of psychology concerned with framing and evaluating models of human nature. Personality psychology has a curious position in modern thought; although the public sees it as the most crucial and interesting part of psychology, academic psychologists seem to take the opposite view (cf. Kagan, 1988). Consistent with this trend, textbooks and review articles in industrial and organizational psychology (e.g., Guion, 1965) often report that personality measurement is not very useful for selecting employees or forecasting performance on the job.

Outside academic psychology, however, matters seem different. Most organizations use some form of personality assessment to hire and promote employees. Coaches, hostage negotiators, venture capitalists, and political columnists all spend a major part of their time trying to analyze the personalities of their occupational counter players. The primary ingredient of most novels, motion pictures, and stage plays is their character development, while most of the fascination in biographical writing lies in the clues it provides to the personalities of its subject.

This chapter argues that developments in personality psychology over the past 20 years suggest that people can be characterized in terms of their enduring dispositional qualities and that applied psychologists can take advantage of this information in ways that have significant consequences for employee development and organizational effectiveness. Moreover, personality is implicated in a surprising number of topics in industrial and organizational psychology. These include absenteeism

(Mowday, Porter, & Steers, 1982), employee reliability (Sackett & Harris, 1984), employee satisfaction (Staw & Ross, 1985), goal setting (Campbell, 1982), job scope (Hackman & Oldham, 1976), leadership (Ghiselli, 1971), organizational climate (Schneider, 1985), performance variability (Kane & Lawler, 1978), and work motivation (Korman, 1976). Consequently, a measured appreciation of modern personality psychology should be useful for many industrial and organizational practitioners.

The chapter is organized in six sections, beginning with some definitions to ensure a common understanding of terms for the rest of the discussion, followed by a brief review of the recurring criticisms of personality psychology perpetuated by our textbooks. In this review, I will suggest ways in which these criticisms miss the mark. The second section concerns personality from the observer's perspective—type and trait theory. The third section discusses major views of personality from the actor's perspective. The fourth section addresses the relationship between sections two and three. The fifth section deals with personality measurement as applied to personnel selection. Finally, the last section of the chapter discusses future trends in personality research and their implications for industrial and organizational psychology.

Personality Defined

Psychology as a discipline is characterized by a high level of methodological sophistication and an indifferent regard for definitional rigor. The conceptual confusion caused by this indifference may explain why progress often seems so slow. The word *personality* is a good case in point. The word has two very different meanings, and the failure to keep them separate leads to considerable confusion. On one hand, it refers to a person's social reputation and to the manner in which he or she is perceived by friends, family, co-workers, and supervisors. This is personality from the observer's perspective and concerns the amount of esteem, regard, or status that person has within his or her social groups. *Personality* in this sense is public, relatively objective, and can be described in terms of a common vocabulary—that is, in terms of trait words like *dominant, passive, considerate,* and *ruthless.* Moreover, because reputations summarize a person's past behavior, and because many writers believe that the best predictor of future behavior is past behavior, reputations (which are encoded in trait words) may be a useful way to forecast trends in a person's performance.

On the other hand, *personality* may also refer to the structures, dynamics, processes, and propensities inside a person that explain why he or she behaves in a characteristic way. The vocabulary used to describe these inner dimensions changes from writer to writer and forms the terminology of the various personality theories that have been developed over the years.

Thus, *personality* refers both to a person's social reputation and to his or her inner nature: The first is public and verifiable; the second is private and must be inferred. From the perspective of the philosophy of science, the conceptual status of these two meanings is quite different—a person's reputation is the empirical phenomenon that we want to explain, and we use the hypothesized inner structures to explain or account for that reputation.

The word *trait* also has two meanings, and they correspond to the two meanings of personality. On one hand, *trait* refers to recurring regularities or trends in a person's behavior; for example, to say someone is aggressive means that he or she has periodic episodes of hostile behavior, which usually include verbal and/or physical abuse. Note, however, that in this sense the word *trait* is theoretically neutral and purely descriptive. It tells us what we may expect the person to do but indicates nothing about why we should expect the person to behave that way. Thoughtful modern writers use the word in this sense (cf. Buss & Craik, 1983).

But *trait* also denotes psychological features—attitudes, emotions, and ways of perceiving and thinking—that exist inside a person and explain the recurring tendencies in that person's behavior. Allport (1961), the most vigorous spokesperson for this meaning, is regarded as the major trait theorist in the discipline. This second use of the term is unfortunate because it confounds description with explanation and makes the meaning of the word ambiguous. In this chapter, the word will be used to denote stylistic consistencies in a person's social behavior; the cause or explanation for this consistency remains to be illuminated by further research and theory. The word *trait* will not be used to denote structures or systems inside people.

Personality Criticized

For a while some psychologists regarded Mischel's 1968 book as a definitive critique of personality theory and assessment. A complete discussion of the implications of personality and personality measurement for industrial and organizational psychology must, therefore, at least review the major claims of that book. This turns out to be less difficult than one might think because the debate inspired by it has reached some resolution (cf. Kenrick & Funder, 1988; Snyder & Ickes, 1985). Essentially, Mischel's book makes four claims:

- If personality is an important concept, then individual differences in behavior should be consistent across situations and over time.

- A review of the literature provides no evidence for this consistency.

- Validity coefficients for personality measures rarely exceed .30.

- Because personality measures explain only nine percent of the variance in social behavior, situational variables must account for much of the remaining variance in social conduct. These situational variables, therefore, command the majority of our attention.

On closer analysis, each of these claims turns out to be flawed. Let me examine them briefly in turn.

With regard to the first claim, it is an assertion with which only a behaviorist would agree. Behavior need not be consistent across situations; it need only be "functionally equivalent" to allow inferences to be made about the existence of stable personality structures. As Weiss and Adler (1984) remark, "Rather than focus on consistency in behavior, we should focus on coherence.... We need to search for coherence of behavior at the mediating level and should not be deferred by inconsistency at the reaction level" (p. 37). Another problem concerns how to define consistency—one of the oldest questions in philosophy—and how much consistency is necessary before one can infer that stable personality structures guide overt behavior. Computer-driven robots may "behave" consistently, but people never do; actually, to be consistent we must change our behavior to fit whatever circumstances we find ourselves in. Consequently, the first claim is too vague to be useful.

Mischel's (1968) second claim is based on the extensive behaviorist literature from Thorndike (1906) to Mischel (1968), which points out that the correlations between behavior at different times are usually small (see Epstein & O'Brien, 1985, for a review of

this literature). But if behaviors are seen as items on a test, then the Spearman-Brown prophecy formula tells us that the correlation between any two single behaviors is necessarily low. Drawing on this well-known principle, Epstein (1979, 1980, 1983, 1984) shows that, when properly aggregated, the correlations between various behaviors at two points in time vary between .75 and .93. Similarly, McGowen and Gormly (1976) find correlations in excess of .70 between personality measures and behavior aggregated across several acts. Thus, Mischel's second claim seems to be an artifact of the unreliability of the measures used to evaluate stability; behavior may be situationally specific at the level of a single act but cross-situationally stable when correctly aggregated (cf. Epstein & O'Brien, 1985).

Ozer (1986) provides an interesting analysis of the consistency issue. He argues that the entire "person-situation" debate was wrong-headed because behavior is a function of persons, situations, response modalities, and time of assessment. This means that there are 12 different ways to talk about consistency (e.g., person x situation, person x response mode, person x time, situation x response mode, etc., plus the higher-order interaction terms), but the consistency debate has so far only dealt with the first two. In Ozer's view, the consistency debate has been inconclusive because it has been uninclusive.

Concerning Mischel's third point, the research literature contains many studies reporting correlations between personality measures and criterion behavior that exceed .30 (cf. R. Hogan, DeSoto, & Solano, 1975).

There are several responses to Mischel's fourth point, which maintains that because personality measures account for nine percent ($r = .30$) of the variance in social behavior, situations must account for the remainder. One response is that the correlations between well-constructed and self-validated personality measures and nontest behavior often exceed .30 (R. Hogan, DeSoto, & Solano, 1975).

A second response concerns the fact that some of the best-known "situational effects" in the history of social psychology, when converted to correlations, yield coefficients on the order of .30 to .40 (Funder & Ozer, 1983), and this may be the upper limit.

Third, it is hard unambiguously to define a "situation." Beyond such physical characteristics as temperature, air quality, and noise level, situations are largely defined in terms of our perceptions of the expectations of the people with whom we must interact. This point, incidentally, was stated explicitly by W. I. Thomas in 1918 (Berger & Luckmann, 1966) and was a truism of gestalt psychology in the 1930s (Krech & Crutchfield, 1948). More recently, Weick (1979) makes the same point in the context of organizational psychology—situations are our cognitive constructions of the environment. We bracket a section of the stream of experience, impose structure on it, and then assign meanings to the components of that structure. Our construct of the environment *is* the situation. Consequently, as Weick notes, it often makes little sense to speak of situations as distinct from personality.

Finally, this entire discussion has taken on a historical cast. Most knowledgeable reviewers believe that people can be characterized in terms of stable and enduring dimensions of individual differences in social behavior. Consequently, it seems safe to conclude that personality and personality assessment, despite occasional rumors to the contrary, are alive and well.

Personality From the Observer's Perspective

Type Theory

Personality from the observer's perspective concerns the categories or units that we use to sort, classify, perceive, and describe other people. The most important and dangerous part of our everyday environment is other people, and the success of our plans and aspirations depends to some degree on our ability to anticipate and predict their reactions. In order to make other people's behavior more interpretable, we tend to sort it into categories so that we can then classify people. These classifications result in types that we use when we talk and think about others. We might, for example, describe someone as a "health freak" or an "airhead" and expect health freaks to be physically active, mildly hypochondriacal, and fussy about their eating and drinking habits and airheads to be disorganized, self-absorbed, and suggestible. Note that type categories usually break down into trait lists.

Types are syndromes or trait conglomerates. Two persons in the same type category will only share roughly the same traits; rarely will they share precisely the same traits. The first systematic type theory is attributed to Galen, a Greek philosopher from the second century A.D., who proposed that there are four types of people in the world: the *sanguine,* who is cheerful and upbeat; the *choleric,* who is hot-tempered and self-dramatizing; the *melancholic,* who is lugubrious and fretful; and the *phlegmatic,* who is stolid and unflappable. Galen's types were based on a crude biochemical theory framed in terms of four humors: black bile, yellow bile, phlegm, and blood. The melancholic, for example, was said to have an excess of black bile and the choleric too much yellow bile (Roback, 1927).

This simple theory has persisted through the centuries with only minor changes; along the way it has been endorsed by some notable people. Immanuel Kant's *Anthropologie* (1798) revived Galen's type theory and became the best known psychology text of the late 18th century. Wilhelm Wundt (1874) restated Galen's theory by suggesting that the four types were caused by neurological mechanisms rather than humors. H. J. Eysenck (1981) proposes that certain neurophysiological mechanisms will produce a modern version of Galen's types.

Modern personality assessment reflects the influence of several type theories. For example, Jung's (1923) well-known theory of psychological types stimulated the development of the *Myers-Briggs Type Indicator* (MBTI; Myers & McCaulley, 1985). Spranger's (1928) theory of types led to the development of the *Study of Values* (Allport, Vernon, & Lindzey, 1951). Holland's theory of personality and vocational types led to the *Self-Directed Search* (SDS; Holland, 1985). Moreover, correlations among the scales on these inventories suggest that they overlap quite substantially. Finally, these type theories also resemble Galen's model as reflected by Wundt's and Eysenck's circumplexes (cf. R. Hogan, 1982).

Type theories are the oldest means we have for classifying the personalities of other people. Furthermore, there are interesting conceptual and empirical convergences in the type theories that have evolved over the past 50 years. Holland's work shows that these models can be surprisingly useful (Holland, 1985). In his well-known RIASEC model, Holland proposes six ideal personality types, each defined in terms of a distinctive pattern of interests, competencies, vocational choices, and problem-solving styles. The *Realistic* type (an engineer or technician) is mildly introverted and conforming, has concrete, practical interests, and prefers traditionally masculine careers. The *Investigative* type (a scientist or researcher) is mildly introverted and nonconforming, has abstract theoretical interests, and enjoys intellectual work. The *Artistic* type (a writer or musician) is unconventional and sometimes nonconforming, and enjoys working on open-ended design problems. The *Social* type (a minister or human resource person) is unconventional, extraverted, idealistic, and enjoys helping people. The *Enterprising* type (a salesperson or manager) is extraverted, ambitious, and enjoys leadership positions and manipulating others. The *Conventional* type (an accountant or data processor) is conforming, orderly, and pragmatic, and enjoys problems that have clear-cut solutions.

Holland overcomes the inherent vagueness of type theory by describing individuals in terms of their resemblance to two or more of his six pure types (for example, an industrial and organizational psychologist is a rare IE—investigative and enterprising—type).

Holland has shown that jobs and tasks can be classified on the basis of their psychological demands using his system (see also Driskell, R. Hogan, & Salas, 1987). This classification provides a straightforward way to match a person to a job on the basis of that person's personality and the psychological requirements of the job.

Jung, Eysenck, and Holland also explain where their types come from. Jung does this in terms of habitual styles of information processing; Eysenck does it in terms of neuropsychological mechanisms; Holland traces types back to individual learning experiences. All in all, type theories are a surprisingly robust way of describing and grouping other people, and the modern versions have some interesting uses in applied psychology (e.g., in career choice, person-environment fit, and personnel selection; cf. J. Hogan & R. Hogan, 1986).

Trait Theory

Despite Allport's deeply humanistic orientation, he initiated an influential line of empirical research. In the early 1930s, he (Allport & Odbert, 1933) began an important taxonomic effort by compiling a *trait lexicon*, a listing of English trait words. That reference list contains all the terms that English-speaking people use to describe one another.

It seems likely that language evolves in response to social reality. If so, then language should mirror that reality, although not necessarily in a precise way (Wittgenstein, 1953). From this assumption, it follows that ordinary language, when properly analyzed, can tell us something about the way the social world works. In particular, the structure of the trait vocabulary is probably related at some level to the structure of personality—from the observer's perspective.

Cattell (1947) put Allport's trait list together with factor analysis in an initial effort to identify the structure of personality. Using a 140-item subset of the 23,000 trait terms in Allport and Odbert's original listing, Cattell obtained ratings for several samples of people. Cattell's analyses of the correlations among these ratings revealed 16 factors (actually, item clusters) underlying the correlation matrix. Fiske (1949) advanced this line of analysis by showing, without the aid of a computer, that the structure of personality ratings could be parsimoniously expressed in terms of five factors (which will be described below). These findings have been replicated over and over in many different populations, languages, and age groups, using a variety of peer and self-ratings (cf. Borgatta, 1964; Botwin & Buss, 1989; Digman & Takemoto-Chock, 1981; Goldberg, 1982; John, Goldberg, & Angleitner, 1984; McCrae & Costa, 1985; Peabody & Goldberg, 1989).

What are these dimensions or factors? How factors are interpreted is a topic about which psychometricians love to quarrel, but there is reasonable agreement regarding the meaning of the recurring five. The first, *Neuroticism* or *Adjustment*, is defined at one end by terms like *nervous*, *self-doubting*, and *moody* and at the other by terms like *stable*, *confident*, and *effective*. The second factor, *Extraversion* or *Sociability*, is characterized at one end by such terms as *gregarious*, *energetic*, and *self-dramatizing* and at the other by such terms as *shy*, *unassertive*, and *withdrawn*. The third factor is usually called *Conscientiousness*. It is anchored at one end by traits like *planful*, *neat*, and *dependable* and at the other by *impulsive*, *careless*, and *irresponsible*. The fourth factor is generally called *Agreeableness*. One end is marked by such words as *warm*, *tactful*, and *considerate*; the other end reflects a combination of hostility and unsociability and is denoted by words like *independent*, *cold*, and *rude*. There is some disagreement

about how to label the final factor, which combines elements of creativity and school success. The convention is to call it *Culture* and then to agree that this term is somewhat misleading. At one end, *Culture* is defined by trait terms such as *imaginative*, *curious*, and *original*; it is defined at the other end by terms such as *dull*, *unimaginative*, and *literal-minded*.

These five dimensions can be reduced to three through higher-order factor analyses. Conversely, each factor quickly breaks down into a set of more specific facets; the components of Neuroticism, for example, include guilt, low self-esteem, depression, anxiety, somatic complaint, and poor sense of identity, among others. Because people seem predisposed to think about others in terms of these factors and to detect them even in ambiguous behavioral data (Norman & Goldberg, 1966), it seems reasonable to suppose that they are midlevel *cognitive prototypes* (Cantor & Mischel, 1977) or *cognitive schema* (Fiske & Linville, 1980). They can be seen as prewired categories of social cognition used to sort the behavior of others and to give some predictability to social life.

Moreover, note that these five dimensions are inherently evaluative; each presupposes a value judgment, a comparison with an unspecified standard of performance. R. Hogan (1987) suggests that, because people evolved as group-living animals, because all human groups must do the same kinds of things to survive (i.e., acquire food, construct shelter, and organize defenses), and because the welfare of the group depends on the collective efforts of its members, trait terms reflect observers' evaluations of others as potential contributors to or exploiters of the group's resources. Reputations, which are encoded in trait words, tell us about a person's possible contribution to the economy of his or her social groups.

I have described the modern view of the structure and function of trait words. The question of where they come from and what determines their use is a matter of some dispute. It is also what personality theory is all about, and more will be said about this shortly.

Practical Implications

Type and trait theory as described in this section are often useful heuristic devices for understanding the adequacy of certain organizational procedures.

Consider, for example, John Holland's theory, which postulates six pure vocational types defined in terms of a distinct set of motives, values, and interests. The theory provides a taxonomy of the types of persons found in the work force—for example, Gottfredson, Holland, and Ogawa (1982) and Viernstein (1972) show that the Holland codes can be used to classify and recover every entry in the *Dictionary of Occupational Titles*.

Holland's model should provide an efficient way to appraise person-job fit; extraverted people (in Holland's terms, Social and Enterprising types) should be in jobs requiring social interaction; introverted people (Realistic and Investigative types) should be in technical and analytical jobs; conforming people (Conventional types) should be in jobs where conformity is an asset; and nonconforming people (Artistic types) should be in positions where they can exercise their imagination. Organizations often put the wrong type of people in the wrong jobs, but individuals also make bad career decisions. Adventuresome and nonconforming people, for example, seem fascinated by law enforcement, a line of work normally requiring compulsiveness, attention to detail, and the ability to tolerate boredom. Despite their fascination they do poorly. Johnson and R. Hogan (1981), using a sample of 50 suburban Baltimore police officers, report a correlation of .34 between Holland's Artistic scale and number of citizen complaints; in the same sample, the Artistic scale correlated −.22 (and the Conventional scale correlated .23) with supervisors' ratings.

With regard to trait theory, job analyses typically reveal that certain personal attributes are necessary to perform a particular job adequately. Salespeople, for example, generally should be extraverted and agreeable, whereas truck drivers, who need to avoid accidents and make timely deliveries, should be conscientious, introverted, and focused in their interests (cf. J. Hogan & R. Hogan, 1986). Similarly, although many performance appraisal procedures seem job specific, most of them require judgments about interpersonal performances—these judgments are often what we mean by personality from the observer's perspective. Consequently, it might be useful to consider the Big Five theory to ensure the consistency and precision of the terminology across performance appraisal procedures.

Personality From the Individual's Perspective

What is it that causes people to behave so that observers classify them in certain ways or ascribe certain trait terms to them? Although it all depends on whom you ask, the answers generally can be found in personality theory.

Generally speaking, personality theories are intended to explain what people are like "way down deep." Most are designed specifically to explain the origins of neurotic or disordered behavior. If you want to understand why someone is erratic, moody, depressed, anxious, or stressed, then these theories may be useful. But they are not especially useful for understanding social competence, as in, for example, leadership, interpersonal effectiveness, or social insight. The absence of neurosis does not necessarily imply the presence of anything useful—i.e., ambition, tact, originality, or political acuity. Consequently, traditional personality theory is not always valuable in helping us understand the behavior of normal individuals in most organizations.

Many personality theories have been proposed over the years, but they can be usefully sorted into four categories which I will call *psychoanalytic, humanistic, cognitive social learning,* and *interpersonal.*

Psychoanalytic Theory

Freud is one of the most important social theorists of the past 100 years, and the intellectual tradition he inspired has influenced Jung, Adler, Fromm, Adorno, Marcuse, Rank, and others, all of whom are well worth serious study in their own right. Some useful lessons can be gleaned from the psychoanalytic tradition, stemming largely from the social theory of Freud and his distinguished contemporary interpreter, Erik Erikson (1968).

There are two themes in psychoanalysis with which most writers agree. The first concerns the notion that social behavior is symbolic, that people's actions carry disguised meanings, and that these meanings can be discovered by careful inquiry and investigation. Consider, for example, a manager who says that he or she values initiative and imagination in subordinates. Before taking this statement at face value, a prudent subordinate will find out exactly what the manager means by initiative and imagination. The popular study of body language is also based on the psychoanalytic notion that overt behavior has symbolic meaning. Although correct about this, psychoanalysts have been unable to provide systematic rules or generalizations for interpreting the symbolic meanings of social behavior. Their insight is valid, but how one deals with it is a matter of interpretation.

A second theme from psychoanalysis about which there is widespread agreement is the notion that people are often unaware of the reasons for their actions, that people sometimes deceive themselves, that rationality regarding crucial life choices is hard to achieve or maintain. Freud maintained that we never choose our mates or our vocation for rational reasons. If we reflect for a moment on how we got into our current relationship or employment circumstances, more often than not we will find that these circumstances somehow evolved, and for reasons that were only dimly understood at the time.

What are people like way down deep? According to psychoanalysis, people are motivated by forces they often don't understand. These unconscious desires typically can't be fully satisfied in reality (e.g., most of us want wealth, power, and world-class sex, but few of us have them). Consequently, we develop indirect ways to achieve these goals—we find ways to acquire as much power and love as we can in the circumscribed conditions of our lives. What we often see when we watch others, and what they often see when they watch us, are attempts to satisfy these basic and largely unconscious strivings for love, power, and survival. These attempts have been molded by experience during development; behaviors that were learned early in life—responses to paternal authority, maternal affection, or sibling competition—form the basis of adult social behavior. The wise person, according to psychoanalysis, will spend some time trying to understand the childhood origins of his or her present behavior.

Freud and Erikson make additional observations about which agreement is less complete but which are nonetheless relevant to this chapter. In a series of monographs starting with *Totem and Taboo* (1913), Freud argued that every human group is composed of a leader, some people who would like to be leaders, and a larger group of followers. According to Freud, an effective leader must be able to generate in followers the same feelings of loyalty and submission that they felt toward their own fathers, in essence, becoming a sort of surrogate father figure for the group. This will produce social conformity and cohesion among the group members. Freud also pointed out that effective leadership depends on the ability to deal with challenges from group members who are would-be leaders. Life in social groups, according to Freud, is characterized by periodic conflict and power struggles, and competent leadership requires dealing with these inevitable challenges and crises. Freud's point is that the way people react to authority—that is, with submission or defiance—is perhaps the most crucial aspect of their personalities. These reactions are the primary source of both stability and conflict in social organizations.

Erikson (1968) writes about human development over the life cycle and describes eight stages of personality growth, each of which is defined by a particular developmental challenge. Two of these stages are important for understanding peoples' behaviors in organizations. According to Erikson, some time in late adolescence people must decide who they are, what they stand for, and what their lives mean—they must develop a sense of identity. Life will go on whether or not the problem is solved, but unless it is, the person will be stunted and incomplete. Identities are normally formed by adopting the dominant mythology or ideology of one's culture, which is usually encapsulated in a political philosophy (e.g., Marxism) or a religion. But, says Erikson, the pace of life in modern industrial society prevents many people from developing an identity. The next developmental challenge concerns starting a family and becoming a productive member of society—choosing a mate and a vocation. Because many people entering the labor force lack well-defined identities, they are (according to Erikson) alienated and less than productive employees. Enlightened management will try to help those employees see that being a productive member of their organization can provide a sense of identity.

Among the best-known programs of empirical research based on Freud's ideas were the "Authoritarian Personality" studies carried out at the University of California at Berkeley in the 1940s. Individuals with authoritarian personalities are unconsciously hostile toward authority in general (their fathers), but overconform when dealing with superiors and demand strict obedience from their subordinates, whom they tend to treat with little respect. Authoritarians also tend to be politically conservative and nationalistic, to favor law and order, and to come from working-class backgrounds (cf. Adorno, Frenkl-Brunswik, Levinson, & Sanford, 1950).

Authoritarian tendencies can be assessed with the California F-Scale; a vast literature has grown up around this measure (cf. Aronoff & Wilson, 1985), and it is much too large to review here. Nonetheless, one of the more interesting generalizations to come from that literature is that groups composed of persons with authoritarian tendencies tend to have less agreement and participation among their members than nonauthoritarian groups. Authoritarian types also dislike participatory leadership and favor structured leadership. In both laboratory and field research, authoritarian people tend to use power coercively, especially if they are in a position of higher status; they reward ingratiating subordinates and exert strong personal control over group activities. Conversely, groups composed of low authoritarian members tend to prefer a participatory management style and are stressed by authoritarian leadership (cf. Dustin & Davis, 1967; Haythorn, Couch, Haefner, Langham, & Carter, 1556a, 1956b).

The literature on authoritarianism is based in psychoanalysis and concerns flawed leadership. Freud also had a theory of and an explanation for charismatic leadership: Charismatic leaders capture the superegos of their followers because they are archetypal father figures (Freud, 1913). Examples of charismatic leadership are easy to find, and such people can cause considerable mischief. For example, think of Adolph Hitler and the Ayatollah Khomeni; these men made a dreadful impact on world history, and it is insufficient to explain their careers in terms of historical circumstances or neurotic afflictions. Among the major social theorists Freud alone predicts the occurrence of such persons and provides a detailed psychological explanation for their charisma. Freud's leadership theory is one of the more interesting aspects of psychoanalysis, yet it is one of the most frequently ignored (except see Marcuse, 1955; Rieff, 1958; Roazen, 1968).

Humanistic Theory

Humanistic theories developed as a reaction against both psychoanalysis and behaviorism. German Romanticism in the 19th century celebrated individual freedom and encouraged people to take control of their lives by developing and realizing their innate potential, usually by exploring their unconscious tendencies. Freud regarded individual freedom as potentially dangerous; he considered human nature to be essentially selfish, wanton, and undependable. In contrast, Carl Jung, who was in the mainstream of Romanticism and much more optimistic about human potential, successfully imported a romantic vision of human nature into personality psychology.

This has proved to be a popular import, and Gordon Allport, Viktor Frankl, Carl Rogers, and Abraham Maslow became the best-known psychological advocates of the view of human nature initially expressed by Jung. If modern textbooks are a guide, Maslow also became one of industrial and organizational psychology's most frequently cited motivational theorists, although within this group there are some critics (cf. Wahba & Birdwell, 1976). Maslow is perhaps best regarded as a synthesizer rather than an original thinker; nonetheless, in that role he had some interesting things to say.

In particular, Maslow (1970) argued that, despite the different vocabulary, there is much convergence in psychological theory regarding the nature of human motivation, and that this convergence could be expressed in terms of five themes. The first is that all human motivation is physiologically based. At the lowest level, these motives concern purely physical needs—food, water, sleep, oxygen—and

physiological damage occurs when these needs go unmet.

At the next level, people need predictability and control. Should these "safety needs" be frustrated, people become anxious, fearful, and guilty and develop self-defeating behaviors designed to give them a sense of control and reduce anxiety. For example, a person may become passive and dependent or fussy and compulsive in order to feel in control.

Assuming that physiological and safety needs are met, people must then address needs for intimacy, social contact, and human relationships. Adults in particular develop elaborate methods for gaining attention and approval from others. Such methods might include agreeing with others and acquiescing to their wishes, allowing others to take advantage of them, provoking others just to see what they will tolerate, swearing loyalty to someone else's values, entertaining others, and doing them favors. The point of these strategies is to gain inclusion in group activities, to be noticed, and to be well regarded.

Maslow (1970) argues that once people have achieved a measure of social acceptance, esteem needs become important. These take two forms. They include first

> the desire for strength, for achievement, for adequacy, for mastery and competence, for confidence in the face of the world, and for independence and freedom. Second,... the desire for reputation and prestige (defining it as respect or esteem from other people) status, fame, and glory, dominance, recognition, attention, importance, dignity, or appreciation. (p. 45)

We have here, then, a need for achievement and a need to have that achievement recognized.

The fifth need in Maslow's hierarchy is self-actualization. He is most widely known for promoting this concept, which refers to the desire for self-fulfillment once more fundamental needs have been met. The need for self-actualization is expressed in ways that are idiosyncratic and unique to each person.

The self-actualization part of Maslow's motivational theory is largely ignored by modern personality psychology, and this is so for three reasons. First, it is difficult to find a biological or evolutionary justification for Maslow's need for self-fulfillment. Second, Maslow's most sympathetic modern interpreters agree that self-actualization is an unnecessary addition to his motivational theory (Aronoff & Wilson, 1985, p. 56). Finally, the concept of self-actualization is more readily seen as a sociopolitical ideal than a scientific concept (Smith, 1986); it provides a vantage point from which to criticize organizations rather than to explain the behavior of individuals. Maslow was clear about the political intent of this concept. There are many reasons for suggesting that organizations should treat their employees well; however, to criticize an organization for stultifying workers' self-actualizing tendencies is to appeal to humanistic rhetoric rather than to a well-grounded scientific principle.

Setting aside the need for self-actualization, the rest of Maslow's motivational theory reflects concepts that are sensible and capture important elements of personal and social dynamics. But Maslow's writing tends to be humanistic and political rather than scientific; consequently, his work is not influential in modern personality psychology.

Cognitive Social Learning Theory

Cognitive social learning theory is perhaps the most active area of research in modern personality psychology. Any generalization about this movement will necessarily misrepresent the views of some who take this perspective. If we define the perspective in terms of the viewpoints of Kelly (1955), Mischel (1968), and Bandura (1977), we can convey the flavor of this popular modern tradition.

Kelly argued that there is little point in talking about human motivation (Kelly was deliberately criticizing Freud, Jung, and Maslow). Motivation is a pointless explanatory concept because everyone who is alive is motivated. Social behavior is best understood in terms of how people think about the world—that is, the *cognitive strategies* that they develop to make sense out of their lives and interpret the behavior of others.

According to Kelly, cognitive strategies, rather than biological motives, form the core of personality; these strategies explain why people act as they do. Because cognitive strategies are learned, they can be unlearned and new ones can be acquired. Consequently, personality is always changeable, and this is the basis for Kelly's most provocative claim: Personality is like a suit of clothes— if you don't like it, then change it.

Bandura and Mischel develop these themes in several ways, linking cognitive strategies to specific situations—that is, the strategy a person uses will reflect the situation he or she is performing in. In addition, Bandura analyzes the sense of *efficacy*, the feeling of competence to deal with the demands of a particular situation. His more recent research concerns the origins and consequences of this sense of efficacy. Mischel identifies various components of the social information processing system and analyzes how people use trait words, concluding that trait words at certain levels of abstraction are more prototypical of the underlying personality concept and are therefore more likely to be used than others.

Cognitive social learning theory is concerned with how social and behavioral strategies are learned, which has implications for training. For example, behavior modeling, inspired by Bandura's theory, seems to be a promising technique for supervisory training (Latham & Saari, 1979).

Because cognitive social learning theory emphasizes social information processing, it is compatible with the modern emphasis on cognition, and this may explain its popularity. At the same time, most of the research is conducted in laboratories, there is little interest in individual differences, and it may have less relevance to industrial and organizational psychology than other major traditions in personality theory.

Interpersonal Theory

Psychoanalysis, humanistic theory, and cognitive social learning theory all focus on the intrapsychic processes and problems of individuals. These theories are individualistic rather than social or interpersonal: They deemphasize the importance of relationships. In contrast, interpersonal theory regards personality as arising from social relationships and as meaningful only in that context.

Interpersonal theory is a blend of clinical and social psychology, and it is also an active movement in modern personality psychology. Major contributors from the clinical tradition include Sullivan (1953), Leary (1957), Carson (1969), and J. S. Wiggins (1979). From social psychology, the contributors include Mead (1934), Goffman (1958), Snyder (1974), Jones and Pittman (1982), and Baumeister (1982; see especially Schlenker, 1985). R. Hogan (1982) and Snyder (Snyder & Smith, 1982), among others, try to integrate these movements. The basic assumption is that people need social approval, social status, and predictability—as Maslow suggested—and that these needs are satisfied through interaction with others. Social interaction, from the most casual to the most formal, is structured by situational norms, by the roles that people choose or are assigned, and by their self-presentational styles. Self-presentational styles or behaviors are in turn guided by each person's self-concept or identity. To close the conceptual loop, a person's identity is developed during social interaction.

Social skill is a key concept in interpersonal theory and includes social insight, role-taking ability, social acuity, and the capacity for effective interpersonal performances. Research associated with Machiavellianism, self-monitoring, and empathy—all constructs involving social skill—shows that role-taking and self-presentational skills are associated with a variety of positive social outcomes (cf. Aronoff & Wilson, 1985).

Interpersonal theory concerns roles, strategic interaction, and social competence. These notions are a natural part of organizational behavior; negotiation, bargaining, and behavior in organizational rituals that depend on ceremonial adequacy are easily interpreted in these terms. Insofar as managerial effectiveness entails reading social cues and using that information to guide one's behavior, then interpersonal theory is also relevant to the management process. Finally, interpersonal theory emphasizes individual differences in social competence, and many of the writers in this tradition have been involved in assessment research (cf. Gough, 1948; Leary, 1957; Sarbin, 1954; J. S. Wiggins, 1979).

Actions, Observations, and Their Connections

I attended an executive committee meeting chaired by a well-known psychologist; he was pompous and authoritarian and annoyed everyone at the meeting. Afterward, at a hotel bar, he remarked expansively on his special talent for conducting meetings. The discrepancy between his view of his performance and the group's view is the point of this section.

During social interaction, people often have different agendas. While one person tries to make a point, the other, barely listening, may be formulating a counterargument. During employment interviews, job candidates may try to demonstrate their energy, productivity, and overall suitability, while the interviewer may probe for inconsistencies in that performance. And so it goes for police interrogations, marriage proposals, loan applications, courtroom cross-examinations, and every conceivable form of negotiation. These interactions are usually double-contingency situations wherein people attempt to guide their behavior by what they think the observer may expect. The situation is something like: "I think that he expects me to do X. But if he believes that I think he expects me to do X, then perhaps I should do Y. But what happens if what he expects me to do is different from what he wants me to do?" In any case, there will always be differences between a person's own view of his or her social behavior and the way different observers perceive it. This discrepancy leads to the issue of social acuity or accurate social perception.

Traditional psychoanalytic theories focus on self-perception and self-understanding; they regard perceptions of others as projections of our own unconscious desires and fears. Cognitive social learning theory views social perception as a form of social cognition and studies the process itself rather than accuracy—which is seen as a meaningless concept (cf. Hastorf, Bender, & Weintraub, 1955). In contrast, humanistic theory (e.g., Allport, 1961; Maslow, 1970) concerns itself with accuracy in social perception and for an interesting reason: Both Allport and Maslow thought accurate social perception was a sign of psychological health, maturity, and self-actualization. Consequently, in their view, not everyone is capable of accurate perception; rather, accuracy depends on a particular organization of individual personality. From the perspective of interpersonal theory, social perception is one of the most crucial preconditions for social behavior—the social-perceptual act precedes most interpersonal exchanges, and the perceptual act defines the framework in terms of which an interaction will be conducted. Perceptual errors necessarily lead to flawed interactions, whereas accuracy is advantageous in the pursuit of a person's social goals.

The relevance of social perception to industrial and organizational psychology should be obvious. It is the basis on which most procedures in industrial psychology depend: rating techniques, interviews, performance appraisals, and assessment center evaluations (cf. Kane & Lawler, 1979). Accurate social perception is also thought to be related to managerial effectiveness (cf. Dansereau, Graen, & Haga, 1974; Kenny & Zaccaro, 1983). Moreover, a long tradition of social perception research exists in industrial and organizational psychology, including a keen awareness of the accuracy issue (cf. Guilford, 1936). This issue is relevant also to the practice of clinical and counseling psychology, but various historical trends since about 1960 have turned clinical researchers away from the topic (for an interesting review, see Sarbin, Taft, & Bailey, 1960).

Personality psychologists began studying accuracy in social perception more than fifty years ago, and it was an active area of research for many years (Dymond, 1949; Estes, 1938; Taft, 1955; Vernon, 1933). However, a series of methodological critiques (Cronbach, 1955; Hastof et al., 1955) essentially brought research in this area to a halt. The issue concerned how accuracy was defined. Often it was defined in terms of the difference between a self-rating and an observer's rating of that person, where the person's self-rating was taken as correct. Alternatively, a person's rating of a target actor might be compared with a group consensus of that person. Either way, accuracy was defined in terms of a simple difference score. The complaint was and is that these difference scores are, from a components of variance perspective, quite complex: Accuracy could be achieved by at least three different means, all of which were confounded in the difference score. The accuracy research based on these scores is therefore uninterpretable as well.

The Process of Social Perception

Research into the determinants of accurate social perception stopped in the mid-1950s. But three other areas in social perception research continued unabated. The first concerns the process of social perception. Heider (1958) suggested that people know a lot about themselves and other people and that they use this knowledge to organize their relations with others. Drawing on Heider's analysis, Jones (Jones & Davis, 1965) began an influential series of studies designed to analyze the cognitive categories and methods people use to explain the behavior of others. As a result, the study of social perception soon became largely identified with attribution theory. As Ross and Fletcher (1985) note:

> In the 1970s…social psychology was dominated by attribution theorists and researchers…. Most attribution theorists are not concerned with the validity of the attributions that the lay person produces. Instead, theorists focus on the cognitive processes involved in forming attributions. (p. 73–74)

Perhaps the most useful lesson to be gleaned from attributional studies of social perception is the importance of distinguishing between one's own view of one's actions and the observer's view of those actions. This is necessary because the perceptual units used by actors and those used by observers are fundamentally and qualitatively different, probably as a consequence of their different goals. The second lesson may be less useful; according to attribution theory, observers explain actors' behavior in terms of the actors' traits (i.e., personality), whereas actors explain their behavior in terms of situational contingencies. This claim, which has been questioned (Monson & Snyder, 1977), means that observers believe that actors are more responsible for their own behavior than the actors do. The third lesson is even more problematic and concerns what is called the *fundamental attribution error*. Because personality exists more in the eye of the beholder than in the psyche of the person (Jones & Davis, 1965), observers invariably underestimate the degree to which a person's behavior reflects situational demands.

The concept of the fundamental attribution error contains two implicit generalizations whose empirical validity is not well established. The first is that situations determine people's actions more powerfully than personality; attribution theory argues that traditional personality variables lack explanatory power. The second implicit claim is that observers' judgments about other people's traits are often in error—because attribution theory believes that human social judgment is fundamentally biased or flawed, and thus research would be most profitably directed at analyzing the sources of inaccuracy (cf. Cook, 1985; Schneider, Hastorf, & Ellsworth, 1979).

The Units of Social Perception

The research inspired by Heider's (1958) book largely concerns the *process* of social perception; a second tradition addresses the *units* of social perception. Miller, Galanter, and Pribram (1960) popularized the idea that people develop mental models or schemas to represent reality, which are then used to organize behavior. This argument leads to an analysis of the categories of social judgment (Cantor & Kihlstrom, 1981), and this research shows that people organize their thinking about others by using trait words; there is an orderly hierarchical structure to these words—i.e., trait words vary in terms of their prototypicality (Hampson, 1982; John, Goldberg, & Angleitner, 1984).

What do we perceive when we watch other people? Or, more accurately, what do we *report* having seen, and what is it that organizes our reports? The most general answer is that it depends on what we're looking for. A police officer interrogating a criminal suspect, a woman responding to a social invitation from a male stranger, and a banker taking a loan application are looking for very different things. In general, however, they are looking for *signs* or indications that the other person has certain tendencies. Although the raw perceptual data may be behaviors, people attempt to discern themes in those data, and these themes are normally behavioral tendencies. Consequently, people tend to report their perceptions in terms of trait words—trait words are the natural language of social perception.

This point has important implications for industrial and organizational psychology. Many personnel procedures depend on ratings, for example, results of interview and performance appraisals. These ratings are often provided by nonpsychologists, and the format may be a behaviorally anchored rating scale (Smith & Kendall, 1963). But the research suggests that people don't perceive behaviors, they don't organize their thinking about others in terms of behaviors, and they don't normally report their perceptions in terms of behaviors: They perceive, think, and report in trait terms. Murphy, Martin, and Garcia (1982) provide an excellent example of this point in the familiar context of performance ratings. They show that nonpsychologists conceptualize and evaluate the performance of others in trait dispositional rather than behavioristic terms. Focusing on behaviors rather than traits is not only odd conceptually, it is inefficient as well. Moskowitz and Schwartz (1982) show that it takes 1,440 direct measurements of behavior over 8 weeks to yield a score with the reliability and validity of the average trait ratings of 3 knowledgeable informants. People seem able to abstract consistencies from the flux of behavior; they can do this easily, and their knowledge of these consistencies can be put to important practical uses.

The Organization of Social Perception

When we describe another person, our descriptions have a kind of structure or coherency of their own. What organizes these descriptions? There are four general answers. The first is that they are influenced by the response format used to obtain the description. There are significant differences in peoples' descriptions depending on whether they use fixed or free response formats (McGuire & Padawer-Singer, 1976), and people make different and finer distinctions at a researcher's request than they normally make on their own (Funk, Horowitz, Lipshitz, & Young, 1976).

A second and more disconcerting answer is provided by the *systematic distortion hypothesis* (cf. Berman & Kenny, 1976; Bourne, 1977; Chapman & Chapman, 1967; and especially Shweder & D'Andrade, 1980). This hypothesis maintains that observers' descriptions of others are organized by the semantic relationships among the descriptive words themselves so that descriptions are essentially unrelated to the actual behavior. The systematic distortion hypothesis

> asserts that judges on personality inventories, interpersonal checklists, and questionnaire interviews unwittingly substitute a preexisting model of conceptual association for a description of correlational structure. Thus the correlational structure of ratings replicates preexisting beliefs about what is like what with little sensitivity to the correlational structure of actual behavior. (Shweder, 1982, p. 67)

This view contradicts our common-sense notions about the validity of social perception. Not surprisingly, a number of writers have challenged both the logic of the argument and the data on which it is based (cf. Block, Weiss, & Thorne, 1979; DeSoto, Hamilton, & Taylor, 1985; Hampson, 1982; Romer & Revelle, 1984). In an especially telling critique, Weiss and Mendelsohn (1986) devised rating procedures that either permit or preclude the systematic distortion effects defined by Shweder and D'Andrade, then showed that target persons are described in essentially the same way regardless of the degree to which distortion effects could have operated. Weiss and Mendelsohn conclude that there is no evidence that the systematic distortion effect operates when describing real people.

A third model maintains that social perception is organized in terms of categories that reflect core activities of the culture. Goldberg

(1982) remarks that "those individual differences that are of the most significance in the daily transactions of persons with each other will eventually become encoded into their language" (p. 204). This, he argues, is how trait terms originate. Hampson (1982) and Hampson, John, and Goldberg (1986) show that personality trait words are categories that have a surprisingly clear hierarchical structure. John, Goldberg, and Angleitner (1984) trace the similarities in these structures through English, Dutch, and German. I suggested earlier in this chapter that the so-called Big Five theory (J. S. Wiggins, 1973) provides a heuristic for thinking about the structure of trait words. In a widely cited paper, Passini and Norman (1966) show that the well-known five factors can be found even when people rate virtual strangers. After reviewing the foregoing, Digman (1990) concludes that these five factors are midlevel cognitive schemas or prototypes that tend to structure social perceptions.

A final account of how social perceptions are organized is provided by implicit personality theory. According to Kelly (1955), people perceive and respond to others in terms of their own *personal construct theory,* that is, in terms of their private notions of what others expect of them during social interaction. These constructs (i.e., role constructs) guide social behavior and make social interaction possible. This view is highly plausible (e.g., see Mischel, 1973), but it doesn't lead to a clear research agenda, largely because of its idiographic nature—each person has a unique perceptual model; it has the status of a conceptual promissory note that has yet to be cashed in.

Distortions of Social Perception

Distorted social perception should always bias social interaction, and sometimes in unfortunate ways. Stagner (1948) argued that flawed perceptions were a major contributor to labor management problems. That misjudgments spark miscommunication in human affairs is a widely shared assumption among organizational psychologists (Alderfer, 1984). This assumption was verified in an interesting series of studies. Snyder, Tanke, and Berscheid (1977) show that women talking on the phone with men who, unbeknownst to the women, believe them to be attractive, behave in a more "positive" way than women talking to men who believe them to be unattractive. Snyder and Swann (1978) show that game players who believe their opponents are hostile and competitive adopt strategies that subsequently elicit hostile behavior from the opponents. Wilder (1986) shows that perceiving a person to be an "insider" or an "outsider" to the group leads people to treat that person differently, even when the group has been arbitrarily composed. Finally, Lewicki (1986) shows that people need not be aware of their perceptions for those perceptions to affect their behavior; people make choices on the basis of influences that are, and remain, nonconscious.

Other research shows that some people display consistent or traitlike biases in social perception. For example, a person's self-image seems to act as a filter that screens social information. The self-concept predicts the kind of information a person seeks about others (Riggs & Cantor, 1984); people have better developed schemas about those traits they believe characterize themselves (Markus & Smith, 1981); people favor trait terms they think describe themselves when they are describing others (Hirschberg & Jennings, 1980); and traits perceived as relevant to the evaluation of oneself are more often used in free descriptions of others (Shrauger & Patterson, 1974).

In a perhaps more nomothetic vein, persons with authoritarian tendencies seem especially sensitive to other people's official social status (Jones, 1954), whereas nonauthoritarians are sensitive to other people's "personal power cues" (Wilkens & deCharms, 1962). In a well-replicated study, Scodel and Mussen (1953) showed that authoritarians consistently see others as similar to themselves;

nonauthoritarians are more variable in their perceptions. Another well-replicated finding is that persons with an external locus of control (poor adjustment in Big Five terms) consistently describe others in more negative ways and recall more negative information about themselves than do people with an internal locus of control (good adjustment; cf. Bryant, 1974). In a fascinating study, Jones and Daugherty (1959) found that Machiavellians (i.e., high dominance, low conscientiousness in Big Five terminology) used negative terms to describe strangers with dominant characteristics whom they thought they would meet later in competitive circumstances. Assor, Aronoff, and Messe (1981) replicate this using the Dominance scale of the *California Psychological Inventory;* that is, persons with high Dominance scores describe high Dominance strangers negatively if they think they are future competitors. After reviewing the literature on personological biases in social perception, Aronoff and Wilson (1985) wisely conclude that

> most dispositional variables won't have a general effect on social perception across a broad range of persons and social contexts; rather…dispositions should affect impression formation only when there are factors in the situation that affect that disposition so as to evoke a subjective response that can stimulate adaptive cognitive reconstruction of the social impression. (p. 143)

Accuracy Revisited

Despite early interest in the determinants of accurate social judgment (e.g., Vernon, 1933), research on this topic came to a halt in the mid-1950s. Research then began to focus on the process of social perception and on the errors that erode accuracy. As Funder (1987) remarks, "The psychology of social judgment has been dominated in recent years by a flood of

research on the subject of 'error'" (p. 76). These studies, Funder observes, appear at a "prodigious" rate and are widely cited. Despite the conceptual and methodological problems, and the torrent of error articles, interest in the accuracy issue has returned.

With regard to modern error research, Funder (1987) points out that this research is "almost completely irrelevant to the accuracy of social judgment" (p. 76) because an error is not the same thing as a mistake. In psychological research, errors are judgments made by individuals about social stimuli that differ from the experimenter's view of the correct response. A mistake, however, is an incorrect judgment made in the real world. Funder then shows in detail how the errors that people make in laboratory studies of social perception would not necessarily be mistakes outside the laboratory. The errors are caused by people bringing into ambiguous laboratory situations assumptions and information that are valid in the real world. As an example, Funder describes a study by Ross, Amabile, and Steinmetz (1977), wherein undergraduate students were randomly assigned the roles of "questioner" and "contestant" in a mock quiz show. The questioners devised questions for the contestants. After the quiz, the contestants—who were at an obvious disadvantage in the situation—rated themselves as inferior to the questioners in terms of general knowledge. Naive observers, watching reenactments of this situation, also rated the questioners as having more general knowledge than the contestants. Funder argues that this study only shows that the contestants and the naive observers imported an assumption from real life to make their ratings: Namely, we all know that people who have trouble answering questions are probably not very well informed, and this tacit knowledge biased the study's results. In a subsequent study, Block and Funder (in press) show that, among 14-year-olds, susceptibility to the foregoing mistake is a function of social competence so that the better-adjusted youngsters were more susceptible to the mistake. Once again, Funder's point is that laboratory research on errors in social judgment is largely irrelevant to the study of accuracy in real-world situations.

Although some people are skeptical regarding the accuracy issue, evidence regarding the existence of stable individual differences in accuracy has been accumulating for years. Cline and Richards (1960), in a curiously ignored paper, provided solid evidence for individual differences in generalized accuracy using Cronbach's (1955) computational formula. Other studies include papers by Bernstein and Davis (1982), DePaulo (1978), DePaulo, Kenny, Hoover, Webb, and Oliver (1987), Harackiewicz and DePaulo (1982), R. Hogan and Briggs (1984), Jackson (1982), Mills and R. Hogan (1976), and Pryor, Gibbons, Wicklund, Fazio, and Hood (1977). These studies define accuracy in different ways (e.g., how well one can judge a person relative to a group's consensus about that person, how well one can judge how one is perceived by others, etc.), and it may be that accuracy at one judgment task is only moderately related to accuracy in another. Borman, Hough, and Dunnette (1976) sensibly suggest that certain individual differences may be consistently related to interpersonal accuracy across a wide range of situations, whereas other differences may correlate with accuracy only in certain specific contexts.

Industrial and organizational psychologists have always been interested in the relationship between social judgment and overt behavior; specifically, they have studied how well social judgments can forecast job performance. In general, peer ratings are consistently useful predictors of future performance (see Kane & Lawler, 1978, for a review). Further, Borman (1979) studied accuracy in evaluating performance effectiveness. He developed "true" measures of performance

on a managerial and a recruiting task, then had college students judge the same performance. Using a variety of other measures, Borman found that persons who were accurate judges of performance in this typical organizational task were bright, well adjusted, self-controlled, and likable. This profile of accurate judges of performance effectiveness is consistent with findings from academic research regarding the characteristics of good judges in general (cf. Grief & R. Hogan, 1973; R. Hogan & Briggs, 1984).

Personality Measurement

Personality measurement has traditionally been used to solve applied problems. Clinical psychologists use it to assign clients to treatment programs, and industrial and organizational psychologists use it for selection purposes. The potential contribution of personality measurement to these problems has been obvious for a long time. For example, Eysenck (1949), in his review of the 19-volume report of the Army Air Force's aviation psychology research program, notes that the success of this selection program was "indisputable and stands as a monument to what scientific psychology...is capable of doing" (p. 143). The best-weighted combination of air crew classification tests with attrition versus graduation in flight training was .69 ($N = 1,143$), which is stunning given the underlying complexity of the criterion. A detailed followup of the outliers—high-scoring persons who failed and low-scoring persons who succeeded—revealed that the differences were in the areas of motivation, emotional maturity, and self-discipline. This prompted Eysenck to note that "the weakest point of the Army Air Forces Aviation program [was] its failure to deal adequately with the problems of temperament and character" (p. 144). The point of this section is to argue that personality measures can contribute significantly to the prediction of important real-world criteria.

Personality Theory and Personality Measurement

In principle, personality measurement should sample elements or aspects of an individual's behavior that are diagnostic of important characteristics of people in general. These diagnostic behavior samples should, on the one hand, allow us to compare different people against the same standard and, on the other hand, allow us to interpret what a person has done and predict what he or she will do in other important nontest situations. Both processes—comparisons among people and interpretations of individual cases—are important tasks in industrial and organizational psychology.

The goals of personality measurement often reflect a researcher's theoretical orientation. Psychoanalytic theory assumes that the core of personality is a set of unconscious structures designed to protect individuals from anxiety, self-criticism, and loss of self-esteem. Personality measurement from the psychoanalytic perspective is intended to reveal these unconscious structures and forecast the disordered behaviors arising from them. Two well-known and widely used tests that serve these purposes are the Rorschach (1921) and the *Thematic Apperception Test* (TAT; Murray & Morgan, 1935).

Humanistic theory evolved in part as a reaction against the tendency to explain personality in terms of a small number of universal, unconscious, neurotic categories. Humanistic theory seeks to capture individual uniqueness in terms of variables that reflect growth, health, mastery, and development. The solution to this problem requires a compromise; humanistic theory, to the degree that it tries to be scientific, must use measures that are only relatively idiographic. Examples include the TAT (Morgan & Murray, 1935), the *California Q-Sort* (Block, 1961, 1978), and the *Adjective*

Check List (ACL; Gough & Heilbrun, 1983). The Q-Sort is a particularly good example; although everyone is described using the same item pool, the pool can be configured uniquely for each person, and the resulting configuration can be treated quantitatively.

Cognitive social learning theory (Mischel, 1973) adopts Allport's (humanistic) agenda for personality measurement and focuses on person-centered, as opposed to norm-centered, measurement. A norm-centered approach compares people against one another on a trait continuum. In contrast, a "person-centered focus…tries to describe the particular individual in relation to the particular conditions of his life" (Mischel, 1977, p. 248). Consequently, the research agenda concerns the study of cognitive and behavioral construction competencies, categorization preferences, expectancies, values, and self-regulatory systems—with the intent of characterizing specific individuals in specific situations. No measurement methods have been developed, and so far this line of personality research has developed no direct applications to industrial and organizational psychology.

Interpersonal theory (Leary, 1957; Wiggins, 1979) has always had a strong quantitative orientation. The goal is to assess the personality factors that underlie the full spectrum of interpersonal exchanges, including leader-subordinate relations, group dynamics, and intergroup relations. Wiggins' model is based on his *Interpersonal Adjective Scales* (IAS), which contain two major dimensions, hostility-affection and dominance-submission. In a psychometric tour de force, Wiggins and Broughton (1985) show that these two dimensions, which define a circumplex, can encompass the Murray need system (Murray, 1938) as defined by either Gough and Heilbrun's (1980) *Adjective Check List* or Jackson's (1967) *Personality Research Form*. Digman (1990) and R. Hogan (1987) suggest that trait terms, including the well-known five factors that come out of peer rating studies, reflect crucial dimensions of interpersonal evaluation. Specifically, they reflect the structure or profile of a person's reputation within his or her peer or work group.

Objective Personality Measurement. In a paper on the history of measurement in psychology, Ramul (1963) suggests that Christian Thomasius (1655–1768), a German lawyer and philosopher well known during the Enlightenment, developed the first system of personality measurement. This system consisted of rating scales for "reasonable love," "voluptuousness," "ambition," and "greed," which, argued Thomasius, produce all the inclinations of the human mind. Goldberg (1971) points out that modern personality measurement began with the symptom check list of Heymans and Wiersma (1906), although Galton used questionnaires at his anthropometric laboratory in 1884, and G. Stanley Hall used questionnaires in his early (1904) developmental research. From 1906 until the end of World War II, personality measurement was primarily used to assess psychopathology, largely stimulated by the need to screen army recruits during World War I. Woodworth's (1918—see Symonds, 1931) *Personal Data Sheet* was the first of a series of psychopathology measures that led to the development of the *Minnesota Multiphasic Personality Inventory* (MMPI; Hathaway & McKinley, 1943). The MMPI is the most widely used objective personality test in the world; in the United States it is used to screen applicants for jobs in which emotional stability is considered crucial, such as law enforcement and nuclear reactor operation.

During the period immediately after World War II, several major inventories designed to measure normal personality were published. Among the best known of these are the 16-PF (Cattell & Stice, 1957), the *Guilford-Zimmerman Temperament Survey* (Guilford, Zimmerman, & Guilford, 1976), the *Comrey Personality Inventory* (Comrey, 1970), and the *California Psychological Inventory* (Gough, 1987). Despite the early promise of these

measures, personality measurement went into a decline during the 1960s for reasons discussed below. The field seems only now to be recovering, due largely to the success of some narrowly defined measures (locus of control, self-monitoring, sex role orientation, and type A behavior). A conference and a book by Bernardin and Bownas (1985) suggest that there may be a renewed interest in personality research within industrial and organizational psychology.

Projective Personality Measurement. Most objective personality measures contained fixed stimuli (e.g., printed statements) and fixed response options (e.g., true or false). Projective measures, in contrast, have fixed stimuli (pictures, abstract designs, sentence fragments, a structured in-basket), but the response options are open-ended.

Galton introduced the free association technique at his anthropometric laboratory in 1884. This was elaborated on by the German psychiatrist Kraepelin and used with psychiatric patients. Carl Jung formalized this methodology in his 1910 paper. Rorschach's (1921) book, *Psychodiagnostics*, popularized the ink blot test, and Rorschach's cards are the most widely used projective test in the world. The *Thematic Apperception Test*, developed by Murray at the Harvard Psychological Clinic (Morgan & Murray, 1935), has been widely used for selection purposes and in the study of management and entrepreneurship (Cummin, 1967; McClelland & Boyatzis, 1982; McClelland & Burnham, 1976; Morris & Fargher, 1974).

Scale Construction. Two key decisions guide the process of personality scale construction: (a) what to measure and (b) how to measure it. The first point is determined largely by the researcher's theoretical orientation and the problems in which he or she is interested; these are largely matters of scientific taste. The second point is what scale construction is all about.

There are essentially three steps in the scale construction process. The first step concerns assembling an item pool, largely an intuitive procedure in which the researcher puts together a set of items that seem to reflect, embody, or capture the essence of the construct, theoretical dimension, or phenomenon to be assessed. Subsequent research may reveal gaps or shortcomings in the item pool; if so, those gaps will be filled by a reiteration of the intuitive process. The success of this first stage depends in part on the psychological insight of the researcher.

The second and third steps are logically distinct but procedurally confounded. These steps concern choosing a final item pool and defining a scoring key—the rules by which item responses are quantified. The process of establishing a scoring key usually defines the final set of items to be included on the scale or measure.

Scoring Keys. Personality measures differ in terms of item formats, that is, written statements versus unstructured stimuli such as ink blots or incomplete sentences. They also differ in terms of response formats—structured (true or false) versus unstructured (free response). Either item format may be used with either response format. Finally, and perhaps most critically, personality measures differ in terms of how the responses are scored. There are essentially three methods for composing scoring keys, and all existing personality measures have scoring keys based on one or more of these methods (they are not necessarily mutually exclusive). These three methods are called *rational, factor analytic,* and *empirical.*

In the *rational* method, items are scored on the basis of a researcher's intuition about the psychological meaning of the item content. As naive as this may sound, it is a surprisingly popular and widespread method for constructing scoring keys, particularly among researchers who have limited experience with psychological measurement. Consider what

the *Jenkins Activity Survey* (Jenkins, Zyzanski, & Rosenman, 1979), the *Locus of Control Scale* (Lefcourt, 1976), and the *Self-Monitoring Scale* (Snyder, 1974) have in common: They are popular in research applications, and their item pools and scoring keys were defined on a rational or a priori basis. Finally, these three scales share the common fate of many rationally constructed scales—other researchers sooner or later examine the internal structure of these scales and find them to be complex. Specifically, using a large sample of subjects, researchers compute the matrix of correlations among the items on the scales and put that matrix through a factor analytic procedure. This often reveals that the items chosen on an a priori basis form clusters, some of which are negatively related to the others. When a scale contains item clusters that are unrelated statistically, it is very difficult to interpret scores on that scale.

The *factor analytic* or *internal consistency* method of scale construction has just been described. It is a refinement of the rational method wherein the correlations among the items in the initial item pool are evaluated through factor analysis. Items that form a statistical cluster, that is, items that cluster together on the basis of their intercorrelations, are used to define a scale. Scales defined in this way have a thematic unity that facilitates the interpretation of scale scores.

The positive feature of scales constructed through factor analytic or internal consistency procedures is that scores on such scales reflect a single theme and can therefore be more easily interpreted. The bad news is that interesting psychological phenomena are usually complex rather than thematically unified, so that such scales may pick up one aspect or facet of the phenomena but miss others. In addition, some researchers who rely on the factor analytic method seem primarily interested in the internal statistical properties of their scales and thus pay less attention to validity—the nontest correlates of scale scores. A scale with high internal consistency may or may not have interesting or useful nontest correlates. Well-known examples of tests developed in this manner include the 16-PF (Cattell & Stice, 1957), the *Guilford-Zimmerman Temperament Survey* (GZTS; Guilford et al., 1976), and the NEO-PI (Costa & McCrae, 1985).

In its pure form, the *empirical* method of scale construction is very different from the rational or factor analytic methods. In the empirical method, a researcher develops an initial item pool, then administers the items to a sample of people. These people are known to differ along a dimension of interest (e.g., academic performance or leadership) for which there are objective indicators of performance. Item scores are compared with scores on the dimensions of interest, and those items signifcantly associated with the external scores are retained for the final set of items that form the scale.

Scales developed using the empirical method have one useful distinguishing feature—validity is guaranteed. When scales are developed for practical purposes, this is a powerful benefit. On the negative side, scales developed in this way will almost always have less internal consistency than scales based on factor analysis, making scores harder to interpret. Well-known tests developed by the empirical method include the MMPI (Hathaway & McKinley, 1943) and the CPI (Gough, 1987).

In reality, the foregoing distinctions tend to blur. Both the MMPI and the CPI, prime examples of inventories developed by empirical keying methods, contain rational scales purified by factor analysis. Moreover, papers by Hase and Goldberg (1967) and Goldberg (1972) suggest that none of the methods described above has a necessary advantage in terms of final scale validity—that, when carefully done, all three methods lead to scales of comparable validity. If so, then future scale development efforts ought to pay attention to rational considerations, internal consistency, and external validity simultaneously.

The Validity of Personality Measures in Personnel Selection

Objective Measures. Many psychologists seem to believe that personality measures have limited utility in selection contexts. One reason may be that the MMPI is often seen as the prototypical personality inventory. As an extraordinarily rich source of information about individual personality, the MMPI is particularly useful as a prophylactic screening device. The MMPI was initially designed for hospital populations as a tool for studying aspects of mental illness, and the items were chosen to reflect themes in the verbal behavior of psychiatric patients. The scales were then developed in the empirical manner by comparing the item responses of persons with various psychiatric diagnoses (e.g., depressed, schizophrenic, or manic) with the responses of "normal" people. The MMPI also contains three scales designed to identify people who may have answered the test items in a way that disguises their "true" scores. The MMPI was *not* designed to predict job performance in normal populations and in fact doesn't do this very well. More importantly, the MMPI samples only one area of personality—adjustment—which is an important but necessarily restricted domain of personality. People can be well adjusted but unimaginative, dishonest, lazy, and socially inept; conversely, maladjusted people can be creative, honest, ambitious, and socially adroit. There is more to personality than what is mapped by the MMPI, and it is a mistake to equate personality measurement with this one venerable inventory.

Skepticism regarding the validity of personality measurement may also reflect the fact that there are a plethora of published personality measures whose quality differs dramatically. Because it is so easy to write questionnaire items, the research literature contains hundreds of personality scales and inventories, many of which are conceptually deficient or lacking in internal psychometric qualities or demonstrated external validity.

Finally, Guion and Gottier's (1965) review was quite influential. Many industrial and organizational psychologists have taken to heart its principal conclusion that the evidence for the validity of standard personality measures for personnel selection is so poor that their continued use seemed unwarranted.

Not everyone agrees with this assessment. For example, Ghiselli (1973) reviewed the validity of the major categories of measures for personnel selection. He organized his review in terms of occupational category (managerial, clerical, sales, protective service, trades and crafts, and industrial occupations) and summarized the findings for personality constructs he judged relevant to an occupational category. Validity coefficients varied by occupational category; although they were unimpressive for clerical and service occupations, they were encouraging for sales and managerial jobs. In the most comprehensive review of this topic to date, Hough, Barge, Houston, McGue, and Kamp (1985; see also Hough, Eaton, Dunnette, Kamp, & McCloy, in press) surveyed civilian studies on the validity of personality measures in selection contexts going back to 1960 and military studies going back to 1940. They classified the results of the research in terms of the personality construct employed (using 10 categories) and the criterion predicted (using 5 categories). Validity coefficients varied by personality construct across criterion category, with Achievement being the best predictor (r between .24 and .33 across 21 studies) and Agreeableness the worst predictor; Adjustment at Work was the most predictable criterion (significant with 4 of 9 predictors over 171 studies) and Job Involvement was the least predictable. Hough et al. (1985) remark that their conclusions are similar to Ghiselli's (1973) positive findings but differ from Guion and Gottier's (1965) review. The difference, they suggest, reflects the fact that Guion and Gottier didn't

group studies according to a taxonomy of either constructs or criteria.

The empirical literature concerning the relationship between personality and occupational performance is relatively positive, yet so extensive that I can only briefly note some representative results based on the best-constructed inventories of normal personality. For example, the most recent version of the *Guilford-Zimmerman Temperament Survey Manual* (Guilford, Zimmerman, & Guilford, 1976) reports 23 separate studies of managerial performance; three longitudinal studies are especially noteworthy. In the first, the Harrells and colleagues (Hanson & Harrell, 1985; Harrell & Harrell, 1971, 1984; Harrell, Harrell, McIntyre, & Weinberg, 1977) tested 336 MBA students who graduated between 1961 and 1964, and the class of 1966, using the GZTS and seven other measures. Personality test scores predicted earnings 5, 10, and 20 years after graduation. Particularly important were the GZTS scales for Energy and Ascendance; Sociability predicted compensation only for persons working in large companies. The correlations between compensation, Sociability, and Ascendance averaged about .20 across all three follow-up periods and were the most stable coefficients in the study. Harrell and Harrell (1984) note that personality predicted success better than academic aptitude; they thought this was because "business success is usually...dependent upon relating effectively with people, rather than solving a scholastic puzzle" (pp. 29–30).

In a second large-scale study, Sparks (1983) tested 2,478 men in a large oil company with the GZTS and found consistent relationships between scale scores and indices of job success, job effectiveness, and managerial potential. Finally, Bentz (1985) describes 20 years of research designed to identify "general executive competence" using a test battery selected by L. L. Thurstone in the early 1940s. Included here was an early version of the GZTS. In 33 different tables, Bentz shows that Sociability, Energy, and Ascendance are modestly but steadily and significantly correlated with a surprising variety of criterion data (e.g.,ratings, nominations, compensation level, and promotability) across a large number of samples. His report is a treasury of objective data on executive performance and contains two conclusions worth noting. The first is that the

> psychological factors predicting effectiveness of female executives are not markedly different from those predicting effectiveness of other executives. It seems that "an executive is an executive is an executive" rather than there being differential concepts of executive behavior appropriate to gender identification. (1985, p. 109)

The second is that, after surveying 30 years of research with thousands of executives and real-world performance criteria,

> it has been demonstrated that personality measures are reliable over a considerable time span; tests taken years ago predict both job progress and current performance. From the perspective of this research it is…appropriate to conclude that the pervasive academic bias against paper-and-pencil personality assessment is unjustified. (p. 143)

Cattell's 16-PF also seems to work in practical situations. For example, Bernardin (1977) studied absenteeism and turnover in a sample of 51 sales personnel; he found correlations between the 16-PF Conscientiousness and Anxiety scales and absenteeism and turnover varying between .21 and .40. The sample of results listed above is interesting because these tests were constructed by internal consistency methods with little concern for external validity; the fact that they yield valid results testifies to the general robustness of personality measurement.

In contrast with the Guilford and Cattell tests, the CPI (Gough, 1987) was empirically developed and designed to forecast practical

life outcomes. Over the years, the CPI has been successfully used in a wide range of practical applications. Among the more consistent findings are the CPI correlates of performance in law enforcement (cf. R. Hogan, 1971; R. Hogan & Kurtines, 1975; Spielberger, Spaulding, Jolley, & Ward, 1979). Mills and Bohannon (1980) used the CPI in a study of 49 highway patrol officers; for 6 scales and 2 criterion ratings, they found 9 significant correlations varying between .26 and .43. There is also an interesting CPI literature concerned with forecasting educational performance (Gough, 1966, 1968). More recently, Gough has published CPI scales designed to assess individual differences in devotion to the work ethic and in managerial effectiveness (Gough, 1989).

The *Gordon Personal Profile* (Gordon, 1963) is a forerunner of inventories based on the five-factor model of personality; like the CPI, this device was designed for practical applications, and it too seems to work rather well. For example, Dodd, Wollowick, and McNamara (1970) report significant correlations between the Gordon Ascendancy scale and a criterion measure of progress for 396 maintenance technician trainees over 9 years and 103 sales trainees over 11 years. Spitzer and McNamara (1964) divided a sample of 102 manufacturing managers into four groups. In three of the four groups, Ascendancy correlated .28, .27, and .31 with peer ratings for managerial potential. Palmer (1974) corroborates these results with both versions of the instrument in a different sample.

R. Hogan (1986) developed a structured inventory, the *Hogan Personality Inventory* (HPI), based on the Big Five theory and designed to forecast performance in practical settings. J. Hogan and R. Hogan (1986) report 15 studies using 24 different samples ($N = 2,227$) in which the HPI correlated with job performance in the military, in hospitals, and in insurance firms and other occupational

settings. The cross-validated zero-order correlations in some cases are in the .5 to .6 range,
and they are for the most part psychologically
sensible.

Although some industrial psychologists will
know about pertinent recent developments
in personality research, few personality psychologists will have read Ghiselli's (1971) research using personality measures to predict
occupational performance. Ghiselli's (1971) *Self
Description Inventory* was developed as an interesting experiment wherein he tried, with
some success, to combine in a single inventory
the most promising scale construction techniques of the early 1960s. He developed a set of
64 items, each of which contained two forced-
choice adjectives matched for their social desirability values; he then composed scales from
these items in a purely empirical manner. This
exercise in brute empiricism produced 13
scales, which Ghiselli (1971) used to study
"managerial talent"—"those human properties which determine the quality of performance in all executive and administrative jobs"
(p. 17). The best of these 13 scales is Supervisory
Ability; this scale had an average correlation of
.55 with rated performance in four samples (*N*
= 152). In a study of 81 stockbrokers, 7 of the 13
scales were significantly correlated with the
criterion of retention versus nonretention, with
coefficients ranging from .26 to .53 (the latter
coefficient was for Supervisory Ability).

Summary. Structured personality measures,
when competently developed, are reasonably
valid predictors of occupational performance.
The variables or dimensions of most importance depend on the job in question. For most
blue collar jobs, imagination, ambition, and
sociability tend not to be significant and are
sometimes even negatively related to performance, whereas adjustment, conscientiousness,
and agreeableness are relatively important for
such jobs (cf. R. Hogan, J. Hogan, & Busch,
1984). For managerial positions, however,
imagination, ambition, and sociability are crucial. That this isn't more widely recognized is at

least partly the fault of personality psychologists, who, under the spell of what Freud called
the "narcissism of minor differences," insist
on giving the same variable different names
(extraversion, sociability, ascendancy, and gre-
gariousness, for example, all mean the same
thing). Nonetheless, if personality is defined
from the observer's perspective—that is, as the
actor's reputation—and if structured inventories are seen as a convenient mechanism for
taking a snapshot of that reputation, and if
reputation reflects past behavior, then we see
that there are sound practical reasons for expecting objective personality measures to predict job performance.

Projective Measures.   As noted above, projective personality measures differ from so-called
self-report measures in that the response format is open-ended. Proponents of projective
testing tend to regard item response dynamics
in a fundamentally different way from those
who work on self-report measures. McClelland
(1980), for example, argues that responses to
projective measures are *operants*—behaviors
that are somehow freely emitted—whereas
responses to self-report measures are *respondents*—behaviors that are elicited by antecedent conditions. McClelland also argues that
self-report measures assess values, whereas
projective measures assess needs. It follows
from his argument that projective and self-
report measures are assessing fundamentally
and categorically different phenomena. That,
in turn, suggests that it is a mistake to see the
two kinds of measures as being in competition;
to ask which is better is like asking whether a
hammer is better than a screwdriver.

Many advocates of projective measures
argue that the purposes of a self-report measure are transparent whereas those of a projective measure are disguised. This is in fact an
empirical question, the answer to which is
not obvious. However, projective tests were
originally developed in part because investigators didn't trust people's self-reports.
Moreover, many psychologists believe that

scores on self-report measures are susceptible to conscious manipulation. For those concerned about the faking problem in assessment, projective measures may be an alternative to standardized inventories.

L. K. Frank (1939) published the first clear statement of the theory of projective testing. According to Frank, people's responses to ambiguous stimuli are a kind of point-for-point rendering, or projection outward, of the contents of their psyches. Today, however, many people believe that projective tests are an avenue to the workings of the unconscious mind (cf. Cornelius, 1983, p. 131). This seems to be needless speculation; suffice it to say that responses to projective measures often contain material the subject may not realize he or she is disclosing. The same, however, is true of responses to self-report measures (Meehl, 1945).

In a spirited defense of projective techniques in personnel selection, Cornelius (1983) remarks that many people believe "that projective devices are 'subjective' and 'clinical' in nature, and that skill in interpreting responses is more art than science" (p. 133). What this seems to mean is that projective measures are scored in arbitrary and idiosyncratic ways. It is true that individual practitioners sometimes use and score projective protocols according to their own private rules, but this reflects on the scientific integrity of the practitioner rather than on the intrinsic merits of projective procedures. The best-known and most empirically useful projective measures are scored for well-defined categories, the scoring rules are carefully codified in scoring manuals, and interrater reliabilities are routinely in the .80 to .90 range (cf. Grant, Katovsky, & Bray, 1967).

It is also worth noting that many projective measures are like the MMPI item pool in that they can be keyed against any criterion of interest. The number of variables assessed by a projective procedure depends on the goals and the ingenuity of the investigator. Sentence completion tests tend to be narrowly focused, but the Rorschach cards elicit a wide range of responses that are susceptible to an equally wide range of interpretations.

This discussion is intended to give the reader some insight into understanding projective measures. The fundamental question, however, is how well do they work, and how well do they work in selection situations. The answer is that they seem to work when objective scoring procedures are developed to assess reliable criteria. Cornelius (1983) provides an interesting, lively, and partisan review of the utility of projective procedures and makes three important points. First, he notes that Guion and Gottier (1965) overlook a major finding in their early review; namely, of the 11 studies presented in their Table 2, 8 contain significant results, and the magnitude of the 17 validity coefficients ranges from .17 to .73. Second, Cornelius suggests that an influential review by Kinslinger (1966) is also unduly pessimistic. Of the 42 papers cited by Kinslinger, only 20 were competent studies of actual job performance; 16 of these report positive findings, and some contain cross-validated validity coefficients in the .50 to .80 range. Finally, Cornelius reviews all 34 papers appearing in *Personnel Psychology* and the *Journal of Applied Psychology* between 1960 and 1981 that mention projective devices. In this group, there were 14 "prediction studies" with quantifiable results; 10 of the 14 studies report significant validity coefficients.

There are some interesting convergences within the literature on projective testing and job performance. Two seem particularly noteworthy. First, Miner (1965) proposed that successful managers in "bureaucratically organized" business firms must (a) have positive attitudes toward authority, (b) be competitive, (c) behave in an assertive, self-confident manner, (d) find it easy to exercise power over and direct others, (e) be willing to take stands, and (f) deal responsibly with routine administrative details. Miner then wrote 40 incomplete sentence items, 35 of which tap the foregoing propensities; the content and keying of these sentence stems were based on a number of item analyses. Miner (1978) reports that the median interscorer reliability using the manual for the *Miner Sentence Completion Test* (MSCS) is .92. Miner (1978) also reports 21 studies in which the MSCS was used in bureaucratic organizations: The test yielded significant results in every case. The most robust subscales were those dealing with competitiveness, attitudes toward authority, and willingness to exercise power (Miner, 1985, provides a more up-to-date review of results using the MSCS).

Murray (1938) proposed a theory of personality that is loosely based on a list of needs. Morgan and Murray (1935) developed a series of pictures about which persons were to construct stories; these stories could be coded for the presence of the various needs. The entire procedure is called the *Thematic Apperception Test* (TAT), and it has been used extensively by McClelland and his colleagues to study entrepreneurship and management potential. Careful scoring procedures are available for five of Murray's needs: Achievement, Power, Affiliation, Activity Inhibition, and Intimacy. Achievement is used in entrepreneurship research; the contribution of Power, Affiliation, and Activity Inhibition form what McClelland (1975) calls the *leadership motive pattern*, which is used to study management. The need for intimacy (McAdams, 1982) has not been used in personnel selection.

Cummin (1967) reports that, in a sample of 52 Boston area businesspersons, TAT-based Achievement scores significantly predicted salary level (adjusted for longevity) using a chi-square test. In a sample of 60 Australian owner-operators of small firms, Morris and Fargher (1974) found that Achievement scores predicted the rate of individual business growth. Varga (1975) studied 118 Hungarian managers of 17 research and development projects in the chemical/pharmaceutical industry and found that Achievement scores predicted the judged technical success of a project as well as its economic return. Wainer and Rubin (1969) tested 51 technical entrepreneurs for Achievement and found that scores were significantly related to a transformed score reflecting each

firm's growth rate. Grant, Katovsky, and Bray (1967) gave the TAT to 201 AT&T managers participating in an assessment center; they scored the TAT stories for 10 variables of their own devising and found that their variables of Achievement, Leadership, and Dependency predicted salary progress 7 to 9 years later about as well as intelligence measures administered at the same time. Finally, McClelland and Boyatzis (1982) compared the leadership motive patterns (Power, Affiliation, and Activity) of 237 AT&T managers and found them to be significantly associated with managerial success after 8 and 16 years. This replicated Winter's (1979) earlier unpublished study of naval officers.

Summary. The foregoing suggests that projective measures can be used to assess aspects of personality related to performance in business and the world of affairs. Because they are only modestly correlated with self-report measures, they add another dimension to the appraisal process. There are, however, three problems associated with projective tests that should be mentioned. The first concerns internal consistency reliability. Sentence completion measures normally have good internal consistencies, but measures like the TAT do not (cf. Entwisle, 1972). This problem would probably disappear if the tests had more items. In any case, the more serious question from a test user's perspective concerns test-retest reliability. Sentence completion measures are quite satisfactory in this area; again, however, measures like the TAT routinely yield only very modest test-retest reliabilities and that *is* a problem for users. Finally, scoring projective measures of all types is laborious and time consuming.

Reliability issues are, however, mechanical problems that can usually be fixed with some psychometric tinkering. The more fundamental question concerns predictive validity. In this area, projective measures seem to work about as well as many standardized psychometric tests—much better than many psychologists realize.

Recent Developments and Future Tasks

Item Response Theory

I believe that further advances in personality assessment will be based on a better understanding of the processes that mediate the way people respond to personality test stimuli. Clearer understanding of these processes should lead to improvements in the reliabilities and validities of standard assessment procedures. Moreover, understanding these processes should allow interpretation of moderator variables, a topic discussed in a later section of this chapter.

Five theories of item response dynamics reside in the assessment literature. The first and by far most popular theory proposes that item responses are *self-reports*. On this view, a person reads an item on a personality measure (e.g., "I often have strange and unusual thoughts"), reviews his or her memory, compares the item to the relevant memory trace, decides whether the item matches the memory trace, and then endorses or rejects the statement as being self-descriptive. This is a pretheoretical account of item response dynamics that rests on a naive notion of how memory seems to work. Modern research suggests that memories are not objective facts, but are constructed and shaped by important personality processes (Tulving, 1985). In the context of this view of memory, to say that item endorsements are self-reports begs the question of why certain items are perceived as self-referential in the first place. Johnson (1981) presents data using the CPI item pool showing that the more valid items have more ambiguous content; this finding is inconsistent with a self-report view of item response dynamics.

The notion of *response styles* (Cronbach, 1950) provides a second theory of item responses. In this view, people are predisposed to agree or disagree with written statements (e.g., "I often have strange and unusual thoughts"), and this trait or tendency to agree is more important in determining item endorsement than the content of the item (cf. Jackson & Messick, 1962). The acquiescence theory of item response has been seriously questioned (Rorer, 1965); nonetheless, it is more sophisticated than self-report theory, and it takes seriously the problem of what processes mediate item endorsement.

A third theory holds that item responses are determined by individual differences in the need for social approval or the need to be perceived as socially appropriate. Whatever the motivational basis, it is claimed that the *social desirability* of items (which can be measured quite accurately), not their content, is the primary influence on item endorsements. Edwards (1957) demonstrated, using the MMPI item pool, that the rated social desirability of the items correlated above .80 with their known endorsement frequency (see also Jackson & Messick, 1962). For example, most people would rate a positive response to the item "I often have strange and unusual thoughts" as socially undesirable; at the same time, relatively few people in the population say "true" to this item. Edwards' influential (1957) monograph set off a debate within personality assessment that paralyzed and finally exhausted the field (Craik, 1986). In retrospect, the obsession with the problem of social desirability response set seems curious because the concept is inherently ambiguous (Messick, 1960; N. Wiggins, 1966) and because content is demonstrably more important than social desirability in determining item endorsement (Block, 1965). Although textbooks continue to warn us about the dangers of social desirability response set, most assessment researchers regard Block's (1965) book as a definitive analysis of the problem. Nevertheless, social desirability response set is an advance over self-report theory as an account of item response dynamics.

A fourth viewpoint, called the *deviant response hypothesis* (Berg, 1955), maintains that individual differences in the tendency to endorse extreme statements determine item responses. After a period of intense investigation, most assessment researchers concluded that the deviancy hypothesis, although interesting, is largely unsupported empirically (Goldberg & Slovic, 1967).

Whatever the empirical merits of these four theories, they are unrelated to the major theoretical perspectives in personality psychology. They are not inconsistent with these perspectives; rather, they are independent of them. On the other hand, interpersonal theory provides a relatively explicit account of item response dynamics, and a surprising amount of research has accumulated that generally supports this account. Interpersonal theory proposes that item responses are *self-presentations* rather than self-reports—in other words, what drives the response is the kind of statement a person wants to make about him or herself. N. Wiggins (1966), for example, suggested that the MMPI item pool can be seen as a communication device, as a medium for self-presentation. Carson (1969) subsequently proposed that the consistency among MMPI item responses reflects neither the influence of indwelling traits nor the influence of response sets. Rather, he believes that consistency is the result of a particular communicative process in which items are chosen so as to express information about the self. Taylor, Carithers, and Coyne (1976) expand on this argument by suggesting that people hold a variety of self-concepts and that responses to specific items may be mediated by these more abstract self-conceptions, where each self-concept is a criterion against which items are evaluated. Drawing on the theories of William James and George Herbert Mead, Taylor et al. (1976) argue that an individual's self-concepts are a source of consistency in everyday behavior and that item endorsements are

a specific example of social behavior guided by self-images. To demonstrate their point, they construct a set of self-concept scales that parallel J. Wiggins' (1966) MMPI content scales, administer both to two separate samples, and show that this allows for the identification of an unusually well-differentiated MMPI factor structure (10 factors versus the usual 3 factors).

Rogers, Kuiper, and Kirker (1977) make the same argument, but from an information processing framework, then provide experimental data consistent with this view of item response dynamics. R. Hogan (1982) modifies the foregoing argument slightly by suggesting that (a) in everyday social interaction people's behavior is guided by their efforts to maximize approval and status; (b) approval and status are sought through self-presentations organized in terms of individual conceptions of identity; (c) some people have made better identity choices than others, and some people are more competent at self-presentation than others; and (d) these processes tell us how to interpret item responses and test scores—i.e., item endorsements reflect automatic and often nonconscious efforts on the part of test-takers to negotiate an identity with an anonymous interviewer (the test author). Cheek (1982), Johnson (1981, 1986), Mills and Hogan (1976), and Penner and Wymer (1983) present data that generally support this line of reasoning.

Consider for a moment the item, "I often have strange and unusual thoughts." How do we interpret a "true" response to this statement? From the perspective of interpersonal theory, the interpretation depends on the image an actor typically projects. An endorsement of this item may signal a schizophrenic asking for help or a nonconformist advertising his or her potential creativity. In trying to choose between these interpretations, it may be helpful to remember Meehl's (1945) caution that the most useful way to interpret an item's meaning is to examine its nontest correlates. Far from being a naive form of "dust bowl empiricism," this view is consistent with Wittgenstein's (1953) very subtle analysis of the problem of meaning—the meaning of a word, Wittgenstein argues, is given by its use rather than by the more abstract conceptual category that it belongs to. In the same way, the meaning of an item is primarily reflected in the pattern of its nontest correlations and only secondarily in the test author's theory.

Faking

One question that people often ask about personality measures in selection contexts is, "Can't people fake their scores?" This is a reasonable question for which there are interesting and dependable answers. The question breaks down into five related issues, and the first of these concerns whether people can raise their scores on standardized or objective personality measures. Here the answer is clearly yes. Studies by Borislow (1958), Dicken (1959), Stollack (1965), and Orpen (1971), using Edwards' (1959) *Personal Preference Schedule* (EPPS), show that scores can be deliberately altered to convey a more favorable self-image for specific purposes. That this was shown for the EPPS is especially interesting because the EPPS was constructed specifically to minimize possible distortion due to social desirability response bias. Grayson and Olinger (1958) show that, when under instruction, some psychiatric patients can improve their scores on the MMPI. A number of studies (e.g., Abrahams, Neumann, & Githens, 1971) show that vocational preference scores can be deliberately altered. Dicken (1960), Canter (1963), and Johnson (1986) show that people can consciously improve their scores on the CPI, and Hough et al. (1985) report that army enlistees can, when asked to do so, improve their scores on a personality inventory constructed for the army. On this first point, then, there is little dispute—people can consciously enhance the image conveyed by scores on a personality inventory.

A second issue concerns how much conscious dissembling takes place in an employment or selection context. Given that people can consciously change their scores in a more positive direction, do they in fact do this? Again the data are clear regarding this issue. As part of the selection process in a large insurance company, Orpen (1971) used the EPPS to test 30 men and women applying for clerical positions. Several weeks later, he tested the same people again with the same instrument as part of a research project. During the same time period, he had a "matched" group of undergraduate students complete the EPPS under straight and fake-good ("assume you are applying for a job and want to make the best possible impression") conditions. Orpen computed two indices of consistency and found that although the students' item endorsements and scores changed significantly over the two conditions, the applicant sample's scores changed only slightly.

Abrahams et al. (1971) conducted a similar study using the *Strong Vocational Interest Blank* (SVIB). In one sample, they compared the mean SVIB profiles of 46 high school students applying for a scholarship with the profile of a matched sample of 46 students who completed the test under routine conditions; the profiles were virtually identical. A second analysis compared the scores of 56 students who completed the SVIB as part of a scholarship application and then again later as part of routine college testing; the correlation between the two mean profiles was .98, and the overall test-retest correlation for the individual scales was .71. The authors conclude that "simulated faking designs do not provide a particularly appropriate estimate of what occurs in selection, instead they provide only an indication of how much a test *can* be faked" (p. 12).

The best study of this issue to date was completed by Hough et al. (1985, in press). Two-hundred forty-five soldiers were randomly distributed across four groups, each of which completed a personality inventory twice as follows: (1) Fake good–Honest; (2) Honest–Fake good; (3) Fake bad–Honest; (4) Honest–Fake bad. This was a repeated-measure, counterbalanced design, in which faking good on the inventory was defined as trying to get into the army and faking bad was defined as trying to avoid selection into the army. The Honest condition was defined as directions to respond "honestly." Scores under these conditions were compared with those of 276 persons who had gone through the testing at an army processing station but who had not yet been informed about whether they had been accepted. Hough et al. found that (a) soldiers could, when so instructed, distort their responses; (b) the distorted protocols could be detected with a validity key; but (c) regular army applicants did *not* distort their responses. Hough et al. (1985) conclude that "intentional distortion does not appear to be a problem in an applicant setting" (p. 33; see also Hough et al., in press). All of the empirical data converge on the finding that the incidence of faking on personality inventories in real-applicant populations is low.

A third issue concerns individual differences in the ability to consciously manipulate scores on personality inventories. Although people can change their scores when instructed, some people can change their scores more than others, and these people turn out to be distinctive. Dicken (1960) asked students to complete the CPI twice—once in a "natural" way and then again in such a way as to simulate a good profile. He found that the change scores were positively correlated with measures of psychological sophistication and technical knowledge. Grayson and Olinger (1958) asked a group of psychiatric patients to "fake good" on the MMPI. As always, there were individual differences in the ability to do this, and that ability was positively related to a patient's prognosis for discharge—that is, those most able to "fake good" were also those judged by the staff as psychologically most adequate. Canter (1963) asked 50 male

alcoholics and 50 male applicants for a hospital aide job to complete the CPI. The alcoholics had been involuntarily admitted to the hospital and were anxious to be discharged. After a period of time, both groups were asked to take the CPI under fake-good instructions. The aides and the alcoholics were closely matched in terms of age, IQ, and SES. On the basis of staff ratings, the alcoholics were divided into better and poorer adjusted groups. All groups were able to improve their scores, but the aides improved more than the better-adjusted alcoholics, who in turn improved more than the poorer-adjusted group. Canter concludes that

> under standard conditions of administration and where there is presumed motivation on the part of the subjects to present themselves as normal or well adjusted, there is a positive relationship between the ability to present a good picture on the CPI and the actual life adjustment of the subject. (p. 255)

From these studies, it seems reasonable to conclude that the ability to enhance scores on a personality inventory is itself a personality variable, one that is also associated with good adjustment. In this light, dissimulation, when it exists, becomes less serious as a problem to overcome and instead becomes an important individual differences variable.

A fourth issue concerns what Paulhus and Levitt (1987) call *automatic egotism.* In an ingenious experiment, they show that under emotionally arousing conditions, people not only endorse more positive traits as self-descriptive and do so more quickly, but deny more negative traits and do so more quickly than under emotionally neutral conditions. Because this process occurs very rapidly, Paulhus and Levitt conclude that under arousing circumstances, self-perception automatically becomes more egotistical and that automatic egotism may underlie a variety of self-presentational phenomena, which would include item responses. According to this analysis, some self-enhancement is automatic and outside conscious control.

A final issue on the topic of faking concerns the distinction between what Paulhus (1984, 1986) defines as self-deception on one hand and impression management on the other. According to Paulhus, *self-deception* is the process of giving positively biased responses to questionnaire items when these responses are not true but the respondent actually believes that they are. In contrast, *impression management* is defined as a conscious dissimulation in responding to test items. Although discussions of social desirability response bias tend to confound these two forms of biased responding, several studies have factor analyzed matrices of correlations between scores on social desirability scales. They find two distinct factors, one representing self-deception and the other impression management (cf. Edwards & Walsh, 1964; Jackson & Messick, 1962; Paulhus, 1984; J. S. Wiggins, 1964).

For persons who worry about the problem of faking on personality inventories, the literature surrounding the distinction between Paulhus' dimensions of self-deception and impression management contains two lessons. The first concerns what happens if one tries to control for self-deception—which can be assessed by Edwards' Social Desirability (SD) scale or the K scale of the MMPI. The answer, quite simply, is that one loses valid variance because self-deception is correlated with adjustment. There is a large and replicated literature showing that well-adjusted people have positively biased self-images; consequently, well-adjusted people tend to ignore minor criticisms, discount their failures, avoid negative thoughts, and expect to succeed in most of their undertakings. Self-deception contributes to stress tolerance and self-esteem and protects against anxiety and depression; in addition, self-deceivers tend to say overly positive things about themselves. Consequently, when one

controls for self-deception, measures related to well-being and adjustment lose some of their predictive power (Amelang & Borkenau, 1986; Edwards, 1970; McCrae & Costa, 1983).

Impression management, on the other hand, refers to the effort to consciously alter scores in a positive direction. This tendency is a trait or individual differences variable, and there are scales to assess this tendency—e.g., Snyder's (1974) Self-monitoring scale and Crowne and Marlowe's (1964) Need for Approval scale. Persons with high scores on these scales are alert to the social expectancies operating in the various social contexts through which they pass, and they try to fit in. Scores on these measures are negatively correlated with adjustment. In addition, it is useful to distinguish the desire to create a good impression from the ability to actually do so. Paulhus (1986) suggests that the Crowne and Marlowe scale measures the desire, whereas the Self-monitoring scale measures the ability. Potential users of personality measures in selection contexts might include scales of this type as a prescreening device and be alert for persons with high motivation and low skill—such persons crave social approval and are inept in pursuing it (Danheiser & Paulhus, 1981).

Moderator Variables

Allport (1937) drew a distinction between nomothetic and idiographic traits. *Nomothetic traits* are terms that psychologists use to describe people in general, while *idiographic traits* are terms that people use to describe themselves. Allport also argued that not all nomothetic traits are relevant to all people; it is possible, in fact likely, that some concepts used by psychologists are irrelevant as descriptions or explanations of the behavior of some people. Two very different conclusions about how to do research have been drawn from this reasonable premise. The first, which Allport favored, is that we should stop studying people in general and start trying to capture the concrete uniqueness of each individual person. Allport's preferred form of personality description is useful for biographers but impractical for applied research (and makes the cumulative development of knowledge impossible); nonetheless, some recent researchers (e.g., Kenrick & Stringfield, 1980) have advocated a modified version of this position. The alternative conclusion that follows from Allport's analysis is that we should look for *moderator variables*—concepts or processes that systematically modify the relationship between predictor and criterion measures so as to identify more and less predictable people. Ghiselli (1956, 1960) introduced the notion of a moderator variable to modern psychology, but the concept has had a spotty history since then (cf. Chaplin, in press; J. S. Wiggins, 1973, chap. 2). Nonetheless, over the past 10 years there has been a surprising amount of research on moderator variables in personality psychology.

In contrast with Allport's romantic humanism, Ghiselli's original insight was scientific in the best sense of the word. For any given plot of test and criterion scores, there will be persons with high scores on the test and low scores on the criterion and persons with low scores on the test and high scores on the criterion. Ghiselli (1956, 1960) showed that, in different settings with different tests and with different criteria, moderator variables could be discovered that would enhance the predictability of "off-quadrant" scorers. Ghiselli's search process was empirical rather than guided by theory; nonetheless, as Gough (1986) points out, Ghiselli established the principle that *discrepancies between scores on well-developed tests and reliable criteria are lawful.*

Snyder and Ickes (1985) provide a useful framework for thinking about moderator variables, suggesting that they can be sorted into four classes or categories, which concern *predictors, criteria, persons*, and *situations*.

Specification of Traits That Are Good Predictors. Bem and Allen (1974) studied *self-reported consistency* as a moderator variable.

They asked people, "How much do you vary from one situation to another in how friendly and outgoing you are?" Separating the groups into high and low self-reported consistency, they found a correlation of .51 between scores on Eysenck and Eysenck's (1964) Extraversion scale and actual friendliness for the high consistency group, and a correlation of .31 for the low consistency group. Their paper attracted considerable attention, but recent evidence suggests that their findings should be interpreted cautiously. Borkenau (1981) shows that self-rated variability is unreliable over time. More importantly, Chaplin and Goldberg (1984) and Amelang and Borkenau (1986) conducted careful, large-scale replications of the Bem and Allen study and report no significant results. The information derived from asking people how consistent they are with regard to a trait dimension seems not to yield a reliable moderator effect; one reason may be that people just aren't very good at judging how consistent they are with regard to various trait dimensions.

Kenrick and Stringfield (1980) studied *self-reported observability* as a moderator variable. They asked people to rate on a 7-point scale the extent to which their behavior in each of Cattell's 16 trait dimensions was publicly observable. For example, on the emotionality dimension, they asked, "If it is easy for others to tell how emotional you are all or almost all of the time, mark a high number; if others can never or rarely tell how emotional you are, mark a low number." For those traits on which people rated themselves as observable, correlations between self-ratings and other ratings were significantly higher (.68 vs. .49) than for those traits on which people rated themselves as not observable. In replicating and extending the Kenrick and Stringfield study, Amelang and Borkenau (1986) conclude that "observability" is a weak but significant moderator and that it is traitlike; that is, some people are more consistently "observable" than others. This is an important point to which I will return shortly.

Amelang and Borkenau (1986) studied *self-reported appropriateness* as a moderator variable, asking individuals to rate traits in terms of how appropriate they were for describing them. Using this data, they found that appropriateness ratings are a moderator variable—that is, correlations between self- and peer ratings are higher for those traits people regard as being appropriate as self-descriptors. They conclude that when subjects are given an inventory, items asking about the appropriateness of several trait dimensions as descriptors of their personality should be incorporated. Moreover, subjects should be asked which traits they would use to describe themselves.

Self-reported observability and appropriateness seem to be useful as a way of specifying, on a person-by-person basis, the traits that will be the best predictors of a person's behavior. This finding is potentially valuable as a method for systematically boosting validity coefficients and predicting the behavior of "off-quadrant" persons.

Specification of Criterion Behaviors That Are Maximally Predictable.   Not all criterion behaviors are equally predictable, even when they are equally reliable; some behaviors are inherently more predictable than others. Furthermore, multiple acts or aggregated behavioral measures are more predictable than single behaviors. Fishbein and Ajzen (1974) demonstrate this quite nicely for the relationship between attitudes and behavior. For example, they found a measure of attitudes toward religion to correlate about .10 with single-act criteria of religious behavior but over .60 with a multiple-act measure of the criterion. Epstein (1979, 1980), Jaccard (1974), and McGowen and Gormly (1976) have actively promoted this well-known psychometric principle in personality research. For example, Jaccard (1974) studied the relationship between scores on a measure of dominance and self-reports of 40 dominant behaviors (e.g., interrupting, controlling conversations, etc.). The average correlation between Dominance

scale scores and single dominance behaviors was .20, whereas the scale correlated .60 with the sum of the single acts.

The foregoing application of the Spearman-Brown prophecy formula should be familiar to most industrial and organizational psychologists. Buss and Craik (1980) provide a more interesting and conceptual analysis of the problem of differential predictability of criteria. They were concerned with predicting dominant behaviors with scores from personality measures of dominance. They found that the predictability of dominant behaviors was a function of the prototypicality of the behavior for the category of dominance. For example, taking charge of a situation was much more predictable with CPI Dominance scale scores than was flattering someone in order to get one's way. The application to selection research is straight forward. Assume, for example, that one were developing a set of measures to predict performance as a police officer. Law enforcement officials tend to regard neatness of appearance as an essential aspect of the job; official preferences notwithstanding, neatness is not a prototypical element of police performance and will necessarily be hard to predict using measures of self-confidence, masculinity, and social tact—which *are* aspects of overall performance.

Specification of Persons Who Are Maximally Predictable.   Gough (1986) postulates that (a) when discrepancies exist between a valid test and a meaningful criteria, these discrepancies are sensible and lawlike and that (b) certain kinds of people are consistently mismeasured, misrated, or misjudged. The first point is an article of faith but one that is central to scientific inquiry; the second point is a verifiable empirical claim. Drawing on an unpublished dissertation by Baker (1961) and data of his own, Gough shows that persons rated higher than suggested by their test scores (false positives) tend to be guarded and self-protective but overeager to conform to external cues. (This resembles Snyder's description of a high self-monitor; cf. Snyder, 1974.) Such persons are necessarily hard to judge. Persons who are rated lower than suggested by their test scores (false negatives) tend to be talented but skeptical and taciturn; they also are hard to judge. Note that, according to these notions, both false positives and false negatives tend not to express their "true" reactions to situations; recall also that self-rated "observability" is traitlike. Gough's data suggest that two very different kinds of persons may form that group of persons who give themselves low ratings for "observability." In any case, Gough shows clearly that certain kinds of people are consistently misrated and misjudged and that the discrepancies are caused by a guarded and defensive interpersonal style.

If a group of people rate themselves on a series of trait dimensions, each person can then be assigned a score based on his or her variance across the ratings. Amelang and Borkenau (1986) show that this intraindividual variance is relatively stable across traits—that is, the same people will be more (or less) variable across all traits; thus, variability is a trait. Moreover, this variability functions like a moderator variable. Variability scores were used to designate people as "traitlike" or "trait free," and validity coefficients were significantly higher for persons designated as traitlike. Baumeister and Tice (1988)) replicate this finding. They introduce the notion of *traitedness*, which they define in terms of low interitem scale variances; they find significantly higher validity coefficients for persons who are traited for a dimension. Amelang and Borkenau (1986) conclude that cross-situational consistency may be a trait itself—that is, some people are generally more consistent than others—but how such consistency is assessed is critical. Simply asking people how consistent they are doesn't seem to work because people aren't very good at estimating this about themselves; individual differences in consistency must be assessed in more indirect and behavioral ways.

We may extend Gough's (1986) analysis and ask what kinds of people are hard to predict. The empirical literature points to three kinds, who may be similar at a deep level. The first type are persons who describe their behavior as dependent on "the situation." They are characterized by *situationality* or external locus of control, and like external locus of control, it is associated with low self-esteem. The second type is called *defensive*. Amelang and Borkenau (1986) show that persons with high scores on measures of social desirability will consistently attempt to do what is socially desirable and will therefore be more variable and less predictable with trait measures. Social desirability, therefore, may also be a moderator variable.

Snyder (1974) introduced the notion of self-monitoring as a personality variable and developed a short scale to assess individual differences in self-monitoring tendencies. Consistent with interpersonal theory, Snyder (1974) argues that people in social settings try to act in a way appropriate to that setting. People differ in terms of what they use to guide their behavior. High self-monitoring people, who endorse such items as "In order to get along and be liked, I tend to be what other people expect me to be rather than anything else," behave quite differently across situations. The behavior of such persons is hard to predict (Snyder, 1974). The neurotic conformity and unpredictability of persons with high scores on the self-monitoring scale suggests that they are also characterized by what Amelang and Borkenau (1986) call *defensiveness*. That is, measures of situationality, defensiveness, and high self-monitoring may be facets of the same construct.

Finally, certain personality scales can be used to identify people who are generally more predictable than others. Interpersonal theory predicts that people with well-developed self-presentational skills should be more predictable than other people. Mills and Hogan (1976) show that women with high scores on the CPI Empathy scale (a measure of role-taking and role-playing ability; R. Hogan, 1969) describe themselves in ways that are more congruent with peer descriptions than persons with low scores. Cheek (1982) and Penner and Wymer (1983) use a measure of private self-consciousness (Fenigstein, Scheier, & Buss, 1975) and the Acting subscale of Snyder's self-monitoring scale as moderator variables. They find that people who are self-reflective (high private self-consciousness) and expressive (high acting) yield higher validity coefficients (correlations between scale scores and peer ratings) than other people.

The preceding discussion can be quickly summarized by saying that some people are more predictable than others. Predictability seems to be a function of a lack of defensiveness, self-knowledge, and good self-presentational skills.

Specification of the Situations in Which People Are Most Predictable. Mischel (1977) distinguishes between strong and weak situations. Strong situations are constraining because everyone sees the situation the same way, understands what the behavioral expectations are, and knows what the sanctions are. For example, if a traffic light is red, virtually all motorists will stop. In such cases, situational cues, expectations, and sanctions tend to suppress individual differences. Conversely, situations that are ambiguous, containing few cues to action or information about behavioral sanctions, should allow for a greater expression of individual differences (Price & Bouffard, 1974; Schutte, Kenrick, & Sadalla, 1985). Monson, Hasley, and Chernik (1981) show that by varying the strength of a situation, one can systematically vary validity coefficients from low (.13) to moderate (.32) to substantial (.42). Ickes (1982) has developed a method for composing weak situations that he uses to study the effects of personality on social interaction and that yields good validity coefficients.

The literature regarding the impact of situational strength on validity coefficients has immediate practical relevance. For example, in employment situations requiring surveillance, the validity of honesty measures will necessarily be reduced. The research by Ickes and by Monson concludes that individual differences in personality will have their strongest impact on behavior in relatively unstructured, psychologically weak situations.

Conclusions

Although much information has been presented in this chapter, there are six major points that I hope the reader will take from this discussion. I shall restate them as a way of concluding the chapter.

- The critique of personality psychology mounted by Mischel and others in the 1960s is no longer regarded as valid. Some of the criticisms have been shown to be empirically false (e.g., .30 is not the upper limit for validity coefficients for personality measures); others have been shown to be a function of faulty methodology (e.g., unreliable criteria based on single behaviors). The "person-situation" debate is now seen in historical terms (cf. Kenrick & Funder, 1988; Snyder & Ickes, 1985).

- Traditional personality psychology was based on clinical practice and was designed to explain the origins of psychopathology. Consequently, traditional personality theory may not be relevant to many of the concerns of practicing industrial and organizational psychologists. Modern interpersonal theory, however, is concerned with the dynamics of everyday social behavior and is therefore relevant to such topics as leadership, performance appraisal, and personnel selection.

- Factor analytic research since the early 1960s converges on the view that ratings of others can be described in terms of five broad dimensions (cf. Norman, 1963). Consequently, when a researcher decides to "measure" personality, he or she should include measures of at least these five primary dimensions of interpersonal evaluation. On the other hand, it is insufficient to define personality in terms of simple, off-the-shelf measures of convenience, such as anxiety, locus of control, self-monitoring, or self-esteem.

- Academic research regarding the determinants of accurate interpersonal perception stopped in the early 1960s, but it is presently enjoying something of a renaissance. Because social perception is implicit in a large number of personnel procedures, e.g., in interviewing, selection, and performance appraisal, this is a significant area of overlap between personality research and industrial and organizational psychology. Future research in this area will have considerable relevance for applied psychology.

- Despite the pessimistic conclusions of reviews published in the 1960s, evidence gathered over the past three decades suggests that personality inventories can make valid contributions to personnel selection and assessment. Moreover, in many cases personality measures are race- and gender-blind. The criticism that these measures are easily faked has less force than is typically believed.

- Moderator variables are still with us. Research regarding what kinds of measures, what kinds of people, what kinds of criteria, and what kinds of situations are most predictable has yielded some findings regarding systematic constraints on validity coefficients. This modern research on moderator variables has implications for applied

psychology, especially in the area of personnel selection and appraisal.

References

Abrahams, N. M., Neumann, I., & Githens, W. H. (1971). Faking vocational interests: Simulated versus real life motivation. *Personnel Psychology, 24*, 5–12.

Adorno, T. W., Frenkl-Brunswik, E., Levinson, D. J., & Sanford, N. (1950). *The authoritarian personality*. New York: Harper & Row.

Alderfer, C. P. (1984). An intergroup perspective on group dynamics. In J. Lorsch (Ed.), *Handbook of organizational behavior*. Englewood Cliffs, NJ: Prentice-Hall.

Allport, G. W. (1937). *Personality*. New York: Holt.

Allport, G. W. (1961). *Pattern and growth in personality*. New York: Holt.

Allport, G. W., & Odbert, H. S. (1933). Trait-names: A psycho-lexical study. *Psychological Monographs, 47*, 171–220 (1, Whole No. 211).

Allport, G. W., Vernon, P. E., & Lindzey, G. (1951). *Study of values*. Boston: Houghton-Mifflin.

Amelang, M., & Borkenau, P. (1986). The trait concept: Current theoretical considerations, empirical facts, and implications for personality inventory construction. In A. Angleitner & J. S. Wiggins (Eds.), *Personality assessment via questionnaire* (pp. 7–34). Berlin: Springer-Verlag.

Aronoff, J., & Wilson, J. P. (1985). *Personality in the social process*. Hillsdale, NJ: Erlbaum.

Assor, A., Aronoff, J., & Messe, L. A. (1981). Attribute relevance as a moderator of the effects of motivation on impression formation. *Journal of Personality and Social Psychology, 41*, 789–796.

Baker, B. 0. (1961). *The personological significance of constant errors in inventory measures*. Unpublished doctoral dissertation, University of California, Berkeley.

Bandura, A. (1977). *Social learning theory*. Englewood Cliffs, NJ: Prentice-Hall.

Baumeister, R. F. (1982). A self-presentational view of social phenomena. *Psychological Bulletin, 91*, 3–26.

Baumeister, R. F., & Tice, D. (1988). Metatraits. *Journal of Personality, 56*, 571–598.

Bem, D. J., & Allen, A. (1974). On predicting some of the people some of the time: The search for cross-situational consistencies in behavior. *Psychological Review, 81,* 506–520.

Bentz, V. J. (1985). *A view from the top: A 30-year perspective of research devoted to the discovery, description, and prediction of executive behavior.* Paper presented at the annual meeting of the American Psychological Association, Los Angeles.

Berg, A. (1955). Response bias and personality: The deviation hypothesis. *Journal of Psychology, 40,* 60–71.

Berger, P. L., & Luckmann, T. (1966). *The social construction of reality.* New York: Doubleday.

Berman, J. S., & Kenny, D. A. (1976). Correlational bias in observer ratings. *Journal of Personality and Social Psychology, 34,* 263–273.

Bernardin, H. J. (1977). The relationship of personality variables to organizational withdrawal. *Personnel Psychology, 30,* 17–27.

Bernardin, H. J., & Bownas, D. A. (Eds.). (1985). *Personality assessment in organizations.* New York: Praeger.

Bernstein, W. M., & Davis, M. H. (1982). Perspective taking, self-consciousness, and accuracy in person perception. *Basic and Applied Social Psychology, 3,* 1–19.

Block, J. (1965). *The challenge of response sets.* New York: Appleton-Century-Crofts.

Block, J. (1961, 1978). *The Q-sort method in personality assessment and psychiatric research.* Palo Alto, CA: Consulting Psychologists Press

Block, J., & Funder, D. C. (in press). Social roles and social perception: Individual differences in attribution and "error." *Journal of Personality and Social Psychology.*

Block, J., Weiss, D. S., & Thorne, A. (1979). How relevant is a semantic similarity interpretation of personality ratings? *Journal of Personality and Social Psychology, 37,* 1055–1074.

Borgatta, E. F. (1964). The structure of personality characteristics. *Behavioral Science, 9,* 8–17.

Borkenau, P. (1981). *Intraindividuelle variabilitat und differentielle vorhutsagbarkeit.* Heidelberg: Dissertation der Fakultat fur Social-und Verhaltenwissenschaften.

Borislow, B. (1958). The Edwards Personal Preference Schedule and fakability. *Journal of Applied Psychology, 42,* 22–27.

Borman, W. C. (1979). Individual difference correlates of accuracy in evaluating others' performance effectiveness. *Applied Psychological Measurement, 3,* 103–115.

Borman, W. C., Hough, L. M., & Dunnette, M. D. (1976). *Performance ratings: An investigation of reliability, accuracy, and relationships between individual differences and rater error.* Minneapolis: Personnel Decisions Institute.

Botwin, & Buss, D. M. (1989). The structure of act report data: Is the five factor model of personality recaptured? *Journal of Personality and Social Psychology, 56,* 988–1001.

Bourne, E. (1977). Can we describe an individual's personality? Agreement on stereotypes versus individual attributes. *Journal of Personality and Social Psychology, 34,* 863–872.

Bryant, B. K. (1974). Locus of control related to teacher-child interperceptual experience. *Child Development, 45,* 157–164.

Buss, D. M., & Craik, K. H. (1980). The frequency concept of disposition: Dominance and prototypically dominant acts. *Journal of Personality, 48,* 379–393.

Buss, D. M., & Craik, K. H. (1983). Act prediction and the conceptual analysis of personality scales. *Journal of Personality and Social Psychology, 45,* 1081–1095.

Campbell, D. J. (1982). Determinants of choice of goal difficulty level: A review of situational and personality influences. *Journal of Occupational Psychology, 55,* 79–95.

Canter, F. M. (1963). Simulation on the California Psychological Inventory and the adjustment of the simulator. *Journal of Consulting Psychology, 27,* 253–256.

Cantor, N., & Kihlstrom, J. F. (Eds.). (1981). *Personality, cognition, and social interaction.* Hillsdale, NJ: Erlbaum.

Cantor, N., & Mischel, W. (1977). Traits as prototypes: Effects on recognition memory. *Journal of Personality and Social Psychology, 35,* 38–48.

Carson, R. C. (1969). *Interaction conceptions of personality.* Chicago: Aldine.

Cattell, R. B. (1947). Confirmation and clarification of primary personality factors. *Psychometrika, 12,* 197–220.

Cattell, R. B., & Stice, G. F. (1957). *Handbook for the Sixteen Personality Factor Questionnaire.*

Champaign, IL: Institute of Personality and Ability Testing.

Chaplin, W. F., & Goldberg, L. R. (1984). Predicting some of the people some of the time: An attempt to replicate and to extend the Bem/Allen study of individual differences in cross-situational consistency. *Journal of Personality and Social Psychology, 47*, 1074–1090.

Chapman, L. J., & Chapman, J. P. (1967). Genesis of popular but erroneous psychodiagnostic observations. *Journal of Abnormal Psychology, 72*, 193–204.

Cheek, J. M. (1982). Aggregation, moderator variables, and the validity of personality tests. *Journal of Personality and Social Psychology, 43*, 1254–1269.

Cline, V. J., & Richards, J. M. (1960). Accuracy of interpersonal perception—A general trait? *Journal of Abnormal Psychology, 60*, 1–7.

Comrey, A. L. (1970). *EITS manual for the Comrey personality scales.* San Diego, CA: Educational and Industrial Testing Service.

Cook, M. (1985). *Issues in person perception.* London: Methuen.

Cornelius, E. T., III (1983). The use of projective techniques in personnel selection. In *Research in personnel and human resource management* (Vol. 1, pp. 127–168). Greenwich, CT: JAI.

Craik, K. H. (1986). Personality research methods: An historical perspective. *Journal of Personality, 54*, 18–51.

Cronbach, L. J. (1950). Further evidence on response sets and test validity. *Educational and Psychological Measurement, 10*, 3–31.

Cronbach, L. J. (1955). Processes affecting scores on "understanding others" and assumed similarity. *Psychological Bulletin, 52*, 171–193.

Crowne, D. P., & Marlowe, D. (1964). *The approval motive.* New York: Wiley.

Cummin, P. C. (1967). TAT correlates of executive performance. *Journal of Applied Psychology, 51*, 78–81.

Danheiser, P., & Paulhus, D. L. (1981). *Self-monitoring and need for approval as impression management styles.* Atlanta, GA: Southeastern Psychological Association.

Dansereau, F., Graen, G., & Haga, W. J. (1974). *A vertical dyad linkage approach to leadership within the formal organization.* SUNY–Buffalo: Unpublished manuscript.

DePaulo, B. M. (1978). Accuracy in predicting situational variations in help-seekers' responses. *Personality and Social Psychology Bulletin, 4*, 330–333.

DePaulo, B. M., Kenny, D. A., Hoover, C. W., Webb, W., & Oliver, P. V. (1987). Accuracy of person perception: Do people know what kind of impressions they convey? *Journal of Personality and Social Psychology.*

DeSoto, C. B., Hamilton, M. M., & Taylor, R. B. (1985). Words, people, and implicit personality theory. *Social Cognition, 3*, 369–382.

Dicken, C. F. (1959). Simulated patterns on the Edwards Personal Preference Schedule. *Journal of Applied Psychology, 43*, 372–377.

Dicken, C. F. (1960). Simulated patterns on the California Psychological Inventory. *Journal of Counseling Psychology, 7*, 24–31.

Digman, J. M. (1990). Personality structure: Emergence of the five-factor model. *Annual Review of Psychology* (Vol. 41, pp. 417–440). Palo Alto, CA: Annual Reviews.

Digman, J. M., & Takemoto-Chock, N. K. (1981). Factors in the natural language of personality. *Multivariate Behavioral Research, 16*, 149–170.

Dodd, W. E., Wollowick, H. B., & McNamara, W. J. (1970). Task difficulty as a moderator of long-term prediction. *Journal of Applied Psychology, 54*, 265–270.

Driskell, J. E., Hogan, R., & Salas, E. (1987). Personality and group performance. In C. Hendrick (Ed.), *Personality and social psychology review* (pp. 91–112). Beverly Hills, CA: Sage.

Dustin, D. S., & Davis, H. P. (1967). Authoritarianism and sanctioning behavior. *Journal of Personality and Social Psychology, 6*, 222–224.

Dymond, R. F. (1949). A scale for the measurement of empathic ability. *Journal of Consulting Psychology, 13*, 127–133.

Edwards, A. L. (1957). *The social desirability variable in personality assessment and research.* New York: Dryden.

Edwards, A. L. (1959). *Edwards Personal Preference Schedule.* New York: Psychological Corporation.

Edwards, A. L. (1970). *The measurement of personality traits by scales and inventories.* New York: Holt, Rinehart & Winston.

Edwards, A. L., & Walsh, J. A. (1964). Response sets in standard and experimental personality scales. *American Educational Research Journal, 1,* 52–61.

Entwisle, D. R. (1972). To dispel fantasies about fantasy-based measures of achievement motivation. *Psychological Bulletin, 77,* 377–391.

Epstein, S. (1979). The stability of behavior: I. On predicting some of the people much of the time. *Journal of Personality and Social Psychology, 37,* 1097–1126.

Epstein, S. (1980). The stability of behavior: II. Implications for psychological research. *American Psychologist, 35,* 790–806.

Epstein, S. (1983). Aggregation and beyond: Some basic issues on the prediction of behavior. *Journal of Personality, 51,* 360–392.

Epstein, S. (1984). The stability of behavior across time and situations. In R. Zucker, J. Aronoff, & A. I. Rabin (Eds.), *Personality and the prediction of behavior* (pp. 209–268). San Diego: Academic Press.

Epstein, S., & O'Brien, E. J. (1985). The person-situation debate in historical and current perspective. *Psychological Bulletin, 98,* 513–537.

Erikson, E. (1968). *Childhood and society.* New York: Norton.

Estes, S. G. (1938). Judging personality from expressive behavior. *Journal of Abnormal and Social Psychology, 33,* 217–236.

Eysenck, H. J. (1949). *Dimensions of personality.* London: Routledge.

Eysenck, H. J., & Eysenck, S. J. (1964). *The manual for the Eysenck Personality Inventory.* San Diego: Educational and Industrial Testing Service.

Eysenck, H. J. (1981). General features of the model. In H. J. Eysenck (Ed.), *A model for personality.* New York: Springer-Verlag.

Fenigstein, A., Scheier, M. F., & Buss, A. H. (1975). Public and private self-consciousness. *Journal of Consulting and Clinical Psychology, 43,* 522–527.

Fishbein, M., & Ajzen, I. (1974). Attitudes toward objects as predictors of single and multiple behavioral criteria. *Psychological Review, 89,* 51–74.

Fiske, D. W. (1949). Consistency of the factorial structures of personality ratings from different sources. *Journal of Abnormal and Social Psychology, 44,* 329–344.

Fiske, S. T., & Linville, P. W. (1980). What does the schema concept buy us? *Personality and Social Psychology Bulletin, 6,* 543-537.

Frank, L. K. (1939). Projective methods for the study of personality. *Journal of Psychology, 8,* 389–413.

Freud, S. (1913). *Totem and taboo.* New York: Norton.

Funder, D. C. (1987). Errors and mistakes: Evaluating the accuracy of social judgment. *Psychological Bulletin, 101,* 75–90.

Funder, D. C., & Ozer, D. (1983). Behavior as a function of the situation. *Journal of Personality and Social Psychology, 44,* 107–112.

Funk, S. G., Horowitz, A. D., Lipshitz, R., & Young, F. W. (1976). The perceived structure of American ethnic groups: The use of multidimensional scaling in stereotype research. *Sociometry, 39,* 116–130.

Ghiselli, E. E. (1956). Differentiation of individuals in terms of their predictability. *Journal of Applied Psychology, 40,* 374–377.

Ghiselli, E. E. (1960). The prediction of predictability. *Education and Psychological Measurement, 20,* 3–8.

Ghiselli, E. E. (1971). *Explorations in managerial talent.* Pacific Palisades, CA: Goodyear.

Ghiselli, E. E. (1973). The validity of aptitude tests in personnel selection. *Personnel Psychology, 26,* 461–477.

Goffman, E. (1958). *The presentation of self in everyday life.* New York: Doubleday.

Goldberg, L. R. (1971). A historical survey of personality scales and inventories. In P. McReynolds (Ed.), *Advances in psychological assessment* (Vol. 2, pp. 293–336). Palo Alto, CA: Science and Behavior Books.

Goldberg, L. R. (1982). From ace to zombie: Some explorations in the language of personality. In C. D. Speilberger & J. N. Butcher (Eds.), *Advances in personality assessment* (Vol. 1, pp. 203–234). Hillsdale, NJ: Erlbaum.

Goldberg, L. R., & Slovic, P. (1967). Importance of test items content. *Journal of Counseling Psychology, 14,* 462–472.

Gordon, L. (1963). *Gordon Personal Profile manual.* New York: Harcourt Brace Jovanovich.

Gottfredson, G. D., Holland, J. L., & Ogawa, D. K. (1982). *Dictionary of Holland occupational codes.* Palo Alto, CA: Consulting Psychologists Press.

Gough, H. G. (1948). A sociological theory of psychopathy. *American Journal of Sociology, 53,* 359–366.

Gough, H. G. (1966). Graduation from high school as predicted from the California Psychological Inventory. *Psychology in the Schools, 3,* 208–216.

Gough, H. G. (1968). College attendance among high-aptitude students as predicted from the California Psychological Inventory. *Journal of Counseling Psychology, 15,* 269–278.

Gough, H. G. (1986). *Some implications of noncorrespondence between test scores and ratings.* Paper presented at the annual meeting of the American Psychological Association.

Gough, H. G. (1987). *Manual: The California Psychological Inventory.* Palo Alto, CA: Consulting Psychologists Press.

Gough, H. G. (1989). The California Psychological Inventory. In C. C. Niemark (Ed.), *Major psychological assessment instruments* (Vol. 2, pp. 67–98). Boston: Allyn & Bacon.

Gough, H. G., & Heilbrun, A. B., Jr. (1983). The Adjective Check List manual: 1983 edition. Palo Alto, CA: Consulting Psychologists Press.

Grant, D. T., Katovsky, W., & Bray, D. W. (1967). Contributions of projective techniques to assessment of management potential. *Journal of Applied Psychology, 51,* 226–232.

Grayson, N. M., & Olinger, L. B. (1958). Simulation of "normalcy" by psychiatric patients on the MMPI. *Journal of Consulting Psychology, 21,* 73–77.

Grief, E. B., & Hogan, R. (1973). The theory and measurement of empathy. *Journal of Counseling Psychology, 20,* 280–284.

Guilford, J. P. (1936). *Psychometric methods.* New York: McGraw-Hill.

Guilford, J. S., Zimmerman, W., & Guilford, J. P. (1976). *The Guilford-Zimmerman Temperament Survey handbook.* Palo Alto, CA: Consulting Psychologists Press.

Guion, R. M. (1965). *Personnel testing.* New York: McGraw-Hill.

Guion, R. M., & Gottier, R. F. (1965). Validity of personality measures in personnel selection. *Personnel Psychology, 18,* 135–164.

Hackman, J. R., & Oldham, G. R. (1976). Motivation through the design of work. *Organizational Behavior and Human Performance, 16,* 256–279.

Hall, G. S. (1904). *Adolescence.* New York: Appleton.

Hampson, S. E. (1982). Person memory: A semantic category model of personality traits. *British Journal of Psychology, 73,* 1–11.

Hampson, S. E., John, O. P., & Goldberg, L. R. (1986). Category breadth and hierarchical structure in personality. *Journal of Personality and Social Psychology, 51,* 37–54.

Hanson, B. A., & Harrell, T. W. (1985). *Predictors of business success over two decades: An MBA longitudinal study* (Research paper No. 788). Stanford, CA: Stanford University, Graduate School of Business.

Harackiewicz, J. M., & DePaulo, B. M. (1982). Accuracy of person perception: A component analysis according to Cronbach. *Personality and Social Psychology Bulletin, 8,* 247–256.

Harrell, T. W., & Harrell, M. S. (1971). The personality of MBAs who reach general management early. *Personnel Psychology, 26,* 127–134.

Harrell, T. W., & Harrell, M. S. (1984). *Stanford MBA careers: A 20-year longitudinal study* (Research paper No. 723). Stanford, CA: Stanford University, Graduate School of Business.

Harrell, M. S., Harrell, T. W., McIntyre, S. H., & Weinberg, C. B. (1977). Predicting compensation among MBA graduates five and ten years after graduation. *Journal of Applied Psychology, 62,* 636–640.

Hase, H. D., & Goldberg, L. R. (1967). Comparative validities of different strategies of constructing personality inventory scales. *Psychological Bulletin, 67,* 231–248.

Hastorf, A. H., Bender, I. E., & Weintraub, D. J. (1955). The influence of response patterns on the "refined empathy score." *Journal of Abnormal and Social Psychology, 51,* 341–343.

Hathaway, S. R., & McKinley, J. C. (1943). *Manual for the Minnesota Multiphasic Personality Inventory.* New York: Psychological Corporation.

Haythorn, W., Couch, A. S., Haefner, D., Langham, P., & Carter, L. F. (1956a). The behavior of authoritarian and egalitarian personalities in groups. *Human Relations, 9,* 57–74.

Haythorn, W., Couch, A. S., Haefner, D., Langham, P., & Carter, L. F. (1956b). The effects of varying combinations of authoritarian and egalitarian leaders and followers. *Journal of Abnormal and Social Psychology, 53,* 210–219.

Heider, F. (1958). *The psychology of interpersonal relations.* New York: Wiley.

Heymans, G., & Weirsma, E. (1906). Beitrage zur speziellen psychologie auf grund einer massenuntersuchen. *Zeitschrifte fur Psychologie, 43,* 81–127.

Hirschberg, N., & Jennings, S. J. (1980). Beliefs, personality and person perception: A theory of individual differences. *Journal of Research in Personality, 14*, 235–249.

Hogan, J., & Hogan, R. (1986). *Manual for the Hogan Personnel Selection System.* Minneapolis, MN: National Computer Systems.

Hogan, R. (1969). The development of an empathy scale. *Journal of Consulting and Clinical Psychology, 33*, 307–316.

Hogan, R. (1971). Personality characteristics of highly rated policemen. *Personnel Psychology, 24*, 679–686.

Hogan, R. (1982). A socioanalytic theory of personality. In M. Page (Ed.), *Nebraska symposium on motivation* (Vol. 30, pp. 56–89). Lincoln: University of Nebraska Press.

Hogan, R. (1986). *Manual for the Hogan Personality Inventory.* Minneapolis, MN: National Computer Systems.

Hogan, R. (1987). Personality psychology: Back to basics. In J. Aronoff, A. I. Rabin, & R. A. Zucker (Eds.), *The emergence of personality* (pp. 141–188). New York: Springer.

Hogan, R., & Briggs, S. R. (1984). Noncognitive measures of social intelligence. *Personnel Selection and Training Bulletin, 5*, 184–190.

Hogan, R., DeSoto, C. B., & Solano, C. (1975). Traits, tests, and personality research. *American Psychologist, 6*, 255–264.

Hogan, R., Hogan, J., & Busch, C. (1984). How to measure service orientation. *Journal of Applied Psychology, 69*, 157–163.

Hogan, R., & Kurtines, W. H. (1975). Personological correlates of police effectiveness. *Journal of Personality, 91*, 289–295.

Holland, J. L. (1985). *The SDS professional manual— 1985 revision.* Odessa, FL: Psychological Assessment Resources.

Hough, L. M., Barge, B. N., Houston, J. S., McGue, M. K., & Kamp, J. D. (1985). *Problems, issues, and results in the development of temperament, biographical, and interest measures.* Paper presented at the annual meeting of the American Psychological Association, Los Angeles.

Hough, L. M., Eaton, N. K., Dunnette, M. D., Kamp, J. D., & McCloy, R. A. (in press). Criterion-related validities of personality constructs and the effect or response distortion on those validities. *Journal of Applied Psychology.*

Ickes, W. (1982). A basic paradigm for the study of personality, roles, and social behavior. In W. Ickes & E. Knowles (Eds.), *Personality, roles, and social behavior.* New York: Springer-Verlag.

Jaccard, J. J. (1974). Predicting social behavior from personality traits. *Journal of Research in Personality, 7*, 358–367.

Jackson, D. N. (1967). *Personality Research Form manual.* Goshen, NY: Research Psychologists Press.

Jackson, D. N. (1982). Some preconditions for valid person perception. In M. P. Zanna, E. T. Higgins, & C. P. Herman (Eds.), *Consistency in social behavior.* Hillsdale, NJ: Erlbaum.

Jackson, D. N., & Messick, S. (1962). Response styles on the MMPI. *Journal of Abnormal and Social Psychology, 65*, 285–299.

Jenkins, C. D., Zyzanski, S. J., & Rosenman, R. H. (1979). *Manual for the Jenkins Activity Survey.* New York: Psychological Corporation.

John, O. P., Goldberg, L. R., & Angleitner, A. (1984). Better than the alphabet: Taxonomies of personality descriptive terms in English, Dutch, and German. In H. C. J. Bonarius, G. L. M. van Heck, & N. G. Smid (Eds.), *Personality psychology in Europe: Theoretical and empirical developments* (Vol. 1, pp. 83–100). Lisse: Swets & Zeitlinger.

Johnson, J. A. (1981). The "self-disclosure" and "self-presentation" views of item response dynamics and personality scale validity. *Journal of Personality and Social Psychology, 40*, 761–769.

Johnson, J. A. (1986). *Can applicants dissimulate on personality tests?* Paper presented at the annual meeting of the American Psychological Association, Washington, DC.

Johnson, J. A., & Hogan, R. (1981). Vocational interests, personality, and effective police performance. *Personnel Psychology, 34*, 49–53.

Jones, E. E. (1954). Authoritarianism as a determinant of first-impression formation. *Journal of Personality, 23*, 107–127.

Jones, E. E., & Daugherty, B. N. (1959). Political orientation and the perceptual effects of an anticipated interaction. *Journal of Abnormal and Social Psychology, 59*, 340–349.

Jones, E. E., & Davis, K. E. (1965). From acts to dispositions: The attribution process in person perception. In L. Berkowitz (Ed.), *Advances in experimental social psychology* (Vol. 2). New York: Academic Press.

Jones, E. E., & Pittman, T. S. (1982). Toward a general theory of strategic self-presentation. In J. Suls

(Ed.), *Psychological perspectives on the self*. Hillsdale, NJ: Erlbaum.

Jung, C. G. (1910). The association method. *American Journal of Psychology, 21,* 219–269.

Jung, C. G. (1923). *Psychological types.* New York: Harcourt Brace Jovanovich.

Kagan, J. (1988). The meaning of personality predicates. *American Psychologist, 43.*

Kane, J. S., & Lawler, E. E., III (1979). Methods of peer assessment. *Psychological Bulletin, 85,* 555–586.

Kant, I. (1974). *Anthropology from a pragmatic point of view* (M. J. Gregor, trans.). The Hague: Nijhoff. (Original work published 1798)

Kelly, G. A. (1955). *The psychology of personal constructs.* New York: Norton.

Kenny, D. A., & Zaccaro, S. J. (1983). An estimate of variance due to traits in leadership. *Journal of Applied Psychology, 68,* 678–688.

Kenrick, D. T., & Funder, D. C. (1988). Lessons from the person-situation debate. *American Psychologist, 43,* 23–34.

Kenrick, D. T., & Stringfield, D. O. (1980). Personality traits and the eye of the beholder: Crossing some traditional philosophical boundaries in the search for consistency in all of the people. *Psychological Review, 87,* 88–104.

Kinslinger, H. J. (1966). Application of projective techniques in personnel psychology since 1940. *Psychological Bulletin, 66,* 134–149.

Korman, A. K. (1976). Hypothesis of work behavior revisited and an extension. *Academy of Management Review, 1,* 50–63.

Krech, D., & Crutchfield, R. S. (1948). *Theory and problems of social psychology.* New York: McGraw-Hill.

Latham, G. P., & Saari, L. M. (1979). Application of social learning theory to training supervisors through behavioral modeling. *Journal of Applied Psychology.*

Leary, T. (1957). *Interpersonal diagnosis of personality.* New York: Ronald Press.

Lefcourt, H. (1976). *Locus of control: Current trends in theory and research.* Hillsdale, NJ: Erlbaum.

Lewicki, P. (1986). *Nonconscious social information processing.* Orlando, FL: Academic Press.

Marcuse, H. (1955). *Eros and civilization.* New York: Beacon.

Markus, H., & Smith, J. (1981). The influence of self-schemas on the perception of others. In N. Cantor & J. F. Kihlstrom (Eds.), *Personality,*

cognition, and social interaction (pp. 233–262). Hillsdale, NJ: Erlbaum.

Maslow, A. H. (1970). *Motivation and personality.* New York: Harper & Row.

McAdams, D. B. (1982). Intimacy motivation. In A. J. Stewart (Ed.), *Motivation and society.* San Francisco: Jossey-Bass.

McClelland, D. C. (1975). *Power: The inner experience.* New York: Irvington.

McClelland, D. D. (1980). Motive dispositions: The merits of operant and respondent measures. In L. Wheeler (Ed.), *Review of personality and social psychology.* Beverly Hills: Sage.

McClelland, D. C., & Boyatzis, R. E. (1982). Leadership motive pattern and long term success in management. *Journal of Applied Psychology, 67,* 737–743.

McClelland, D. C., and Burnham, D. (1976). Power is the great motivator. *Harvard Business Review, 25,* 159–166.

McCrae, R. R., & Costa, P. T., Jr. (1983). Social desirability scales: More substance than style. *Journal of Counseling and Clinical Psychology, 51,* 882–888.

McCrae, R. R., & Costa, P. T., Jr. (1985). Updating Norman's adequate taxonomy: Intelligence and personality dimensions in natural language and questionnaires. *Journal of Personality and Social Psychology, 49,* 710–721.

McGowen, J., & Gormly, J. (1976). Validation of personality traits: A multicriteria approach. *Journal of Personality and Social Psychology, 34,* 791–795.

McGuire, W. J., & Padawer-Singer, A. (1976). Trait salience in the spontaneous self-concept. *Journal of Personality and Social Psychology, 33,* 743–754.

Mead, G. H. (1934). *Mind, self, and society.* Chicago: University of Chicago Press.

Meehl, P. E. (1945). The dynamics of structured personality tests. *Journal of Clinical Psychology, 1,* 296–303.

Messick, S. (1960). Dimensions of social desirability. *Journal of Consulting Psychology, 24,* 279–287.

Miller, G. A., Galanter, E., & Pribram, K. H. (1960). *Plans and the structure of behavior.* New York: Holt, Rinehart & Winston.

Mills, C. J., & Bohannon, W. E. (1980). Personality characteristics of effective state police officers. *Journal of Applied Psychology, 65,* 680–684.

Mills, C. J., & Hogan, R. (1976). A role theoretical interpretation of personality scale item responses. *Journal of Personality, 46,* 778–785.

Miner, J. B. (1965). *Studies in management education.* New York: Springer.

Miner, J. B. (1978). The Miner Sentence Completion Scale: A reappraisal. *Academy of Management Journal, 21,* 283–294.

Miner, J. B. (1985). Sentence completion measures in personnel research: The development and validation of the Miner Sentence Completion Scales. In H. J. Bernardin & D. A. Bownas (Eds.), *Personality assessment in organizations.* New York: Praeger.

Mischel, W. (1968). *Personality and assessment.* New York: Wiley.

Mischel, W. (1973). Toward a cognitive social learning reconceptualization of personality. *Psychological Review, 80,* 252–283.

Mischel, W. (1977). On the future of personality measurement. *American Psychologist, 32,* 246–254.

Monson, T. C., Hasley, J. W., & Chernik, L. (1981). Specifying when personality traits can and cannot predict behavior. *Journal of Personality and Social Psychology, 43,* 385–399.

Monson, T. C., & Snyder, M. (1977). Actors, observers, and the attribution process. *Journal of Experimental Social Psychology, 13,* 89–111.

Morgan, C. D., & Murray, H. A. (1935). A method for investigating fantasies. *Archives of Neurology and Psychiatry, 34,* 289–306.

Morris, J. L., & Fargher, L. (1974). Achievement drive and creativity as correlates of success in small business. *Australian Journal of Psychology, 26,* 217–222.

Moskowitz, D. S., & Schwartz, J. C. (1982). Validity comparison of behavior counts and ratings by knowledgeable informants. *Journal of Personality and Social Psychology, 42,* 518–528.

Mowday, R. T., Porter, L. W., & Steers, R. M. (1982). *Employee organization linkages: The psychology of commitment, absenteeism, and turnover.* New York: Academic Press.

Murphy, K., Martin, C., & Garcia, M. (1982). Do behavioral observation scales measure observation? *Journal of Applied Psychology, 67,* 562–567.

Murray, H. A. (1938). *Explorations in personality.* New York: Oxford.

Myers, I. B., & McCaulley, M. H. (1985). *Manual: A Guide to the development and use of the Myers-Briggs Type Indicator.* Palo Alto, CA: Consulting Psychologists Press.

Norman, W. T. (1963). Toward an adequate taxonomy of personality attributes: Replicated factor structure in peer nomination personality ratings. *Journal of Abnormal and Social Psychology, 66,* 574–583.

Norman, W. T., & Goldberg, L. R. (1966). Raters, ratees, and randomness in personality structure. *Journal of Personality and Social Psychology, 4,* 44–49.

Orpen, C. (1971). The fakability of the Edwards Personal Preference Schedule in personnel selection. *Personnel Psychology, 24,* 1–4.

Ozer, D. J. (1986). *Consistency of personality: A methodological framework.* New York: Springer-Verlag.

Palmer, W. J. (1974). Management effectiveness as a function of personality traits of the manager. *Personnel Psychology, 27,* 283–295.

Passini, F. T., & Norman, W. T. (1966). A universal conception of personality structure? *Journal of Personality and Social Psychology, 4,* 44–49.

Paulhus, D. L. (1984). Two-component models of socially desirable responding. *Journal of Personality and Social Psychology, 46,* 598–609.

Paulhus, D. L. (1986). Self-deception and impression management in test responses. In A. Angleitner & J. S. Wiggins (Eds.), *Personality assessment via questionnaires* (pp. 144–165). Berlin: Springer-Verlag.

Paulhus, D. L., & Levitt, K. (1987). Desirable responding triggered by affect: Automatic egotism? *Journal of Personality and Social Psychology, 52,* 245–259.

Peabody, D., & Goldberg, L. R. (1989). Some determinants of factor structure from personality trait descriptors. *Journal of Personality and Social Psychology, 57,* 552–567.

Penner, L. A., & Wymer, W. E. (1983). The moderator variable approach to behavioral predictability. *Journal of Research in Personality, 17,* 339–353.

Price, R. H., & Bouffard, D. N. (1974). Behavioral appropriateness and situational constraint as dimensions of social behavior. *Journal of Personality and Social Psychology, 30,* 579–586.

Pryor, J. B., Gibbons, F. X., Wicklund, R. A., Fazio, R., & Hood, R. (1977). Self-focused attention and self-report validity. *Journal of Personality, 45,* 513–527.

Ramul, K. (1963). Some early measurements and ratings in psychology. *American Psychologist, 18,* 653–659.

Rieff, P. (1958). *Freud: The mind of the moralist.* New York: Anchor.

Riggs, J. M., & Cantor, N. (1984). Getting acquainted: The role of the self-concept and preconditions. *Personality and Social Psychology Bulletin, 10,* 432–445.

Roazen, P. (1968). *Freud: Political and social thought.* New York: Random House.

Roback, A. A. (1927). *A bibliography of character and personality.* Cambridge, MA: Sci-Art Publishers.

Rogers, T. B., Kuiper, N. A., & Kirker, W. S. (1977). Self-reference and the encoding of personal information. *Journal of Personality and Social Psychology, 35,* 672–688.

Romer, D., & Revelle, W. (1984). Personality traits: Fact or fiction? A critique of the Shweder and D'Andrade systematic distortion hypothesis. *Journal of Personality and Social Psychology, 47,* 1028–1042.

Rorer, L. G. (1965). The great response style myth. *Psychological Bulletin, 63,* 129–156.

Rorschach, H. (1921). *Psychodiagnostics.* Berne: Haber.

Ross, L., Amabile, T. M., & Steinmetz, J. L. (1977). Social roles, social control, and biases in social-perception processes. *Journal of Personality and Social Psychology, 35,* 485–494.

Ross, M., & Fletcher, G. J. O. (1985). Attribution and social perception. In G. Lindzey & E. Aronson (Eds.), *Handbook of social psychology* (3rd ed, vol. 2, pp. 73–122). New York: Random House.

Sackett, P. R., & Harris, M. M. (1984). Honesty testing for personnel selection. In J. Bernardin & D. Bownas (Eds), *Personality assessment in organizations.*

Sarbin, T. R. (1954). Role theory. In G. Lindzey (Ed.), *Handbook of social psychology* (Vol. 1). Reading, MA: Addison-Wesley.

Sarbin, T. R., Taft, R., & Bailey, D. E. (1960). *Clinical inference and cognitive theory.* New York: Holt.

Schlenker, B. R. (Ed.). (1985). *The self and social life.* New York: McGraw-Hill.

Schneider, B. (1985). *The people make the place.* Presidential address presented at the annual meeting of the Society for Industrial and Organizational Psychology.

Schneider, D. J., Hastorf, A. H., & Ellsworth, P. C. (1979). *Person perception.* Reading, MA: Addison-Wesley.

Schutte, N. A., Kenrick, D. T., & Sadalla, E. C. (1985). The search for predictable settings: Situational prototypes, constraints, and behavioral variation. *Journal of Personality and Social Psychology, 49,* 121–128.

Scodel, L. A., & Mussen, P. (1953). Social perceptions of authoritarians and nonauthoritarians. *Journal of Abnormal and Social Psychology, 48,* 181–184.

Shrauger, J. S., & Patterson, M. B. (1974). Self-evaluation and the selection of dimensions for evaluating others. *Journal of Personality, 42,* 569–585.

Shweder, R. A. (1982). How relevant is an individual difference theory of personality? *Journal of Personality, 43,* 455–485.

Shweder, R. A., & D'Andrade, R. G. (1980). The systematic distortion hypothesis. In R. A. Shweder (Ed.), *Fallible judgment in behavioral research.* San Francisco: Jossey-Bass.

Smith, M. B. (1986). Toward a secular humanistic psychology. *Journal of Humanistic Psychology, 26,* 7–26.

Smith, P. C., & Kendall, L. M. (1963). Retranslation of expectations: An approach to the construction of unambiguous anchors for rating scales. *Journal of Applied Psychology, 47,* 149–155.

Snyder, C. R., & Smith, T. W. (1982). Symptoms as self-handicapping strategies. In G. Weary & H. L. Mirels (Eds.), *Integrations of clinical and social psychology.* New York: Oxford.

Snyder, M. (1974). The self-monitoring of expressive behavior. *Journal of Personality and Social Psychology, 30,* 526–537.

Snyder, M., & Ickes, W. (1985). Personality and social behavior. In G. Lindzey & E. Aronson (Eds.), *The handbook of social psychology* (pp. 883–947). New York: Random House.

Snyder, M., Tanke, E. O., & Berscheid, E. (1977). Social perception and interpersonal behavior. *Journal of Personality and Social Psychology, 35,* 656–666.

Snyder, M., & Swann, W. B. (1978). Behavior confirmation in social interaction. *Journal of Experimental Social Psychology, 14,* 148–162.

Sparks, C. P. (1983). Paper and pencil measures of potential. In G. F. Dreher & P. R. Sackett (Eds.), *Perspectives on employee staffing and selection* (pp. 349–368). Homewood, IL: Irwin.

Spielberger, C. D., Spaulding, H. C., Jolley, M. T., & Ward, J. C. (1979). Selection of effective law enforcement officers. In C. D. Spielberger (Ed.), *Police selection and evaluation: Issues and techniques*. New York: Praeger.

Spitzer, M. E., & McNamara, W. J. (1964). A managerial selection study. *Personnel Psychology, 17*, 19–40.

Spranger, E. (1928). *Types of men*. Halle: Max Niemeyer Verlag.

Stagner, R. (1948). Psychological aspects of industrial conflict: I. Perception. *Personnel Psychology, 1*, 131–144.

Staw, B. M., & Ross, J. (1985). Stability in the midst of change: A dispositional approach to job attitudes. *Journal of Applied Psychology, 70*, 469–480.

Stollack, G. E. (1965). EPPS performance under social desirability instructions. *Psychological Reports, 16*, 119–122.

Sullivan, H. S. (1953). *The interpersonal theory of psychiatry*. New York: Norton.

Symonds, P. M. (1931). *Diagnosing personality and conduct*. New York: Appleton-Century-Crofts.

Taft, R. (1955). The ability to judge people. *Psychological Bulletin, 52*, 1–23.

Taylor, J. B., Carithers, M., & Coyne, L. (1976). MMPI performance, response set, and the "self-concept" hypothesis. *Journal of Consulting and Clinical Psychology, 44*, 688–699.

Thorndike, E. L. (1906). *Principles of teaching*. New York: Seiler.

Tulving, E. (1985). How many memory systems are there? *American Psychologist, 40*, 385–398.

Varga, K. (1975). N Ach, N Power and effectiveness of research and development. *Human Relations, 28*, 571–590.

Vernon, P. E. (1933). Some characteristics of the good judge of personality. *Journal of Social Psychology, 4*, 42–57.

Viernstein, M. C. (1972). The extension of Holland's occupational classification to all occupations in the Dictionary of Occupational Titles. *Journal of Vocational Behavior, 2*, 107–121.

Wahba, M. A., & Birdwell, L. B. (1976). Maslow reconsidered: A review of research on the need hierarchy theory. *Organizational Behavior and Human Performance, 15*, 212–240.

Wainer, H. A., & Rubin, I. M. (1969). Motivation of research and development entrepreneurs:

Determinants of company success. *Journal of Applied Psychology, 53*, 178–184.

Weick, K. E. (1979). *The social psychology of organizing* (2nd ed.). Reading, MA: Addison-Wesley.

Weiss, D. S., & Mendelsohn, G. A. (1986). An empirical demonstration of the implausibility of the semantic similarity explanation of how trait ratings are made and what they mean. *Journal of Personality and Social Psychology, 50*, 595–601.

Weiss, H. M., & Adler, S. (1984). Personality and organizational behavior. *Research in organizational behavior* (Vol. 6). Greenwich, CT: JAI.

Wiggins, J. S. (1964). Convergences among stylistic measures from objective personality tests. *Education and Psychological Measurement, 24*, 551–562.

Wiggins, J. S. (1966). Substantive dimensions of self-report in the MMPI item pool. *Psychological Monographs, 80* (22, Whole No. 630).

Wiggins, J. S. (1973). *Personality and prediction*. Reading, MA: Addison-Wesley.

Wiggins, J. S. (1979). A psychological taxonomy of trait-descriptive terms: The interpersonal domain. *Journal of Personality and Social Psychology, 376*, 395–412.

Wiggins, J. S., & Broughton, R. (1985). The interpersonal circle: A structural model for the integration of personality research. In R. Hogan & W. Jones (Eds.), *Perspectives in personality* (Vol. 1, pp. 1–48). Greenwich, CT: JAI.

Wiggins, N. (1966). Individual viewpoints of social desirability. *Psychological Bulletin, 66*, 68–77.

Wilder, D. A. (1986). Social categorization: Implications for creation and reduction of intergroup bias. *Advances in Experimental Social Psychology, 19*, 291–355.

Wilkens, E. J., & deCharms, R. (1962). Authoritarianism and response to power areas. *Journal of Personality, 30*, 439–457.

Winter, D. G. (1979). *Navy leadership and management competencies: Convergences among tests, interviews, and performance ratings*. Boston: McBer and Company.

Wittgenstein, L. (1953) *Philosophical investigations*. New York: Macmillan.

Wundt, W. (1874). *Principles of physiological psychology*. Leipzig: Engelmann.

Credits

Name Index

Subject Index